THE NEW
CAMBRIDGE MODERN HISTORY

ADVISORY COMMITTEE

G.N.CLARK J.R.M.BUTLER J.P.T.BURY

THE LATE E.A.BENIANS

VOLUME VI

THE RISE OF GREAT BRITAIN
AND RUSSIA

1688–1715/25

THE NEW CAMBRIDGE MODERN HISTORY

VOLUME VI

THE RISE OF GREAT BRITAIN
AND RUSSIA
1688–1715/25

EDITED BY

J. S. BROMLEY

CAMBRIDGE
AT THE UNIVERSITY PRESS
1970

Published by the Syndics of the Cambridge University Press
Bentley House, 200 Euston Road, London N.W.1
American Branch: 32 East 57th Street, New York, N.Y.10022

© Cambridge University Press 1970

Library of Congress Catalogue Card Number: 57-14935

Standard Book Number: 521 07524 6

Printed in Great Britain
at the University Printing House, Cambridge
(Brooke Crutchley, University Printer)

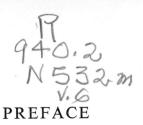
PREFACE

For delays in the production of this volume, which has extended over
rather more than a decade, the editor takes full responsibility. Its preparation has required more than the straightforward commissioning and
writing of the contents, difficult as these tasks can be: a collective effort
of this kind rather resembles a conference in permanent session, except
that it never meets. Many of the contributors have been good enough to
peruse each other's work, and all have patiently put up with some revision.
They should be thanked in this place, as also should Mrs Wendy Block
and Mrs Pauline Kemp, formerly of the Arts Faculty office in the University of Southampton, who typed or retyped a large proportion of the
chapters. Other personal acknowledgements, as inadequate as these, are
made in the footnotes as they arise.

In accordance with the practice of the series, all dates are given in New
Style—ten days, from 1700 eleven days, later than Old Style—unless
otherwise indicated by the letters O.S. In either case the year begins on
1 January. The styles peculiar to Sweden and Russia have been ignored.

The spelling of East European place-names has presented some difficulty, since frontiers were changing rapidly at the time and many territories
have since developed a national status of their own. No rigorous consistency can be claimed for this volume. While we have usually chosen
the forms most familiar in English-speaking countries, it has sometimes
seemed courteous, as well as more realistic, to respect local spellings. To
retain 'Thorn' for the Polish 'Toruń', for example, must now appear
plainly unhistorical to anyone who has been there, not least if he is a
student of the Teutonic Knights. In a work like this the opportunity must
surely be taken to accustom western readers to absorb a modicum of East
European terms in general, even if we are not yet ready to do the same for
the whole wide world, of which this series was never intended to be the
history. Where any ambiguity might arise in such cases, two forms are
given on first mention.

Unless otherwise stated, places of publication are London and Paris
respectively for book titles in English and French cited in footnotes.

J.S.B.

July 1969

CONTENTS

CHAPTER I
INTRODUCTION

By J. S. BROMLEY, *Professor of Modern History in the*
University of Southampton

Periodization and changes in political geography	*page* 1–2
The Baltic and the Levant	2–3
Russia and Europe	3
The Northern kingdoms and the Western powers	3–4
The Habsburgs between East and West	4–6
Decline of the Ottoman empire	6–7
Hungary and the Habsburg lands	7–8
Rivalries in Spain; the Bourbon rule	8–9
Rivalries in Italy	9–10
The Mediterranean	10–11
Rivalries in America	11–12
War and peace in North America	12–14
The balance of trade; merchants and governments	14–15
World trading; the South Sea and Canton	15
Britain and the Peace of Utrecht	16–17
William III's European aims	17–18
Strategy in western Europe	18–19
Privateering war	19–20
The strain on manpower	20
Mercenaries and conscripts	20–1
Care of soldiers	21
Upkeep of navies	21–2
The strain on finance	22–3
Profiteers and projectors	23–4
Tensions in Church and State	24–5
Significance of the English Revolution of 1688	25–6
Louis XIV: the question of 'decline'	26–8
Louis XIV: domestic legacy in European perspective	28–9
Economic distress; climate and harvests	29–30
Social distress; mobility of populations	30–1
Town and country	31
Aristocratic and middle-class tastes	31–3
The scientific movement	33–5
Europe and the world overseas	35–6

CONTENTS

CHAPTER II

THE SCIENTIFIC MOVEMENT AND THE DIFFUSION
OF SCIENTIFIC IDEAS, 1688–1751

By A. C. CROMBIE, *Senior Lecturer in the History of Science in the*
University of Oxford
and MICHAEL HOSKIN, *Lecturer in the History of Science in the*
University of Cambridge

Change in scientific movement . . . . *page* 37
The Royal Society and the *Académie des Sciences* 38
The Royal Society at home and abroad 38–40
The *Académie des Sciences* and the State 40–2
Societies in other countries 42
Teaching and research 42–3
Science in the universities 43–4
The new German universities 44–5
Diffusion of scientific knowledge: journals and other publications . . 45–7
Emphasis on measurement; Political Arithmetic 47–8
An aggregate of autonomous movements 48
Advances in mechanics and related branches of mathematics . . . 49
The Newtonian–Cartesian debate 49–50
Newtonian physics attacked by Leibniz and Berkeley 50–1
Spread of Newtonian ideas 51–2
Astronomy; optics; sound 52–3
Chemistry: 'phlogiston' 53–4
Improvement in instruments and apparatus 54–5
The calculus: Newton and Leibniz 55
Biological sciences in search of theoretical principles 55–6
Collection and classification in botany and zoology 56–8
Ray and Tournefort 58
The 'sovereign order' of Linnaeus 58–60
Geology: fossils and the Flood 60–1
Evolutionary ideas; Maupertuis, Buffon, and the microscope . . . 62–4
Rival theories of reproduction and heredity 64–5
Physiological experiment and its competing models: Réaumur, Hales, Boerhaave
and von Haller 65–7
Technology 67
Problem of longitude at sea 67–8
The New Husbandry 68–9
Organization of manpower 69
Inventions 69–70
Science and society: the 'scientific revolution' 70–1

CHAPTER III

CULTURAL CHANGE IN WESTERN EUROPE

I. TENDENCIES IN THOUGHT AND LITERATURE

By W. H. BARBER, *Professor of French Literature in the University of London*

Anglo-French co-dominance 72
Spain and Italy 72–3

CONTENTS

Germany . . . . *page* 73–4
The Netherlands 74–5
Russia 75
The reading public 75–6
Academies and journals 76
The *salon* and the coffee-house 76–7
International contacts 77–8
Publication and distribution of books 78
Orthodox literary canons 78
Classical standards in England 79
French literature: ancients and moderns 79
'Reason' 80–1
Aristocratic conceptions 81–2
Effect of rationalist attitude 82–3
Effect of scientific thought 83–4
The growing prestige of science 84–5
The religious motive in popular science 85
Science and metaphysics 85–6
Historical scholarship 86–7
Scepticism 88
Biblical criticism 88–9
Restoration comedy of manners 89–90
The prose portrait 90–1
Towards the novel 91–2
The philosophical approach 92–3
Fénelon 93
The periodical essay 93–4
French drama 94–5
Contacts with the wider world 95
Narratives of travel 95–6
Oriental studies 96–7
The invented travel narratives 97–8
Contacts with non-Christian religions 98–9
The Noble Savage 99–100
Repercussions on political thought 100–1

2. MUSIC, 1661–1752

By FREDERICK W. STERNFELD, *Fellow of Exeter College and Lecturer in Music in the University of Oxford*

Early histories of music 101–2
Later histories 102–3
Absolute and programmatic music 103–4
Public concerts 104–5
Music printing and publishing 105
Opera at the court of France; Lully's *tragédies lyriques* . . . 105–7
Handel in London; oratorio 107–8
Lully's influence 108–9
The opera at Venice and Naples 109
The orchestra 110
The libretto: Zeno and Metastasio 110–12
Alessandro Scarlatti 112–13

CONTENTS

Purcell. . . . . *page* 113–14
English attitudes to opera 114–15
Purely instrumental compositions: overtures and concertos . . . 115–16
Johann Sebastian Bach 116–18

CHAPTER IV

RELIGION AND THE RELATIONS OF
CHURCH AND STATE

By THE REVEREND J. MCMANNERS, *Professor of History in the
University of Leicester*

The threat of Catholic domination 119–20
Growth of the spirit of toleration 120–1
Isolation of Geneva 121–2
Religious freedom in Holland 122–3
Limits of toleration in England 123
'Reasonable' religion 124
The right to resist tyranny 124–6
The English bishops 126
Church and State in England 126–7
Missionary enterprise: Protestant, Orthodox, Catholic 128
Jesuit, Capuchin and Franciscan in the New World 128–9
The Far East; the Jesuits at Peking and the Propaganda in Rome . . . 129–30
Relations between the papacy and rulers; papal elections 130–1
Regalism in Spain and the Spanish Indies 131
Gallican liberties 131–2
Jansenism at Port-Royal 132
Unigenitus 132–3
Political Jansenism 133–4
'Jansenists' outside France; the Church of Utrecht 134–6
Intellectual tensions 136–7
A crisis within Christianity 137–8
Reason and revelation: scepticism and fideism 138–9
'Natural' morality 139
Biblical criticism 140
Oecumenical scholarship 140–1
Bossuet 141
Religion and Science: the Creation 141–2
Predestination 142–3
The problem of evil 143–4
Religion and the arts 144–5
Ethical stereotypes; the 'Christian hero' in England 145–6
The 'honnête homme' in France 146–7
Madame Guyon and the conference of Issy: the Quietist controversy . . . 147
Bossuet and Fénelon 147–9
Quietism and Quakerism 149–50
Faith and Works: German Pietism 150–1
Pietism and education 151
The State and moral standards in England 151–2
Christian principles in the economic world: Baxter and Steele . . . 152–3
Compromises 153

CONTENTS

CHAPTER V

INTERNATIONAL RELATIONS IN EUROPE

By ANDREW LOSSKY, *Professor of History in the University of California, Los Angeles*

Tripartite division of Europe	*page* 154–5
Britain in Europe	155
The principle of 'balance of power' and its origins	155–7
Applications of the principle; the northern balance	157–8
South-eastern Europe	158–9
Equilibrium in Italy: the place of Savoy in 1713	159
The problem of the Spanish monarchy	159
France and Spain	159–60
France and the Italian States	160
France and the Netherlands	160–1
Louis XIV and the papacy	161–2
William III and the Mediterranean	162
The Austrian Habsburgs in Italy	162–3
Diplomatic rivalries at Turin and Lisbon	163–4
Humiliations of the papacy	164
Consequences of Italian disequilibrium	165
The western powers and the German princes	165–6
The Emperor's influence	166
Bavaria and Cologne: the Wittelsbachs	167
Effects on the structure of the Empire	167
'Europe' and 'Christendom'	167–8
Influence of dynastic ties	168–9
Legitimist sentiment and aid to rebels	169
The hierarchy of States; diplomatic etiquette	169–70
Methods of negotiation	170–1
Difficulties of coalitions and of mediation	171–2
The art of diplomacy	172–3
International law and diplomatic procedure	173
Contraband and neutral rights	174–5
Conventions between belligerents	175
William III's control of foreign policy; Heinsius and Marlborough	176–7
Vienna's delays	177
Louis XIV's methods and the development of the *Affaires Etrangères*	177–8
Communications, codes and ciphers	178–9
Ambassadors, envoys and residents	179–80
The cost of being an ambassador	180–2
Collecting information: secret agents	182–3
'Gratifications' and subsidies	183–4
The efficacy of gifts and pensions much exaggerated	184–5
The protection of nationals: consuls	185–6
Increasing importance of commerce in diplomacy	186–7
Economic motives not decisive	187
William III and commercial interests	187–8
Religious motives in international affairs	188–9
Louis XIV as defender of the Catholic faith	189
Louis XIV and William III compared: basic assumptions and views of the world	190–1
William and 'the liberty of all Europe'	192

CONTENTS

CHAPTER VI
THE ENGLISH REVOLUTION
By E. S. De Beer, c.b.e., d.litt., f.b.a.

Significance of English constitutional dispute in European politics . . *page* 193
Charles II and the House of Commons; the borough charters 193–4
Character of James II 194–5
Changes of ministers 195
James II and Louis XIV 195–6
The Parliament of 1685; situation of the English Catholics 196
Army commissions granted to Catholics 196
The standing army enlarged 197
James II and the Church of England 197–8
James II and William of Orange 198
Dijkvelt's embassy to England, 1687 198–9
The Declaration of Indulgence of April 1687 199
Preparations for a new parliament 199
William's predicament and decision to invade 200
The Seven Bishops acquitted 201
The invitation to William, July 1688 201
Birth of an heir to the throne 201–2
William perfects his invasion plans; German princes, Dutch provinces . . 202
Louis XIV and the Cologne election 202–3
William's declaration of 10 October 203–4
James II's attempts to reverse his policy 204
The landing at Torbay on 15 November 204
James leaves England 205–6
The Convention Parliament 206
The constitutional problems 206–7
William and Mary as joint sovereigns 207
The Declaration of Rights: William III and English institutions 208
William III's character 208–9
The Nonjurors 209
The Toleration Act 210
Freedom of the press by default 210–11
The state of Scotland: William and Mary accepted 211–12
Church and State in Scotland; growth of Scottish separatism . . . 212–13
The state of Ireland 213
The battle of Ireland; Treaty of Limerick (October 1691) 213–14
William III and the English parties 214–15
Discontent in England: the Whigs in power 215–16
The Revolution in political thought; theories of kingship 216–18
French absolutism attacked and defended: Jurieu 218
Locke's *Two Treatises of Government* 219–20
A conservative revolution 220
Increasing influence of English thought 220–2

CONTENTS

CHAPTER VII

THE NINE YEARS WAR, 1688–1697

By Sir George Clark, D.Litt., F.B.A., *Fellow of All Souls College, Oxford*

A question of nomenclature. . . . . *page* 223
Strategic advance and military growth of France since treaties of Nymegen. . 223–4
Importance of Cologne and Liège: a disputed election 224–5
The French invade the Rhineland 225
French diplomatic calculations: fall of Belgrade; James II 225–6
William of Orange in England 226
War declared against the United Provinces: the alignment of forces in the Empire 226–7
Bearings of the Turkish war on the West 227–8
The Austrian army 228
The Dutch and British armed forces 228–9
Characteristics of the fighting and war aims 229–30
Restraints on operations; war casualties 230–1
Differences between the belligerents in discipline, training and equipment . . 231–2
Operations in the Rhineland, autumn 1688 232
The importance of the Spanish Netherlands; war declared on Spain, April 1689 232–3
Devastation of the Palatinate 233
The Emperor, the Turks and the Maritime Powers in 1689 233–4
British and Dutch co-operation: naval agreements 234
Extension of belligerent rights at sea 234–5
British and Dutch attitudes to conquests in America 235
The French in Catalonia, May 1689 235
King James in Ireland, March 1689 235–6
French naval initiative; William III and sea power 236
Opening of the Irish campaign; the siege of Londonderry 236–7
French reverses in the Rhineland 237
William III's 'congress' at The Hague; Habsburg influence in Germany . . 237–8
Savoy: Victor Amadeus II between France and the Allies 238
The prospects for 1690; William III goes to Ireland in June . . . 238
French victory at Fleurus in July 239
Tourville fails to exploit victory off Beachy Head on 10 July . . . 239–40
The Boyne, 11 July: King James returns to France 240
Savoy joins the Allies: the battle at Staffarda, 18 August 240–1
The Turks recover Belgrade: effect on the German war 241
Sweden and Denmark assert neutral rights at sea 241
1691: end of Irish campaign 241–2
William III in the Spanish Netherlands; fall of Mons in April . . . 242
Operations elsewhere; Catinat takes Nice 242–3
The strain on French resources; death of Louvois 243
French plans to invade England: La Hougue to Barfleur, 29 May–3 June . . 243–4
French privateers 244
Luxembourg captures Namur in June; battle of Steenkerk, 3 August . . 244–5
1692: French superiority on the Rhine; abortive invasion of France from Savoy. 245
Loosening of the Grand Alliance; Swedish offers of mediation . . . 245–6
1693: The Smyrna convoy; William defeated at Landen-Neerwinden, 29 July . 246–7
French successes in Catalonia and Piedmont 247
1694: French on the defensive in all theatres except Catalonia . . . 247–8
Failure of Allied landing near Brest in June 248

CONTENTS

Naval operations in the Mediterranean: William orders Russell to winter there *page* 248–9
1695: Campaign in the Netherlands: William recaptures Namur in September . 249
Peace-feelers: Callières at Maastricht 249–50
1696: abortive plans to invade England 250
The Treaty of Turin (29 August) and the neutralization of Italy in October; effects
   in the Balkans and in Spain 250–1
Financial exhaustion of both sides 251
War in North America and the Caribbean, 1689–97 251
1697: French advances in the Netherlands and capture of Barcelona, 10 August 252
The Peace of Ryswick, 20 September–30 October 252–3
Recognition of William III by Louis XIV 253

CHAPTER VIII

THE EMERGENCE OF GREAT BRITAIN AS A WORLD POWER

By the late DAVID OGG, *Fellow of New College, Oxford*

Transformation of Britain between 1660 and 1714 254
English and French war-making resources compared 254–5
The Jacobite menace 255
Ireland and Scotland 255–6
The French use of Ireland and Scotland 256–7
England's natural advantages 257–8
The human element: social change in the countryside 258
A wide range of craft skills; 'the poor' 259–60
The fiscal factor and economic policy 260–1
The balance of trade and the chartered companies 261–2
London 262
The 'new rich' and new luxuries 262
The status of women 263
Predominance of southern England 263
The Revolution survives 263–4
A régime of toleration: religion, treason and blasphemy . . . 264–5
The judges: Sir John Holt 265
Limitations on the prerogative 265–6
The control of foreign policy 266–7
The importance of the Act of Settlement 267
Towards cabinet government; the Junto 267–8
Queen Anne's ministers: Godolphin and the Marlboroughs . . . 268–9
Queen Anne turns to the Tories: Dr Sacheverell 269–70
Harley and Bolingbroke, their characters and political outlook . . . 270–1
Death of Queen Anne and succession of George I; the 'Fifteen' . . . 271–2
Composition of the House of Commons 272–3
Whigs and Tories 273–5
Tory opposition to full-scale hostilities 274–5
The Union with Scotland: Scottish parties 275–6
The Estates of Scotland throw down the gauntlet 276–7
Negotiations for union; the treaty of 1706, ratified in 1707 277–8
Consequences of the Union; Highlanders and Lowlanders . . . 278–9
The Augustan Age in England; the new journalism 279–80
Attacks on Marlborough 280
Swift as a pamphleteer: *The Conduct of the Allies* 280–1
The liberalism of Defoe 281–2
Addison's eulogy: an enlarged and unified Britain 282–3

CONTENTS

CHAPTER IX

WAR FINANCE, 1689–1714

By P. G. M. Dickson, *Fellow of St Catherine's College and Lecturer in Modern History in the University of Oxford*, and John Sperling, *Associate Professor in Humanities, San José State College, California*

Neglect of the financial side of war . . . . *page* 284–5
The English financial system before and after 1688 285
Mounting war expenditure 285–6
Limitations of tax revenue 286
Long-term borrowing; the Tontine of 1693 286–7
Excessive reliance on short-dated borrowing; depression of credit by 1697 . . 287
Lottery loans and long annuities; the lenders 287
Technical developments in the City of London: the insurance market . . 288–9
The Bank of England and the Exchequer: tallies 289–90
Waning of public credit in 1696 290
The Bank saves the situation 290–1
Origin and development of Exchequer Bills 291–2
Over-issue of bills by Navy and Victualling Boards: the South Sea Scheme . 292
Problem of remitting money to 'the forces abroad': several false starts . . 292–3
Bank of England office at Antwerp; competing syndicates 293
Godolphin's exchange system survives the Spanish Succession War . . 293–4
Defects of public finance in the United Provinces 294
Financial machinery of the central government; federal revenue . . . 294–5
The military budget and naval finance 295–6
Cost of two wars chiefly met by increasing provincial contributions . . 296
Direct and indirect taxes in the province of Holland 296–7
Growth of public debt in Holland; loan facilities at Amsterdam . . . 297–8
France: the *Contrôle Général*; strength and weaknesses of Colbert's example . 298–9
Scale of war expenditure; direct and indirect taxes 299–300
Long-term loans and sales of offices 300–1
Types of short-dated bills; their over-issue after 1704 301–2
Dearth of specie 302–3
Foreign remittances: the experience of Huguetan 303–4
Samuel Bernard's system: Protestant bankers and the Payments of Lyons . . 304–5
Crisis of 1709; Desmarets and the Caisse Legendre 305
Deficiencies in Habsburg financial organization 305–6
Estimates of revenue and expenditure 306–7
Limits to dishonouring commitments; transference of military obligations . . 307
Loans on Dutch market and from England 307–8
Internal borrowing: great nobles and Jewish financiers; Samuel Oppenheimer . 308–10
Financial crisis of 1703; proposals for a State Bank 310–11
Ineffectiveness of the Imperial *Banco del Giro* (1703) 311
Success of Vienna City Bank (1706); funding operations 311–13
Unprecedented scale of government expenditure 1689–1714: comparative fiscal records 313
Cost and efficiency of State borrowing: comparisons between countries . . 313–14
International elements 314
Social and economic consequences of war finance 314–15

CONTENTS

CHAPTER X

THE CONDITION OF FRANCE, 1688–1715

By JEAN MEUVRET, *Director of Studies at the Ecole Pratique des Hautes Etudes, Paris*

Louis XIV his own first minister after 1691 . . . . . . *page* 316
More obedience to government by 1688 316–17
Colbert's concern with short-term needs; tax abuses 317–18
The reorganization of 1661–88 in other branches of administration . . . 318–19
Two instruments of power: the intendants and the army 319
Limitations of the royal power; its opportunism 319–20
A stagnant economy: corn prices. 320
Economy distorted by demands of war; the circulation of money . . . 320–1
The crisis of 1693–4 321–2
Movement of corn prices after 1694 and the famine of 1709 . . . 322–3
Repercussions of food scarcity 323
Financial makeshifts of the Crown 323–4
Riots; the contribution of salt-smuggling to violence 324–5
The Camisard rebellion in Languedoc, 1702–4 325
The army as an element of disorder; characteristics of recruitment . . . 325–6
Criticism of royal policy; the influence of Beauvillier, Chevreuse and Madame de
  Maintenon 326–7
Fénelon's ideas on reform: 'Letter to Louis XIV' (1693/4) and *Télémaque* (1699) 327–9
Other critics: Boisguilbert's economic analysis; Vauban's fiscal proposals . . 329–31
The Controllers-General from 1689 to 1715 331
The *capitation* and the *dixième*; reasons for partial failure 332–3
Social forces: the clergy and the increasing authority of the bishops . . . 333
Gallicanism and the new Jansenism 333–4
The Parlements 334–5
The Provincial Estates 335–6
The financiers: Legendre, Bernard, the Paris family 336–7
International contacts of the 'new converts': the Crown and the Huguenots . 337–8
Proliferation of offices for sale 338
The administrative nobility; social distances in general 338–9
Prospects of social advancement 339–40
Importance of the larger towns; the Parisian *mondain*. 340–1
A shift in mental attitudes 341–2
Growing cosmopolitanism and sense of cultural superiority. . . . 342

CHAPTER XI

THE SPANISH EMPIRE UNDER FOREIGN PRESSURES, 1688–1715

By the late ROLAND DENNIS HUSSEY, *Professor of History in the University of California, Los Angeles*, and J. S. BROMLEY

The question of decline 343–4
Towards recovery; foreign elements in the population. 345
Public finance; the Church 346–7
The seigneurial system and the grandees 347–8
Shifting cabals at the court of Carlos II; his character. 348–9
Overseas possessions: the Philippines, the Canaries, the Indies . . . 349

CONTENTS

Foreign penetration: contraband, piracy, the Asiento . . . . . *page* 349–50
Territorial threats in North, Central and South America 350
Second marriage of Carlos II (1689): Maria Anna of Pfalz-Neuberg . . . 350–1
The new queen's increasing influence: dismissal of Oropesa. 351
Austrophils and Francophils: importance of the *Despacho Universal* . . . 351–2
Government economies and other reforms 352
Max Emmanuel of Bavaria and the hereditary government of the Spanish
   Netherlands 352–3
Administrative reorganization: the *Junta dos Tenientes* (1693) 353
Proposals to curb the Inquisition, 1696 353–4
The Nine Years War overseas: *flotas, galeones,* corsairs 354
Skirmishes in Hispaniola; Anglo-Spanish attack on Saint-Domingue, 1695. . 354–5
Cartagena captured by Pointis and Ducasse, 1697 355–6
Defensive counter-measures and missionary expansion in the Indies: California,
   Amazonia, the Philippines 356–7
Catalonia in the Nine Years War 357
Franco-Austrian rivalry at Madrid: Cardinal Portocarrero and the queen . . 357–8
First Partition Treaty; anti-Habsburg manifestations in Madrid 358
Hostilities in north Africa; the French in the South Sea and Louisiana . . 359–60
The 'Darien Company' of 1695: the Scots in Darien 1698–1700 360
Second Partition Treaty: Carlos wills his kingdoms to Philip of Anjou . . 360–1
Death of Carlos II (1 November 1700): Louis XIV accepts the will . . . 361
Philip V in Madrid: attitudes of the grandees and of Aragonese realms . . 361–2
Reactions in Catalonia and Valencia 362
Philip's character. 362–3
The problems he had to face; constitutional diversity 363
Louis XIV at first displays tact towards Spain 363–4
Growth of French trading in the Indies: the Asiento 364–5
Increasing French influence: Jean Orry sent to Spain in 1701 365
Orry proposes a French-style administration; his financial reforms . . . 365–6
Renovation of the Spanish army 366–7
Marriage of Philip to Maria Luisa of Savoy (1701); influence of the princess
   des Ursins 367
Philip in Saragossa, Barcelona and Naples, 1701–3 368
Maria Luisa as Lieutenant of the Realm; her popularity in Madrid . . . 368–9
French disputes at Madrid: Louis XIV recalls Orry and Madame des Ursins, 1704 369
Reinstatement of Madame des Ursins and Orry, 1705 369–70
Portocarrero retired; appointments of Amelot and Grimaldo 370
Catalonia and Valencia in revolt after the arrival of Archduke Charles on
   22 August 1705 370–1
Criticism of 'Charles III' 371
1706: Philip temporarily evacuates Madrid; second recall of Orry . . . 371–2
The war overseas; French convoy protection; Campeche, the Canaries, Florida,
   Colonia do Sacramento 372
The Manila galleon: Dampier and Woodes Rogers 372–3
After Almanza (1707): destruction of the Aragonese *fueros* 373–4
Breach between Spain and France: the peace-talks of 1709 374–5
Resistance to French economic pressures 375–6
Breach with Rome, 1709 376
Philip and the peace negotiations; the return of Orry in 1713 . . . 376–7
End of the old system of government in Spain 377
Death of Queen Maria Luisa in February 1714 377–8

CONTENTS

Church and State: Melchor de Macanaz and the Inquisition . . . *page* 378
Fall of Barcelona in September 1714: Berwick's rule in Catalonia . . . 378–9
Settlement of Catalan government, 1715–17. 379–80
Philip's marriage to Elizabeth Farnese opens a new era 380

CHAPTER XII

FROM THE NINE YEARS WAR TO
THE WAR OF THE SPANISH SUCCESSION

By Sir George Clark

Ryswick treaties in reality an armistice 381
Max Emmanuel in the Spanish Netherlands; Dutch garrisons 381–2
Weakness of the Spanish forces 382
Run-down of Dutch and English armies 382–3
Austrian and French forces not substantially affected 383
The difference between 1698 and 1688 383–4
Much dependent on the death of Carlos II; the Spanish attitude . . . 384
Attitudes of the Maritime Powers and of the House of Habsburg . . . 384–5
French interests in Spain and her possessions 385
The Spanish succession: legal issues and the claimants 385–6
The Habsburg interest; the secret partition of 1668 386–8
The Bavarian claim 388
Dutch supporters of partition 388
Preliminary moves for a revised partition; Tallard in London, 1698 . . . 388–9
Policy of Louis XIV: military dispositions in southern France . . . 389–90
Position of Max Emmanuel and Bergeyck's plans for Ostend . . . 390–1
William III's proposals; the slurs on his motives 391–3
First Partition Treaty, 11 October 1698: its merits 393–4
The death of Joseph Ferdinand of Bavaria (February 1699) . . . 394
The new situation 394–5
A balance between France and Austria 395
Second Partition Treaty, 25 March 1700; Leopold I prepares for war . . . 395–6
Philip of Anjou made heir to Carlos II: Portocarrero and the pope . . 396–7
Louis XIV accepts the will on 10 November 1700 397
Philip V recognized in Milan and Brussels 397
1701: French military measures 397–8
French troops admitted into the Spanish Netherlands: withdrawal of the Dutch
and of Max Emmanuel 398–9
Archbishop Joseph Clement of Cologne and his chapter 399–400
Philip V recognized by the United Provinces and England, February–April 1701 400
The English parliament persuaded by William III; the emperor's position . . 401
Competition for allies in Germany between Leopold I and Louis XIV . . 401–2
Outbreak of the Great Northern War: the Peace of Travendal, 18 August 1700 402–3
The emperor determined to withstand French claims 403
1701: French troops in north Italy (January); attitudes of Italian States . . 403
Military and naval preparations in the west; attitudes of German States . . 404–5
Austrians in Italy: Eugene defeats Catinat and Villeroi 405
Marlborough and the Treaty of the Grand Alliance (7 September) . . . 406
Franco-Polish negotiations broken off 406
German accessions to the Grand Alliance 406–7
Portuguese treaties with France and Spain (June) 407

CONTENTS

Louis XIV recognizes the Old Pretender (September) and proposes cession of
Spanish Netherlands (30 October) . . . . *page* 408
1702: the emperor's uncertain strategy: preference for a Mediterranean war . 408–9
Death of William III on 19 March; declarations of war, 8 April–15 May . . 409

CHAPTER XIII

THE WAR OF THE SPANISH SUCCESSION IN EUROPE

By A. J. VEENENDAAL, *formerly Secretary of the State Commission for
Dutch History at The Hague*

Aims of the Grand Alliance. 410
German States and the Alliance 410–11
Strength of Allied forces in 1702 411–12
French advantages 412
Situation in the Spanish Netherlands: reforms of Count Bergeyck . . . 412–13
Support for Louis XIV in the Empire: Bavaria and Cologne 413–14
William III's continental policy continued under Queen Anne . . . 414
Effects of William's death on the United Provinces; Dutch war aims . . . 415
Problem of the supreme command: Marlborough 415–16
Initial successes of the Allies on Rhine and Meuse, 1702–3 416
Marlborough's preference for a mobile strategy frustrated by the Dutch . . 416–17
1703: Villars breaks through to Bavaria; Tyrol attacked on two sides . . 417
The war in north Italy; Savoy joins the Allies 417–18
Cadiz and Vigo, 1702; Portugal joins the Alliance: the Methuen treaties (May–
December 1703) 418–19
Anglo-Dutch interdict on trade with Spain and France (1703–4) . . . 419–20
1704: the threat to Vienna; Marlborough's march to the Danube: Blenheim
(13 August) 420–2
Stalemate in the Netherlands and north Italy 422
Opening of Allied campaign in Spain (March): Gibraltar captured on 3 August . 422–3
The battle of Malaga on 24 August 423
1705: Emperor Joseph I, Bavaria and Transylvania 423–4
Marlborough's abortive Moselle advance; differences between Marlborough
and the Dutch 424
The plight of Savoy; Barcelona capitulates on 14 October to the Allies . . 425
Louis XIV's first secret peace offers rejected 425–6
1706: Ramillies (23 May) and the Belgian revolution 426–7
The Dutch Barrier; Marlborough and the government of the south Netherlands. 427
Anglo-Dutch Condominium in the south Netherlands; the upper Rhine . 428
The relief of Turin (7 September) and French retreat across the Alps . . 428–9
Allies' successes in Spain followed by evacuation of Madrid . . . 429–30
Favourable position of the Allies: 'No peace without Spain' . . . 430–1
Frustration of Dutch Barrier diplomacy 431
1707: Charles XII in Saxony: Marlborough goes to Altranstädt in April . . 431–2
Sterile campaign in the Netherlands; Villars forces the Lines of Stollhofen . . 432
The Austrians move into Naples 432–3
Allied failure before Toulon (22 August) and defeat at Almanza (25 April) . 433
1708: English successes—Sardinia and Minorca 433–4
Austrian reinforcements for Catalonia. 434
Netherlands the principal war theatre: Oudenarde (11 July) . . . 435
The murderous siege of Lille: fall of the citadel on 9 December . . . 435–6

CONTENTS

1709: failure of peace negotiations . . . . *page* 436–7
Louis XIV appeals to his people; Malplaquet (11 September) a pyrrhic victory . 437–8
Allies on the defensive in Spain 438
Anglo-Dutch Treaty of Succession and Barrier of 29 October: resentments aroused by it 438–9
1710: failure of further peace negotiations (March–July) 439–40
The 'Ne Plus Ultra Lines'; Allied *débâcle* in Spain 440
Tory government in England: a new foreign policy 440–1
1711: the invasion of France again frustrated 441–2
Negotiations between St John and Torcy 441
Disavowal of the Barrier Treaty 442
Swift's *The Conduct of the Allies*; Anglo-Dutch recriminations . . . 442–3
1712: Congress meets at Utrecht, 29 January: the British 'restraining orders' of 21 May 443
The Dutch defeated by Villars at Denain on 24 July 443–4
1713: the new Barrier and the Peace of Utrecht (March–April) . . . 444
1714: Treaties of Rastatt and Baden 444
The fate of Catalonia 444–5
1715: the Third Barrier Treaty (15 November) 445

CHAPTER XIV

THE PACIFICATION OF UTRECHT

By H. G. PITT, *Fellow of Worcester College and Lecturer in Modern History in the University of Oxford*

Early movements towards peace, 1706–8 446–7
Differences about Spain: change in French attitude 447–8
Attitude of Whigs: Britain and Austria opposed to partition . . . 448
Pressure put on the Dutch in return for a Barrier 448
Conflicting aims of the powers: the Preliminaries of 1709 448–9
Lack of a coherent policy in Vienna; Wratislaw's Italian policy . . . 449–50
The negotiations of March–May 1709: Dutch demands stepped up . . 450–1
French concessions; the question of compensation for Philip V . . . 451–2
The 4th and 37th articles rejected by France; causes of misunderstanding . 453–4
Vienna's intransigence. 454–5
Significance of the first Barrier Treaty: a diplomatic triumph for the English . 455
Further negotiations at Mardyck and Geertruidenberg (1710) . . . 456
Break-up of Godolphin's ministry the turning-point 456–7
War-weariness brings support to St John's policy; the English press . . 457–8
Secret Anglo-French *pourparlers* begin in August 1710: the propositions of April 1711 458–9
The Mesnager Convention of 8 October 1711 459–60
Dutch reluctantly accept this as a basis 460
Parliament approves the Convention 460–1
The Congress of Utrecht: agreement between Britain and France the deciding factor 461
The 'Specific Demands' of the Allies: British and Dutch 462
Emperor's refusal to consider partition of the Spanish inheritance . . 462–3
Possibility of Philip V inheriting French crown: Philip's attitude . . 463–4
Deterioration in Anglo-Dutch relations: trading rights and the Barrier . 464–5
The claims of Prussia: Upper Guelderland and Neuchâtel 465–6
Portuguese gains and disappointments 466

CONTENTS

Settlement with Savoy: Sicily and an Alpine barrier . . . . . *page* 466-7
Habsburg isolation: the emperor negotiates over Spain 467-8
French claims against Austria: the Italian princelings 468
Louis XIV removes the Old Pretender to Lorraine in February 1713 . . . 469
Parliament rejects Bolingbroke's commercial treaty with France 469-70
Britain and France settle American questions 470
Signing of peace treaties with France, 11 April 1713 470
Britain's major war aims achieved 470-1
Dutch forced to acquiesce 471
Divergences between the emperor and the German princes 471-2
Negotiations conducted between Villars and Eugene (November 1713-January 1714) 472
Treaty of Rastatt, 6 March 1714 473
The German settlement; religious divisions in the Empire 473-4
The Treaty of Baden, 7 September 1714 474
Comparative instability of the German settlement 474-5
Political and commercial negotiations between England and Spain: the Asiento . 475-6
Anglo-Spanish peace treaty signed on 13 July 1713 476
Treaty between United Provinces and Spain signed on 26 June 1713 . . . 476
Treaty between Spain and Portugal of February 1715: Colonia do Sacramento . 476
Second Anglo-Dutch Barrier Treaty, 30 January 1713 476-7
Austro-Dutch Barrier Treaty, 15 November 1715 478
Later history of the Dutch Barrier 478
Value of the pacification of Utrecht 478-9

CHAPTER XV

FRANCE AND ENGLAND IN NORTH AMERICA, 1689-1713

By PHILIP S. HAFFENDEN, *Lecturer in American History in the University of Southampton*

Repercussions of the Glorious Revolution in North America 480
The background of revolutionary disturbances; the rôle of Boston . . . 480-1
Massachusetts: a compromise with independence 481
New York: Jacob Leisler 481-2
Maryland: dissatisfaction with proprietary government 482
Virginia and East Jersey 482-3
The Massachusetts charter of 1691 483
Changes outside New England 483-4
French Canada: State and Church 484-5
Long-range control from Versailles 485
Character of French Canadians 485-6
The French and the American Indians; Frontenac 486
Failure of the Phips expedition to Quebec (1690) 487
Frontenac borrows the methods of Indian warfare 487-8
French successes in Newfoundland and Hudson's Bay 488-9
The French chastise the Iroquois and procure their neutrality (1701) . . . 489-90
The Navigation Act of 1696 and the Board of Trade 490-1
The Crown and the colonial charters 491-2
The Puritan theocracy at bay: the Salem trials; Quakers and Anglicans . . 492-3
Religion in other colonies; French and German sects 493-4
Effects of war on moral behaviour 494

CONTENTS

Education: Harvard, Yale, William and Mary . . . . . . *page* 494–5
Printing press and libraries 495
Social structure and urban consciousness 495–6
New France: social services, education and culture 496–7
The missionary frontier 497–8
The upper Mississippi and Louisiana: Jesuits and Seminarists . . . 498–9
Origins of Louisiana, 1684–98 499–500
Its early vicissitudes: the Le Moyne brothers and Crozat 500–1
The War of the Spanish Succession in New England 501–2
Vaudreuil and Dudley consider regional neutrality 502
Massachusetts fails to capture Port Royal, Acadia 502–3
Rapid changes of fortune in Newfoundland. 503
Carolinian attacks on Florida missions 503–4
Indian politics and the defence of Louisiana 504
Capture of Port Royal (October 1710) and the 'Glorious Enterprise'. . . 505
Fiasco of the Quebec expedition of 1711 505–6
Seeds of imperial disintegration; the passing of a generation . . . 506–7
American attitudes to the Peace 507–8
New France retains its vigour 508
Effects of war on population; increase of English preponderance . . . 508

CHAPTER XVI

PORTUGAL AND HER EMPIRE, 1680–1720

By V. Magalhães Godinho, *Docteur ès Lettres, Sorbonne*

Slump and boom in Portuguese Atlantic economy; the course of prices, 1668–1728 509–10
Crisis of production in Brazil: sugar, spirits, and tobacco 510–11
Restricted money supply 511
Anti-mercantile feeling: the Inquisition 511–12
Fall in re-exports. 512
Industrial investment projects and new manufactures, 1670–92 . . . 512–13
Sumptuary laws to cut down imports 513
Monetary policy: success of the revaluation decree of 1688 513–14
The slave trade: the Cacheo Company and the Asiento of 1696 . . . 514–15
Mozambique: fresh colonizing efforts 516
Goa and Macao: new East India companies merged in 1700 . . . 516–17
Revival of Eastern trade; profits and cargoes 517
The Omanis capture Mombasa (1698); the Zambesi delta 517–18
Decay of Portuguese cities in India; migrations of Indo-Portuguese . . 518–19
Trade boom during and after the Nine Years War 519–20
Extension of olive groves and vineyards 520–1
Collapse of policy of industrialization 521–2
Interests of the nobility in growth of wine exports 522
A watershed in economic policy: the cycle of port, madeira, and gold. . 523
Expansion of trade with England after 1688; significance of the Methuen treaty
of 27 December 1703 523–4
A strictly defensive foreign policy orientated towards France . . . 524
Frontier problems in the Peninsula and South America 525
Treaties with Spain and France, 18 June 1701 525
Anglo-Dutch sea power and the Methuen treaties of 16 May 1703 . . 525–6
The army in relation to a slow population rise 526–7
The ravages of war, 1704–12: food supplies 527–8

CONTENTS

Shrinkage of silver supply; contradictory results of Succession War . . *page* 528
Brazil: the Buenos Aires trade before and after 1670; convoys to Lisbon . . 528–9
Expansion in Brazil: Colonia do Sacramento, 1680–1715 529–30
Developments in Amazonia: the Maranhão and Gran Pará 530
The Jesuits in Upper Amazonia; the French of Cayenne 531
Cattle-raising and the penetration of the interior 531–2
The great cattle domains: growth of the leather trade 532
Expeditions from São Paulo: the bandeirantes in quest of gold 532–3
Systematic exploration of the interior from 1674; the gold rush after 1700 . . 533–4
The export of Brazilian gold, 1699–1755 534–5
European destinations of Brazilian gold 535
Renewed fall in Portuguese price levels, 1712–30, and new attempts to foster
  industry 535–6
Crown revenues before and after 1716; a mercantile monarchy 536–7
Landed wealth and the religious Orders 536
The wealth of the nobility 537–8
Forms of property and of rights over the land and its produce 538–9
State and society in Portugal 539–40

CHAPTER XVII

THE MEDITERRANEAN

By JEAN MATHIEX, *Agrégé de l'Université, Paris*

Unity and diversity; eastern and western Mediterranean 540
Coastal traffic and innumerable ports; shipping hazards 540–1
Populations of cities 541–2
Cadiz, Leghorn, Genoa, Marseilles 542–3
Plague: a stern quarantine system 543
Corsairs, Muslim and Christian 543–4
The power of Algiers: prizes and prisoners; the redemption of slaves . . . 544–5
France and the Barbary Regencies; Christian corsairs; Malta 545–6
Privateers and merchantmen; neutral flags 546–7
Naval forces a limited deterrent 547–8
Economy of the Mediterranean; corn trade; imports and exports . . . 548
Muslim overland trade-routes 548–9
The Levant trade; the Capitulations and consular organization . . . 549–50
English, Dutch and French in the Levant; French Barbary companies . . 550–1
The balance of East–West trade; Levantine industries 551
The means of payment; the specie trade; cloth exports 551–2
The French lead by 1715–20 552–3
The empires of Spain and Turkey: methods of rule compared 553–4
Morocco under the Sultan Muley Ismael 554
The decline of former Mediterranean powers: Venice 554–6
Changing nature of Venetian economy; the *terraferma* 556
Spanish dominions in Italy: Naples and Sicily, the Milanese . . . 556–8
The culture of Naples; music and the arts 558–9
The achievement of Victor Amadeus II of Savoy 559–60
Limited resources of Piedmont–Savoy 560
Administrative, fiscal and legal reforms; the royal supremacy 560–1
Negative aspects of reform in Piedmont–Savoy 561–2
Shipbuilding in the Mediterranean: the Ottomans and Venice . . . 562
Naval manpower and galley slaves; the French galley corps 562–3

CONTENTS

The uses of the galley: its passing . . . . *page* 564–5
Collapse of Spanish sea power 565
The revival of Ottoman sea power: Mezzomorto 565–6
The irruption of English sea power: Gibraltar 566–7
The French navy in the Nine Years War: Toulon and Brest . . . 567–8
The Anglo-Dutch in the Mediterranean, 1694–6: the balance-sheet . . 568–9
The Mediterranean and the Partition Treaties 569
The War of the Spanish Succession in the Mediterranean 569–70
Spain's losses mainly attributable to defeats on land 570
The Allies fail to exploit naval superiority; the Camisards 570–1
Naval war subsidiary to war on land; French commercial supremacy . . . 571
From Mediterranean to Atlantic power rivalries 571

CHAPTER XVIII

THE AUSTRIAN HABSBURGS

By J. W. STOYE, *Fellow of Magdalen College and Senior Lecturer in
Modern History in the University of Oxford*

Court and government in the Hofburg 572
Vienna: burghers and noblemen 572–3
The growth of autocracy: the central treasury and the court chancery . . 573
Resistance to autocracy: the Estates and office-holders 573–4
The defects of government at the centre: overlapping committees . . . 574–5
Habsburg devotion to the Catholic Church and to 'Our House'. . . . 575–6
Conflicts of priority between widely scattered hereditary claims . . . 576
The reconquest of Hungary, 1685–8 576–7
Strength of the Habsburg position in the Balkans by 1689 577–8
Pressure from western Europe 578–9
Conflict between two fronts; breakdown of peace talks with the Turks . . 579
Habsburg thrusts into Macedonia and Rumania 579–80
Revival of Turkish power in 1690; military deadlock after 1691 . . . 580
The battle of Zenta (11 September 1697) and the Peace of Carlowitz (1699) . 580–1
Habsburg government in the newly conquered lands; population movements . 581–2
Transylvania: Michael Apafi surrenders his title, 1697 582
Hungary: the policy of Cardinal Kollonich 582–3
Taxation leads to peasant unrest 583
The Hungarian rebellion of 1703: Rákóczi and Berczényi 583–4
Rákóczi's military successes and recognition by the Transylvanians . . 584–5
Suppression of the rebellion: battles of Zsibó (November 1705) and Trenčin
(August 1708) 585
The peace settlement at Szatmár and the Diet of 1712–15 585–6
Relations between the emperors and the German princes 586–7
The influence of Habsburg patronage in western and central Germany . . 587–8
Shadowy character of the Imperial authority itself 588
Bavaria before and after Blenheim 588–9
Habsburg and Wittelsbach 589–90
Friction with Brandenburg–Prussia and friendship with Hanover . . 590
Forward policy in Italy: the Spanish succession 590–1
Habsburg reluctance to embark on hostilities in Spain 591
Agreements within the family on Spanish partition, 1703 592
The agreement with Victor Amadeus of Savoy, November 1703 . . . 592–3

CONTENTS

Archduke Charles between the Maritime Powers and Vienna; devotion to his
Spanish title . . . . *page* 593
Austrian campaigning in Italy, 1701–7; contributions levied on the principalities 593–4
Habsburg disputes with the papacy 594–5
Defeat of Clement XI in the War of Comacchio, 1708–9 595
The claims of Victor Amadeus in Lombardy: Habsburg distrust . . . 595–6
The attitude of Emperor Charles VI to Victor Amadeus II and Philip V . . 596–7
Austrian rule in Italy compared with the Spanish 597
Italian cultural influences at Vienna 597–8
The Austrian Netherlands: old liberties confirmed 598
The return to ambitions in the Balkans, 1716–18. 598
Economic and social conditions in the old possessions; lord and peasant in
Bohemia, Moravia and Silesia 598–600
Impact of war taxation on the agricultural classes 600
A wealthy nobility expressed in architectural magnificence 600–1
The nobility a unifying force in the Habsburg lands 601
The entrenched position of the Church and its influence 601–2
A static landlocked economy; production in the towns and on the larger estates. 602–3
A tight gild-structure; court purveyors and privileged manufactures . . 603
Government and mineral resources: the *Innerberger Hauptgewerkschaft* . . 603–4
Development of trade with south-east Europe: the policy of Charles VI . 604–5
Importance of Silesia; shifts in trade-routes of the Austrian lands . . 605–6
Projects of economic reform frustrated before 1714 606–7
Charles VI loses interest in them after 1720. 607

CHAPTER XIX

THE RETREAT OF THE TURKS, 1683–1730

By A. N. KURAT, *Professor of History in the University of Ankara,*
and J. S. BROMLEY

Extent of the Ottoman empire and its administrative divisions 608
Contraction in Asia; Mesopotamia, Syria and Lebanon 608–9
Importance of Egypt: political clans and military insurrections 609–10
The Red Sea and the Black Sea; Tatars and Cossacks 610
Frontier defence and the system of fortresses 610
Communications; internal and external commerce 610–12
Industrial crafts: gildsmen and janissaries 612
Town and country; the growth of tax-farms 612–13
A stagnant agriculture and peasant migration 613
Military manpower, territorial and professional; the janissaries and other corps. 613–14
The navy: galleys and sailing-ships 615
Sultan and grand vizier; importance of the efendis 615–16
Influence of the ulema; the intrigues of the Seraglio 616–17
Self-criticism and the distrust of western influences 617
The Patriarchate of Constantinople 617–18
Religion, race and poverty 618
1683: the retreat from Vienna; the Holy League of 1684 618–19
The struggle for Hungary; fall of Nové Zamky (1685) and of Buda (1686) . . 619
Turks driven out of the Morea (1685–7); the defeat at Nagyharsány (12 August
1687) 620
Army revolt of 8 November 1687 and the dethronement of Mehmed IV . . 620–1
1688: the Austrians capture Peterwardein and Belgrade; failure of peace parleys 621

CONTENTS

The crisis of 1689 and Fazil Mustafa Pasha: a turn in the tide . . . *page* 621–2
The slaughter at Zálankemén (19 August 1691) and attempts at mediation . . 622–3
The Venetians in Chios, 1694–5 623
Resilience of Ottoman war effort; financial dislocation and social evils . . 623–5
Russian attacks on Azov, 1695–6; their implications 625–6
The battle of Zenta (1697) and the agreements at Carlowitz (26 January 1699) . 626
Many-sided significance of the Peace 626–7
Threats of Venice and Russia to the Dardanelles and Black Sea 627–8
Reforms of Hüseyn Pasha; the armed forces 628–9
Conflict between grand vizier and Mufti of Constantinople 629
'The Adrianople affair' of August 1703: abdication of Sultan Mustafa II . . 629
Character of Sultan Ahmed III: Chorlulu Ali Pasha grand vizier . . . 630
Poltava, 1709: Charles XII in Turkey 630–1
Increase in anti-Russian feeling: Devlet-Girei Khan and the Bender circle . . 631–2
Baltaji Mehmed Pasha: Turkey at war with Russia, 20 November 1710 . . 632
Tsar Peter appeals to the Balkan Christians; their relations with Moscow . . 632–3
Antagonism between Orthodox and Catholic; Moldavia and Wallachia . . 633
Russian advance to Moldavia 633–4
Russian surrender on the Pruth, 21 July 1711; criticism of Baltaji Mehmed . 634–5
Peter abandons Azov and Taganrog 635
A Greco-Turkish régime: growing influence of the Phanariots 635–6
Russia and Poland: further declarations of war by the Porte 636
Peace of Adrianople, 5 June 1713; Charles XII leaves Turkey, September 1714 . 636–7
Plans to recover the Morea from Venice: Silahdar Ali Pasha 637–8
Campaign in the Morea, 1715; Corfu threatened, 1716 638
Vienna decides to intervene: confusion in the Divan 638–9
Eugene routs Silahdar Ali Pasha at Peterwardein, 5 August 1716, and takes
    Temesvár on 12 October 639
Fall of Belgrade, 16 August 1717; Venetian defeats at sea 640
Treaty of Passarowitz, 21 July 1718 640–2
Reasons for military inferiority of the Ottoman 642
Ottoman desire for peace: Ibrahim Pasha and 'the Age of Tulips' . . . 642–3
Cultural developments 643–4
Epidemics, dear food, and unemployment 644
The Afghans invade Persia: Tsar Peter moves to the Caspian, 1723 . . . 644–5
The Turks and Russians dismember Persia, 1724–30 645
Janissary rising in Constantinople, September–November, 1730 . . . 645–6
Sultan Mahmud I murders Patrona Halil and his associates 647

CHAPTER XX (1)

CHARLES XII AND THE GREAT NORTHERN WAR

By RAGNHILD HATTON, *Professor of International History*
in the University of London

The war of 1700–21 seen as the climax of historic rivalries 648
Swedish theory of empire 648–9
Shifting balance of power in the Baltic 649
Reassessments and reforms under Charles XI 649–50
Sweden's neutrality in the Nine Years War: a prosperous interlude . . . 650–1
1697: accession of Charles XII: omens and dangers 651–2
Holstein-Gottorp and Livonia: the coalition between Denmark, Saxony and
    Russia 652–3

CONTENTS

Augustus of Saxony-Poland attacks Livonia in February 1700 . . . *page* 653–4
The Swedes attack Denmark: Peace of Travendal, August 1700 654–5
Swedish success over the Russians at Narva, 30 November 1700 . . . 655–6
Decision to attack Augustus; the crossing of the Dvina, 19 July 1701. . . 656
The situation in Poland and Lithuania 656–8
Charles XII's Polish policy and its critics 658
Stanislas Leszczyński crowned king of Poland: the Treaty of Warsaw, 1705 . 658–9
Poland as a base for a campaign against Russia or as a buffer-state . . . 659–60
Swedish victories at Kliszów (1702) and Fraustadt (1706) 660–1
Character of Charles XII 661–2
Charles moves into Saxony, 1706; Treaty of Altranstädt, 24 September 1707 . 662–3
Marlborough's visit to Altranstädt 663–4
1708: preparations for the invasion of Russia 664
The Russians forced out of Poland 664–5
The routes to Moscow 665
Russian defence plan: costly Swedish victory at Hołowczyń, 14 July 1708 . . 665–6
Failure of Lewenhaupt to join the main Swedish army: battle of Lesna, 9 October 666–7
Winter quarters and scorched-earth tactics 667
1709: Swedish diplomacy in search of a military success 667–8
The defeats at Poltava and Perevolochna, 8–11 July 668–9
Charles in Turkey for four years; schemes for a coalition at Bender . . . 669–70
Sweden invaded from Denmark and Norway: attitude of the Maritime Powers,
1710. 670
Charles XII at Bender: his plans for reforms in Sweden 671
Stenbock's victory at Gadebusch (December 1712) and surrender at Tønning
(January 1713). 671
Failures of Swedish diplomacy 671–2
The 'tumult' of Bender, February 1713; Charles reaches Stralsund on 21 November
1714. 672–3
The diplomatic situation; Prussia and Hanover join Sweden's enemies, 1715 . 673–4
The fall of Stralsund (23 December 1715) and of Wismar (19 April 1716) . . 674
Administrative reforms in Sweden; Görtz and the Jacobites 674–5
Negotiations with Peter the Great and George I of England 675–7
The succession question; struggle between the Holstein and Hesse parties . . 677
1718: the invasion of Norway and death of Charles XII on 11 December . . 677
What he had had in mind 677–8
Treaties of Stockholm and Frederiksborg, 1719–20 678
The Peace of Nystad, September 1721 679
Sweden no longer a great power; the question of Charles XII's responsibility . 679–80

CHAPTER XX (2)

THE ECLIPSE OF POLAND

By JÓZEF GIEROWSKI, *Professor of Modern Polish History*, and
ANDRZEJ KAMIŃSKI, *Lecturer in Modern European History*,
in the Jagiellonian University, Cracow

'Eclipsis Poloniae' 681
Causes of paralysis; the basic malaise; a pessimistic generation 681–2
John Sobieski and Augustus of Saxony 682–3
Polish participation in the War of the Holy League: meagre results . . . 683–4
Sobieski's succession strategy and family dissensions 684–5
Lithuanian opposition to Sobieski's dynasticism spreads to Poland . . . 685–6

CONTENTS

The interregnum of 1696–7: the contested election at Wola, 27 June 1697 . *page* 686

Frederick Augustus I of Saxony crowned king of Poland as Augustus II,
15 September 687

Possibilities and weaknesses of the Polish-Saxon Union 687–8

Failure of duke of Conti to oust Augustus 688

Resumption of war with the Ottoman, 1698: setbacks for Augustus . . . 688–9

Dispute with Prussia over Elblag, 1698–1700 689–90

Civil war in Lithuania: the Sapieha family capitulate, December 1698. . . 690–1

The Sejm of 1699 and the withdrawal of Saxon forces from Poland . . . 691–2

The anti-Swedish coalition and the invasion of Livonia, 1700 692

Augustus tries to limit the conflict with Sweden, 1700–1 692–3

Charles XII cultivates a pro-Swedish faction in Poland 693

Renewed civil war in Lithuania (1700) and appeal for Russian help . . . 693–4

Opposition groups within Poland; James Sobieski 694

The Sejm of 1701 and the Swedish invasion of Lithuania 694–5

Charles XII calls for the deposition of Augustus II and occupies Warsaw, 1702. 695

Conditional support for Augustus in Poland 695–6

Cossack rising in the Dnieper Ukraine, 1702–4 696

Swedish successes in 1703; the Sejm meets at Lublin 696–7

Anti-Saxon confederacy of Warsaw, 1704 697

Charles XII has Stanislas Leszczyński crowned king in Warsaw, 12 July 1704 . 697

Support for Augustus: General Confederacy of Sandomierz, 1704 . . . 697–8

Russo-Polish alliance: the Treaty of Narva, 30 August 1704 698–9

Charles XII imposes the Treaty of Warsaw, 28 November 1705 699

Difficult position of Charles XII in 1706: the Swedes devastate Poland . . 699–700

The Swedes invade Saxony while the Russians advance into Poland . . . 700–1

The Treaty of Altranstädt: Augustus deprived of the Polish Crown . . . 701

Tsar Peter and the confederates of Sandomierz: alternative candidates for the
Polish throne 701

Charles XII returns to Poland (1707) and moves into the Ukraine (1708) . . 702

Augustus pressed to return: Leszczyński withdraws beyond the Vistula . . 702–3

Battle of Poltava; Augustus finally decides to return in 1709 703–4

Growth of Russian influence in Poland 704

The devastation and depopulation of Poland 704–5

The decay of the towns and decline of the gentry 705–6

Creeping disintegration of Poland; growing independence of provincial diets . 706

Republican tendencies in reform: ideas of Szczuka and Karwicki . . . 706–7

The General Council of Warsaw (1710) and the Sejm of 1712 707–8

Ascendancy of Peter the Great and revival of the Leszczyński party . . . 708–9

Augustus intent on ensuring succession to his son: absolutist schemes. . . 709–10

Attitudes of foreign powers to these plans: the French treaty of August 1714 . 710

Extremist policy of Charles XII fatal to Augustus and to Poland . . . 710–11

Polish discontents exploited by Peter the Great 711

Violent agitation against Saxons in Lithuania and Poland: the General Confederacy of Tarnogród, 1715 711–12

Augustus gives way to the confederates in November 1716 712

Russian diplomacy at a loss; the Silent Sejm of 1717 712–13

Military, economic and ecclesiastical reforms proposed to the Sejm of 1718 . 713–14

Successful opposition of the hetmans supported by Russia and Prussia . . 714

Poland the second major victim of the Great Northern War 714–15

CONTENTS

CHAPTER XXI

RUSSIA UNDER PETER THE GREAT AND THE CHANGED RELATIONS OF EAST AND WEST

By M. S. ANDERSON, *Reader in International History
in the University of London*

Russia in the seventeenth century . . . . *page* 716
The education of Peter the Great; his character and interests 716–17
Conflict with the Tsarevna Sophia, Prince V. V. Golitsyn and the *strel'tsy*, 1689 717–18
The capture of Azov (1696): Peter's Black Sea policy 718–19
Peter's 'great embassy' to western Europe, 1697 719
Suppression of *strel'tsy* revolt, 1698 719–20
A series of great innovations, 1699–1724 720
The reorganization of the army; the training of officers 720–1
The construction of a fleet 721–2
Development of economic life: Peter's 'mercantilism' 722–3
Industry and industrial labour: successes and failures 723–4
Failure of commercial policies: a merchant marine and commercial treaties . 724–5
Agriculture resistant to change despite some innovations 725
Administrative changes: the *prikazy* (1699–1701), the Senate (1711), the adminis-
trative colleges from 1718 725–6
Bureaucratization of the provinces: strengthening of central control . . . 726
Intellectual life and education 726–7
Books, the theatre, science and the arts 727–8
The conservatism of the Orthodox Church; end of its autonomy. . . . 728–9
Structure of society: landowners and peasants; the 'Table of Ranks'. . . 729–30
A forced evolution 730–1
Intolerable physical and financial burdens laid on the peasants 731–2
The rebellion of the Don Cossacks (1706–8) and destruction of the Zaporozhian
sech' 732
Religious dissent and the tragedy of Tsarevich Alexis 732–3
Poltava a turning-point in Russia's relations with Europe 733–4
Bids for Russian support: the Northern War and the Spanish Succession . . 734–5
The Western powers and the North after 1713 735–6
Peter and the Balkans: the Russo-Turkish war of 1711 736
Fears of Russian domination of the Baltic and north Germany, 1716–22 . . 736–7
Russia politically part of Europe: Peter's second journey to the West, 1717 . 737
Diplomatic and dynastic relations established with the European states . . 737–8
Contemplated marriage alliances 738
Expansion in Asia: China and Siberia; Persia and the Caspian . . . 738–9
Growing interest of the West in Russia 739–40
Peter's contemporary standing as a monarch 740

CONTENTS

CHAPTER XXII

ARMIES AND NAVIES

1. THE ART OF WAR ON LAND

By DAVID G. CHANDLER, *Senior Lecturer in Military History
at the Royal Military Academy, Sandhurst*

Limited and total warfare . . . . *page* 741
Growth in size of armies 741–2
International elements; mercenaries and adventurers 742
Similarity between armies: French and Swedish influences 742–3
Ottoman army relatively backward 743
The Swedish 'military revolution' 743–4
Military administration in France: Le Tellier and Louvois 744–5
The *Ordre du Tableau* (1675) and other command-structures 745–6
Developments in infantry weapons; flintlock musket and bayonet . . . 746–8
Importance of the infantry soldier enhanced 748
The effects on tactics and tactical formations 748–9
Increase in casualty rates 749
The art of fortification and siege-warfare; Vauban and Coehoorn . . . 750–1
Use of permanent lines of defence: Stollhofen, Brabant and 'Ne Plus Ultra' . 751
Defensive caution of generals and governments 751–2
Exceptions: Charles XII, Marlborough, Eugene and Villars 752–3
Limiting factors on operations: terrain and weather 753
Four main war-theatres in western Europe 753–4
The Baltic lands and the Balkans. 754
General features of field operations: the assembly-camp 754–5
March-formations and field administration; Marlborough's night-marches . . 756–7
Battle-formations; fire control 758–9
Types of cavalry and their uses 759–60
Artillery: types and uses; the siege-train 760
Little progress in organization of ordnance; status of gunners and engineers . 760–1
Rudimentary staff systems: the commander in battle 761–2
Contemporary records and comments 762

2. SOLDIERS AND CIVILIANS

By J. W. STOYE

The seasonal rhythm of war and politics; winter quarters 762–3
Recruiting and redrafting; poverty the great provider 763–5
Foreign contingents: the case of the Swiss cantons 765–6
The theory of conscription by government 766
Conscription and militia service: the example of Piedmont 766–7
The French *milice* of 1688: substitutes and exemptions 767–8
Conscription in Germany 768–9
The German trade in soldiers 769
The British army: mercenaries, volunteers and conscripts 769–70
Recruitment of cavalry and dragoons easier than raising foot-soldiers. . . 770–1
The Scandinavian systems; discontent in the Baltic States 771–3
The demands of Charles XII, before and after Poltava 774
The Danish militia: the order of 24 February 1701 and its social repercussions . 774–5
Mobilization of manpower in Russia; breakdown of old Cossack organization . 775–6

CONTENTS

Poland's military weakness . . . . *page* 776–7
Officers: the bond between Peter's army and Russian landowners . . . 777
Brandenburg-Prussia: the Cadet Corps and the winning of the Junkers . . 777–8
The military career in German families; commoners and noblemen in Prussia . 778–80
Household Guards in England and elsewhere 780
Policy of Louis XIV: royal pressures and social conventions 780–1
Aristocratic attitudes to military service in Italy and Spain 782–3
Army and militia in England; the Scottish influx; purchase of commissions . 783–4
The 'half-pay' officer; old soldiers 784
Other soldier–civilian relationships 784–5
Varied rôle of intendants in French frontier provinces: Flanders, Artois, Alsace 785–6
Supply of armies in southern Netherlands and western Germany . . . 786–7
Billeting and barracks 787
Municipal oligarchies and war contractors 787–8
Profits of war: fortunes and failures 788–9
The armed forces as a reflection of social structures 789
Growing distinction between military organization and civil society in the West;
  social transformation in Russia and Prussia 789–90

3. NAVIES

By J. S. Bromley and A. N. Ryan, *Senior Lecturer in Naval History
in the University of Liverpool*

Changes in relative strengths of navies; rise of British predominance . . . 790–1
The line-of-battle: capital ships and others 791–2
Building programmes: English, French and Dutch before and after 1688 . . 792–3
Design of warships; ship science in France 793–4
Levelling influence of the line-ahead: the importance of numbers . . . 794
Factors governing the size and structure of navies; conflicts of use . . . 794–6
Pressures of mercantile opinion: English and Dutch assumptions . . . 796
American versus European strategy: navies subordinate to armies . . . 796–8
Conflict between sea and land requirements in the Dutch Republic: its naval
  decline 798–9
Dutch naval organization: the Admiralty Colleges 799–800
The Zeeland privateers; the privateering war 800–2
Vauban and the *guerre de course*. 802–4
Economic warfare; rights of neutrals 804–5
The Swedish and Danish navies 805
Character of naval warfare in the Baltic; Tsar Peter's galleys 806–7
Rapid rise of Russian sea power 807
Limited endurance of warships; naval bases in the Baltic 807–8
Mediterranean bases; Cadiz and Lisbon 807–8
Bases overseas; the West Indies 809
Defence problems and naval difficulties in the Caribbean 809–10
Dockyards in England; the problem posed by Brest 811
French arsenals: Dunkirk, Rochefort, Brest and Toulon; their supplies . . 811–13
Forest policies in France and England; timber imports from the Baltic, Germany
  and North America 813–14
Dockyards and contractors: shipbuilding and naval stores 814–15
The State and its contractors in France and England 815–17
Problems of victualling: English and French compared 817–19
Dockyard labour: the expansion in England 819
Labour discipline in dockyards; irregular employment and pay 819–20

CONTENTS

Manning problems: the *Inscription Maritime* . . . . . . *page* 820–1
The Marines in France and England 822
French impressment and the system of classes 822–3
The English press gangs and the voluntary register of 1696–1710. . . . 823–4
Danish and Swedish methods of manning 824–5
Sickness; hospital ships and naval hospitals. 825–6
The formation of officers 826–7
Emergence of the regular naval officer: rank and post; flag officers . . . 827–8
Naval ethics. 828–9
'Gentlemen' and 'tarpaulin'; the warrant officers 829
Administrators, naval and civilian 829–31
Spending and borrowing in England and France 831–2
Naval finance in the United Provinces and Scandinavia 832
Administrators and statesmen 832–3
Political priorities: unique situation of the English navy 833

CHAPTER XXIII

ECONOMIC ACTIVITY

I. THE MAP OF COMMERCE, 1683–1721

By JACOB M. PRICE, *Professor of History in the University of Michigan*

International aspects of production and exchange over the short term . . 834
Wars and economics; mercantilism old and new 834–5
Growth of international finance; an age of speculative creativeness . . . 835–6
Inter-regional exchanges of goods and commodities 836
Baltic grain exports; the Amsterdam market 836–8
Other corn-exporters: the transformation of England 838
Corn production and market conditions in France 838–9
The timber trade; masts 839–41
Pitch and tar: Russia and North America break the Swedish tar monopoly . 841–2
Turpentine and rosin: the French Landes 842
Flax and hemp: Riga and Archangel 843–4
Ash and potash for the soapmakers; tallow and wax 844–5
Salt production in Europe: Dutch dominance in Baltic imports . . . 844–5
European vineyards: French, Spanish and Portuguese wines 846–7
The victory of Oporto in England; expansion of the Dutch entrepôt favours
  Bordeaux 846–7
Spirits: growth of brandy distillation in France and of gin in England . . 847
European fisheries: decline of the Dutch herring-fleets; the Scots . . 847–8
The whale fishery: Dutch supremacy in Greenland and the Davis Strait . . 848
The cod fisheries of Iceland and Newfoundland; the New England fishery . 848–9
The French fisheries; importance of the Banks; post-war recovery . . 849–50
Other overseas commodities: the North American fur trade and its European
  markets 850–1
The sources of tobacco; blending at Amsterdam; European competition . . 851–2
Increase of smoking in Russia and France; the French tobacco-farm learns to
  buy British 852–3
Sugar as an empire-builder 853–4
Rice; dyestuffs 854–5
The African slave trade: the English outdistance their competitors . . 855–6
East India trade: its special features 856

CONTENTS

The Dutch predominance decreases; French disappointments in the East . *page* 856–7
Sugar, pepper and spices; Dutch selling policy 857–8
Coffee and tea: the new trades to Mocha and Canton. 858–9
Raw silk: competition between Persia and Bengal 859–60
Wrought silks and cottons from India compete with European textiles; calico-
    printing in Europe 860–1
Outward cargoes: the shipment of specie; decline of Dutch purchases of gold
    and copper in Japan 861–2
Specie in the Levant trade: Spanish silver and Brazilian gold 862–3
The woollen industry in France: imports of Spanish wool; centres and types of
    production 863–4
The Dutch woollen industry depressed; growth of Silesian and German
    manufactures 864–5
The great English woollen and worsted industry: centres of production and
    export markets. 865–6
The linen trade: manufactures in western and eastern Europe 866–7
European silk manufacture: expansion in France; a new industry in England . 867–8
Coal-mining: growth of English ascendancy 868–9
The iron industry in Liège, England and Sweden: Swedish pre-eminence . . 869–70
English and French foreign trade compared: their principal orientations . . 870–1
The 'map of commerce': preponderance of the Baltic-Iberian artery; the Sound
    statistics 871
Dutch foreign trade and shipping: its pattern in 1740 and in 1670 . . . 871–2
Dutch and English shipping activity compared; post-war growth of French
    tonnage 872–3
Incidence of the wars on international business cycle 873–4
The most striking changes in the general map of commerce. 874

2. PRICES, POPULATION AND ECONOMIC ACTIVITIES IN EUROPE, 1688–1715: A NOTE

By JEAN MEUVRET

Prices as an index of economic activity: contours of 1690–1714 874–5
Cereals: variations in rye at Amsterdam, Lyons and Carpentras 875–6
Olive oil, wines, peppers 877–8
Examples of price rigidity in textiles 878–9
The building industry: bricks and wages 879
Mutations in money values 879–80
Relative rigidity in prices of non-foodstuffs in relation to soaring food prices . 880–1
Variations in intensity of food crises: France and northern Europe . . . 881
Prices of raw wool compared with corn prices at Castelnaudary 881
The meaning of a fall in pewter valuations 881–2
'Rigidity' of wages 882
Population trends; sources of demographical statistics and their limitations . 882–3
English population in the eighteenth century 883–4
Evidence for Venice, Sicily, Munich, Augsburg, Zürich, Catalonia, central Sweden 884–5
A relatively stationary situation: examples from England and France . . . 885
Factors determining population: family limitation, war, morbidity . . . 885–7
Morbidity and food shortages 887–8
Crises in birth and death rates; French demographic geography . . . 888–9
Subsistence and mortality elsewhere: Piedmont, London, Finland . . . 889–90
Agricultural returns: an example from the Paris region 890–1
The effect of low prices on producers 891–2

CONTENTS

Industry linked with agriculture . . . . *page* 892
Activity in urban crafts: output and changes in the quality of manufacture . 892–3
Danish Sound tolls compared with port dues of Amsterdam; East India sales . 893
Transformation of English foreign trade 894
Underlying buoyancy of French external trade 894–5
Depression of inland centres: boom and slump at Geneva 895
Tight money and interest rates in France; *rentes constituées* 895–6
Solidity of the Amsterdam Exchange Bank 896
The National Debt in England 896–7
Wars the main cause of higher price level in 1690–1714 897
TABLES A–J 898–902

INDEX 903

CHAPTER I

INTRODUCTION

THE phase of European experience studied in the present volume, and to some extent in its predecessor,[1] has elastic chronological boundaries and no such recognizable identity as may be claimed for ages of reformation or revolution, though it contained features of both. Nor does a single figure bestride it. The conventional description which fixes on the decline of France is at best a half-truth, and then only for the West. Even in characterizing 'The Age of Louis XIV' from 1661, the editors of the 'old' *C.M.H.* were aware of 'the long, and seemingly remote, history of the Ottoman Power in Europe' as a main determinant of a period which lacked 'the organic unity which belongs to our Napoleon volume'; and as soon as this 'question of life and death' had been settled at Carlowitz in 1699, 'a large division of the canvas is filled by the great Swedish or "Northern" War',[2] formally closed at Nystad in 1721, six years after the *Roi Soleil* had gone to his grave but more than three before Peter, the great tsar, was to follow him.

If we consider the political geography of these years (ch. v), it is the changing map of eastern Europe which impresses us first. By 1716 Sweden was stripped of her trans-Baltic provinces, the basis of her great-power position (ch. xx(1)), with a commerce and revenues that had long been her answer to Danish control of the Sound and Dutch domination of the trade which passed through it.[3] Sweden's loss was chiefly to the advantage of Russia, which staked out claims also in the direction of the Black Sea and the Caspian and was able for a time to station troops in Denmark and Poland, to send caravans to Peking and work up feeling against Islam in the Balkans. There, the Peace of Passarowitz in 1718 added Transylvania and Little Wallachia, with much of Serbia and Bosnia, to the war-trodden wastes of Hungary acquired by the House of Habsburg at Carlowitz. Some of these developments, it is true, proved ephemeral. The Turks were to recover Belgrade, the key to their position in Europe, and over half a century was to pass before the Russians occupied the Crimea; Tsar Peter's ignominious surrender to Turkish forces on the river Pruth in 1711 was as great a sensation as had been his destruction of King Charles XII's brilliant expeditionary force at Poltava and Perevolochna in 1709.

[1] See Preface to vol. v, p. v. Below it has been judged useful to carry the surveys of science, music and Ottoman affairs well into the eighteenth century.
[2] *The Cambridge Modern History*, vol. v (1908), ed. A. W. Ward, G. W. Prothero and Stanley Leathes, Preface, pp. v–vii.
[3] For the larger perspective see Folke Lindberg, 'La Baltique et l'historiographie scandinave', *Annales (Economies, Sociétés, Civilisations)*, 16e année (1961), 425–40.

I

But 'the Turkish menace' was a thing of the past and 'the Eastern Question' had been noisily announced. Several features it had in this period, however, which were not to concern the future. Carlowitz ended the last war which had at least begun, with the Holy League of 1684, as a crusade. In effect, it also marked the end of a persistent Polish interest in the Rumanian principalities of Moldavia and Wallachia, although the Polish hold on neighbouring Podolia was now restored. Passarowitz likewise put a term to Venetian ambitions in the Aegean: they had seemed to threaten Constantinople itself when the republic stood in possession of the Morea for a generation. During the interval between these historic settlements the viking Charles XII, who dreamed of attracting Ottoman and Persian trade to a Swedish Baltic and who for five years established his own nominee on the Polish throne, was to scheme in vain for a vast combination of Swede and Turk, Pole and Cossack, against the victor of Poltava.

Charles's fertile imagination, especially in exile on Turkish soil, drew together the strands of Baltic and Levantine affairs, but he was not the only ruler capable of conceiving an eastern Europe utterly different from that which took shape in this period. Frederick Augustus of Saxony, soon after his controversial election to the Polish throne in 1697, entertained the vision of a trading power which would extend from Riga to the Caspian, as well as of a territorial link between Poland and Saxony along the middle Oder—a link which Brandenburg seemed willing to encourage in return for concessions in the Vistula delta. It was a Saxon thrust into Swedish Livonia, as much as Danish pretensions to Sleswig-Holstein, which opened two decades of war in the North and drew the Swedes into the Penelope's web of Polish politics (ch. xx(2)). The Polish-Saxon Union turned out to be disastrous to the strengthening of central government in Warsaw because it led to foreign intervention, invited by dissident noblemen who feared for historic liberties or by Augustus II himself, whose best intentions were suspect of absolutism and compromised by the behaviour of his Saxon troops. Yet Charles XII's determination to break that Union at any price—thus involving the Polish-Lithuanian Commonwealth in his own ruin[1]—should warn us not to read its history backwards. Like Sweden's own bid to retain domination of the eastern Baltic, and indeed to extend it to the Arctic, the potentialities of the Polish-Saxon Union were a major issue of the Great Northern War, which can only be understood in the light of these contemporary options and not simply as a stage in the

---

[1] Paradoxically, nevertheless, in resolving to fill the throne with a Polish subject, Charles was anticipating one of J.-J. Rousseau's principal recommendations for the preservation of the Commonwealth's independence. Rousseau's *Considérations sur le gouvernement de la Pologne*, though written in 1772 with conscious modesty, remains a remarkable diagnosis of the strength and weaknesses of this unique nation, whose spiritual vitality and originality he recognized. Since the tendency of historians has been to underline its factiousness, it is interesting that Rousseau saw the constitutional resort to spontaneous confederation as 'a political masterpiece'.

expansion of Muscovy. Although Peter was to enjoy Russia's familiar privilege of *tertius gaudens* in the end, at least as arbiter in Polish and Lithuanian party conflicts, the first twenty years of his reign must be seen as a struggle for survival (ch. xxi). The Dnieper frontier itself had been settled as recently as 1686; and even this 'perpetual peace', with its provision for a tsarist protectorate of the Orthodox religion in Poland, could not be taken in Moscow as permanent proof against Polish irredentism in the Ukraine.

Muscovy's humble value in Western eyes in 1689 was repeatedly confirmed at the hand of Sweden's young warrior-king until Poltava dramatically resurrected the anti-Swedish coalition of 1698–9 and restored Augustus II to the Polish throne. The tsar had still to survive his humiliation on the Pruth, and his most drastic administrative reforms, till then subsidiary to the Swedish conflict, belong to his last decade; but by the time of Charles XII's return to Sweden, in 1715, the 'maritime powers' of Britain and the Netherlands, with a western balance of power only just attained, were uneasily aware of the need to contain 'a kind of northern Turk' (p. 735), who threatened to turn the Baltic into a Russian lake, much as the Ottomans regarded the Black Sea as their *mare clausum*. When Peter first visited the West in 1697, he came to acquire its technology; in 1717 he returned as a conqueror and reformer, the greatest ruler of the age. At the Russian celebration of the Peace of Nystad he was congratulated on joining his newly created Empire to the comity of political nations. East and West remained indeed far apart in understanding: for all his realism, Peter had some of the pride of his Orthodox churchmen (whose dislike of westernizing policies rivalled that of their Ottoman counterparts, the *ulema*) and he may have intended Holy Russia to turn her back on the West after several decades of apprenticeship. But when he died, in 1725, the chancelleries of the West were amply represented at his handsome new capital of St Petersburg, with its German architects and Dutch printing-presses (ch. xxi).

It had not been Russian friendship, however, but rather Sweden's and Denmark's, or at least the use of their troops, that the western powers competed for in their own protracted wars of 1688–97 and 1701–14 (ch. vii and xiii). For the British and the Dutch, the perseverance of distrust between the Northern Crowns was a tiresome irrelevance. Stockholm was nervous of Danish irredentism in Scania, while Copenhagen feared Swedish pressure through the duchy of Holstein-Gottorp, whose lands and fortification rights mingled confusedly with those of Denmark in Sleswig and Holstein. This dispute, no more than patched up by the Treaty of Altona in 1689, largely explains Denmark's participation in the Northern War; it was only the concerted attack from two other new kings, Augustus II and Peter I, that took Charles XII by surprise. As they had tried to straighten out the Holstein question, so the western powers would have stopped the larger struggle if they could, especially when the death of the childless King Carlos II[1] of Spain in 1700 opened the possibility of another ordeal by arms in the West itself. In the event, the Spanish Succession War was never to merge with the Northern War, although Augustus II more than once sought allies among the western belligerents, while fears of a Swedish diversion westwards contributed to the mission of the commander-in-chief of the Maritime Powers, Marlborough, to Charles XII in camp at Altranstädt in 1707. Western diplomacy had been altogether more active at Stockholm during the Nine Years War, when both sides found supporters among the Swedish magnates and set value on the arbitration of Charles XI in the deadlock into which their hostilities entered from 1693; but Danish troops in the pay of the Maritime Powers then played a more direct rôle than anything the Swedes ever did. The record of these years shows the breakdown of the classical French 'eastern barrier' in Sweden as in Poland. At the same time, neither Sweden nor Denmark—where French influence tended to predominate in proportion as it lost ground in Stockholm—relished an Anglo-Dutch command of the seas, and the Northern Crowns were capable of sinking their differences in defence of their rights as neutral traders against attempts by the Maritime Powers to dictate to them. The most constant interest of all the western powers in the Baltic was their commerce, particularly their naval supplies and the corn and timber of the Polish and north German plain (ch. XXIII (1)), however hard they sought to snatch political advantages for themselves and deny them to their rivals. The court of Stockholm cost more in 'gratifications' than most others,[2] but nothing in the baffling silences of Charles XII's personality rings truer than his refusal to take foreign subsidies at the expense of his freedom of action. Has any sovereign, placed in succeeding situations of extreme difficulty, preserved a single-minded independence for so long? When he crossed the Sound in 1700 to knock Denmark out of the coalition which sought to take advantage of his youth, he was protected by an English fleet; but this did not prevent him from depriving England of essential Finnish tar at a critical moment in her fortunes, nor later from risking her friendship when he badly needed it by unleashing his privateers against ships trading with Swedish ports in Russian occupation.

In such manner did the course of events in northern Europe impinge on the West. Subsidy-troops apart, Brandenburg-Prussia was the only Baltic power to become involved in Western hostilities. A more direct and continuous reciprocity is discernible between the middle Danube and the upper Rhine. The dramatic thrusts of the Habsburg armies over Hungary

---

[1] Contrary to the general practice of this *History*, his name and that of Louis XIV have not been anglicized, for we know them best as they called themselves.

[2] See the contribution by R. Hatton to *William III and Louis XIV: Essays 1680–1720 by and for Mark A. Thomson* (ed. R. Hatton and J. S. Bromley, Liverpool and Toronto, 1968), ch. 5.

and deep into the Balkans, after the Turkish failure before Vienna in 1683, were virtually halted by 1692 because the Emperor Leopold I had increasingly to divert resources to the defence of western Germany, where the devastation of the Palatinate in 1688 had been followed by similar if less systematic acts of French ruthlessness. The defensive organization of the Empire, at least of its western Circles, had been slowly improved since 1681 and German troops were to play a notable if subordinate part in all the main war theatres of the West throughout the period: what is more, many officers and their best leaders—Charles of Lorraine, George of Hesse-Darmstadt, Lewis of Baden, Eugene of Savoy—were formed in the hard school of the Balkan campaigns, the greatest common enterprise of the Imperial princes since the days of Charles V.[1] Inevitably, however, as was always crystal clear to the managers of French policy, this crusade weakened the Imperial contribution to anti-French coalitions. To these the Austrian Habsburg as such had also become a principal party in 1673, but the siege of Vienna had reintroduced a conflict of priorities between the House of Austria and the Habsburg as emperor (ch. XVIII). Hence the momentum of the *Drang nach Osten* was not immediately halted by the series of crises—in particular, the first of the many succession disputes of the period, those of Cologne–Liège and of the British Isles— which touched off the Nine Years War, nor even by the early French successes in it (ch. VII). The emperor's allies had to carry on that struggle in the knowledge that he might at any moment desert them. Conversely, every attempt to assist the allies by terminating the Balkan hostilities broke down until the rout of the Turkish army at Zenta in 1697—a battle as decisive as Poltava, but only made possible by Habsburg evacuation of Italy in the previous year.

In the Spanish Succession War, again, the emperor was bitterly accused of withholding troops needed by his allies, this time in a costly attempt (until 1712) to impose his own terms on Francis Rákóczi and the Hungarian rebels. Imperial perfidy, like Habsburg debts, thus became a byword in London and The Hague. Most selfish of all from the Anglo-Dutch stand-point was the decision of Emperor Joseph I (1705–11) to overrun Italy when, with Prince Eugene's rescue of Turin in 1706, it was the turn of the French to withdraw across the Alps. An Austrian Milan and an Austrian Naples may be said to have been the price of Eugene's assistance on Marlborough's great battlefields; but in 1707 the advance on Naples ruined the siege of Toulon, success in which was to have ended the war in the West—years before the British left the Emperor Charles VI and Eugene, by an act of poetic justice, to work out their own settlement with Louis XIV and Marshal Villars at Rastatt. There, and in the ensuing negotiations of 1714 at Baden, which settled the claims of the Imperial

---

[1] The internal affairs of the Empire in the period of the present volume are treated in vol. V, ch. XVIII and XXIII; but cf. below, ch. V and XVIII.

princes against France, Habsburg interests were preferred to the idea of a Rhenish 'barrier' against a repetition of French incursions—such a barrier as was devised in 1713 and in 1715 for two other areas exposed to them, Savoy and the Netherlands (ch. xiv). Disappointed of the Spanish monarchy and its overseas possessions, which he strongly felt to be as much a portion of his legitimate family inheritance as the old Spanish Habsburg holdings in the Netherlands and Italy, Charles VI was induced to turn back to operations on the Danube in 1716. Free from other obligations but enriched by war experience in the west, Eugene stormed Belgrade and forced the sultan to a peace within two years.

The meaning of this for the Ottoman empire was manifold and profound. Acutely aware of a novel danger from Muscovy, the Turks had already accepted in 1699–1700 the loss of large territories, including such holy places of war as Buda and Azak (Azov). Despite their remarkably resilient war effort, at Carlowitz they had for the first time formally acknowledged defeat, and by the treaty with Peter next year they obliged themselves to receive a Russian envoy. Later, in 1711 and 1714, they provoked fresh trials of strength with the tsar and then Venice, in each case victoriously; but they had not sought revenge against Austria. Now, in 1718, the whole future of European Turkey was placed in doubt by the sacrifice of Belgrade and Temesvár, while the House of Austria apparently assumed the vocation of liberating the Balkan Christians, instead of remaining a defensive outpost of Christendom. The blow to Muslim pride was felt at all levels of Turkish society. It hardened the xenophobia of the exponents of the Koran and of the turbulent people of the capital. At the same time intelligent men were led to reconsider the relations of Islam with Christendom and what they must stoop to learn from infidel techniques, most obviously in the modernization of diplomacy and the armed forces. Carlowitz was the first treaty ever signed by the Porte with a European coalition and it showed the rising influence of members of the Greek and Jewish communities with knowledge of the West, just as the Ottoman navy, which underwent major reforms *ca.* 1700, owed much to renegade European captains who had served with the Barbary corsairs. Even a flavour of the French rococo seems to have reached the Golden Horn in 'the Age of Tulips', for tulipomania was only the symbol of a reaction among the well-to-do after 1718 in favour of an extravagant hedonism. It came to an end with the appalling riots of 1730 in Contantinople. These displayed more luridly than had earlier risings in that crowded city—the largest in Europe—the domestic insecurity of the Ottoman State. Violence, as the overthrow of sultans and the brevity of most grand vizierates during the previous half-century testify, was never far from the surface of Turkish politics. The democratic susceptibilities of the janissaries and their penetration of civilian life alone guaranteed a chronic restlessness, and this was fed by a run of shameful reverses and the enormous social cost of long campaigns, reflected in deserted homes and soaring prices. An observant traveller could already prophesy in 1701 some strange revolution in this great empire: a generation later, the idea of its decay was a commonplace in the West (ch. xix).

If Russia had returned to Europe, it is equally true that the Habsburgs (ch. xviii) were now irrevocably though less abruptly committed to the East. Neither Italy, where except in Lombardy their acquisitions were to prove ephemeral, nor the unloved south Netherlands, where they had to accept the intrusion of Dutch garrisons, presented problems comparable with those of the impoverished and often empty areas down the Danube. Here it was imperative to evolve a system of government and defence, promote the true faith and impart new economic life. The ambitious plans of Charles VI for the development of trade with the Balkans damaged Venice without promoting Trieste for some time to come, and Belgrade was lost again in 1739; but the repopulation of the Hungarian plain, of Transylvania and the Banat of Temesvár—often by organized immigration from Slovakia, Croatia, Serbia and Germany—was energetically undertaken, especially the military colonization of the frontiers, which bears broad resemblance to the measures used by Peter for subsisting garrisons and border militias on the Don Steppe (ch. xxii (2)). A stern test of statecraft began when the Habsburgs received the Crown of St Stephen at Buda in 1687. The ensuing suppression of Hungarian Protestantism and Hungarian liberties, as tenaciously prized as those of Catalonia or of Scotland, forms the background to one of the toughest rebellions of the period, although it has to be added that Rákóczi and others of its leaders were also great lords defending a mass of properties against a centralizing treasury and war commissariat in the Habsburg apartments at Vienna.

Attempts to weld the heterogeneous collection of departments, councils and committees sitting in the Hofburg were never wholly successful in this period, partly because efficient authority in the French style was held of lesser account than the accumulation of territories and the religious unity of the Counter-Reformation. But two tendencies are to be remarked: technical advances in Austrian public finance (pp. 305–13) and the encroachment of the Habsburg chancery on the functions of its Imperial counterpart (ch. xviii). Outside Bohemia the *Hofkanzlei* was becoming the most powerful instrument of Habsburg government. This meant that all major decisions were to emanate from the ruler in accordance with the family law, even if in practice Habsburg officers shared administrative control of the principalities with proud Estates, dominated by landowners who in Bohemia and Moravia were often the royal office-holders as well. The negotiation of the Pragmatic Sanction in 1720–2 with each of the constituent territories of the monarchy is of deep significance as a bid for converting the loosely knit *Hausmacht* into a *Machtstaat*—but only on the basis of the ruler's personal authority, not by crushing old and distinctive institutions. After the cement of the Roman faith, it was the social sympathies between the various territorial nobilities, forged in a common Viennese culture, which best gave coherence to the most diverse populations under a single sovereign to be found anywhere in Europe. The multiplication (and complication) of these populations must be seen as a major development of the age, even in comparison with the rise of Russia and Great Britain. It was accompanied by a certain loss of interest in the affairs of the Holy Roman Empire, and this was to open the way in time for the *rapprochement* of 1756 with France—a diplomatic revolution already recommended by Louis XIV before he died. Yet the insatiable Habsburg appetite for accumulation made it unlikely that they would write off any loss for ever: Alsace was not to be forgotten even when the filching of Silesia, by a Prussia of little account in these years,[1] was a fresh wound. On the whole, as one surveys the action and inaction of Vienna in the age of Leopold I and his sons, one may be impressed by a certain hesitancy in contrast with the daring that drove Sweden and Russia.

It seems unlikely that Charles VI, the most enterprising of these German emperors, would have produced better solutions for the many-sided problems of the humiliated Spanish monarchy, had he made good the Habsburg claim to the whole inheritance of Carlos II, than did the successful Bourbon claimant, Philip V. As Charles III of Spain, he would have depended no less on alien merchants to sustain the country's colonial commerce. He would certainly have shown more tenderness towards established forms and regional particularities. Leaving aside the consequences of remote control from Vienna after 1711, when the death of Joseph I compelled him to abandon his devoted Catalans, the later record of Charles's rule in Milan and Naples scarcely suggests a strong will to overhaul the established machinery of government. By contrast, Philip V's gradual introduction of French methods into Spain, contentious and frustrated though they were, did offer a line of escape from the political dominance of the grandees. Habsburg notions of caste were a good deal more congenial to this small, wealthy and privileged body, as events showed (ch. xi), than was the radical revision of administrative habit undertaken by Philip's closest advisers, not all of them French. True, despite early measures in French favour, Philip belied expectations that he would take all his instructions from Versailles, which in any case did not speak with one voice in Spanish affairs;[2] and when, in 1709, a European peace could have been purchased at the price of his abdication (ch. xiv), his Spanish loyalties proved stronger than his French origin. Nevertheless, by 1714, when all the powers concerned in the succession

---

[1] See vol. v, ch. xxiii.

[2] It is important for the understanding of contemporary diplomacy that this was not obvious even to close observers; see (e.g.) the otherwise perceptive report of the marchese di Trivié from Barcelona to Turin (1711) in C. Morandi (ed.), *Relazioni di ambasciatori sabaudi, genovesi e veneti, 1693-1713*, vol. I (Bologna, 1935), p. 41.

had come in effect to acknowledge him, Philip was king of a Spain constitutionally more homogeneous than the several kingdoms, with their ancient liberties, which had received him in 1701. Gone were the Aragonese *fueros* and the *Diputació* of Catalonia, which in 1716 suffered a wholesale assimilation of its institutions to those of centralizing Castile; only Navarre and the Basque provinces still kept a degree of autonomy. Local power over the municipalities as well as the countryside of Aragon, Catalonia and Valencia—the kingdoms least sympathetic to the new régime—had been one foundation of rule by the grandees. At the centre this was rooted in the old Councils, now giving way to secretaries of state on the French model. In addition, the Gallican assumptions of Philip's advisers were hostile to the parasitism of ecclesiastics on Spanish life. The influence of the Holy See had grown considerably during the reign of Carlos II and was strikingly exemplified in his last years by Cardinal Portocarrero, a determinant influence on the Bourbon succession. An opportunity for readjusting Church–State relations came when Habsburg pressure in Italy forced Pope Clement XI to side against Philip, who in 1709 broke with Rome and inaugurated those essays in 'regalism' which were to culminate in the Concordat of 1753 and the later expulsion of the Jesuits. But the disgrace of Melchor de Macanaz, the Crown lawyer who drafted the programme of regalism in 1713, shows the limitations of the new monarchy in face of a traditional force like the Inquisition, especially when the king's marriage to Elizabeth Farnese reintroduced Italian influences at court (ch. xi).

At the outset of the new century a close observer of Vienna could write that it 'looked upon the kingdom of Spain as a mere carcase scarce worth the having unless accompanied with the Dominions in Italy, which were supposed to be the flesh and vitals'.[1] In spite of an industrial decline recalling that of Spain, the duchy of Milan was after all richer and easier of access. Established on the Lombard plain, furthermore, the Habsburgs could hope to sway the policies of Venice, an ally against the Turks, and of Piedmont-Savoy, the indispensable but enigmatic custodian of the Alpine passes against the French. In possession of Naples and Sicily, with their populous and strategically situated ports, the emperor's influence would be extended through Italy and especially in Rome; Naples, with its brilliant culture, enjoyed close connections with the grand duchy of Tuscany and the republic of Genoa. Since Italy was of major interest to Louis XIV also, if only as a reserve of States which might be used in exchange for Lorraine or Savoy,[2] it is not surprising that Bourbon–Habsburg hostilities took place in north Italy as well as the Rhineland, or that Duke Victor Amadeus II of Savoy found himself in a strong bargain-

[1] Stepney to Vernon, 26 April 1702, quoted A. D. Francis, 'Portugal and the Grand Alliance', *Bulletin of the Institute of Historical Research*, vol. XXXVIII (1965), p. 76.
[2] J. Meuvret, 'Louis XIV et l'Italie', *XVIIᵉ Siècle: Bulletin de la Société d'études du XVIIᵉ siécle*, nos. 46–7 (1960), pp. 98–102.

ing position: the domestic statesmanship designed to support his freedom of choice has an interest of its own (pp. 560–2). Of the other Italian states only the Papacy really counted, although its influence was challenged by more than one Roman Catholic sovereign outside Italy (ch. IV). After the rupture brought about by his uncompromising Gallicanism in 1688, Louis XIV's relationship with the Holy See nevertheless returned to normal from 1693; indeed, it evolved so far into one of mutual aid as to bring the French Crown into a paradoxically Ultramontane position with the publication of the anti-Jansenist Bull *Unigenitus* in 1713—an event pregnant with trouble for Louis's successors (ch. x). The support of the Papacy was worth having for the weight it exercised on other Italian States, but also in a solution of the problem of the Spanish succession. There is reason to believe that the main effort of French diplomacy was already moving from northern to southern Europe as a whole by 1685 (ch. v).

During the partition diplomacy of 1698–1700 and the intense phase of negotiations which followed the French king's acceptance of the testament of Carlos II in breach of it (ch. XII), the distribution of Spain's possessions in Italy presented the chief stumbling-block. A section of English opinion was certainly more interested in the trading opportunities of the Spanish Indies, particularly in those afforded by the official contract for the supply of African slaves, the Asiento, now a serious object of international competition; the French Asiento of 1701 was one of the first-fruits of the Bourbon succession in Spain and the British were to bargain for it a decade later. Yet in 1700 the eyes of statesmen and of many merchants were fixed on the future of the Mediterranean (ch. XVII). Is this surprising? Besides the Bourbon–Habsburg jealousy, something must be allowed for the fascination exerted by Italy over the imagination of northerners. The culture of ruling groups was still deeply suffused by Roman antiquity and the prestige of Italian artists, good and bad, who from the 1680s looked increasingly beyond the Alps for their larger commissions: the whole notion of 'nobility', so powerful a yeast everywhere in this period, demanded the luxury of grand decorative schemes which the Italians of Rome and Bologna, Naples and Venice, were best able to satisfy. From Italy and from the Levant, moreover, came many of the silks, wines, fruits and other necessities of the patrician way of life. Although the Mediterranean basin, like the Baltic, was a net importer of precious metal, its markets were important to cloth-manufacturers, cod-fishermen and grain-carriers alike. Southern Europe as a whole still absorbed greater quantities of British and French exports than the transatlantic world, while for the Dutch southern Europe (including western France) was the essential complement of their basic Baltic trade. The map of European commerce between 1680 and 1720 (ch. XXIII (1)) shows the persistent priority of the old North–South axis, extending from Riga and Danzig to Leghorn and Smyrna. At the same time, economic considerations were secondary to political and strategic arguments in the diplomacy of William III. The grand strategy of encircling France herself was sketched out when the main fleet of the Maritime Powers was sent to the Mediterranean in 1694 and ordered to winter there, with Cadiz as its base. It achieved little enough, even in support of the long-suffering Catalans and Piedmontese, but the precedent was to govern the naval history of the following war, at the expense of operations in American seas; and then it resulted in the acquisition of Gibraltar and Minorca to the British Crown, as well as providing indispensable coverage for the Habsburg cause in Spain and Italy (ch. XIII) and enabling the British to intervene with greater effect in Mediterranean politics.

This permanent British presence in southern Europe was one of the most striking innovations of the time, plain for all to see, like the Habsburg presence in the Balkans and the tsar's in the Baltic. Without any one of these the diplomacy and war-making of the eighteenth century would have taken a different course, although in neither was Britain destined to take consistent advantage of her new position as a Mediterranean power— partly no doubt because sea power alone did not confer a continental preponderance (ch. v). It can be argued that by 1715, already, France was again the strongest political influence in the Mediterranean, as hers was incontestably the most vigorous commercial impulse, in that mosaic of ancient cities and centrifugal provinces whose populations contrived to make a living in time-hallowed ways, less disturbed by the clash of navies than by endemic scourges of drought, disease, pauperism and more or less licensed piracy (ch. XVII). With their network of consuls and experienced Provençal traders, their high standing alike in Malta and Algiers, Seville and Cairo, the French were well placed to act as the most efficacious and congenial link between Islam and the West. Surprising only is the indifference displayed by Louis XIV for Morocco, whose extraordinary ruler, Muley Ismael, suggests a comparison with Peter the Great (p. 554).

By 1715, on the other hand, it may be said that the Mediterranean had given way to the Atlantic as the centre of economic calculation. American territories, indeed, had become the object of power rivalries more explicitly related to commerce than could be claimed for any other large region—even for the Eastern Seas, which at this time were much less affected by wars in Europe than by the collapse of the Mughal empire, the advance of the Omani Arabs to Mombasa, the opening of a free-for-all trade with Canton and Mocha, and the high summer of piracy between Madagascar and the Red Sea.[1] This last had itself an American as well as an indigenous element; it gave as much concern to the English and French governments as the West Indian *flibuste* or 'buccaneering' had

---

[1] Far Eastern developments in this period are summarized in vol. v, ch. XVII; cf. below, ch. XVI and XXIII (I).

done, with its extension across the Isthmus of Panama to the South Sea. The whole phenomenon calls for fresh investigation, but its connections are clear enough with the long past of privateering against the Spaniard as with the power vacuum left by the decline of Portugal in the Indian Ocean, with the harsh circumstances that attended the slave trade and the foundation of European colonies in the tropics, together with the imperfections of all government in the Americas (ch. xi, xv, xvi). The *cause célèbre* of Captain Kidd links the pirate coasts of Malabar and Madagascar with respectable circles in New York and Boston.

Once the colonial powers were formally at war with one another, much lawless energy was absorbed in privateering under official sanction. Thus in 1689–97 the *flibustiers* of Saint-Domingue could continue operations against the inter-colonial shipping of the Spanish Indies with the satisfaction of knowing that they served their king, who in fact made use of them for an attack on Cartagena. In the next war, when they had to live off the English and Dutch alone, they shifted their base to Martinique without change of name and often ran up to Port Royal in Acadia—a perfect northern base in relation to Boston and Newfoundland—and sometimes across to West Africa, where the English trading fort on the Gambia was twice held to ransom. Conversely, the Jamaican privateers could add Spanish to French prey in 1702–13, contrary to the strong British interest in smuggling to the Spanish Creoles, for which purpose Jamaica (only less than Dutch Curaçao) was well placed. In both wars, moreover, small English naval squadrons came out to attack French sugar islands and cod-fishing villages, without achieving more than a destruction which the French, usually without naval assistance, were able to repay with interest, especially in Newfoundland waters. There, and in Hudson's Bay and along the northerly borders of New York and Massachusetts, much deadly hole-and-corner skirmishing took place. In general the French had the best of it, their corsairs and *coureurs de bois* displaying an audacity and skill as guerrillas usually superior to that of the farmers and traders of the North American seaboard. In the wilderness warfare of the 1690s, Count Frontenac's use of the Canadian Indians made an impression on the New England mind that gave resonance to its neurotic dread of popery for years to come. Yet the Carolinians, during the next round of fighting in North America, did not hesitate to negotiate Indian alliances in order to clear northern Florida of Spanish soldiers and missionaries.

The larger strategical problem of North America was best understood, and of course most urgently felt, by Americans (ch. xv). Frontenac, who must surely count as one, and the Le Moyne brothers, who founded Louisiana, recognized in the expulsion of the English from New York and Carolina, respectively, the only guarantee of French survival on the continent. Nor did clear heads in Charleston, whose Indian trade depended on controlling the play of intertribal relations south-west of the Appalachians, welcome a competitor on the lower Mississippi. The 'reduction' of Canada had been suggested only to be dismissed in 1666, as it appeared to require an overland march through difficult country; but very early in the Nine Years War the New Englanders launched this godly undertaking themselves, up the St Lawrence, and when they failed they kept up pressure on London to take it seriously. The postponement of help from Europe in this 'glorious enterprise', together with its abysmal sequel in 1711, implanted a distrust of British sincerity which found an echo among French Canadians vis-à-vis their own distant metropolis. In truth, neither the British nor French governments had resources to spare for major operations in America so long as a military decision was sought in the Netherlands, Rhineland, Italy or Spain; their navies were fully stretched— within limits imposed by men, money, stores and bases—in support of European operations, by plans or fears of invasion, not least by continuous pressure on the maritime nerves of commerce. It is equally true that neither government yet regarded colonial friction as primary in their dispute with one another. They had attempted in 1686 to secure that any conflict in Europe should not spread to North America, although French aggression in Hudson's Bay and the return of Frontenac to Quebec made certain that it would. So far from sharing Frontenac's ambitious vision, however, Louis XIV ordered the abandonment of the western outposts of New France in 1696, thus returning to Colbert's preference for concentrating the colony's small manpower in the St Lawrence valley. This policy was contradicted by the foundation of the first settlement near the Mississippi outlets in 1699—a posthumous triumph for La Salle and Frontenac stimulated by fears of a British preemption; yet it cannot be said that Louis was easily persuaded to this further commitment to the American interior (which also alarmed the Spaniards), or that Louisiana would have survived early disillusionment had it not attracted the interest of his minister for the navy and colonies, the younger Pontchartrain, and later of Antoine Crozat, one of the outstanding entrepreneurs upon whose financial strength the French State increasingly depended to sustain a war economy. William III, the stadholder-king who directed the war effort of the Maritime Powers in 1689–97, did not press colonial issues at the Peace of Ryswick or award them any prominence in his efforts to avert a Spanish succession war, notwithstanding the superiority of Peruvian and Mexican silver to Caribbean sugar and Canadian beaver as an attraction to mercantilist statesmen, at a time when the piece-of-eight was the nearest thing to a world currency.

It says something for the originality of St John, Viscount Bolingbroke, who was responsible for the British attempt to capture Quebec in 1711, that he placed colonial claims high on his agenda in the peace-making of 1711–13, which resulted in the British acquisition of Acadia and all of St Christopher, to say nothing of the hard-fought exclusion of the French cod-fishermen from their customary bases in Newfoundland and of the *coureurs de bois* from the shores of Hudson's Bay (ch. xiv). This contrast between Ryswick and Utrecht is in part a recognition of what the English colonists had accomplished for themselves, in part the exploitation of a stronger bargaining position by a brilliant intelligence imbued with late Stuart conceptions of government. The flight of James II in 1688 had brought down the Dominion of New England by which James sought to blend his proprietary possessions of New York and the two Jerseys with their recalcitrant Puritan neighbours, for better defence and enforcement of the navigation laws: the advent in James's stead of a Protestant Dutchman, deliriously celebrated in Boston, spelt a return to provincial particularism and bitter faction fights in some of the seaboard colonies (ch. xv). Bolingbroke apparently contemplated 'putting the whole Empire of North America on one uniform plan of government',[1] once the conquest of Canada had improved his standing with tough American assemblies, and with influential proprietors who had successfully held out against proposals to annul their charters. Between Ryswick and Utrecht, moreover, as so acute a politician well understood, the organized forces of commercial opinion had come into fuller play on the political stage.

During these years there were evident signs of impatience with conventional mercantilist restrictiveness precisely when the British and French governments, and even the Spanish and Austrian, showed a disposition to improve the techniques of economic regulation and to allow economic factors more weight in policy-making. It is true that the new Board of Trade and Plantations created by parliament in 1696 proved its value chiefly by the many fresh inquiries which it stimulated, and that sound information was Louis XIV's characteristic expectation of the *Conseil de Commerce* set up in 1700 in response to the restlessness of merchant circles in the chief French ports, which were represented on it. Nevertheless, the activity of these bodies, like the extension of consular representation (ch. v), reflects a mounting official concern with the old problem of ensuring a favourable 'balance of trade'. The wars placed an almost intolerable strain on national economies at the same time as new commercial opportunities beckoned. In the trade balance, which began to be measured more scientifically by the English from 1696, the re-export of colonial produce—above all sugar, tobacco, cod and furs (ch. xxiii (1))—figured largely. Hence wartime irregularities in shipments and payments, or saturated markets and low prices, were a worry not only to overseas planters and merchants. These men, however, could do more than influence colonial governors and intendants. Whether or not their interests coincided, they had family and business connections with powerful circles at home, which in turn were relevant to the interests of ministers and

---

[1] St John to Governor Hunter, 6 February o.s. 1711, in G. S. Graham (ed.), *The Walker Expedition to Quebec, 1711* (1953), p. 278.

of the managers of parliamentary majorities no less than to the borrowing facilities of governments. Good examples of organized political pressure are the campaigns mounted against overseas trading monopolies in both England and France during the 1690s. 'Free-trade' demands may not have been novel, in direction or intensity; but they were delivered now on a wider scale, more fully ventilated in pamphlet and petition, memorandum and debate. The merchant's outlook, as well as the merchant, was counting for more. His business figured more frequently not only in the House of Commons but at Versailles, where his advice was more often sought and honours more often accorded to him. France had no Defoe, but she had more than one Josiah Child. Her chambers of commerce fulfilled a necessary function in the give-and-take which lay beneath the surface of the absolutist State. Colbertism had certainly been attacked at many points since Colbert died in 1683: for his successors, however, the growth of exports and the supply of specie were not of lesser importance— only more elusive. It is true that 'the City' did not make its full impact on the foreign policy of William III, who had the tastes of a prince and had learnt to distrust the political foresight of commercial men in his long quarrel with pacific Amsterdam: even so, the diplomacy of his last years suggests clearer understanding that the co-operation of English Commons and Dutch States alike depended on a tenderness for trading interests.

The expansive potential of world trading (ch. XXIII (1)) was most dramatically suggested by rising expectations of both sides of the Pacific Ocean. The South Sea furore, so striking a feature of post-war Britain, had been long preparing. In England William Dampier and in France J.-B. de Gennes were early links between the buccaneers of the 1680s, who brought back valuable charts of the Pacific coasts of the Spanish Indies, and the companies launched in 1695 by William Paterson of Edinburgh, which issued in a short-lived Scottish colony on the Isthmus of Darien, and in 1698 by Jean Jourdan of Paris and Noël Danycan of St Malo, whose captains showed what sensational profits could reward the carriage of suitable cargoes direct to Chile and Peru, at a time when the Spanish-American convoys were functioning less and less regularly (ch. XI). Some of these French ships went on to Canton, which after the wars was to attract wide European interest. This South Sea trade was an embarrassment to the none too successful French Asiento in the Caribbean; but by 1712, when French policy called for the suppression of both, heavy losses showed that it had been overdone. Meanwhile, blind to the inelastic consumption of Spanish-American markets, but anticipating in the Asiento rosy prospects of converting England's naval debt into a more remunerative share of the Spanish colonial trade than had been practicable through the established clandestine channels, the English minister Harley, colleague and rival of Bolingbroke, established the South Sea Company in 1711.

Like Bolingbroke's sketch of a new colonial policy—it was Bolingbroke too who obtained the British Asiento, for the unprecedented contract period of thirty years—Harley's plan belongs to a conception of England's interests widely at variance with that which had determined the contours of her strategy and diplomacy down to the Tory election victory in 1710— a volte-face in Britain's attitude to Europe as it was in the fretful course of her domestic politics (ch. VIII). The new Tory ministry of 1710 sought disengagement. For this purpose ministers had to break through the impasse reached in the peace negotiations of 1709, when their predecessors insisted not merely that the Spanish Crown should go to a Habsburg but that Louis XIV should himself expel his grandson from Spain. By admitting the necessity of a Bourbon Spain, the new masters of British policy returned to what had in fact been the formal Anglo-Dutch position *ante bellum* and made a long overdue acknowledgment of the impotence of Allied arms in the harsh Spanish war theatre, where most of the population was against them. But since the formation of the Grand Alliance in 1701, which had not guaranteed a Habsburg Spain, Britain had entered into pledges—with Lisbon and Barcelona as well as Vienna and The Hague—incompatible with the bilateral Anglo-French agreement which became the main foundation of the peace settlement at Utrecht (ch. XIV).

That Peace was the fruit of an English realism which at this distance of time may be admired, but the bitterness it engendered has much to do with the image of *perfide Albion*. Uneasy English consciences might point to the selfishness of the emperor in Italy and even that of the Dutch in the south Netherlands, where their Barrier was connected in English eyes with commercial advantages. Of these, however, in return for the 1709 Barrier (scaled down in 1713–15), England insisted on a full share, despite the unilateral advantages she had secretly wrung from the Habsburg candidate for the Spanish throne, and those Bolingbroke's diplomacy was to obtain from Philip V, in the Indies. The very treaty, negotiated by John Methuen with Portugal in 1703, which had committed the Allies to war in Spain against the better judgment of Vienna and The Hague, in order to purchase a naval base at Lisbon, was followed by a commercial treaty which helped to make Portugal an English economic satellite for years to come, as well as by naval operations in the Mediterranean which brought no solid gains for the Dutch. It is against this background, which includes the definitive eclipse of Holland's naval reputation in wars which overstrained her public finances (pp. 294–8) by an all-out effort on land, that the humiliation of the United Provinces is to be pondered. In relation both to their seventeenth-century greatness and to the new strength of their old enemy across the Narrow Seas, the Dutch lost more by these wars than France herself, especially as they failed to display the economic resilience of the defeated power. The coincidence of wars in North and West went particularly hard with them, tenacious as their hold remained on some of their traditional trades (ch. xxIII (1)). The Peace was also a disappointment to the crown of Portugal, although its army had done little enough to help achieve that Habsburg victory in Spain which had been its price for joining the Grand Alliance against Louis XIV, an old ally. Economically, the supremacy of English naval power, which dictated the reorientation of Lisbon's foreign policy in 1703, was now underwritten by the triumph of Portugal's wine-exporting interest at the expense of an earlier industrial policy that had been directed against the importation of English cloth (ch. xvi). Had Bolingbroke's draft commercial treaty with France been ratified by parliament, the Portuguese landowners would in turn have had cause to reconsider their deference to London. As matters were left in the Peninsula, the hard fate of the Catalans (ch. xi) was a more unpleasant monument to Tory peace-making. All in all, however, the bilateral origins of the Peace struck contemporaries as shabbier than the substance of the preliminary Anglo-Bourbon agreements which the powers had to accept at Utrecht. In the Nine Years War, many members of the anti-French coalition, including the emperor, tried to make separate terms with Louis XIV and some of them did so; but until 1711–12 the Grand Alliance of 1701 had held together against his characteristic efforts to divide it.

The nationalist drift of British foreign policy in Queen Anne's last years had long been anticipated by criticism of the whole European strategy of William III and his political heirs: the Lord Treasurer Godolphin, the Grand Pensionary Heinsius, and the duke of Marlborough. At the start, William of Orange had not risked the invasion of England in 1688 to save the liberties of Englishmen, or Anglican intolerance, from his Roman Catholic father-in-law, but rather to put an end to James II's neutrality in the war of nerves between Orange and Bourbon which followed the *Réunions* and the so-called Truce of Ratisbon.[1] William possessed a view of the whole European scene comparable only with that of Louis XIV, who had the advantage of a model diplomatic service but was trapped in the toils of his own maxims of policy, based on a low opinion of human nature and a record of successful aggression (ch. v). William and his intimate circle had won through to a sense of the European common weal more generous, if in some ways more old-fashioned, than Louis's concept of France's civilizing mission—a notion which preceded and outlasted the *grand roi*, but one which it was understandably difficult for Louis to detach from his personal *gloire*. In this respect, even more than in his stubborn refusal to know when he was beaten or in his good faith as a monarch (ch. viii), lies William's title to greatness. It was William who took the lead in the partition-diplomacy which sought to settle the Spanish succession without an appeal to arms. Disabused of Louis's good faith, it was he again who took the essential steps to con-

[1] Vol. v, pp. 219–20.

clude the Grand Alliance of 1701 and to condition Anglo-Dutch thinking towards it (ch. xii).

In 1688 the English navy, in particular, clearly promised to be a vital factor in open hostilities with a France whose line of battle could be out-gunned only by the Maritime Powers in partnership. Large-scale naval operations indeed proved unavoidable in order to consolidate William's hold on English and especially on Irish soil (ch. vii); and it is a mistake to think that his admirals could afford to neglect the squadrons of Brest and Toulon after the rout of Barfleur in 1692. On the other hand, the English could only get their Revolution (ch. vi) accepted by Louis XIV, for whom it was both a strategic reverse and a blasphemy, by throwing in all their resources with the loose coalition of small land powers which it had been their new king's life-work to knit and re-knit against the unpredictable aggressions of the *Roi Soleil.* As these were backed by well-organized armies on an altogether unprecedented scale—not far short of half a million men at maximum mobilization—it became necessary, by recruitment at home and abroad, for England to intervene in continental military warfare to an extent unknown since the Hundred Years War. Had she realized it, this was only the first round in such another epic. At the time, to men like Harley, it came to appear a wasteful deflection of the country's true genius for maritime empire: instead, the English found themselves mainly committed to a military effort and this was centred in the Nether-lands, where alone in William's thought could the French power be decisively broken but where movement was impeded by a system of cunningly designed fortresses. There the military engineering of Vauban—a great Frenchman also by the test of his radical criticism of the *ancien régime*—had endowed the most vulnerable of French frontiers with defences which ultimately withstood, though by a fine margin, even the initiatives of Marlborough and Eugene, who shared the preference of Charles XII for mobile campaigning more than did King William or any Dutch general. France was thus saved by the kind of strong barrier which it became the over-riding aim of the United Provinces to achieve for them-selves. It is suggestive indeed that so much importance was attached to barriers by other governments at the peace-making of 1712–14. There was foundation for it in the fact that the art of fortification had outstripped that of the gunner, and also in certain geographical circumstances like those of the Piedmontese Alps; yet the barrier mentality was to prove as deceptive in the long run as did the Maginot Line in 1940, while in the short run it drugged strategic imagination (ch. xxii (1)).

The Nine Years War, bitterly but indecisively fought in half a dozen theatres, should have ended in 1693–4, when the first of the two most terrible harvest failures of this period in France added to the financial strain on the combatants. That war continued until 1697 was as much due to French reluctance to recognize King William as the prolongation of the

18

next war after 1709–10, the years of the second major food and credit crisis, is attributable to Allied obstinacy on the subject of King Philip V. The two wars bear a certain resemblance in that the broad areas of fighting were much the same, except for Ireland and in Spain; in 1702, however, the French started by having to defend the Spanish Netherlands instead of trying to overrun them. In each case early victories failed to produce a strategic decision, although the French battle honours of Catinat and Luxembourg, the 'tapissier de Notre-Dame', in 1690–3, were matched only at a late stage in the succeeding struggle, by Villars at Denain; this time it was the Allies who at first had the best of it, at least in 1704–6, when the lightning marches of Marlborough and Eugene saved Vienna and Turin. There was more mobility of armies in the Spanish Succession War, if nothing like as much as in the Northern War, which also contained longer spells of military inactivity. As the events which culminated at Blenheim and Turin testify, the French desired to avoid that confinement of the main issue to the Netherlands which had caused them in the Nine Years War repeatedly to divert troops from the Rhineland and accordingly to practise frightfulness there. Yet their generals were hampered by remote control from Versailles, as was Eugene by his duties with the Austrian War Council and Marlborough by the obsession of his Dutch colleagues with defence. Marlborough's sharpest disappointment, however, came with the failure of Eugene's attack on Toulon, which was to have opened the way to Paris in 1707. He had King William's eye for combining land and sea forces, and in Shovell the rare phenomenon of an active admiral who expected success.

Until the 'miscarriages' of British shipping led to a redeployment of naval strength in home waters from 1708, Mediterranean operations absorbed it more consistently than in the previous war, when the defence of the British Isles was a constant preoccupation, despite the influence of anti-navalists at the French court after Barfleur and the increasing concentration of French frigates against the enemy's rich and vulnerable seaborne commerce. Except for the 'alarm from Dunkirk' in 1708, the only French naval initiative during the Spanish Succession War was the attempt to recover Gibraltar and its sequel in the drawn battle off Malaga in 1704. On the other hand, the damage wrought and the windfalls won by French corsairs owed more than in the past to the co-operation of the king's dockyards, which helped to equip roving squadrons capable of disrupting the Dutch whale-fishery at Spitzbergen or the transport of troops to Lisbon, and thus of giving background support to the very numerous smaller privateers (ch. xxii (3)). The Dunkirk of Bart and Forbin was foremost in this business, so that the demolition of its fortifications and harbour works became a major article in the British peace terms; the celebrated Malouin *course* had faded by 1706, although some of its promoters continued to nourish the expeditions of Duguay-Trouin from Brest and it was then that a combination between Marseillais capital and Toulon's unemployed naval talent began to flourish. It was from home ports too that Iberville and Cassard sailed to carry out their depredations in the Antilles in 1706 and 1712. With these multifarious but speculative enterprises only the dreaded *Commissievaart* of Middelburg and Flushing offers any comparison on the Allied side, even if the Channel Islanders were a plague on the coastal navigation of the Bretons, while the Jamaican privateers made an intermittent nuisance of themselves. The legislative encouragement of British privateers in 1708 was essentially the counterpart of panic measures to protect England's own sea-approaches by statutory cruisers and convoys. The art of the *guerre de course*, which called for speed and ruthlessness rather than gun-power and courage, was most naturally fostered in narrow seas. In the Mediterranean, where some small naval powers were permanently at war with Islam, it was endemic (ch. xvii).

The intensity and duration of the wars told severely on both manpower and public finance. If the social upheaval entailed by war in Peter's Russia was an exceptional case on the one hand, so on the other was Sweden's ability (down to 1709) to make war pay for itself. Wastage of men, by sickness and desertion as much as by enemy action, was ultimately less of a limiting factor than the national debts, but every winter the problem of replacements strained the ingenuity of recruiting officers. This is one reason why contemporaries deplored the heavy slaughter at Malplaquet (1709) nd indeed the 3,000 dead at Steenkerk (1692); nor was it only cumbersome field-guns and the art of fortification that encouraged commanders and governments to evade full-dress en-counters, for the widespread adoption of flintlock musket and socket bayonet, with their implications for tactics (ch. xxii (1)), made battles more murderous.

Poverty might be the great provider of soldiers (ch. xxii (2)), but even in the West it did not preclude semi-coercion or the necessity of supplementing national forces with mercenaries hired from German princes and Swiss cantons. The sizeable Dutch army of 1702 was largely composed of subsidy-troops, apart from the independent Prussian infantry and Danish cavalry, both of which, in the pay of the Maritime Powers, earned the gratitude of Marlborough and Eugene; the Imperial army itself was raised by the Diet to the unprecedented figure of 120,000 in 1702, but in practice this amounted to a much smaller army of the Rhine. The grand polyglot army of Louis XIV, which always enjoyed the advantage of fighting on interior lines, filled some of its gaps in Italy and Spain with militiamen from the French parishes. The development of militias, ostensibly for local defence under local landlords, is a feature of the period in France and elsewhere. It is important because it involved the principle of conscription, most widely used by Tsar Peter, who also dragooned civilian labour on far more drastic lines than did, for example, the intendants of the French frontier *généralités*. Beside this development, which in the extreme cases of Russia and Brandenburg-Prussia meant the progressive articulation of society for the needs of war, the period saw the maturing of the Scandinavian systems for producing and supporting men and officers from villages and properties assigned to these purposes. On the other hand, the Poles continued to rely too much on a species of feudal levy, so that a larger Crown army became the focus of all their efforts at constitutional and financial reform (ch. xx (2)).

Beyond the Elbe and down the Danube all armies lived more or less on the country of passage. In the West, on the contrary, the tendency was to liberate them from day-to-day dependence on civilians: billeting remained to burden the unprivileged—and was not without its uses as a sanction for promoting obedience to government—but there was less unofficial pillage and clumsy requisitioning. This is a tribute to the more sophisticated logistics of western armies, if not to better discipline. Indeed, when the equipment and tactics of the belligerents differed so slightly, the issue of victory or defeat might turn on quite marginal superiorities of that kind. The successes of Marlborough and Charles XII, like the devotion they aroused in their men, reflect the personal care they gave to fodder and footwear. Eugene's victories over the very large Ottoman field-armies, while they owed much to his own genius, were also the reward of a more efficient staff organization, even in an age when this was still rudimentary (ch. xxii (1) and (2)).

Relatively to the numbers of men mobilized, dockyards and warships cost even more than fortresses and siege-trains. They also depended on a more elaborate range of skills and supplies, some of them only available in quantity from the Baltic; the Ottoman navy was exceptionally fortunate in being able to rely on materials produced at home, whereas the Dutch and English were least well placed in this respect. It needed long experience, zealous administrators, good craftsmen and reliable contractors to build the ships and keep them seaworthy. Despite many abuses, all the naval powers possessed these in good measure except Spain and Russia. Peter's visits to Zaandam and Deptford in 1697-8 were to acquire shipbuilders besides direct experience for the new navy which was his most personal achievement—and the least sympathetic to the genius of his people (ch. xxi). France, on the other hand, despite naval intendants of the quality of Bégon of Rochefort, builders like Blaise of Toulon and a great admiral in Tourville, lacked a ruler with an unwavering belief in naval power. The Dutch Republic, in turn, relied on the grudging co-operation of five admiralty colleges and after William's death most of the burden fell on that of Amsterdam alone, with the result that the Dutch fleet diminished like the French. The explanation in both cases is basically a financial one. Britain alone, among the western powers, proved able to carry to the end the enormous cost of war simultaneously on land and sea. She did so thanks to the willingness of her parliament to run up a national debt horrifying in its novel dimensions, but also by making individual creditors wait for their money. Of these the seamen suffered worst. Arrears and discounts of pay were aggravated by the much-criticized new practice of turning sailors over from ship to ship to economize manpower and limit desertions, thus confusing the books and exposing the men too long to sickness and deprivation: a vicious circle was completed between harsh treatment and failing recruitment. It was during the Nine Years War, precisely, that English pamphleteers first assailed the wickedness and inefficiency of impressment, now occurring on an unprecedented scale. They admired the superior smoothness and humanity of Colbert's *Inscription Maritime*, even if it scarcely sufficed to man the squadrons of Brest, Rochefort and Toulon in years when these were at full stretch. Parliament's half-hearted attempt to imitate it, by means of a national register, failed largely because its full bureaucratic implications were misunderstood or rejected. In spite of a greatly expanded marine, therefore, the English often experienced difficulty in getting their ships to sea promptly. Yet this period of growth, which included the establishment of new bases in Jamaica and Minorca as well as at Plymouth and temporarily at Cadiz, showed that the English admiralty and navy board were generally equal to the new problems posed by wars with France. Apart from manpower, the chief weakness lay in the quality and cost of sea-rations, which jeopardized the health of seamen at the same time as the victuallers' debts absorbed supplies voted for the navy's other expenses (ch. xxii (3)).

As the wars went on, the western powers were driven into heavier and ever more ingenious borrowing, to meet State expenditures several times their dimensions before 1688 (ch. ix). Significantly, the budgets of the Maritime Powers rose proportionately more than the French, which at the outset enjoyed an ordinary revenue five times larger than the English, although the French fisc was far less centralized. England doubled her tax yield between 1688 and 1697, and nearly did so again in 1702–14, largely at the expense of her country gentlemen, many of whom were ultimately forced off their highly mortgaged properties and naturally disposed to believe that they were lining the pockets of war-profiteers (ch. viii). Further, a fourfold rise in the general level of English import duties may be said to have founded a system of industrial protection, although this was not its purpose.[1] Stiff excises were more important to the Dutch, who yet relied most of all on the unrivalled though by no means inexhaustible loan-market of Amsterdam. Vienna also drew heavily on Dutch financiers, but developed banking institutions of its own which

[1] R. Davis, 'The Rise of Protection in England, 1689–1786', *Economic History Review*, 2nd ser. vol. xix (1966), pp. 306–17.

mark an epoch in Austrian history. French revenues, notably the tax-farms, in the end fell off drastically. The poll and income taxes of 1695 and 1710 introduced the king's claim to tax all his subjects, at least in principle (ch. x); but in France, as in the Habsburg dominions, which borrowed at ruinous rates of interest, it was principally the peasants who carried the tax load. It is remarkable how long the 'absolutism' of Louis XIV contrived to live from hand to mouth, especially during the Spanish Succession War, when the sale of public offices and other *affaires extraordinaires* were inflated to lengths that would have been ridiculous had they not been so odious; mint bills and successive short-dated paper 'promises' circulated at rising discounts, so that the State came to depend on the credit of private financiers like Legendre and Bernard—all the more since it counted on them to manage its remittance business abroad. In this complex matter, however, the expulsion of the Protestants proved paradoxically a solid asset, for it extended the international banking network at French disposal. The first generation of Huguenot émigrés remained deeply French in feeling and the English treasury, for one, burnt its fingers with them in the Nine Years War, when substantial remittances to the Continent were as novel a technical problem for it as was the manipulation of public credit on the scale required (ch. ix).

In both respects, the wars crystallized an English financial miracle. In 1688 James II had no machinery for long-term borrowing: by 1714 widows and country parsons might be familiar with tontines, annuities, exchequer bills and the notes of the Bank of England. Thanks above all to Godolphin, one of the ablest statesmen of the age, English finances as a whole were better managed in the Spanish Succession War, although the big innovations belong to the first and more hazardous period. Average annual expenditure in 1702–13 ran half as high again as during the Nine Years War and Britain now found two-thirds of the Allied subsidies, but interest rates were down. Between 1689 and 1715 Britain underwent one recoinage, whereas the hard currency of France was revalued forty times as her stock of specie dwindled and her government tried to stave off bankruptcy. Moreover, the *Contrôle Général* was far from possessing that oversight of military and naval spending which to some extent the Treasury gained in Whitehall (ch. ix).

War loans and contracts, the mere handling of large sums of pay and subsidies, called for the special knowledge, connections and capital of many entrepreneurs, some of whom derived large fortunes from these transactions. They included warlords like Marlborough and Eugene, but also a Dauphiné innkeeper, Paris la Masse, and a Dutch bookseller, J. H. Huguetan. We witness the definitive arrival of the Court Jew in Germany, the 'moneyed interest' in London, the *Banque Protestante* operating between Rouen and Amsterdam, Lyons and Geneva. Habsburg and Bourbon pride was obliged to accommodate and even to ennoble financiers, whatever playwrights or pamphleteers might say. Noblemen and magistrates had never despised a bargain; now, for all the survival power of big landowners and urban patricians, they more frequently took the merchant and banker, though seldom the industrialist, into partnership and marriage. But it was the mass of lesser speculators who gave the tone to what Defoe dubbed an 'age of projects'—and none more inventive than he. It was they, in warehouse and coffee-house, who worked up the expanding trades to China and the slave coasts of Africa, fresh markets in marine and life insurance, more sophisticated routines of investment and exchange. These were the men of action whom the early eighteenth century idealized as the friends of the human race; even their egoism was socially useful, in contrast with the traditional aristocratic honour of the duel and gambling-table. They shared too in the refinement of manners symbolized by the porcelain teapot and the walnut chair; and doubtless, with the scientists, they contributed much to that subtle change of ethos which sought more rationality and tolerance, perhaps more charity, in what was still the first interest of this generation, its religion.

The 'age of reason' did not arrive with a fanfare and it would be a grave mistake to schematize the period here under review as in any simple sense its prelude. Even for educated men the old Christian cosmos underwent adaptation and renewal, rather than surrender to the small number of sceptics who denied the divinity of Christ or (more commonly) the assistance of divince grace. Clearly these heresies were not new, although Arian and Pelagian viewpoints were reinforced as Christian belief was deprived of many superstitious trimmings at the hands of scientists and historians, themselves usually devout men. But for many believers, also, the seventeenth century had been one of growing spritual insecurity, for it was Galileo who destroyed the music of the spheres and Descartes who produced a fully mechanistic universe. During the years 1680–1715, which a brilliant book[1] has stereotyped as that of a crisis in the European mind, the critical work of Simon, an excluded Oratorian, and of Bayle, an exiled Huguenot, weakened confidence in revelation and rationality alike, while the logical rigour of Newton and Locke demanded stricter proofs of reason itself. Above all, new perspectives of space and time were offered to a generation already oppressively aware of the corruption in human nature; moral pessimism stamps the classicism of Boileau as well as Calvinist and Jansenist. Could 'reasonable religion' or 'natural morality', however constructively intended, be kept clear from libertinism in a world so sensitive to the evil that men do? Had Providence withdrawn from it? Had the capitalist a duty to prosper, the valet a hope of regeneration? Was the intrusive ego of the Stoic answered by the self-abandonment of the Quietist, the resignation of the Epicure by Pietist missions and

---

[1] P. Hazard, *La Crise de la conscience européenne, 1680–1715* (1935).

charity schools, the honest Pyrrhonist by the Jesuit call to submission to pope and king? These are some of the uncomfortable questions debated at this time, by men of every temperament and persuasion, with a depth of insight and an intellectual subtlety which speak to the present day. To a robust traditionalist like Bossuet, the enemies were as much within the Roman Catholic body as in the luxuriant 'variations' of Protestant Churches without, while the erudite guardians of the New England Way strove desperately to preserve their covenant theology not only against Papist, Anglican and Quaker, but from more insidious contamination by ministers willing to admit 'half-way members' to the Lord's Supper. On this level the age of Malebranche and Spener, Bayle and Leibniz, was one of doctrinal revision, daring in theodicy (a new word) and fecund in casuistry. Yet the combined forces of secularism, latitudinarianism and natural theology were slowly evolving the religious temper of 'Christianity not mysterious', in circles which could afford it, despite occult elements in the new science and the continued hold of magical practices even on persons in high places.[1] So the optimism of the scientists eventually spread to theologians and moralists, and the life went out of old controversies such as Predestination, Passive Obedience and 'cujus regio, ejus religio'—controversies, nevertheless, which in many countries had come to a bitter and menacing climax as recently as the 1680s (ch. IV).

It is necessary to keep all these developments in mind if the explosive implications of the English Revolution of 1688 (ch. VI) are to be understood. Its inner logic only became apparent during the three following decades of national self-adjustment to a new rôle in Europe and to a new structure of power at home. The rapid sequence of events in 1688–9 was indeed more than a defeat for the religious policy initiated by James II or attributed to him, for it also reversed the absolutist trend which pre-dated his accession; the argument between divine right and contractual kingship had produced its fundamental documents, after all, in writings by Filmer and Locke respectively published and drafted in 1680–3. Yet the statutory contract of 1689—the maximum area of agreement between the politicians that was acceptable to a new king whom they needed even more than he did them—left residual prerogative powers which were the root of much subsequent anguish, whether exercised by a warrior-king of unconventional methods or delegated by a devout queen to the leaders of parliamentary coalitions, meeting regularly in what was beginning to be called the Cabinet. Decades were to pass before a smooth working relationship was hammered out, after many false starts, between this limited monarchy and a House of Commons which learnt in these years to feel its strength even in the conduct of foreign policy. Consequently, the very framework for settling party differences without civil war was itself, like

[1] See J. Ehrard, *L'Idée de Nature en France dans la première moitié du XVIIIe siècle* (2 vols. 1963), vol. I, ch. I.

the intrinsically sensitive questions of war and religion, an open invitation to partisanship (ch. vIII). This extended to the relations of parliament and convocation, Lords and Commons, electors and elected, government and the press. The upshot was a classical 'mixed' constitution, entrenched in landed property, civil liberties and political consent. It was to be long admired as the model domestic counterpart of that 'balance of power' which was contemporaneously becoming the first axiom of international statesmanship (ch. v). And yet 'the late happy revolution' would hardly have cast the spell it did on Whig mythology (on both sides of the Atlantic), or on French Anglomania, had it not seemed to explain, as it did for Macaulay,[1] how England's 'opulence and her martial glory grew together': this 'auspicious union of order and freedom' was held to be ultimately accountable for the Bank of England and industrial primacy, toleration of Nonconformists and freedom of the press, the Union with Scotland of 1707, the conquest of North America and an empire in Asia. While its authors preferred to regard it as a restatement of immemorial legal liberties, the Revolution also released economic energies which the conciliar government and monopolies of the previous régime had checked. The Revolution, moreover, owing to the international context in which it was enacted and consolidated, stimulated an appetite for political information and commentary—reflected in the rise of a vigorously polemical newspaper press which itself contributed not a little to the notorious English 'heats of faction'—and so inaugurated one of this people's most enduring traits.[2] With it went a sense of having arrived to first rank among the nations, strikingly declaimed in the palace Vanbrugh built for Marlborough at Woodstock.

English neutrality had been a condition of Louis XIV's continental 'preponderance', so that the English succession of 1689 was at once acknowledged as a major defeat for him. Equally, his recognition of William III as king 'by the grace of God' at Ryswick cost him a loss of face at home. But by perseverance Louis later won the main point for his grandson, if not for himself, over the Spanish succession. Neither Peace cost him important territorial concessions, although Newfoundland and Hudson's Bay represented appreciable economic sacrifices at Utrecht. Above all, he retained Alsace and Strasbourg, the strategic key to his kingdom when Franco-Imperial relations were habitually at the centre of his calculations. The 'decline' of France in these years denotes primarily the loss of a military and diplomatic ascendancy. Even at its zenith in the 1680s however, Louis had never been able to take this for granted: an eternal vigilance all over Europe was the price of quite modest territorial

---

[1] *History of England from the Accession of James the Second*, vol. I (1848), p. I.
[2] That 'a feeling for the interconnection of European events' was not confined to the English is well suggested by G. C. Gibbs, 'Newspapers, parliament, and foreign policy in the age of Stanhope and Walpole', *Mélanges offerts à G. Jacquemyns* (Brussels, 1968), pp. 293–315.

advances along the French frontiers, especially as their security was still felt to depend on the possession of bridgeheads, a Trarbach or a Casale, beyond them. Such outposts were a dangerous encouragement to the aggressive if precautionary military moves in the war of nerves which preceded open hostilities in 1688 (ch. VII). For this freedom of initiative there was substituted the European balance of 1713–14, with its barriers and renunciations. Yet France was shortly to be an indispensable partner in the Anglo-French and Quadruple Alliances devised to maintain that balance, and by 1735 Cardinal Fleury had restored her diplomatic leadership in Europe.

By that time, too, the subjects of Louis XV looked back with respect on the great reign which had closed, unmourned, in 1715. How, therefore, are we to interpret its 'sunset' years? Real military adversity and financial disaster are features of the last decade only, when the king's family bereavements echoed the distresses of his people. That the régime survived these terrible years shows how far it had travelled since the Fronde. Even in 1710, for all the fiscal racketeering to which he had stooped (but for which the financiers were scapegoats), Louis could still evoke an all-out effort from his subjects against humiliating peace terms. The sins of James II were surely trifling in comparison, but he had kept for less than four years a Crown which at his accession seemed to have attained an unshakeable predominance, whereas Louis's boldest critic could write at the crisis of the reign: 'The King's affairs have become violently our own... the nation must save itself.'[1] Disillusionment notwithstanding, the *Roi Soleil* had come to represent the French nation far too successfully for it to be able to translate any sense of divergent interest or separate identity into revolution. There were seditious outbreaks enough in France, especially when the harvests failed, but only the revolt of the Protestant Cévennois was difficult to put down. Much as they had to complain of, solid townsmen feared their own distressed neighbours more than they hated royal policy and its agents.[2] If there was less obedience in 1713 than in 1688, this was due to the alarm created among magistrates and clergy— more sensitive indicators of public opinion than courtiers starved of power or pleasure—by the king's desertion of Gallicanism (ch. IV), rather than to his war-making. Nevertheless, a long war marked the failure of diplomacy in Louis's own eyes, and war itself had become a wickedness to moralists close to him. Although Louis was no more directly responsible for the hunger of 1693 than for the economic stagnation which preceded it, Fénelon was already driven into a blistering attack on the king's whole European record and domestic extravagance alike; Beau-

---

[1] Fénelon to Chevreuse, 4 August 1710, quoted G. G. Van Deusen, *Sieyès* (New York, 1932), p. 149.
[2] Compare the articles by J. Gallet and G. Lemarchand in *Revue d'histoire moderne et contemporaine*, vol. XIV (1967), pp. 193–216 and 244–65.

villier, a member of Louis's small cabinet, condemned his breach of faith in tearing up the Partition Treaty; and in the succeeding years such criticism became more outspoken still. Significantly, however, it came from noblemen who wanted above all a return to the feudal order, an end to 'ministerial despotism' and luxury industries, the revival of provincial Estates (ch. x). Political liberty was identified with the privileges of the higher orders and of the historic provinces, economic salvation with the demise of Colbertism.[1] Louis XIV's absolutism is no more than an episode in the long history of these tensions, which it was never part of his programme, opportunist as it was at heart, to resolve frontally: the projects of an Abbé de Saint-Pierre, whose precocious modernity reminds us of Defoe, would have seemed chimerical to a heavily burdened king and ministers who lived on the whole from day to day. Their means of action, though comprehensive by most contemporary standards, fell short of those already available to the new Prussian kingship.[2] Yet their administrative tutelage, which little by little had sapped the resistance of centrifugal forces—incorporated in a heritage of institutions amazing in its variety—might have been extended but for the wars. In the event, Estates and *parlements*, Church and municipalities recovered enough of their earlier vitality to frustrate the reforming monarchy of the eighteenth century.

In the light of tendencies elsewhere in Europe, too, it may be possible to avoid a facile condemnation of Louis XIV's domestic legacy. The growth of bureaucracies notwithstanding, government and society were not at all points antithetical and the eighteenth century was to be the high noon of the European nobilities, elusive of definition though they remain. Even the service nobilities of Sweden and Russia came to merge, like robe and sword in France, with the territorial magnates. In southern Europe these were often the urban patricians as well or overlapped with them, hostile as the land might be to banking in Genoa, sharp as was the genealogical competition in the zones of Spanish influence—long deprived of a military class but lush in new titles. It is true that a social fissure between *noblesse de race* and newly ennobled, familiar to us from the Memoirs of Saint-Simon, was to be found from the Mediterranean to the Baltic, least of all in the Habsburg lands but emphatic in Prussia and Sweden and wherever dynastic service depended more than did Vienna on appointments and promotions outside land and lineage; in the Prussia of Frederick I, in fact, ennoblement came more abruptly to ministers of state than in France, whose *noblesse administrative*—Saint-Simon's 'vile bourgeoisie'—emerged gradually through the high robe and the *Conseil d'Etat*.[3] Yet

---

[1] See the interesting thesis of L. Rothkrug, *Opposition to Louis XIV* (Princeton, 1965).
[2] See vol. v, ch. xxiii.
[3] For a sociological analysis see H. Rosenberg, *Bureaucracy, Aristocracy and Autocracy: The Prussian Experience, 1660–1815* (Cambridge, Mass., 1958).

Crown employment, civil and military, necessarily expanded under the pressure of the long wars and there are signs that it was increasingly sought by old families, who enjoyed more of a monopoly of it afterwards. The conception of State service as the up-to-date basis of nobility was not permanently realized even in Russia, where Peter sought to make it the only basis (ch. xxi), in clean contrast with birth or wealth. The traditional status of landed patrimony still had a long future before it and in some countries conferred national political power. In England and Sweden, as in Hungary and Poland, the smaller nobility or gentry shared in this, usually under the leadership of territorial magnates, although a certain opposition between court and country long survived in England and Hungary—where it was reinforced by the Germanization of the greater families—and almost everywhere there was a very large 'provincial' nobility which lacked the means or tastes for national politics. Often its circumstances no longer matched its pride of ancestry, and it was accordingly insistent on making the most of status and privilege.

Except in Britain and the Dutch Republic, where regent office-holders and politicians nevertheless leaned more and more to the luxurious way of life typical of the southern senatorial families, the pleasures or just the pride of eighteenth-century nobilities were supported by privileges which bore hard on the mass of peasants—Vauban's 'menu Peuple de la Campagne', Shaftesbury's 'poor rural animals', the Magyars' 'misera plebs contribuens'. From the Balkans to Denmark, the period under review witnessed the depression of all these except the 'coqs de village' and a few mountain communities (outside Savoy and Switzerland). However we distinguish the varieties of freeholder and tenant, or western day-labourer from eastern serf, it may not be too much to say that nine-tenths of the population of the Continent was worse off in 1715 than it had been in 1690. Against more remunerative price-levels apparently arising out of the wars (ch. xxiii (2)) we must set much hardship which the wars did not cause but might aggravate. The second part of the reign of Louis XIV turned out to be very largely a period of climatic adversity.[1] No European economy, least of all the French, was made to withstand such a cataclysm as overtook Europe in and after the winter of 1708–9, one of the hardest ever known; even in England, relatively healthy under William and Anne, burials and riots increased. The cold wet summers of the 1690s hurt spring sowings from Scotland to Finland as well as the vintages of the South. Mediterranean countries were stricken by the frequency of drought and cattle disease between 1699 and 1723; in 1713–20 rinderpest reached the Netherlands from Russia. The loss of livestock or cereals threatened famine to rural populations whose normal diet was a bare subsistence. The old and the very young were particularly vulnerable to the sickness which accompanied—if it did not anticipate—such scarcities as gripped France in

---

[1] E. Le Roy Ladurie, 'Histoire et Climat', *Annales (E.S.C.)*, 14e année (1959), p. 21.

1693–4 and the whole of the North from 1696 to 1699. In addition, abrupt rises in the price of food quickly reacted on industrial demand, credit, employment and wages—inelastic as these were in relation to changes in the cost of living.

There was, of course, a differential geography of mortality as of prices, in what appears to have been demographically a relatively stable period (ch. XXIII (2)), and *a fortiori* the same is true of the incidence of fighting. To the increase of *corvées*, billeting and conscription in many lands, to the hardening of serfdom across the Elbe, to higher taxation combined with uncertainties of money supply and the growing indebtedness of villages, we must add the direct effects of the passage of armies in Spain and the Balkans, in the eastern Baltic and southern Netherlands, the 'scorched-earth' tactics of the French in the Palatinate and of the Russians in the Ukraine, the pillage of Bavaria after Blenheim, of Portuguese frontier districts after 1704, of Saxony in 1706–7 and of Poland throughout the Northern War—not to mention raids on West Indian and Aegean islands, New England homesteads and Florida missions. For half a century to come, the depopulated towns and deserted villages of Poland would bear witness to the movements of Swedish, Russian and Saxon soldiers, whose necessities spared neither bourgeois nor nobleman (ch. XX (2)). Although military administration in the West was increasingly capable of limiting the impact of hostilities on civilians, it is a mistake to suppose that any belligerent exercised restraint unless it advanced his cause. In any case, the dislocation of peacetime trading patterns by the mere fact of hostilities—much as governments might try to accommodate the two by special licences to enemy merchants or by the encouragement of neutral carriers (ch. V)—could affect thousands of producers, especially when the Great Northern and Spanish Succession wars coincided. When great ports like Riga and Lisbon changed masters or allies, when shipping movements were delayed and distorted, the repercussions would be felt far from the open sea, in continental markets like Geneva, in ill-lit cottages where woollens and linens were spun or woven, in modest vineyards and tobacco plantations. From this point of view, there is clear evidence (ch. XXIII) that the first decade of the eighteenth century was more disruptive than the last of the seventeenth.

These compound pressures, along with those aimed at stricter conformity in worship and allegiance, added numbers of fugitive agriculturists, prisoners and deserters of war, debtors and sectarians, to that large segment of the population which was habitually on the move: the herdsmen, shepherds, squatters, pedlars, journeymen masons and carpenters, waggoners and boatmen, strolling players and professional adventurers, smugglers and bandits. The exodus of southern Serbs into Hungary, the mass flight of Old Believers from Tsar Peter's long arm, the semi-voluntary exile of Irish Jacobites, Palatine Germans and Catalans—these are only epic instances of the widespread displacements which await study. The indications are that they were most numerous in Russia and the Ottoman empire, not least on the Black Sea steppes where Tatar and Cossack horsemen contested one of the many zones of friction which eluded the shaping power of the 'political' States, as did the brigandage endemic on the rivers and caravan-trails of the East. It was against tsar and sultan that the bloodiest revolts of the time took place—of Cossacks and janissaries. But over the rest of Europe there was raiding and rioting enough to match the high-seas piracies of those who had opted out of Western civilization altogether.

Except under siege or occupation, earthquake or bubonic plague—which scythed a memorable path through central and northern Europe between 1706 and 1714—the towns were best organized to protect themselves and even to strike advantageous bargains in hard times, when the rural poor made for their gates in hope of a relief all too often denied to them. There were cities, like Milan and Berne, which regularly exploited their dependent countrysides. There were municipal oligarchs among the war profiteers. French communities subscribed to State taxation on the cheap; Hungarian, Belgian and even some German boroughs strengthened their franchises; many were the town halls built in England in these years. The feeding of Paris and Constantinople was a major concern of statesmen, while London's coal prices could alarm parliament. The long-term drift of industries away from the towns, with their restrictive craft gilds almost everywhere, certainly provided thousands of peasant families with an indispensable money income; but the profits of the entrepreneurs were largely spent in the towns, like the interest payable on the debts of rural communes and that antique mixture of rents, dues, tolls, tithes and fees which composed so large a portion of seigneurial and ecclesiastical revenues. Except in Russia, which at Peter's death had only some three hundred towns (averaging no more than a thousand inhabitants), and in the lands beyond the Elbe generally, the bourgeoisie was continuing to extend its hold on the countryside. Especially was this true of farms, vineyards and parklands within easy reach of the centres of business and administration, whether it was London or Vienna, the Venetian *terraferma* or the Côte d'Or of Burgundy. As long as the wars lasted, few princes could afford to compete with the building mania of their richer subjects, even if the growth and embellishment of Turin and Düsseldorf, Berlin and Dresden, were nursed by their sovereigns, while Peter conjured St Petersburg out of the Neva marshes at enormous cost in life as well as money.

The broad contrast of wealth and poverty which was increasing the social distance between town and country was paralleled, of course, by secular differences in levels of literacy, and these were overlaid by the promise of a cosmopolitan urban culture. It is true that the cultivation of

3-2

music still depended most of all on court and church, but the public concert was gaining ground in London, Paris and Hamburg. Londoners were acquiring from Handel an enduring taste for a new musical form, the oratorio, as a Lenten substitute for the opera. Of opera itself, which continued to dominate the development of music (ch. III (2)), Venice and Naples remained the capital cities. It was likewise to poverty-stricken Italy that German princes and English peers looked for artists to produce that Baroque decoration, replete with goddesses and warriors, which best satisfied a virile self-importance[1]—unlike the French aristocracy, which was feeling its way towards the caprice of rococo and finding in the guitar-hushed trysts of Watteau, the one great painter of the age born north of the Alps, hints of release from Louis XIV's later austerity. At the same time, the civic rulers of Paris were sitting to the fluent brush of Largillière, English journalists and admirals to the genial Kneller. Although Thornhill's Painted Hall at Greenwich, begun in 1708, still drew heavily on the allegorical resources of the seventeenth-century Italian schools, as Verrio had done for William III at Hampton Court, the artistic tide was setting towards the more intimate, episodic vision of the departed Dutch masters.

A sometimes prosaic concreteness was strikingly evident in the more accessible literary genres, whereon bourgeois interests made a strong mark (ch. III (1)). The picaresque novels of Defoe and Lesage dealt in the stuff of common life, gave fiction the verisimilitude of historical memoirs, and taught the values of prudential endeavour. Addison and Steele endowed the sagacious merchant with a moral dignity worthy of European emulation. Even if in France he still craved nobility, the style of 'vivre noblement' was changing under the influence of the philosophe[2]—pleasure-loving and free-thinking, but well informed and fundamentally humble, after the pattern of the delightful and long-lived Fontenelle, the central figure in the passage of French culture from Descartes to Voltaire. The stock jokes of the French theatre might still be at the expense of the nouveau riche, but Dancourt in 1700 portrayed bourgeois types with sympathy, while the English comedy of manners derided the vices or follies of the courtier. In both countries the edifying moral and the sentimental ending made headway. Fénelon's Télémaque, the best-seller of 1699, is only the most celebrated title in a whole literature of revolt against luxury and licence; the songs and broadsheets of France point to the existence of a discontented public which was returning under pressure of great hardship to dreams of rural solitude, not without the tears which herald Manon Lescaut and perhaps suggest the influence of many translations from English.[3] English and French taste alike was veering

[1] See F. Haskell, *Patrons and Painters* (1963), ch. 7.
[2] Defined by the Académie in 1694 as 'one who applies himself to the study of the sciences, and who seeks to know effects by their causes and by their principles.'
[3] See G. Atkinson, *Le Sentiment de la Nature et le retour à la vie simple, 1690–1740* (1960).

from the grand universal generalizations of classicism towards a more intense absorption in the passing scene, including political news and popular science.

While the contemporary world thus recovered the prestige which had been slighted by orthodox classicism, historical research in the lifetime of Mabillon and Hearne, Rymer and Muratori, continued to document specific phenomena, often in support of contemporary polemics and with new refinements of technique. The unique philosophic genius of Vico, labouring obscurely in Naples, was as alien to this age as to the next, though in a different way. The classicist emphasis on the typical and recurrent, so apparent in historiography with Montesquieu and Voltaire, is discernible as early as 1703 in the work of a London doctor who explained cultural diversity by a historical anatomy of government, but Locke was one of the few to notice him.[1] The philosophizing spirit of French classicism,which had always been a crusade against the culture of a majority, only came to full maturity after Racine, who died in 1699. The later history of French taste was to show that it would not easily be emancipated from the aristocratic canons of the *grand siècle*, none the more because the very triumphs of the classicists enabled the Moderns to measure its claims against those of the Ancients (ch. III (1)). There was a relative but short-lived failure of energy here in Louis XIV's later years which has much to do with the stereotyped picture of a sunset. Yet the French language, and the *bienséances* which it had come best of all to express, were conquering the rulers of Europe. Paradoxically, the Huguenot diaspora made a timely contribution to this result, particularly through the international press which its pastors established in Holland for the dissemination of knowledge. Bayle's *République des Lettres*, in particular, was the cultural counterpart of the stadholder-king's European commonwealth (ch. III (1)). If the vitality of the Augustans suggests a fresh self-assurance among the English, their debt to French culture is nevertheless apparent from Dryden onwards. Mr Spectator indeed advocated the simple life, but by enlivening morality with wit and rendering learning polite he was inviting his readers to emulate the decorum of the *salons*. In turn, Addison was widely read on the Continent.

This cross-fertilization of French and English letters, attaining a 'co-dominance' over Europe (p. 72), bore marks of the much wider scientific movement (ch. II). The established national scientific societies of England and France, in their very different ways, were the prototypes for others—recognized in these years as essential to the equipment of a modern State. Important work was still done in Holland and in Italy, while Germans, Swiss and Scandinavians contributed major discoveries to that understanding of nature which even at the time was recognized as an

[1] J. A. W. Gunn, 'The *Civil Polity* of Peter Paxton', *Past and Present*, no. 40 (1968), pp. 42–57.

intellectual revolution. The number and variety of investigators involved can make it rather difficult to represent them as a single movement: and yet some such character is bestowed on them by the increasingly well organized channels for the transmission, indeed the vulgarization, of new knowledge, even in war-time, and by a common faith in the rewards of systematic research. This had already yielded so much that it is tempting to regard the age as empirically minded. In fact, scientific thinking was also impregnated with dogmas, not always very old, which distorted the direction of much inquiry or delayed the reception of new truth. The outstanding example of this dogmatism is the continued prestige enjoyed by the Cartesian universe, so alluringly exhaustive as to impose a barrier of prejudice, especially in France, to Newton's more modest mathematical demonstration of the laws of matter-in-motion. Newton's principle of 'attraction', while leaving vastly more scope for the direct intervention of Omnipotence in the natural world than did the fully determinist system of Descartes (or Leibniz's revision of it), seemed at first to be a regression to Aristotelianism in the way it blurred the boundaries between the natural and supernatural orders. Precisely this spiritualization of Nature, which theologians were quick to distrust, was to characterize the Enlightenment. Outside England and Holland, however, Newtonian science did not triumph until about 1740. A decade later, Diderot's *Encyclopédie* was to come down on the side of positivism against total explanations based on speculation, incidentally providing science with that explicit creed which justifies us in describing it as a 'movement' or even as a 'revolution'.

Newton's theoretical physics thereafter remained unchallenged almost until the present century. His procedure, moreover, grounded in new standards of accuracy in measurement, distinguished theory from hypothesis with an unprecedented austerity, even though his methods, like the questions he answered, were largely inherited from the empirical habit of the half-century preceding publication of his *Principia*, and especially from the dramatic advances in mathematics. In 1687 the scientific scene was dominated by the intimate union of mathematics and mechanics with the crude atomism of corpuscular physics. The mechanical model long prevailed in the study of physiology, sidetracking the doctors; Boerhaave, who made the reputation of Leiden's medical school, turned to chemistry, which at last began to discover a theory of its own through the fertile error of 'phlogiston' but in this period remained largely the domain of soap-makers and other craftsmen. The career of Boyle is particularly instructive in this connection. In breadth of culture and in his willingness to converse with artificers, he perhaps had no peer: yet his very desire to unify the 'new philosophy' led him to harden the subjection of chemistry to physics. On the other hand, botanists and zoologists and geologists were struggling to classify the specimens which piled up in their cabinets, from near and far, at an ever more formidable rate. The labo-

rious prerequisites of collection and systematics alone explain why the
biological sciences were slow to find an independent theoretical framework; from Ray to Linnaeus, botanical taxonomy developed faster than
its less tractable material allowed to zoology, in spite of great advances
made by the microscopists in the study of physiological functions and of
the minutest of living creatures. What is more, the sensational finds of
geology and palaeontology were slow to break down the *a priori* notion of
the immutable fixity of species, reinforced as this was by the biblical
account of the Creation and by Linnaeus's 'sovereign order of nature'
of 1735. Less than a decade later, however, anticipations of Charles
Darwin can be found in the essays of Maupertuis and Buffon, whose
ideas on heredity also put an end to the revival of ancient theories of
reproduction; the whole 'preformationist' controversy shows the real
limitations of the boasted empiricism of the new philosophy. In more
than one direction the great *Encyclopédie* thus coincides with an epoch in
the history of science. What is most striking in the record of the preceding
half-century is less the modernity than the momentum of discovery. But
this was both cause and consequence of an intellectual outlook which was
to change the world.

While science was unveiling a new universe and seeking the origins of
life, the minds of thoughtful Europeans were also digesting, more consciously and courageously than ever before, some of the facts of strange
polities and beliefs described by missionaries and other travellers to the
Asian courts and American forests. A large travel literature had already
accumulated but there was now an unmistakably larger public for it, as
the publishers of 'Relations', 'Voyages' and map collections were quick
to realize. These made an intellectual impact more far-reaching than the
influence of cargoes from Canton and Mocha (ch. XXIII (I)) upon manners
or that of the Brazilian gold discoveries upon the money market, even if
the true pioneering explorations of these years—the sensational penetration of the Brazilian interior by the *bandeirantes* from São Paulo
(ch. XVI) and the stubborn Jesuit advances down the Amazon and up to
California (ch. XI)—made less impression at the time than the exploits of
the Fathers at Peking (ch. IV) and the prying of foreign sea-captains around
the secret places of the Spanish Indies (although Dampier, in particular,
achieved more than that). At bottom we are confronted as much with
another indication of the contemporary zeal for amassing curious knowledge, from Saxon antiquities to Indonesian herbs, as with a dilettante
thirst for the exotic and the primitive, proper to a *fin de siècle* which saw
the scrapping of so many familiar signposts to the kingdom of God upon
earth. And yet, although many items in the news from overseas were
intended for practical use, whether details of the topography of Darien
or of the wars of Aurangzeb, much else took the form of disinterested
accounts of the appearance, diet, economy, government, religious and

sexual practices of tribes and civilizations which challenged the assumptions of the European visitor and caused the candid reader to reconsider his moral and political bearings (ch. III (I)). He was disturbed and might be shocked. In this period certain Christian tenets lost their uniqueness and a new respect was born for alien explanations of the phenomena of pain and evil—so much so that efforts to assimilate them to European historical and cosmological schemes had to be abandoned. Later, the *philosophes* and the Physiocrats were to order this information and derive instruction from it, especially from China: but already a rudimentary anthropology was reinforcing the questions posed by Spinoza and Simon, Bayle and Locke, about the authority of Church and Bible, the intellectual foundations of sovereignty, the nature of knowledge itself.

Tahiti and the sources of the Nile belonged to the future, Terra Australis Incognita and the North-West Passage would yet tempt speculation. The world known even to the small élites of Europe, at a moment of culture when no gentleman's library was complete without a globe, lay rich in secrets long after the speed of light had been determined. To the generations reared on Mother Goose and Robinson Crusoe there were still far horizons where anything might happen. In their taste for the imaginary voyage, in the satire of *Gulliver* as in the astonishments felt by Montesquieu's Persian visitor to Paris, Europeans were proving their civilization by laughing at it and inventing better ones.

CHAPTER II

THE SCIENTIFIC MOVEMENT AND THE DIFFUSION OF SCIENTIFIC IDEAS, 1688–1751

THE years following publication of the *Principia Mathematica* in 1687 saw a gradual but definite change in the character and spirit of the European scientific movement. Newton's masterpiece showed for a fact that the 'new philosophy' could solve the most imposing of problems. No longer was it necessary, as in the heroic days of Bacon, Galileo and Descartes, to convince contemporaries by argument of the power of experimental and mathematical science. Scientific deeds had spoken for themselves. At the same time the *Principia* brought to a conclusion the great cosmological debate opened by Copernicus, and established mechanics as a model for all the sciences.[1] With these developments, a period of adventure in ideas and organization gave way to one of systematization, fact-collecting and the diffusion of scientific ideas. Science became for a time distinctly less original. In 1698, Gottfried Wilhelm Leibniz (1646–1716) and the aged John Wallis (1616–1703), discussing in the *Philosophical Transactions* of the Royal Society 'the cause of the present languid state of Philosophy', found that among their younger contemporaries 'Nature nowadays has not so many diligent Observers'.[2] Two years later the Council of the Royal Society regretfully recorded that neglect and opposition had thwarted their plan to produce a series of useful inventions. Yet at this very time the influence of science was spreading as never before. A new profession had grown up. Scientific societies of high technical standards were soon to multiply, governments investing in science with the expectation of a profitable return. An expanding scientific journalism was spreading a new philosophy among a wide lay public. The culture of educated Europeans was changing. Science and its methods began to take the place of traditional metaphysics as the normative intellectual discipline. At the same time the geographical centres of intellectual influence shifted. English ideas penetrated the rest of Europe as never before, and this was before all else a triumph for the English empirical outlook.

To the scientific societies of the seventeenth century had fallen the task of organizing science as a profession. In general, the universities as such made little provision for scientific education or research; the societies, like the literary societies before them, were established, primarily by

[1] See vol. v, pp. 52–8, 63–5.　　　　[2] No. 255, pp. 281, 273.

university men, as a home for the new learning outside the conservative university system. The earliest had been Italian, but by 1700 these had ceased to exist. Elsewhere, however, two major national institutions had emerged to provide centres for organized scientific enquiry: the Royal Society and the *Académie Royale des Sciences*.[1] They reflect the intellectual leadership of Europe then coming to be divided between England and France. There were also two minor scientific societies in Germany, but no national academy there as yet. It was the Royal Society and the *Académie des Sciences* that furnished the prototypes of the numerous later academies in Europe and America. But they were two very different prototypes. The Society was a private body, entirely self-governing, controlling the election of its Fellows, embracing amateurs as well as professionals; it had no financial support or physical accommodation from public sources, no obligation to undertake work for the Crown. The *Académie*, from the start, was a State institution. The members were all professional scientists appointed by the State, well paid and accommodated, provided with adequate funds for research; in return they were expected to carry out any projects, usually with some technological application, requested by government. Both societies, indeed, endorsed Francis Bacon's insistence that science be useful as well as enlightening, and both emphasized the experimental character of research. But whereas the Crown soon learnt to leave the Royal Society free to pursue without interference its investigations for the relief of man's estate, the French scientists realistically decided that the good of humanity began at home and that the only way to raise funds was to appeal to their king's interests. In terms of work published, it is not easy to decide which policy paid best in the first half of the eighteenth century, for into the balance must be thrown the imponderable of the abilities of individual members. But certainly it was the French example of a national academy with public support, though not necessarily under governmental control, that was followed by most other countries; and during the second half of the eighteenth century the *Académie* completely outdistanced the Society, as a direct consequence of its professional character and adequate endowment.

In 1688 the Society was in the middle of the most difficult period of its early history. The average number of Fellows for 1686–95 fell to about 115 —little over half the average for 1666–75—and its finances were more than usually embarrassed. But its fortunes began to improve with the election of Sir Robert Southwell (secretary of state for Ireland and an amateur chemist) as president in 1690 and of Dr Hans Sloane as joint secretary in 1694. Newton himself was elected president in 1703. Throughout his long period of office (lasting until his death in 1727) and that of his successor, Sir Hans Sloane, both the membership and professional character of the Society increased steadily. Sloane was one of the leading naturalists and

[1] For their origins see vol. v, pp. 50–1.

physicians of his day; his zoological and botanical collection, begun while serving in 1687-9 as physician to the governor of Jamaica, was to become (together with his collection of manuscripts) the nucleus of the British Museum. When he declined re-election in 1741 he had served the Society continuously for 47 years. To him is due much of the credit for its progress throughout this period.[1]

It was the discoveries of Newton and the mathematical physicists that had first made the Society's reputation and towards 1700 they dominated its outlook. The work discussed or published by it nevertheless reflects fairly enough the extremely varied scientific activity of the age. Hooke continued to present experiments on mechanics, magnetism and optics, as well as observations made with a large telescope erected in the quadrangle of Gresham College. In 1703, after waiting for Hooke's death, Newton presented his *Opticks* to the Society. His versatile friend Halley, whose interests extended to demography and Arabic, continued to make outstanding contributions to many branches of astronomy, his *Synopsis of Cometary Astronomy* being communicated in 1705. Colin Maclaurin, one of the brilliant young mathematicians who gathered round Newton after his creative career was spent, extended his mathematical work: his *Treatise on Fluxions* (published in 1742, the year of Halley's death) is 'probably the most logically perfect and rigorous treatment of the calculus on Newtonian principles'.[2] In the 1720s Abraham

---

[1] Some idea of the Society's institutional history can be gained from the following statistics contained in Sir Henry Lyons, *The Royal Society, 1660-1940* (1944), App. II:

Percentages of scientific Fellows
representing different subjects

Year	Total number of Fellows	Proportion of scientific to non-scientific Fellows	Medicine and surgery	Mathematics and astronomy	Experimental and observational sciences (chemistry, botany, zoology, geology, optics etc.)	Number of foreign members
1663	137	1:2·1	55·1	34·9	10·0	0
1698	119	1:2·3	54·3	20·0	25·7	28
1740	301	1:2·04	63·0	19·0	18·0	146

[2] C. D. Broad, *Sir Isaac Newton* (British Academy, 1927). In 1712 the Society appointed a committee to report on the dispute between Newton and Leibniz over priority in the invention of calculus. Newton was not a member of the committee but not surprisingly it found in his favour. The officers also found themselves involved in disputes with the Astronomer Royal, John Flamsteed, when in 1710 they were appointed Visitors of the Royal Observatory at Greenwich. Good relations between the Observatory and its Visitors did not exist until Halley succeeded the petulant Flamsteed in 1720. For later developments see A. Armitage, *Edmond Halley* (1966) and E. G. R. Taylor, *The Mathematical Practitioners of Hanoverian England, 1714-1840* (1966).

de Moivre developed probability theory. The first announcement of the important discovery of the aberration of light was made in the *Transactions* for 1728 by James Bradley, who succeeded Halley as Astronomer Royal. The influence of the new physics was no less truly reflected in the work of Stephen Hales on blood pressure and the rising of the sap in plants. The Fellows also made a large contribution to early discoveries in electricity. One experiment published in 1731 showed for the first time that electricity can pass great distances through conductors; on a later occasion a current was passed across the Thames at Westminster Bridge. The Society's interest in botany, zoology and geology was maintained by Sloane, Ray, Woodward and their fellow naturalists. Leeuwenhoek sent much of his work with the microscope for publication in the *Transactions* and left a cabinet of his instruments to the Society, which also acquired specimens from various parts of the world, especially in gifts of the East India Company (in which it held stock) and from North America. The earliest maps of the Great Lakes were exhibited at the Society in 1688. In 1725 it sent barometers and thermometers to correspondents overseas to encourage meteorology. The Turkish practice of inoculating for smallpox was discussed as early as 1714, before the fashionable example set in 1718 by Lady Wortley Montagu dramatically reduced the death-rate from this disease. Yet it was as individuals that the Fellows achieved most of this diverse research. As Voltaire said, Newton was its glory but it did not produce him. It could afford to keep as paid officials only its Curator of Experiments and later its Secretary. Its accommodation remained modest.[1] It could occasionally assist scientific expeditions, but never finance one of its own. It never, in fact, carried out any large-scale research project. Even its publications had more than once to be abandoned. The *Transactions*, begun as a private venture by Henry Oldenburg, its first Secretary, were not published by the Society until 1753.

In contrast, the official character of the *Académie des Sciences* was underlined by its dependence on the interest of the minister in charge. From 1683 this was Louvois, who did not share Colbert's regard for pure science and determined that academicians should be set to answer practical questions about public works: La Hire and Picard about the surveying of Versailles; Thévenot about aqueducts; Mariotte and Sauveur about hydraulic problems at Chantilly; and Perrault, Roemer, Mariotte and Blondel about ballistics. The *Académie* wilted under this régime. But in 1692 its affairs became the responsibility of a new minister, Louis Phélypeaux de Pontchartrain, who reorganized it under his nephew, the Abbé Bignon. In 1699 it was given a new constitution with an increased membership, transferred from its old quarters in the *Bibliothèque du Roi* to spacious apartments in the Louvre, and equipped with a library,

---

[1] Rooms in Gresham College until 1710, when it moved to a house in Crane Court, Fleet Street.

physical and chemical apparatus, and biological collections. There, a neighbour of four other academies, it became the chief instrument of French scientific leadership until its suppression in 1793. The new constitution regulated the composition and functions of the *Académie* precisely. There were 70 members: 10 honorary, 20 stipendiary, 20 associate (including 8 foreigners), and 20 student members. The stipendiaries comprised trios of geometers, astronomers, mechanicians, anatomists, chemists, and botanists, with a permanent secretary and treasurer. They were elected only for distinguished published work. At first a student was attached to each stipendiary, but later the distinction between these classes was abolished. Stipends and other expenses were paid direct from the treasury, increments depending on the work produced; the paid members were obliged to live in Paris and their holidays were regulated. The king nominated Bignon president, Fontenelle (1657–1757) perpetual secretary. Their co-operative investigations being declared a failure, members were to return to individual research. But they had to make an annual report of plans and results; to demonstrate their discoveries at meetings, held twice a week; to report on books submitted for publication in their fields, and on all new inventions and machines; to correspond with foreign scholars and inform the public of their investigations by publishing memoirs and holding two open meetings annually. In the new *Académie* science found itself accepted as a department of the modern State.

The history of science in France becomes, at once, virtually that of the *Académie*. Its stipendiary membership included European leaders in many fields: the geometers Gallois and Varignon, the astronomers La Hire and G. D. Cassini, the anatomists Duverney and Méry, the chemists Lémery and Etienne Geoffrey, the botanist Tournefort. Among others who later joined them were the physicist and naturalist Réaumur, the botanist brothers de Jussieu, the anatomist and geologist Daubenton, the mathematician and geneticist Maupertuis, the mathematical physicist Clairaut. The association of different specialists on full pay and with proper equipment provided conditions of work found nowhere else. Thus physiology could develop in proximity with chemistry and physics. The *Académie* was also able to send substantial expeditions abroad—to Cayenne (near the equator) in 1672, Lapland in 1736–7, Peru in 1735–44.[1] Under this professional and critical régime, the reporting of observational and experimental techniques and results improved greatly. New standards of precision were established for scientific instruments. The Paris Observatory under G. D. Cassini (1625–1712) became the best equipped in Europe. Under Bernard de Jussieu (1699–1777), the *Jardin du Roi*—established by Louis XIII as a garden of medicinal plants, where anatomy

---

[1] Maupertuis was sent to Lapland, and Godin, Bouguer, La Condamine and Joseph de Jussieu to Peru, primarily to check Newton's theory of the shape of the earth and provide more accurate maps, but they brought back a variety of valuable information and specimens.

and surgery as well as botany were taught—began to play its profoundly important part in the development of the biological sciences. Harvey's doctrine of the circulation had been taught there from 1673 by order of Louis XIV.

Two main factors came into play in determining how other countries followed English or French example: the *de facto* condition of scientific activity awaiting organization, and the interest of rulers in such an accession to the equipment of a modern State. The first imitation came in Berlin in 1700, on a plan drawn up by Leibniz, providing for the ideals of both pure research and immediate utility. Yet the early years of the Prussian Academy were difficult: it was without proper resources, and a quarrel with Leibniz, shedding no credit on his colleagues, robbed it of its moving spirit: it did not really come to life until 1745, when Maupertuis finally took up residence in Berlin to carry out Frederick II's design for an institution based on Newtonian philosophy that would rival the *Académie des Sciences*. Leibniz hoped to cover Europe with such research institutions, but succeeded only in Prussia and Russia. In 1711 he met Peter the Great and discussed with him a plan for an Imperial Academy— eventually started at St Petersburg in 1725 when both were dead. It played an important part in the westernizing policy of the tsars. Its 15 salaried members supervised education, the book trade, and the principal techno- logical activities of industry. One of its main contributions was to survey Russian natural resources; for these members made long journeys to the ends of the empire. Russia having no advanced scientific tradition of her own, however, the early membership was composed largely of foreigners, including such leading scientists as Daniel Bernoulli (1700–82) and Leon- hard Euler (1707–83), both from Basle. But as early as 1741, when the great chemist Mikhail Lomonosov (1711–65) was elected, the Russians had a representative of equal standing. Russian jealousy of the foreign members, combined with inadequate financing, made difficulties for some time; but the work published from 1728 in the *Commentarii* of the Academy is among the most interesting of the period. Other nations and cities went on to found their own scientific societies: for example, Seville as early as 1697, Edinburgh in 1705, Uppsala 1710, Stockholm 1741, Copenhagen 1743, Göttingen 1751. The American Philosophical Society was promoted by Benjamin Franklin at Philadelphia in 1743. The number of scientific societies in provincial cities also increased rapidly: beginning with Bordeaux in 1712, there were at least 37 in France alone by 1760. The larger societies carried out serious research and published their own journals. Societies for particular sciences also appeared. There could be no better evidence for the wide diffusion of the scientific movement.

The main functions of the academies being research and its communica- tion, scientific education was left to the universities. Not until the nine- teenth century did they become the normal institutions for both teaching and research. In the seventeenth and eighteenth centuries there was even some antagonism between these two functions. Teaching tended to be traditional, whereas research, by definition, was always breaking new ground. In 1700 the basis of university education was still the traditional arts course, leading to the higher faculties of theology, law and medicine. Neither curricula nor methods of teaching—by lectures and disputations—could easily accommodate the new content and aims of the developing experimental and mathematical sciences, with their emphasis not merely on acquiring knowledge but also on advancing it. Bacon's criticism was to be repeated in much the same terms by d'Alembert and Diderot: the universities failed in their teaching to take account either of the advances in scientific knowledge or of the practical requirements of the new professions in technology, engineering and medicine; they also failed to encourage research.

But the state of the universities was not, of course, the same everywhere. The early eighteenth century saw changes in some that mitigated these criticisms. The steady creation of new professorships in mathematics, astronomy, physics, chemistry, anatomy, botany, geology, and other specialized sciences might mean much or little. More significant was the making of university observatories, anatomy theatres, botanical gardens, even physical and chemical laboratories. Distinguished scientists who were attracted to chairs usually gained more fame by their discoveries than by the numbers of their students, but the research they brought into the universities eventually influenced the curricula. The most favourable situation was a close connection between university and academy. Through professors such as (notably) Newton and Roger Cotes at Cambridge, or Wallis, Halley and Bradley at Oxford, the English universities kept strong links with the Royal Society, as did the Scottish. Oxford and Cambridge accepted Cartesian philosophy in the seventeenth century, but lectures were given in both on the Newtonian system early in the eighteenth; an important consequence was the introduction of the mathematical tripos at Cambridge, although this gave no encouragement to *experimental* science.[1] By contrast, the most striking example of the separation of teaching from research appears in France. French universities failed to develop close contacts with the *Académie des Sciences*; while the *Académie* was assuming a European leadership, they gave the scientific movement as little recognition as possible. Under strict ecclesiastical control and insulated from changing public opinion, the University of Paris began to admit Cartesian physics at about the same time as the French scientific world recognized that Newton had proved it false: the arts course, to which natural science belonged, remained elementary and out of date. Although some up-to-date natural science was taught at Montpellier, the great flowering of scientific life in France took place almost entirely

---

[1] See W. W. R. B., *The Origin and History of the Mathematical Tripos* (Cambridge, 1880).

outside the universities. But in fact the most advanced attempts to teach the new disciplines were made neither in England nor in France, but at Leiden, Edinburgh, Glasgow, Göttingen and Uppsala.

Of these, the influence of Leiden on medical education, and that of Göttingen on the development of the research mentality in the faculty of arts, may be singled out, for it had been in the faculties of medicine and arts that science had had its traditional place. Since the thirteenth century, the only systematic and advanced scientific education available had been that offered in the medical faculty; indeed, most scientists had a medical training until the nineteenth century. Leiden had been a pioneer in attempting to introduce the new science into medicine, and after the appointment of Herman Boerhaave (1668–1738) as a professor in 1709 its medical school led Europe. The programme there was twofold: first, a thorough grounding in anatomy, the current mechanistic and chemical physiology, chemistry, the relevant branches of physics, and botany; there followed instruction in clinical medicine (for which some beds were reserved in the hospital), including diagnostics and therapeutics, pathological anatomy, surgery, and specialized work in obstetrics, children's diseases and other subjects. In all this the experimental discoveries of Harvey and the clinical methods of Sydenham served as an example. Outside Holland, Leiden's most immediate influence was felt at Edinburgh, Vienna and Göttingen. These four universities came to dominate medical education *ca.* 1750. All owed their effectiveness to the same features: teaching began to be brought into contact with research, largely through the modern principle of specialization; specialized chairs were established, and working facilities provided in botanical gardens, chemical laboratories and hospitals; examination standards were raised. The provisions of the arts faculty at Göttingen initiated an analogous reform in the position of the mathematical, physical and social sciences in universities. The new style of arts faculty, empirical in outlook, emphasizing research as well as teaching, and providing advanced work in its own right instead of a mere introduction to the traditional higher faculties, was essentially a German innovation. It began at the new university founded at Halle by the elector of Brandenburg in 1694, and was extended by the elector of Hanover when he founded the university of Göttingen in 1734. Both universities, especially Göttingen, carried to the extreme the principle that education was a State affair. The new German universities were no longer self-governing. In contrast with the medieval conception of an independent corporation of masters of arts, they were denied the ancient privileges of electing to posts and controlling their own revenues. The government appointed professors like other civil servants, obliged them to swear loyalty to the sovereign, supervised instruction, demanded reports on lectures and attendance. Organized into faculties, the professors had only two duties, teaching and research, intimately connected. Thus grew up the system of the general course of public lectures and the private research seminar. In addition to offering favourable salaries, pensions for professors and scholarships for students, Göttingen provided excellent conditions of work. Professors were given freedom in teaching, which included the complete range of the natural sciences, economics and other social sciences, and such technical subjects as agriculture, certain branches of chemistry and metallurgy, as well as the various specialized medical sciences. The university library became the best in Europe. There were physical and chemical laboratories, an observatory, a botanical garden, an anatomy theatre, a university hospital. The Royal Society of Sciences of Göttingen, composed of professors, also became the means of insisting on the research principle and exerted a wide influence through its journals. Raised to the highest level of intellectual distinction by such men as the physiologist and botanist Albrecht von Haller (1708–77), Göttingen became a model for the modern university.

Besides the academies and certain universities, another institution, closely connected with them, bound the scientific profession together. This was the scientific press. For scientists themselves, growing specialization imposed regular communication. Nor did the communication of general conclusions now suffice. Increasingly precise standards of observation demanded that methods and results be reported in detail. Hence the publication of scientific treatises became a recognized function of academies and even universities. But the quickest and most regular means of publishing individual investigations was the journal, of which the *Philosophical Transactions* was the model. From 1665 also, original investigations had found a place in the *Journal des Sçavans*, an independent enterprise closely affiliated with the world of the scientific societies—in 1702 it was placed in the care of a committee by Bignon—but one which did not neglect the wider public. The first successors of the professional prototype were medical journals, which appeared in Germany, Denmark, Holland and elsewhere from 1670; dealing with the general range of sciences in relation to medicine, they are another reminder of the privileged position of the medical faculty in organized scientific research. More influential, however, was the *Acta Eruditorum*, which appeared regularly in Latin at Leipzig from 1682. Besides announcing new books, it published papers on all branches of science and mathematics (and on law and theology) by leading scholars from all over Europe; it was in the *Acta* that Leibniz published his papers on the calculus. Other professional publications were the *Miscellanea curiosa* or *Ephemerides* (1670) of the *Academia Curiosorum* at Nuremberg and the *Miscellanea* of the struggling academy at Berlin, brought out first by Leibniz in 1710. Far more important was the decision of the reorganized *Académie des Sciences* to follow the Royal Society in publishing regular proceedings. Hitherto the *Académie* had published only occasional *Mémoires* and a *History* in Latin

(1697) by its secretary, J. B. Du Hamel. In 1720 and again from 1732, Fontenelle (secretary, 1699–1741) brought out a long series of *Histoires et Mémoires* covering all years from its foundation and continuing with current work; in addition, he composed a series of *Eloges* on great scientists of all nations as they died, adding others from the recent past—invaluable sources for the contemporary feeling of the scientific profession. The professional standards set by Society and *Académie* became an example for the published proceedings of other principal academies. At the same time international contact was maintained by the journals' practice of printing each other's scientific news, and by translations of articles and reviews, as well as by foreign editions of scientific books. The success of the scientific journal reflected both the general journalistic vogue of this period and that of science itself. Even the *Mercure Galant* printed scientific news and opinion, while a number of new periodicals imitated the *Journal des Sçavans* in catering for laymen and professionals alike. Italy had its various *Giornali dei litterati* from 1688. In Holland, Pierre Bayle brought out in 1684 his *Nouvelles de la République des Lettres*, which continued under different titles and editors until 1718 and gave rise to later imitations. For those who read French the Dutch press also produced journals specializing in the translation of English and German writings— among them the *Bibliothèque anglaise* (1717–28), *Bibliothèque britannique* (1733–47) and *Europe savante* (appearing with changes of title from 1718). In reply to Bayle came the remarkable *Journal de Trévoux*, published 1701– 62 (with interruptions) under Jesuit editorship, in a small principality within France as a means of getting round the official privilege of the *Journal des Sçavans*: conservative in science, theology and politics, it was a major instrument for bringing scientific matters—from the great theoretical controversies between Cartesians and Newtonians to experiments on ballistics, electricity and magnetism—to the knowledge of a wide public which would never see the professional periodicals.

These years saw the growth of a number of other agencies for the diffusion of scientific knowledge. Of fashionable expositions, often brilliant in execution, the learned and witty Fontenelle, the model *philosophe*, was the acknowledged master. Other notable contributions to this genre, in very different ways, included Maria Sibylla Merian's attractive books on entomology,[1] Moitrel d'Element's *Expériences sur l'air et l'eau* (1719), Abbé N. A. Pluche's *Spectacle de la nature* (1732), the writings of Abbé J. A. Nollet, William Jacob 'sGravesande and Pieter van Musschenbroek on physics, and Voltaire's account of English science in *Lettres philosophiques* (1734). Voltaire remarked in his dedication of *Alzire* (1736) that

[1] Her *Metamorphosis insectorum Surinamensium* has been called 'one of the finest books that has ever come from a printing-press' and her work in Surinam compared in originality with that of George Rumphius, whose *Amboinse Rariteitenkamer* was also published in 1705: C. R. Boxer, *The Dutch Seaborne Empire* (1965), pp. 181–3.

Merian, Réaumur, Maupertuis and others set out not only to cultivate science but 'by making it agreeable, to render it necessary to our nation. We live in an age, I venture to say, when a poet must be a philosopher and when a woman may dare to be one openly.' Serving much the same public were the new encyclopaedias. In England these were at first primarily technical, notably John Harris's *Lexicon Technicum* (1704) and Ephraim Chambers's *Cyclopaedia* (1728); by contrast, French encyclopaedias echoed Bayle's *Dictionnaire* (1697) in spicing information with theoretical and social criticism. A further means of satisfying curiosity was the popular lecture and demonstration. Early in the eighteenth century, distinguished scientists like John Keill and J. T. Desaguliers at Oxford, Roger Cotes and William Whiston at Cambridge, taught physics through experiments; Desaguliers and Whiston later taught in London. From 1719 their example was followed in Manchester and other provincial centres. In Holland popular lectures with demonstrations were given by 's Gravesande and Musschenbroek. In Paris, J. G. Duverney (1648–1730) is said to have made anatomy so much the fashion that one lady fitted up her boudoir with wax models and corpses, while another took with her in her coach a corpse to dissect as one might read a book. The most celebrated of all such lecturers was Nollet, who opened a free course under the aegis of the *Académie* in 1734 and was later given a chair at the University of Paris; he achieved special success by repeating in public the most recent experiments in physics, giving spectacular performances based on Franklin's discoveries in static electricity. For such demonstrations a large collection of apparatus of all kinds had to be brought together to form a *cabinet de physique*. Other scientific tastes encouraged a vogue for the cabinet of natural history. And serving both lay and professional interests was the development of yet another characteristic institution, the science museum.

The general unity of outlook imparted by the scientific movement meant, in the broadest sense, that it was agreed that all questions, whether or not concerned with natural philosophy, should be decided by observation and reason alone. Thus Locke, on the explicit model of Sydenham, Boyle and Newton, made a freshly empirical approach to epistemology, psychology, ethics, social and political theory, treating them as problems in the 'natural history' of man.[1] Voltaire described him as the anatomist of the soul, and followed his example in becoming an anatomist of society. More specifically, science laid increasing stress on quantity and measurement, in place of a rational discussion that remained merely impressionistic. New kinds of problem were brought within range of quantitative measurement. Thus England's population in 1688 was estimated by Gregory King in *Natural and Political Observations* (1696), while from 1686 Vauban had been breaking similar ground in France.[2] The first official census in Europe

---

[1] See vol. v, pp. 91–4.   [2] For Marshal Vauban cf. below, pp. 329–31 and 750.

was of Iceland in 1703. Developing the statistical demography pioneered by John Graunt in 1662 and by De Witt's annuity calculations of 1671, Halley drew up in 1693 a table of life-expectations based on data for Breslau. From these beginnings, aided by advances in the mathematics of probability, the actuarial basis of modern insurance was worked out during the eighteenth century. Vital statistics developed more soundly than the ambitious 'political arithmetic' associated with the name of Sir William Petty (1623–87). From 1696 England had an inspector-general specially concerned with commercial statistics and ten years later, in William Fleetwood's *Chronicon Preciosum*, produced the first serious price-history. John Arbuthnot's *Essay on the Usefulness of Mathematical Learning* (1701) expresses the high hopes then held of a quantitative social science and goes so far as to identify statistics with 'the true political knowledge'.[1]

Nevertheless, in spite of genuine broad agreement on methods of approach and philosophical outlook, what we have called the scientific movement consisted, in reality, of a number of different activities by no means all logically or causally connected. They were all bound together, it is true, by the social framework that kept individuals and institutions in close communication; but within this framework the problems of each separate field gave rise to further problems mainly by their own internal logic. Related sciences—e.g. mechanics and astronomy, chemistry and physiology—of course made contact; but others did not, and their methods remained distinct. Thus mathematics had no application in natural history or geology. Controlled experiment could not be used in astronomy, and only with difficulty in the study of human beings. Technology made contact with science only at specific points, the commonest being the design of instruments. Such developments as the early steam-engine and the new methods of crop rotation, or of animal husbandry and breeding, owed nothing to scientific knowledge of heat, plant and animal nutrition, or genetics. In fact, such knowledge scarcely existed. Philosophy likewise followed its own problems in epistemology, psychology and politics, using science only as a general inspiration and deriving from it old questions in a new guise. All these activities, like the contemporary changes in theological and political opinion, industry and commerce and social organization, were strongly marked by the scientific spirit; but all had their independent histories as well as their connections with it. The scientific movement itself was less a *bloc* than an aggregate of autonomous movements, carried out by men who were united by broad intellectual agreement, and by institutional contact, rather than by any close logical or technical connection between their separate activities.

[1] (Sir) G. N. Clark, *Science and Social Welfare in the Age of Newton* (Oxford, 1937), ch. v, where the non-scientific antecedents of political arithmetic are also discussed.

The most striking general characteristic of science in this period was the dramatic advance of mechanics and related branches of mathematics, in contrast with the lack of powerful theories and mathematical techniques in most other fields, where collecting and classifying facts usually proved of more immediate value than trying to explain them by the inadequate theories available. This very deficiency, however, encouraged a remarkable growth of observation. Thus science became increasingly empirical, not only in its practice but also in its attitude to theory. There was an attempt to exploit mechanical ideas—especially Newtonian attraction—for theories in biology and chemistry as well as physics; but it was precisely in the growing empiricism that even a mathematician and theoretician like d'Alembert saw a true expression of the Newtonian spirit.

The outstanding question of the half-century after 1687 was the great Newtonian-Cartesian debate over physics and cosmology. The issues were ultimately theoretical and methodological, but involved discussion at every scientific level. In making headway against the widely accepted Cartesian system, Newton and his followers had to show convincingly that their mechanics gave a greatly superior account of the known facts, but also that Newton's methods and conception of scientific explanation generally were more appropriate than those of their opponents. Controversy was keenest over these last, fundamental issues. Thus an anonymous reviewer in the *Journal des Sçavans*, seeing science as a deductive exercise in the Cartesian sense, conceded that Newton's conclusions followed from his assumptions, but claimed that his assumptions had not been *proved*— i.e. not deduced from necessary propositions: they could serve 'only as the foundations of a treatise on pure mechanics',[1] as a mathematical exercise. A more eminent critic was Christiaan Huygens (1629–95). He agreed that Newton's assumption of forces acting between members of the solar system was fully justified by the correct conclusions that followed from it, and that Newton had demolished the Cartesian explanation of the motion of the planets and comets as due to the circulation of a vast vortex or whirlpool of matter with the sun at its centre. But Huygens could not go one step further to accepting attraction as the mutual interaction, not merely of pairs of planets and stars, but actually of every pair of particles, however small, 'because I think I see clearly that the cause of such an attraction can be by no means explained by any principle either of mechanics or of the laws of motion'.[2] It was the pride of the natural philosophers that they had banished for ever the 'occult qualities' of Aristotelian physics—mere names that explained nothing—and replaced them with mechanical explanations, in principle as clear as the explanation a clockmaker might give of the working of the great clock of Strasbourg.

[1] 2 August 1688; quoted R. Dugas, *La Mécanique au XVIIe siècle* (Neuchâtel, 1954), p. 445. On Newton's philosophy and its impact see A. Koyré, *Newtonian Studies* (1965).
[2] *Traité de la Lumière* (Leyden, 1690), p. 159. For Huygens, cf. vol. v, ch. III.

For Huygens, Newton had demonstrated the mathematical pattern under-lying the motion of the solar system, but the mechanical causes at work must now be found. Huygens held that these could not be associated with the mutual attraction of particles: Newton's own work had discredited every explanation along such lines. In any case, mechanical explanations of the once-mysterious gravity had been given since the time of Descartes: Newton surely could not be turning his back on these and making gravity once more 'a property inherent in corporeal matter'? On this particular point Huygens was interpreting Newton correctly:

That gravity should be innate, inherent, and essential to matter, so that one body may act upon another at a distance through a vacuum, without the mediation of anything else, by and through which their action and force may be conveyed from one to another, is to me so great an absurdity, that I believe no man, who has in philosophical matters a competent faculty of thinking, can ever fall into it.[1]

In other words, there must be an *explanation* of gravity: it 'must be caused by an agent acting constantly according to certain laws, but whether this agent be material or immaterial, I have left to the considera-tion of my readers'.[2] Gravity may be due to the action of an 'aether', consisting of 'parts differing from one another in subtility by indefinite degrees';[3] or it may be 'an original and general law of all matter impressed on it by God. We ought no more to enquire how bodies gravitate than how bodies first began to be moved.'[4] Whatever the cause, a force de-scribed as gravitational attraction was at work. But this force was not to be explained simply as 'essential' to matter in the Aristotelian sense. Although Newton's position, so easy to misunderstand, needed clear and careful expression from the start, the first edition of the *Principia* was not sufficiently explicit on this point. For the second edition Newton made a number of changes to meet the criticism that the work 'deserts mechanical causes, is built upon miracles, and recurrs to occult qualitys'.[5] Yet many natural philosophers on the Continent continued to believe that Newtonian attraction represented a return to Aristotelian physics.

Newton was attacked on other grounds by Leibniz and Berkeley.[6] Each felt that some philosophical features of Newtonianism—e.g. his views on space and time—were opposed to natural religion. In an ex-

---

[1] Newton to Bentley, 25 February 1693, *Principia*, ed. F. Cajori (Berkeley, 1934), p. 634.
[2] *Ibid.*   [3] Newton to Boyle, 28 February 1679, *ibid.* p. 633.
[4] As Dr Samuel Clarke, Newton's champion in his later controversy with Leibniz, wrote on p. 82 of his notes to his translation (2nd edn. London, 1702) of the *Physique* of Jacques Rohault.
[5] Cotes to Newton, 18 March 1713, reporting the criticisms of Leibniz, in I. B. Cohen, *Franklin and Newton* (Philadelphia, 1956), p. 136. Newton's changes included the addition of the *General Scholium* to Bk III, with the famous passage making it clear that he would not be driven into speculations: 'hitherto I have not been able to discover the cause of those properties of gravity from phenomena, and I feign no hypotheses' (Cajori edn. p. 547).
[6] On the philosophy of Leibniz see vol. v, ch. IV; for George Berkeley (1685–1735), cf. vol. VII, p. 110.

change with Clarke, Leibniz in particular accused Newton of representing God as an inferior clockmaker, requiring God to intervene in the world 'and even to mend it, as a clockmaker mends his work'.[1] In fact, for all his doubts as to the divinity of Christ, Newton, like most scientists of his age, was deeply religious. He held that his work provided new evidence for the providence of God, reaffirming in the *General Scholium* to Book III of the *Principia*: 'this most beautiful system of the sun, planets and comets, could only proceed from the counsel and dominion of an intelligent and powerful Being'.[2]

Granted Newton's methods and conception of scientific explanation, natural philosophers had still to be convinced that his mechanics gave an account of the facts superior to the Cartesian. This occupied several decades. Although the first edition of the *Principia* was limited to a few hundred copies, the second did not appear for over a quarter of a century; and even those who owned copies of the first found themselves confronted with an austerely mathematical treatise of great complexity. Non-mathematicians might be forgiven if they found the inverse-square law a poor substitute for the Cartesian vortex that carried the planets round the sun. It is not surprising, then, that when in 1693 Whiston went up to Cambridge, where Newton had been teaching for many years, it was to study 'particularly the Mathematicks, and the Cartesian philosophy: which was alone in Vogue with us at that time'.[3] For some years Newtonian theory was taught in the universities of England and Scotland only by isolated mathematicians. The further spread of Newtonian physics in these universities came about in a curious way. The outstanding textbook of Cartesian physics was Rohault's *Traité de Physique* (1671). Clarke felt that, as long as the teaching of Newtonianism was hampered for want of a suitable text, the continued use of the *Traité* was justified, and as late as 1697 published a new translation. To bring the *Traité* up to date he added a number of 'annotatiunculae'—mostly concerned with the work of later Cartesians such as Perrault, but with references to Boyle, Hooke, Newton and others of the Royal Society. Newton's work on prisms and his theory of comets (one of the weakest features of the Cartesian system) are treated at length; but Clarke hesitates to depart too radically from the original text. In the second edition (1702; Amsterdam 1708) the notes— now 'annotata'—have grown to a fifth the length of the original text. Clarke expressly states that they are taken from Newtonian philosophy and there are frequent, undisguised attacks on Cartesian physics: the notes are now the work of a partisan of Newton, and this is still more so with the third edition (1710). In this way the outstanding Cartesian

---

[1] First letter to Clarke, November 1715, in H. G. Alexander (ed.), *The Leibniz–Clarke Correspondence* (Manchester, 1956), pp. 11–12.
[2] Cajori edn. p. 544. For a full and acute analysis of these controversies see J. Ehrard, *L'Idée de Nature en France pendant la première moitié du XVIIIᵉ siècle*, vol. I, esp. ch. III.
[3] *Memoirs* (1749), pp. 35–6.

textbook became the vehicle for the introduction of Newtonian ideas.[1] On the Continent too, Newton's work was becoming better known during these decades, although long unacceptable. To Moreau de Maupertuis (1698-1759) belongs the honour of being the first in France to defend Newton's right to use a principle the cause of which was unknown. In 1732 he subjected the Cartesian concepts to a logical analysis as hostile as, though much more subtle than, the attacks on Newtonian attraction. An influential disciple of Maupertuis was Voltaire, who defended Newton in his *Lettres philosophiques* and published *Eléments de la philosophie de Newton* in 1736. Henceforward Newtonianism rapidly gained ground. It proved impressively successful—e.g. in dealing with the complicated analysis of the motion of the moon, and in predicting the shape of the earth and the return of Halley's comet. The last time the *Académie des Sciences* 'crowned' a Cartesian work was in 1740. For the rest of the century, when in England there were no outstanding men to continue Newton's work, the Continent produced a series of mathematicians of the first rank who did so: Clairaut, Euler, d'Alembert, Lagrange and Laplace.

Besides being the most advanced theoretical science of the period, astronomy led the way in the drive for more and better observations. Telescopes and micrometers were fitted to existing instruments; the telescopes grew to enormous lengths, sometimes 100 feet. Accurate time-measurement became increasingly important. The new search for accuracy led to important collections of data such as Flamsteed's *Historia Coelestis Britannica* (1712), the 1725 edition listing nearly 3,000 stars, and to such practical benefits as improved navigation. It led also to a number of far-reaching theoretical discoveries: in particular, the proper motions of some of the 'fixed' stars and the secular acceleration of the moon, both discovered by Halley, and the aberration of light and the nutation of the earth's axis discovered by Bradley.

To other fields of physical science mathematics was less obviously applicable. The theoretical interpretation of experiments was dominated by the 'corpuscular' philosophy, which sought to interpret all phenomena in terms of the motion of particles—discussed more often than not in qualitative terms. The most developed theories related to optics, a controversial subject long before Newton's early experiments with prisms. His *Opticks* (1704) had a great influence, thanks partly to the emphasis on proof by experiments, which appealed to non-mathematicians; but more important still, whereas in the *Principia* Newton 'seems to have exhausted his Argument, and left little to be done by those that shall succeed him',[2] in the *Opticks* he wrote that 'to communicate what I have tried, and leave the rest to others for farther Enquiry, is all my Design in publishing these

---

[1] Further editions continued until 1735. By then popular accounts of Newtonianism, like H. Pemberton's *View of Isaac Newton's Philosophy*, were available.

[2] Halley, *Phil. Trans.* no. 186 (1687), p. 291.

Papers'. He even added a list of 'Queries', which grew with succeeding editions and indicated to later researchers how his thought had been running. Newton is guarded in his remarks on the nature of light, though he seems to favour a corpuscular theory in contrast to the wave theory of Huygens: 'Are not the Rays of Light very small Bodies emitted from shining Substances? For such Bodies will pass through uniform mediums in right Lines without bending into the Shadow, which is the Nature of Rays of Light. [Query 29.]' On the other hand, certain phenomena, such as 'Newton's rings', seemed to be periodic in nature; and this led Newton to bring in the medium of aether, in which the light is propagated and which by vibrating itself will bring about periodicity.

The study of sound, though less advanced theoretically, afforded ample scope for simple experiment—as with overtones, the velocity of sound in air, and the effects of atmospheric conditions. Francis Hawksbee the elder (d. 1713?), extending earlier experiments with the air pump, showed that sounds are louder when produced in air at greater than atmospheric pressure; he also studied the transmission of sound through water. Electricity, in contrast, was mysterious and difficult to control. No true science of electricity was created until the second half of the eighteenth century; meanwhile, discoveries were often the result of haphazard experiments with electrical machines. The earliest were quickly forgotten, but soon after 1700 Hawksbee made a systematic study of 'barometric light'— the mysterious glow produced by shaking the mercury in a barometer.[1] The tempo of discovery accelerated twenty years later with the work of Stephen Gray (d. 1736) and Charles Dufay (1698-1739), who between them, from a number of somewhat random experiments, hit upon several important phenomena: the conduction of electricity, induced charges, conductors and non-conductors, and two opposite kinds of electricity (positive and negative static) which Dufay called 'vitreous' and 'resinous'. The mid-century saw big improvements in electrical machines; about 1745 two experimenters made the accidental and alarming discovery of the powerful shock to be obtained from what has since become known as the Leyden jar. From this time the science of electricity began to take shape.

In the second half of the seventeenth century Boyle, who died in 1691, had helped to make chemistry a respectable part of natural philosophy by interpreting chemical experiments in terms of the motion of corpuscles.[2] But although it seemed to some that chemical changes might be explained in terms of attractive forces between particles, as Newton had suggested in the last 'Query' of the *Opticks*, in fact the first unifying theory came from Germany. Although not entirely independent of Boyle's work, it was derived from a much older tradition: the sulphur–mercury–salt theory

---

[1] *Physico-Mechanical Experiments* (1709), Section 1. Hawksbee also describes experiments with his machine for producing electricity by friction, but the possibilities of such machines were generally ignored for some thirty years.

[2] Cf. vol. v, pp. 58-60.

of Paracelsus. The 'sulphur' was 'whatever burns', so that combustion was a process of decomposition. This theory, with modifications, was put forward by Joachim Becher in 1669; at the turn of the century, his pupil G. E. Stahl (1660–1734) used the inflammable principle, which he named 'phlogiston', to explain a wide variety of chemical phenomena: thus combustion and calcination both involved a loss of phlogiston. The calx was the metal deprived of its phlogiston, but the metal could often be restored by heating the calx along with a substance like charcoal that was highly combustible and so contained a large proportion of phlogiston, some of which might unite with the calx. As now understood, the success of this theory was due partly to the fact that the supposed gain in phlogiston often corresponds to loss of oxygen. In various forms, it survived the study of air and gases which began with Stephen Hales's invention of the pneumatic trough, described in his *Vegetable Staticks* (1727), and it found supporters of note even after Lavoisier's execution in 1794. The theory served a useful purpose, however, in encouraging and directing specifically chemical research throughout the first half of the eighteenth century, at a time when confusion was so great that some of the most valuable contributions were mainly empirical, like the tables of affinity of Geoffroy and others, which indicated pairs of substances that reacted with each other.

We have already noticed several examples of the way in which scientific advance was linked with developments in instruments and apparatus. In many cases—the telescope, microscope, barometer, thermometer, hygrometer, air pump, even electrical machines—the original inventions came decades earlier, but for various reasons their exploitation was delayed. For instance, the earliest thermometers were sensitive to changes in air pressure; even when this had been remedied by the *Accademia del Cimento*, the development of 'absolute' scales essential to their full exploitation had to await the work of the Prussian G. D. Fahrenheit (1686–1736) and of the Frenchman Réaumur.[1] The telescope and microscope, both used by Galileo, involved major problems of mechanical design even when properly shaped lenses of good glass were available; the instruments were not widely made until *ca.* 1670 and then serious difficulties had to be overcome, such as those caused by chromatic aberration, which led Newton to devise the first reflecting telescope. An achromatic lens was invented in 1729 by Chester Moor Hall, but such lenses were not effectively used in telescopes or microscopes before the next century. The air pump and electrical machines were developed thanks to the mechanical skill of men like the two Hawksbees in the early eighteenth century. Fortunately, the development of the necessary practical arts, on which instruments and apparatus so much depended, was encouraged by the spread of scientific

---

[1] The Fahrenheit scale takes melting ice as 32° and steam from boiling water as 212°; for Réaumur these were 0° and 80° respectively. Various other phenomena had been suggested from 1665 as suitable for use as 'fixed points'. On the *Accademia del Cimento* of Florence (1657–67) cf. vol. v, p. 49, and for Réaumur below, p. 65.

interest among amateurs, and by the speed with which improvements became known. To satisfy the demand, instrument-makers increased in numbers and narrowed their range of product; their artistic standards dropped, but the all-important mechanical standards improved.

Significant as were these developments, it might be doubted whether they match in importance the mathematical tools introduced about this time, above all the calculus, invented by Newton in 1665–6 and Leibniz in 1673–6, independently. Newton's customary neglect in publishing his discoveries led to a bitter quarrel with Leibniz over priority, which had the unfortunate effect of making the inferior Newtonian notation a matter of national prestige, with disastrous consequences for later mathematics in Britain. A second controversy over the calculus, this time with a happier ending, began with Berkeley's criticisms of the logical foundations of the method—that it deals with 'the ghosts of departed quantities'.[1] The calculus was already too much part of the mathematician's equipment to be disturbed by philosophical attack, but Berkeley's remarks evoked replies that in turn led to further developments of the method.

In contrast with contemporary physics, biology appears *ca.* 1700 to be still largely at a stage of empirical exploration.[2] The great diversity of types of living things and the complexity of their physiological processes, even as so far revealed, hindered the formulation of general theories with anything approaching the precision achieved in physics. Yet effective experiment would have been impossible without guidance from some theoretical ideas, and in fact two such had emerged to lay down the main programme for biology: the idea of searching for a 'natural' classification that would order and display the 'real' relationships between all the different types of livings things; and the idea that the nature of their complex physiology could be discovered and explained by analysing them into the simpler processes known to physics and chemistry. The first idea sought a principle of order that would establish the relationship between fixed species, regulated for all time in a state of unchanging harmony. The second, dating effectively from Descartes, looked for the built-in mechanisms that enabled each organism to maintain its functions in its environment; this gave rise to some excellent experimental physiology as well as to some of the most wasteful speculation. Both ideas belonged to the Newtonian model of an essentially unchanging clockwork universe, but both became incorporated into a new model, based on yet a third theoretical idea. Unlike Newton, Descartes had been concerned with the genesis as well as the present state of the universe: beginning tentatively in Newton's own lifetime, the idea developed that the explanation of the present state of things, including the relationships between the different

---

[1] *The Analyst* (1734), in *Works*, ed. A. A. Luce and T. E. Jessop, vol. iv (1951), p. 89.
[2] Cf. vol. v, pp. 66–71.

species of living creatures, was to be sought in their descent in time. Thus the first half of the eighteenth century was to see the first essays in the idea of organic evolution, involving geological change and a complete sketch of a mechanistic explanation of genetics and survival, as an alternative guide to biological speculation.

The problem of classification had been made acute by the growing accumulation of data since the sixteenth century. By 1700, naturalists were moving into many different regions of the Old and New Worlds and into many different types of organisms. Descriptions of flora, often beautifully illustrated, were covering the main parts of western Europe from Sicily to Lapland. Leading naturalists, such as John Ray (1627–1705) and the Provençal Pitton de Tournefort (1656–1708), travelled widely to collect. These two laid out the main outlines of European plant geography; and Tournefort, as professor at the *Jardin du Roi* from 1683, put together the beginnings of the famous herbarium of what was to become the *Muséum d'Histoire Naturelle* in the *Jardin des Plantes*. The journeys of naturalists overseas, often following national routes of trade and colonization, sometimes had the practical purpose of discovering new plants with medicinal properties. At the same time new living plants were introduced into botanical and large private gardens, especially in England and the Netherlands, with far-reaching effects on botany. Whatever their immediate object, the result by the 1720s was that naturalists—medical men, priests, professional scientists, sailors and explorers like Dampier—had brought home collections and published descriptions of plants from the Americas, the East Indies and Australia, southern Asia from Persia to Siam, China and Japan: a prelude to the large expeditions of the second half of the eighteenth century.[1]

The problem of preserving animal specimens, many of which decayed quickly and could not simply be pressed and brought home to be kept like a herbarium, made zoology more difficult. Nevertheless, naturalists did bring home stuffed specimens, skeletons and hard parts that gave a fairly extensive idea of the zoology of the globe; menageries were added to botanical gardens; systematic dissection became standard practice. Following the lead given by Malpighi, Swammerdam and Claude Perrault, marked progress was made in collecting materials for a comparative anatomy and physiology of the vertebrates and of invertebrate groups such as those now called molluscs and arthropods. Particular attention was given to the comparative method by the anatomists of the *Académie des Sciences*, especially by Duverney, who dissected a range of vertebrates including an elephant, a panther, a viper, an ostrich and a hedgehog. In England, Martin Lister (1638–1712), Nehemiah Grew (1641–1712) and above all Edward Tyson (d. 1708) made outstanding use of the comparative

[1] For the contributions of the Dutch East India Company and its servants, see vol. v, p. 411.

method; in his important monographs on the anatomy of the porpoise and the 'Orang-Outang' (really a chimpanzee), Tyson initiated the comparative study of man and the apes.[1] Zoological investigation ranged over the rest of the animal kingdom. In skilful hands, the simple microscope could reap a harvest from a drop of pond water, or a slice of tissue, as great as any that Galileo and his successors had gathered by sweeping their telescopes round the sky; and the possibilities of the new compound microscope were only beginning to be explored. Greatest of all the microscopists was Anthonie van Leeuwenhoek (1632-1723).[2] Outliving Hooke and the other pioneers, he continued almost to the end to publish a brilliant series of discoveries which included the red blood corpuscles, the transverse striation of muscle fibres, the circulation of the blood in the capillaries, the spermatozoa of man and other mammals and of fish, snails and oysters, as well as rotifers, infusoria with their vibrating cilia, and bacteria. With or without the microscope, the number of studies of the structure, biology and habits of particular creatures steadily increased. Specially interesting were those by a Marseilles doctor, J. A. Peyssonel, who in 1725 discovered to his astonishment that corals were not plants but animals; by Réaumur on the structure and biology of insects; and by Pierre Lyonet in his monograph on the caterpillar of the goat moth—a *chef d'œuvre* in the genre of skilled minute dissection and illustration. These and other published studies of many individual organisms began to show in accurate detail—again beautifully illustrated with the aid of new refinements in printing—the wide variety of different types making up the invertebrate world.

Down to the publication (1735) of the *Systema Naturae* of the great Swedish naturalist, Carl Linnaeus (1707-78), the main effort to order all this accumulating material was concentrated on devising practical systems of classification, in which each type could be exactly located and named, and which would also express the intuitively grasped 'natural' relationship between different types. The great collections of 'natural curiosities' could not be made scientifically effective without systems of naming and indexing which would enable specimens to be found in their proper cupboards and cabinets. Linnaeus's first great service was to provide such a system. Until this practical problem had been solved, it was not easy to investigate the deeper theoretical problem arising from comparative anatomy of which biologists were increasingly aware—the meaning to be given to 'natural' or 'real' relationship or affinity. Yet this problem appeared immediately any system of classification was proposed that was more than a mere artificial convenience: in fact, theoretical ideas on the constitution of the natural order run through all the main systems, above

---

[1] *Orang-Outang, sive Homo Sylvestris: or, the Anatomie of a Pygmie* (1699); cf. M. F. Ashley Montagu, *Edward Tyson* (Amer. Phil. Soc., *Memoirs*, vol. xx, Philadelphia, 1943).
[2] Cf. vol. v, pp. 68-70.

all those of Linnaeus himself, apart from his avowedly artificial 'sexual system' for plants.

The problems of systematics were first seen clearly in botany, where important reforms were attempted by Ray and Tournefort. In his monumental *Historia Plantarum* (1686–1704), Ray—while retaining some old commonsense practices such as the division between trees and herbs—tried to base a rational classification of more than 18,000 plants on the constitution and differentiation of the flower and fruit. This led him to make explicit the fundamental distinction between the monocotyledons and the dicotyledons,[1] and enabled him to give reasons for distinguishing intuitively recognized natural families such as the *Umbelliferae, Asperifoliae* (i.e. *Boraginaceae*), and so on. Ray also used the old logical term *species* for the first time in its modern restricted biological sense and tried to make it precise by attaching to it the notion of a community of origin. Tournefort, basing his classification also largely on the floral parts, made a more explicit, though hardly more successful, attempt to make his system objectively 'natural' and introduced the important idea of the *genus* as a definable group of related species. In his *Elémens de botanique* (1694) and the better-known *Institutiones rei herbariae* (1700), he gave botanical classification a degree of order never seen before: many of his *genera* and other 'natural' groups still survive in modern taxonomy. Yet another important step in the search for a natural classification was taken by Pierre Magnol, director of the botanical garden at Montpellier, who in 1689 introduced the term *family* for major groups of plants.

The immediate impression given by Linnaeus's *Systema Naturae* was of a retreat from the goal of establishing a natural classification. He adopted a general classification based on apparently arbitrarily chosen floral characteristics—number and arrangement of the stamens, number of pistils. The extreme artificiality of this 'sexual system' caused much controversy, but Linnaeus used it with such methodical skill—and popularized it so alluringly with such metaphors as 'the loves of the plants'—that it soon imposed itself at the expense of all rivals. His triumph was due above all to his own wide scope; he set out to provide means of identifying all organisms wherever found. This success led to the acceptance of his second and most lasting innovation, a consistent binomial nomenclature for species, each being given a dual name—e.g. *Rosa Carolina*—first the generic name shared with other species of the same genus, then the name belonging only to the species. His systems and methods established the main lines of organization of the descriptive biological and other classificatory sciences, as Newton's conceptions had done for mechanics and optics. Linnaeus himself tried to construct a natural system but for practical purposes had to adopt an artificial one.

---

[1] Monocotyledons are flowering plants in which the seed leaf or cotyledon is single; dicotyledons are flowering plants in which it is double.

His successors, especially A. L. de Jussieu and Michel Adanson, who rejected the sexual system and likewise tried to make classification once more explicitly natural by basing it on a wide range of defining characteristics, nevertheless worked within a generally Linnaean structure.

In contrast with botany, no classification was worked out before 1800 that coped adequately with the much more intransigent data of zoology. The main problem was that of finding both unifying and differentiating characteristics which would apply over more than a limited range of types—a search vitiated by the then rudimentary understanding of the range of fundamentally different types that make up the animal kingdom. The combined force of these difficulties can be seen by contrasting the relative progress made in vertebrate systematics with the almost total lack of it as regards the invertebrates. The rationalization of vertebrate anatomy was greatly assisted by the possibility of taking the human body as the standard of comparison and terminology. As a result, Ray and Willughby were able to attempt a classification of the vertebrates based not only on the existing practice of using externally observable features—the presence of hair, feathers or scales, the birth of the young as eggs or as infant animals—but also on the internal anatomy of the respiratory system, the heart, and other organs. Linnaeus adopted this excellent method, and was able to set out the vertebrates according to their main natural orders. But when these zoologists attempted to put the rest of the animal kingdom into some sort of rational order they found themselves frustrated by the unsuitability of the human body as a standard, except very generally and vaguely, and by the lack of any other standard. They had not yet reached a position from which the possibility of a comparative zoology comprehending even all the then known types could be grasped. All that Linnaeus could do was to offer the crude and retrogressive division of the invertebrates into Insects and Worms, a rag-bag containing all the other groups; and there was scarcely any improvement on this before Lamarck.

Progress in taxonomy before publication of the *Systema Naturae* was achieved on the assumption that species remain fixed. This had the great strength of imposing a formal structure on the chaos of existing biological knowledge—a structure into which new knowledge could expand. Moreover it was an assumption based—explicitly by Ray and Linnaeus—on the sound principle that all organisms come from eggs or seeds of the same species. Although Linnaeus had used some very artificial criteria in devising a practical taxonomic system, he fully shared with nearly all his contemporaries the view that the ultimate goal must be the construction of a 'natural' system, such as would truly display the real relationships between the fixed species of beings forming 'the Sovereign Order of Nature'.[1] This had three outstanding characteristics, all belonging to a non-

---

[1] Caroli Linnaei *Systema Naturae* (13th edn. Vienna, 1767), vol. I, p. 13.

evolutionary view of the organic world. First, Linnaeus himself believed, under the influence of Aristotle and the sixteenth-century naturalist Andrea Cesalpino, that the fixed order of things was maintained by the transmission, in the process of generation, of the 'specific essence' from parent to offspring. It was because of this intimate connection with the specific essence that he chose the sexual parts of the flower as the basis for his botanical classification. His first opinion was that the same species had existed from the day of creation and that any differences between parent and offspring, as also occasional monstrosities, were purely accidental and transient; following Ray, he attributed these phenomena to the aberrations of 'nature' and not to the Divine Wisdom that had established the eternal species. After 1742, when he examined an aberrant form of toad-flax (*Linaria vulgaris*) which he called *Peloria* (the monstrosity) and regarded as a 'mutant' (*mutata*) produced by fertilization with foreign pollen, Linnaeus came to admit the possibility of changes of species taking place by sudden variations or by hybridization, and thus of permanent new species coming into existence; but this scarcely affected the main picture of massively stable order which his system presented. A second characteristic of the 'sovereign order', also coming ultimately from Aristotle and reinforced by Leibniz's principle of continuity,[1] was that organisms were conceived as forming a scale of nature, descending from man down to lowly plants scarcely distinguishable from dead matter. In Linnaeus's time the scale was essentially linear; later it was made to branch like a tree. Such schemes provided the data which theories of evolution set out to explain. As Tyson presciently asserted in discussing his conception of 'gradation' from one form to another, by making 'a comparative survey of this animal with a monkey, an ape and a man...we may the better observe nature's gradation in the formation of animal bodies, and the transitions made from one to another'.[2] Thirdly, the order of nature was held to exist in a state of divinely established harmony. The parts of each organism—e.g. the structure of a fly's eye, so much admired by Newton—were held to be perfectly adapted to their functions, the organisms of each region perfectly adapted to their surroundings. Thus (in an example given by Linnaeus) the plants fed on the soil, the insects on the plants, the birds on the insects, the larger birds on the smaller ones, and so on; and all lived together in a perfect harmony which maintained an exact equilibrium of population. In the words of Ray's title, the whole of nature was a living proof of 'The Wisdom of God manifested in the Works of the Creation'.

This conception of an unchanging order of nature lasted into the nineteenth century. But already information had begun to be accumulated, and

[1] 'It is one of my great maxims, and one of the most completely verified, that Nature makes no leaps: a maxim which I called the law of continuity.' *Die philosophischen Schriften von G. W. Leibniz*, ed. C. J. Gerhardt (Berlin, 7 vols. 1875–90), vol. v, p. 49.

[2] *Orang-Outang*, preface, p. vii.

a rethinking of ideas to take place, which exposed it to criticism at several different levels. Descartes had popularized the notion that the earth had a history; that its present state was the product of a long series of geological changes, occurring as it cooled from its original state as a star like the sun. This theme was developed further by both speculation and observation. Of the speculative developments, those of Leibniz have a particular interest. Charged to write a history of the House of Hanover and the duchy of Brunswick, Leibniz had gone to Italy to look for documents and there met the Danish naturalist Niels Stensen (Steno, d. 1686), the founder of modern stratigraphy. One of Stensen's greatest contributions had been to recognize the formation of strata by marine sedimentation, with different fossils in different strata. Charmed by these ideas, Leibniz decided to begin his history by placing Hanover and Brunswick in the history of the earth; the result was his *Protogea* (résumé 1693, in full 1749), in which he envisaged a series of geological transformations produced by the earth's cooling and by the action of fire, wind and water, one of them being the biblical Flood. (By this time igneous and sedimentary rocks had been distinguished by naturalists.) In the *Nouveaux Essais*, published in 1765 but written in 1703, Leibniz provided ideas on the nature and transformations of biological species that run through all the succeeding discussions. 'We define species by generation so that similar creatures that come or could come from the same origin or seed are of the same species', but 'we cannot always assign fixed boundaries to species': for 'species are all bound together and differ only by imperceptible degrees'; 'everything happens by degrees in nature and nothing by jumps'.[1] Perhaps, he concluded, species had gradually changed and did so still.

Meanwhile, observers in many countries were filling in further details of the earth's actual history. In Britain Edward Lhuyd published in 1699 a remarkable description of 1,600 animal and plant fossils; both he and John Woodward noted the presence of different fossils in different strata laid down by marine sedimentation. Antonio Vallisneri (d. 1730) made a study extending over the whole of Italy, concluding that much of the country had once been covered by the sea. In France a remarkable explanation given by Réaumur of the presence inland of marine shells, which he ascribed to deposition by former ocean currents, led Fontenelle to suggest the idea of making a geological map.[2] In Switzerland, J. J. Scheuchzer (1672–1733), perhaps the greatest geologist of the time, compiled over a period of nearly fifty years a series of monographs on the largest number of plant and animal fossils yet described. But these field geologists by no means always kept pace with the theoretical implications which some of their more speculative contemporaries were drawing from their work. The notions that fossils were the skeletons of victims of the Flood

---

[1] *Nouveaux Essais*, vol. III, p. vi; *Die philosophischen Schriften*, vol. v, pp. 285–8.
[2] The first such map worthy of the name was made of France, by J. E. Guettard (1746).

or 'sports' of nature were going out of fashion; but Scheuchzer was not alone in using his observations to try to trace the course of the biblical catastrophe. Perhaps it was such pious uses of basically sensible geological analysis that led Voltaire to put himself into the ridiculous position of rejecting the geologists' story altogether. In any case, it was in presenting Scheuchzer's work at the *Académie des Sciences* in 1710 that Fontenelle made his classic declaration: 'Here are new species of medals of which the dates are, without comparison, more important and more certain than those of all the Greek and Roman medals.'[1] Fontenelle became impressed with the geological and genetical evidence showing that biological species had changed in the course of the earth's history: fossils were historical documents. By 1710, clearly, a good many naturalists would probably not have found the tentative suggestions that had been made by Hooke in a letter of 1687 too outrageous: 'That there have been many other species of creatures in former ages, of which we can find none at present; and that...there may be divers new kinds now, which have not been from the beginning.'[2] These suggestions gained support from a second main quarter besides geology: from observations on albinism in negroes (a case was cited by Tyson), polydactyly and other human anomalies, fancy breeds of dogs and pigeons, and the varieties of decorative and useful plants, such as tulips and strawberries, in which horticulturists were showing much interest.[3]

Towards 1750 these lines of enquiry led to a reappraisal of the whole accepted Linnaean conception of the order of nature and to the development of a rival kind of interpretation. The most radical alternatives were those offered by Maupertuis and the great naturalist Buffon (1707–88). In a series of essays written *ca.* 1741–51, Maupertuis put forward, for the first time, a completely evolutionary explanation for the whole existing range of organisms by differentiation from common ancestors. Moreover, disregarding the Linnaean and Leibnizian conception of a self-regulating harmony established by divine providence at the Creation, he offered a thoroughly mechanistic explanation, postulating that order was produced out of fortuitous variations by the automatic selection through survival of individuals better adapted to their environment. No break with the accepted view of the 'sovereign order of nature' could have been sharper. Approaching the whole question through genetics, Maupertuis showed an extraordinary insight into the formal character required by evolutionary theory as it was to be developed much later. The genetical hypothesis he

---

[1] *Histoire de l'Académie Royale des Sciences*, 1710, p. 22.

[2] 'A Discourse of Earthquakes', *Posthumous Works*, ed. R. Waller (1705), p. 291.

[3] A case made celebrated by Fontenelle was the discovery by the French botanist Jean Marchant of two unknown types of the plant mercury in his garden; Marchant wrote in 1719 that he believed he had seen the birth of new species and he proposed an hypothesis of partial evolution within the limits of the genus. *Mém. de l'Acad. Royale des Sciences*, 1719, pp. 59–66; cf. Fontenelle, *Hist. de l'Acad.* 1719, pp. 57–8.

adopted was that the mechanism of reproduction is provided by 'seminal molecules' from each parent which combine to produce the offspring:

Cannot we explain in this way how, from only two individuals, the multiplication of the most diverse species could follow? They would owe their first origin only to chance products in which the elementary particles would not keep the order they had in the father and mother animal: each degree of error would make a new species, and from the force of repeated deviations would come the infinitive diversity of animals that we see today, which will perhaps go on increasing with the passage of time but to which each century will add only an imperceptible increment.[1]

Commenting on the observation that of these chance products of Nature only those with certain adaptive features could exist, and that in fact such features are found in all those that do exist, he accounted in the new style as follows for the providential order:

We could say that chance had produced an innumerable multitude of individuals; a small number were so constructed that the animal's parts could satisfy its needs; in the other, infinitely greater part there was neither adaptation nor order; all these latter have perished: animals without mouths could not live, others without reproductive organs could not perpetuate themselves. The only ones that have remained are those in which order and adaptation were found, and these species, which we see today, are only the smallest part of those which a blind destiny had produced.[2]

Buffon's critique of Linnaean biology concentrated on somewhat different issues and reached rather different conclusions. Maupertuis did not question the Linnaean *genera* and families; he aimed simply to give them a different explanation. Although Buffon wrote, in his *Histoire de la Terre* (1749), the first synoptic essay on the succession of fossil forms found in the different geological strata, he did not accept the hypothesis of general evolution advanced by Maupertuis. His purpose, in the famous article on 'The Ass' which appeared in volume IV (1753) of his *Histoire Naturelle*, was to attack the whole Linnaean conception of the family. He regarded it, along with the principles of Linnaean nomenclature, as thoroughly unjustified and misleading. Buffon discussed the possibility of the ass and the horse (or man and the apes) belonging to the same family only in order to dismiss it, along with the explanation by common descent, and so bring biology back to its true method. This he held to be the search for causal laws, on the Newtonian model, by keeping close to observation. Thus he concluded that 'families' existed only in imagination, and that in nature there were only individuals belonging to species defined strictly in terms of genetic continuity. But Buffon discussed the possibility that natural families were produced by descent with variation. His causal approach made him interested in artificial selection, the geographical distribution of the quadrupeds, the causes of variation, the extinction of species, and the exceptions to the rule of hybrid sterility. Thus he was to

---

[1] *Système de la Nature* (1751), in *Œuvres* (Lyon, 4 vols. 1756), vol. II, p. 148.*
[2] *Essai de Cosmologie* (written before 1741, publ. 1750), in *Oeuvres*, vol. I, pp. 11-12.

become the inspiration of Lamarck and Saint-Hilaire; Darwin himself acknowledged Buffon as a forerunner.

A major difficulty for evolutionary theory was the lack of accurate knowledge of the elementary facts of biological reproduction and heredity. Yet there was progress in investigating these and other problems of basic biology, not only by ingenious experiment but by speculation, which usually ranged far beyond the known facts and yet was sometimes fruitful. The microscope and the mechanistic hypothesis combined to provide the basic facts, conceptions and controversies that came into play in the question of generation towards 1700. By this time, the generalization that all animals reproduce themselves by means of eggs had been elucidated for oviparous forms such as birds, amphibia, fish and insects by Redi, Swammerdam, Malpighi, Vallisneri and others, and extended to viviparous animals by the discovery of the ovaries of selachian fish by Steno and of mammals by De Graaf. Meanwhile Hartsoeker and Leeuwenhoek had discovered spermatozoa, though without understanding their function, and in flowering plants Grew had observed pollen grains and suggested that the flower-parts were the sexual organs. In 1691 an Italian Jesuit, Buonanni, published drawings of pollen grains adhering to the styles of different species, but the first experimental proofs of plant sexuality were given in 1694 by the German botanist R. J. Camerarius.

The controversies into which these important discoveries were immediately caught up are a good example of the extremely formalistic character of biological speculation throughout this period. Reviving three ancient theories in modern form, a bitter argument arose between the so-called 'ovist' school which claimed that the egg alone gave rise to the offspring, the 'animalculists' claiming the same for the sperm, and a third school (including Maupertuis and Buffon) which argued from the facts of heredity that there must be seed from both parents. A second controversy raged between the 'preformationists', who asserted that each individual born had been pre-formed either in the egg or in the sperm of its parents (so that the generations literally unfolded themselves mechanically), and the 'epigeneticists', who maintained a true development in the form of the embryo. The absurdity to which this controversy went reached its extreme form in the *homunculus*—a little man said to be visible fully formed within the sperm and illustrated in a celebrated drawing (1694) by Hartsoeker. In the dialogue between theory and observation these ideas scarcely ever suggested new experiments; as a rule they were simply manoeuvred to fit old ones.[1] Exceptions occurred chiefly in the testing of

[1] A good example is provided by the shifts of Charles Bonnet (1720–93), a leading protagonist of ovism with preformation, to adapt his theory, first to his own important discovery of parthenogenesis in the aphis (1745), and then to the difficulties produced by the dramatic experiments *ca.* 1740 of Abraham Trembley (1700–84) with the aquatic polyps *Hydra* and *Plumatella*. Trembley showed that from each of the pieces into which he cut one of these animals a complete small polyp would become regenerated, and also that asexual reproduction occurred by budding.

theories of the origin of life by spontaneous generation,[1] and of new species by hybridization. Among the different theories, preformationism tended to go with a rigid conception of the fixity of species and against spontaneous generation, epigeneticism with belief in spontaneous generation and evolution.

Perhaps the best example of an acute, sagacious grasp of the most fruitful biological problems then within range of solution is the work of R. A. Ferchault de Réaumur (1683–1757), a great biologist by any standard. Trained originally in jurisprudence and mathematics, Réaumur worked first in engineering and in 1706 entered the *Académie des Sciences* as a pupil-mechanician. But soon, with a stipend of 12,000 *livres* a year, he installed himself in the Faubourg St-Antoine with a large garden, a laboratory, and his collections. His outstanding contribution was to realize that it was not sufficient to study only the structure and classification of animals: biology must also investigate their physiology and behaviour in relation to their environments. His major achievement here was the *Mémoires pour servir à l'histoire des insectes*—six magnificent volumes published in 1734–42. It was in the investigation of particular physiological processes that the interchange between experiment and hypothesis yielded its most lasting results. Since Harvey's day experimental physiology had steadily improved in range and precision. The new discoveries provided a notably fruitful succession of models—mechanical, chemical, and later electrical—such as physiology has always demanded for the analysis and explanation of living processes; the new apparatus made possible the quantitative determination of new biological constants. Except in the study of the nervous system, non-medical scientists were more active in experimental research; the medical professors were mainly responsible for the development and criticism of theoretical ideas and systems. Yet the great medical physiologists—Boerhaave at Leiden, Stahl and Friedrich Hoffmann (1660–1742) at Halle, von Haller at Göttingen— all aimed at basing their explanations firmly on experiment, and the last two made a point of treating physiology as a science of bodily functions independent of its practical applications in medicine.

The theoretical framework and much of the inspiration for physiological experiment was provided by three great competing models. The first was the mechanical model, derived from Descartes and Harvey and characterized by emphasis on measurement. Thus a number of investigators tackled the problems of measuring the quantity, speed and pressure of the blood, and of the force exerted and work done by the contraction of the heart. In *Vegetable Staticks* Hales showed that the sap of plants did not circulate in the manner suggested by a widely accepted analogy with animals. He made an important contribution to plant physiology by measuring the

---

[1] Thus, in 1748, John Needham found 'animalculae' in boiled broth which he had kept in a supposedly airtight container.

upward pressure of the sap from the roots and its daily variations, the amount of water absorbed by the roots and transpired by the leaves, and various other quantities. In his *Haemastaticks* (1733), he adapted these techniques to measuring the pressure of the blood in animals, using a long tube into which the blood was led in different experiments from the carotid or crural arteries or the jugular vein of a horse, a dog, a sheep and a doe; he established that blood pressure varied in different species and at different times in the same animal. A few years later Daniel Bernoulli showed by hydrodynamical analysis how to measure cardiac work correctly. Haller showed that the heart's force extended to the capillaries. And so the circulation became the first physiological function in which quantitative measures of biological constants were made with reasonable accuracy. The analysis of physiological function in purely mechanical terms was clearly a fruitful guide in studying the dynamics of the circulation, in the mechanics of the entry of air into the lungs (of which Haller gave a correct account), and the mechanics of movement and locomotion generally. But for many physiological functions the mechanical model alone was inadequate and misleading, as the progress of chemistry showed. Hales himself made important discoveries in chemical physiology: thus, having designed an apparatus for collecting gases, he proved by measurements that plants enclosed over water 'fixed' one-seventh of the air in which they were confined; but perhaps his obsession with mechanical explanations often prevented him grasping what he had found. In opposition to the extreme mechanical point of view, Boerhaave became the leading advocate of the second great source of physiological explanation. The main area of experimentation inspired by the chemical model was the study of digestion. Different mechanical and chemical explanations had been offered for this process, and Boerhaave raised a basic chemical problem by asserting that the acidity of the gastric juice was its product, not its cause. Réaumur began his analysis by ingeniously taking advantage of the buzzard's habit of regurgitating its food, making it swallow perforated tubes containing food thus protected from mechanical action, and showing that meat but not grain became digested; he also made the buzzard swallow small pieces of sponge from which he squeezed drops of liquid to try to effect artificial digestion outside the bird, and on its death pursued his experiments with a dog and some ducks. He was unable to determine the rôle of the gastric juice, but he introduced the technique of studying digestion both *in vivo* and artificially outside the animal.

Both the mechanical and the chemical models, if carried to extremes, involved the 'mechanistic' assumption that the phenomena of life could all in the end be reduced to physics and chemistry. Against this the organic or 'vitalist' model was advanced—a challenge and an invitation to biologists to forge their own principles of explanation. In the early eighteenth century its principal advocates were Stahl, who founded a vitalism of principle on his metaphysical beliefs, and Haller, who in contrast based a vitalism of fact on the observation that organic actions and reactions are *sui generis* and not immediately explicable by concepts borrowed from other sciences. This model was most fruitful in the analysis of the neuromuscular system, in terms more empirically adequate than the mechanistic schemes derived from Descartes. It supplied physiologists with specifically organic concepts based on observation, such as Stahl's concept of muscular *tonus* and of the co-ordinating function of the nervous system, or again Haller's concepts of 'irritability' (contractility) as the specific property of muscle and of 'sensibility' (conductivity) as that of nerves, thus distinguishing the domains of 'sensibility' and sensation. Haller's ingenious experiments, in particular, analysed the relations between the different parts of the central and peripheral nervous system in involuntary movements. The organic model also led to a renewed grasp, first by Jean Astruc of Montpellier and then in 1751 by Robert Whytt of Edinburgh, of Thomas Willis's fundamental concept of the reflex (1670) and an understanding of the function of the spinal cord. Later, this analysis of levels of neurological control was used by comparative anatomists to give a new facet to the scale of nature and eventually of evolution. At the same time the models of speculative mechanism in most important branches of physiology began to give way to models provided by the new empirical sciences of chemistry, electricity and heat.

To those who practised it, the new approach to natural science was, above all, experimental. As Bacon had said, 'the secrets of nature reveal themselves more readily when tormented by art than when they go on their own way'.[1] In science this active attitude was comparatively (though not of course entirely) novel. But technology, thanks to this approach, had been advancing steadily and on a broad front since medieval times. The advent of the 'experimental philosophy', then, meant that the spirit of technology had spread to pure science, and it is not surprising that many scientists were also very much interested in practical problems. As we have seen, the two great scientific societies of the seventeenth century made a point of cultivating practical matters. Yet the intimate union between pure science and technology that we know today did not come about overnight.

Although scientists were now keenly aware of technological problems, it was not often that their scientific knowledge could be applied. There were of course exceptions. Perhaps the most important (if only a partial) exception was the problem of navigation at sea. Position in latitude could be obtained by direct observation of the celestial pole, but there was no satisfactory method for ascertaining position in longitude; yet an error might be disastrous in bad visibility or on a long voyage, and from the

[1] *Novum Organum*, Bk I, Aphorism XCVIII.

sixteenth century large rewards were offered by governments of maritime nations for a practical solution to the problem. The chief methods of attack were of three kinds. The first depended on covering charts with lines along which the magnetic variation was constant: by measuring the local magnetic variation the ship's position would be known to lie along a given line, and a knowledge of the latitude would (in theory) allow the position to be determined uniquely by its intersection with that line. In 1698 Halley was put in command of an Admiralty pink, the *Paramour*, with orders 'to improve the knowledge of the Longitude and Variations of the Compasse'; in 1701–2 he published charts of magnetic declination of great value for navigators, without solving the main problem. The second method depended on the nearness of the moon and the rapidity of its motion: Greenwich Observatory was set up in 1675 expressly to make the necessary observations, but the practical and computational obstacles were not overcome until the publication of Nevil Maskelyne's *British Mariners' Guide* (1763) and the *Nautical Almanac* from 1767. The third method regarded differences in longitude as differences in local time. The problem here was to determine whatever time was taken as standard, for seventeenth-century clocks, despite the great improvement in timekeeping efficiency that followed the substitution (*ca.* 1660) of the new pendulum for the old balance wheel, were hopelessly inaccurate after some time at sea. Galileo had suggested that a seaman observing an eclipse of one of Jupiter's satellites might read off the standard time for the eclipse from tables, but again practical difficulties proved insuperable. In the end, the problem was solved not through any theoretical developments but through the technical excellence of the marine timekeepers made by a Yorkshire carpenter's son, John Harrison (1693–1776), the first of which was tested in 1736. It embodied two original inventions, the 'gridiron' pendulum and the 'grasshopper' escapement, which largely overcame the defects of earlier chronometers by compensating for changes of temperature and working with a minimum of friction.[1]

In the absence of a guiding theory, problems of technology, like those of the most primitive fields of science, had to be solved empirically. An excellent example is the so-called New Husbandry, which introduced fodder-crops into the rotation system of the light soils of Norfolk, where clover, wheat, turnips and barley were grown in turn. This was done because it had been noticed that wheat seemed to grow best on ground previously occupied by clover, turnips on ground where wheat had grown, and so on. Why this should be so was not understood until the nineteenth century; but a classical illustration of the value of observation is the discovery by Jethro Tull (1674–1741) that pulverizing the soil is to some

---

[1] See R. T. Gould, 'John Harrison and his Timekeepers', *The Mariner's Mirror*, vol. XXI (1935), pp. 115–39. On the techniques for marine survey *ca.* 1700, cf. A. H. W. Robinson, *Marine Cartography in Britain* (Leicester, 1962), pp. 40–60.

extent a satisfactory substitute for manuring it. Tull's horse-hoe and seed-drill were among the few major additions to the farmer's tools between 1669 and 1758. He had studied the intensive husbandry of the Netherlands and elsewhere before 1700, about the time when mention first appears of the Brabant plough, a foot-plough combining mouldboard and plough-share in a single concave iron piece, which turned the soil in the furrow completely over and required little tractive power.[1]

Although we associate the industrial revolution with the later eighteenth century, certain activities in this period prepared the way for its technological, organizational and economic procedures. Thus the growing scale of merchant and naval shipbuilding, even if it evinced no striking innovations in technique, called for the organization of a complex of skills and in the naval dockyards for a large labour force. In France, the vast fortification and canal-cutting programmes of the seventeenth century demanded manpower and materials on a still bigger scale—in 1669 more than 8,000 men were at work on the Languedoc canal alone—and the organizational methods so required contained lessons for the later building of roads and railways, and for industry. All this was dwarfed by the enterprise of erecting St Petersburg.[2]

Of the technological problems, some of the most important centred round the search for new sources of power and prime movers, especially in mining. A seventh of all patents for inventions issued in England between 1561 and 1668 had been connected with problems of flooding; in 1660–1700, out of a total of 236, no less than 30 were for draining land or mines. The old methods of horse-, wind- or water-power were too expensive for use in the deep copper-mines and collieries. The possibilities of steam had been glimpsed in the ancient world, and throughout the seventeenth century attempts were made to apply steam-power, in conjunction with the piston and cylinder, to the problem of clearing the mines of water. Thomas Savery's pump (1698) made a laborious and dangerous use of steam in combination with atmospheric pressure; an interesting variation of this idea, proposed by Huygens, involved the explosion of gunpowder.[3] But the first effective machine to convert heat into mechanical energy was not developed till the first decade of the eighteenth century: by 1720 the 'fire' engines of Thomas Newcomen (1663–1729), a Devon blacksmith, were in general use in England (for mines, canal-locks and reservoirs) and beginning to be exported. Another important problem was the transport of coal on the surface. As early as 1600 wooden rails were used in two places in England, the loaded waggons moving downhill

[1] G. E. Fussell, *The Farmer's Tools, 1500–1900* (1952), pp. 218–22, and B. H. Slicher van Bath, 'Agriculture in the Low Countires', *Relazioni del X congresso internazionale di scienze storiche*, vol. IV (Florence, 1955), pp. 189–91.
[2] Below p. 731–2.
[3] Denis Papin, who anticipated the idea of Savery's water-raising machine in 1687, when he was assistant to Huygens, applied it in 1707 to move a boat by means of a paddle-wheel.

under their own weight and being brought back empty to the pitheads by horses; in the eighteenth century the carriage of coal over short distances by horse-drawn railway was to become general in Britain. Meanwhile, the pressure of war stimulated new applications of coal to the production of metals, beginning with the development at Bristol in the 1690s of the reverberatory furnace for copper-smelting. At Coalbrookdale (near Wolverhampton) Abraham Darby (d. 1717), who had worked in Bristol as a brass-caster, established the coke-smelting of iron on a commercial basis about 1709. His process produced only an inferior pig iron, but by 1750 his son was to succeed in refining it into bars that could begin to compete with charcoal pig in the making of quality wares which required a metal less brittle than cast iron.

By the eighteenth century science had acquired a unity of outlook and activity, of formulated natural expectations and practical aims that placed it among the dynamic influences at work in western civilization. The attitude to nature and society associated with it was based on the concrete achievements of the previous century; but it was made explicit by writers, mostly not scientists themselves, who were prominent in organizing communication and publicity. In the French Enlightenment, notably, the empirical methods and rational conceptions attributed to science were made the standards for all civilized principles, the ground of action.

Before 1700 the recent progress of science was being used in a famous literary debate to dispose of the claim for the superiority of Greece and Rome in the arts and sciences.[1] William Wotton and John Dryden saw the scientific revolution as the most important part of the revival of the West after the centuries of medieval barbarism. Fontenelle filled in this picture with further ideas. A recurrent theme of his *Eloges* is the rational inspiration provided by reading Descartes, although Fontenelle distrusted Descartes's extreme use of *a priori* reasoning and his belief in the possibility of rational certainty. A complementary theme is Fontenelle's praise for exactitude of observations and attention to facts: here the model is the *Opticks*, Newton's experimental masterpiece, known in France before the *Principia*. Fontenelle's characterization of the scientific approach as one that aimed at rational explanations in all questions but accepted the experimental method, with all its difficulties and uncertainties, as the only method of discovering truth, now became a commonplace. With this he combined a more general scepticism, derived not from the scientists but from Lucretius and Montaigne. The result was a view of things corrosive of religious authority while yet respectful of the mysteries of existence.

Fontenelle's interpretation of the general meaning of the 'scientific revolution' was translated into a view of history by Voltaire. In his

[1] Below, pp. 79 ff.

Siècle de Louis XIV (1751) and *Essai sur les mœurs* (1756) Voltaire set out to give an example of history written *en philosophe*—an historical analysis that would discover the causes of the progress and decline of civilizations, yield principles as natural science did, and teach by its results. In these works Voltaire wrote the first full comparative history of civilization. He included in them a brief comparative account of the history of science and technology. He defined an attitude to the past and an evaluation of human activities that made Newton greater than Alexander, Caesar or Cromwell, because Newton had enlightened men's minds by the power of his understanding whereas these great soldiers had enslaved men by violence. For Voltaire, the climax of the progress of the human mind, after its escape from 'superstition' through the sceptical philosophy of the Renaissance, was the discovery of 'the true philosophy' by Galileo, Descartes, Bacon and Newton. Other eighteenth-century writers—Diderot, Hume, Robertson, Gibbon, Condorcet—also gave prominence to the scientific movement in their view of history. At the same time specialized histories of science began to appear. A history of medicine by Daniel Le Clerc was published as early as 1696 and the subject was taught at Göttingen. J. E. Montucla's great *Histoire des mathématiques* (1758) was followed by a succession of other works. By this time the scientific revolution had been recognized as a great event in world history, the history of science had found a place in the development of modern historiography, and the norms of scientific thought had become the norms of rational thinking in general.

CHAPTER III

CULTURAL CHANGE IN WESTERN EUROPE

I. TENDENCIES IN THOUGHT AND LITERATURE

THE factors involved in the relationship between the artistic achievement of a nation and success in its other endeavours are complex and often obscure: there have been great powers with little culture, more rarely great cultures with little power. There can be few periods in history, however, in which the cultural influence of the major European nations corresponded as closely to their political standing as the last decades of the seventeenth century and the first two of the next. The France of Louis XIV reached the summit of its power soon after 1680, and its ascent had been accompanied by a coruscation of literary and intellectual brilliance which continued to light up the European scene long after the decline of French political domination and the death of the *Grand Monarque*. The literary tradition perfected by Molière and Racine, La Fontaine and Madame de la Fayette, La Rochefoucauld and Bossuet, provided aristocratic standards of taste which dominated the polite literature of Europe for the best part of a century: and the intellectual qualities of rationality, clarity and order implied by that tradition themselves lie at the root of much in the Enlightenment, however deep the gulf may seem between the piety of Fénelon and the irreverence of Voltaire. Alongside continuing French predominance, however, there emerges at this time a new intellectual and literary influence, that of England, characterized by a strong emphasis on factual observation and a new deference to middle-class tastes, which runs parallel with the steady growth of British wealth and power. The period, indeed, sees the establishment of the pattern of intellectual and literary forces in Europe from which were to spring all the later developments of the eighteenth century.

Beside this major phenomenon of French cultural hegemony, ultimately developing into an Anglo-French co-dominance—in itself involving many fertile conflicts—other countries contributed little of significance. The decline of Spain was reflected in her failure to throw up any successor, even in the drama, comparable with Calderón, who died in 1681; revival, when it began, came in the form of response to the new French and English influences, and the next major figure in Spanish letters, Feijóo (1676–1764), while firmly rooted in the Spanish tradition, was primarily a bearer of the message of the Enlightenment.

In Italy, learning continued to flourish and the intellectual tradition of

CULTURAL CHANGE IN WESTERN EUROPE

Galileo and the Renaissance thinkers was not extinct, as is shown by the scientific achievements of Cassini and Malpighi, and by the seminal work of Vico as jurist, philosopher and sociologist.[1] Nor were foreign developments in the field of thought neglected. At Padua the traditional Aristotelianism was replaced by the Cartesian 'new philosophy' in the teaching there of Michelangelo Fardella da Trapani, a disciple of Malebranche, during the years 1700–9. The French revival of Epicurean doctrines also attracted interest, as appears from the publication in 1727 by the grand ducal press at Florence (at the behest of the last Medici to rule there, Giovan Gastone) of a handsome folio edition of the works of Gassendi. Imaginative literature, however, remained largely overshadowed by past greatness, and perhaps also impeded by the ultimately sterile excesses of the Baroque taste which had dominated the seventeenth century. A first movement towards renewal is discernible in the foundation in Rome, in 1690, of a poetic academy, the 'Arcadia', intended as a continuation of the literary gatherings sponsored there by Queen Christina of Sweden, who had died in 1689. This body, which attracted members from many other cities and developed into the first truly Italian literary society, had as its object the purification of taste, appealing against the mannered extravagances of the previous hundred years to the relative sobriety of the Renaissance masters and classical antiquity. But in practice its cultivation of the humble simplicity of the pastoral was as artificial and self-conscious as the 'barbarities' it rejected. The neo-classical revival, however, was to bear better fruit in the rise of the Italian theatre: in the tragedies of Scipione Maffei (1675–1755; *Merope*, 1713), the operas of Metastasio,[2] and the new comedy of Goldoni (1707–93).

Germany lacked even the memory of a golden age. In the general poverty of cultural life since the Thirty Years War, stimulus necessarily came chiefly from abroad. The poetry of the Silesian school—the predominant influence for thirty years until the death in 1679 of its acknowledged leader, C. Hofmann von Hofmannswaldau—found its models primarily in the mannered verse of such Italian poets as Marino (1569–1625), with its baroque exuberance, and also in the polished gallantry and wit of the French court and salon poets of the preceding generation. Later, the more austere classical standards associated with Boileau led to some reaction against preciosity and Italian extravagance, in the work of such poets as the Prussian F. R. von Canitz (1654–99), whose *Satiren* reflect those of Boileau, and the Saxon J. U. von König (1688–1744). Similarly, Grimmelshausen's *Der Abenteuerliche Simplizissimus* (1668), though it owes its continuing vitality[3] to the freshness of its picture of the German scene during the Thirty Years War, is cast in the mould of the

[1] For Vico see vol. VII, pp. 94–5. [2] Below, p. 111.
[3] A new translation by W. Wallich, *The Adventures of a Simpleton*, appeared in 1962 (London, New English Library).

73

earlier Spanish and French adventure novels of low life. The influence of the French episodic prose fiction of the period of Louis XIII is again visible in the long heroic and didactic novels of Duke Anton Ulrich of Brunswick-Wolffenbüttel (1633–1714) and in the most popular German novel of the whole first half of the eighteenth century, *Die Asiatische Banise* (1689), by H. A. von Ziegler und Kliphausen (1663–96). The widespread acceptance of French models and standards culminates in the criticism of J. C. Gottsched (*Critische Dichtkunst*, 1730). It led in the end nevertheless to a healthy reaction, which gave birth to a truly national German literature in the latter half of the eighteenth century. Of this only the first indications are detectable in our period—in the prevalence of satire against the slavish imitation of French manners, and in the efforts of the best German minds to endow their country with a more dignified and independent attitude in matters of art and taste, and with a more vigorous intellectual life. Of these, the two most influential were Christian Thomasius (1655–1728), a disciple of Pufendorf[1] and an outspoken opponent of all prejudice and superstition, who was the first Leipzig professor to lecture in German; and Leibniz, the intellectual genius not only of Germany but of Europe in his generation, whom only Newton can be considered to rival. Leibniz's career was personally in some ways unsuccessful, and none of his more grandiose projects came to full fruition, but he nevertheless exercised a profound influence on German intellectual life in the first half of the eighteenth century, especially through the systematic university teaching of his philosophical disciple Christian Wolff (1674–1754). What is more, by his telling interventions in some of the philosophical controversies occasioned in France by Cartesianism, by his rôle in the international negotiations for ecclesiastical reunion in the 1680s and 1690s, and by his wide reputation as a jurist and scholar, he made a deeper mark upon the life of Europe than any private German had done since Luther's day.[2]

The chief literary and intellectual significance of the northern Netherlands at this period is that by reason of the relatively wide toleration which obtained there, and of its highly developed printing trade, the country was something of a European clearing-house: a home for political and religious exiles from many countries, a centre for the international collection and dissemination of literature and scholarship. Dutch literature itself did not escape these foreign influences. The decline from the peak of achievement, in letters as in the arts, is marked by the death in 1679 of Vondel, the outstanding poet and dramatist of the seventeenth century. The wealthier classes, consolidated by the increased prosperity of the country, now tended to cultivate aristocratic tastes, and so to look beyond the essentially middle-class and popular tradition of their native literature

---

[1] See vol. v, pp. 110–14.
[2] See vol. v, pp. 82–5, 114–17, 145–6.

to the nobler artistic notions of Paris and Versailles. A major force in spreading French classical ideas in Holland was the literary society 'Nil Volentibus Arduum', founded at Amsterdam in 1669 and particularly influential during the 1670s in encouraging the translation and imitation of French classical drama—a field in which the most successful practitioners were Lucas Rotgans (1654–1710) and Sybrand Feitama (1694–1758). The novel, similarly, was strongly influenced by such French models as *L'Astrée* (first complete Dutch translation 1671) and Scarron's *Roman comique* (tr. 1678), while pastoral poetry was revived a little later chiefly by the works of J. B. Wellekens (1658–1726), the translator of Tasso's *Aminta* (1715). Some writing in the older national tradition nevertheless continued: while Molière had his imitators among the younger generation, such as Pieter Langendijk (1683–1756), the comedies of Thomas Asselijn (*ca.* 1620–1701) successfully continued in the earlier and earthier native manner (*Jan Klaaz*, 1682). But by 1700 literature in Holland, like other creative pursuits, had largely fallen victim to that mood of comfortable passivity which was to characterize Dutch life until the upheavals of the revolutionary era.

Finally, Russia at this date is barely on the horizon of the European intellectual world. That horizon was crossed by the young Tsar Peter when he first travelled to the West, but the contacts he established remained largely at the technical and practical level.[1] It was not till later that the spread of secular education among the new Russian aristocracy opened the way to Western cultural influences, and ultimately to the founding of a new polite literature based on Western, especially French, models.

To say that in 1680–1720 the European scene was dominated by established French and developing English cultural and literary influences is not to say, however, that the spectacle is in any way a simple one. In many of its apparently novel aspects it exhibits primarily a revival or continuation of developments discernible in the sixteenth century and subsequently driven underground, by the Counter-Reformation in Catholic countries, to a lesser degree by the new Protestant orthodoxies elsewhere. The period bears witness to the continuing prestige of classicism, with its aristocratic and authoritarian overtones: but in addition it contains the seeds, not only of that general rejection of authority in the name of reason which is known as the Enlightenment, but even of the later Romantic reassertion of the claims of feeling and imagination. These conflicting intellectual and literary forces reflect the underlying tensions of the age. They are also related to widespread developments in the organization and extent of cultural life, of which something must be said before considering their literary manifestations.

The proportion of the total population which could be described as

[1] Below, pp. 726 ff.

the reading public is of course undiscoverable in any precise sense, though it is clear that by modern standards it was extremely small. In such countries as England and Holland it was perhaps greater than elsewhere; certainly Protestantism provided a stimulus to literacy whose effects must, for many, have extended beyond the reading of the Bible and of devotional and controversial works, important as these were as the bread-and-butter of the publishing trade. It seems generally true, however, that throughout Europe the reading public was steadily extending down the social scale to embrace ever larger numbers of the middle classes. This widening of the area of cultural life, also, was accompanied by a number of developments that helped quicken its tempo and increase its fruitfulness. The foundation of national literary and scientific academies had begun earlier in the century: the Académie Française (1635), indeed, was mature enough to complete its first great project with the publication of the *Dictionnaire de l'Académie* in 1694, by which time both the *Académie des Sciences* and its English forerunner, the Royal Society, had been influential for a generation. In France, too, this movement spread to the provinces with the inauguration of the *Académie de Bordeaux* in 1712. The foundation of the Academy of Sciences at Berlin in 1700 and of the *Real Academia* at Madrid in 1714, amongst others,[1] attests at least the desire of governments to extend the benefits of science, learning and literature. A further development, ultimately perhaps of greater influence, was the learned and literary periodical. Of these the earliest, the *Journal des Sçavans* and the *Philosophical Transactions*, had begun to appear in 1665. In Italy, from 1668, various *Giornali dei letterati* appeared in imitation of the *Journal des Sçavans*; in 1710 a more authentically native periodical, the *Giornale dei letterati d'Italia*, began publication in Venice. The first such periodical in Germany, the *Acta Eruditorum* of Leipzig, dates from 1682. Huguenot immigration led to similar journals in Holland, of which Pierre Bayle's *Nouvelles de la République des Lettres* (1684–87) is both the earliest and the most celebrated.[2] Such periodicals rendered a quite new service to serious readers by filling the greater part of their space with reviews—informative rather than critical—of scholarly works, and by including, often at length, lists of new and forthcoming books contributed by correspondents in the major European publishing centres. In a rather lighter vein, Donneau de Visé's *Mercure Galant* (1672–1716) offered comment on contemporary literary, theatrical and scientific events as part of its general chronicle of the life of the court and of Parisian society. To such new intellectual stimuli must be added the continuing activity of the *salon* as a focal point of literary, and increasingly of intel-

---

[1] See above, p. 42.

[2] Only less so was Jean Le Clerc's *Bibliothèque universelle et historique* (1686–93), which had the distinction of first persuading John Locke to appear in print: see the contribution by R. L. Colie to J. S. Bromley and E. H. Kossmann (eds.), *Britain and the Netherlands* (1960). From 1687 Bayle's title was appropriated by others. Cf. above, pp. 45–6.

lectual, discussion in France, and the emergence in both France and England of a new amenity, the coffee house, which provided facilities for the exchange of ideas of a more informal and socially less restricted kind.

Opportunities for the spread of knowledge and opinion, for contact between writer and public, were thus improving considerably in each country: but there was also a corresponding improvement, ultimately perhaps even more far-reaching in its effects, in international contacts of this sort. The learned world had preserved something of the intellectual unity of medieval Europe through its use of the Latin language, and the international correspondence of great scholars is a familiar feature from the Renaissance onwards; but there was now a marked increase in the volume and tempo of such exchanges. The learned correspondence of such men as Bayle, Leibniz and Huygens, or even of a secondary figure like the Florentine librarian Antonio Magliabecchi, reached voluminous dimensions and extended all over Europe, occasionally (as with Leibniz) even beyond it. The demand for contacts of this sort was indeed sufficiently great, it seems, to enable at least one relatively obscure scholar, the Abbé Nicaise of Dijon, to constitute himself a private clearing-house for learned correspondence and earn a modest European fame as 'le facteur du Parnasse'. The Republic of Letters, which Bayle's periodical professed by its title to serve, was no empty phrase. It acquired fresh meaning in the later years of the seventeenth century thanks to political developments in France that provoked scholarly migration. The first was Louis XIV's deliberate policy of enhancing the glories of his capital and court by offering strong inducements to foreign savants to settle in Paris. His major successes here lay in the scientific field, with Christiaan Huygens and the astronomer Cassini; Leibniz himself, who spent three years in Paris, was deterred from accepting a permanent position there only by religious scruples. Louis undoubtedly succeeded by this means in making Paris an intellectual centre of European importance. London was less so, but the reputation of the Royal Society exercised a strong attraction, and many distinguished foreign visitors were admitted to its fellowship. A second act of French policy stimulated intellectual cosmopolitanism in an exactly opposite way. The Revocation of the Edict of Nantes created in every major city of Protestant Europe groups of Huguenot refugees (a high proportion of them ministers), many of whom were forced to support themselves by teaching and writing. Not only were the Protestant countries thus brought into a new and more immediate contact with the French language and French culture; the refugees themselves, in addition to maintaining by their writings the intellectual life of their community in exile, and especially its theological vigour (to use no harsher word), also took up the task of acquainting the French reading public with the most significant of what they found in their countries of adoption. It was by this means, to cite only one example, that French readers were introduced to Locke's *Thoughts concerning Education* (1693) and *Essay concerning Human Understanding* (1690), and to Newton's *Opticks*, in translations by Pierre Coste published respectively in 1695, 1700 and 1720. Again, the first periodical ever founded specifically to acquaint one country with the intellectual life of another, the *Bibliothèque anglaise* of 1717, was the work of a Huguenot refugee in England, Michel de la Roche. Of such men Bayle alone has left a permanent mark on intellectual history, but the collective efforts of his less distinguished fellow exiles provided in their day a powerful stimulus to the cosmopolitan movement which reached such extensive proportions during the later eighteenth century.

This movement, however, depended for its success at practical level upon the existence of an adequate organization for the free publication and wide distribution of books. During our period the Dutch publishing trade was largely successful in meeting this need. Not only did it enjoy a large degree of freedom from official censorship: it was situated at a centre of European communications, with relative ease of access to all northern Europe, and in spite of much opposition from French governments it seems to have maintained a clandestine trade with France in pirated editions and banned books which even war did not wholly extinguish. It is thus scarcely surprising that in 1699, while publishing in England was largely confined to London and Oxford, in France to Paris and Lyons, and in Germany to Leipzig, there were no less than five Dutch cities where it flourished—Amsterdam, Rotterdam, The Hague, Leiden and Utrecht, with *ca.* 400 printers and booksellers in Amsterdam alone.[1] The new forces making for a wider and freer circulation of ideas thus found at their disposal a centre already well equipped to meet their demands.

The literary canons established in France by about 1650 were unquestioned orthodoxy by the 1680s. Their best-known formulation, Boileau's *L'Art poétique* (1674; E. T. by Sir W. Soames, 1683), notwithstanding the legend—encouraged by Boileau himself in his later years—that makes its author 'the legislator of Parnassus', is essentially a recapitulation of accepted opinions rather than a manifesto. The movement developed slightly later in England, but the common starting-point in both countries—respect for the achievement of antiquity and a desire for clarity and order—led naturally enough to an English acceptance of the basic attitudes already formulated in France, to the respectful study of the work of such men as Rapin, Boileau and Bouhours. It is significant, however, that in both countries the period which saw the establishment of classicism was the heyday of the literary theorist.

Public taste, in the broadest sense, was in some respects slower to

[1] See H. J. Reesink, *L'Angleterre et la littérature anglaise dans les trois plus anciens périodiques de Hollande* (1931), p. 93.

appreciate the full merits of the classical achievement, often reluctant to abandon old habits or restrict its pleasures to what the critics approved. Molière himself had crossed swords with the pundits who wished his audiences to laugh only 'selon les règles': the classical austerity of Racinian tragedy was counterbalanced by the scenic splendours of the *pièce à machines* and the operas of Lully:[1] in England, Bunyan's work, which scarcely ranked as literature, appeared in the same years as the classical tragedies of Nathaniel Lee, and Samuel Butler's eccentric *Hudibras* was completed in 1678, only three years before the appearance of Dryden's *Absalom and Achitophel*. In England, moreover, the acceptance of classical standards had encountered stronger resistance than in France, from the very vigour of the existing literary tradition, which before the Restoration had largely ignored them. In France the poetry of the *Pléiade* was little known or valued by 1680, and no play earlier than *Le Cid* (1637) held the stage; but in England Shakespeare, Spenser and Milton remained to be reckoned with. In spite of the more narrowly prosaic of the new classical theorists, such as Thomas Rymer—for whom *Othello* was no tragedy but 'plainly none other than a Bloody farce, without salt or savour'[2]—the literary stature of the older writers, though it defied the rules, could not be denied; indeed, it seemed to prescribe a group of models in rivalry with those writers of the ancient world upon whose practice the classical orthodoxy professed to be based. A compromise naturally began to emerge. John Sheffield, earl of Mulgrave's exhortation concerning Shakespeare and Fletcher—'Their Beauties imitate, avoid their faults'[3]—was perhaps a naïve solution: but others, beginning with Dryden in his *Essay of Dramatic Poesy* (1668), saw that the English literary tradition, if it could learn polish and balance from French classicism, was no less valid for being an independent creation of the national genius. Dryden thought that Chaucer often failed to make his verse scan; but he none the less regarded him as the Homer of English poetry.[4]

If French literature saw no 'Giants before the Flood' (in Dryden's phrase) with whom it had to come to terms in this way, the very triumphs of the classical age itself created an essentially similar problem. The foundation of classicism in literature, as of the Renaissance in general, had been respect for the achievements of a past civilization, one which was looked back upon as a distant peak whose height man was now again struggling to attain. By the late seventeenth century in France, however, some were coming to feel that that height had not merely been reached, but surpassed. Descartes had already shown the way in philosophy; the idea of progress was in the air and national self-confidence, not un-

[1] Below, pp. 106–10.
[2] *A Short View of Tragedy* (1693), in J. E. Spingarn, *Critical Essays of the Seventeenth Century* (Oxford, 3 vols. 1908–9), vol. II, p. 255.
[3] *An Essay upon Poetry* (1682), in Spingarn, vol. II, p. 292.
[4] *Fables, Ancient and Modern* (1700), Preface.

supported by royal propaganda, now engendered the view that French civilization, especially French manners and French art, was more polished, more perfect, than anything in antiquity. Since, at least in theory, artistic creation continued to be conceived in terms of the imitation of models, it then seemed logical to substitute the more perfect contemporary achievement for the ruder product of antiquity. It is this line of thought, and the opposition it aroused among the more traditionally minded, that underlies the 'quarrel of the ancients and moderns', the most celebrated literary controversy of the period in both countries. With the details of this dispute we cannot here concern ourselves, and its outcome was in any case inconclusive, but the issues involved are worth further analysis, since they bring out with some clarity the essential characteristics of the classical outlook, and also disclose profound conflicts within classicism itself. These, once revealed, were perhaps a factor in the decline of its creative achievement which is apparent in our period.

Respect for the literature of antiquity was a principle in some ways parallel with scholastic respect for authority in philosophy and theology, and no doubt it derived some force in men's minds thereby. But it was widely regarded, in a rationalist age, as being in itself grounded in reason: a rational appreciation of the excellence of the ancient masterpieces was what, in the last resort, provided the foundation of their authority. The rôle of the critic was, then, to deduce from them 'rules' of universal validity which the creative artist had but to follow faithfully. 'Reason' thus appeared to be paramount. In matters of style, certainly, it had promoted a new clarity, harmony and simplicity in both French and English writing. Nevertheless, it remained in other respects a vague concept, frequently amounting to little more than common sense: and common sense, in aesthetic questions, is all too often simply common prejudice. In this way, mere contemporary taste becomes a criterion of universal, because 'rational', validity. An unhistorical and unimaginative attitude towards Homer and Virgil, for instance, made it easy for the moderns to find their works gross, ill-planned, full of ludicrously implausible episodes, especially where interventions by the gods were involved. Yet precisely such an attitude was facilitated by the nature of much seventeenth-century reasoning itself, with its preference for the *a priori* and the abstract, its penchant for arguing about 'man', 'reason', and 'good taste', as though these were universal and unchanging concepts capable almost of mathematical definition. Pope, in his *Essay on Criticism* (1711), deplores the ingratitude of certain critics: they had deduced their precepts from the ancient writers, but nevertheless

> Against the poets their own arms they turned,
> Sure to hate most the men from whom they learned.[1]

[1] Part I, ll. 106–7.

But he himself, in an earlier passage in his poem, had shown by what line of thought such a rejection of antiquity could come. The writer's constant guide must be a universal principle, which he here calls Nature but which Boileau, in a parallel passage in *L'Art poétique*, had called 'la raison':

> First follow nature, and your judgement frame
> By her just standard, which is still the same:
> Unerring nature, still divinely bright,
> One clear, unchanged, and universal light,
> Life, force, and beauty must to all impart,
> At once the source, and end, and test of art.[1]

Such views reflect ultimately the underlying conviction of the age that the universe is rationally ordered: the unusual or extreme (or even unfamiliar) is a deviation from normality and therefore unnatural, unreasonable, to be avoided or corrected. Here, possibly, is one factor in the very pronounced bent which the period shows for comedy in general and satire in particular. The most enduring product of the quarrel of the ancients and moderns is Swift's burlesque prose epic describing its English repercussions, *The Battle of the Books* (1704), the first of a series of satirical masterpieces which culminated in *Gulliver's Travels* (1726); and some of the finest verse of the age, from Dryden's *Absalom and Achitophel* (1681) to Pope's *Rape of the Lock* (1712–14) and later *Dunciad* (1728–42), is also satirical in intent.

One conflict within classicism itself thus consisted in the opposition between, on the one hand, a respect for ancient literature founded partly on tradition and partly no doubt (for many) on a genuine sympathy and understanding, and on the other hand a progressive rationalism that wished to impose its intellectual norms upon art as well as thought. A further conflict also arose between ancient literature and its modern critics in the field of taste. However ready the latter may have been to equate the taste of their contemporaries with 'nature' and 'reason', it was inevitably a product of historical and social forces. French classical literature was written primarily for an aristocratic and urban élite, 'la Cour et la Ville',[2] and its standards and assumptions reflect those of its public. Hence it is hardly surprising that the ancient distinctions between literary genres, to be found in Aristotle and Horace, were developed into the conception of a literary table of rank and precedence, with epic and tragedy at the top and comedy immediately below them, followed by the ode, the elegy and the lesser verse forms, and finally descending, beyond the pale of nobility, to prose fiction and the crudities of farce. Misalliances were frowned upon: tragicomedy, a flourishing dramatic form earlier in the century, did not survive, and Molière's obstinate addiction to farce was deplored by purist critics.[3] More important, the notion of rank in

---

[1] *Essay on Criticism*, pt. I, ll. 68–73.   [2] Cf. below, pp. 341–2.
[3] Including his admirer Boileau (*Art poétique*, chant III, ll. 393–400).

literary forms led to the idea that in the noble genres *all* should be noble. Concrete references to the commonplace, trivial and vulgar should be excluded; the language should exhibit a due refinement and elevation of tone. The resulting 'style noble' which characterizes classical writing in these genres, with its tendency to favour the abstract and the general, and its occasionally over-obvious desire to allude to a spade without actually mentioning it, has sometimes irritated modern readers as mere artificiality. It springs chiefly from the wish to create a unified tone, ensure that each genre preserves its appropriate level of style, and so maintain in noble literature that refinement which was expected in noble company. In lesser genres, of course, the concrete detail, banal or gross, may have its part to play; the handkerchief which Rymer jeers at as ludicrous in *Othello* is in its properly repulsive place in Boileau's satire on women:

> Attends, discret mari, que la belle en cornette,
> Le soir, ait étalé son teint sur la toilette,
> Et dans quatre mouchoirs, de sa beauté salis,
> Envoie au blanchisseur ses roses et ses lis.[1]

Such emphasis upon a particular aristocratic conception of refinement was a natural reflection of the cultivated public's awareness of itself as an élite of relatively recent growth in a society still largely uncouth;[2] but it found little to correspond with its standards in the ancient literature it was traditionally expected to admire. Before the ungentlemanly simplicity of Homeric manners and the homely concreteness of Homeric vocabulary it was possible indeed to maintain, as Racine did, that calves and cows, though shocking in French, were not so in Greek[3]—in a dead language they lost their familiarity. It was doubtless easier for those without Racine's feeling for antiquity to reject Homer as untutored. A middle way, pursued by many translators, was to modify the ancient by reinterpreting it in terms acceptable to the modern reader, but this inevitably displeased those who admired the ancient for its own sake: Bentley's comment on Pope's *Iliad* is a just one—'a very pretty poem, Mr Pope, but you must not call it *Homer*'.[4]

The strongly rationalist attitude which infused the whole classical conception of literature made considerable achievements possible, especially in the matter of style. Whatever the pedantic follies of the more unimaginative theorists, it at least set firmly before the literary novice models of real, if sometimes uncomprehended, merit. Above all, it encouraged an assiduous attention to the details of craftsmanship viewed in the light of rational criteria of clarity, simplicity, sobriety and harmony;

---

[1] *Satires*, no. x, ll. 196–200 (1692). [2] Cf. below, p. 94.

[3] 'Ces mots de veaux et de vaches ne sont point choquants dans le grec, comme ils le sont en notre langue, qui ne veut presque rien souffrir': Racine, *Remarques sur l'Odyssée d'Homère*, in *Œuvres*, ed. Mesnard, vol. vi, p. 163.

[4] S. Johnson, *Lives of the English Poets*, vol. iii (ed. G. B. Hill, 1905), p. 213, note 2.

and this effected a stylistic revolution in both English and French writing. Theorists tended to imply that successful writing was primarily the result of following their precepts. The age, indeed, tended to regard inspiration with some mistrust, just as it looked upon imagination as deception[1] and enthusiasm, especially in the forms of religious emotionalism and mys-. ticism, as unreason.[2] In the first twenty lines of *L'Art poétique*, the aspiring poet is informed that without inspiration he can hope for nothing, and Boileau feels no need to revert to the subject in the rest of his treatise. Of course, the greatest artistic achievements of classicism are as profoundly original, and as profoundly the reflection of individual genius, as those of any other age; but it is certainly true that its rationalism unduly encouraged the uninspired and the merely derivative. For all their classical regularity, no previous author had ever written a play like Racine's *Phèdre* or a poem like Dryden's *Absalom*: yet a purely academic composition such as Addison's tragedy *Cato* (1713) also won great praise in its day because of its scrupulous formal correctitude, and one detects a certain air of bafflement in Voltaire's later admission that *Cato*, though regular, is a frigid work and has none of the emotive power of certain passages in the 'barbaric' Shakespeare.[3]

This is perhaps enough to suggest that the intellectual superstructure of classicism was in some ways at odds with, or at least tended to obscure, the emotional foundations of all art. Yet the potential harmfulness of this contradiction was mitigated in fact by the creative energies of the major writers, and by the general acceptance of the view that the essential function of imaginative literature was to please, to move the reader. The purpose of classical literary theory, of having rules at all, was of course originally to facilitate precisely that task for the poet; and this meant that the ultimate appeal lay, not to the theorists, but to what the public liked. As Racine himself wrote, 'La principale règle est de plaire et de toucher'.[4] And the public itself, though its taste by this time had been deeply influenced by the current of classicism, was impatient of pedantry and academic squabbles. In practice, it was dissuaded neither from enjoying great works which the pundits held to be defective, nor from patronizing forms of art which lay beyond their scope or beneath their attention— spectacle-play, *comédie-ballet*, farce and prose fiction.

The orthodoxy of classicism, with its clarity, harmony and universality, might at first glance appear to offer a favourable milieu for the movement of critical scientific thought which developed so strongly at this period. In certain directions, indeed, the two forces certainly move together.

[1] Malebranche, *De la recherche de la vérité* (1674).
[2] Shaftesbury, *A Letter concerning Enthusiasm* (1708).
[3] *Lettres philosophiques* (1734), eighteenth letter.
[4] Preface to *Bérénice* (1671).

Both, to take the most obvious instance, were strongly aware of the value of a clear and precise use of language. As early as 1664–5 the Royal Society had set up a committee to examine the English language and suggest improvements which would fit it better to serve the Society's work; what was aimed at was 'a close, naked, natural way of speaking'.[1] This is perhaps to emphasize scientific austerity, but the description is not altogether inapplicable to the prose of La Rochefoucauld, and it is apt enough for that of Montesquieu at the end of the period. Fundamentally, however, the new scientific movement ran in an opposite direction to much in the classical outlook. Where classicism still preserved something of the traditional respect for ancient authority as such, the spirit of critical enquiry demanded the rejection of whatever did not rest solely upon demonstrable fact and valid argument. Classicism tended to concern itself with the analysis of human nature in its general and recurrent aspects, setting aside particularity and concrete detail as at best irrelevant and at worst degrading; whereas the new empiricism saw in the minute verification of isolated and sometimes apparently casual phenomena the necessary starting-point for such generalizations as might prove possible. The effect of the new science was thus ultimately to direct men's minds back to the material and the specific, to precise observation of the external world in all its aspects, to the critical examination of the factual basis underlying established beliefs and generalizations.

The foundation of this movement was, of course, the new and growing prestige of science itself. In France, the scientific aspects of Cartesianism were attracting public attention by 1670. Rohault's *Physique* was published in 1671 and his activities as a writer and lecturer, together with those of other Cartesians such as Du Hamel and Régis, drew a wide following both in Paris and the provinces, arousing enough fashionable enthusiasm to provide material for satire in Molière's *Femmes Savantes* (1672). Though based upon the *a priori* thinking of Descartes, the work of his scientific disciples tended in practice to lay increasing emphasis upon experiment, as English scientific thought had done consistently since Bacon's time; and the scientific academies had a considerable experimental bias from the start. The revolutionary progress in many scientific fields is described elsewhere (ch. II). Much of it, certainly, remained outside the grasp of the general public, and travelled slowly across national frontiers; the conflict between the systems of Ptolemy and Copernicus was still an unsettled issue for many Frenchmen, as contemporary academic teaching shows,[2] and the prestige of Cartesianism in France delayed any general acquaintance with Newton's theories there until the 1730s. Nevertheless, science was impinging on the public consciousness to a quite new extent,

---

[1] T. Sprat, *History of the Royal Society* (1667), p. 113.
[2] Bayle's *Systema totius philosophiae*, delivered as lectures at Sedan and Rotterdam, 1675–93, expounds both theories impartially.

as is reflected in the emergence of a literature attempting a popular exposition of scientific knowledge.

The major motive behind one type of scientific popularization was a religious one. For many of the most distinguished minds of the time, the pursuit of scientific knowledge was an activity of essentially religious significance, the understanding of God through his works. And this view drew new strength from the great successes of the century in discovering rationally comprehensible laws at work governing the phenomena of nature—phenomena which to earlier centuries had seemed those of a corrupt, fallen Creation which was the passive plaything of supernatural, and chiefly evil, forces. At a time when the possibility of serious conflict between science and religion was not generally envisaged, it was consequently natural that the new knowledge should be seized upon as a valuable support for religious truth: the Psalmist's cry, 'The heavens declare the glory of God', seemed to have acquired a fresh and compelling significance. Thus the naturalist John Ray in his *Wisdom of God* (1691) demonstrates God's existence, not only by the orderliness of Copernican astronomy, but also by the evidence of order and purpose in the animal and vegetable kingdoms which his own studies had revealed to him. Similarly, William Derham, an Anglican divine who was also a scientist, published *Physico-Theology, or a Demonstration of the Being and Attributes of God from his Works of Creation* (1713) and a parallel volume entitled *Astro-Theology* (1715), both frequently reprinted. This attitude continued to find favour, indeed, throughout the eighteenth century, as the widespread literature testifies, from the Abbé Pluche's *Spectacle de la Nature* to Paley's *Evidences*. In France, however, the first impulse towards scientific popularization came less from theological zeal than an extensive fashionable interest, though this was also to be found in England and elsewhere.[1] Fontenelle's *Entretiens sur la pluralité des mondes* (1686; E. T. 1702) is a series of lively dialogues between a philosopher and, significantly, a marquise. It offers some interesting speculations concerning life on other planets, mingled with a clear (though in some details inaccurate)[2] account of the facts of astronomy as then available, with the motions of the heavenly bodies explained according to the current Cartesian theory of vortices—the whole suitably adorned with conventional gallantries and presented in the elegant but simple terms which the fashionable lay public would expect.

The effect of this increasing public interest in the orderly world of natural phenomena which the scientists were revealing was in the long run more profound than the facts so far mentioned might suggest. While contemporary theologians found valuable apologetic material in the new knowledge, its ultimate philosophical implications soon appeared

[1] Above, pp. 46–7.
[2] See the introduction to R. Shackleton's edition (Oxford, 1955).

as far from favourable to religion. In the first place, the new understanding of the physical universe deprived it of much of its mystery and even engendered a little contempt for it. Man seemed now to be emancipated from his age-old superstitious terror of inexplicable natural forces; that ancient harbinger of doom, the comet, was shown by Halley to be subject to laws of motion as regular as the sun and moon. The Cartesian emphasis upon mechanical causation made the universe appear a mere machine. Fontenelle compares the world of nature, with all its mystery and splendour, to an operatic spectacle: all is done with ropes and pulleys, did the spectator but know;[1] or it is a watch—intellectually speaking, man can hold the universe in the palm of his hand. Secondly, such analogies led to the conclusion that the world, far from being permeated with corruption and chaos since the Fall of Man—Thomas Burnet's *Sacred Theory of the Earth* (1681–9) still accepted this view—was the perfect handiwork of a God envisaged as the Supreme Reason. The step towards a natural religion, free of all reference to a Christian redemption, was thus an easy one for Deists to take. The problem of evil inevitably arose in acute form, however, as is shown by the extensive literature of the subject in the first half of the eighteenth century, of which Leibniz's *Essais de Théodicée* (1710) and, at a more popular level, Pope's *Essay on Man* (1733–4) were the most influential. Sweeping inferences of this kind, all-embracing metaphysical and moral systems, were indeed still typical of much of the philosophical thought of the time; from Descartes to Leibniz, the seventeenth century is the golden age of systematic metaphysics. But in fact it was already beginning to be felt in some quarters that such *a priori* thinking was invalid because it had no basis in factual knowledge. What was commonly known at the time as 'natural philosophy' begins to fall into its modern divisions of 'science' and 'metaphysics', when Newton is content to demonstrate the laws governing the behaviour of gravitational attraction without offering any philosophical explanation of its nature: to Cartesian objections that attraction is an incomprehensible occult force, a notion in the medieval manner, his reply is merely the celebrated 'Hypotheses non fingo'.[2] The same unwillingness to go beyond the facts, the same scepticism about the merely speculative, also infuses the philosophy of Locke in his *Essay concerning Human Understanding*, with its insistence that there are no 'innate' ideas (as the Cartesians maintained): everything in the human mind has its starting-point in sense experience, and what lies beyond the range of the senses cannot truly be known.

While factual study of nature was thus leading to great extensions of knowledge and beginning to exercise a profound intellectual influence, a similar movement developed in the field of historical scholarship. The Renaissance tradition conceived historiography as having two functions.

---

[1] Fontenelle, *Entretiens*, premier soir.
[2] For this controversy, see above, pp. 49–50.

Either it provided a compendium of edifying anecdotes concerning the actions of great men, and thus was chiefly moral in purpose, rhetorical in manner, and to be judged by primarily aesthetic criteria; or else it served some fairly immediate partisan end—the establishment of a dynastic claim, the support of a sectional attitude, the encouragement of party enthusiasm by hagiographical means. Much continued to be written in both these veins well into the late seventeenth century, and partisan history in particular produced some very notable works, such as Clarendon's *History of the Rebellion* (1702–4)—an inquest on failure for the warning of future governments—and Bossuet's *Histoire des Variations des Eglises Protestantes* (1688). More characteristic is a growing interest in the recovery of the facts of the past by the collection and investigation of the surviving documentary evidence, instead of the traditional reliance for information upon either the writings of previous historians or, at best, a restricted and uncritical use of early chronicles. The starting-point of such an interest was sometimes the desire to establish personal or family rights and privileges, as in the case of Leibniz's vast documentary researches for the history of the House of Hanover which his employer, the elector, commissioned from him. But the collective outcome was to transform historical scholarship by endowing it with a huge range of source material made accessible and systematically presented for the first time. In England, where pioneer work had already been done by Camden and other Elizabethan antiquaries, the medieval ecclesiastical documents published in Dugdale's *Monasticon Anglicanum* (1655–73)[1] were supplemented by Henry Wharton's assemblage of chronicles in *Anglia Sacra* (1691–5); important work on the cataloguing of medieval manuscripts in the Bodleian and Harleian collections was done by Humphrey Wanley, and the study of English foreign relations was given a new basis by the fifteen volumes of Thomas Rymer's *Foedera* (1702–13)—a work which in its original inspiration apparently owed much to Leibniz's similar collection, the *Codex Juris Gentium Diplomaticus* (1693). In France, the outstanding names are those of the Benedictine Congregation of St Maur: Jean Mabillon (1632–1707), whose *De Re Diplomatica* founded the study of diplomatic in 1681, and Bernard de Montfaucon (*Palaeographia graeca*, 1708). The Maurists of St-Germain-des-Prés, unlike the Jesuit Bollandists at Antwerp—compilers of the *Acta Sanctorum*—were not confined to a single great work of scholarship in the field of Church history.[2] In Italy, the comparably vast labours of L. A. Muratori (1672–1750) did not begin to bear fruit until 1723.[3]

The first result of this attention to an ever-widening range of fact was

---

[1] Much of the work was compiled by Roger Dodsworth: see D. Douglas, *English Scholars, 1660–1730* (rev. edn. 1951), pp. 33–41.

[2] See M. D. Knowles, 'Great Historical Enterprises', I and II, in *Transactions of the Royal Historical Society*, 5th ser. vol. VIII (1958), pp. 147–66, and vol. IX (1959), pp. 169–87.

[3] Below, pp. 558–9.

dismay. Examined in the critical light of reason, the facts often appeared not merely to destroy existing historical beliefs, but by their mutual contradictions to make any historical belief at all seem dangerous. Scepticism appeared the only justifiable approach to the study of the past —an attitude most characteristically reflected in Bayle's very influential *Dictionnaire historique et critique* (1697, 2nd edn. 1702). Here, in a work which in its original conception was intended merely to correct mistakes in an earlier historical dictionary by Moreri, Bayle systematically exposes the elements of deception, credulity and error which have gone to make up man's supposed knowledge of the past. In the course of the methodical confrontation and analysis of historical evidence which is undertaken for this purpose, however, Bayle arrives at valid criteria for the assessment of such material, so that the small area of historical fact which he is able to accept as established is nevertheless established with a new degree of certainty.[1] The parallel here with the scrupulous modesty of a Newton in science, or a Locke in philosophy, seems inescapable.

Such an examination of what had long passed for factual truth was a process which, once set in motion, was bound to extend beyond the range of the professional interests of the scholar. The Christian religion itself rests upon historical evidence, and the critical exegesis of the Bible, begun, to the general horror, by the execrated Spinoza in his *Tractatus theologico-politicus* (1670), was continued in the work of the French Oratorian Richard Simon, whose *Histoire critique du Vieux Testament* (1678) was followed by similar studies on the New Testament in 1689–93. Significant as such developments are as a prelude to the frontal attack which the eighteenth century was to see launched against the factual bases of Christianity, the social and religious environment of the period was scarcely favourable to a direct rationalist challenge of this sort.[2] There were, however, a number of popular beliefs, of a kind which might be described as the outworks of religion, which were immediately vulnerable to factual criticism. Of these there are two notable French examples. Bayle's *Pensées diverses sur la Comète* (1683) is a scrutiny, undertaken ostensibly on the occasion of the appearance of a comet in 1680, of the persistent superstition that comets are divine warnings of impending human disasters. Bayle has little difficulty in demonstrating that there is, in fact, no historical evidence for this belief; but his argument also has wider implications. Not only is he here attacking ways of thinking in which tradition or 'universal consent' were still accepted as valid grounds for belief; he is also undermining the old confidence, profoundly religious in origin, that God concerns himself directly and immediately in human affairs, that the universe is anthropocentric. Fontenelle's *Histoire des*

---

[1] See E. Labrousse, 'La Méthode critique chez Pierre Bayle et l'histoire', *Revue Internationale de Philosophie*, vol. XI (1957), pp. 450–66, and idem, *Bayle* (1965).
[2] See below, ch. IV.

Oracles (1687), adapted from a larger work by a Dutch scholar,[1] is similarly concerned with a time-hallowed Christian superstition—that the pagan oracles of antiquity were indeed supernatural, though diabolic and not divine in origin, and that they were all silenced by the birth of Christ. Here, again, a critical analysis of the facts suffices to show that both these beliefs are groundless. But in explaining the pagan oracles as deliberate frauds practised by a crafty priesthood on a gullible public, Fontenelle was clearly inviting his readers to infer that Christians too are similarly deceived; and such an exposure of the foolish credulity of the ancient world was a further blow to its prestige, from a distinguished leader of the 'modern' party.

This widespread preoccupation with the collection and critical analysis of factual knowledge in the realms of science, thought and scholarship is perhaps paralleled by certain developments in the sphere of imaginative literature. There appear during the last decades of the century the beginnings of a new and immediate awareness of the contemporary scene and its external details. In England, the resurgent vitality of the theatre at the Restoration achieved its most successful and characteristic expression in a new comedy of manners. While frequently relying upon the stock devices of comic tradition for its plots, and borrowing extensively from the French theatre in particular, this comedy is chiefly concerned with presenting an essentially realistic, though often bitterly sardonic, picture of aspects of the contemporary London scene. Its rakes, fops, coquettes, scheming matrons and boorish country squires are primarily caricatures of observed reality, not presentations of universal humanity in its comic aspect, as are the great figures of Molière's plays. The purely satirical element seems to be strongest in the early exponents of the manner. Wycherley's *The Country Wife* (1672) is not only more grossly priapic than most later plays in this notoriously uninhibited genre; it seems to spring from a passionate detestation of contemporary hypocrisy, as does also *The Plain Dealer* (1674). Such strength of feeling, out of place no doubt in a drama whose subject was its patrons, is absent on the whole from the more urbane work of the group of dramatists who produced the finest examples of this comedy at the turn of the century: Congreve (*Love for Love*, 1695), Vanbrugh (*The Provoked Wife*, 1697) and Farquhar (*The Constant Couple*, 1699). Here, the follies and affectations of London society are on the whole treated with a kindlier mockery: the comic emphasis is placed upon the flash of wit and repartee, particularly in the sophisticated and artificial plays of Congreve, whose *The Way of the World* (1700) is the masterpiece as well as the quintessence of the genre. In France, comedy remained very much under the shadow of Molière,

---

[1] A. van Dale, *De Oraculis Ethnicorum* (1683). Another Dutch work of the period attacking superstition is Balthasar Bekker's *De Betoverde Weereld* (1691): below, p. 123.

and the non-realistic conventions of the *commedia dell'arte* continued to exercise some influence, but a similar trend towards concern with the contemporary scene is also discernible. Comedy of manners had been of course an important, if subsidiary, part of Molière's own work; and comment on topical themes had been occasionally attempted by other comic writers. What is new in the period, however, is that, while purely topical comedy of a fairly trivial sort continues, a new element of social satire of a profounder kind emerges. In particular, the growing cynicism of upper-class society, its increasing infiltration by wealthy and unscrupulous parvenus, the breakdown of old social barriers before the new power of money, provide the theatre with a vein of comic material not accessible to Molière. This world appears in the 1680s in the comedies of Michel Baron (*L'Homme à bonne fortune*, 1686) and Florent Dancourt (*Le Chevalier à la mode*, 1687): it is used as a background for a renewal of comedy of character by J. F. Regnard in his *Joueur* (1696). Perhaps the best-known example of this realistic comedy of manners, however, though it is scarcely superior to others which have sunk into obscurity, is Lesage's *Turcaret* (1709), a harsh picture of a rich, gross and ruthless financier and of the parasites, from lackeys to baronesses, who attempt to exploit him.

This new element of realism, of observation of the externals of the contemporary scene, is not confined to the drama. One of its most interesting literary manifestations is perhaps to be found in France in the development of the prose *portrait*. The interest taken by the society of the *salons* in the 1650s and 1660s in the succinct but penetrating description of human character, as a party entertainment, had literary repercussions; collections of such portraits were published, and in the novels of the time increased care was given to such analyses of individuals, which now became set-pieces. In the classical manner, however, the interest in them is almost exclusively concentrated on the psychological. Physical description is usually perfunctory or, in fiction, merely conventional and largely unrelated to the personality of the subject; it is clearly regarded as irrelevant to the main purpose. In La Bruyère's *Caractères* (1688–94) something very different appears. The work is much more than a collection of maxims and portraits: the subtitle, *Les Mœurs de ce siècle*, correctly describes its full and perspicacious account of the contemporary French scene as closely observed by a keen-eyed moralist who enjoyed a specially favourable point of vantage. And it presents men and women in such a way that, as in real life, the externals of their appearance and behaviour provide the key to our understanding of their personality. We are allowed to observe, first Giton's fresh complexion and portly figure, then his self-assurance, his ill-mannered contempt for others, the deference with which he nevertheless is treated; only in the last sentence of his portrait does La Bruyère confirm our inference: Giton is rich.[1] More daringly, La Bruyère

[1] *Les Caractères*, 'Des Biens de Fortune', 83.

begins his portrait of Onuphre[1] with a description of his bed which makes it a symbol of religious hypocrisy: externally, it is ascetical and severe, with its covering of coarse grey serge; within, all is soft down and fine cotton. To see such artistic possibilities in the use of observed or imagined physical detail is to reveal the first signs, at least, of an approach to art and imagination profoundly different from the classical.

A further direction in which a heightened interest in the factual manifests itself during the period is one of great importance for the future development of the novel. A taste for an authentic, or supposedly authentic, glimpse of past reality manifests itself in the extensive literature of memoirs and pseudo-memoirs which was published in the latter part of the seventeenth century. The line, indeed, is unbroken and full of infinitesimal gradations which leads from serious general history written by a participant, such as Clarendon; through the genuine personal memoirs of public men, such as those of La Rochefoucauld (1662) and de Retz (published 1717) concerning the Fronde; to the invented but supposedly authentic narratives published, for example, by the ingenious and fertile Courtilz de Sandras, whose *Mémoires de M. d'Artagnan* achieved the distinction of being treated as a serious historical document by Bayle,[2] as well as eventually providing the material for Dumas's *Trois Mousquetaires*; and so to the avowed fiction of the historical novel, which was also very popular and had by this date largely usurped the place of the long heroic novel in the tradition of La Calprenède and Scudéry. Pseudo-memoirs of this sort seem to have achieved popularity in England too, since in 1709 *The Tatler*, lest its readers be deceived, felt impelled to impress upon 'all booksellers and translators whatsoever, that the word "Memoir" is French for novel';[3] and it was in England that they found their most masterly exponent, in Daniel Defoe. Defoe never admits to writing novels: *Robinson Crusoe* (1719) and *Moll Flanders* (1722) are presented as genuine autobiographical documents; others, such as the *Memoirs of a Cavalier* (1720), have sometimes been seriously accepted as such by critics. And Defoe's great artistic innovation is his technique of creating this air of authenticity by a careful accumulation of circumstantial details, so realistic that the reader is convinced that they could have originated only in memory, not in imagination. His journalistic experience undoubtedly played a great part here; he is the only writer of the period to traverse the whole range from factual reporting to pure fiction. The upshot of this, however, and of the general public interest in memoirs and pseudo-memoirs, is to give prose fiction a new orientation. Where in the seventeenth century it had been conceived as prose epic (the heroic novel), or sometimes as non-dramatic farce (the comic novel of low life), it now

---

[1] *Ibid.* 'De la Mode', 24.
[2] *Dictionnaire historique*, art. 'Louis XIII', notes F, X, V, Z.
[3] No. 84 (22 Oct. 1709).

begins to emerge as primarily an evocation of observed reality: of human experience, past or present, seen and presented in the round. Lesage's *Gil Blas* (1715–35), though primarily in the older Spanish tradition of the picaresque novel, already moves in this direction in its introduction of historical characters and its use of the autobiographical form. In later novels, in Prévost and Marivaux, Smollett, Fielding and Richardson, the development continues, and the novel first begins to assume its modern shape.

Profound as the conflicts thus were between the new sceptical empiricism and factual realism, on the one hand, and the older forces of orthodoxy and traditional classicism on the other, both forces had this in common, that they were primarily intellectual in preoccupation and approach, and that their literature was for the most part directed towards an educated public, and reflected a predominantly aristocratic taste and outlook. In this period, however, a reaction against this state of affairs begins to be apparent from two quarters, the first philosophical, the second moral and social in origin.

The characteristic philosophers of the mid-seventeenth century, Descartes in France and Hobbes in England, had conceived of the material universe in purely mechanical terms: as passive matter subject to exclusively physical forces. Such an attitude destroyed the basis of the older way of thinking which, in the middle ages, had delighted in endowing nature with spiritual significance, in seeing symbol and allegory everywhere. In its turn, however, it provoked a reaction. In the latter half of the seventeenth century the group of thinkers known as the Cambridge Platonists, liberal theologians who wished to harmonize the new scientific knowledge with Christian belief, took issue in particular with Hobbesian materialism, and propounded a neo-Platonic conception of the universe which restored spiritual significance to the material world by seeing it as a symbolic representation of an underlying supernatural reality. The rational patterns which scientists were discovering in nature thus became reflections of the rationality of the divine mind, and it was possible to explain those phenomena which could not be fitted into a scheme of purely mechanical causation by postulating the existence of a creative principle of organic growth, or 'plastic nature' in Cudworth's phrase, which was ultimately divine in origin. Such views had far-reaching implications for art, even if contemporary artists did not greatly feel their influence. Not only did they renew the validity of artistic symbolism by thus allotting a cosmic rôle to the symbolic: they made it possible to see God in the guise of a supreme poet, communicating through his poem, Creation, intimations of his own reality which could be conveyed only through symbolism. The poet, similarly, becomes truly a creator: his function is not primarily that of a craftsman aiming at formal perfection in the imitation of models or of nature, but rather to impose an ordered pattern upon his material, and so to create a beauty which has a symbolic significance parallel with that of the beauty of nature. Shaftesbury's *Characteristicks* (1711) was the most influential work to develop an approach of this sort. For him the true poet is 'indeed a second Maker: a just Prometheus, under Jove'.[1] The highest function of man is the creative propagation of beauty, moral and physical, of which God remains the fountainhead.[2] Beauty and goodness, in fact, are one; and to be moved by natural beauty, as by a work of art, is to achieve some awareness of its ordered harmony, imposed upon a formless raw material by the mind of the artist—by the mind of God. The emphasis in aesthetic matters is thus once again laid upon emotion: 'enthusiasm', for all Shaftesbury's distrust of it in religion, is a worthy state of mind when it arises from the contemplation of beauty, for it is then in a sense divinely inspired (and consequently not in any way contrary to reason). And the apostrophe to the sublimity of nature in all its aspects, even the most awe-inspiring and untamed, which Shaftesbury introduces into *The Moralists*, is perhaps a first step in the general movement towards admiration for the primitive and uncivilized which later became a characteristic of eighteenth-century feeling, with its ready acceptance of the poetry of Ossian, its cult of the 'Gothick', its discovery of the pleasure of mountain scenery. 'La poésie', Diderot was to say, 'veut quelque chose d'énorme, de barbare et de sauvage.'[3]

The influence of such ideas was for the most part for the future, especially in France, where it appears that Shaftesbury remained little known. But it is not altogether implausible to see a similar approach to a freer sensibility in art in the work of Fénelon (1651–1715), the most sensitive and distinguished mind among French churchmen of the period, who was also strongly influenced by Platonism.[4] Fénelon's affinities with an effusive mysticism in religion are paralleled, in his didactic novel *Télémaque* (1699), by an unmistakable lyricism in the descriptions of scenes such as Calypso's island grotto, or of the arcadian life of idyllic simplicity led by the people of La Bétique.[5]

A reaction of a stronger and more immediately telling kind is that engendered during this period, especially in England, by the emergence of a new class of readers, of rather different taste and outlook. The rise in wealth and social importance of the middle classes naturally created a newly influential element in the reading public, and one whose preferences came to be reflected in contemporary literature. Puritan and indeed religious influences in general were stronger among such readers than among the courtly public which had previously set the tone. It was con-

---

[1] *Characteristicks*, Bk. III, 'Advice to an Author', I, 3.
[2] *Ibid.* Bk. v, 'The Moralists', III, 2.
[3] *De la Poésie dramatique* (1758), ch. XVIII.
[4] See J. L. Goré, *L'Itinéraire de Fénelon* (1957).
[5] Bks I, VII. On Fénelon's interest in Quietism see below, pp. 147–9.

93

sequently to be expected that there should be something of a reaction against the cynicism, for instance, of the established Restoration comedy. Jeremy Collier's pamphlet, *A Short View of the Immorality and Profaneness of the English Stage* (1698), found some echoes in public opinion and exercised considerable influence, on playwrights at least. The preference for an edifying moral and for a sentimental appeal in drama finds early expression in Colley Cibber, whose *Love's Last Shift* (1696) ends with the reform of the rake-hero, and also in some plays by Farquhar; but the new genre of moral and genteel comedy, intentionally improving in tone and making a deliberate break with the Restoration manner, is perhaps most to be associated with Steele (*The Funeral*, 1701; *The Conscious Lovers*, 1722). The most influential English vehicle for such views, however, was the periodical essay, a relatively new form which achieved wide popularity through the work of Steele, Addison and some lesser collaborators in *The Tatler* (1708–11) and *The Spectator* (1711–14). Here the didactic intention is quite explicit: Addison remarks in *The Spectator* that 'Discourses of morality, and reflections upon human nature, are the best means we can make use of to improve our minds, and gain a true knowledge of ourselves, and consequently to recover our souls out of the vice, ignorance and prejudice which naturally cleave to them. I have all along professed myself in this paper a promoter of these great ends.'[1] These periodicals succeeded in reaching an extensive public, of both sexes, by the appeal of their discursive comments on the contemporary scene, lively and critical, but humorous and kindly in tone, and endeavouring always 'to enliven morality with wit, and to temper wit with morality'.[2] Their effect was not only to civilize social conduct by spreading standards of gentility among new and wider sections of society, but also to infuse Christian morality into the concept of gentlemanliness itself. The character of Sir Roger de Coverley, presented in *The Spectator* as the ideal figure of a country squire, benevolent and humane, himself symbolizes the transformation, for in youth he was a Restoration rake.[3]

This English emphasis upon social morality and delicacy of feeling, though it owed much to French politeness and was in turn to be influential in France later in the eighteenth century, has no real French parallel during our period. There was, indeed, some French hostility to the theatre, of which Bossuet's *Maximes et réflexions sur la comédie* (1694) is the best-known formulation; but this attack, supported by a minority of devout rigorists in Church and nobility, was directed not against moral laxity or impropriety on the stage—such things had been virtually unknown in France for half a century—but against the drama itself, as by its nature morally harmful in its emotional impact on the spectator. It is possible, however, to find there the first beginnings of a new sentimen-

---

[1] No. 215 (6 Nov. 1711).   [2] *Spectator*, no. 10 (12 March 1711).
[3] No. 2 (2 March 1711).

talism which undoubtedly contributed to the later French cult of 'l'homme de sentiment' and of the pleasures of virtue. The tragedies of the elder Crébillon (1675–1762), while observing the letter of the classical convention, appear to cater for a new taste which prefers a superficial and melodramatic sensationalism, of an ultimately sentimental kind, to the authentically tragic. His *Atrée et Thyeste* (1707) has a final scene in which Thyestes *almost* drinks a goblet of his own son's blood, while in *Electre* (1708) the ancient tale is embroidered with amatory entanglements for Electra and Orestes, and a mystification concerning the latter's identity. But the strongest indication of the new direction in which French taste was moving is supplied by the great success of La Motte-Houdard's tragedy *Inès de Castro* in 1723, with its trial scene in which the judges weep when the hero, Don Pedro, is condemned, and with its pathetic dénouement in which the king, his father, is moved to forgive his rebellion by the touching sight of Pedro's children, the offspring of his secret marriage to Inès. Such works look forward to the sentimental virtue of Nivelle de la Chaussée, Marivaux and Rousseau, but also to the violent passions of the Abbé Prévost's ill-starred heroes.

We have so far been concerned with developments which, whatever their diversity, all have their being within the body of western European civilization as it had evolved from its Mediterranean origins. A further distinguishing feature of our period, however, is a more general awareness that European man is not the sole inhabitant of the globe: that the wider world may have much to offer that is not merely curious, but also challenging. The growing intimacy between maritime Europe and the Americas, together with the multiplication of commercial and missionary contacts in Asia and Africa, not only increased public curiosity about unfamiliar regions; they also increasingly provided the means to satisfy it, both by notable additions to the already considerable literature of travel, and by stimulating scholarly interest in the languages and history of the civilizations of the East.

Attention had been most strongly concentrated upon the Muslim East, to a lesser degree on what lay beyond it. Bernier, in 1675 the popularizer of Gassendi's philosophy, had published a penetrating account of contemporary India in 1660–71 (E. T. 1671), after some years in Mughal service. The later narratives of Tavernier and Chardin[1] paid more attention to the practical details of travel, commerce and everyday life in Turkey, India, and especially Persia, where both spent long periods. Travellers beyond India were rare; but two French accounts of Siam appeared, in 1686–7,[2]

[1] J. B. Tavernier, *Les Six voyages…en Turquie, en Perse et aux Indes* (1st edn. 1676, E. T. 1678); J. Chardin, *Journal du voyage…en Perse et aux Indes Orientales* (1st edn. 1686, E. T. 1686). For François Bernier, who died in 1688, cf. below, p. 99.
[2] G. Tachard, *Voyage de Siam des Pères Jésuites…*(1686, E. T. 1688, Dutch tr. 1687); F. T. de Choisy, *Journal du voyage de Siam fait en 1685 et 1686* (1687).

and China, described in Louis Le Comte's *Nouveaux mémoires sur l'état présent de la Chine* (1696), became widely familiar through the controversial activities of the Jesuit missionaries there, reports from whom began to be published regularly in 1702. These *Lettres édifiantes et curieuses*, full of praise for Chinese morals and government, were to be the main source of a philosophic cult, especially in France, that for half a century was to make Confucius a patron saint of the Enlightenment. By 1705 Leibniz looked forward to an exchange of knowledge with China that would be more useful than the study of European antiquity. But materials for the later picture of Chinese tyranny and bad faith can be found in the *Giro del Mondo* (Naples, 1699–1700) of Gemelli Careri and the *Journal* (Leiden, 1726) of Lorenz Lange, a Swedish Protestant engineer sent to China by Peter the Great. The impressions formed by merchants who did business at Canton also differed widely from the reports of the Fathers in Peking.[1]

By the later seventeenth century a picture of the primitive peoples of the Americas had long been established in the public mind. New collections of voyages were published, such as Sir Tancred Robinson's *Account of Several Late Voyages and Discoveries to the South and North* (1694) and the *Collection of Voyages and Travels* (1704) edited by the brothers Awnsham and John Churchill. Further travel narratives continued to appear, but their novelty, where it existed, was to be found either in an unorthodox point of view, such as that of Lahontan's strongly anti-clerical *Nouveaux Voyages ...dans l'Amérique Septentrionale* (1704),[2] or in the renewed glamour of adventure in the South Sea, as in Dampier's *Voyages* (1687, etc.), the narratives of Woodes Rogers's circumnavigation of 1708–11 (1712), and earlier in the still more famous *De Amerikaensche Zee-Rovers* of A. O. Exquemelin (Amsterdam, 1678, translated into German 1679, Spanish 1681, English 1684, and French 1686).

The value of the information which travellers to remote regions could obtain was appreciated in scientific circles. The *Philosophical Transactions* of January 1665/6 published some 'Directions for Seamen, bound for far Voyages' which contain the Royal Society's advice on collecting and recording 'such observations abroad, as may be pertinent and suitable' for the Society's purposes and would increase its 'Philosophical stock'.[3] Linguistic and historical studies of the Near East also attracted attention; for example, the humanist tradition of the study of Arabic, in the major European universities, was reinforced by a new practical interest. This was reflected in France by the measures initiated by Colbert to establish a

---

[1] Louis Dermigny, *La Chine et l'Occident: le commerce à Canton au XVIIIe siècle, 1719–1833* (4 vols. 1964), vol. I, pp. 22 ff. Cf. Basil Guy, *The French Image of China before and after Voltaire* (Geneva, 1963). Cf. below, p. 130 and vol. v, ch. XVII (1).

[2] For the bibliography of Lahontan, see the edn. of his *New Voyages to North-America* by R. G. Thwaites (Chicago, 2 vols. 1905), vol. I, pp. li–xciii.

[3] *Phil. Trans.* I, no. 8, p. 141.

regular system of training in Arabic, Turkish and Persian for young men aiming at the position of *secrétaire-interprète du Roi*. Historical studies remained more limited in geographical scope at this period: while Turkish history came to be comparatively familiar to the general reader by the turn of the century, thanks to such widely known works as those of Sir Paul Rycaut,[1] remoter countries for the most part had to wait a decade or two longer for their European historians. The appearance of translations into European languages of something of the literature of the East was a further manifestation of such interests. The Koran was available in the major European languages by 1650 and frequently republished; some Turkish, Persian and Arabic chronicles were also translated; but the vogue for the Oriental in literature was launched among the wider public by a more immediately attractive genre, the Eastern tale. The *Arabian Nights* began to appear in French in 1704 and shortly afterwards in English. It was followed by a flood of further tales either genuinely or supposedly translated from an Eastern tongue—a flood which continued late into the eighteenth century and was to include works by Voltaire and Diderot, not to mention that remarkable Anglo-French hybrid, Beckford's *Vathek*. The immediate appeal of such reading lay, of course, in its exotic colour, in the strangeness of the world of sultan and harem, vizier and eunuch, which it revealed; in its violence and freedom from the conventional restraints of European society; and in its atmosphere of fantasy that mingled the magic carpet and the genie with mundane affairs. Such qualities were precisely those which the orthodoxies and proprieties of the classical tradition could not offer.

This ready welcome for an imaginative literature which depicted the Orient as revealed by the travel literature of earlier decades gives clear proof of the growing European awareness of other continents. The imaginative possibilities of the Voyage itself, however, did not go unnoticed. The invented travel narrative is as natural a development from the authentic one as was the fictitious from the genuine memoir; and, as with the literature of memoirs, there are examples, such as the *Aventures de Monsieur de Beauchêne*, published by Lesage in 1732, whose status has been matter for controversy. The European masterpiece in this genre, *Robinson Crusoe*, though it drew for its material to some extent on travel literature and also on the actual experiences of the castaway Alexander Selkirk (whose adventures had attracted much attention in England on his return with Captain Woodes Rogers in 1711[2]), is above all a great imaginative creation in its own right. Here Defoe employs his vast talent for realistic detail in order to depict an individual at grips, unaided, with the forces of nature and coming to terms perforce with solitude. Other

---

[1] *The Present State of the Ottoman Empire* (1668 and many subsequent edns: Fr. trans. 1670, Ger. 1694, Polish 1678); *The History of the Turkish Empire from 1623 to 1677* (1680).
[2] Below p. 373.

fictional voyages owed less to human experience. Utopian literature had always involved some account of the journey, however fantastic, by which Utopia was reached; but the growth of travel literature naturally offered writers a new resource, now that their imaginary country could be made more credible by a circumstantial account of the voyage to it and of its geographical location. Denis Vairasse's frequently reprinted *History of the Sevarites or Sevarambi* (English version 1675, French 1677), like Foigny's *La Terre australe connue* (1676), is set in an Australia which, however imaginary its inhabitants, is intended to be identified with the southern continent whose existence had been confirmed by Tasman. And Swift in 1726 was to employ the same device, though with mocking perfunctoriness, in *Gulliver's Travels.*

Utopian literature, however, was now in rivalry with the factual travel narrative, so far as its intellectual function was to encourage critical reflection on the state of European man, religious, moral, or political. Travellers' revelations concerning human beliefs and customs in a range of widely differing societies increased the general tendency of the period towards a critical self-awareness, towards a rational examination of all traditionally held assumptions. Just as astronomy had now questioned the earth's unique status in the universe, so the evidence of travellers tended to undermine the European's confidence in the unique value of his religion and civilization. Such a situation, too, offered a new possibility to writers who felt the need of a vehicle for social and moral satire. A reversal of the direction of travel, an account of the experiences of foreigners visiting Europe from afar, gave opportunities for introducing a critical viewpoint by presenting the European scene through the eyes of observers whose fundamental assumptions were quite alien. The pioneer work here was G. P. Marana's *L'Espion du Grand Seigneur* (1684), frequently reprinted and widely translated, and Addison contributed a brief sketch in the genre to *The Spectator*;[1] but the outstanding achievement is Montesquieu's *Lettres Persanes* (1721), which interlards critical discussion of the French scene with descriptions of life in a Persian harem, and draws extensively for its details of oriental customs, and its itinerary of the journey from Ispahan, upon the travels of Tavernier and Chardin.

In the religious world, new contacts and the opportunity to hear non-Christian views of his own beliefs discouraged the European's traditional assumption of the evident superiority of Christianity. The Chinese authorities, he could now learn from the Jesuit missionaries, had proclaimed Christian doctrines to be 'without foundation, pernicious and absurd', Christian practices a violation of 'all the laws of nature and of friendship', and Christian miracles merely fraudulent.[2] More important

---

[1] No. 50 (27 April 1711).
[2] F. Pallu, *Relation abrégée des Missions...*(1668) and A. Greslon, *Histoire de la Chine* ...(1671), quoted by G. Atkinson, *Les Relations de voyages du XVIIe siècle et l'évolution des idées* (1924), pp. 151–2.

than such direct criticisms, however, were the subversive implications of the accounts of other religions given, often with the best of Christian intentions, by the travellers themselves. The evils of priestcraft, the trickeries practised by mullah, brahman, bonze and witch-doctor upon the gullible heathen, were frequent subjects of comment, especially by Protestant travellers who saw in such practices merely a confirmation of their own attitude towards the Catholic priesthood. And the miracles accepted in alien religions were often subjected to a stringent critical examination which would have been widely regarded as inadmissible in a Christian context. Bernier, in his account of Mughal India, describes the allegedly supernatural feats of fakirs and yogis, but insists with scrupulous care that he personally has witnessed none that he could not satisfactorily explain as trickery.[1] Similarly, such discoveries as that traditions of divine incarnation and of resurrection existed among the Red Indians of New York, that belief in the virgin birth of the founder of a religious sect flourished in Japan, and that a faith in immortality was not confined to adherents of revealed religions—all these could perhaps be accepted by the pious as evidence of the spread among the heathen of garbled fragments of Christian truth; but inevitably they suggested to some inquiring minds an interpretation less favourable to the uniqueness of Christianity.

Further difficulties also arose on specific points of doctrine. Was the unashamed nudity of many primitive peoples, the freedom of their women from pain in childbirth, to be interpreted as a denial of the universality of original sin? Or were such races not in the descent from Adam? And what was to be made of the fact that the ancient peoples of the East— Chinese, Hindus, Chaldeans—preserved accounts of human history that were incompatible with the Old Testament and differed widely from its chronology? The problem was serious enough to engage the attention of Newton, whose *Chronology of Ancient Kingdoms amended* appeared posthumously in 1728.

The theological questions raised by the literature of travel clearly played a part in loosening the hold of religious orthodoxy on men's minds. They pointed the way to Deism, seen by so many writers of the eighteenth century as the highest common factor of all religions—the kernel of truth within the brittle shell of useless dogma—and so also to the need for religious toleration, that other major preoccupation of eighteenth-century thinkers. It was not only in the sphere of dogma, however, that the new European awareness of the wider world created difficulties; in the sphere of morals they were also acute. The widespread assumption that the European Christian was necessarily the moral superior of the heathen received, indeed, considerable support from the many gruesome tales in the travel narratives of the cruelty of the American Indian or the brutishness of the Hottentot; but the earliest discoverers had also frequently

---

[1] *Histoire...des Etats du Grand Mogol*, vol. III: 'Lettre à M. Chapelain', pp. 65–6.

remarked upon the many virtues they observed among primitive peoples, and by the end of the seventeenth century such comments had become a familiar commonplace for the reader. The typical picture of the savage, and especially of the American Indian, was of a man who, if vindictive towards his tribal enemies, was full of a spontaneous benevolence and affection towards his family and other members of his tribe, and who was even-tempered, honest and contented: a man free, above all, from the besetting European vices of envy, avarice and ambition.[1] Such a view seemed to lend support to the suggestions to be found in Bayle and Shaftesbury that morality was not inseparable from revealed religion, that mankind was universally endowed with a natural 'moral sense'—ideas of major import for the Enlightenment. This picture of the inherent virtues of primitive man had a further significance. Not only did many travellers draw attention to the fact that primitive man seemed happier, more contented and more virtuous than the supposedly superior European; it was also noted that contact with the European frequently resulted in the deterioration of the savage. The contrast thus seemed to be firmly established between the vices of civilization and the virtues of the simple life— virtues which gained in prestige from being seen as the surviving modern equivalents of such familiar ideals as the ancient Roman hero and the early Christian saint. The way was clear for the development of the cult of the Noble Savage.

Finally, in the political sphere, the new knowledge of remote countries provided equally significant grounds for European self-criticism. On the one hand, primitive man's apparent lack of political institutions seemed to make his communities enviable examples of liberty, equality and fraternity, where constraint was unknown and public spirit prevailed—an ideal crystallized in Montesquieu's celebrated description of the Troglodytes in the early pages of Les Lettres Persanes. Such a picture, indeed, formed the basis of an attack of revolutionary violence upon French religious, political and social traditions in the 'Dialogues d'Adario' which conclude Lahontan's Nouveaux Voyages. On the other hand, Oriental societies (with the exception of China) came to be identified in the public mind with the worst extremes of capricious tyranny, with the cruel and ruthless despot reigning by fear over an abject population of virtual slaves. It is within the area bounded by these extremes, both depicted in the travel literature, that the political thinking of the eighteenth century moves. While the attraction of the political freedom of primitive society is apparent in Rousseau's Discours, as is that of its supposed sexual freedom in Diderot's Supplément au Voyage de Bougainville, hatred of despotism produced a certain tendency to identify the European monarch with the Oriental tyrant—a tendency favoured by the widespread use of exotic

---

[1] Considerable evidence is quoted by Atkinson, op. cit. and R. W. Frantz, The English Traveller and the Movement of Ideas (Nebraska Univ. Studies, vols. XXXII–III, 1934).

settings by political satirists in need of a suitable veil for their attacks. Here again an early example is provided by the *Lettres Persanes*, in which Montesquieu employs his descriptions of Oriental despotisms as a means of indicating the dangers for France which he feels to be inherent in the authoritarian tendencies of the French monarchy of his day.

To the many stirrings of new thought which we have earlier discussed, and to the fertile conflicts with more traditional conceptions which they engendered, the growth of knowledge of distant lands thus added a further stimulus. The period, in fact, is one in which European man not only reaches out to new and wider horizons but also acquires a new critical self-awareness, a new ability to weigh evidence, make comparisons, and understand as temporary and local what had previously been accepted as permanent and universal.

2. MUSIC, 1661–1752

The rise of historicism which distinguishes the end of the eighteenth century yielded, among others, the first great histories of music. Works of corresponding comprehensiveness were slow to follow in the wake of these initial achievements, and for this reason a proper understanding of the musical scene in the age of Louis XIV has not been possible until the comparatively recent past. The writings of Charles Burney and John Hawkins, when set in this perspective, become the more remarkable for their precocious sweep and penetrating insights. Burney, in particular, amazes one by his ability to bring to completion the task he set for himself—an account that runs from ancient Greece to his own day. This cannot be said of his distinguished successors in the nineteenth century: the antiquarian completeness of F. J. Fétis and the independent judgments of A. W. Ambros unfortunately were never brought to bear on the seventeenth and eighteenth centuries; like their fellow romanticists, these scholars were much too fascinated by the more remote past. Lacking modern tools of research to aid him, Burney's narrative, on the other hand, suffers from a disproportionate treatment of the eighteenth century, to the neglect of earlier periods. One cannot wholly blame his enthusiasm for Handel: the paucity of available documents concerning earlier composers like Lully and Scarlatti precluded a corresponding consideration of their achievements. No work comparable in scope with that of Burney appeared until the beginning of the present century, when Henry Hadow edited the *Oxford History of Music*.[1] By this time the writing of comprehensive histories was no longer committed to a single hand, and the various periods were allotted each to its own specialist. Accordingly,

---

[1] Burney, *General History of Music* (4 vols. 1776–89); Hawkins, *General History of the Science and Practice of Music* (4 vols. 1776); Fétis, *Histoire générale de la musique* (5 vols. 1869–76); Ambros, *Geschichte der Musik* (Breslau, 5 vols. 1862–82); *Oxford History of Music* (6 vols. 1901–5).

the volume on the seventeenth century in the Oxford series was entrusted to Sir Hubert Parry who, in common with Burney, had that rare combination, a true avidity for knowledge and an awareness of the relative values underlying a mass of data. No more than Burney, however, had Parry readily available to him an account of musical life at the courts of Louis XIV, Charles II and Queen Anne. Nor was the music of that time within the range of taste of their respective contemporaries. But their perseverance was in each case well rewarded; the results were not merely catalogued, they were also discussed and evaluated. That there should be a bias in their judgments was natural. The European leadership of Lully, that 'Frenchified Tuscan' and favourite composer of Louis XIV, and the Frenchification of English culture under Charles II could only elicit an aloof disdain from an English historian. Nevertheless, once we discount the bias, we find in Burney and Parry alike genuine stylistic comparisons between the singing opera of the Italians and the orchestral opera of the French, between the contrapuntal style of Palestrina, the thorough-bass style of Lully and Scarlatti, and the melodic style of Haydn, since renamed 'classical'. These comparative studies exposed the characteristic elements peculiar to certain periods, such as the all-pervading thorough-bass in the works of Lully, Corelli and Purcell, to which Hugo Riemann gave due recognition when he entitled the relevant volume of his *Handbuch der Musikgeschichte* (1901–13) 'The Age of the Thorough-Bass, 1600–1700'. The title was, if nothing more, both a vice and a virtue. Praiseworthy was the attempt to isolate a conspicuous element of musical style, in contrast to Parry's chronological title, *Music of the Seventeenth Century*. To emphasize thus a technical means of expression, the 'thorough-bass', was undoubtedly a necessary though still a tentative stage in the evolution of musical historiography.

Historians in the decades following Riemann and Parry have endeavoured, with increasing success, to go beyond the purely technical aspect and to include music as part of the general nexus of civilization and its history. By the mid-twentieth century there were available three significant histories of music. First, in 1929, there appeared Robert Haas's *Die Musik des Barocks*, one of ten volumes of the *Handbuch der Musikwissenschaft*, edited by Ernst Bücken (Potsdam, 1928–34). The novelty of the volume, as of the entire series to which it belongs, was the recognition on the part of its authors, professional historians of music, of the notion of a European mind expressing itself in the meanderings of political and cultural history. This general concept, derived from Dilthey and others, was applied with great conviction and in considerable detail to the unravelling of the thread of musical history. To the compositions of the seventeenth century were attributed such traits as 'sweep', 'massiveness', and 'theatrical character', and an attempt was made to measure the extent to which these features were equally applicable to the literary and visual arts. Particular attention was paid to the visual arts, which were exemplified in seventeenth-century depictions of operas and concerts. Above all, having edited the works of Monteverdi and Gluck, Haas was able to discern the position of opera as the central spectacle of the age of Louis XIV. His investigation of the social and artistic events of this age led him to borrow the descriptive term 'baroque' in order to characterize the music of the seventeenth century and the opening decades of the eighteenth. This designation was so convincing that later scholars in Germany, Italy, France and America adopted it: gone were the days when 'barocco' was a term of disparagement as it had been with the great nineteenth-century cultural historian, Burckhardt. Further, a chapter on the baroque, again written by Robert Haas, was included in the revised edition (Berlin, 1930) of the *Handbuch der Musikgeschichte* which appeared under the editorship of Guido Adler. This work was less lavish in the space and illustrations allotted to the concept of general cultural history: Adler stressed to a greater degree than had been done hitherto the evolution of musical styles. Lastly, in 1940, the American publishing house of Norton initiated a history of music which included Manfred Bukofzer's *Music in the Baroque Era* (1947). This series as a whole[1] marks a return to the idea of cultural history and gives limited space to technical analysis. Thus Bukofzer resolutely refrains from restricting his discussion to sharps and flats. It was his belief that 'music does not, as legend has it, lag behind the other arts. The dominant trends in baroque music correspond to those in baroque art and literature...' Nor was he oblivious of the inevitable consequences that the Italianism of Mazarin and the protectionism of Colbert would have for the style, and even for the eventual fate, of French opera. He is careful to trace not only analogous procedures in the musical and visual arts,[2] but also the effects of the patronage of nobility and clergy.

The cleavage between nineteenth-century taste and that of the age of Lully, Purcell and Handel grew out of the continued ascendancy of absolute over programmatic music—that is, of music which moves the heart and mind by its own sonorous means rather than by extra-musical associations. Set against the aesthetic and emotional enjoyment of pure sound, the naïve tone-painting of François Couperin (1668–1733) and the French *clavecinistes*, for instance, might seem a frivolous desecration of music's profound and hieratic powers. Styles and preferences in music seem to yield more readily to the tides of fashion than do tastes in literature and painting. Moreover, the time-art of music has the disadvantage of a written notation intelligible only to the few, so that much depends on the possibilities of maintaining live performances, in the past necessarily

[1] It also includes: C. Parrish and J. Ohl, *Music before 1750* (1952); P. Láng, *Music in Western Civilization* (1952); O. Strunk, *Source Readings in Music History* (1942).

[2] Cf. Bukofzer, 'Allegory in Baroque Music', *Journal of the Warburg Institute*, vol. III (1939–40), pp. 1–21.

restricted and usually expensive. This is notably the case with the music written for the stage by Cavalli and Scarlatti, Purcell and Handel. Widespread opportunities to hear it had to await the achievement of sound recordings, which have brought the discoveries of the music historians to the notice of a larger public. These considerations apart, any real understanding of the composers who appear as protagonists on the cultural stage of Europe in the century after 1660 must be related to the contemporary setting, particularly as that setting was affected by notions of public taste, the advent of public concerts, and the activities of the publishing centres.

In the age of Louis XIV the arts were still experiencing the benefits and drawbacks of the patronage system. The nobility, secular and clerical, distributed commissions and thereby governed taste. Singing and dancing, with their spectacle and rhythmic drive, were the order of the day. Louis XIV's preference for ballet, dancing and lavish spectacle quickly became an international vogue. To be sure, a new art form, the sonata, was insinuating itself and even becoming fashionable in certain circles. But to the average audience sonatas were tedious instrumental 'sound-pieces', for solo instrument or orchestra: Fontenelle expressed the general attitude when he cried out in a fit of impatience, 'Sonate, que me veux-tu?'. Not until the end of the eighteenth century did German symphonies triumph in Paris and Europe.

That triumph was largely established in public concerts. Indeed, the gradual rise between the 1680s and the 1780s of this new form of entertainment transformed many aspects of music-making and listening. England was the first country to offer public concerts. John Banister, formerly one of the king's violinists, initiated a series at Whitefriars in 1672 and Thomas Britton, coal merchant, began his series in Clerkenwell in 1678. It has often been remarked that these concerts betrayed a middle class rather than an aristocratic cast: 'The first attempt was low; a project of old Banister, who was a good violin, and a theatricall composer. He opened an obscure room in a publik house in white fryars; filled it with tables and seats...'[1] Events of this kind, open to all paying customers and not merely to invited guests, were the harbingers of modern concert life, even though most audiences remained largely aristocratic. Many series of concerts were given in metropolitan surroundings; others were academic in their habitat, such as the Public Concerts in the Sheldonian Theatre at Oxford (under Pepusch, 1713) and those in the Holywell Music Room, Oxford (under William Hayes, 1748).[2] Here Handel played a prominent part, at Oxford as well as London. But the prestige of a leading composer did not suffice to give these English concerts the

[1] R. North, *The Musical Grammarian* (ed. H. Andrews, 1925), p. 30.
[2] J. H. Mee, *The Oldest Music Room in Europe* (1911); M. Tilmouth, 'Some Early London Concerts...1670–1720', *Proc. Royal Music Assoc.* vol. LXXXIV (1957–8), pp. 13–26.

far-reaching reverberations of the Parisian *concert spirituel*, a series founded in 1725 and continuing until 1791. They were intended to relieve the tedium of Lent when the theatres were not free to produce opera; indeed, many of the so-called public concerts down to the middle of the century, like Handel's oratorios, were largely substitutes for opera. We must, then, view the first public concerts[1] as containing the root of a new audience and of new programming, though not as yet effecting a break with aristocratic custom and taste—an event to be signalized by the American and French revolutions.[2]

The state of music printing and publishing in this age was similarly balanced between traditional and progressive elements. Not that the distribution of manuscript copies had ceased: but by Louis XIV's reign music had to be printed if it were to make a noticeable impact abroad. That Paris and London should become important publishing centres in the eighteenth century was a natural circumstance, but the Revocation of the Edict of Nantes furthered the position of Amsterdam as an influential purveyor of printed music. There the enterprise and initiative of publishers were sustained to the advantage not only of the concertos and trio sonatas of Corelli and Vivaldi, but of the works of Haydn and Mozart much later. Suffice it to say that a new genre, namely the concerto, could not have risen to its European stature in the early part of the eighteenth century but for the new methods of printing and the editions published in Holland, notably those of Estienne Roger. The main impetus was not technological; Amsterdam, now one of the intellectual centres of Europe, showed superior artistic judgment in musical matters. On the other hand, the rather spectacular revolution in the matter of casting musical type, initiated by J. G. I. Breitkopf in 1755, helped to establish Leipzig as the eventual international capital of music publishing.[3] The importance of printing for the promulgation of musical compositions is inversely exemplified by the case of Bach's Brandenburg Concertos, composed between 1718 and 1721. The fifth of these is often hailed as the first modern piano concerto and erroneously labelled the model for later composers, but there is no evidence that any of them were known to Haydn, Mozart or Beethoven, or that they were played in any of the major cities outside Germany: the Brandenburg Concertos did not appear in print until 1850.

In the later seventeenth century Paris was still queen of the musical world. The spectacles presented at the French court cast a spell over

---

[1] For the rôle of Hamburg, which supplemented those of London and Paris, cf. E. Preussner, *Die bürgerliche Musikkultur* (2nd edn. Kassel, 1950).

[2] See M. Brenet, *Les Concerts en France sous l'ancien régime* (1900). Cf. R. Schaal, 'Konzertwesen', *Die Musik in Geschichte und Gegenwart* (ed. F. Blume, Kassel, 14 vols. 1949–68), vol. VII, pp. 1587–1605.

[3] In England John Walsh introduced the use of punches into the engraving process before 1730—a means of music-printing still in use. Walsh was the original publisher of Handel's English compositions and provided English reprints of the most fashionable Italian music of the day.

Europe which lasted well over a century after the accession of Louis XIV. In fact, the *Roi Soleil* owes this title to one such spectacle, the famous *Ballet de la Nuit* of 1653, in which both the monarch and the young composer Giambattista Lulli participated. The contribution which Lulli, or Lully, made to the splendour of entertainments at Paris and Versailles has scarcely ever been surpassed in the history of drama and music. Born in Florence in 1632, he came to Paris at the age of fourteen. Between 1653 and 1657 he contributed some of the music to several ballets of Benserade, among them the *Ballet de la Nuit*. Still more important was his collaboration with Molière, encompassing *L'Impromptu de Versailles* (1663), *Le Bourgeois Gentilhomme* (1670) and *La Comtesse d'Escarbagnas* (1671). Yet, though he had been superintendent of the king's music since 1661, the ultimate glory of Lully's career was still to come. In 1672 he purchased from Pierre Perrin the 'privilege' for the *Académie Royale de Musique* which Perrin had obtained from the king in 1669.[1] This institution, which across various vicissitudes still exists as the Opéra in Paris today, was to nurture Lully's *tragédies lyriques* from *Cadmus et Hermione* in April 1673 to the posthumous *Achille et Polyscène* in November 1687. His style was carried to England by Pelham Humfrey (1647–74), to southern Germany by Georg Muffat (1645–1704), to northern Germany by Johann S. Kusser (1670–1727); and the first opera presented at the Spanish court was Lully's *Armide* in 1693.

The subject-matter of the operas, whether derived from the Bible or from the ancients, was invariably refashioned in the spirit of the age. As an influence in establishing the temper of this spirit the importance of Racine can hardly be overestimated. Librettists carefully studied his works; in fact, it was the chief merit of Quinault, Lully's librettist, that he purveyed Racinian tragedy in a manner peculiarly well suited to musical composition. The attraction of the theatre in public entertainment was such that, directly or indirectly, new musical compositions were involved with dramatic presentations. Lully moved from the orbit of Molière into that of Racine when he chose to devote himself, from 1673 until his death in 1687, to an annual production of a *tragédie lyrique* for presentation at the *Académie Royale de Musique*. The new tone and style quickly found their way across the English Channel. In 1674 the court of Charles II was treated to *Ariane, ou Le Mariage de Bacchus*, with music by Louis Grabu, the 'Master of the King's Musick' from 1666 to 1674, and text by Pierre Perrin. It was the opening opera at London's short-lived 'Royall Academy of Musick', which was named after its Paris model and domiciled at Christopher Wren's Drury Lane Theatre. *Ariane* had a French text: More than a decade passed before we hear of an English text with continuous music. Dryden's *Albion and Albanius*, also set to music by

---

[1] See H. Prunières, *The Musical Quarterly*, vol. XI (1925), pp. 528–46, who makes clear that it was Colbert who induced Lully to take the *Académie* in hand.

Grabu, and performed in Dorset Gardens in 1685, was the first public performance of what may legitimately be termed an English opera. But nothing more explicitly acknowledges the attraction of French drama for English playwrights and librettists than the prefaces to Dryden's plays—for example, his famous observation that Racine had sent the *Hippolytos* of Euripides 'from Athens to Paris, taught him to make love, and transformed [him]...into Monsieur Hippolyte'.[1] The gallicization of Hippolytos required the creation of Aricie as the object of his affections—an apt addition from an operatic point of view. Full use of this innovation was made by Rameau's librettist Pellegrin when he adapted *Phèdre* in 1733 and named the opera *Hippolyte et Aricie*. Such was the order and symmetry that Racine imposed on Greek mythology.[2]

Likewise, across the Channel, Handel derived his *Esther* (1732) and *Athalie* (1733) from the same French source. When the German Handel succeeded the German Pepusch as chapel-master to the duke of Chandos, he raised the position to a new dignity. The Chandos anthems are well known to English-speaking congregations, but of particular interest here is Handel's *Haman and Mordecai, a masque*. This work, presented at the duke's palace in 1720, was an adaptation by Alexander Pope and John Arbuthnot of Racine's *Esther*. As a musical spectacle, harking back to Stuart England, it was properly termed a masque, though in the current European sense *Haman* was really an opera. The splendid *entrée* for the arioso 'Jehova crowned' (in the manner of Lully) and the operatic style in which this arioso precedes the Chorus of the Israelites, 'He comes', establish the work's true place in musical annals. It is of a piece with the oratorios which were meant for the stage, not for the Church, and which, through Handel's genius and showmanship, became the English substitute for opera. The series of Handel's London oratorios began with a revision of the Chandos masque, presented at the Haymarket Theatre in 1732 as 'The Sacred Story of Esther: an Oratorio in English. Formerly composed by Mr Handel, and now revised by him...'[3] The announcement continued: 'There will be no action on the stage, but the House will be fitted up in a decent Manner for the Audience'. The ingenious Handel realized that music in the grand manner required scenery, even if deprived of accompanying action. According to Burney, also, the bishop of London opposed the performance of a sacred story on the stage. Handel's oratorios were entertainment for Lenten time. Yet the operatic character of the first presentation of his *Esther* is as obvious from the scenery as from the cast of singers, which included the famous castrato Senesino. As a composer of opera to Italian texts Handel was firmly established in London as early as 1711. His first bid to rank as an English composer, successor to Purcell,

[1] *All for Love* (1678), Preface.
[2] Cf. C. M. Girdlestone, *Rameau* (London, 1957), p. 195, for detailed comparison between *Phèdre* and *Hippolyte et Aricie*.
[3] *Daily Journal*, 19 April 1732.

occurred in 1713 with the *Birthday Ode* for Queen Anne and the *Te Deum* for the celebration of the Peace of Utrecht. Both were settings of English texts, ceremonious rather than fashionable, and they pointed the way to the future. In fact, the performance of the Utrecht *Te Deum* at St Paul's set Handel on the way to becoming a national institution.

The wide diffusion of Lully's style invites consideration of the qualities by which his works succeeded, for a time, in eclipsing Italian opera as the exclusive model for other European countries. The proverbial short-comings of the Italians, with their almost exclusive reliance on solo singing, were freely castigated when Mazarin brought his countrymen's compositions to Paris. As a matter of historical record, the French, English and Germans tend to be more concerned with dramatic probability; they usually favour a poised work which balances the arias and recitatives with orchestral and choral numbers. A familiar example of this aversion from the almost exclusive predominance of arias is the abundance of choral and ballet music in Purcell's *Dido and Aeneas* (1689), which exhibits the influence of Paris as well as the native English fondness for choral singing. But with due allowance for these considerations and the towering social prestige of the French court, there were yet further reasons for the absorption of the French style. The rhythmic élan of Lully's music was particularly admired. All the composers of London 'strained to imitate Babtist's vein...But the whole tendency of the ayre had more regard to the foot than the ear; and no one could hear an *entrée* with its starts and *saults*, but must expect a dance to follow...'[1] And Voltaire observed of the melodies that 'they are short simple tunes, more in the style of our Noëls, or Christmas carols, and Venetian ballads, than opera songs...the more artless the music, the easier it was retained'.[2] This reference to the *Noëls* which, like the carols, pulsate with dance rhythms, is an astute comment that aptly complements many other contemporary assessments of French music.

Lully's organization was equally admirable. The appeal of his *tragédies lyriques* in the 1680s lay in the integration of ballet into the dramatic structure. When the pioneering operas of Monteverdi's pupil Cavalli (1602–76) were presented in Paris, the French love of ballet had to be satisfied by the insertion in the intervals of Lully's *divertissements de danse*. This was true both of Cavalli's *Xerxes*, performed in 1660 for the marriage of Louis XIV, and of *Ercole Amante* in 1662. Lully's ingenuity further led him to temper French rationalism by relying on the universal human appeal of the marvellous. His *tragédies lyriques* and those of his immediate successors—Colasse (his secretary), Marin Marais and J. P. Rameau—abound in spectacular scenic effects which add a popular element to Racine's dramatic scheme. On Molière's death in 1673, Lully

[1] *Roger North on Music*, ed. J. Wilson (1959), p. 350.
[2] Burney, vol. III, p. 593.

moved with his troupe into the Palais Royal and there inherited the famous and expensive stage machinery which Giacomo Torelli had built for Luigi Rossi's *Orfeo* (1647), the first Italian opera expressly written for the French capital. Willing enough to dispense with Italian vocalism, the French operatic public nevertheless thoroughly enjoyed Italian stage tricks. Movable scenes had appeared in Europe's first opera house, San Cassiano at Venice, opened in 1637; and a few years later Giacomo Torelli (1608–78) invented a method of scene-shifting by means of a winch for use at the Teatro di S. Giovanni e Paolo at Venice, opened in 1639. Italian stage-designers migrating to Paris, or brought there by enterprising composers, introduced the element of the fantastic which caught the imagination of producers all over Europe and is still to be found in such later works as Weber's *Freischütz* and Verdi's *Aïda*. The innovations brought to Paris by Torelli and pursued by Gaspare Vigarani, and eventually by Vigarani's son Carlo, engendered a fashion for the miraculous which offended the aesthetics of some Frenchmen as well as calling down censure over the extravagant costs of such scenic diversions. On the other hand, La Bruyère hotly denied that 'machinery is only an amusement fit for children'. He criticized the astute Lully for yielding to anti-Italian sentiment and a need for economy by reducing such stage effects:

Machines increase and embellish poetical fiction and maintain among the spectators that gentle illusion which is the whole pleasure of the theatre, and they also add a feeling of wonder. There is no need for flights, for chariots, or for changes of scene in the Berenices [of Corneille and Racine]...but there is a need for them in operas.[1]

Great as was the influence of French opera, however, it was only an interlude in an essentially Italian art form. From the time that Peri's *Euridice* was performed at Florence in 1600, the Italians never lost their lead for long in supplying mellifluous specimens of the new musical art, and there was now, beside the exemplar of French opera, a new and brilliant Italian lodestar to attract attention. When Lully died in 1687 Alessandro Scarlatti (1660–1725) had already been active in Naples for some three years: he it was who complemented Lully, if he did not supersede him, in teaching European composers how to write an opera. His commanding musicianship was such that Neapolitan opera was to remain the leading model well into the second half of the eighteenth century. French opera was never indeed completely set aside: Handel's oratorios and Gluck's operas bear eloquent testimony to the lasting influence of the *tragédie lyrique*. Nor does the art of the elder Scarlatti—not to be confused with his famous son Domenico, born at Naples in 1685—mark a complete break with Lully's school, two features of which notably persisted: the expansion of the orchestra and the Racinian dramatic treatment.

[1] *Les Caractères*, in *Œuvres*, ed. R. Radonant (1925), p. 81.

The prestige of French music undoubtedly owed something to the accomplishments of the *grande bande* (or *Vingt-quatre violons*) of Louis XIV. Lully had set up his own orchestra, the *petits violons*, and eventually he gained control of the *grande bande* as well. Individual players were no longer encouraged to add embellishments of their own. By ruthless drilling Lully achieved an intermingling of the eloquently expressive style of the Italians with the rhythmic vitality of the French. His ability to exploit Europe's finest string band, judiciously including from time to time the famous Parisian oboes (as well as other wind instruments), provided a means of orchestral expression without which his ballets, recitatives and arias would be greatly impoverished. Naturally enough, this instrumental technique, modified by national traditions, was imitated in Italy, Germany and England. In Italy the increased rôle of the orchestra led to a change in the accompaniment of the arias. The older method of supporting the voice merely by a harpsichord—a string bass doubling the bass line—became progressively rarer. Scarlatti, in his development as an operatic composer, both influenced and reflected the new trend, as the following chronological tabulation of harpsichord and orchestral arias shows:

	harpsichord	orchestra
Cavalli, *Giasone* (1649)	18	9
Cesti, *La Dori* (1661)	27	7
Scarlatti, *Statira* (1690)	25	26
Buononcini, *Camilla* (1696)	24	25
Handel, *Agrippina* (1709)	9	31
Scarlatti, *Telemaco* (1718)	0	41

Much of Scarlatti's finest work is concentrated in the strings, without harpsichord. But whereas strings were the backbone of his technique, he could on occasion make excellent use of the French horn, as in *Telemaco*, and even introduce a 'noise of bagpipes and castanets and rattles in the manner of barbarous nations' to endow his Carthaginians with local colour, as in *Attilio Regolo* (1719). The emphasis on string technique was abetted by contemporary developments: significant progress in the art of violin-building on the part of Stradivarius in Cremona (*ca.* 1690), and the new standards of excellence for performers and composers set by Corelli, whose string concerts in Rome spanned three decades, from 1681 to 1713.

It would have been strange indeed had the schools of Corneille and Racine, and the subsequent achievements of Quinault and Lully, left no imprint on Scarlatti's libretti or on Italian opera as a whole during the eighteenth century. To the Venetian, Apostolo Zeno (1668–1750), must go the credit for applying the principles of French dramaturgy to the construction of opera. He it was who supplied Scarlatti with libretti for several of his operas: *Gl'inganni felici* (1699), *Odoardo* (1700), *Scipione nelle Spagne* (1714) and *Griselda* (1721). Zeno's characterizations and his understanding of the requirements of the art of music were of such excellence that his plots were used by composers throughout the century (Porpora, Caldara, Handel, Hasse, Traetta, Jommelli) and even beyond (Zingarelli's *Berenice*: Rome, 1811). But neither the viceroy of Naples nor the cardinals of Rome could provide a patronage comparable with that of Louis XIV. From 1718 to 1729 Zeno was attached to the Habsburg court, where he functioned as historian and poet to Charles VI. When he retired to his native Venice he was permitted to select his successor, Pietro Metastasio (1698–1782), one of his own followers who was to continue and extend Zeno's reforms. Metastasio's libretti were set to music by Gluck, Mozart, Rossini and Meyerbeer, and thus Zeno's influence was prolonged far beyond his own time. As historian and poet, he was affected by the rationalism of his age and an awareness of literary propriety. Yet his reforms sprang primarily from an admiration for Racine. Opera should focus on heroic emotions and these would be more powerfully delineated if the unities of French classicism were observed. Tragedy, the keynote of grand opera, was rigorously maintained, except for the final scenes when the customary happy ending would make its mechanical bow to the commissioning court—and even this convention Metastasio ventured occasionally to ignore, as in his *Didone* and *Attilio Regolo*. The comic element was severely reduced: with Zeno it usually appeared toward the end of the act; in the case of Metastasio it disappeared altogether.

Zeno's curtailment of the comic seems to spring from the same preoccupation with consistency that prompted Voltaire's criticism of Shakespeare's defiance of the classical unities. This Venetian nevertheless understood the requirements of music. He established the rule of division between librettist and composer, the compromise which governed operatic composition from Scarlatti's time to that of Mozart. Dramatic development was conveyed in the fast-moving recitative with harpsichord accompaniment, and at its climax the salient emotion (or reaction) found lyrical expression in full-fledged melody, the aria. It was an obvious requirement of drama that the *recitativo secco*, with its bare chords, should accommodate a good deal of necessary action, and Zeno and Metastasio jealously guarded their rights when composers overstepped their bounds: too many *recitativi stromentati* (or *accompagnati*) resulted in an excess of full-scored music overwhelming the dramatic value of the plot. The French orientation of Zeno, however, is evident in his rigid characterization as well as in the organization of his plots. If his models, the tragedies of Racine, were in themselves static by comparison with eighteenth-century drama, the transformation of a spoken drama into an opera would tend to emphasize this limitation. Zeno's noble heroes, his suffering heroines—in short, his stock characters—were obvious targets for ridicule by quick-witted critics; more than once they provided material for the comedians of Neapolitan *opera buffa*. When, occasionally, he departed from the traditional three-act structure of Italian opera to write five acts, as Racine and Quinault had done, his classical leanings were unmistakable (*Meride*, Vienna, 1722; *Gianguir*, Vienna, 1724).

Alessandro Scarlatti wrote over a hundred operas, the majority for Naples. At the Neapolitan court work had to proceed rapidly, necessitating composition in a facile manner that made for immediate popularity. But the very mass and popularity of these productions resulted in creating the prototype of eighteenth-century opera, for Scarlatti's main vehicle of expression was the *da capo* aria. The *a-b-a* pattern—a melody which, after a contrasting middle section, returns to its beginning—is beyond question the oldest of all musical forms, but Scarlatti transformed the occasional into the usual and typical. It was Scarlatti's musical formula—sensuous melody and lucid *da capo* form—in combination with Zeno's literary treatment of the aria, restricting it to the end of the scene (after which the singer left the stage), that together proved the most successful theatrical mode of presentation. So much, in fact, did this formula appeal to the eighteenth-century imagination that opera made serious inroads into the popularity of spoken drama.

Already by the 1690s the noise Scarlatti made at Naples was being heard abroad, and the poignancy of his melody and harmony were quickly emulated by the composers of other lands. Contrary to the demands of the Neapolitan court, however, the commissions Scarlatti received from Venice and Rome afforded him an opportunity to experiment with new ideas.[1] His *Mitridate Eupatore* (Venice, 1707) profits from a libretto by G. Frigimelica Roberti (1653–1732) which reaps the full benefit of Zeno's reform: no comic scenes, not even *mirabile dictu* a love scene, but a steady unfolding of intense and poignant emotions, lucidly conveyed within the structure of five acts. Scarlatti's last works were commissioned for performance at Rome and included *Telemaco* and *Griselda* (1721), the latter after Zeno's libretto. His *Griselda* illustrates both the vices and the virtues of Racinian opera. The long-suffering patience of the heroine and the cruelty of her villainous tormentor are static in the extreme: yet it is precisely from this rationalistic casting of human types that the musical poignancy of the scene between heroine and villain is born.[2] In the later works, there is an increasing tendency to vary the succession of solo arias by an occasional ensemble. *Griselda*, for instance, boasts both a trio and a quartet, neither of them envisaged in Zeno's original draft. But *opera seria* did not offer the same scope for

---

[1] Regarding the nature of the Venetian audiences in the last quarter of the century and the rôle of Venice as the centre of a cosmopolitan society, see S. Towneley Worsthorne, *Venetian Opera* (Oxford, 1954; reprinted 1968), p. 120.

[2] Cf. E. J. Dent, *A. Scarlatti* (1905; rev. edn. 1960), p. 165; A. Schering, *Geschichte der Musik in Beispielen* (Leipzig, 1931), p. 374. For Scarlatti's idiomatic handling of the orchestra in this opera, cf. the reprint of the overture in A. T. Davison and W. Apel, *Historical Anthology* (1950), p. 155.

development of the ensemble as did its more humorous counterpart, *opera buffa*. Scarlatti's single comic opera, *Il Trionfo dell'onore* (Rome, 1718), is historically important, for its libretto foreshadowed the plot of Mozart's *Don Giovanni* and its 'ensemble of perplexity' became the prototype for later composers. The real development of *opera buffa*, however, followed Pergolesi's *La Serva Padrona* (1733) and so belongs to a later part of the century.[1]

Henry Purcell was born only a year before Scarlatti, in 1659, but he died at the age of thirty-six. Nevertheless, he was able to absorb the guiding influences of France and Italy and to graft them upon his native tradition—Tudor polyphony and Stuart masque. Alas, the glories of English music were entombed with him in Westminster Abbey; in a European sense, his country did not recover its position until the arrival of Elgar and Vaughan Williams. The opera, *Dido and Aeneas*, and the semi-operas—*Dioclesian, King Arthur, Fairie Queen, Tempest*—which flowed from Purcell's pen in the last six years of his life were unknown on the Continent in his lifetime. But in sheer genius, both dramatic and musical, they stand proudly beside Scarlatti and musically they dwarf Lully. Like Mozart a century later, Purcell was one of the great learners of history. In the dedication of the score of *Dioclesian*, published in 1691, he laments that 'musick is yet but in its nonage' and advises that the method to make the child a man is 'learning *Italian*, which is its best Master, and studying a little of the *French* Air, to give it somewhat of Gayety and Fashion'. The mode of expression is Dryden's, for it was he who penned the dedication to the duke of Somerset on Purcell's behalf, but the sentiments are the composer's. Purcell availed himself of the latest advantages of French orchestral music and Italian aria. In all branches of music he seems to gather the development of decades into a few years. In chamber music he proceeds from the old 'fancy' (fantasia) to the modern trio sonata; in church music, from the full *a cappella*[2] anthem to the newfangled verse anthem with solo singing and orchestral ritornelli.[3] Charles II was determined to have his band of twenty-four violins in emulation of the splendour of the *vingt-quatre violons*, and to have them in church, as his countrymen were shocked to learn. To observe Purcell and his age at their best, however, one must return to the theatre. Purcell's development, beginning with his setting of Nahum Tate's *Dido and Aeneas* (1680), to be followed by Dryden's *King Arthur* (1691) and Shadwell's adaptation of *The Tempest* (1695), is nothing short of astounding. *Dido and Aeneas*, written for a girl's school in Chelsea, takes a mere hour to perform. Within that compass is the gaiety of French dance, the Italian chroma-

---

[1] Cf. vol. VIII, p. 85, for the first performance of Pergolesi's comic opera as an interlude to his grand opera, *Il Prigonnier Superbo*, and its great success in Paris in 1752.
[2] I.e. for unaccompanied choir.
[3] A ritornello is the purely instrumental section which opens a vocal composition and frequently 'returns' both in the course of the composition and at the end.

ticism of Dido's lament,[1] and a peculiarly English way of handling ground bases. *The Tempest*, with its profusion of *da capo* arias, is more up-to-date in the Italian fashion;[2] but from an *entrée* in Lully's first *tragédie lyrique*, *Cadmus et Hermione* (presented in London 1686) Purcell fashioned one of the dances in *The Tempest*. Shakespearean semi-operas with spoken dialogue, such as *The Tempest* and *The Fairie Queen* (adapted from *A Midsummer Night's Dream*), met the compromise between drama and music for which the age was groping. In his preface to *Albion and Albanius*, Dryden, the *arbiter elegantiarum* of England, makes a distinction between the arias, whose function it is 'to please the Hearing, rather than to gratify the understanding', and the recitative, which supplies the dialogue. But Anglo-Saxon common sense has never wholeheartedly accepted the hybrid of speech-song called recitative.

The doom of English opera was sealed when the court insisted on opera in the Italian tongue and Handel was imported to provide Italian opera. Between the performances of *Rinaldo* (1711) and *Deidamia* (1741) Handel wrote thirty-six Italian operas for London, but the genre was too alien for English soil and even Handel's musical genius could not succeed in making it thrive there. Though Lully had been a foreigner in France, his *tragédies* had been French and his great talent for adaptation and organization were responsible for a continuous French national opera from Louis XIV to Louis XVI. London and Vienna, on the other hand, subsisted on Italian importations. This is not to say that the aesthetic argument for the singing of Italian opera in Italian is negligible; it has been ably advanced from the days of Queen Anne to the foundation of the Glyndebourne Trust, and by none better than Dr Burney:

Music is a Manufacture of Italy...and its no more disgraceful...to import it than wine, tea or any other production of remote parts...The vocal music of Italy can only be heard in perfection when sung to its own language...There is as much reason for wishing Italian music performed in this genuine manner, as for the lovers of painting to prefer an original picture of Raphael to a copy.[3]

But the historical evidence suggests that connoisseurs, craving for perfection but lacking a substratum of popular support, are not a potent cultural force. The story of Handel's operas in London is well known: the rivalries between composer and star singers, the fraudulent managers, the bankruptcies. Taken as a whole, these events document the English attitude towards Italian opera as 'an exotic and irrational entertainment'.[4] Handel's Royal Academy of Music, founded in 1720, was no more destined than its predecessor of 1674 to reach the mature age of its French prototype and was obliged to close its doors in 1728, the year in which

---

[1] Cf. the music examples from Purcell and Cavalli in J. A. Westrup, *Purcell* (rev. edn. 1965), p. 122.
[2] Its attribution to Purcell has been contested: *Proc. Royal Music Assoc.* vol. xc (1963–4), pp. 43–57. [3] E. J. Dent, *Opera* (2nd rev. edn. Penguin Books, 1949), p. 174.
[4] Burney, *History*, vol. iv, p. 221.

The Beggar's Opera—whose folk tunes and airs were arranged by C. J. Pepusch, interspersed with dialogue by John Gay—parodied so effectively the serious, the grand and the foreign. Handel's own operas are less well known than the gossip which surrounds them. For one thing, they lack the magnificent choruses of his oratorios. It is true that his arias, in the Italian style, possess some exquisite passages; but, as in the case of the famous *Largo* (originally a Larghetto in Handel's only comic opera, *Xerxes*), it is a beauty independent of dramatic context. In his best vein, Handel disdained composition of one aria-scene after another and created dramatic complexes of larger musical dimensions: one instance is the mad scene from *Orlando* (1733), while *Alcina* (1735) contains a good deal of ballet music in the French manner, intermingled with choruses. The production of *Esther* in 1732, billed as an oratorio but fitted up with stage scenery, marked the beginning of nearly a decade of vacillation and transition for the composer. Handel ran with the hare and hunted with the hounds, fluctuating between opera and oratorio until, in 1741, his tenacity gave way to public demand and he henceforth devoted himself to oratorio composition. In the decade to follow he composed such masterpieces as *Messiah, Samson, Judas Maccabaeus* and *Jephtha*, which led to the veneration of Handel later in the century.

By the 1730s there were firmly established throughout Europe three types of purely instrumental composition, all derived from the genre of opera but independent of the operatic stage: Lully's French overture, Scarlatti's Italian overture, and Vivaldi's concerto. Lully's overture has a mixed pedigree and many ancestors: some French, with their profusion of dotted rhythms; some Italo-French, such as the great *Canzoni alla Francese* (1645) of Frescobaldi; while the Venetian overtures of Cavalli provide a pure Italian strain. Lully's ability to fuse these elements, combined with his good fortune in the support and prestige of Louis XIV, established the form, which was to last well over a century. The gradual transformation of French pomp and circumstance, from Lully's overture for the ballet *Xerxes* (1660) to the slow introductions of Haydn's London symphonies (1790–5), embraces in its intermediary stages the overtures to Purcell's *Dido*, Handel's *Messiah* and J. S. Bach's *Overture after the French Manner* (1735). The technical peculiarities of the overture were marked, whether attention was focused on the slow beginning, on the dotted (*saccadé*) rhythm, or on the harmonic connection between the slow and the fast section. Composers knew the fashion, and they knew it to be French. About ten years after Lully's death Scarlatti established his own type of overture. Although it never wholly displaced the older model, this Italian overture eventually became even more popular. Its main characteristic was the initial fast tempo and the tripartite pattern, fast-slow-fast. These attributes were also present in the concerto which, about 1710, had developed into a three-movement form with the slow movement in the middle. Whilst the concert-overture sprang from the festive opening of operas, the concerto, at least in its later stages, emerged from the rivalry between an operatic singer and the orchestra (or, more rarely, the chorus): thus the taming of the orchestra by the soloist in Beethoven's G Major Piano Concerto has been iluminatingly compared with the taming of the Furies of Gluck's *Orpheus*.[1] But the foundations of the Mozart and Beethoven piano concertos were laid much earlier in certain of Giuseppe Torelli's *Concerti* (op. 6, 1698; op. 8, 1709) and more decisively in the *Concerti* (op. 3, Amsterdam, 1712–13) of the Venetian Antonio Vivaldi (1675?–1741). This latter work, subtitled *L'Estro Armonico*, established Vivaldi's European reputation and with it a new musical form, in which Vivaldi was prolific. The *Concerti grossi* of Arcangelo Corelli (1653–1713) are earlier in date as well as in style; although they were not in print until Estienne Roger published them in Amsterdam in 1714, we have the reliable testimony of Georg Muffat that Corelli rehearsed his concertos in Rome as early as 1682.[2] Corelli usually began his alternating movements with a slow movement, a pattern which Handel favoured. Nevertheless, European composers preferred, on the whole, to emphasize animation and rhythmic vitality with an opening quick movement. Corelli taught his admirers the new Italian violin technique and the new mastery of the orchestra, but it was the formal pattern of Scarlatti and Vivaldi that tended to shape the concertos and later the symphonies of Europe.

That the greatest composer of the age, and one of the greatest of all time, should have remained obstinately outside the main stream of music is a phenomenon that can only be explained by his deliberate refusal to accommodate himself to the fashions of his epoch. Had he chosen so to do, Johann Sebastian Bach (1685–1750) might have catered for contemporary taste with compositions everlastingly in the vein of his French and English Suites, Orchestral Suites and 'Capriccio over the Departure of a Beloved Brother'. Ironically enough, a contest between French elegance and German thoroughness, arranged in 1717 by the elector of Saxony, was won by Bach, such was his prowess as a performer. Needless to say, the outcome did not affect the popularity of the French style in Europe in the first half of the eighteenth century; but when Bach's devoted pupils compiled his famous obituary they took occasion to refer to the incident and to contrast the programmatic and elegant art of his French rival with the timeless greatness of Bach's absolute music:

Bach always gladly admitted that Marchand deserved praise for his beautiful and very neat playing. Whether, however, Marchand's Musettes for Christmas Eve, the composition and playing of which are said to have contributed most to his fame in Paris, could have held the field before connoisseurs against Bach's multiple fugues: that may be decided by those who have heard both men in their prime.[3]

[1] D. Tovey, *Essays in Musical Analysis*, vol. III (1936), p. 81.
[2] M. Pincherle, *Corelli* (Paris, 1954), pp. 18, 169 ff.
[3] A. Pirro, *Bach* (tr. B. Engelke, 2nd edn. Berlin, 1919), pp. 40 ff.

To compose a musette[1] for keyboard was a trick of composition well known to Bach. He did not choose to compose many such pieces, however. In fact, he did not choose to impinge upon the European scene at all during his own lifetime. He resided in a peripheral country and never composed an opera. Moreover, his style was considered old-fashioned and heavy even by his compatriots. The famous *Well-Tempered Keyboard* of forty-eight preludes and fugues did not appear in print until the nineteenth century. To compose sacred music and lofty fugues *sub specie aeternitatis* was to court immortality at the price of temporal obscurity.

To understand Bach's position in his own time one must consider the works he himself chose to publish. In a dictionary of music compiled by J. G. Walther (one of the composer's relatives) the account of Bach's works specifically mentions only those in print and appears to stress the technical aspects of printing:[2] 'Of his excellent Clavier works there have appeared in copper engraving: Anno 1726 Partita in B Flat Major...' Seventy years later, in 1802, J. N. Forkel pointed out in a book that functioned as one of the mainsprings of the Bach renaissance:[3] 'At the appearance of his first work he was over forty years of age. What he himself, at so mature an age, judged worthy of publication has certainly the presumption in its favour that it is good.' The number of works printed in Bach's lifetime amounts to eight if we include the *Art of Fugue*, the printing of which was supervised by the composer, though it appeared posthumously. It is significant that, one and all, these compositions are instrumental. Why, then, did Bach not choose to publish his sacred cantatas or motets, *The Passion according to St Matthew* or even the *Mass in B Minor*? The fact that church music in his day rarely travelled beyond the church where the composer held office may be a partial answer. But since Bach did sanction the publication of some of his sacred music for organ, it may be that this obstinate German foresaw the future development of the art over which German composers were to assume the hegemony. After the triumphs of Haydn's symphonies in Paris and London, the history of music was to be no longer pre-eminently that of opera, which was overtaken in importance by instrumental compositions, just as the heyday of opera in the seventeenth and eighteenth centuries had been preceded by the glories of the mass and motet. Of Bach's sacred vocal music we need say only that he grafted the fashionable techniques of his day, like the French overture and the Italian *da capo* aria, on to the trunk of the Lutheran liturgy; in his Cantatas and Passions these devices remained subservient, however, to a larger purpose, and the operatic origin of his means may be obscure to present-day listeners.

[1] A musette, literally bagpipe, usually imitates the drone bass of the bagpipe and has a dance-like character.
[2] H. T. David and A. Mendel, *The Bach Reader* (New York, 1945; rev. edn. 1966), p. 46.
[3] *Ueber Johann Sebastian Bach: Leben, Kunst und Kunstwerke* (1802): E. T. (1820) probably by A. C. F. Kollmann.

Bach's Opus I was fashionable both in title and content. It was published in 1731 as *Clavierübung* [Keyboard Practice] and consisted of 'Preludes, Allemandes, Courantes, Sarabandes, Gigues, Minuets, and other Galanteries [better known today as *Partitas*]'. One is not surprised to discover that the second partita opens with an overture in the manner of Lully. The French names of the dances are a further indication of Bach's models. The title of the second volume (1735) speaks for itself: *Second Part of the Clavierübung, consisting of a concerto after the Italian taste and an overture after the French manner.*[1] The third part of the *Clavierübung* (1739) was, on the whole, dedicated to sacred music, namely, chorale preludes for the organ: clearly, this Protestant music could hardly have been fashionable in Paris or Rome, Vienna or Dresden. The fourth and final instalment of the *Clavierübung* appeared in 1742 and contained the *Goldberg Variations*, great music but too lengthy to have any contemporary vogue. In 1747 Bach published *Six Chorales of diverse kind, to be played on the organ.* This, again, was a collection of sacred chorale preludes similar to the third part of the *Clavierübung*, with the difference that its six chorales consist primarily of transcriptions of vocal work for organ solo. Since the *Musical Offering* appeared in the same year, it is a fair supposition that Bach wished to record for posterity his achievement in the realm of chamber music.

Of the *Art of Fugue* (1752) there exist twentieth-century arrangements for orchestra, for string quartet, and for other combinations, though one surmises that the composer himself would have played it on the organ. How indicative of the taste of the eighteenth century that only thirty copies were sold between 1752 and 1756! In 1758 Bach's son, C. P. Emanuel Bach, felt obliged to sell the copper plate for metal, in an effort to recover some of the cost of printing. Bach's final masterpiece is a great but forbidding work, a creation offered at the end of the composer's career which is neither of his own age nor, indeed, to the taste of the frivolous or hurried or uncharitable of any age. In this respect it invites comparison with Goethe's *Faust*, Part II. Some portions are less moving than others, but the great passages touch the divine in so far as man may reach it.

---

[1] Titles are here translated except for *Clavierübung*—a comprehensive term applying to any keyboard instrument, whether harpsichord, clavichord, organ or the modern pianoforte.

CHAPTER IV

RELIGION AND THE RELATIONS OF CHURCH AND STATE

IN 1678 Giant Pope did not greatly affright the celestial pilgrims: but eight years later, Protestants trembled. The emperor was bringing the Calvinist nobles of Hungary under Catholic domination, an aggressive papist was on the throne of England, a Catholic elector had succeeded to the Palatinate, Louis XIV had revoked the Edict of Nantes and persuaded the duke of Savoy to march once again into the valleys of the Vaudois. There were those who feared that the morale of the disunited forces of Protestantism would be unequal to the trial. 'If God have yet any pleasure in the Reformation', wrote Burnet from his exile in Holland in 1686, 'He will yet raise it up again, though I confess the deadness of those Churches that own it makes me apprehend that it is to be quite laid in ashes.'[1] This pessimism was soon confounded and Burnet proceeded to an Anglican bishopric, though for long he remained apprehensive on the score of popery.

It is true that the years 1688–1715 saw the completion of an intolerant Catholic domination in France and Poland. After some vacillation, Louis XIV reaffirmed his ruthless policies in a declaration of March 1715 by which Protestants were deprived of all legal status, the mere fact of continued residence in France being taken as 'proof that they have embraced the Roman, Catholic and Apostolic religion'.[2] Five months later, as Louis lay dying, nine men, practically all that was left of the Calvinist pastorate, met in a quarry in Languedoc to hold the first synod since the Revocation and to initiate the secret and painful rebuilding of the churches of the 'desert'. Like the French declaration, the Polish edict of 1717, prescribing the demolition of more recently erected Protestant churches, merely confirmed an intolerance which had already achieved its ends: the Lutherans and the *Unitas Fratrum* had declined: only in Lithuania did Calvinism remain a force. This subjection of the Protestant, along with the Orthodox, minority was to prove politically disastrous; already the idea of foreign intervention on behalf of these 'dissidents' was mooted.[3] For the moment, however, Russia and Prussia remained deaf to proposals of joint action, and Catholic dominance in Poland was undisturbed. Yet these developments were not typical of Europe generally. Most

---

[1] T. E. S. Clarke and H. C. Foxcroft, *A Life of Gilbert Burnet* (Cambridge, 1907), p. 214.
[2] Cf. below, pp. 337–8.
[3] L. R. Lewitter, 'Peter the Great and the Polish Dissenters', *Slavonic Review*, XXXIII (1954), 75–101.

Catholic rulers found it wiser to come to terms with their Protestant subjects, at least to recognize that proselytizing enthusiasm was not for export. The duke of Savoy was reconciled to the Vaudois in 1694. By 1705 the elector palatine had seen the wisdom of toleration, though Englishmen supported Palatine immigrants in the belief that they were victims of active persecution. Louis XIV himself found that an aggressive foreign policy needed religious moderation as its counterpart. In Alsace, Catholics enjoyed more than their share of public offices and favourable conditions for propaganda, but Lutherans were allowed the substance of their rights as guaranteed by the letter of treaty obligations. After the formation of the League of Augsburg France ceased to encourage the 'bishop of Geneva', resident at Annecy, in his intrigues to reincorporate the city of Calvin into his diocese; it was enough now to keep Geneva isolated and neutral, to prevent it admitting Bernese garrisons or joining the Helvetic Confederation. As a secret unratified agreement of May 1715 with the Catholic cantons shows, Louis would have been glad to intervene in Switzerland, but the compulsions of foreign policy restrained him, and the Protestant cantons won the civil war of 1712 without foreign interference.[1] Like his enemy at Versailles, the emperor found that necessity imposed moderation. Though Vienna did its best to introduce Catholic immigrants from south Germany, Hungary did not go the way of Bohemia after 1648. The Calvinist nobles demonstrated that, if driven to desperation, they would choose the cynical quasi-toleration of the Turk rather than lose religion and liberty under the Habsburg, and intransigence won a grudging recognition of their religious freedom.

Once the peculiar circumstances of 1685-8 were past, Protestants returned to complacency about their divisions. German Lutheranism, in particular, remained parochial and introspective. The multitude of state-churches (*Landeskirchen*) ruled by princely magistrates 'resembled a series of inland pools, stagnant save for exceptional inundations'.[2] A rigid loyalty to an unhistorical 'Byzantine' Luther divided his followers from their fellow Christians; in a church in Leipzig, an English visitor claimed to have seen a picture of the Devil, Loyola and Calvin, all standing together as 'the three great enemies of Christ'.[3] Yet the hard shell of Lutheran intolerance was cracking. The political fragmentation which imposed itself on churchmen proved an advantage to the universities, for teachers and students could migrate to the centres which offered the widest freedom. Pietists insisted that the life of virtue is a bond between

---

[1] Berne and Zürich had fought the Catholic cantons in 1656 in the 'First Villmergen War': the 'Second Villmergen War' began in 1712, when Berne and Zürich were provoked by the construction of a 'Catholic highway' from Schwyz to the Austrian border, and by the unreasonable conduct of the abbot of St Gallen. See E. Bonjour, H. S. Offler and G. R. Potter, *A Short History of Switzerland* (Oxford, 1952), pp. 196-7.

[2] A. L. Drummond, *German Protestantism since Luther* (1951), p. 177.

[3] F. G. James, *North-Country Bishop; a biography of William Nicolson* (Yale, 1956), p. 11.

Christians which dogmatic differences cannot cancel—a tolerant doctrine which found expression in Veit von Seckendorff's *Historia Lutheranismi* (1692), where praise was awarded even to the reformed post-Tridentine Roman communion. When the prince was enlightened, his power over the Church was not always a disaster. For two generations the Hohenzollerns, striving to weld their heterogeneous subjects together in the service of the State, had adopted a policy of religious toleration: its justification was now appearing in the attraction which their dominions exerted upon industrious Huguenot refugees, and in the successful absorption of new territories with a predominantly Catholic population. It was in Brandenburg, in 1665, that Locke had received his first object lesson in the value of toleration; in Berlin that D. E. Jablonski, grandson of Comenius and leading exponent of the oecumenical ideal, found refuge and headquarters for his prolonged (but eventually unsuccessful) negotiations to reconcile Lutheran and Calvinist by common acceptance of a German translation of the English Prayer Book. That hoary maxim, *cujus regio, ejus religio*, which had served its turn as a formula for circumscribing intolerance within political frontiers, had implied that a ruler was absolute in his own dominions, even over consciences: the Hohenzollerns demonstrated that absolutism was best served by leaving consciences alone. In 1708, Queen Anne considered proposals for a general agreement that the subjects of a prince who changed his religion should suffer no hardships in their 'worship or revenues'.[1] Such a ruling might have been of use for dealing with the irresponsible fringe of minor princelings, like Eberhard Ludwig of Württemberg, who was proposing to drive his Lutheran subjects back to Rome if the pope would relieve him of inconvenient marriage vows, but elsewhere in Germany Queen Anne's principle was already tacitly accepted. When Augustus of Saxony became a Catholic in 1697 to obtain the Polish throne, no one expected his subjects to reconsider their theology; the Catholic minority in Saxony remained under civil disabilities until the beginning of the nineteenth century. It was now a case of *cujus religio, ejus regio*, if the prize was great enough.

In the 1670s an observer in touch with Holland and Geneva, the two fortresses of Calvinism, might have suspected that the Reformed were doomed to become as hidebound and introspective as the Lutherans. In Holland, the brutal French invasion had unleashed passions as devastating as the bitter flood-waters, amid which the intolerance of the orthodox clergy, for whom the Synod of Dort was the culmination of the Reformation, seemed likely to prevail. And in 1679 the pastors of Geneva had resolved, however reluctantly, to require subscription to the *Formula Consensus Ecclesiarum Helveticarum* (adopted four years earlier by the Reformed Cantons of Switzerland), which proclaimed extreme forms of the doctrines of predestination and biblical inspiration. Then came the

[1] W. A. Knittle, *Early Eighteenth Century Palatine Emigration* (Philadelphia, 1936), p. 23.

dramatic threat to international Protestantism from 1685 to 1689, the psychological impact of a stream of refugees, the rise of England as Europe's shield against the ambition of Louis XIV, and the arrival of a new generation of theologians in touch with the intellectual tendencies of the day—a combination of circumstances which undermined the forces of intolerance. Surrounded by the military might of Catholic powers, the Genevan pastors were haunted by their isolation: news of a few satirical verses in the university of Oxford drove them to pathetic protest of their 'very honourable sentiments' towards episcopal government: 'did we dwell among you we should readily appear at your congregations'.[1] Huguenot refugees—many brusquely removed to avoid French reprisals— were a humiliation to their consciences and a witness to a tragedy which dwarfed the disputes of dogmatic precisians. This proud city-state stood at a cross-roads in the intellectual life of Protestantism, a resort for foreign schoolboys and tourists, a centre of the ecclesiastical printing trade which, when the French market for Protestant books collapsed, turned to primers of theology and devotion for Catholic Spain and Italy. Liberal ideas found quick entrance, even into the inner circles of academic theology with professors like J. A. Turrettini. In 1708, two years after the *Formula* was abandoned in Geneva, Turrettini and two other foreign members of the English missionary societies met to draw up a plan for Protestant reunion on the basis of those fundamental beliefs which are clearly revealed and essential to pious living. These generous spirits, like Jablonski at Berlin, were aware that the Anglican Church was the keystone of their hopes; and like Jablonski, but unlike the sympathetic English divines who were their correspondents, they were blind to the harsh realities of the political situation. Yet their efforts bore some fruit, for the idea, as old as Calixtus, that there are but few basic truths necessary to salvation, which was meant to lead to religious unity, led more certainly to religious toleration.

In Holland, where the idea of religious freedom had been developing for half a century and where the impact of the refugees was intellectual as well as emotional, liberal tendencies were more obvious still. Heterodoxy, Arminianism and Cartesianism continued to undermine the sacred Synod of Dort. It is true that a resolution of the States of Holland in 1694, exhorting to 'brotherly harmony', also urged the universities to teach conformably to the conclusions of Dordrecht and not 'according to the rules of philosophy'; the object, however, was to outmanoeuvre the strictly orthodox Voetians, who were demanding yet another national synod, this time to destroy the Cocceians, supporters of the allegorical interpretation of the scriptures. William III, himself a Voetian, insisted that both sides show moderation in their controversies, and the theologians of Franeker and Leiden gave learned support to his politic attitude.

[1] E. Carpenter, *The Protestant Bishop: Henry Compton, 1632–1713* (1956), pp. 346–9.

Suspect professors found protectors in high places; the urbane magistrates of Amsterdam continued Balthasar Bekker's salary for life after the North Holland Synod had deposed him for his onslaught on superstition in *De Betoverde Weereld* (1691). The established Calvinist Church was unable to suppress the Pietists, the Collegiants who still flourished at Rijnsburg, theosophists and other newer sects; and the laws against the Catholics remained unenforced. The Walloon Church, linked to the State Church but quasi-independent and tolerant, was strengthened by the recruitment of French refugees and families of the upper bourgeoisie. As the reading public of Europe became familiar with the names of Bayle, Jurieu, Le Clerc, Benoist and Basnage, it became evident that the persecutions of Louis XIV had enriched Calvinist Holland with the leadership of the 'republic of letters'. And amid the babel of sects and the clatter of printing presses commerce flourished, not perhaps by mere coincidence. Holland, wrote Penn, had become great by toleration: 'it is the union of interests and not of opinions that gives peace to kingdoms.'[1]

Even as Penn wrote, the English Protestants, divided in opinions, were uniting to defend their interests.[2] Once James II had gone, the relationship between Nonconformity and the Establishment had to be changed. Persecution had been justified not so much on religious as on practical and political grounds: the old arguments that lawful authority can command in things indifferent, and that the sects had kindled flames of civil war, looked unconvincing now that lawful authority had been misused and a respectable revolution taken place. That 'due tenderness to Dissenters' which the bishops had promised when they refused to read James's Declaration of Indulgence must now be implemented. There were two possible courses, comprehension and toleration. At first it seemed likely that the Presbyterians would be brought back into the established Church: one side recognized that its ideal of a national Church could only be achieved within the Establishment; the other saw hope of reconciling Scotland, Ulster, and the socially significant elements of Dissent in England. But the scheme for a comprehension was never submitted to the Lower House of Convocation. At a time when the Nonjurors would have 'pretended that they still stuck to the ancient Church of England',[3] High Churchmen would not risk concessions. Comprehension was abandoned and a limited toleration granted by parliament. It was a realistic settlement, but one lacking in generosity and imagination.

Thus toleration came in England, Holland and Brandenburg as the

---

[1] *A Persuasive to Moderation to Dissenting Christians* (1686), quoted W. C. Braithwaite, *The Second Period of Quakerism* (1919), p. 128.

[2] Below, ch. VI.

[3] Burnet, quoted N. Sykes, *From Sheldon to Secker* (Cambridge, 1959), pp. 88–9. The Anglican practice of admitting foreign Protestants to communion became the basis of the Act of Settlement: N. Sykes, *William Wake, Archbishop of Canterbury, 1657–1737* (Cambridge, 2 vols. 1957), vol. II, p. 20. Cf. below, pp. 209–10 and 212.

offspring, primarily, of economic prudence, political necessity, and weariness with sectarian controversy and fanaticism; even so, theoretical arguments in its favour were accumulating concurrently. 'Reasonable' religion tended towards the idea of the invisible Church, which could easily decline into Locke's 'voluntary society of men joining themselves together of their own accord to the publick worshipping of God...'[1]—an unmysterious religious club which could hardly invoke terrors divine or human. Protestants sought unity on the basis of a minimum of fundamentals, accepting and indeed glorying in Bossuet's accusations of 'variations', and leaving themselves open to Bayle's question: why then forbid Socinian speculations? If Locke was right in rejecting innate ideas (though he did not reject 'natural antipathies'), differences between men were mainly the result of education—a conclusion which left compulsion a logical possibility, but not hatred. Naturally enough, it was among the exiled Huguenots that the debate over toleration waxed keenest. Pierre Jurieu, making lurid propaganda against Louis XIV and yet clinging to the right of the true religion to suppress false teaching, found his own arguments turned against him by Bayle and the more liberal refugees. In a famous commentary,[2] Bayle wrecked the procedure of debate from proof-texts by insisting that no isolated statement can stand against the general sense of the Gospels and natural decency. While Locke excluded atheists from toleration, and Penn laid down a moral code for Pennsylvania which Locke thought tyrannical, Bayle went beyond both—and beyond his age—in defending the rights of the erring conscience, which even an atheist was obliged to follow—an argument that was turned full circle when Jurieu added that he supposed the zealous persecutor ought also to follow his. It is interesting that Bayle attacked Jurieu precisely at the point where the latter was most generous, in his theory of the Church. Down to *ca.* 1670 ecclesiologists had taken the view that Christians must opt for one among the churches claiming to be the true one: Jurieu, however, defined the Church as the totality, the 'confederation', of those Christian communities which preserved a minimum of doctrinal identity, a visible community whose boundaries extended to include the unbaptized children of believing parents and all who accept the fundamental verities, even in schism.[3] Bayle ridiculed this view as making the Reformation an unnecessary incident. He had seen that comprehension was a potential danger to toleration: if few were left out, they could more easily be persecuted.

In the other great dispute that divided the Huguenots of the Refuge—

[1] *A Letter concerning Toleration* (1689).
[2] *Commentaire philosophique sur les paroles de Jésus-Christ: Contrains-les d'entrer* (Amsterdam, 1686–8).
[3] R. Voeltzel, *Vraie et fausse Eglise selon les théologiens protestants français du XVIIe siècle* (1956), pp. 25–6, 32, 73, 78–9; G. Thils, *Les Notes de l'Eglise dans l'apologétique catholique depuis la Réforme* (Gembloux, 1937), pp. 167–83. For Jurieu cf. below, p. 218.

the right to resist tyranny—Bayle and the moderates remained French patriots, while Jurieu passionately supported the English Revolution and looked forward to the ruin of France on the way to a Protestant victory. Before James II compelled a revision of the generally held (though vaguely defined) doctrine of civil obedience, both Catholics and Protestants stood by the famous text in the Epistle to the Romans (xiii. 1): 'the powers that be are ordained of God'. It was conceded that all forms of government could be legitimate and that the monarch lies under God's judgment, but these qualifications tended to be theoretical. Bossuet subscribed to them and in practice revered the 'miracle' of kingship, a majestic conservatism which was reflected prosaically in the *Christen Staat* (1685) of the Lutheran Veit von Seckendorff, who held that prayer is the Christian's only weapon against a wicked ruler. Submission to the sovereign, ruled the university of Oxford in 1683, 'is to be clear, absolute and without exception', a doctrine which English divines urged upon Monmouth on the eve of his execution. One of them was William Lloyd, bishop of St Asaph—three years later one of the Seven Bishops in the Tower. 'Is this your Church of England loyalty?' But in truth there was little excuse for this famous outburst of James II to the Fellows of Magdalen College. Non-resistance did not preclude non-co-operation; as the bishops said, they taught 'obedience, and suffering when they could not obey'. Non-resistance might be simply an unenthusiastic duty owed by a Christian to any established government. This was Sherlock's defence in accepting the deanery of St Paul's from William III; 'a providential king in possession', said his enemies unkindly, 'hath bishoprics and deaneries at his disposal.'[1] The old formulas of divine-right monarchy did not have to be abandoned: instead of applying them to a hereditary king, they could be attached, with a little revision, to a king owing his throne to God's providential election. Different groups of churchmen completed their self-justification by adopting different formulas: Sacheverell and the High Churchmen preferred the fiction of James's 'abdication'; Stillingfleet argued that an oath is not binding against the public interest; Lloyd followed Hobbes in denying obedience to a sovereign who could no longer give protection; Burnet and Compton (who appeared for the Protestant cause in buff coat and jackboots, with sword and pistols) took their stand on the laws of England, whereby supreme authority rests not in the king's person but in king and parliament, and which guarantee the religion of the subject as part of his property. English churchmen did not need the full theoretical scope of Jurieu's arguments—that government is a result of the Fall and is necessarily founded on contract, that in that contract religious duties can never be sacrificed, that final sovereignty rests in the whole people. But both Jurieu's abstractions and the revision of divine-right theories were, at bottom, complicated ways of appealing to simple

[1] J. Hunt, *Religious Thought in England* (3 vols. 1871), vol. II, p. 65.

common sense; political events themselves, as well as Descartes and Locke, were forcing men into an age of 'reason'. It was absurd, said an archdeacon, to cite Scripture against a people's liberties: 'there be prime laws of Nature and Reason and civil government, which our Blessed Saviour came not to destroy but to fulfil'.[1] May a king be deposed? 'I will suppose him', says Swift, warming to his theme, 'to murder his Mother and his Wife, to commit Incest, to ravish Matrons, to blow up the Senate, and burn his Metropolis.'[2] Poor James! Swift was still willing to submit to the crimes of the 'Legislature'. On the other hand, like Berkeley, one could go on insisting on 'absolute unlimited non-resistance' to the 'supreme civil power' with the proviso that in extreme cases the claim of any authority to be that supreme civil power should be submitted to examination.[3] Reason, rather than the literal words of Scripture, became the clue to Christian conduct in politics.

If there are divinely approved limitations on the sovereign, presumably they will apply particularly in defence of the Church. Yet in Catholic and Protestant Europe alike, the alliance between Church and State was weighted in favour of the secular power, which normally had a decisive voice in the appointment of higher ecclesiastical officials. The English bishoprics had not gone the way of the French and become morsels chiefly reserved for the nobility, perhaps because there were so few of them, but 26 prelates were a strong voting force in the House of Lords and their nomination was therefore a matter of high politics. Here was a crucial incidence of patronage which could not be left to the religious convictions of the wearer of the Crown; in 1707 Queen Anne found herself obliged to promise that she would always consult her ministers when making episcopal appointments. While the higher clergy of France enjoyed their quinquennial assemblies, in which (under the shadow of royal tutelage) they voted benevolences to the Crown, in England the Church had surrendered its right to tax itself and the Crown had consequently suspended sitting Convocations, a policy resumed after the failure of the Convocation of 1689 to deal with comprehension.

Though this sort of erastian control was generally accepted in most countries, churchmen occasionally grew restive. In Sweden, when the royal absolutism broke in 1719, the lower clergy won their fight for a genuine voice in episcopal nominations. In 1711 Fénelon was dreaming of the fantastic prospect that the Gallican Church would surrender its property to regain its freedom. The Church of Ireland proudly insisted that it was not just an appanage of the Church of England but the successor of the ancient Celtic Church, which had never made submission

[1] Quoted K. G. Feiling, *History of the Tory Party, 1640–1714* (Oxford, 1924), pp. 491–2.
[2] *The Sentiments of a Church-of-England Man, with Respect to Religion and Government* (1708): *Prose Writings*, ed. H. Davis, vol. II (Oxford, 1940), p. 22.
[3] A. A. Luce, *The Life of George Berkeley* (1949), p. 53.

to Henry VIII. Even in Russia, where Peter was determined to allow no more patriarchs, Stefan Yavorsky, the deputy on the patriarchal throne, complained that 'Christ did not entrust his Church to the Emperor Tiberius, but to the Apostle Paul'.[1] It was in England, however, that the most significant discussion of the relationship of Church and State was to take place, the issue being stated trenchantly in the famous manifesto, *A Letter to a Convocation Man* (1697) that touched off the controversy: 'The Church is a Society instituted in order to a supernatural end; and as such, must have an inherent power in it, of governing itself in order to that end.' The point had already been made by the Nonjurors, when challenging the deposition of bishops who refused the oaths to William and Mary: if the State could remove the rulers of the Church, 'this will perfectly overthrow the Church as a society distinct from the state, and perfectly disable it to subsist as a society in time of persecution'.[2] Though the Nonjurors had widespread influence and George Hickes carried the controversy into the next generation, they won few converts on the specific matter in dispute. But when Atterbury used the spiritual independence of the Church as an argument for the restoration of sitting Convocations, he struck a chord among the lower clergy and received factitious applause from political interests. His attempt to demonstrate that Convocation must meet to transact business whenever Parliament does so relied upon a fallacious appeal to precedent, which Wake demolished. Yet there is force in Atterbury's riposte: 'These are sad stories, but (God be praised) they were done a great while ago, and do not therefore much concern us.'[3] From 1701 the controversy moved on to new ground, Atterbury and his supporters concentrating now upon the rights of the Lower House of Convocation, the 'Commons spiritual'. Once again, Atterbury's history was proved fallacious, this time by Gibson, and once again his strongest argument was drawn from natural reason, which he invoked against the weight of precedent; he was asking for powers 'necessarily involved in the *Notion* of a *House*' and had nothing in his favour, as Gibson put it, but 'uncertain inferences from the nature of things'.[4] When reviewing their ideas of the divine sanction which fortifies government, when discussing the problem of a transfer of allegiance, and when manoeuvring to limit the Royal Supremacy in the Church as it was limited in the State, or to give lower clergy their due against Whig and latitudinarian bishops, the effective arguments of churchmen were drawn, not from Scripture or precedent, but from natural logic. They were ushering in the age of Reason.

[1] J. Serech, 'Stefan Yavorsky and the Conflict of Ideologies in the Age of Peter I', *Slavonic Rev.* vol. XXX (1951), p. 57. Cf. below, pp. 728–9.
[2] Henry Dodwell, quoted G. Every, *The High Church Party, 1688–1718* (1956), pp. 71, 84.
[3] H. C. Beeching, *Francis Atterbury* (1909), p. 58.
[4] N. Sykes, *Edmund Gibson, Bishop of London, 1669–1748* (Oxford, 1926), p. 37.

The transition from the vivid controversies of Protestant London to the capital of Catholicism is abrupt, for in the political and intellectual life of Europe Rome had become a peripheral provincial city. Yet in another sense she was more than ever the centre of the world. The great missionary expansion of Protestantism had barely begun; the foundation of the Society for Promoting Christian Knowledge in 1698 and of the Society for the Propagation of the Gospel three years later, the arrival of Pietists from Halle at Tranquebar, and the activities of a few teachers among the North American Indians were the small beginnings of a movement whose great days lay another century ahead. In the Russian Church, Philotheus Leszczyński, metropolitan of Tobolsk, was almost alone in taking an interest in evangelizing the tribes of Siberia. Outside Catholicism it required the genius of a Leibniz to visualize the whole planet as a single field of destiny, an insight which was a routine assumption at the Congregation of Propaganda and at the Jesuit headquarters in Rome. While Jansenist, Gallican and Quietist disputes raged and popes troubled diplomats about their feudal suzerainty over Parma and Piacenza, from China to Peru the frontiers of Christianity were being pushed forward.

Seen from the Propaganda at Rome, the northward defences against Protestantism were the only boundary where advance was no longer possible. Though the developing links between the Anglican and the Eastern Churches caused some concern, it seemed reasonable to hope for new gains at the expense of the Orthodox and the lesser Eastern Churches, especially after the Synod of Jerusalem (1672) had repudiated the 'Calvinist' confession of faith of a former patriarch of Constantinople, Cyril Lukaris. In Poland, Orthodox bishops were transferring to the Uniat Church. Negotiations were under way that were eventually to bring over a patriarch of Antioch to form the Melkite branch of Byzantine Uniats. Jesuit preachers were winning Nestorians into communion with Rome as Chaldeans. The Maronites of Syria, who had given their allegiance to Rome in the Middle Ages, were now the object of special solicitude by the Roman Congregations.

Much more important than these skirmishes on the frontiers with Protestantism and Orthodoxy was the war against paganism in America and Asia, the brunt of which was borne by the religious Orders, not the least prominent being those which in Europe were becoming bywords for worldly finesse or obscurantism. In the New World, the Propaganda naturally looked to the empire of Spain as the centre of expansive power. It is true that the French and Portuguese possessions were rising in significance: the bishopric of Quebec was founded in 1674 and two years later Bahia, till then the only diocese in Brazil, became a metropolitan see. But the religious establishments of the French and Portuguese did not become bases for dramatically successful missions. In New France the heroic Jesuits worked north, west and south of the Great Lakes; but wars and the liquor trade among the nomadic Indians compromised the continuity of conversion, while the highly developed paganism of the Iroquois tribes, along with Anglo-French rivalry for their allegiance, continued to limit the penetration of Christianity into the confederate villages. The Church in Brazil was stagnant: what life there was came from the Jesuits, now inspired by Fr António Vieira, a fashionable preacher in Europe and founder of native townships north of the Amazon, who died in Brazil in extreme old age in 1697. In the Spanish dominions as in the Portuguese, the Indians were kept in tutelage and little attempt was made to build up a native priesthood. Yet the religious Orders continued to adventure and explore. Although the Capuchins (whose stronghold was Venezuela) withdrew from Darien in 1689 and the christianized Indians of Chiapas revolted in 1712–13, Franciscan perseverance sometimes won spectacular if ephemeral rewards in other parts of Central America, while their missions in Texas and Florida, held up by the Apaches, were moving forward again. From Mexico also, the Jesuits pushed towards California, settling the nomadic Indians into agricultural communities as they went. Between the rivers Paraná and Paraguay the famous Jesuit 'reductions', that remarkable experiment in theocratic paternalism, were successful in rescuing some 15,000 Guaraní Indians from their own idleness and European exploitation alike. By contrast, many of the Christian communities established by Jesuit and Franciscan in the jungle of Upper Amazonia, among less docile Indians and great diversity of speech, were destroyed by pagan or Portuguese attacks early in the eighteenth century.[1]

In the Orient, where European nations were trading round the edge of ancient cultures not yet in disintegration, the problems for missionaries were different.[2] Preachers could not follow in the wake of military conquest, mass conversions were improbable, the dense indigenous populations were far removed from the American tribes to whom Christianity could be offered as synonymous with civilization. One exception illustrates the rule: native society in the Philippines was too primitive to offer resistance to the Spanish Church, as firmly established there as in America. Elsewhere in Asia, Christianity had to make its way unsupported by material force and in debate against established philosophies and civilized customs. This was understood by the Propaganda in Rome, which had appointed two vicars-apostolic for the Far East in 1658, with instructions to remain under the ordinary law of the land where they found themselves, in accordance with the policy advocated by the Jesuit Alexandre de Rhodes —the establishment of a network of vicars-apostolic who would build up a native priesthood able to act independently of European patronage. Difficulties were created by the hostility of the regular Orders to this policy (and to each other), and by the Portuguese and Spanish rights to oversee all Catholic missions in the East. Nevertheless, the resources of

---

[1] Below, pp. 356–7.   [2] Cf. vol. v, pp. 403–9.

French Catholicism were enlisted in Siam, Tonking and Cochin China; and other apostolic vicariates were set up to take over Chinese areas from the nominal sway of the Portuguese dioceses of Macao, Peking and Nanking. The Propaganda aimed to push reconnaissance to the furthest boundary. Even Tibet was taken over on the ground that the missionaries of the Portuguese *Padroado* had abandoned it: two Capuchins struggled to Lhasa in 1708, and Desideri the Jesuit left the palaces, grapes and lilies of Srinagar in 1714 for the 'black mountains' and the wild road to the Tibetan capital, which his *confrère* Grüber had reached half a century earlier from the Great Wall of China. But the greatest prize was the vast Chinese empire. For nearly a century the Jesuits had maintained a mission in Peking, and in the reign (1669–1722) of the Emperor K'ang-hsi they rose to unparalleled influence, as scientists, artists, gunfounders, diplomats and administrators. When the Belgian Fr Verbiest, Director of the Bureau of Astronomy and Mandarin of the Sixth Order, died in 1688, the emperor's guards marched behind images of the Virgin and the Child Jesus in his funeral cortège. In 1692 K'ang-hsi approved a decree allowing his subjects to worship in the European churches: it must have seemed as if the mission was in sight of its goal. Yet long before the death of this tolerant emperor the golden days of the Jesuits were over. It had been their policy to annex Confucius (as in their colleges in Europe they had annexed Cicero), and to accept without question the rites of the scholar-official class and the general ancestor-worship of the common people. The Jesuit position in these matters had been challenged since the mid-seventeenth century. The dispute came to its crisis when in 1703 Rome sent Maillard de Tournon as *legatus a latere* to the Indies. De Tournon, bound before ever he set sail by a secret decision of the Propaganda, in 1707 condemned the Jesuits on all counts—on the rites and on the appropriate Chinese terms for the Christian God. The emperor, who had given his assurance that the rites were purely civil and was enraged at the intervention of foreigners who could not even read Chinese characters, ordered the expulsion of all missionaries who obeyed the Roman decisions and did not promise to stay in China all their lives, as some did. The details of this dispute are unedifying, often trivial; yet a major decision had been taken. We are, perhaps, still too close to the event to reflect upon its full significance in the history of the relations of Christianity with other religions.

'The age of crusades is over', said Cardinal d'Estrées, when Innocent XI offered in 1682 to crown Louis XIV emperor of Constantinople in return for intervention against the Turks. Catholic monarchs conducted foreign policy without deference to Rome, where their ambassadors acted with an arrogance inconceivable in any other major capital. Papal protests against the royal title acquired by the elector of Brandenburg and against provisions of the Peace of Utrecht, for instance, went unheeded. The emperor at times treated Rome as an Italian principality in league with his enemies; the nuncio was expelled from Vienna in 1705 and Imperial troops later violated the papal territories. When Clement XI changed sides in 1709, it was Philip V's turn to be offended and he encouraged 'regalist' doctrines in his dominions. Nevertheless, the Catholic sovereigns still expected Rome to do them favours. The Medici must have a cardinal in the family, were it Francesco Maria, brother of Grand Duke Cosimo of Tuscany, a homosexual and a sybarite; Louis XIV must have Forbin Janson raised to the purple, a prelate notorious for his activity in persuading the Turks to attack the emperor. At a papal election, the Crowns insisted upon their power of 'exclusion', a claim said to have become a definite right at the conclave of 1691 :[1] at the next conclave (1700), the French cardinals agreed to the election of Albani, a candidate of the *Zelanti* (the party which claimed to act on purely ecclesiastical motives), only after sending to their ambassador for instructions. Fortified with this power, the sovereigns treated the choice of a pope as if it were as purely a political matter as that of a king of Poland, and often as not they looked for a pliable candidate, incapable of rising to the heights of his great office. Such was the septuagenarian Alexander VIII (1689–91), who rushed down his relatives from Venice to give them employment before death could take him. Yet he was not typical. Innocent XII (1691–1700), though advanced in years, was firm and honourable; Innocent XI (1676–89) and Clement XI (1700–21) were good men with elements of greatness. But to rule a corrupt Italian principality, outface the Catholic sovereigns who used religion for their own ends, direct a missionary empire and give an intellectual lead in this period of crisis, would have required a Hildebrandine courage and energy—more than they had to offer.

The Catholic monarchs were even more determined to prohibit Roman intervention in their internal affairs. If Spain's regalist doctrines were only to reach full and harsh definition in the Concordat of 1753, they were already highly developed in her colonies, where the clergy—weakened by rivalries between Spanish dignitaries and Creole subordinates, and overshadowed by the owners of the big *haciendas*—showed little inclination to resent dictation by the civil authorities. Although the Propaganda claimed oversight of foreign missions, Church affairs in those immense and often isolated dioceses were directed by the Council of the Indies.[2] Under Philip V Spain was strengthening her own traditions by imitating France, whose history, more than that of any other Catholic country, provides the classical examples of legal barriers to ecclesiastical encroachments upon the sphere of the State. The famous Gallican 'liberties' enshrined in the

---

[1] L. von Pastor, *History of the Popes*, vol. XXXII, (tr. E. Graf, 1940) p. 565.
[2] E. Préclin and E. Jarry, *Les Luttes politiques et doctrinales aux XVIIe et XVIIIe siècles* (2 vols. 1955–6), vol. I, pp. 91–9. For regalism in Spain, cf. below, pp. 363, 376, 378.

law-books were underscored by Bossuet's eloquence, the researches of the Dominican historian Noël Alexandre, and the far-reaching implications of the Fourth Article of the 1682 Declaration.[1] By autumn 1688, indeed, no further compromise between Roman and Gallican standpoints seemed possible: Louis XIV lay under a secret excommunication and France was on the verge of schism. Yet five years later the feud was patched up, although nothing very conclusive was determined about the two great subjects in dispute, the *régale temporelle* and the Articles of 1682; so far as he went to Canossa (or rather, sent his bishops there) the French king acted from political motives—to neutralize Italy in the interests of his foreign policy.[2] With the Gallican Articles reduced to unofficial status but not disavowed, the dispute between Church and State took a new turn, its overt tensions being forced underground, to reappear in the complications of the renewed Jansenist controversy.

Reconciled to Rome, Louis expected the pope to aid him in settling accounts with the Jansenists.[3] It would be satisfying to ensure they reaped no ultramontane reward for defying the Crown in the matter of the *régale*, and the government was still obsessed by phantom dangers of theological cabals. In 1704 Germain Vuillart—the harmless editor of the works of Arnauld, Nicole and Le Nain de Tillemont—was interrogated in the Bastille, no less than twenty times, on the strength of a few puerile code-words in his correspondence with Pasquier Quesnel, a companion of Arnauld in exile. In 1705, under pressure from Louis, Clement XI issued the bull *Vineam Domini*, which forbade mental reservations when taking the Formulary. The few remaining nuns at Port-Royal accepted this Bull only so far as it did not derogate from the 'Peace of the Church' under Clement IX. It was absurd, as Sainte-Beuve says,[4] for twenty-two old ladies who claimed to be humble to refuse an order solicited by the king, accepted by the Assembly of Clergy and the Faculty of Theology, registered by the *Parlement* and published by all the bishops; one must agree, too, when he adds that it is a spectacle that fills us with compassion and respect. The upshot of their defiance was the notorious *journée* of 29 October 1709, when the Lieutenant of Police and his *archers* arrived at Port-Royal with a dozen carriages to remove them all, and the subsequent visitations of demolition squads and drunken gravediggers to erase the last vestiges of Jansenist memories.

There was to be a different *dramatis personae*, a different atmosphere, in the new act of Jansenist drama which was preparing. On 24 September 1713 the courier from Rome arrived at the French court bearing the bull *Unigenitus*, which condemned 101 propositions in a devotional manual

---

[1] See vol. v, pp. 135–9.
[2] J. Meuvret, 'Les Aspects politiques de la liquidation du conflit gallican, 1691–1693', *Rev. de l'hist. de l'Eglise de France*, vol. XXXIII (1947), pp. 257–70. Cf. below, pp. 161–2.
[3] For the earlier history of this quarrel, see vol. v, pp. 132 ff., and below, p. 133, note 2.
[4] *Port-Royal* (ed. M. Leroy), vol. III (1955), p. 622.

written long ago by Pasquier Quesnel. It is not entirely obvious why this exiled septuagenarian and the five editions of his treatise became a centre of controversy. The best explanation is probably that which sees the whole affair as originating in a manoeuvre to discredit Cardinal Noailles, archbishop of Paris, who had fallen foul of the Jesuits—a manoeuvre which got out of hand to the point where means became ends in themselves. Unlike the worldly and cynical Harlay, his predecessor, Noailles was no time-server but an honest man who vacillated continuously in face of a labyrinthine dispute which baffled his conscience. As bishop of Châlons, in 1695 he had publicly approved the latest edition of Quesnel's *Réflexions Morales*; as archbishop he condemned a work of the Jansenist Abbé Barcos, a nephew of Saint-Cyran. A fanatical Jansenist controversialist[1] inadvisedly pointed out that the theology of Barcos was indistinguishable from that of Quesnel and convicted Noailles of inconsistency. The Jesuits took up the attack. Ostensibly complaining about Quesnel, their arguments struck indirectly at the archbishop, and led to fifteen years of controversy culminating in *Unigenitus*. Louis XIV, who had solicited such a condemnation two years before, enforced acceptance of the Bull by the *Parlement* of Paris, the Sorbonne and the episcopate.

Unigenitus proved a meeting-place for many discontents, the cave of Adullam where opponents of royal and papal power alike could rally. Hitherto, the Jansenist challenge had been focused on the issue of 'fact': was it reasonable to enforce the view that certain Latin propositions were embodied within a theological work, like thorns in a great faggot, upon those who maintained that by diligent research they had been unable to find them?[2] Now, it was a question of a multitude of propositions in straightforward French and authentically from Quesnel, some obviously open to official review but others, to all seeming, of unexceptionable orthodoxy: what could be wrong with statements that all must study the Scriptures, or that fear of an unjust excommunication ought never to prevent us doing our duty? To defend the Bull in such cases, one must distinguish the condemnation of propositions from the imposition of a belief in their opposites, and concede that they must have been censured in *odium auctoris*—on the supposition that Quesnel had put them forward with some dark design in mind.[3] Not unnaturally, Jansenists were un-

[1] Dom Monnier, of the Benedictine congregation of St-Vannes, wrote the notorious *Problème ecclésiastique* (1698), but was not responsible for its publication: R. Taveneaux, *Le Jansénisme en Lorraine* (1960), pp. 156–8.

[2] The anti-Jansenist Formulary approved by Alexander VII and imposed by the Assembly of the Clergy of France, 1657–61, committed signatories to condemning 'the five propositions of Cornelius Jansen contained in his book entitled the *Augustinus*' and denying that their doctrine was that of St Augustine. Jansenists had subsequently declared that the Five Propositions were not to be found in the *Augustinus*—the famous 'issue of fact'.

[3] J. F. Thomas, *La Querelle de l'Unigenitus* (1950), pp. 60–1, argues that the Church was not entitled to prejudge the subjective opinions of the author; on the other side see J. Orcibal, *Revue Historique*, vol. CCVIII (1952), p. 321. Cf. vol. VII, pp. 114–15.

willing to go out of their way to make the Bull reasonable by admitting this possibility. A devotional manual praised by a generation, used even by the Jesuits, had been damned, without allowing its author to appear in his defence, by a Roman congregation of which only one member knew the language it was written in, and that in a document which piled up accusations unrelated to any individual proposition. These circumstances lent force to the Jansenist demand that the Bull be made explicit, so that those who were supposed to accept it could know what they were doing. In reply, Languet, bishop of Soissons, the ablest of orthodox controversialists, urged that the pope, like a shepherd, owes no explanations to his flock: if he sees poisonous weeds in a certain pasture, he simply moves them elsewhere. In short, papal authority was at stake, and thanks to Louis XIV the authority of the Crown with it. The future of Jansenist agitation in France was to lie with the Gallicanism of the *parlements*, delighted to find an opportunity of resisting the pope in the king's interests and the king in his own, and that of a lower group in the clerical hierarchy than the aristocratic episcopate. Parish priests already resented the maldistribution of wealth and honours in the Church, and the growing power of the episcopate.[1] Minds thus prepared turned readily to views which exalted the independence of the parochial ministry and the rôle of the synod in diocesan affairs. It is the diffusion of these 'Richerist' ideas among the 'second order' of clergy, the alliance of the *curés* with the lawyers, and the amalgamation of their joint protests with the grievances of Jansenists against 'episcopal despotism' that together form the central history of the 'political Jansenism' of the eighteenth century.[2] The theological past of Jansenism was becoming an associative myth. Before *Unigenitus* it had been to some extent an 'imaginary heresy', invented by the enemies of those who held its tenets; to some extent afterwards, it became an imaginary orthodoxy, kept alive by parties who found in it their only bond of unity, their chief argument against arbitrary power in Church and State.

Any summary account of Jansenism inevitably does violence to the complexity of the factors involved. According to Cardinal Aguirre in 1688, there were a few obstinate supporters of the Five Propositions and two much larger and less definable groups of potential sympathizers, the moral rigorists and the opponents of the Jesuits. This was an analysis limited to ecclesiastical groupings. In France, there were also political forces ready to come in behind the façade of the theological issues. Elsewhere, in each area where a 'Jansenist' contretemps is recorded, the particular kind of 'Jansenism' involved—and possibly the motives for saying that it existed at all—needs separate analysis. At Rome there were cardinals, Augustinians or Thomists, who deplored the division of the

---

[1] Cf. below, p. 333.
[2] See vol. VII, chs. vi and x.

world into 'Molinists'[1] and 'heretics' and who were sometimes regarded as crypto-Jansenists. Among the Catholic minority in England, allegations of Jansenism were levelled at the 'Blackloists', followers of Thomas White (the friend of Hobbes), who denied papal infallibility. At Liège in the 1690s, the prince bishop tried to replace 'Jansenist' teachers in his seminary by Jesuits, evoking an avalanche of pamphlets and a long dispute, in which the bishop received moral support from Fénelon.[2] But this furore had little to do with doctrine: Canon Denys, the leading 'Jansenist', was to make no difficulties over *Unigenitus*: his offence consisted in preferring Austria to France. As for the motives of Joseph Clement, who occupied four episcopal sees in addition to Liège, it is enough to say that he held them all by papal dispensations without the encumbrance of holy orders, until in 1707 he made a quick leap into sanctity because Marlborough's victories were jeopardizing his tenure. His personal position and foreign policy alike compelled him to put on a show of orthodoxy. In the Netherlands the bases for a 'Jansenist' dispute had existed even before the *Augustinus*, for the Jesuits wanted Catholic activities put under the Propaganda, while the local clergy wished to remain under their own episcopate and in this were abetted by the civil authorities, anxious to keep the Catholic minority independent of Rome. Archbishop Neercassel (d. 1686) of Utrecht had been a friend of Arnauld, a rigorist theologian, an enemy of the Jesuits; his successor, Peter Codde, who refused to subscribe the Formulary, was summoned to Rome in 1699 and suspended in 1702. The episcopal pro-vicars and the chapter refused to accept Theodore de Cock as Pro-Vicar Apostolic, and the States of Holland forbade Cock to exercise his office within their territories. Thenceforward, the Church of Utrecht—the Old Catholic Church still in being—carried on independent of Rome, sympathetic bishops in Ireland and France ordaining its priests until in 1724 opportunity occurred to obtain the consecration of a new archbishop. Though it rejected *Unigenitus*, it regarded itself as breaking with Rome on the subject of ecclesiastical jurisdiction. In Utrecht, as in France, the dispute about Jansenism came to involve the question of the nature of ultimate authority in the Church. The scholars who searched the Bible and St Augustine to demonstrate that Christian doctrine breaks all human canons of 'reason' found themselves conscripted to fight the battle of 'reason', against the exponents of total obedience in both Church and State. In this way, though there was a fundamental

---

[1] Followers of the doctrine of grace of Luis de Molina (1535–1600), who had emphasized the fact of free human co-operation. The Jesuits had widely adopted Molinism, and the term had come to be used (not very appropriately) as a sort of theological antithesis to Jansenism. For the position at Rome see E. Appolis, *Entre Jansénistes et Zelanti: le 'Tiers Parti' catholique au XVIII⁰ siècle* (1960), pp. 28 ff.

[2] G. Simenon, 'Le Jansénisme au pays de Liège', *Rev. ecclés. de Liège*, XVI (2) (1924), 87–99; R. Bragard, 'Fénelon, Joseph-Clément de Bavière et le Jansénisme à Liège', *Rev. d'hist. ecclés.* vol. XLIII (1948), pp. 473–94.

opposition between Jansenism and the Enlightenment, there was paradoxically an indirect Jansenist contribution to 'la crise de la conscience européenne'.

In that famous phrase Paul Hazard[1] summed up the critical intellectual tensions of the transition from the seventeenth to the eighteenth century. Scientific progress involved adjustments to a new picture of the universe within which there was no obvious place for miracles, since 'the course of things goes quietly along, in its own channel of *Natural Causes* and *Effects*'.[2] A great movement of historical scholarship was under way; legends, including those of the saints, were destroyed; the biblical documents themselves came under scrutiny.[3] Bossuet, unlike Malebranche and Arnauld (who found in Descartes an ally for Christian apologetics), scented danger. 'A great battle against the Church', he wrote in 1687, 'is being mounted, under the flag of the Cartesian philosophy.'[4] Socinian books from Holland, where fugitives of this persuasion from eastern Europe found refuge, cast doubts upon the Trinitarian and sacramental mysteries, doubts originally drawn from scriptural literalism but now achieving the status of difficulties suggested by pure reason. The French *libertins* were being read again in the 1680s, and there was a revival of interest in some of their original sources, the Epicurean philosophy and the *De rerum natura* of Lucretius. Religious apologists were also concerned about newer dangers, the writings of two highly individual philosophers not long dead: the shadow of Hobbes, sinister and ambiguous, who had wreaked his worst havoc with unexceptionable biblical propositions, darkened the path of the theologians; Spinoza's pantheism and determinism and, above all, his attitude to the Bible were exerting an influence masked only by his readers' reluctance to admit alarm or indebtedness. Since in Locke's philosophy there were no innate ideas, the inference might be drawn that in the confused and possibly accidental early history of man's acquisition of beliefs lay the explanation of all religion, though Locke himself proved that Christianity was 'reasonable' with limpid contemporaneity. But Reason, or rather a certain opinion of what is reasonable, led to John Toland's *Christianity not Mysterious* in 1696. Already the principal challenge of English Deism to revelation had been formulated by Charles Blount: 'That Rule which is necessary to our future Happiness ought to be generally made known to all men.'[5] Bayle was

[1] *La Crise de la conscience européenne, 1680–1715* (1935).
[2] T. Sprat, *History of the Royal Society* (1667), ed. J. I. Cope and H. W. Jones (Washington Univ. Studies, 1959), p. 340.
[3] Cf. above, pp. 87–8.
[4] *Œuvres complètes de Bossuet*, ed. Migne, vol. XI (1865), col. 974. For suspicions that Cartesianism led to materialism see A. Vartanian, *Diderot and Descartes: a study of scientific naturalism in the Enlightenment* (Princeton, 1953), pp. 50–73, 228.
[5] *The Oracles of Reason* (1693); extracts in J. M. Creed and J. S. Boys Smith, *Religious Thought in the Eighteenth Century* (Cambridge, 1934), p. 23.

simultaneously compiling his *Dictionnaire*, its readers driven to reflect that they could only indulge their reason at the expense of religious belief: Manichean dualism explained the world of good and evil better than the doctrine of Creation; God could not be good if he foresaw the Fall, nor omniscient if he did not. And there were other authors—famous like Fontenelle, or little noticed at the time like John Trenchard, whose *Natural History of Superstition* (1709), an account of the origin of religion in fear, was to be welcome to d'Holbach. When English and French thought coalesced, when rationalism and scepticism were brought into temporary alliance, cemented by anti-clericalism and adorned with literary talent, we reach the age of Voltaire.

But it was only in August 1711 that Voltaire left the classes of the Jesuits, his mind indelibly stamped with their 'catholicity' but closed to their Christian convictions. The future still held many alternative possibilities. Though in retrospect we can see that this generation had amassed weapons for the use of future opponents of Christianity, it is an abuse of hindsight to summarize these years simply as the prolegomena to an intellectual conspiracy. As yet, no one thought in terms of the nineteenth-century antithesis of religion and science, and most scientists were convinced Christians; if Newton lacked the confidence of his colleagues in the divinity of Christ, he kept his secret to himself and wrote his *Principia* with 'an eye upon such principles as might work with considering men for the belief of a deity'.[1] The great historical scholars, almost to a man, were ecclesiastics—non-juring divines and latitudinarian bishops, Jesuits, Oratorians, Maurists. So too were Malebranche and Berkeley, while of lay philosophers Locke sincerely desired to find rational grounds for religious assent, and Shaftesbury received the Sacrament blessing Providence for keeping the Church of England in a religion of decency and charity, free from 'monstrous enthusiasms'.[2] Socinian propagandists in England hoped to be allowed to stay in the Church, even in its ministry, without too many questions asked. Among the Huguenots who dominated the republic of letters in Holland, if Le Clerc fell from Trinitarian orthodoxy, his theology was sound in other respects and far from Socinianism; and Bayle, who made such reckless use of the double-edged weapon of scepticism, was yet an austere practising believer.[3] With a Calvinist view of human nature, a despair of rationality, a sad conviction that men use arguments merely as a cloak for following their passions, Bayle turned inwards to a religious illumination which was all there was to live by. It was a pale cold flame, but his devotion to it made him nearer than he imagined to the Quietists, whom he detested. Thus, while from one

[1] Quoted R. C. Jebb, *Bentley* (1882), p. 26.
[2] R. L. Brett, *The Third Earl of Shaftesbury* (1951), pp. 46–7.
[3] A. Barnes, *Jean Le Clerc et la République des Lettres* (1938), pp. 237 ff.; P. Dibon (ed.), *Pierre Bayle, le philosophe de Rotterdam* (1959), pp. vii-xvi.

point of view 'la crise de la conscience européenne' may be regarded as a prelude to Voltaire, its total significance is better seized if we realize that it was essentially a crisis within Christianity itself. The ideas conveniently grouped within the portmanteau words 'reason', 'scepticism' and 'science' were being used to explain, defend and reinterpret religion. Moreover, the measure to which these efforts succeeded can easily be overlooked in face of the heterodoxies which sprang up in a thousand places and of the arguments scattered abroad for the use of agnostics and anticlericals. The terminology of warfare is often inappropriate to describe tensions of belief. In more senses than one, for apologists as well as for opponents of Christianity, this period marks the beginning of the modern world.

What rôle does reason play in religious belief, and what are its limitations? Locke's and Tillotson's reply—revelation has independent status, but reason must judge what may properly be termed revelation—was simply the traditional teaching of Hooker and the Anglican theologians, as of the Puritans. English Protestantism was reluctant to concede that the Fall had irremediably tainted the human intellect and preferred, with Milton and the Cambridge Platonists, to see the primeval tragedy as consisting in the overthrow of reason by the passions of self-interest. To seek enlightenment, therefore, was to contribute to the restoration of fallen humanity, which by knowledge and repentance was being led to a new interior Paradise, 'happier far' than the simplicities of Eden. Anglican and Puritan alike accepted the obligation to provide rational proofs of religion. The more devious path of apologetics, the argument from scepticism, was left in the main to Catholic apologists, who made use of doubts about human reason to throw their readers back to fideism. The papists, Burnet recorded angrily, 'went so far even into the argument for atheism as to publish many books in which they affirmed that there was no certain proof of the Christian religion, unless we took it from the authority of the Church as infallible'.[1] But reason, no less than scepticism, had its dangers. When Locke observed that any credit given to a proposition in excess of its proof is 'owing to our inclinations that way and is so far a derogation from the love of truth as such', he had crossed a frontier,[2] beyond which the attempt to prove the existence of God encouraged those who believed only in the sort of God who was susceptible of proof. Controversy among the orthodox, culminating in Clarke's *Scripture Doctrine of the Trinity* (1712), was a further help to the Deists, who set forth the minimum of Locke's 'reasonable' Christianity as a maximum. Yet the English Deists, who were to have considerable influence in France, never gained great honour in their own country, where the age of reason was

---

[1] *History of My Own Time* (1839 edn.), p. 129. Cf. L. I. Bredvold, *The Intellectual Milieu of John Dryden* (Ann Arbor, 1956), pp. 73–91.

[2] D. G. James, *The Life of Reason: Hobbes, Locke, Bolingbroke* (1949), pp. 101–3.

always more concerned with finding the limits of reason than with deifying it. 'The Philosopher's Business', wrote Defoe in 1703, 'is not to look through Nature, and come to the vast open Field of Infinite Power... The Christian begins just where the Philosopher ends.'[1]

Along with the idea of a 'natural' religion went that of a 'natural' morality, which also took its rise within 'reasonable' Christianity. Before Shaftesbury said that virtue ought to be its own reward, Cudworth had said so, in the course of refuting Descartes, the Calvinists, Hobbes, and all who claimed that good and evil are the results of God's arbitrary choice, rather than implicit in the very nature of things.[2] The hypothesis of a primitive monotheism, generally accepted by religious apologists as a link in the proof from universal consent, helped to fortify natural morality; so too did the propaganda of the Jesuits. On the main doctrinal issue, Jesuit theologians would have agreed with Arnauld that predestination is *ante praevisa merita*—so far, in fact, the quarrel of Jesuit and Jansenist was a quarrel of words. But when one asked if unbaptized infants were damned, or if pagans who loved justice thereby loved God, Arnauld gave the rigorist answer—let human reason say what it will. By contrast, the Jesuits praised the 'noble savage', a fiction as they well knew, but one which served as their defence against Jansenist attacks on their missionary methods and against the ruthlessness of colonial authorities and brandy-selling fur-traders.[3] Above all, they evoked the shimmering mirage of China, an unbaptized civilization which had known the true God for 2,000 years and had developed a religious code and vocabulary which could be assimilated to Christianity. It was a tragedy for Catholicism that the clash between revelation and natural religion should have come at this point. The condemnation of Fr Le Comte's *Nouveaux Mémoires sur... la Chine*—by a committee of the Sorbonne packed with Jansenists— and the papal constitution *Ex illa die* of 1715 possibly averted a threat to doctrinal integrity; yet the disavowal of the Jesuits became a classical instance of intolerant stupidity to the Enlightenment. Meanwhile Bayle carried the discussion about natural morality and natural religion to its logical conclusion, by his contention that morality need have no connection with religion at all, natural or revealed. Spinoza was as virtuous as his doctrines were vicious; as for the mass of mankind, they live according to their passions, in a fashion which makes religious belief or unbelief morally irrelevant. But few in this age of reason wished to accept Bayle's desperate conclusion. Men preferred to reflect on the freethinker of Swift's parable who, hearing that one of the proof-texts for the Trinity had a variant reading in an ancient manuscript, 'most logically concluded:

---

[1] Quoted B. Dobrée, *English Literature in the Early Eighteenth Century* (Oxford, 1959), p. 17.
[2] Cudworth's major ethical treatise, 'Eternal and Immutable Morality', remained in manuscript until 1731: see J. A. Passmore, *Ralph Cudworth* (Cambridge, 1951), pp. 40–1.
[3] G. R. Healy, 'The French Jesuits and the Idea of the Noble Savage', *William and Mary Quarterly*, 3rd ser. vol. xv (1958), pp. 143–60.

"Why, if it be as you say, I may safely whore and drink on, and defy the Parson"'.[1]

The manoeuvres of Catholic scepticism which so angered Burnet were principally directed towards undermining Protestant reliance on the Bible. Simon, who followed the way pointed by Spinoza, being the first to apply critical scholarship to the structure of the Pentateuch, was a Catholic polemicist, not a precursor of Renan. Jesuit writers used similar tactics to weaken the Protestant appeal to the Fathers.[2] But there were others interested in the weaknesses of Scripture, like Toland, who compared the problem of the authorship of the New Testament documents to that of *Eikon Basilike*, and like the Quakers, who welcomed the discovery of errors which drove men from the letter that killeth to the inner witness of the Spirit. The design to throw men forward from the Bible to the Roman tradition might easily miscarry, serving the interests of enthusiasts, Deists or unbelievers. It is little wonder, then, that Bossuet condemned Simon's writings or that French theologians applauded the reply of Anglican divines to Jesuit doubts about the Nicaean Fathers.

This rapprochement between Anglican and Gallican churchmen was based on stronger ties than their common hatred of sceptical legerdemain and of the Jesuits. The intellectual leaders of both Catholic and Protestant worlds were being drawn together, even in their controversies, by a common respect for disinterested scholarship. Dom Mabillon recommended the works of Anglican theologians for monastic libraries; Anglicans defended the validity of their orders by using the researches of the Oratorian Jean Morin; Le Clerc entered the lists in defence of Huet, bishop of Avranches, who had incurred the enmity of Boileau over a point of Hebrew scholarship; Daniel van Papenbroeck, the Bollandist, demolished St George's dragon and the portable head of Denys the Areopagite amid the applause of learned men on both sides. When Scipione Maffei discovered that he had offended Clement XI with his *Della scienza chiamata cavalleresca* (1710) he refused to withdraw: the pope, he said, was the judge of religion and morals, 'but where erudition and philology are concerned... he becomes once again a man exposed, like other men, to be mistaken'.[3] The English historians and antiquaries—Hickes and Wharton, Stillingfleet and Collier—were anxious to prove, as against the papists, that their Church retained its continuity from Saxon times and, as against the Nonconformists, that it had been continuously governed by a diocesan episcopate; yet the fascination of their studies absorbed their

---

[1] *An Argument to prove that the Abolishing of Christianity in England, may... be attended with some Inconveniencies*... (1708): *Prose Writings*, ed. Davis, vol. II, p. 38.

[2] H. Fréville, 'Richard Simon et les Protestants d'après sa correspondance', *Rev. d'hist. mod.* VI (1931), 30; O. Chadwick, *From Bossuet to Newman: the idea of doctrinal development* (Cambridge, 1957), pp. 50–8.

[3] G. Maugin, *Etude sur l'évolution intellectuelle de l'Italie de 1657 à 1750* (1909), pp. 110–11.

polemical interests, which tended to become pious excuses for indulgence in learning. Awareness of Simon's conspiratorial aims did not deter Protestants from following his lead in biblical scholarship. Le Clerc outdid him in daring hypotheses about the authorship of Genesis; Campegius Vitringa, an orthodox Dutch Calvinist, perfected some of the techniques which finally enabled Astruc to separate the main strands of the Pentateuch in the mid-eighteenth century; and Thomas Burnet won the applause of the wits as having proved

> That all the books of Moses
> Were nothing but supposes.

When Bossuet condemned Simon, he was being clear-sighted so far as he regretted the opportunities that scholarship would present to unbelievers. In the long run, however, 'la crise de la conscience européenne' was more significant for creating a learned world in which historians and theologians of all parties could debate with common presuppositions and standards of intellectual integrity. In the context of a more distant future, Bossuet's triumph was both temporary and disastrous.

Rejecting Simon's scholarship and the apologetics of scepticism, Bossuet himself used erudition in an honest, unsubtle and momentarily effective fashion against the Protestants. His *Histoire des Variations des Eglises Protestantes* (1688) is a monument of the age of reason, a superbly logical edifice constructed by a methodologist indifferent to the complexities and ironies of history. Its basic postulate, that the doctrine of the true Church never varies, was a rationalistic assumption on a level with the Deists' principle that what is necessary to happiness must have been revealed to all men simultaneously; indeed, both Bossuet and the English Deists were constructing syllogisms in an abstract world where there was no allowance for development or for the idea that truth may be many-sided. Apocalyptic speculations and the 'new philosophy' had already predisposed Protestant apologists to theses of progress and development, and they now replied to Catholic and Deist opponents alike by rejoicing in differences of opinion, accepting the possibility of doctrinal evolution, and outflanking the scandal of particularity by insisting that 'God dispenseth not all his Favours together...The manifestations of his Will grow greater and greater successively.' John Edwards, who wrote these words,[1] was a Calvinist divine of the Church of England. The idea of inevitable progress was not solely the result of the rejection of original sin by the Enlightenment.

This affinity between apocalyptic and scientific visions of a millennium was characteristic of the time. Though their methods differed, religion

---

[1] *A Compleat History...of All the Dispensations...of Religion* (1699): see R. S. Crane, 'Anglican Apologetics and the Idea of Progress, 1699–1745', *Modern Philology*, XXXI (1934), 284. Cf. E. L. Tuveson, *Millennium to Utopia* (Berkeley-Los Angeles, 1949), pp. 75 ff.

and the 'new philosophy' were regarded as complementary aspects of a single universal enquiry; in areas where conflict threatened, churchmen were usually up-to-date and cautious, as when Bayle was sarcastic about prognostications, Bekker about witchcraft, or Shaftesbury about the French prophets of London. Proofs from miracle were used with restraint. Providence was reconciled with a mechanistic universe by the assumption that Nature in its ordinary workings was the best mirror of the glory of its Creator. Fénelon's God, who guides the wandering stars as a shepherd his flock, and John Ray's opening sentence—'How manifold are thy works, O Lord!'—are typical expressions of the central theme of religious apologetic, and of the concordance of religion with science. If problems troubled this concordance they were, generally, old problems newly magnified. What if the planet had a fortuitous origin? Lucretius had suggested it, on the evidence of irregularities in the earth's crust. Another old problem which gained a new intensity was the possibility of a plurality of worlds: what, then, of the uniqueness of Christianity? Against a plurality of worlds were arguments going back to Augustine and Aquinas—if other worlds were the same as this they would be superfluous. If different, imperfect. Scripture is silent about their existence; the Atonement cannot be repeated. The argument for multiplicity, dominant towards 1700 among both theologians and secular thinkers, was based upon the old principle of 'plenitude', according to which God's creative activity would necessarily abhor a vast and useless emptiness, and would choose to fill it with infinite gradations of being, all in the end (as Ephesians i suggests) destined to be gathered into one in Christ.[1]

Significantly, this particular view of divine creative activity was prevailing just when the extreme interpretation of predestination was being abandoned. This doctrine had, indeed, outlasted the nominalist philosophy within whose framework its rigours could be defended as necessary consequences of God's omnipotence. Dutch Arminians and Cambridge Platonists, the 'federal' theologians of Old and New England, Milton and Vondel (and even Bunyan, if Part II of Pilgrim's Progress be our guide), Baxter and Tillotson, all agreed in repudiating a doctrine which made the exercise of divine power inexplicable by the ethics of ordinary reason —in Cudworth's phrase, 'a blind, dark, impetuous self-will running through the world'.[2] In 1693, after controversy over a posthumous work of Dr Tobias Crisp (d. 1643), the English Presbyterians and Independents went their separate ways—the Independents, a small minority, being the last adherents of extreme 'antinomian' predestinationism. The titles of the two most famous works by last-ditch defenders of the iron Calvinist

---

[1] G. McColley, 'The 17th-century Doctrine of a Plurality of Worlds', Annals of Science, vol.1(1936),pp.385–427; A.O.Lovejoy, The Great Chain of Being (Harvard, 1936),pp.99ff.; R. S. Westfall, Science and Religion in Seventeenth-Century England (Yale, 1958), pp. 82–6.
[2] Quoted H. J. C. Grierson, Cross Currents in English Literature of the XVIIth Century (1929),p.230.Cf.G.R.Cragg, From Puritanism to the Age of Reason(Cambridge,1950),ch.III.

tradition are significant: *Christ Exalted and Dr Crisp Vindicated* and *The Glory of Christ Unveiled*. They were defending the exaltation, glory and majesty of God. By now, however, most contemporaries saw that majesty, not in acts of arbitrary will incompatible with natural laws and human reasoning, but in the glittering complexities and orderly design of the created universe. In strict logic, these two contrasting views of reality, divine predestination and the web of general causes, were not irreconcilable. Yet they appeared to be so, even to subtle Cartesian predestinarians like the French Jansenists, bitterly hostile to Malebranche's thesis that God rested the seventh day and henceforward rules by *volontés générales* rather than by particular interventions. In spite of the qualifications with which Malebranche surrounded his theory, and of his intensely spiritual view of the universe, wherein all perception is through union with God and there is a continual ministry of angels, Arnauld censured him as one who disputed on beyond the point where reason ought to be annihilated in worship.

For those who reasoned and those who worshipped, alike, there was one inescapable stumbling-block. As Bayle well knew, the problem of evil destroyed every rationalist theodicy—as in the end it was to destroy the thought of the Enlightenment. Two imaginative answers were given in this period, breaking through the assumption that total omnipotence is necessarily a quality of divine perfection and action. Le Clerc[1] and Ray used Cudworth's conception of a 'plastic nature', which is God's 'drudge' to carry out the routine process of moving matter. Malebranche similarly justified goodness at the expense of power by emphasizing that Christ's human nature has not an infinite capacity, so that in his heavenly work as Mediator his dispensation of graces must be partial and arbitrary. However, the main tendency of Christian philosophers in their discussion of evil was to bind God in a sense more acceptable to Reason: evil exists by the very nature of things. Among other arguments, Malebranche held that evil followed from God's design to rule by general laws; it was, in fact, the ransom paid for the universe's superb simplicity. William King, bishop of Derry, in his *De origine mali* (1702), emphasized the necessary 'defect' which must exist once created things are differentiated from God and from each other; he used the principle of plenitude to show that God is obliged to create a full universe, and fullness inevitably involves clashes of interest. Similarly, in his *Essais de Théodicée* (1710), Leibniz refuted Bayle and made theology 'reasonable' by placing the origin of evil in the eternal truths, so that, taking into account the condition of the whole universe (and not just human welfare), this is the 'best of all possible worlds'. In this phrase we see how far Reason was destined to move away from Christianity—not because the words are unduly optimistic, but

[1] At the expense of a great quarrel with Bayle: R. L. Colie, *Light and Enlightenment: A Study of the Cambridge Platonists and the Dutch Arminians* (Cambridge, 1957), pp. 117, 129.

because they can lead to a total pessimism beyond redemption. If all partial evil is universal good, then whatever is, is right.

While the period saw patterns of thought crystallize that challenged Christianity, theological issues remained at the centre of debate, though perhaps only because religion itself was being subjected to compromise and reinterpretations. Something like this might also be said of the relations of religion to the arts, which were put to ecclesiastical use with a lavishness, sophistication and worldly brilliance rarely equalled. The mental inhibitions that made the artist instinctively conscious of unyielding differences between styles appropriate for the church, on one hand, and court or theatre, on the other, were breaking down. Appropriately enough, it was in the royal chapel at Versailles that the fusion of French and Italian musical styles took place which introduced histrionic and secular inspirations into devotion;[1] but similar tendencies can be seen in architecture, from the smooth, unequivocally baroque classicism of Carlo Fontana in Rome to the sumptuous rebuilding of the Benedictine monasteries along the Danube. The charm of the fashionable *putti*, the weakening of gesture in the figures on papal mausoleums, the English tombs where reference to mortality is limited to conventional symbols, the gleaming white and gold of the high altars of Fischer von Erlach, the amazing inventiveness of the brothers Asam that was to fill German churches with a riotous perfection of gilt and scarlet too vivid for an opera house—these examples demonstrate the 'secularization' of religious art and hint at the decline of unselfconscious piety behind the splendid façade. Yet this is only half the truth. As indicated elsewhere (ch. III (2)), the age which began with Purcell and ended with J. S. Bach produced some of the greatest religious music ever written. Wren designed his London churches with a high seriousness and a Protestant concern for preaching and seating of the poor; the best work of the great builders and decorators of the Continent was far from being merely theatrical. For the Middle Ages the symbol of sanctity had been miracle; for the seventeenth century it was ecstasy. Bernini died in 1680, but works like his St Theresa remained models for artistic aspirations, to draw the beholder into the orbit of mystical rapture, to the edge of an abyss, by every device of illusionism and play of light and shade. The ceilings of the Gesù, S. Pantaleo and S. Ignazio at Rome are not only masterpieces of perspective technique, peopling a sky with figures in celestial hierarchy: they are expressions of a yearning for infinity, for a luminous eternity reaching down through the wastes of space that had haunted Pascal. The new Nativities and Annunciations, lacking in the naïve simplicity most suited for their theme, with the ox and ass banished from the manger-side out of

[1] N. Dufourcq, 'La Musique religieuse vocale en Ile-de-France', *Etudes*, vol. CCLXXXVIII (1936), pp. 247–55; W. Mellers, *François Couperin and the French Classical Tradition* (1950), pp. 323–4.

respect to scholarship and refinement, are nevertheless vivid expressions of the divine incursion, a glimpse of a world of angels in the shafts of radiance that pierce our mortal gloom.

This 'last great building age of Christianity' was the last when religious belief dominated artistic expression.[1] Despising former attempts to realize the same aim—the 'cut-work and crinkle-crankle' of Gothic[2]—artists went their own way to express man's yearnings for eternity. Yet the artistic interpretation of religion must always be selective and partial. The Italian Jesuits—patrons of Gaulli and Pozzo, the creators of luminous empyreal infinities—recommended meditation with curtains drawn in the presence of a skull. One is tempted to speculate that the differing artistic atmospheres of succeeding Christian generations spring from different ways of picturing the divine transcendence, while their basic sameness derives from inescapable awareness of the facts of our human condition.

It is a truism that religion aims to affect that condition. It is equally true, if less obvious, that the moral guides of any particular generation have always taken social circumstances and intellectual presuppositions into account, so that each tends to have its own stereotypes of Christian conduct—idealized figures of the gentleman, tradesman, soldier or divine, built up by preachers, casuists, pious biographers, religious publicists generally. To such interpreters of Christian life in our period, it seemed that the man of fashion or superior education was faced by one particular overwhelming temptation. Stoicism, as the Renaissance had revived it, offered a noble but inadequate morality which a man might cleave to, leaving the Gospel to take care of the life to come. Christian moralists insisted that the pagan virtues were founded on secret pride, and that the passions, necessary and natural, are to be harnessed by the will rather than suppressed by the reason. When Cato was struck, he denied that he was hurt in his essential being: when Christ was struck, he pardoned. So Malebranche summed up the contrast between Renaissance neo-Stoicism and Christianity.[3] It was in terms of this contrast that the ideal of honourable conduct was pictured for Continental Protestants by Jacques Abbadie, and for Englishmen by Timothy Nourse, Captain Ayloffe, above all Steele. In *The Christian Hero* (1710) Steele specifically warns his readers that his is no 'Stoical rant'; a man should do good for conscience' sake, unmoved by desire for fame except so far as the precept, 'Let your light so shine before men' makes publicity an obligation.[4] In England and

---

[1] Sacheverell Sitwell, *German Baroque Art* (1927), p. 102. Cf. vol. v, ch. VII and R. Wittkower, *Art and Architecture in Italy, 1600–1750* (1958), pp. 292–4.

[2] John Evelyn (1697), quoted A. O. Lovejoy, *Essays in the History of Ideas* (Baltimore, 1948), p. 138.

[3] H. Gouhier, *La Philosophie de Malebranche et son expérience religieuse* (1926), p. 397. For Malebranche (1638–1715), cf. vol. v, pp. 78–9.

[4] See R. Blanchard's edn. (Oxford, 1932). Jacques Abbadie (1654–1727), a Huguenot exile, had enormous influence as a Christian apologist; his *L'Art de se connoître soi-même* was published in 1692 (E. T. 1694).

later, under Pietistic influences, Germany, the Christian ethical stereotype was enriched by what might be called the autobiographical tradition of Puritanism, which influenced many whose churchmanship was far removed from Puritan connections. The Quakers published journals (including that of George Fox, 1694) and collections of death-bed testimonies out of reverence for the inner light that shines in every man. Bunyan overflowed in gratitude for the certainty of his election. Baxter wrote out of love for his wife and 'that young Christians may be warned by the mistakes and failings of my unriper times', by the stolen fruit, 'romances, fables and old tales' which, in his naïveté, he always regretted.[1] For their writers, these works were a Protestant variety of the confessional; for their readers, a substitute for the lives of saints that still sustained Catholic piety. They were, too, in their accounts of moral dilemmas faced and overcome, a substitute for technical casuistry: as Jeremy Taylor had observed, Protestants were deficient in this respect and 'cannot be well supplied out of the Roman store-houses; for although...many excellent things are exposed to view, yet have we found the merchants to be deceivers'.[2] English theologians never produced a comprehensive guide to casuistry for the 'gentleman'. It is tempting to suggest that this was ultimately to be found in literature, with Addison.

In France, the Christian stereotype for the aristocrat had to be more subtle than the Englishman's 'Christian hero'. Although in 1685 Fr Héliodore the Capuchin was still concentrating his fire on Stoicism, there were other fashionable tendencies competing with Christianity: 'pleasure' was being redefined and spiritualized, Epicurus replacing Seneca. There was, too, the complication of the alternative of that total renunciation of the world which Catholicism retained and Protestantism had rejected. If Malebranche was right and the general vocation of all Christians was retreat, so that a man needed a particular vocation to stay in the world, the *honnêtes gens du monde* were walking ever on slippery paths. They did well, then, to seek discipline in methods of prayer—wherein Baxter admitted the papists were greatly superior—and in continual guidance from confessors skilled in casuistry. To be just to 'la religion belle, aimable et auguste' of Fénelon's educational treatises, to the whole tradition of devotion which angry Jansenists termed Molinist, one must remember that it presupposed an austere background of guidance and penitence. This tradition, the conventional piety of high society, stemmed from St François de Sales, whose *Introduction* (for readers who stopped short of his *Traité de l'amour de Dieu*) provided a picture of the *honnête homme* frankly accepting the honours of the world, as an adventurer from Peru,

[1] *The Autobiography of Richard Baxter* (ed. J. M. Ll. Thomas, 1931), p. 5; *Breviate of the Life of Margaret...wife of Richard Baxter* (1681). Cf. M. Bottrall, *Every Man a Phoenix: Studies in 17th century Autobiography* (1958).

[2] *Ductor Dubitantium* (1660), Preface, quoted F. R. Bolton, *The Caroline Tradition of the Church of Ireland* (1958), p. 132.

laden with silver, might add curious monkeys and parrots to his cargo.[1] This concept of Christian urbanity, however, was losing its religious value, even as a staging-point to true devotion. Versailles was a morally destructive place, all the more when Louis XIV changed to piety. In 1688 La Bruyère noted the transformation of the typical courtier: 'Il est dévot: tout se règle par la mode.' But apart from the debasement of values at Versailles, the stereotype of the Christian *honnête homme* was doomed when the essential presupposition of his Christianity, the austerity of the confessional, became suspect. Pascal had dealt the casuists, bad and good, a paralysing blow; he had created the atmosphere of lingering suspicion in which Rome (in 1679) and the Assembly of the Clergy of France (in 1700) condemned laxist propositions, and in which Tirso González, General of the Jesuits, fought and defeated the supporters of 'Probabilism'[2] within his own Society in the 1690s. Whether Christianity was rescued from a compromise with worldliness, or deprived of the machinery for providing moral direction in the face of new social conditions, or whether both these conclusions are valid, is matter for argument; but it is important to notice that it was in this context, and against this background of panic concerning a threat to moral standards, that Fénelon clashed with Bossuet over the nature of Christian devotion. In the very year of La Bruyère's cynical description of the courtier *dévot*, Fénelon met the mystic Madame Guyon; and in 1694, when González's book against Probabilism was infuriating his fellow Jesuits, the theologians' 'Conference' at Issy (near Paris) began, in an attempt to find a formula to reconcile the friends and opponents of Madame Guyon's Quietism.

Although in March 1695 Fénelon acceded to the Articles which the theologians of Issy—Bossuet, Noailles bishop of Châlons, and Tronson the Superior of Saint-Sulpice—had drawn up, their agreement was from the start founded upon ambiguities. Yet if some further disagreement was inevitable, the relentless battle which ensued—publications and counterblasts, the appeal to the judgment of Rome in 1697, and the intrigues leading to the condemnation of propositions in Fénelon's *Maximes des Saints* (1699)—calls for explanation. There was a clash of two dramatically opposed temperaments, the one four-square and bourgeois, the other sensitive and aristocratic; there was an underlying and obscure struggle for power over the mind of the ageing and superstitious king, in which the forces were aligned by the fears, hopes and insincerities of Madame de

---

[1] J. A. Calvet, *La Littérature religieuse, de François de Sales à Fénelon* (1956), pp. 14 f., 50 ff.

[2] The rule in moral theology by which a solidly established 'probable opinion' may be followed, even though the opposing opinion be 'more probable'. As against this doctrine, predominant among the Jesuits, the Dominicans in the seventeenth century developed the contrary view, 'Probabiliorism'. González published his *Fundamentum Theologiae Moralis* (1694) in support of the more rigorous Probabiliorism. 'Laxism', condemned by Rome in 1665 and 1679, may be described as a perversion of Probabilism. See F. L. Cross (ed.), *The Oxford Dictionary of the Christian Church* (1957), pp. 791–2, 1108–9.

Maintenon;[1] there were misunderstandings, like the premature publication of the *Maximes*, that made Bossuet suspicious and exasperated. Yet the bitterness of it all can only be understood if the issues at stake are referred to the deepest religious aspirations of the two warring prelates. Theologically, the essence of their dispute lay in the question whether, when a soul surrenders to God in an act of pure love, it can consciously exclude all hope of its own eternal happiness. To Bossuet—slenderly versed in the language of mysticism, proclaiming a religion for everyday use, unsympathetic to a spirituality apparently moulded for an aristocratic coterie—Quietism threatened Christian morality. Thirty years before, he had begun his great career by courageous denunciation of court wickedness; now, more than ever, morals were in danger. At the time of the Conference of Issy, he was excoriating the stage and committing to his private manuscripts terrible reflections banishing poetry, even laughter, from the Christian life. If Fénelon's qualifications and reinterpretations are ignored, the doctrines of the single act of love, of the acceptance of sin as a source of humiliation, of the willingness to abandon hope of salvation, could be made to appear mere refinements of the perfumed spirituality which had made Miguel de Molinos the fashionable confessor of Italian society. Madame Guyon, Fénelon's inspiration, was accused of immorality, though on flimsy evidence. To a prelate accustomed to rule and in combat with tangible evils, this strange woman, with her realism and her hallucinations, her meek obstinacy and her humble self-righteousness, was a pious nuisance, a purveyor of esoteric consolations in place of the straightforward rules of Christian duty.

And yet Madame Guyon gave Fénelon the inspired formula which brought coherence to all his strivings, new depth and originality to his work as a spiritual director of the great; the beginning of her influence coincides with his appointment as tutor to the duke of Burgundy.[2] How could one direct the consciences of great nobles and form the soul of a royal pupil amid the hypocrisies of Versailles? And this at a time when the ideal of the *honnête homme* and the casuistry which was its underlying prerequisite were falling into discredit? Perhaps the answer was very simple. Fénelon was greatly moved by Madame Guyon's warning to cast down the 'interior statue'—that mental picture of the self towards which the Stoic continually casts sidelong glances—and to embark on the mysterious current of grace. By self-abandonment, his pantheistic yearning for absorption into the divine might be sublimated into a form compatible with Christian theology; the dark fear that Omnipotence must be responsible for evil was exorcized if he could adore the inscrutable will that allows men to sin for their humiliation; and here, too, the periods of spiritual dryness

---

[1] The essential authority is L. Cognet, *Crépuscule des mystiques: le conflit Fénelon-Bossuet* (Tournai, 1958).

[2] See below, p. 327.

which made a mockery of the proofs from interior certainty could also be accepted, patiently, as divine visitations. Above all, Fénelon was haunted by the shade of La Rochefoucauld, by the knowledge that *amour propre* enters into all human actions, even the highest. In this he was at one with Jansenists and Calvinists, his doctrine of abandonment filling the same psychological need as did theirs of election. The complexities of Versailles, of salvation itself, were to be annihilated in a love towards God of child-like simplicity. In this deceptively naïve method, which Fénelon defended with arguments of labyrinthine subtlety but which Bossuet feared was undermining morality, the intellectual and ethical aspects of 'la crise de la conscience européenne' were brought to a focus. The victory of Bossuet—though, indeed, the Roman condemnation of Fénelon (March 1699) was of the lightest possible kind—meant, like so many of Bossuet's victories, something resembling a defeat for Catholicism. The only gainers, it was said, were the pope, who had enlarged his authority by judging the case, and the unbelievers, who could rejoice to see the doctrine of pure love being the occasion for so much uncharitableness. Certainly, there is something oblique about Fénelon's feline deftness at keeping himself in the right and his masterly use of the 'coquetry of humility'. Worse still is the spectacle of Bossuet with his insinuations and unpardonable use of confidential documents—the Eagle of Meaux feeding scraps of gossip to that carrion-bird[1] his nephew, his agent at Rome. In its intellectual implications, too, the dispute was a misfortune for religion. With Fénelon, the attitudes to life implied by 'individualism' and 'sentiment' were being incorporated into Catholic devotion and patterns of behaviour. Left undisturbed, he might have done the work of a St François de Sales in linking the way of the mystics with the devotional practices of ordinary people; he might have grafted *sensibilité* on to the Christian moral stereotype in place of the withered *honnêteté*. Bossuet prevented this. *Sensibilité* appears again in the course of the eighteenth century, in lay dress and serving ends which would have been anathema to the archbishop of Cambrai, whose intuition had detected its emotive power half a century before Rousseau.

Quietism was not limited to one religious community or social milieu. The mental attitude which seemed to Fénelon to provide a remedy, by sheer contrast, for a world of gilded sophistication and moral compromise, in other circles won its way by simple affinity. In her later years Madame Guyon received pilgrims from Scotland, who had come to Quietist beliefs with great sincerity, under inspirations even more eccentric than her own. In Germany, Fénelon's doctrines met with some favourable notice in Pietistic circles. But the only considerable body in Protestant Europe to be deeply affected was the Friends, whose inspiration came from within their own community. In his *Apology* for 'the People called in

---

[1] In Ronald Knox's striking metaphor: *Enthusiasm* (Oxford, 1950), p. 346.

Scorn Quakers', Robert Barclay tried to align Fox's elementary theology with orthodoxy by introducing the concept of original sin, arguing that man's corruption was such that he was unable, of his own volition, to stir up the gift of the inner light which Christ had conferred: thus worship was essentially a passive waiting upon the divine intervention. This view was for a time accepted in the assemblies of the Friends and did something towards weakening their unconventional prophetic fervour.[1]

The diffusion of Quietism in Protestant circles was limited by the existence of a more compelling alternative. In the endless debate between Faith and Works, moderate men had always agreed that both were necessary: the dispute was about emphasis. Granting this, Quietism was on the side of Faith, and at the end of the century Protestantism was determined to rehabilitate Works. Reason and right conduct were to be, if not the heart of religion, at least its pillars of support, its most obvious evidence. Pietism satisfied this need, as well as possessing those qualities of simplicity, individualism and emotionalism which gave Quietism its charm. Though the movement had forerunners here and there in Dutch and German Calvinism, and in the little sect of followers of Jean de Labadie in the Palatinate, its central tradition arose in Germany as a reaction against the aridity of official Lutheranism, while owing a good deal to the tradition of hymnology which went back to Luther himself, and to Catholic mystical poets like the Jesuit Friedrich von Spee. The *Pia Desideria* (1675) of P. J. Spener (1635–1705) became its basic document, the new Prussian university of Halle its intellectual centre. Under the name of 'tokens of pure faith', Spener rescued Works from belittlement; together with prayer they became signs of a 'saving light' within us, in which all Christians, whatever their dogmatic differences, can share. A. H. Francke (1663–1727), Spener's disciple and first professor of Greek at Halle, led the way in drawing practical inferences; he founded a Bible Society, encouraged schools and orphanages, initiated foreign missions. Essentially a doctrine of personal regeneration, Pietism did not intervene directly in the great intellectual debates of the age, but its very presuppositions were themselves an important contribution to the cause of 'reasonable' religion. Spener was tolerant. Baptism, faith and good works united all Christians in the one invisible community which was the only true Church: human authority, whether of the pope or of Luther, bound no one if its orders could not be substantiated 'from the clear word of God': doctrine is always at root the same, yet continually developing under pressure of new situations. Tolerant, universalist, rejecting human authority, Pietism embodied ideas which, in laicized form, were to triumph in the *Aufklärung*; emotional and individualistic, it also embodied forces that were to react against the Enlightenment. Its powerful emphasis on

---

[1] A. Lloyd, *Quaker Social History, 1669–1738* (1950), pp. 123 ff. Cf. G. D. Henderson, 'Un Mouvement Quiétiste en Ecosse', *Revue de littérature comparée*, vol. XXVII (1953), pp. 263–73.

individual conversion was to be transmitted to Wesley, at a time when in Germany itself the movement was beginning to disintegrate into the narrow enthusiasm of private coteries. This complicated destiny is a measure of the lucid spirituality and insight that enabled Spener to provide simultaneous satisfaction to so many of the deepest urges of his religious contemporaries.

Pietism was sincerely concerned with the workaday world and the lives of ordinary folk. The 'Histories of the Reborn' and the 'Biographies of Holy Souls', its standard sources of edification, included the spiritual experiences of peasants and maidservants. Francke insisted on the education of the children of the poor with some success, especially in Prussia, where it must be admitted that Frederick William I was aware of the military utility of literacy as of the religious value of the *Volksschule*. This Christian concern to advance educational opportunity to a wider section of the population was evident also in other European countries. England had her Charity School movement; in France J.-B. de la Salle (d. 1719) founded the *Frères des Ecoles Chrétiennes* to teach mathematics, navigation, surveying, book-keeping and manual arts to the children of poor and lower middle-class families. But if Pietism emphasized education, there were other problems of immense potential significance about which it had little to say, partly because it had no institutional frame and no corporate responsibility, partly because the circumstances of German life presented no new challenge. It was in a Britain of political upheaval, of rapid social and economic change, that religious thinkers were attempting to answer essentially 'modern' questions.

In a self-styled Christian country, what is the State's proper rôle in maintaining moral standards? Tuscany, under the bigoted Cosimo III, and Geneva, where the *Chambre de la Réforme* still enforced sumptuary laws, were anachronistic survivals. In theory, coercive powers of moral discipline abounded in England, where the existing laws could deal with blasphemy, bawdy-houses, swearing and profanation of the Lord's Day, and where the Church courts (with powers of excommunication) had been reinstated at the Restoration. But these rusty instruments, all still in occasional use, seemed to make little difference, except one day out of seven. 'This is, I suppose,' said a foreigner in 1710, after a gloomy Sunday in London, 'the only point in which one sees the English profess to be Christians.'[1] The collective consciousness of Englishmen registered the fact that vice was rampant just at the epoch of the Glorious Revolution, when the reaction against the rule of the saints had run its course and the popish menace smacked of a divine visitation; it was also a time when the licentiousness of the stage provided an obvious public challenge. Since the congregational control which the Friends still exercised over marriage, trading, dress and amusements (extending even to the prohibition of golf

[1] D. W. R. Bahlman, *The Moral Revolution of 1688* (Yale, 1957), p. 61.

at Aberdeen) was out of fashion, it was inevitable that suggestions for the more efficient use of the police power of the State in moral questions should be made. With encouragement from royal exhortations, various societies were formed—some of them private meetings for edification, like the Oxford gathering to which the Wesleys belonged; others, the 'Societies for the Reformation of Manners', avowedly repressive, using informers to set the antiquated machinery of the law in operation. High Churchmen like Archbishop Sharp disapproved of this substitution of delation for true ecclesiastical discipline, and Dr Sacheverell owed some of his popularity to his defence of the rights of drinking Englishmen against these 'troublesome wasps'. But the Societies for Reformation of Manners represent merely the less attractive side of a movement of religious co-operation, reform and lay endeavour which had a great future. Besides the Charity School movement, which Addison described as 'the glory of the age we live in',[1] the period saw the foundation of the S.P.C.K. and its offspring the S.P.G. by Thomas Bray, in 1698 and 1701. A beginning had been made within Protestantism towards the erection, alongside the clerical hierarchy, of great religious corporations for education, missionary work and propaganda which were to fulfil something of the rôle of the religious orders in Catholicism. These developments were taking place to meet a new situation, in an age which was reading with shocked fascination Bernard de Mandeville's doctrine that the love of luxury is the root of all progress. The idea that the State should suppress vice, solely because it was vice, was dying.

The other great issue for English religious thinkers was the relevance of Christian principles to the expanding economic world. They shared with all their contemporaries the assumption that society was necessarily hierarchical. Dives, said Tillotson, was damned for refusing to succour Lazarus, not for his sumptuous table and rich apparel, for 'this of itself, if it be according to a man's estate and quality, and without intemperance ...is a commendable virtue'.[2] It was accepted, also, that the man of affairs moved in a world of buying and selling which imposed its own necessities, in which lending at interest was normal practice and precautions had to be taken against rivals; the excommunication of Richard Haines by a Baptist church for 'covetously' taking out a patent for an invention was an anachronistic incident. There was a duty to prosper in the place of one's vocation. 'The tradesman's care and business', according to a popular religious handbook, 'is to serve God in his calling and to drive it as far as it will go.'[3] But what Christian writers gave the world with one hand they took away with the other, for they held that those callings must be chosen as tend most to the salvation of the soul and the

---

[1] M. G. Jones, *The Charity School Movement* (Cambridge, 1938), p. 59.
[2] Quoted R. B. Schlatter, *The Social Ideas of Religious Leaders, 1660–88* (1940), pp. 121–2.
[3] Rev. Richard Steele, *The Tradesman's Calling* (1684).

public good. While admitting that a man did well to live up to his station, they insisted he was no more than the steward of his riches. As Baxter wrote in 1691, in condemnation of the worldly: 'The atheistical misconceit of their property hardeneth them. They thinke they may please themselves with their owne as they list. As if they knew not there is no absolute propriety but God's.'[1] Thus wealth brought obligations, of charity to all in need, of personal interest in the lives of employees. From this concept of privilege balanced by obligation, books like Baxter's *Christian Directory* and Steele's *Tradesman's Calling* built up a detailed casuistry, for one class of society, such as English divines had never developed for the Christian life as a whole: the casuistry of commerce. On supply and demand, the 'just price', the buyer's 'fantasy', necessity and 'unskilfulness', on window-dressing and the limits of usury, Baxter and Steele were intelligent, realistic, high-minded. But the path they trod was narrow, with the sloughs of worldly compromise, of a religion that brings in customers, lying close on either hand. When Defoe dramatized the casuistry of domesticity and commerce, the product was coarser as well as lacking in the genius which he brought to his other venture in laicization, the transformation of the Puritan autobiography.[2]

Yet one cannot pretend that the answers to the problems arising from the relationship of religion to life were straightforward, nor refuse sympathy to those who, like Defoe and Jesuit probabilists, operated too near the margin. Fénelon failed at Versailles, and it is unlikely that Baxter was closely followed by London tradesmen. Ordinary Christians pay lip-service to the saints and find guidance a little lower down the hierarchy, creating that series of compromises, necessary or unjustifiable, which we study as the history of religion and of the relations between Church and State. Caught in the toils himself, Swift surveyed the sum total of the compromises of his own age with masochistic irony. He was, he said, defending 'nominal' Christianity, not '*real* Christianity, such as used, in primitive Times (if we may believe the Authors of those Ages) to have an Influence upon Men's Belief and Actions', and which has now, for some time, been 'wholly laid aside by General Consent, as utterly inconsistent with our present Schemes of Wealth and Power'.[3]

---

[1] 'The Poor Husbandman's Advocate', ed. F. J. Powicke, *Bulletin of the John Rylands Library*, vol. x (1926), p. 194.

[2] Cf. above, p. 91. Defoe regarded vice as unreasonable rather than sinful: R. G. Stamm, 'Daniel Defoe: an Artist in the Puritan Tradition', *Philological Quarterly*, xv (1936), 229–32.

[3] *An Argument to prove, that the Abolishing of Christianity...*, in *Prose Writings*, ed. Davis, vol. II, pp. 27–8.

CHAPTER V

INTERNATIONAL RELATIONS IN EUROPE

MOST of the changes in the political structure of Europe between 1688 and 1721 arose in connection with five great wars: the Nine Years War, the War of the Spanish Succession, the Turkish wars of 1683–99 and 1714–18, and the Great Northern War. That these wars never merged into one European conflict suggests a tripartite division of Europe into west, north and south-east. Of course there were no hard and fast partitions between these regions. A number of States belonged to two or more: for example, Hanover and Brandenburg to both west and north, the Habsburg monarchy and Venice to west and south-east, Russia and Poland to the north and south-east. Nor was it uncommon for countries of one region to get involved in the affairs of another—almost always to redress the balance of forces in it or prevent innovations deemed harmful: as examples we can cite William III's rôle in the Altona settlement of 1689, Charles XII's in the Empire in 1706–7, the Habsburg intervention in the Turco-Venetian war in 1716. Yet attempts to call in the forces of another region in order positively to upset the existing order elsewhere, or to break a military deadlock nearer home, usually miscarried. The decline of French influence in Sweden and Brandenburg, Poland and Turkey, amounting to a breakdown of the classical 'eastern barrier' in the 1680s, indeed tended to sharpen the tripartite division of Europe. In the Nine Years War Louis XIV was no longer able to summon his northern allies to fight on his side, while William III was not strong enough to secure more than a few auxiliary troops from them. In 1700 William, more or less supported by Louis, was able to impose a *status quo* settlement between Sweden and Denmark; but all their combined efforts were of no avail when it came to inducing the Northern Crowns to guarantee the Second Spanish Partition Treaty in that year. During the Succession War, the French were usually interested in bringing the Northern War as far west into the Empire as possible: conversely, their enemies mostly strove to keep the wars well separated, thereby accentuating the existing division of Europe. In this they succeeded, at least down to 1710, although it is only fair to mention that the peculiar bent of Charles XII's mind came to their aid at a decisive moment in 1706–7.[1] We can trace a parallel development with regard to Turkey. Allied diplomacy helped to keep the Turks out of the Succession War, when Louis had to content himself with aiding Rákóczi's followers against the emperor in Hungary. Whatever be true for 1688–1714, however, a tripartite division of Europe afterwards would

---

[1] Below, pp. 662–3.

be hard to postulate. The European capitals, including even Constantinople, then came to form a single indivisible political structure. The end of French preponderance, the consolidation of the Habsburg monarchy in central Europe, together with the emergence of Britain and Russia, led to a more even distribution of power—or of weakness—on the Continent. Instead of one preponderant power, there were now five of the first rank: Great Britain, France, Spain, the Habsburg monarchy, Russia. Savoy and Prussia were rising. A slow decline had settled on the Dutch Republic; it was more marked in Venice, quite precipitous in the case of Sweden.

By 1700, most States had built up more or less efficient administrations at the centre, but about 1714–15, and for some years thereafter, many were afflicted with the same malady: in Great Britain, France, Spain, the Habsburg State, Russia, Sweden, Tuscany and Parma, the succession to the throne was either disputed or uncertain, to say nothing of the chronic problems of papal and Polish succession. The resulting dynastic weakness of the chief States was not conducive to a bid for political hegemony by any one of them. It is true that on the seas Great Britain now reigned supreme. Between 1688 and 1713, moreover, she had taken part in two great land wars almost from start to finish, on a scale not seen since the Hundred Years War. This was indeed a novel experience for Britain and the continental powers alike, but the significance of this new element in European politics was not immediately apparent to all the elder statesmen; it took Louis XIV about twenty years to realize that it was more than a passing phenomenon. The Regent Orléans and Abbé Dubois suffered no illusions on this score. By their time it was clear that Britain was to stay in Europe, and not only because of the Hanoverian predilections of George I. Nevertheless, it is misleading to say that the Peace of Utrecht ushered in an age of British 'preponderance' in the sense of Spanish or French preponderance earlier, based as these had been mainly on a superiority of continental land forces. Britain's pre-eminence was ultimately maritime in nature and could not be exerted effectively on the Continent without allies; her most effective diplomatic weapon was the freedom of action in distant lands that command of the sea affords. Without conscious design, however, this helped to combine all Europe into one political system.

The new order was founded on the balance of power between the leading States. This was no accident. The avowed purpose of the Utrecht settlement was 'to confirm the peace and tranquillity of the Christian world through a just equilibrium of power (which is the best and most secure foundation of mutual friendship and lasting agreement in every quarter)'.[1] The peace instruments were replete with variations on this theme. A kind of 'equality' and 'political equilibrium' between the powers

---

[1] Anglo-Spanish treaty of 18 July 1713, in Dumont, *Corps universel du droit des gens*, vol. VIII, pt. i, p. 394. Cf. below, ch. XIV.

was to be 'the foundation of public safety'.[1] Within a few years 'the balance of Europe' became a hackneyed diplomatic phrase, invoked to explain and justify many different arrangements, ranging from adjustments in the Dutch Barrier to the Pragmatic Sanction in the Habsburg lands. We need not scrutinize the sincerity of every profession of faith in it, but it is significant that the phrase quickly acquired the character of an incantation with which to conjure up consent, or at least weaken the mental resistance of opponents: in later times a similar prestige was reserved, in turn, for 'legitimacy' and 'national self-determination'. Such usage implies wide acceptance of a principle among the people who mattered politically. To what extent it was furthered by the imagery of Newtonian mechanics among the educated is a question beyond the scope of this chapter; but the early eighteenth century certainly tended to calculate the balance of power in precise mathematical terms, for which the new science of 'political arithmetick' already supplied a warrant.

The idea did not spring from a brainstorm at Utrecht. It already had a long history. But hitherto it had seldom been applied to more than a relatively small area like Italy. As to its immediate antecedents and the manner in which it was propounded and accepted, it seems certain that this latest version had not originated at Versailles. To Louis XIV 'equality of power' between States appeared almost as preposterous as equality of honour between them. On occasion, certainly, Louis was ready to admit a kind of condominium. In 1698–1700, to preserve peace by the Spanish Partition Treaties, he sought a close association with William III: if William were in agreement with him, they 'could together lay down the law to the rest of the world'.[2] In 1715 Louis apparently again entertained the idea of a condominium, this time with the emperor, to resist the Maritime Powers who were encroaching on 'the true gods of the earth'.[3] It is also true that he understood that a fusion of the French and Spanish monarchies (which he probably never seriously contemplated), or of the Austrian and Spanish monarchies, would occasion much 'jealousy' and lead to war. But all this does not add up to an acceptance of the balance of power principle. Some support for it could be found in the writings of Fénelon; but the court of Versailles did not embrace it wholeheartedly until after Louis died. More surprisingly, one searches in vain for any clear statement of the principle in William III's correspondence with his political confidants—Heinsius, Portland, Waldeck. William thought mainly in terms of 'the liberty of Europe', endangered by the overweening ambition of Louis XIV, whose victory would have brought on 'the slavery of all

[1] See the renunciations of Philip V, Orléans, and Berry in H. Vast, *Les Grands traités du règne de Louis XIV*, vol. III (1899), pp. 50–4, 68–159.
[2] Portland to William, 26 March 1698, N. Japikse, *Correspondentie van Willem III en...Bentinck* (The Hague, 5 vols. 1927–37), vol. I, pt. I, pp. 266–8. Cf. below, ch. XII.
[3] See the dispatch of Mandat quoted by E. Lainé, 'Une Tentative de Renversement des Alliances sous Louis XIV', *Revue des études historiques*, vol. CLXVII (1933), p. 183.

Europe'. William strove above all to preserve the independence of numerous European states, large and small, and to safeguard certain old institutions: only in such a Europe could the Protestant religion be safe. Like Louis, he often used the term 'balance' in discussing various 'equivalents' in exchanges of territory; later, the general principle of balance did involve 'equivalents', but these two concepts should be distinguished. Thus the Partition Treaties, though based on the notion of 'equivalents', did not invoke the general balance of Europe, some of whose proponents, like Charles Davenant, could claim that these treaties were the greatest crime against that principle. The Treaty of the Grand Alliance of 1701, inspired by William, contained no mention of any 'balance', but spoke of the danger that France and Spain would arrogate to themselves 'the empire over all Europe' in order 'to oppress the liberty of Europe'; similarly, the Dutch declaration of war in 1702 merely raised the spectre of Louis XIV's 'universal monarchy'.[1] William's English subjects, however, sounded a new note. In December 1697 the Commons thanked him for having restored to England 'the honour. . .of holding the Balance of Europe'.[2] Queen Anne's declaration of war on 4/15 May 1702 explained that William had concluded the Grand Alliance 'in order to preserve the liberty and the balance of Europe and to curtail the exorbitant power of France'.[3] Already English political writers, notably Defoe and Davenant, had often employed the term. By 1713, Anne's government claimed for itself a constant adherence to 'the same principle . . . [which is] to preserve the equilibrium in Europe'.[4] On the Continent, nearly all the early official references to the 'balance of Europe' gave credit to Anne as its sponsor. Thus it is not unreasonable to regard the spread of this concept in the early eighteenth century as an English victory, and to connect it with the general vogue for English ideas then beginning. It is only fair to add that it hardly ever included any notion of the balance of naval power.

In practice, the application of the balance principle meant that the French and Spanish monarchies were to be kept for ever separate. Further, the House of Austria, excluded from Spain, was to rest content with acquiring most of the Spanish lands in Italy and the southern Netherlands: while these would constitute a general barrier against any revival of French expansionism, they would also ensure the continued presence of the Habsburgs in western Europe. The Dutch, in turn, were to be secure behind their own Barrier in the Austrian Netherlands.

It looked at one time as though the spread of Russian influence in the Baltic and Germany might seriously upset the northern balance. But Peter pursued a strictly limited objective in the Northern War: he wanted

[1] Dumont, vol. VIII, pt. I, pp. 90, 112.   [2] Cobbett, *Parl. Hist.* vol. v, col. 1667.
[3] Dumont, vol. VIII, pt. I, p. 115.
[4] G. de Lamberty, *Mémoires pour servir à l'histoire du XVIIIᵉ siècle* (The Hague, 14 vols. 1724–34), vol. VIII, p. 29.

a stretch of the Baltic shore sufficient for secure communications between his country and western Europe. North Germany was for him a theatre of military operations, never of territorial expansion. Thus, when different coalitions were formed to check him in Germany, he could easily afford to limit his activity there in favour of Frederick William of Brandenburg-Prussia. Russia displaced Sweden as the chief northern power, but her ascendancy was never absolute and did not even equal the earlier Swedish predominance. Moreover, Peter himself believed in the balance of power for both western and northern Europe; this eventually facilitated an understanding between the Maritime Powers and Russia. While the Northern War was yet in progress, he contemplated a Russo-Swedish alliance; he wished to avoid laying Sweden too low for the same reason as induced him to champion the House of Holstein-Gottorp—fear of strengthening Denmark unduly. Thus Russia's emergence complicated, but did not destroy, the northern balance. With the Maritime Powers intent on maintaining it, it was quite secure.[1]

In south-eastern Europe, the upheavals accompanying the Turkish wars of 1683–1718 tended to obscure the operation of the balance. The last Ottoman onslaught on Christendom caused Russia and Poland to lay aside old hostility and join the Holy League of 1684 with the emperor and Venice. The Christian coalition, however, did not survive its victorious peace at Carlowitz in 1699. For Turkey, the most dangerous consequences of defeat were the Venetian occupation of the Morea, Russia's approach to the Black Sea, and the extension of Russian influence in Poland during the Northern War. But in 1711–13 the Turks pushed back the Russian threat and in 1715 reconquered the Morea. When laid low by the Austrians at Passarowitz (1718) and threatened by an extension of Habsburg influence in Poland, Russia (aided by France) came temporarily to sustain them; and in 1739, even when Vienna and St Petersburg co-operated, the Turks were able to reclaim their Passarowitz losses. These developments[2] suggest that local jealousies played a large part in maintaining a balance in the south-east. Venice and to a lesser extent Poland, Hungary and the Balkan Slavs had to foot the bill for this balance. In 1689–99 and 1718, the Maritime Powers mediated between the Habsburgs and Turkey, and in 1710–13 they worked for peace between Turkey and Russia; their main purpose was to make Habsburg or Russian forces available in the west or north. The French traditionally backed both Turkey and Venice—to direct Ottoman energies against the Habsburgs, to bolster Venice as a

[1] See below, pp. 675 ff. The northern powers, for their part, liked to see a balance of naval and commercial power between the countries of the west, so as to avoid falling into too close a dependence on any one of them. In this respect the threat of Louis XIV's preponderance loomed smaller than on land. Sweden and Denmark agreed they would lose much of their freedom of action if the English and Dutch joined forces and the French navy declined. Peter seems latterly to have shared this attitude.

[2] See below, ch. XIX, and vol. VII, pp. 407–8.

counterweight to them in Italy. These interventions by the western powers do not reveal any conscious preoccupation with the south-eastern balance; nevertheless, their effect was favourable to it.

It was in Italy that the new system needed most to be shored up, for there it was endangered by the local preponderance acquired after 1707 by the House of Austria. Appropriately enough, the greatest benefits accrued to the House of Savoy, long tried in the art of double-dealing with Bourbon and Habsburg, and in 1713 made heir presumptive to the Spanish Bourbons and officially recognized as the pivot of the balance ensuring 'equality' and 'equilibrium' between France, Spain, and Austria. To support Savoy in her new rôle, the peacemakers gave her Sicily (exchanged in 1720 for Sardinia) and recognition of the royal title of her sovereign. She also received most of Montferrat, and the French conquests in Nice and Savoy were restored to her, though she lost the Barcelonette valley to France. Henceforth a long stretch of her frontier with France was to follow the main crest of the mountains. These territorial adjustments favoured the Italian future of Savoy and discouraged her aspirations to carve out a kingdom in southern France.

The increased importance of Savoy reflected a larger trend which had set in in the 1680s—a shift of the main game between the Bourbons and the House of Austria from north to south, from Germany to Italy. One explanation lies in the problem of the Spanish monarchy, the chief preoccupation in Louis XIV's foreign policy after 1685. Over a period of years, neither Louis nor the emperor followed a consistently intransigent line with regard to Spain: at one time or another each sacrificed principle to expediency. Nor yet were they interested in all the Spanish lands in equal measure. This becomes apparent when we consider Louis's various partition schemes in the 1690s, his reversion to the partition programme when fortune had abandoned him in the Succession War, and the Italian preoccupation of the court of Vienna.

No matter what line Louis followed, he knew that the dauphin and the duke of Anjou would stand a better chance of acceptance in Spain if Franco-Spanish differences were laid aside. The task of wooing Spain was long and arduous, for (as Louis had previously remarked) the two monarchies were so constituted that reciprocal hostility was natural, indeed 'essential', to them. Yet Louis came to believe that a lasting settlement, as a prelude to alliance, could be reached if Spain would cede her Netherlands to France in exchange for Roussillon: 'such an accommodation would be the most important service that any of my subjects could ever render me'.[1] To make the scheme more attractive he was ready to abandon his traditional ally, Portugal, and even to subsidize a Spanish

[1] To Rébenac, 11 Jan. 1689, A. Legrelle, *La Mission de M. de Rébenac à Madrid* (1894), pp. 61–4; cf. *ibid.* pp. 51–2.

war against Portugal. A distinguished diplomat, Feuquière, went to Madrid in 1685 to prepare the ground for recognition of the dauphin's claim; after his death in 1688 he was succeeded by his even more skilful son, Rébenac. In support of this diplomacy, the bulk of the French navy was in the Mediterranean in 1688—a fact of moment for the course of events in England and the Dutch Republic. Of all the powers arrayed against him in the Nine Years War, Louis wanted to fight Spain least. He had made every effort to negotiate a treaty of neutrality with her, even if limited to only part of her territory. Only after all these manoeuvres had failed, and the Viennese influence had begun to prevail at Madrid after the death of Queen Marie Louise of Orléans, did he declare war on Spain. But even the outbreak of war did not deter him from seeking local suspensions of hostilities with Spain in both Italy and the western Pyrenees.

Italy, if only for geographical and strategic reasons, was bound to count in any Habsburg–Bourbon contest; but not until the Nine Years War did Louis evolve a comprehensive, consistent Italian policy. In 1691 two experienced diplomats, Baron d'Asfeld and Rébenac, were sent to Germany and Italy respectively, with roving commissions to obstruct Allied progress. The German mission yielded meagre results, but in Italy Rébenac's work eventually enabled Louis to break up the anti-French coalition. Nearly all the Italian states, except possibly Savoy, had reason to fear that hostilities on the peninsula might endanger their independence. The contingent of Imperial troops there, inadequate for a major operation against France, sufficed to alarm the Italians. By playing adroitly on their fears Louis could build up a group of benevolent neutrals, provided he himself forswore open aggression in Italy. In 1692 Rébenac negotiated treaties with Parma, Modena, Mantua and Tuscany; these duchies undertook to allow free passage to French troops and were promised French aid in the event of invasion by the emperor or his allies. Venice and the pope, who stood to lose most from an increase of Habsburg power in Italy, looked on with approval. To reap the full benefit, it remained for Louis to win the duke of Savoy. Victor Amadeus was pursuing well-defined and limited objectives in the Nine Years War: to reconquer lands overrun by the French, drive them out of Casale, and get Pinerolo—a long tongue of land pointing straight at Turin.[1] Louis could satisfy these aspirations at a moment of his own choosing, and this is precisely what he did when his other peace-feelers failed; the Treaty of Turin of 29 June 1696 exploded the anti-French coalition.

As Louis fixed his gaze on the south, his aims in the north gradually became more flexible. In 1693 he was ready to allow Max Emmanuel of Bavaria to become lord of the Spanish Netherlands; in 1685 a mere rumour of such a possibility had roused him to threaten war. After 1693, in spite of French military successes in the north-east, Louis agreed, with

[1] On the background of Franco-Savoyard relations, see vol. v, pp. 471–3.

surprising ease, to give up many of his conquests and *réunions* of the 1680s; he consented to let the Dutch have their Barrier; he gave up Luxemburg and almost abandoned Strasbourg. This new disposition helped to smooth the ground for the Peace of Ryswick in 1697.

At the end of 1697 Louis revived his threat of 1685, but this time over Milan, not the Netherlands, for there had been talk of installing the Austrian Archduke Charles as governor of the Milanese. For some years Louis had been convinced that the emperor was seeking to extend his dominion in Italy. When, in March 1698, Pomponne first broached the subject of the Spanish succession to Portland, he called his attention to the danger that if the emperor were to get Spain, 'he would then make himself master of all Italy, and [make his power] so absolute in the Empire, that we should all have to fear his excessive might'.[1] In the negotiations that led to the Partition Treaties of 1698 and 1700 there was remarkably little dispute over Spain, her Netherlands or colonies; nearly all the bargaining was over the Spanish lands in Italy. There the dauphin was to have his share of the Spanish inheritance; and even schemes for exchanging portions of it for Lorraine, or Savoy and Piedmont, called for a strong French position in Italy. In 1710, when Louis was suing for peace on almost any terms, out of the entire Spanish monarchy he sought to retain only Sicily and Sardinia for Philip V; it was not his fault that Philip would not listen. Perhaps political considerations were reinforced by sentiment: once at least he had referred to Italy as 'the fairest land on earth'.[2] But he had another reason—perhaps the most compelling—for focusing attention on Italy. Dissensions within the French Church, together with the pope's refusal to send bulls of investiture to the French bishops nominated since 1682, threatened to wreck the internal unification of his realm. Above all, the Jansenist movement (as he saw it) presented Louis with the thorniest of problems; he could not hope to settle it without the pope's aid. Papal help was also highly desirable in building up a pro-French party in Spain. Moreover, early in the Nine Years War Louis assumed the posture of the defender of the Catholic faith 'against the leagues formed by the Protestant princes for its destruction'.[3] In the circumstances, he could ill afford to pursue his quarrels with the Vatican. His threat to use armed force against Innocent XI had availed nothing against this man of integrity, and after Innocent's death (12 August 1689) he applied gentler methods in dealing with the Papacy. At the conclaves of 1689 and 1691 French cardinals helped secure the elections of Alexander VIII and Innocent XII. These two popes were willing to come to terms

[1] Portland to William III, 15 March 1698, in Japikse, *Correspondentie*, vol. I, pt. I, pp. 259–60. On the diplomacy of the Spanish succession, cf. below, ch. XII.
[2] To Amelot, 4 May 1687, A. T. de Girardot, *Correspondance de Louis XIV avec le marquis d'Amelot...1685–1688* (Nantes, 1863), p. 352.
[3] To Rébenac, 6 Dec. 1688, Legrelle, p. 54. On Louis XIV's breach with the papacy, see vol. V, pp. 135–9; for Spanish court politics, below, ch. XI.

with Louis; however, the Vatican now held all the trumps in negotiations with the French court, and the settlement reached in 1693 was a barely disguised surrender by the French king. At least Louis knew how to derive maximum advantage from his submission. Innocent XII became the foremost champion of Italian neutrality and supported French peace proposals; later, he imparted to Carlos II his opinion that the dauphin was his lawful heir; and he was no friend of the Jansenists. His successor, Clement XI, on the whole favoured the Bourbons in the Succession War, supported the Old Pretender, and was an avowed enemy of Jansenism.

Louis was of course not alone in looking southward. As early as 1689 William III spoke of sending a naval squadron to the Mediterranean, chiefly to protect Allied trade. As the Nine Years War progressed and he despaired of a favourable decision in the Netherlands, the plan of invading France through Savoy appealed to him more and more. Such an operation required an Allied fleet in the Mediterranean, which would also help to sustain Spain's half-hearted war effort, offset French diplomatic successes in Italy, overcome the vacillations of Savoy, and incite Vienna to a more vigorous prosecution of the war. William saw the war as a whole and discerned the significance of lands and waters far from the sphere of his personal command. He was thus fully armed for the negotiations leading to the Partition Treaties, in the course of which he could appreciate the value of places like Gibraltar; and the ground was prepared for later enterprises like the Portuguese alliance, operations in Catalonia, the capture of Minorca. William's political disciples, Marlborough and Heinsius, never hesitated to give their utmost support to Mediterranean ventures. It was this comprehensive vision, probably even more than their economic strength, that gave the Maritime Powers ascendancy in the counsels of the Grand Alliance. By far their most important ally was the emperor. In concluding his treaty of 1689 with the Austrian Habsburgs William had to promise to fight for a return to the settlements of West-phalia and the Pyrenees, promote the election of Archduke Joseph as King of the Romans, and back the Austrian claim to the entire Spanish succession. He consented to these terms without enthusiasm but was in no position to bargain, for he needed the emperor's support, military and diplomatic. Imperial troops became especially desirable for an invasion of France through Savoy; moreover, William counted on Leopold to restrain the Vatican when the pope began to promote the movement for Italian neutrality and other measures favourable to France. Vienna, having secured recognition of its claims by the Maritime Powers, sent 12,000 men to fight in the west and then promptly turned back to the Turks. The Peace of Carlowitz was not concluded until the emperor felt his western claims endangered by negotiations for partition of the Spanish monarchy. Then he offered military aid to Carlos II to help guard his lands in Italy. When, in 1701, it became necessary to revive the Grand Alliance, Leopold set his heart on obtaining the Italian possessions of Spain; after much wrangling, the Maritime Powers acquiesced in his claims, apparently at Marlborough's instance. In spite of successive dangers to the heart of the Habsburg lands from other directions, Leopold and his successor Joseph I (1705–11) concentrated on the war in Italy, virtually abandoning Archduke Charles to the care of the Maritime Powers when in 1703 the latter undertook to put him on the Spanish throne.

As early as 1700, Leopold had set in motion an inquiry into the historic Imperial suzerain rights in Italy, and Joseph I displayed even greater interest in them than his father. These proceedings found an echo in the curia of Clement XI. In his private life Clement was pious, austere, given to scholarly pursuits; as a public figure, he was above all an efficient administrator of the papal domain; and he dreamt of retrieving the ancient suzerain rights of the Roman Pontiff in Italy, which at that time were as musty from disuse as those of the Holy Roman Emperor.[1] These imperial and papal excursions into feudal history could not fail to alarm the Italian states—already frightened by the prospect of Bourbon supremacy— and they go far to explain the political instability in the Italian theatre of war, which was of crucial importance for the solution of the Spanish succession.

Acceptance of the testament of Carlos II severely strained French diplomacy. Before 14 November 1700 it had been geared to an exact execution of the Partition, most French envoys being instructed to act in consultation—wherever possible in concert—with their British and Dutch colleagues. After that date these ties were quickly relaxed and most of the treaties then in force, or in various stages of completion, had to be renegotiated. Henceforth French diplomacy was hampered by the prospect of Louis XIV's unmeasured success, later by the apparent imminence of his collapse. Apart from verbal assurances of continued goodwill, Louis did little to allay apprehensions of Bourbon hegemony conceived by his Italian friends and Portugal. In 1701, fear induced Savoy and Portugal to conclude treaties of alliance with France; but their value for Louis XIV was doubtful, since the emperor could relieve the pressure of fear on Savoy, and the Maritime Powers could inspire greater fears in Portugal. Soon Louis's high-handed treatment of Savoy threw Victor Amadeus into the ranks of his adversaries, at the end of 1703, and threatened the strong French military position in north Italy. Portugal presented a somewhat different problem: recent gold discoveries in Brazil made her more sensitive than ever to Allied squadrons in the Atlantic. Moreover, Louis probably realized it was impossible to extend the Portuguese frontiers in Galicia or Estremadura (as he had thought of doing in 1692) without courting rebellion in Spain. Still, he need not have waited until April 1703 with his offer of neutrality for Portugal, which was all that King Peter II had really

---

[1] Cf. below, p. 595.

wanted. As it turned out, Louis exposed his offer to the chance of a postal mix-up: it was mistakenly sent to Madrid, returned to Paris, then to Lisbon, just as the First Methuen Treaty was being completed.[1]

The Portuguese and Italian mistakes of Louis enabled the Allies to hit the Bourbons in Spain and Italy. Yet Louis could probably have forced a military decision in Italy (as apparently intended) but for Marlborough's victory at Ramillies in May 1706 and Philip V's reverses in Spain in 1705–6. By sacrificing Italy in 1707, however, Louis was able to help Philip tide over a crisis; the loyalty of Philip's Spanish subjects did the rest. Further, the removal of French pressure from Italy almost broke up the Grand Alliance. Dutch and English trading circles wanted to concentrate on the Iberian war, while Victor Amadeus was incensed by the Imperial occupation of the Milanese and Montferrat—a marquisate belonging to Louis XIV's client, the duke of Mantua, which the duke of Savoy coveted for himself. Vienna was bent on a speedy conquest of Naples, letting the rest of the war take care of itself. The particularist policy of the Habsburgs changed radically only when 'Carlos III' became Emperor Charles VI in 1711. This very transformation, however, made the rest of the Allies ask whether they were fighting to restore the monarchy of Charles V.

Meanwhile, the pope was left virtually alone to resist the triumphal Habsburg progress in Italy. Even more than his predecessors, he was sensitive to every move that strengthened their position there. Clement XI's own Italian policy, however, had vitiated his attempts to form an Italian league. In 1708, when ecclesiastical weapons had failed, he attempted armed resistance, but in the end recoiled from the prospect of German soldiers (many of them Protestant) capturing Rome as in 1527. Early in 1709 he was forced to recognize 'Carlos III', and several years later he suffered another humiliation when the peacemakers disposed of the papal fiefs of Naples, Sicily and Sardinia without reference to him. Subsequently, the Turkish renewal of war against Venice in 1714 offered an opportunity to salvage his political leadership: but Queen Elizabeth Farnese of Spain and her minister Alberoni, a priest from Parma, made use of the pope's plans to cover Spanish attacks on Sardinia and Sicily in 1717–18. This eighteenth-century version of the Fourth Crusade compromised beyond repair the political aspirations of the Papacy. Venice, most venerable of the secular Italian states, could do no more to check the Habsburgs than the pope. Only Eugene's victories in the Balkans in 1716–17 enabled the republic to escape Turkish revenge merely with the loss of the Morea. Henceforth she was at the mercy of the Habsburgs, who confronted her in Mantua and Milan, in the north, even in Dalmatia. Worse still, Charles VI began to develop the port of Trieste. Savoy, for all her gains at Utrecht, was not yet in a position to counterbalance the Habsburgs in Italy.[2]

---

[1] Below, pp. 525–6. [2] On Venice and Savoy see below, pp. 555–6, 559 ff.

The failure to establish effective balance in Italy after Utrecht, and the determination of Charles VI to vindicate his Spanish title, had far-reaching consequences. First, these factors were largely responsible for the miscarriage of Louis XIV's plans to conclude a Bourbon–Habsburg alliance in 1715: the great 'diplomatic revolution' had to wait until 1756. Second, though most of the political combinations of the Italian States to weaken the Habsburgs were quite ineffective, Italy provided excellent ground for the dynastic proclivities of Elizabeth Farnese, chief disturber of the European balance until Frederick the Great switched the lights on in Germany.

The great powers took an interest in the component parts of Germany according as the German states provided troops or possessed potential nuisance value in impeding the Habsburg war effort. In this respect both Louis XIV and William III were growing disappointed with the German princes and the Northern Crowns, who tended to overstrain their credit in bargaining for advantageous terms. In 1685 the young Torcy, travelling in Germany, wrote to his father that in the final test all the German states would range themselves willy-nilly with the emperor—a forecast on the whole borne out in the Nine Years War. On 8 July 1700 Louis wrote to Tallard that the princes should not be armed, for 'they change sides easily, and often the troops they raise are employed against those from whom they have received the means to levy them', while a memorandum of 1700 (possibly by Torcy) played down the importance of leagues which could be formed in Germany:

The forces of the Empire cannot act by themselves; in the last war they were moved to action by the banks of London and Amsterdam; the same is true of the Northern Crowns. Therefore, just as one could expect only feeble assistance from them, which would have to be dearly bought, so one need not fear them should they appear to be hostile to us.[1]

In 1697 Louis had brushed aside the pretensions of the elector of Brandenburg to a separate peace, ostensibly forgetting that the elector had been at war with him as anything but a prince of the Empire. In short, Louis was departing from the German policy of Richelieu and Mazarin, which he had followed during the first half of his reign.

For rather different reasons, William III was moving in the same direction. In 1689 he was reluctant to guarantee the existing order in the Lower Saxon Circle for fear of offending the emperor; he also opposed the admission of minor princes to full membership of the Grand Alliance so as not to complicate the future task of peace-making. In 1690 he told Heinsius that if subsidies were accorded to Denmark and Savoy, then 'all the princes of Germany would want to be treated in a like manner; and if

[1] Paris, Arch. du Min. des Affaires Etrangères, Corresp. Polit., Angleterre, t. CLXXXVI, fo. 192, and t. CLXXXIX, fo. 273. For the German background, see vol. V, chs. XVIII and XXIII.

we refuse them, they will change sides'. In the next war we can detect the same scepticism in Marlborough's complaint:

You can have noe troupes from any prince in Germanie but by paying dearly for them...You see how backward the Princes of Germany are in sending their contingent and that will alwais be soe, when thay can flatter themselves, that you must help them...for I am veryly persuaded, if you can't put an end to thes solicitations, the warr will at last be soe very chargable, that you will not bee able to goe throe itt.[1]

The general disappointment of the main western powers, however, did not cause them to renounce an active rôle in German affairs. Louis continued to pursue a twofold aim: to erect strategic barriers between the emperor and his main allies; to create maximum political embarrassment to the Grand Alliance. In pursuit of the first aim he took a special interest in Cologne, Münster and the Palatinate in the Nine Years War, and supported the neutrality of the southern Circles in the early stages of its successor. As for stirring up trouble, he was handicapped during the Nine Years War by lack of active military allies in Germany and had to be content with supporting neutral 'third parties', dissatisfied for some reason with the emperor or his allies. The emperor, aided by William, could take the sting out of such opposition by satisfying its leader with new titles and privileges. The French would then seek to organize the smaller fry. These manoeuvres forced French diplomacy to descend down the princely ladder, one rung at a time, until it reached the level of the margraves of Baden-Durlach and Brandenburg-Culmbach. The affair of the ninth electorate well illustrates this process. In 1688 Duke Ernest Augustus of Hanover was one of the most prominent princes in the French interest. In 1692 Leopold won him by the electoral dignity; in exchange, Ernest Augustus undertook to provide 6,000 troops, cast his vote for the Habsburg candidate at Imperial elections, and help erect a tenth electorate in favour of the House of Austria. Louis proceeded to incite the princes to resist such innovations. The noisiest objection came from the senior branch of the Guelph family, the dukes of Brunswick-Wolfenbüttel, but they were much less powerful than the junior (Hanoverian) branch. The opposition of Christian V of Denmark, as duke of Holstein, was more important; but he too wanted to continue to receive rent-money for troops loaned to the Allies, while William's project to send a squadron to the Baltic in 1693 also, possibly, had a moderating effect on him. The opposition to the Hanoverian electorate, lasting about ten years, made the new elector cling that much closer to the emperor, who later applied substantially the same technique in recognizing the royal title of the Hohenzollerns and supporting the Saxon candidacy to the Polish throne.

---

[1] Dijkvelt to Heinsius, 13 Sept. 1689, H. J. van der Heim, *Het archief van...Heinsius*, vol. 1 (1867), pp. 166–7; William to Heinsius, 19/29 Sept. 1690, British Museum, Add. MS. 34,504, fos. 37–8; Marlborough to Heinsius, 21 April 1703, B. van 't Hoff, *The Correspondence of...Marlborough and...Heinsius* (The Hague, 1951), pp. 61–2.

Amid the generally unsatisfactory results of Louis XIV's German policy, one major exception stood out: on the eve of the Spanish Succession War the French had managed to lure Max Emmanuel, elector of Bavaria, into their camp, and with him his brother, Joseph Clement of Cologne. Despite his adherence to the Habsburg cause in the 1680s and 1690s, Louis had never ceased to woo him, believing the interests of Vienna and Munich to be incompatible. Indeed, the Wittelsbachs were dangerous rivals to the House of Austria, whom for almost a century they had aspired to supplant as leaders of Catholic Germany and as emperors. Moreover, the centre of their power lay close to the main Habsburg lands; they had territorial ambitions in Tyrol and the Palatinate. The emperor could not satisfy Max Emmanuel's desire for a royal crown, or any of his other major pretensions, without endangering his own position; their negotiations broke down in 1702. Marlborough's victory at Blenheim, however, was an object-lesson to all the German princes of what to expect from an association with Louis XIV. When the bustle of Emperor Joseph I aroused an uproar among many of the princes, they did not turn to Louis, but to Charles XII of Sweden, as a possible deliverer from imperial high-handedness.

The policies of the great powers had a marked effect on the structure of the Empire. First, they helped raise the prestige of the emperor in Germany: at Ryswick he negotiated in the name of the princes, and in 1714 the members of the Empire merely subscribed at Baden to the conditions of the emperor's peace at Rastatt. Second, these policies, by placing the major princes of Germany in a favourable bargaining position, tended to widen the gulf between the greater and the lesser German powers, thus preparing the ground for the 'mediatization' of Germany by Napoleon. It was also during this period that German princes began to mount thrones outside the Empire in impressive numbers. At the same time the Habsburgs acquired several Italian crowns. This new development prevented German politics from becoming altogether parochial in the first half of the eighteenth century and helped to knit Germany into the European system.

Long before this period there had emerged the concept of 'Europe', side by side with the older medieval concept of 'the Christian Commonwealth'. By 1700 statesmen and publicists often used 'Christendom' and 'Europe' interchangeably to denote the community of sovereign Christian kingdoms, principalities and republics adhering to what we now call 'Western civilization'. Yet certain other considerations and distinctions were associated with these notions. European colonies overseas, which of course were part of 'Christendom', were sometimes loosely included in 'Europe'; but in the language of the treaties 'Europe' had come to mean a geographical area. Balkan Christians under Ottoman rule were generally excluded from both 'Europe' and 'Christendom'. On the other hand, Russia, the only sovereign State professing Eastern Christianity, was usually included in 'Christendom' but often excluded from 'Europe'. She gained full admittance into the European community only after the Romanovs had begun to intermarry with the princely families of Germany at the beginning of the eighteenth century: it had become an established custom that a European sovereign had to be related to other European sovereigns.

Family ties between the ruling houses became an increasingly important element in maintaining the European community, especially after religious bonds had begun to weaken. A few examples must suffice. William III was not only a nephew and son-in-law of James II but also a son of a first cousin of Louis XIV and a first cousin of Frederick I of Brandenburg-Prussia who, in turn, was a brother-in-law of George I of Britain and Hanover. Louis XIV and Leopold I were first cousins and brothers-in-law, as were Louis XIV and Carlos II, whose first wife (Marie Louise of Orléans) was a niece of Louis and a first cousin of William. Victor Amadeus II of Savoy was the son of a first cousin of Louis XIV and married to Louis's niece, herself a first cousin of William; he was also a second cousin and brother-in-law of Carlos II, father-in-law of Philip V, grandfather of Louis XV, and a first cousin of Max Emmanuel. Max Emmanuel was a second cousin and son-in-law of Leopold, son of a first cousin of Louis XIV, brother-in-law of the dauphin, and uncle of both Philip V and the Regent Orléans. Philip William of Neuburg, the elector palatine, counted among his sons-in-law Leopold I, Carlos II, and Peter II of Portugal. An elected native king, like John Sobieski of Poland, sought to enter the family of rulers by arranging suitable marriages for his children: Sobieski's son married a daughter of Elector Philip William. The pope, as a temporal sovereign, was in a somewhat delicate position in this respect: he could improve it by elevating junior members of the dynasties to the cardinalate: many a scion of the princely houses of Italy received the red hat. Republics like Venice and Genoa, and free cities like Hamburg, were also somewhat handicapped by being left out of the sovereigns' connection. In the Dutch Republic, however, this deficiency was offset by the House of Orange-Nassau. Most rebel governments, of course, laboured under a severe disadvantage.

It can be argued that dynastic ties gave rise to claims which could be settled only by resort to arms. This argument is plausible, especially if we think of the Spanish succession; but it is valid only so far as the protagonists sincerely clung to their claims as a matter of principle, as Louis and Leopold so often did. Moreover, it is misleading to speak of 'dynastic wars' in an age when princely matches were dictated primarily by reason of state. Dynastic ties certainly did not avert wars, although they did exert a certain influence on war aims. No matter what schemes a sovereign might lay to harm his relative, no matter how unceremoniously he would chase him from his lands in time of war, he hardly ever sought to compass his total ruin and the destruction of his State. It was expected that at the end of a war, the same *dramatis personae*, or their lawful heirs, some of them rather crestfallen, would still be there to make peace. The ban of the Empire imposed on the Wittelsbach brothers after Blenheim was not intended to outlast the Succession War. In 1708 the Habsburgs retained Mantua simply because Duke Charles IV, the last Gonzaga, died in 1708 without lawful issue. Even in war, the ruling houses continued to notify one another of births, marriages and deaths, and messages of congratulation and condolence went back and forth between them. No one thought it odd that in the middle of the Succession War Versailles should go into mourning for an Austrian archduchess. These marks of civility did not make the wars any less serious, but they helped to keep open the channels of communication and to re-establish normal relations as soon as hostilities ceased.

This frame of mind was reinforced by considerations of legitimacy which, as Louis XIV and Leopold I grew older, loomed larger at their respective courts. Even William III was a legitimist at heart though, being a Calvinist, he would admit of more frequent direct interventions by God to alter the course of human events than would most of the Catholic sovereigns. Legitimist sentiment was also quite strong in Queen Anne and her friends. Its precise influence on international affairs is impossible to assess. Some rulers, like Victor Amadeus or Charles XII, were less affected by it than others. Although it impeded the fomenting of rebellion abroad, temptations of expediency often proved too strong even for the most delicate legitimist scruples: necessity induced Emperor Leopold to recognize William as king of Great Britain in 1689; Louis XIV received Rákóczi at Versailles. Yet influential voices at every court denounced aid to rebels; for example, among Queen Anne's ministers, Nottingham opposed Marlborough's intentions of helping the Camisards in the Cévennes. Perhaps the most interesting case of a political step at least partly induced by legitimist sentiment was Louis XIV's recognition of the Old Pretender as James III of England in September 1701. Louis explained that he had no right to refuse James a title which was his by right of birth and cited precedents: but he went on to proclaim his determination to observe faithfully the Ryswick treaty, referred to William III as 'King of England' and disclaimed any intention of aiding James 'with troops, money, or ships'.[1] To dismiss this as sheer sophistry would be to misjudge Louis's attachment to the principle of divine right.

There was a general consensus that the states of Europe were not all equal in rank, though they might be in point of sovereignty. Republics,

[1] To Chamilly, 15 Sept. 1701: Arch. du Min. des Aff. Etr., Corresp. Polit. Danemark, t. LXVI, fos. 393–4.

besides dukes and other inferior princes, willingly conceded the superior status of the 'crowned heads', and Catholic sovereigns recognized a certain pre-eminence in the pope. Beyond this there was much quarrelling over precedence, for the contestants could neither find common ground for classifying the sovereigns nor agree on the merits of each claim. Thus the emperor would barely concede the title of 'majesty' to the king of France, while Louis sought to justify on many grounds his pretension to be at least the equal of the Holy Roman Emperor: his realm was an 'empire', his crown the oldest hereditary crown in Christendom, and above all his power within his kingdom was the most absolute. Thus in drawing up the Ryswick treaty Louis objected to the use of the same terms to describe his own and William III's relationship to their respective realms. Every State, even the lowliest barony of the Empire, quarrelled over rank. England had such contests with Spain, Portugal, Denmark and other Crowns. The Dutch Republic and Venice each claimed precedence over the other, and both clashed with the German electors. Outwardly, the hierarchy of States was reflected in the ceremonial surrounding their representatives abroad as well as in royal titles. In practice, each State established its own procedure for dealing with foreign diplomats; and the enormous tomes compiled to serve as manuals of protocol—still more the fat bundles of correspondence about it in the archives—point to a state of anarchy in this field as a whole.

Generally, ceremonial was almost as much of an impediment to effective diplomacy in the seventeenth century as publicity in the twentieth. Two States might agree on the mode of negotiating with each other, but to convene a peace congress of many powers was a formidable undertaking in itself. It was the chief task of the mediating power to set up a message-station through which the parties could communicate with one another.[1] Proceedings were so cumbersome that a congress could produce results only when it served as a screen for real negotiations, or when called on to register agreements arrived at elsewhere. Thus the groundwork for the Ryswick settlement was laid in 1694–6 in secret talks between Callières, Louis's emissary, and Dijkvelt and Boreel, who were in the confidence of William III and Heinsius. Later we encounter both Callières and Dijkvelt among the plenipotentiaries at Ryswick. There, when unexpected difficulties arose, the conference marked time while they were being ironed out in five private meetings held in the Spanish Netherlands between Portland and Boufflers.

Whenever possible, the powers preferred to treat of important matters through trusted individuals and without intermediaries. The Utrecht treaty between Anne and Louis explicitly stated that it had been concluded with-

---

[1] Only seldom would mediators get directly involved in the substance of negotiations, although at Carlowitz and at Passarowitz the British ambassadors tried to hasten peace by pressing both sides to moderate their demands.

out a mediator. There was none at the Peace of Nystad between Russia and Sweden. The secret treaty of Turin of 1696 was worked out by Count Tessé, a subordinate French military commander, and Gropello, Victor Amadeus's minister of finance, disguised as a Savoyard peasant. In 1709, when Louis wanted to end the war quickly, Torcy, the French foreign minister, himself went to The Hague, disguised as a private gentleman, to confer with Heinsius, Marlborough and Eugene. The Treaty of Rastatt was arranged in direct talks between Eugene and Villars, the two commanders-in-chief, who were personal friends. Rules of polite intercourse between equals, rather than ceremonial, prevailed in such negotiations. Contemporary writers on diplomacy recommended more use of second-rank negotiators—less shackled by protocol than ambassadors—while maintaining that ceremonial seldom prevented a resourceful diplomat from transacting important business. Here we should note a comment by Louis XIV, whom no one could suspect of negligence in matters of protocol. In 1710 his efforts to promote union between the Italian states were hampered by a rupture between Venice and Tuscany. Venice had sent to the Florentine court two successive residents whose gout was so severe that the Grand Duke allowed them to sit in his presence; when he refused to extend this privilege to their perfectly healthy successor, the two States severed relations. Louis observed: 'One cannot see without astonishment that...minor difficulties of ceremonial should hinder the union of powers that have a common interest in averting their impending ruin.'[1]

The working of coalitions was impeded by divergent interests rather than by ceremonial. In August 1689 William III, worried by dissension between the Allies and haunted by memories of his last war and the Nymegen Conference, proposed a congress at The Hague. He recoiled from making the minor princes full partners in the alliance of 'the four great powers', but there was need for some central co-ordinating body. The congress finally opened on 16 March 1690 and was still in existence in 1697. Nobody, not even William, had a clear idea as to what it was supposed to accomplish. Before it met, William decided that its main task would be to work out the Allied order of battle for the next campaign, and that its session should be short. The emperor had meanwhile been won over to the idea of a permanent congress, but his representative, Count Berka, was insufficiently instructed on the military views of his superiors and had to refer everything to Vienna. The Hague Congress was somewhat more successful in dealing with questions like the distribution of winter quarters, and it seems to have had a hand in settling the plans for the 1691 campaign, but in 1692 a separate conference had to be called at Cologne to concert measures for the defence of the Rhine. Certain political questions—even conditions of the future peace—also came

[1] To Gergy, 18 Sept. 1710, *Recueil des Instructions données...Florence* (1912), p. 89.

up for discussion at the congress, but could hardly be resolved in so large a gathering. In any case, not all the diplomats were in the full confidence of their masters. The congress was further undermined by the growth of a rival body at Vienna, where several members of the emperor's council began to sit in conference with a group of Allied diplomats to discuss both military operations and peace plans. The Vienna meetings were more loosely organized and better suited to run the coalition than were the plenary sessions at The Hague. They became more important and frequent as the main interest of the belligerents shifted south. By the end of 1695 Heinsius complained that peace measures concerted at The Hague were being altered at Vienna.

This rivalry between Vienna and The Hague was sharpened by Swedish mediation. William was not opposed to it in principle, but he considered communications through Stockholm too slow and objected to working with the Swedish envoy Lillieroot, whom he believed to be in the French interest. Moreover, Charles XI disliked the prospect of Anglo-Dutch maritime supremacy, though he was also rather hostile to Louis XIV and ready to render a service to the emperor. William, apparently, did not fully understand the reasons for the equivocal attitude of the Swedes; he attributed undue weight to French gold and the machinations of the pro-French party at Stockholm. Swedish mediation was not officially accepted by the Allies until the autumn of 1696—that is, after the Peace of Turin. Nevertheless, beginning with 1693, French peace proposals were being made through Count d'Avaux, the French ambassador at Stockholm, and were transmitted by the Swedish foreign minister, Count Oxenstierna, to Leopold's minister, who forwarded them to Vienna, whence they were passed on to The Hague and Madrid. Such an arrangement put Vienna in control of these negotiations on the Allied side. William then pinned his hopes on the Dijkvelt-Callières talks and proposed that the Allies agree on peace terms at The Hague. The Hague Congress was incapable of fulfilling this task.

During the Succession War the frequent travels of Marlborough, Wratislaw and Eugene were far more effective in maintaining the bonds between the key allies. In the Northern War the travels of Tsar Peter played a similar rôle in holding the anti-Swedish coalitions together. As for the anti-Turkish coalitions, it seems that apart from the regular diplomatic intercourse no mechanism was devised to co-ordinate the actions of the allies.

The changes in Europe's political structure had relatively little immediate effect on international law, the organization of diplomatic services, or the manner of negotiating. Diplomatic usage reflected the social order of the European community as well as of the individual States; and since this was not an age of great social upheaval, no urgent need was felt to overhaul it. In Russia, where such an upheaval did take place, Peter reformed the diplomatic service by combining patterns used in several western States. Nevertheless, Antoine Pecquet, in a treatise written about 1720,[1] noted that diplomacy now embraced many more matters than of old. By 1720, the Dutch and Venetian republics were no longer virtually alone in considering matters of trade and public opinion fit for diplomatic attention. Nearly all governments had come to take a more systematic interest in them. Emphasizing the complexity of the diplomat's task, contemporary manuals built up an image of a 'perfect ambassador' whose accomplishments included a knowledge of Latin, French, Italian, Spanish and German; a thorough study of history, ancient and modern, and especially of all the treaties since the Peace of Westphalia; an understanding of military, naval and mercantile affairs; extensive travel; sharp powers of observation and comprehension; command of a graceful style; and a host of other attributes, both mental and physical. Needless to say, such paragons were rare, though a few men like Torcy came close to the ideal.

For international law and diplomatic procedure Abraham de Wicquefort's *L'Ambassadeur et ses fonctions* (1680) was the standard manual, treated with great respect until the mid-eighteenth century. This rambling work is a vast collection of materials on the diplomatic practice of the previous hundred years; if it has any unifying theme, it is the defence of diplomatic immunity. The brilliant essay by François de Callières, *De la manière de négocier avec les souverains* (1716), was immediately translated into English, Italian and German; but, like the writings of his contemporaries—Leibniz, Rousseau de Chamoy, and Pecquet—it contained little that was new for the theory of international relations. Samuel von Pufendorf's *De jure naturae et gentium*, which went through 17 editions between 1688 and 1717 (in Latin, English, French and German), was a landmark in the history of the natural law concept, but for international law Pufendorf relied mainly on Grotius. We should note, however, his explicit statement that a sovereign was bound by a treaty only so far as it did not conflict with the interests of his State, for his bond with his own subjects was paramount to all other engagements.[2] The early work of the Dutch lawyer, Cornelius van Bynkershoek (1673–1743), *De dominio maris dissertatio* (1702), foreshadowed Vattel's theory of territorial waters: they were to extend as far as weapons could shoot from the shore.[3]

---

[1] *Discours sur l'art de négocier* (first published in 1737 in Paris).

[2] Book VIII, ch. IX, para. 5. For a bibliography of Pufendorf (1622–94) see J. B. Scott's edn. of *De jure naturae et gentium libri octo* (Oxford, 2 vols. 1934), vol. II, pp. 59 a–62 a. Cf. vol. V, pp. 109–14.

[3] See J. B. Scott's edn., New York, 1923; Bynkershoek's masterpiece, *Quaestionum juris publici libri duo* (1737) was republished in facsimile at Oxford in 1930, with E. T. by T. Frank and Introduction by J. de Louter in vol. II.

The problems of contraband and neutral rights at sea proved thorny, as always. In the Nine Years War, William III's drastic efforts to curtail neutral commerce threatened to involve the Northern Crowns in open hostilities in the west. In the next war these disputes were less acrimonious after 1705, when general disillusionment with the measures to restrict neutral trade with the enemy is discernible. The law and custom of the sea varied from country to country. Generally, the Dutch took the view that war should interfere with commerce as little as possible; the English were inclined to restrict commerce, both enemy and neutral; the French, in theory, were very severe toward both enemy and neutral. But in practice considerations of policy often tempered the rigour of the prize courts. The Dutch feared the competition of neutral commerce more than the British, and the Zeeland privateers at times handled it harshly; but William III relaxed the application of his own measures whenever it suited his diplomacy, and so did Heinsius. The French needed both Dutch and Irish trade so much that they were usually liberal in granting special passports to enemy ships; the *Conseil des Prises*, like the States-General, was also in a stronger position than the English High Court of Admiralty to act on extra-legal considerations. This state of affairs produced litigation and diplomatic correspondence on a massive scale. Much friction was caused by inconsistencies and impracticalities in the great series of bilateral commercial treaties which since 1648 had established rules for ships' papers and defined contraband of war.[1] As the terms of these agreements reflected not only the special economic circumstances of each party but also the facts of power, especially naval power, the results for international law were contradictory.

The notion of neutral status remained somewhat nebulous, chiefly because the practice of the times had blurred the line separating war and peace. A neutral abstained from direct acts of hostility; but he could send auxiliary troops to a belligerent (under a previously made treaty) without compromising his neutrality, and could allow the troops of a belligerent 'innocent transit' through his territory to attack the enemy. However, he was generally expected to prevent fighting in his waters. So difficult was this to prevent at times that the Danes and Portuguese contemplated closing their harbours to belligerent warships; the grand duke of Tuscany often had occasion to complain of breaches by belligerent captains of the neutrality of Leghorn, though this did not save him from accusations of favouritism. There was a growing belief that a neutral had to accord the same treatment to both sides. Special 'neutrality treaties' tried to define this treatment in individual cases: for example, in May 1689 Louis XIV made such a treaty with the Swiss cantons: he promised not to send French

---

[1] See P. C. Jessup and F. Deák, *Neutrality: the Origins* (New York, 1935); J. S. Bromley, 'Les Corsaires zélandais et la navigation scandinave pendant la Guerre de Succession d'Espagne', M. Mollat (ed.), *Le Navire et l'Economie Maritime du Nord de l'Europe* (1960), pp. 93–109.

troops through Swiss territory, and the Swiss undertook to deny passage to the troops of any other power. The concept of neutrality was sometimes applied to a geographical area rather than to a power: belligerents would agree not to fight in it. Thus on 7 October 1696 Victor Amadeus concluded with the emperor and Spain the convention of Vigevano, to which Louis XIV immediately acceded, providing for the neutrality of Italy for the rest of the war. Neutrality was also contemplated for the Baltic in 1691–3, the Aegean in 1697, and the Holy Roman Empire with respect to the Northern War in 1710. Louis XIV's desire for a local neutrality accommodation with Spain prompted the 'treaty of commerce and good correspondence' of 1694 between the Bayonne–Labourd district and the province of Guipúzcoa.[1] Not only a geographical area, but certain classes of population, such as fishermen, might also be given formal protection.

Conventions between belligerents were quite common, dealing usually with technical matters like postal communications, commercial transactions, safe-conduct, and exchange of prisoners. Most peace treaties, even some treaties of alliance, on the other hand, envisaged a possible future state of war between the contracting parties, specifying a period of six months or longer during which enemy subjects would be allowed to wind up their affairs. There was nothing extraordinary about the case of Abbé Gaultier (chaplain to the French ambassador Tallard) who stayed in London throughout the Succession War, finally helping to arrange the secret talks that ended it. A state of war usually began with a proclamation in which the sovereign expounded his reasons for taking up arms, enjoined all his subjects to fall upon the enemy and forbade any communication with him on pain of death. Like so many ordinances of that time, however, it was made only to be broken. In a curious letter addressed to the governor-general of the Spanish Netherlands in 1689, Louis XIV argues that the words of his declaration are, in effect, but an empty formula: it would be unjust to deprive of their livelihood those subjects who do not bear arms, and belligerent princes usually exempt them from the penalties of the law either by granting special passports or simply by not interfering with their pursuits.[2] Passports and discriminations mitigated the rigours of war, fed treasuries, and enlarged the means of government control over the movements of persons and goods—friend, enemy and neutral. Conversely, the customs of the time, not being charged with nationalist emotion, rendered the transition from war to peace relatively simple and helped to preserve the European system. Amnesty clauses in the peace treaties took care of those who had broken wartime ordinances.

[1] Dumont, vol. VII, pt. II, pp. 342–5.
[2] C. G. Picavet, 'Etat de paix et état de guerre au temps de Louis XIV', *Rev. d'hist. dipl.* vol. XXXVIII (1924), pp. 436–7. Sometimes there was a considerable time-lag between two reciprocal declarations: Louis XIV declared war on the Dutch 26 November 1688, the Dutch on him 9 March 1689.

Though virtually all States had in some measure modelled their diplomatic practices on the Venetian, they varied widely, even from reign to reign. They were not yet hardened by bureaucracies and electorates. The idiosyncrasy of even a mediocre statesman could determine the foreign policy of his State. General statements about the diplomatic services are therefore difficult to make with confidence.

Even in the Dutch Republic—with an intricate diplomatic tradition of long standing—William III was able gradually to take foreign policy into his own hands, chiefly by influencing appointments to the States-General, its Committee on Secret Affairs, and diplomatic posts. Dutch representatives abroad were expected to correspond with the States of their province—the distribution of diplomatic posts was mainly in the hands of the States of Holland and of Zeeland—and with the States-General and the Committee on Secret Affairs through the Greffier of the States-General. In practice they also corresponded with the Stadholder, the Grand Pensionary of Holland (the real minister of foreign affairs) and key personages in the city of Amsterdam. It is doubtful whether William could have assumed control over Dutch diplomacy without the personal friendship of Grand Pensionaries Fagel and Heinsius, or without an understanding with Amsterdam. When William was in England, Heinsius acted as his *alter ego*; to him the king poured out his innermost thoughts. In England, William's two Secretaries of State were confined mainly to routine correspondence; it was to Blathwayt, the Secretary at War, who usually accompanied him on his travels, that English and Dutch diplomats wrote on questions requiring William's decision. If the matter was very secret, as often happened, the diplomats were instructed to address themselves to Heinsius or William direct. When the First Partition Treaty was being negotiated, only William, Heinsius and Portland, on the Anglo-Dutch side, knew what was afoot. In effect, William was his own foreign secretary, frequently negotiating with foreign ambassadors alone and penning his more important letters himself in the seclusion of his cabinet —sometimes in too great a hurry to summarize the contents for his own future reference, as he regretfully admitted. It is not surprising that he preferred to concentrate all negotiations of any consequence at The Hague or in London. With few exceptions, his envoys gathered and transmitted information rather than negotiated. Under William the British and the Dutch diplomatic services were one, concerting their measures and frequently sharing their information; sometimes their respective envoys deputized for each other. Despite murmuring on both sides, this union worked with increasing efficiency and greatly expanded William's diplomatic resources. With William gone, the two services parted company, especially after Ramillies had put the Maritime Powers out of immediate danger. That the dissolution was gradual and (at least in its early stages) not acrimonious was largely due to Heinsius and Marlborough, who worked closely together. However, though Heinsius continued to direct Dutch foreign policy, he could not command all the loyalties attaching to the magic name of Orange; imperceptibly at first, some of the Dutch groups, especially in Amsterdam, began to diverge from the Grand Pensionary. This tended to make him more rigid and to cling that much closer to Marlborough. Marlborough, though not a secretary of state, was so much in control of British foreign policy that in 1707 he was able to decide on his own authority to visit Charles XII. His fall severed the last link between the British and the Dutch diplomatic services.

The methods of the stolid Emperor Leopold were in striking contrast. On one occasion, when the Dutch envoy had broached peace plans, Count Kinsky replied that the matter was 'too delicate to be taken up with the Emperor between four eyes' and proposed a conference.[1] Convinced of the superior wisdom of committees, Leopold made it a rule to abide by the decisions of the majority of his Council even when he disagreed with them. Some of his ministers thought him rather dull, though other observers, including Villars, credited him with having more brains than his counsellors. Not surprisingly, contemporary correspondence complains much of Vienna's delays. The Polish–Lithuanian Commonwealth presented yet another pattern: the two chancellors and vice-chancellors carried on routine diplomatic correspondence, but Polish ambassadors were responsible to the Diet, which handled the more important affairs. The king made use of his 'small privy chancellery' for his personal policy —often distinct from that of his realm. Each magnate pursued a foreign policy of his own, indeed, so that any power with a real interest in Poland, if it could afford the expense, had to maintain two ambassadors and a host of minor agents there, as was sometimes done by Louis XIV.

Compared with the usages so far sketched, French procedure was a model of regularity. Louis himself laid down his foreign policy after free discussion in the *Conseil d'en haut*, whose secret no outsider could penetrate. The foreign secretary then worked out the details in daily consultation with the king, who frequently altered his minister's drafts. The foreign secretary was also present at the audiences of foreign diplomats; the very few occasions on which Louis alone received an ambassador gave rise to much comment. Wishing to ensure secrecy and the greatest possible freedom of action, Louis disliked the presence of foreign diplomats at his court for other than decorative purposes, preferring to entrust important negotiations to his own representatives abroad. In the second half of his reign, he relied on them more and more to deal with unforeseen situations according to their knowledge of his views. He hardly ever disgraced an ambassador for an honest mistake. Throughout, he demanded that his

[1] Heemskerk to Heinsius, 2 Jan. 1696, G. von Antal and J. C. H. de Pater (eds.), *Weensche Gezantschapsberichten*, vol. 1 (The Hague, 1929), p. 615. Cf. below, pp. 572 ff., for administrative organization at Vienna.

ambassadors write to him with the utmost candour, and the dispatches of men like d'Avaux or Tallard show that at least the top diplomats took him at his word. It is clear that Louis's system put a premium on accomplished negotiators; it also charged the foreign secretary with a heavy load of work. By 1715, however, the foreign secretary had a competent staff of several first secretaries and a number of translators and clerks—his personal employees. It is unlikely that they exceeded thirty, even after the establishment of a separate archival section under Saint-Prest in 1710. Even before the Succession War several propagandists were attached to the ministry, partly to combat hostile publications: as in England, there was increased awareness of public opinion as an instrument of foreign policy. The foreign secretary could also consult experts outside his department on matters like trade, but he often clashed with other ministers, particularly the secretaries of state for war and the navy. Foreign trade came within the purview of the latter, and in 1698 the king tried to give the foreign secretary more exclusive control over French representatives in Europe by confining the navy's direct correspondence with diplomats abroad to those in Spain, Portugal, Constantinople and Barbary, and to the consuls. It was far more difficult to settle the quarrels with the secretary for war, who had his own network of informants and could not be prevented from meddling in foreign policy. Moreover, military commanders in the field, like Villars, were usually charged with diplomatic missions.

Diplomacy clearly required rapid and secure communications. The bulk of diplomatic correspondence was sent by 'ordinary' post, travelling between most capitals usually once or twice a week. Only an extremely urgent or secret message would warrant the expensive use of an 'express' courier, for whom an ambassador frequently had to pay out of his own pocket.[1] No statesman better appreciated good postal connections than William III: an interruption in the timely receipt of news or in his correspondence with Heinsius would have slackened his grip on negotiations. London, The Hague and Paris were normally four days apart, but England's communications were at the mercy of the winds, and even an express might take a week or longer to reach The Hague or Paris. Overland couriers also were often delayed by bad weather, sometimes by unstable political conditions, occasionally by highwaymen, genuine or feigned. It was a wise precaution to send several copies of a letter by different routes. An outbreak of hostilities made communications even more

[1] A letter by ordinary post from Paris usually reached Madrid in 10 or 11 days; Lisbon (via La Rochelle) in about 5 weeks; Vienna in a fortnight; Venice in 13 days, Rome in 17, Berlin in 11, Stockholm in 16–17, and Warsaw in 19 days. An express could get to Madrid in 8 days, to Vienna in 9–10, and to Rome or Warsaw in 11. From The Hague to Vienna the postal distance was 11–12 days, to Copenhagen 7–9, to Stockholm 13, and to Moscow about 5 weeks. From Vienna, the post usually took 4 or 5 weeks to Madrid, 4 to 6 weeks to Constantinople; a courier could reach Madrid in 18 days, Turin in 5 or 6.

uncertain, but as Europe settled to a state of war normal postal service would usually be resumed even between enemy countries. In 1703 the Habsburgs and the Maritime Powers prohibited postal and other relations with France, but this provoked such an outcry among the Dutch that the interdict was not resumed a year later.[1]

Contemporaries differed in evaluating the efficacy of the various codes and ciphers employed. Wicquefort said there was no such thing as an unbreakable cipher, while Callières believed it was possible to devise one that would be impenetrable without the aid of treason. A few experts, like the mathematician John Wallis, were credited with the ability to crack almost any cipher; the papers of a French intelligence agent caught in north Germany in 1691 were at once sent to London for his examination. In war especially, regular diplomats as well as secret agents often enclosed reports in envelopes addressed to a merchant or banker, real or fictitious; the addressee or the postmaster would then forward to the proper destination. Besides providing a plausible cover for government correspondence, this device had the advantage that postmasters were reluctant to tamper with merchants' and bankers' mail: to have done so excessively would have diverted their correspondence into other channels, causing considerable pecuniary loss to the postal route. Nevertheless, it was extremely difficult to prevent interception of the mails or conceal any important negotiation. Thus the general tenor of the secret treaty of Turin (June 1696) was known in Vienna four days before it was concluded, and William III seems to have had an even earlier inkling of what was going on.

Many different titles designated diplomatic representatives. They can be reduced to three basic ranks: ambassadors, envoys and residents. Only fully sovereign States could be represented by ambassadors. Even so, some were reluctant to appoint them, whether to save expense or avoid quarrels over precedence. In practice, however, there was little difference between an ambassador and an envoy; though an envoy was surrounded by less elaborate ceremonial and received less pay, it was no disgrace for a former ambassador to serve as one. But between the growing number of envoys and the diminishing class of residents there was an ever-widening gap, enlarged by the tendency to appoint as residents deserving members of relatively obscure families—sometimes (as by the lesser German princes) without any real function. In the French service it was becoming extremely difficult for a resident to rise to an envoyship. The British and the Dutch custom remained less rigid for the time being.

Differences in rank notwithstanding, diplomats in every capital were beginning to form a distinct community, held together by similar practices and privileges, so that any infringement of the rights of one member was felt by the entire corps. By general agreement the law of nations made the

---

[1] On the interdict of 1703–4, see below, pp. 303 and 420.

person and household of a representative inviolable; but its interpretation varied from place to place, and the problem of competent jurisdiction over 'public ministers' and their possessions exercised some of the best legal minds of the day. The law of nations did not permit an ambassador to foment cabals and rebellions in the country of residence; yet he could properly suborn the local ministers and clerks for information. Foreign diplomats might be expelled, while such incidents as the arrest in 1717 of Gyllenborg and Görtz, the envoys of Sweden in London and The Hague, were not uncommon. The injured party usually retaliated: thus, in 1703, on hearing that his ambassador in Savoy was being held virtually incommunicado, Louis XIV prescribed a similar régime for Savoy's ambassador in Paris.

As a rule, a diplomat negotiated orally or in writing with the foreign minister or *ad hoc* commissioners. He could not succeed without reliable information and the support of key personages. No matter how he went about it—by flattery, bribery, or plain persuasion—he could not gain their confidence without sharing their interests and conversing as their social equal. As personal representative of his sovereign, he must in any case cut a figure at the foreign court. A man of inferior social standing, however talented, would have been at a serious disadvantage. Hence most diplomats were members of the military nobility; some came from the legal aristocracy; a few were ecclesiastics. Even in the Dutch service many ambassadors and envoys were nobles, while the rest were recruited among the 'regents'—from families which had withdrawn from direct business transactions to devote themselves to governing the Dutch polity. Venetian ambassadors were also of patrician origin. In designating a representative, it was unnecessary to seek approval by the foreign court but advisable to consider the mode of life he would be expected to lead. For example, Callières thought that an ambassador to a northern court should be able to consume large quantities of alcohol without ill effects. A nobleman of the highest rank, with a large fortune, was most appropriate for Rome. Envoys to the minor German courts might find it useful to be versed in the intricacies of law. The aristocratic austerity of Feuquière's life made him much appreciated in Spain. Monks were effective on highly secret diplomatic or intelligence missions in Catholic courts, especially the Spanish, thanks to the ease with which they could penetrate unnoticed into almost any household. Yet a Catholic dignitary would be no more suitable for a Muslim than for a Protestant country.

An ambassador or envoy had to recruit his staff. It was especially important to find one or two good secretaries, for the secretary copied out the dispatches in legible hand, had access to codes and ciphers, was often employed on minor diplomatic errands, and in the ambassador's absence carried on routine correspondence. In the British, Spanish and Swedish services a secretary was supposed to be appointed and paid by the king;

in the French, the ambassador himself selected his secretary, usually from among his clients, and paid him out of his own funds. In addition, an ambassador had to have a chaplain, several gentlemen in attendance, a number of cooks, lackeys, footmen, pages, coachmen, stablemen, and other domestics. Where court life was relatively simple, as in Holland, some thirty people might suffice; at Rome the French and Spanish ambassadors usually carried over a hundred in their retinues. An ambassador also had to provide himself with a suitable mansion, plate, at least two coaches, and horses. Mourning, festivities, and movements of the court entailed additional outlays. Usually he met his own postal expenses. Occasionally he advanced his own money 'for the king's service'. A recall or a new mission could be embarrassing, for it meant that he would have to settle accounts with his local creditors and raise additional funds. 'They are sending me on a difficult, dangerous, and costly journey, but they do not tell me where I am to find the money for it', wrote the Dutch envoy at Vienna on receiving orders to proceed to Constantinople.[1] Many a diplomat could have said the same. Louis XIV's representatives were, on the whole, better paid than others.[2] But the salary or ordinary allowance never sufficed to defray even ordinary expenses. Worse still, it was seldom paid on time, and as much as a quarter of it was sometimes consumed in arranging a banker's advance and in currency exchange. Some diplomats tried to supplement their income by speculation in currency exchange, or by stockjobbing, if their posts offered facilities; a few went so far as to use their customs exemption to carry on underhand retail trade. In the exceptional case of the western embassies at Constantinople, ample consulage dues supplemented salaries, themselves largely paid by the merchants. Otherwise, there was little choice but to get into debt; many family fortunes were lost in the diplomatic service. Modest perquisites of office, a lump sum (equipage) on first appointment, and an allowance for 'extraordinaries'[3] might ease but not remove the burden. An occasional extraordinary grant was awarded in all services, but a diplomat was well advised to solicit one during the critical phase of a negotiation: thus Briord at The Hague, on hearing that Carlos II was dead, at once informed Torcy that he was in desperate straits. Some governments sought to alleviate hardship by allowing a diplomat, now and then, to retain the emoluments of an office held at home: an ecclesiastic with a rich benefice was an excellent candidate for service abroad. Yet it would be exaggerated

[1] Heemskerk to Heinsius, 17 Sept. 1692, von Antal and de Pater, vol. I, p. 522.
[2] The French ambassador at Rome normally received 72,000 *livres* a year; in England, 48,000; at The Hague, Madrid and Stockholm, 36,000; in Savoy, 30,000; and in Portugal and Venice, 24,000. An envoy would draw 12,000–24,000 *livres*; a resident, 6,000–12,000. A British ambassador drew £100 a week in Paris, Madrid, and Vienna, £10 a day in other capitals; an envoy extraordinary received £5 a day, a resident £3.
[3] In England a regular scale of 'extraordinaries' was drawn up by order-in-council on 9/19 Jan. 1690; it was not revised till 1789. Cf. D. B. Horn, *The British Diplomatic Service, 1689–1789* (Oxford, 1961), chs. III–IV.

to suppose that good diplomatic performance went unrewarded. Often it brought some mark of distinction, military or civil promotion, or ecclesiastical preferment, although there was a widespread conviction among the diplomats that friends at home received all the choice appointments. All too many looked upon diplomatic service as an honourable but ruinous exile, preferring to treat it as a temporary occupation rather than a career. This in itself was enough to frustrate the efforts of the writers on diplomacy, who unanimously urged the creation of a regular corps, trained from early youth. Only in France was an attempt made to set up a 'political academy' for the training of future diplomats. In 1712 Torcy entrusted Saint-Prest with the education of a dozen young men: his disciples helped to order the archives of the foreign ministry and produced some interesting historical memoranda: otherwise the results were meagre, and the 'academy' died a natural death by 1720. The training of diplomats everywhere remained largely a matter of chance and of family connections.

A major task of the diplomat abroad was to gather information from every available source. Informal personal intercourse with the local dignitaries and fellow diplomats afforded the best opportunity. An ambassador was well advised to keep open house; next to his secretary, his cook was his most valuable assistant. But to draw out his companions he himself had to impart news to them. The post from his government brought him 'news-letters', extracts from dispatches of other envoys, texts of new laws and ordinances, letters from friends; he also had direct correspondence with other diplomats stationed abroad. Dutch representatives were notably well supplied with information by their government; they also corresponded with many merchants abroad. The French, before Torcy's ministry, seem to have been rather negligent in supplying current information; Louis had earlier frowned upon news-letters from his court. Most diplomats also had secret and semi-secret informants. Some clerks and postal officials sought to supplement their meagre and irregular pay by selling copies of the papers they handled; here and there a secretary of legation was not above this temptation. It was probably through such channels that Marlborough procured a copy of Louis XIV's instructions to de Ricous, who was to have gone on a special mission to Charles XII in 1707. An enterprising ambassador like d'Avaux gathered information from men of all classes, down to ships' carpenters. A foreign diplomat lured into one's secret service could obviously be invaluable, especially in war. Those in the service of minor German princes were notoriously susceptible to this kind of employment. During the Nine Years War, the bishop of Münster's deputy at Ratisbon kept the French fully informed of proceedings there. During the next war Petkum, resident of Holstein-Gottorp in Holland, was a French spy, supplying copies of Dutch dispatches from Portugal and similar documents. At this time the French apparently employed many Danes and almost persuaded von Stöcken,

Danish envoy to the Dutch Republic and to England, into joining their secret service; they had better luck with Stiernhök, Swedish resident at Vienna. William III and Heinsius had a secret intelligence network in no way inferior. The diplomat normally kept in touch with secret agents through an intermediary, usually his secretary, but sometimes met them in person, in cloak-and-dagger fashion: thus Amelot, in Portugal, occasionally contrived a 'chance encounter' at the Capucin Friars' with his best informant, the Dame du Verger, a confidante of Infanta Isabella. Available evidence indicates that minor agents received a mere pittance. Those on special errands, like Pastor, whom the French sent to Vienna in 1706, would agree to work for 40 *écus* a month; star spies like Petkum could command a yearly salary of 3,000 *livres*, which Petkum seems to have supplemented by drawing sums from the Allies for services rendered to them. The Dame du Verger refused to take money, but in 1686 asked for ecclesiastical preferment for her son in France; her daughter in Portugal took a liking to Amelot's carriage and the ambassador, before leaving Lisbon in 1688, made her a present of it.

Pensions and 'gratifications' to foreign statesmen and courtiers were intended, as a rule, not to procure information, but to build up a party and influence policy. Often these outlays were not even clandestine. Whenever a great prince concluded a treaty, he was expected to honour the ministers of the other party with some valuable gift. In most instances the lesser princes at least surmised that their ministers were receiving pensions from a foreign power. So long as it did not impair the minister's loyalty to his master, they saw no harm in it; many German princes even encouraged such practices, which helped economize on ministers' pay. For that matter many a prince relied on foreign subsidies himself, usually for his army. Astutely applied, these methods helped an Ernest Augustus of Hanover to improve his posture with his neighbours and also his bargaining position with the great powers. Of the lesser princes, only Charles XI of Sweden openly tried to defy this fact of political life: for most of the others the question was not whether to receive financial aid but from whom to receive it—a question usually resolved, however, in accordance with their political interests.

In the 1680s Louis XIV was by far the most generous provider. The Dutch were reputed to be rather parsimonious and often in arrears. Charles II and James II were experienced only in receiving subsidies. Spain and the emperor might promise but could seldom give them. Russia was only a beginner, subsidizing Sobieski's war against the Turks. All this changed radically within the next decade. Louis was still capable of massive financial effort—in Sweden and Denmark in the 1690s, for example, and later in Spain—but could no longer scatter resources all over Europe. The Maritime Powers, under pressure from William and Heinsius, were able eventually to outdo the French on this battlefield. Meanwhile,

Tsar Peter became paymaster of the anti-Swedish coalitions. Louis, William, Peter, Leopold, and most of their ministers had an implicit faith that, next to Divine Providence, money was the most powerful agent in the world—against all evidence. Between 1688 and 1721 it seems impossible to find a single instance of a subsidy or pension determining a State's foreign policy. More often than not, a subsidy enabled a prince to pursue the policy that he desired but lacked means of his own to finance. It is doubtful whether the king of Denmark could have maintained his excellent navy, necessary as it was to the very existence of his realm, without subsidies; it is unlikely that Augustus II of Poland would have stayed long in the Northern War without Russian finance. A subsidy could perhaps delay, but could not prevent, a shift in policy to the detriment of the giver. It could even render such a shift highly profitable and tempting to the recipient. In 1692 Louis XIV was punctually paying Ernest Augustus of Hanover a monthly subsidy of 109,000 *livres*: so far from deterring him from joining the Allies, this bounty enabled him to make such a nuisance of himself, as Louis's henchman in the Empire, that he managed to extort the electoral dignity from the emperor.

The efficacy of gifts and pensions to foreign statesmen was much exaggerated by contemporaries. Nowhere was the tradition more ingrained than in Sweden, where from 1691 Louis XIV tried to rebuild a pro-French party for joining the neutralist 'third party' in the Empire.[1] In 1692 Swedish ministers received 150,000 *livres* in gratifications, in 1693 another 43,000; the Francophile Senator Bielke, an enemy of Count Bengt Oxenstierna, also drew a yearly pension of 20,000 *livres*—his two sons sharing 24,000 more—while Oxenstierna was to have been promised up to 50,000 *livres* for acceding to a formal treaty of neutrality. Sweden, however, did not join the 'third party'. Though her auxiliaries no longer fought with the Allies after 1692, even this modest result should probably be ascribed to Charles XI's and Oxenstierna's fear of Anglo-Dutch maritime supremacy. Likewise, the pensions William III assigned to Oxenstierna's daughters in 1694 apparently had little effect on the count's policy of neutrality and mediation. He and Carl Piper would receive gifts only for measures in which they believed or which had already been decided by their masters: in any case, Charles XI and Charles XII were both strong-willed men who did not feel themselves bound by ministerial advice. In 1707 Marlborough induced Piper to accept a pension of £1,500, while secretaries Hermelin and Cederhielm were to receive £500 a year each; his purpose was to move the Swedish army out of the Empire—something that Charles had already decided to do. At the same time Piper remained as impervious to French offers as before: by 1707 Louis was

---

[1] See R. Hatton, 'Gratifications and Foreign Policy: Anglo-French Rivalry in Sweden during the Nine Years War', R. Hatton and J. S. Bromley (eds.), *William III and Louis XIV* (1968), pp. 68–94.

willing to pay him 300,000 *livres* for a successful Swedish mediation in the war in the west.

Perhaps the best example of an apparently effective use of money in diplomacy was provided by Peter Tolstoy and Shafirov, the tsar's ministers at Constantinople in 1701–14. Tolstoy not only bribed high Turkish dignitaries, like everyone else, but even managed to put the British ambassador, Sutton, and the Dutch resident, Colijer, on the Russian payroll.[1] No doubt this whetted the zeal of these capable mediators between Russia and Turkey in 1711–12; but at that time it was in the interest of the Maritime Powers to prevent a Russo-Turkish conflict, for they had been provoked by Charles XII's rejection of the neutrality treaty for the Holy Roman Empire. It is hard to assess the rôle of Russian subornation in the palace intrigues at Constantinople. In 1700–9, few Ottoman statesmen desired any involvement in the Northern or Spanish Succession wars: if there was a war party, it resented chiefly the Venetian occupation of the Morea. After Poltava, however, the threat of Russian influence in Poland loomed larger than Russian bribes, and the Turks fought. Shortly after Peter's disaster on the Pruth, in 1711, whether or not his bribe to the grand vizier was large or not, Peter accepted the main Ottoman demands, although Russo-Turkish peace was not secure till after 1713, when it appeared that Peter meant to honour most of its conditions. Only then could the Turks turn on the Venetians.

One need not infer from these disappointing results that subsidies and gratifications were altogether useless. The donor of subsidies greatly expanded his field of political manoeuvre—provided the recipient government was already inclined to follow a course advantageous to him—while gifts and pensions promoted a friendlier personal disposition among politicians, without which it would have been hard to expedite even the simplest business.

A diplomat's chief duty, of course, was to 'maintain correspondence' between two courts. He was also expected to protect his nationals, notably merchants. Nearly all Dutch, most British, and some French diplomats took this instruction seriously, though Louis XIV's government, sceptical of the probity of French merchants abroad, urged caution in taking up their cause. Consuls also protected and furthered merchants' interests, but their primary function was to judge lawsuits arising between their own protégés; it reflected a lingering medieval notion that a man carried his law about him wherever he went. A sovereign like Louis XIV looked askance at projects to set up foreign consuls within his State; nor were the Dutch eager to receive them; the Franco-Dutch commercial treaty of Ryswick did away with Dutch consuls in France and French consuls in

---

[1] In 1714–19, when the Turks would not allow a permanent Russian representative in their capital, Colijer acted for the tsar.

Holland. Most often a consul was a merchant settled, even naturalized, in the country where he resided; his native origin, whatever country he served, was immaterial. Some French consuls in the North were Huguenot refugees. Consuls were not 'public ministers' and could claim no diplomatic immunity. They were seldom salaried by their governments. With commercial negotiations livening up, however, their status was gradually improving and some diplomatic privileges began to be extended to them by courtesy. In the Mediterranean, where consular service had a longer history than elsewhere, they were already diplomatic agents, chiefly because commerce had always been a main subject of negotiation with the Porte, but also because the sultan's vassals, and even some of the provincial pashas, enjoyed considerable latitude in foreign relations. Certain commercially important ethnic groups—Greeks, Armenians and Jews— also influenced the foreign policy of the Porte, with the result that a consul who mixed with them not only produced valuable intelligence but was inevitably drawn into semi-public negotiations.

In the increased prominence they gave to commercial questions in the conduct of diplomacy, Britain and France had of course long been anticipated by the Venetians and Dutch; they were followed by the Scandinavian kingdoms and Brandenburg, later by Emperor Charles VI, Tsar Peter, Spain and other powers. In commercial negotiations most rulers and diplomats still found themselves treading unfamiliar ground. Thus Tallard, when sent to negotiate the Partition Treaties with William III, had to ask for a commercial expert to be attached to his embassy. William himself was liable to be ill at ease in matters of this sort: realizing that he was 'not too well acquainted' with the question of the Spanish Indies, which Tallard had broached, he merely mentioned Havana and then put off the discussion to a later date.[1] From 1696 the Board of Trade gathered commercial information abroad more or less systematically. Some English diplomats developed a thorough knowledge of trade, as in Stockholm, Danzig and Hamburg did Dr John Robinson, later concerned with the economic discussions at Utrecht; the poet Matthew Prior, who specialized in economic negotiations with the French in 1711–13, was a commissioner of customs and had served on the Board of Trade. Many statesmen, Marlborough included, had a personal stake in trading companies. In France, the *Conseil de Commerce* (1700) included the secretary for the navy, the controller-general and other officials, besides deputies from the chief French towns: one of them, Mesnager, later treated with Robinson and the Dutch as a French plenipotentiary at Utrecht. The career of d'Usson de Bonrepaus also reflects the new trend: as a naval intendant he had become proficient in commercial matters, and then proved a capable ambassador, serving at Copenhagen during the Nine Years War and later at The Hague. A few versatile men like d'Avaux and

[1] To Portland, 12 May 1698, Japikse, vol I, pt. I, p. 304.

Amelot were at home in all spheres, but most French diplomats needed advisers. Everywhere the volume of consular correspondence increased, and consuls fell into the habit of giving economic intelligence (occasionally advice) to governments and ambassadors. In 1662 Colbert was unable to ascertain the names of all French consuls. Fifty years later such a predicament would have been unthinkable anywhere in Europe.

The upsurge in international economic activity and negotiation did not signify that major political combinations were made, or wars fought, from economic motives. To those who decided the issues of war and peace, or alliance, economic measures were instruments of policy, never its aim. For instance, the French tariffs of 1688 and 1701 were meant to intimidate the Dutch by stirring political dissension in the Republic. Towards the end of the Nine Years War, Louis did not hesitate to sacrifice what he regarded as French commercial interests to win Dutch political co-operation. In spring 1701 he dangled before the Danes the prospect of a commercial treaty, desired by the Danes and likely to benefit French commerce, but his avowed purpose was to induce them not to send troops to a possible anti-French coalition and the proposal was dropped as soon as they promised auxiliaries to the Maritime Powers.

At the helm of the Maritime Powers, William III had more complex problems of management than Louis. He knew from experience what a nuisance a powerful mercantile group could be in opposition. His leadership in the Dutch Republic largely depended on his understanding with Amsterdam; in England he drew much of his support from mercantile groups whose interests did not necessarily square with those of the Dutch; and to keep the coalition going he needed money badly, English or Dutch. The moral was that he must accord some protection to commercial interests. He was willing to use naval squadrons to safeguard trade, support Dutch commercial demands at Ryswick, insist on provisions for securing English and Dutch trade in the Mediterranean in the Partition Treaties. But William also wished to inflict the pinch of scarcity on Louis. The war on French trade unleashed in 1689 was calculated to hurt France, not to further Allied trade: the strongest opposition to measures prohibiting all trade with France came from the Dutch, to a lesser degree from British merchants. To strengthen this measure, but also allay Anglo-Dutch fears of neutral competition, he sought to stop all neutral commerce with France as well; when the neutrals forced him to retreat from this extreme position, he persisted in trying to suppress all Allied trade with the enemy under their flags. One might suppose that he would have favoured privateers: yet he quarrelled with them bitterly when they failed to comply with his policy, and at one time contemplated revoking all letters of marque issued to the Zeelanders.[1] Thus, at bottom, William's

---

[1] To Heinsius, 16/26 Feb. 1694 (B.M. Add. MS. 34,504, fos. 139–40). See G. N. Clark, *The Dutch Alliance and the War against French Trade* (Manchester, 1923), ch. v.

attitude to commerce did not much differ from that of Louis. Most other statesmen shared their predominantly political standpoint.

While economic questions nevertheless intruded increasingly into foreign policy, religion occupied a less conspicuous place in it. No connection is discernible between these two phenomena. The growing separation between religion and international politics presents a paradox: for in their personal lives many statesmen of the early eighteenth century had more religion in them than they or their predecessors thirty years before. Yet some very religious men, like William himself, were probably reacting against the injection of religious passion into foreign policy in the 1680s, when, if left unchecked, fear of a colossal Catholic plot could have produced crusades which would have wrecked the political structure of Europe. In October 1697 William wrote: 'I have always been afraid of a war of religion, fearing that France and the Emperor might come to a secret understanding.'[1] He did what he could to restrain the wave of anti-Catholic feeling in England at the time of the Revolution, while trying to persuade the emperor that he had no intention of fighting the Catholic religion. The devout Habsburgs, on their part, needed Protestant allies against both France and Turkey: at their court, it is true, voices were always decrying Protestant alliances, but they became loud only in 1707–8, when the Grand Alliance had begun to fall apart. Nowhere did Louis XIV's suggestion that the Nine Years War was a religious conflict meet with greater contempt than in Spain.

If religious interest was usually checked by reason of state, then it could also be used for political ends. The Spanish government was ready to use a Protestant weapon when it proposed in 1689 that the Vaudois subjects of Savoy be brought into play against France; it was only several months afterwards that William pleaded for the Vaudois with Victor Amadeus, who agreed to restore their old liberties.[2] Upon the outbreak of war with Turkey in 1711, Tsar Peter appealed to the Christians in the Balkans, for whose fate, at other times, he had little interest. Peter, however, was a man of sincere religious convictions; the same can hardly be said about Augustus of Saxony, who became a Catholic solely to become king of Poland. But whenever interests of state allowed it, the princes gave rein to their religious inclinations. For instance, in 1692 the emperor was able to insist on freedom for the Catholics in Hanover and Celle; in 1707 Charles XII took up the cause of the Lutherans in Silesia and tried to intercede for the Huguenots in France. Towards the end of his reign, Peter championed the freedom of Eastern Orthodox worship in the Polish-Lithuanian Commonwealth. Such action, however, was often inhibited by

---

[1] *Archives...de la Maison d'Orange-Nassau*, 3rd ser. (ed. F. J. L. Krämer, Leiden, 3 vols. 1907–9), vol. II, p. 2.

[2] Later the Allies formed a corps of Protestant volunteers, who operated in Italy with Spanish, Imperial and Savoyard forces. To most of these volunteers, as to many other Protestants, the war was of course one of religion.

the belief that each State should be fully master at home. Thus Louis XIV withheld his protection from Catholics abroad whenever he thought that it might bring on an intercession for the Huguenots in France.

There were moments when religious belief played a conspicuous part in Louis's policy. In 1688 he claimed to be the defender of the Catholic faith, but failed to impress his Catholic adversaries, except perhaps Elector John William of the Palatinate, who disapproved of the emperor's war against France because it advanced the Protestant interest. It was John William who suggested that provision be made at Ryswick for the dominant position of the Catholic Church in the lands that France ceded back to the Empire. Louis, with Leopold's connivance, forced the insertion of this stipulation into the treaty. But this point of agreement between Leopold and Louis in no way helped resolve their dispute over the Spanish succession. On the whole, Louis's Catholic policy in the Empire was un-rewarding. What it did for him in the Mediterranean is harder to deter-mine: probably he would have failed miserably there had he not followed a pronounced Catholic policy. In this area his political interests and religious convictions did not clash. When they did so elsewhere, there is much to suggest that even in his later years Louis subordinated religion. The champion of the Catholic cause assured Protestant princes that he intended no harm to their faith. After Ryswick he interceded for the Palatine Protestants, and in 1712 he tried to allay religious strife between the Swiss cantons. During the Succession War he showed annoyance with the dukes of Burgundy and Beauvillier for constantly dragging in questions of morality and religion into politics.[1]

Since Louis XIV and William III contributed more than anybody else to the emergence of the European order of the early eighteenth century, we should consider the relation of some of their basic beliefs to policy. Louis's opportunism did not affect his belief in stable principles of foreign policy and of human behaviour. His aim was quite simple: to increase the grandeur of his State and of his House, so that his own pre-eminence as 'the greatest king in Christendom' would be beyond dispute. This pre-eminence rested on the natural order of things: provided he did not overstep the bounds of this order, the good of his State coincided with the good of the world. Louis conceived of the world as an orderly place, directed indeed by divine providence, but mainly through intermediary agencies. Only during the disasters of 1710–12 did he seriously think of direct divine intervention in human affairs. He believed that each country had its own 'true maxims of state', rooted in the natural order whose ultimate author was God. Good statesmanship consisted in following these maxims. Without knowledge of one's own and everybody else's true maxims no sound policy was possible; even occasional successes would turn out to be ephemeral. Only an absolute monarch stood a chance of

---

[1] Cf. below, pp. 326 ff.

following the true maxims consistently. Wherever kingly power was limited, it was virtually certain that private interests would becloud the real interest of the State; the only exception was Venice—a curiosity of nature. Here and there, in such circumstances, an individual statesman like William or Heinsius might rise to an understanding of the true maxims, but his efforts would be doomed in the end. Men were actuated by fear and hope. Yet intimidation was a dangerous weapon, for it was apt to produce the opposite of the desired effect: Louis's instructions to his diplomats in later years abound in admonitions against using threats. Hope was a more pliable instrument, if only because adaptable to each person according as ambition, greed, or vanity was his dominant passion. Though there were many variations, princes and high nobles were swayed mainly by ambition; ministers of more lowly origin, merchants and domestics, by greed; women by vanity; ecclesiastics by all three vices. It was not always possible to satisfy the ambition of a foreign prince or statesman, and vanity had a rather limited application, but greed could be put to the utmost use. Money was thus the factotum of Louis's diplomacy.

Louis's view of the world was conducive to careful planning based on a dispassionate analysis of the interests of every State and of reliable information; it also gave a certain stability to his course. At the same time, his pursuit of perfection often led to periods of indecision, and in all his calculations there was too little room for the unexpected. Most of his mistakes were not due to ignorance, but to a doctrinaire reading of excellent information. As late as 1712, he could assert that Queen Anne had had to carry on a long war 'useless to her realm' because British policy was guided, not by reason of state, but by private interests.[1] Someone who failed to react properly to the standard stimuli, like William III, baffled him. Exasperated by this strange phenomenon, Louis finally built a mental image of William as a man of insatiable, indeed monstrous, ambition—the more dangerous because he was so able.

William was in many respects a more complex person than Louis. His aims, and even many of his beliefs, changed considerably with time. In the last fifteen years of his life, he seems to have lived and thought on several planes simultaneously. On the highest was his religious world, where those whom God had elected went about in their appointed courses at the bidding of their Lord. Here William was the chosen instrument of God to curb the pride of Louis XIV, and it was here that the two men were locked in single combat. Victory was not assured in William's lifetime; but, if he persevered, he would show himself a worthy servant of God. On earth, this divine drama was reflected in the realm of hard-headed politics, where power, computed in mathematical terms, was paramount. Here there was room for political alliances based on reason of state, conciliation

---

[1] C. G. Picavet, *La Diplomatie française au temps de Louis XIV* (1930), p. 156.

of pressure groups, skilful negotiation. Strange as it may seem, William's view of human motives resembled Louis's. On this plane operated William the politician, cautious and daring at the same time. Still lower was the plane of everyday action. Here miracles were a daily occurrence, and God arranged the issue of every battle, the success or failure of every diplomatic move, the weather, and William's safe arrival at Loo. Having lived through 1672 and 1688, William had every reason to believe in miracles. But miracles did not happen in a wholly arbitrary fashion: they would not come unless one exerted oneself to the utmost and took care of every detail: thus it was best to keep one's powder dry and leave the rest to the inscrutable wisdom of God's ways. Behind the cold and forbidding exterior—like Louis, he was a master of dissimulation—lurked a man of passion, beset by cares and doubts. Whenever he contemplated the consequences of an impending setback, such as the fall of Mons, it seemed that final collapse was approaching, and he was often on the verge of despair. The worst usually happened: but the end would not come: and William would carry on, sustained by his belief in Providence.

William had acquired diplomatic caution after his premature attempts to aid Spain in 1683–4 had brought the Dutch Republic to the brink of ruin. Yet, unlike Louis, he was at times prepared to run great risks. His early experience in the field may have contributed to this trait, but its real source was his belief in divine help and in miracles. It required much courage to enter into the Partition Treaty of 1698, which could have brought him disaster at home and abroad. Here William performed an act of faith; in 1698–1700 he worked on the assumption that Louis was a chastened and reasonable man, and that henceforth such friction as might occur would be of the normal type between any two powers. In other words, William's work had been done, and it only remained to consolidate it. William was not shackled by any 'true maxims' in his understanding of the interests of States; there was more room for change in his world than in Louis's. Yet the tendency to see his contest with Louis in the light of eternity had earlier impaired his vision. Together with many contemporaries, he had been inclined to impute to Louis the dream of a 'universal monarchy with universal religion'. This distorted image of the *Roi Soleil* died hard and probably added to the difficulties of peacemaking in the Nine Years War, although William had come to desire peace as early as 1692. At the same time, seeing the struggle on an exalted metaphysical plane helped him attain to that comprehensive view of the war, and eventually of all Europe, which made him natural leader of the coalition. He ceased to belong to any one country. He sacrificed Dutch interests to English, English to Dutch; when necessary, he was ready to sacrifice the interests of both to those of the coalition; and towards the end he preferred the welfare of all Europe to the smooth running of the coalition.

The correspondence of William and his narrow circle of friends frequently contains expressions like 'the general interest of Europe' and 'the public good'. These are no mere phrases: often the writer is aware of a conflict between 'public good' and State interests, and he invariably sides with the former. Louis, probably, would have resolved such a conflict the other way round, had he been aware of its existence anywhere except in the imagination of misguided men. But then Louis was a more modern man than William, who was inspired by some of the ideals of the Middle Ages, buttressed by Calvinist theology. The 'liberty of all Europe' that William championed was not the liberty of Rousseau or of Mazzini; it was a set of medieval 'liberties' which ensured the continued existence of what were, by the test of absolutism, anachronistic States like the Dutch Republic. There were in William III vestiges of a medieval baron defending his rights and privileges against the encroachments of central authority.

In the duel between Louis XIV and William III neither side emerged full victor. Louis had failed to establish a hierarchy of States based on reason as he saw it. William III's concept of the public good was soon forgotten. Nevertheless, each in his own way helped to bring forth that unified order of Europe which, while it maintained the independence of many States, was rational, cosmopolitan, and civilized.

CHAPTER VI

THE ENGLISH REVOLUTION

LOUIS XIV, in his conflicts with Spain, the United Provinces, the emperor, and the German princes, had to consider England as a possible factor in them. His relations with Charles II ranged from open hostility to alliance; generally Charles was benevolently neutral. But this was the king's policy: as the reign advanced, English public opinion became increasingly opposed to France. This difference of outlook was linked with an enduring subject of constitutional dispute, the relations between king and parliament. The accession of James II brought to England a further and inescapable subject of dispute, the mutually hostile views—on what was the matter of greatest importance to all thinking men—of a Roman Catholic king and a Protestant nation. The religious advanced the constitutional dispute to a point where only force or abject submission could provide a settlement. Nor was it only for England that the outcome would be decisive. The settlement of the dispute was therefore a matter not only of pre-eminent interest to Continental governments, but also in varying degrees for their participation. What was achieved was more than the transfer of a crown from one prince to another, or a decisive change in the grouping of the European powers, or the emergence of Great Britain as a major power in world politics, or a new polarization of European culture. It was also the permanent establishment of effective constitutional government, and of the general principle that government exists for the governed.

When Charles died unexpectedly on 16 February 1685 the kingly power appeared to have attained a preponderance in the State such as it had not held since the coming of the Stuarts. This was in part due to Charles's efforts to provide efficient government. For the work of administration, so far as it then extended, he had brought together a body of able men; he had also built up a standing army strong enough to protect the government in all ordinary emergencies. These were advances such as any government must have desired. Charles, however, went much further. During much of his reign he, like his father and grandfather before him, had been in violent conflict with successive Houses of Commons. As the Houses were normally constituted he could do little with them; but if he could control the electorate he could obtain an adequate number of members favourable to himself. This control he was winning in the last four years of his reign by forcing many of the boroughs (which returned most of the members) to surrender their charters, and by issuing new ones which brought them directly under royal control.[1] At the same time he struck down his leading opponents among the Whigs and enforced rigorously the laws against the Protestant Nonconformists.

The means adopted by Charles to secure his objects were so violent, if not positively illegal, as to alienate moderate opinion; the frequent changes in the judiciary are symptomatic. Despite his advantages Charles would not face parliament. He was degenerating morally; he could obtain subsidies from Louis provided that parliament did not sit; above all he knew that, however loyal a future House of Commons might be, divergences which would ultimately raise constitutional issues must exist so long as Louis persecuted his Protestant subjects and seized the territories of his neighbours. Parliament, if it met, would demand strong measures and perhaps force Charles into war, with its sequels of inquiries into miscarriages and financial control. Fortunately for him, Louis's fear of parliament matched his own: much as he distrusted Charles, he was willing to pay him enough to enable him to dispense with parliamentary supplies. Charles gladly postponed the evil day, even though it involved the breach of an ineffectual statute.

Where Charles had been supple, unstable, astute and venal, James II was rigid, proud, single-minded and self-centred. Converted to Roman Catholicism at about the age of thirty-five, he had now all the proverbial convert's ardour and was encouraged by his devout queen, Mary of Modena. He had two paramount interests, to render the English Catholics permanently secure and to assert the royal power in the constitution. He probably never distinguished them one from another, or set any limits to his aims; he seems indeed to have confused what he believed to be right with the realities of religion and politics; and, whatever he might say, he showed little regard for other men's convictions. He was morally obtuse. He was on bad terms with Pope Innocent XI; while this might be attri-

---

[1] The total figure has never been established. The House of Commons at this time consisted of 513 members, returned by 40 English counties (two members each), 2 universities (two each), and 204 English parliamentary boroughs (two each, apart from 5 which returned one each and London, which returned four); and 12 by Welsh counties (one each) and 12 Welsh parliamentary boroughs (one each). Of the English parliamentary boroughs about 153 were incorporated by charter, the governing body established by the charter generally having an important, if not a controlling, power in parliamentary elections. Between February 1682 and March 1687 new charters were granted to about 116 parliamentary boroughs, affecting the elections of about 229 members. (By the beginning of May 1685, 100 parliamentary boroughs, returning 197 members, had received new charters.) Five of these, and perhaps more, were probably first charters of incorporation for the boroughs; on the other hand London, and perhaps some other places, did not obtain new charters in place of those which were forfeited. Of the chartered parliamentary boroughs not affected some were obviously under Crown influence or controlled by James's adherents. The unincorporated parliamentary boroughs ranged in size from Westminster and Southwark to Bramber and Old Sarum; most of them were probably small. In 1688 James issued about 35 charters to English parliamentary boroughs; some of them replaced or modified charters of the preceding six years. (I am indebted to Mrs Sonia M. F. Knecht for some of the above statements.)

buted in part to James's adherence to Louis XIV, it was principally due to his choice of an ambassador to the pope and to his pertinacious claims. For his ministers he wanted not advisers, but agents; from his judges he demanded subservience.

Public opinion, weary of Charles II, welcomed the new king, and James improved on this when, immediately after his accession, he declared to his Council that he would maintain the existing constitution in Church and State. He soon began to change the ministers who had served his brother. The liberal-minded and free-spoken Sir George Savile, marquis of Halifax (1633–95), was dismissed after some months. Laurence Hyde, 1st earl of Rochester (1641–1711), James's brother-in-law and second son of the great earl of Clarendon, a devout Anglican but an intriguer rather than a politician, was advanced to be Lord Treasurer. Robert Spencer, 2nd earl of Sunderland (1641–1702), thoroughly versed in court politics but inexpert in public opinion, a gambler too intent on success to have scruples of any kind, continued with steadily increasing powers as Secretary of State; in 1686 he became Lord President of the Council. These two were soon joined by the new Lord Chancellor Jeffreys (1648–89). Brutal by nature and trained in a bad school, he was a willing servant of the two kings, ready at all times to make the law serve their claims to absolutism. These three executed the king's wishes; his advisers were the queen and Fr Edward Petre, a Jesuit, inexperienced, rash, and perhaps ambitious. The queen disliked him and the Catholic nobility distrusted him, but he joined forces with Sunderland. While the nobles, who would have been content with freedom from persecution, advised caution, the queen and Petre alike hurried James forward.

In his endeavours for Roman Catholicism and absolutism James looked to his first cousin, Louis XIV, for encouragement and for protection against his subjects. France was now incomparably the strongest power in Europe, and Louis was in complete command. His two principal enemies were impotent to harm him: the emperor was engaged in driving the Turkish invaders from his territories; William III, prince of Orange, the stadholder of Holland and Zeeland, was unable to arouse the United Provinces to their danger. But the great days were passing. Louis was engaged in a series of quarrels with the pope; Protestants everywhere were horrified by his treatment of his Protestant subjects; the German princes were beginning to league together for protection against him; Brandenburg was abandoning his alliance; Leopold was gaining ground against the Turks; the senators of Amsterdam were losing their distrust of William. These changes amounted to little as yet, but Louis was ready to accept what James offered. There was at no time a formal alliance between them. Though he accepted a subsidy from Louis at the time of his accession, James avoided financial dependence on him. He occasionally showed some independence and there were local differences in North

America.[1] Nevertheless, common interest generally kept the two kings close together.

James called a parliament for 29 May. To give it a lead he called a Scottish parliament for 3 May. The Scottish parliament was an institution far more subordinate to the Crown than the English. The present body indeed confirmed all the existing statutes securing the Protestant religion; but it granted supplies more than adequate, endorsed the doctrine of hereditary succession, and decreed fierce penalties against the extreme Presbyterians. In England the Commons were elected mainly by the recently reformed boroughs, and royal influence was used freely in county elections; as a result, of the 513 members of the House, there were not more than forty of whom James disapproved. James believed that with some plain speaking he could obtain everything that his father and grandfather had claimed. Swallowing his harsh words, the Commons granted him an ample revenue for life. Before parliament could do much more its sitting was interrupted by the rebellions of the earl of Argyle in Scotland and of the duke of Monmouth, Charles II's eldest son, in the west of England. Both leaders appealed to the victims of Charles II's repressions; in neither case was there much response and the risings were easily suppressed, leaving James more powerful than before.

James raised additional forces to meet the emergency. The English Catholics were a small minority, probably far less than a fiftieth of the population.[2] They were oppressed by two groups of statutes: first, the older penal laws, enacted at various times from Elizabeth's reign onwards to extirpate Catholicism, but since the Restoration generally in abeyance —they were partially enforced only during the Popish Plot crisis; secondly, the two Test Acts, designed to protect the Protestant majority against the establishment of a Catholic ascendancy. By the first Test Act (1673) Catholics were debarred from civil or military office under the Crown; by the second (1678), from sitting in either House of Parliament. James was little concerned with the penal laws, for it was unlikely that any future government would enforce them; but he was determined to abolish the Test Acts, as a restriction on the royal power. Now, when raising forces, he granted commissions to Catholics in defiance of the first Test Act.

Parliament met again on 19 November, a month after Louis XIV had formally revoked the Edict of Nantes. It was prepared to grant James a further supply and to indemnify the Catholic officers for their breach of

[1] Cf. vol. v, pp. 366–7.
[2] Estimates of their number have gone as high as 10 per cent and above (B. Magee, *The English Recusants*, 1938); this may include crypto-Catholics, a meaningless term at this date. The population of England in 1685 is generally believed to have been rather more than five million. A relatively large proportion of the peers were Catholics, and in some areas Catholics were numerous; but the whole course of James's reign shows that there cannot have been half a million Catholics to require spiritual provision or to supply him with manpower.

the Test Act; but it was divided on James's proposal to replace the militia by a standing army and was resolute against the retention of their commissions by the Catholic officers. On receiving the Commons' protest James prorogued parliament. In 1686 a collusive action at law—Godden v. Hales—validated his dispensations from the Test Acts. Thenceforward he could dispense with statutes as he pleased.

The standing army at Charles II's death numbered about 9,000 men. James increased it in 1685 to 20,000 and by the end of his reign to about 34,000. He believed that it would give him security and enable him to enforce his wishes upon his subjects. He reckoned without two factors. He forgot, or was unaware, that since Cromwell's time Englishmen dreaded military government. In the three summers succeeding Monmouth's defeat he formed great encampments on Hounslow Heath; intended to intimidate London, they aroused hatred of the government which established them. And James could not find troops who would serve him as he required. His men were almost entirely Protestants who remained loyal to their creed and to the homes from which they came; illegal commissions granted to Catholics hardened existing antagonism. In default of a sufficient number of English Catholics to fill the ranks James introduced Irish recruits. By the end of the reign there was widespread disaffection in the army.

As king, James was also Supreme Governor of the Church of England. An important section of the Church had always identified its interests with those of the Crown and since about 1681 this section had predominated. Now it was to be put to the test. Relying on its promises of passive obedience James would inflict on the Church such burdens as he chose; at the same time he was beguiled by the more facile bishops into believing that the Church might be won over to his creed. By way of courtship he continued to persecute the Protestant Nonconformists; but perhaps more was to be gained by harsher measures. To two sees that fell vacant he appointed subservient divines; the archbishopric of York was kept vacant—perhaps, should all go well, in favour of Petre. When Henry Compton, bishop of London, refused to silence without due process a divine who had preached against Rome, James appointed the first of a series of ecclesiastical commissions. With Jeffreys at its head, it could be relied on to subject the Church to the king's will, more especially as William Sancroft, archbishop of Canterbury, refused to take part in its proceedings. It suspended Compton from discharging his episcopal functions. The Church remained steadfast. At this time it included many divines capable of defending its positions against all attack and, although the press was under control, they were sure of utterance because one of the licensers was the archbishop of Canterbury's chaplain. Hence there appeared a prolific and brilliant Anglican controversial literature. Writings of this class rarely convince opponents; they instruct believers about the points at issue and confirm the hesitant. The clergy might be forbidden to preach on controversial issues, but sermons on almost all doctrinal subjects were likely to bear on the great dispute. Whatever inducements James could offer, there were few conversions to Rome. Protestants became more sure of the grounds of their belief; the controversy perhaps taught Anglicans and Nonconformists to appreciate what they had in common. To that they were further encouraged by Louis XIV's persecution of the Huguenots, which was made widely known in 1686 by a national collection for the refugees.

William of Orange's position was now improving. Frederick William, the Great Elector, formed an alliance with the United Provinces in 1685; in August 1686 he and William met at Cleve. In the course of this year William's wife, Mary, had intimated to him that, should she as James's elder daughter ever succeed to the English throne, William should be king in name and in fact. So far he had kept on good terms with James II. He had advised Monmouth to enlist under the emperor against the Turks and tried to prevent his sailing for England; on the outbreak of the rising he had sent to England the six English and Scottish regiments in Dutch service. In August 1685 James renewed all the treaties made between England and the United Provinces since 1667.

Mary was disturbed by the attack on the Church of England and more especially by the treatment of Compton, who had been her tutor. About the end of 1686 William decided to send an extraordinary ambassador to England, Everard van Weede, lord of Dijkvelt. He was to expostulate with James about his domestic and foreign policy and to question him about a reported alliance between himself and Louis; he was also charged to observe the state of England, and to declare the prince's views on religious issues to the Anglicans, the Nonconformists, and the Catholics. The embassy came too late to influence James. On 15 January 1687, the day on which Dijkvelt's appointment was announced, he dismissed Rochester from the treasurership, replacing him by five commissioners, of whom two were Catholics. About the same time Rochester's brother Henry, 2nd earl of Clarendon, was superseded as Lord Lieutenant of Ireland by an Anglo-Irish Catholic, Richard Talbot, earl (later duke) of Tyrconnel (1630–91). In March Clarendon was succeeded, this time as Lord Privy Seal, by another Catholic. James's two brothers-in-law were too obstinately Anglican to be continued in his service. Meanwhile, in person, he was questioning members of parliament about their views on the Test Acts; the office-holders among them, if opposed to his wishes, were apt to lose their offices. On 22 February he issued a Declaration of Indulgence to Scotland. Dijkvelt had his first audience on 3 March. James laughed at the report of an alliance between himself and Louis, but paid no heed to Dijkvelt's representations. Dijkvelt therefore took up the other parts of his instructions. He possessed extremely pleasing manners. The leading politicians who opposed James met at his dinner-table; there they discovered what they had in common and learnt to trust one another. There was no conspiracy; a great political alliance was forming. When Dijkvelt returned home in June he carried to William letters from leading men of all parties, all expressing their confidence in the prince.

James issued a Declaration of Indulgence on 14 April, granting complete liberty of worship and annulling the Test Acts; at the same time he promised to maintain the Church of England and stated that holders of former monastic lands would not be disturbed; he trusted that parliament would concur in his views. The Nonconformists had been too long oppressed not to be grateful for the relief and many of them presented addresses thanking the king for his declaration. They were soon warned by Halifax in *A Letter to a Dissenter*, a remarkable tract published in August, of the folly of accepting the Indulgence. While Halifax urged the common cause of all Protestants James was showing the value of his protection of the Church of England.[1] The bishop of Oxford was the compliant Samuel Parker and Catholicism had made a slight advance in the university. The presidency of Magdalen College fell vacant in March. James decided to secure the college for his Church. His first candidate was not qualified according to the statutes of the college and was too disreputable even for James; ultimately a new ecclesiastical commission appointed Parker as president, and on 26 November expelled the recalcitrant Fellows.

Having ascertained in the spring that the existing parliament would not give up the Test Acts, James dissolved it on 12 July and set to work to obtain a House of Commons favourable to his projects. The borough constitutions were again tampered with, to replace Tories and Anglicans by Whigs and Nonconformists. To secure knights of the shire, agents questioned the lords lieutenants of the counties and justices of the peace. The replies were generally unsatisfactory; prospective candidates declared that their votes must depend on the debates of the House. As a result of their answers many lords lieutenants and justices were replaced by Catholics and other adherents of James.[2]

There were other ways in which to proclaim the triumph of his Church. In January 1687 a splendid chapel was opened for worship in his palace of Whitehall. His subjects might regret, but could not cavil at this. The public reception of the papal nuncio was more objectionable; indeed it was only unwillingly that Innocent had conferred on his representative the rank of nuncio. James had by now publicly surrounded himself by Catholic peers and other advisers (Sunderland himself, though he did not announce it until 1688, may have already turned Catholic); then in November he showed his complete disregard of the laws, his subjects'

---

[1] Cf. above, p. 125.
[2] J. P. Kenyon, *Robert Spencer, Earl of Sunderland, 1641–1702* (1958), pp. 171–4, 187–90.

feelings, and his own interests, by appointing Petre a Privy Councillor. But by this time he had a fresh hope of complete and permanent success. In November it was rumoured that his queen was pregnant; in January 1688 the pregnancy was officially announced.

William and Mary of Orange were in a difficult position. The contact which Dijkvelt had established between William and the king's leading English opponents was maintained by other agents, so that William knew how near English opinion was to breaking-point. On one issue he and Mary announced their views: they disapproved of persecution for conscience' sake but, while they would welcome the repeal of the penal laws, they insisted on the retention of the Test Acts. So much moral support they could give to the king's opponents. It would, however, be invidious for them as James's son-in-law and daughter to head a rising against him and they were further bound to him by domestic affection. Yet, if they left England to herself, there might ensue a civil war like that which had divorced England from European affairs for a decade in the mid-century; or Louis might intervene and so make James his vassal; or James, wishing to distract his subjects, might even join Louis in a repetition of the attack made on the United Provinces in 1672. William was further pressed to intervene by the European situation. English opinion had long since shown its hostility to Louis: it was essential that the full strength of the country should be turned against him, to maintain peace or to conquer in war. If James would change his whole policy, all would be well. It is probable, however, that at some time between Dijkvelt's return to Holland and the end of 1687 William envisaged intervention. He and three or four friends or associates appear to have worked out what forces would be required by land and sea, and how they could be raised or obtained: a complete plan was drawn up. But nothing was put in writing; there were no secretaries; absolute secrecy was maintained. Any warnings that Count d'Avaux, the French ambassador to the United Provinces, sent to Louis were such as he had sent long since and were based on his general distrust of William. Early in 1688 William began to make active preparations. The States-General, stung by a new French tariff on imports from the United Provinces, and alarmed by James's demand that they should send home the English and Scottish regiments in their service, voted strong defensive forces over and above their usual summer guard. While these forces were essential for the defence of the country, they could be used for a future expedition to England. In view of the uncertain attitude of Amsterdam (though that also was changing, thanks to the French tariff), William's preparations were made as inconspicuously as possible; they were thus largely hidden from d'Avaux as well as James. They were so far advanced that when, towards the end of April, an agent of James's leading English opponents, Edward Russell (the future admiral), asked William what he could do on their behalf, he replied that, given an adequate invitation from England, he could be ready to sail by the end of September.[1]

On 7 May 1688 James reissued his English Declaration of Indulgence, and on 14 May ordered it to be read in all churches and chapels throughout the kingdom. On 28 May a petition signed by Archbishop Sancroft and six other bishops was presented to the king: the Declaration, they said, was founded on an illegal dispensing power, and they asked James not to insist on their reading it. As William foresaw, the issue went to extremes. The great majority of the clergy failing to read the Declaration, James decided to act. The seven bishops appeared before him on 18 June and were sent to the Tower of London. Two days later his queen gave birth to a son. On 9 and 10 July the bishops were tried and acquitted by the court of King's Bench on a charge of seditious libel. From Westminster Hall, where the trial took place, the cheering which hailed the verdict echoed throughout London and beyond. At Hounslow, where he was inspecting the camp, James heard the shouting of the troops and was stiffened in his resolution against the Church.

On that night Arthur Herbert (earl of Torrington 1689) left London in disguise, carrying a letter to William signed by seven leading opponents of James II, Tories as well as Whigs: men of political experience, wealth, popularity and influence. In the plainest manner they informed William that nineteen out of every twenty 'of the people throughout the kingdom' wanted a change; they set out circumstances favouring an immediate invasion and the perils of delay; and they promised, on William's landing, to join him.[2]

In the course of the invitation the leaders mentioned the disaffection in the army and navy. In the following months their agents so organized this disaffection that, when the moment came, James's forces would be ready to abandon him—a task made easier by James's introduction of Irish Catholics into his English regiments. How William financed his expedition is imperfectly known; while he drew on the money voted by the States-General for defence, the English leaders perhaps remitted considerable sums to him. They also helped in another way. The queen's pregnancy was from the start a matter of dispute: Catholics augured that the child would be a son, Protestants suspected papistical fraudulence. From various motives the queen never allowed Princess Anne to examine her. The child was born unexpectedly early and the queen's labour was short. Anne, who was next in succession to the princess of Orange, was absent at Bath and Archbishop Sancroft, one of the principal *ex officio* witnesses to the

---

[1] G. Burnet, *History of My Own Time* (1833 edn.), vol. III, pp. 240–1, 276–7. Burnet's original account, written by October 1688, is printed in *A Supplement to Burnet's History*, ed. H. C. Foxcroft (Oxford, 1902), pp. 288–90.

[2] The text of the invitation is to be found in Sir J. Dalrymple, *Memoirs of Great Britain and Ireland*, vol. II (1773), pp. 228–31. It was signed by Devonshire, Danby, Shrewsbury, Lumley, Bishop Compton, Russell, and Henry Sidney.

birth of an heir to the throne, was a prisoner in the Tower; almost all the witnesses of the birth were Catholics who had never possessed, or Protestants who had forfeited, public confidence. William and Mary had accepted the child as genuine, but the invitation to him said that it was generally regarded in England as spurious. The circumstances of the birth were such as were consonant with fraud. William and Mary cannot have believed that James himself could be concerned in anything of the kind, but in compliance with the invitation William stopped the prayers for the prince in Mary's chapel.[1] In England the belief that James had attempted fraud perhaps weighed heavier against him in popular esteem than any of his real misdemeanours.

As soon as he received the invitation William put his invasion plans into execution. A private agent whom he had already sent to Vienna was to convince the devout and strait-laced emperor that the object was to safeguard Protestantism and not to start a holy war against Catholicism.[2] Some 7,000 seamen and 5,000 soldiers were enlisted. Hans Willem Bentinck (1st earl of Portland 1689), William's closest friend, went to the German courts to obtain troops who would protect the United Provinces when the Dutch troops went to England: 13,000 men were provided by Brandenburg, Hesse, and the princes of the House of Brunswick—except Ernest Augustus at Hanover, who had recently concluded a conditional treaty of alliance with Louis XIV.[3] William had sounded the Holland provincial councillors early in the year, when they reminded him of Monmouth's fate. Now he must persuade the various governing bodies in the United Provinces to support his expedition. Busy as he was with his preparations, the late summer was a period of acute anxiety for him. He had known long periods of adversity; his expedition, if it set sail, must trust to the chances of weather and of war. What harassed William most was the thought that the course of events on the Continent might preclude its sailing.

Louis played into his hands. Seeking recognition of his exclusive sovereignty in the territories seized from the Empire by the *Réunions*,[4] Louis had obtained only a guarantee for twenty years by the truce made at Ratisbon in 1684. He now hoped to secure a gateway through Cologne into Germany.[5] Late in 1687 he tried to install a supporter of his own, Cardinal W. E. von Fürstenberg, as coadjutor to the archbishop-elector. When the archbishop died on 3 June 1688 there were two candidates to

---

[1] They were resumed after a time to avoid an open breach with James.

[2] Leopold had conscientious difficulties in recognizing William as king: O. Klopp, *Der Fall des Hauses Stuart* (Vienna, 14 vols. 1875–88), vol. IV, pp. 424–37. It has been said that Innocent XI supported or had some knowledge of the expedition, but the documents generally adduced for this assertion are forgeries. It was impossible for Innocent to associate himself in any way with a Protestant against a Catholic prince; while he cannot have been surprised by James's catastrophe, he was deeply grieved by it: L. von Pastor, *Geschichte der Päpste*, vol. XIV, pt. ii (Freiburg-im-Breisgau, 1930), pp. 1032–6.

[3] G. Pagès, *Le Grand Electeur et Louis XIV* (1905), p. 601.

[4] See vol. v, pp. 219–20.   [5] Cf. below, pp. 224–5.

succeed him: Joseph Clement of Bavaria, whose brother, the Elector Maximilian Emmanuel, was at this time an adherent of the emperor's, and Fürstenberg. The election took place on 19 July. Despite intrigue, bribery and threats neither side carried the day, and the decision was transferred to Innocent XI, who in his turn referred it to a special congregation. Innocent had however already shown his aversion to Fürstenberg; he had several quarrels with Louis on hand already, and saw no reason why Louis should intervene in the affairs of the Empire; this the less as Leopold was the champion of a cause on which Innocent had set his heart, the expulsion of the Turks from Christendom. Indifferent to Louis's offers and threats, he announced on 18 September that Joseph Clement was elected. Louis had decided on his policy some three weeks earlier. He paid little heed to d'Avaux's warnings, while his ambassador in England could tell him little about English opinion. William's expedition could scarcely sail before the spring; James had adequate forces with which to defend himself; in addition, Louis had promised him that some ships should be available at Brest in case of need. In any case James was so unsatisfactory an ally that, should he be compelled to appeal to Louis for aid, the lesson would be salutary. Moreover, a show of French force would be valuable elsewhere. Now, while James appeared to be in little immediate danger, Leopold was driving back the Turks; Louis was not an ally of the sultan, but the Turks must be encouraged to fight on, so as to prevent Leopold from throwing all his forces into the western conflict.[1] Louis had suffered diplomatic defeats at Ratisbon and Cologne; Brandenburg had changed sides; if he was not to have to contend with the entire strength of the emperor and with some of the German princes, he must act immediately. On 9 September d'Avaux declared to the States-General that the alliance between France and England would oblige Louis to regard the first demonstration against James as a breach of the peace. James, infuriated by this patronage, denied the existence of any alliance with France, and the brusque disavowal confirmed Louis in his decision to attack Leopold. On 24 September he issued manifestos, threatening to appeal to a General Council against Innocent and vindicating his conduct towards Leopold. Three days later his troops laid siege to Philippsburg in the bishopric of Speyer, some 160 miles as the crow flies from the nearest Dutch territory. He had already missed one prize; Brandenburg and other German troops had already occupied Cologne.

D'Avaux's declaration had not intimidated the Dutch. As the danger of invasion receded, the senators of Amsterdam, the States of Holland, and the States-General all pledged their support to William. On 10 October he issued a declaration, enumerating the illegal acts of James's ministers and explaining Mary's and his concern; the purpose of his expedition was the assembling of a free and lawful parliament, which should safeguard

[1] Maréchal de Villars, *Mémoires* (ed. de Vogüé, 6 vols. 1884–1904), vol. I, pp. 99–102.

Protestantism and establish a just settlement of religious questions. The expedition was ready to sail a few days later, and waited only for a favourable wind.

Immediately after the trial of the bishops James dismissed the two judges who had pronounced in their favour, and instituted inquiries about the reading of his Declaration of Indulgence; he also declared that parliament would meet on 7 December. It was not until the first week in October that he realized that William intended to invade England. He immediately countermanded the writs for parliamentary elections, prepared as fast as he could to defend himself, and tried to enlist popular support by cancelling some of the obnoxious acts of his own and of the preceding reign. There was a general restitution of the old borough charters, with London at the head; the Commission for Ecclesiastical Affairs was abolished and the Fellows of Magdalen were reinstated. It would not do; these were the first fruits of the invasion; men fixed their hopes on it and not on the king, who, they noted, still kept Fr Petre about him. At a plenary meeting of the Privy Council on 1 November witnesses testified to the prince's birth. Four days later Sunderland was dismissed. Meanwhile the London mob destroyed two Catholic chapels.

William's expedition consisted of some 50 men-of-war and 200 transports, carrying 9,000 foot and 4,000 horse. After a fortnight's delay it set sail on 29 October, but was driven back by a storm with little loss. It sailed again on 11 November. It was probably intended to make for Yorkshire, where the earl of Danby, a signatory of the invitation to William, would raise the county; but the wind drove the expedition southward through the Channel. Wind and tide prevented James's fleet from leaving its station, and so saved William from the greatest risk, a fight with the English fleet, by then fully mobilized. The French ships which should, according to Louis's promise, have been at Brest had failed to leave the Mediterranean. On 15 November the expedition put into Torbay. Landing next day, the troops started to march towards London. During the first few days they were welcomed only by the country people; then the gentry began to come in, and William soon had a distinguished gathering about him. James, fearing riots against Catholics on 27 November, the day of Queen Elizabeth's accession—the great day for Protestant celebrations— and with plenty to do in London, sent forward his army, and himself reached Salisbury on 29 November. There had already been some desertions. Now the north was rising. Rendered impotent by prolonged bleeding at the nose and not daring to risk a battle, he began to retreat on 4 December. On the previous night John, Baron Churchill (earl of Marlborough 1689, duke 1702), the ablest of James's commanders, his trusted favourite, had deserted him. On the night of the 4th he was followed by Prince George of Denmark, husband of Princess Anne, and on the succeeding night by Anne herself and Sarah, Lady Churchill, who left

Whitehall to join Danby and the rebels in the north.[1] James had strong family affections; when he reached London on 6 December he was a broken man.

Meanwhile William advanced with ever-increasing strength; only one or two small skirmishes disturbed his march. James had planned to make Portsmouth a place of refuge and sent the infant prince there when he went to Salisbury. Now he decided on flight. To gain time he promised a parliament for 25 January and sent three commissioners to negotiate with William: Halifax, Daniel Finch, 2nd earl of Nottingham, and Sidney, Baron Godolphin. They met William at Littlecote, some 65 miles from London, on 18 December, and obtained terms next day. James was to dismiss all Catholic officers, civil and military; the Tower and the fort at Tilbury were to be entrusted to the City of London; during the sitting of parliament James and William, with their Guards, were both to be in London, or both equally distant from it; and both armies were to remove to 40 miles from London. On that night (19–20 December), before the report of the terms could have reached him, James had sent his queen and son to seek refuge in Paris and promised to follow within 24 hours.[2] He wrote a farewell letter that led his commander-in-chief, the earl of Feversham, to disband the troops who remained with him. Very early on 21 December, after burning the writs for the promised parliament, he left Whitehall, carrying with him the Great Seal which, with insane logic, he dropped into the Thames. Parliament could not lawfully meet unless summoned by writs certified by the Great Seal; no new Great Seal could be made without his authorization; his enemies could now do nothing without him.

The country was thus left without a government. James's closest adherents, Catholic and Protestant, took to flight. The press immediately sprang into action. Throughout the reign pamphlets had been published surreptitiously; now, between 21 and 25 December, four newspapers were started. On two nights there were riots against the Catholics. But the peers who were then in London met at Guildhall on 21 December; next day they met in Whitehall and elected Halifax their chairman; on the following day order was completely restored. Meanwhile James had been taken at sea near Faversham on the night of 21 December; he returned to London on the 26th.[3] There he was well received by the populace; after the anxiety of the last few days the way seemed open for a settlement.

[1] The northern rising is described by A. Browning, *Thomas Osborne, Earl of Danby and Duke of Leeds* (3 vols. 1944–51), vol. I, pp. 386–418. Resistance in England probably ceased with the surrender of Carlisle Castle on 25 December.

[2] In January 1689 Louis XIV installed them in the royal château of St-Germain-en-Laye (a few miles from Versailles), where Mary resided until her death in 1718.

[3] These are New Style dates; by this reckoning the English Christmas would fall on 4 January.

William was not prepared for James's flight. Until it took place he envisaged James as king and as chief governor of the country. By the time that James returned to London William's attitude had changed. It is probable that he was strongly affected by the disbandment of James's army without provision for its subsistence—a dereliction of duty. What had gone before was mistaken policy; now James had shown his moral incapacity for rule. James's former commander, when bringing William a message from James, was arrested. William advised James to remain at Rochester, but the message miscarried. On 27 December William, who was coming to London, ordered James to remove to Ham, some ten miles up the Thames from London. James preferred to return to Rochester. He left London on 28 December; William arrived there later in the day. The peers continued to meet. While they co-operated with William they sought James's consent to the summoning of a parliament. But James had escaped from his lodgings early on 2 January and was now making his way to France. A legal parliament could not meet without his consent; the peers therefore advised William to summon a Convention, and invited him to assume the administration until it should meet. On 6 January the surviving members of Charles II's Houses of Commons, with some representatives of the City of London, presented a similar address. On 7 January William agreed to carry on the administration until the Convention should meet on 1 February.

The need for settlement was urgent. France had declared war against the United Provinces on 26 November; Ireland under Tyrconnel was asserting its independence; although William had been invited to assume the administration of Scotland until a Convention should meet, James had many supporters there. To maintain what had been won England needed a stable government, Protestant, and strong to resist France. Though men are primarily concerned with political, religious, and economic issues, and not with constitutional, which are too abstruse for them, the first task of the Convention was to decide the constitutional problems which James had forced on the country. In theory, the existing constitution would provide the requisite government: hence the largely conservative character of the settlement. The immediate problems were to lodge the executive power in trustworthy hands, and to ensure the holder's trustworthiness. Four courses were open. First, James might be recalled on conditions. There were few advocates of this course, and James's own pronouncements soon showed its impracticability. Secondly, James and his direct heirs might retain the crown, but be regarded as infants or lunatics, while the executive power would be entrusted to regents. This course would do least harm to the monarchy as an institution and would save the oaths of allegiance which many of his subjects had sworn to James; hence its attraction for the Lords, of whom many had been closely associated with him, and for the clergy. But whatever his errors, James was not a lunatic; so long as he was legally recognized as king, whatever his actual powers, many of his subjects would not transfer their loyalty to a regent—more especially as, if they did so, they would not be protected by the law which exempted adherents of the king in possession from the penalties of treason. The third course was to regard James's flight as a demise of the Crown, in which case his elder daughter, the princess of Orange, would succeed him automatically; the newborn prince's claims being set aside for sufficient reasons. This course was supported by Danby, but neither Mary nor William would consent to it. Fourthly, James might be held by his flight to have dissolved the government; it would then be the duty of the Convention to settle the executive power as it thought fit, and to provide rules for its maintenance and exercise. This view, if rather rough and ready, corresponded fairly well to the situation created by James. It was supported by a large majority in the House of Commons, which resolved

That King James II having endeavoured to subvert the constitution of this kingdom, by breaking the original contract between king and people, and by the advice of Jesuits and other wicked persons, having violated the fundamental laws, and having withdrawn himself out of this kingdom, hath abdicated the government and that the throne is thereby vacant.[1]

The Lords proposed to substitute 'deserted' for 'abdicated', but the crucial question was whether the throne was vacant; the Lords voted to expunge the final clause of the resolution, the Commons stood fast. At length William intervened. He had so far refrained from any interference with the Convention, whether in the elections to it or in its proceedings. Until it met he favoured the plan for a regency; the debates showed how unsatisfactory it would be in practice. He therefore informed Halifax and some other peers that, if he were to exercise power in England, it must be as king in his own right and for life; if the Convention made any other settlement, without repining he would return to his own country.[2] The Houses at once reached agreement. The crown was to be offered to William and Mary jointly and to the survivor of them, William alone having the executive power during their joint lives; after their deaths it was to pass to Mary's children, then to Princess Anne and her children, and then to William's children by any wife other than Mary. Mary had been delayed in Holland by weather. She arrived in London on 22 Feb-

[1] *Journals of the House of Commons*, 28 Jan. O.S. 1689.
[2] N. Japikse dates William's conviction that he must have the crown between James's second flight on 2 January and a conversation with Halifax on 9 January: *Prins Willem III* (Amsterdam, 2 vols. 1933), vol. II, pp. 271–3. William's letters to Waldeck suggest a later date. On 3 or 4 January he fears that the Convention will force the crown on him; Waldeck, in reply to a letter of 20 January, hopes that the Convention will appoint him regent; on 24 February William writes that he had considered the matter thoroughly and could not avoid the crown: P. L. Müller, *Wilhelm III von Oranien und Georg Friedrich von Waldeck* (The Hague, 2 vols. 1873–80), vol. II, pp. 126, 130, 137.

ruary. On the following day she and William accepted the crown and a Declaration of Rights[1] which accompanied it.

In the seventeenth century a constitution was generally believed to be something static, an artifact more or less connected with the manners and customs of a particular nation. It was assumed that England already possessed a constitution of this nature; there was therefore no need to draw up a written constitution; in any case there was no time to do so, and there could have been no agreement in definition. That the ruler should conform henceforward with the nation's views was secured partly by enactment, partly by implication; much was taken on trust. It was agreed that Protestant England could not be governed by a Catholic prince. The Declaration of Rights stated what was believed to be the law, or the spirit of the law, on the principal issues in recent disputes; the new coronation oath pledged rulers specifically to observe the laws agreed on in parliament. That parliament should meet every year was effected principally by means of supply: apart from the requirements for war, William was deliberately kept short of money for the ordinary expenditure of the government; further control was secured through the legislation requisite for disciplining the army, which was provided in a succession of 'Mutiny' Acts, each of short duration.

But much was left to a general idea of contract between ruler and people, to the common interest and necessity of William and England, and to trust in his character. Before the Revolution his knowledge of the English polity was based on Stuart practice. He attributed too much power to the Privy Council, too little to parliament. He wished to retain the prerogative as his predecessors had held it, and used the royal power of veto to reject parliamentary bills on four occasions. But the rough treatment which he early received from the House of Commons changed his views, and his conflict with Louis XIV was so much more important to him than the prerogative that he soon learnt to comply with parliament's terms for its support. For counsel in these matters he was greatly indebted to Halifax who, in *The Character of a Trimmer* (published 1688), had set out the constitutional aspirations of the great middle body of English opinion—of those, neither monarchists nor republicans, who might in periods of stress or in everyday issues take sides as Royalists or Parliamentarians, Whigs or Tories, but who had at length signally asserted their common demand. Having acquired the crown William was resolved to be king of England, so far as the circumstances of the Revolution would permit, and not the king of a party. His essential moderation rivalled that of Halifax; his choice of ministers and his dislike of vindictiveness disappointed and safeguarded Whigs and Tories alike.

His sense of duty and his reliability linked him to his new subjects. At

[1] Later incorporated in a statute and commonly called the 'Bill of Rights'.

first there was distrust on both sides. There was widespread dislike of the transfer of the crown, where men should rather have disliked the need for the transfer, and this dislike was visited on William. Because he had ultimately obtained the crown it was easy to believe that his earlier professions of disinterestedness were hypocritical, a view which affected many persons who, while not adherents of James, pitied his misfortune. Where Charles II had an easy, friendly manner, William was reserved, if not morose; he found it difficult to take part in general conversation; and he obviously preferred his fellow-countrymen to his new subjects. William regarded some of these as self-seeking and treacherous: Rochester and Clarendon were knaves; Danby had shared in Charles II's French intrigues; Churchill was using Anne for his own ends and William perhaps also disrelished his desertion of James II, to whom he owed everything. In his relations with his subjects he was helped by Mary, who softened the effect of his manner, was familiar with English character, and as a Stuart brought a semblance of continuity to the new system. In course of time, as William and his subjects gained experience of one another, the situation became easier. With parliament some disagreement was inevitable. Parliament sat every year, and in any one harvest-year sat longer than it had done in the whole eight years preceding the Revolution. It thus gained in strength and widened its interests, the more so as fresh sources of information became available for its members. While William's conduct of affairs, rather than his policy, occasionally led to noisy disputes with it, he had long been accustomed to opposition and knew that in political life conviction by argument is more fruitful than proscription; if he could not have his way, despite his strong language in private he would yield; although he was sometimes censured, he never forfeited parliament's trust. His character contributed greatly to that public confidence which became manifest in the National Debt and the Bank of England.

For the general settlement of the country there were two urgent tasks. First, the transfer of the crown necessitated the imposition of a fresh oath of allegiance on all office-holders, including all holders of ecclesiastical dignities and other benefices. An Act enforcing the oath, on pain of forfeiture for refusal to take it, was passed in May. Comparatively few men refused, but among them were Archbishop Sancroft, six other bishops, and about 400 other clerics. Distinguished as Nonjurors, they claimed to be the true Church of England; but they had little following among the laity, apart from the Jacobites, the adherents of the exiled king. They were more important in political and ecclesiastical controversy than in politics. The second task was one to which the leading men in Church and State were more or less explicitly pledged: to provide legal toleration for the Protestant Nonconformists. It was an intolerant age, and if men's aversion from Catholicism had recently been inflamed by James's and Louis's conduct, they could not forget the real or imagined wrongs to which the Puritans had formerly subjected them or their fathers; as Anglicans they must maintain the external splendour of the Church of England and its paramountcy in the State, as well as its spiritual integrity. On the other side persecution was clearly impotent to make good converts; it was argued that it was incompatible with the teaching of the New Testament; men in general disliked seeing it exercised against their neighbours; the leaders of an important section of the Church, the Latitudinarians, were opposed to it; the new king had declared that he would have no part in it. Two measures were adopted to benefit the Nonconformists. By one, the Comprehension Bill, the Anglican liturgy was to be so modified that a majority of the Nonconformists could conscientiously accept it. This failed to pass in the House of Commons, partly because few Anglicans favoured it, partly because of the success of the other measure, the Toleration Act. This Act exempted the Protestant Nonconformists from all penalties to which religious dissidents were liable (apart from the disabilities imposed by the Test Acts), gave some privileges to their ministers, and allowed them to meet for worship. Most of them were willing to comply with the Test Acts, if occasion required, by receiving the Anglican sacrament. They were free to educate their children as they pleased. While William and the Latitudinarians prevailed they maintained their position; attempts made in Anne's reign[1] to restrict them to the narrowest indulgence were short-lived. Henceforward their difficulties would be social rather than political. The Toleration Act also provided for the Quakers, but excluded from its benefits the Catholics and all persons not believing in the Trinity. The Catholics were again liable to all the penalties and disabilities imposed on them by the penal laws and the Test Acts; theoretically their position was worse than before 1685 because they were almost necessarily Jacobites, and as such disloyal to William and Mary. Another statute expelled from London those of them who were not employed or permanently resident there, and they were also subject to double the usual rate of land tax. But in general they enjoyed greater security and freedom of worship than they had known before 1685. In this period they developed the use of foreign ambassadors' chapels in London as regular places of worship. Their prosperity ultimately contributed to the enactment in 1700 of an extremely harsh but mainly inoperative law against them. The worst feature of their position was that there was little prospect of its improvement; so long as they remained Jacobites no government would attempt much for their relief.

The more liberal outlook of the new reign appears not only in its connivance in religious matters, but also in its conduct towards the press. The accepted theory of the time required, and almost all States exercised, control over it. The principal exception was the United Provinces, where

---

[1] Below, pp. 264, 273–4.

it had long been free. In England it had generally been controlled by Licensing Acts or other means, but control had broken down during the Civil War and in the year preceding the Restoration, during the crisis of the Popish Plot, and in the interregnum created by James's flight. At other times there was no free discussion, apart from what was provided by surreptitious pamphlets—for example, Halifax's *Letter to a Dissenter* (1687) was not licensed—or in certain particular fields, as in the religious controversies of James's time. The Licensing Act of 1685 was still in force in 1689. Badly as it worked after the Revolution, it was renewed in 1693; by 1695, when it was again about to lapse, it had become so discredited that it could not be renewed. As there was no alternative plan available, the press, despite widespread belief in the need for its control, became free, subject only to the risk of prosecution for criminal libel. Several capable and long-lived newspapers started immediately, while innumerable pamphlets discussed everything of public interest.[1]

The English Revolution was in a narrow sense complete when William and Mary accepted the Crown on 23 February 1689. At first Louis did not realize the magnitude of James's disaster. When his queen and their son arrived in France he decided to use them as sureties for James's future good behaviour. James's second flight showed that England was lost. There was so little fear of civil war that early in the new year William sent home the Dutch contingent in his expedition; the Dutch fleet had returned long since. Although England did not declare war against France until 17 May, Louis already expected her to join his enemies; it was possible, however, that Scotland and Ireland might resist William successfully, and might even help James to recover England.

At this time Scotland had about a million inhabitants. The Highlands and Islands comprise rather more than half the country. The population was sharply divided. The Highlanders, perhaps a third of the total, spoke Gaelic; the Lowlanders, Scots English. By contemporary English standards the Scots were poor. Civilization was advancing as best it might in the Lowlands, despite backward political and economic systems, and the misgovernment of the Stuarts. The Highlanders were divided into clans, each owing obedience to its chief, who had jurisdiction of life and death over his followers; the poor living which they could wrest from their land was supplemented by lifting the cattle of their Lowland neighbours. While the majority of the Highlanders were nominally Scottish Episcopalians, Catholicism prevailed in a few areas; there was probably much crude superstition. Most of the Lowlanders were Presbyterians. The Stuarts had tried to force an episcopalian system upon them, but with little success; in the south-west, where feeling ran highest, repression and

---

[1] E. S. de Beer, 'The English Newspaper from 1695 to 1702', in *William III and Louis XIV*, pp. 117–29.

persecution, broken by occasional risings, had continued ever since the Restoration. The extremists, the Field Conventiclers or Cameronians, had been excluded by King James (in Scotland, James VII) from his Indulgence.

In October 1688 James summoned his forces in Scotland to the defence of England. Shortly before his first flight the Edinburgh mob attacked the Catholic chapel at Holyrood. On the old-style Christmas Day Presbyterians in the west began to evict the Episcopalian clergy. In January thirty Scottish noblemen and eighty gentlemen who had come to London requested William to undertake the government of their country and to summon a Convention of Estates. The latter met on 24 March. James permitted his adherents to attend, but they were outvoted from the beginning. Eventually, on 21 April, the Convention put forward a Claim of Right, declaring that James had forfeited the crown on account of his misdeeds and offering it to William and Mary. They accepted it on 21 May. Long before this James's adherents had left the Convention, and one of them, James Graham of Claverhouse, Viscount Dundee, was raising the Highlanders for his cause. On 6 August he routed a force of government troops at Killiecrankie, but was killed in the action. Without him the Highlanders could do little. About three weeks later they were repulsed by a regiment of Cameronians at Dunkeld. Resistance ceased in 1690, and in the course of 1691 the chiefs were compelled to swear allegiance to William.

Scottish parliaments had hitherto been controlled in the Crown's interest by a standing committee, the Lords of the Articles. This was abolished in 1691; parliament could henceforward initiate legislation. Largely on account of Anglican feeling William wanted to retain Episcopalianism, but the Scottish bishops were irreconcilable. Presbyterian government was therefore established by law in 1690. The Church remained subject to the king in parliament, much to the dissatisfaction of the Cameronians, who seceded. The Episcopalian clergy fared ill, though William did what he could for those who submitted to the new government; many of them continued as Nonjurors, especially in Aberdeenshire and along the borders of the Highlands. Industry and commerce began to expand, as is shown by the foundation of the Bank of Scotland in 1695 and by the attempt to found an overseas trading company; but so long as England protected her own industry, colonies and overseas trade against Scottish as against all foreign competition, there was slight prospect of much development. As a result of this and of more general causes national feeling ran high against England; it was strengthened by the Massacre of Glencoe[1] and by the failure of the Scottish venture to colonize Darien.[2]

---

[1] Macdonald of Glencoe having failed in due time to swear the oath required for the pacification of the Highlands, the king signed a conditional order for the extirpation of his clan. This was used to further private revenge, and led to the treacherous murder of 38 of the Macdonalds.

[2] Below, pp. 360 and 392.

Before the end of William's reign it was clear that there must be either complete separation between the two kingdoms or a parliamentary union.

While the Scottish Lowlanders quickly repudiated James II and closed their country to him, Ireland offered hope of recovering his lost kingdoms. The population, probably about double that of Scotland, was divided by nationality, religion, and the disputed ownership of the land. The native Irish and many of the English settlers in the Pale were Catholics. The Irish, the great majority of the population, still held a large part of the land west of the Shannon; elsewhere they were dispossessed, poverty-stricken labourers; the Catholic Anglo-Irish were relatively wealthy. The remainder of the Anglo-Irish and some more recent English settlers and colonists belonged to the Church of Ireland, which was identical in doctrine, government and worship with the Church of England. Other English colonists, former Cromwellian soldiers, were Protestant sectaries. In Ulster, as a result of confiscations in James I's time, there were colonies of Scottish Presbyterians.[1] Charles II had done little to right the wrongs of the native Irish but, as an unintentional effect of English protectionist legislation, the Irish developed a woollen industry on their own account, with the result that the country enjoyed twenty years of prosperity. There was also a remarkable amount of religious freedom.

This did not satisfy the natives. Their day dawned when Tyrconnel succeeded Clarendon. He apparently proposed, should the Crown devolve on a Protestant, to free Ireland from English control, even at the cost of French protection. Meanwhile he transferred civil and military power from the colonists to the natives. When James fell, Tyrconnel played for time with William, while he invited James to Ireland. He controlled the whole country except parts of Ulster, where the colonists formed centres of resistance at Londonderry and Enniskillen. James arrived on 22 March 1689, bringing with him arms and money provided by Louis, as well as French officers and d'Avaux as ambassador.[2] He had not recovered much energy or spirit. He disliked Ireland; just as formerly he regarded it as a source of Catholic soldiers who should coerce his English subjects, so now it was a means of recovering England; in his concessions to the Irish he was fearful of alienating English opinion. Here he was at variance with his two principal advisers—Tyrconnel, who wished Ireland to throw off the English yoke, and d'Avaux, who ignored English opinion and Irish suffering. James summoned a parliament which sat at Dublin from 17 May to 28 July. In the House of Lords four bishops and a few temporal peers formed an appreciable Protestant minority. In the Commons, thanks to Tyrconnel's handling of the electorate, there were few Protestants. Most of the 230 members were of Anglo-Irish descent, only about sixty

[1] See J. C. Beckett, *Protestant Dissent in Ireland, 1687–1780* (1943): the Independents (Congregationalists) were relatively unimportant (*ibid.* p. 136).
[2] On the Irish campaign, see below, pp. 235-7, 240, 241-2.

bearing Irish names; few had any parliamentary experience and most were concerned only to assert their rights and avenge their wrongs, without knowing how to achieve their ends. The Act of Settlement (1662) was repealed and the land restored to those who had owned it before 1641, or to their representatives, while a wide-ranging Act of Attainder declared some 2,400 persons guilty of high treason. James was obliged to assent to both measures, ruinous as they were to his prospects of returning to England.

The resistance in the north continued. Irish forces besieged Londonderry and nearly reduced it by starvation. William, who would have preferred to encounter Louis's forces on the Continent, but who was compelled by the English parliament to undertake the reconquest of Ireland, dispatched ships and troops. Londonderry was relieved on 10 August, the greater part of Ulster recovered later in the year. William himself came in 1690. On 11 July his army met and routed that of James at the Boyne; James, almost the first to fly from the field, immediately returned to France. William failed to capture Limerick in this campaign; it capitulated to an English force on 13 October 1691, and the subjugation of Ireland was complete.

The terms of the Treaty of Limerick amounted to a general indemnity for the Irish participants in the war and a return to the conditions of Charles II's reign. Those who wished might leave Ireland to seek their fortunes abroad: 12,000 men did so by December. But the Protestants in Ireland wanted security, land and revenge. As regards land the terms of the treaty seem to have been kept.[1] But an Act of the English parliament excluded Catholics from the Irish parliament; then in 1695 the Irish parliament passed the first of a new series of penal laws against the Catholics. Although William opposed this course, he was obliged to assent to some of the Acts, and further penal laws were enacted by his successors. At the same time the English parliament attacked the reviving woollen industry. Although the penal laws were never fully enforced, the Revolution led to a period of Irish history which for Englishmen must always be shameful.[2]

With the Revolution, the constitutional conflict in England ceased to be a fight to the death between king and parliament. The future was uncertain. William and Halifax alike hoped that parties as they had known them would disappear. In this they were mistaken. Soon there would be an habitual contest between parties which accepted the rule of king in parliament, the limited monarchy; and, though the parties were loosely organized and disciplined, it would soon be necessary for the king to govern through whichever of them could command the support of the House of Commons—to form a ministry based on party, with all the

[1] J. G. Simms, *The Williamite Confiscation in Ireland, 1690–1703* (1956), p. 161.
[2] Cf. below, pp. 255–6.

patronage and corruption requisite in this period for the stability of such a ministry. In 1689 William drew his ministers from all sides, but was restricted by his dislike of Rochester and the latter's High Church followers, and by the lack of suitable Whigs. While the Tories made difficulties about the religious settlement, the Whigs alienated him by their efforts to avenge the wrongs they had suffered since 1681. Their vehemence caused William to dissolve the Convention and to call a new parliament early in 1690; it also drove Halifax from office, leaving as principal minister the Tory Danby, now marquis of Carmarthen (1631–1712), whom William and Mary both disliked. William made some further changes, generally preferring Tories to Whigs; but, when he went to Ireland in the summer of 1690, the councillors whom he left with Mary were appointed without regard to party.

Louis was now at war with the emperor, Bavaria, Brandenburg and other German states, Spain and Savoy, as well as with the United Provinces, England, and Scotland. He had no allies, but the attack on Philippsburg had succeeded in keeping the Turks in arms. Strong as his enemies were, he was able to hold his own in the field and at first was equally successful at sea.[1] But Louis and his advisers had little idea of exploiting their victory off Beachy Head, while Mary showed by her firmness that the new government need not rely for its endurance entirely on William. She remained in charge when William went abroad in the following years, until her death in December 1694. There were, however, continuous attempts by the Jacobites to spread disaffection and to win to James's cause politicians who considered themselves slighted by William. The discovery of a Jacobite conspiracy led William in 1691 to enforce the laws against the Nonjurors.

By 1692 there was wider discontent in England with William's government. Many participants in the Revolution were disappointed by its outcome. Numerous clerics and some laymen had refused their allegiance to the new government, or paid it only grudgingly; there was some disaffection in the navy; the French were seizing or destroying English merchantmen; taxation for the war was heavy; and the war seemed endless. Exaggerated reports reached James, who persuaded Louis that the time had come to invade England. French and Irish troops gathered on the Norman coast, where James joined them; but Tourville's fleet, ordered to cover their voyage to England, was defeated early in June at La Hogue (La Hougue).[2] Although from this time the new government was secure against military overthrow, by attacking a large convoy bound for Smyrna and the Levant in 1693 Louis inflicted a heavy loss on London.[3] An Allied attack on Brest in 1694, moreover, proved a costly failure. In these years it had been difficult to find suitable men to serve as ministers.

[1] For the course of operations on the Continent and at sea, see below, ch. VII.
[2] Below, p. 244 and note.   [3] Below, p. 246.

Until late in 1693 William continued to divide appointments between the parties. Then, on the advice of Sunderland, who had returned from exile to a twilight existence at his country house, he decided to trust mainly to the Whigs. The Tory Nottingham had been a Secretary of State since 1689; the other secretaryship had been held by a series of Whigs. As a result of his dispute with Admiral Russell, Nottingham was dismissed in November and replaced by a Whig, Charles Talbot, earl of Shrewsbury, who had already served as secretary in 1689-90. Another Whig, Charles Montagu (earl of Halifax 1700), who had been appointed a Commissioner of the Treasury in 1692, was soon to emerge as a great finance minister. In 1693 Sir John Somers (Baron Somers 1697), also a Whig, was appointed Lord Keeper of the Great Seal (Lord Chancellor 1697). These three men were all fairly new to political life, with no rankling memories of 1683. They organized the resources of the country for war. The campaigns of 1694, the year of their accession to power, were the first which ended with the advantage to the Allies rather than to Louis.[1]

The Revolution brought foward a major problem in political thought. The theories prevalent or officially encouraged in France and England were those of monarchic absolutism and the divine right of kings. If the supersession of James by William and Mary on the English and Scottish thrones was to be regarded as anything more than a successful crime, some moral basis for it must be found and stated.

Absolute monarchy and Divine Right involve independent theories, but readily associate with one another. They had only recently attained full stature. In France, thanks to earlier discord and the brilliance of Louis XIV's autocracy, absolutism was widely accepted.[2] In England Divine Right, with the unlawfulness of resistance, was introduced by James I. Most of its leading advocates were clerics, but immediately before the Revolution its chief exponent was Sir Robert Filmer. He composed his principal work, *Patriarcha*, shortly before the Civil War. It was first published in 1680 in order to invigorate Charles II's supporters against the Whigs. Divine Right was about at its zenith in 1683, when the University of Oxford solemnly burnt a number of books which expounded principles incompatible with or contradictory to it. There was also much antagonism to the theory. One of its principal corollaries, the duty of passive obedience (that is, patiently enduring the penalties for refusing to obey the king's commands when they are contrary to God's law), which was inculcated by some of the clergy and accepted by many of them, was repugnant to most laymen; for the energetic and enterprising, non-resistance was absurd. They were constitutionalists; even if they made

---

[1] For England in William's later years, see below, ch. VIII.

[2] The most elaborate exposition is by Bossuet, *Politique tirée des propres paroles de l'Ecriture Sainte*, begun in 1677 and published posthumously in 1709: see vol. V, pp. 99-102.

some concessions to Divine Right, they held that the king was bound by the laws of the land. In this they were supported by the unimpeachable authority of Richard Hooker, who moreover had found a sufficient basis for the State in the natural sociability of mankind, and who denied that government must necessarily be monarchic. Recently Halifax in his *Character of a Trimmer* had warned Charles II against any breach of the constitution, eloquently declaring his own great admiration for it. Other writers were far more averse from Divine Right. Hobbes satisfied neither side: *Leviathan* was too secularist, not to say atheistic, for the supporters of monarchy, and too absolute for its opponents; it was among the books burnt at Oxford. But the pyre also included, with several less notable books, the *Vindiciae contra Tyrannos* and George Buchanan's *De Jure Regni apud Scotos*, which had both been translated into English.[1]

The general conception of the constitutional monarchy emerges clearly in a passage in an orthodox political year-book. The king is absolute and can do what he pleases; should he seize arbitrarily the property of any particular subject, there is no redress. But he is restrained by his conscience; by his coronation oath and by 'the Law of *Nature, Nations*, and of *Christianity*' he holds himself bound to protect his people, to do justice and maintain order, and 'to allow them their just Rights and Liberties':

Two things especially, the King of *England* doth not usually do without the consent of his Subjects, *viz*, make *New Laws*, and raise *New Taxes*, there being something of *odium* in both of them, the one seeming to diminish the Subject's Liberty, and the other to infringe his Property.[2]

In England, where men's minds were so open and so much printed discussion was available, the issues of the Revolution could be dealt with partly by reprints, partly by ephemeral pamphlets; only one major work was published to justify it, and that had been written for another purpose and went far beyond immediate requirements. The practical need was to show that subjects possess a right to resist the supreme authority in the State, and to define that right. The most notable of the pamphlets is by Gilbert Burnet, the future bishop of Salisbury, *An Enquiry into the Measures of Submission to the Supreme Authority*. This apparently originated in 1687 in discussion between Burnet and Princess Mary and was first published in the Netherlands, probably a few weeks before William

---

[1] The *Vindiciae* in 1680, Buchanan in 1648: both were reprinted in 1689, when there appeared an English translation of Spinoza's *Tractatus theologico-politicus* and an altered version of Milton's *Tenure of Kings and Magistrates*. The history of the theory of contract is given by J. W. Gough in *The Social Contract* (Oxford, 2nd edn. 1957).

[2] E. Chamberlayne, *Angliae Notitia*, I believe in all editions prior to 1689; here quoted from 1679 edn. vol. I, pp. 92–4. The passage was altered after 1689. Henry Care's *English Liberties: or, The Free-Born Subject's Inheritance* (1680 and later) sets out the rights of the individual as established by Magna Carta and later statutes, and by the 'work and power' of parliaments. Constitutionalism is implicit, if not explicitly avowed, in many of the political pamphlets of Charles II's reign, as well as in speeches in parliamentary debates.

sailed. As author of *The History of the Reformation of the Church of England* (1679–81) and as a keen observer of contemporary affairs, Burnet had a ready command of his subject. Here he states explicitly and without argument that civil society is based on contract; the contractors distinguish between the power of making laws for the control of society and that of executing them; the executive power, when acting separately from the legislative, is a trust accountable to it. The obligation to obey the government thus established is set out, and then the limits of its powers. Burnet then turns to England, where the constitution limits the king's powers, and easily finds a right of resistance.

What was easy for an English writer was difficult for a Frenchman. The Huguenots had held strong views on absolutism. In 1685 Elie Merlat stated them in uncompromising form. The State originates in man's sinful nature; to restrain that nature God created sovereign powers, and in course of time made them absolute and unlimited. The sovereign cannot control men's consciences, but has power over external forms; men who cannot obey him for conscience' sake must suffer in patience or fly.[1] After 1688, unless they repudiated William, the Huguenots must establish a moral right of resistance. French absolutism was attacked at practical level in *Les Soupirs de la France esclave*,[2] and at theoretical level early in 1689 by Pierre Jurieu in three issues of his *Lettres pastorales*. Jurieu had fled from Sedan in 1681 and was now professor of theology at Rotterdam. He was a fiercely orthodox Calvinist. The *Lettres pastorales*, which appeared from 1686 to 1689, were written to console the Huguenots who remained in France. From views similar to Merlat's he was forced by the Revolution to adopt a new position. Governments are established by contract; when they are established they are entitled to complete obedience. Jurieu is mainly concerned with absolute monarchies. He now employs an old distinction between absolute and unlimited power. The contractors cannot confer the latter because they do not possess it over themselves. They give their rulers sovereignty only for the preservation of their property, their lives, their freedom, and their religion. When the monarch exercises unlimited power his subjects, on certain conditions, are entitled to resist him. In practice Louis XIV has revoked a perpetual and irrevocable edict; his subjects may therefore resist him. Jurieu's views, and especially the right of resistance, were attacked alike by the Huguenot Bayle and the Catholic Bossuet. They are not worked out fully enough to rank high as a contribution to political philosophy. Appearing in a surreptitious periodical, they were quickly lost to sight. A few months later there appeared a far more adequate statement of the rights of the individual.

---

[1] *Traité sur les pouvoirs absolus des souverains*: see G. H. Dodge, *The Political Theory of the Huguenots of the Dispersion* (New York, 1947), pp. 7–10.

[2] Fifteen *mémoires*, Amsterdam, 1689–90: cf. below, p. 317.

This is the work of John Locke, in the second of his *Two Treatises of Government*.[1] In or about 1681, on the publication of *Patriarcha*, Locke set to work to refute Filmer's views. But negation alone would not suffice; he therefore added to the refutation a second treatise setting out a satisfactory political system. He probably completed the book before he left England in 1683. When six years later he decided to publish it, part of the refutation of Filmer was lost; but Filmer counted for little in 1689. The second treatise was probably revised and expanded, but in conception and general execution it belongs with Shaftesbury and the Exclusion crisis of 1680–1, not with the Revolution and the preparations for it in 1688. It is a moral argument for constitutional monarchy; the right of resistance is an integral part of the argument but not its main feature. If Jurieu's and Locke's views on individualism are not to be regarded as parallel developments from a common stock of ideas, then it is probably Jurieu who derives from Locke, and not the other way about. Like Hobbes, Locke believed in the secular origin of the State by means of a contract; in all other respects he differs from Hobbes. Men in the state of nature have various rights, but not enough security in the enjoyment of them; they therefore agree to unite 'for the mutual *Preservation* of their Lives, Liberties and Estates, which I call by the general Name, *Property*'.[2] To achieve union every man agrees to surrender his right of punishing those who injure his property. He retains all the rights which he does not expressly surrender, and civil society exists solely for the preservation of those rights: the State exists for the individual, not the individual for the State. The contractors appoint a legislative, which is concerned with the making of laws and which may appoint an executive to enforce them. The legislative is a trustee for the contractors. The individual must obey the government thus established, but it is dissolved if the legislative or the executive break their trust.

Locke thinks too much in terms of the English constitution as it existed in his own time for his system to claim universal validity.[3] Such passages as the contractual origin of government have always aroused criticism. Much of the treatise is too vague. Thus, in 'governments, where part of the legislative consists of representatives chosen by the people', 'the people' is not defined; Locke probably intended the customary parliamentary electorate of his own time rather than anything approaching manhood suffrage but, if he had considered it practical, would perhaps have welcomed the wider interpretation. The book was valued on account of its success in finding a moral basis for the new settlement of the constitution and for the support which it gave to

---

[1] The first edition is dated 1690 but was advertised in November 1689; the best is that by Peter Laslett (Cambridge, 1960).

[2] II, § 123.

[3] Cf. vol. V, pp. 119–21.

current ideas of liberty and property; its essential liberalism was probably more important in a later period. Although there were new editions of Locke's *Two Treatises* in 1694 and 1698, and others in the eighteenth century, he did not enjoy an immediate triumph over Filmer, whose works were reprinted in 1696. But there was no serious criticism of Locke's views, and they were generally accepted in England by the time of the Sacheverell trial in 1710. A French translation and an analysis of the book in French both appeared in 1691, but its diffusion in France came later; nine new editions of the translation appeared between 1724 and 1802.[1]

The Revolution was due to political and religious, and only in a very general sense to social and economic causes. Its object was essentially conservative, to maintain institutions and practices which had recently been attacked on questionable or improper grounds. The Declaration of Rights called for redress, not reforms. Recognized abuses were left untouched. Thus no attempt was made to reorganize the parliamentary constituencies, and while a general widening of the existing franchise was not demanded and was scarcely desirable, some of the existing anomalies might have been removed. The limited scope of the Declaration was due, apart from the probable lack of will, to the need for haste. As deficiencies came to light they were supplied by the Triennial Act of 1694 and the Act of Settlement of 1701; thereafter the only fundamental changes in the law of the constitution for over a century—the Act of Union of 1707 and the Septennial Act of 1716—were largely safeguards of the achievement of 1689. The Revolution had solved so completely the more visible problems of its own time that men only gradually became aware that the new life in the conditions provided by it was in its turn creating new problems.

Among its products must be counted the place taken by England in European thought and culture in the eighteenth century. In the last quarter of the seventeenth century the culture of Louis XIV's court was declining from its noontide splendour; in his last years, with other discontents to arouse them, Frenchmen themselves became increasingly aware of its shortcomings. The Revocation of the Edict of Nantes had directed many Huguenot refugees and other French-speaking Protestants to England as the potential saviour of Protestantism. These men were admirably suited for the work of diffusing English ideas; there were few great original thinkers among them, but translators, extractors, compilers, publicists, without number. In place of the old international scholarship based on the use of Latin for learned works, their periodicals—the *Nouvelles de la République des Lettres* and the like, consisting as a rule of critical summaries of books—engendered a new international scholarship;

---

[1] Locke also wrote on religious toleration: *Epistola de Tolerantia,* 1689 (E. T. also 1689). For Dr Sacheverell, see below, p. 270.

through them books written in a little-known language reached a European public. Where the Protestants had sought security, Frenchmen about the time of Louis XIV's death began to seek liberty. England's power of mobilizing her resources during the wars had proved greatly superior to that of France; the stability and the strength of the new government evoked increasing curiosity. For a decade there was comparatively little inquiry; the change comes with the publication of B. L. von Muralt's *Lettres sur les Anglois et les François* in 1725 and of Voltaire's *Lettres philosophiques* in 1734. By the mid-century the English language was being studied in France. English literature attracted attention and there were many translations; it was readily assimilated because the authors chosen for translation were themselves strongly influenced by France, whether through the predilection of Charles II or through contact with the Huguenot refugees, many of whom found employment as tutors. Through the Huguenots, through France, occasionally through foreign visitors, English and (later) Scottish culture and thought penetrated to Germany and Italy, and became the predominant strain in European culture in the third quarter of the eighteenth century.

The influence of English political ideas is at its strongest in Montesquieu's *L'Esprit des Lois*. Montesquieu was in England from 1729 to 1731. He was in contact with Bolingbroke and the Tories rather than with the Whigs, but he found everywhere, despite much corruption, the effects of liberty as he conceived it, the result of particular political institutions. In two famous chapters he describes and analyses the constitution; here he was helped by Locke's second *Treatise*. *L'Esprit des Lois*, published in 1748 at Geneva, ran through perhaps 22 editions in its first 18 months. From the time of the Seven Years War it lost its primacy. Montesquieu is aristocratic, urbane, retired. He was concerned rather with the means by which liberty is maintained than with liberty itself, or the everyday political life of the citizen. In Great Britain the new age was aware of failings which he overlooked. Society had developed rapidly in numbers, wealth and complexity; the inherited administration, in its best days less than adequate, survived almost unchanged; many old abuses awaited reform; the anomalies of the parliamentary electorate, which had been noticed long before 1689, became a glaring injustice as great towns arose in new industrial areas. But for all its deficiencies the British government accorded with national requirements, and Montesquieu strongly influenced later political thought. In France, where government and people clashed, his views were too moderate; England, with its many visible evils, could not serve as an example; what was needed was provided by Rousseau, a passionate restatement of the rights of man. Yet this was not completely new ground. These rights, which were to inspire or to ennoble the American[1] and

---

[1] For the immediate repercussions of the English Revolution on the American colonies, see below, pp. 480 ff. Its economic sequels are discussed below, ch. viii, ix and xxiii (1).

French Revolutions and the liberal constitutions of the nineteenth century, are already implicit in Locke. Without the Revolution of 1688 they could scarcely have advanced beyond theory. For this reason, though appeals were constantly made to the new statement, with only occasional references to the old achievement—or to Locke and Montesquieu, its expounders—the Revolution continued, and continues, indirectly or directly, to exercise a strong and distinctive influence.

CHAPTER VII

THE NINE YEARS WAR, 1688-1697

FRANCE was at war from November 1688 until October 1697, so that the name of the Nine Years War accords almost exactly with the facts. It is also less likely to mislead than the other names which have been used. 'The War of the League of Augsburg', which originated with French writers, seems to impute responsibility to the Augsburg alliance of 1686. This alliance was, indeed, one of the preliminary steps towards the organizing of a coalition against France but, strictly speaking, it was abortive. Its signatories never acted upon it. A third name, 'King William's War', may be misunderstood to mean that King William III was chiefly responsible for the outbreak of the war.

Except for the short war with Spain in 1683-4, France was legally at peace or in truce with all the states of Europe for the ten years following the treaties of Nymegen in 1678-9; but during these years Louis XIV took possession of various towns and territories beyond his borders. His methods were various; they ranged from the legal pretexts of the *Réunions* to the purchase of Casale from the duke of Mantua; but the lordships and revenues so acquired were not as miscellaneous as might appear. The French moved forward from the points where their armies had halted at the peace settlement. They acquired three first-class fortresses. Strasbourg, with Kehl to support it, commanded the crossing of the Rhine on the road to the Danube; Luxemburg was the *point d'appui* on the left flank of the defence of the Spanish Netherlands; Casale stood on the Po, above the point where it entered the Spanish duchy of Milan. Others of the places were by no means negligible. The acquisition of Dinant, in the bishopric of Liège, removed an obstacle in the way of an attack on Namur, the next great fortress to the west of Luxemburg. The French built forts at Hüningen on the Rhine, immediately below Basle; at Mont Royal near Trarbach on the Moselle, between Trier and Coblentz; and at other points in the territories of friendly German princes.

These strategic advances were part of a general activity of the war-machine. The fortresses in Flanders, Alsace and Franche-Comté were strengthened under the orders of Vauban, the most famous of all masters of fortification; magazines were stocked; 36 battalions of infantry were ready for service, and the cadres of the 140,000 men disbanded at the peace were kept on foot so that the units could be raised quickly to their full complement.[1] There were changes in organization. Louvois formed the

---

[1] Throughout this volume the numbers given for military and naval forces are only approximate. More precise figures would need to be accompanied by much explanation of

compagnies des cadets, training corps for younger sons of noble houses who were to serve as officers, although it was announced that evidence of noble descent would not be scrutinized too severely. In 1688 a new kind of militia service was introduced: local *milices* serving for two years, equipped and paid by the parishes of certain *généralités*, exercised on Sundays and holidays under paid officers drawn from the local *noblesse*. Their establishment amounted to 25,000 men. In war they served as second-line troops, returning to their homes when the army went into winter quarters.[1] Naval preparations were as active as those of the army. Between 1678 and 1688 the number of ships of the line increased only from a nominal 116 to a nominal 120, but all the dockyard services and the system of compulsory enrolment for seafaring men were brought up to a higher standard of efficiency.[2] The fleet gained experience chiefly in the Mediterranean and especially in using its newly invented bomb-ketches against shore-defences, as at Genoa (1684), Tripoli (1685) and Algiers (1688); French squadrons had gone into action against Spanish as well as Algerine ships. Besides these military and naval measures, the French used strong economic pressure in disputes with their neighbours. In the 1680s, they and the English and Dutch engaged in a three-cornered tariff war. In this, however, France was not the aggressor, except in the sense that she was the newcomer in the competitive exporting of manufactures and was trying to gain markets by vigorous protectionism.

In 1688 three chains of events converted this undeclared war into open and recognized war. Cologne had a Francophil archbishop and elector, Maxmilian Henry, a member of the Bavarian electoral family of Wittelsbach. Early in this year his health was failing. The ground had long been prepared for the election of a successor devoted to the French interest, by the appointment of Cardinal Fürstenberg, bishop of Strasbourg, as coadjutor to the archbishop. This would confirm French influence at a vital point. The territory of the archbishopric lay along the left bank of the Rhine and included three fortresses of the river-line—Bonn, Rheinberg and Kaiserswerth—besides Cologne itself. Moreover, the archbishop was also prince-bishop of Liège. That bishopric lay astride the Meuse, itself a strategic highway, and contained the industrial district, the coalfield and the ironworks from which the Dutch army drew most of its munitions. A candidate was available whose election would remove Cologne and Liège from French influence, namely Joseph Clement, a son of the archbishop's nephew, and brother of the reigning elector of Bavaria, Maximilian Emmanuel. This Max Emmanuel was the successor of a French ally; but he had married the emperor's daughter. In 1685 the emperor had

their exact meaning, and in many instances could only be established by research that has not yet been undertaken.

[1] Below, pp. 767–8.

[2] Cf. below, pp. 811 ff. for the arsenals and pp. 821 ff. for the *Inscription Maritime*.

proposed that the Spanish Netherlands be given him as an appanage. At the moment he was commanding the victorious Imperial army against the Turks. Even if he had been personally insignificant, the election of his brother would have been most unwelcome to Louis XIV. On 3 June the old archbishop died. There was a disputed election. The pope refused Fürstenberg a dispensation and the emperor refused to confirm him in the electoral dignity. Late in August, 16,000 French troops, with the promise of an equal number to follow, occupied Bonn, Kaiserswerth and the open country of the electorate. Cologne itself received Imperial troops, chiefly provided by the elector of Brandenburg who, in his duchy of Cleves and county of Ravensberg, was a close neighbour lower down the Rhine.[1]

The movement of French troops was not unsupported. More than a hundred miles further south a much larger force advanced with the intention of deterring the German princes from offering opposition. After preparations of which the objective was a well-kept secret, three French corps, numbering some 80,000 men, crossed the virtually undefended Imperial frontier on 24 September. In a declaration which was not in form a declaration of war, Louis justified his action with a separate pretext for each of the States whose territory he violated. The principal objective was the fortress of Philippsburg, which belonged to the elector of Trier and had an Imperial garrison. Philippsburg, Mazarin's gateway into southern Germany, had been recovered from the French by the Imperial army under the duke of Lorraine in 1676. In addition to it the French now occupied Worms, Speyer, Mainz, the Palatinate fortresses of Heidelberg and Frankenthal, and Mannheim. They threatened Frankfurt and also Coblentz, the 'residence' of the elector of Trier, at the junction of the Moselle and the Rhine.

The French diplomatic calculations on which these movements were based seemed to be confirmed by the second train of events, the victories of the Imperial forces on the Danube. On 6 September Belgrade, the key to the European possessions of the Turks, surrendered to Max Emmanuel.[2] It was to be expected that the German princes, who often supported the emperor in adversity, would either turn against him in his success or at least sit still. In a third direction, however, the French had miscalculated grossly. During the period of undeclared war they had tried to foment ill-feeling between the English and the Dutch and also, at times, between the kings of England and their political opponents at home. King James II's policy was a revised version of the programme which he and his brother Charles II had attempted in 1672. He again risked dividing his subjects acutely about religion. He raised the English and Irish military establish-

---

[1] The papal decision was in favour of Joseph Clement, who did not obtain full possession of the territory until some years later. In Liège John Lewis van Elderen was elected, to the exasperation of Louis. On his death in 1694 Joseph Clement was chosen.

[2] See below, pp. 621 ff. for the Ottoman war in these years.

ments from 20,000 to about 34,000 men, and he had some 37 ships of the first four rates[1] either in commission or ready to be fitted out for sea with little delay. But, although he accepted a French subsidy, he eluded Louis's attempts to pin him down to the external policy of 1672, alliance with France against the Dutch. As he could not be counted upon to support France in the event of war, it seemed advisable to allow him to be weakened at home. Before the end of August—that is, before Louis was finally committed to his German sally—intelligent diplomatists had divined that an expeditionary force which the Dutch were forming was destined for England. It could only be intended to enforce the English policy of its commander, the captain and admiral general, William III of Orange. During the summer his intimate friend Hans Willem Bentinck was in north Germany making agreements for the hire of troops. He used the argument, that, unless William intervened in arms, there might be civil war in the British Isles, ending either with a victorious monarchy subservient to France or an anti-Dutch republic. Except in the Hanoverian court of Celle, William's approaches were successful. The expedition was adopted as an official enterprise of the Dutch Republic. By moving into Germany the French army cleared the way for it psychologically as well as geographically.

William sailed with about 50 ships of war, escorting a composite force of about 9,000 foot and 4,000 horse, troops partly already in Dutch service and partly hired for the occasion. The naval commander was Sir Arthur Herbert, formerly Rear-Admiral of England. To sail as they did with an unbeaten English force of 32 ships off the Essex coast was a gamble, but gales and the tides kept the English squadron out of action and on 15 November William made an unopposed landing in the west of England. Before the end of the year William took control of the British army, the navy and whole machinery of government. His revolution is illustrious in the history of civil and religious liberty. From the point of view of the history of war, it has a less familiar aspect. By his combined operation William achieved on an enormously greater scale something which Louis had effected many times, though hitherto none of his opponents had ventured to imitate him: for William now occupied a crucially important piece of territory in time of peace. Both in the country and outside he carried opinion with him more successfully than Louis ever did; he effected his purposes in the three kingdoms and he brought their full resources to bear in the war which Louis had declared against the States-General on 26 November.[2] It did indeed take years of fighting to con-

---

[1] Ships were classified in rates according to size, and the first four rates according to the English reckoning (which went by the number of guns) were considered strong enough to take their places in the line of battle. See below, pp. 790 ff.

[2] William, as administrator of Great Britain, broke off diplomatic relations with France on 2 January; but Great Britain was not included in the French declaration because Louis regarded James II as king until 1697. William, having in the meantime become king (above, pp. 206 ff.), declared war against France on 17 May.

solidate this double revolution, but the character and outcome of the struggle were more than half imposed by the success of the invasion. Thus the cardinal event of the war occurred before it began, to be followed by nine years of anticlimax.

This was the second coalition war against Louis XIV, but it was the first in which France met Britain as an enemy. The British fought the French on land for the first time since 1629. British contingents had served in Continental wars on various occasions, of which the most recent was in 1674; but since the union of the English and Scottish Crowns the island had never intervened on the Continent as a major military power. For the French the hostility of Great Britain was the only great strategic novelty of the war. They had not only faced a European coalition; once already they had also fought as a naval power, and their ships had operated both in the Mediterranean and outside the Straits. They had long experience of co-operating with a half-circle of Northern and Eastern allies in the rear of their Habsburg opponents. There were contemporaries who said that Louis was now making a western diversion to relieve the Turks from the weight of the emperor's pressure on the Danube: this was indeed plausible whether the French thought mainly of weakening the Emperor Leopold before he became more formidable, or of attacking him while his army was tied down in the East and his control of Germany open to challenge. Louis did what he could to resuscitate his old ring of allies. Sweden, however, had been alienated from him since 1681, so much so that William in 1688 hoped to gain both Sweden and Denmark as allies, and could have done so if these Crowns had been stronger and more stable and less distrustful of one another. As it was, Denmark hired out auxiliaries both to William and to the emperor throughout the war, and in the earlier years Sweden supplied the contingents due from her German possessions; but the two Northern Crowns remained neutral, and this was disappointing for the belligerents on both sides.

Louis could do no more with Poland than with Sweden, for Poland was at war with the Turks and could not be induced to make a separate peace. For the time being Leopold had mastered the Hungarian national resistance. Nor could Louis, even if he had offered them something more than diplomatic encouragements, induce the Turks to do anything beyond what they were doing in their own interests. The only quarter where he could repair his outer ring was in North Africa. In 1689 he reversed his policy towards Algiers and made a treaty of peace which lasted until the nineteenth century. The Turks were at war with the emperor's allies, Russia and Venice, and derived some maritime help from Algiers, Tunis and Tripoli. This was the only direct advantage to the Turks from the diversion. The relations of the Maritime Powers with the North African states were complicated. Tripoli was nominally at war with France for a period in 1692; Dutch and British men-of-war seem to have operated on opposite sides in the hostilities between Morocco and Algiers which began in 1691; but strategically all this was unimportant. North Africa was not seriously involved in the war. The Turks, in effect, were making a diversion in the East for the benefit of the French.

There were two wars, not one, but the Empire was engaged in both. The two were connected by transferences of troops, subtracted from time to time from one front and added to the other. The western war made available for the emperor Dutch financial aid; although not great in amount, the loan of 1695, secured on the exports of the quicksilver mines, was an earnest of reform in Austrian finance.[1] In general, however, neither the Habsburgs nor the other German states undertook any changes of organization. The Austrian administration remained as it was, cumbrous and corrupt. The army supply-services worked badly, and perhaps the hospital service was the only well-organized branch. The men, both Germans and Slavs, were good soldiers, many of them veterans, and the cavalry had a high reputation, but the higher ranks had dangerous shortcomings. The colonels exercised the power of life and death in their commands and in this the sovereign could not overrule them. The generals were ill-disciplined: their moods and personal interests counted for too much. The number of regular troops which the Austrian government raised during the war appears to have risen from about 30,000 towards 50,000.

The Dutch went through the war without seriously modifying their military, naval and administrative system, which had carried them through a critical war in 1672–8. The strength of their army remained fairly steady at about the level of 1689—some 11,000 cavalry, 2,000 dragoons, 60,000 infantry. Their Guards regiments were in British pay, since they counted as personal guards to William III. Besides three English and three Scottish infantry regiments of old standing, their army included 'subsidy-troops' from up to a dozen states of the Empire, of which Brandenburg and Sweden supplied the largest numbers. The relations between the civil power and the armed forces worked well, though when William was not in personal command he had to provide against a tendency of the Dutch States to interfere unduly by means of their field-deputies. All through the war the Dutch were under severe strain. The Grand Pensionary, Anthony Heinsius, with William's other faithful supporters, overcame more of the obstructions of the federal machinery than had been thought possible; but, even at the cost of heavier financial burdens than any of the other allies carried, the Republic repeatedly failed to be ready by land or sea by the appointed dates, and sometimes fell short of its appointed quotas.

The one great change in the distribution of European military and naval

---

[1] The mines at Idria in Carniola were at that time the world's most important source of mercury; cf. below, pp. 307–8.

resources was that Great Britain, compelled to make greater efforts than ever before, and to strike in new directions, developed her strength for war. This change was gradual, and in each sector it underwent setbacks. It was the less appreciated because almost to the last months of the war there seemed to be a possibility that it would be undone by a Stuart restoration and the return of Great Britain to the French orbit. But, in spite of many misadventures, the latent forces were brought into action. The army was built up. Nothing was done, indeed, to turn the militia into a useful fighting force. It had a nominal establishment in England and Wales of 74,000 foot and 6,000 horse. As in France and Holland,[1] on occasions when there was a fear of invasion it was embodied in the threatened districts, but it was fortunate enough never to come under fire. The regular army establishments were more than doubled. The troops raised for the war were predominantly recruited in Great Britain; when they reached their greatest numbers, in 1694, out of a total of 93,635 men there were 32 foreign regiments. The navy had in theory numbers of men afloat which grew from 22,000 in 1689 to a maximum of 48,000 in 1695, though these figures were only reached in the summer season when the largest ships were at sea. On shore the navy was the largest single employer of labour and consumer of materials in the country. Its organization was rudimentary, and it was starved of money; but it accomplished a great work of readjustment to the new strategic requirements. In 1688 the greatest dockyard in the country was at Chatham, and there were no docking facilities west of Portsmouth. By the end of the war there was a well-balanced dockyard at Plymouth; there were additions and improvements at Portsmouth, Deptford, Chatham and Woolwich: the bases needed for war against France were in existence. All these improvements in the British military and naval systems were founded on constitutional and administrative changes of a kind which was new, not only there but in Europe. They were promoted and controlled by the king in parliament. The appropriation of supply, the auditing of accounts, and the responsibility of commanders to the Crown were shaped in annual parliaments. The upshot of innumerable debates and committee meetings was that the country discovered by trial and error how a parliament, including an opposition, could clench its strength against an enemy.

Before we trace the course of events year by year, it will be convenient to discuss some characteristics of the fighting. First is the question how far the belligerents were animated by a will to destroy the armies and fleets of their opponents, and how far they were restrained by some conscious limitation of their political aims or their use of force in the field. So far as it relates to political aims the question is not difficult to answer.

---

[1] The French body here referred to was the *arrière ban*; the Dutch, the levies raised under the obligation of *tocht en wacht*. Cf. J. R. Western, *The English Militia in the Eighteenth Century* (1965), ch. III.

The four leading powers—the French, Austrians, British and Dutch—did not limit their aims. There were, of course, elements in each country which would have preferred to do so; but they were ineffective. Louis XIV, his minister Louvois, and even the comparatively unenterprising successors of Louvois hit as hard as they could. Leopold I and William III both regarded the war as an opportunity for reducing the power of France to a level which should be tolerable to the rest of Europe. Leopold was personally slow and conservative, but he had the quality of his defects; he was obstinate. William expressed the spirit of attack in everything that he did or wrote or said. Among the minor allies, however, it was not so. Few if any of them were steadily devoted to their common cause; all watched their own interests jealously. Only one of them succeeded in changing sides twice to his own advantage; but the others sometimes calculated what they might gain at least from neutrality, and never hesitated to exact a stiff price for continuing their support, whether as allies or as lenders of auxiliary troops.

It is harder to answer the question whether there were restraints on the conduct of operations.[1] There were some features of warfare on land which tended to hamper movement. The fortresses, especially in the Low Countries, blocked traffic along the rivers, the only highways for heavy burdens like siege-artillery. They were so strong that siege-operations were very costly. There were too many strongpoints and too many men were tied up in garrisons. The magazines did away with the necessity of collecting food and provender before the beginning of each campaign and so made it possible to make an earlier start in the spring; but the habit of depending on them seems to have made it unusual for commanders to move more than five marches—sixty miles or so—away from them. An army moved all in a piece and deployment was cumbrous. It needed hours to take up a battle-formation, and therefore it was easy to evade an attack before it developed. Battles were seldom fought except by mutual consent. Pursuit was difficult and rare, so that generals sometimes fought without keeping their lines of communication behind them. The bad habit of protecting an army by long lines of field-fortifications was resorted to both in Germany and in Flanders. Originally intended to keep out enemy parties raiding for contributions, they easily came to be regarded as lines of strategic defence and so tempted commanders to inactivity.

In spite of all this, it does not seem that there was a recognized system in which limited objectives, material gains of ground and fortresses, were preferred to victorious combat. Some of the best military writers on both sides argued the case for the combat strongly. Vauban himself believed

---

[1] The affirmative answer is given by Sir John Fortescue, *History of the British Army*, vol. I (1899), pp. 354-7. For the less familiar negative answer see J. Colin, *L'Education militaire de Napoléon* (1901), pp. 1–28; *L'Infanterie au XVIIIe siècle* (1907), pp. 2, 3, 30; *Les Transformations de la guerre* (1911), pp. 162, 169–72. Cf. below, ch. XXII (1) and (2).

that fortresses served only a temporary purpose, and that the resistance of each of them had its limit of duration; he even mentioned a general standard of 48 days before honourable capitulation. There were generals, such as the Margrave Lewis of Baden, who had the reputation of sacrificing their troops too lightly; but this does not necessarily imply that the others conserved them too cautiously. The pageantry which accompanied Louis XIV when he took the field in person did not make siege-warfare cease to be costly of life. The war as a whole was bloody. Landen was believed to have caused more casualties than any other battle of the seventeenth century and Barfleur more than any other recorded naval encounter. Disease killed many soldiers, and at sea it often rendered fleets completely inactive. In 1689 it forced the English battle-fleet into harbour; in 1690 it drove the victorious French from the Channel; and it forced the English West India squadrons home from every one of their expeditions. There were indeed instances of operations languidly conducted: in Germany, for instance, there was only one considerable battle, that of Speirbach in 1692. But the reason for this is to be sought in the policy of the princes, not in their notions of military science.

Another preliminary question is that of the effects of differences between the belligerents in discipline, training and equipment. It was generally agreed that the French had the best discipline both in action and in quarters. Differences in quality between the troops of the different countries were well known, as were the differences between the *corps d'élite* and the other troops within each army; but they seem to have been of less practical importance than might have been expected. In the British army there were mutinies, connected with both politics and shortage of pay, in the first year of the war; and there were chronic unrest and desertions in the navy, where the seamen were abominably treated in the matter of pay. The Spanish troops in the Netherlands suffered badly from similar disorders. But the battle of Staffarda seems to have been the only occasion when the poor quality of one of the armies made a serious difference to the outcome of a major operation. In Piedmont, Dauphiné and Spain regular troops were harassed by guerrilla fighting, but not in the Netherlands and Germany, where the better-organized armies were engaged.

Differences in equipment and training seem to have counted neither much more nor much less than differences in discipline and morale. At sea the divergences of ship construction and armament were unusually slight and in battle the individual performances of ships mattered much less than numbers. On land the war fell within a period of inventiveness and rapid improvement; but new devices were imitated from one army to another quickly enough to forestall any one of them from acquiring an irresistible superiority. The flintlock was displacing the matchlock by degrees; the cartridge was coming in; the bayonet was displacing the pike;

Vauban invented the socket-bayonet in 1687.[1] From 1690 each French infantry regiment had a company armed with rifled carbines. Louvois integrated the artillery into the army. Luxembourg earned the reputation of handling the new mass-armies more skilfully than any other general, and he worked towards the divisional system, the system of self-subsistent formations of all arms, which later enabled armies to move more quickly. But none of these changes gave the French a decisive lead. On land as at sea, numbers and generalship seem to have been the decisive factors.

After these preliminaries we may return to the continental position in the summer of 1688, when the French invaded Germany while the Dutch were preparing to invade England. The emperor stood firm, which was not surprising in view of the prosperous state of his Turkish war. The princes stood firm too. There was no Imperial army on foot in Germany; and on 2 October the French commander, the marquis de Boufflers, took Kaisers-lautern. But at Magdeburg on 15 October the electors of Brandenburg and Saxony, with Ernest Augustus, duke of Brunswick-Lüneburg (whose capital was Hanover), and the Landgrave of Hesse-Cassel, signed an agreement for the common defence of the middle and lower Rhine which is known as the Magdeburg Concert. Together they represented a considerable force of well-trained and well-found troops. The Great Elector of Prussia, who died on 9 May 1688, had left his successor a good army of about 30,000, the strongest of the four. The neighbouring 'circles', which consisted of ecclesiastical and minor princes who did not maintain armies, entered into definite obligations to provide winter quarters and contributions. Germany showed a stronger front against France than ever before. Ernest Augustus led a force of 8,000 to the middle Rhine; John George of Saxony followed; Max Emmanuel brought Bavarian and Austrian troops from the Danube. Before the end of October an army of 20,000 was assembled about Frankfurt, and Boufflers had to retire from his position before Coblentz. It was too late to save Philippsburg, which was poorly provided and surrendered to the French after a defence of four weeks; but it was evident that Germany would not submit. On 11 December came the first of a series of decrees by which the Empire declared France its enemy.

Down to this point the French military machine was not fully in action: levies of men had been joining the colours to bring the units up to their full strength. Now there was a clear prospect of European war on the full scale. In the autumn Louis had hoped that Spain would stand aside as a neutral, in which case France could not be attacked between Luxemburg and the sea. Spanish policy, however, was turning against France. William III believed that the Dutch and their prospective allies could not break the French power on any front except the Spanish Netherlands, and from the first days of 1689 or earlier it was certain that Spain would be

---

[1] The tactical implications are discussed below, pp. 748-9.

involved. The Spaniards indeed were in no position to defend their Netherlands by themselves. Their fortresses were in disrepair; there were no magazines, no system of compulsory recruiting, no money for pay. The government was on bad terms with the population. It was believed that unless the Spanish Netherlands were defended the territory of the Dutch Republic would be indefensible; yet no one could defend them except the Dutch and their allies, and the Spaniards were willing to enter the war with their support. The Dutch equipped a field-army to serve under their field-marshal,[1] George Frederick, count of Waldeck-Pyrmont. On 15 April 1689 France declared war on Spain. Since either side could win or lose the war in the Low Countries and only there, the Rhine would now be a secondary theatre.

This meant that the French had to withdraw troops from that quarter and would be unable to maintain active operations on the whole length of the front they had occupied. The French ministers agreed to a plan, originally proposed by their military commanders, for releasing their troops without allowing German forces to re-occupy the positions thus evacuated. In the winter of 1688–9 they began the systematic devastation of the Palatinate and the neighbouring districts, burning towns and villages and destroying all stores that could not be removed. Churches were not spared. Heidelberg and the three ecclesiastical capitals—Trier, Worms and Speyer—were destroyed. The damage was much more severe than when Turenne ravaged the Palatinate in 1674. Fierce and widespread indignation, fanned by able and honest propaganda, strengthened the unity of feeling in Germany and in the European coalition that was forming. The military results of the devastation fell short of what was expected. But it did at least contribute to the absence of serious fighting in this region in the following years. Nor can it be affirmed that the protests had any marked effect on the action of the French or other armies, at least in the immediately ensuing years. In 1690 French officers recommended the destruction of Newry and even of Dublin when they were about to fall into the hands of their enemy. Catinat used the same methods in Piedmont. There were to be terrible examples of them in the Great Northern War, and they were not unknown in the War of the Spanish Succession.

During the winter and early spring the powers opposed to France made their preparations for the campaign of 1689. The first great question was whether the emperor, instead of fighting on two fronts, would make peace with the Turks and turn all his efforts to the West. William III did all he could to bring this about. He rightly believed that it would give a better chance than there had ever been before of a decisive blow against Louis. He also believed that Leopold had it in his power to impose terms satisfactory to himself and to his allies, Poland and Venice. Some historians

[1] This was not a rank but an appointment, at this time that of second-in-command under the captain-general, William III.

dispute this. However it may be, Leopold did not make peace with the Turks, and no such favourable opportunity of making it occurred until after the end of the western war. There remained the questions to be settled between the three principal allies. On 12 May 1689 the emperor's plenipotentiaries made an alliance with the Dutch, the declared aims of which were to restore the territorial and religious settlements of the treaties of Westphalia and the Pyrenees, to undo the *Réunions* and to restore Charles of Lorraine to his duchy. The emperor was to invite the king of Spain to adhere to this treaty; the English were to be invited to adhere not only to it but also to a secret clause regarding the Spanish succession.[1] This they, or rather William III, who did not take parliament into his confidence, duly did on 9 September. The Allies agreed in general terms to make war with all their resources and not to make peace separately.

Meanwhile, the British and the Dutch had settled the principles of their co-operation by sea and land. For the land service it was merely a question of fixing contingents: William was already constitutionally the commander-in-chief of both armies. The Dutch forces which had sailed with him were needed at home and returned in the course of the winter; the Danish auxiliaries remained. The British were obliged by their treaties of 3 March and 26 July 1678 to send a force of 10,000 infantry to succour the Dutch on the Continent. This clause was allowed to stand and more or less exactly complied with. At sea the quotas set in the treaties of 1678 were thought to ask too much of the weaker power; so they were now fixed at three Dutch to five English ships. As the French fleet was estimated at 80 of the line, this meant in practice at least 50 English and 30 Dutch, with smaller craft in proportion. These were to be divided into two squadrons, one of 50 for the Channel and the Irish Sea, the other of 30 for the Mediterranean, each with the same proportions from the two navies. The French fleet had bases on both coasts, but neither its dockyards on the Channel nor those on the Atlantic were adequate by themselves to maintain the entire fleet: French strategy would thus hinge on uniting their 'Levant' (Toulon) and 'Ponant' divisions, and the plan of dividing the Allied fleet was meant to prevent such a union. Difficulties were to be expected in the command of the Allied fleets, and it was only after acrimonious arguings that William settled this point. The English, by virtue of their larger contribution, were in effect to have the command of joint fleets. In the event this had the result, detrimental to Dutch naval efficiency, that the higher Dutch commanders always served in subordinate capacities.

Another naval agreement shows that the Maritime Powers began the war with high hopes of what they could compass by the exercise of sea-power. France did not depend as much as they did on seaborne commerce; but like them she needed to import timber and naval stores. The English

[1] Below, p. 388.

persuaded the Dutch to abandon their traditional indulgence to neutral commerce and to join in giving notice to their allies and to neutrals that they would make prize of all vessels of whatever flag sailing to French ports or carrying goods to French subjects. This was a bold extension of belligerent rights, or rather a repudiation of treaties which had been held to bind the two powers: as William III remarked succinctly, 'C'est droit du canon.'[1]

In one direction the English rejected Dutch proposals for joint action. Like the French, both countries had colonies in America. The Dutch proposed an expedition for the protection of these and the advancement of the interests of the two States. The English, taking this to mean that the Dutch, unlike themselves, aspired to fresh conquests in America, replied that their interests in that quarter did not agree. No closer co-operation was provided for there than that each power should grant the protection of its ships to the other's West Indiamen and 'plantations, colonies ou autres états'.

When the war began in earnest the French were on the defensive, but they had not lost their central position and that enabled them to decide where the fighting was to be. Their method of pushing armies forward over the frontiers, and of provisioning them as far as possible from the enemy territory which they occupied, was a standing temptation to open more theatres of war than the central supply of money and munitions could easily cope with. In 1689 they did not act offensively in the Spanish Netherlands. Their troops were commanded by Marshal d'Humières, who was unequal to his task and suffered a minor reverse at Waldeck's hands in a cavalry affair at Walcourt; but Waldeck was not strong enough to attempt any major operation. The French brought pressure to bear on the Spaniards in a second theatre, where they were more sensitive than in the distant Netherlands. If in this they indulged in political strategy, the political result was to be valuable to them and to outweigh the loss from the dispersal of forces. Catalonia had been restive under Castilian rule for generations. In 1687 its frontier districts had been the scene of a dangerous peasant rising which, although apparently settled in 1688, broke out again in the spring of 1689. In May the French general Noailles crossed the frontier with 9,000 men. He appeared before Camprodon and it surrendered. The French army remained on Catalan soil.

A fourth theatre of war had opened in Ireland. King James II, as a fugitive in France, became a piece in Louis's game. On 22 March 1689 a French squadron of 13 ships set him ashore at Kinsale, and in the summer he was in uneasy control of Ireland, except for the province of Ulster, where the Protestant population of the island formed themselves into an irregular defence force. They held Londonderry, the chief port of

[1] See G. N. Clark, *The Dutch Alliance and the War against French Trade, 1688–1697*, ch. v.

northern Ireland; but it was invested by land. William had been disposed to treat Ireland as a side-issue. He had overcome his opponents in Scotland by the summer of 1689 with the use of minor forces, and he only reluctantly yielded to the pressure of English parliamentary opinion by forming an army for service in Ireland. Its strength was nominally 20,000. It was commanded by the celebrated duke of Schomberg, 74 years old, a Protestant prince, half German and half English, who had been a marshal of France.

For both British and French, the Irish campaign had to be reached by sea and the most significant movements of the fleets were connected with it. The French naval administration proved the more efficient, at least in making its fleet ready for sea, with the result that the Toulon ships made their junction with the Brest fleet. There was no longer any question of action against Toulon or the French Levant trade. The Allies were reduced to defending their own coasts, their transports in St George's Channel, and their trade in home waters. The French, however, did not attempt any great stroke, and there was only one encounter of squadrons. In Bantry Bay on 11 May Sir Arthur Herbert, with 19 ships much stronger in guns, engaged 24 French ships which had been carrying troops. Though scarcely a victory, the result was good enough to justify his promotion to the peerage as Viscount Torrington. Both sides landed their troops in Ireland without serious loss.

Both have been blamed, however, for not making more of their opportunities, and this has been associated with a wider criticism of William III that he did not appreciate the importance of sea power. It has been written that he regarded the fleet only as an alternative factor in a campaign, and that he seems always to have had at the back of his mind that the best way to use a fleet was to send it where armies could not be sent.[1] On this occasion he did at least see that James could be prevented from landing. Embarrassing though the possibility was, William gave precise orders that if James were captured he should be landed in Dutch territory. There are few general expressions or directives about naval matters in William's correspondence; but the explanation may be that he left them to the sailors as he left siegecraft to Menno van Coehoorn, the Dutch rival of Vauban, even when he himself was present at a siege. In earlier life, as admiral-general with De Ruyter under his command, he had formed the habit of trusting his subordinates. It would be difficult to say what his conception of sea power was, or to prove that it fell short of the requirements of the time.

When James landed in Ireland his army there amounted to some 40,000 troops, but they were not an efficient army and he could do no more than make a ring round Ulster and besiege Londonderry. The city held out for 105 days: 590 bombs were thrown into it and there were thousands of

---

[1] J. Ehrman, *The Navy in the War of William III* (1953), p. 259.

deaths from hunger. On 31 July O.S., after needless and tormenting delays, Colonel Kirke relieved the city from the sea, sending in a frigate and three ships with provisions. The same night the duke of Berwick raised the siege and marched off. On 23 August Schomberg landed on the coast of County Down near Bangor. The actual strength of his army was only about 14,000, and except for the foreign regiments it was ill trained and ill led. Its supply-services were abominably bad. Schomberg started well enough by capturing Carrickfergus and moving forward to Dundalk, but there he stuck. Wet weather and disease pinned him down, but the opposing army was in no better case, and indeed was even less fit to take the offensive. Throughout the autumn and winter the two faced one another inactive.

In 1689 the French were on the defensive in Germany. They were inferior in numbers, and their troops, especially their raw cavalry, inferior in quality. There were three Imperial armies. The smallest protected Swabia and Franconia, holding the Lines of Stollhofen, north of Stras-bourg, from the Rhine to the Black Forest. This was originally commanded by Max Emmanuel, but in the course of the campaign he moved to the second and largest of the three armies, which operated on the middle Rhine. Here, besides the Bavarians and 13,000 Austrian troops from the Danube, were the Saxons and Hessians—in all 50,000, under the best of the Imperial generals, Charles duke of Lorraine. They cleared away the French threat from Frankfurt and laid siege to Mainz. After a vigorous defence of 52 days the marquis d'Huxelles, running short of powder, capitulated: a notable reverse, indeed the only great success of the Allies in Germany in the whole war. On the lower Rhine they also scored successes, but the conduct of the elector of Brandenburg, who commanded his own troops and the Hanoverians to the number of 40,000, was not of good augury for the alliance. He had no difficulty in recapturing Kaisers-werth and clearing the electorate of Cologne. William III, constantly hoping to drive blows home against France, wanted him then to join the army of the duke of Lorraine; but the elector preferred to stick to his own sphere of interest about the lower Rhine. He invested Bonn and reduced it to ruins by bombardment; it was poorly provided and surrendered on 10 October. William's recapture of Bonn in 1673, dislocating the com-munications of the French army in Holland, had been a famous victory; but in this war Bonn had no strategic value. The result was that, when the campaign ended, the French still held Philippsburg, but the Allies con-trolled the Rhine from there to Rheinberg.

In the winter of 1689–90 William III collected the heads or represen-tatives of the Allied states in a 'congress' at The Hague, as he had done in the 1670s, to concert measures for the coming year. He continued this practice in the succeeding winters. It did something to co-ordinate action and to settle the problems of armed coalitions, but it also revealed the divergences of interest between the Allies and, as the years went on, it became less useful.[1] The two major diplomatic negotiations of this winter had their centres elsewhere. In November, after considerable difficulties, the emperor gathered the electoral college in Augsburg and procured its assent to the election and coronation of his elder son, Joseph, as king of the Romans. Thus he assured the continuance of the Habsburg primacy in Germany and checked the dwindling ambitions of France in that direction; but he strained the concord of the princes and strengthened their misgivings about Habsburg power. The other negotiation concerned Savoy. The duke, Victor Amadeus II, was married to a niece of Louis XIV. The French garrisons in Pinerolo and Casale left him little of his nominal independence, and he conformed to French policy (deeply as he resented his mother's subservience to it), particularly by persecuting his Protestant subjects.[2] The French, however, distrusted him and in 1689 demanded as a guarantee of his fidelity that he should limit his forces to 2,000 men. With this also he professed to comply, but he passed men through training so that his reserves exceeded the prescribed limit. He entered into negotiations with Spain and the emperor.

The prospects for 1690 were much more favourable to the French than for 1689. The emperor intended to leave the West to his allies and devote himself to the Turkish war. A French offensive was coming in the Netherlands, and British troops were detained in Ireland. At sea so many British ships had been lost in the previous year that the merchants demanded more protection, especially for the Mediterranean trade, and this was provided at the expense of the home fleet. By June a critical position had developed. Without meeting any opposition the French landed 6,000 troops and a large quantity of supplies in Ireland. Schomberg advanced from his winter quarters and took Charlemont, but it was not until 24 June that William landed to take command in person. With an army of something under 40,000, including six Dutch, eight Danish and three Huguenot battalions—together, the major part of his infantry—he faced a smaller force in which there were seven French battalions. He could look forward to the Irish campaign with reasonable confidence; but the European scene was changing to his disadvantage. The united French fleet was in the Channel and England feared an invasion. Torrington's ships had made their junction with the Dutch, but another Anglo-Dutch squadron of 24 ships under Vice-Admiral Henry Killigrew was out of touch to the west, making its way from Cadiz after escorting outward-bound merchantmen. Torrington, with the unanimous support of his council-of-war, judged that his inferior force should evade battle until Killigrew could join him. The ministers in England took it upon themselves to send him peremptory orders not to fall back further but, if the sea and weather permitted, to engage the French fleet.

---

[1] See above, pp. 171–2.   [2] See vol. v, pp. 472–3.

At the beginning of the campaign there were two French armies in the Netherlands. The smaller was in the east, between the Meuse and the Moselle, and the commander in this region, as before, was Boufflers. In the west was the ablest of the French generals, the marshal duke of Luxembourg, a veteran of Rocroi, who knew that country as few men knew it. There was no enemy opposite Boufflers, and Luxembourg moved both forces towards one another to unite them. On the other side Waldeck was waiting for the Brandenburg troops; but, in spite of pressing admonitions from the Hague Congress, they did not come. The two French armies joined and Waldeck was outnumbered by 40,000 to 30,000, but he decided to fight and marched forward till he reached a position on 30 June between Fleurus and St-Amand. On 1 July there was fighting all day. By evening Waldeck had no cavalry left. His Dutch infantry were armed with the pike, and suffered for it; but it was they who made the last attack. Then they withdrew, nine regiments, defeated but unbroken. It was believed that the French casualties were of the same order of magnitude as the 7,000 killed and wounded in the Allied force. This was the last pitched battle of the war in which Spanish troops fought in defence of the Spanish Netherlands. After it the two armies relapsed into inactivity. The Brandenburg reinforcements arrived in August.

The news of Fleurus reached England in a dark hour. The naval battle on which so much depended came about on 10 July off Beachy Head.[1] Torrington with his 56 ships obeyed his orders; the French were to the west of him and he had the weather-gauge, so that he could have molested them and fallen back towards the Downs without engaging closely. The English, in accordance with this intention, held off; but the Dutch, who were on the right, closed with the enemy. The English did not give them close support; they suffered heavily and then the whole fleet retreated. The French did not lose a single ship; by the time the Allied fleet anchored at the Nore, the English had lost one and the Dutch four. These figures do not represent the gravity of the defeat. The Dutch and the king were angry, and Torrington, though acquitted by a court-martial, was never employed again. On the question of his personal responsibility in the battle opinions still differ. It is separate from the larger strategic question, which is equally disputed. After the battle the French did not invade England. William, as he wrote to Marlborough, had never believed there was much danger of that, since they carried no troops. Tourville judged it impossible to attack Killigrew in Plymouth Sound, so they merely burnt the fishing-village of Teignmouth. The minister Seignelay showed how completely they commanded the Channel by bringing round the galleys— oared vessels which could not defend themselves against ships of the line— from the Mediterranean; but the victorious Tourville had 7,000 sick on

---

[1] The battle is known to the French as Béveziers and to the Dutch as Bevesier, which are said to be forms of 'Pevensey'.

board and he retired to his harbours. When it was all over Torrington wrote a sentence which has been the text for much confused discussion: 'Most men were in fear that the French would invade, but I was always of another opinion, for I always said that whilst we had a fleet in being they would not dare to make an attempt.' These words may be understood in two different senses. Some writers regard them as expressing a mistaken reliance on *matériel* instead of combat, on a fleet rather than a victory. On the other hand, they may be taken to mean that the French would not dare to do what Torrington himself apparently did in 1688, when he invaded England and left Dartmouth's fleet in being behind him.[1] On this view, they compendiously state the opinion expressed by Nelson in the different conditions of 1805, namely that any French plan for invasion must be presumed to include the defeat of the British fleet as a prerequisite of that command of the sea which was necessary for transporting an army. This interpretation is the more probable.

If the French had been able to exploit their victory, invasion or no invasion, they could have interrupted the communications of the British army in Ireland. That army won a notable victory on 11 July at the crossing of the Boyne. King James held a good, entrenched, defensive position on the south bank of this river, scarcely more than a day's march north of Dublin. William attacked frontally and also turned the left flank. James's army, after suffering some 1,500 casualties, retreated in good order westwards towards the Shannon. James left his army, as he did in 1688, and returned to France. William secured the ports from Dublin to Waterford, but failed to take Limerick. The Irish war was not over and it still locked up British troops, but the odds were now on a British win. In the autumn John Churchill, earl of Marlborough, came by sea to take Cork by storm and Kinsale by siege. The French and Irish troops were now cooped up in the west with no useful ports except Limerick and Galway.

In the meantime a new, fifth theatre had been opened in Savoy. Victor Amadeus rejected the final French terms and joined the Allies. In addition to the inevitable subsidies, they offered the duke handsome terms, including the recognition of Savoy as a sovereign State and the return of Casale to Mantua and of Pinerolo to himself. His adhesion roused high hopes, for it opened the chance of invading France through Dauphiné and Provence, where Toulon lay. With longer lines of communication it was much more costly for the French to maintain troops there than in the Netherlands or Germany. On the other hand, the French might march through Savoy and Piedmont to attack the duchy of Milan and the

---

[1] For two opinions, respectively favourable and unfavourable to Torrington's judgment, see Admiral Sir Herbert Richmond, *The Navy as an Instrument of Policy* (Cambridge, 1953), pp. 213–19, and J. C. M. Warnsinck, *De Vloot van den Koning-Stadhouder* (Amsterdam, 1934), pp. 101–44. For a detailed account of Torrington's behaviour, see Ehrman, pp. 341–56.

emperor's lands beyond it. The Spanish administration in Milan was incapable and the governor, Fuensalida, torpid, but the Spaniards talked of sending up 10,000 troops. The emperor who, like the French, now had too many fronts to think about, contemplated providing 5,000-6,000. The French army was commanded by Nicolas de Catinat, an exceptional man in many ways, among others in not belonging to the high military caste; he was the son of a judge in the *Parlement* of Paris and had himself abandoned a career in the law. His initial dispositions for the campaign may not have been very enterprising but, as it turned out, that did not matter. Victor Amadeus insisted on fighting a battle before his dilatory allies arrived. On 18 August Catinat beat him at the abbey of Staffarda,[1] south of Pinerolo, and followed up his victory by easily capturing Saluzzo and Susa. After that the Imperial troops came up, so that nothing of moment happened for the rest of the year except French exactions and ravaging, followed by reprisals.

For the emperor and the German princes the most serious fact of 1690 was that the Turks were victorious on the Danube. They recovered Belgrade in October. Bavaria, Brandenburg and Brunswick-Lüneburg had to send troops to stiffen the army. That and the recalcitrance of other princes changed the face of the German war. Early in the year the duke of Lorraine died and no more satisfactory successor as commander-in-chief could be found than the elector of Bavaria. After Fleurus, and after the emperor's 6,000 had set out for Italy, the French brought the strength of their army up to 40,000. The Imperialists could effect nothing on the lower Rhine, nor on the upper, where the emperor hoped to prepare for an offensive in some future year by attacking Hüningen. The troops of electoral Saxony went home after two months in the field, and those from the German possessions of Sweden after one month.

The heavy fighting at sea and in Flanders, and the smaller but expensive operations in Ireland and Savoy, had left the war undecided and the balance of forces still substantially unaltered; but this year, the first in which the two sides had exerted their full strength, had proved that the coalition could not succeed either easily or soon. The withdrawal of the Swedish troops was symptomatic. Sweden also took advantage, as did Denmark, of the continuing uncertainty of the naval war. After the experience of the first two campaigns, the Maritime Powers gave up their attempt to extinguish neutral rights, and for the remainder of the war they made concessions, sometimes under the threat—not, it is true, very formidable in itself—of combined naval action by the neutrals. The effect of these agreements was to restore for good the old position that neutrals might carry on such seaborne trade with belligerent States as they could bargain for in the changing course of hostilities.

The year 1691 was no more decisive than 1690. The Irish episode was

---

[1] This was the only major engagement in which French militiamen took part.

indeed concluded. William left the command there in the hands of his capable Dutch general Godard, baron van Reede-Ginkel, afterwards earl of Athlone. The French did not altogether neglect their opportunity: they landed men and supplies in Limerick—the largest consignment, in May, consisting of over 1,200 men and 800 horses, with arms for 26,000 and also engineers and stores of every kind. But the new French minister of marine, Phélypeaux de Pontchartrain, was not equal to the situation. In May Ginkel crossed the Shannon at Athlone and won an action at Aughrim, where the French commander, Saint-Ruth, was killed. After a siege of two days Galway surrendered on easy terms, and nothing remained to conquer except Limerick. Here a siege in form was necessary. The city held out for half of August and the whole month of September. Even without help from the French fleet its brave commander, Patrick Sarsfield, might have kept up his resistance through the winter. Ginkel offered not only honourable military articles but terms of settlement in the religious and agrarian issues for which the Irish were fighting.[1] These terms were not ungenerous; the soldiers were not to blame for the bad faith which marred their execution, and it is remarkable that there was no sequel of guerrilla warfare.

While Ginkel was in Ireland, William, for the first time in this war, took command of the Allied army in the Netherlands. The Allies made a great effort, and they intended to put 80,000 into the field there besides 40,000 on the Rhine. But the French, as usual, were first in the field. They drew off the Brandenburgers by a diversion against the Cleve duchies. William was still at Brussels when Luxembourg laid siege to the great fortress of Mons. It surrendered on 8 April. After that there was desultory fighting, in which William failed to bring the French to battle. Early in June Boufflers attempted a blow at Liège, but succeeded in doing no more than bombard it, destroying (it was said) 3,000 houses. The defence of the Spanish Netherlands now depended almost wholly on the Allies, and William insisted on the removal of the Spanish governor, the marquis of Gastañaga—as it turned out, the last of the Spanish governors. His successor was Max Emmanuel of Bavaria, whose ambition was rather stimulated than satisfied by the position of a Spanish viceroy.[2] He was still inferior in rank to William, who had been far below his electoral station three years before. He was the emperor's son-in-law, but also brother-in-law to the dauphin. For three years he had been a jealous and exacting ally; it soon appeared that he was not even dependable.

In this year the emperor fought hard and not unsuccessfully on the Danube, as well as in Transylvania and Croatia, and the Poles and Venetians were also pressing the Turks. On the Rhine there was no important fighting. In Catalonia, where the Spanish army was supposed to number 18,000, the French did not attempt much, but they did what they

---

[1] See above, p. 214 and below, p. 256. [2] Below, pp. 352–3.

set out to do. They captured Urgal and their galleys bombarded Barcelona —a mere demonstration since they carried no weight of guns. The Allies planned a stronger effort in Italy. Prince Eugene of Savoy-Carignan (1663–1736) was rising in influence and reputation in the Imperial service; he was a great-grandson of Duke Charles Emmanuel of Savoy, a grand-nephew of Mazarin, a first cousin of the great Turenne and of Lewis of Baden.[1] He urged that the Italian front should be either reinforced or abandoned. It was decided to form an army of 40,000, including (besides Spaniards and Savoyards) 12,000 Bavarians and 5,000 Austrians, with a contingent of Huguenots and Swiss paid by the Maritime Powers, which were also to pay subsidies to Bavaria and Savoy. This army was far stronger than the French forces opposed to it. But the Allies had too many generals; the Austrians under their Italian general Caraffa were ill disciplined; Catinat out-generalled them all and, though he was not uniformly successful, the net result was that he captured Nice (with support from the sea), Villafranca and, as late as December, Montmélian, the pivot of the defence.

Thus the French did well in the main theatre, and not badly anywhere except in Ireland; but in this year there were plain indications that they were beginning to strain their resources. The king stopped work on his great buildings. The sale of offices was extended to the navy, which meant that inefficient men would acquire a vested right to administrative places. The harvest of this year was not bad; but taxation was so heavy that even substantial peasants had to sell what they reaped instead of storing it.

Although there were no great events at sea, the English and the Dutch had been out as soon as the French, and in greater numbers than ever before; and the English were carrying out a great programme of ship-building and naval reorganization. It was in 1691, on 16 August, that Louvois died. In spite of these ominous signs, it was to be in 1692 that the French reached their maximum of armed strength. In more ways than one, 1692 saw great changes in the main character of the war. Before the fighting began William III expressed his opinion about the terms on which peace might be made; but he abated nothing of his original purposes, and he also said that the Allies must take the offensive on all sides.

Each party now intended to make use of sea power for the invasion of enemy country. The Allies were the first to be ready, but they cancelled their own plan in order to frustrate that of the French. The French concentrated a force of 24,000 men in the Cotentin, where James II joined it and collected transports for it. The great French admiral Tourville received an order from Pontchartrain that he was to put out from Brest

---

[1] He was the son of Olympe Mancini and the comte de Soissons; though the latter was a hereditary enemy of Louis XIV, 'Eugenio von Savoye' (as he signed himself) had been brought up at the French court, which he had quitted in time to take part in the battle for the relief of Vienna in September 1683. For his service against the Turks, see below, ch. XIX.

on 25 April and, if he met the enemy, to engage them with whatever ships he had. Louis XIV wrote his own confirmation on the order; the admiral knew that the order was senseless and the minister, discovering this too late, sent counter-orders which never arrived. Tourville with 44 of the line met the Anglo-Dutch fleet under Edward Russell numbering 79. The battle began on 29 May. It lasted six days, running along the coast from Barfleur to La Hougue:[1] 15 French ships were destroyed. A large part of the French force escaped to St Malo, where the English and Dutch sailors wanted to attack it. But the English ministers were as inept as the French: 23 battalions no longer needed in Ireland had embarked in May and now was the time to use them; they were sailed and marched uselessly about, and nothing was done except a bombardment of Dunkirk. Russell wrote: 'Burning a town in France is no more consequence to them than an accidental fire in Knightsbridge is to us.' As a defeat, therefore, Barfleur was incomplete; in itself it was no heavier than Beachy Head had been for the other side. Yet the French navy was unable to recover as the Allies had done, and the consequences were momentous.

The French did not learn their lesson immediately, nor abandon the idea of fleet-actions altogether; but from 1695 they severely reduced their naval expenditure and their chief purpose now was commerce-destroying. Their privateers operated from Dunkirk, St Malo and the smaller ports with skill and daring, often assisted with government stores and loans of ships. Jean Bart, the comte de Forbin and René Duguay-Trouin, the most famous of their captains, were not simply guerrillas of the sea. They set their opponents the difficult task, in which they sometimes failed badly, of convoying their merchant fleets. They threatened and even impaired British and Dutch import and export trade, capturing or destroying some hundreds of vessels.[2] French losses at sea were also heavy; 1,296 enemy vessels of all sizes were condemned by the English court of admiralty alone.

In the year of Barfleur there was an eventful campaign in the Netherlands. The Spaniards were no longer able to pay for the troops of Brandenburg and Hesse; the emperor would have liked them for the Rhine and for offensive action there; but the Maritime Powers took them into pay, and so were able to build up a numerical superiority to the French in infantry. Luxembourg, however, succeeded in holding their army off while he besieged Namur. In June it fell, and thus the French gained the

[1] French and some English writers call the battle 'La Hougue', most English writers 'Barfleur' or, using an older French spelling, 'La Hogue'. Two engagements were fought: one off Barfleur (off Cape La Hague), the other in the bay of La Hougue. Cf. Ehrman, p. 397, n. I.

[2] See the statement of the Lord High Admiral to a committee of the House of Lords in 1707/8 (Cobbett, *Parliamentary History*, vol. VI, p. 646). The figure there given of 'near 4,000' British ships lost is not authoritative: it is derived from an anonymous pamphlet and does not square with other figures, such as those of the number of prisoners returned by the French.

whole length of the river Sambre. On 3 August, at Steenkerk, William at last succeeded in bringing the main French field-army to battle. He found it in a strong position, but by surprise he seized a height which commanded its right flank. Four hours of desperate fighting followed, and William believed that he very nearly won. The Allies admitted 7,000 casualties, the French probably suffered almost as heavily. In the end William called his troops off, and they retired in good order to their former position. The British officers accused their allies, especially William's kinsman Count Solms, of failing to support them. Steenkerk was Waldeck's last battle: he died later in the year, aged seventy-two.

On the Rhine the French certainly had the upper hand. In the spring they were weakened to provide troops for the Netherlands, but the Imperial army assembled slowly and by the time it reached 47,000 men, in June, the French troops were back again. The Imperial forces were under divided command. Twice, part of them crossed the Rhine westwards only to withdraw again; they lost Pforzheim and they failed to take Eberenburg. The duke of Württemberg was taken prisoner. Marshal de Lorge levied contributions, spreading terror far and wide, in Swabia and Franconia.

The emperor's attention was elsewhere, but he gained no compensating advantage. In Savoy, at last, an invasion of France was launched. Catinat was weakened by sending some of his troops to the Netherlands; the Allies had half as many men again, although (with 100 battalions and 40 squadrons) he was the stronger in infantry. The Allies lacked equipment to besiege Pinerolo, so they left a force of 5,000 to watch Catinat, encamped between there and Susa, and another 6,000 to block Casale. The main army of 29,000 crossed the Alps in three columns—one by Cuneo to Barcelonette, the second by Saluzzo and Castel Delfino, the third by Luserna and Queyras. All three converged on Embrun in Dauphiné; it capitulated on 16 August. Finding Gap deserted, they sacked and burnt it. Then everything went wrong. Victor Amadeus fell ill. The three major allies wanted to hold Embrun, but it did not appear to be tenable. With Catinat's troops about, supplies would be precarious. The army, especially the troops of the Austrian general Caprara, ravaged the country, sparing only the churches. The Spaniards wanted to go; nothing had come of their promise to send ships to the coast in support. On 12 September it was decided to withdraw. The fortifications of Embrun and Guillestre were slighted. For the remainder of the war French soil was free from insult.

The strain of the war was telling heavily on the French. Their finances were sustained by such desperate remedies as sales of the royal domain, and they had difficulties with recruiting. The harvest was poor over most of western Europe.[1] This hit the Allies too, and for other reasons their

---

[1] Cf. below, pp. 320 ff. for the effects on France.

cohesion was weakening. In the spring the emperor had made sure of regular contingents of 6,000 men from the two related princes of Brunswick-Lüneburg and Brunswick-Wolfenbüttel, but this meant a worsening of his strained relations with the elector of Saxony, and it was bought at the price of promising to erect Hanover to be a ninth electorate. Early in 1693 an association of German princes was formed to oppose this innovation,[1] thus encouraging French hopes that some members of the Empire, if not Leopold himself, might be detached from the Grand Alliance. In furtherance of this policy Louis sent one of his best diplomats, Count d'Avaux, to Stockholm. Sweden offered to mediate in the general war and after 1692 there were no more Swedish contingents in the Imperial armies. French diplomacy failed in the event to achieve its object of isolating William III, but by May 1693 William made up his mind that no more could be hoped for than to find a middle way between the *status quo ante bellum* and the treaties of Westphalia and the Pyrenees. His diplomacy became defensive. The full programme of the Grand Alliance was abandoned. During the remainder of the war an increasing number of diplomatists and secret agents busied themselves over questions of peace terms. An important result was to excite suspicions between the allies and loosen their military cohesion.[2]

The year 1693 was unpromising for them. Although the economic position was worse in France, where it amounted to famine, in the fighting both by sea and by land the French did well. The Maritime Powers again threw away their chance of using their fleet to any purpose. St Malo was bombarded with poor ammunition; an 'infernal machine', a ship stuffed with explosives, was loosed against the defences and made a complete fiasco. In June came the worst shipping disaster of the war. The Toulon squadrons had prevented sailings to the Levant in the two previous years, and it was now decided to provide a strong protecting escort, eleven English and five Dutch warships, for 400 merchantmen. The naval authorities wanted to hold the ships back until they knew the whereabouts of the French, but they were badly served with intelligence and the ministers ordered the convoy to sail. Off Lagos on 27 June they met the united French fleet, with 70 of the line. As many as 80 merchantmen fell into the hands of the French intact, and the loss in cargo was enormous.

On land the Allies had 220,000 men at their disposal: 120,000 in the Netherlands, 58,000 on the upper Rhine, 40,000 in Piedmont. The French

---

[1] This league of the 'Corresponding Princes' was formed at Ratisbon on 26 January by Denmark, Brunswick-Wolfenbüttel, Saxe-Gotha, Hesse-Cassel and Münster; others joined it later.

[2] William's insistence on French recognition of his kingly title was a theme of serious negotiations between French and Dutch agents every year from 1693, while the emperor was ready to approve a settlement favourable to the Stuarts throughout his negotiations with the French from 1692 to 1696: see M. A. Thomson, 'Louis XIV and William III, 1689–97', *Eng. Hist. Rev.* LXXVI (1961), 37–58, and H. Ritter von Srbik, *Wien und Versailles, 1692–1697* (Munich, 1944).

armies in the Netherlands were slightly smaller: Luxembourg had 47,000 infantry and 21,000 cavalry, concentrated between Estines and Givet; Boufflers, in the neighbourhood of Tournai, had 31,000 infantry and 17,000 cavalry. As early as January the French seized Furnes, and the neighbouring town of Dixmude was abandoned to them. The Spaniards and Max Emmanuel insisted that Flanders should be covered, and it was necessary to defend Liège against Boufflers, so William divided his forces. Luxembourg outmanoeuvred him. On 29 July William's entrenched position between Landen and Neerwinden was attacked. The defenders were superior in artillery: this was the first time that the Dutch brought howitzers of their own manufacture into action. Both sides fought hard. Both had more killed and wounded than at Steenkerk. The Allied army was broken and driven out of its trenches. The line of retreat was open and William fell back to Brussels. It looked as if Luxembourg could move against Louvain, cutting William's communications, and against the arsenal of Mechlin (Malines), or against Nieuwpoort and Ostend. He contented himself with besieging Charleroi. After a stout defence it fell on 13 October.

On all the three other fronts the French scored advantages. In northern Catalonia Noailles besieged and captured the small seaport of Rosas with its valuable, protected bay. On the Rhine the French were only temporarily weakened by detaching troops to the Netherlands: in spite of the discontent among the princes, the response to the call for their support was satisfactory. Lewis of Baden evaded the French and on the one occasion when they were in a favourable situation they did not venture to attack him. But they carried out a demonstration, a second sacking of Heidelberg, which caused renewed indignation. In Piedmont, after the fiasco of the previous year, Prince Eugene had a better plan. First, Pinerolo should be captured; then there should be an invasion, either through the Alpine passes or, with Spanish or Anglo-Dutch naval support, along the Riviera. But the dilatoriness of the Austrians ruined the plan. The army did not concentrate at Carignano until June. The siege of Pinerolo was a failure. Catinat, with timely reinforcements, won a crushing victory at Marsaglia on 4 October. The military results were not the worst of this battle. Victor Amadeus, still in control of most of eastern Piedmont, judged that there was less to gain by standing firm than by changing sides: in the winter he was secretly in touch with the French general Tessé.

After all this it may well seem surprising that the next year, 1694, was the most favourable for the Allies since 1689. The reason was that the economic and financial strain hit them less hard than the French, whose harvest had failed again in 1693. Both sides at times ran short of money for pay in the field, but the Allies had more for other purposes. Luxembourg still had 100,000 men; but he was outnumbered and he had not sufficient supplies to mount any attack. William intended to cross the Meuse from east to west and operate on the Flemish coast. Luxembourg kept him back, but failed to prevent the recapture of Huy. For the first time the Allies held their own on the main front. The French remained on the defensive in all the theatres except Catalonia.

At sea there were two great changes. The English and Dutch began with an attempt on the heart of French naval strength, the arsenal of Brest. The start was delayed by the same administrative faults which had spoiled so many of their naval efforts. There was no secrecy. In June, with the main fleet cruising in the Channel and a squadron in tactical support, a force of 7,000 men set sail, only to find the fortress strengthened for the occasion by Vauban and French troops in position to receive them. They landed in Camaret Bay and were driven back with heavy loss. Thus ended the plans for invading France with which the English admiralty had been occupied from 1691. Dieppe, Le Havre and Dunkirk were bombarded. Jean Bart convoyed Baltic corn-ships through the blockade.

Since the previous winter, however, William III had taken a direct interest in naval strategy, and he was concerned about the Mediterranean. The Spanish army in Catalonia was about 16,000 strong; but Noailles had 26,000 against it, and he could be supplied from the sea as he advanced down the coast. The Brest fleet appeared off Barcelona. The Anglo-Dutch squadron in the Mediterranean was far too small to meet it. On 17 May Noailles won a battle on the Ter and on the same day the squadrons from Brest and Toulon joined company in the bay of Rosas. On 7 June Noailles stormed Palamos; on 19 June at Gerona he took the oath as viceroy of Catalonia, a well-calculated threat against Spanish rule in the province. In June the English and Dutch fleets were ordered to the Mediterranean. On 10 July they concentrated off Gibraltar—41 English, 24 Dutch and 10 Spanish ships of the line, none of them with less than 50 guns. By 8 August they in their turn appeared off Barcelona. The French had not even waited to sight them, but were making for their harbours. Noailles, deprived of his naval support, retreated. The Spanish army was too weak to attack any fortified town, but the French were harassed by guerrillas.

It was too late for the new masters of the Gulf of Lions to affect the course of events in Italy. There was no longer any chance of invading southern France. An attack on Toulon needed a land-army, but of that there was no hope. William, indeed, was unaware of this. He did not know that the duke of Savoy was actually working for the French. The Imperial troops did not concentrate, at Orbassano, until May, and Victor Amadeus only joined them in July. They did nothing except to blockade Casale, a blockade which was maintained through the winter. On 24 August Russell (now Lord Orford), commanding the Allied fleet, decided not unnaturally to make for home.

On 14 September he received the king's orders, overruling the admiralty, that the fleet was not to return to its home ports for the winter, but to refit in the Allied port of Cadiz, to which store-ships would be sent. This meant that a difficult administrative operation, altogether new in kind, could be undertaken, thanks to the general administrative progress in England and to the initial loan from the new Bank of England, more than half of which had been assigned to the navy. It also meant that the Maritime Powers could use their ships to bring pressure all the year round on the Mediterranean states—a new phase in European warfare.

When the campaign of 1695 began, therefore, the prospects of the Allies were good. France was still short of food until the harvest at last ended the famine. The Levant trade of Marseilles had its first bad year since the war began. In January Luxembourg died, to be succeeded by the incompetent Villeroi, with Boufflers's army, as before, on the right. Again the French were unable to mount an offensive in the Netherlands, and for the first time they suffered a major defeat. Villeroi's army was stretched along the Lines of Ypres, from the Scheldt to the sea. William made a feint towards the coast, coming within 25 miles of it. He threatened Dunkirk, Ypres and Tournai—to all of which the French hurried provisions—and then, turning back and joining the electors of Bavaria and Brandenburg, he began the siege of Namur. The French attempted diversions in the west and bombarded Brussels, Max Emmanuel's capital, where they are said to have destroyed 3,830 houses. After nearly three months of siege Namur surrendered. The left flank of the Allied defence was thus restored to the position of 1691. More important, French military prestige was shaken.

The year was not indeed decisive. The Maritime Powers expended more shells in vain on St Malo, Granville, Calais and Dunkirk: likewise on Palamos in Catalonia. There Noailles was succeeded by one of Louis's best generals, the duke of Vendôme. The Spanish army still amounted to very little indeed, but the Austrians sent three German regiments under the capable Prince George of Hesse-Darmstadt, a cousin of the queen of Spain. The Spaniards relinquished their attempts to give naval support, however, and in the autumn the greater part of the Allied fleet returned to its home ports. The great Mediterranean plan was abandoned. Victor Amadeus was inactive and the Allies, with good reason, distrusted him.

During the summer, the French diplomat Callières, in conversations with Dijkvelt and Boreel (a burgomaster of Amsterdam) at Maastricht, offered William III unconditional recognition after a general peace had been concluded. This concession was not satisfactory to William, who mistrusted its sincerity; yet in May 1696 Callières categorically rejected the suggestion that William should be recognized at the outset of a general peace conference. As the discussion of peace terms became increasingly realistic, however, disagreements between the Allies sharpened. Some of the German princes were placated and new plans made for their co-operation, but it was evident that this might easily break down and that peace was on the way.

Against this background neither side expected or attempted anything in 1696 on the scale of the preceding years. Instead of an effort in the Netherlands, the French made ready for an operation which might be called a parody of William III's expedition of 1688. The Toulon division came to Brest. The signal was to be given from England, not by a powerful group of statesmen, but by a knot of conspirators who included in their programme an old-fashioned device, the assassination of William. There was not to be any naval force strong enough to control the sea: 20 ships of the line were to cover the crossing of the transports. An army of 14,000 all told—that is, of about the same strength as William's army in 1688—was brought from the main front. King James joined it at Calais on 2 March. The only other fact of importance about the expedition is that a week later 60 English and Dutch sail took up their stations in the offing. That was the end, although Louis did not cancel the operation until April. In the meantime, 20 battalions were withdrawn from the Netherlands for the defence of Great Britain. In spite of this reduction of his forces the prince of Vaudemont, who had a command in the Spanish service, sent Coehoorn in the middle of March to destroy the magazine at Givet, from which alone the French might have drawn the stores for an attack on one of the fortresses of the Meuse. But during the remainder of the year there were no more excitements in the Netherlands, although that theatre deprived Lewis of Baden on the Rhine of the troops of Hesse and Münster. His other contingents came in very slowly; only the Swabian and Franconian circles, being in danger, showed energy. Heavily outnumbered, Lewis maintained his defence by manoeuvre. The emperor was dissatisfied with the division of resources between the Netherlands and the Rhine. He was also anxious that his allies should support Spain, but William distrusted the Spaniards, who seemed to be making no exertions to defend Catalonia.

Savoy William had trusted too long. Victor Amadeus needed to have Pinerolo in his own hands and Casale dismantled. There was little chance that the Allies would satisfy him in these immediate matters, and none at all that the Austrians would countenance his claim to the eventual inheritance of Milan. He now openly proposed a neutrality for Italy. Prince Eugene and the British and Spanish representatives thought the Allies could go on in Italy without him, so he joined the French. The French collusively admitted his troops into Casale, and by the Treaty of Turin on 29 August (as they had secretly agreed on 29 June) they surrendered Pinerolo and concluded peace. There was nothing to do now but accept the neutralization of Italy, to which the Allies agreed at Vigevano on 7 October. The

French troops, 30,000 of good quality, returned to southern France on their way to Barcelona. The intentions of Spain were so doubtful, and the problems of transport so difficult, that the Austrians, instead of heading in the same direction, went to the Danube, where Eugene's overwhelming victory at Zenta in the following year was ultimately to end the Turkish war.

Great Britain, the Dutch Republic and France were all economically and financially exhausted. In 1696 Britain endured a grave financial emergency, which rendered her seamen and soldiers more obstinately mutinous than at any time since 1689. The peace negotiations had reached a point where almost the only question was whether there would be a general settlement or further defections like that of Savoy. Still there was one more campaign, and the fighting of 1697 was different in one respect which pointed to the future. For the first time America was the focus of the naval fighting.

There had, of course, been war in America for all the nine years.[1] The Anglo-French Treaty of 1686 for neutrality in America was inoperative because France did not recognize the government of William III. In the Caribbean the French started with the great advantage of owning, in Martinique, a naval base and headquarters for the whole region; but the support sent from Europe for the local forces of the two sides was the main factor. Until 1697 neither could send enough ships and men to win more than minor or precarious successes. The Spaniards brought plate fleets home unmolested.[2] In 1689 the French took St Kitts and marched from Canada into the Hudson valley as far as Schenectady. In 1690, after a year's delay, a small squadron with a regiment of infantry reached Barbados and enabled the elder Christopher Codrington, governor of the Leeward Islands, to retake St Kitts; but the French re-occupied Acadia, and Sir William Phips failed in an attack on Quebec and Montreal. In 1691 Codrington and Commodore Ralph Wrenn unsuccessfully attacked Guadeloupe. In 1693 Sir Francis Wheler with eight of the line and 1,500 troops made an unsuccessful attack on Martinique and then, following orders, went on to Newfoundland, where he was able to effect nothing. This failure was made in London. Next year no English squadron went out and the French marauded at will among the islands. In 1695 Commodore Wilmot, in concert with Spanish ships, collected considerable booty in Saint-Domingue.[3] In 1696 there was no money for any English squadron. Then came the last campaign. Baron de Pointis, in command of ten ships with 1,500 soldiers thought to be destined for a descent on England, crossed the Atlantic, followed by six English and four Dutch ships under Admiral John Neville. On 20 April, reinforced by privateersmen from Saint-Domingue, Pointis reached Cartagena, the richest of the Spanish

---

[1] For the fighting in North America see below, pp. 486–90.
[2] Cf. below, p. 354, n. 1.   [3] Below, p. 355.

colonial ports, and on 4 May he captured it. This was the worst Spanish disaster overseas since Piet Hein captured the silver-fleet in 1628; but it had no influence on the outcome of the war. The same is true of all the other fighting overseas, such as the winning and losing of forts on Hudson's Bay and the taking of Pondicherry by the Dutch in 1693.

In the last summer of the war, also, the French pressed on in the Netherlands, taking Ath and Alost, both on the river Dender. It was now the emperor and the Spaniards who were reluctant to make peace. The French, irresistible by sea or land in what had been the least important of the theatres of war, settled the matter on 10 August by taking Barcelona. By October the peace was made. The emperor signed on 30 October; the others had done so on 20 September.

The terms finally fixed at Ryswick, after the main difficulties had been thrashed out privately between two old friends, Portland and Boufflers, seemed to the more fiery of Louis's subjects humiliating to France and needlessly so. Pinerolo had gone to Savoy already. A new marriage alliance between France and Savoy might mean much or little. With one great exception, the territorial settlement was the *status quo ante bellum*. The French had to march out of Philippsburg and Breisach, Freiburg-im-Breisgau and their fort at Kehl; all their fortifications on the Rhine—La Pile, Fort Louis, Trarbach—were to be destroyed. At this price, at last, they gained the legal title to Strasbourg. They cunningly sowed ill-feeling between the emperor and his Protestant allies by making him agree to deprive the Strasbourg Protestants of their rights. Some of the German princes took pickings and the duke of Lorraine was restored to his duchy, though on conditions which left it strategically at the mercy of France. But the Spaniards, who had done so little to help themselves, now received what their allies had failed to win for them. The list of fortresses was long: Luxemburg and Chimay, Mons, Courtrai, Charleroi, Ath, Barcelona. Dinant went back to Liège. It soon began to be said that Louis, having shown the Spaniards how easily he could ruin them, now wanted them as friends with an eye to their succession question.

The Maritime Powers asked for no territory. The Dutch were given a favourable commercial treaty, of which the most important provision was for a return to the French tariff of 1664. The British ambassadors were instructed to arrange for an eventual commercial treaty, and their new Board of Trade had actually worked on a draft treaty similar to that of the Dutch; but the plenipotentiaries put forward no proposal, holding that 'the balance of trade, as it now stands, is evidently on the English side'.[1] The British were content to allow their tariff war with France to continue. Whereas the French merchant marine was supposed to have declined from 750 sizeable ships in 1688 to 533 in 1698, that of England was larger at the end of the war than at the beginning. In the absence of

---

[1] Historical Manuscripts Commission, *Bath Papers*, vol. III (1908), p. 127.

commercial and industrial statistics for the earlier years of the war, it is impossible to estimate its permanent economic effects, and it was followed by a 'replacement boom' which effaced many of its temporary results; but it made great changes in the borderland where economic merges into political power. The Empire indeed was still at war against the Turks, and Spain was sunk in poverty. The Dutch were hard hit financially. In France economists diagnosed the defects of the wasteful, unjust and ineffective financial system, but there was no reform. More than 40 m. *livres* had been raised by the sale of offices in and over trade, and the holders of these offices inevitably damaged it to a far greater amount. There were no more State subsidies or other favours for industry. In Great Britain, on the other hand, the foundations of reform had been well laid. The results appeared in a lasting improvement of the navy. Its shore establishments had been greatly improved. At the beginning of the war it had 100 ships of the line, at the end 130, the increase being mainly in the lower rates which were useful for more varied services, notably 'convoys and cruisers'.

Above all, William III had achieved his primary war aim. He was recognized by the French as king of Great Britain and Ireland. His three kingdoms were thus united with the Dutch, in a partnership which was almost certain to be enduring, to uphold the balance of power against France.

CHAPTER VIII

THE EMERGENCE OF GREAT BRITAIN
AS A WORLD POWER

IN the summer of 1714—when Her Majesty's effective government consisted of Abigail, Lady Masham, Robert Harley, earl of Oxford, and Henry St John, Lord Bolingbroke—the duke of Buckingham, on his dismissal from office, penned this summary of English history in the preceding half-century:

Good God, how has this poor Nation been governed in my time! During the reign of King Charles the Second we were governed by a parcel of French whores; in King James the Second's time by a parcel of Popish Priests; in King William's time by a parcel of Dutch Footmen; and now we are governed by a dirty chambermaid, a Welsh attorney, and a profligate wretch that has neither honour nor honesty.[1]

The frankness of these words well illustrates the freedom permitted to dukes and denied to pedants. Looking back from the standpoint of the year 1714, the last of Stuart rule, the observer must have been impressed by the variety of race, religion and occupation among those who, in succession, had come to possess the confidence of the Crown; surely, there can be few periods of history abounding in such mutations of colour as these fifty-four years between the eager, joyful accession of a young, restored king and the last pathetic moments of a dying queen. Can it be wondered at that these kaleidoscopic externals have concealed the matter-of-fact but momentous changes which transformed the insular England of 1660 into the Great Britain of 1714?

These changes were intimately connected with the two great wars of 1689–1713. In 1660 England, with a population of just over five million (to which may be added about a million for Scotland and just over two million for Ireland)[2], had recently emerged from her first naval war with the Dutch; but for twenty-eight years she was to remain still untested in the full-scale, nearly continuous warfare, on land and sea, in Europe and elsewhere, which was brought into existence by Louis XIV, who had the backing of a population three times as large and the services of proven admirals and generals, as well as of the most efficient ministers in the world. Indeed, in 1689, when England was obliged to take up the challenge of Versailles, it must have seemed that the struggle was hopeless, because

---

[1] Quoted by Winston S. Churchill, *Marlborough: His Life and Times* (1947 edn. 2 vols.), vol. II, p. 1008.

[2] K. H. Connell, *The Population of Ireland, 1750–1845* (Oxford, 1950), p. 25. Gregory King's well-known figures for England relate to the last decade of the seventeenth century and are analysed in D. V. Glass, *Population Studies*, vol. II, pt. 4 (1950), pp. 338–74.

she had no army worthy of the name; her shipping offered innumerable targets to enemy privateers; and neither financial nor material resources seemed likely to last as long as the French. The total cost of the second Anglo-Dutch war had amounted to little more than £5 m., a sum which proved to be less than the average *annual* cost of the nearly twenty years of war waged in the period 1689–1713, with a breathing space of only five years. Nor were these the only matters which might have dismayed observers. France had the advantages of unity of governmental control, which ensured concentration on the war effort, no matter what sacrifices might be demanded of the large submerged portion of the population; whereas in England the Revolution had imposed parliament on the sovereign, with all the possibilities of pressure from the representatives of public opinion; moreover the English landed classes were likely to be less tolerant of increased taxation than the peasants of France. The enemy, fighting on interior lines, well able to suppress discontent at home and to destroy English resources at sea, was in a position not unlike that of Germany in 1914 and 1939, when it appeared that all the cards were in his favour.

There were other, long-term factors impeding the British war effort. Most prominent was the Jacobite menace. Here it is necessary to distinguish: for, while many supporters of the exiled James Stuart came out into the open for his cause, a larger number remained at home, many of them in office and all determined—whether by treachery, dishonesty or mere incompetence—to damage the new régime. For years after 1689, patriotism meant loyalty to the king over the water; for years before 1714, prudence meant keeping in the good graces of the courts of both Hanover and St Germains.[1] William was threatened with removal by assassination and invasion; Anne would be succeeded by the Elector or the Pretender. For neither of these stopgap sovereigns could Englishmen feel that devotion which they willingly accord to an established line of kings. A truculent Dutchman and the prospect that he would be succeeded by a boorish German—these were the chief assets of the Stuart cause in England.

Jacobitism was for long a popular cause in Catholic Ireland and in the western Highlands of Scotland, where the loyalty of the clansmen to their chiefs was reinforced by the survival of feudal jurisdictions. Moreover, these two neighbours stood in a somewhat ambiguous relationship to England. While Ireland was nominally a kingdom, she was treated as a plantation, having her subordinate position within the old empire; yet Scotland, actually a kingdom until joined with England in 1707 in the United Kingdom of Great Britain, was forbidden the plantation trade and so, until that date, not strictly a part of the empire at all. Both these countries retained their own legislatures, the Irish remaining largely

---

[1] The royal residence at St-Germain-en-Laye, about 10 miles west of Paris, placed at the disposal of James II and later of the Old Pretender by Louis XIV. Mary of Modena died there in 1718.

dependent on the supervision of the English Privy Council, the Scottish enjoying an independent existence (after 1603) only between 1689 and 1707. In each country the racial configuration was roughly that between Saxon east and Celtic west, except that the south-west of Scotland was closely linked with northern Ireland. After the defeat of James II in Ireland the Catholic Irish were subjected to a nominal proscription, considerably mitigated in its enforcement; but exports of cloth and cattle were prohibited by the parliament at Westminster, with the result that the export trade in provisions became Ireland's only commercial staple. After the Treaty of Limerick the attitude of the greater part of Ireland was one of resentful submission, while that of Ulster (to which the Toleration Act of 1689 did not apply) was one of indignation against the exercise of the Episcopalian monopoly.[1] So, too, Scotland had her grievances. Her chief exports were salmon, hides, coal, salt and coarse cloth, and her best customer was Holland; hence her economic interests had been seriously prejudiced by enforced participation in the three Anglo-Dutch wars. Population and economic activity were greatest along the eastern seaboard, especially on the Firth of Forth and in the mining area connecting the Forth and Clyde estuaries—a reflection of the fact that the commercial and cultural relations of the older Scotland were with Scandinavia, Holland and France, rather than with England. Already a change was taking place in this orientation, for there was considerable clandestine trade with the American plantations and for that purpose Glasgow was much better situated than Leith, then the chief seaport. The Clyde at Glasgow was still too shallow for any but the smallest vessels; nevertheless, merchants were sending their goods by road to Greenock and Port Glasgow for shipment to the west. But this did not compensate Scotland for her exclusion from the plantation trade and so, as in Ireland, there was much bitterness against the predominant partner. By 1702, when it was obvious that neither William nor Anne would have an heir, there was, until the matter was settled by legislative union, a real possibility that the northern kingdom would confer the crown on someone other than the person named in the English Act of Settlement (1701).[2]

Strategically, Scotland and Ireland were both an advantage and a disadvantage to England. It was obviously an advantage to have access to their ports in war-time; on the other hand, these might be open to the enemy. While the east coasts offer few opportunities for concealment, the western, with their innumerable sea lochs and estuaries, offer secrecy to the invader, and it was on this side of Scotland and Ireland that the friends of the Stuarts were to be found. Hence the best port of departure from the Continent was Brest, with its easy access to the south-west of

---

[1] J. C. Beckett, *Protestant Dissent in Ireland, 1687–1740* (1948), p. 41. Cf. L. M. Cullen, *Anglo-Irish Trade, 1660–1800* (Manchester, 1968).

[2] Below, pp. 266–7. Cf. T. C. Smout, *Scottish Trade on the Eve of the Union, 1660–1707* (1963).

Ireland, an opportunity freely exploited by French and Jacobites in the earlier years of William's wars. The inlets of the western Highlands provided still more ideal landing-spots, as well as a population likely to sympathize with a losing and even a lost cause: this is why the '15 and '45 rebellions were initially so successful. By contrast, the attempt of March 1708 did not even have a chance, because the French commander sailed from Dunkirk to the Forth, a part of Scotland distinguished more by trade with the Dutch than by widespread sentiment for the Stuarts.[1] Louis XIV had made the usual mistake of assuming that all Scots are Highlanders. Only by the good fortune of the wind and Forbin's seamanship did the French succeed in making their escape.

The natural conditions prevailing in England were more genial, more favourable to a diversity of occupations. This was especially true of the area which the geologists call the English Plain, an area bounded roughly by the Tyne and the Pennines on the north; on the west, by a line stretching south from Cheshire, skirting the Welsh marches and reaching the Channel on the Dorset coast; on the south and east, by the sea. This zone was distinguished not so much by fertility of soil as by comparative ease of cultivation, since it includes no mountains and the soil consists mostly of those (geologically) newer substances, as marl or clay, which could be easily ploughed with primitive implements. This region was also better served by navigable rivers than the north and west. Hence it was natural that population and industry were more concentrated here than outside the Plain. The deepening and widening of rivers provided one of the most common 'improvements' of the later seventeenth and early eighteenth centuries. Here England had the advantage of France; not only had she as good a network of streams, but these were free from the numerous and vexatious tolls which impeded French transport. Generally, England's natural advantages may be summarized in the negative statements that there are no great or prolonged extremes of temperature and no vast stretches of territory devoted to the same product or activity; deposits of the metals, again, are seldom far from deposits of coal and the centres of population never far from a navigable stream. It may be doubted whether any seventeenth-century State of similar size offered such variety of climate and product within such short distances; and it may be added that English good fortune in coal and iron, though not then fully exploited, was soon to prove a determining factor, whereas France remained rich mainly in products—such as corn, wine and textiles—characteristic of an older, more self-contained economy. Lastly, there are the long continuous coastlines of England and Scotland. New harbours could be developed, as on the west, to meet new requirements; the tides in these waters are more usually a help than a hindrance; there is no great land mass as in France dividing one sea from another, no danger of ice blockage as in the Baltic.

[1] For this 'alarm from Dunkirk', see below, p. 435.

Ireland shields a large part of England's west coast from the Atlantic, as the islands of the west coast shield Scotland's. Britain's duty to be great she owed as much to the sea as to herself.

Equally important was the human element. The countryside was dominated by the landed freeholder, the unit of society, whose land provided a guarantee of independence as well as an obligation to perform unpaid local service—whether in the county lieutenancies, on the grand juries, on the bench as a justice, as an officer in the militia, sometimes even as a lord of the manor. He was not influenced by class prejudice, because his was the only class; his main objects were to keep rents up and rates down; his chief complaint was that he had to shoulder most of the Land Tax and accordingly he detested the merchant and townsman, who in this respect got off lightly. Within the large class of landowners, however, there were numerous long-term changes.[1] At one end of the scale, more of them were becoming independent of agriculture as they derived incomes from trade, ground-rents or public office. But there was also a continuous flow of capital from the towns to the country, chiefly within easy reach of London, since many who had prospered in trade or the professions bought estates; after 1688, moreover, possession of land came to have a greater political value. At the other end of the scale, copyholders and leaseholders were often becoming tenant farmers and wage labourers. Intermediate between these extremes were the poorer gentry and the substantial yeoman, a steadily diminishing group, well exemplified by Addison's 'hundred pounds a year man', who 'knocks down a dinner with his gun twice or thrice a week' and so lived more cheaply than his poorer neighbours, whom the Game Act forbade to shoot:[2] already, sporting rights were becoming the monopoly of the rich. The small farmer was also prejudiced by the cheapening of corn, but this benefited farm labourers and workers in the towns. At the same time the larger tenant farmer was making his appearance on the estates of the new rich. In general, extremes of wealth and social position were becoming more sharply accentuated. At least one interesting social change may be connected with this development, namely, the gradual mitigation and obsolescence of those manorial rights which still survived. Had these been exacted, they might have yielded a modest revenue; but English lords of the manor, in their comparative prosperity, were usually able to ignore them.

[1] See the articles of H. J. Habakkuk: 'La Disparition du paysan anglais', *Annales* (*E.S.C.*), 20ᵉ année (1965), pp. 657–63; 'English Landownership, 1680–1740', *Econ. Hist. Rev.* 1st ser. vol. x (1940), pp. 2–17; 'The English Land Market in the Eighteenth Century', *Britain and the Netherlands* (ed. J. S. Bromley and E. H. Kossmann, 1960), pp. 154–73. The development of a market in long-term mortgages, together with lower interest-rates and the legal device of the 'strict [marriage] settlement', tended to reduce land sales from the 1680s, against the tendency of the high wartime Land Tax, which drove many of the smaller gentry off the land by 1730.

[2] *The Spectator*, no. 122 (20 July 1711). The Game Act of 1670–1 prohibited the use of guns or sporting dogs by persons having an estate of less than £100 per annum.

As the freeholder was the unit in the countryside, so in the corporate towns the unit was the worker 'free' of his craft. At this time many journeymen and apprentices were neglecting to take out their 'freedom' because of the expense, and the companies themselves were becoming the great charitable institutions which we know today. Increasing specialization of industry made it impossible for them to control their crafts. Nevertheless, the apprenticeship system still conferred two benefits. First, it protected one class of worker against exploitation, as can be seen by contrasting conditions in the old 'regulated' industries with those in newer and 'unregulated' occupations, such as coal-heaving, and with industries employing cheap female labour. Second, apprenticeship ensured the maintenance of a strict standard of workmanship, manifested not only in textiles old and new but in silverware, leatherwork and the making of mechanical devices, such as watches and clocks, the reputation of which was so high that there were many foreign counterfeits. In these and some other respects English craftsmanship had the best reputation in the world. Englishmen were also distinguished for their inventiveness. This was stimulated by the shortages of war-time, when people had to 'make do' with native materials where formerly they had used imported ones— Breton canvas, for example—while the operations of war encouraged inventors to contrive such appliances as primitive 'tanks' and landing apparatus.[1] More generally, enterprise was stimulated by the influx of Huguenot skills and capital, and by the greater security of status accorded to Dissenters by the Toleration Act of 1689. The Dissenters, still excluded from the universities, schools and professions, were bound to find an outlet in trade and industry, as was true not least of the Quakers, who excelled in the making of hardware, cutlery and agricultural implements.[2] In the skilled crafts, therefore, England had the advantage of a large and diversified body of men who took pride in the integrity of their products, a fact which goes far to explain the expansion of the English export trade.

There was also the large class known as 'the poor'. The Protestant Reformation, which had introduced the two new virtues of respectability and the possession of a fixed address, was intolerant of poverty and unemployment, on the assumption that these misfortunes must have arisen from moral defect. The 'poor' now were not a class but a residue, consisting of those who had no accredited place in society. They included all who were neither landed freeholders nor in a profession nor 'free' of a craft; and so the term extended to soldiers and sailors, labourers and cottagers, besides paupers, unemployed and vagabonds, indeed all who were either on the rates or considered likely to be: a great reservoir of cheap, unorganized labour and potential liability. Everyone was agreed

[1] Thomas Puckle's revolving (machine) gun was not patented till 1718; it is illustrated in W. Y. Carman, *A History of Firearms* (1955), p. 81.
[2] On their prominence in the iron industry in this period see A. Raistrick, *Quakers in Science and Industry* (1950), pp. 89–160.

that their wages must be kept down to the minimum level of subsistence —only thus could England undersell her competitors—and so the white worker at home was in some sense the counterpart of the black labourer abroad. Not much commiseration was spent on either of these residues. On the contrary it was objected, somewhat illogically, that neither was a great consumer of English products: for the scantily dressed slave in the West Indies lived largely on half-rotten codfish supplied by enterprising New England merchants in exchange for molasses which, when converted into rum, helped to buy more slaves; and at home the ragged labourer and pauper had scarcely an ounce of English wool on his back, while his diet of potatoes and water was obviously of little advantage to the farmer, not to speak of the landlord and his rent.[1] But before we lose patience with such reasoning we should remember that it was this callousness which helped to make England rich, and that she had less of it than most contemporary societies.

The fiscal factor is another of the many reasons why England held her own and eventually defeated a much richer nation. The most productive of the direct taxes, the Land Tax, reassessed in 1692, yielded £2 m. a year at the usual wartime rate of 4 shillings in the pound. The most dependable of the indirect taxes by this date was the excise, whose increasing yield conformed fairly closely to the expansion of wealth and population; hence its value for the payment of interest on the many loans which also had to be raised for war purposes. It was dependability that encouraged public confidence, the essential condition for the success of English schemes of public credit in the wars against France.[2] The great developments in public finance provide one of the many striking contrasts between the England of the Revolution and that of the last male Stuarts. From whatever angle they are interpreted, however, whether as a more adequate exploitation of national resources or as a logical development of administrative progress, they cannot be divorced from the expansion of maritime enterprise in the later seventeenth century. The full-scale war initiated in William's reign made this of even more pressing moment than before; the nation, intent on developing its advantages for industry and commerce and on limiting its disadvantages, became (as it were) economically self-conscious. The elucidation of economic policy enlisted the co-operation of some of the greatest minds of the age, including Newton and Locke, with whom must be associated such specialists as Gregory King, Josiah Child and Charles Davenant, whose intelligent analysis of wealth and poverty did much to prepare the way for Adam Smith. Generally, they helped to popularize a policy which aimed at full employment, low wages

---

[1] Martyn's essay 'On Mendicity' in *The Spectator*, no. 232 (26 Nov. 1711). For a more favourable opinion of attitudes to the poor see Charles Wilson, 'The Other Face of Mercantilism', *Trans. R. Hist. Soc.* 5th ser. vol. IX (1959), pp. 81–101.

[2] For English and French public finance see below, ch. IX. The excise on beer is discussed in P. Mathias, *The Brewing Industry in England, 1700–1830* (Cambridge, 1959), ch. X.

and maximum exports, with imports limited as far as possible to raw materials and to products capable of a further manufacture at home. The ideal, seldom realized, was exchange with those countries which might export bullion; in any case, overseas trades were classified according as they produced a favourable or unfavourable 'balance', a distinction not unlike that between areas of 'hard' and 'soft' currencies today. Thus, from the point of view of the balance, the Baltic countries were 'unfavourable', although English imports from them were essential. Trade with France was entirely 'unfavourable' because the imports therefrom were considered luxuries, such as wine and silk, not compensated for by any adequate admission into France of English manufactured goods; consequently, this trade was condemned by patriots.[1] The fact that Bolingbroke was mainly responsible for the draft commercial treaty of 1713, which gave France 'most favoured nation' terms for her exports to Britain, accounts partly for the attempt to impeach him in 1714. In contrast, Portugal fulfilled the requirements of orthodox mercantilism, for she took English woollens (despite efforts to do without them) and paid for them in bullion and port.[2] The bullion helped to put Britain on the gold standard; the port, as a test of robust virility, gained by contrast with the supposedly effeminate claret, the beverage of Frenchmen, Jacobites and Tories. Portugal had another claim on British affection because Lisbon could be useful to the fleet for operations in the Mediterranean and her coast flanked an artery of sea-trade. Trade with most of the Mediterranean countries was considered 'favourable', especially with Spain, which took even the heavier varieties of cloth as well as Newfoundland codfish. Above all, the rich and (nominally) closed empire of Spain in the west was clamouring for European goods and African slaves: hence, in large degree, English and Dutch opposition to a Bourbon on the throne of Spain.

In these years there was evidence both of greater control over the direction of foreign trade and of more freedom in its pursuit. The first tendency is best illustrated by the comprehensive enforcement clauses of the Navigation Act of 1696 and the institution a month later of the Board of Trade and Plantations, whose main function was to collect the information necessary for the shaping of policy, and to make recommendations, many of which were embodied in legislation.[3] On the other hand, there was more freedom in the conduct of overseas enterprise. The Royal African Company had at once recognized that the flight of James II meant an end to monopoly based on royal charter;[4] in 1698 the slave trade was opened to all who paid dues to the Company. The Hudson's Bay Company

---

[1] For contemporary criticism of this view by Davenant and others, see W. J. Ashley, 'The Tory Origin of Free Trade Policy', *Surveys Historic and Economic* (1900), pp. 268–93. Cf. below, ch. XXIII (1) and M. Priestley, 'Anglo-French Trade and the "Unfavourable Balance" Controversy', *Econ. Hist. Rev.* 2nd ser. vol. IV (1951), pp. 37–52.

[2] Below, pp. 523–4 and 535.   [3] Cf. below, pp. 490–1 ff.

[4] K. G. Davies, *The Royal African Company* (1957), p. 123. Cf. below, pp. 855–6.

and the looser, 'regulated' Levant Company still retained their privileges; but the 'old' East India Company, having lost its monopoly in 1694, was finally obliged to come to terms with a rival New Company when reconstituted as the United Company in 1709. With Russia there continued to be open intercourse. Many old companies, like the Russia and Eastland (Baltic) Companies, were moribund.[1] One of the earliest Acts of William's reign lifted the restrictions on the export of woollens and finally put an end to the old Merchant Adventurers' monopoly, thus stimulating a tendency for the outports to obtain a larger share of foreign trade from London, which had been responsible for up to nine-tenths of England's legitimate overseas trade between 1500 and 1650.

Even in the newer Atlantic trades on which the western ports chiefly prospered, however, London retained overwhelming predominance. Its vitality was most evident to contemporaries in the thickening forest of masts which crowded the river—a growth matched by the development at this time of markets in marine and fire insurance.[2] The new opportunities provided by many government-sponsored loans, an attractive alternative to the traditional investment in land, encouraged successful merchants and others to keep their homes in town, and so helped to develop a resident patrician class like that of London's chief rival, Amsterdam. The population of the capital, over 400,000 in 1700, was to double in the succeeding century and far to outdistance that of Paris.[3] By 1689 the rebuilding of the City after the Great Fire was near completion. On 2 December 1697, in thanksgiving for the Peace of Ryswick, the choir of St Paul's cathedral was opened for public worship. Wren's masterpiece consecrated the disappearance of the half-medieval City, its place taken by an increasingly more spacious London, worthy to be the capital not only of a nation but of an empire.[4]

Of this increase of national wealth two broad social consequences were discernible in the reigns of William and Anne. The first was the emergence of a group of 'new rich', able to afford those imported articles and commodities which stamped the age with so much of its style: mahogany and satinwood, lacquers and porcelain, coffee and tea. It was usual to store porcelain in cabinets made of fine woods, and to use the china for serving tea. In this way the 'withdrawing room' came into existence, where the

[1] R. W. K. Hinton, *The Eastland Trade and the Common Weal in the Seventeenth Century* (Cambridge, 1959), pp. 156–61.

[2] See below, pp. 289 and 855–6.

[3] R. Mols, *Introduction à la démographie historique des villes d'Europe* (Louvain, 3 vols. 1955–6), vol. II, p. 47. It is salutary to remember that in 1700 Japan already had three cities of comparable size—Yedo, Kyoto and the expanding commercial centre of Osaka: Sir G. Sansom, *A History of Japan*, vol. III (1964), p. 113.

[4] For Wren's successive designs and difficulties see J. Lang, *Rebuilding St Paul's* (1956); cf. John Summerson, *Georgian London* (1945), chs. III–VII. On the whole, these were boom years in the erection of houses and other buildings, as Oxford and Bath alone testify: T. S. Ashton, *Economic Fluctuations in England, 1700–1800* (1959), pp. 91–2.

lady of the house could maintain a dominion not so easily attainable amid the odours of tobacco and beer. Nor was the drawing-room only an avenue to the emancipation of women; it was an institution which, especially when developed into the *salon*, served to stimulate and often to refine the expression of opinion by men of intelligence. A modulation of literary expression—less pedantic, less technical, more easily under-standable—may have owed something to the Stellas and Vanessas of the Augustan Age. There was another indication of a subtle change in the attitude of men to women. In the past, women had provided the inspira-tion of sonnets and odes; now they were brought down to earth as the recipients of worthwhile correspondence, often of high literary value, because the writers treat the women as of similar or equal intelligence. Hitherto they had been in the clouds or in the kitchen.

A second social consequence of expansion may be suggested. In medi-eval times and during the Civil Wars the north of England had enjoyed periods of national pre-eminence, but certain natural features ensured the predominance of the midlands and south. This predominance was now to be accentuated by greater exploitation of coal and metal resources; by increased profits from wholesale and overseas trade; and by the many fortunes made from the wars. The first of these developments indeed affected mainly the districts to the north of Trent and Severn, but the profits and the fortunes were spent mainly in the Thames Valley and the south-east—in the heart of the English Plain, where were to be found the metropolis, the residences of the Court, the legislature, the two universities. There was, of course, also the difference that the north was more sparsely populated and less fully represented in parliament; but there was deve-loping a more subtle distinction in this, that while northern occupations and products were coming to be associated with manual labour and grime, those of the south could be handled without soiling one's hands, indeed often without physically handling them at all. Coal, tar and soot were helping already to bring two Englands into existence, the one 'eligible', the other less so. A further contrast can be seen in political leadership. Under Charles II, Yorkshire indeed was responsible for such notable personalities as Danby and Halifax; but the later political leaders came almost entirely from the south, until Grey and Peel, Cobden and Glad-stone brought Lancashire and the north again into prominence.

Such were among the more important natural and human characteristics that helped determine the course of British history after 1692, when it could reasonably be assumed, for the time being at least, that England, Scotland and Ireland were won for the Revolution. The first serious threat to the Revolution settlement occurred in 1696, when there was an attempt to murder William and when an invasion threat from France was again forestalled by English sea power. The Peace of Ryswick provided no more than a breathing space, but by 1697 many Jacobites had given up James's cause because they realized that his success would mean domination from Versailles; moreover, many Englishmen had invested their money in the Revolution, and the regularity with which they received their dividends contrasted strikingly with the speculative character of Stuart investments. The direct burdens on the poor were not increased, as they were in France; the middle classes benefited by war loans and contracts; the influential made fortunes in many and devious ways. There was less debauchery in high places than under the preceding régime, but a more widely diffused materialism and a more matter-of-fact attitude to life.

But that civilization is best which has fewest disadvantages. The Revolution was followed by a régime of toleration which in practice extended far beyond the limits of the Act of 1689,[1] and this must be numbered among the invisible assets of England in her struggle with the intolerant France of Louis XIV. In a total Dissenter population of perhaps a quarter of a million, some 14,000 voted at parliamentary elections. Many, especially the Presbyterians, were willing to qualify for office in the corporations by receiving the Anglican Communion from time to time; not until 1711 did the Whig Lords cease, for reasons of political manoeuvre, to block bills for the suppression of 'occasional conformity'. In respect of Nonconformist teaching at any rate, the Act of Uniformity (1662) was at most times and places a dead letter. The specially delicate legal position of the Quakers was somewhat alleviated. Distraints, especially in kind, on the property of the poorer among them for non-payment of tithe and church-rates could still be ruinous, but they were less frequent than before 1688; prosecutions for sums under £10 might after 1696 go before the local justices, instead of to the exchequer and ecclesiastical courts, where the expense had been such as to drive many Quakers to neglect their testimony against tithe. The Affirmation Act of 1696, whose passage owed even more to the personal intervention of King William than to the already precocious political organization of the 50,000 Friends, substituted affirmations for most of the oaths still required of them.[2] The Roman Catholic clergy also constantly risked fine and imprisonment, but the laity now suffered more from civil disabilities than downright persecution. The priest who solemnized a papist marriage might be heavily fined: the parties were none the less lawfully married and the heirs, though with some technical difficulties, might succeed to property; it proved difficult to enforce a badly drafted Act of 1700, which aimed at destroying their position as landowners.

While English civilization was the poorer by its ostracism of its Roman Catholic community, the practice of toleration became more deeply entrenched than in any other European society. Unlike the position in France

---

[1] Above, pp. 209–10.
[2] N. C. Hunt, *Two Early Political Associations* (Oxford, 1961), chs. III–IV.

for almost another century, torture in criminal proceedings was unknown; the Habeas Corpus Amendment Act (1679), though parliament suspended it during short periods of crisis, as in 1689 and 1715, ensured that (except for treason and felony) a person under detention could claim to be released on bail, while nobody could be detained indefinitely without trial. From 1696, persons accused of treason acquired the right to retain counsel and were given a copy of the indictment ten days before trial—a humane measure which made it more difficult for the Crown to obtain convictions against the disaffected. This was all the more important in view of the extended definitions of treason to which the dangers of the time give rise: in 1692, for instance, it was made treason to go to France without a licence, and in 1706 to affirm in writing that the Succession could not be altered by statute. As with treason, so with blasphemy. On the Continent and in Scotland the penalty for blasphemy was death; in England, Christianity was considered to be so strongly established that the State could afford to impose much milder penalties for denial of its truth. Under an Act of 1698 blasphemy was punishable by civil disabilities and not more than three years in prison; and even these penalties were seldom enforced, perhaps because it was difficult in practice for lawyers to determine at all precisely when learned heresy became a crime. In practice the age was remarkable in England for the vigour and boldness of theological discussion.

As there was a change in the laws, so there was a change, even more striking, in the character of the judges. Neither William nor Anne interfered with the conduct of the judicial bench, with the result that Westminster Hall regained some of the repute it had lost under the Stuarts. Of the judges of these two reigns, the most notable was Sir John Holt, Chief Justice of the King's Bench, whose legal learning and acuity were such that many of his judgments have passed into the very substance of English jurisprudence. He maintained the independence of the Bench, not against the Crown—there was less need for that[1]—but against a much more formidable institution, the House of Lords. In many of his judgments, particularly in those cases which came to him by appeal from a local Poor Law authority, where the very humblest were concerned, he showed a humanity strikingly new; and not only did he disallow trials for alleged witchcraft, but he ordered the prosecution of those who sought to initiate such trials. Of the judges immediately before the Revolution, the most notable had been Jeffreys.

In practice, as in theory, the royal authority remained a strong force in government. The Bill of Rights had declared illegal the exercise of the suspending power without consent of parliament, and of the dispensing power as wielded by James II. More serious limitations of prerogative

[1] The Act of Settlement of 1701 finally gave the judges a security of tenure (except upon a demise of the Crown) which they had not enjoyed under Charles II or James II.

were that the king must summon parliament regularly and that its proceedings could not be questioned outside. But the king retained the right
to veto legislation. In fact, William vetoed only four public bills of
importance; although afterwards placed on the statute book, they did not
long remain there in their original form. The important thing is not the
number of laws he disallowed, but the number he observed.

Control of foreign policy was another ancient right left to the Crown
intact. Its exercise involved some complicated issues, among them that
William was known to have a more intimate knowledge of foreign affairs
than any of his ministers or secretaries; and so, for a time, there was at
least acquiescence in the royal exercise of this right. Moreover, William's
war with France was for some time accepted as an inevitable consequence
of the Revolution and approved by both Houses of Parliament. But there
was increasing dissatisfaction with his conduct of it, and a critical spirit
spread to his control of foreign policy, especially his share in the Partition
Treaties.[1] There was resentment against the Dutchmen, Portland and
Heinsius, who enjoyed his confidence to the exclusion of all English
ministers but Somers and Sunderland. In 1701 the Commons impeached
Somers, with Orford and Halifax, for their alleged responsibility in the
signing of the Partition Treaties, brushing aside their plea that the king
can do no wrong. The impeachments failed, but the victory was really
with the Commons, for their action conveyed a clear hint to the king that,
in all major matters of foreign policy, he must act only with the advice of
his accredited ministers; equally, it was a warning to the ministers that
they could no longer evade responsibility by trying to transfer it to the
person of the sovereign. But for the bitter disputes between the two
Houses at this time, a formal scheme might have been devised to ensure
that in all great matters of state the king would act only on the advice of
agents responsible to parliament. By 1701 William himself had shown
some realization of this important change in the situation, for he communicated copies of his treaties to both Houses; in effect, he had abandoned
the old prerogative right to control foreign policy in person. Thus, in
regard to the exercise of the vast prerogative with which he was still
endowed, it can be claimed that William acted with moderation and good
sense. To these qualities can be added a good faith far more efficacious
than strictly legal limitations. The fact that his successor was a woman, and
that she conducted her foreign policy on the advice of her ministers,
served to ensure the establishment of that parliamentary sovereignty to
which the Hanoverians succeeded in 1714. The Act of Settlement, which
in June 1701 declared the Protestant Electress Sophia of Hanover (granddaughter of James I) next heir after William and Anne, marked the first

---

[1] Below, ch. XII. Cf. M. A. Thomson, 'Parliament and Foreign Policy, 1689–1714',
History, new ser. vol. XXXVIII (1953), pp. 234–43, and 'Louis XIV and William III, 1689–
1697', *Engl. Hist. Rev.* vol. LXXVI (1961), pp. 37–58.

statutory encroachment on royal control of foreign policy, in providing that no sovereign after them should engage in war for the defence of any foreign territory, nor leave the country, without parliamentary consent.

In some other respects this fundamental statute, significantly entitled 'An Act for further limitation of the Crown and for better securing the rights and liberties of the subject', was a commentary on the constitutional behaviour of King William. As soon as it should come into force, on the death of Anne, no foreigner was to hold public office, sit in parliament, or hold land of the Crown. Just as this clearly condemned William's largesse to Dutch favourites, so a further criticism was implied of his use of Court influence, in a wider sense, by the 'place clause' prohibiting office-holders and pensioners of the Crown from sitting in the Commons—a provision which in principle has come to govern the modern civil service but which, had it not been modified in 1706 (by a distinction drawn between offices created before and after 25 October O.S. 1705), would have inhibited the development of the cabinet system as we know it. Indeed, by ruling also that all important matters of state should be transacted by the Privy Council, and its advice tendered in writing with the signatures of those who gave it, the parliament of 1701 showed how little it liked the recent innovation of a small and elusive cabinet unknown to the law. Although this clause too was repealed as unworkable in 1706, the essential principle of ministerial responsibility which it sought to establish was nevertheless enhanced, once and for all, by the provision of 1701 that no royal pardon should be pleadable in bar of an impeachment by the Commons.

There remained intact other elements in the prerogative, notably the powers to dissolve parliament and to create peers, which were to prove of real political value in 1710 and 1712 respectively. Above all, there was the right to appoint and dismiss ministers. In both reigns much difficulty and controversy was occasioned by the exercise of this right. To a large extent William acted as his own first minister; as he spent about half his reign outside England, however, he was obliged to entrust some responsibility to ministers at home. He had no preference for Whigs; indeed, he came to regard them as republicans, for whom Dutch experience had taught him distaste. But, as so many Tories were loyal to the wrong monarch and as so many Whigs, particularly those in office, supported the war, he was obliged to show the Whigs some confidence and, in general, to select his ministers from those who would further his objects and who could claim to have a considerable backing in the Commons. In so doing he may have been influenced by his confidant Sunderland;[1] only thus can we explain the appointments of Godolphin and Rochester in the later years of his reign. The one English statesman for whom William showed any real regard, however, was John, Baron Somers (1651–1716), who for three years after 1695 was the unofficial head of a small body of Whigs known

---

[1] J. P. Kenyon, *Robert Spencer, Earl of Sunderland*, chs. VIII–IX.

as the Junto, which included Charles Montagu (baron 1700 and earl of Halifax 1714), Admiral Russell (earl of Orford 1697), and Thomas, Baron Wharton (earl 1706 and marquis of Wharton 1715). It was this informal council of ministers that guided the nation through the last, critical years of the war. Its existence happened to coincide with a period when the Whigs and their allies had a majority in the Commons; but it is notable that Somers's appointment as Lord Keeper preceded the general election of 1695, which returned so many Whigs, and that his tenure lasted until 1700, two years after his party had lost preponderance in the Commons. The only implication that the Junto had any corporate existence was the fact that three of its members were impeached in 1701 for their supposed part in the Partition Treaties. Nevertheless, the Junto has a special interest in the history of the cabinet for these reasons: because its members were Whigs, and even gloried in the name; and because two of them, Montagu and Russell, the heads respectively of the Exchequer and Admiralty, represented a newer type of minister, responsible to parliament as well as to the king for the conduct of a great department of state, in contrast with the older type, holding a household or conciliar office and responsible only to the Crown. Somers, it is true, held the office which in the past had entailed pre-eminence in State affairs, but that pre-eminence was now coming to be associated rather with the Treasury than with the Chancery.[1] Wharton does not fit into any of these categories, but he was a useful colleague, an electioneering expert and the owner of boroughs in Yorkshire and Buckinghamshire. Between them, the members of the Junto controlled about sixty seats—the largest single *bloc* in the reign of Anne. Before the end of the century these four men were in the Lords, a fact which weakened them in their corporate capacity, though their influence re-emerged in 1705 and they were joined by Charles, 3rd earl of Sunderland (1674–1722), whom they were strong enough to impose on the administration in 1708. By that time the conception of cabinet government had become established, and its procedure was becoming formalized.[2]

Nevertheless, the existence of some kind of cabinet, dependent on the support of the Commons, did not seriously interfere with the royal right to choose and dismiss ministers. Just before his death William dismissed Rochester, uncle of Princess Anne; as soon as the princess became queen she reinstated him, though he had the prudence to resign in 1703. Anne's exercise of this prerogative was marked by the caprices of an obstinate woman, given to strong prejudices and resolved that, if she had to give way, she would be 'terrible in the rebound'. An added complication was that she was dominated in succession by two women—first by that

[1] Cf. Stephen B. Baxter, *The Development of the Treasury, 1660–1702* (1957).
[2] J. H. Plumb, 'The Organisation of the Cabinet in the Reign of Queen Anne', *Trans. R. Hist. Soc.* 5th ser. vol. VII (1957), pp. 137–57.

termagant Whig, Sarah, duchess of Marlborough, and then by that demure lady's companion, Abigail Hill, 'Mrs' Masham. So long as the duchess was in the ascendant, the queen was content to rule with the help of Marlborough in the field and of Godolphin, Lord High Treasurer, at home. These two, acting in close co-operation, came to be more and more dependent on the Whigs and their associates after 1705, even though both captain-general and minister were loosely regarded as Tories. In this way, the state of war and the need of good administration to win it tended, for a time, to blur party alignments among those who believed in them. Sidney Godolphin (1645–1712), who was never out of office for long during four reigns and a revolution, was the most competent and self-effacing minister of his age; with Anne, as previously with Charles II, he was 'never in the way and never out of it'. Marlborough's position was assured so long as the queen submitted to the tantrums of his duchess. Such was the curious partnership which achieved the great series of victories following the battle of Blenheim—a partnership having no counterpart in English history, for while the Lord Treasurer obtained the supplies and skilfully kept the attention of parliament on the prosecution of the war, the general made the British army a force to be reckoned with in world politics. This Godolphin–Marlborough–Sarah partnership may, somewhat loosely, be described as a ministry. It lasted from 1702 to 1710, with Harley as its fourth influential member from 1704 till 1708.

The manner of its termination reveals how Anne exercised her all-important prerogative of choosing and dismissing ministers. By 1708, tired of Sarah's domination, she was eagerly seeking emancipation. In this receptive state she welcomed the advice of Lady Masham, who fomented the royal indignation against the duchess and the ministry and insinuated the claims of her cousin Harley as the potential deliverer of the queen from her oppressors. At that time Harley was under a cloud, owing to suspicion of his complicity in the treasonable correspondence of his clerk, William Greg: the ministry had finally induced Anne to dismiss him in February 1708 from his secretaryship of state. Her sympathy flowed out to the very man whom she had been obliged to remove from office, the more since she had little liking for his hot-tempered successor, the young Sunderland—no respecter of royalty—whom the Junto had nominated as the price of their support for the ministry. As for Harley's alleged disloyalty, was not that really a recommendation in his favour, since Anne was by no means enthusiastic for the Hanoverian succession? Already Harley himself had insinuated that the ministry he served was backed only by Whigs and infidels: the Church was in danger: only with a 'sympathetic' minister like himself could the queen fulfil the object dearest to her heart—the maintenance of the monopoly of the Church of England. The queen took her time, but an incident in the spring of 1710 may have encouraged her to strike: the impeachment of Dr Sacheverell. In a sermon preached before the lord mayor and corporation of London in 1709, under the transparent guise of a defence of the doctrine of non-resistance Sacheverell had intimated that the Revolution of 1688 was really a usurpation. Unwisely, the ministry impeached him and secured a conviction. The punishment was enough to make him a national martyr. Just as in 1679 an ecclesiastical mountebank, Dr Titus Oates, had rallied round him all the forces of whiggery and anti-popery, so in 1710 an ecclesiastical clown, Dr Henry Sacheverell, became the focus of a great resurgence of High Tories, High Churchmen and all who wished to penalize Dissent. This national movement swept the Whigs from power in the general election of the autumn of 1710. But already the queen had acted. In August she dismissed Godolphin, much to that statesman's surprise and disgust; she dealt in more leisurely fashion with Marlborough, who was not dismissed until January 1712.[1] Long before that, Harley was in office as treasurer and earl of Oxford, with Henry St John (created Viscount Bolingbroke in July 1712) as a secretary of state. These were the ministers who deserted Britain's allies and brought the Spanish Succession War to an end.[2]

Seldom has there been a more ill-assorted ministry. Robert Harley (1661–1724), the inheritor of Whig and Dissenting traditions, was probably the first politician to achieve prominence by sustained opposition to government in the Commons; in William's reign, as leader of the 'new' Country party, he was insistent in his demand for a higher standard of purity in public life. The success of this campaign was not hampered by the reputation of 'Robin the Trickster' for double-dealing. Like his Whig opponent, the able financier Halifax, he had intimate knowledge of the moods and traditions of the House and was one of the most skilful parliamentary managers of the time; like Halifax and Somers, he acquired some prestige by patronage of letters and intelligent collecting of books and manuscripts. Professing to be of no political party, he had the less difficulty in winning the support of those clans and groups which, when united round a personal nucleus, were the arbiters of power. But his almost lack total of good faith prevented him from retaining their allegiance for long. As informal prime minister, he was shuffling and procrastinating. In particular, when the queen's failing health made the delicate question of the succession more urgent, he was unable to make up his mind. He backed both horses, but at the critical moment he could not decide on which horse to put the extra bet that would win him a political fortune. Still worse, he abused the queen's confidence; he neglected business; he was slovenly and disrespectful in his demeanour; his statements,

---

[1] 31 December 1711, O.S. As captain-general he was succeeded by James Butler, 2nd duke of Ormonde, who was to take a leading part in the Jacobite rebellion of 1715. Cf. below, pp. 440–1.
[2] Below, pp. 440 ff. and 457 ff.

when they could be understood, could not be relied on; and in the royal presence he was often completely incoherent. These were the reasons assigned by the queen when she dismissed him on 7 August 1714. A year later he was in the Tower, awaiting trial for treason and other high crimes, which the rancour of his enemies nevertheless failed to prove against him even by 1717. By that date his younger colleague and rival had long since taken refuge in France. Bolingbroke (1678–1751) was a politician of less devious and more spectacular type—one of those almost fantastic libertines whose sceptical wit and impetuosity give an impression of intellectual brilliance; plausibility, indeed, he carried almost to the height of genius. Like the elder Sunderland, he gambled for high stakes; but, unlike his predecessor, he never retrieved his losses, and never quite lost a sense of honour. More deeply committed than Oxford to the Stuart cause, he appears to have thought that a strong, organized Tory party might succeed in bringing in the Pretender on the queen's death, a project to which Anne herself may have been sympathetic. The chief obstacle, after the Pretender's refusal to abjure his faith, was Harley's dilatoriness and bibulous associations with the leading Whigs. Acrimonious quarrels between the two ministers in the royal presence hastened Anne's death, which took place on 1/12 August 1714.

Her death was preceded by four of the most anxious days in English history—the four days following the dismissal of the Lord Treasurer. When, on 9 August, the doctors pronounced the queen's life to be in danger, Bolingbroke was faced with the necessity of taking the plunge. Freed from the incubus of Oxford, he had taken steps for the creation of a Jacobite ministry which would restore the Stuarts; in six weeks, he claimed, he could have completed the necessary preparations. But he was not allowed as many days. The initiative was suddenly snatched from his hands by the intervention of two men who, as they had recently been dismissed from office and never figured prominently in the queen's counsels, appeared singularly unfitted to lead the nation in this crisis. But the dukes of Somerset and Argyle were not only endowed with the power of rank and wealth; both, the one in England, the other in Scotland, had been among the most consistent advocates of the Protestant succession. Still more, as members of the Privy Council, they were constitutionally entitled to offer their advice to the Crown. Acting with them was another great lord, Charles Talbot, duke of Shrewsbury (1660–1718), Lord Lieutenant of Ireland, now (in spite of earlier hesitation) committed to the Hanoverian cause. When these three magnates entered the Council chamber on 9 August they took charge of the situation. Having received the assurance of her physicians that the queen was in grave danger, the Council resolved that a Lord Treasurer be appointed and that Shrewsbury be recommended. Queen Anne's last act of state was to place the white staff in the duke's hands. This act, as events showed, sealed the fate of Bolingbroke and of the Stuart cause. It is said that he had been the first to suggest Shrewsbury's appointment: if so, it can be claimed that the gesture which terminated the first part of his career was that of a sportsman. His dismissal was one of the first acts of George I, as was the reinstatement of Marlborough in his military offices. Later, when it was said that the early months of a German reign had done more to foment the spirit of Jacobitism than four years of Tory government, the ever-resilient Bolingbroke again confused British discontents with support for the Pretender. Yet the prompt counter-measures of the new king's ministers showed that they apprehended a real danger. There was evidence enough of Jacobitism among different ranks of English society, especially in the north and west, to justify the retention of most of the armed forces in England itself, as a precaution, while the Highland clans gathered slowly round the earl of Mar at Perth. Better led and co-ordinated, or less vigorously anticipated by the new government, the rising of 1715 might have attained the dimensions of civil war.

Neither the forces of pseudo-Jacobitism nor the comparative instability of Queen Anne's administrations can be understood outside the context of the often virulent struggles between political parties in her time; nor these, in turn, without the parliamentary framework in which they were chiefly, though by no means exclusively, brought to a focus. The two Houses were custodians of the sanctity, not of human rights, but of free-hold property; as the Lords, the greatest freeholders in the State, re-presented themselves, so the Commons, in a mystic way, were supposed to represent, not the voters who returned them, but all the freeholders of England. By modern standards they were unrepresentative, because so many were returned by a mere handful of electors; but, in a less arith-metical sense, they were representative in so far as so many national 'interests'—the land, the professions, the mercantile classes, the armed services, the civil service—had exponents in the House. Generally, it has been estimated that, of 513 members, over 200 were business or profes-sional men.[1] Of the others, the majority consisted of squires, younger sons of peers, holders of Scottish or Irish peerages, and numerous hangers-on who, whether by marriage with an heiress or by other connections, or by their own assiduity, had commended themselves to a borough or borough-owner.[2] The only large class left out was the lower clergy, which

---

[1] William's last House of Commons contained 58 common-law barristers, 2 admiralty lawyers, 2 Chancery lawyers, 15 'henchmen' (mainly legal representatives of magnates); 43 merchants, 7 bankers, 4 brewers and 7 other members of the 'commercial' interest; 39 army and 9 naval officers; 113 holding offices of profit under the Crown, mostly of minor importance and including some sinecures: R. Walcott, *English Politics in the Early Eighteenth Century* (Oxford, 1956), pp. 161–77. *Ibid.* pp. 91–3 and 156–9, the author argues for use of a fourfold framework in the analysis of party at this time—i.e. in terms of Court and Country as well as Whig and Tory.

[2] On the interplay between local and national affairs see J. H. Plumb, *Sir Robert Walpole*, vol. I (1956), ch. II, which draws attention to the rising cost of elections in this period—a

in this period can be described as consistently Tory, in contrast with the bishops in the Lords who, in many cases appointed by William, were as consistently Whig. The fiction was still maintained that the lower clergy were represented in their Convocations. Had they been represented in the Commons, the history of these years might have been very different.

Because a straightforward distinction of party was not always clearly evidenced in the shifting combinations of parliamentary management it cannot therefore be assumed that this is the end of the matter, for Westminster is not England. Nor were politicians always representative of the best elements in the nation; indeed, as their motives were often selfish, their conduct was sometimes too clever for reduction to consistent principles. But that such principles existed is indubitable. From the time of the Popish Plot and the Exclusion controversy there had emerged a distinction of opinion about matters of public importance, a distinction which, as it constantly reacted to the course of events, can be associated almost as much with temperament as with opinion. The Tories were more tardy in accepting their nickname than the Whigs, because they for long laboured under imputations of Jacobitism, Divine Right, and even willingness to subordinate the national interests to the behests of Versailles. Not unnaturally, and in proportion as the Revolution settlement was consolidated, the Whigs took pride in their name, while the Tories preferred to describe themselves as 'gentlemen distinguished for their quality, principles and estates', the second of these being more difficult of assessment than the other two.[1] Such, in broadest outline, was the fundamental distinction which justifies the postulation of two parties in this age. However inadequate it is to describe the behaviour of everyone in politics, or indeed that of any Englishman on every specific public issue, it penetrated into many spheres of national life. Thus the Protestantism of the Whigs ensured them the support of Dissenters, who were Protestants in that strict sense of the word which could not be applied to Anglicans; on their side, the Tories, in the first three sessions of Anne's parliaments, passed Occasional Conformity Bills which were rejected by the Whig House of Lords, and in 1714 Bolingbroke managed to steer through parliament a Schism Act intended to prevent Dissenters from earning a

reflection no doubt of the growing demand for parliamentary seats—as well as to the effect of frequent elections, following the Triennial Act of 1694, in contributing to the animosities of political life.

[1] Plumb (*ibid.* p. 65) puts the number of independent country gentlemen in the Commons at nearly 200, but of course they were not necessarily all of them Tories. Granted that in the counties, where the political struggle was most acute, party spirit might be grafted on to family antagonisms that had endured for centuries, he allows more significance to traditional party conceptions than does Walcott, who prefers to emphasize the influence of faction (*English Politics in the Early Eighteenth century*, esp. pp. 198–232). The best full-scale treatment is by G. Holmes, *British Politics in the Age of Anne* (1967), which appeared after this chapter was written.

living by teaching.[1] So, too, the Tories objected to the naturalization of foreigners, whether Huguenots or Palatines,[2] not so much on economic grounds as because these foreigners were more likely to associate with Dissenters than with Anglicans. This antipathy between Church and Chapel had more remote consequences. Tory devotion to the Church of England involved not only the exclusion of Dissenters from the universities, but also a refusal to modify those statutes of Oxford and Cambridge colleges which required a large proportion of their Fellows to take Holy Orders—an excessive clericalism that greatly impeded the progress of the two universities. By contrast, its absence in Scotland helps to account for the great prestige of the four northern universities in the eighteenth century.

The old contest between parliamentary sovereignty and Divine Right kingship had a number of consequences: notably, that the Whigs were the first to insist on ministerial responsibility, enforced by impeachment in parliament; while there still remained, even in Anne's reign, the Tory opinion that, as the Crown should be unfettered in its choice of ministers, so the primary allegiance of the minister is to the sovereign. The conduct of war accounted for another crop of differences. The Revolution had committed England to full-scale hostilities against Louis XIV, but dissatisfaction with William's leadership caused many to regard his war as a Whig war. Moreover, the manoeuvres of armies abroad, often apparently purposeless, cost a lot of money, and the Tories objected that this was raised by the legerdemain of public credit, so that the nation maintained a war by 'annually pawning itself', a process bound to lead to bankruptcy. As Swift wrote bitterly, after nine years of the Spanish Succession War,

It will, no doubt, be a mighty Comfort to our Grandchildren, when they see a few Rags hung up in *Westminster-Hall*, which cost an hundred Millions, whereof they are paying the Arrears, and boasting, as Beggars do, that their Grandfathers were Rich and Great.[3]

At this point the fiscal system underlined an ominous antithesis, for the Land Tax fell most heavily on the smaller landlords and lower clergy, almost all of them Tories, and left the townsman and merchant—often, though not always, Whig—almost untouched.[4] Curiously enough, no Tory government thought of amending the Land Tax so that it would fall on personal property as much as land. Instead, Tories insisted that, as far

[1] This stillborn measure was repealed in 1719, as was the Occasional Conformity Act of 1711.
[2] By July 1709 some 10,000 refugees from the Lower Palatinate were encamped at Blackheath and Camberwell, not all of them Protestants; famine and the lure of America also caused the emigration, which greatly embarrassed the English and Dutch authorities.
[3] *The Conduct of the Allies* (1711): text from *The Prose Writings of Jonathan Swift* (ed. H. Davis), vol. VI (1951), pp. 55–6. Cf. below, pp. 442–3.
[4] W. R. Ward, *The Land Tax in the Eighteenth Century* (Oxford, 1953), pp. 7, 39–41. In general, the north and west came off more lightly than the counties nearer London (*ibid.* pp. 7–10).

as possible, England should avoid full-scale hostilities and confine herself to naval operations. For many years after the Revolution, the Tories were for the most part in opposition, and they necessarily adopted much of the technique characteristic of opposition. As they did not profit so much as their rivals from the spoils of office, they naturally demanded a higher standard of public morality and the exclusion of placemen from the Commons. Handicapped by outworn doctrines, they had to borrow more up-to-date ones from the Whigs, such as the idea of annual or at least short parliaments; but posterity has endorsed the wisdom of the Septennial Act (1716), based on the view that frequent elections are dangerous and expensive, and that some measure of continuity is desirable, particularly in foreign policy. On the whole, it can be claimed that the Tories were more insular and—if such a difficult term be allowed—less 'progressive' than the Whigs. It was said that the usual toast drunk by the ultra-Tory October Club[1] was 'Damnation to foreigners!' Among the largely rural Tory rank and file there was considerable distrust even of English-speaking people not domiciled in England, as was seen in their attitude to Scotsmen, most of whom were Presbyterians and therefore detested on religious if on no other grounds. That this objection was surmounted was possibly the greatest achievement of Godolphin and his Whig supporters.

Several proposals for a legislative union with Scotland had been made in the later seventeenth century, but these had not matured, mainly because England was unwilling to admit Scotland into the plantation trade, while Scottish nationalism resented any loss of independence. Meanwhile, with the Revolution settlement in Scotland, the Scottish parliament could be regarded as a sovereign body and at last the country was free, if not from intolerance, at least from persecution. But William was never popular in the north. He was blamed for the massacre of Glencoe and the Darien disaster, when Scottish opinion was inflamed by the fact that the English government instructed its plantation governors to refuse help to the Scottish refugees.[2] Then, with the accession of Anne and the revival of the High Church party in England, many Scots came to believe that a union would be the destruction of their Church. Equally serious was the revival of Jacobitism and the recurrence of many obscure plots, fomented by St Germains and involving the most eminent personages. Indeed, in the opening years of the eighteenth century there seemed a chance that

---

[1] 'So called because of their ardour and because the strongest beer is brewed in the month of October': Robethon to the elector of Hanover, 21 March 1711, quoted Churchill, *Marlborough* (1947 edn.), vol. II, p. 800.

[2] Hist. MSS. Comm. *House of Lords MSS.*, new ser. vol. IV, pp. 68–9. Cf. below, p. 360. The depth of Scottish feeling was again shown by the arrest in 1704 of an English East India vessel in the Forth, followed by the judicial murder of her captain and several of his colleagues on 11 April O.S. 1705: see R. C. Temple, *New Light on the Mysterious Tragedy of the "Worcester"* (1930).

Scotland might develop as a politically independent nation, having her own legislature, her own foreign policy, her own kings. That it might even become a republic, or at least a strictly controlled monarchy, was the solution popularized by one of the ablest publicists of the time, Fletcher of Saltoun, who (with Lord Belhaven) did most to create a strong body opposed to the loss of independence. Scotland's first free parliament sat from 1690 to 1703: the general election in 1703 showed this change, that a number of Jacobites and Episcopalians took the oaths and entered parliament, intent on placing the Pretender on the Scottish throne, while leaving Anne undisturbed. They were sufficient to form a third party, ranged alongside the Court and Country parties. The last-named, mainly Presbyterians, were natural enemies of the Jacobites; but, for a time, these two were united in hatred and distrust of England—the Presbyterians, because the Kirk seemed in danger, the Jacobites, because they believed that a union would consolidate the Revolution settlement in Britain and so exclude them permanently from power. There were similar complications in the leadership of Scottish politics. Since the Revolution, pre-eminence had been contested by two representatives of the House of Douglas: James, 4th duke of Hamilton (1658–1712), premier peer of the kingdom and a possible candidate for its throne; and James, 2nd duke of Queensberry (1662–1711), who in 1706 did more than any other Scottish statesman to effect the Union. Hamilton, an opponent of the Revolution, was a force because of his great prestige and possessions, but he was arrogant and inscrutable; nor had he the tact necessary for holding a party together. In contrast, Queensberry, an upholder of the Revolution, was an expert in management, always able to attain his ends by concession and diplomacy. His personal experience of the uncertainties of Scottish politics may well have convinced him that his interests would be best secured by union. He was ably assisted by the Chancellor, James Ogilvy, 1st earl of Seafield (1664–1730), whose farewell to the old order, 'the end of an auld sang', revealed regret rather than cynicism.

The last parliament in Scottish history met in May 1703 and began by passing an Act 'securing the true Protestant religion and Presbyterian government', a conjunction of expressions that offended Anglicans and Episcopalians. Two Acts followed that implied defiance of England—one admitting French imports, another to the effect that Anne's successor should not drag Scotland into war without the Scottish parliament's consent. Even stronger evidence of the new nationalism was the Act of Security (1704), providing that on Anne's death the Scottish Estates should declare a Protestant successor of the Stuarts other than the person designated by the English parliament, unless securities were meanwhile given for Scottish religion, government and trade. At the same time orders went out to raise the old semi-feudal levy. This created a situation of extreme difficulty for Godolphin. The Jacobite threat had to be met by an army, but to be effective it must be in Scottish pay, and so a supply by the Scottish Estates was essential. For this reason Godolphin induced Anne to assent to the Act of Security, although its terms were tantamount to a declaration of independence. Many contemporaries believed that in so doing he made a serious mistake from which he was afterwards obliged to extricate himself, but it should be recalled that the battle of Blenheim had not yet been won. Meanwhile, the English legislature accepted the challenge and passed a measure declaring that, unless the succession question in Scotland was settled by the end of 1705, all Scotsmen in England would be deemed aliens and Scottish imports forbidden. But this same Act empowered the queen to name commissioners for effecting a Union. After much manoeuvring and the defection of Hamilton from the Jacobites, the northern Estates were induced to pass a Bill for exactly that purpose.

Negotiations began late in 1705, when the two countries appeared to be on the brink of war. The leaders on the English side were Godolphin and Somers. That they succeeded, and so quickly, is striking testimony to the good sense and restraint which, on both sides of the Border, underlay a surface of faction and resentment. The Commissioners, at their meetings in London, began by accepting two essentials: namely, the two countries were to be joined as the United Kingdom of Great Britain, and the Crown was to devolve on the House of Hanover. The Scots Commissioners, knowing the temper of their countrymen, favoured a federal union; but to prevent a breakdown this had to be abandoned, although only on condition that freedom of trade be granted at home and abroad. Acceptance of this condition provided a third basic principle. Finance caused some difficulty. In Scotland the taxes yielded much less, for the obvious reason that there was much less to tax and because it had been possible, in large measure, for the king to live of his own; on the other hand, her national debt was insignificant when compared with England's and so an actuarial adjustment had to be made when Scotland assumed responsibility for a share of the English debt. It was agreed to moderate, for a time, the imposition on Scotland of taxes already exacted in England; and it was arranged to pay Scotland an 'Equivalent' of about £398,000 as compensation for shouldering her share of the other partner's debt, a portion being paid to the creditors of the Darien company and another to recoup individuals for losses incurred by the change of coinage. Scotland retained her native jurisprudence and courts: as that jurisprudence is not easily capable of addition or amendment by statute, it presents the interesting phenomenon of a dying system of law. It was arranged that the Scots should be represented in the new parliament of Great Britain by 61 members—45 in the Commons and 16 elective peers in the Lords. The last of the twenty-five articles of Union contained guarantees for the two established Churches, Anglican and Presbyterian. So vital was this matter considered in the north that in November 1706, when the clauses of the Union were being hotly debated, a second Act of Security was passed, this time for the maintenance in perpetuity of the Church of Scotland as it had been established at the Revolution.

Numerous petitions and widespread riots showed that the impending Union was not at once palatable to the Scottish people. Most ominous was the prospect that enemies hitherto regarded as irreconcilable would unite to prevent it; when the Cameronians (extreme Covenanters) talked of association with the Jacobites, it was clear that the old alignment of parties was gone. Seldom have two governments carried out such an important measure against such bitter opposition. Yet it was ratified by the legislatures of the two countries early in 1707 and the first parliament of Great Britain met in October. Inevitably, the suggestion of bribery is made. It was an age of bribery in both countries; at least since 1703, money from the English treasury had gone to members of the Scottish Estates, nominally on the score of 'expenses'. But to say that the Union was secured by bribery is to single out one parliamentary achievement for condemnation and to leave unscathed all the others, such as the legislative support of William's war, which was made possible only by offices and pensions. Financial irregularity often acquires an immunity in direct proportion to its magnitude: the real difference between English and Scottish politicians was that, owing to their better standard of living, the former had a much higher price. Nevertheless, as early as 1715, Seafield (now earl of Findlater) moved in the Lords for the dissolution of the Union, on the grounds that the nation was deprived of its Privy Council, that the English treason laws had been extended to Scotland, that Scottish peers were incapable of being peers of Great Britain, and that the Scots were subjected to the English malt tax. His motion was lost by only four votes—71 to 67. The grounds adduced for repeal are of interest because of their comparative insignificance. The real sacrifice made by Scotland was the loss of her own legislature. Such a concession suggests how retarded was the political development of a country—emancipated only during the eighteen years preceding the Union—where parliament was overshadowed by other institutions, notably by the General Assembly of the Church of Scotland. By its handling of secular as well as ecclesiastical matters, the General Assembly more truly approximated to a national legislature than did the Estates. That is why the Scots insisted so vehemently on the security of their Kirk; once that was guaranteed, the still medieval Estates, so unlike the English parliament, might easily be surrendered. For long, at Westminster, the 45 Scottish members of the Commons normally voted *en bloc* for government measures; how much they came to be out of touch with their constituencies was to be shown in the War of American Independence, when the great majority of the nation, in contrast with its representatives, supported the American cause. It was the Lord Advocate of Scotland who led the Scottish delegation in the House, and it was thought essential that he should be a tall man, so that his henchmen could see on which side to vote.

The immediate consequence of the Union was that the United Kingdom presented a more solid front to the enemy. There were threats, like the attempted Franco-Jacobite landing in 1708 and the risings of the '15 and the '45; but the two countries became more conscious of their need for each other, and of the fundamental things which they shared. These fundamentals were derived from the essential Protestantism of their laity, and from their common elements of race. The first was associated with enterprise, thrift and probity; in regard to the second, Scotland was to enjoy this additional advantage that, after the mid-century pacification of the over-populated Highlands, there was to be a steady infiltration of Celtic blood into the Lowlands, so that today there can be few Scottish townsmen who do not boast at least one Highlander in their ancestry. Rightly or wrongly, this Highland strain is reputed to contribute an imaginative or at least an emotional element to the more stolid qualities of the Lowlander. Such integration contrasts with the hostility which Stuart kings had sought to excite between these two main divisions of the Scottish people, and also with the bitter segregation which for so long has divided Ireland. Scotland's good fortune in this respect was soon to be manifest. Within less than a century Scots were to be found in responsible positions throughout the empire—men not always of approved pedigree but usually endowed with education and intelligence. The Scottish universities, among the foremost in Europe, attracted many Dissenters from England and America; they provided a good, cheap education for men of practical and speculative intellect alike. It is significant that only in music was the North deficient. There were, it is true, many beautiful folk songs, whether in Scots or Gaelic; but the exclusion of music from the churches had denied Scotsmen much of the tradition and training which elsewhere encouraged concerted musical effort.

The progression of the seasons in Scottish civilization does not appear to have followed a normal course. A springtime of literature in the fifteenth century, when the Chaucerian tradition was perpetuated, succumbed to the icy blasts of the Reformation and the seventeenth century; with the eighteenth, there came an autumnal flowering, always so beautiful in the north. England has enjoyed more continuity. Her Augustan Age is numbered with her greatest achievements. Of newspapers, pamphlets, journals and lampoons there was no end; the Popish Plot had created a demand for rogue stories and ghost stories; the wars of William and Anne brought gazetteers, atlases and accounts of foreign countries, eloquent of a new and wider reading public, anxious for diversion or information. The cessation of censorship in 1695 partly explains this development. Though criticism of government still constituted seditious libel, there emerged a frank and usually intelligent discussion of domestic and foreign affairs—clear evidence that, after her comparative insularity, England was emerging as a world power. A new type was coming into existence—the literate (as distinct from the learned) Englishman, well informed about public events and able to debate them without coming to blows. It is true that the official *London Gazette* was limited to scraps of home and foreign news, but some newpapers were introducing a novelty, the leading article, which by analysis of a critical situation purports to guide as well as inform. Nor was this all. By 1698 the 'paperback' was appearing, price sixpence; a more ambitious shilling series offered short national histories. Such manuals must have proved serious rivals to the almanacs and funeral sermons. In these ways the nation, though still unenfranchised, was becoming more mature, and a relatively well-educated public opinion came to characterize the English-speaking world.

In 1710, the turning-point of Anne's reign, the new journalism came into special prominence. A number of events combined to create a revulsion of public opinion, clearly reflected in the general election of that autumn. The costly victory of Malplaquet (September 1709), where Allied losses greatly outnumbered the French, was followed in 1710 by decisive defeats in Spain. Meanwhile, a favourable peace offer from Louis XIV had come to nothing when the Allies insisted that he should himself expel his grandson from Spain. Louis won esteem abroad as well as at home by rejecting this unreasonable demand. It could therefore be charged against Godolphin and Marlborough that they had failed to accept a good opportunity for making peace. But these events,[1] even when reinforced by the 'Church in danger' cry, do not in themselves explain the violent explosion of party feeling in 1710. On such occasions there is usually needed a prominent personality who, as it were, crystallizes the amorphous elements around him into definite shape. Such a person was the duke of Marlborough. His reputation for meanness is one of the most insistent things in historical literature; his critics could not have known of his many acts of private generosity. More serious, there seemed reason to think that the days of his great victories had ended with Malplaquet, and that the war in Flanders would return to the wearisome siege-warfare of William's time. The year 1710 was the critical point in the duke's career. Unwisely, he had applied in 1709 for his appointment as captain-general to be secured to him for life, and was refused. This was seized on with alacrity by one of the most disordered geniuses of English literature, the Anglo-Irish clergyman Swift, temperamentally the complete antithesis of the great general. Taking over main responsibility for *The Examiner* in November 1710, he mercilessly pilloried his victim, concentrating on the many public tokens

---

[1] See below, pp. 436 ff. and 448 ff.

of gratitude which Marlborough had received from the nation,[1] and contrasting them with the meagre rewards accorded to conquerors in the past. This was a telling point because it was true. There was less truth in the insinuations that the general was continuing the war for his own enrichment and aiming at a dictatorship of Cromwellian dimensions. The establishment of the Oxford-Bolingbroke ministry did not stem the spate of political literature. Marlborough had been fairly easy game: it was a greater test to indict the general conduct of the war and even the policy which had initiated it. This was done by Swift in *The Conduct of the Allies*, one of the most brilliant party pamphlets ever penned. He attacked on three main fronts. First, England should have fought only as an auxiliary, since not directly menaced by Louis XIV save in his recognition of the Pretender, which might have been no more than a formality; English interests would have been better served by naval war in the West Indies against French and Spanish possessions. Second, the war was piling up a colossal national debt that would one day overwhelm us and was already ruining the country gentry, to the advantage of contractors and stock-jobbers. Third, England was the catspaw of her allies. The emperor had cheated us of Toulon and diverted troops to crush a revolt in Hungary; the Dutch, whittling down their own obligations, expected Britain to bear the brunt of the expense and the human sacrifice. Superb journalist that he was, Swift directed his appeal to a war-weary nation, suspicious of foreigners and convinced that the Dutch invariably got the better of a bargain.

By contrast, a precocious liberalism saturates the polemic of Daniel Defoe. As a Dissenter, denied full citizenship, he stood as it were on the margin of events and could survey them more impartially than could the participants. In a host of pamphlets and journals he castigated social evils often imperceptible in his day because so generally condoned: sending unseaworthy ships to sea for the sake of the insurance money; 'wrecking' on the south coast; imprisoning debtors; imposing savage sentences on wretches who had pilfered from sheer necessity. A profound and fertile concern for the public welfare, a hatred of the 'heats' of faction, inspires the commentary in his *Review*,[2] begun early in 1704 when he was in prison —imprisoned because of *The Shortest-way with the Dissenters* (1702), wherein, with desperate irony, he had proposed that the problem of the Nonconformists be settled by hanging the lot. In *The True-born Englishman* (1701) he had ridiculed the excesses of nationalism and pleaded for a

[1] Notably a grant of £240,000 towards the building of Blenheim Palace. See D. Green, *Blenheim* (1951) and L. Whistler, *The Imagination of Vanbrugh and his Fellow Artists* (1954), pp. 83–123.
[2] See W. L. Payne (ed.), *The Best of Defoe's Review: an Anthology* (1951). The range and novelty of his interests are best presented by J. R. Moore in *Daniel Defoe, Citizen of the Modern World* (Chicago, 1958) and *A Checklist of the Writings of Daniel Defoe* (Bloomington, 1960).

more intelligent attitude to foreigners, including Scotsmen. Indeed, before and after 1707, he did much to create a more friendly feeling on both sides of the Border: of all the men of letters of his time, he had far the most intimate knowledge of conditions in the northern kingdom and the fullest realization of the imperative necessity of bringing it into partnership with its neighbour. In striking contrast with Swift, who scorned commerce, Defoe believed in the future of Britain. He thought that its soil and climate were unduly disparaged, and that it possessed workmen, well paid and fed, who 'are not used to work slight and superficially', with a genius for improving the inventions of other races even if their temper was 'gay, ostentatious, vicious, and full of Excesses'.[1]

But the man of genius is often less representative of his age than men of lesser mould. Of this new England—prosperous, secure and complacent—Joseph Addison was the best interpreter. Here is his eulogy of the Royal Exchange in 1711:

There is no Place in the Town which I so much love to frequent as the *Royal-Exchange*. It gives me a secret satisfaction, and, in some measure, gratifies my Vanity, as I am an *Englishman*, to see so rich an Assembly of Country men and Foreigners consulting together upon the private Business of Mankind, and making this Metropolis a kind of *Emporium* for the whole Earth...I am wonderfully delighted to see such a Body of Men thriving in their own private fortunes, and at the same time promoting the Public Stock...by bringing into their Country whatever is wanting and carrying out of it whatever is superfluous...Almost every *Degree* produces something peculiar to it. The Food often grows in one Country, and the Sauce in another. The Fruits of *Portugal* are corrected by the Products of *Barbadoes*: the Infusion of a *China* plant sweetened with the Pith of an *Indian* cane...The single Dress of a Woman of Quality is often the Product of an hundred Climates. The Muff and the Fan come together from the different Ends of the Earth...[2]

Forty-five years earlier Dryden had handled a similar theme, but then it was the Dutch, not the English, who held the world in fee:

> For them alone the Heavens had kindly Heat,
> In Eastern Quarries ripening precious Dew;
> For them the *Idumaean* Balm did sweat,
> And in hot *Ceylon* spicy Forests grew.

> The Sun but seemed the Labourer of their Year;
> Each waxing Moon supplied her watery Store
> To swell those Tides, which from the Line did bear
> Their brim-full Vessels to the *Belgian* Shore.

The contrast between the slick rhetoric of Addison and the poetry of Dryden is a sharp reminder of what England lacked in her Augustan Age.

[1] *A Plan of the English Commerce* (1728; reprinted Oxford, 1928), pp. 32, 144, 224.
[2] *The Spectator*, no. 69 (19 May 1711).

But, in these forty-five years, the fortunes of the island kingdom had been transformed. The year 1666, the 'Annus Mirabilis', was a year when England, already visited by plague and tested by fire, was bitterly engaged with her most formidable rival on the seas. The year 1711 brought with it the certainty of a victorious peace with her new enemy on the Continent, as well as of an enlarged and unified Britain, about to take preeminent place among the nations of the world.

CHAPTER IX

WAR FINANCE, 1689–1714

'W HENEVER this war ceases,' wrote the English pamphleteer Charles Davenant in 1695, 'it will not be for want of mutual hatred in the opposite parties, nor for want of men to fight the quarrel, but that side must first give out where money is first failing.'[1] This was an opinion from which few statesmen, generals, administrators or contractors on either side during the wars of 1689–1714 would have dissented. At this time financial capacity, not economic capacity, was, in the last resort, the limiting factor which decided the length, and modified the intensity, of war. Because a bankrupt government, unable to coax or force its citizens' wealth into its exchequer, or to make financial innovations with speed and skill, would be compelled to make peace, the rival powers tended to count each others' losses from bad coin, internal revolt, unfilled loans, unfavourable exchanges, the flight or bankruptcy of important financial agents, and so on, rather than losses in lives or war materials. As Richard Hill, the English envoy at Turin, wrote to Lord Treasurer Godolphin in 1705:

The French King's treasury begins to fail him. He is already bankrupt for 25 millions...Do you continue, my Lord, to beat Mons. Chamillard [the Controller General] a year or two more, as you have done, and leave the rest to the Duke of Marlborough.[2]

Yet the financial side of war, so pressing to contemporaries, has been relatively neglected by historians. There are great difficulties in reconstructing it, partly because of the complexity and obscurity of surviving records, partly because their volume and utility vary considerably from one country to another. Only for England are the financial statistics reasonably certain. For other States the edges of the picture are blurred. Moreover, most of the questions which an economist would ask about the 'real' aspects of war finance must, in the absence of reliable data, remain at best imperfectly answered: the extent to which war was paid for by foreign borrowing or by cutting down investment or consumption, or by all three; the effect of deficit borrowing on economic growth; the changes in the pattern of demand caused by government contracting, and so on. It is also necessary for practical reasons to limit the scope of the present survey to the four major powers engaged on either side in Louis XIV's later wars. Nevertheless, the attempt to describe and compare in main outline the financial systems of England, France, the United

[1] 'Ways and Means', *Works* (ed. Whitworth, 5 vols. 1771), vol. I, p. 15.
[2] *The Diplomatic Correspondence of the Rt. Hon. Richard Hill*, vol. II (1845), p. 490.

Provinces and Austria, under the stress of war, is worth making for the light it throws on the decisive influence of public finance on the history of this period.[1]

The English government's financial system on the morrow of 1688 must have seemed to many unlikely to be able to provide for a long and costly war.[2] Ordinary revenue was only about one-fifth that of France, and there was no machinery of long-term borrowing to cover deficits, as there was in France and the Dutch Republic. Further, the traditional hostility between Crown and Parliament in financial matters had often imperilled or prevented the raising of supplies, and might do so again. But there were favourable features too. The abolition of the Crown's feudal dues, recognized by statute in 1660, had removed the grievances caused by royal rights of wardship, marriage, purveyance, etc., and placed the revenue on the relatively certain basis of excise and customs dues, supplemented by direct taxes agreed to in parliament. One effect of this had been to double the revenue between 1660 and 1688. The Church had given up her right to tax herself shortly after the Restoration. Between 1660 and 1685 the Treasury had gained an effective control over the entire collection of revenue, abolished tax-farming, and centralized receipts at the Exchequer. By the end of Anne's reign it was exercising a similar control over expenditure, and the holder of the treasurership became the most important man in the government. This trend, which continued after the office went permanently into commission in 1714, was partly concealed from 1688 to 1702 because the Treasury was then in commission and William III himself took a close interest in finance; but it became fully apparent during the treasurership (1702–10) of Godolphin, who showed an aptitude for public finance and an appreciation of the importance of public credit upon which his successors were to look back admiringly for a century.

Native abilities, exemplified by Godolphin, were put to severe test, for during the long wars England's public expenditure, like that of her allies and enemies, mounted to unprecedented levels. Before the Revolution it had been under £2 m. per annum; between 1689 and 1702 it totalled £72 m., and between 1702 and 1714 no less than £99 m. About 40 per cent of this was spent on the army and 35 per cent on the navy. Subsidies to other powers, though useful in tying the coalitions together, were considerably less than in later conflicts: the figures for the 1690s are uncertain, but between 1701 and 1711 England and Holland undertook to pay roughly £8 m. to eight members of the coalition.[3] Although this burden

---

[1] For brief considerations of Spanish and Russian finance, see below, chs. XI and XXI, and of Savoy-Piedmont, pp. 560–1.

[2] Much of this section is based on P. G. M. Dickson, *The Financial Revolution in England. A study in the development of public credit 1688–1756* (1967).

[3] *House of Commons Journals*, vol. XVII, p. 48.

should have been equally borne, England in the event paid about two-thirds of the whole, as the Tory government complained in 1711. As we know from Swift's pamphlets, the dislike felt at home about these payments to foreigners was reinforced by the fact that a much more considerable part of English war revenue was spent abroad.

The extra money for the war came partly from increasing tax revenue which doubled between 1688 and 1697 and went up by a further 75 per cent between 1702 and 1714. The main direct tax was the Land Tax, first imposed in 1692, though recognizably derived from previous taxes, including the Monthly Assessment of the Commonwealth period. Originally levied on all income from money, goods and offices, as well as land, it soon came (like similar taxes in other countries) to be charged on the latter only, at a standard wartime rate of four shillings in the pound. The assessment valuation, and therefore the income, soon became stereotyped; but despite the grumbles of the landed classes the tax compared very favourably with its French equivalent, the *taille*, both in basic equity and in yield, computed in this period as just over £2 m. a year. It was supplemented by miscellaneous stamp, house and window duties. The principal indirect taxes were those of customs and excise, which formed approximately half the tax income of the State by the end of the war. The structure of both became extremely complicated, largely because parliament settled new duties nearly every year to pay interest on long-term loans, and soon abandoned its earlier attempts to restrict excise duties to 'luxuries' like wine, beer and spirits.[1] Few articles of common consumption were left untaxed by 1714 and the complexity of the resulting excise and customs tariff was such that, like modern income tax, only experts could understand it in more than bare outline.

The substantial increase of a normally inelastic revenue was a considerable achievement, but it went only part of the way towards meeting government needs. The gap had to be filled by borrowing. Here England was at a disadvantage, for her credit machinery in 1689 was limited to loans made each year in anticipation of taxes and paid off when they came in. Heavy capital commitments had traditionally been met by selling royal lands and rents. However, this procedure had been so often resorted to that the yield on the royal estates was nugatory by 1702, when further sales were forbidden by statute. Parliament was obliged soon after the Revolution to consider a different and more important expedient. Early in 1692 a committee of the House of Commons, presided over by Charles Montagu, the able Chancellor of the Exchequer, invited proposals for raising £1 m. 'upon a perpetual Fund of Interest', and these, though at

---

[1] Malt was added in 1697; candles in 1710; hops, hides and water-borne coal in 1711; soap, paper, starch, printed calicoes, hackney chairs, cards and dice in 1712. On the effect of the quadrupling of the general level of import duties between 1690 and 1704 see R. Davis, 'The Rise of Protection in England, 1689–1786', *Econ. Hist. Rev.* 2nd ser. vol. XIX (1966), pp. 306–17.

first abortive, resulted eventually in a plan for a tontine loan for £1 m. at 10 per cent which was approved by the House in January 1693.[1] Excise duties were settled for 99 years to pay interest *pro rata* and tax-free among the subscribers, during their own lives or those of nominees, until the number of nominees was reduced to seven.[2] If £1 m. was not lent on this basis, the balance was to be raised by the sale of ordinary life annuities carrying 14 per cent interest. Wary investors, mostly in London, thought the tontine too complicated and uncertain, and in the end it realized only £108,000, as against £892,000 in life annuities. Its importance, however, lay not in its form—seldom copied later—but in the fact that it was the first stone in a massive edifice of long-term borrowing, which was to enable Great Britain to finance war and conquest on a scale that 'surprised and astonished Europe'.[3]

The Tontine of 1693 was followed by other long-term loans in 1694, 1697, and 1704–14. The total borrowed during the 1690s was about £7 m., not more than a tenth of expenditure. During the Succession War borrowings rose to nearly £35 m., about a third of total expenditure. The difference between the two proportions was largely due to parliament's initial unwillingness to pledge sections of the revenue in virtual perpetuity to pay interest. This proved short-sighted, for it led to excessive reliance on short-dated borrowing, so helping to create a high discount on short-term paper, about £7 m. of which had to be extended between 1697 and 1702 to later dates of payment.

As befitted a period of experiment and uncertainty, types of government long-term bonds varied considerably. Lottery loans, previously used by private persons in England, and by government in the Netherlands and France, were floated in 1694, 1697, 1711 and 1712.[4] The lottery of 1697 was largely unsubscribed, owing to a severe depression of credit, but the others proved very popular, as indeed public lotteries were until their suppression in 1826. Their use at the end of both wars suggests that the Treasury considered them most suitable in difficult times, when investors' jaded palates needed tickling with the lure of speculative gains. Earlier, the greater part of the money was raised by selling annuities for terms of years, again a type of borrowing long familiar in the Netherlands and France. Between 1695 and 1702 the life annuities of 1693 and 1694 were largely converted into long annuities, in return for further payments by the annuitants; between 1704 and 1708, £8 m. was raised by long annui-

---

[1] Tontines—a form of annuity which increases to survivors as subscribers die off—were so called from their inventor Lorenzo Tonti, one of Mazarin's advisers. They had been used in Holland in the 1670s and 1680s by town governments and by syndicates of private persons. The interest on the loan of 1693 was 10 per cent until 1700, then 7 per cent.

[2] Income from British government stock was free of tax until 1799, despite numerous proposals for taxing it.

[3] Isaac de Pinto, *Traité de la circulation et du crédit* (Amsterdam, 1771), p. 42.

[4] There were two lottery loans in 1711 and two in 1712. A small lottery loan for the queen's Civil List was floated in 1713.

ties; and another annuity loan was floated in 1710. Apart from the latter (which was for 32 years), these annuities were for between 89 and 96 years and therefore tied up substantial parts of the revenue until the 1790s. It is true that the average rate of interest offered on these loans fell from over 8 per cent in the 1690s to about 6½ per cent during the Succession War, and that this reflected a genuine increase in investors' confidence in the State's good faith, 'large sums' (as Walpole observed in 1712) being 'constantly advanc'd, and almost forc'd upon the Government at Five or Six per Cent'.[1] Nonetheless, the fact that about one-third of the £40 m. National Debt by 1714 was in the form of annuities, which could not be paid off or reduced to a lower rate of interest without their owners' consent, was to prove a grave embarrassment to the government for some years after the war.

Long-term loans raised by subscription from the general public, and managed by the Exchequer, were supplemented in 1694, 1698, 1709, and 1711 by loans from chartered companies. In 1694, £1·2 m. was borrowed at 8 per cent from a group of subscribers who were incorporated as 'the Governor and Company of the Bank of England'. In 1698 the New East India Company was chartered, against the bitter hostility of the Old East India Company, on condition that it lent the State £2 m., also at 8 per cent. In 1709 the two were run together as the United East India Company, paying a further £1·2 m. into the Exchequer. In 1711 Godolphin's successor, Harley, arranged for the owners of £9 m. of short-term debts, which the government could not immediately pay off, to be incorporated as 'The Governor and Company of Merchants of Great Britain trading to the South Seas'. The holder of securities received an equivalent sum in South Sea Company stock, and the money market was thus freed at a stroke from a large floating debt, even though the former discount on short-term securities was transferred to the new stock, which only reached par in 1715.

The evidence about subscribers to this and the other government loans of the period suggests that there was an important top-dressing of nobles and politicians and a long tail of small lenders, but that the bulk was subscribed by the London bourgeoisie, including an influential minority of Jews, Nonconformists and Huguenots. Only small sums appear to have been placed from abroad in long-term loans; the most important sum which the government negotiated abroad was a loan of £150,000 from the canton of Berne in April 1710.[2] There may, however, have been a considerable flow of foreign funds into short-dated loans.

The innovations in public finance, including the chartering of the Bank and the other companies, must be seen against the background of major

---

[1] [R. Walpole], *The Debts of the Nation Stated...in Four Papers* (1712), p. 7.
[2] The English government also borrowed on short term in Holland to pay troops in 1695 (£220,000) and 1697 (£280,000).

technical advances within the City of London itself. Marine under-writing was developing at Edward Lloyd's coffee house, and (after earlier projects had failed) marine insurance companies were inaugurated in 1720—the Royal Exchange Assurance and the London Assurance. Life assurance was starting on a small scale, principally at the Amicable Office founded in 1706. Fire insurance was growing steadily: Barbon's Office of 1681 was followed by the Friendly in 1683, the Hand-in-Hand in 1696 and by the Sun Fire Office in 1710, which swiftly outdistanced its rivals and acquired first place in the national market.[1] Partnership bank-ing, which had begun to flourish after the Restoration, was expanding. At the same time a market was growing up in the securities of the govern-ment and the chartered companies, centred on Garraway's and Jonathan's Coffee Houses in Exchange Alley, opposite the Royal Exchange. The period thus saw the first stages of a financial revolution, during which the institutions were established which would dominate the City for two centuries.

Among these the Bank of England takes first place. Its rise was bitterly deplored by its enemies. An abortive scheme for a Land Bank in 1696, and to some extent the creation of the South Sea Company in 1711, were regarded by Tories as counterstrokes to its predominance; and the view that it was gradually making the Treasury merely the West End branch of its own headquarters in Threadneedle Street found many adherents down to the present century. Early critics regarded it as a credit monopolist and, agreeing with Harrington that 'where there is a Bank ten to one there is a Commonwealth',[2] hinted that it derived from Whig leanings towards a republic. However, in view of its services to the stability of public finance and the improvement of public borrowing from the year of its foundation, it is hard to resist the conclusion that no institution contributed more to the stability of the Revolution settlement or underwrote more effectively the liberties that Englishmen enjoyed during the eighteenth century. The Jacobites who planned in 1715 to take and burn it showed a nice appreciation of its importance.

During the thirty years after 1713, the Bank gradually took over the administration of long-term borrowing from the Exchequer, substituting its own cheap and efficient methods for the latter's antique routine. Before 1714, however, its chief assistance to the State was in short-term finance. Here, as in long-term borrowing, there were important innova-tions after 1688, but serious mistakes were also made which led in 1696–7 to a crisis of such severity that the entire conduct of the war was imperilled. Anticipation of revenue at this date was largely effected by taking in loans at the Exchequer secured on a particular tax. The lender

---

[1] P. G. M. Dickson, *The Sun Insurance Office 1710–1960* (1960).
[2] *Works* (ed. J. Toland, 1737), p. 247.

was given half a wooden tally[1] and a paper Order of Repayment, which was assignable and bore interest until the tax came in and it could be redeemed. This system was relatively foolproof provided all the loans could be punctually discharged from the taxes, which were normally imposed only for a short term of years. Unfortunately, prospective yields were frequently miscalculated, and several groups of taxes therefore became due to expire before the loans secured on them could be repaid.[2]

Furthermore, tallies were frequently issued to departmental paymasters inscribed as though the latter had lent money in anticipation of a given tax. They had in fact lent nothing, but they could use these 'tallies of fictitious loan' either by discounting them for cash or by paying them directly to government creditors. Theoretically, on receipt of the tax tally-holders would get their money; in practice, the Treasury appears to have exercised very ineffective control over the amount of such tallies discounted by the departments and over the rates at which they were discounted. The situation was aggravated by bad harvests and increasing deterioration of the coinage, which finally impelled the government in 1696 to carry through a complete exchange of the old worn, light and clipped coins for new specie—a step which, though it roused admiration on the Continent as an expression of England's resolve to honour her commitments, was drastically deflationary during a short but critical period. Thanks to the combination of economic discontent, deficient tax funds, over-issue of tallies, and the adverse state of specie, the foreign exchanges moved against England, credit rapidly waned, contractors refused to meet their obligations until they were paid, and there seemed grave danger that the entire war machine would grind to a halt. A contemporary noted that the year 1696 was 'very likely to have proved many ways fatal to England'.[3] By the spring of 1697 fifteen tax funds were deficient, and tallies of loan amounting to over £5 m. secured on them were at such high discounts that they yielded up to 10 per cent.

Decisive remedies were made possible by the co-operation of the Bank, which had already taken over the exchange contracts for the forces in Flanders, and agreed in April 1697 to open a subscription for an unlimited amount of new stock, payable as to four-fifths in tallies and one-fifth in Bank notes. The subscription realized just over £1 m., including £800,000 in depreciated tallies. At the same time, Parliament settled eight sets of customs and excise duties until 1706 to pay the principal and interest of

---

[1] The tally, a relic of medieval methods of accounting, remained in use at the Exchequer until the 1830s. It was a notched wooden stick which, on receipt of money at the Exchequer, was divided between the payer (who retained the stock or greater portion) and the Exchequer, which kept the foil or minor portion. Two main kinds of tally were used in loan business at this period; the commoner of these was the tally of 'sol' referred to in the text.

[2] According to Davenant, 'The Projectors of most new Funds have hitherto been generally mistaken two parts in three': *Discourses on the Publick Revenues* (1698), p. 27.

[3] *Some Remarks on the Bill for Taking...the Public Accounts of the Kingdom* (1702), p. 7.

all the outstanding tallies, including those now held by the Bank. These measures, soon followed by the Peace of Ryswick, revived short-term credit, and 6 per cent tallies were again at par by 1700. A director of the Bank later claimed with some justice that without its assistance this crisis could not have been weathered at all.[1] During the next war, thanks to Godolphin's skill and prudence, the tally system was much more carefully managed and the discount bargains of paymasters strictly supervised. A further factor making for stability was the large annual advances regularly made by the Bank, either by discounting tallies for paymasters or on security of deposits of tallies. By then, moreover, the Treasury was making increasing use of a new instrument for short-term borrowing which by 1763 was to supersede the tally—the Exchequer Bill.

Exchequer Bills originated in the crisis of 1696–7, when an issue was authorized of £1·5 m. in bills bearing 4·6 per cent interest, encashable at the Exchequer on demand.[2] This early experiment, partly derived from discussions in Charles II's reign, was not well timed or planned. Only £158,000 of the bills authorized went into circulation; most were cancelled by 1697. A year later a further £2·7 m. were issued. Their interest was raised to 7·6 per cent; they could be used to pay taxes; and arrangements were made with a group of merchants to provide funds for their encashment.[3] The circulation was successful and the Treasury, remembering the fate of tallies in 1694–7, was careful to retire the bills, which were nearly all redeemed by 1710. After 1697 there was no further creation of Exchequer Bills until 1707. Between 1707 and 1713 no less than £5·6 m. were issued, bearing interest at just over 3 per cent and charged on specific groups of taxes. Because some of these tax funds were already encumbered, additional bills were made out to pay interest until the funds were clear. At the same time the Bank undertook the task of 'circulating' the bills by cashing them under agreed conditions, and in 1709 funded £1·7 m. of them which the Exchequer found itself unable to discharge. The Bank financed its services by a call of 50 per cent on its stock in 1707, by doubling its capital in 1709,[4] by calls of 15 per cent and 10 per cent in 1709–10, and then by special annual 'subscription for the circulation'. By 1710 these operations had increased its nominal capital (roughly equivalent to the sum which the State owed it) to £5·5 m., at which it remained until 1722.

---

[1] [Nathaniel Tench], *A Defence of the Bank of England* (1707), pp. 8–9.

[2] The issue was authorized by a statute for the establishment of a Land Bank. It was provided that if the subscription for the latter failed to realize £2,564,000 (which its promoters had undertaken to lend at once to the government), the deficiency might be raised by short-dated loans, of which £1.5 m. might be in Exchequer Bills. The Land Bank subscription was a complete failure.

[3] There were at first twelve 'trustees for the circulation' but by 1702 their number had fallen to three, who continued to act until 1710. They evidently only cashed bills for payees at the Exchequer who had refused to accept them. Their funds came from an annual subscription, the subscribers being given an equivalent sum in Exchequer Bills.

[4] The subscription was for £2.2 m. and the books were filled 22–25 Feb. 1709.

Owing to the Bank's help, the Exchequer Bill by the end of Anne's reign had become an efficient instrument of short-term credit, readily accepted by the investing public—a far cry from the doubtful days of its infancy. It is true that no systematic provision had been made to discharge the bills of 1707–13, £4·5 m. of which were still outstanding in 1713; but the way was already open for the gradual supersession of tallies by Exchequer Bills in the anticipation of annual revenue.

The bills issued by the spending departments, principally the Navy and Victualling Boards, were an important factor in short-term finance, and the regulation of their volume was a constant problem for the Treasury. During the Nine Years War both army and navy were partly run on credit. Vouchers ('debentures') were given out for arrears of army pay and clothing, and were only partly satisfied by exchanging them for forfeited Irish lands in 1697–1702; the residue (£987,000) was exchanged for South Sea stock in 1711. Attempts were also made in the 1690s to pay regiments in depreciated tallies—a desperate expedient which invited mutiny. Godolphin was careful to prevent the recurrence of these risks in the following war, when the army was punctually paid in cash, and in 1713 army debts were negligible. The Navy Board's contractors were less fortunate. They were paid by 6 per cent bills registered and paid 'in course', in order of priority—a practice businesslike enough in normal times but one which deteriorated during the Succession War, partly owing to parliament's failure to grant sufficient naval supply, and partly because the time within which new bills would be paid—the 'Course of the Navy'—steadily lengthened.[1] By 1711 the combined volume of Navy and Victualling bills was £4 m., and the bills at the end of the course, which had about three years to run, were at over 30 per cent discount. Their holders, many of whom were London merchants and bankers who had discounted them for contractors, put pressure on the Treasury for satisfaction, and it was largely in response to this that Harley laid his South Sea Scheme before parliament, the Act receiving the royal assent in June 1711. The existing Navy and Victualling debts, as well as a variety of other short-term paper, some of it dating from the 1690s, totalling in all about £9 m., were exchanged for 6 per cent stock in the new company—an operation recognizably similar to the Bank's 'ingraftment' of tallies which had saved the day in 1697.

The task of remitting money for the payment of 'the forces abroad' always presented considerable difficulties. In 1709, for instance, £3 m. had to be remitted to the various theatres of war, a sum probably not much less

---

[1] A number of factors combined to raise the Navy debt between 1702 and 1710. They may be summarized as parliament's failure to vote the full estimates or provide for the interest on bills; under-issue by the Treasury of sums voted for naval supply; overspending (on credit) by the Navy and Victualling Boards; and a general rise in the price of naval provisions. The number of ships in pay varied slightly from year to year, with some tendency to decrease as the war went on. Cf. below, ch. xxii (3).

than the favourable balance of the country's payments; there was clearly need for great care lest the exchange should swing against England, with disastrous consequences. On this, as on other sectors of the financial front, the period was one of learning from costly mistakes. In 1689 there was no machinery for military remittances in London and little under-standing of the problems involved in them, particularly of the difficulty of harmonizing the seasonal needs of the campaign with the seasonal fluctuations in trade, which upset most *ad hoc* exchange contracts.

Unable to rely on English experience, William III turned at first to Dutch paymasters; but by 1691 this arrangement, which allowed little Treasury control, had proved so unsatisfactory that he fell back on syndicates of London merchants, sometimes working in competition with each other. By 1695 this system had succumbed in its turn, owing to the deterioration of the government's credit, and the Treasury, faced with a crisis which imperilled the very maintenance of the army in the field, turned for help to the newly founded Bank of England. Negotiations began in September 1694, and early in 1695 Godolphin, then a Treasury Commissioner, was in touch with the Court of Directors about 'some of their number going into Holland to establish a credit there for supplying the army in Flanders and raising the Exchange (now so low) and agreeing at a certain rate for the time to come'.[1] The Bank set up an office at Antwerp (1695–7) and undertook first a year's contract at a fixed rate, then from 1696 to 1697 shared the remittances with private merchants. The Bank's help was very costly to it—it estimated a loss on the whole transaction of nearly £130,000—but was invaluable to government. The completion of the recoinage, revival of short-term credit, and above all the decline in remittances with the approach of peace, restored a favour-able exchange by the end of 1697, leaving Godolphin and his two prin-cipal allies in the Bank, Sir Henry Furnese and Sir Theodore Janssen, to ponder what they had learnt.

Early in the next war (1702–4) the Treasury again used competing syn-dicates, many of whose members, like Janssen himself, were Huguenots belonging to a complex of family firms which managed the remittances of Holland and France as well. Increasing suspicion of the activities of this informal consortium, as of the negotiation of French commercial paper by Amsterdam and London merchants, both of which were said to sustain French credit and prolong the war, played an important part in the English government's decision in 1703 to bully the Dutch into an agreement for a complete embargo on trade and correspondence with France. The advice of the principal French remittance agent, Jean Huguetan, who fled to England in 1705, confirmed Godolphin's suspicion of the London syn-dicates and his determination to concentrate all remittance business in the capable hands of Janssen (handling Italy and the Empire) and Furnese

---

[1] British Museum, Portland Loan 29/45, 8 May O.S. 1695.

(handling the Low Countries, Portugal and Spain). Their exchange system remained intact and efficient until the end of the war, despite Godolphin's dismissal in 1710.

Throughout the seventeenth century the United Provinces, 'so respected in Europe and so formidable in Asia', as Montesquieu was to write of them in 1721,[1] had led the rest of Europe in commercial and financial technique. It was to Amsterdam, with its Bank and its Bourse, to Dutch commercial law and registration of land, to the structure and attitudes of Dutch society, that foreign pamphleteers looked for the true model of a mercantile state. The contemporary observer might therefore have expected that the richest, most urbanized and most cosmopolitan nation in Europe, accustomed from daily use to the latest business methods, would have constructed a simple and effective system of taxation, with duties clearly apportioned, easily raised and accounted for, fully adequate to the needs of the State in war and peace. This was not so. The finances of the Republic, though greatly superior in their administration to those of any other country except England, were characterized by uncertainty, delay and insufficiency. Nor were they free from waste and fraud. The explanation lies chiefly in the strong provincial feeling which dominated Dutch life and politics. The most logical basis for a financial system—a central treasury administering 'federal' taxes—was one which the provinces were determined at all costs to avoid.[2] Instead, they clung obstinately to their own financial machinery, voted the budget for the central government with marked reluctance, and tried, particularly in peace-time, to foist the burdens of the Republic off on each other in a way which—as the States-General complained bitterly in 1721—imperilled its very existence.[3]

Owing to the decentralization resulting from provincial jealousies, the financial machinery of the central government was relatively simple. The Public Treasury (*Comptoir Generaal*) at The Hague, with its Chamber of Accounts (*Rekenkamer*), was largely a book-keeping office which kept track on paper of the sums voted by the States-General and received and paid by the provincial treasuries. The actual revenue entering the coffers of 'the Generality' (from the *Landen van de Generaliteit*)[4] was only of the order of 0·75 m. guilders at the end of the wars, and was disbursed to cover the interest on federal loans and the administrative expenses of the central government, including those of the *Comptoir Generaal* itself.[5] In

---

[1] *Lettres Persanes*, no. 136.

[2] Federal excise dues were imposed at the Union of Utrecht in 1579 but later given up. For valuable help in this discussion thanks are due to Dr Simon Hart of the Gemeente-Archief, Amsterdam.

[3] The Hague, Algemeen Rijksarchief, Collectie Fagel, no. 1146.

[4] Parts of Brabant, Flanders and some other territories, largely Catholic in population and not having the same rights (e.g. representation in the States-General) as the Seven Provinces.

[5] Coll. Fagel, no. 1138. Division by ten gives a rough sterling equivalent.

these circumstances the General Treasurer and the Receiver General of the Republic, who were charged with superintending and checking this machinery and reporting regularly on financial matters to the Council of State (*Raad van Staat*), were not of equivalent importance to the English Lord Treasurer, the French Controller-General or the President of the Austrian *Hofkammer*.[1]

The bulk of the federal revenue derived from the contributions (*Quoten*) of the provinces. The needs of the Union for the coming year were estimated in advance by the Council of State at The Hague and submitted to the States-General, which approved them generally after much debate and exchange of information and advice with the provincial and town governments. Since each provincial delegation had to approve its own contribution, consent had in practice to be unanimous, and this procedure made quick decisions on urgent cases virtually impossible. The Council of State's estimates took the form of a Military Budget (*Staat van Oorlog*) and, in time of war, of an additional Extraordinary Military Budget, which specified in minute detail the troops to be levied and maintained by the respective provinces. The size of the military budget steadily increased as the wars continued. The ordinary peacetime establishment in the 1680s was of the order of 9 m. guilders; in 1695 the estimates amounted to 23·4 m., in 1703 to 24·4 m., in 1708 to 27·7 m., and in 1712 to 29 m. guilders.[2] These were staggering figures compared with previous years, and help to explain why the naval expenditure of the Republic (like that of France) declined during the Spanish Succession War.

Naval needs were estimated by the Council of State in consultation with the five Colleges of Admiralty, headed by the college at Amsterdam. These administered the import and export dues (*Convoöien en Licenten*), nominally imposed as federal taxes but in practice under provincial control. The proceeds, although not sufficient to cover naval war needs, were by no means insignificant; between 1689 and 1714 the income of the Amsterdam college was between 1 m. and 1·75 m. guilders a year. The Council of State raised additional money for naval purposes by agreement with the provinces, generally only after considerable haggling and obstruction.[3] Extraordinary expenditure financed by the provinces for the navy between 1688 and 1701 amounted to about 78 m. guilders. This was a period when the battle fleet rose to more than 100 of the line. No similar accounts have survived for the Succession War, towards the end of which the effective Dutch fleet evidently fell to as few as thirty ships; but it is

---

[1] The *Thesaurier Generaal der Unie* from 1666 to 1699 was Cornelis Burgh, and from 1699 to 1725 Jacob Hop. The *Ontvanger Generaal der Unie* from 1674 to 1707 was Cornelis de Jonge van Ellemeet, and from 1707 to 1740 Gijsbert van Hogendorp.

[2] Algemeen Rijksarchief, Staaten van Oorlog and Extraordinaris Staaten van Oorlog.

[3] The sums eventually agreed upon were sometimes set off against the provincial *Quoten*: Coll. Fagel, nos. 1123, 1135; J. C. de Jonge, *Geschiedenis van het Nederlandsche Zeewesen*, vol. III (Zwolle, 1869), app. IX.

clear that the mounting military budget made the provinces more and more unwilling, if not less and less able, to pay for the Dutch share (three-eighths) of the Allied fleet,[1] particularly since England, with her apparently bottomless purse, seemed well in charge of the war at sea.

If the average military budget of the Union is taken as *ca.* 20 m. guilders a year during the Nine Years War, and as *ca.* 25 m. during its successor, the total *estimated* military costs of the whole period were of the order of 450 m. guilders, to which (say) 150 m. may be added for naval expenditure. In the absence of precise accounts, it cannot be stated how far these sums were actually raised: it seems unlikely, owing to delays and frauds, that the full total was ever realized. Even so, the two wars must have cost the Republic somewhere between 500 m. and 700 m. guilders (say £50–£70 m.). Of this total, long-term loans floated by the central government accounted for only a small part. They were of two kinds: those raised 'at the cost of the Generality' and financed from its revenues, and those raised 'at the cost of the Provinces' and financed from their revenues. The former totalled 24·5 m. guilders in 1715, the latter 56·6 m.[2] In addition, allies were allowed to raise loans in Holland. Austria's are considered separately.[3] Other States were allowed to raise about £1 m. in all in the Nine Years War and about £1¼ m. in the Succession War. The heaviest borrowers were Carlos II and Charles III of Spain, charging their Netherlands revenues.[4]

The major part of Dutch war costs was covered by increasing the provincial contributions. The proportion of the financial burden borne by each province had originally been decided early in the seventeenth century, though it was subsequently the object of much disagreement. Holland, as the richest and most populous, was expected to provide a much larger contribution than the others; between 1689 and 1714 she had to meet 57 per cent of the Republic's military expenditure. Holland's ordinary revenue in 1689, based on taxes voted by the States of Holland and West Friesland, was about 13 m. guilders.[5] Of this sum, 2·6 m. came from house and property taxes (*verpondingen*) and 9·6 m. from excise duties on over 20 articles. These excises—regarded as the Public Taxes *par excellence*—had grown up piecemeal over many years. Their collection was farmed out to syndicates of private individuals, who provided the Receivers of Public Taxes at the various tax offices of the province. Tax-farming, as usual, bought security of revenue at the expense of elasticity, causing

---

[1] Cf. above, p. 234. [2] Coll. Fagel, no. 1138.
[3] Below, pp. 307–8.
[4] Indexes to the *Resolutiën van de Heeren Staten van Hollandt*... for 1687–1700 and 1701–13. According to this source, Spain borrowed about £317,000 in the first war and £603,000 in the second. Other borrowing powers were Brandenburg-Prussia, England, Hesse-Cassel, the Palatinate, Portugal, Saxony, Trier, the Swabian Circle and Württemburg.
[5] Algemeen Rijksarchief, 3de Afdeeling, Financie—Holland, no. 797; Amsterdam, Gemeente Archief, Collectie Huydecoper.

great public bitterness against the farmers and allowing a considerable amount of fraud; but it was not abandoned until the mid-eighteenth century. One of its effects during the period of the wars with France was to hold down the revenue from indirect taxation just when it should have increased; thus the yield of the Public Taxes was of the order of 10·25 m. guilders per annum in the 1690s, and fell to about 9·5 m. from 1700 to the 1730s. An attempt was made to compensate for this failure to expand revenue from indirect taxes by increasing the burden of direct taxes on property. The scope of the *verpondingen* widened during the war, the goods of the knights and nobles being taxed for the first time in 1689 and imposts falling on the income from government securities (which in England were not taxed), East and West India Company shares, manors and manorial goods, land and houses. Thanks to this additional taxation, the income of the province of Holland had risen by the 1720s to about 19 m. guilders.

This was quite insufficient, however, to meet war costs. In 1712, for example, the *Quote* which Holland had to pay was over 16 m. guilders. The gap between revenue and expenditure—proportionately greater for Holland than for the Republic itself—had to be closed by borrowing, the extent of which is shown by an increase of the province's interest payments on long-term loans from 7·1 m. to 14·5 m. guilders per annum between 1678 and 1720. The Grand Pensionary of Holland told the States of Holland and West Friesland in 1727 that he estimated that 28 m. guilders had been added to the provincial debt between 1689 and 1697, and no less than 128 m. between 1702 and 1714.[1] From one point of view this was an ill-considered policy, for it left the finances so encumbered that for many years the strength of the province (and so of the Republic itself) was seriously impaired. 'In the last war', complained the Finance Committee of the States of Holland in 1728,

people seem to have been determined not to lose the advantages gained with so much blood and money in the earlier years, so they overwhelmed the already burdened finances with such vast capital commitments that it is now extremely difficult to remedy the situation.[2]

From the opposite point of view, as English experience also proved, the increase in the debt showed how successfully a limited revenue could be used by a rich country as a 'fund of credit' for loans which would bring in the additional sums that people would not pay in taxes. A poor country like Austria could not do this on a comparable scale, however much she might have liked to, and had to pay ruinous interest on the sums she did borrow.

Holland's ability to float public loans on an unprecedented scale was due to her immense wealth, based on the world trade centred in Amsterdam, and to the habit of borrowing and dealing in credit, of which

[1] *Secrete Resolutiën...van Hollandt ende West-Vrieslandt*, vol. VII, p. 836.
[2] *Resolutiën van de...Staten van Hollandt...*, vol. for 1728, p. 468.

willingness to lend to government was a natural consequence. The province had been accustomed to borrow on long terms for part of its requirements since the sixteenth century. By the later seventeenth, its system of loans was well established and its securities were regularly dealt in on the Bourse at Amsterdam, together with those of the Dutch and English East India Companies and the Dutch West India Company. Price-lists of stocks, including government stock, were issued by brokers, and securities could be bought spot or for time.[1] The three chief types of loan floated between 1689 and 1714 were thus already familiar to the investing public. Redeemable annuities (*losrenten*), which the State was entitled to repay at will, were the best known and most important; there were also life annuities and lotteries. Lotteries, more and more popular as the wars went on, were held every year (as in England) between 1711 and 1714. In view of the very large loans negotiated, it is not surprising that their terms became increasingly generous. In 1711, for example, when the States of Holland wished to raise a loan of 4 m. guilders, they decided to offer 20-year annuities which were either at 9 per cent tax-free or at 10 per cent for ten years and then taxable. None the less, such was the availability of funds in Amsterdam that the charge on the whole debt of about 250 m. guilders by 1714 was not greatly in excess of 4 per cent.

The receipt of loans was decentralized. Lenders' names were entered in registers by the Receivers at the *comptoirs* of the province at which they paid their money, and the lender was given a formal document obliging the provincial government to pay his interest and capital. A general oversight was provided by the *Comptoir Generaal van de Provinciën* at The Hague; it also kept accounts of the totals of revenue and expenditure. The much more efficient book-keeping methods of the Dutch East India Company, which kept ledgers of shareholders' accounts and transferred shares by transfer books in exactly the same way as the Bank of England, were not taken over by the Dutch government—as they were in England shortly after the war—until the Napoleonic era.

When Colbert acquired control of the French financial system in 1661, he found it one which, as he said, 'the cleverest men in the realm, concerned in it for forty years, had so complicated in order to make themselves needed that they alone understood it'.[2] Unfortunately, despite his important reforms, much the same could have been said of it at any time down to 1789. Under Colbert and his immediate successors as Controllers-General—Le Pelletier (1683–9), Pontchartrain (1689–99), Chamillart (1699–1708) and Colbert's nephew Desmarets (1708–15)—financial control was strengthened by the reconstruction of the *Conseil Royal des Finances*, and by the development of the *Contrôle Général*, which did most of the

---

[1] That is, for cash now or for a future date on credit.
[2] P. Clément, *Histoire de...Colbert* (2 vols. 1846), p. 438.

day-to-day financial work. It kept in close touch with the intendants and with the other components of the financial system, such as the royal exchequer (*Trésor Royal*). With the growth of business its Chief Clerks became of considerable importance, although it never acquired the institutional preponderance of the English Treasury; its strength reflected the Controller's personality.[1] It was Colbert who created the General Farm of the Taxes (1681). He also tried to abolish venal offices and establish efficient audit. For the first time there was effective knowledge of receipts and issues; fraud was reduced, charges cut down. Further, he instituted legal process against many State creditors, which enabled him to cancel the debts due to them on the grounds that they had been contracted dishonestly. All this helped to balance the budget and simplify financial administration.

But Colbert's policy had grave weaknesses. The inequity of the fiscal system, which discriminated blatantly in favour of the upper Estates, was not remedied. Decentralization of receipt and issue, effectively ended in England during this period, remained to plague successive French governments until 1789. Colbert, moreover, who had the limitations as well as the virtues of the private householder, concentrated on teaching the State, in the person of the king, to live within its income. He not only paid little serious attention to developing a system of public credit which would facilitate a smooth increase of expenditure in war-time: he actively alienated the *rentier* class by his attacks on it, and he maintained old practices of State repudiation that were to prove deadly to the monarchy's fortunes.

French public expenditure in 1689 was about 130 m. *livres* (roughly £9 m. sterling). Moving up to 211 m. in 1698, it rose to a peak of 264 m. in 1711, then fell to 213 m. in 1714. Total expenditure over the period was of the order of 5,000 m. *livres*—say £300 m. sterling, only slightly less than the combined expenses of France's three chief opponents. In the Nine Years War the army absorbed about 65 per cent of expenditure, the navy little more than 9 per cent; in the Succession War the corresponding figures were 57 and 7 per cent. Debt service and administrative costs took up most of the remainder.[2] Revenue was based in 1689 on the *taille*, which formed about 30 per cent of tax revenue and, like the other direct taxes, was collected by a body of General Receivers. Though resembling the English land tax it was much less satisfactory, since for one reason or

---

[1] M. Antoine, *Le Fonds du Conseil d'Etat du Roi aux Archives Nationales* (1955) and 'Les Conseils des Finances sous le règne de Louis XV', *Rev. d'hist. mod. et contemp.*, vol. v (1958), pp. 161–200.

[2] Estimates of public revenue and expenditure are mainly taken from Véron de Forbonnais, *Recherches et considérations sur les finances de France* (2 vols. Basle, 1758), and A. de Boislisle (ed.), *Correspondance des contrôleurs généraux des finances avec les intendants des provinces* (3 vols. 1874–97). Exchange-rates between *livres* and pounds sterling fluctuated considerably, partly owing to numerous revaluations of the *livre*. The average number of *livres* to the pound sterling was 15·3 in 1688–97, 17·2 in 1702–7, 18·3 in 1708–14.

another nearly half the land in France was exempt from it. The *capitation* (1695) and *dixième* (1710) were attempts to tax the property of all classes, but as such misfired;[1] although introduced only as wartime measures, they had to be retained after 1714. Besides these main direct taxes, there were the *dons gratuits* (benevolences) paid by the clergy[2] and the Provincial Estates in lieu of them; the *étapes et secondes parties* (an augmentation of *taille* levied as military taxes); the *parties casuelles* levied on venal offices; and the forest dues. By this period the royal domain no longer produced a significant income, though still an important administrative complex.

There were literally hundreds of indirect taxes, customarily grouped as the *gabelles* (on salt), the *tabacs* (on tobacco), the *traites* (internal and external dues on commerce), the *aides* (sales-taxes and stamp duties) and the *domaines* (primarily registry taxes on legal documents). Save for the tobacco tax, which was leased separately, each was a complex of several duties rather than a single levy. They were called collectively 'the receipts of the General Farms' and were nearly all administered by the General Farmers, a group of capitalists who ran an elaborate network of provincial agencies from their headquarters in Paris. Since the taxes were largely charges on commerce, their yield declined during the wars as business activity decreased. In the period 1689–91, the government was able to charge the farmers 66 m. *livres* a year for their lease; by 1703 it was forced to reduce this to below 50 m.; in 1709 the farmers refused to take a new lease at any price.[3] By the end of the war indirect taxes were contributing no more than 5 per cent of the State's revenue.

Faced with soaring war costs, the government might have been expected to increase its rates of taxation as sharply as possible. Instead, it largely resorted to loans and to the sale of offices baited with tax concessions. Its motive was simple. It hoped each year for peace, and such expedients aroused less resistance, and produced more immediate results, than tightening the already vicious screw of taxation. The effect of this short-sighted policy was so drastically to increase charges (in the form of interest and salaries) that by the end of the wars they absorbed nearly the whole ordinary revenue of the State.[4]

By 1713 the capital of State long-term loans, mostly raised during the wars, amounted to 1,360 m. *livres* (say £75 m. sterling).[5] The largest part

[1] See below, pp. 332–3.

[2] Below, p. 333. According to A. Cans, *La Contribution du clergé de France à l'impôt* ...*1689–1715* (1910), the clergy paid 6·4 m. *livres* a year from 1690 to 1715. This was 5·8 per cent of their income though only 3 per cent of government revenue.

[3] G. T. Matthews, *The Royal General Farms in the Eighteenth Century* (New York, 1958), p. 58. Cf. also J. F. Bosher, *The Single Duty Project. A Study of the Movement for a French Customs Union in the Eighteenth Century* (1964), chs. 1 and 2.

[4] Memorandum of Desmarets, Jan. 1715, in Boislisle, vol. III, p. 621.

[5] See A. Vührer, *Histoire de la dette publique en France* (2 vols. 1886); A. Vuitry, *Le Désordre des finances...à la fin du règne de Louis XIV...*(1885); and L. Germain-Martin and M. Bezançon, *L'Histoire du crédit en France sous le règne de Louis XIV* (1913).

(1,280 m.) was administered by the Hôtel de Ville of Paris. According to Forbonnais, the princes and nobility held about 10 per cent of this, members of the bureaucracy and law courts 29 per cent, ecclesiastical corporations 7 per cent, merchants and bankers 6 per cent, artisans and tradesmen 4 per cent, foreigners 4 per cent.[1] There is unfortunately no indication of the geographical spread of ownership, but it seems likely from the evidence of later periods to have been concentrated in and around Paris. The loans from which this debt had been built up were of various kinds. Tontines were floated in 1689, 1696 and 1709, lotteries in 1704 and 1705. But the greater part of government long-term bonds was in the form of redeemable and life annuities (*rentes perpétuelles* and *rentes viagères*). By 1709 these accounted for nearly half the interest paid on the *rentes* administered by the Hôtel de Ville.[2] The need to convert short-term paper into *rentes* between 1709 and 1714 further increased their amount.

The sale of new offices, on a colossal scale, supplemented the capital derived from long-term loans and was the more tempting for investors owing to the State's poor record as a borrower. It was to these sales in particular that the description 'affaires extraordinaires', often applied in official circles to all war-time financial expedients, became firmly attached in general usage. The disadvantage of the system from the public's stand-point was that offices were not sold direct to investors but were marketed through syndicates of office-jobbers (*traitants*), who paid the treasury a fixed price and resold at a profit; it has been estimated that probably no more than two-thirds of the 500 m. raised by this means between 1689 and 1714 ever reached the government. A further expedient was to compel office-holders to pay a capital sum in return for an increase in salary: these *augmentations de gages* brought the State a further 120 m.[3] The *traitants*[4] themselves were a small and powerful group, overlapping in personnel with the tax-farmers, war contractors and royal office-holders; and they showed a fertile ingenuity both in suggesting expedients to the treasury and in fleecing their clients. The bitter comments of contemporaries show that they were a much-hated group. For the government the *vénalité des offices*, while temporarily useful, was ultimately damaging. It increased the burden of (often useless) posts, reduced tax-yields by the grant of exemptions, and further weakened the bourgeoisie's readiness to invest in public loans.

Besides the sums raised by taxes, long-term loans and the sale of offices, the government financed its expenses by issuing short-dated bills on a large scale. They were to prove a major source of confusion as the

---

[1] Forbonnais, vol. II, p. 385. Most of the records of the *rentes* were destroyed in 1871.
[2] Interest due in 1709 on this section of the debt was 38·7 m. *livres*, of which *rentes perpétuelles* formed 14·5 m. and *rentes viagères* 558,000 *livres* (Paris, Arch. Nat., G7/1594).
[3] Vuitry, p. 45. [4] As members of syndicates they were often called *partisans*.

wars went on. There were three chief types of bill. The first were promissory notes (*promesses*) charged on the Caisse des Emprunts, a deposit bank established by Colbert in 1674, suppressed after his death but restored in 1702. The second were assignments on the future revenue. The third were the *billets de monnaie*, mint bills originally issued as receipts for specie during the recoinage of 1701 but subsequently put into enforced circulation, partly to redeem the discredited notes of the Caisse.

Down to 1704 treasury control of the various types of bill seems to have been adequate, but it largely collapsed after Blenheim, owing both to a rush to encash bills and to their reckless over-issue to cover immediate expenses. By 1706, 173 m. of *billets de monnaie* alone were in circulation at ruinous discounts, virtually paralysing credit.[1] As a first step towards remedying the situation, 50 m. were converted into 5 per cent bills issued by the General Farmers and General Receivers, repayable after five years (*billets de cinq ans*). These quickly went to 80 per cent discount. A further 51 m. were exchanged against *promesses* of the Caisse des Emprunts or turned into *rentes*. In 1709, 43 m. *billets de monnaie* were discharged in cash. The remaining 29 m. was either paid in this way or forcibly converted into *rentes* in 1711–12. Meanwhile the *promesses* of the Caisse des Emprunts had increased from 60 m. in 1708 to 147 m. in 1715. Like the other bills, their market price was no more than 20 per cent of their face value. Further bills amounting to 61 m., issued by the War Office, Artillery and Marine, were funded in 1715. A renewed attempt in 1710 to put the service of short-term paper on a better footing, the Caisse Legendre, enjoyed only partial success and broke down shortly after the peace. It is clear that by the close of the wars repayment in cash and conversion into *rentes* had failed to do more than palliate the chaos caused by the over-issue of bills. It was estimated in 1715 that paper in circulation amounted to 600 m. *livres* (say £33 m. sterling), while an equal sum was due from the government for wages and salaries. This was in addition to the long-term debts of *ca.* 1,000 m. *livres*. The total long- and short-term indebtedness was placed by Desmarets at 2,382 m. *livres*, the equivalent of over thirty years' ordinary revenue. As he pointed out, it would take twenty years to redeem the situation.[2]

Over and above the difficulties caused by falling tax-yields, reluctant creditors, and over-issue of short-dated paper, the government had to deal with a virtual disappearance of specie from circulation. Whether the result primarily of the Dutch drawing off gold and silver owing to its undervaluation in France,[3] or of a general shortage of world specie in relation to the volume of trade, or of outright hoarding in face of the

[1] Boislisle, vol. III, pp. 616, 620; Vuitry, ch. VII.
[2] Boislisle, vol. III, pp. 673–82; Vuitry, ch. VII (in which he draws on sources destroyed in 1871).
[3] Paris, Arch. Nat., G7, nos. 722 (undated *mémoire* of Sieur Cazier on specie and exchange (?1706)) and 1119 (*mémoire* of F. Léonard, 1715).

government's punitive fiscal policies, there is no doubt that the stock of coin was shrinking. The banker Huguetan estimated that French specie totalled 534 m. in 1689 but only 125 m. by 1705.[1] This famine created the gravest difficulties. They were accentuated by over forty revaluations of the *livre* between 1689 and 1715, worth about 140 m. to the treasury at the cost of finally destroying public confidence in the currency.

One view of the dearth of specie was that it was due largely to the massive remittances for the French armies in Flanders, Germany, Italy and Spain. However this may be, there is no doubt that these remittances were so important that much else had to be sacrificed to them, and that they had to continue even on terms ruinous to the treasury. The business had developed considerably during the 1690s, and by the end of the Nine Years War its main centres outside France were Amsterdam and Geneva. In Amsterdam the chief French agents were Pierre Gott, Andreas Pels—one of the greatest merchants in Europe—and the bookseller-merchant Jean Henri Huguetan. In Geneva the international houses of Calandrini and Fatio were the most prominent, though there were several others. Inside France the Genevan bankers had close connections with Lyons, many of whose financiers were either converted Huguenots or foreign Protestants. In Paris, Samuel Bernard was beginning to move into this field which, though it formed only part of his mercantile empire, he was to dominate until 1709.[2]

Huguetan's work for the French treasury was so successful by 1703 that the English government brought pressure on the Dutch to expel him. He therefore moved to Geneva. There—working closely with the houses of Calandrini, Fatio, Saladin, Tourton, Guiguer and their Lyons correspondents, and with Bernard in Paris—he continued to play a key rôle in the French remittances, which by 1704 were running at roughly 80 m. *livres* a year. This system was, however, an improvised reply to the Anglo-Dutch trading Interdict of June 1703,[3] which effectively stopped the negotiation of bills through Amsterdam. Before long the whole consortium of financiers was under heavy stress. Bernard's correspondence with the *Contrôle Général* describes a rising curve of anxiety, culminating in July–August 1704, when some of his bills were noted for protest owing to Treasury delay in paying him and he was on the verge of bankruptcy. If he perished (as he was careful to point out), forty others would perish with him—and with them the State's credit.[4] The situation was retrieved in the nick of time by the ending of the Interdict on 1 June 1704, which enabled the consortium to resume negotiation of long-dated bills in Amsterdam. This success partly offset the difficulties caused by the

---

[1] Ibid. 'Memoire touchant les finances de France', July 1705.
[2] See H. Lüthy, *La Banque Protestante en France*, vol. I (1959); J. Saint-Germain, *Samuel Bernard* (1960). Cf. below, p. 336.
[3] See below, p. 420.
[4] Arch. Nat., G7, no. 1120, Bernard to Chamillart, 6 August 1704.

depreciation of government short-term paper after Blenheim in August. The immediate consequence of this depreciation was, unexpectedly, to ruin not the treasury but Huguetan, and thus to concentrate remittance business in Bernard's hands. The treasury proposed to pay Huguetan in *billets de monnaie* without allowance for the heavy discount. When he countered by threatening to stop remittances, the government lured him to Paris and forced him to draw bills on his foreign correspondents for nearly 8 m. *livres* (December 1704). Escaping from Paris, however, before his bills were due, he reached Amsterdam ahead of his pursuers, stopped the bills, drew 6 m. or 7 m. *livres* on his French correspondents (causing several houses to go bankrupt) and pocketed the proceeds. Having thus dramatically turned the tables on his old employers, he prudently retired to England in April 1705 and placed his considerable financial knowledge at the disposal of the English government.[1]

After this Bernard and his partner Nicolas, working with their Protestant correspondents in Geneva and the financiers of Lyons, virtually controlled the whole of French remittance business until the later years of the war, although even at the height of their power they were unable to edge successive members of the Hogguer family out of the contracts for Alsace. The rates Bernard charged varied from 8 to 25 per cent, increasing as the war went on; but it is fair to add that he owed considerable sums abroad on which he had to pay 10 per cent, while he also had to run the risk of dangerous fluctuations in the exchanges.

His system, while it lasted, centred on the negotiation of very large quantities of bills at the quarterly Payments of Lyons. These had survived the decline (since 1660) of the Lyons fair with which they were historically connected, and at the beginning of the eighteenth century were still, next to Amsterdam, the most important market in commercial bills in Europe. They acted as a clearing-house in which debtors and creditors could set off their exchange liabilities against each other, either paying the final balance due on the spot or continuing it for settlement at the next Payment. This mechanism was workable only so long as the volume of bills bore some relation to real commercial transactions. The vast increase of bills drawn for payment of the French armies—and backed, in effect, only by the promises of a bankrupt treasury—placed increasing pressure on it. At the beginning of 1709 it was computed that half the bills drawn on Lyons were those of Bernard and Nicolas. But the Geneva houses who were Bernard's principal helpers were, by this time, too deeply committed to withdraw. Later in the same year it was explained that all their assets were locked up either in this business or in English govern-

---

[1] Lüthy, vol. I, pp. 150–62; A. E. Sayous, 'Le Financier Jean-Henri Huguetan à Amsterdam et à Genève,' *Bull. de la Soc. d'hist. et d'arch. de Genève*, vol. VI, no. 3 (1936–7), 270–3. In 1707, on a return visit to Holland, Huguetan was kidnapped by French agents, but again escaped. In 1711 he moved to Denmark. French agents were still following him in the 1720s.

ment securities, which they were unable to sell owing to the adverse rates of exchange.[1]

The market had thus become dangerously vulnerable. In the financial crisis of 1709 it collapsed. This crisis had a threefold origin: the mounting total of State debts which could not be paid; the appalling winter of 1708–9, which froze the rivers and paralysed commerce; and the disastrous corn and wine harvests of 1709, which completed the ruin already started. Mortality, food prices and the rate of bankruptcies soared.[2] Pressed by his creditors, who were unable to give him further time, Bernard was unable to meet his bills at the Payments of 1709, thus triggering off a chain of bankruptcies among his French and Swiss correspondents. Thanks to government action assigning him 1 m. *livres* a year in *rentes* and imposing a three-year moratorium on part of his bills, Bernard himself survived the crash and by the end of 1711 had met most of his vast obligations. But his system, centred on Lyons, had been completely discredited—and with it his central position in French remittance business. Although he continued to undertake contracts for the treasury until the war ended, the main share fell into other hands, nor was its scale again so ambitious as in the days of his ascendancy.

After 1708 the new Controller, Desmarets, though a clever financier, could do little more than shore up the tottering fiscal structure. The *dixième* and Caisse Legendre palliated the Crown's troubles, and projects for a State bank were studied in the critical years 1708–10; though without immediate effect, they pointed the way to John Law's financial innovations.[3] Meanwhile it was clear that French financial weakness precluded any large-scale offensive after 1709.

Compared with England, France and the United Provinces, the Habsburg dominions in 1700 were in general poor and backward, their wealth concentrated in few hands, the structure of government still largely medieval; in addition, many areas were subject to constant internal as well as external dangers or tensions. Given this setting, it is not surprising that the monarchy's financial system was corrupt, inefficient, laborious to an extent unsurpassed elsewhere. Already severely strained by the Turkish war, and before there was time to reform it (as several critics desired), it was forced to meet the vast expenses of the wars against Louis XIV which on several occasions nearly broke it. For this reason, although various changes were made during the wars, substantial financial reform was largely delayed until the coming of peace—and in some important respects until the 1740s.

Central financial control was provided, though in theory rather than

[1] Lüthy, vol. I, p. 223.   [2] Cf. below, pp. 322–3.
[3] Boislisle, vol. III, app. iii; A. P. Herlaut, 'Projets de création d'une Banque Royale en France à la fin du règne de Louis XIV', *Rev. d'hist. mod.* vol. VIII (1933), p. 143.

practice, by the *Hofkammer* (court treasury) in Vienna, under which were separate Payment Bureaux (*Zahlamten*) for court and administrative finance, on the one hand, and military purposes on the other.[1] Hungarian revenues were separately administered at Pressburg. Provincial exchequers (*Landkammern*), staffed by professional bureaucrats, collected the court and administrative revenues (*Camerale*); these came from the royal domain and from taxes on wine, beer, salt, etc. The military revenues (*Militäre*), which came primarily from house and property taxes, were voted by the provincial Diets, annually as a rule, but in Hungary, where the Diet sat only every three years, for three to four years at a time. The military budget was divided into three parts: Ordinary, Extraordinary, and Recruit and Remount money. Payments assigned from the previous year formed a prior charge on the sums voted.[2] The minimum to be voted by each Diet was specified by the *Hofkammer*, but often bitterly contested.

The size of the civil and military revenue at the end of the seventeenth century is conjectural. Estimates vary from 12 m. to 20 m. florins per annum:[3] the range of disagreement (contrasting significantly with the more precise figures available for the Maritime Powers and France) arises from the excessive decentralization of the system, in which each kingdom or province collected and disbursed the section of revenue under its care, and ran up and paid off its own debts. In these circumstances the *Hofkammer*, however laboriously it minuted its own discussions and collected accounts, could do little more than make estimates and drafts whose imperfections it candidly acknowledged.[4]

It was very difficult to wring an increased revenue out of a poor and sullen body of taxpayers with this creaking machinery, but the emperor's ministers were driven to the attempt by the cost of prolonged war. As the years passed, the annual estimates of military expenditure drawn up by the Imperial Conference mounted alarmingly. In 1701, before war broke out, they totalled 14 m. florins; by 1703 they had risen to 28 m., and averaged over 20 m. per annum until the conclusion of peace in 1714. Another 6–8 m. should have been found annually to cover the expenses of court and administration. Over the Succession War alone, therefore, estimated expenditure was of the order of 350 m. florins.[5] If 150 m. are added for 1689–97, the total *estimated* cost of the two wars was around 500 m.

[1] The *Hofkammerpräsidenten* in this period were Wolfgang Andreas, Count Rosenberg (1683–92); Seifried, Count Bruener (1694–8); Gotthard, Count Salaburg (1700–3); and Gundaker Thomas, Count Starhemberg (1703–15). At intervals there was no formal president. For the reorganization under Joseph I, see below, p. 573. Cf. J. W. Stoye, 'Emperor Charles VI: the early years of the reign', *Trans. R. Hist. Soc.* 5th ser. vol. XII (1962), pp. 64–73.

[2] [Vienna,] Ö[sterreichisches] S[taatsarchiv], Hofkammerarchiv Hs. 217.

[3] The official exchange rate was 6¼ Austrian florins to the £ but the real rate, used here, was about 8½.

[4] The *Hoffinanz-Akten* run to four thick volumes a year during this period; the indexes are slender and of little use.

[5] F. von Mensi, *Die Finanzen Oesterreichs von 1700 bis 1740* (Vienna, 1890).

(about £59 m. sterling). It is extremely unlikely that these estimates were ever fully met; indeed, the gap between them and the revenue actually received was probably wider than for any of the other great powers. Committees of Ways and Means (*Mittelskonferenzen*) from among the emperor's councillors anxiously studied the situation from year to year. They drafted proposals for the increase of old taxes and the raising of new ones. The basic rates for house, property and excise taxes were increased, and an entry tax on Jews (1708), a tax on offices, and a poll-tax were all introduced. In December 1710 an attempt was made to levy 10 per cent on gambling profits, though the yield disappointed its proposer's sanguine expectations. Although the Church and nobility remained insufficiently taxed, these expedients did increase the total revenue.[1] In the period just after the war, for instance, the civil ('cameral') income, which in the 1690s was only of the order of 4–5 m. florins, had increased to 8 m., and the military revenue had risen in the same proportion. Nevertheless, this was quite insufficient to cover the monarchy's expenses.

The situation could partly be relieved by the simple expedient of non-payment. But though the government allowed its courtiers' pensions and bureaucrats' salaries to fall into arrears, and delayed payment to its troops until there was grave risk of mass desertion, there were limits to open dishonouring of commitments if Austria was to remain a great power. Tribute from occupied enemy states was a second expedient; it was practised successfully in Bavaria from 1706 and in Italy from 1707. It probably produced about 5 m. a year. It was also possible to persuade the Maritime Powers to take over part of the monarchy's military obligations in Savoy, Italy and Spain, thus effecting a considerable saving of revenue, though England and Holland were not prepared to go beyond this and pay direct subsidies, as they did to other members of the Grand Alliance.[2]

Besides such indirect aid, the Maritime Powers, with their accumulated capital and relatively advanced systems of credit, could be persuaded to lend. The more promising of the two capital markets was still in Holland, where loans to the emperor, secured on the produce of the quicksilver mines at Idria in the Julian Alps, had been floated as early as 1669. In 1695, and again in 1698, fresh loans on this security were negotiated for the Imperial government by Jean Deutz van Assendelft, a well-known banker in Amsterdam, who held the office of Imperial Quicksilver Factor. Repayment was guaranteed by the States-General and interest secured by shipment of the mines' produce for sale by Deutz in Amsterdam. Further advances on this basis were arranged in 1702, 1704 and 1706, though only

---

[1] Both church and noble lands were subject to direct taxes except in Hungary, but there were numerous exemptions and under-valuations. All classes, of course, paid indirect taxes.

[2] For a recent discussion see G. Otruba, 'Die Bedeutung englischer Subsidien und Antizipationen für die Finanzen Österreichs 1701 bis 1748', *Vierteljahrschrift für Sozial- und Wirtschaftsgeschichte*, vol. LI (1964), p. 192.

after much haggling—Deutz refusing to do business unless the States-General provided a guarantee, and the latter refusing to give one for some time (1701–2) on the grounds that Sweden and the Palatinate were also trying to raise capital sums in Holland. The suspicion of the Dutch government—and of Dutch investors—was understandable, for payments of interest quickly fell into arrears[1] and the loans were only liquidated in 1724. Advances on the security of the Hungarian copper revenues, also floated through Deutz (1700, 1703), and on the contributions of the princes and Estates of Silesia (1713, 1714), supplemented these quick-silver loans. The last two, handled by Cliffords of Amsterdam, were punctually repaid; the copper loans drifted on until repaid in 1736. The total sum raised for the emperor's account in the Dutch market between 1689 and 1714 seems to have been of the order of 10·8 m. Dutch florins (about £1·1 m.), at an average rate of 5 per cent.

Loans from England were to become of some significance in the eighteenth century. In this period, however, they were less important than the Dutch. In 1705 there was a small loan of £66,000. In 1706 a larger loan of £250,000, repayable in five years, was negotiated in London at 8 per cent, despite French sneers that the subscription was bound to fail. The Bank of England administered it; the prince of Denmark and the duke of Marlborough headed the subscription lists.[2] Two years later an attempt to borrow a further £250,000 was abandoned, after the Imperial ambassador had explained that owing to the emperor's poor reputation as a debtor the stock of the existing loan was quoted at 12 per cent discount and found no buyers.[3] In 1710 a renewed attempt met with only partial success, £100,000 being asked for and £87,000 being subscribed. Besides these English and Dutch loans, the monarchy also made attempts to tap the capital market in Genoa, Germany and Switzerland, without great success. The total amount borrowed abroad between 1689 and 1714 was roughly 12 m. florins (about £1½ m.). These figures, though admittedly uncertain, suggest that only 4 to 5 per cent of Austrian war costs in this period was covered by foreign loans and subsidies.

Taxation, the accumulation of arrears, tribute and foreign loans helped to close the yawning gap between Austria's financial needs and her normal revenue, but they did not by any means close it entirely. Like other powers, she was therefore forced to rely increasingly on internal borrowing. The machinery of Imperial credit around 1700 seems to have changed little since the days when the Fuggers had underwritten the wars of Charles V. Formal loans were acknowledged by Royal Obligations

---

[1] Owing partly to the difficulties Deutz experienced in marketing the Idrian quicksilver; e.g., in 1705–6, the English East India Company exported Chinese quicksilver to Amsterdam and undercut the market price.

[2] Cf. H. L. Mikoletzky, 'Die grosse Anleihe von 1706', *Mitteilungen des Österr. Staatsarchiv*, vol. VI (1954), p. 268. The subscription ledgers are in the Bank of England Record Office.   [3] *Feldzüge des Prinzen Eugen*, vol. X (Vienna, 1885), p. 57.

(*Kaiserliche Obligationen*), elaborate sealed instruments issued to named persons, and by Treasury Receipts (*Cassa-Amtsquittungen*), issued blank. The first were used for long-term, the second for short-term borrowing. Both were secured generally on the royal treasure and specifically on particular sources of revenue; both bound the emperor personally to repayment. The circle of borrowers prepared to take up these securities was limited, an important segment of it consisting of high officials of state. For example, the great nobles who played a leading rôle in Habsburg government were prepared to lend it part of their vast wealth. Thus Gundaker, Count Starhemberg, as vice-president of the *Hofkammer*, advanced 790,000 florins in all between 1698 and 1701; in 1701 Count Salaburg's outstanding loans amounted to 310,000 florins; in 1704 Count Tschernin advanced 1·2 m., the largest individual loan of this period. These operations were probably inspired by patriotism rather than greed, for their security was doubtful and the interest asked was generally well below the current rate. Supplementing the loans of the nobility, there were advances charged on individual offices (*Amtsdarlehen*) and forced loans from laity and Jews.

The sums so raised, by appeals to duty or to fear, could not keep pace with the rising curve of war expenditure, and larger sources of credit had to be found. The first remedy adopted was desperate and proved expensive. Like some needy aristocrat of ancient lineage, unable to wring from encumbered estates and unwilling friends the means to cover his extravagances, the monarchy gave itself into the hands of the Jews, who bled it white. It was said later that at the death of Leopold I in 1705 the financial system was in chaos, with 18 per cent interest allowed on new loans and profits of 30 per cent being made by the Jewish army contractors.[1] That this picture, though lurid, is probably not overdrawn, is suggested by the rise of the great Jewish house of Oppenheimer and Co. to a central place in the Habsburg war machine during the 1690s. Its chief, Samuel Oppenheimer, accumulated the lion's share of Habsburg contracting and short-term lending in this period.[2] An account of his total advances for 1695–1703 shows interest of 15·7 m. florins allowed on a capital of 30·7 m. (a rate of roughly 50 per cent) and it may safely be assumed that his contracting profits—he was freely charged with selling bad goods and short measure—were not very much lower. He was, of course, obliged to run the risk of default on the government's part, so his extortionate terms were partly a form of insurance premium. Nevertheless he was feathering his nest nicely at the State's expense, and the same was true in less degree of other Jewish financiers who were allowed to live in Vienna at this time: for example, Samson Wertheimer, Lazarus Hirschl and Simon

---

[1] H. I. Bidermann, 'Die Wiener Stadt-Bank', *Archiv für Kunde österreichisches Geschichtsquellen*, vol. XX (1859), pp. 415–16.

[2] On the 'Court Jews' generally, cf. below, pp. 788–9.

Meichl. Popular opinion of them, in the intensely anti-Semitic atmosphere of the city, is shown by the mob's storming of Oppenheimer's counting-house in July 1700, a summer of dear bread.

However distasteful the services of Oppenheimer's and similar firms might be, the court could not do without them. The extent to which it relied on them was shown dramatically in May 1703 when Samuel Oppenheimer died. 'All the merchants are so involved in this business', wrote Prince Eugene to Count Guido Starhemberg in May 1703, 'that they refuse to enter into any contracts before the Jew's affairs are in some degree adjusted.'[1] Worse was to come, for shortly afterwards the firm, pressed for payment by its creditors, and with its assets largely locked up in advances to the government, went bankrupt. A contemporary commented: 'This is so deadly a blow that France herself could not have contrived anything more advantageous to herself and harmful to the Emperor.'[2] The armies in Germany and Italy were on the verge of collapse for want of pay. 'Money matters have reached a crisis', wrote Margrave Lewis of Baden to the emperor on 15 June 1703, 'and I can hardly raise a hundred guilders even on my own property.'[3] An urgent appeal for a loan of 400,000 crowns (about £100,000) from the Maritime Powers to pay the army in Italy foundered on the resistance of the States-General.[4] Clearly, this desperate situation required a new and bold stroke to remedy it.

One attempt had already been made to improve the government's financial position. In 1701 the provincial Diets had agreed to assume and repay from their own revenues 16 m. of the treasury's total debts, computed at 22 m. florins. But this was little more than a palliative—and one which further impaired both the provinces' willingness to vote additional taxes and public confidence in the treasury's good faith. Moreover, it was an expedient which could hardly be repeated. Arguing on these lines, in 1703, a special commission under Hans Adam, prince of Liechtenstein, came out in favour of a more sophisticated and radical project: the creation of a State bank. Plans to found banks of one kind or another had long been discussed in Austria as elsewhere, the general aim being to stimulate economic growth by a liberal use of credit. Johann Joachim Becher and Wilhelm von Schröder, the two principal advocates of an Austrian bank in the later seventeenth century, argued that credit and paper money would lessen dependence on gold, expand trade and industry, and ease business conditions. Schröder added that a bank could only be founded by private persons because the monarchy's credit was so bad, but hinted that a wise prince might adopt it once it became a going concern. These discussions, which reflect growing preoccupation in governing circles with the relatively backward state of the economy, were given

---

[1] Quoted Bidermann, *loc. cit.* p. 418.
[2] F. von Mensi, *Die Finanzen Oesterreichs*, p. 140.
[3] Quoted Bidermann, *loc. cit.* p. 353.   [4] *House of Commons Journals*, vol. xv, p. 247.

point by the increasing deterioration of Habsburg finances. Perhaps a bank could be made both to stimulate the economy and disembarrass the Treasury. This duality of purpose is reflected in the foundation of the Imperial *Banco del Giro* at Vienna in August 1703. Its principal aims were declared to be the provision of war supply and the development of trade on the lines followed by the Banks of Venice, Amsterdam, Hamburg and Nuremberg.[1]

In practice, the first object transcended the second. Nor was it initially so much a question of supplying the war as of satisfying government creditors. The latter were given credit in the bank's books for the sums due to them (totalling about 6 m. florins) and the right to make transfers by assignable notes. A revenue computed at 4 m. per annum from the contributions of the hereditary lands was settled on the bank, to be used to pay off this and subsequent debts by instalments over a period of years, at 4 to 6 per cent. It was clearly intended to increase the original sums charged on the bank almost at once. Besides this primary aim, the bank was allowed to receive contributions from private depositors, and the fatal provision was added that all commercial bills of exchange should be cashed there. It was to be administered by a *Banco-Collegium* of Imperial councillors presided over by Prince Liechtenstein. This first essay at grafting modern practices into the antiquated structure of Habsburg finance was completely unsuccessful. It appears to have been foisted on the government by the creditors of Samuel Oppenheimer, working through their man of straw, Abbé Norbis, who sat on the commission which devised it; certainly the Oppenheimer debts of around 5 m. formed the principal part of the total liabilities taken over.[2] Within a year of its foundation the bank's notes were at 60–70 per cent discount and it was barely able to pay its servants' wages. An irritated Viennese contemporary complained that it was all the fault of the Jews, who were jobbing its notes down, and suggested a levy on the Jewish community in the city to repay the whole debt.[3] A revised charter (July 1704), raising the endowment to 5·5 m. florins a year, failed to improve the bank's situation. The new emperor, Joseph I, appointed a commission headed by Count Georg Martinitz to consider the establishment of another bank. The result was the creation of the Vienna City Bank (*Wiener Stadt-Bank*), which was to play an important part in Imperial finance for the rest of the century. It opened its offices on 1 April 1706.

This bank's main feature was that, like the Bank of Amsterdam, it was administered by the city, not the government; its formal head was the

---

[1] Giro-banks were established at Venice in 1584, Amsterdam in 1609, Hamburg in 1619 and Nuremberg in 1621. In a giro-bank depositors of coin or precious metals are allowed to make and receive payments by book-keeping entries; but no credit operations are allowed.

[2] Ö.S., Hofkammerarchiv Hs. 646.

[3] Ö.S., Hofkammerarchiv Hs. 650, fo. 1259—a memorandum in Italian, strongly hostile to the Oppenheimers.

burgomaster of Vienna, its business was done in the Rathaus. The revenues which the State settled on it, largely derived from excise duties levied in Vienna and computed at 600,000 florins per annum, were to be under its control for fifteen years. In return, the bank contracted to pay off the whole State debt within this period. Assignable notes were to be made out to creditors, carrying 5 to 6 per cent interest till redeemed. It was also agreed that further government debts might be charged on the bank provided its endowment was proportionately increased. The attempt of 1703 to force the mercantile community to cash its bills of exchange in bank paper was not repeated. A link with the government was provided by creating a standing committee of the *Hofkammer*, the ministerial *Banco-Deputation*, over which Gundaker Starhemberg presided until the reign of Maria Theresa.[1]

These arrangements proved workable for a number of reasons. First, they had the backing of the corporation of Vienna, whose credit was good and whose administration was efficient. From the start this weighted public opinion in its favour. Second, the fact that the revenues forming the endowment were, in effect, assigned to the city government, gave the bank a sure and independent basis which its predecessor had lacked. Third, the endowment was reasonably certain in amount. The revenue of the Giro Bank (1703–4) had formed so large a part of the total income of the State that it was intrinsically improbable that it could be fully raised. The City Bank's more modest income was relatively punctually paid, averaging 1·4 m. from 1705 to 1709.[2]

So far as the State's debts were concerned, the whole episode was a funding operation—a conversion of short-term into long-term debts—analogous to those carried out in England in 1697 and 1711. The first charge on the new institution was 6 m. florins due to the creditors of the Giro Bank, whose paper appreciated 100 per cent almost at once. This initial success enabled the treasury to charge further debts and advances to the bank, so that by 1707 the total sum which it owed the latter amounted to 13·8 m. florins, of which over 5 m. was in respect of debts due to Oppenheimer's creditors in the form of Giro Bank paper.[3] By 1711, the total due to former Giro Bank creditors had been reduced to 3·2 m., but other items brought the total to 23·9 m. This increase was partly due to funding of new short-term debts and partly to straight advances to the government for salaries, military wages, etc., in return for an increase in its endowment.

The Vienna City Bank was the Habsburgs' most successful financial experiment in this period, and obviously did a great deal to loosen the usurious hold which Jewish financiers had acquired on the machinery of

---

[1] A separate *Justiz Banco-Deputation* handled lawsuits involving the bank.
[2] Ö.S., Hofkammerarchiv Hs. 646. The endowment was increased to service new debts charged on the bank in this period.
[3] *Ibid.*

loans and contracting in the later seventeenth century. It is true that it was a State credit institute, rather than an effective bank in the sense that Becher or von Schröder would have wished, and that its rôle in fostering Austrian commerce and industry in the eighteenth century was therefore limited. None the less it was a step towards a more coherent and centralized system of finance than had previously existed in the Habsburg dominions. Arguing from its success, Starhemberg proposed in 1711 that other banks should be set up in all the provincial capitals. In 1712 a special financial commission drafted a much more radical plan for financial and administrative reform, centred on a 'reform commission' containing representatives both of the Diets and of the common people. The emperor and his advisers, needless to say, rejected this daring initiative. The effective reshaping of Imperial finance was to take place on more conservative lines in the age of Maria Theresa.

European government expenditure from 1689 to 1714 had run at a level never reached in earlier wars. Taking the estimates put forward here with all due reservations, the total was not less than five to six hundred million pounds sterling, of which probably three-quarters was due to war. The capacity of each of the powers to meet its share of this vast bill from revenue varied greatly; none was able to do so completely. In England revenue trebled between 1689 and 1714. In Holland, the backbone of the United Provinces, and in the Austrian dominions, it increased by half. In France it actually decreased. Taxes were extremely complex in detail, but had certain common features. On the whole they relied heavily on consumption duties and fixed levies on houses and landed property; lack of bureaucratic skills and organization precluded effective taxes on incomes. Exemption of the Church and nobility from direct taxes was widespread in France and Austria, but not in England or Holland. The system of farming indirect taxes stood up badly to war stresses in France and Holland; England's abandonment of it in the 1680s was probably one cause of her financial success.

The gap between revenue and expenditure was bridged by borrowing larger in scale and, in England in particular, better devised than any in the previous history of Europe. France and Holland covered a half to a third of their outlay in this way; England about a third; Austria, the poorest, about a tenth. At the end of the wars the combatants were indebted to the extent of five to seven years' revenue, debt service absorbing between a fifth (Austria) and two-thirds (Holland) of net revenue. This put a premium on attempts to reduce indebtedness, and thus pointed the way to Law's Mississippi Scheme and the South Sea Bubble. The indebtedness of the powers was also a factor of some importance in preserving Europe for the generation after 1713 from any major war.

State borrowing varied greatly in cost and efficiency. The main contrast here was between England and France. The former, starting as a virtual newcomer in the field of long-term lending and international finance, established the Bank of England, worked out a viable system of long- and short-term government loans, including a nascent stock exchange, and brought rates of interest on State bond issues down from 10–14 per cent in the 1690s to 5–6 per cent by the early 1700s. In France, by contrast, the monarchy's credit was impaired by frequent, unscrupulous violations of public faith; proposals for a central bank were rejected; and the wars ended with the whole financial machine in such confusion that it never really recovered before 1789. England's achievement was almost matched by that of the United Provinces, which successfully raised vast sums in what was still the world's leading capital market. It did so, however, only at the cost of allowing the country's wealthy financiers, interlocked by business and family ties, virtually to turn the State into a joint stock company whose dividends were distributed amongst them. A tougher taxation policy might, by limiting this process, have accelerated Dutch economic growth during the eighteenth century. In Austria, despite the successful establishment of the Vienna City Bank in 1706, economic backwardness made considerable expansion of State borrowing impracticable, but the financial confusion induced by the war put a high premium on reform in this field, which could and did lead logically to reforms in a whole series of others. It is to be noted that the descending scale of efficiency of the powers' mobilization of public credit corresponds to, and is clearly connected with, that of their military effectiveness.

Government bond issues seem largely to have been subscribed by nationals of the powers concerned, and transfers of long-term capital by loans and subsidies were limited in amount. There was, however, a considerable flow of short-dated funds through Lisbon, London, Paris and, in particular, Amsterdam and Geneva, without which the armies of Marlborough, Villars and Eugene could not have fought. The financial coteries which ran this network were international in character and strongly Huguenot and Jewish in origin, though containing important outside figures like Samuel Bernard, Sir Joseph Herne and Sir Henry Furnese. Religious freedom in England and the United Provinces helped their activities, though it is clear that even in France and Austria the State's financial needs made it temper its official policy of religious uniformity when dealing with the financial classes.

The social and economic consequences of war finance in this period cannot be traced with certainty, owing to the absence of statistics, but certain points may be suggested. Thanks to considerable under-employment of resources in each of the States concerned at the start of the wars, it is unlikely that heavy government borrowing diverted capital to any great extent from existing enterprise. Indeed, it can be argued that government spending may have accelerated economic development, by stimulating investment in industries like iron, textiles and shipbuilding, which were directly responsive to war contracts. The poorer classes were affected by the rise in prices due to taxation and scarcity, but probably secured increased employment thanks to the general wartime increase in economic activity. Minor owners of property, particularly small landowners, seem to have fared worst, squeezed between rising prices and heavy taxes, and generally without access to the social and political circles in which they might have recouped their fortunes. Those who belonged to these circles— the great landowners, the financiers, the large contractors, the professional bureaucrats—were able, owing to their opportunities, not merely to keep their heads above water but in many cases to make princely fortunes. The social conflicts ensuing from this situation in England have long been familiar from the writings of Swift, Addison and Defoe. It is interesting to speculate how far both the situation and its consequences were of European and not merely of English extent, leading, at the expense of the smaller gentry and peasantry, to consolidation of the great landowners, financiers and merchants, and of the state bureaucracies which everywhere in Europe after 1715 were extending their scope and power.

CHAPTER X

THE CONDITION OF FRANCE, 1688–1715

No matter what aspect of the condition of France in these years we consider, it cannot be understood apart from the behaviour of the machinery of state. The present survey may usefully begin, therefore, by summarizing the strong and the weak elements in the monarchical government about the year 1688. Colbert died in September 1683, Louvois in July 1691. The disappearance of these two ministers left a real void. Admittedly the king had taken control of affairs in 1661, but for the first thirty years of his personal rule, in practice, many important decisions, and *a fortiori* most laws and ordinances, had been the work of one or other of his councillors. It was only from 1691, in effect, that Louis XIV became effectively his own first minister. Even then, however, anything affecting war or foreign policy retained a special interest for him; in these two fields his routine labour involved him in every detail, and he had acquired undisputed ability in handling them. Questions of justice, finance and commerce, to which he attended as in duty bound, certainly occupied his mind a great deal less. The organization of power at the centre corresponded with these personal inclinations. The *Conseil d'en haut*, an extremely restricted cabinet, dealt with scarcely more than those 'foreign' affairs of which the king had made a kind of speciality. The other councils had far less effective importance: as a rule, they merely ratified decisions taken elsewhere. Responsibility for home affairs was, on the one hand divided geographically between the four secretaries of state—each, as of old, having a fraction of the kingdom in his department—and, on the other hand, was more or less systematically divided between the various ever-encroaching departments of the Controller-General of Finance. The running of 'home' affairs thus stood to be more strikingly influenced by the disappearance of the two chief ministers than did foreign. Nevertheless, without belittling the rôle they had played, we have above all to take account of the condition in which they had left the complex machine inherited from their predecessors, for it was precisely to this that their successors were going to have to adapt themselves.

French historiography very soon endowed both Colbert and Louvois with a prestige partly compounded of legend. The least controversial fact about them is that the joint effort to which they contributed, each in his own fashion, had by 1688 broadly and decisively attained its principal object. It would be ingenuous indeed to suppose that thenceforward every government order was always and everywhere punctually carried out: but obedience was now far more complete than ever before. From another angle it can be said that the monarchical system of centralization, though it always displayed gaps and imperfections, had taken firm root. What is more, the authority on which it rested was now safe from any conceivable hazard. The significance of this outcome must be defined, however, and not exaggerated. The ultimate consequences that historians and philosophers may be tempted to derive from the actions of Louis XIV's ministers are doubtless far removed from what those ministers most likely intended. To furnish their master with money, thanks to more regular and reliable revenues, and to provide him with armed forces effectively at his disposal—these were concrete and limited aims, achieved by unrelaxing effort but expressed through a series of detailed measures. If the outcome of it all was indeed a kind of 'system', this was simply because there had necessarily to be some co-ordination of the means employed. Had this system been pressed to its logical conclusion, no doubt a 'revolution from above' might well have come of it. But it was not at all to the taste either of the king or of his ministers to thrust forward in any such direction.

By 1688 Frenchmen had gradually become resigned to paying the king every sort of tax. No one any longer expected that he could or should henceforth live of his own. On the contrary, slowly but surely, the principle of taxation was taking shape as an indispensable factor in financing public services. Yet there are many indications to show the survival of the old attitude according to which any imposition was at best an extraordinary expedient, and more often than not plain extortion. The most notable example, occurring at the outset of our period, is a very curious passage in *Les Soupirs de la France esclave*, where the author betrays his shock at the fact that the seigneurs can no longer extend fiscal protection to their dependants—to their tenants in particular—as they had formerly done.[1] This passage strikingly reveals the regressive nature of much of the opposition to the monarchy of Louis XIV. It is of even greater interest as testimony to the efficacy of the administration of the intendants. But it must at once be added that it implies no real spirit of innovation. What Colbert and his collaborators had contrived to bring about was the enforcement of decrees that had been drawn up and promulgated before ever they came to office. By securing in country districts, for example, from those who held farms of privileged persons, payment of direct taxes in a more regular manner than earlier (even if not strictly in proportion to their taxable capacity), the scope of privilege was remarkably well kept in check, because in such cases the tax liability was reflected in the terms of the lease: indeed, since it was generally the better-off countrymen, the *coqs de village*, who farmed seigneurial properties, the extent of this step forward may have been considerable. And yet, to achieve it, no

---

[1] *Les Soupirs de la France esclave qui aspire après la liberté* (Amsterdam, 1689), 2ᵉ *mém.*, p. 27.

modification of existing law had been necessary; it sufficed simply to give effect to long-standing rules. Grouped under the generic description of *taille*, these direct taxes remained essentially the same as in 1661. Thanks to closer and stricter supervision various abuses had been checked, but no direct attack had yet been made on privilege in principle. Again, neither the basis of assessment nor the methods of tax collection had been modified. It was still, of course, a question of taxation apportioned territorially and collectively (*répartition*), not of taxes graded according to individual incomes (*quotité*). Within each *communauté*—a group of townsmen and villagers held collectively responsible for the payment of a round sum fixed for them in advance—taxpayers were surcharged with what was due from those who failed to meet their individual liabilities. Thus the *taille* weighed heavily on the average peasantry—at once the victims of the poor from whom nothing could be required, of the many who were exempt, and of the arbitrary manner of tax assessment. A similar inertia is to be seen in other directions. The tax on salt was notoriously unpopular: yet Colbert's ministry ended without the least reform of the *gabelle* having been introduced. The same negative verdict has to be returned on the subject of the *aides*. Essentially these last were taxes on the distribution of wines and spirits, and it goes without saying, in a country where cultivation of the vine was so astonishingly widespread, that taxes of this kind affected not only merchants and innkeepers but a large section of the rural world as well. Yet here again nothing had been changed. More original, at first sight, was the great minister's work regarding import and export duties. He did indeed bring some order into the chaos of taxes levied here and there by the various agencies; but it could hardly be claimed that he created anything like our modern customs organization. It is true that he entertained the idea of moving all the customs offices to the frontiers of the kingdom, and of subjecting merchandise to a single tariff of import and export duties, but this never got beyond the stage of an idea. The fact is that Colbert had been primarily concerned with pressing short-term needs—to improve the revenue from Crown lands, negotiate more advantageous leases with the tax-farming companies responsible for collecting the indirect taxes, and so on. Little by little, the different *fermes*[1] had been united, although in 1688 the great administrative structure that was to become the *ferme générale* of the eighteenth century had not yet assumed its definitive form.

In reality, the whole effort of reorganization carried out between 1661 and 1688 can be seen to have been limited to improvements of a practical kind, not only in finance but in all the branches of administration. However remarkable the great ordinances of Louis XIV were in themselves, they were scarcely more than codifications summarizing existing laws without adding significantly to them. Whether one examines the Civil Ordinance

[1] Above, p. 300.

of 1667 or the ordinance regulating the administration of the *Eaux et Forêts*, very few provisions will be found that had not been anticipated in earlier legislation. They were now, admittedly, much more rigorously observed. Nevertheless, could it be said of a single minister of the time that he had any clear notion of the sweeping, inevitable changes implicit in the way the State was evolving? French historians have long sought to trace step by step the evolution in the seventeenth century of the *commissaires départis* in charge of *généralités* or provinces. Several features distinguish the intendancy of the age of Colbert and Louvois from that of Richelieu's time: its now regular instead of sporadic character; routine correspondence with the central authority; investigations more and more methodically carried out. But on one essential point there reappears the conservative mentality which acted as a brake on its development. Even on the eve of his death, Colbert was still quarrelling with those intendants who retained permanent assistants (*subdélégués*). The minister was willing enough to let the intendants obtain help from men upon whom they could rely in the sub-districts of their immense jurisdictions, but he would not tolerate the growth of new and specialist functions as a result of such an arrangement.[1] Any intendant who used such help too freely was suspected of idleness. The improvements made in that other great instrument of power, the army, call for similar comment.[2] Here again nearly all the measures taken have their origin in the period of Louis XIII or even earlier. Le Tellier's iron hand in a velvet glove, followed by the more brutal authority exercised by Louvois, had in the end at least made sure that directives were respected. The soldier, better fed and better clothed, came under tighter discipline. Officers more or less gave up cheating over payroll musters. But because command of a company or a regiment was purchased, it remained a kind of personal property, in the same way as legal or financial offices: an officer who drew his men's pay kept accounts in his own fashion, and he continued to answer for their recruitment. Barracks were still few and far between. In peace or war, in quarters or on the move, troops were generally billeted on the local inhabitants. As to the disagreeable consequences of this practice, it is enough to remember how keenly exemption from the obligation of billeting was sought: it was a mercy that contributed not a little to the sale of many a minor office. Ultimately, moreover, the threat of billeting could be used to bring pressure, at need, against the recalcitrant subject.

That in all this king and ministers showed a certain empirical opportunism, rather than true audacity, should cause us no surprise. The majestic bearing, the display of prestige, the judicious inflections of the royal voice—now courteously benevolent, now curt and haughty—these were

---

[1] Circular letter to the intendants of 15 June 1682, in P. Clément, *Lettres, instructions et mémoires de Colbert*, vol. VII (1882), p. 315.
[2] See below, pp. 744 ff.

very often a mask for great prudence, well aware of the real weaknesses of the régime, anxious to avoid a head-on collision with traditional patterns of behaviour, tender in handling vested interests. Failing revolutionary measures, important reforms at least could have been effected had the monarchy commanded the necessary financial means. What is more, some reforms would have paid well in the long run, by enlarging the resources of the treasury far beyond the temporary sacrifices entailed. This is what gives dramatic significance to the years 1661–83 in particular. For a time, Colbert had succeeded up to a point in setting limits to the young king's exacting demands—to his thirst for 'la gloire' even more than to his taste for magnificence—and could thus flatter himself that, in stimulating the country's economic life while lightening the taxpayer's burdens, he was really watching the growth of taxable wealth. But the future had very soon had to be sacrificed to the present. The same fatal logic, of course, was bound to be accentuated by the renewal of hostilities in 1688 and their prolongation through two long wars, in which France was to find herself virtually alone against almost the whole of Europe.

For several decades the general movement of prices had been tending to decline, and the economic life of the country in general to stagnate. Other countries, it is true, had experienced similar phenomena; but in France they persisted beyond the quite marked international recovery of the 1680s.[1] As regards cereals, in particular, prices fell to their minimum levels in 1687 and 1688. The chief landowners, stewards of country estates and big tenant-farmers—whose interests were far from identical with those of the mass of peasants—bemoaned the low return on foodstuffs. But the price increases that followed brought many fresh calamities in their train. In one part of the realm the harvests of 1689, 1690 and 1691 were indifferent or poor; in Limousin a real dearth (*disette*) was already felt in the autumn of 1691, and fear of it was spreading through other provinces. Yet there were marked differences as between one region of France and another at this time. Whilst in one region prices rose excessively, elsewhere they stayed quite low. The royal administration had therefore to face this dilemma: should it forbid certain districts to export corn at the risk of depriving others of precious supplies, or should it grant permission at the risk of letting a surplus area drain itself of its resources? Circumstances made this a hard choice. Because of the war, stocks had been moved towards the frontiers. The number of men under arms had grown to a size which, by the standard of the century, was something quite new; their needs led to the channelling of food supplies and the commandeering of transport to the places where they were concentrated. Accordingly, a large part of State expenditure flowed into these same districts, while

[1] J. Meuvret, 'Les Mouvements des prix de 1661 à 1715 et leurs répercussions', *Journal de la Société de statistique de Paris*, vol. LXXXV (1944), pp. 109–18. Cf. below, ch. XXIII (2).

elsewhere trade languished. The economic geography of France, complex enough in itself, was thus artificially distorted.

In addition, there was an acute monetary problem. The country's natural dependence on foreign supplies of the precious metals made itself felt more cruelly than ever. The efforts of the last thirty years to improve the balance of trade had yielded no more than indifferent results, to say the least. Persecution of the Protestants had ruined, or injured, many activities. It had also led to a large exodus of capital. To all this, from the end of 1688, were added the difficulties of maritime trade arising out of a conflict in which the English and the Dutch were at last allied against France. Finally, the increased weight of taxation made the country's lack of specie more acutely felt. Heavy taxes on the distribution of food and goods slowed down trade and consequently the circulation of money. At the same time direct taxation, in its turn, absorbed most of what cash was left in the country districts. After good coin had found its way to the public chests, it usually finished up by being redistributed at the expense of just those regions, and of those social classes, which had most need of it. It should also be noticed that the scarcity of minted metals of good weight and sound alloy, although an endemic evil, was particularly dangerous in times of food shortage. Normally the inhabitants of the 'plat pays', the mass of countryfolk, bought few products outside their own neighbourhood; such exchanges as were indispensable for currents needs were maintained by dint of various systems of deferred barter and payments in kind.[1] But when it was foodstuffs that had to be procured outside their own neighbourhood, people could no longer dispense with payment in coin. Hence the lack of hard cash became fatally serious when any sizeable deficiency of corn had to be faced. Such a situation occurred more often in the country than in the towns.

Such is the background against which we should recall the dramatic events of 1693 and 1694. They were the cumulative result—as nearly always in such cases—of two very bad harvests in succession, those of 1692 and 1693; but the circumstances outlined above lent them a peculiarly sombre significance. After one critical year (summer 1692 to summer 1693) came a really terrible one (summer 1693 to summer 1694). As regards the effect on population, the decrease observed in the number of births, which fell off considerably from 1693, is today regarded by demographers as equally characteristic of such a crisis as the increase in deaths:[2] but it was this last phenomenon, of course, that struck the imagination of contemporaries most forcibly. Doubtless the sensitivity of seventeenth-century people towards these calamities, to which they were after all no

---

[1] J. Meuvret, 'Circuits d'échanges et travail rural dans la France du XVIIᵉ siècle', *Studi in onore di Armando Sapori* (2 vols. Milan, 1957), vol. II, p. 1127.

[2] J. Ruwet, 'Crises démographiques: problèmes économiques ou crises morales? Le pays de Liège sous l'Ancien Régime', *Population*, vol. IX (1954), p. 451.

strangers, differed from our own. Hardened as they might be to them, however, they could scarcely be left stone cold by the extremity of want. It was in the 1689 edition of La Bruyère's *Caractères* that appeared the often-quoted passage: 'Certain wild animals, male and female, are scattered over the country...they live on black bread, water, and roots; they spare other men the trouble of sowing, tilling the ground, and reaping...and, therefore, deserve not to be in want of that bread they sow themselves.'[1] These words antedate by four or five years the crisis of 1693–4, but they struck men at the time as the most shattering commentary on it. If one sensational detail or another can always be questioned, scepticism hardly survives the entries in the parish registers—not that by any means all the dead are there listed, for destitution drove many country-folk away from their homes and often, on the way to seek help elsewhere, they died unknown on the road or at the gates of places to which they were strangers.

Corn prices remained rather high down to 1700. In the year 1698–9 they even approached the figures for the years of crisis; indeed, fear of a repetition of the catastrophes of 1693 and 1694 again set in motion the usual sequence of measures to meet such a contingency. In fact, the circumstances were very different. War had ended in September 1697. On the other hand, a real famine gripped the Baltic countries. It was the turn of the Amsterdam corn market, usually so stable, to endure some quite abnormal months.[2] The French price increases, by comparison, appear at this juncture simply as reflections of the international situation; local dearths apart, they could have no very serious repercussions. More painful in the long run was the return to low prices in 1700 and their persistence down to 1707. These years saw a renewal of that series of unprofitable sales of which there had been such frequent complaint before 1690. Considering the generally straitened condition of the economy, indeed its partial paralysis, it is certainly not easy to say how far this low price-level is attributable to the factor of poor sales, especially as this was one that powerful interests tended to exaggerate. It is true that the resumption of war in 1701 favoured certain branches of production and certain middlemen, thanks to abnormal State expenditure; but then the State's financial difficulties attained proportions so large that the very management of its expenditure forced it to use means which themselves clogged activity in other spheres. The last great famine crisis of the reign is also the most famous. It was unleashed by a cataclysm not so much French as European, but France was the country that suffered most from it. The 1708 harvest had been very poor; price quotations rose in the autumn. But the decisive event occurred in January 1709. It was a meteorological one. An altogether exceptional degree of frost, sudden in its onset, destroyed all

---

[1] *The Characters of Jean de la Bruyère* (tr. Henri van Lann, 1929), p. 318.
[2] See J. G. van Dillen, *Mensen en Achtergronden* (Groningen, 1964), pp. 193–226.

hope of harvests to follow. At once panic began to spread. Nearly everywhere corn prices reached, or far exceeded, the record heights of spring 1694, and they were followed by the same inexorable chain of consequences. Even the court ate wretched bread. Till the beginning of summer 1710 men lived in anguish. Few harvests in the history of any country have been so momentous as that of the year 1710. Fortunately, it turned out to be satisfactory.

The sharp price-rises attributable to a dearth of corn no more stimulated the economy than the long-term tendency to low prices. Both had broadly the same effect, in fact, paradoxical as this may seem. Nowadays we are fairly well accustomed to regarding low-price phases as periods of economic difficulty, yet apt to forget that an abrupt and steep rise in corn prices used formerly to aggravate a recession: so far from correcting it, such rises converted it into a far-reaching depression. Outside the corn sector prices stagnated and indeed weakened, as trading slowed down. All available stocks were engrossed to deal with the immediate necessity of feeding the population, or from fear of not having enough to do so. Even in Paris, which was relatively well protected, demand and employment were sensitive to these restrictive measures: the accounts of the *Hôpital des Incurables*, for example, show that building activity perceptibly contracted in 1693 and 1694 and that builders' wages declined.[1] In northern France the output of textile fabrics, the staple manufacture of several provinces, fell off considerably; at Tours the silk manufacture was so badly damaged as never to recover, and at Lyons the same thing occurred for a time.[2] In the small provincial centres and humblest villages, craftsmen and labourers went without work just when it cost them far more to live. Those who profited from these crises were few enough by comparison with the number of victims. Stocks of corn were quickly multiplied, but they were scattered and usually very modest in amount; many were accumulated less with a view to lucrative sale than to provide against the risk of total want in the event of a prolongation of the famine. Landowners and their agents were forced to allow loans of corn to the peasants, so that they might both feed themselves and see to the sowing; but everywhere there were reports of fields deserted by their desperate tenants. On all sides, in fact, private and public incomes alike were reduced, and all payments in arrears.

Thus the financial history of France from 1688 to 1715 is a long succession of ever-growing troubles. The men who held the public welfare in their keeping were not incapable of thinking out reforms, and we shall see that in fiscal matters they did at least sketch out what should be done. Working with the fever at its height, however, they had to fall back on a variety of

[1] Paris, Archives de l'Assistance Publique, Fonds des Incurables, pièces comptables.
[2] M. Van Haeck, *Histoire de la sayetterie à Lille* (2 vols. Lille, 1910), vol. II, p. 203; letters of Miromesnil, intendant at Tours, March–April 1697, in A. de Boislisle (ed.), *Correspondance des contrôleurs généraux*, vol. I, no. 1614; letter of the *recteurs de l'aumône générale de Lyon*, 22 Dec. 1693, *ibid.* no. 1259.

makeshifts, often ingenious enough, but useful only in the short run. In this domain of expedients, credit ruled. One major difficulty here was the lack of confidence among those who could ultimately lend to the government and who yet doubted its capacity strictly to honour its undertakings. The only men to risk business dealings with the Crown were those who could hope for, or simply grasp for themselves, some indirect benefit—were it only a sop to vanity—or else, more likely, extract what amounted to a usurious rate of interest by virtue of schemes to which a blind eye had to be turned. As State indebtedness mounted up, bankruptcy came to appear unavoidable.

The Controller-General wrote on 26 August 1709 to the king: 'For four months now not a week has passed without there being some seditious outbreak. Troops have been needed in nearly every province to keep them under control.'[1] Reading these lines and taking note of the number of such disorders, in other years besides 1709, we may well be surprised that the monarchy should have come out of them unscathed. Nevertheless, it is necessary to distinguish between the different kinds of disorder. One category consists of disturbances directly due to the high price of corn. As to these, it has to be said that the sick and dying could hardly be dangerous to authority: if a town resisted invasion by poor wretches from the countryside, it was not from fear of violence, but from terror of the diseases they brought with them. It was really in the biggest centres of population, precisely where there was much less suffering than elsewhere, that popular movements most alarmed the public authorities. In Paris, during the periods of very high prices, the Lieutenant of Police and the officials of the Châtelet were constantly on the alert. Sometimes writings or drawings were seized that were violently provocative. At bottom, however, though incidents were common enough, they were unquestionably spontaneous and short-lived outbursts. In the markets where bread was sold, or at places where it was being given away, mobs dominated by women would become inflamed with sudden rages. In 1709, it even happened that the dauphin's carriage was surrounded by a crowd as he arrived at the Opera. Yet a promise was enough to pacify it: the presence of mind of Marshal Boufflers stopped an affray that looked as though it must end in tragedy, and he was even cheered by the rioters. In the provinces there were innumerable gatherings to prevent the movement of corn. Boats and farm-carts were stopped, and those in charge of them forced to sell their loads; there were cases of local authorities being more or less accomplices to such deeds. But none of this was the result of propaganda, still less of any regular plot. Age-old habits seemed to awaken with the same traditional reflexes. As was said at the time, they were not so much 'émeutes' as 'émotions'.

All in all, the rioting and other unlawful conduct prompted by the

[1] *Ibid.* vol. III, appendice, p. 603.

machinery of taxation and its agents were often more serious. Here the salt tax must be accorded a quite peculiar importance. The highly complex organization for the sale of salt and the collection of the *gabelle* upon it implied different rules and widely varying prices side by side in neighbouring provinces. Virtually tax-free and cheap in one province but in another subject to strict monopoly and vastly more expensive, this article of prime necessity gave rise to abuses, protests, incessant racketeering. As in the past, the mere rumour of the introduction of the *gabelle* was enough to bring the humble and the well-to-do together, as happened at Aubusson in 1704. On a wider scale, thanks to fairly general public sympathy and even connivance, smuggling was rife. The tax-farmers had at their disposal organized *brigades*, permanently at war with the *faux-saulniers*. Yet the audacity of the salt-smugglers increased with the years; they were not deterred even by the fact that arrest meant condemnation to notoriously hard service in the king's galleys. In Champagne as in Normandy, they went about in armed bands of sixty or eighty, with guns and ammunition, under the squire's command. And yet the intendant who supplied this information (in 1706) was careful to add that it carried no political implication whatsoever.

The only disturbances that might have developed into civil war came from an altogether different direction. Since October 1688 the government had been at pains to disarm the new Catholic converts, and in any case it is a fact that the most ardent and energetic Protestants had generally fled. Languedoc, almost alone, retained an indomitable element, in the mountains of the Cévennes. The dauntless faith of the *Camisards*[1] may suffice to explain why so many troops should have been deployed against a mere two thousand guerrillas, and why the diplomatic as well as tactical cunning of Marshal Villars should have been called upon. A further explanation is to be sought in the government's anxiety to subdue a revolt which, though limited to no more than two present-day *départements*, could easily spread further and, worst of all, invite and aid a foreign intervention. On the other hand, the critical phase in the episode of the *Camisards* dates from 1702 to 1704, and so it would seem to have had no vital connection with the subsistence crisis, or even with the latent economic crisis which characterizes the whole period.

In the case of towns rioting against the *gabelle*, a hint that the dragoons were coming would be the beginning of wisdom. To reinforce the shock troops against the *faux-saulniers* the king's own regular companies might be detached. Troops were also detailed to escort convoys of corn. Thus the army was constantly being called upon for the maintenance of civil order. And yet, often enough, it was itself an element of disorder. For this the methods of recruitment were partly to blame. The last attempts, in 1690 and 1693, to obtain from the nobility as a class the military service it

[1] So called from the white shirts worn as a uniform.

owed under feudal law were a complete fiasco, but in 1688 the *milice* had been established.[1] In theory, the drawing of lots in each parish was to settle who were to be these new-style soldiers. It soon happened that those who served were the poor and the good-for-nothings whose families no longer wanted them; well-to-do peasants bought their sons off. The bulk of the army, on the other hand, was still obtained by what amounted to press-gang methods. Theoretically, recruits signed on of their own free will; in practice, the recruiting officers used cunning devices to ensnare simple souls by false promises and convivial drinking; failing all else, they seized hold of whom they could. These manhunts took place even in Paris. Apart from such perfectly normal methods, poverty was the great provider. Given this background, it is not surprising that deserters were numerous and that many a tramp, smuggler or robber had once been a soldier. Yet soldiers who stayed faithfully at their post inspired hardly less fear in the people among whom they lived. If the task of supplying the troops with their bread ration grew ever more crushing, it also became exceedingly hard to issue the pay needed for the rest of their upkeep and discipline. At times they had even to go without boots. During the critical years that all but settled the Spanish Succession War, the correspondence of military headquarters with the *Contrôle Général* repeats the same cry time and again: shortage of corn, shortage of cash.

Towards the end of spring 1693 the Ministers of State, the permanent members of the *Conseil d'en haut*, drew up memoranda on the general situation. In the very first line of his memorandum[2] the duke of Beauvillier affirmed the absolute necessity of peace. He added, however, that no one was more convinced of this than the king himself; and, as the argument developed, the idea was put forward that peace would allow king and ministers to concern themselves with the 'internal' state of the realm. The duke was not in charge of a department of state, though he had long been at the head of the *Conseil Royal des Finances*. As Governor of the Royal Children and (since the death of Louvois) as a Minister of State and First Gentleman of the Royal Bedchamber, his influence rested on his deep piety and complete integrity. His opinions were dominated by his conception of Christian morality. In 1700 he was to be the one man not only to advise, in his anxiety for peace, that the will of Carlos II be rejected, but to remain faithful to the undertakings of the Partition Treaty. At that time he was, with his brother-in-law the duke of Chevreuse (1646–1712), 'at the zenith of the king's confidence and that of Madame de Maintenon'. Madame de Maintenon 'dined regularly once and sometimes twice a week at the private houses of Beauvillier or Chevreuse...

[1] See above, p. 224 and below, pp. 767–8.
[2] Text dated 16 June 1693 in G. Lizerand, *Le Duc de Beauvillier, 1648–1714* (1933), pp. 577–85.

with a bell on the table, so that they need have no servants about them and could talk without constraint'.[1] But about this time, according to Saint-Simon, a newcomer had been introduced into this 'sanctuary'. This was the Abbé de Fénelon (1651–1715), whose 'play of mind' enchanted them all. Chosen by Beauvillier in September 1689 as tutor to the king's three grandsons, Fénelon was going from strength to strength. He was elected member of the Académie Française in March 1693; at the end of 1694 he was to be provided with one of the richest abbeys in the realm; and in 1695 he was to become archbishop of Cambrai, with an income of roughly 100,000 *livres* a year, thanks to a special 'indult' obtained from the pope by the court of Versailles.

The celebrated document known as the 'Letter to Louis XIV' is in Fénelon's hand,[2] and from internal evidence we can date it towards the end of 1693 or beginning of 1694. The vehemence of its tone has often caused surprise: 'All France is but one great hospital, desolate and without maintenance.' Much later Voltaire was to say, with more balanced judgment and greater justice: 'Men were dying of hunger to the sound of Te Deums.' Doubtless the king never set eyes on the text of this letter, but it is not impossible that Madame de Maintenon and Beauvillier, to whom it clearly alludes, knew about it. It praises their goodness of heart, but reproaches them for want of energy in bringing their influence to bear on the king; and it was perhaps chiefly to stir up their zeal that Fénelon put pen to paper. Be that as it may, the justification of his strictures on the king lay entirely in the fact that he spoke as a priest of the Church: 'You love not God.' This was precisely what it was Fénelon's duty as a priest to point out. All the rest, however daring it strikes us, was weak by comparison. His whole policy was simply an extension of his priestly office, the policy of a *directeur de conscience*. What makes for the greatness of his indictment, therefore, is what also sets limits to its value. For Fénelon attributes all the evils of the realm to Louis XIV's personal psychology. Some of those evils are movingly recalled; but the only remedy proposed is the conversion of the king to true religion, and the only practical advice to emerge at all clearly is to make peace at once.

From 1696 to 1699 Fénelon lived through the years of the Quietist storm.[3] In 1699 Rome condemned his apologia, *Les Maximes des Saints*. But he disarmed his adversaries by his submission. After that he was still archbishop of Cambrai and the man who had educated and continued to advise the young duke of Burgundy, the eldest of the royal grandchildren. From the moment that trouble had first threatened, Madame de Maintenon (1635–1719) had taken the side chosen by most of the bishops and consequently by the king himself. In 1697, moreover, her position at court

---

[1] Saint-Simon, *Mémoires* (ed. A. de Boislisle), vol. II, p. 342.
[2] First published 1825, with a facsimile of the handwriting; new edn. (Neuchâtel, 1961), ed. P. Guillemain. [3] See above, pp. 147 ff.

had been consolidated; already the king's lawful wedded wife for probably the last twelve years,[1] from 1697 she was officially recognized by the royal family as queen, although never formally proclaimed. Louis XIV's rather childish anxiety not to be ruled by anybody, least of all by a woman, set limits to what she could do, as did the natural prudence of a former lady-in-waiting. In 1698 she openly abandoned Fénelon and Beauvillier. Nevertheless, she could still be an extremely useful if only an occasional ally for the Beauvillier–Chevreuse–Fénelon trio, whose influence in fact acquired greater weight as the duke of Burgundy grew up. It increased still further when the calamities of the Succession War seemed to be reproducing, in aggravated form, the miseries of the preceding years. During this second period Fénelon could no longer push audacity as far as he had done in his Letter of 1693–4. Yet he remained the passionate champion of peace, ready to conclude it at any price if need be. As opportunity offered, he sketched out for the use of his old pupil a portrait of the ideal monarch. It was a portrait which forcibly challenged comparison with the ruling king. In this manner, from the starting-point of his rôle as tutor, he insinuated his way into politics. His didactic novel, *Les Aventures de Télémaque*, had been printed in 1699 without his authorization, but he had allowed the work to achieve a limited publicity in the form of manuscript copies. Within the artificial setting of Homeric antiquity, Télémaque is unquestionably Louis XIV's grandson, and the wise old man who guides him under the name of Mentor is no more difficult to identify. Criticism of the actual reign is also to be discerned behind the moral commonplaces, although it is couched in very general terms. Another work, the *Examen de conscience sur les devoirs de la royauté*, was to remain unpublished until 1734. It is written in a livelier vein and its counsels are more directly formulated. Beyond condemning certain shocking abuses, however, this 'Examination' is scarcely more realistic or explicit than *Télémaque*.

The death of the *grand dauphin*, in April 1711, appeared to herald the accession of his son, Fénelon's disciple, at no distant date. In November, at Chaulnes, our Mentor set down in writing a summary of his political ideas.[2] This time it really was a question of drafting a programme containing the outlines of State reform. In each diocese the bishop was to preside over a small assembly with the task of allocating the taxes voted for the whole province by 'Etats particuliers', composed of members of the three orders of clergy, nobility, and third estate. The system working in Languedoc would thus have been extended over the whole of France. The taxes were to suffice for all civil and military expenditure. This, of course, presupposed substantial budgetary cuts and the maintenance of peace. Over and above this, for the kingdom as a whole, 'Estates General' were

---

[1] L. Hastier, *Louis XIV et Madame de Maintenon* (1957) discusses the question again, but I do not accept the author's conclusions about the date of the marriage.

[2] Fénelon, *Ecrits et lettres politiques* (ed. C. Urbain, 1920), pp. 97–124.

to meet every three years, with power to prolong their sessions and to take cognizance of almost every department of public affairs. Economically, the principle of 'free trade' was affirmed, and it was specifically noted that merchandise of Dutch or English origin was to be admitted. Such are the features of Fénelon's programme that may be allowed to justify the title of 'precursor' sometimes bestowed upon him. By contrast, it is easy to discover others which serve chiefly to show up his patrician prejudices. The 'Estates General' as conceived by him would have been less representative of the nation as a whole than those which had sat for the last time in 1614. In effect, they were to consist of the bishops, joined in each diocese by a seigneur 'of ancient and high nobility' and an 'important' commoner. Thus the first two orders would have been confined to the most exalted elements in the hierarchy of each: the clergy would have been represented legally by their bishops and by them alone. Again, the real significance of Fénelon's proposal to abolish the sale of offices lies in the preference to be given to nobles over commoners, not merely in military employments but as far as possible in judicial functions also. Formal prohibition of 'misalliances' and restriction of ennoblement to exceptional cases complete the archaic tints that colour these suggestions as a whole. Even so, in comparison with the other great nobles, the archbishop of Cambrai had a mind of uncommon range. Taking up his pen in order to complete Fénelon's text, Chevreuse added a clause providing for the suppression of the intendants in favour of the military governors, whose powers he would have restored. Similarly, a Boulainvillier or a Saint-Simon could devote his learning to reconstructing what he imagined the government of France to have been in centuries gone by.

Totally different in kind were the works of Boisguilbert (1646–1714) and Vauban (1633–1707). Here the real core of the French problem was attacked. As lieutenant of the *bailliage* of Rouen, Pierre le Pesant de Boisguilbert was a law officer of medium rank. A relative of the Corneille family and author in his youth of literary compositions, he lived in a town where the bourgeoisie, by the nature of its economic life, constantly had dealings abroad. The Legendre family, the richest, had very close ties with Holland.[1] Its head, Thomas Legendre, newly converted and ennobled in 1685, had a pastor brother who was a refugee with Basnage de Beauval at Rotterdam. Nor should it be forgotten that the Normandy of trade and manufactures had a firm basis in agriculture: in this country of lush meadows and great stretches of arable, merchants as well as magistrates owned fine estates. Boisguilbert's ideas reflected at once the preoccupations of commercial circles and the interests of landed proprietors. His masterpiece, the *Détail de la France*, was published in 1695. In form the little work is part satire, part prospectus. Like many a *donneur d'avis* of the

---

[1] J. Meuvret, 'Une Famille de grands négociants au XVIIᵉ siècle: les Legendre de Rouen', *Bull. de la Soc. d'hist. mod.* 49ᵉ année (June–July, 1950), pp. 7–9.

sixteenth and seventeenth centuries, Boisguilbert claims to possess a prompt and sovereign cure that will restore the public finances. His satirical verve, which in this book enlivens what was usually a rather clumsy style, combines a sharp eye for certain facts with obvious exaggerations—notably as regards the statistics he plays with. For all that, there is an element of genius in the *Détail*. Nobody before Boisguilbert had so well explained, and nobody has since described in such a concrete way, how an economic crisis develops. Nobody has shown better how the losses suffered by a single social group, through the restriction of its purchasing power, can depress the sales and hence the incomes of other groups, causing each in turn to retrench. 'Defective consumption' is thus at the root of the evil. On the other hand, there is nothing new in this defect. It does not stem from the severe scarcity that the country has just suffered, but goes back to the years 1660–90, during which all foodstuffs were selling at low prices. It is this slump which has been the real cause of the impoverishment of the realm and indeed, because it discouraged cultivation, of the famine itself. In this way Boisguilbert treats some of the topics that he was to take up again some ten years later in his *Traité des Grains*, in which he called for free trade in corn.[1] But in 1695 he inveighs above all else against the fiscal system: indirect taxes interfere with the movement of trade: direct taxes ruin the producer. By the light of his lively and often pertinent criticisms, however, the solutions envisaged by Boisguilbert strike one as weak, his only innovation amounting to a chimney tax. He is clearly reluctant to formulate the question of privileges openly.

Nor was Vauban, at that time, any less reluctant to do so. As early as 1694 he had written a *Projet de capitation* which abundantly illustrates his interest in the question of taxation even at that date, although it stressed the temporary character that an extraordinary imposition like the poll-tax must have, involving as it did the 'honour' of the sovereign. With a less sprightly but a more methodical and disinterested mind than Boisguilbert, the marshal was to mature his great design for tax reform during the following years. His chief merit lay in the care he took to inform himself thoroughly. Not only did his 'wandering life' allow him to observe for himself a great variety of matters; he also set on foot real quantitative as well as qualitative investigations. The questionnaire circulated to the intendants in 1697 by Beauvillier was in line with Vauban's statistical work, and the famous *mémoires* in response to it served him well; but in addition he made use of his own personal research, of which a concrete example is his *Description géographique de l'élection de Vézelay* (1696). On the eve of his death, in 1707, he brought out his *Projet d'une Dixme royale*,[2] in which was proposed a complete reform of the fiscal system. It involved

---

[1] *Traité de la nature, culture, commerce et intérêt des grains*, n.d. This work and the *Détail* were reprinted in E. Daire (ed.) *Economistes financiers du XVIIIe siècle* (1851) pp. 323–71 and 163–247   [2] E. Coornaert's edn. (1933), pp. 274–95, adds the *Description*.

suppressing all existing duties and replacing them, not exactly by a single impost, but by a series of taxes based on as accurate an assessment as possible and levied on each income in exact proportion to its amount. It was no longer a question of some simple expedient, but of definitive reform. The system was technically rather utopian. But the marshal wrote in utter good faith, his care for the public good was transparent, and the whole fiscal problem was treated for the first time by a great servant of the State whose moral authority was beyond question.

Louis Phélypeaux de Pontchartrain, who headed the *Contrôle Général* from 1689 to 1699, held the post in plurality with his position as the secretary of state responsible for both the navy and the royal household. Historical tradition has given us no very clear picture of the man, but his court manners and conversation probably concealed a very shrewd practical wisdom. In a passage intended to sing his praises, Saint-Simon cannot help observing that he 'had enriched himself exceedingly in the positions that he had occupied'.[1] He and his family certainly had close relations with the world of maritime commerce—with shipowners and privateering captains as well as merchants. During his administration, again, the practice of giving courtiers a stake in financial schemes seems to have been somewhat extended, although of course there was nothing new in this and it long outlived Pontchartrain. On becoming Chancellor in 1699, he handed over his secretaryship of state and the naval administration to his son Jérôme, while the *Contrôle Général* fell to Michel Chamillart, who held it along with the war department. Contemporaries agreed that Chamillart was a man of good intentions but a second-rater. Behind him, however, a much stronger personality was already to be perceived. Nicolas Desmarets (1648–1721) was a nephew of the great Colbert, who took him away from school at the age of sixteen to apprentice him to office life: intendant of finances at 29, he was 34 when his uncle died. Nevertheless he did not succeed Colbert. Compromised by a fraudulent issue of 4-sol coins, he was kept away from court for more than twenty years after the discovery of this peculation of 1683. During the whole period of his exile, however, he never ceased to enjoy prestige as an expert, or to be consulted by ministers and businessmen alike. Chamillart obtained permission to use him from the outset of his ministry, and in 1703 Desmarets was again given an official post, as 'director of finance', which in effect made him the principal figure in the department. Five years later the title of Controller-General itself was his. Physically 'a big, well-built man' and 'very hard-headed'[2], he was the last Controller-General of the reign.

Under this direction the administration lived, and managed to make the

---

[1] Saint-Simon, 'Ecrit sur les chanceliers et gardes-des-sceaux' (Paris, Arch. du Ministère des Aff. Etr., Mémoires et Documents, France 200), of which an extract was printed by Boislisle in his edition of Saint-Simon's *Mémoires*, vol. VI, app. 14.
[2] *Ibid.* vol. VII, pp. 129 and 394.

country live, on expedients. Many of them were traditional in character. Nevertheless, two innovations may be taken as signs of things to come. These were taxes of a new kind, the *capitation* (poll-tax) of 1695 and the *dixième* of 1710. Their names remind us of Vauban's projects, but in fact they were net additions to the rest of the fiscal machinery, not substitutes. The edict of January 1695 divided Frenchmen into 22 classes, all members of the same class having to pay the same sum. The sums involved were scaled down from 2,000 *livres* to one. In the text of the edict[1] it was written that no subject of the king should be exempt 'of whatever quality and condition he might be, secular or regular priest, noble, army officer, or any other person whatsoever'. Following almost at once on this statement of principle a large exception was made in favour of the clergy, who were invited to vote a substantial free-will offering in lieu of the tax. But at any rate everyone else figured in the 'Tarif contenant la distribution des classes'. In the first of these classes were to be found, side by side, the dauphin, the princes of the blood royal, the ministers, the *gardes du Trésor*, the *trésoriers de l'extraordinaire des guerres*, and the General Farmers. Thus 'the order of the nobility', as the *Gazette d'Amsterdam* ironically pointed out, 'was confounded with the commoners and some of these last elevated, by the accident of wealth, to the honour of belonging to the first in the land'.[2] Moreover, this summary classification was far from achieving a just proportion between taxation and income: 'It is just as silly to have decreed that lawyers or merchants shall pay the same sum as it would be to require that every lame person must pay the same amount.'[3] But this criticism, however sensible in itself, could not outweigh government anxiety for an immediate yield; and only a classification which accorded with people's outward station in life could provide that with any reasonable facility.

It must be admitted that the poll-tax proved disappointing in practice. Corporate bodies were allowed *abonnements*—that is, payments of an agreed annual sum assessed and levied by themselves—which enabled them to compound cheaply in advance. Remissions of tax in the case of those individuals who were in any case the least heavily burdened further served to falsify the principle, and so lessen the effectiveness, of the tax. From 1695 to 1698, in the *généralité* of Paris, the share paid by the nobility diminished each year, by comparison with the sum paid by those who were subject to the *taille*. The *capitation* was suppressed after Ryswick, but reappeared in 1701 and remained permanent thereafter. On this occasion, however, so far as the main body of taxpayers was concerned, the registers compiled for payment of *taille* were accepted as the basis of assessment, entirely separate registers being prepared for those who paid no *taille*.

---

[1] Boislisle, *Corr. des contrôleurs gén.*, vol. I, app. 10.
[2] Quoted in Saint-Simon, *Mémoires* (ed. Boislisle), vol. II, p. 464.
[3] Boiusgilbert, *Factum de la France* [Rouen, 1706], reprinted in E. Daire (ed.), *Economiste financiers du XVIIIe siècle* (1851), pp. 248–322.

And so it turned out that the capitation of the privileged became lighter, while the burden on everybody else grew heavier. The second great fiscal innovation, the *dixième* of 1710, rested on a totally different basis. Every subject was now invited to make detailed declarations of his whole income, whatever its sources. We are familiar enough with all the objections raised two centuries later to a tax dependent on declarations of this kind: to suppose in 1710 that you could effectively get possession of a tenth of all incomes by this means would have been pure chimera. But doubtless neither Desmarets nor his collaborators had any illusions on that score. In effect, negotiations took place with the privileged classes and they escaped more or less lightly: as for others, the *taille* registers were once again pressed into service. Nevertheless, the partial failure of these two experiments should not obscure their historic importance. In making them, the king had definitively asserted his right to require tax from all his subjects.

Between 1688 and 1715 the royal authority was led to make concessions to various social forces which at other times it would have handled in a less conciliatory fashion.

In the quinquennial Assemblies of the clergy, the members of the 'first order', the archbishops and bishops, enjoyed indisputable preponderance. But the ordinary *dons gratuits* that were regularly voted by these assemblies were getting larger and larger. To these were added further extraordinary *dons gratuits*—4 m. *livres* in 1695, 8 m. in 1711. In return, the archbishops and bishops obtained the support of authority for decisions made at the expense of the lower clergy. To enable country priests to live, an 'appropriate stipend' (*portion congrue*) was assured to them of at least 300 *livres*. Many priests preferred to take this sum entirely in cash, and so be quit of the burden of collecting the few tithes which were traditionally their due but which were poor and uncertain in yield. The royal declaration of 30 June 1690 abolished this freedom of choice. It specified, moreover, that no priest would any longer be exempt from the taxes that the clergy as a body levied on its members. In yet another respect, the episcopacy was able to strengthen its authority over the whole Church in France. The edict 'regulating ecclesiastical jurisdiction' of 11 April 1695 compelled every priest, secular or regular, before he could preach or hear confession, to obtain a licence from his bishop, whose authorization could at any moment be revoked. In December 1698 diocesan bishops received power to order any parish priest, without reason given, to make a three-month retreat in a seminary. The Assembly of 1700 resolved that the 'second order' delegates—that is, the representatives of the majority of the clergy—should have no say in deliberations on doctrine and morals.

By these last measures the episcopacy committed itself to paths that were to bring it into conflict with some powerful currents of opinion. For several reasons, foreign policy among them, Versailles had done its best since 1693 not merely to keep clear of any conflict with Rome, but to associate the pontifical court as far as possible with the king's undertakings.[1] Bossuet's death in 1704 deprived episcopal Gallicanism of its main protagonist, and it also deprived Church and State of a moderating influence in the struggle between Jesuit and Jansenist that was breaking out again. Since theology in Louis XIV's eyes was the province of specialists, moreover, and the pope's authority in dogmatic questions beyond question, the rôle of the temporal power was to make that authority respected: accordingly, to resuscitate doctrines already officially condemned was an act of rebellion. In characterizing the Jansenist Quesnel as 'seditious', the Jesuit Lallemant was adopting precisely the same standpoint. When Rome and Versailles were in agreement, then Catholics had only to obey. But this agreement—given concrete form in the bulls *Vineam Domini* (July 1705) and especially *Unigenitus* (September 1713)— was the occasion for a regrouping of opposition forces of whose strength neither king nor pope seems to have taken a correct measure. From now onwards the strictly theological problem of divine grace—'efficacious' or 'sufficient'—was widely forgotten. And yet the dispersion of the nuns of Port-Royal in 1709, the razing of the convent in 1710, and the exhumation of the mortal remains of the nuns and solitaries in 1711, all this made clear to the Catholic world how brutal was the intervention of the temporal power. The use of *lettres de cachet*—of arbitrary imprisonment orders made out by government—against priests suspected of Jansenism seemed to hand over the Church of France to police rule. The second order of clergy and parliamentary circles alike reacted against this threat. Such clergy were not merely the scores of priests who made up the lower clergy: the second order also included abbots, deans and canons, many of them learned men, often of good middle-class stock, and some of them strongly independent spirits with a legal turn of mind, like Jacques Boileau (brother of the famous writer), who found himself presiding over the Faculty of Theology of the Sorbonne at the moment when *Unigenitus* was published. Nor could the attitude of the majority of the *parlementaires* be much in doubt. The new Jansenism and its cognate Gallicanism were to find their most stubborn and ablest defenders in the Parlements.[2]

The royal power, which had every reason to distrust these formidable corporations and had kept them in check during the first years of the reign, had nevertheless not merely relaxed its attitude towards them but even allowed them to strengthen their position. How had this come about? Multiplication of offices diminished their selling value, both by splitting the profits to be made from their exercise and by upsetting the balance of supply and demand. Here was one serious cause of discontent among the *parlementaires*—the office-holders *par excellence*—and hence the necessity

---

[1] See above, pp. 131–2, 161–2.   [2] See above, pp. 132–4 and vol. VII, pp. 230 ff.

of trying to provide them with compensation. Thus the Breton Parlement, exiled to Vannes ever since the rebellion of 1675, was allowed to return to Rennes under an edict of October 1689 which created one new presidential office and six more counsellorships. Further, as appeals came before a Parlement, subordinate magistrates looked to the *parlementaires* as their natural leaders. This was important because justice and 'police' were intimately connected, so that it seemed natural for magistrates to intervene in all questions bearing on public order, especially in economic regulations during times of crisis: *arrêts de parlement* controlled the corn trade, and the Parlements also held the whip-hand over the *assemblées de police* which grouped together representatives of each local body. The years 1693–4 and 1709–10 provided occasions for giving new life to these old practices. In the big provincial towns far from the court, moreover, in contrast with many gentlemen whom army service had not enriched, these high magistrates maintained their social position with ease. When, as was sometimes the case,[1] they were not of noble origin, the *parlementaires* acquired *noblesse* by the mere fact of holding office. In general, besides the capital invested in their offices, they possessed large fortunes in land, which they often managed with more systematic care than did other nobles. The rich vineyards of the Bordelais and the Côte d'Or were largely in the hands of members of the Bordeaux and Dijon Parlements who themselves supervised their cultivation and cunningly propagated their reputation, for these expert gastronomes were also shrewd businessmen. Frequently, too, the intendants would make the First President of a Parlement their chief collaborator. In Provence, from 1690 to 1704, Pierre Cardin Lebret was simultaneously intendant and First President, as his son (bearing identical names) also became by 1710. The largest jurisdiction, of course, was that of the Parlement of Paris, extending over a third of the kingdom, and the most important cases came before it. The fact that the princes of the blood and the peers of both Church and Realm could take their seats there—and sometimes in fact did so—strengthened the theory that it was affiliated to the ancient *curia regis*. Still less were those precedents forgotten that made of it the guardian of the 'fundamental laws' of the kingdom.

Wherever they had survived, the Provincial Estates had a certain part to play that was not only fiscal but administrative in a wider sense. Here again circumstances lent fresh vigour to old institutions. The intendant Basville, who had won the confidence of the people he administered in Languedoc, took care not to come into open conflict with the Languedoc Estates during the years of crisis; their sessions, which in the past had lasted only a few days, now went on for several weeks, sometimes for more than two months. In Brittany the struggle to maintain and develop an autonomous financial administration, of which the Estates had the

---

[1] J. F. Bluche, *L'Origine des magistrats du Parlement de Paris au XVIIIe siècle* (1956).

mastery, won some unquestionable successes. The Estates also influenced some of the towns. When, in 1692, the office of mayor-perpetual in every town was created by edict, it seemed that whatever was left of the old municipal liberties must be blotted out: in the event, the towns themselves bought back the office thus put up for sale and often it was the Estates which saw to this, so that in effect the municipal magistrates became agents of the provincial administration—a development particularly characteristic of Burgundy.

The financiers, otherwise known as *partisans et traitants*[1] and *gens de finance*, were a highly miscellaneous group. Among those who were office-holders figured *trésoriers* and *receveurs* of all kinds: at the very end of the reign, it was a syndicate of twelve receivers-general that guaranteed the mass of notes which for the time being met the most pressing payments. Alongside, often in association with them, were men who had an interest in the tax-farms and the *munitionnaires*, who supplied food to army and navy after tender of contract. But nearly all these enterprises were backed by the credit of a few substantial men of business. On all alike the administration conferred special advantages and honorific distinctions. Thomas Legendre (1638–1706), for example, came of a long line of merchants who had been prominent in sixteenth-century Rouen: in 1700 he received the title of Inspector-General of Commerce, which was worth an income of 12,000 *livres*, without ceasing to look after his own business and without having any official work or responsibility: on his death the semi-official *Mercure* recalled the fact that he had been ennobled 'in consideration of his scrupulous integrity and of the loans he had advanced on several occasions'.[2] Samuel Bernard (1651–1739), the son of a fairly well-known painter, belonged to a middle-class Parisian family, though one that attended the Protestant Church at Charenton.[3] We do not know how he came to be a banker, but from the 1690s the part he played in public business was one of capital importance and it developed still further during the Succession War. Saint-Simon has a celebrated story of the king personally showing him round his gardens with a view to persuading him to accept the proposals of Desmarets: certainly he was protected in 1709 from his creditors' demands and this 'respite' allowed him to restore his position. The most remarkable case among the *munitionnaires* is that of the Paris family. In 1690 Paris la Masse, hotel-keeper at Moirans in Dauphiné, had a hand in supplying the army of the Alps; his sons assisted in this task and one of them, Paris la Montagne, particularly distinguished himself in 1691 by managing to get together a thousand mules loaded with corn, whose arrival at Grenoble saved the royal troops from starvation.[4] In the

---

[1] Above, p. 301.   [2] *Mercure Galant*, April 1706, p. 226.
[3] *Acte de baptême* of 28 Nov. 1651 (Paris, Bibliothèque de la Soc. hist. du protestantisme français).
[4] Paris, Bibl. de l'Arsenal, MS. no. 4494, 'Discours de Paris la Montagne à ses enfants', pp. 5–6.

following years this family's share in the business of food supply expanded greatly and we find them again, with a vast capital behind them, during the Succession War. Under the Regency, it was they who were to wind up Law's system.[1] Although these examples are exceptional, measured on the scale of success, they are none the less suggestive. In the world to which Legendre, Bernard and the Paris belonged, the latest parvenus mingled indiscriminately with men who had enriched themselves yesterday or the day before and with men of old and established family fortunes.

The case histories of Legendre and Bernard raise a further question: the situation of the 'new converts'. When we look into their activities, it is clear that recourse was had to them because of their Huguenot origin rather than in spite of it. The services expected of them were what they could perform precisely because of their connections with their former co-religionists. The network of their contacts abroad, in countries with which France was often at war, was in fact the foundation of their trading and financial power. Similar cases on a more modest scale are to be found by cross-relating Dutch and French archives. Within families theoretically sundered apart it could happen that personal ties were not severed, even though some members became converts to Catholicism and stayed in the kingdom whilst others took refuge abroad. They were ties of affection, but of mutual advantage too. The royal administration was well aware of them, and tried to profit from them. In 1698 there appeared in the *Gazette d'Amsterdam* the following news item: 'Monsieur Legendre, the well-known Rouen banker, arrived here [Paris] today by order of the Court to make contact with the two commissaries of the Estates-General ...who are here for business reasons.'[2] When the *Conseil de Commerce* was created in 1700, Legendre took part in its labours whenever he liked by virtue of his office of Inspector-General of Commerce. Among the deputies from the chief commercial towns who were summoned to the *Conseil*, to sit with the government commissioners, was Nicolas Le Baillif Mesnager, another Rouen merchant, Catholic by birth but associated on occasions with Legendre. This same Mesnager was one of the negotiators of the Peace of Utrecht: and it is worth remark that the well-known Protestant theologian, Jacques Basnage, a refugee from Rouen, served as a go-between in the conversations preliminary to the treaty. Apart from all this, some of the intendants had drawn attention to the economic consequences of the revocation of the Edict of Nantes and there was always the fear that important men, useful to the State, might leave France. At the time of Ryswick the government had refused to yield to demands from abroad and had met revolts at home by force. Nevertheless it was prepared to reverse policy without too openly proclaiming it. By the declaration of 13 December 1698, and above all by the explanatory

[1] See vol. VII, pp. 223–4.
[2] No. 7, 23 Jan. 1698, 'Correspondance de Paris du 17 janvier'.

circular of the following January, it tolerated non-enforcement of the harshest measures enacted against the Protestants, while refusing at the same time to rescind them. Henceforward the degree of enforcement depended on the local authorities, and on the local opinion with which those authorities had to reckon. In the larger towns and especially Paris, converts, if they could not practise their old religion, could at least cut down their observance of the new to the strict minimum. Of course, scrupulous consciences might be shocked by these compromises and mental reservations; but emigration had sifted out the Protestants of yesterday, and that section of the Huguenot middle class which stayed in France was very far from sharing the state of mind that aroused the Cévenol peasants to revolt.

A witticism attributed to Pontchartrain—that the king had only to create an office for some fool to want to buy it—applied to a great many modest or even trivial offices. Their proliferation was doubtless due to the ease of finding a purchaser among men with a limited amount of capital. Yet it mortgaged the future: though it is true that some offices were suppressed, it was hardly likely that all could be bought back. Hence the formation of an extensive social class consisting of men who were part rentier, part civil servant and yet neither quite one nor the other. In many cases, obviously, the creation of an office was useful only for the 'finance' paid up by the purchaser before taking over his charge: only this immediate advantage can explain such innovations as the twenty 'packers' created in March 1690 for Paris, or again the 'sworn funeral-criers'. Thus the French economy came to be burdened with a mass of public servants whose main activity was simply to register and to tax. Sometimes, however, it did happen that expediency was combined with an effective reform. In October 1691, the creation of the offices of registrars of births, marriages and deaths made it possible to obtain, from the priests who compiled the registers, duplicate certificates intended for safe-keeping by the royal courts. This was no new provision, but hitherto it had been very poorly observed. Henceforward it was well observed, thanks to the registrars, who profited by the sale of franked paper to the parish priests.

And so, as best it could, the newly-born bureaucracy adapted itself to institutions inherited from a period that had not known it, and to the recent growth of new privileges and new monopolies which, under pressure of circumstances, it had been forced to create.

Controllers-general, secretaries of state, counsellors of state and in-tendants nearly all belonged by birth to the class from which came the law and finance officers; but they formed, within that mass of privileged men, a group with its own rather special characteristics. Amongst the nobles, whose ranks they had now joined, often bearing the titles of count or marquis, they figured as some of the richest in lands and seigneuries.

Their brothers and cousins had their substantial share of bishoprics and the more important abbeys. Often the splendour of their lineage went back two or three generations, perhaps even a century or two, though seldom further—little enough, of course, in the eyes of a Salignac de la Mothe (as Fénelon was born) or a Rouvroy de Saint-Simon, proud of their origins in medieval chivalry. On the other hand, the large clan of *officiers de robe* was more or less jealous of these too successful relatives who had grown away from them and who were suspect, also, of defending interests not always the same as those of the robe.

An enormous gulf divided members of the higher clergy, whose benefices might be worth thousands of pounds a year, from the priest in charge of a country parish, cut down to his 'appropriate stipend'. As vast a distance separated the millionaire financier from the wage-earner working for five *sous* a day. Nor, though different, was the gap any narrower between a famous writer, even one of modest means, and a peasant who could not sign his name, who might speak no tongue but Breton or some southern dialect. On the other hand, prelate, financier and poet, nobleman and senior magistrate, could meet in the same *salon*, or within the precinct of some learned society, on a footing of relative equality. The governing classes, despite squabbles over precedence and other mutual jealousies, formed a group of people who mixed socially. No doubt the merely moneyed man was looked down upon in theory. In actual fact he could become somebody by getting himself a title in return for services rendered. Often he could ensure that his descendants climbed several rungs of the social hierarchy simply by marrying off his daughters well. Samuel Bernard was to die a counsellor of state and count of Coubert; a granddaughter of Thomas Legendre was to become duchess of Cossé Brissac. Then again, many of the magistracy and clergy had literary pretensions, trying their hand at genres often far removed from jurisprudence or religious writing. A successful author, even of humble origin, was after all a fellow writer.

These few thousand persons, combining prestige and power and wealth, flattering themselves that they assisted in the progress of the arts, science and letters, were precisely those who set the tone of good society. Hundreds of thousands of folk had their eyes fixed upon them. Craftsmen and tradesmen who gained their livelihood by supplying the various luxuries made up a world in themselves, from cooks and wigmakers to famous painters and architects. In the nation at large, though some severe souls deplored the decadence of beliefs and manners, many individuals were set on winning positions they coveted, for themselves or their children. In this respect, the end of Louis XIV's reign marked the last period of the old monarchy when it was easy to gain certain kinds of social advancement. Below the upper middle class, itself ready to infiltrate high society, there existed a mass of medium and small climbers. These could hope that their own families would one day, by stages, rise to the positions which they saw the most successful attain. Below them, again, the lackey, the rustic polished up a bit, dreamed that some lucky fate would give him a push forward. Besides Lesage's well-known comedy *Turcaret*, many scenes from the plays of Dancourt and Dufresny testify to the cupidity aroused by the occupations opened up by the world of finance. Commoners thought still better of posts they could buy, and thus make the traditional progress up the hierarchy of public office, sometimes to reach the top rungs of the social ladder as well. For the time being, too, a military career offered another path of advancement. Marshals, it is true, tended to come only from a few great families, but the ranks of lieutenant-general or brigadier were not inaccessible to new men: more generally, the officer cadres in the army were pretty well open to men of all vocations during Louis XIV's last wars because of the exceptional needs that had then to be met. No less noteworthy was the case of the Household Guards (*Gardes du Corps*), who to the end of the reign remained what the king had intended them to be from the beginning—at once an élite of experienced soldiers and a nursery of future commanders:[1] and yet these companies, surrounding the king's person as they did and loaded with privileges as they were, have been described as having at this time 'a plebeian character'.[2] In this respect the contrast with what the institution of the *Gardes du Corps* was later to become is very marked indeed.

With cunning and luck, but also by personal merit, one could hope to get on—even to the extent of entering circles sufficiently sure of themselves, sufficiently blasé or intelligent or polite, to pretend to overlook distinctions of birth. Developments of this kind in the France of 1700 were not altogether novel; but they were already beginning to take on a new importance. We may properly link them with the part that was being played by the big towns. Small townships of a few thousand souls were already sleeping behind the ruins of their now pointless city-walls—their economic life declining, their municipal franchises crumbling or vanished. The great ports, on the other hand, were ready to take advantage of the revival of international trade. Towns which were the seats of royal courts —*parlement, cour des comptes, cour des aides*—were already prominent in literary and scientific history. Some of the best brains lived in them. For instance, it was at Dijon that Bernard de la Monnoye (1641–1728), *maître des comptes*, published his popular *Noëls Bourguignons* in 1701; and it was there too, about 1715, that Jean Bouhier (1673–1746), a parliamentary *conseiller* at the age of nineteen and a *président* at thirty, reached the prime of life and the peak of his many-sided intellectual activities.

[1] See below, pp. 780–1 for the military section of the *Maison du Roi* generally.

[2] A. Corvisier, 'Les Généraux de Louis XIV et leur origine sociale' in *XVIIᵉ siècle: Bull. de la Soc. d'études du XVIIᵉ siècle*, nos. 42–3 (1959), pp. 25–53, and 'Les Gardes du Corps de Louis XIV', *ibid.* no. 45 (1959), pp. 265–91.

Montesquieu himself was one of the members of the Bordeaux Parlement from 1711. But the 'town' *par excellence*, the town that La Bruyère could set in antithesis with the court, meant Paris. It was there, by a process that one might describe as the co-optation of like-minded men, in exclusive circles which nevertheless had contacts with one another, that 'le monde' was forming and that already a very modern kind of man, the *mondain*, could be distinguished. He was not unlike the *honnête homme*, as preceding generations had tried to define him, but he bore the stamp of changed habits of mind and manners. Two characteristics at least were now particularly prominent in him: the practice of a wide tolerance and the cult of the art of living.

Long ago Gustave Lanson sought the origins of the eighteenth-century 'philosophical spirit' in the writings of the end of Louis XIV's reign. More recently Paul Hazard carried the idea further and generalized the problem: he saw fit to write of 'la crise de la conscience européenne', born (he thought) around 1680. Today perhaps we should wish to employ terms at once more precise and less positive to describe that age. So far as France is concerned, it is permissible to trace the fundamental changes in men's consciousness back to Descartes and Pascal—those two uniquely strong figures of the preceding age. All the same, with a writer like Fontenelle we are a long way from the all-conquering enthusiasm of the *Discours de la méthode*, or from the tragic confrontation of faith with reason to be found in the *Pensées*. In his *Histoire des Oracles* (1687), Fontenelle—a man of letters acquainted with science and a wit—slipped in an ironical comparison between the oracles of pagan antiquity and the Christian miracles. But he did it in a light tone, free from passion—the tone that he had adopted a few years previously in his *Entretiens sur la pluralité des mondes*. Moreover, it was arguable that the scepticism with which men's minds were thus imbued would not necessarily destroy all Christian belief. The faith of Richard Simon, for example, whose sincerity does not seem open to question, was compatible with a rational exegesis of the Old and New Testaments. Basically far more dangerous was the work of the Protestant Bayle, a refugee in Holland but a refugee who remained profoundly French. Bayle very quickly took sides against Jurieu, in favour of a policy of negotiation with Versailles.[1] In that monument to a remarkable erudition, the *Dictionnaire historique et critique*, his philosophical position sheds light on his practical standpoint. Without denying the value of faith and its efficacy, Bayle makes a clean cut between faith and morality. As early as 1686 he had revealed the direction of thought by invoking 'the light of natural religion—the primal law and source of justice'. The appeal of all these writings to a fairly wide public lay in the fact that they were presented, not as abstract systems, but as discussions about facts. As theology lost ground, so metaphysics commanded less

[1] Cf. above, p. 218.

341

interest. Study the texts and expound them by common sense: that was the prevailing taste. In history as in philosophy, people went straight for the clearest and easiest explanations. The moral of it all was toleration. To this end worked men's weariness with religious quarrels, the influence of the new converts, and the desire of the *mondains* to be left in peace. It seemed as absurd to rebel for one's faith as to harass people in order to coerce their inmost feelings.

This easy-going wisdom often went with a very keen sense of the pleasures that wealth and leisure could bring to a polite and cultivated society. Everywhere a certain amount of reckless gambling went on, and hunting was passionately pursued. But these were a heritage from the past. In polite society the pleasures of conversation were more and more appreciated. From 1698, in her new home at the Hôtel de Nevers, the marquise de Lambert set the pattern for the society hostess of the new century. Education for life in society, which had begun in the days of the *précieuses* and the *femmes savantes*, was now complemented by the style and bearing to which the king accustomed his courtiers. Those curious brutalities and coarse jokes, so common amongst the preceding generation of the *noblesse d'épée*, were slowly disappearing. Men were moving towards the ideal that the Abbé Gedoyn, himself the very type of the worldly cleric, was to try to define in his dissertation of 1718 on 'urbanity'.[1]

Peace was passionately desired. Peace alone would allow the sweetness of life to be tasted to the full. A certain cosmopolitanism, too, was growing up. Thus Holland was so strongly attached to France that even war hardly weakened the links between the two countries. The mass of French publications printed in Holland included the work of authors who lived in France and preferred to avoid troubles with the censorship at home. Interest in the exotic countries of eastern Europe or of Asia was no more than superficial; but travel-books and volumes of foreign literature were multiplying in private libraries. Over against this, the French had the feeling that a cultural rôle could double or even succeed to the political rôle of their country. The quarrel of the Ancients and Moderns, opened by Perrault in 1688, had ended in general acceptance of the fact that the age of Louis XIV had known some very great writers, worthy of the Augustan age. Abroad—where Parisian fashions were partly adopted and French artists employed, where Protestant émigrés found refuge and by their mere presence helped to spread the French language—this conviction seemed to be shared. At home in France, this same conviction was henceforward elevated to the status of a national dogma.

[1] 'De l'urbanité romaine', *Mémoires de l'Académie des Inscriptions*, vol. VI, p. 208.

CHAPTER XI

THE SPANISH EMPIRE UNDER FOREIGN PRESSURES, 1688–1715[1]

IN 1688 a Spanish octogenarian could have remembered when Spain was the first nation of Europe. Although in his youth the royal finances were already in ruinous state, no Spaniard at that time need reasonably have dreaded the future. Yet the octogenarian would have lived his remaining years amid disasters. From 1620 until the Truce of Ratisbon Spain was at war, with one or many nations, for 58 of the 65 years. By 1684 she had lost critical areas in Europe and much that she claimed in the Americas. Her naval reputation had perished at the Dunes and her infantry never recovered from the humiliation of Rocroi. Her economy now lay in ruins. Only her culture retained vestiges of its former vitality. Disillusioned by the success of the Neapolitan Luca Giordano at court, the last great painter of the Madrid school, Claudio Coello, was to die in 1693; but native architecture flourished in the ornate work of the Churriguera family.[2] Except for the works of the Mexican nun-poetess, Sor Juana Inés de la Cruz, who died in 1695, few books of great literary worth were published in Spain during the last decades of the century, when political satire, significantly, was the liveliest manifestation of Spanish ingenuity. From 1685 to 1693 Francisco Bances Candamo wrote subtle political plays for the court, striving to revive the drama which, as he saw, had declined since the death of Calderón in 1681. The greatest of Spanish bibliographers, Nicolás Antonio, died in 1684, but his *Bibliotheca hispana vetus* was not published till 1696. The decadence of the universities was indeed marked, although Spain could still produce, in Omerique, a geometrician whose work impressed Newton, in Cardinal Aguirre a historian and theologian who was praised by Bossuet, and in Manuel Martí a classicist and antiquarian whose international reputation was to survive. If on the whole it is true that Spain stood apart from the scientific and philosophical currents which were stirring across the Pyrenees, a Royal Academy of Medicine was established in Seville before the end of the century and in 1714 it was to be followed by the Royal Spanish Academy, which marks the beginning of a new and more enterprising era of Spanish culture.

The general phenomenon of Spanish 'decadence' may be seen in better perspective when certain subjective factors are kept in mind. The story generally told applies mainly to Castile, but America and Catalonia con-

---

[1] Professor Hussey did not live to complete this chapter himself. The editor is grateful to Messrs Brian Roud and Duncan Moir for advice on certain points.

[2] See vol. v, p. 174.

stituted considerable exceptions. Thus the notorious decline of population was in part only a shift, as men moved from rural areas and the harsh Castilian plateau to cities on the maritime periphery. Much that has been written by Spaniards, moreover, derives from looking back to a Golden Age which never existed, or never existed for long;[1] complaints of the later seventeenth century, in fact, often echo those of the late sixteenth or early seventeenth, for which 'decadence' has never been suggested. Throughout the seventeenth century *arbitristras* (projectors) anatomized their country's *malaise*, but their analyses were more often of symptoms than of basic causes; in general, they advocated only better enforcement of existing regulations and, rather like the Ottoman critics of disorders in Turkey, invited sinners to sin no more. Much of the common picture, again, comes from the letters of foreign diplomats, or from travellers and French memoir-writers (usually anti-Spanish at the start), or from the guesswork of contemporary Spaniards, optimistic or pessimistic according to temperament and motives. Even a good many quantitative details turn out to have originated in the complaints of people decrying their ability to pay taxes, resenting abler competitors, or seeking royal aid; and financial data are vague as to whether they are in units of sound currency or in the debased copper coinage (*vellón*). 'Decadence' has also been inferred from Spanish failure to match the economic growth of northern Europe. Nevertheless, it is impossible to doubt either that the seventeenth century saw a great deterioration in conditions of private life and national strength, or that much of that decline can be understood as an outgrowth of policies followed in the sixteenth century. It is true that Spanish economic policies did not appreciably differ from the mercantilism of parts of Europe which prospered, but there was certainly an overstraining for world empire; the use of American treasure to pay for war and subsidies to foreign courts, instead of to strengthen domestic manufactures and transportation; the subordination of agriculture, under the influence of the privileged *Mesta* (sheepmen's association), to production of wool for export; the exaltation of religion at the expense of economic sanity and intellectual freedom; and the intermarriage of cousins as a method of territorial and dynastic gain. This last was probably not the least important weakness. Children of the seventeenth-century Habsburgs had an extremely high death-rate. Carlos II, who ended the Spanish line, had a mother who was her husband's niece and so first cousin to her son. By 1665, the opening of his long reign, Spain had pretty well exhausted her resources. The succeeding years of bad government accelerated her material and spiritual ruin. The level-headed marquis de Villars, who knew the court by three embassies, remarked after his third:

[1] The Catalan historian, Capmany y Montpalau, already showed a healthy scepticism about this at the end of the eighteenth century. Cf. J. H. Elliott, 'The Decline of Spain', *Past and Present*, vol. xx (1961), pp. 52–73.

Fifteen years ago one still found Ministers of reputation in the Councils: one saw in the King's finances and in the trade of his subjects enough silver to remind one of the riches which the Indies gave them under a better government. But [in 1671–3]... I found few remains of the old Spain, either public or private.[1]

Some of the seventeenth-century writers read as though Spain of the 1680s must have passed its nadir—as though, perhaps, Spaniards had so sunk in hopelessness that they now had no way to go but upwards.

In this they were correct. Governmental inertia during Carlos's later years at least proved beneficial in granting a period of monetary stability, after the cycle of inflation and deflation culminating in the devaluation of silver in 1686. This decree, which was followed by a steady rise in non-agricultural prices down to 1715,[2] may be said to have paved the way for economic recovery under the Bourbons. There was no repetition of the plague after the terrible visitation of 1683–5. But for this setback,[3] it looks as if the population was slowly increasing after the mid-century trough. In 1688 peninsular Spain may have had between six and seven million inhabitants—probably not greatly different from the figure of 1500, though 2 m. less than in 1600.[4] But it was a population notably uprooted from its earlier homes and work, living under stress of new economic patterns without finding adequate employment in its new centres. Poverty and degradation were widespread. Many workers, like many of the controlling figures in trade, finance and the scanty luxury industries, were foreign: French, Genoese and Flemings in large numbers and some from other countries, including English and Dutch. In 1680 Villars estimated the number of French artisans, pedlars and agriculturists at approximately 65,000; they came from all parts of south-western France and often went home after a time.[5] French merchants were particularly prominent in the large foreign colony at Cadiz. The indirect taxes were frequently farmed by Genoese bankers, whose ready cash had supported Spanish troops in Flanders as well as Italy, and some fiscal functionaries were even illegally repatriated Jews, thinly disguised as Christians (conversos), who could be allowed to make money and then squeezed.

---

[1] *Mémoires de la Cour d'Espagne...1678–1682* (London, 1861), p. 4.
[2] See Earl J. Hamilton, *War and Prices in Spain, 1651–1800* (Harvard Econ. Studies, 1947), p. 31.
[3] Attention is drawn to it by H. Kamen, 'The Decline of Castile: the last crisis', *Econ. Hist. Rev.* 2nd ser. vol. xvii (1964–5), pp. 70–4.
[4] All estimates are very uncertain. For a probability of 5–7 m. *ca.* 1500, see R. B. Merriman, *The Rise of the Spanish Empire in the Old World and the New* (New York, 4 vols. 1918–34), vol. ii, p. 93, n. 3. Cf. T. González, *Censo de población de...Castilla en el siglo XVI* (Madrid, 1829); A. Girard, 'Le Chiffre de la population de l'Espagne', *Rev. d'hist. mod.* vol. iii (1928), pp. 420–36, and vol. iv (1929), pp. 3–7; J. R. Almansa, *Población de Galicia, 1500–1945* (Madrid, 1948); J. Vicens Vives, *Historia social y económica de España y América* (Barcelona, 5 vols. 1957), vol. iii, pp. 251–71; J. Nadal and E. Giralt, *La Population catalane de 1553 à 1717* (1960).
[5] Cf. A. Poitrineau, 'Aspects de l'émigration...en Auvergne, *Rev. d'hist. mod. et contemp.* vol. ix (1962), pp. 5 ff.

The greater part of the royal revenues, which came from Castile and America, never reached the treasury, partly because the yield of so many taxes had been assigned for years ahead to meet loans from financiers, above all because of a swollen national debt in the form of *juros* (government annuities). The royal income from the Indies, after meeting the heavy expenses of America and the Philippines, averaged annually between 1 m. and 2 m. *pesos*. Total expenditure was officially assumed as 8 m. *escudos* a year after 1683, of which a half went for inadequate payments on the public debt.[1] Spanish diplomats notoriously lacked money for buying secrets; the servants and even the ladies of the royal household were as likely as the populace to suffer want; the king could not always afford the customary summer visit to Aranjuez. The sale first of fee-earning and finally of salaried offices in both Spain and the Indies, where it now amounted to 'an abdication of control',[2] ultimately impoverished the Crown and burdened the public: no reform was more widely requested than a reduction in the number of office-holders. Chronic penury had also driven the dynasty to sell rights of jurisdiction by creating new *señorios* (seigneuries). Like tax-farms and the sale of offices, such transactions corroded a patrimony and sovereign power already limited by numerous historic franchises. The coveted status of *hidalguía* (nobility), with its resonance of chivalry, was obtainable through financial 'services'.

The Church enjoyed revenues enormously greater than those of the Crown, along with many immunities. Consequently, the priesthood could attract men without a vocation, who merely asked to be fed and housed. Some of the diocesan chapters and religious orders were wealthier than even the great nobles, who indeed, being commonly in debt, were as apt to complain of dire poverty as anyone. Critics fastened on the swollen numbers and worldliness of the clergy, all too often poorly educated and disciplined. It was said in 1683 that the city of Valladolid contained no less than 53 convents, as compared with 17 parishes.[3] There was strong feeling against the Inquisition, not because it burnt an occasional Jew, but because it had power to confiscate property outside the law of the land; it frequently did so, causing indirect damage to third parties. On the other hand, the Jesuits, who could handle remittances of any size to any foreign exchange, were trusted by many merchants (and of necessity by all who did business with the Philippines), since no one expected the Society to go bankrupt. The banking functions of religious institutions might prove a rewarding study, but there was a notably persistent demand in

---

[1] The (silver) *peso* was the Spanish dollar or piastre or piece of eight (i.e. of 8 reals) and had a sterling value at this time varying in Europe between 4s. 6d. and 5s.; it contained 26·5 to 27·2 gr. silver from 1686. The (gold) *escudo* of full weight was equivalent to 16 reals during the three decades preceding the devaluation decree of 26 Nov. 1686, when it would exchange for 20 devalued reals. See Hamilton, *War and Prices*, pp. 24 ff., and below, p. 514.

[2] J. H. Parry, *The Sale of Public Office in the Spanish Indies under the Habsburgs* (Berkeley-Los Angeles, 1953), p. 73.

[3] Kamen, *loc. cit.* p. 70.

these years for credit banks (*montes de piedad*). It is certain that the very large amount of land held in ecclesiastical mortmain constricted the market and discouraged agricultural improvement, as did the spread of *mayorazgo* (entail) among even small lay families

Well over half the little towns and villages of Spain were subject to lay and ecclesiastical *señorios*, the former being perhaps twice as numerous. Contrary to French experience, the seigneurial system had tended to expand in recent times. So far as our limited knowledge of its later history goes, however, it never gave rise to that maximization of manorial claims associated with the French *feudistes*; there were indeed many *señorios*, especially in Castile, which conveyed no title to jurisdiction; and even in the more usual case which mingled landed estate with the profits of justice, a number of ancient monopolies and more especially services had fallen into disuse. Lord and peasant might be on good terms; in fact, the protection of a magnate could attract immigrants when the royal administration was in decay.[1] The *señor* commonly retained possession of woods and pastures, but his property in ploughlands had often been converted into emphyteutic leases. As in Portugal,[2] his income was fed by a miscellaneous array of tolls and taxes, infeudated tithes and monopolies of mill, oven, winepress, inns, etc., to say nothing of levies (*laudemios*) on the sale of land or house and of other survivals of medieval law. The monetary perturbations of the past had discouraged the commutation of rents and of dues (which were much more frequently payable in kind than was now the case in France). The *señor* could normally lay claim to something between a seventh and a twelfth part of his vassals' produce, but in Valencia this could rise to as much as a third. The character of the system varied greatly from one kingdom to another. It had made comparatively slight inroads in Biscay and Guipúzcoa, and the royal domain (*realengo*) was also extensive in Galicia, which was nevertheless 'the classical region of abbey lands',[3] contrasting in both respects with Valencia, a land of lay lords with a bad reputation for extortion. Conditions could also be harsh in Andalusia, where the largest estates were to be found, but they seem to have been much more oppressive round Cordoba than in the Sevillian area; and there were villages in Old Castile where tenants were more exposed to sudden eviction than elsewhere. Until 1716, the lords of Aragon were unique in possessing power of life and death over their dependants, at least in law. The Catalan *señorio* was not by comparison oppressive, although the lay nobility of Catalonia had acquired an unusually large share of the tithes. Nor was seigneurial rule limited to the countryside in Spain, for a great

---

[1] A. Domínguez Ortiz, *La Sociedad española en el siglo XVIII* (Madrid, 1955), p. 327.
[2] Below, pp. 537 ff.
[3] Domínguez Ortiz, p. 335. Paradoxically the proportion of noblemen to the rest of the population was much higher in Biscay and Guipúzcoa than anywhere else: in 1797 these provinces, with Asturias, accounted for more than half the hidalgos in Spain, though it has to be remembered that everyone claimed *hidalguía* in Guipúzcoa (*ibid.* p. 78).

number of small boroughs were run by noblemen and their nominees. In all this rich medley of profit and influence one general characteristic seems to predominate: it has been said that the real economic crime of the nobility was 'a desire not to be bothered with the running of their estates'.[1] More keenly felt at this time, no doubt, was the servility of most of them—and for that matter of clergy and lawyers as well—towards the small and exclusive caste of grandees, the death of whose political ambition supplies a key to much of the confused history of the period with which this chapter is concerned.

In Castile the Crown was absolute at least in theory, the only limitation on the king's authority being the oath, taken at his accession, to maintain the fundamental laws of the kingdom. The various Cortes, of which six survived in 1700, had little political power: in 1700 the Cortes of Castile had not been summoned since 1665; that of Catalonia had last met in 1640, of Valencia in 1645, of Aragon in 1686. On the other hand, the kingdoms of Aragon and Navarre, the principality of Catalonia and the Basque provinces had other representative institutions which were still vigorous. These lands possessed their own entrenched liberties (*fueros*) and a certain control over taxation. Yet it was Castile, more heavily burdened, which dominated national policy with the permanent seats of the king and his councils. When the sovereign was weak there was a dangerous power vacuum, filled by a turmoil of intrigue among grandees and churchmen. During the 1680s, shifting cabals formed about the Queen Mother Mariana of Austria (1634–96) and Queen Marie Louise of Orléans, whose young and not very independent mind was infused with distrust of her mother-in-law before she even reached Madrid in 1679,[2] a rather pathetic prisoner of her chief lady-in-waiting, the designing duchess of Terranova. As *camarera mayor*, the duchess remained even more influential than the royal confessor in the backstairs contest for power and pelf. Amid the gossip, the hurt vanity, the calculated slanders of the court, the succession question was always present. Carlos, four years old at his accession, was never sure of life nor competent to rule. He was amiable, pious, vaguely desirous to govern well; he showed occasional shrewdness in judging people. But he was irresolute and superstitious; he had been dominated by his mother; his education had been superficial. His illnesses suggest epilepsy; he was almost certainly impotent; probably he suffered from severe malnutrition, as he certainly did from chronic indigestion, the extreme deformation of his Habsburg jaw causing him to bolt his food unchewed. He hardly had amusements or interests: he hunted a little, as if from a sense of duty, but mostly wandered gloomy, listless and withdrawn through his palace, except for conscientious

---

[1] R. Carr, in A. Goodwin (ed.), *The European Nobility of the Eighteenth Century* (1953), p. 53. Cf. R. Herr, *The Eighteenth-Century Revolution in Spain* (Princeton, 1958), ch. iv.
[2] Villars, *Mém.* pp. 40 ff. Villars showed sympathy with the queen mother and some disappointment with the queen.

attendance at religious services and brief, restless sessions with his ministers.

Spain's overseas possessions on the whole offer a less gloomy scene.[1] It is true that the Philippines and the newly missionized Marianas (Ladrone Islands) had never been prosperous; it was only from 1696 to *ca.* 1736 that the Philippines, for the first time, were to contribute more than their keep.[2] The Canaries were injured by the success of the Andalusian merchants in restricting their trade with America: they had some legal trade there and more with Europe, but in fact this was often the cover for a foreign contraband trade with the Indies which had grown to enormous dimensions through many devices. For this reason alone the presence of several alien nations in the Antilles created problems. French, English and Portuguese settlements also threatened some mainland frontiers, where the officially supported missions and *presidios* (garrisons), usually sufficient to control local Indians, were to prove inadequate against European invaders and interlopers. Spain's own trade with America had declined: the *flotas* to Vera Cruz—as distinct from the *galeones*, whose principal destination was Cartagena—had once averaged 8,000 tons per annum or more, but now only about 3,000 every two years. Yet the widespread evasion of the Spanish navigation laws implies that such shrinkage could take place without necessarily indicating a decline in American economic activity. American currency was sound and American governments paid their bills. Moreover, while the penetration of *contrabandistas* was accompanied by the terror of *filibusteros* (freebooters), these two scourges were now seen to be mutually inimical, so that by 1688 the French and English governments no longer encouraged the *flibustiers* at Saint-Domingue, the buccaneers at Jamaica. Mixed parties still cruised as pirates, and as privateers in war-time, but Spain's use of privately financed coastguards (*guardacostas*)—adopted by 1674 after years of reluctance to allow this built-in incentive to take prizes—helped stifle the worst dangers from that quarter.

Many Spanish colonial problems were still to figure in European diplomacy and none more so than that of foreign 'asientists'—for long a necessary evil. Never having African territory from which to draw slaves other than Moorish prisoners, Spain had bought them through *asientos*—contracts which in Spanish America meant contracts for a slave-trading monopoly over a short term of years. The Crown would have preferred not to allow any major power to participate, least of all non-Catholic ones, dangerous to its monopoly and to the Faith. Yet Portugal, the traditional supplier, was experiencing difficulties in reviving her own slave trade,[3] while Genoese and Spanish contractors had been unsatisfactory in

---

[1] Cf. vol. vii, ch. xxi (1).
[2] P. Chaunu, *Les Philippines et le Pacifique des Ibériques (XVIe, XVIIe, et XVIIIe siècles)* (1960), pp. 132–3, 261–2. [3] Below, pp. 514–15.

the 1660s and 1670s, having obtained their slaves from the Dutch, Danish or English West Indies. The heart of the problem was that the slave trade necessitated facilities ashore that gave foreigners legal contact with Spanish colonists; and once this took place illicit trade in other wares was harder to prevent. By 1685 Spain had decided that the Dutch were not more dangerous as legal asientists than as hidden suppliers, and Balthasar Coymans, a Dutch merchant domiciled in Cadiz, was allowed a receivership for the *asiento* held by a Spaniard, Nicolás Porcio. Dutch factors were now established in Caribbean ports and Dutch ships proceeded thither until the end of the contract, although from late 1689 Porcio was partially back in control and the Netherlands government was exerting its diplomacy to recover debts claimed by Coymans's heirs.[1] Thus the Asiento was already a factor in the relations between States.

Down to 1688 Spain had lost very little territory in the New World which she had ever tried to settle—chiefly Jamaica and western Hispaniola (Saint-Domingue),—but there were huge tracts of isolated country along her Caribbean coasts where foreign traders, pirates and logwood-cutters did much as they liked. The Dutch at Curaçoa had an interest in the tobacco and cacao production of Venezuela, the trade of whose back-country they tapped from Guiana through their Carib allies. The mahogany, cedar and dyewood forests from the Bay of Campeche to the Mosquito Coast of Nicaragua had long since attracted West Indian buccaneers and North American shippers: here and there, among swampy creeks shielded by the cays or coral reefs, small parties of logwood-cutters formed more or less permanent settlements over which the governors of Jamaica exercised a kind of protectorate. Early in 1680, after sacking Portobello, a party of English adventurers hacked their way across the Isthmus of Darien and inaugurated a new phase of buccaneering in the South Sea. They were too undisciplined to hold together for long, but their example was followed in the succeeding years by others, including some of the French *flibustiers*. Spanish counter-measures, though effective on the whole, could not entirely prevent the loss of isolated ships or attacks on small coastal towns. If this South Sea piracy was less significant than the publicity accorded to it, it nevertheless broke out at a time when the Spanish imperial frontiers were threatened at widely separated points. On 1 January 1680 the Portuguese pushed the southern limits of Brazil as far as the Plate river by establishing Colonia do Sacramento, to divert the trade of Buenos Aires with Chile and Peru. In North America, the Carolina English were already disturbing the northern borders of Florida, while the Canadian French reached the Gulf of Mexico in April 1682.

On 12 February 1689 Queen Marie Louise died. She had intimated to Louis XIV that the king's childlessness was due to his own incapacity, but

[1] G. Scelle, *La Traite négrière aux Indes de Castille* (2 vols. 1906), vol. I, pp. 641–93.

a new queen could still be an influence for one or another claimant to the succession. Pressed hard against his own wishes to choose among possible spouses, Carlos dutifully married Maria Anna of Pfalz-Neuberg, daughter of the elector palatine and sister of the empress, on 15 June. His new queen and the Spaniards soon discovered a violent dislike for each other as the queen's avarice and choice of associates revealed themselves.

Soon after the marriage Spain was involved in the Nine Years War (ch. VII), which must be kept in mind if we are to understand the concentration and exhaustion of national energies which it caused in Spain. In particular, the French invasion of Catalonia in May 1689, though it did not at once penetrate deeply, revived the widespread unrest of 1687 among the peasants, now provoked by their Castilian viceroys in the quartering of troops and the levies of supplies and men. Here the Catalans had the law, in the form of their cherished *fueros*, at least partly on their side; but there was in these years a marked increase of brigandage and other crime in the principality, where it was customary to carry arms.

The prime minister, since 1685, had been Don Manuel Joaquín Alvarez de Toledo y Portugal, count of Oropesa (1642–1707), able and honest by the debased standards then current, 'Austrian' by inclination. The king, kindly treated by Oropesa, supported him, though he cautiously declined the title of *Valido* (favourite), rendered odious by the experience of Nithard and Valenzuela earlier in the reign.[1] He had revalued the currency and suppressed some of the worst taxes, pensions and offices. But the revaluation was severe, the revenue largely pledged to the service of the public debt. Bankrupt merchants and outraged creditors joined extruded officials and pensioners in attacks on Oropesa. When wartime costs and privations also made themselves felt, the queen, the queen mother and the royal confessor lent themselves to a cabal of grandees which forced the ill and irresolute king reluctantly to dismiss Oropesa on 24 June 1691. The queen was now supreme, at least in all that concerned court patronage; Austrian interests were still in the ascendant. Councillors and noblemen continued to plot for influence. Details of their intrigues would often seem more probable in comic opera if one could overlook what issues hung upon them. One truly light touch appeared in the great conflict over the *golilla* or Spanish ruff: 'Austrians' wore it, their opponents favoured the dress of the French court. Prominent among the contestants were the Admiral of Castile,[2] an ambitious Francophil with a good knowledge of Italian affairs, and the more retiring duke of Montalto,

---

[1] Vol. v, pp. 380–1.
[2] Don Juan Enríquez de Cabrera, duke of Medina de Ríoseco, succeeded his father in September 1691 as the last *Almirante de Castilla*; he died in 1705. There are interesting judgments on his character and those of other members of the Council of State in the report of Count Vernone to Turin (1696) in C. Morandi (ed.), *Relazioni di ambasciatori sabaudi, genovesi e veneti, 1693–1713*, vol. I (Bologna, 1935), pp. 33 ff. Cf. *ibid.* pp. 143–8 for a Genoese account of the court in 1693.

whom the king often consulted privately. Carlos, not daring to fall back on a favourite minister, tried fitfully to direct affairs. In 1692, in a moment of independent decision, he brought into the government Manuel Arias, the capable and trustworthy ambassador of the Order of St John, who remained a strong influence until 1704. But for seven years the government was without an effective leader. Ambassadors accredited to Madrid all complained of the difficulty of getting business done and described the Councillors of State in terms of their accessibility or lack of it. Such commands as Carlos issued were communicated to the *Secretaría del Despacho Universal* (General Secretariat), ably and honestly served by Alonso Carnero; it provided a degree of co-ordination between the various departments of government, but there was trouble if the king's orders failed to cohere with those of the Council of State. With the king, the final depository of power, increasingly ill and melancholy, sometimes inaccessible to anyone, the real explanation of how government worked, of how a war was fought and overseas affairs conducted, lies in the conciliar system. Cumbersome and procrastinating it was, but beneath the Councils worked an experienced bureaucracy which at least got some of the routine business done.

A surprising number of reforms, indeed, were instituted even after Oropesa's fall. The continued attack on pensions and extravagant living became a jest, it is true, as people saw widows and orphans deprived of pensions while the duke of Osuna, described by Stanhope (British minister at Madrid 1690–9) as the wealthiest man in Spain, get a new one of 6,000 pesos annually. But other administrative efforts had more effect. A series of decrees in 1691 slashed the number of conciliar and military officials and set up provincial superintendents to consolidate the revenues. On 25 December the *Real y General Junta de Comercio* was revived to consider means of promoting the economy. A decree of December 1692 amplified a law of 1682 which allowed noblemen to participate in trade and industry without derogation. Then and later, also, various groups favoured the creation of chartered companies for trade to the East or West Indies. Both areas, in addition to the Mediterranean, were embraced in a scheme of Flemish origin whose promoters anticipated John Law in undertaking to combine trade with the administration of the national debt, the revival of industries and even the upkeep of naval forces. This project for a General Company of Spanish Trade is said to have been vetoed by the Dutch and by the Biscayan merchants who dominated the *Consulado* of Seville. It was one of many defeats for the elector of Bavaria as governor-general of the Spanish Netherlands.

The creation of Emmanuel, son-in-law of the emperor and nephew-in-law of Carlos II, as hereditary ruler of the Spanish Netherlands had long been under consideration. It had been partially promised at his marriage in 1685 to the Archduchess Maria Antonia of Austria, whose son would be close to the Spanish throne. By May 1691 William III was urging it, for he saw that an hereditary governor with large powers could aid the defence of the Low Countries, overcoming the weaknesses which arose from changing governors every three years and from delays in getting decisions from Madrid. Some of the Council of State deplored the added expense of appointing a prince of the blood and doubted if the elector would return the province if his wife should die. Carlos made the appointment on 12 December 1691, but the elector got neither autonomy nor hereditary title. When Maria Antonia died on 24 December 1692, after bearing the desired heir Joseph Ferdinand, his acts were often interfered with from Spain and he had no assurance of permanence. Nevertheless, till March 1701 he exercised more power in practice than had his predecessors.[1]

From 1692 to 1694 Crown orders had some effect on the defence of the realms. On 16 February 1693 the militia was restored to the system of Philip II, mainly with a view to coastal and frontier defence. The years 1693–4 also saw a strenuous though less sound effort to improve administration and defence by the creation of a *Junta dos Tenientes*, a small committee of the more powerful ministers such as had been advocated by the Imperial ambassador Lobkowitz in 1692, when there were fears even for the safety of the capital. In September 1693 Montalto persuaded the king to divide the country under these three *Tenientes Generales*: Montalto himself to govern Navarre, Aragon, Valencia and Catalonia, while his main rivals, the Constable and the Admiral of Castile, dealt with Galicia and the two Castiles, and with Andalusia and the Canaries, respectively. Their authority overrode that of all the regional tribunals, councils, and captains-general or viceroys, thus violating every tradition and 'liberty' of the various kingdoms. The chief result was confusion; but one of the Junta's orders suspended all pensions for 1694 and exacted a third of all official salaries, together with a 'donation' from everyone according to his status.

Even the best 'reforms', of course, meant less in execution than on paper. In any case, they could not overcome the general misery. Some indeed added to it. Thus the forced contributions and military conscription caused widespread flight from homes; many, perhaps a majority, of those who were drafted soon became vagabond deserters. By 1696 the effort to raise money or pay bills was virtually abandoned. And yet it was in that very year that an effort was made to grasp a fundamental constitutional problem which had nothing directly to do with war. There had been bitter disputes over the Inquisition's abuses of temporal jurisdiction under the two previous kings, but the breakdown of royal authority under Carlos emboldened its tribunals still more. Someone having found

---

[1] The elector made his solemn entry into Brussels on 26 March 1692. See F. van Kalken, *La Fin du régime espagnol aux Pays-Bas, 1693–1713* (Brussels, 1907), ch. I.

the courage to bring charges, Carlos formed a special committee of two men each from the five great Councils, including that of the Indies since that body alleged similar abuses in the colonies. On 21 May 1696 this Junta indicted the Inquisition for having incessantly stretched its powers over civil and criminal cases properly belonging to the ordinary royal courts, and for having evoked from these courts any cases which even remotely concerned its own personnel; its penalties, also, were allegedly without rule or moderation. The Junta proposed limits to the temporal jurisdiction of the Holy Office; when a case had no concern with religion the accused was to benefit from the same rules as prevailed in the ordinary courts. Nothing was done. Yet it is remarkable that with so weak and superstitious a king anyone dared even to advocate such changes.

If exception can be made for the hard lot of the slaves and some of the Indians, and for endemic vagabondage, the misery in Spain had no counterpart overseas. Until 1697 the French navy left Spanish possessions alone and local hostilities were on a small scale, although (as always) the mere fact of war created widespread tension in the Caribbean, where raiding was facile and marginal damage could take years to repair. The supposedly annual convoys to Vera Cruz and Cartagena were not much more irregular than they had been;[1] but inter-island traffic and the like was interrupted and coastal towns made unsafe by corsair raids. Some of the *flibustiers*, who had been looking for the Manila galleon off southern California in 1687–8, moved south in 1690 to plunder the Peruvian coast and a residue was still in the Pacific as late as December 1693. It was first-hand if somewhat fabulous reports of their activities which inspired J.-B. de Gennes, a naval officer, to try South Sea privateering in 1695–6 with a squadron of six vessels armed at La Rochelle, though he turned back at Magellan's Strait. To offset these nuisances, Spain had some successes in the Caribbean against illegal settlers, ejecting 200 men from strategic Crab Island in 1689 and mounting several expeditions against the loggers in Campeche and in the Belize area in 1695–6.

In Hispaniola, French and Spanish settlers had long clashed along an undefined frontier. The scattered French population of the 'Coast of Saint-Domingue' included some 1,500 fighting men, the *flibustiers*, but they much preferred privateering to the discipline of regular war. Lack of supplies and men prevented Governor de Cussy from protecting nascent plantations against Spanish pillage and from attacking his neighbours until the summer of 1690.[2] Then his troops were ambushed, after they had

---

[1] *Flotas* sailed for Vera Cruz in 1688, 1689, 1692, 1695, 1696, 1698, 1699, 1701, 1703, 1706, 1708, 1711, 1712, 1715; the *galeones* in 1690, 1695, and later under French escort (below, p. 372) but much more rarely, according to R. Antuñez y Acevedo, *Memorias históricas sobre la legislacion y gobierno del comercio de los Españoles con sus colonias en las Indias Occidentales* (Madrid, 1797), apendice VII, pp. xxvi–vii and xxxiii.

[2] The population of the eastern or Spanish part of the island was estimated in 1717 at 18,410, including 3,705 combatants, but this may be an exaggeration: D. L. Ropa, 'La

burnt Santiago de los Caballeros on 8–9 July. Next January Spanish land forces, combined with the *Armada de Barlovento* (Windward Squadron) sent by the Mexican viceroy, defeated the French decisively and raided Cap Français on the north coast. In 1695 a joint Anglo-Spanish expedition attacked this settlement. The English were supposedly under Lt-Governor Beeston of Jamaica, who had asked for protection, but the orders were loosely drawn and the commanders ignored him. Captain Robert Wilmot and Colonel Luke Lillingston sailed from England with five frigates and 2,000 soldiers, after a personal interview with William III, who showed his foresight in ordering detailed instructions for the division of plunder.[1] This force joined the *Armada de Barlovento* and 1,600 troops from Mexico and Hispaniola. The project had long been known to the French, but their new governor, the experienced Jean Ducasse, had only 2,000 men and they were dispersed in four small towns, north and south. In May the combined fleet appeared off Cap Français, from which the settlers fled. The fort of Port-Paix, the governor's residence 40 miles to the west, withstood a fortnight's siege, the allies leaving in mid-July with booty valued at £200,000 in addition to 140 captured guns, 1,000 slaves and 900 prisoners: this, the first French foundation in Saint-Domingue, was no more than a score of earthen houses and a wooden church in 1701, when Fr Labat toured the Coast.[2] Both towns were burnt, but the visitors did not follow up their advantage. The English had many sick and the allies distrusted one another, the Spanish governor being warned lest England conquer for herself instead of for Spain; and Wilmot, who was out to make his fortune, treated Lillingston as badly as he did the Spaniards. These two centres of the northern quarter of Saint-Domingue menaced Cuba as the southern quarter did Jamaica, where Ducasse had inflicted losses estimated at £500,000 (including the destruction of 50 sugar mills and the abduction of 1,800 slaves) in 1694. During this war the exploits of the *flibustiers* brought large quantities of Spanish coin to Saint-Domingue, whose rapid growth as a tropical producer dates from these years.[3]

Sickness and dissension also shadowed the French capture of Cartagena in 1697. The attack was planned by a privateering company in which Louis XIV had a share and the French navy contributed ten ships of 36 to 90 guns, with lesser craft, under Baron Jean de Pointis. He was joined

Société coloniale de Santo-Domingo à la veille de l'occupation française', *Rev. française d'hist. d'outre-mer*, vol. XLVI (1959), pp. 162–3. An official census gave Saint-Domingue 8,000 inhabitants, white and black, in 1687: 30 years later they probably outnumbered the population of Santo-Domingo.

[1] N. H. Moses, 'The British Navy and the Caribbean, 1689–1697', *The Mariner's Mirror*, vol. LII (1966), p. 33.

[2] *Nouveau Voyage aux Isles de l'Amérique* (The Hague, 2 vols. 1724), pt. v, ch. v.

[3] Colonization was proceeding most actively on the fertile plain round Léogane on the west coast, where sugar plantations were beginning to challenge the established crops of indigo, cacao and tobacco: G. Debien, 'Aux Origines de quelques plantations des quartiers de Léogane et du Cul-de-Sac, 1680–1715', *Rev. d'hist. et de géog. d'Haiti*, vol. XVIII (1947), pp. 11 ff.

by a thousand *flibustiers* under Ducasse. Each group despised the other. The Cartagena forts and walls were badly armed and manned, however, and after two weeks the governor asked for terms. The French entered on 4 May. Early in June, having gathered huge spoils but suffering great losses by sickness, Pointis sailed. In Saint-Domingue he had agreed that the privateersmen should share equally with the naval crews, without revealing that the shares of the speculators and the king would leave those crews only a trivial percentage. On learning how they had been misled, the *flibustiers* brutally sacked Cartagena again.

The course of Spanish colonial life was little changed by the war, though Mexico City suffered a serious hunger riot in 1692. Contraband trade continued, even with the enemy. Some forts, as in Campeche, were hurriedly finished and the Gulf coasts reconnoitred several times to ward off danger from the French or English. The move into eastern Texas, begun in 1686 in reaction to La Salle, was abandoned in favour of Pensacola Bay (western Florida) in 1693, although for five years no more was done here than on the decision in 1694 to fortify the Orinoco. On the other hand the count of Monclova (viceroy of Peru 1689–1705) usefully continued his predecessor's efforts to fortify the Pacific Coast ports and to strengthen the South Sea Fleet (*Armada del Sur*) with ships built at Guayaquil. There were Indian questions on many frontiers. In southern Chile the Araucanians were persuaded to accept missionaries again in 1692, though this effort was abandoned some eight years afterwards. From 1692 to 1696 Governor Vargas of New Mexico reconquered and resettled the Pueblo Indians who had rebelled there in 1680; and between 1695 and 1697 a joint effort initiated in Guatemala and Yucatan, with royal encouragement, subjected the Lake Peten Indians. Under the indomitable Tyrolese, Fr Eusebio Francisco Kino (1645?–1711), a Jesuit drive, begun shortly before the war in northern Sonora, moved up the Gulf of California into Pimería Alta (Arizona), and in 1697 Fr Juan María de Salvatierra was licensed to move across the Gulf into Lower California: the first mission there, Loreto, was founded in October. In Upper Amazonia, Fr Fritz (1654–1724) established the first mission-stations in 1686–9 among the Omaguas and Jurimaguas, near the Amazon–Napo confluence;[1] but they were wiped out by the advancing Portuguese between 1700 and 1711, in which year the Audiencia at Quito had to refuse funds for the further defence of the Marañon missions, though the Jesuits held on to La Laguna—an earlier foundation, on the lower course of the Rio Guallaga in modern Ecuador. It was to ward off aggression that the Jesuits in these years pioneered a road-river link between the Chiquitos missions in

---

[1] Fritz's map of the Amazon (1691) was the first to contain a roughly 'correct delineation of the main stream of that river and of the mouths of its affluents': G. Edmundson (ed.), *Journal of the Travels and Labours of Father Samuel Fritz in the River of the Amazons between 1686 and 1723* (Hakluyt Society, 1922). Cf. below, p. 531.

eastern Bolivia and Asunción on the Paraguay. When the Spanish government closed the Chiquitos road in 1717, it here sacrificed the defensive system of the mission frontier, which normally it recognized an obligation to support, in favour of lay colonists, in Tucumán and elsewhere, who were resentful of the Jesuit economic empire and of the protecting hand which it threw over Indian labour.[1] Settler competition for water rights in the cattle country of northern Mexico is a further reminder that the missions had powerful enemies among Spaniards, not excepting the secular clergy.

Except for a visit by Barbary corsairs in June 1690, the Canaries might hardly have been at war. The Philippines—always disorderly, with scandalous disputes among the religious orders, the archbishop and the governor-general—were now better off, since a despotic archbishop died about the same time that a good governor-general arrived. He supported a Dominican effort (1693) to expand missionary work into Cambodia and a Jesuit attempt (1697) to evangelize the Palaos (Pelew Islands), resumed without success in 1708–12.

In the Peninsula itself, the impact of the Nine Years War was most directly felt by Catalonia, where there had been fighting every year since 1690 and where the French slowly but steadily pressed forward after going on the defensive in other theatres. Like its successor, this war culminated in a siege of Barcelona, a city with about one-third the population of Madrid,[2] an efficient artisan militia, and by Spanish standards a strong citadel. Barcelona succumbed to Vendôme's army of 26,000 on 10 August 1697. The French evacuated it only on 4 January 1698, after exacting a final tribute. The Catalans, though they had long liked the French and detested Castilian interference, had suffered so heavily during the invasion as to welcome the return of Spanish troops with sincere joy. Loyalty to Carlos mounted when he accepted their objection to a proposed viceroy and sent them, instead, Prince George of Hesse-Darmstadt, a cousin of the queen and an attractive personality, who had latterly distinguished himself in the Catalan war in command of 5,000 Imperial troops. He took the oaths in Barcelona on 9 February. This had great significance for the future.

In essence, the political history of Spain from 1697 to 1701 embroiders the international struggle over the succession (ch. XII). The Imperial, British and French ambassadors took part in Spanish court politics as though engaged in their own. The marquis d'Harcourt proved the most skilful intriguer of them all. In his favour was the fact that the long misery of the war had been suffered under 'Austrian' maladministration, with the result that the idea of a French succession had not been unpopular,

[1] E. M. L. Lobo, *Caminho de Chiquitos ās Missões Guaranis de 1690 a 1718* (S. Paulo, 1960), pp. 51–6.
[2] Cf. below, p. 542, for estimates of the size of some Mediterranean cities.

outside Catalonia, even while the war with France went on. The Austrian faction was headed by Queen Maria Anna herself. It was opposed to the king's longstanding preference for an heir who would be neither Austrian nor French but Bavarian, and to the privately tendered advice of the archbishop of Toledo, Luis Fernández de Portocarrero (1635–1709), underrated by the Savoyard envoy as 'a man of good intentions but of little influence'.[1] In May 1696 the death of the queen mother, who had supported Carlos and the small Bavarian party, removed a principal check upon the queen. It is true that in the following September, while recovering from what had seemed his mortal illness, the king was persuaded by Portocarrero to recognize Prince Joseph Ferdinand of Bavaria (1692–9) as his heir. At the same time he found the courage to recall Oropesa, an enemy of the French party. On both occasions, however, Carlos acted while the queen herself was seriously ill: upon her recovery, a month or so later, Oropesa was again dismissed and the king's will cancelled. In the autumn of 1697 the emperor asked her to procure Oropesa's return in order to have an Austrian supporter in high place. Disliking him as she did, the queen delayed until, on 2 March 1698, Portocarrero, who was now a cardinal and had switched to the French faction, got the royal confessor replaced by one with French sympathies. Thus alarmed, the queen then hastily beseeched the king to recall Oropesa, which he did. But Portocarrero now had his advocate at the ear of the royal conscience. On 9 October, before the court arrived and while the queen had gone to church, Portocarrero, the nuncio and others met with the king, convincing him that the presence of regular troops in Madrid endangered the public peace: those troops were a German cavalry regiment, raised by Hesse-Darmstadt for the Catalan war, and their presence violated a tradition of civilianism, but the real objection was that the queen's party might use them to thwart any pro-French movement. When the queen returned, Carlos proposed that to save the landgrave's face, she suggest that he ask to have the regiment sent to Barcelona. She went into hysterics and the king gave way. But her supporters warned her of her danger if such a scene in future should kill the king, and she made no serious objection when Portocarrero ordered the regiment to Toledo, thus leaving only the three companies of part-time royal guard in Madrid.

Yet the triumph of the French party was still uncertain, for Oropesa had espoused the cause of Joseph Ferdinand. When the king heard of the First Partition Treaty (signed on 11 October), Oropesa persuaded him again to name Joseph Ferdinand as sole heir: and when, on 6 February 1699, the boy died, Oropesa was expected to swing Carlos to the Habsburg Archduke Charles. The answer was given by the Spanish people, or at

---

[1] Relazione del Conte di Vernone, 17 Feb. 1696 (Morandi, vol. I, p. 36). In 1693 (*ibid.* p. 146) the Genoese envoy found Portocarrero affable but boastful: his deeds did not always match his words.

least by the population of Madrid. There public order had virtually ceased to exist. Carlos left his palace to go among the people as little as possible. When he did, 'according to the very gentlemen of his chamber, the washerwomen of the Manzanares and small children ran after him calling him *maricón* [catamite, sex invert]...And the most foul insults were hurled at the queen, without there being a single guard by her coach to punish the infamies'.[1] The diary of Count Harrach, the Imperial ambassador, records that in August 1698 a guitarist sang infamous couplets in the streets against the queen and Oropesa. Disrespect for the 'Austrian' queen had long been undisguised and even before her time rioters had shouted under the palace windows: 'Viva el Rey, muera el mal govierno!'[2] Now famine, bad government, and Carlos's long seclusion through illness had created a really dangerous mood in Madrid. The famine resulted in part from manipulation by the food contractors, possibly with the connivance of municipal officers, and rumours had been spread that Oropesa was the culprit. A small incident on 28 April 1699 set off a riot, an attack on the minister's house and a demonstration before the palace. This was quieted only by the immediate appointment of a new *corregidor*, Francisco Ronquillo of the Portocarrero group, and by promises of other changes. Once more the king sorrowfully exiled Oropesa and others of the anti-French party. Thereafter Portocarrero was supreme.

Events overseas also reflect foreign awareness of Spain's weakness. The sultan of Morocco, who had taken several of the *presidios* in North Africa, kept up attacks on Ceuta, though the fortress held.[3] In the Indies foreigners traded more openly. When the Flemings, under their Bavarian governor-general, revived old projects or originated new ones for entering the trade of the Indies and of Guinea, some of them were seriously considered in Madrid as being less harmful than the interloping of complete foreigners. The Dutch were again everywhere in the Caribbean, often with a Hamburg investment in their cargoes. In the summer of 1698, ominously, the French government chartered a South Sea Company, with a 30-year privilege to trade with Pacific coasts and islands not possessed by another European power. The directors included highly placed naval administrators and financiers, notable among these being Jean Jourdan of Paris, who had just launched a China Company, and Noël Danycan of St Malo. The result was the successful trading expedition of Gouin de Beauchesne in 1698–1701 to Chile and Peru.[4] After the Nine

[1] *Mémoires secrets...extraits de la correspondance du marquis de Louville, gentilhomme de la chambre de Philippe V* (2 vols. 1818), vol. I, p. 72.

[2] 'Long live the King, death to bad government': cf. Villars, *Mém.* p. 154.

[3] Below, p. 554. The Mediterranean shipping of Spain continued to suffer losses to the Barbary privateers, which often hung about the poorly protected coasts.

[4] The complex background of this departure was unravelled by E. W. Dahlgren, *Les Relations commerciales et maritimes entre la France et les côtes de l'Océan Pacifique*, vol. I (1909), pp. 115 ff.

Years War the French also resumed their interest in the Gulf of Mexico. Iberville's Louisiana preparations were known in Spain and the viceroy of Mexico rushed an expedition to Pensacola Bay, to establish the *presidio* of San Carlos de Austria there in November 1698. Two months later Iberville appeared. Spain's friendship being at this juncture important to Louis, Iberville moved on, founding a small fort on Biloxi Bay, west of Pensacola and Mobile.[1]

Meanwhile, the Scots invaded Darien. The 'Darien Company', chartered by the Scots parliament in 1695, had started as a combination of London and Scottish capital, under the leadership of William Paterson. It hoped, under the authority of the kingdom of Scotland, to circumvent the monopoly of the English East India Companies. The storm raised by those interests, however, stopped most English backing and influenced King William, so that Paterson diverted his effort to the Isthmus. In July 1698 five ships sailed with 1,200 men, first to Golden Island in the Bay of Acla, now known as Caledonia Bay (in Spanish, Bay of the Scotsmen). Early in November they founded New Edinburgh on the mainland and began trading and establishing protective relations with the Indians. But William III had no desire to cause gratuitous offence to Spain. On 2 January 1699 he ordered the English colonies to boycott the Scottish colony. The Spaniards, for their part, had quickly prepared an expedition against the settlement and some small-scale fighting occurred in February. Internal jealousies, hunger, sickness, injured trade and news of Spanish movements alarmed the settlers and many deserted; on 20 June 400 survivors left. A relief expedition resettled the colony in August and September, but in February–March 1700 a dozen Spanish ships and over 1,000 men threatened it. After honourable capitulation the Scots sailed away on 11 April.[2]

By now, in Spain, the end was near. The king, nearly bedridden, had suffered medical treatments that might have killed a man of robust constitution, while his mental health was destroyed by an episode of exorcism springing out of the factional pressures and importunities which surrounded him. The Second Partition Treaty infuriated him, and the French partisans ruthlessly assaulted his emotions through clerical admonitions to his conscience.[3] On 2 October he signed a will leaving everything to Philip of Anjou (1683–1746), on condition that the Crowns of France and Spain never be united in one person; a pathetic codicil three days later expressed the wish that his successor accomplish his life-long desire to place his kingdoms under the protection of St Teresa. On 29 October he named a

[1] Below, p. 500.

[2] See G. P. Insh (ed.), *Papers relating to the Ships and Voyages of the Company of Scotland trading to Africa and the Indies, 1696–1707* (Edinburgh, 1924).

[3] Portocarrero, having accused the 'Austrians' of casting spells on the king, obtained a new confessor, Froilan Diaz, who invoked the aid of visionary nuns and was then imprisoned by the Inquisition on a charge of sorcery himself.

Regency Junta composed of the queen as presiding officer (with a limited vote), Portocarrero, Arias, the Inquisitor-General (Balthazar de Mendoza, bishop of Segovia), and three others. On 1 November 1700, a worn old man of thirty-nine, he died.

The will was read, the Imperial ambassador mocked, a courier sent to Louis XIV. Disputes quickly appeared within the Junta, however, and it did little until it heard from Versailles, apart from such precautions as an order on 18 November for the Mexican fleet to remain in the safety of Vera Cruz or Havana harbour until further word. Louis, having decided to accept the will,[1] introduced his grandson by his new style at Versailles on 16 November. He began with equal diligence to prepare Philip for his future status and to direct the Junta in Spain. His first instruction, offering his army and navy for the defence of all the Spanish realms, reached Blécourt, his chargé d'affaires in Madrid, on 21 November. Philip was formally proclaimed there on the 24th. He left Versailles on 4 December and reached Madrid on 18 February 1701, having wisely dismissed nearly all his French retinue at the frontier.

Louis now took over the affairs of Spain, offering advice through Harcourt, the able and experienced ambassador who enjoyed the confidence of the grandees and who was able to impose restraint on his compatriots at Madrid.[2] Before Philip entered Madrid Maria Anna of Neuberg had been removed to Toledo, Oropesa's exile had been confirmed, the Inquisitor-General retired to his seat in Segovia, and a reshuffle begun among officials of uncertain loyalty. Just before or after Philip's arrival, the Regency Junta was replaced by a new cabinet council, the *Junta del Despacho Universal*. The new king being a timid youth of only seventeen years, a continuation of the system of Carlos's last five years, when the king gave his day-to-day orders to the *Secretaría del Despacho Universal* in a private conference, was obviously undesirable. In the new cabinet, therefore, the secretary of the *Despacho* was joined at his meeting with the king each morning by Portocarrero, Arias and (from September 1701) the French ambassador. At the same time, reforms were made in the royal household, now resident in the Buen Retiro palace.

Castilian sentiment had been reasonably favourable. The people as a whole disliked Frenchmen; but the dead king's will was clear, Philip made a good appearance, and his accession laid the ghost of a partition of Spanish possessions. The grandees and perhaps a majority of the higher nobility would have much preferred a Habsburg. They knew the political impotence to which Louis had reduced the older nobility of France. Many feared reprisals on former Austrian partisans, and some already could complain of harassment and deprivation of office by Portocarrero.

[1] Below, p. 397.
[2] A. Baudrillart, *Philippe V et la cour de France, 1700–1715* (2 vols. 1889–90), vol. I, p. 55.

Nevertheless the Castilian nobles expressed approval or kept quiet. The Aragonese realms more clearly preferred the House of Habsburg, but even there opinion was divided; and in any case it is impossible to know how much Aragonese dynastic preferences were influenced by devotion to the ancient privileges and cherished forms.[1]

Barcelona had learnt of Carlos's death on 8 November 1700. Following custom, the administration of justice was suspended and the *Consell de Cent* (Council of One Hundred) met. A fissure at once appeared. Devotion to the Bourbon was found mostly within the Audiencia and among others whose position depended on, or would make them prime targets of, the Crown. Members of the *Corts* and the Barcelona municipality, mostly firm defenders of the *fueros*, judged them safer under a Habsburg. But no responsible people contemplated revolt. Extreme feeling was apparently confined to the peasants, herdsmen and semi-nomadic reapers of Catalonia and Valencia. On 30 November Barcelona received the Junta's demand to celebrate the newly proclaimed king. The city firmly reminded the viceroy that this was against usage until the new king should come personally to take his oath as prince-count; it afterwards complained when the Audiencia recognized Philip's status on 9 January 1701. Late in January Philip replaced Hesse-Darmstadt as viceroy. This was understandable in view of the landgrave's family connections and his leniency towards Catalan protests; but he was popular, and dismissal or appointment by a sovereign who had not yet taken the Catalan oaths was against the liberties. When Philip's decree was read in the *Consell* on 2 February, an angry exchange began. On the 24th, Philip wrote menacingly of the liberties, but promised to come later and comply with the formalities. On the 28th the Council decided to admit the swearing-in under protest, for which there was precedent. The new viceroy, Palma, assumed office on 2 March.

The Spanish nation now had a leader. Even if at this stage control lay ultimately in Versailles, the tug of forces there depended on rival influences from Madrid, some of which counselled caution. Yet it was expected from the start that the young king personally would be a negative factor in policy-making. He was intelligent, gentle, well-meaning, but also volatile, naïve, easily flattered. Deep melancholy and fits of listlessness

[1] Most histories of Spain have been written from the Castilian viewpoint. That of the Aragonese realms has been utilized throughout this chapter. Among recent works are: J. Carrera Pujal, *Historia política y económica de Cataluña* (Barcelona, 4 vols. 1946–7); F. Duran i Canyameres, 'Catalunya sota el govern dels reis absoluts de la Casa de Borbó', *Rev. jurídica de Catalunya*, vol. XL (Barcelona, 1940), pp. 195–231, 283–366; J. Mercader Riba, 'La Ordenación de Cataluña por Felipe V', *Hispania*, vol. XI (Madrid, 1951), pp. 257–366; J. Mercader Riba, *El siglo XVIII. Els capitans generals* (Barcelona, 1957); J. Reglá Campistol, *Els virreis de Cataluyna* (Barcelona, 1956); F. Valls-Taberner and F. Soldevila, *Historia de Cataluña* (Madrid–Barcelona, 2 vols. 1955–7); P. Voltes Bou, *El Archiduque Carlos de Austria, rey de los Catalanes* (Barcelona, 1953), and 'Felipe V y los fueros de la Corona de Aragón', *Rev. de estudios polít.* vol. LV (Madrid, 1955), pp. 97–120; P. Vilar, *La Catalogne dans l'Espagne moderne* (Paris, 3 vols. 1962), vol. I, pp. 638–704.

were soon conspicuous in him, although he later gave proof of a tenacity which was not always the perverse stubbornness of the weak. On any point of his royal status he was as sensitive and opinionated as the haughtiest grandee; he owed no less to his peoples, especially in standing up to his grandfather, as he soon did.

The terrifying problems confronting him in this backward but complicated land, so full of hatreds, had been the subject of French diplomatic correspondence for many years. Most urgent were problems of public order, finance and defence, but two others impressed the French in particular. The first was ecclesiastical: papal intervention in Spanish politics and justice (through the nuncio and his tribunal); papal collection of Spanish revenues; papal control over appointments, dispensations, grants, pardons and the sale of Bulls of Crusade (indulgences). Together with the dispute over the *Pase Regio* (prior royal validation of new papal bulls, briefs and letters), such questions had all concerned the Bourbons as much as the sixteenth-century Spanish Habsburgs. The Inquisition presented a stranger face, shocking in its public burnings to a king who avoided bullfights. Secondly, the untidy constitutional situation was bound to offend the Bourbon absolutist mind. 'Spain' was an assemblage of sovereign jurisdictions, each with its own laws and forms of government, and a differing status for its Crown, bound by a merely personal union under Philip. The question was not so much diversity of laws—there was great diversity in France—as the survival of too many organs of regional resistance to royal control. It is true that the Basque provinces and the kingdom of Navarre, though technically independent, had long been as satisfactorily controlled as if they were part of Castile, and their constitutional status was never attacked; Philip twice (1702, 1704) confirmed Guipúzcoa's liberties, as he did those of Navarre in 1701. Yet Aragon and Valencia still had large control and Catalonia almost full control of taxes, contributions to the Crown, troops and the quartering of 'foreign' troops, and of their own justice; in the filling of public offices and in other respects, Aragonese exclusiveness had gained ground in the time of Carlos II. In Castile itself the French disliked the swollen councils, which fostered delays and permitted evasions of responsibility: to reformers they resembled a complex of strongholds inside which the conservative Castilians could manoeuvre to defeat the royal will.

The proud and sensitive Spaniards would have resented even the most tactful intervention, but few of the new French advisers tried to adapt themselves to Spanish attitudes. They were often to blame for the clumsiness of French policy in these years. Louis XIV—advised by Harcourt, Chamillart and their protectress, Madame de Maintenon—better understood the need to flatter Spanish susceptibilities. In February 1701, for instance, when he sent a French fleet to America under the marquis de Coëtlogon, at Harcourt's suggestion he ordered Coëtlogon to serve under the Spanish commander, Pedro Fernández de Navarrete; later, when he wished Coëtlogon to rank above Navarrete, he added another ten ships and promoted him lieutenant-general so that he could command without offending.

The little that was done in Philip's first months in fact concerned America. Spanish officials had protested against an order of 5 January admitting French warships to American ports, with rights to buy necessary supplies for cash. Louis unblushingly assured Spain that he would severely punish any of his officers who dared trade in her ports, but his ships needed a dispensation to sell 'bagatelles' for necessary supplies, as was done in the French Antilles. This was accepted by the Council of War and a decree of 28 March broke the news to American officials. It made the trade laws unenforceable. Since Spanish officials could hardly search or mount guard on a French warship or privateer, such ships thereafter took enormous amounts of trading goods to America and sold them openly. In 1702 two Malouin ships armed by Danycan reached the Pacific coast, whither at least 150 French ships are believed to have followed before Madrid's repeated protests were backed by a punitive expedition in 1717 —for which it is significant that three French warships, under a French commander, were chartered.[1] In 1707–8 the French government promised to stop these expeditions, but its need of specie to fight the war always got the better of its diplomacy; a more serious ban in 1711 proved as ineffective as earlier ones, though by that time the trade was showing signs of having been overdone commercially. Most of these ships returned, sometimes (from 1708) after crossing the Pacific to China. This South Sea traffic was always prohibited to the French Asiento Company, whose interests it to some extent injured. On 27 August 1701 the French Guinea Company took over for ten years the *asiento* of the Portuguese Cacheo Company, which had obtained a six-year contract in July 1696 against the objections of the Council of the Indies.[2] Frenchmen already had large interests in this Company: in the reorganized French company the kings of France and Spain each held a quarter of the shares. Its contract contained a new provision allowing the use of all Atlantic ports, thus for the first time opening Buenos Aires to legitimate slave imports; and its vessels, which might be French men-of-war, were permitted to discharge their cargoes in French ports. Both points were conceded in face of opposition from the Council of the Indies, although they left ample scope for detailed interpretation, which was not always resolved in the Company's favour. In fact, only three of Louis's major objectives in the Indies were wholly frustrated: a French Pensacola, a boundary in Hispaniola,

---

[1] E. W. Dahlgren, 'Voyages français à destination de la Mer du Sud avant Bougainville', *Nouvelles Archives des Missions Scientifiques*, vol. xiv (1907), pp. 423–568. A full account is given in Dahlgren's *Relations commerciales et maritimes*: for a convenient summary, cf. C. Dunmore, *French Explorers in the Pacific*, vol. i (1965), pp. 7–25.

[2] Below, p. 515.

and a legal share in the American convoy system.[1] As early as 23 March 1701 he claimed that France must take over Pensacola, at least temporarily, to keep the English out; in July he emphasized Spain's inability to defend it. The Spanish councils admitted the danger, but replied with queries about French rights in Cayenne. Early in 1702 Louis fortified Mobile Bay, between Biloxi and Pensacola, as the best that he could do, Spain merely protesting. He was no more successful in regard to Hispaniola and the convoys, despite years of negotiation and occasional permits for individual ships.

By June 1701, as the threat of a European war drew nearer, Louis's letters and envoys were already using imperatives. He began dealing direct with the marquis of Bedmar, the new governor-general of the Netherlands, to the exclusion of the Council of Flanders, which he caused to be suppressed in 1702. He also forced Madrid reluctantly to sign a treaty of alliance with Portugal on 18 June 1701, at the price of surrendering Spanish claims north of the Plate.[2] Again, it was at Louis's wish that the *ducs et pairs* of France were established on an equal footing in Spain with the grandees. The fury of the latter did not prevent them from soliciting Versailles for favours, as Louis insisted on reviewing nominations to all the more important positions in Church and State. He was not indeed responsible for all the Frenchmen who flooded Madrid in search of jobs, but he interposed so often in cases which did interest him that he must accept blame for those which did not: according to the marquis de Louville, Philip's personal confidant and the nominee of Beauvillier, the first good impression made by the French owed much to the fact that they were few in numbers and restrained their tongues.[3] Harcourt's illness removed his influence; he returned to France in November. Above all, on 22 June Louis chose the strong-minded financier Jean Orry (1652–1719), rather than Desmarets, as the adviser for whom Portocarrero and Louville had asked. The cardinal misled the French about Spanish pliability, and at Versailles both Torcy and Beauvillier urged an energetic forward policy under the impetus of the impatient Louville, whose letters abounded in contempt for the Castilians.[4]

Orry's urgent task was to prepare a memorandum showing how the

[1] In order to protect French merchants at Seville against the bad faith of members of the *Consulado* who covered French-owned cargo, Colbert had made a strong effort in 1680–2 to obtain the explicit right to ship it under French names on board the *flotas*, using the Spaniards simply as factors who could then be prosecuted for malversations. The Spanish government, which habitually requisitioned the returns of silver, realized that juridical recognition of foreign merchants in the Indies trade would enable their governments to claim damages on their behalf. The financial penalization of French merchants and alleged breaches of privilege gave rise to many incidents after 1667 and led to a strong French naval demonstration at Cadiz in 1686. See A. Girard, *Le Commerce français à Séville et à Cadix au temps des Habsbourg* (1932), chs. vi–vii.

[2] Below, p. 525.   [3] *Mém. secrets*, vol. I, p. iii.

[4] Baudrillart, vol. I, pp. 82, 131. Cf. *ibid.* p. 90, for Torcy's proposal that Spain should cede the Netherlands in recompense for French services.

royal revenues were to be improved, but without proposing anything to Spanish ministers until Louis had approved it. His report was ready by the end of 1702. His proposals amounted to nothing less than the total introduction of French administrative methods. He maintained that the chief obstacle to effective government was the conciliar system itself: the councils, while remaining the principal instruments of royal policy, had been taken over by the grandees under Carlos II and were a positive hindrance to reform. Orry judged a direct assault on their powers too dangerous for the new dynasty, but advised a large increase in their membership. This would permit the introduction of new officials loyal to the king and yet serve as a screen behind which other desirable changes could be made. At the same time, the councils should be replaced as the main executive organ by creating new ministers patterned on the French secretaries of state, within the framework of the existing *Secretaría del Despacho Universal*, to which Louis XIV strongly advised his grandson to reserve major policy decisions. This was indeed to be the growing-point of the later Bourbon administration, although for the moment Orry could only try to lubricate the existing machinery. More immediately he opened proceedings to recover for the Crown thousands of leases and other property rights alienated or stolen over the years. Carlos had ordered such proceedings in 1674 and 1695, without result. In 1707 Philip created a *Junta de Incorporación* which lasted for a decade, although it did not venture to touch the really difficult question of the abolition of *señorios*.[1] He also reorganized the tax-farms and in 1706 increased the yield of the tobacco farm fivefold. Salt and stamp duties were raised, as were those on the export of wool. The Castilian excise (the hated *millones* that Olivares had wanted to abolish)[2] was doubled and large sums extracted from *donativos* (voluntary only in form, but related to taxpaying capacity) or saved by the suspension of annuity payments (*juros*). Inevitably there was much recourse to old expedients, like the sale of titles and American offices, and as in France there were gross inequities built into the incidence of taxation. Yet in a few years, with her finances in better trim, Spain had a real army—organized, uniformed, armed and trained on the French model.

Little was left in 1700 of the crack Spanish regiments, in spite of the soldierly qualities of Andalusians, Estremadurans, Galicians and others. The best of the infantry, withdrawn from Flanders, fought gallantly and suffered heavy losses in the effort to recover Gibraltar in 1704–5. The principal weaknesses resulted from arrears of pay and lack of exercise, but also from the distribution of commissions by favour to officers not always humble enough to serve the necessary apprenticeship. In a country where social prestige counted so much, military service had fallen into low esteem.

[1] Domínguez Ortiz, p. 339.
[2] J. H. Elliott, *Imperial Spain, 1469–1716* (1963), pp. 323–4. This book, though slight on the period after 1665, offers a thorough treatment of fiscal questions earlier.

Philip succeeded in remedying much of this, though he could not produce inspiring officers nor bring his infantry up to the standard of his well-officered and aggressive cavalry, which made a stronger appeal to the hidalgos. His fundamental innovation was contained in the decree of 8 November 1704, which rendered military service obligatory on all males of 20–50 years, while permitting a long list of exemptions, from schoolmasters and the larger peasants to notaries and certain members of the Inquisition; noblemen were not included because they were expected to serve 'con armas y caballos' in the traditional manner. This was the foundation of the later Bourbon army, however disappointing in the short run.[1] As late as 1711 a Savoyard critic[2] noted a certain rawness among the infantry, which then numbered 116 battalions, rather less than a quarter being of foreign extraction; he remarked, too, on the wasteful annual replacement of about half the excellent Andalusian horses, numbering about 20,000 for cavalrymen and dragoons. Philip also financed a household guard with aid from the French Asiento Company, which was in fact expected to meet a good many miscellaneous expenses of the royal household, including pensions to the French ministers and advisers.[3] Even in 1706, when the Company was unable to meet its obligations to the Spanish treasury without having itself to borrow, it was unable to resist pressure from the French government, as in previous years, to send cash for the pay of Philip's troops.

It was Louis who decided, for diplomatic reasons, that Philip should marry Maria Luisa of Savoy, sister of the duchess of Burgundy and then aged 13. She very soon displayed a precocious tact, courage and decisiveness. Hoping to detach her from the influence of her shifty father, Victor Amadeus, and of Portocarrero and the Spanish grandees, Louis chose as her *camarera mayor* the elderly Anne-Marie de la Trémoille, princess des Ursins (1635?–1722). The princess, perhaps the ablest woman in European public life, with a long experience of politics in Rome,[4] soon gained the queen's affections and later those of Philip. She did her best to introduce a little gaiety into the dull monotony of the Spanish court: there were French plays and in 1703 the first visit to Madrid of the Italian opera, inexpensive 'adjustments' to the comfort of the royal apartments and improvements in the garden of the Buen Retiro. Like the queen's, however, her interests were entirely political. The two women supplied the firmness and vitality which Philip lacked. Above all, though neither had much use for the stiff Spanish etiquette, they were loyal to Spain. The princess desired to serve French interests, but never at the expense of Spanish—as she saw them.

---

[1] Domínguez Ortiz, pp. 371–3.
[2] Marchese di Trivié, in Morandi, vol. I, pp. 73–5.   [3] Scelle, vol. II, pp. 428 ff.
[4] Her second husband had been Prince Flavio Orsini, duke of Bracciano, and she probably had some influence, through Portocarrero, on the Spanish succession: A. Geffroy (ed.), *Lettres inédites de la princesse des Ursins* (1859), pp. xxi ff.

Because of his long delay in visiting them, the Aragonese kingdoms had begun to suspect that Philip had no intention of observing their customs. The Catalans were particularly alarmed, for Philip, having announced his departure for 16 August 1701, had convoked the *Corts* for the 9th: he could not lawfully do this before taking the oaths in person as count of Barcelona, nor could the *Corts* function unless its prince was there to open its session. The Catalans therefore prepared for his reception, but put off their *Corts*. Philip had probably been badly informed rather than badly intentioned. He took the oaths in Saragossa on 17 September, but postponed the Aragonese Cortes until his return. On the road to Barcelona and after arriving there on 2 October he observed all the customs. He was now the legal ruler. These transactions took place against the background of a Neapolitan conspiracy. Philip sent troops, but other action had to wait till he had satisfied the *Corts*. After long and angry exchanges he agreed to nearly everything they asked. In particular, he abandoned his claim to quarter troops upon them. He also granted titles and gave Barcelona a free-port sector, with the right to send two ships a year to America 'so long as that may not injure the rights of the city of Seville'. Barcelona then voted him 6 m reals payable over six years.

Philip turned to Naples. Since the abdication of Charles V no Spanish king had visited the kingdom of Naples. Spaniards were reluctant to allow their sovereign out of the Peninsula, but Philip wished to deal personally with the restlessness in Naples, whose distressed and impressionable people had responded to the appeal of the prince of Macchia and his fellow conspirators in the riots of September 1701. Their revolt had been hatched in Rome with the full knowledge of Vienna, and Austrian sympathies remained strong in Naples, which was to welcome the arrival of an Imperial army in 1707. While Philip was there, a second conspiracy was discovered and this aimed at his life.[1] To his journey, in the first place, there were strong objections at Versailles as well as Madrid. Louville went to Versailles to overcome Harcourt's opposition, and Louis finally agreed on condition that Philip left without the queen. He sailed on 8 April with a French fleet. It has been suggested that his distrust of the French government dates from this stormy episode.[2]

Maria Luisa, new Lieutenant of the Realm, proceeded to Saragossa where on 27 April, having sworn to uphold the laws and liberties, she opened the Aragonese Cortes. She found that body as exigent as the

---

[1] P. Voltes Bou, 'Aportaciones a la historia de Cerdaña y Nápoles durante el dominio del Archduque Don Carlos de Austria', *Estudios de Historia Moderna*, vol. I (1951), p. 94. The prince of Macchia was only the figurehead of a genuine reforming movement among a section of the aristocracy, which desired a resident ruler and the confinement of public offices and ecclesiastical benefices to Neapolitans, as well as the suppression of the Inquisition and freer trade with other countries. For a fresh assessment of this radical programme and its background see R. Colapietra, *Vita pubblica e classi politiche del viceregno napoletano, 1656–1734* (Rome, 1961), esp. ch. iii.

[2] G. Lizerand, *Le Duc de Beauvillier*, p. 229.

Catalan had been. Discussions were still in train when she received her husband's orders to press on to Madrid, where ill-feeling had intensified. She therefore prorogued the Cortes for two years, though not before it had voted 100,000 *pesos*. She was personally satisfied, but the French were shocked at the thought of discussing grievances before voting subsidies. The Aragonese Cortes never met again. Maria Luisa reached Madrid on 30 June 1702, characteristically forbidding a formal welcome. She soon won the hearts of the Madrileños by her simple friendliness—for example, by personally reading her husband's dispatches to the crowd from a palace balcony. She was unable, it is true, to overcome popular hatred of Portocarrero, especially of his truckling to France, or discontent among the grandees. Almost alone, however, she rallied Castile against the Anglo-Dutch attack on Cadiz in July, which came at a time when troops and money had been diverted from Andalusia to Naples. This was the first serious display of Spanish national feeling under Bourbon rule.[1]

The Succession War (ch. XIII) dominated a decade of Spain's domestic history and left upon it the scars of a civil war. But operations in the Peninsula were inconsiderable before mid-1704. Philip returned from Italy in January 1703, after visiting the Milanese war-front. On the other hand, the complaints and passive resistance of the Spanish nobles and bureaucracy multiplied and hardened. Resentment of French manners and pressures was sharpened by the tactless energy of Louville, who was also on bad terms with the Camarera. Nor was Louis fortunate in his choice of ambassadors. Seeking to use their seat in the *Despacho* as virtual prime ministers, they clashed with the rival power of Orry and his patroness, Madame des Ursins, who in 1703 developed a major quarrel with the overbearing Cardinal d'Estrées and got rid of Louville. Estrées was duly replaced by his nephew, but he too showed less deference to the princess than she had hoped. Tired of these scandalous disputes between the French at Madrid and provoked by the conduct of Maria Luisa's father,[2] Louis XIV recalled the princess in March 1704 and Orry six months later. Spain's now desperate need of French military aid helped Louis to have his way, but Maria Luisa remained inconsolable. Marshal Tessé, who had taken over the command of the Spanish army from the duke of Berwick after the latter's breach with the queen in November, humanely intervened on her behalf, while the princess received powerful support at Versailles from Madame de Maintenon.[3] In April 1705 Louis finally gave in, summoning the princess to Versailles for fresh instructions: it was agreed that in future she use her own discretion in the choice of Spanish ministers and disregard recommendations from the French court unless

---

[1] See N. Rodolico, 'Alcuni documenti sulla Regina di Spagna, Maria Luisa Gabriella di Savoia', *Estudios de Hist. Mod.* vol. I, pp. 33–46.

[2] Victor Amadeus joined the Allies in November 1703 (below, p. 417).

[3] Their friendship went back to youth but was to come under strain from 1708, when Madame de Maintenon wanted peace at any price (Baudrillart, vol. I, pp. 378–82).

they came from Louis personally. Seeing how he distrusted female influence on government, this was a remarkable tribute to her statesmanship. In August she was back in Madrid. Now not only Orry, who had returned in May, but also Michel Amelot, the cool and resourceful new ambassador (who stayed till 1709), were subordinated to her. Portocarrero had been retired to his seat at Toledo in March. New men, satisfactory to the princess, entered the government. On 11 July 1705 a second secretaryship of the *Despacho*, with responsibility for war and finance, had been created and was filled by José de Grimaldo—a first step in implementing Orry's plan for the reform of the central administration. The same year inspectors of the army and military intendants were appointed, while the place of the Admiral of Castile was left unfilled on the death of the incumbent. Other grandees were soon to be disgraced and the new régime began to achieve more solid results. Yet in 1706, when Philip had to evacuate Madrid and send his jewels to France to raise money, it touched the lowest point of its fortunes.

Until 1705, despite the activity of Imperial agents and strong local resentment at the persecution of people identified as 'Austrian' in 1700, the eastern realms had been securely Philip's. Even Hesse-Darmstadt failed to rouse the Catalans when he came ashore near Barcelona, with a party of English and Dutch marines, in May 1704. On 22 August 1705, however, when the Archduke Charles landed there,[1] revolt flared up among the rural classes. In September and October, while Barcelona resisted the Anglo-Imperial attack, outlying Catalan towns were declaring for Charles. Leadership came from the bourgeoisie of Barcelona (which hoped for better results of English sea power than of the competition of French merchants) and from the smaller noblemen, who were able to rally peasants and herdsmen, monks and lower clergy; in the end, relatively few others stood by Philip in either Catalonia or Valencia—only the higher clergy, a few great nobles and senior officers. In Valencia, where rent-strikes had broken out as recently as 1693, the Succession War had more the character of a social struggle; but by 16 December, when the city of Valencia proclaimed Charles III, some of the magnates had joined in. Feeling in Aragon was less strong, but a revolution in favour of Charles spread there too and he was proclaimed king in Saragossa in June 1706—less than a month after the battle of Ramillies had delivered Brabant and Flanders to the Allies. Later in the year Alicante, Cartagena, Ibiza and Majorca capitulated to the English fleet. The English did not seize Sardinia and Minorca for Charles III until August–September 1708, but at Barcelona in 1706 the *Corts* reaffirmed the ancient attachment of Sardinia, Sicily and Naples to the Crown of Aragon. The horizons of Catalan businessmen, who had prospered since 1688, extended even beyond the Mediterranean.

[1] Below, p. 425.

They created a company to trade with Gibraltar and undermine Cadiz. The Catalans, in short, aimed at imposing their claims and ideas on the rest of Spain and no longer, as in 1640-52, at secession.[1]

The young archduke, who had entered Barcelona on 23 October 1705 and been proclaimed by the *Corts*, erected a government within the old forms but with new personnel. He maintained a brilliant little court of Viennese style, granted a score of titles, and repeatedly displayed a largesse which accorded ill with his means and which sometimes, as later in Sardinia, contradicted his general instructions.[2] On the other hand, he and his circle had the reputation of being ungrateful friends. They continually complained of the climate, of Spanish character and abuses, of their allies who did not bring them enough support to conquer Spain in a single campaign. At least one good observer at Barcelona thought that Charles failed to make the best of the goodwill available to him in Aragon and Valencia, and that German methods of command were ill suited to Spanish soldiers,[3] although the Catalan guerrilla bands known as Miqueletes were scarcely susceptible to regular discipline of any kind.

The Castilian people remained loyal to Philip, in response to the proud determination of the queen whom they adored, when the Portuguese under Galway temporarily occupied Madrid, Toledo and other places in June 1706.[4] Many of the nobility, on the contrary, whose preference for Habsburg ways had been confirmed by contact with French, openly showed their joy, if they did not prudently vanish to their distant estates. Portocarrero at Toledo intoned a *Te Deum* for the Austrians and Maria Anna of Neuberg came out of mourning. Later, when they had recovered central Castile, Madame des Ursins and Amelot advised severe punishments. Philip accepted his grandfather's admonitions to avoid these, pardoning some who had already been disciplined and making allowance for many others. He treated Portocarrero gently, as an old man who had rendered valuable services; he exiled the dowager queen to Bayonne, but continued her pension; he proscribed only some of the more prominent leaders. But he seized the occasion to get rid of disloyal members of the Councils of Castile and of War, and to abolish one of the two secretaryships of the Council of State. A decree of 21 November 1706 extended to the grandees Orry's programme of recovering alienated fiefs. Orry himself, however, who had gone to Versailles in the summer, was not allowed to return to Spain until 1713. Amelot had advised that the feeling there against his ruthless methods made him too heavy a liability to the French

---

[1] Vilar, vol. I, pp. 670-3; cf. idem, *Le 'Manual de la Compañya Nova' de Gibraltar, 1709-1723* (1962).

[2] P. Voltes Bou, 'Aportaciones a la historia de Cerdaña y Nápoles', pp. 72-3. Cf. Vilar, *Catalogne*, vol. I, pp. 685 ff. for the taxes and loans raised by Catalonia, the issue of new coinage (the first *peseta*) and the price-rise in 1708-12 there.

[3] Relazione del Marchese di Trivié (1711), in Morandi, vol. I, pp. 43 f., 75 f.

[4] Below, p. 429.

cause. Berwick, who had resumed command of Philip's army from the unsuccessful Tessé and reoccupied Madrid in August, also distrusted Orry.

The overseas possessions, on the whole, were not severely affected by the war. The Allies began with exaggerated hopes of persuading the Creoles to declare for Charles III, and fear of this was real enough for the Council of the Indies to tolerate armed French ships in the South Sea, which in 1706–7 included several warships sent expressly to stiffen the colonial authorities against disaffection. Bourbon influence was decisively asserted in 1706 by the appointment, at Louis XIV's behest, of the marquis of Castel-dos-rios as viceroy of Peru. Interruptions of coastal and oceanic trade were the main features of the war. The disaster at Vigo in 1702[1] deprived Spain of valuable cargo, but most of the bullion had been got ashore. Further French convoys enabled shipments of treasure to reach Cadiz intermittently. Ducasse brought the galleons home in 1703 (after fighting Benbow's squadron off Santa Marta on 18 August 1702) and the Mexican fleet (with some rich English prizes) in 1708. In that year, however, Commodore Wager destroyed several of the Isthmian galleons coming out of Cartagena, where Commodore Littleton was to enjoy a similar though less lucrative success in 1711. In 1706–12 four fleets sailed to Vera Cruz and one to Cartagena, always under French convoy and sometimes, as in 1708, consisting mainly of French ships.[2]

The war overseas took the form of minor clashes, but in many places. At an early stage the English raided Trinidad in Cuba. Against that, the Campeche loggers were assaulted five times from 1702 to 1712. The Canaries repulsed a light attack by Admiral Jennings in November 1706, and South Carolina a Franco-Spanish raid the following August. More seriously, in 1702–4 the Carolinians entered Florida, taking the town (but not the fort) of St Augustine and destroying mission-villages.[3] In 1702 Spain had withdrawn the century-old missions far up the coastal islands and the English now began to control the debatable lands south of the Savannah. But in 1703 a Franco-Spanish fleet surprised New Providence in the Bahamas and later raids forced the English to abandon their first effort to maintain a colony there.[4] Meanwhile, as Portugal turned to an English alliance, troops from Buenos Aires descended upon Colonia do Sacramento, forcing evacuation of the fort on 14 March 1704 after a three-month siege. Early in 1704 Dampier had privateered up the Pacific coasts of America, but failed to take the rich Manila galleon *El Rosario*.

---

[1] Below, p. 418.

[2] R. Du Casse, *L'Amiral Du Casse, 1646–1715* (1876), pp. 250 ff., 343 ff.; R. Bourne, *Queen Anne's Navy in the West Indies* (New Haven, 1934), ch. v; C. H. Haring, *The Spanish Empire in America* (Oxford, 1947), p. 335.

[3] Below, pp. 503–4.

[4] The island became a principal resort of pirates until the governorship (1718–21) of Woodes Rogers.

Returning to England in 1707, he acted as pilot next year to a Bristol privateering squadron commanded by Captain Woodes Rogers. Bound for the South Sea, they called for supplies at the Canaries—an essentially peaceable call, consistent with the plea of resident English wine merchants that the Canaries lay outside European wars—and in 1709 cruised up the Pacific coasts, ransoming Guayaquil and taking prizes. On 22 December, off Lower California, Rogers captured the frigate *Encarnación* from Manila, although her larger companion afterwards beat off his three ships. He then crossed the Pacific to Batavia, stopping at Guam, which had been missionized by the Spanish Jesuits in the 1660s. This was England's most remunerative privateering venture[1] and the last episode of the war in Spain's American possessions.

The turning-point at home came in 1707. Philip was hurt by his grand-father's decision to withdraw from north Italy in March and by Louis's refusal to contest the Habsburg occupation of Naples and Sicily. Yet Berwick's victory at Almanza on 25 April[2] did more than reverse the tide of disasters to the Bourbon cause in Spain. In opening the way to Philip's recovery of most of Aragon and Valencia by 14 November, when the heroic garrison of Lérida surrendered after the town had been destroyed, it also provided the opportunity to remodel the Aragonese constitution. Philip of course had some vengeful motives, as was seen in his humiliation of Aragon's *Justicia* (chief justice and custodian of Aragonese liberties), in the erasing of the notably contumacious city of Játiva even to its name, in the very language of the new decrees, and in the reasons given for imposing a general contribution on all the towns and for requiring the quartering of troops—obligations from which even the clergy were not exempted. But neither vengeance nor French example seems fully to account for the steps taken with regard to the *fueros*. Philip knew that the leading rebels had escaped into Catalonia, and that there was danger in adopting excessively punitive measures against the Aragonese at large. Much of the responsibility for the constitutional revolution falls upon Amelot and Madame des Ursins, as also upon Berwick, to whose officers in the crisis of the peninsular war much local government effectively fell.[3] Other influences at Madrid—including that of Francisco Ronquillo (the former *corregidor*) as president of the Council of Castile and of Melchor de Macanaz (1670–1760),[4] an able Murcian in his service—evidently

---

[1] The Spanish evidence on this controversial voyage has been used by B. Little in *Crusoe's Captain* (1960).   [2] Below, p. 433.

[3] The duke of Orléans, who had joined the army on the morrow of Almanza and was not without hopes of the Spanish throne for himself, cultivated friends among the defeated by promises which greatly embarrassed Madrid (Baudrillart, vol. 1, pp. 291 f., 390).

[4] Macanaz was sent to Valencia on 20 June to reform the administration and to carry out confiscations, out of which he received substantial grants. For his many services to the Crown and for an assessment of his career, see H. Kamen, 'Melchor de Macanaz and the foundations of Bourbon power in Spain', *Eng. Hist. Rev.* vol. LXXX (1965), pp. 699–716. On 11 Feb. 1711 Macanaz was to become the first *intendente general* of Aragon.

seized the chance to end an inequality of constitutional status which had long rankled among Castilians, although they were opposed in this by most of the noblemen in Philip's immediate entourage. His decree of 29 June 1707 abolished 'all the *fueros*, laws, usages, and customs of the kingdoms of Aragon and Valencia', including the Council of Aragon, and submitted those realms in all things to the constitution of Castile. The broad language of the decree embraced even private law, with which the Crown was not really concerned. Having learnt more of the facts, however, Philip recognized that most of the towns, indeed most civil and clerical persons of all ranks, had been victims of circumstance who had suffered for their loyalty. On 29 July he clarified his intentions by confirming to them all their private liberties and privileges,

this not being extended so far as to the mode of government, the laws and *fueros* in the said kingdom...since the difference of government was in great part the occasion of the past disturbances...[1]

The Valencians petitioned against this interpretation of their ancient constitution. Amelot angrily held the petition to be illegal, exiled two of its authors and sent in harsher governors. From then on, wherever Philip ruled, matters of criminal law, taxes and troops were handled under Castilian law. By the *Nueva Planta* (new plan) of 3 April 1711, the Aragonese realms were given a captain-general and an Audiencia of the Castilian type.

Domestic events in Spain after 1707, as before, cannot be understood without reference to foreign relations. For the time being, it is true, Philip felt less need of Louis's aid than earlier, while French troops were in serious difficulties in other war theatres. As early as 1706, however, Louis had begun to manoeuvre for peace at Spanish expense, and there was not a year thereafter when Philip or Spain could feel secure against being sacrificed to a European settlement (ch. xiv). The negotiations of March–May 1709[2] marked an open breach between the two courts. In April Louis told Amelot that he had decided to abandon Spain to its own devices, and Philip instructed Bergeyck[3] to impress on the Dutch that his ideas about a settlement differed from those of the French. After their rejection of the obnoxious Peace Preliminaries in June French ministers counted on Philip's voluntary abdication, which was to be encouraged by the withdrawal of French troops from Catalonia. Friction steadily increased between the soldiers and merchants of the two nations; by the autumn the two armies were on the point of fighting each other. Amelot, who had become virtually the chief minister, was recalled to France in September in view of Spanish restlessness, and the *Despacho* was turned over to Spanish noblemen, headed by the duke of Medinaceli. Sending

---

[1] The decrees are printed in J. Ortiz y Sanz, *Compendio cronológico de la historia de España*, vol. vii (Madrid, 1801), pp. 129–32.
[2] Below, pp. 450 ff.　　　　　　　　　[3] For Count Bergeyck see below, pp. 390, 413.

most of the French officers home, after he had tried in vain to retain 20 battalions of their infantry, Philip left for the Catalan front. But he held most of the cards in his own hands and at least to the Spanish mind played them under French influence.

The new *Despacho* did poorly with what little authority it had. The finances and administration began to deteriorate again, and there were further desertions of Philip's cause among the abler Spaniards. Medinaceli himself was arrested in April 1710, on a mysterious charge of treason. This further convinced Louis XIV and his ministers of the hopelessness of Philip's cause. While still refusing the Allied demand that they should use French arms against him unconditionally, they now offered money and soldiers if another kingdom were found for him. After the failure of the summer talks at Geertruidenberg,[1] it is true, Louis agreed to send Marshal Vendôme to make good the deficiencies of Spanish generals and French troops began to flow back into Navarre, where they had continued to garrison the fortresses. In September, however, with Aragon recovered for the archduke and the Spanish court forced to retire from Madrid to Valladolid, Louis made an effort to persuade Philip to give up Spain in exchange for Sicily and Sardinia. Instead, the duke of Noailles, military governor of Roussillon and Languedoc, who had been charged with this delicate mission, returned with supplications for more help. These included a solemn address signed by 32 grandees. Fearing above all that French diplomatic schemes might succeed in dividing Spain, the grandees had now resigned themselves to a Bourbon king of their own and begun to rally about his government. Noailles predicted a turn in the tide and his forecast was soon proved correct, at Brihuega and after Villa Viciosa in December—successes for Vendôme's generalship and for Spanish and French arms combined.[2] Moreover, the French king had personally succumbed at last to his grandson's pleas for an attack on Catalonia from Roussillon: on 24 January 1711 a French army of 20,000 under Noailles stormed Gerona. By the autumn of that year, when the archduke had acceded to the Imperial title and so transformed the international problem of the Spanish succession, only the Catalan war challenged Philip's hold on the Peninsula.

Even during their earlier troubles, Philip and his advisers had shown how little they identified Spanish interests with French. They had been much occupied by French efforts to penetrate the American trade system, where the Spaniards wanted to end what the French were already doing, legally or not. A new committee for the revival of trade (1705) became a Committee of Trade, Money and Mines on 15 May 1707—a larger but no more successful version of the *Junta de Comercio* of 1691. Yet it cannot be claimed that either Spaniards or French achieved much more after 1707 than previously of their objectives in the Indies. While the Malouins

---

[1] Below, p. 456.   [2] Below, p. 440.

and others continued to trade with Chile and Peru, French diplomats were not always successful in obtaining the facilities required by the Asiento Company. Orry himself had disliked it. Not until 1704–5 did it obtain the right to set up its own warehouses and to sell prize goods away from Portobello; not until 1708 was it allowed to send French vessels other than slavers to pick up returns for which the latter had no room. All these concessions expanded the possibilities of contraband and aroused resentment. Yet no amount of French pressure could persuade the Spanish government to open the profitable tobacco and cacao trades, each the subject of a tax-farm, to the Company's shipping. Its factors also met with much obstruction from officials in the Indies and occasional mob violence there. No doubt they, and still more the Company's captains, gave legitimate ground for complaint: they made the smuggling profits, while the directors were forced to open their pockets to Philip.[1] The attempt to establish regular trade with Buenos Aires, though welcome to the people there, was contested with particular bitterness because it threatened to outflank the established control of Lima and Panama over South American trade. All this had much to do with the bad feeling between the two allies in 1709–10.

Meanwhile, relations between State and Church had come to a crisis. Philip's native Gallicanism was strengthened by the advice of Orry and Amelot, who were especially hostile to the financial immunities of the clergy. In 1705 Philip had forced the resignation of the Inquisitor-General, Bishop Mendoza of Segovia, in face of the support he enjoyed from the Curia. The Inquisition ostentatiously supported Philip thereafter, but neither this nor a large 'loan' extorted from the clergy before Almanza much softened the king's views or those of his advisers. Thus a rupture with Rome had long been developing. It came when Clement XI, under Habsburg pressure, was driven on 15 January 1709 to recognize Archduke Charles as the Catholic King, although not in terms as king of Spain.[2] Louis having refused to advise him, the enraged Philip consulted a committee of theologians and on 22 April expelled the nuncio, closed his court, barred the sending of funds to Rome, sequestered clerical revenues, and ordered the clergy to turn in to the royal officials any briefs, bulls or letters from Rome without giving the least effect to them. This theoretically restored the situation to what it had been before the nunciature had been established. The breach was not healed until 1717.

In the negotiations which slowly crystallized in the Peace of Utrecht (ch. XIV) Philip usually allowed his grandfather to speak for him. Yet he protested against French willingness to acknowledge, even as an empty form, the new emperor's continued use of his Spanish titles, and he consistently refused to buy Imperial recognition himself at the price of leniency

---

[1] Scelle, vol. II, pp. 339–450.   [2] Below, p. 595.

to the Catalans. In particular, he embarrassed his grandfather by refusing to make peace with the Dutch, his object being to get them to guarantee a principality for the princess des Ursins; he gave way in May 1714, only because he needed French troops for the siege of Barcelona.[1] While sympathizing with Philip's desire to be master in his own realms, Louis was often criticial of his attitudes, which he judged not only ungrateful but maladroit.[2] Once again he regretted the influence of the tempestuous Orry, who returned to Spain in 1713 and was given plenary powers as *veedor* [inspector] *general*. This time Philip and Madame des Ursins resisted all French efforts to recall him. They also disgraced several opponents of Philip's obstinate policy towards the peace-making, including the admirable Ronquillo, whose elevation to the presidency of the Council of Castile had earlier caused so much consternation since he was not a nobleman.

Meanwhile, besides the introduction of the New Plan in the Aragonese realms, changes of great significance were taking place in Castile. In November 1712 the Cortes of Madrid was called to approve a modified Salic Law, intended to make it nearly impossible for some future marriage of a Bourbon princess to lead to the accession of a scion of the Houses of Savoy or of Austria. The new rules were promulgated by the Pragmatic of 10 May 1713. The Councils of State and of Castile had given their approval with reluctance, however, since the new law reversed one which was centuries old and hence cast reflections upon the process that had brought about the Habsburg succession in the sixteenth century, and to some degree that of Philip himself. The opposition thus manifested by the Councils gave fresh cause for attention to their reform. A decree of 10 November 1713 carried into effect Orry's proposals of 1702. The Councils of Castile, Indies, Finance, Military Orders and Inquisition were reorganized and their membership, in general, greatly increased. A separate decree of 23 April 1714 dealt with the Council of War. It is true that these changes were reversed in the summer of 1715, in the course of a reaction following the advent of Elizabeth Farnese and Orry's dismissal; but their effect in destroying conciliar power to obstruct the royal will was permanent. They marked the end of the old system of government in Spain.

The death of Queen Maria Luisa on 11 February 1714, after a long illness, nearly deprived Philip V of his wits. He leaned more than ever upon the princess des Ursins, while she and Orry pushed reforms faster than before. One of the most important was the decree of 30 November 1714. By dividing the *Despacho* into four departments—so that separate ministers now dealt respectively with War, with Marine and Indies, with Justice, Police and Foreign Affairs, and with the Treasury—it at last carried into effect Orry's scheme for introducing a system of secretaries of state. This reform, like that of the Councils, did not survive for long in

---

[1] Marquis de Courcy, *L'Espagne après la Paix d'Utrecht, 1713–1715* (1891), p. 201.
[2] *Ibid.* pp. 198, 205.

exactly the form in which Orry cast it, but it proved of great consequence for the future government of Spain.

Prophetic and comprehensive, though ineffective in the short run, was the handling of Church affairs. Louis XIV having offered his services to reconcile the Crown of Spain with the Papacy in 1712, Melchor de Macanaz, noted for his prolific pen and for his championship of prerogative, produced on 19 December 1713 a memorial in 85 heads which has been described as 'the first great statement of eighteenth-century regalism, in its complete exaltation of the royal power over the Church'.[1] Calling amongst other things for the suppression of Roman fiscal rights in Spain and of temporal jurisdiction in the hands of ecclesiastical tribunals, the memorial was so radical as to shock many in the Council of Castile who would have liked to accept its basic intention. The Council, of which Macanaz had recently become fiscal (attorney) general, hastily returned the paper to Philip. But Amelot, Orry, the princess and (with reservations) the royal confessor all supported Macanaz, with the result that Philip referred the memorial back to the Council, requiring each member to present his written opinion. This time it seems to have given a qualified consent. But someone betrayed the memorial into the hands of Cardinal Giudice, the Inquisitor-General, who passed it to the Holy Office. To remove his influence, Giudice was hurried off to France as ambassador; but on 31 July 1714 he published an inquisitorial condemnation of the memorial and announced it in full court at Marly. He was at once recalled and Philip angrily ordered the Council of Castile to report its advice. On 5 November it recommended the total abolition of the Spanish Inquisition. Apparently, only the problems connected with the reduction of Catalonia, and then the changes brought about by Philip's marriage to Elizabeth Farnese, saved that body from extinction in 1714. As it happened, the decree was not signed and in March 1715 Philip was forced to make public disavowal of the 'pernicious advice' which had led to it. Macanaz, a victim of the Italian clique now dominant at court, was banished in February.[2]

On 11 September 1714, after a terrible siege, Barcelona had fallen to Berwick. Four days later the marshal wrote:

When I had disarmed the inhabitants and abolished by decree the Deputation and all the ancient form of government...[I] established a new one...ordering that the police in future should be regulated according to the laws of Castile.[3]

---

[1] Kamen, *loc. cit.* p. 707.

[2] In exile, mainly in France, he revealed himself as a furious anti-Jansenist and in 1734 embarked on a *Defensa crítica de la Inquisición*, published in 1788. He spent the years 1748–60 in a Spanish prison, dying shortly after his release. For a brief conspectus of his voluminous writings, see Kamen, *loc. cit.* pp. 711–15. As most of these remain in manuscript, it seems ironical that Macanaz played a leading part in establishing the royal library which is now the Biblioteca Nacional.

[3] *Memoirs* (London edn., 2 vols. 1779), vol. II, p. 178. The *Diputació*, originally a small committee of the *Corts* for collecting the subsidies it voted, had long been the most powerful and vigilant guardian of Catalan liberties.

Berwick's new creation was the Royal Junta of Government and Justice, which also served as a temporary high court. Prominent members included José Patiño (1667–1736),[1] a Galician born in Milan who had been climbing to prominence under Amelot, and various Catalans who had stood for Philip in 1701 and been persecuted as a result: among these the most important was Francesc Ameller, once the fiscal of the Audiencia of Catalonia, who in exile had become a member of the Council of Castile. On 16 September Berwick dissolved the Council of One Hundred, substituted sixteen local 'Administrators', and ordered the officials of the old government of the *Corts* to tear down all insignia, turn in all keys, and cease discharging their duties. On 2 October, remembering (as he later wrote) 3,000 dead and wounded, he proceeded against the clergy who had supported the archduke: 'I likewise embarked the Bishop of Albarazin and 200 priests and monks for Genoa, forbidding them on pain of death ever to set their foot in the dominions of His Catholic Majesty.'[2] Berwick himself then left for Madrid: but orders against the bearing of arms, imprisonments, confiscations, debarments from office-holding, the tearing down of city and castle walls, and other forms of punishment continued for years. In 1715–18, to build a citadel in the maritime district (*Ribera*) of Barcelona, as a threat and humiliation, 4,000 people were evicted from their homes.[3] About the same time Philip completed the suppression of the six old Catalan universities, replacing them in 1717 with that of Cervera. Majorca, which had supplied Barcelona during the early stages of the siege, surrendered with no real struggle on 2 July 1715 and came under the same régime as Catalonia.

Final settlement of the Catalan government was not reached until 1717. In 1715, on the king's orders, the Council of Castile sought written opinions from Patiño and Ameller, who is said to have had considerable influence in moderating the execution of the final decree. The ideas of Patiño seem most clearly to have been followed in drawing it up. His judgment of the Catalan character was harsh: 'They respect the precepts of the king and justice now, not for affection nor love, but from the superior force of arms.'[4] Nevertheless, he too advocated moderation. He had no desire to have Catalan law changed in fields which were not of direct concern to the Crown, and he recommended that the decisions of the Audiencia should not be subject to appeal to the Council of Castile. He got his way. When the Audiencia of Barcelona was set up, on 9 October 1715, its decisions were to be final. By the decree of 16 January 1716,

---

[1] See vol. VII, pp. 278–80.   [2] *Memoirs* (1779), vol. II, pp. 179–80.
[3] See Vilar, vol. I, pp. 679 ff. for an estimate of the social and economic effects of the war in Catalonia, whose total population did not now exceed 400,000. It seems clear that until 1712 the business classes did well out of the price-rise brought about by an afflux of English and Portuguese specie, the archduke's monetary policy, and the spending of his court and army.
[4] Quoted J. Mercader Riba, 'La Ordenación de Cataluña por Felipe V: la Nueva Planta', *Hispania*, vol. XI (1951), pp. 257–366.

establishing the whole of the New Plan, political power was to rest in the Audiencia, presided over by the captain-general, and it also held the judicial power; royal *corregidores* were substituted for the earlier Inspectors; proceedings were to be in Castilian; only the king might coin money; and the municipal organization was fundamentally reshaped. But there was a realization throughout that the preservation of the old laws was desirable when it did not injure a royal interest: 'In all the rest', said the king, 'I order that there be observed the Constitutions which there were formerly in Catalonia, understanding that these are established anew by this decree, and that they have the same force and vigour.'[1] As to both criminal and civil affairs, therefore, Catalan private law mostly continued, like the Catalan language.

The marriage of Philip late in 1714 to Elizabeth Farnese[2] also ended an age. Her ejection of Madame des Ursins and Orry from Spain, her ambitions to provide thrones for any future sons, and her reliance on a new favourite, Alberoni, gave a new direction to Spanish policy.

[1] Quoted *ibid.* p. 272.
[2] They were married by proxy on 16 September, but the new queen did not reach Spain till 23 December: E. Armstrong, *Elisabeth Farnese* (1892), pp. 11 ff., discusses the marriage negotiations.

CHAPTER XII

FROM THE NINE YEARS WAR TO THE
WAR OF THE SPANISH SUCCESSION

IN the treaties signed at Ryswick the clauses which formally terminated the war show differences of phraseology. Between the French and the Dutch there was to be a good, firm, fruitful and inviolable peace; between Louis XIV and William III as king by the grace of God of Great Britain, a universal and perpetual peace was to be inviolably, religiously and sincerely observed. The peace made by France with Spain was to be good, firm and durable; that with the emperor Christian, universal and perpetual. Whatever significance these variations may have had, none of them implied any reservation. None of the leading contemporaries seems to have suggested, at least in writing or in reported conversation, that the official phrases were hypocritical or over-optimistic, or that this peace of exhaustion was a mere armistice. Yet less than four years later the French were fighting the Austrians in Lombardy, and in the spring of 1702 the emperor, Queen Anne and the States-General declared war against France. This was the result of two processes. The first and more difficult to trace was the economic and administrative recovery which enabled the powers to take the field again. Such recovery was a normal concomitant of peace; it was usually quicker than seemed possible at the moment when peace was made, and statesmen were liable to miscalculate when they estimated how far it had proceeded in their own or in other countries. The other process was the building-up of antagonisms, some inveterate and others new.

One of the main provisions of the Ryswick settlement was insufficient for its purpose. The surrender by the French to the Spaniards of their conquests in the Netherlands did not satisfy the need of the Dutch for a secure southern frontier. The war had proved over again that the Spaniards could not defend their Netherlands. The governor there, Maximilian Emmanuel, elector of Bavaria, was an ambitious prince who wanted to make something of his provinces. The obvious course for him was to work with the Spaniards and their recent allies, the Maritime Powers of Great Britain and the United Provinces. He therefore made an informal agreement under which the Dutch established garrisons, amounting to 25 battalions, in eight barrier-fortresses: Nieuwpoort, Courtrai, Oudenarde, Ath, Mons, Charleroi, Namur and Luxemburg. This did not make a strong barrier. The French held the upper waters of all the rivers and there was no Spanish fortress on the Scheldt or the Lys. The French army had captured six of the eight fortresses before. On the seaward flank, Dunkirk was intact and capable of inflicting damage on Dutch and British shipping. But with the Dutch garrisons the places would be able to stand the first shock of a new invasion.

The Spaniards acquiesced in this agreement, but otherwise behaved as if the peace was indeed to be perpetual. They made no pretence of keeping up forces sufficient to defend their frontiers in the Peninsula. The governor of Catalonia, Prince George of Hesse-Darmstadt, still had three German regiments, but there scarcely existed any Spanish forces. There were not horses enough to mount any body of cavalry; the royal guards were part-time units of no military value; the navy consisted of two warships in Spanish harbours and thirteen in Italy, of which seven were on hire from Genoa.

Except for sending their garrisons to the barrier-fortresses the Dutch likewise made no preparations for an eventual renewal of war on land. They needed relief from financial strain, and William III as stadholder did not obstruct the reduction of the forces to a peace-footing as he had done in 1684. Though low, this footing seemed provisionally sufficient. Almost all the troops raised since 1688 were paid off, which left 41,440 infantry and 4,100 mounted troops. The fleet, however, in response to strong representations from William was strengthened. The war-losses in frigates were made good and, though the big ships were laid up, eighteen new ships of the line were built, to which twelve more were added from 1701.

In Great Britain there were the same reasons as in Holland for limiting expenditure and taxation; there was the same desire to get back to peaceful commerce, and there were mingled currents of opposition to William's policy in general and to the maintenance of a strong army in particular. Continental warfare had been costly and at times inglorious. The prejudice against it had been reinforced by arguments that it could not serve national purposes so well as war at sea and in the colonies. According to the Declaration of Rights of 1689 it was illegal to maintain a standing army in time of peace. Now that peace had come, large numbers of politically minded Englishmen were genuinely, if stupidly, afraid that such an army might be used as an instrument of despotism. The king was partly to blame for this suspicion. He had excluded not only parliament but most of his English ministers from the secrets of his foreign policy. A few months before the peace he had given high office to the earl of Sunderland, the most widely distrusted of the former servants of his despotic uncle. These and other causes led the House of Commons in December 1697 to resolve on a drastic reduction of forces, the disbanding of all the land forces raised since 29 September 1680. That would have brought the strength of the army down to about 10,000, among whom there would have been no foreign units. When parliament met again in December 1698 it found that this programme had not been carried out. After a tussle the king had to agree that before 26 March 1699 all troops in England should be disbanded except 7,000, all of whom were to be natural-born subjects. All alien regiments in Ireland were to be disbanded and all other troops in excess of 12,000.

There remained two great powers which did not disarm. The emperor was still at war with the Turks, and in spite of their financial embarrassment the Dutch made him a small loan in 1698. His efforts were now concentrated on this war, which turned decisively in his favour when Prince Eugene won the battle of Zenta on 11 September 1697.[1] Thus the military situation was somewhat as it had been when Louis XIV set his armies in motion in 1688; but the emperor's financial situation was bad, and no considerable improvement resulted from certain modest measures of financial reform which began in 1698. The dissatisfaction stirred by the raising of Hanover to electoral rank had impaired the emperor's influence in Germany. The Protestant princes blamed him for the religious clause of the Peace of Ryswick.[2] Having no fleet he could do nothing in the Mediterranean. Altogether there was no likelihood of his taking a military initiative in the West. Yet France did not disarm either. William III distrusted the intentions of the French from the first weeks of the peace; he feared that they would not carry out the cessions agreed upon in the treaties. They did indeed effect a reduction of their army. It numbered 150,000 foot and 30,000 horse. Each company sacrificed five men, a small proportionate reduction the total effect of which is hard to calculate; but the cadres remained intact. All the militia regiments were disbanded; but they were second-line troops, which had been of very little use as reserves for the field-army. On 14 March 1698 William told the Austrian ambassador in London, Count Auersperg, that the conduct of France was already similar to what it had been after the Peace of Nymegen. A fortnight later, at The Hague, Heinsius told Count Stratmann that the forces of France were almost on the same footing as during the war.[3] This comparison was true, but it was a comparison with the last years, not the earlier years, of the late war. The French were not yet making ready to equip a battle-fleet again.[4]

Not only did the French cut down expenses and limit their ambitions at sea: they did not contemplate a renewal of that pressure in all directions which gave its special character to the period of the *Réunions*. This time the show of force was related to one specific political aim. By March 1698 the statesmen of the Maritime Powers saw clearly what it was, and on 16 June Louis stated it plainly. There is no reason for doubting either

---

[1] Below, p. 626.
[2] Below, pp. 473–4.
[3] O. Klopp, *Der Fall des Hauses Stuart*, vol. VIII (1879), pp. 56–7.
[4] In 1700 their ships of the line numbered 107, but this includes those which were not in commission, of which several were probably not fit for general service: J. H. Owen, *War at Sea under Queen Anne* (1938), p. 279.

the sincerity or the soundness of his judgment that the peace 'can only be upset, apparently, by the eventuality of the King of Spain's death'.[1]

On no other occasion in the history of modern Europe have so many questions of vital concern to its peoples depended on the death or survival of one man. When the king of Spain should come to die the Spanish line of the Habsburgs would die with him; and whoever succeeded him in all or any of his dominions, there was no Spaniard who could do so. His enfeebled empire was still the richest and by far the most populous aggregation of human beings that owed allegiance to any European sovereign, and its ruling classes were proud of its historic greatness. The first certain factor in its future was that, at least in Old Spain, their pride and conservatism would be on the side of holding the great empire together and transmitting it as an unbroken whole. With the nation behind them, they would frustrate any attempt by the head of another State to rule Spain through a viceroy. Like all conservatism, this drew its strength not only from pride and sentiment but also from vested material interests.

Among the other European powers interest and sentiment were unstably mixed. For the Dutch the choice of a new master for the Spanish Netherlands was a matter of political life or death. They needed a buffer-state to protect them from France, and they had undertaken a large share in making the buffer-state viable for defence; but, if it became strong enough to carve its own fortunes, it might revive the great dormant port of Antwerp and ruin their own position as the greatest inlet and outlet of European trade.[2] In Dutch business overseas the Spanish colonies absorbed exports and provided silver, as they did also for England, and these two Protestant trading-states, once Spain's historic enemies, were not only reconciled with her beyond the Line, but had good reasons for wishing her lax imperialism to continue undisturbed. Their trade with the colonies was substantial, but nominally illegal; no energetic régime would connive at so much smuggling, through monopolistic paper barriers. Here again the interest of the Maritime Powers was only to preserve the Spanish empire, not to see it once more strong and self-reliant. A different kind of conservatism ruled in Vienna. The younger branch of the Habsburg line, separated more than a century before, had intermarried with the elder in such a way that, but for the uncertainties of births and deaths, it should have succeeded as a matter of course in any vacancy. Its relations with Spain had been purely political and consistently friendly. There had been disagreements, especially about when and whether and how to resist the

---

[1] Instructions to Villars for his mission to Vienna, quoted in A. Legrelle, *La Diplomatie française et la succession d'Espagne*, vol. II (1889), p. 514. The correspondence printed in Legrelle's book is of great importance; but his account of French policy is less satisfactory than that given by the late M. A. Thomson in an acute and learned article in *Trans. R. Hist. Soc.* 5th series, vol. IV (1954), pp. 111–34.

[2] Cf. vol. VIII, pp. 272–3 for Joseph II's attempt to reopen the Scheldt in 1782–4.

attacks of France, but there had been no conflicting territorial ambitions and no colliding economic encroachments.

France was Spain's next neighbour on two frontiers: if the Dutch and the English in their time had wrested away Spanish lands, the French had done it more recently and nearer the heart of the empire. In the Nine Years War they had almost mastered both the Netherlands and Catalonia. Their expanding seaborne commerce was involved in the Spanish empire at many points. They did not trade directly with Spanish colonies like the English and the Dutch; but the trade which they carried on under cover of Spanish names in Cadiz was equally clandestine and had the same ultimate destinations. It amounted to perhaps a quarter of the Cadiz trade, and Louis XIV had protected it with a high hand. All over Spain, and especially in Andalusia, there were colonies of French merchants and shopkeepers, besides more or less migratory labourers. To the prevailing economic thought of the time, however, the most desirable kind of trade was the direct trade with the colonies, and the French government was turning its thoughts in the direction of South America. In 1695–6 six French ships tried unsuccessfully to round Cape Horn and in 1698 the newly founded *Compagnie de la Mer du Sud* sent out three ships and a corvette, which returned from the Pacific in August 1701. Conjectures about the future of the Spanish empire may have had little to do with these adventures; but such conjectures were very relevant to the Levant trade of Marseilles. This was the greatest branch of French maritime commerce. The British and to a lesser degree the Dutch were competitors here too, and in 1695 they had been backed up by their fleet; but if France could control the Spanish coasts of Naples and Sicily, and the Balearic Islands, and the Spanish ports in North Africa, the future might be very different. That was an economic prize not much less tempting in its way than the strategic domination which might accrue to France from the control of Spain itself, with its Atlantic and Mediterranean coasts and the Straits of Gibraltar. By a fateful chance the control of all this, and of all the rest of the Spanish dominions, had come within the ambit of what the French king and his ministers considered to be not merely legitimate aspirations but justifiable claims.

At the time of the Peace of Ryswick King Carlos II was nearly thirty-six years old. His health, always feeble, was deteriorating and he neither had nor could be expected to have any child. The prospect of his death therefore raised in the first place the legal problem of who would be entitled to the succession. If this had been a mere matter of law it need not have proved very difficult. The Spanish Crowns could descend through females; for that there were good and sufficiently recent precedents. Carlos had two sisters. Before he was born, the elder, Maria Theresa, had become the wife of Louis XIV and by him she had a son, Louis the dauphin, who was five days older than Carlos. In 1666, when the king of Spain and the dauphin were five years old, the younger sister, Margaret Theresa, became the first wife of the Emperor Leopold. If it had been merely a matter of heredity the dauphin would have been heir presumptive to the Spanish monarchy from his birth.

There were, however, other legal issues besides that of heredity, and they left openings for contradictory interpretations. Some jurists believed that a monarch, in particular a Spanish monarch, had only a life-interest in his dignity and could not alter the rules by which it passed from one holder to another. Outside Spain and France the more commonly accepted opinion, on the other hand, was that an absolute monarch could alter this constitutional rule as he could any other.[1] Philip IV, when he died in 1665, left a will by which he bequeathed the reversion of the whole of the Spanish dominions, if he should die childless, to his younger daughter, the empress. Under this will her grandson, the son of Max Emmanuel of Bavaria, stood to inherit. If a king had the right to dispose of the succession by a will, then anyone in the line of succession had an equal right to renounce the inheritance, at least for himself, though perhaps not for his posterity. Both of the two daughters of Philip IV actually did exercise this right at the time of their marriages. There was a difference between the two renunciations. That of the younger, the empress, was absolute and its effectiveness was not questioned; but the queen of France made her renunciation as part of a marriage-treaty which contained other stipulations. Some of these other conditions were not fulfilled; for instance, the king of Spain did not pay the promised dowry, and therefore French lawyers maintained, reasonably enough, that the whole treaty, including the renunciation, was invalidated. Further, there were at least some authorities who held that to be effective a renunciation required the assent of the Spanish Cortes, and in this case no such consent was sought. The emperor, for his part, did not recognize the will of Philip IV as valid. He claimed the whole inheritance for himself as the grandson of King Philip III.

Besides the wills and renunciations other legal questions were involved. Some of the Spanish possessions, the duchy of Milan and the marquisate of Finale (which gave access to Milan from the Gulf of Genoa), were Imperial fiefs. The emperor had the right to invest the successor to them, and if no successor could be found, to provide one. For the Milanese to fall into French hands would be dangerous to Austria: it would make the French virtually her neighbours. They would be separated from Tyrol, Carinthia and Carniola only by the Venetian republic, which was insignificant as a military power. Only weakness could prevent the emperor from resisting such a transference. As early as 1667 there were signs that

---

[1] According to J. A. Maravall, *La Philosophie politique espagnole au XVIIe siècle* (1955), p. 152, the only Spanish writer of the period who expressed this opinion was Rodríguez de Lancina, in a book published in 1697 and influenced by the circumstances of that time.

Austria must beware of the French. In that year Louis XIV invaded the Spanish Netherlands, claiming that part of the inheritance of Philip IV for his wife on the pretext that it was due to her by the right of devolution.[1] This pretext for aggression implied a further danger. It was no secret that Louis was keeping the dauphin's claim to the Spanish succession in good repair. Leopold as yet had no son; his only child was an infant daughter. The future of his own dominions might well become, and in the eighteenth century did become, an international problem. Louis conquered the Spanish Netherlands almost without fighting. On 19 January 1668 Leopold did a good turn to Spain and provided against trouble for himself in the future by concluding a secret treaty with Louis, which remained secret for a generation. It provided for an eventual partition of the Spanish empire: if Carlos II should die without heirs, the emperor was to succeed to Spain itself (save for an adjustment of the frontier with France), to the Balearics, Sardinia and the Canaries, Milan, Finale, and the Italian *presidii*,[2] to the whole of Spanish America; France was to take the Netherlands, Franche-Comté, Spanish Navarre and its dependencies, the Catalan port of Rosas, the *presidii* of the North African shore, Naples and Sicily and the far-away Philippines. An attempt to put this treaty into effect would have brought the risk of local conflict in many sensitive places. Success in the attempt would have precipitated still greater dangers. France would still have been compact and centrally placed, but richer and stronger, mistress of the western Mediterranean. The Austro-Spanish empire would have spread out as widely as that of Charles V, but without adequate strategic communications between Germany, Spain and Italy. It is scarcely conceivable that a conflict between the two great agglomerations could have been deferred for long. Nor would the Maritime Powers have been easily reconciled to the plan. Six months earlier they had concluded the Treaty of Breda (31 July 1667), which ended the second of their mutual wars. It was too soon to appreciate that this treaty had gone far towards eliminating the causes of rivalry between them, but for the time being their disputes were suspended and they were acting together in the question of the Spanish Netherlands, which concerned their trade and their safety. It was evident that their great fleets might be combined to maintain their common interests. As things then stood the two powers would have been irresistible at sea, and there were clear signs in the diplomacy of the year 1668 that they might find allies among the continental States.

All this was well known to the French and the Austrians when they made the partition treaty of 1668. They knew that this first essay in secret and hypothetical diplomacy for the disposal of the Spanish empire

---

[1] See vol. v, p. 210.

[2] The *Stato dei Presidii*, constituted by Philip II in 1557, included Porto Ercole, Orbitello, Telamone, Monte Argentaro, Porto Santo Stefano, Porto Longone and Piombino, all on the coasts of the Tyrrhenian Sea. The same Italian form might be used for the garrisoned ports (in Spanish, *presidios*) in North Africa—Ceuta, Melilla and Oran.

could never be put into practice without great efforts of conciliation, or fighting, or both. The course of events was such that the programme soon ceased to have any attractions for either of the contracting parties. The hostility between them, deepened by two wars, became one of the most obstinate of the divisions between the European powers. In the Grand Alliance of 1689 the Maritime Powers and their continental allies pledged their support to the emperor's full claim under the will of Philip IV and, though this clause was not repeated in the renewed alliance of 1695, it was not withdrawn.

By the time of the treaties of Ryswick, after an interval as long as we usually reckon for a generation, not only the European, but also the personal relationships of the Habsburgs and their relatives had altered completely. The dauphin had married a sister of Maximilian Emmanuel of Bavaria, and they had two sons: Louis, duke of Burgundy, who was fifteen years old, and Philip, duke of Anjou, who was nearly fourteen. The emperor's daughter Maria Antonia had been married unhappily to the same elector of Bavaria. She had died in 1692 in Brussels (her husband being, as we have seen, governor of the Spanish Netherlands) in giving birth to a son, the electoral prince Joseph Ferdinand. The emperor himself had now two sons by his third wife—Joseph, who was twenty-one, and Charles, a boy who reached the age of twelve on 1 October 1697. Thus in Vienna, Brussels and Versailles there were young male descendants of King Philip IV of Spain. In Madrid there was no heir and the king's health was failing.

As the Nine Years War drew to its close, and Louis tried to divide the coalition, some of his agents tried, without any chance of success, to tempt the Austrians with hints of a return to the policy of partition. The peace made all the interested States once more accessible to French addresses under the normal conditions of diplomacy. While the Ryswick Congress was still sitting the French plenipotentiary François de Callières, author of a famous treatise on the diplomatic art,[1] sent home a report from which it appeared that two Dutch representatives, Jacob Boreel and Everard van Weede, lord of Dijkvelt, were personally in favour of partition. Boreel spoke for Amsterdam and Dijkvelt belonged to the inner circle of William III, so there was evidently a chance of inducing the Maritime Powers to agree to this principle. The combination which was manoeuvring the Habsburgs into the Peace of Ryswick might continue and sponsor this further scheme.

Immediately after the conclusion of peace a series of exchanges began. They bore some resemblance to the secret conversations between Marshal Boufflers and William's most intimate friend, Hans Willem Bentinck, earl of Portland, which had virtually settled the peace terms. Boufflers indeed

---

[1] Above, p. 173.

was one of Portland's first callers when he arrived early in 1698 in Paris as ambassador, with secret instructions to open the Spanish question. His mission as a whole was executed clumsily and he did not succeed in raising this question; but Pomponne and his son-in-law Torcy had a preliminary talk about it with him in March, on the day before another military man, Camille Hostun, comte de Tallard, went to London to discuss it with the king himself. Neither the English nor (outside William's immediate circle) the Dutch were consulted: nor were the Spaniards, whose diplomatic relations with the Maritime Powers had been broken off in consequence of a personal incident: nor the Austrians, whose attempts to obtain a full renewal of the agreement of 1689 were politely but firmly discouraged by William in November. He did not admit that the Spanish clause in the Treaty of the Grand Alliance was still binding; but the Austrians proposed to make arrangements for enforcing it without informing Spain and without taking precautions against provoking a new war against France. They proposed to dispatch 8,000 to 10,000 troops to Catalonia, for transporting whom they would need the assistance of the Maritime Powers.

Although they did not take the Spaniards into their confidence, the Austrians intended to make full use of any influence which dynastic tradition and diplomatic pressure might give them at the court of Madrid.[1] They wanted the emperor's younger son, the Archduke Charles, to whom he intended to pass his claim, to be admitted to the duchy of Milan. This might have been a prelude to partition. There was only one thing of any importance that anyone in Spain could do: the king could still make a new will in favour of one or other of the claimants. Louis XIV commissioned to Madrid an able diplomatist, Henri marquis d'Harcourt, later duke and marshal of France, who was to advocate the French claim and convince the Spaniards of Louis's goodwill. There was a more certain way of demonstrating his power. On 16 March 1698 he informed Harcourt that he was holding 30 battalions of infantry and 3,000 horse ready to assemble immediately for the march to the Spanish frontiers. If necessary he would add to this force. On the side of Catalonia his magazines were full; on that of Navarre, if it appeared more appropriate, they could easily be stocked in a short time. French troops could enter Spain long before any others could arrive to dispute the dauphin's right. Against the emperor these rights would be maintained by arms, not only because he had no just claim, but also because the union of the Spanish and the Austrian dominions would be contrary to the interests of the whole of Europe. Louis understood, he said, that all Europe would similarly be jealous of a union of his own Crown with those of Spain, and therefore he proposed that the dauphin's rights should pass to whichever of his two sons should be selected by the Spanish Cortes, with the condition that the Crowns of France and Spain should never be united.

---

[1] The court factions are discussed above, pp. 357 ff.

There were many influential opponents of France at the Spanish court, and among them not only Spaniards true to the longstanding national policy. There were supporters of the Austrian Habsburgs, chief among them the queen, Maria Anna of Neuburg, who was the sister of the elector palatine and also of the empress. But the French were formidable and their offers seductive. In the summer of 1698 things went well for them in Spain. In May, indeed, an offer of support by their galleys against the Moors, who were attacking Ceuta and Oran, was refused; but from July to September d'Estrées cruised about the south-west coast of Spain, putting in at Cadiz among other places, ostensibly operating against the Sallee corsairs.[1] Galleys from Rochefort and Marseilles paid visits to ports on the Spanish coast and on that of Italy as far as Naples. By the end of July, besides the 30 battalions and 50 squadrons in Roussillon (with a reserve of 20 battalions and 20 squadrons behind them in Dauphiné) there were 30 battalions and 30 squadrons in French Navarre. The only sign of military counter-measures came from Portugal, where new levies were raised which the French found merely laughable. In August Prince George of Hesse-Darmstadt, the Viceroy of Catalonia, was the object of a French diplomatic campaign which did much to discredit him.[2]

The Maritime Powers had other things to think of besides the policies of France, Spain and the emperor. First there was the demeanour of Max Emmanuel. He was not content with his status as a Spanish official; a hereditary governorship, or at least a secure tenure for life would have suited him better, and might have been a stage on the way to sovereignty; but his masters understood this so well that they kept his actual powers within bounds. He was not allowed to nominate the commanders of the principal fortresses, and a governor of Luxemburg was appointed against his wish. The government in Madrid regarded with suspicion the one able administrator in the Netherlands, Count Bergeyck, who was *trésorier général*.[3] It had refused its support to earlier plans for a Company of the Indies in the Netherlands, but by a decree of 7 June 1698 Bergeyck and Max Emmanuel forced its hands and created the *Compagnie Royale des Pays-Bas, négociant aux places et lieux libres des Indes Orientales et Guinée*, based upon Ostend. Carlos II gave his approval, but there was not enough capital and the Dutch helped to stifle the company at birth. Bergeyck also equipped five ships in 1696–8 to trade with the Spanish colonies in America, and he obtained grants of land in Santo Domingo. He aroused Dutch jealousy by planning new canals to link Ostend with Antwerp and the Sambre and Meuse. All this made Max Emmanuel a source of anxiety, his dynastic position apart. This too was ambiguous.

---

[1] On Morocco in these years, see below, p. 554.

[2] For the moves against his regiment in Madrid later in the year, see above, p. 362. In August it was rumoured that he planned to bring additional troops to Madrid and kidnap Portocarrero, and that he had been forced to resign.

[3] See below, p. 413, for his later reforms.

His own son, the electoral prince Joseph Ferdinand, had no real claim to the Spanish inheritance. He was the grandson of the younger sister of the dauphin's mother. This younger sister had renounced her rights when she married and, resenting her husband's unfaithfulness, she had renounced them again on her deathbed. Nevertheless Max Emmanuel might look forward to making some claim for his son. His alliance was the more desirable for either side precisely because he was untrustworthy and restless.

By the beginning of April 1698 William III made up his mind that, if diplomacy could prevent these calamitous alternatives, neither the Bourbons nor the Habsburgs should acquire the whole Spanish inheritance, or make war for it. He was ready to negotiate with Louis and to press the principle of partition on the emperor and on Max Emmanuel. His position, however, was not that of a mediator: if he was to carry the British and the Dutch along with him he must see that their own direct interests were protected. In the early stages of the negotiations he put forward three points. The Dutch barrier in the Netherlands must be enlarged; for the sake of commerce it would be necessary to have places in the western Mediterranean, perhaps Port Mahon or the whole of Majorca, and some places on the African shore; it would also be necessary to acquire some port in the Indies—that is, in America.[1] None of these points was new. The first demand was essentially defensive. The second also was related to the experience of the recent war. Since the evacuation of Tangier in 1684 the English had possessed no base of their own from which they could operate in the Mediterranean; the Dutch had never possessed any. During the war the two States had used the ports of their Spanish ally to good purpose, but in an uncertain future it was natural that they should not wish to depend on Spain. The idea of acquiring a port in America arose from the peculiarity of trade with Spain. As no successor could be expected to indulge smuggling so handsomely as the Spaniards, trade must have an assured place of entry.

Some historians have supposed that the second and third of the demands indicated by William were not defensive but represented a resumption of the longstanding British policy of commercial expansion and overseas annexations. The idea of a base or bases in the Mediterranean had been mooted at intervals by the ministers of Charles II: they had mentioned Majorca and Sardinia. In 1670 Sir Thomas Allin's fleet made use of Port Mahon in its operations against the Algerines. In the Nine Years War Orford's fleet had protected British and Dutch commerce, but it had done much more; it had been a major strategic and political force. Nor were indications lacking that British colonial ambitions were more alive than they had been in 1689, when the English had refused to agree to a

---

[1] To Portland, 7 April 1698, *Correspondentie van Willem III en van...Bentinck*, vol. I, pt. I, p. 278: it is not specified which of the two powers was to acquire the several places, but only Britain was willing to take a Mediterranean base.

joint expedition to the West Indies with the Dutch. During the war, in 1693–5, the Scottish parliament had founded the Company of Scotland trading to Africa and the Indies. English capital had supported the venture. In spite of the alliance with Spain, the first expedition to the Isthmus of Darien set sail in July 1698. It was not until the next year that there was an armed collision between the Scots and the Spaniards;[1] but the probability of such a collision was implicit in the whole enterprise. Here, then, as in the Mediterranean, it has been maintained that William III used the Spanish succession crisis as an opportunity for furthering British ambitions, which should have been suspended if he had sincerely desired the peace of Europe. It has even been insinuated that he was planning a war for colonial conquests.

So far as the Darien Company is concerned this argument cannot be reconciled with the facts. In its first phase the Company threatened the strongest of English commercial interests, that of the East India trade. The king dismissed the ministers who had procured his assent to the foundation, and the English shareholders withdrew. In the second phase, when the Spanish ambassador protested in London, the king, in January 1699, sent a circular letter to the governors of the English colonies ordering them to refuse all aid or countenance to the Scottish colonists. The Darien Company was not a manifestation of William's policy, but an obstacle to it. Another incident of 1698 scarcely deserves mention: a British battalion was sent to Jamaica. There is no reason for doubting William's explanation to Heinsius that its purpose was purely defensive. Nor is it justifiable to maintain, as some have done, that William excluded the English from the discussions of partition because fundamentally he cared only for Dutch interests. In one of their conversations Tallard propounded an economic argument against the granting of an American port to the British and the Dutch. William replied that, having been brought up in Holland he was well informed about Dutch commercial interests, but not about those of England; he would 'prendre les lumières nécessaires pour cela'; he thought Havana would suit them, but he was not saying anything positive.[2] Many mutually inconsistent slurs have indeed been cast on William's motives. Perhaps the most absurd was that of his former minister the earl of Nottingham, in many ways an estimable man, who had lost office because he was incompetent as secretary of state in time of war. At Ryswick and in the partition-negotiations William relied on the word of Louis, who had so often deceived him and the world, and Nottingham compared him with Hezekiah, who meanly comforted himself and said 'Is it not good if peace be in my days?'.[3] William did not indeed conceal his wish for peace in the short span of life that he was allowed to

---

[1] Above, p. 360.   [2] Legrelle, vol. II (1889), p. 320.
[3] *The Conduct of the Earl of Nottingham*, ed. W. A. Aitken (1941), p. 137. For Hezekiah see II Kings xx. 10 and Isaiah xxxix. 8.

expect, and he knew perfectly well that the negotiations were slippery and even dangerous; but his purpose was to maintain what he valued above all else, the liberties of the States of Europe.

After six months of close bargaining, while the French troops and ships were in motion as we have seen, a Partition Treaty was signed on 11 October 1698. Unlike that of thirty years before, it did not divide the Spanish empire into a French and an Austrian portion, each by itself overwhelmingly stronger than any other State which would remain in Europe. It attained its end, desirable from any general European point of view, by assigning the metropolitan kingdoms of Spain and the richest share of its subject possessions to the one claimant who was not tied to a great power, the child Joseph Ferdinand, electoral prince of Bavaria. He was to have Spain, the Indies, the Netherlands and Sardinia. Enough remained to give great accessions of territory to the other claimants. The dauphin was to take Naples, Sicily, the Basque province of Guipúzcoa, Finale and the Tuscan *presidii*. The emperor's second son, Archduke Charles, was to have the duchy of Milan.

It is hard to imagine a scheme of partition better suited to the requirements of the time. The dynasties of France and Austria were offered possessions on which they could enter without exciting one another's fears and jealousies at once or intolerably. The Maritime Powers would have their Barrier in the sufficiently competent military hands of Max Emmanuel. He, with his electorate of Bavaria and with his brother, the Archbishop-Elector Joseph Clement, established in Liège and Cologne, would be strong enough to prosecute ambitions of his own and to maintain his independence against France. Secured in this way in the strategic keypoint, the Maritime Powers relinquished the hope of guarantees for their Mediterranean navigation, for it was proposed to give France so much of the Italian coasts that she had a prospect of aggrandizement in the eastern as well as the western Mediterranean. No one was to surrender any actual possession; each of the claimants and no one else was to have an accession of power.

The real problem, however, lay not in devising a just partition but in prevailing on the powers to accept any partition at all. The treaty provided that as soon as it was signed the Maritime Powers should impart its contents to the emperor and the elector of Bavaria. If the king of Spain should die without issue these two should be invited to accept the treaty. If they or anyone else refused to comply, in the last resort the signatories should impose it by making war. Louis XIV, however, procured a change in this programme before there was any change in the circumstances. Rumours of the treaty were spreading from France before it was ratified, and no one expected it to remain strictly secret when it should come before the Dutch States-General for approval; but Louis persuaded William to postpone the official notification of the emperor until January 1699. This was a date to which, as it was then thought, the king of Spain could not survive. In effect the emperor was isolated, and he was not unaware of it, which was an obstacle to any renewal of cordial relations between him and the Maritime Powers. William not only agreed to this; he also refrained from helping the emperor to come to any understanding with Max Emmanuel. The elector accepted the proposals, as well he might, with high hopes. Spain itself could not be expected to tolerate the treaty. Her government protested. The king took the only step by which he could still resist partition: on 14 November he made a will. Spanish resentment against the treaty-makers turned him against the dauphin's claim; the emperor, it seemed, would be unable to take advantage of a bequest which France and the Maritime Powers would oppose. In disregard of the four great powers the whole great inheritance was therefore willed to the electoral prince of Bavaria. Legally this will was as much open to cavil as the will of Philip IV. If Louis and William were to hold together and insist on the treaty, they might still prevail on the emperor to brush aside the Spanish recalcitrance. Their determination was never put to the test. After an illness of less than a week, the child Joseph Ferdinand died on 6 February 1699.

The statesmen of Europe reacted to the shock according to their respective natures. In Spain there were some who believed that the integrity of the empire had been saved by a miracle. After an interval Max Emmanuel endorsed the opinion that his son had been poisoned at the instance of the emperor. Louis XIV fulfilled the requirements of official grief, but on the same day when the news reached Versailles he dispatched couriers to Madrid and London to keep the situation in control. The contingency of the prince's death had not been provided for. According to a secret clause of the Partition Treaty, Max Emmanuel was to be treated as heir presumptive to his son, and William III would have been satisfied to allow this arrangement to take effect now; but Louis pointed out truly enough that the elector had only been designated to succeed to what his son should take, and not to his unfulfilled expectations. Apart from this legal objection the new situation was more dangerous for France than the old, but it offered greater prizes to bold ingenuity. Now, as in 1668, there was no third claimant; the Spanish succession was disputed between France and Austria alone. There was no possibility of a direct compromise with the emperor. Since 1689 he had never budged from his claim to the whole, and now at last he was free to use his power in the West as he had never been in those eleven years. On the day of the electoral prince's death the news reached The Hague that a peace for 25 years had been concluded at Carlowitz between the emperor, the Poles, the Venetians and the Turks, with time allowed for the Russians to come in.[1] A year earlier it might

[1] Below, p. 626.

have kept William clear of the entanglements of negotiating with Louis. Now it was too late. William, his reserve and self-control unbroken, entered on negotiations for a new partition.

It took rather more than a year to reach agreement, during which time the health of the king of Spain declined from bad to worse. No other name, such as that of the king of Portugal, proved acceptable to fill the place of the electoral prince. The only principle on which the Spanish empire could be divided into two portions, with France and Austria behind them, was to make each so strong that neither would be tempted to attack the other. Portland used the word 'balance' to Tallard in March 1699, but he meant the balance of two units, not a general European balance in which all the probable allies of either side were taken into account.[1] In this negotiation the Maritime Powers did not revive any of the proposals for cessions to themselves which had been discussed and eliminated before the first Partition Treaty. They did, however, hold out for a satisfactory disposition of the Netherlands Barrier. From the very beginning King William said that it would be intolerable for any French prince to succeed to the Netherlands. Neither did he wish them to go to the emperor. Even if the emperor were a constant ally of the Dutch, and content to leave the Scheldt closed to foreign trade, the Netherlands would have been involved in any eventual conflict between the emperor and France, and therefore the Maritime Powers would again be involved as they had been before. There were other possibilities. The first was Maximilian Emmanuel, but his chance had gone. He was no longer acceptable to either side. Bergeyck's protectionist measures had led to Dutch and British reprisals and diplomatic protests, and to angry resistance from the gilds, which had been supported by the Spanish authorities. Bergeyck fell from office, and Max Emmanuel, frustrated in his economic and political plans, veered to the French, although they were fundamentally even less favourable to such plans than the Spaniards. At one point Louis suggested through Tallard that, if that would be a means of settling all differences, he would not be averse from seeing the Netherlands fall into the hands of the queen of Spain. William thereupon promptly remarked: 'If it were not for my religion I should ask for them myself.'[2] Tallard reported this with inappropriate gravity. In the end there was nothing for it but to assign the Netherlands to an Austrian prince.

The second Partition Treaty was not as ingenious as the first. Its scheme was to give the Netherlands, with the rest of what would have been the electoral prince's share—that is, Spain and the Indies—to the emperor's younger son, Archduke Charles. The frontier between France and Spain was to be modified as in the former treaty. The dauphin was to take Finale and the Italian *presidii* in addition to the Two Sicilies allocated to

---

[1] On the emergence of the idea of a European balance, see above, pp. 155 ff.
[2] Legrelle, vol. III, p. 37.

him then; but Milan was to pass to the emperor's nephew, the duke of Lorraine, in exchange for his duchy, which was to go to the dauphin. Since the Peace of Ryswick Lorraine had been disarmed. It was allowed no fortresses and French troops had the right to march through it. It was ready to be annexed whenever the opportunity came.

As before, the problem lay not in the terms of the treaty but in its reception. This time there was no secrecy: even if secrecy could have been kept it would have created suspicion. The Maritime Powers were again charged with the task of informing the emperor and this time they had to propose that he should allow the French to take the Milanese. The experienced Dutch diplomatist Jacob Hop was instructed to secure his adhesion. He did not succeed. The Maritime Powers did not press the emperor very hard; indeed they were not in a position to do so. He may have known or inferred or guessed that the treaty allowed time for him to come in even after the eventual death of Carlos II. He stood to gain nothing from abating his claim before that event and he had no mind to do it after. The treaty was concluded on 25 March 1700. Instead of agreeing, Leopold discussed the measures he would take if there was no partition. In the summer of 1700 he promised to send two more regiments to Catalonia, and to have 30,000 men ready for the defence of Italy. The Maritime Powers protested in Vienna. The queen of Spain about the same time succeeded in having some expenditure on pensions suspended in order to provide money for the defence of Catalonia. But the queen was only enjoying one of her intermittent spells of influence. There were competitors who could bring Spanish policy back to its moorings and the strongest influence was that of Cardinal Portocarrero, the archbishop of Toledo, who believed that the monarchy could be preserved from partition by no other power than France. The Regency Junta[1] recommended that the dauphin's second son, Philip duke of Anjou, should be sole heir. The aged Pope Innocent XII was consulted, as was indeed proper if only because the kingdom of the Two Sicilies was a papal fief. He was asked how the new will which the king must make should be drawn in the interests of the Church and the Spanish monarchy. He took advice from a special committee of three cardinals and replied as Portocarrero had wished.[2] The French knew what was going on in Rome, and they knew that Carlos had not long to live. Whether they believed there was still a chance that they could agree on any solution with the emperor may be doubted. On 4 October[3] they began to augment their army, before they knew that two

---

[1] Above, pp. 360-1.

[2] Pope Innocent died on 27 September and his successor, Clement XI, denied the authenticity of French reports to this effect. Although the originals of the Spanish request and the papal reply have not been discovered, and there are obscurities in the story of events, the main point is not seriously open to question. See L. von Pastor, *History of the Popes*, vol. XXXII (1940), pp. 686-8.

[3] For this instructive date see G. Girard, *Racolage et milice, 1701–1715* (1921), pp. 4-5.

days earlier the king had made his will. It was such as the pope and the cardinal had recommended. The whole inheritance was bequeathed to the duke of Anjou. If neither he nor his younger brother would accept it, it was to go to the Austrian Habsburgs. The king died on All Saints' Day.

The French king and his ministers did not hurry unduly; they considered the crisis in all its aspects, and they were not unanimous. They preserved the forms of politeness in communicating their decision to the other powers. The decision was to accept the will. The marquis de Torcy, a nephew of the great Colbert, had succeeded his father-in-law Pomponne as foreign secretary, and in November he smoothly stated the case for this decision in a memoir to King William. The happy tranquillity which everyone desired would now be assured. The two monarchies of France and Spain were to remain separate as they had been for so many years. The even balance which all Europe desired would be much better established than it would have been under the Partition Treaty, which contemplated additions to the strength of France itself.

This line of thought received a commentary from events in various quarters. The governor of Milan, appointed in 1698, was Charles Henry, prince of Vaudemont. This old comrade-in-arms of William was an illegitimate son of the great Imperial general Charles V of Lorraine, to whose House according to the Partition Treaty the duchy of Milan would ultimately fall. Before November was out Vaudemont proclaimed King Philip V of Spain as duke of Milan. The most important of all the Spanish governors, Max Emmanuel, would certainly try to pursue his own ambitions, but he recognized King Philip as his new master: on 7 December a *Te Deum* was sung at Ste Gudule in Brussels. There was no public promise that the merchants of other countries would enjoy their freedom of commerce in the Spanish dominions, or of navigating freely through the Straits of Gibraltar or the Sicilian narrows, both of which would be effectively under French control. There was not even any announcement in France to assure the rest of the world that the Crowns of France and Spain were never to be united. In order to exclude other branches of his own family from the French succession Louis expressly reserved the right of the Spanish house of Anjou to succeed to the French throne in default of heirs. This laid itself open to a sinister interpretation by hostile propaganda.

For the first two months of 1701 Louis XIV supposed, and not without reason, that he might carry out the policy of the will without provoking a general war and without having to meet any armed resistance except such as the emperor might maintain in Italy. But the diplomacy of these months, and indeed of the whole year 1701, is unintelligible unless account is also taken of the concurrent French and Austrian military measures. We have seen that the augmentation of Louis's army began before the king of Spain died. Each of the French companies of infantry received the considerable addition of ten men. In January 1701 the militia was reconstituted, and this time, to make it more effective, the militia units were attached to regular battalions. By February the reinforcement of the infantry was complete. In November the granting of discharges from the colours was stopped. Before January 1702 the regular army numbered 220,502 men, a larger number than in 1688. Along with intense diplomatic activity to isolate the emperor, Louis moved his troops to be ready for fighting or intimidation much as he had done then; indeed he seems to have followed that precedent too closely. He acted as if France had recovered from the exhaustion of 1697, but there were difficulties and deficiencies which showed that this was not the case. Nor was the European situation as favourable as it had been then to his efforts to attract support in Germany, in Italy, in northern and eastern Europe. He counted too much on the temporary embarrassments of his former enemies.

In the Netherlands the decrepit Spanish government was now on Louis's side. His troops stood on the frontier and by moving in they could easily overpower the Dutch garrisons of the barrier-fortresses or cut them off from their supplies. The fortresses indeed were in poor condition; there was a shortage of engineers; there were no stores worth mentioning; the guns were of different calibres from the French; and the Spanish and Bavarian troops, about equal in numbers, only amounted to about 10,000 infantry altogether, with 1,500 Spanish cavalry, mostly unmounted, all of them ill-disciplined and ill-paid. French money was immediately made available for setting all this to rights. On 4 February William III, as captain-general, ordered the Dutch troops to withdraw; but he left it to the local commander to choose his time, and the order came too late. On 6 February the Spanish commanders admitted superior French forces to each place. The Dutch troops were kept in humiliating uncertainty and not released to return to their own country until the French had reinforced the northern frontiers of the Netherlands. When their withdrawal was completed at the end of March, much had been done—for instance at Antwerp, Lierre and other fortresses. Max Emmanuel, however, was no longer there. On 9 March 1701 he made a treaty of alliance with the French in which they guaranteed the debts owed him by Spain, and promised to support him as a candidate for election as emperor; but they extinguished his hopes of a great future in the Netherlands. When Bergeyck came back into office as *surintendant des finances* it was to work with the French, much as the Spanish military commander, the marquis of Bedmar, worked with Boufflers. Max Emmanuel was packed off to his German territories. There he was to remain neutral but he was to raise 8,000 infantry and 2,000 cavalry, a contingent which was increased by a new agreement a few weeks later to 15,000.

The agreement with Max Emmanuel appears indecisive because it touched the most delicate point of the French diplomatic network. Louis had once more carried out the manoeuvre which he had often practised before: he had pounced upon a territory in time of peace. This time it was not only the inhabitants of the Spanish Netherlands that he had acquired, with their resources and ports and the great commercial advantages that a strong power might obtain from them. He had also pushed his frontier forward so that the Dutch could have no forward bases outside their own territory and Antwerp was lost to the Maritime Powers. This enormous advantage did not mean, however, that he had the same strategic problem as in 1688 and was in a better position to turn it to account. The difference was that then he was committed to fighting in Germany, and wanted to prevent it from spreading to any other region, but now he was committed by the emperor's attitude to fighting in Italy and equally anxious to prevent it from spreading thence. For the time being the best service his German supporters could render him was to remain neutral, while at the same time arming in order to deter the emperor from acting north of the Alps. This task did not appear too much for them. Closely linked with Maximilian Emmanuel, and even more amenable, was his brother Joseph Clement. As bishop of Regensburg, Joseph Clement counted for something in the south; as bishop of Liège, he counted for more in the direction of the Netherlands; and as archbishop of Cologne, he held the Rhine above the Dutch frontier fortresses, including the bridges by which the French could join hands with Bavaria and the Corresponding Princes[1] in the north.

Joseph Clement, however, had to be handled carefully, not so much because he was shifty as because overt action on his part might easily touch off explosions in Germany. His fortresses were in need of repair. The elector palatine coveted Kaiserswerth, and the elector of Brandenburg Rheinberg. In the spring of 1701 the archbishop made an agreement with France: he was to receive a subsidy and to hire 4,000 men and 1,000 horses, numbers which were increased later in the year. No sooner was the treaty made than he began to raise the troops, and he rashly revived old quarrels with the chapter of Cologne, with the result that in August the Estates, led by the chapter, refused to vote him supplies and he announced that he would raise taxes by force. The chapter appealed to the emperor. The emperor was willing to support them and also to forestall wider dangers by occupying the elector's fortresses; but the Maritime Powers would not agree. The defences of the Dutch frontier, for instance at Bergen-op-Zoom, were not ready. The French were close enough to Cologne for their immediate purposes, and they were equipping Namur, Venlo and Guelders as magazines for an offensive. Fifteen French battalions and fifteen squadrons were dispatched to Spanish Gelderland, where

---

[1] See above, p. 246, n. 1.

the Dutch held Maastricht, nominally as a pledge for money owed them by the Spaniards. It looked as if this fortress on the Meuse, or the land between the Meuse and the Rhine, would be the French objective.

In the Netherlands and on the lower Rhine, by the end of March 1701, things were visibly moving as if the French intended to begin an offensive war. They were, however, still negotiating with the Maritime Powers, and until this time these negotiations on both sides were much more like a last attempt to reach a peaceful settlement than a device to gain time for military preparations. The news that France had accepted the will of Carlos II was a blow to William III. He had been deceived by French promises; the Partition Treaty was dead; he had no agreement with the emperor and no certainty that the emperor would not as soon agree with the French as with the Maritime Powers. The Spanish Netherlands, the strategic key to Europe, were under French control. Worst of all, the French arguments in favour of a general acceptance of the will told heavily both in London and in Amsterdam, where many, or even most, of the influential men believed that trade in the Mediterranean and the Spanish colonies was not threatened by anything except a possible war. In England the indifference was more stubborn than in Holland. The last session of the parliament which was dissolved on 19/29 December 1700 was the most factious that William ever had to contend with. He wrote to Heinsius in November that he thought the blindness of the English to their continental interests was a punishment for them from Heaven. But he also wrote:

It is my extreme mortification to be unable to act in this important matter with the vigour which it demands and to set a good example of going forward; but it must happen through the republic (*den staet*), and I hope with prudent management to engage the people here insensibly, without their being aware of it.[1]

When it became evident that nothing could be arranged with Max Emmanuel, the next possibility to be tested was that the French might allow Spain to hand over some of the towns—such as Ostend and Nieuwpoort to the English, and Luxemburg, Namur and Mons to the Dutch—as guarantees for the independence of the Spanish Netherlands. In order to placate their own commercial opinion, and also in order to negotiate jointly and show a common front, the two States—the Dutch in February, the English in April—conceded a major point, at the risk of offending the emperor, by recognizing Philip V as king of Spain. Tallard was in London and the famous Count d'Avaux was in The Hague; couriers galloped to and fro and conference followed conference. William's new parliament seemed to most observers as perverse as the old. The country members inveighed against the defunct Partition Treaties, impeached the former ministers, and struggled in party feuds; but the king treated them with imperturbable courtesy and with a new confidence. Silently abandoning his claim to the control of foreign affairs, he put

[1] *Archives de la Maison d'Orange-Nassau*, 3rd ser. vol. III (1909), pp. 206, 249.

before them all the treaties since 1677 and all the available information about current events. He left it to them to judge what action was needed. Simultaneously and with scarcely any contact two series of debates ran side by side, in one of which William was obstructed, while in the other parliament moved into line behind him. Spontaneously or not, a popular agitation out of doors demanded measures against the French, and though this ruffled the self-esteem of the Commons the upshot was exactly what William had begun to work for in November. In February he told Heinsius that the opinion of the nation was changing. The Commons resolved that they would support the interests and safety of England and the Protestant religion and the peace of Europe. Three days later they requested the king to open negotiations for sending succours to the Dutch on the basis of the treaty of March 1678. Next day Tallard wrote that he considered war inevitable, and Louis replied that he was right. Before the session closed on 14/25 June the Commons had given the king *carte blanche* to make his alliances; they had voted more money than had ever been voted in time of peace, and they had done it 'for the advantage of the common cause'. Tallard stayed in London for another week, d'Avaux in The Hague rather longer, but there was no real business for them to do.

There was a common cause against France, but it was not yet clear who was engaged in it besides the Maritime Powers, or on what terms. First there was the question of the emperor. When the king of Spain died the emperor had an army of 75,000 men on foot, and he could augment it if he would. The court of Vienna was always slow to move. Its finances had been exhausted by the Turkish war, and though something was done to improve them in 1701, it was not until two years later that reform got well under way.[1] The emperor wanted the Maritime Powers to fight the French, indeed to be the first to do so; but they not unnaturally thought that it was for him, the claimant, to lead the way into war over the Spanish succession, not for them, the frustrated advocates of partition. And they wanted him to pitch his claim high. If he confined himself to the Imperial fiefs, Milan and Finale, he might conquer these and be satisfied, or Louis might buy him off by surrendering these and then concentrate his efforts elsewhere. To break 'the exorbitant power of France' it was necessary to have the emperor fully committed, with all the allies he could muster, and for that the best leverage would be his old full claim to the whole Spanish inheritance. William, however, expressed himself as doubtful whether the clause embodying this claim in the Grand Alliance treaty of 1689 was still binding; in any event new agreements on war-aims and contingents were needed, and the emperor's decisions would depend on events both in Germany and in Italy.

In both countries there were likely to be allies for both sides and also neutrals. In Germany there were no Spanish possessions. France might

---

[1] Cf. above, pp. 310 ff.

renew her schemes of hegemony and territorial encroachment, and the new understanding with Bavaria might drive a wedge into south Germany. Bavaria, however, was geographically cut off from the French by Württemberg and Baden. Max Emmanuel had not yet declared his change of sides and Louis was studiously avoiding any sign of aggressiveness. For the four greater powers the German problems were subsidiary to those of Italy, the Netherlands and Spain, but Germany could not be ignored.

For the first two years after the Peace of Ryswick the emperor had serious embarrassments there; but after that his position became stronger. Two of the lay electors gave him no anxiety, his brother-in-law John William of the Palatinate and Augustus of Saxony, whom he had assisted to the throne of Poland in 1697. The strongest elector, Frederick of Brandenburg, was also the most exigent, but on 16 November 1700, after the Second Partition Treaty, the emperor agreed to his price, recognition as king in Prussia, in exchange for an auxiliary force of 8,000 men. Frederick placed the crown on his own head at Königsberg on 18 January 1701. Hanover, the Hessian States and Waldeck were unconditionally with the emperor. The Corresponding Princes, on the other hand, continued to give trouble, chief among them Anton Ulrich of Brunswick and the duke of Gotha. On 5 August 1700 a group of them even applied to Louis XIV for his support. Another combination of princes, which had been formed in 1697, also impeded the emperor's designs. The six Hither Circles which touched the Rhine were associated together, and until 1701 Baden and Württemberg tried to persuade them to organize a common army. In November 1700 the Franconian and Swabian Circles made an agreement with Max Emmanuel. In December Louis XIV informed the electors on the Rhine that if they concerned themselves with the Spanish succession he would regard this as a rupture of the peace. By this time, however, the emperor was able to assert himself in Germany with more vigour.

In 1699 the peace with the Turks had freed him from the burdens of war. A year later the Great Northern War broke out. During the Nine Years War the rivalry of Sweden and Denmark had prevented them from playing a part of any importance. Now they were at war with one another. Their first cause of quarrel, the *status quo* in Sleswig–Holstein, might easily involve the princes of north-west Germany. Moreover the Danes had joined a coalition which aimed at destroying the Swedish power in Germany and the Baltic lands: the future of Denmark, Poland and Russia was at stake. Charles XII of Sweden crushed the Danes, and compelled them to recognize the full sovereignty of the duke of Holstein; but the Maritime Powers sent a fleet to restrain him from further exploits against Denmark, and after the Treaty of Travendal (18 August 1700) the Northern War no longer threatened the entry to the Baltic.[1] Charles succeeded in

---

[1] For these events, see below, pp. 652 ff.

removing danger from the Saxon and Russian forces later in the year, and in December he promised the French his armed guarantee for the will of Carlos II.

In Vienna the Swedish victories caused great anxiety. It was natural, though groundless, to suppose that Charles XII, like Gustavus Adolphus, was acting in concert with the French. The old discontent of Hungary stirred again, and Louis XIV sent agents to work with Francis Rákóczi.[1] Leopold, however, with his sons and the now famous Prince Eugene, firmly withstood the peace-party among his counsellors. In December 1700 it was announced that Lewis of Baden would command an army on the Rhine; that the emperor would raise men in Hungary and take eight regiments of the Palatinate into his service. Newspapers credited him with the intention of raising the army to 100,000 in the spring. The action of Louis in the Netherlands and his intrigues with the Wittelsbachs raised support for the emperor in Germany. In March 1701 there were unsuccessful attempts to bring together the Corresponding Princes in a conference; thenceforward Louis could only negotiate with them individually, and only two promised to raise troops—Brunswick-Wolfenbüttel 8,000 and Saxe-Gotha 6,000. But the French had no intention of starting a fight on the lower Rhine. Further south they strengthened their existing fortifications. Instead of interfering with Germany the Swedish king had crossed the Baltic to save Ingria from the Russians: he won his victory at Narva on 30 November 1700. Everything concurred to indicate Italy as the theatre where French and Austrian would come to blows.

In Italy the French had an initial advantage in the adhesion of Vaudemont. Tessé went there in December 1700 and soon discovered that the governor of the Milanese was the only man in all Italy whom they could trust. To begin with, Tessé was anxious not to alarm the other Italian States and so he asked for only a small number of French troops—24 battalions, three squadrons of cavalry and three of dragoons. At the end of December and the beginning of January they embarked at Monaco, Antibes and Toulon, and landed at Finale, Vado and Alassio. Their status was to be that of auxiliaries for the Spaniards: their coming did not imply war between France and the emperor. In February 1701 the emperor's preparations convinced Vaudemont and Tessé that they would need more, and they asked for the whole army of Italy, which was to amount to 40 battalions and 56 squadrons. In March the princess of Mirandola surrendered her city to the French, and the duke of Mantua, a more genuine supporter, also received French troops. The duke of Savoy—'ce prince incompréhensible', as Tessé rightly called him—bargained enthusiastically with both sides. In the end he came to terms with the French: he was to allow their troops to pass through his dominions, to provide 10,000 men and to have the nominal command-in-chief. One

[1] Below, p. 584.

of his daughters was to be married to Philip V of Spain. Among the other powers Tuscany adhered to the emperor; Venice was bound by treaty to allow Austrian troops to pass through her territories but might be expected to allow the French to do the same within decent limits; and all the others favoured the pope's plan of neutrality for the Spanish possessions in Italy. In the spring Marshal Catinat arrived in Milan. It did not yet appear whether the emperor would confine his efforts to north Italy or also strike at Naples by sea from Trieste.

By these processes it came about that by the beginning of April, 1701, the time of year when the fighting season normally began, there was undeclared war. The kings of France and Spain, with the electors of Bavaria and Cologne and the duke of Savoy as allies, were building up armies in the Low Countries, on the lower Rhine and in Italy, while the emperor and the Maritime Powers made their counter-preparations. No one had fired a shot; there was still no formal coalition against France. But neither side felt sure that the other might not go into action that summer, in any of the theatres where the last war had been fought except Catalonia, which now lay between two friendly powers. The middle and upper Rhine seemed likely to be spared; and the military preparations everywhere were less advanced than the powers wished them to appear.

During the summer both sides were openly busy with military concentrations and the financial and diplomatic groundwork for them. In England the money was voted for 90 ships and 40,000 seamen 'new raised'. The Dutch, by increasing the number of effectives in their existing units, set about raising their army to 75,000 men. They were making 50 ships ready for sea. They took two regiments into pay from Hesse-Cassel in May, and agreed to hire troops from Mecklenburg-Schwerin. By July these, with the contingents from Brandenburg, Brunswick-Lüneburg, the Palatinate and Ansbach, brought the Dutch land-forces up to about 100,000. Their principal camps were near Maastricht and at Goch on the Niers (near Nymegen). A force was stationed in the neighbourhood of Guelders to resist any French attempt in that quarter. Boufflers had his headquarters at Diest, while Tallard assembled a separate force on the Moselle. In the Netherlands, however, the French preparations savoured of territorial and defensive strategy: there was little to indicate that offensive operations were intended. The French court agreed, after some hesitation, to Spanish proposals for the construction of long lines of earthworks. One line was to run from Antwerp to Namur; another, to cover the Pays de Waes from the old Bourg of Ghent to the Franc de Bruges. By the end of August, Boufflers and Tallard together had 147 battalions and 225 squadrons. The lines from the sea to the Meuse were almost complete. On 12 August Marlborough felt sure that the French had abandoned any thought of opening a campaign in Flanders that year.

They were indeed soon planning their winter quarters, and it was decided to leave a third of the army in the Netherlands and withdraw two-thirds of it to French Flanders. Louis made up his mind, by 22 September, that fighting in the Netherlands would not begin that year.

By parallel stages it became certain that Germany also was to have a respite in 1701. The emperor contracted for a regiment from Bayreuth in the spring, and another from Hesse-Darmstadt, which also sent reinforcements to the bishop of Osnabrück. The bishop of Würzburg contributed two regiments of infantry and one of cavalry. In August, indeed, the south German Circles, Franconia and Swabia, with the upper Rhine, the electoral Rhine and Bavaria, declared that they would stand neutral and agreed to form a common army. This was a success for French diplomacy; but it was not followed by any other successes, and it did not foreshadow a French offensive. There were many who pressed the emperor to keep troops on the Rhine for the defence of Germany; but there was no immediate threat from the French or their friends, whereas unless something was done to save the Milanese it would be lost.

Eugene took command in December 1700 of an army which began its march from the Austrian duchies in February, growing as it marched. Late in May it entered Venetian territory and early in June it was drawn up on the river Adige to the number of 32 battalions and 26 squadrons, with five mounted regiments on the way to join them. The emperor decided to add to their strength by withdrawing 10,000 men from the Rhine. Catinat asked for reinforcements. They were too slow in coming, and when they did come consisted only of three Spanish battalions, with one regiment of cavalry and one of dragoons. On 19 June shots were exchanged across the Adige. The Italian fighting had begun and, in spite of appearances, the French were not ready for it. They had pushed their troops forward without a proper provision of supplies, and they had long lines of communication running through unfriendly country where the peasants were not averse from shooting at stragglers. Catinat was uncertain of success in battle and he left the initiative entirely to Eugene. The result was startling. Eugene had a smaller army, no magazines and no proper respect for his opponent's scientifically correct manoeuvres. He crossed four rivers unopposed. On 9 July he won a battle at Carpi. Before the middle of the month the French had no longer any river in front of them. In August Marshal Villeroi arrived from the Netherlands to supersede Catinat, and with positive orders to fight. He kept Catinat with him for the time being, and threw himself into restoring French discipline and morale. On 1 September, in difficult hill-country at Chiari, an engagement on the French left flank developed into a big battle in which 20 French battalions went into the attack. They suffered thousands of casualties and their attack was a failure. King Louis reversed the order to fight.

None of the military movements of the summer gave French diplomacy any advantage and none of them impeded the building of the coalition. The Italian victories of Eugene assisted it. There was one momentous personal change. King William knew from his doctors that his health was now failing fast. Little strength remained to him except his clear purpose and his unbreakable will. In 1698 he had fully restored to favour the earl of Marlborough, who was not only the favourite of the heiress presumptive, the Princess Anne, but also a most dexterous politician and a first-class military commander. He now promoted Marlborough to offices which enabled him to fill the king's own place so far as office could qualify an Englishman to fill it, those of commander-in-chief of the British forces destined for Holland and ambassador extraordinary to the republic. In July Marlborough was installed in the Mauritshuis while the king paid his summer visit as stadholder; he stayed behind when the king returned to England, and in completing the treaties of alliance he showed that he had the personal qualities that were needed. The central agreement, the Treaty of the Grand Alliance, was signed on 7 September 1701. It did not ostensibly make the arrangements for a war that was bound to happen. It provided that from the date of ratification two months were to be spent in attempting to obtain the purposes of the alliance by amicable negotiation with the king of France. Nor were these purposes closely defined. The principle of partition was accepted. The emperor was to receive a satisfaction for his claims to the Spanish inheritance. At his insistence Naples and Sicily were specified as well as Milan. On the other hand, he had to agree that the Maritime Powers were to retain any conquests they might make in the Spanish Indies. The southern Netherlands were to be a barrier for the Dutch; but the sovereignty over them, which the emperor did not desire for himself, was still an open question. Nothing was said about the future of Spain. This, however, was enough to go on with, and the alliance now had a solid nucleus.

The king-elector of Brandenburg-Prussia came in as an ally. Besides the contingent of 6,000 men which he supplied in the next year to the Imperial army, he retained a substantial force which he could have used, but in fact did not use, to intervene in the Northern War. Augustus the Strong of Poland and Saxony was already deeply involved in that war, and he might have compassed large ambitions with French support. When the Spanish succession question came to a head, the only attraction of Augustus for the French was that he might become an ally if France could mediate successfully in the North. In May 1701 he promised to attack the emperor with 30,000 men in that event; but nothing came of the French mediation. In January 1702 the Polish-French negotiations were broken off, and the king-elector signed an offensive and defensive alliance with the emperor. Hesse-Cassel had been near to acting with the Corresponding Princes, but contracted with the Maritime Powers in the spring of 1701 to supply two infantry regiments (each of 1,000 men) and went on in the summer to further negotiations which ended in his joining the alliance with 9,000 men, of which two-thirds were to be entirely paid and supplied, and the remainder provided with maintenance and ammunition in the field, by the Maritime Powers.

France had promised heavy subsidies to Bavaria and Poland, heavier than she could easily have paid, and in dealing with the minor German princes she was hampered by shortage of money. Her diplomatists could do little more than appeal to the princes to join with the French in asserting their own true interests; but the course of events, as well as the solvency of the Maritime Powers, led them to think the emperor the more likely to understand where these interests lay. There was a movement of German opinion in his favour. The elector of Mainz, who was also prince-bishop of Bamberg, was won over, with his neighbour of Trier, to a subsidy-treaty in October 1701. By March 1702 the whole of the Associated Circles except Bavaria came to an agreement with Austria and joined the Grand Alliance. In May Trier joined the Grand Alliance, promising to garrison its places and allow the Allied troops freedom to march through its territories. The formal declaration of war by the Empire as a body, and the plans for forming an Imperial army did not follow until the autumn of 1702; but in the spring the positions of the German States were already defined. Besides his two main allies, Cologne and Bavaria, Louis had only three States on his side. One was Holstein-Gottorp, which made a subsidy-treaty in October 1701, but changed sides when the duke died a year later. The other two were Brunswick-Wolfenbüttel and Saxe-Gotha, the remnant of the Corresponding Princes. Neither of them was of any use to him. In February 1702 regiments from Hanover and Celle carried out a *Reichsexecution*[1] against Anton Ulrich of Brunswick. The duke of Saxe-Gotha, finding that France could not help him, drew the lesson and let his troops out on hire to the Allies.

The one considerable success of French diplomacy in 1701 related to Portugal. The ancient tradition of Portuguese alliance with Great Britain could not be expected to count for very much, nor the ancient Portuguese enmity with Spain; but the Maritime Powers could exert pressure on the Portuguese ports and commerce, and it was only there that the Allies could find a land-base to invade Spain or a sea-base for the Mediterranean. As the king of Portugal had toyed with the idea of putting forward claims to a share in the Spanish succession, it was surprising that in June 1701 Portugal made treaties of alliance, or more truly of friendship, with France and Spain.[2]

The French preparations in the summer and autumn of 1701 showed

---

[1] That is, the enforcement of an Imperial decision—in this case a decision made by the emperor at the instance of William III.

[2] On Portuguese foreign policy cf. below, pp. 524 ff.

what the strategic outline of the war was to be. In August they had 19 ships rigged in Brest and 24 in Cadiz: in November they convoyed the Spanish plate-fleet home. In November too they were building a fort opposite Sas van Ghent, and in December the Dutch fired on them there. Three French decisions of the autumn show that it was impossible for the undeclared war to end in anything except real war. On 16 September, nine days after the signing of the Grand Alliance, but before Louis knew of it, King James II died at St Germains. In spite of the Peace of Ryswick he had, like other exiled kings, been allowed to use his old titles. If Louis XIV denied these honours now to the 'pretended prince of Wales', he would appear to treat the Stuarts shabbily. If he conceded them, he would gain credit in several quarters, including the Vatican. After some little deliberation he recognized the heir as titular king of Great Britain and Ireland. This chivalrous gesture was believed in England to mean that Louis espoused the Jacobite cause and, as Louis believed war to be coming, this belief was correct. It had the effect of consolidating every possible English resentment against France. In the same month, recklessly arousing English commercial feeling, Spain followed the example given by France a few days earlier and prohibited the importation of British manufactures.

In his dealings with Spain Louis had been careful down to this point to avoid provoking dissatisfaction against Philip, whose position was still precarious; and it is surprising that he now approved of a proposal which, from this point of view, was dangerous. On 30 October Torcy wrote to Count Marsin, a soldier of Flemish extraction who had succeeded Harcourt in Madrid, instructing him to ask for the cession of the Spanish Netherlands to France. It would make war easier to manage, and it would not make peace more difficult to arrange. It would compensate France for the expenses she had incurred and would still have to incur. Marsin answered that such a proposal would be resented by the Spaniards as a blow at the integrity of their empire, perhaps with disastrous consequences. Louis dropped it, but he did not drop the idea of partition, to which he was already reverting as a basis for a settlement. It was plain enough, even from the course of his public conduct, that he regarded the Spaniards and their king as virtually his subjects.

During the winter of 1701–2, preparations for war went forward on all sides without any interruption and without any diplomatic attempt worth mentioning to avert it. In November Joseph Clement of Cologne, alarmed by the appearance of Dutch troops in the Palatinate, prevailed on the French to send troops to his fortresses, including Liège. As an excuse they were called auxiliaries to the Burgundian Circle. William III was still not ready to move, or to encourage the emperor to intervene. He was anxious, however, that the emperor should hold his German supporters[1] together by sending to the upper Rhine the full contingent of his own troops

---

[1] Below, pp. 410–11.

which he had promised in the Grand Alliance treaty. The emperor was tempted to divert troops to Italy, where Eugene's army was weak and ill-provided. On 1 February Eugene narrowly failed in a *coup de main* against Cremona on the Po, and carried away Marshal Villeroi as a prisoner; but there had been an element of the unaccountable in his successes, and even if reinforced he expected to be outnumbered in the spring. The emperor played with the idea of detaching a force for Naples and, equally prematurely, asked the Maritime Powers to send a fleet to the Mediterranean.[1] In spite of William's exhortations and of new offers which he was willing to make, it seemed as if the French might once more, as in the earlier wars, find the Germans too late in the field to take their share in the strain. A good 40,000 men from the Circles assembled, along with Austrians and Palatines, under Lewis of Baden on the upper Rhine.

Fighting had already begun again in Italy when William died on 19 March. Boufflers halted the concentration of his troops and waited for orders. A French diplomatist, Barré, was at The Hague as secretary. He was hastily commissioned as 'agent' and applied to the States-General for new negotiations with them alone. He explained the pacific intentions of France to such of the Amsterdam regents as were thought to be well intentioned. On 8 April the States-General rejected the French advances. The Dutch were firm and by now they were ready. Marlborough, Heinsius and the emperor's ambassador, Count Goes, made the final arrangements. On 16 April the troops of the Dutch Republic, Prussia and the Palatinate invested Kaiserswerth. Since there was still a chance of prolonging the nominal peace with the Empire, Boufflers, stationed in the territory of Jülich, was ordered not to cross the Rhine. On 15 May Austria, Great Britain and the United Provinces simultaneously declared war against France.

[1] A. D. Francis, 'Prince George of Hesse-Darmstadt and the Plan for the Expedition to Cadiz of 1702', *Bulletin of the Institute of Historical Research*, vol. XLII (1969), pp. 58–75, shows that Vienna regarded the capture of Cadiz (below, p. 418) as complementary to a Mediterranean offensive in the same year, in face of the objections of the British admiralty.

CHAPTER XIII

THE WAR OF THE SPANISH SUCCESSION IN EUROPE

THE two great conflicts which ushered in the eighteenth century added up to a real world war. Yet they developed without ever fundamentally influencing each other. Only on rare occasions, as in 1707, were the two European storm-centres in danger of merging. The belligerents of the Succession War stayed neutral in the war against Sweden, as did the Baltic belligerents in the war against France, although Denmark supplied the Maritime Powers with subsidy troops. Prussia joined in the western war even though the Great Northern War really concerned her much more.

The Grand Alliance of 7 September 1701 united the three powers which primarily waged the last and decisive war against the hegemony of Louis XIV: Austria, Britain and the United Provinces. In principle, Emperor Leopold I claimed the whole Spanish inheritance for the House of Habsburg. Without waiting till the treaty was signed, without even declaring war, he had sent an army into north Italy to try to occupy Milan, an Imperial fief which in his view reverted automatically to the Holy Roman Empire upon the death of Carlos II; the French troops acted in Lombardy only as auxiliaries of Philip V.[1] The Maritime Powers, however, were not prepared in 1701 to fight for the strictly legitimist Habsburg claim. They undertook to assist the Habsburgs only to acquire 'a just and reasonable satisfaction' in Italy, the Spanish Mediterranean islands and the Spanish Netherlands, subject in this last case to the provision of 'a dyke, rampart and barrier to separate and keep off France from the United Provinces'. It is therefore clear that the Grand Alliance, William III's last masterpiece, started from the premiss that the Spanish monarchy should be divided. Further, Philip V would be allowed to rule in Spain and the Indies only on condition that the Crowns of France and Spain were never united: even at that, the Maritime Powers decided, at Britain's prompting, that they would retain any possible conquests in the Indies, besides retaining all the commercial privileges in Spanish territories which they had enjoyed under Carlos II.[2]

During the winter of 1701–2 a number of German States adhered to the Alliance, either by separate treaty or through a so-called Act of Inclusion: Brandenburg-Prussia, Hanover, the Palatinate, Münster, Hesse-Cassel,

[1] For the formation of the Grand Alliance and operations in 1701, see above, pp. 405 ff.; for the Habsburg interest in Italy, below, pp. 590 ff.
[2] For the war in America, see above, pp. 372–3 and below, pp. 501 ff.

Baden and some smaller powers. In exchange for the recognition of his new title of 'king in Prussia', Elector Frederick III of Brandenburg had committed himself to support the emperor; the mere prospect of succeeding to the English throne brought in Elector George Lewis of Hanover. These princes were seldom to be allies in the full sense, their regiments being hired out to the Maritime Powers simply as auxiliaries: only Prussia, in addition to this kind of help, made a direct contribution to the war. Thanks to their financial resources, the Maritime Powers possessed in Germany thoughout the war a virtually inexhaustible reservoir of soldiers, whereas French reserves there were giving out. Opinion in the Empire was predominantly anti-French, both out of resentment at the losses incurred under the treaties of Nymegen and Ryswick and from fear of further French aggression.[1] Yet two strategically important powers, Bavaria and Cologne, chose the French side, while Saxony was fully occupied by the Northern War and other princes advocated neutrality. When at last, in September 1702, the Empire as a whole declared war on 'Philip of Anjou', the contingents supplied by the Circles proved to possess only mediocre fighting value.

Of all the Allies, the Dutch Republic was best prepared for war on land. The army created by William III was in excellent form; in 1702 it was rapidly being increased to a total strength of 100,000. Britain was less well prepared, but during 1702 she sent an expeditionary force of 40,000 to the Continent. In the course of the war the Republic increased its army to 137,000, Britain to 70,000. In each case, these large numbers were only achieved by enlisting German and Danish auxiliaries; not a half of either army consisted of national troops. For all that, these figures do suggest what an enormous effort was put out by the tiny Republic in the land war. In the main theatre, the Spanish Netherlands, it was the Dutch who had continuously to carry the heaviest burden. They were responsible for the cost of the many sieges and the supply of heavy guns: the British brought field-guns but no siege-artillery with them. And from the very start the Republic was forced to borrow at high interest to meet the cost of the war; in England, which was financially more stable, the yield of the taxes went much further towards it. At sea the situation was completely different. There, as in the previous war, it was agreed that Britain was to be responsible for five-eighths of the joint naval enterprises, but in practice the Dutch failed increasingly to supply the three-eighths due from them; whereas the English fleet was kept in fairly good condition, the Dutch rapidly deteriorated.[2] Essentially, this was because the Republic had to neglect its other interests for the war on its southern frontier. Nevertheless, its naval shortcomings did much to feed those anti-Dutch prejudices which were still strong in England; nor were English and Dutch naval

[1] See H. Gillot, *Le Règne de Louis XIV et l'opinion publique en Allemagne* (1914).
[2] Cf. below, ch. xxii (3).

personnel always on good terms.[1] Austria, a vast continental power without a fleet, took part only in the land war. The Habsburg army, about as large as the Dutch but less well organized and paid, carried the burden of the war in Italy and a great deal of it on the south German front. It was, of course, an advantage for the emperor to have peace at this time with the Turks; he had, however, to reckon with the discontent of the constitutional party in Hungary, where in 1703 an open revolt sprang up under the leadership of Francis II Rákóczi.[2] In vain did the Maritime Powers urge Leopold and his successor, Joseph I, to make concessions to the Hungarians: for years substantial Habsburg forces were held down by these disturbances. But whatever his military (and financial) weakness, the emperor possessed an asset of the highest value in the military genius of Eugene of Savoy, who in 1701 had already achieved resounding successes in Lombardy.

What could the Bourbon Crowns pit against the Grand Alliance? The weakness of the Spanish monarchy deprived it of any serious military or naval significance, but France alone was militarily almost equal to the entire coalition ranged against her. In 1705 her army was estimated in all at 250,000.[3] Her central geographical position and comparatively short lines of communication, the concentration of her military leadership in one person—these were obvious advantages. To win the war she had no more to do, ostensibly, than to preserve positions already acquired. Her inferiority at sea, however, was soon to be demonstrated: only in the Mediterranean did French sea power at first preponderate, and as early as 1704 it lost even its local supremacy there. The result was that French and Spanish overseas trade was severely cramped by its enemies, and that Spain herself, with her long and vulnerable coastlines, was repeatedly exposed to attack. Above all, the main Anglo-Dutch fleet was at liberty, once in possession of the requisite forward bases, to enlarge the opportunities open to the striking-power of Allied armies, while yet having squadrons to spare for policing the Channel Soundings and vital communications across the North Sea. Nevertheless, as in the Nine Years War, France was in a strong position to wage intensive war on enemy trade: Dunkirk, St Malo and (until 1706) Ostend were only the most formidable of the many nests of privateers which were an object of terror to English and Dutch merchants. Only in 1708 did the activity of the French privateers begin to decline, and it revived in the last year of the war.

Closest partners of the French were the Spanish Netherlands. One of the first royal decisions of Philip V had been to appoint his grandfather as regent of these far-away provinces, and so the fortresses were occupied by French troops—not without the co-operation of Max Emmanuel of

---

[1] D. Coombs, *The Conduct of the Dutch: British Opinion and the Dutch Alliance during the War of the Spanish Succession* (1958), p. 37.   [2] Below, pp. 584-5.
[3] J. W. Wijn, *Het Staatsche Leger*, vol. VIII, pt. I (The Hague, 1956), p. 539.

Bavaria, governor-general in the last years of Carlos II. Louis XIV found a most able and energetic minister in Count Bergeyck, the 'Belgian Colbert', who inaugurated a policy of absolutist centralization. The three Collateral Councils established by Charles V—State, Privy Council, Finances[1]—were replaced by a single *Conseil Royal*, and the two exchequers united. The army was increased and reorganized on the French model; as voluntary enlistment fell short of requirements, civilians were conscripted by lottery. Thanks to the introduction of tax-farming, the central government's revenues from domains, posts, import and export duties were roughly doubled. Bergeyck also tried to farm out the provincial and local taxes; he met with success in Flanders, but not in Brabant. The provincial and local courts were more strictly supervised at the centre. In ecclesiastical affairs, Jansenism was strongly resisted after the French example, its principal leaders being exiled under *lettres de cachet*—a disregard for due process of law in keeping with French absolutism, but utterly opposed to the ideas of the inhabitants of the Low Countries. These new departures were hardly appreciated by a population which, though still without much national consciousness, was yet passionately attached to a great tradition of civil (and notably civic) liberties; many adherents of the House of Habsburg were to be counted among its gilds and corporations, the judicial office-holders and magistrates, and the high nobility. Yet it was, rather, the outbreak of war which prevented Bergeyck's measures from achieving the economic recovery which lay nearest his heart, useful as they were for the conduct of the war itself. The country was put in a posture of defence by the construction of the famous Lines of Brabant—a system of rivers and redoubts stretching in a wide curve from the Scheldt near Antwerp to the Meuse near Namur. The Lines fell short of the high expectations placed upon them, for a strong concentration of troops proved able to push through them. Until 1705, however, they prevented Allied raiding parties from penetrating the country and preserved it from being held to ransom by them.

In the Empire, Louis XIV's only important allies both belonged to the House of Wittelsbach. As governor of the Spanish Netherlands, Max Emmanuel had been on the side of William III and the emperor, but now he looked to Versailles for the realization of his soaring dreams—the title of king and perhaps the sovereignty of the south Netherlands. Bavaria itself could be a strong French outpost in the Empire, seriously menacing Austria; with French subsidies, an efficient army of 21,000 was soon created there. The elector's brother Joseph Clement, archbishop and elector of Cologne as well as bishop of Liège, had also changed front and invited the French to occupy a number of fortresses along the Rhine and Meuse, notably Bonn, Kaiserswerth, Rheinberg, Liège itself and Huy. His

---

[1] Cf. vol. II, p. 445. On Bergeyck see above, p. 390, and R. de Schryver, *Jan van Brouchoven, Graaf van Bergeyck, 1644–1725* (Brussels, 1965). He had been out of office in 1700.

pro-French policy was, however, resisted in both Cologne and Liège by the constitutional parties, which possessed considerable strength in the ecclesiastical chapters and among the urban bourgeoisie. The French position was really stronger in Italy. Victor Amadeus II, duke of Savoy and father-in-law of Philip V, was more dependent on France than he had been earlier, placed as he was between France and a now Bourbon Lombardy: French troops were ready to march across Piedmont and he opened the Alpine passes to them in February 1701. The duke of Mantua, by admitting a French garrison, gave Catinat command of the Po valley. Moreover, it was a major political and moral victory for France that Pope Clement XI, who had been elected in 1700, distrusted the Habsburg more than did his predecessors. He recognized Philip V as king of Spain and duke of Milan, gave a subsidy to help prepare a French expedition against Britain, and until 1709 generally followed a policy of benevolent neutrality towards France. On the other hand, the aggressive Catholicism of the Most Christian King brought him a grave embarrassment at home in the shape of the rebel *Camisards*,[1] although the Allies never succeeded in linking this revolt with their own operations.

On 19 March 1702, when war was on the point of breaking out, William III, the soul of the Grand Alliance, died at Hampton Court. Contrary to French expectation, this did not take the edge off the fighting spirit of Britain or the Republic. The political and commercial interests at stake were too momentous for either country to indulge in apathy. Under an Act of 1696 parliament remained in session, and Princess Anne quietly succeeded to William's throne. On the very Sunday of her accession, the loyal addresses of Lords and Commons expressed a will to wage war with utmost vigour. John Churchill, earl (soon to be duke) of Marlborough (1650–1722), who had long been in her confidence, now became Captain-General of the British expeditionary force and ambassador extraordinary to The Hague. A military leader and diplomatist of rare skill, he was to remain, despite his Tory origins and sympathies, the most convinced advocate of William III's Continental policy. The new government of moderate Tories, centred on Lord High Treasurer Godolphin, supported him wholeheartedly. That most Tories favoured the war at this juncture reflects partly their interest in overseas expansion, but also the anger felt by even the most anti-Dutch among them at Louis's proclamation of the Catholic Pretender as James III in September 1701. Though not the essential reason for England's going to war, this tactless if chivalrous act of recognition endowed the conflict with the aspect of a dynastic and religious war in most English eyes. Even so, it was at first seriously debated whether Britain should go to war simply as an auxiliary, concentrating on the high seas and in the Americas.

[1] Above, p. 325. Cf. a stimulating reconsideration by D. Ligou, 'Forêts, garrigues et maquis dans la guerre des Camisards', *Actes du Colloque sur la Forêt* (Cahiers d'Etudes Comtoises, 12 (1967)), pp. 129–39.

In the Dutch Republic, William's death had important repercussions. In almost all the provinces of the federation the anti-Orangist, republican, traditionally peace-loving party returned to power, although in Zeeland and Gelderland this restoration was not accomplished without local convulsions. Scarcely anywhere was a new stadholder appointed; in any case, no serious candidate was available, for the stadholder of Friesland, John William Friso of Nassau, William's cousin, was not yet of age.[1] This change-over, however, affected only domestic policy. Contrary to early French expectations, the new rulers unhesitatingly endorsed the foreign policy of William III. Any contradiction apparent here is explained by one simple fact: French domination of the Spanish Netherlands was universally regarded as a direct threat to the very survival of the Republic. For half a century already, the idea of building a barrier against French imperialism had amounted to a national aim—not that it was in the least inspired by a feeling of solidarity with the Dutch-speaking inhabitants of Brabant and Flanders, although its effect was indeed to save Dutch civilization in Belgium. The economic interests which counted for so much with the regents and merchants, especially at Amsterdam, dictated the same course as considerations of basic national safety. Philip V's concession of the Asiento to a French company made a deep impression on Amsterdam as well as London. Dutch trade was also hurt at a peculiarly sensitive point by renewed restrictions on French importation of herring and of whale-products. Thus the Republic embarked on war without enthusiasm but with an exceptional unanimity of opinion. All the leading statesmen of William's later years remained in office, the most powerful being the Grand Pensionary, Anthony Heinsius, who held in his hands all the complicated threads of Dutch politics. His excellent personal relations with Marlborough ensured close co-operation between Holland and England during the earlier years of the war.

The first problem before the two Maritime Powers on William's death was that of the supreme command of their combined armies. The nomination of a member of the stronger force would not have been surprising, but the excellent Dutch army was defective in one respect: though it possessed many able generals of great experience, none of them had sufficient personal prestige and political authority for the post of commander-in-chief. The States made what was for them the next best choice: on 30 June 1702 they appointed Marlborough commander-in-chief of their army so far as it would operate in the field in conjunction with the British. This did not mean that he was in command of the Dutch army as such: on all occasions when it acted independently, it was to be commanded by a general in Dutch service.[2] From 1704 this was Nassau-Ouwerkerk,

---

[1] He later became a general and earned many laurels in the fighting; but at the very moment when there was a chance that he might become dangerous to the republicans, in 1711, he accidentally lost his life.

[2] See J. W. Wijn, vol. VIII, pt. I, p. 697.

from 1708 Tilly, who sprang from the famous Belgian military family of the Tserclaes. Even the authority over the Dutch troops which Marlborough did command was not complete, for he was to be accompanied on all his campaigns by political commissioners of the States-General, the so-called field-deputies, who could veto his orders. Still less did this limited unity of command extend to the Austrians, who conducted the war almost independently.[1] On the other hand, Marlborough's appointment committed Britain more deeply to the Continental war than was to the liking of many Tories, with their preference for a purely maritime strategy.

The three great allies declared war on France on 15 May 1702. Britain and the Dutch Republic, having both recognized Philip V, also declared war on Spain; the emperor sent his declaration to Anjou and his adherents. For two years the main fronts lay in the Netherlands, the area of the lower Rhine, south Germany and north Italy. Along the Rhine hostilities had begun shortly before the declaration. The first aim of the locally superior Anglo-Dutch army in the northern sector was to get possession of the outlying posts on the Rhine and Meuse which Joseph Clement had handed over to the French. This was largely effected in 1702, when Kaiserswerth, Venlo, Roermond, Stevensweert and Liège fell in rapid succession between April and October: in 1703 the process was completed by the capture of Rheinberg, Bonn, Huy, and of two fortresses situated between Meuse and Rhine—Limburg and Guelders. Joseph Clement, robbed of both his territories, sought refuge in France. Thus the French lost their excellent forward positions and the United Provinces were freed from the immediate nightmare of invasion. But a plan to occupy Antwerp led only to the drawn battle of Ekeren, in June 1703, when the Dutch under Slangenburg fought an army twice as strong.

Thus far the war had been carried on in the old-fashioned leisurely style—as a siege war, in which Vauban and his Dutch competitor Coehoorn (1634–1704), both still in active service at the outset of hostilities, excelled. Marlborough was the protagonist of a more mobile strategy. Judging a single victory in the field 'of far greater advantage to the common cause than the taking of twenty towns',[2] and full of confidence in the excellent morale of his army, he was disposed to seize every opportunity of fighting a battle. His dynamic conceptions sowed doubt and apprehension among the Hollanders, and for good reasons. The Dutch generals had not yet learnt to put trust in Marlborough's military talents, and the consequences of a lost battle would have been more dangerous for the Republic

[1] Apart from Marlborough's friendship with Eugene (dating from June 1704), contact was confined to diplomatic channels, in which the good understanding between Marlborough and Count Wratislaw (the able Habsburg envoy extraordinary in London 8 Jan. 1701 to 9 May 1703 and 30 Dec. 1703 to 16 April 1704) counted for a great deal, especially in 1704: cf. below, p. 420, n. 4.

[2] W. C. Coxe, *Memoirs of...Marlborough*, vol. I (2nd edn. 1820), p. 250.

than for England. The first signs of opposition to Marlborough appeared in 1703. When he wanted to force the Lines of Brabant and compel the French to give battle, the field-deputies, advised by the Dutch generals, vetoed his decision. He was bitterly disappointed.

The situation on the upper Rhine and in south Germany developed very unfavourably for the Allies during these early years. The Imperial commander-in-chief, Lewis margrave of Baden, had mounted guard on the Rhine at the Lines of Stollhofen, constructed by him some twenty miles north-east of the Kehl bridgehead to prevent the French marching north between the Black Forest and the Rhine. But in September 1702 Max Emmanuel, who until that date had continued to negotiate with the emperor, suddenly declared his hand by tricking the Imperial city of Ulm into surrender; before the next campaigning season opened, Villars laid hands on the fortress of Kehl and then moved audaciously through the Black Forest passes to join the Bavarians in May 1703. This swift and unexpected manoeuvre turned the Lines of Stollhofen and resulted in a double attack on Tyrol—from the north by Max Emmanuel, from Lombardy by Vendôme. The elector got as far as Innsbruck, Vendôme as far as Trent: but the ferocious guerrilla attacks of the Tyrolese peasants forced a rapid retreat from their mountains in July. The elector stood firm, however, in Bavaria, defeated the Imperialists from the Rhine near Höchstädt in September, and overcame Passau on the border of Upper Austria in January 1704. Habsburg prospects thus looked desperate for the next campaign, especially as the Hungarian rebels were approaching Vienna from another direction. Villars had wanted to attack it in the summer of 1703, when the elector's preference for an attempt at gaining control of the Brenner pass marked the beginning of friction between them. In the new emergency, the emperor recalled Eugene from Italy to reorganize the Austrian forces as president of the Court War Council (*Hofkriegsrat*).

Shortly afterwards, the duke of Savoy finally came round to the side of the Allies, with whom he had fought from 1690 to 1696. Just as then he had been in almost continual negotiation with the French, so now, as France's ally, he had been in touch with Vienna since 1701, pressing those claims on the Milanese which Louis XIV failed to satisfy. The French had been able to strengthen their hold on Milan after the drawn battle of Luzzara (August 1702), which marked the limit of Eugene's victorious advance until 1706, and to hamper his supplies by sea from Trieste in 1702–3. Victor Amadeus was increasingly angered by the arrogance shown to himself and his officers by the French; in September 1703, after Vendôme's failure to join Max Emmanuel in Tyrol, Louis XIV ordered the seizure of the Piedmontese contingent at Santo Benedetto. On 8 November, Austria made terms with Savoy, under the guarantee of the Maritime Powers. They were to provide the duke with a monthly subsidy; the emperor was to yield the Montferrat, Alessandria, Valsesia, Valenza and Vigevano at the expense of Lombardy.[1] For some time to come this decision was to involve the duke in serious embarrassment. Tessé quickly snapped up Savoy, for which Swiss protection was unavailable. Part of Piedmont was also occupied and more of her troops disarmed. Vienna made no strong effort to relieve this pressure before Leopold died, in 1705; and it was 8,000 Prussian troops, negotiated by Marlborough, who were to save the duke in 1706. Nor could Victor Amadeus count on the support of the Allied fleet, whose Mediterranean operations were for long subordinated to the needs of a new war theatre in Spain.

The expedition against Spain which the Anglo-Dutch fleet undertook in August–September 1702 had been far from glorious. Its aim, which William III had laid down, was to recover a naval base from which to penetrate the Mediterranean even in winter. The admiral in command, Sir George Rooke, had no faith in his task. A strong expeditionary force of 16,000 infantry and marines, under the duke of Ormonde, went ashore near Cadiz, but did not seriously try to take the town, whose defences had recently been strengthened and whose population displayed no sign of sympathy; any hope that Spaniards would in future grow better inclined to support the Allies was as good as extinguished by the scandalous looting, even of churches, which took place across the bay in Port St Mary. On the homeward voyage in October, however, the fleet recovered some of its prestige by boldly attacking a Spanish treasure-fleet deep in the bay of Vigo and destroying Châteaurenault's squadron which had convoyed it across the ocean. This blow to the French fleet, which also yielded loot and prize goods, made a deep impression at Turin and at Lisbon.

Portugal was nominally an ally of France and Spain: by treaties of June 1701, though not a belligerent, her harbours were closed to their enemies. Once the Maritime Powers had clearly demonstrated their naval supremacy, however, and consequently their power to cut off trade and food supplies, it was not hard for them to induce King Peter II to join the Grand Alliance. But Peter demanded more than military and financial aid. He asked for territorial concessions in Spain and stipulated that the Allies should send to Lisbon, as an earnest of their support, the emperor's younger son Charles, whose presence was estimated to be worth 20,000 men. It was the Englishman, John Methuen, who urged the impossibility of Portuguese neutrality and chiefly forced through the two treaties of alliance of 16 May 1703 (after much Portuguese hesitation), realizing that effective action in the Mediterranean required a naval base near the Straits.[2] The English also expected commercial advantages from the fact

---

[1] Cf. below, pp. 466, 595–6.
[2] Unlike the Quadruple Offensive Treaty, the Perpetual Defensive Treaty did not involve the Habsburgs; it gave Portugal a permanent Anglo-Dutch guarantee against French and Spanish attack.

that the future king of Spain would owe his throne to their help. The Dutch too were interested in commercial advantages, but feared the expense of a Peninsular war and so were inclined to vacillate. The emperor followed reluctantly. He wanted a kingdom for his favourite younger son, but he was primarily interested in Italy, not in Spain, and in any case opposed to any partition of the Spanish monarchy until he had vindicated the claim of his elder son Joseph to the whole Spanish inheritance. The Maritime Powers were left responsible for the territorial concessions required by Portugal, which were included only in a secret article. Even so, when all was agreed, the emperor hesitated to sign the act of renunciation required of him, and remained most reluctant to spare the Archduke Charles personally to face the risks of the journey by sea to Portugal and of a Peninsular campaign.[1]

The Portuguese alliance had far-reaching consequences. In placing the Portuguese harbours at the disposal of the Maritime Powers, it placed them in effect at the disposal of English imperialism. From Lisbon a predominantly English fleet could mount attacks on Gibraltar, Barcelona, Minorca, Toulon. Economically, too, the new alliance offered many advantages to England. On 27 December the 'second' (strictly, the third) Methuen treaty was signed, opening the Portuguese and Brazilian markets to English cloth and the English market to Portuguese wines.[2] For the Grand Alliance as such, however, the Portuguese commitment was disastrous. Substantial Allied forces were drawn off to a new and distant front. Worse still, the whole purpose of the Grand Alliance was radically changed. The principle of dividing the Spanish monarchy was now replaced by the much less realistic prescription: 'No peace without Spain.' It was this formula that was to cause the war to drag on long after the moderate aims of the treaty of 1701 had been fulfilled.

The dealings with Portugal are evidence of the preponderance which Britain had acquired in the Alliance within two years. The Republic

[1] Cf. below, p. 591. The presence of the archduke was essential in Portuguese estimation to a Spanish rising and as a guarantee that the Allies would not leave them in the lurch, once they had forfeited Bourbon friendship. In the 'first Methuen treaty' the archduke's candidature for the Spanish throne thus became a condition imposed by Portugal. Nevertheless, until they encountered Vienna's resistance, the Maritime Powers had taken the proclamation of Charles III for granted and had sometimes used his name, although at Cadiz they spoke only of the House of Austria. Prince George of Hesse-Darmstadt, who had been in touch with Spaniards about a possible invasion, may have mentioned Charles's name in London in April 1702. But as late as November 1702 Waldstein, Imperial ambassador in Lisbon, who in any case felt that a Portuguese alliance could be purchased cheaply, refused to declare himself. In the event, the person of Charles was for long the only Habsburg contribution to the war in Spain, for the emperor's third share of Allied subsidies and troops had to be made good by England. See A. D. Francis, 'John Methuen and the Anglo-Portuguese Treaties of 1703', *Historical Journal*, vol. III (1960), pp. 103–24; 'Portugal and the Grand Alliance', *Bull. Inst. Hist. Research*, XXXVIII (1965), pp. 71–93; and *The Methuens and Portugal, 1691–1708* (Cambridge, 1966).
[2] See below, pp. 520 ff. and 524, n.1.

merely followed Britain's lead, however hesitantly. In 1703, on yet another question, it complied with English demands. At the beginning of the war the English government had forbidden its subjects to trade with Spain and France (though the order-in-council was evaded by smugglers and not adopted by Scotland). On the other hand, only the earnings of trade enabled the Republic to sustain the high cost of war, and Dutch trade with the enemy had continued in face of the indignant protests of England and Austria; nor had Amsterdam stopped remittances to France by bills of exchange.[1] But early in 1703 the English parliament made its willingness to increase its expeditionary force by 10,000 conditional upon a prohibition of all trade, in goods or bills, with the Bourbon countries. The States-General yielded to this pressure, but for one year only and on condition that the Hanseatic ports were subjected by the emperor to a similar ban. On its expiry in the following June the States categorically refused to renew the interdict, partly on the ground that neutral trade had exploited the openings it created:[2] Swedish and Danish attempts to do so had indeed given English and Zeelander privateers an additional pretext to arrest their ships, thereby causing much bad blood not only between the Maritime Powers and the Northern Crowns but also between the province of Zeeland and The Hague. It was to save the Alliance that Marlborough himself argued against his government's wish to renew the interdict.[3]

At the beginning of 1704 the military situation was such that the main theatre could only be south Germany. Vienna was under threat from two sides, the emperor's financial resources exhausted, the condition of the Austrian army poor. Unless the Maritime Powers took vigorous action there was a real risk that Leopold would be forced into a separate peace. Wratislaw worked tirelessly to impress this upon Marlborough, the only man with vision enough to see the interests of the Grand Alliance as a single whole. Marlborough wanted to rescue Vienna by a bold stroke far from his base, overcome Bavaria, and at the same time free himself from the surveillance of the Dutch deputies which had so much frustrated his plans in 1703.[4] Although the States had no wish to allow their army out of

[1] Above, p. 303.
[2] The *Amirauté* records of (e.g.) Bordeaux show that Dutch fears had some foundation, but the total of Scandinavian shipping departures, in the years 1703 and 1704 combined, did not approach the number of Dutch sailings in any single year from 1705 to 1708. Owing to French restrictions, moreover, there had been very little Dutch shipping in the ports of western France during the first war-year. French passports only became available in quantity to Dutch ships in the spring of 1705. They were largely, but not entirely, suppressed after 1710 (J. S. Bromley, 'Le Commerce de la France de l'Ouest et la guerre maritime, 1702–12', *Annales du Midi*, t. LXV, 1953, pp. 49–66).
[3] See G. Van den Haute, *Les Relations anglo-hollandaises au début du XVIII siècle* (Louvain, 1932), pp. 255 ff.
[4] Sir Winston Churchill's researches in the private papers at Blenheim Palace confirm the doubts expressed by G. M. Trevelyan (*England under Queen Anne*, vol. I (1930), pp. 325–6)

the Netherlands, they were persuaded by Heinsius to place strong Dutch forces at Marlborough's disposal—ostensibly for a campaign up the Moselle—with generals devoted to him, but with no commander-in-chief and no political commissioners. In bad weather but in good heart, he undertook a long and audacious march from the Netherlands along the Rhine to Heidelberg, and thence to the Danube, with an army growing during the march to about 40,000—smaller than in former years but with a strong nucleus of British troops which he could command quite independently. As a result of the two former campaigns, the Rhine waterway could be used for the transport of heavy supplies as far as Mannheim. With the rather jealous co-operation of Lewis of Baden, Marlborough's first success was the bloody capture on 2 July of the Schellenberg, a strongly defended hill dominating the town of Donauwörth, which he had chosen to become his forward base for the collection of supplies from central Germany. These last were as much a subject of calculated forethought as the organization of the march itself, and likewise dependent on large credits with the bankers of Frankfurt and Nuremberg.

The Allied army then invaded Bavaria. The countryside was cruelly laid waste in the hope of persuading the elector to change sides, as many of his subjects and advisers had long desired, and of weakening the French who were with him near Augsburg under Villars's successor, Marsin, an inferior but more tactful commander. The elector's own excellent army was mostly dispersed elsewhere, but Louis XIV ordered Marshal Tallard to reinforce him from Strasbourg. Marlborough had deceived the French into expecting attacks up the Moselle and then in Alsace-Lorraine. With a portion of Villeroi's army, which had hastened from the Netherlands (first to the Moselle, then to the upper Rhine), Tallard now slowly brought up 35,000 men in time to cross to the north shore of the Danube at Dillingen, on 10 August, with Marsin and the elector. Between them they commanded some 60,000 troops, stronger in artillery than the 53,000 under the divided command of Marlborough and the margrave. Before the enemy had crossed the river, however, Eugene had reached the north bank at Höchstädt with an additional 18,000 men from the upper Rhine, where he had been guarding the Lines of Stollhofen, now exposed to a possible thrust by Villeroi—a calculated risk which had been pre-arranged with Marlborough. Rather than share command in battle with the vainglorious and touchy margrave, Marlborough and Eugene preferred to reduce their strength by 18,000 for facilitating his pet project of besieging Ingolstadt twenty miles in their rear. Consequently, in the battle that was fought on 13 August, near Blenheim (Blindheim) on the Danube, the Allies had a slight inferiority of numbers. Tallard, who occupied a strong

of the traditional view that this strategic plan originated with Eugene: if Marlborough's conception owed anything to anybody, it was to Wratislaw, its constant advocate, who also accompanied Marlborough to the Continent in the spring of 1704. See *Marlborough: his Life and Times* (1947 edn.), vol. II, pp. 721–2, 727.

natural position, four miles long, protected by the marshes of the river Nebel between the Danube and some wooded hills, did not expect the enemy to dare attack him. All his infantry reserves were locked up in the village of Blenheim on his right, against which the first attacks were directed. Eugene's repeated attacks to the west of Oberglau village tied down Marsin and the elector, whilst Marlborough gradually deployed his centre over the Nebel and launched a devastating attack with fresh infantry and cavalry against Tallard's squadrons, which were supported by only nine raw battalions of infantry. Well over half the French army was destroyed or taken prisoner, including Tallard himself, as compared with Allied casualties of about 12,000. Marsin and the elector, however, were able to withdraw across the Rhine—the elector to Brussels, where he once again took up the lucrative governorship of the Spanish Netherlands. The Allies followed up by taking Ulm in September. Bavaria was occupied by the Austrians and ruled by them until the end of the war. West of the Rhine, the fortresses of Landau, Trier and Trarbach fell in October; during the winter Trier was turned into a major stronghold.

Blenheim was the military turning-point of the war. It rescued Vienna and cost the French the loss of Bavaria, their last ally in Germany. The war in south Germany was all but ended. Trier and Trarbach procured for the Allies the bases needed for invading France along the Moselle— a project already cherished by Marlborough. It was he, in fact, who gained most by Blenheim. The brilliant style of his campaign revealed his genius to the world in a most convincing way. His military prestige in the Allied army was now definitively established, his political position at home immensely strengthened: it is hardly too much to say that it needed Blenheim to give the war on land such popularity as it ever enjoyed in England. The success of the diplomatic missions to all the capitals of the Grand Alliance which Marlborough undertook during the winter added to his authority.

The Netherlands front in 1704 was of only secondary importance; Field-Marshal Ouwerkerk confined himself there to the defensive. In Italy, French preponderance was qualified only by the continued stand of Victor Amadeus in the Alps and in Turin—enough, however, to prevent Vendôme moving against Vienna in the vital months before Blenheim. But a new front was opened in the Iberian Peninsula.

In March an Anglo-Dutch fleet arrived in the Tagus with the 20-year-old archduke and an auxiliary army. The Allied forces, which started the campaign along the Portuguese frontier in May, totalled about 4,000 British, 2,000 Dutch and 20,000 Portuguese (mostly in the pay of the Maritime Powers).[1] The campaign was a failure. No decisive battle was fought, nowhere did the Spanish people choose the side of the Habsburg pretender. Yet there was one great event of which the news ran through

[1] For the war on Portuguese soil see below, pp. 526–7.

the world. Once again the Maritime Powers made use of their naval superiority and the weakness of Spanish coastal defences. On 3 August, without much difficulty, Rooke and Callenburgh took Gibraltar. At this time the Rock itself was not systematically fortified and there were only a few hundred garrison troops in the town. The Allies occupied it on behalf of 'Charles III', but the local population promptly moved away. An almost exclusively British garrison under Prince George of Hesse-Darmstadt, now an Imperial field-marshal who had had charge of Austrian interests in the abortive Cadiz expedition, was given the arduous task of defending the place. In Madrid and Versailles its exceptional importance was well understood. Almost at once the Admiral of France, the count of Toulouse, who a short time previously had succeeded in bringing the Brest squadron to Toulon and was now at Barcelona, sailed out with his entire fleet to recapture Gibraltar. It was on 24 August, off Malaga, that the only battle of this war between the main belligerent fleets was fought. Against a French line of 50 ships, the Confederate fleet numbered 53, but it was short of ammunition after the bombardment of Gibraltar, so that it was perhaps lucky when the French decided not to re-engage after the first day.[1] A tactical stalemate was turned into a strategic victory, however, by the French retreat to Toulon. The French fleet never afterwards reappeared in strength. Though its mere survival constituted a potential threat to Allied operations, the western Mediterranean, in 1702 still virtually a French lake, was more and more abandoned to the Confederate fleet—and this meant, with the growing decay of the Dutch navy, increasingly an English fleet. Soon afterwards, in October, a Franco-Spanish army under Tessé, backed intermittently by a French squadron from Cadiz, tried to succeed where the French fleet had failed. Throughout the winter, with the indispensable support of warships from Lisbon, the Gibraltar garrison heroically withstood a well-conducted and dangerous siege. The Rock of Gibraltar had entered international history.

Allied prospects for 1705 were thus much more promising than they had been a year earlier—none the less so when Emperor Leopold I died on 5 May 1705, for Joseph I pursued his father's anti-Bourbon policy with greater energy. In Bavaria, it is true, discontent with the Austrian occupation led to a fierce peasant rising with the rallying-cry, 'Better die Bavarians than rot as Imperialists'.[2] But this revolt was crushed in December. Both Wittelsbach rulers, Max Emmanuel and Joseph Clement, were then placed under the ban of the Empire and dispossessed of their fiefs, with the concurrence of the Electoral house. In religious matters more tolerant than his father, moreover, the new emperor was inclined to appease the

---

[1] J. H. Owen, *War at Sea under Queen Anne, 1702–1708* (Cambridge, 1938), p. 93, shows why any strict comparison of firepower is difficult to make.
[2] 'Lieber bayrisch sterben als kaiserlich verderben.'

Hungarians by constitutional concessions. After the victory of the Zsibó pass he reconquered Transylvania in November 1705 and opened negotiations with the rebels, although his refusal to restore the elective monarchy meant continuance of the war in Hungary.[1]

Marlborough used the lion's share of his Anglo-Dutch striking force in an attempt to invade France along the Moselle. Allied military circles agreed with him that access to the heart of France was easier this way than across the thickly fortified northern frontier zone—an opinion not corroborated, however, by the further course of the war. They also expected a political success by releasing the duke of Lorraine from the French pressure that had compelled him to stay neutral. The event proved quite otherwise. Marlborough's adventure along the Moselle was short and hardly glorious. Villars, the one French commander whose military talents equalled his own, gave him no opportunity to deliver battle. Nor was the partnership of Lewis of Baden, whose troops were in a deplorable condition, of much value. As early as June, disappointed by the course of the campaign, Marlborough brought the main body of his army back to the Netherlands, never again to return to the Moselle. Trier was reoccupied by the French.

In the Netherlands, on the other hand, Marlborough was initially very successful. By a surprise attack on 18 July he broke through the Lines of Brabant near Heilissem, south-east of Tienen. But after this momentous achievement an immediate march on Louvain and Brussels, which he considered feasible, did not take place. For the loss of this opportunity he blamed the Dutch generals and field-deputies. The campaign ended with bitter wrangling among the allies. The tension came to a head when the deputies, advised by the Dutch generals, prevented Marlborough from fighting a battle near Overijsche, south-east of Brussels, on 18 August; in this unfought battle near Waterloo the French escaped, according to the commander-in-chief, a crushing defeat. Thus the net results of a campaign conducted by a superior Allied army amounted merely to the capture of Zoutleeuw and the partial destruction of the Lines of Brabant, which after 1705 no longer figured in the strategy of the war. The victor of Blenheim now felt strong enough openly to complain to the States-General, especially of General Slangenburg, the head and front of the opposition to him. Public opinion in Holland sided with Marlborough, as did the civil government at The Hague. On the other hand, the States had no thought of giving up control over the powerful instrument constituted by their troops: all their former captains-general, from Maurice to William III, had had political deputies at their side. But the States did appoint deputies personally agreeable to Marlborough, and Slangenburg retired from service. After this we hear no more of sharp differences, over the conduct of military affairs, between Marlborough and the Dutch.

[1] Below, pp. 585–6.

Italy was the sole theatre in 1705 where the military balance was still clearly in favour of the French. They started by investing Turin. Only Eugene's return saved the Imperial army from being driven beyond the Alps by Vendôme in the summer; but even Eugene, when he tried to force his way through to join the hard-pressed duke of Savoy, was beaten off in August near Cassano, where his Prussians were badly mauled. Both the defeat of Savoy and the expulsion of the Austrians from Italy now seemed imminent. A strong armament under the restless earl of Peterborough, with Archduke Charles on board, had been sent to relieve the situation there; but its commanders, though much divided in council, preferred to please the archduke by going to the assistance of the Catalans—only the secondary objective in their instructions—instead of landing troops at Nice, one of Savoy's few links with the sea.

If the archduke had anywhere in Spain some chance of success, however, it was on the Mediterranean coast, where Catalonia, resenting the centralizing policies of Castile, was determined on the preservation of its old privileges. The Allies scored rapid successes there. A large Anglo-Dutch fleet under Sir Cloudesley Shovell and the earl of Peterborough brought 7,000 troops. Fort Monjuic, the citadel of Barcelona, was daringly assaulted on 14 September by Peterborough and Hesse-Darmstadt;[1] the city itself capitulated on 14 October, when an enthusiastic population chose the side of the Allies. All the Catalan towns soon paid homage to King Charles III, who made Barcelona his provisional seat of government. In Valencia and Aragon civil war broke out. Thus, with the Portuguese army (stiffened by 5,000 English and Dutch under the Huguenot Ruvigny, earl of Galway) impinging, however half-heartedly, on his western frontier, Philip V in Madrid seemed to be threatened from two sides. His central position was, on the other hand, an advantage to him, although the Allies had secure lines of communication by sea with Gibraltar and Lisbon.

Their rapid successes in Catalonia led the Allies to believe that the fate of Spain now depended solely on their own will. Indeed, London and Vienna tenaciously stuck to the condition that the entire Spanish monarchy should go to Charles III just when Louis XIV was beginning to resign himself to its partition, for it was in the autumn of 1705 that Louis made his first secret peace-offers. He addressed them to the Dutch in the hope of detaching them from the Alliance.[2] There was, in fact, a peace-party crystallizing under the leadership of Buys, an Amsterdamer, who saw more clearly than Heinsius that the national debt was already rising to a dangerous height. Louis offered to make over the Spanish Netherlands,

---

[1] He was killed in this action, in which other veterans of the siege of Gibraltar also distinguished themselves.
[2] J. G. Stork-Penning, *Het Grote Werk: Vredesonderhandelingen gedurende de Spaanse Successie-oorlog, 1705–1710* (Groningen, 1958), pp. 24–71.

Naples and Sicily to Charles III. If only Milan had been included, this proposal would have been very tempting for the Republic, which was offered certain guarantees for its frontiers. But the Portuguese treaty, in any case, stood in the way of a settlement along such lines. England stubbornly insisted on the conquest of Spain, and Dutch statesmen could not seriously contemplate the possibility of leaving their ally in the lurch; a separate peace was impossible so long as their sea trade was in danger of being compromised by a breach with England.[1] So Buys's peace plan which left Spain to Philip V, stood no real chance and the war went on.

The year 1706, though it opened inauspiciously for the Allies with the duke of Berwick's capture of Nice, was the *annus mirabilis* of the war for them. On every front it brought considerable successes, even in Spain, short-lived as success there was to prove.

In the Spanish Netherlands, as soon as the campaign had started and with the full approval of the Dutch deputies, Marlborough fought his second big battle. Near Ramillies (north of Namur), on 23 May, he beat a Franco-Belgian army of 60,000 commanded by Villeroi and Max Emmanuel. He employed once again the tactics that had broken another battle-line, also four miles long, at Blenheim, drawing the enemy to concentrate at one end by powerful feints and reserving his final thrust for the sector thereby depleted. This victory too, which owed much to the Danish cavalry, had immediate and far-reaching consequences. The French field-army retreated in disorder, first westward, then southward to Lille. Its ignominious retreat brought about a revolution in Brabant and Flanders, the main provinces of the Spanish Netherlands. The pro-Austrian party, never reconciled to the arbitrary government of the French and consequently backed by the democratically minded if archaic urban gilds, held out a joyful welcome to the allies of Charles III. Louvain, Brussels, Antwerp and Ghent were entered without a blow being struck; on 5 and 6 June the States of Brabant and Flanders formally recognized Charles III as their sovereign; the troops of Philip V surrendered the towns they had occupied, deserting in droves to the Allies. The Belgian revolution, a counterpart of the English revolution of 1688, was accomplished in less than a fortnight and without bloodshed. It 'softened the character and speeded the pace of Marlborough's conquest'.[2] It was limited, however, to the Flemish-speaking provinces in the north: the Walloon provinces—Hainault, Namur, Luxemburg—remained loyal to Philip V as their sovereign lord and to Louis XIV as his regent. Max Emmanuel, as governor, removed his residence to Mons, accompanied by Bergeyck. In two Flemish towns, Ostend and Dendermonde, the French garrisons kept the Belgians in hand for a time, but both were taken by the Allies

---

[1] Stork-Penning, p. 64.
[2] G. M. Trevelyan, *England under Queen Anne*, vol. II (1932), p. 123.

after a brief siege. The capture of Ostend, on 6 July, not only delivered English and Dutch navigation from a troublesome nest of privateers, but shortened the lines of communication between England and the front—a fact which in 1708 turned out to have invaluable strategic importance. It also made possible the export of English manufactures to a now re-opened market; Dutch wares poured into it through Antwerp.

The English and Dutch did not treat the Spanish Netherlands as enemy country which had been conquered, but as the territory of an ally which they had recovered. At once, however, a dispute arose between the allies with regard to its future government. A definite construction had now to be put on articles of the Grand Alliance which had deliberately been couched in vague terms. The treaty of 1701 had assigned the Spanish Netherlands to the House of Habsburg, but at the same time declared that they were to be used as a 'barrier' for the security of the Dutch Republic. Charles III, far away in Spain and without any effective power, was unable to take up the government himself. Accordingly, his brother Joseph I insisted, on the strength of the treaty of 1701, that the regency be given to Austria. But the States-General would not hand over such a precious security, to the conquest of which Austria had made no contribution whatever, before they had the certainty of obtaining a good Barrier. It must be emphasized that the Barrier was the overriding and quintessential Dutch war-aim. A good Barrier, however, meant not only the right to occupy the principal fortresses on the southern frontier, but also a financial supply from the new sovereign for paying their garrisons and maintaining the fortifications. The immediate Dutch objective was to make their position so strong as to be able, at the end of the war, to wrest from the Habsburgs an arrangement bound to be highly offensive to that House. This is why the Dutch demanded that for the duration of the war the *de facto* government of the south Netherlands, especially control of the finances, should be allotted to them. England adopted an intermediate standpoint. At first Marlborough's views did not much diverge from the Dutch. But then the court of Vienna, seeing no chance of an Austrian regency, suddenly cast an apple of discord between the two Maritime Powers. Acting on behalf of his brother in Barcelona, Joseph I appointed Marlborough governor-general. The duke, already loaded with gifts and honours,[1] wanted to accept this viceregal office. Dutch statesmen were appalled at the very idea of it and pressed him to decline it. He did so for the time being, hoping that some better occasion might present itself; but his excellent understanding with his Dutch colleagues was for ever impaired by this episode, which sowed seeds of resentment on one hand, suspicions of a pro-Viennese inclination on the other.

---

[1] From the queen he had received, besides his new title, the royal manor of Woodstock; from parliament, a handsome grant for building there; from the emperor, reluctantly, the small principality of Mindelheim—restored in 1714 to Max Emmanuel, from whom it had been confiscated.

A compromise was found which, while letting the Dutch have their way on the main points, did not exclude the English from the government of the south Netherlands. The States of Brabant and Flanders were also allowed to take part in shaping the settlement. From July 1706 the Spanish Netherlands became, for the duration of the war, an Anglo-Dutch condominium. In principle the sovereignty of Charles III was acknowledged, but the government would be exercised on his behalf by a Council of State composed of Belgians under the regency of the Maritime Powers. For the purpose of directing the Council the two powers established at Brussels the so-called Conference, in which each had two plenipotentiaries. England was represented in the Condominium by Marlborough, assisted from 1707 by his quartermaster-general and chief of intelligence, William Cadogan, in some sense the duke's *alter ego*. But it was the Dutch plenipotentiary, Johan van den Bergh, in office from beginning to end of the Condominium, who acquired the preponderant influence in Brussels. For ten years, Brabant and Flanders (together with Hainault after its conquest in 1709) were governed in this way, in accordance with the directives of the Maritime Powers. It cannot be said that this régime was liked in the south Netherlands. The war alone prevented that. The country continued to undergo all the miseries of a frontier-zone, softened as these might be by the more humane methods of warfare at this time—by the system of commuting plunder for taxes, for instance, and of storing army provisions in magazines. The two powers also made use of their authority to remodel the tariffs after the requirements of the Dutch and English export trades. But on the whole the Condominium was characterized by a certain leniency, by respect of the privileges, by the downright rejection of the absolutist tendencies of Bergeyck and the French interregnum. The State Colleges automatically recovered more authority than they had possessed for a long time, while the Council of State at Brussels was able to take advantage of the strained relations between the English and Dutch plenipotentiaries in the Conference. Notwithstanding the activities of a pro-French minority, no serious disturbances took place during the ten years of the Condominium, not even in the critical year 1708. Until the end of the war the Spanish Netherlands made their modest contribution to the Allied effort.

The events in the Netherlands exercised decisive influence on the course of the war elsewhere. In May 1706 Villars had begun an offensive on the upper Rhine, defeated the ailing Lewis of Baden and driven him back across the river. Once again south Germany was threatened by a French invasion. It was also this offensive which frustrated Marlborough's hope of joining Eugene in Italy for the 1706 campaign. Suddenly Villars broke it off: after the catastrophe of Ramillies, he had to send most of his troops to the Flanders front.

In north Italy, where the French had concentrated a record strength of

80,000 troops, the campaign opened with Vendôme's defeat of General Reventlau at Calcinato as early as March, with the result that the Imperialists were driven up to the Trentino valley. In May, La Feuillade opened a systematic siege of Turin. The hard-pressed fortress-capital of Victor Amadeus seemed on the point of falling at last, while the duke himself, with 6,000 cavalry, eluded capture in the foothills of the Alps. These French advantages, which promised to conclude the war in Italy, were reversed by two developments. First, Ramillies compelled Louis XIV to recall the very able Vendôme to defend his now threatened northern frontier. Then, in July, his successors, Marsin and Philip duke of Orléans,[1] had to withdraw from Lombardy when Eugene managed to outflank their river-lines on the Adige, Mincio and Oglio successively. To relieve Turin, Eugene had undertaken an unexpected march from the Trentino at the end of June, moving swiftly across Venetian territory and along the southern bank of the Po. His army, which in the previous year had been disintegrating for lack of money and equipment, was now strongly reinforced by Prussian and other German auxiliary troops in the pay of the Maritime Powers, not all released thus far without difficulty; he now commanded nearly 30,000 men. After joining forces with Victor Amadeus he won the magnificent victory of Turin on 7 September, when Marsin was mortally wounded. Its results were comparable in kind with those of Ramillies. Not only was Turin saved: what was left of the French field-army retreated across the Alps, while the Franco-Spanish garrisons in Italy were cut off. The Allies had in effect won the war there, and the Austrians soon became the preponderant Italian power.[2] It remained to be seen whether Vendôme had prophesied truly when he wrote that 'the loss of Italy would involve the loss of everything'.[3]

For a moment the Allies had appeared to be on the point of winning the war in Spain also. Thanks to the bands of Catalan guerrillas (the *miqueletes*), to the availability of Lisbon for a winter refit of Allied warships, and the initiative of Vice-Admiral Leake in disobeying Peterborough's orders to land troops in Valencia, a serious French effort to recover Barcelona, in May, came to nothing; Tessé withdrew to Perpignan without his siege-train, and the blockading squadron to Toulon. The rival kings both took part in this encounter: Charles III in his temporary capital, Philip V in the besieging army. Meanwhile, Galway and the marquis das Minas succeeded in moving up under difficulties from the west. On 27 June they occupied Madrid, which Berwick's small army evacuated. But they were not supported at the right time from Barcelona, where the command was torn by quarrels that indeed the controversial

---

[1] Orléans (the future Regent) had no real authority: Vendôme had recommended that Marsin (of whose appointment he disapproved) should be accompanied by a prince of the blood to impress the Italian princes.
[2] Cf. below, pp. 593 ff.   [3] Quoted Churchill, vol. II, p. 165.

personality of Peterborough did nothing to heal. In Castile, the proud heart of Spain, feeling flared up against an Austrian king supported by heretical foreigners, by the despised Portuguese, and by the troublesome Catalans: all Spain, in fact, except Catalonia and Valencia, began to identify Philip V with national independence, Charles III with foreign conquest. Galway and das Minas were unable to stand their ground in Madrid against the guerrilla warfare which now broke out in western and central Spain. Some 4,000 Allied troops from the east coast at length joined forces with them early in August at Guadalajara, but only after they had been forced to abandon the capital itself to Berwick, who now had an army of 25,000. Communications with Portugal being cut off, the whole Allied army then retreated to Valencia, while Philip V returned in triumph to Madrid. The one favourable turn in the outlook was that Peterborough was superseded in his command by Galway. Charles III's position even in eastern Spain was far from enviable. Yet the Allies were slow to draw the right inferences from what had happened.

By the end of 1706 the main points of the moderate programme laid down by William III in the Treaty of Grand Alliance had been realized. Louis XIV's hegemony was broken, the balance of power in Europe restored; the claims of the Habsburgs to the Spanish succession in Milan and the south Netherlands were satisfied; the Republic had got a buffer-state between itself and France; Britain had obtained security in the Low Countries and supremacy in the Mediterranean. The Allies, in short, were in a position to wrest from the enemy an honourable peace based on the treaty of 1701. In the course of secret negotiations in Holland the French once again proposed a partition of the Spanish monarchy.[1] During the critical summer of 1706, when Spain seemed lost to Philip V, Louis XIV was even prepared to be content with the Italian possessions for him. But neither England nor the emperor was inclined for peace. Marlborough and Godolphin clung to the 'No peace without Spain' formula, which now meant the entire Spanish monarchy for Charles III. Support for this policy came, above all, from the Whigs, whose position had been strengthened by the elections of 1705. The Marlborough–Godolphin government, which since 1702 had developed into a moderate Tory ministry—joined by Harley and St John in the reconstruction of 1704—relied increasingly on the Whigs, who were strong enough in the autumn of 1706, at a time when the Scottish Union had still to be accepted by parliament, to force the earl of Sunderland upon the queen in place of Sir Charles Hedges, the Tory secretary for south European affairs. In the Republic, on the other hand, a partition of the Spanish monarchy was still considered a satisfactory solution. Realizing that the surrender of Spain would mean an impossible breach with England, the Dutch pressed their ally for some compensation for Philip V in Italy; but the English regarded

[1] Below, pp. 446–7.

430

a French vassal-state in Naples and Sicily as a threat to their Levant trade. For the time being, however, this controversy between the Maritime Powers remained in the background, because Louis XIV, while making several more offers of peace to the Republic in 1707 and 1708, always started from the premiss that Philip V would keep Spain.

Awaiting the secure peace for which they longed, the Dutch tried to obtain England's indispensable support in the Barrier question. It was no annexation which they were striving for in the south Netherlands; territorial expansion did not come naturally to their bourgeois trading spirit, and in any case responsible statesmen at The Hague fully understood that England would never allow it. The Dutch did not even want the south Netherlands to be erected into an independent State; they wanted them to be connected with a power capable of defending them. All the Dutch asked for themselves was the right to garrison a chain of fortresses on the French frontier and the financial means for doing so.[1] This was the system which, on a smaller scale, they already applied on their eastern frontier. In principle, by the Treaty of Grand Alliance, the Habsburgs had accepted the Barrier; but it was a qualification of their sovereignty over the Spanish Netherlands which they wanted to limit as much as possible. Consequently Dutch diplomacy aimed at obtaining from Britain a guarantee that she would help the Republic to acquire, at the final peace settlement, a satisfactory Barrier Treaty from Charles III. In the course of 1706 the Dutch made a first attempt at an agreement with London by which the Republic would guarantee the Protestant Succession in return for a well-defined Barrier. The negotiations broke down on the rock of England's (and Marlborough's) refusal to incorporate in the Barrier either Ostend, the port of entry for English trade, or Dendermonde, the key to Ghent and the upper Scheldt: it was thought in London that the Dutch desired these towns for economic rather than military reasons. Nor was England in any hurry to resume the talks, since the Dutch will to carry on the war would be bound to cool once they had acquired satisfaction with regard to the Barrier. It was all the easier for England to postpone agreement when, on 1 May 1707, England and Scotland were united into one kingdom with the name of Great Britain; a Dutch guarantee of the Hanoverian succession was now less urgent. So the Dutch were compelled to continue the war without their guarantee, and it needed six more years of useless fighting to complete the proceedings which had thus been opened. During those years the Republic was to be completely outstripped by its allies.

The year 1707 brought the Northern War close to western Europe. Charles XII, having conquered Poland and violated Imperial territory, invaded Saxony in the autumn of 1706.[2] His camp near Altranstädt now

---

[1] For earlier arrangements with Max Emmanuel, see above, pp. 381–2.
[2] See below, p. 663.

became the scene of lively diplomatic activity. Louis XIV tried to persuade the Swedish king to attack Austria. There was moreover some danger for the Allies that Brandenburg-Prussia, which had become very nervous, would withdraw its auxiliary troops from the war against France. Allied anxiety was so strong that Marlborough himself went to Altranstädt in April. He encountered no great difficulties there. Charles XII, who looked upon himself as the champion of Protestantism, had reasons of his own for not taking the side of Louis XIV in the western war; he was content with concessions from the emperor in favour of the Protestants in Silesia, on whose behalf he had threatened force. In the summer he broke up his camp in Saxony and went on to meet his fate in the immensity of the Russian plain.[1] The Maritime Powers continued to have the Prussian regiments at their disposal.

The campaigns in the west provided proof enough that the French power of resistance was as yet unbroken, indeed that France was still able even to assume the offensive. In the Netherlands Louis XIV had concentrated an army of 100,000 under Vendôme, whom he ordered to avoid the mistake (which he had himself encouraged Villeroi to make at Ramillies) of fighting a battle. Marlborough's field-army was weaker, and his freedom of movement severely handicapped by the task of covering the great towns of the Spanish Netherlands, above all Brussels. The Netherlands campaign therefore consisted of sterile manoeuvres with no decisive engagement. On the upper Rhine, however, Villars once again demonstrated his genius by a cleverly disguised surprise which forced the Lines of Stollhofen, with ease, in May—a feat which enabled him to overrun south Germany and to screw contributions out of large areas of Swabia and Franconia. Lewis of Baden could probably have prevented this, but he had died in January and his successor as Imperial commander-in-chief, the margrave of Bayreuth, was incompetent.

On the Mediterranean front Marlborough had long cherished a swift but risky stroke, simultaneously by land and sea, on Toulon, not only to paralyse the French fleet there but also to invade France from the south and force her troops to evacuate Spain. This was in full agreement with Victor Amadeus, but the emperor thought it more important first to take possession of the Spanish territories in Italy. Without consulting his allies, he authorized a treaty, signed at Milan on 13 March, for the neutralization of Italy so far as concerned the French, thus allowing their garrisons in the Milanese, which were cut off from their country, to reinforce the armies in Spain and the Netherlands with at least 12,000 men. Further, contrary to Marlborough's grand strategy, an Austrian army

---

[1] Below, pp. 664 ff. It may be significant that he did not stir until the Allied attack on Toulon had failed, and it has been claimed that he brought pressure on Victor Amadeus to make it fail, in the belief that its success would have subjected France to a dictated peace. See, however, R. M. Hatton, *Charles XII of Sweden* (1968), p. 232.

made its easy way southwards under Daun, through the Papal States, to expel the weak Spanish garrisons from Naples; the city of Naples fell without resistance, Gaeta after a siege. Charles III was proclaimed king of Naples. Hence the Dutch desire to leave a kingdom in Italy available to Philip V was rendered virtually illusory.

The Habsburg invasion of Naples first held up and then weakened the attack on Toulon—at best a complex operation requiring the most careful synchronization of movements and supplies along the Riviera. Although an Austro-Savoyard army of 35,000 under Eugene and Victor Amadeus, with the indispensable and ready co-operation of Shovell's warships and transports, eventually appeared before the town, the siege was given up on 22 August. Eugene's heart was not in this design and the delay in his march allowed Tessé to rush enough troops from Dauphiné and Savoy to put up a stout defence. Shovell, the real inspiration of the attack, was unable either to prevent a siege in form or to prolong it. But the French had come so near to expecting disaster to their fleet that they scuttled part of it themselves.[1] Being unable to refloat or refit these ships with any speed, chiefly because of the straitened condition of their dockyard finances, their action left the Mediterranean indisputably to English sea power at last. Victor Amadeus played no further part in the war, beyond a campaign in 1708 to capture the last fortresses held by France in the Alps.[2]

The Allies fared still worse in Spain, where Galway attempted the march from Valencia to Castile with too small an army. Berwick, reinforced by French troops from Italy, intercepted and cut Galway's army to pieces before the walls of Almanza on 25 April. Galway's intelligence had misled him as to the enemy's strength. Besides a general inferiority in numbers, he was specially weak in cavalry; and the Portuguese horse, placed at the insistence of das Minas in the post of honour on the right, let him down badly. With great difficulty, this fine soldier afterwards rallied the broken fragments of the Allied forces, while some of Berwick's troops had to be withdrawn for the defence of Toulon. Almanza was the most serious reverse yet suffered by the Allies in Spain. It destroyed the expectations of the anti-Castilian party in Valencia and Aragon. Nevertheless, when only Catalonia was left to him, Charles III had no thought of giving up the Spanish throne.

The English were no more prepared than Charles to abandon Spain, which they now fancied more than the Netherlands as the vital theatre. In 1708 they achieved indeed some remarkable successes. Thanks to Sir

[1] The damage caused by the invasion to the Provençal communities was estimated at over 6·5 m. *livres*: A. Peyriat, 'Problèmes forestiers en Provence', *Provence Historique*, vol. XVI (1966), p. 48.
[2] Exilles and Fenestrelle. He too wanted a barrier: cf. below, p. 467.

John Leake's fleet, the Allies conquered Sardinia on behalf of Charles III in August. A month later Lieutenant-General James Stanhope took Minorca, with its splendidly protected, deep and commodious harbour of Port Mahon, where the warships could be wintered; the open bay of Gibraltar was of little use for this purpose. The new advance base, whose acquisition was Marlborough's answer to the cautiousness of the admirals, definitely made Great Britain mistress of the Mediterranean: the wonder is that no attempt on it had been made earlier (as the Austrians had urged in 1704): in Stanhope's own words, the island would 'give the law to the Mediterranean in time of War and Peace'.[1] Charles III was now really no more than Britain's puppet king. Some arrangements with her which were kept secret from the Dutch clearly illustrate the extent of his servitude. In January 1708 he secretly yielded to Great Britain the much-coveted Asiento, and later he renewed the promise to give Marlborough the governorship of the south Netherlands. Nor was he in a position to reject Stanhope's proposals for a treaty ceding Minorca to Great Britain.[2] When these dealings became known to the Dutch,[3] they aroused sharp resentment. The British Asiento was in fact a unilateral breach of the Treaty of the Grand Alliance, which had guaranteed commercial parity to the Maritime Powers in the Spanish Indies.

Despite these humiliations, the Habsburgs did better in 1708 than in previous years. Although the Hungarian rebellion went on smouldering until 1711, its main force was broken at Trenčin on 3 August. In Italy the war had come to a victorious end. Clement XI was ultimately induced by Austria and Britain to recognize Charles III as 'The Catholic King' in January 1709.[4] Thanks to these developments, moreover, the emperor was at last in a position to give effective support to his brother in Spain. From 1708 Austrian troops were sent to Catalonia, where the Allied forces were placed under a new commander-in-chief, Count Guido von Starhemberg. They rendered the Habsburg king less dependent on Britain, but they came too late to turn the tide of war for long in that difficult, desolate scene of forlorn marches and empty tactical successes.

On the upper Rhine, George, elector of Hanover and heir to the British throne, now took over command of the Imperial army and found himself confronting his rival Max Emmanuel, who was also striving after a royal title. On the Moselle, Eugene and his small Austrian army faced Berwick. On neither of these fronts, however, did anything of importance occur.

[1] Quoted Sir H. Richmond, *Statesmen and Sea Power* (Oxford, 1946), p. 92.

[2] Stanhope had been British ambassador to King Charles since January 1706 and now doubled this rôle with the command of the British contingent.

[3] As was the case regarding Minorca, and probably the Asiento also, not later than August 1709: see R. Geikie and I. A. Montgomery, *The Dutch Barrier, 1705–1719* (Cambridge, 1930), pp. 151–3. According to B. Williams, *Stanhope* (Oxford, 1932), p. 61, the French captured a copy of the treaty and made it known to the Dutch.

[4] See below, p. 595 for the Austro-Papal war preceding this recognition, which was not made public till October 1709.

The principal scene of war in 1708 was the south Netherlands, where Marlborough with the main Anglo-Dutch army had plans for a new offensive.

His experiences of 1707 had convinced Marlborough that he must not allow his freedom of movement to be again impaired by having to protect the larger towns of Brabant; so he intended to evacuate Brussels and establish the government of the Spanish Netherlands at Antwerp. The French upset this project. For they also, encouraged by the relative success of their 1707 campaign and relying on the friendly disposition of elements in the Belgian population, had conceived a major offensive. First, a diversion in Scotland was to draw off some British troops from the Netherlands. A squadron, with the Old Pretender on board, sailed from Dunkirk in March under Count Forbin, whose seamanship was employed in it against his own better judgment. It appeared off the Firth of Forth, but was unable to effect a landing and returned to Dunkirk 'in parcels';[1] the British battalions sent to Tynemouth were already back in Ostend before campaigning in the Netherlands had begun. When it did start, this campaign was on the grandest scale of the whole war. At first the initiative rested with the French. Vendôme, with the young duke of Burgundy,[2] stood with a strong army north of Mons. Meanwhile Bergeyck, who had secret contacts with Ghent, the key to all the waterways in Flanders, arranged for the surrender of the town by stealth on 5 July. In a rapid march, which took Marlborough completely by surprise, Vendôme advanced to cover this new acquisition. At one stroke the war was brought into the heart of the Spanish Netherlands. There was no longer any question of evacuating Brussels, which now remained the only safe link with Holland. But Marlborough soon recovered from the shock. From the Moselle Eugene hastened to his aid with a few squadrons of cavalry. This move, in turn, brought up Berwick's stronger force from the Rhine, in a race to reach Vendôme first. When the French left their positions near Ghent to take Oudenarde, a bridgehead town on the upper Scheldt, the Allies intercepted them on 11 July, after a forced march of remarkable speed, before Berwick had arrived. The fierce battle which raged in fields and gardens round Oudenarde till nightfall was not fought from prepared positions, but on an improvised front which was extended as more troops came up. It was more of a *mêlée*, and more purely an infantry encounter, than Blenheim or Ramillies. The French were nearly encircled, but the Allies failed to pursue them and they were able to retreat to a strong position behind the canal connecting Ghent and Bruges, which had also surrendered to Bergeyck.

Northern France now lay open to the Allies, Marlborough wanted to

[1] J. H. Owen, *War at Sea under Queen Anne, 1702–1708*, pp. 260–1.
[2] They were not on good terms: indeed, the frequent quarrelling between them had effects on the strategy of this campaign which have yet to be fully considered.

march at once on Paris. More cautiously, with Eugene's support, the Dutch generals refused to by-pass Lille, strongest of French fortresses, the masterpiece of Vauban's art, well supplied and defended by a large garrison under Boufflers. So the murderous siege of Lille began. As the Flemish waterways were blocked by Ghent, siege-artillery and provisions had to be brought by the rivers from Holland to Brussels, and thence in an enormous convoy along the difficult and dangerous overland route to the army before Lille. The French did their utmost to prevent the loss of this important town. Vendôme occupied all the Scheldt crossings from Ghent to Tournai, thus cutting communications between Brussels and the Allies, who were driven to rely on a new supply-line to Ostend, and so by sea to Holland and England. But this route also was in danger. From Bruges and Nieuwpoort the French went into the country, opened the sluices, cut the dikes and inundated a large area round Ostend. A struggle of epic greatness flared up in the submerged polders of western Flanders. A French attack on an Anglo-Dutch convoy, making its way along almost impracticable roads from Ostend to Lille, led to the short but sharp fight of Wijnendaal, near Thorhout, on 28 September, when the English and Dutch, under Webb and Nassau-Woudenberg, demonstrated their moral superiority by beating an army twice as large as their own. In the end, however, the Allies could only maintain their communications by means of a fleet of flat-bottomed boats. Boufflers, after surrendering the town of Lille to the Allies on 22 October, still held out in the citadel, and the French made a last attempt to relieve him. Max Emmanuel, back from the Rhine, marched on Brussels and laid siege to his former capital, in whose defence the civilian population took active part. Marlborough then forced a way through Vendôme's Scheldt line, just in time to relieve the city on 28 November. The French had lost the dramatic struggle. Boufflers surrendered the citadel of Lille on 9 December, the French field-army retreated from Ghent to France, and the garrisons left in Ghent and Bruges capitulated on 1 January 1709.

France was desperate. Her army was disintegrating, while the corrosion of her economic and financial situation, already appalling, was accelerated by the miseries of one of the hardest winters on record in Europe.[1] A famine swept the country; the English navy interfered with the importation of cereals, while even Holland prohibited their export to the enemy. After the fall of Lille Louis XIV was prepared to make peace at almost any price. In the spring of 1709 he sent his foreign minister Torcy, in disguise, to The Hague. But the Allies, having won the war, hopelessly failed in making peace. Responsibility for this can be divided almost equally between Britain, Austria and Holland. The point which led them astray was Spain. They had lost the war there: Philip V was no longer merely

---

[1] Above, pp. 322–3; on the credit crisis, cf. above, p. 305.

the French candidate for the throne, but the national king: after five years of war Charles III was nowhere established outside Catalonia. Yet the Allies refused to accept these facts. England and Austria still insisted on the undivided Spanish monarchy for Charles III. It is true that among the Tories the insight was dawning that this was now an unattainable aim, but they were no longer in power; since the elections of 1708 it was the Whigs who dominated the Godolphin ministry. The Republic was more inclined to peace than its two big partners; the strenuous efforts of 1708 had shaken its credit and increased the already longstanding war-weariness. It is significant that Dutch statesmen were in the habit of calling the peace-negotiations 'the great work'. They had agreed to claim Spain for Charles III only because the alternative was a breach with England, although they were still inclined to seek some compensation for Philip V in Italy. In another respect, however, the Dutch were more exacting than their allies. It soon became apparent that Torcy was aiming at a peace for France alone, but the Dutch feared nothing so much as having to carry on the war in Spain after an agreement with France had given that country the opportunity to recover. It was they above all, though also the Whig government in England, who now insisted that the peace should be general, and hence that France should give some guarantees for the cession of the Spanish monarchy to Charles III. Consequently, the three allies could meet only on the basis of the most exacting claims put forward by each of them. These were laid down in the Preliminary Articles of The Hague, offered to Torcy as an ultimatum in May 1709. The deeply humiliated king in Versailles accepted almost everything: withdrawal of his troops from Spain, surrender of conquests which in his eyes constituted the glory of his reign (including even Lille and Strasbourg), demolition of the Dunkirk defences, cession of Newfoundland. Unhappily, the 4th and 37th articles stipulated in effect that the war would be resumed unless the whole Spanish monarchy were handed over within two months. This he found offensive, and he declared himself unable to comply with it. But for Heinsius, precisely, it was the kernel of the whole negotiation.[1]

To the amazement of Europe, no peace was made. Louis XIV refused to sign the Preliminaries, made with great effect an appeal to his people in June 1709, and once again, with his ebbing strength, prepared for war. But this war, which at first had been inspired by ambitions of absolute dominion and imperial expansion, had now become a national war for the defence of his own territory and honour. Hurriedly a new French army was brought together, hunger acting as a recruiting-officer, and the one soldier who was a match for Marlborough, Villars, was at last given command on the northern frontier. There, from Aire to Douai, Villars constructed the Lines of La Bassée to block the road from Lille to Paris. Marlborough did not succeed in driving him out of this position, although

---

[1] Stork-Penning, pp. 280–313. The negotiation is described below, pp. 415 ff.

his army was reinforced by an unusually large Imperial contingent under Eugene. The expected thrust to Paris did not come. Instead of Marlborough's conception of an outflanking movement by sea and a landing in Picardy, the Allies confined themselves to taking fortress-towns, beginning with the strong city of Tournai on 3 September. When they afterwards turned to Mons, Villars intercepted them. The bloody battle of Malplaquet followed on 11 September—a pyrrhic victory for the Allies which killed the flower of the Dutch infantry. The French army, infused with a new spirit, was beaten but not destroyed; it retreated behind the Lines of La Bassée. Only the fate of Mons was sealed: for the third time Max Emmanuel lost his capital. He removed to Namur, where in 1711 he was rewarded for his loyalty to the Bourbons with the sovereignty of the two provinces remaining to him, Namur and Luxemburg, with the object of giving him a stronger position at the ultimate peace-negotiations.

On the other fronts everything went wrong for the Allies in 1709. An attempt to invade Franche-Comté from south Germany ended with an Austrian defeat. In Spain, the Allies lost Alicante in April; Starhemberg remained on the defensive throughout the year; from Portugal, the marquis of Fronteira, accompanied by the sick Galway, was prevented from advancing in Estremadura by 15,000 Spaniards under the marquis de Bay, a French commander.[1]

In the Republic the Anglo-Habsburg claim that the entire Spanish monarchy go to Charles III continued to be much criticized. Malplaquet, which had cost the lives of many sons of the regent families, made the Dutch more than ever anxious for peace, while Stanhope's secret negotiations with Charles III in Spain, something of which had now leaked out, caused much indignation. Yet the Republic was in no stronger a position than before to detach itself from its powerful ally; even Buys's Amsterdam peace-party realized the impossibility of a separate Franco-Dutch peace. What the Dutch statesmen could do, however, was to make use of the situation by bringing heavy pressure on Britain to provide a guarantee for their Barrier. The Whig ministry, afraid to push the States into the arms of France, was willing to make considerable concessions. In exchange for a guarantee of the Protestant Succession—which possessed for this extreme party government much more value than it had had for the government of 1706—the Dutch obtained all they wanted, not only in the Netherlands but also in the Mediterranean and America. By the Treaty of Succession and Barrier signed at The Hague on 29 October, the Republic promised armed help at need to secure the Hanoverian succession, while Great Britain promised to back the Republic in its attempt to obtain the right of occupying a formidable list of barrier-fortresses—including Lille, Tournai, Valenciennes, Condé and Maubeuge, but not that apple of England's

---

[1] This action on the river Caia, on 7 May, was the last in which the Portuguese army was involved. In October 1710 Galway returned to England.

ye, Ostend—and to annex Upper Guelderland, a territory belonging of old to the Dutch province of Gelderland but severed from it by the Peace of Münster. Moreover, by article 15 Britain promised to share with the Republic all the advantages she might acquire in any part of the Spanish monarchy, which meant that she abandoned Stanhope's agreement with Charles III for the Asiento and Minorca. Once again, however, the Republic emphatically refused to pledge itself to the conquest of the entire Spanish monarchy. It was the Whig ambassador, Townshend, who signed this treaty for Britain. Marlborough, ominously, kept aloof from the negotiations.

The Barrier Treaty of 1709 seemed to be the triumph of Heinsius's policy. In reality, it was an awkward and ill-starred agreement. It aroused the resentment, first, of the emperor, who took offence at so heavy a surcharge being laid upon Charles III's sovereignty over the south Netherlands; then of the king of Prussia, who claimed Upper Guelderland for himself; and finally of the south-Netherlanders themselves, who feared the Dutch economic supremacy which the treaty would establish. But the most unfortunate aspect of the treaty was that it chained the Republic indissolubly, not so much to England—there was nothing new in that—but to the war policy of the Whigs: from the outset, the Tories considered the treaty prejudicial to British interests.

Although France's power of resistance had proved surprisingly strong in 1709, her need of peace was no less urgent. The Northern War, which after Poltava was once again moving westward, brought her no relief, for by the conventions of The Hague, in 1710, north Germany was proclaimed neutral.[1] In that same month two French envoys, Huxelles and the Abbé de Polignac, went to Holland for new talks. They were not allowed to get as far as The Hague, where the three allies were in conference; but at Geertruidenberg they were encouraged to receive the Allied offers brought by Buys and Van der Dussen, both of them still very much for peace. The purpose was primarily to discover some expedient to satisfy article 37 of the Preliminaries. Louis XIV offered cautionary towns in the Netherlands, even a subsidy for the war which the Allies still had to wage in Spain. The Dutch did their utmost to obtain a kingdom for Philip V in Sicily and Sardinia, on condition that France would guarantee that he left Spain; the English were unwilling to yield anything except Sicily. Austria would hear nothing of the partition of Spain and advocated a separate peace with France, while Marlborough made it clear that he was equally prepared to waive article 37 and take the risk of continued war in Spain. Above all, however, the Dutch, prompted by their profound distrust of Louis XIV's good faith, clung fast to the view that the peace must be one and indivisible. In this way their excessive timidity paradoxically led them into recklessness. Heinsius considered France so far gone in

---

[1] Below, p. 670.

economic and financial exhaustion that Louis must ultimately conced everything asked of him. But the French king steadily refused to force hi grandson to leave Spain and content himself with a kingdom in Italy. Fo all these reasons, the Geertruidenberg negotiations were doomed t failure, and in July 1710 broken off. There was no need for France t regret this. At that very time the Whig ministry was already tottering.

During 1710 Villars acted cautiously in the Netherlands and norther France; he could no longer hazard his relatively small army in battles and he even evacuated the Lines of La Bassée when they had become to vulnerable. The result of Marlborough's campaign was the capture, afte expensive sieges, of four fortresses on French territory: Douai, Béthune St-Venant and Aire. Yet the expected collapse of French resistance di not take place. Formidable obstacles blocked the way to Paris, notably th new defence-line built by Villars—the so-called 'Ne Plus Ultra Lines' leaning on Arras and Bouchain.

During the winter of 1709–10 all the French troops, except for garrison in the Navarrese fortresses, had been recalled from Spain. At the sam time Emperor Joseph I, whose position in Hungary was now secure an who was also master of Italy, sent substantial military forces to support hi brother and Starhemberg in Catalonia. Thus reinforced, the Allies resume the offensive, defeating Philip at Almenara in July and again near Sara gossa in August. Once again the way was open to Madrid, which was re occupied on 21 September. For the first time Charles III personally too possession of the city which was intended to be his capital: ironically, i was he who had proposed the wiser course, rejected by his advisers, o by-passing Castile in order to occupy Navarre and the lines of communica tion with France.[1] But Vendôme had left Paris to join Philip at Valla dolid by 17 September; the Castilians remained unshakably loyal t Philip; and it was difficult for the Allies to obtain food and forage. The return of a French army hastily got together by Vendôme finally com pelled them to evacuate Madrid in November. On his way back t Aragon, Stanhope was caught by the French in Brihuega; and although Starhemberg defeated Vendôme at Villa Viciosa the very next day, 10 December, he was forced to retreat to Barcelona. The decision in Spain had arrived. Allied policy was condemned by the very course of events.

The débâcle in Spain confirmed the new course in foreign policy inaugurated by a sweeping change in the character of the British govern ment. During the summer of 1710 a sharp reaction against Godolphin's government had set in, as much for reasons of home as of foreign policy. The population was suffering from the high prices of corn caused by two bad harvests in succession; squires grumbled at the high land tax which paid interest on the National Debt. The widespread enthusiasm accorded

[1] A. Parnell, *The War of the Succession in Spain* (1905), pp. 284–5.

o Dr Sacheverell showed, as early as March, that the Whig ministry no onger had public opinion behind it. Sarah, Lady Marlborough, already or several years estranged from the queen, was banished from court in April. Anne now felt strong enough gradually to dismiss her ministers, ncluding Godolphin himself on 8/19 August. Harley became the leader of the new Tory ministry, St John the principal secretary of state. The general election in October, timed at an earlier date than the constitution equired, brought an overwhelming Tory majority into the Commons. Marlborough, however, was not yet attacked.

The Tories had never favoured Marlborough's continental war. Regarding the Dutch as commercial rivals, still formidable, rather than indispensable allies, they considered Townshend's Barrier Treaty prejudicial o England's interests. The new men in power also wanted peace. As soon as they were in office they embarked on secret and separate negotiations with France, through the medium of a secret agent of Torcy's. They declared themselves willing to abandon Spain to Philip V. This attitude was stiffened when the bad news arrived from Spain at the end of the year, still more after the unexpected death of Emperor Joseph on 17 April 1711. The whole complexion of the Spanish problem was altered when Charles II succeeded to the Austrian hereditary lands and was elected emperor 12 October 1711): the mock king Charles III became as Emperor Charles VI one of the most powerful princes of Europe. The war had already put him in possession of the south Netherlands and the Spanish territories in Italy. If he obtained Spain and her colonies as well, the balance of power in Europe—the real issue of the war—would once again be overthrown, though now in another direction. This new situation urged the Tory government along the path they had already chosen. It was not the rather moderate Harley, however, but the bold and unscrupulous St John who, in the summer of 1711, took control of the secret and bilateral negotiations with Torcy. St John not only wanted peace: he wanted it at the expense of his allies: he wanted to impose England's will on Europe.

While these developments were going forward the war was not halted, but prosecuted in a different spirit. The Tories, who had long complained of the neglect of the colonial war, mounted an elaborate expedition to capture Quebec—an expedition hastily prepared and incompetently conducted, which met with complete failure in August 1711.[1] In Spain no fighting took place. King Charles departed in the autumn of 1711 to take possession of the Austrian hereditary lands and the Imperial Crown, leaving his wife at Barcelona to govern a country which even now he was not willing to give up. He recalled Eugene from the Netherlands to the Rhine because of the impending Imperial election, so that Marlborough alone now confronted Villars. His position also was changed, however. He was no longer the acknowledged leader of the Grand Alliance but only

[1] Below, pp. 505–6.

the commander of the British and Dutch forces. For the last time h
demonstrated his military genius. In August, without losing a single lif
he succeeded by a surprise movement in perforating the Ne Plus Ultr
Lines, behind which Villars had entrenched himself, and laid siege t
Bouchain. But the capture of this small town was not followed up by a
invasion of France, for the way to Paris was still blocked by fortresse:
When he returned to England, the Tory ministry felt strong enough t
attack even him.

The negotiations between St John and Torcy led rapidly to concret
results in the summer of 1711.[1] The French conceded all the specia
advantages Britain wanted: Gibraltar, Minorca, the Asiento, treatmen
as most favoured nation in Spain, demolition of the harbour works an
fortifications of Dunkirk, cession of Acadia and Newfoundland. Thes
concessions were laid down in the Preliminary Articles of London o:
8 October. That they were flagrantly contrary to the treaties, especially t
the Barrier Treaty, did not matter to the Tories. With these Preliminarie
as a working basis, the British government now proposed to its allies
general peace congress, to meet early in 1712. There was a general outcr
of indignation at The Hague and Vienna, and among the smaller allies
for all the articles dealing with their special interests were couched i
vague terms, whereas the British advantages were defined in detail. It wa
chiefly the Dutch who had cause for complaint. This was not because th
London preliminaries left Spain to Philip V: the Dutch had never reall
approved of the 'No peace without Spain' formula: still less could the
wish to see the empire of Charles V restored for the benefit of Charles VI
Even the Barrier question looked quite different now that the sout
Netherlands could be expected not to fall to the share of the wea
Spanish monarchy, but to Austria, the second military power of th
Continent. Yet the States were not prepared simply to shelve the Towns
hend Treaty, whereby they had been promised the same economi
advantages as England might obtain. The disavowal of that treaty pushe
the Dutch over to the side of the one power willing to continue the war t
the bitter end, Austria. It was only with reluctance that these two State
agreed to the peace congress.

The British government brilliantly used pamphlet and newspaper t
rouse public feeling against the Allies, especially against the old Dutc
rival. Grievances and suspicions which had obsessed an earlier generation
were now rehashed. By the end of November 1711 (o.s.) Swift's masterl
pamphlet, *The Conduct of the Allies*, propounded the theme that

no Nation was ever so long or so scandalously abused by the Folly, the Temerity
the Corruption, the Ambition of its domestick Enemies; or treated with so mucl
Insolence, Injustice and Ingratitude by its foreign Friends.[2]

[1] Below, pp. 459–60.
[2] *Political Tracts, 1711–1713* (ed. H. Davis, 1951) p. 15.

It produced an enormous effect, which next year was almost equalled by Dr John Arbuthnot's *The History of John Bull*. There was no lack of opposition pamphlets but they were submerged by the rising tide of Tory popularity. Marlborough was the centre of the opposition, the House of Lords its stronghold. It was ruthlessly broken. A charge of malversations was lodged against the duke, and in insulting terms he was dismissed from all his offices at the end of the year. The great man went of his own free will into exile.[1] The day after his dismissal, the government broke the Lords' opposition by the creation of twelve new Tory peers. Oxford and St John were now completely masters of the situation. A visit paid by Eugene to London, in January 1712, had no effect whatsoever. On 4/15 February the Commons passed a series of resolutions accusing the Dutch of having failed, throughout the war, to supply their proper quota of soldiers, ships and subsidies. This was partly true, but it was unjust. In proportion to the size of their population and to their financial resources, the efforts of the Dutch had been magnificent. They had exhausted themselves in the service of Europe.

The congress of powers met at Utrecht on 29 January 1712.[2] Louis XIV, having come to terms with Britain, raised his demands on his other enemies. But Austria, the Republic and also the smaller allies (especially Hanover) refused to let Britain and France dictate the conditions of peace. While the congress sat, they continued the war. At this point St John did not shrink from the worst possible breach of faith. Marlborough's successor as commander of the British troops in the Netherlands was Ormonde. The campaign of 1712 had hardly begun when he received, on 21 May, the notorious 'restraining orders' which forbade him to take part in any siege or risk any battle. These orders were to be kept secret from the Allies, but St John himself informed the French of their contents. However, the truth came out soon enough. After signing an armistice, Ormonde marched off with all the British national troops on 16 July. Marlborough's veterans felt this as a disgrace. The British occupied Ghent and Bruges, while the French handed over Dunkirk to them, as a pledge for the destruction of its harbour works and fortifications, on 19 July.

On the advice of Heinsius—that old champion of perseverance—the States-General, outraged by the British desertion, decided on a policy of despair. Dangerously overstraining their resources, they took over on their own account the foreign auxiliaries hitherto paid by Britain and went on with the struggle, in conjunction with Austria. Eugene was given the Netherlands command. Before the British withdrawal the Allies had taken Le Quesnoy; but while Eugene was besieging Landrecies, Villars

[1] In the summer of 1714, while Anne was yet alive, he intended to return: he did not arrive till after her sudden death.
[2] Below, pp. 461 ff.

inflicted a painful defeat upon the Dutch covering troops near Denain on 24 July, a defeat which endangered the Allied lines of communication. During the second half of the year the French, their morale rejuvenated, recovered Le Quesnoy, Bouchain and Douai. The Dutch learnt that without Britain they could not hope to carry on the war. Their public finances collapsed. Disappointed and humiliated, they were now willing to submit—the very word used by St John.

The Republic resigned itself to Britain's disavowal of the Townshend Treaty. Instead, it concluded a new Treaty of Succession and Barrier on 30 January 1713. There was now no question of equal trading privileges in Spanish territories, nor of the annexation of Upper Guelderland, which Britain designed for the rising and exigent kingdom of Prussia. The principle of the Barrier was maintained, but the list of garrison towns which Britain promised to help the Republic obtain was about halved. In March and April 1713, a series of treaties could be signed at Utrecht by which Great Britain, the Dutch Republic, Prussia, Savoy and Portugal made peace with France and, in June and July, with Spain. Among the smaller allies it was Prussia and Savoy, the favourites of the Tories, that came off best.

Only Austria and the Empire had yet to acquiesce in the inevitable. Another campaign was necessary to compel Charles VI to submit. The French were now able to bring all their military forces to the Rhine and Eugene was no match for them. In the course of 1713 Villars opened the negotiations which led to the Peace of Rastatt between Austria and France on 6 March 1714, although Charles VI still considered himself at war with Philip V. The Empire became a party to this treaty at Baden in Switzerland on 7 September.[1]

All this was nevertheless an incontestable victory for the coalition against Louis XIV. Although France had finally obtained conditions far more favourable than could have been hoped for in 1709, the partition of the Spanish monarchy meant the triumph of the European balance of power—the leading idea behind the Grand Alliance of 1701. Only two questions remained to be settled, one by force of arms, the other by diplomacy.

The war had a bloody sequel for the deserted Catalans. Most of the British troops in Catalonia and Portugal had been withdrawn in 1712 to Port Mahon and Gibraltar. In the peace treaties with Spain nothing was said about the interests of Catalonia; Bolingbroke declared that the preservation of Catalan liberties was no concern of Great Britain's. But the Catalans refused to resign themselves to their fate. While an English squadron blockaded the port,[2] French and Spanish artillery laid half Barcelona in ruins. After four months' siege and the loss of 6,000 lives, the city capitulated on 11 September 1714. There were no executions, but the

---

[1] Below, p. 474.   [2] Trevelyan, *Queen Anne*, vol. III (1934), p. 357, n. 266.

Catalans were deprived of their political privileges and systematically humiliated.

There was, finally, a diplomatic aftermath also: the definitive arrangement of the Barrier between the Republic and the new master of the south Netherlands, Charles VI. During the phase of bitter quarrelling between Britain and the Republic the authority of the Anglo-Dutch Conference at Brussels had become very weak. The Council of State obstructed its directives and began urgently to insist upon the immediate cession of the provinces to their legitimate sovereign. Only when the Barrier Treaty of January 1713 had restored the two-power unity in some degree could the Dutch reassert themselves in Brussels: the Council of State of 1706 was then replaced by a new one more willing to accept the tutelage of the two powers. After Rastatt it was possible to open negotiations with Austria for a final settlement. With the help of Hanoverian England, where the Whigs were once again in office, the Republic obtained from the reluctant Austrians, by a treaty signed at Antwerp on 15 November 1715, its ardently coveted Barrier. The approval of the Belgian population was neither asked for nor given. Only now was the Condominium terminated. The government was handed over to the Austrians by Van den Bergh, the last remaining member of the Conference, in February 1716. The Spanish Netherlands had become the Austrian Netherlands.

CHAPTER XIV

THE PACIFICATION OF UTRECHT

THE long series of negotiations which led to the Peace of Utrecht had no distinct starting-point and no single concluding date. The Congress at Utrecht, with its sequels at Rastatt and Baden, was but the open avowal of the intention to make peace, a useful clearing-house for the ratification of decisions arrived at by much more devious processes. Much of the difficulty which beset the path to a settlement resulted from differences between the Allies as to how the rather vague objectives of the Grand Alliance would best be secured. Discussion was often as bitter and prolonged between them as with their enemies. Peace was to be made only by common consent, but there was nothing to prevent a party to the Alliance from discussing proposals directly with an enemy, and in fact negotiations of one sort or another were virtually continuous from 1706.

The first significant movements towards peace came in the double approach of France and Spain to the Dutch and English,[1] separately, in July 1706, two months after Ramillies had removed the direct military threat from the Dutch and brought out Allied differences over the administration of the south Netherlands. Louis XIV was ready to dismember the Spanish inheritance if he could so dissolve the coalition against him. Bergeyck approached Bruno van der Dussen, the pensionary of Gouda,[2] with a suggestion that Spain and the Indies should go to Charles III, the Spanish possessions in north Italy to Philip V. The Spanish Netherlands should pass to the Dutch. While Heinsius sounded Marlborough on these feelers, Marlborough himself was indirectly in touch with Max Emmanuel and with Pierre Rouillé, the French envoy accredited to him as governor of the Spanish Netherlands, discussing different disposals of territories: the Netherlands to go to Charles, Hainault to the dispossessed elector. These first serious attempts to treat separately with the uneasy allies ran against their joint insistence that any settlement must satisfy all powers concerned before definite negotiations could open. By the end of

---

[1] On Louis XIV's secret offer to the Dutch alone, in the autumn of 1705, and the pacific views of Willem Buys, pensionary of Amsterdam, see above, pp. 425–6. For a view of Dutch politics in February 1706, see the *mémoire* of the French agent A. E. Helvetius printed by M. van der Bijl in *Bijdragen en Mededelingen van het Historisch Genootschap*, vol. LXXX (1966), pp. 159–94.

[2] Described by Helvetius (*ibid.* pp. 166–7) as a tough and proud republican, hard-working and well-informed, the obvious successor to Heinsius, but extremely suspicious of French sincerity and English ambition alike: 'C'est un homme très dangereux, et qu'on doit surtout ménager si l'on veut tenter quelque négociation avec les Etats Généraux.' For Bergeyck see above, p. 413.

1706, the interchanges had served to show only how difficult that settlement would be. The Allies still agreed that Philip must surrender all his Spanish territories, but England rejected the Dutch suggestion for compensating him with an area so vital to her trade as Naples or Sicily. In Italy, moreover, Habsburg ambitions clashed with those of the French, who hoped that Italian territories might ultimately revert to them from Philip. Already, too, the Barrier had indicated the part it was to play in preventing an easy transition to peace. Vienna proposed that it be sought in territory taken from northern France, thus absurdly stranding Dutch garrisons without land contact with home. London, though more sympathetic, was unwilling to include either Dendermonde, a central town on the Scheldt line of communication between the Dutch and French frontiers, or Nieuwpoort and Ostend, coveted by the English: any of these would have given the Dutch too clear a commercial advantage. Meanwhile, Emperor Joseph I had shown, by the forced surrender to Austria of the duchy of Milan, how lightly he regarded the aim of securing all the Spanish dominions intact for his brother Charles. This first French attempt to divide the Allies produced an advantage only for Savoy: a French proposal to hand the Milanese to Savoy frightened the emperor into a belated fulfilment (1707) of his obligation under the Treaty of Turin to invest the duke with Montferrat.[1] The battle of Almanza made continued French attempts to exploit Allied differences even less promising, for Louis XIV was now less willing to consider the surrender of Spain to the archduke. Nicolas Mesnager, *conseiller de commerce* from Rouen, after talks with Van der Dussen in Rotterdam in January 1708, could offer Heinsius only easier trading conditions with France; he had no powers to discuss any partition of the Spanish inheritance. These *pourparlers* were broken off in March. Difficulties between English and Dutch over the projected Barrier Treaty—which was to contain a guarantee of the Hanoverian succession— did not suffice to tempt Heinsius into a dubious separate negotiation.

Such peace-feelers provided no evidence of a clear policy on the French side. Serious negotiation began only after Oudenarde (July 1708), quickening with the fall of Lille in October, when conversations were opened with Heinsius through Petkum, the Holstein-Gottorp minister at The Hague and a French agent since 1707. How much the French attitude had changed was shown by their willingness now to treat openly on the basis of surrendering Spain and the Indies. By this implicit confession that the whole policy for which he had gone to war was untenable, Louis XIV returned to the idea of the Partition Treaties. But as France abandoned the principle of Spanish integrity the Allies adopted it. Moreover, once Torcy had indicated his readiness to negotiate from the basis of preliminaries agreed between the Allies, the internal stresses within the Grand Alliance

---

[1] This marquisate had been seized by the Austrians in 1701, when Mantua, to whom it belonged, joined the French; cf. above, pp. 417–18 for the Austro-Savoyard treaty of 1703.

16-2

prevented the working out of preliminaries which might have been acceptable to France.

The British election of May 1708 had produced a Whig majority determined on a Dutch guarantee of the Protestant Succession and on lashing the United Provinces to an uncompromising peace plan. The price had to be a firm Barrier Treaty, with or without the emperor's support. The Junto, indeed, was eager to move faster than Marlborough, concerned perhaps more than any single figure on the Allied side with the absolute military destruction of France—now (he thought) not far short of achievement: concessions to the Dutch were therefore unnecessary, whereas the likelihood of their attempting a separate peace would be greater if they first achieved an advantageous treaty with Great Britain, with which they could then bid. The Whigs, on the contrary, feared that the Dutch would make just such a peace unless first promised a strong Barrier. In fact, the risk of Dutch desertion was reduced by military events which lessened the possibility of a peace based on partition. The occupation of Port Mahon, added to the seizure of Gibraltar, made it less likely than ever that Britain would accept the retention of Spain by Philip V, since it was supposed he would claim the return of Minorca. On the other hand, the expansion of Austrian interests in Italy ruled out Dutch suggestions of that peninsula as an area of compensation for Philip and so, indirectly, reduced the possibility that the Habsburgs would be granted Spain itself. Although the pope was forced to abandon 'the absolute neutrality of a common father' and secretly recognized Archduke Charles as Catholic King in January 1709, the Spaniards, forced to choose between Philip V and the papacy, adhered to their king and blamed his breach with Rome (in April) on the hated Habsburg.

With neither Britain nor Austria disposed to partition, a Dutch lead in negotiations wherein they would reap advantage by agreeing to it was ruled out. The Dutch were forced to turn to Britain for their Barrier; in return, they would have to accept all the demands of London and Vienna about the general terms of a peace. Confident of the possibility of absolute victory, but with no clear idea of how to obtain it, the Whigs cajoled the Dutch—until now consistent proponents of partition, as implied in the Grand Alliance[1]—into a solid front with the Austrians. Impotence in the field and disagreement over detail were to be repaired by success in united diplomacy. What the Allied armies could not do in Flanders, the French king should do for them in Spain: he should expel his grandson.

The road to the fatal 'preliminaries' of May 1709 was tortuous in the extreme. Heinsius was unwilling to risk peace without the British, who were unable to make peace without Austria—unless they were to sacrifice Gibraltar, Minorca, and the still secret Asiento provision of the commercial treaty of January 1708 with Charles III.[2] As the emperor never

---

[1] See J. G. Stork-Penning, *Het Grote Werk*, esp. p. 459.　　　　[2] Above, p. 434.

wavered in his intention to obtain the entire Spanish inheritance for the Habsburg, first Britain and through her the United Provinces and the smaller powers, particularly Prussia and Savoy, were brought to accept the only basis on which the Allies could negotiate in concert with the enemy. Once they had found in the Preliminaries a means of avoiding further discussion of their differences, and so transferred the responsibility of fighting their war in Spain to Louis XIV, they were united. Yet Louis was unwilling or unable to procure what the Allies wanted. By June 1709 a deadlock had been reached from which the only possible outcomes, failing complete success in the field, must be either a reduction in Allied aims or a rupture of the Alliance, in which *sauve qui peut* would be restrained only by the basic common interest that a balance of power should be maintained.

The great powers were all internally divided as to the way forward early in 1709. The Whigs, having lost sight of King William's conception of a balanced settlement, were partly brought to their view by the conviction, fostered by Marlborough, that France was *in extremis*. But their confidence of total victory in Spain, through French diplomatic surrender, only served to increase English discontent with the prospect of a new campaign once this proved unfounded; promising more than they could obtain, the Junto, who had taken power with the highest aims just when these aims were no longer attainable, only held on to popular support while there appeared a good prospect of peace. Nor had Heinsius an easy task in persuading the Dutch provinces that more was to be gained of their particular war aim, a perfect Barrier, by following the total demands of Austria and Britain with the implied risk of war alongside Britain against Philip V—while France stood neutral and threatening to the Republic.

In Vienna, a lack of political acumen prevented the formulation of any coherent policy which could relate dynastic ambition to military or diplomatic realities. The perversion by Emperor Joseph of the claims of his brother 'Charles III', in consolidating Viennese interests in Italy and the Low Countries, suited Britain and might be brought to suit the Dutch. But the concomitant support of Charles III in Spain itself—not crucial to Austrian interests—was of no advantage to the Dutch and militarily impossible of fulfilment. Further, it was irrelevant to the interests of those smaller German powers for whom a continued Bourbon–Habsburg war was a direct military menace on the upper Rhine. Blenheim had not prevented further incursions into Imperial territory across the Rhine, and there had been no territorial gains in this area from which the Empire could bargain for a settlement that would restore the losses of half a century of French aggression. A secure settlement in Germany, of prime importance for Vienna since 1648, was now subordinated to Habsburg dynastic interests, whether in Hungary, Italy, the Netherlands or Spain. Faced with the need to formulate German and Austrian demands for the

Preliminaries of 1709, the Secret Conference[1] in Vienna (in February) and the leading Circles of the Empire (meeting at Heilbronn in May) foundered on a lack of common purpose; the negotiations with France were ruptured before the Circles reached agreement on their aims. In Vienna, only Wratislaw had any clear conception of a policy, but his influence was greatly reduced, first by his refusal to join Eugene as plenipotentiary at The Hague for the vital negotiations in May,[2] later by serious illness which removed him to the margin of politics. Wratislaw was concerned, more intelligently than his master, with the consolidation of specifically Austrian power (as opposed to dynastic claims) by acquisitions in Italy and south Germany, perhaps Savoy and Bavaria; he was doubtful, as far back as 1706, of the usefulness of demanding the whole Spanish inheritance once it was clear that, the Emperor Joseph being without a son, the whole Habsburg inheritance might soon fall to Charles. This would create a situation unacceptable to the Maritime Powers and isolate Austria. For the sake of his own Italian policy Wratislaw was eager to work with England and Holland, even to accept their Barrier. He foresaw—what the emperor as a dynast could not foresee—that the Netherlands in Austrian hands, if Charles III should become emperor, would extend the area of Habsburg responsibility without any compensating political or economic advantage. Wratislaw was equally concerned with obtaining a favourable balance of advantage against responsibility in the German settlement. Any recession of the French frontier to the advantage of Austria, rather than of the Empire, would meet with no enthusiasm from the German princes; and any settlement extending Austrian responsibility without effective means to support it would be of little interest to Austria. The final Austrian decision was to claim Strasbourg and a restriction of French rights in Alsace to those laid down in 1648, and it was agreed that any Barrier must be negotiated directly between the United Provinces and Austria. The failure of the Imperial princes to send their own plenipotentiary to the negotiations in 1709, as distinct from the ineffective presence of their individual representatives, threw control over German negotiations to the emperor's agents, Eugene and Sinzendorf, who could free themselves from responsibility by arguing, when it suited them, that the concurrence of the Empire would be necessary.

The negotiations in 1709 were in two phases: first (17 March–21 April), between Rouillé and the pensionaries of Amsterdam and Gouda, Buys and Van der Dussen, at Moerdijk and Woerden; and later (6–28 May) at The Hague between Torcy and (for the Allies) Heinsius, Marlborough, and Eugene.

---

[1] For the central Habsburg institutions, see below, pp. 573–5.
[2] For fear that his control of policy would in his absence be upset by Salm, the intriguing but unintelligent *Obersthofmeister* (senior official of the Imperial household), unwilling to work either with England or with the barrier-seeking Dutch.

In the earlier negotiations, Rouillé was empowered to yield every part of the Spanish inheritance except Naples and Sicily; to agree that the Upper Quarter of Guelderland (part of the disputed Orange succession) should go to the Dutch; to offer commercial concessions to them and negotiate a Barrier. If these bases could be agreed, then all English and German questions could be referred to a general conference—at which it would be the Dutch interest to support the French. Rouillé was instructed to discover how the Dutch proposed to see that the emperor withdrew from Naples. There emerged here in discussion, for the first time, the idea that present enemies should combine to use force against a recalcitrant ally: the idea of a joint Franco-Dutch naval expedition to see Philip V into Naples, in the wake of a Dutch army, was the forerunner of the Allied demand that Louis XIV should expel Philip from Spain. For different reasons, both proposals were fruitless; but that the prior suggestion came from the French must qualify the genuineness of that moral indignation with which the subsequent Allied proposal was greeted in France. The Dutch gradually stepped up the demands for themselves and their allies: even if they agreed Preliminaries alone with France, they could not hope to benefit unless the result was a general peace suitable to their allies. Over the Barrier, they advanced extreme claims for Ypres, Menin, Furnes, Tournai, Condé and Maubeuge, and either Lille or the easterly garrisons at Liège, Huy and Bonn; Rouillé would not concede Lille or Tournai. The Dutch also demanded Neuchâtel and Valengin in Switzerland for Prussia, as the proposed Guelderland settlement ran counter to Hohenzollern claims to the Orange succession; the destruction of Dunkirk; recognition of the Hanoverian succession; and the acquisition by Savoy of her military gains, the Alpine forts of Exilles and Fenestrelle. Throughout these separate negotiations Heinsius was stiffened by the presence of Marlborough and Eugene: the original Dutch offer to the French of 'good offices' in seeing Philip V into Naples was withdrawn once English insistence on total surrender had been made known by Marlborough on 10 April. The French hope for an immediate armistice was taken by Heinsius to indicate Louis XIV's weakness, justifying Dutch co-operation with the Allies for the highest stakes. The desire of Buys and Van der Dussen for a more moderate settlement, especially an English retreat over Italy, gave way before Heinsius's readiness to advance the full Allied demands as the best means of getting the Barrier he could not win from France alone. His refusal to accept separation from his English ally contrasts honourably with Bolingbroke's easy desertion of the Republic after 1710.

The desperate situation of French affairs was admitted by the outcome of the royal council at Versailles on 28–9 April, when the full extent of Dutch demands was debated. It led to the second phase of negotiations with the Allies as a whole, without further attempts to divide them. To speed a conclusion before a new campaign, Torcy himself offered to go to the United Provinces and Louis, in tears, agreed to his mission. He was empowered to yield on every debated marginal issue, except the cession of conquered territory to Savoy. The Barrier might now include even Lille and Tournai. Dunkirk should be destroyed, Queen Anne and the Hanoverian succession recognized, the Pretender removed from French soil, Strasbourg surrendered, the restoration of the elector of Bavaria referred to a general conference. But Torcy still hoped to profit from differences between his opponents over south Italy. He at once warned Heinsius that Louis 'could not, even if he were willing, oblige the king of Spain to resign all his dominions'[1]—an assertion later proved to be truer than Louis liked. But Heinsius was not to be tempted further. When Marlborough joined the negotiations in mid-May, Torcy made one futile effort to seduce England by an offer to destroy Dunkirk and a bribe to the duke. Townshend had now arrived to support Marlborough, and it was made clear finally to Torcy that the Allies would find no compensation for Philip V; if a kingdom was to be found for him, Louis must provide it— they suggested Franche-Comté. On 19 May, the great issue was faced. If Louis was to achieve the peace that France desperately needed, only Philip could now purchase it; Torcy's latest instructions allowed the surrender even of Naples 'so far as it lay in him to make the surrender'.[2] So now discussions turned less on whether France would concede the Allies' demands than on whether she could implement her agreements. From the moment Torcy yielded over Naples and Sicily, peace hinged on the relations of Louis XIV with his grandson. The earlier French insistence that a power offering a settlement must show proof of good intention by providing for its implementation was now turned against Louis. Half a century of mistrust was reinforced by the feeling that France was now but playing for time to recover from the calamities of war and a desperately severe winter. Torcy pressed for a truce: the Allies determined that peace should follow, not precede, the execution of agreed terms. If France was in earnest, she would see Philip safely out of Spain; the Allies were sensibly unwilling to risk giving her peace and then themselves having to embark on a Spanish campaign sustainable only by sea. On 23 May came the demand for an immediate Allied occupation of three French and three Spanish towns as pledges for Louis's good intentions. This was refused. On 24 May Torcy, perhaps hoping to widen their differences, asked the Allies to formulate exactly their full demands.

Count Sinzendorf, the Imperial chancellor, who had just arrived to join Eugene, determined to thrash out every difference between Austria and the Dutch before completing negotiations with France. But that collective

---

[1] Torcy, *Memoirs* (London edn. 2 vols. 1757), vol. I, p. 254.
[2] W. Reese, *Das Ringen um Frieden und Sicherheit in den Entscheidungsjahren des Spanischen Erbfolgekrieges, 1708 bis 1709* (Munich, 1933), p. 222.

peace on which, since their rupture with Rouillé in April, the Dutch had staked their Barrier hopes, would be lost if Allied wrangling were protracted. So Heinsius resolved to turn discussion back to the central and agreed Spanish problem. On 25 May, he presented to the Allied envoys the Forty Articles which he had composed as a basis for a final settlement. Two days later, these Preliminaries were presented to Torcy as their agreed demands. Only two articles were crucial. Article 4 required Louis to concert measures with the Allies to execute the peace terms if, at the end of two months, Philip V had failed to act on them; by article 37, the truce proposed between France and the Allies would continue beyond two months only if the terms of the settlement had been executed. This meant that, with the proposed cautionary towns already surrendered, Naples and Sicily occupied, and the Rhine forts destroyed as required by other articles, the reopening of hostilities would leave France at the mercy of her enemies.

At the last conference, on 27 May, Torcy made clear that the Preliminaries were repugnant to him and impossible of acceptance by Louis XIV. By May 1709 France had already passed the lowest point of her fortunes. Recent arrivals of Spanish silver provided cash for buying grain abroad, replenishing war materials, providing the army with clothes and boots; the misery of the early spring had helped recruiting. How the arguments went in the *Conseil* on 2 June, at which the Preliminaries were debated, is not known. But Torcy had gained sufficient time. Louis XIV, supported probably by Torcy and the dauphin, decided on rejection of the Preliminaries. After the rejection, royal letters were sent out appealing to the population for a last great sacrifice against terms that insulted the dignity of France; this, rather than sympathy for the Bourbon king of Spain, was the keynote.

The rupture of negotiations, effectively because of French refusal to accept the obnoxious 4th and 37th articles, has occasioned much debate as to Allied intentions in putting them forward. Failure to achieve peace when France was at her weakest, and the Allies satisfied in virtually every demand, hastened a reaction in England against the Junto, who were thought to have abetted the Dutch in setting impossible terms so as to continue the war. The truth is probably more complicated. English opinion was genuinely divided as to how peace could best be obtained. Marlborough went further than his colleagues in believing that the total defeat of France was desirable, feasible, and imminent—and that the Allies could easily evict Philip V. But this same view lay, in essence, behind the Preliminaries themselves: if France was at her last gasp, then she must accept terms now. What cannot be certain is whether the Allies envisaged a possible refusal of the Preliminaries by Philip V himself. Had Louis really possessed that control over his grandson which Rouillé had reiterated as late as 11 May, then the 4th and 37th articles would have remained what the Allies probably thought they were—simply an earnest of French good intentions to show Philip he must now give way. But Heinsius had received a hint from Torcy at their first meeting, on 6 May, that Louis might be less the master than the Allies liked to think. It is also impossible to be certain whether Louis was acting in good faith when he undertook to abandon Philip: the assumption of insincerity partly accounts for the repulsive articles in the Preliminaries. Yet it is difficult to believe that Louis was not earnestly pursuing peace after the fall of Lille. Philip's refusal to submit to his grandfather, to whom he owed his crown, was itself wounding to the supremacy of France in the Bourbon alliance; the intractability of the Spanish people in fact gave Philip greater independence of his ally than either Austria or the United Provinces had of England. Thus diplomatic deadlock resulted from an unconsidered commitment by both sides to a proposition neither could execute. Had Louis recognized earlier that no working arrangement with Spain was possible, Torcy might have been prevented from agreeing to the Allied demand for Spain, although the full demand which would make France *solely* responsible for Philip V's good behaviour only emerged slowly—in the Geertruidenberg negotiations next year. In these earlier negotiations the problem had never been considered, so confident did the French envoys appear about Louis's ability to persuade Philip to remove to Italy. Nor had Torcy ever gone beyond the view that France would renounce Philip's right to any part of the Spanish inheritance and withdraw her aid. It was not doubt of Louis's powers, but of his word, that made the Allies demand more: should he prove sincerity by pledging towns or promising military action against Philip, the mere enunciation of these undertakings would suffice to evict Philip, and the 4th and 37th articles would never come into operation. The Allies did not know that Philip was beyond Louis's control and so did not seriously contemplate that the two articles would ever have to be enforced by him. None of the Allies seriously doubted that Louis would submit to their conditions. The remaining articles were considerably less harsh than France might have expected, representing a return to a balanced European system, with France, Britain and Austria (reinforced by a Habsburg cadet in Spain) as arbiters. The three Barriers—in the Netherlands, on the Rhine, and along the frontier of Savoy—were yet to be agreed, but they were unlikely to bar a general settlement. Austria's hope of the Spanish inheritance discouraged her from reasserting Imperial power on the frontier with France: Franche-Comté and much of Alsace were to remain French.

But even the representatives of the Allied powers had achieved only a momentary and precarious agreement. Vienna never accepted the Preliminaries *in toto*. The Secret Conference argued that Eugene and Sinzendorf had gone too far to meet the Dutch, not far enough in claims on the Rhine. Long after the French had rejected the Forty Articles, the Conference continued to debate them; against the warnings of Wratislaw, Eugene and Sinzendorf as to repercussions on the Alliance, the emperor disavowed his envoys' signatures. Fount and origin of the extreme demand which precluded any hope of compromise or partition, Joseph I behaved with such inflexibility towards his allies, at the moment when they had shaped their policies to support his major aim, that they would never again carry their obligations towards Austria further than was useful to them. While Sinzendorf thought the opportunity should now be taken to advance even wider claims, Eugene felt that the repulsive articles had gone farther than necessary. Marlborough agreed: 'If I were in the place of the King of France, I should venture the loss of my country much sooner than be obliged to join his troops for the forcing of my grandson.'[1] Only Charles III in Barcelona had been entirely satisfied with the Preliminaries.

The blame for failure was disputed. At The Hague the negotiators turned on Heinsius, whose hand had designed the Forty Articles, for finding no alternative to the 37th, although they themselves had suggested none. Certainly, Heinsius had failed to secure peace. But he had greatly strengthened the bargaining power of his country. On 29 October 1709 Britain, still fully committed to the Preliminaries, signed the Barrier Treaty[2] she could no longer refuse, cost what it might in Anglo-Austrian relations and in strong differences within English governmental ranks: Marlborough still considered it dangerous. On Dutch insistence it omitted any reference to 'No peace without Spain', while the English agreed to procure similar commercial concessions for the Dutch as for themselves from Madrid. The Dutch were also promised the most extensive Barrier they could have hoped for, including points such as Dendermonde whose importance was clearly commercial. Otherwise, the treaty was a diplomatic triumph for England, containing a guarantee of the Hanoverian succession and a Dutch promise not to make peace until France had acknowledged it. It kept the United Provinces in the war. Politically, however, it boded disaster for both Whigs and Dutch. Heinsius's calculation that Britain was a better guarantor than France for the extended Barrier rested on an imponderable—the survival of the Whig administration long enough to make peace. In the event, the unpopularity of the extensive concessions made by this treaty contributed to English support for its repudiation in 1711. Undoubtedly, it did contain contradictory elements for Britain. Whig insistence on Charles III's full claims had made sense because of the unilateral advantages which she had already gained from him; but to achieve absolute victory for Charles, the Whigs were now willing to let the Dutch share in those exclusive benefits which

[1] To Heinsius, 10 July 1709, quoted R. Geikie and I. A. Montgomery, *The Dutch Barrier, 1705–1719*, p. 131.
[2] Cf. above, pp. 438–9.

Stanhope had obtained, thus weakening the argument that Britain had an overriding interest to establish Charles III.

After the rejection of the Preliminaries, Petkum again became the channel for exchanges. Protracted efforts were made to find satisfactory alternatives to the 4th and 37th articles. The disasters of the 1709 campaign had brought even Torcy to the idea of partition, if Naples or Sicily could be obtained for Philip V. When this was not entirely ruled out, parleys were reopened in March 1710 at Mardyck, then at Geertruidenberg. Little progress could be made: the Allies were adamant on Article 37 as the condition for discussing compensation for Philip. In the later stages, the Dutch revealed that there would be further Allied demands once France signed the Preliminaries; since these would involve her in surrenders that would leave her powerless to resist further encroachments, Louis XIV very sensibly would not sign. He openly admitted to his plenipotentiaries that he could not command Philip V, who would certainly not leave his kingdom voluntarily. His *Conseil* had been divided. Villars, after the Allies invested Douai in April, advocated peace at any price: only Louis's resolution decided against surrender, though he later relaxed to the extent of allowing discussion of how the enemy proposed he should concert with them in Spain. On 5 June he finally agreed to provide soldiers and subsidies to support the Allies there, provided it were first made clear what alternative kingdom Philip should have. Before the Dutch knew of these instructions, they had asked that the whole cost of Philip's eviction be borne by France. By 22 June, the Allies had gone well beyond article 37 to demand that the whole responsibility, in men as well as money, should rest on France. As Torcy wrote, 'They would fain be idle spectators of a war between grandfather and grandson'.[1] The French envoys left Geertruidenberg on 24 July. Contrary to Marlborough's expectation, the Dutch had remained entirely loyal to their allies, while judging their terms too severe. Moreover, they had so disclosed their subservience to London that their last opportunity of an advantageous peace had been lost. Never again did France seriously try to use the possibility of the Republic's defection as a lever to produce general peace. When the Provinces finally came to make peace, they could only salvage from the wreckage of the Grand Alliance what their allies were prepared to demand for them.

The turning-point came with the break-up of Godolphin's ministry. Its promise of a territorial settlement in Spain and Italy, which would free the Mediterranean of commercial rivals and allow the negotiation of uni- lateral concessions in Spanish America, had nearly been achieved by the submission of France. But during the final bout of negotiations at Geertruidenberg, the French had convincing evidence that the English were beginning themselves to show reluctance to resume hostilities.

[1] *Memoirs*, vol. II, p. 86.

It is difficult to discover the moment at which the tide of English feeling turned against the war. The attitudes of politicians were already formed and largely static. The pamphlet war against the Dutch had not yet started. True, the Tory leaders were quite without illusion about the Preliminaries. St John had not wavered from the view expressed in a letter to Harley as early as November 1708: 'For God's sake, let us be out of Spain.'[1] But Tory politicians failed to express their discontent lest they lose public credit and frighten the Dutch, whose views on Spain had throughout the war so much in common with theirs, into a separate peace. As late as March 1709, both Houses passed unanimous resolutions for 'No peace without Spain'. Nevertheless, that the failure of the May 1709 negotiations weakened the Whig hold on the public mind was evident to the less deeply committed politicians. Shrewsbury thought that 'the generality of the nation' wanted peace, St John that 'peace is at this time the most desirable publick and private Good'.[2] The best evidence of growing dissatisfaction with the government, however, came from domestic issues apparently unconnected with the war. The trial of Sacheverell in March 1710 coincided with the reopening of the campaigning season and of Franco-Dutch negotiations; the wild rejoicings accompanying the nominal sentence imposed on him were the first indication to the Tories that their moment had come. A hint of far-reaching political change, reflecting Anne's bitter dislike of the Whigs, came with Shrewsbury's appointment as Lord Chamberlain on 14/25 April and was confirmed by Sunderland's dismissal on 14/25 June, shortly after Louis XIV had agreed to discuss the use of force in Spain. The signs were clearly understood by the Dutch. Sunderland's fall so alarmed them that they were persuaded by the Whigs to warn Anne against a dissolution of Parliament. Her reputed reply— 'it is the greatest insult that ever was offered to the Crown of England'[3]— showed that criticism of her actions only served to convince her of their rightness. A fall in East India stock, a warning from the Bank, a protest from the emperor did not alarm her. Harley was at the same time brilliantly successful in dividing the Whig ministers, many of whom were more concerned to ride out the storm in office than demonstrate solidarity by resignation. By September he was firmly in control. The 1710 election, a two-to-one majority for the Tories, proved his shrewd estimate that the temper of the country was no longer voiced by the Whigs and moneyed elements.

St John now joined the ministry as Northern Secretary and gradually gained power from Harley, more devious but less determined. In February 1711 they quarrelled over the Quebec expedition. In March came Guiscard's attempt on Harley's life. By the summer, St John had British policy in his hands. Harley proposed to secure Britain's allies in an

---

[1] Quoted D. Coombs, *The Conduct of the Dutch*, p. 181. [2] Quoted *ibid.* p. 209.
[3] Quoted *ibid.* p. 224.

honourable and safe peace; and to hold a middle course against High Tory argument for a complete purge of the administration, he played for moderate Whig support. But where Harley would probably have preferred sincere co-operation with the Dutch in peace-making, St John from the start wished to present the Allies with a *fait accompli*. Not only was the Alliance pledged to the impossible Forty Articles, but the Barrier Treaty, whose terms were still unknown to Parliament, was for him a stumbling-block to working with the Republic; he knew that the country, not least the Whigs, would reject the limitations it set on England's trading advantages. The ministry lost no time in working up feeling against the Dutch. In the very week in August when Godolphin fell, the first issue of *The Examiner* appeared; under St John's direction it was to prove a powerful instrument for reawakening old hatreds never far below the surface of an Englishman's mind. St John had to conduct a war on two fronts: against English supporters of the Alliance, whom he had slowly to condition for the desertion he intended, and against the Dutch, who must be kept isolated from both France and the emperor. A press campaign combined with a pretence of openness with the Dutch, an appeal to Britain's special interests, a willingness to retreat from the high pretensions of 1709–10 to the original aims of the Grand Alliance—these enabled him to carry through a brilliant diplomatic plan which gave Europe a less showy, but a more intelligent, peace than could have been reached in 1709. At the same time, he obtained for England those unilateral advantages which the Whigs had lost because they had preferred to steal advantages over their allies without deserting them. St John's ruthlessness was as much the result of overreaching by the previous administration as of his own contempt for the Dutch at their failure to fulfil their naval quota for 1711, and of his preference for negotiating with an enemy. The collapse of Habsburg hopes in Spain at Brihuega (December 1710) made final nonsense of the May Preliminaries, confirming that the war would now go on until one side was willing to alter its peace requirements. Neither Harley nor St John had ever believed in the feasibility or desirability of conquering Spain for Charles III. St John deeply distrusted 'That house of Austria [which] has been the evil genius of Britain. I never think of the conduct of that family without recollecting the image of a man braiding a rope of hay while his ass bites it off at the other end.'[1] The French, now infuriated by Dutch pretensions, were quick to exploit the war-weariness evident in the British political changes.

Torcy's intermediary with London was the Abbé Gaultier, formerly of Tallard's household, who had remained in England in 1701 and become chaplain to the Austrian ambassador, Gallas. As soon as negotiations at Geertruidenberg had been broken off, Torcy suggested he approach the

[1] To Drummond, 5 Jan. o.s. 1710/11, *Bolingbroke Correspondence*, ed. G. Parke (4 vols. 1798), vol. I, p. 59.

new elements in the English ministry, particularly Shrewsbury. Profiting by a hint from a friend, the Jacobite earl of Jersey, Gaultier established contact in August 1710; pending direct negotiations, Jersey acted for Shrewsbury and Harley, giving the French a dangerously misleading impression of how far the new administration would go towards both peace and a Stuart restoration. Not until May 1711 was St John apprised of these conversations, and the French made to realize that the change of government in no way implied a willingness to abandon the Protestant Succession or Britain's commercial interests. But St John did accept the most crucial surrender which Jersey had said could be expected: the throne of Spain, by Charles III. This abandonment of the only demand which had prevented peace in the previous years appeared reasonable when, on 17 April 1711, the entire Habsburg inheritance passed to Charles III. Within three days, death, 'striking with an impartial foot' (as Clement XI put it), had carried off the dauphin and made Philip V fourth in line for the French throne. In that same month, Gaultier's offer of a general peace conference was made subject, by the British government, to a prior agreement on new preliminaries. St John cleverly insisted that these appear as offers from France to provide a basis for discussions, letting it be known that the demand for Spain and the Indies for Charles III would be a formality only. The resulting propositions of 22 April—in fact English demands, but in appearance suggestions from France—were described by St John to Heinsius as indications of a French peace feeler which England wished to explore in concert with the Republic. Differences between Buys and Heinsius, who was suspicious of St John's intentions, led to an indifferent Dutch reaction and an unsuspecting willingness to allow England to go ahead alone. After this exchange, with no ambassador in either country—one was dead, the other on leave—and with only one sight of the propositions in May, the Dutch were not again informed about the negotiations until October, when terms had been agreed between London and Versailles.

The April propositions were to be the basis for a general settlement, securing Britain's interests but without so disregarding those of her allies that they would hold aloof. Britain was to have real securities for her trade with Spain, the Indies and Mediterranean; the Dutch should have such a Barrier, with liberty of trade, as Britain agreed to. Her allies should be satisfied 'by all reasonable methods', the problem of Spain settled 'to the satisfaction of the several parties concerned', and a general conference of plenipotentiaries treat for peace. In July Matthew Prior, an envoy insignificant enough to be disavowed should the bilateral negotiations go awry, was sent with Gaultier to Versailles with more precise and far-reaching demands. Torcy agreed to a more effective barrier for Austria along the Rhine (but no surrender in Alsace), restitutions and grants to Savoy, and a renunciation by Philip V of his rights in the French succession. In August, Prior returned to London, accompanied by Mesnager. Difficulties about Dutch and Austrian interests were set aside until Britain's own claims were settled in more detail. After prolonged conferences with St John, Harley, Dartmouth and Shrewsbury—in which Britain's position was aided by Marlborough's puncture of the 'Ne Plus Ultra Lines' at Bouchain—the secret seven preliminaries known as the Mesnager Convention were signed on 8 October. It was the foundation of the ultimate Utrecht settlement. Anne and the Hanoverian succession were to be recognized, Austria and the Dutch to have their barriers, the fortifications of Dunkirk to be destroyed, the Allies' 'reasonable satisfactions' to be discussed at the peace conference, and measures taken to prevent a union of the French and Spanish Crowns—which left open now who should have the Spanish. It was agreed that the Allies be told of these terms only when it suited the two powers. The advantages to Britain were set out in a separate note; it was clear that she could expect great gains. The prizes which had made her fight to keep Charles III in Spain she was now to receive from Philip V: cession of Gibraltar and Minorca, the Asiento for thirty years, use of trading-stations on the river Plate. Her colonial losses, in Newfoundland and Hudson's Bay, were to be restored. The details were yet to be settled, but from this time forward St John was in direct communication with Torcy.

The secret was soon out. Gallas, from whose household the negotiations had been initiated, released the terms to a Whig journal. Alarmed at their reception, the government, to redress the balance before English opinion, published the terms accorded to Britain. The naked revelation of its clandestine desertion of her allies lowered the government's prestige and endangered its security, which were not restored until Swift's *Conduct of the Allies* won the pamphlet war. Meanwhile, Dutch uneasiness had been sharpened by the cool treatment of Buys on a fact-finding visit to London. His arrival coincided with the disclosures. Clearly the English now attached little importance to the Barrier Treaty undertaking that Britain would seek no unilateral advantage in Spanish trade. Buys met only vagueness when he tried to discover just what had been recently agreed about the Barrier. For his part, St John relied on a new ambassador to The Hague, Lord Strafford, to browbeat Their High Mightinesses into accepting the Mesnager Convention by threat of a separate peace. By the end of November, recognizing their helplessness to fend for themselves, the Provinces accepted a conference on their own soil.

At last it was safe for English ministers to meet Parliament, prorogued from week to week while the Dutch wavered. Close liaison between Torcy and St John had lessened the possibility of the Dutch slipping in ahead; Torcy, indeed, had refused approaches from the alarmed Republic. The Dutch realized that to negotiate a Barrier with either France or Austria, British aid was essential; to resist Britain now might leave them with no

Barrier at all. The Tory majority carried the preliminaries in the Commons on 7/18 December. In the Lords a tactical bargain over Occasional Conformity between High Church Tories and Whig opponents of peace procured a motion that no peace should leave Spain in the hands of Philip V. Within the month, the queen had created twelve new peers and the attempt of the hereditary chamber to block the popular pursuit of peace was broken. Marlborough was dismissed on the last day of the year, now that his retention to deceive the Dutch was no longer necessary; the ensuing outcry was probably due more to the brusqueness of his dismissal than to the policy implied in it. By the beginning of 1712 St John and Harley, now earl of Oxford, had won the domestic battle. The alliance of throne and popular feeling had proved strong enough to carry the administration through the storm of rhetoric and outraged Whig principle which assailed it in the last quarter of 1711. The second stage in the battle for peace opened in the town hall of Utrecht on 29 January 1712.

The fifteen months of negotiations at Utrecht ended in a firm Anglo-French settlement and mutual support for a wider one which all the powers except Austria agreed to accept. The series of treaties which emerged in and after April 1713 was a triumph for the two powers who had most to gain from an unvindictive peace. The initiative throughout was Britain's, and this secured at last her colonial and commercial interests outside Europe by a balanced pressure of the three greatest powers on France and on each other. Much more difficult was the task of forcing her allies to recognize that political aspirations must in the end relate to the means available for achieving them. St John's intention was a balance of power in accord with the terms of the Grand Alliance, not a separate peace, for this would release France to establish that hegemony in Europe which it had been the war's purpose to prevent. Throughout 1712 it was the search for a general settlement which filled his correspondence with the plenipotentiaries, with Prior in France, with Torcy himself. In practice, this meant settling the Spanish succession and bringing one of the major allies, the Dutch, to terms with France—methods involving bitter negotiations with the Dutch and alienation of the emperor. Dutch reluctance to conclude sprang only from their objection to Britain's one-sided advantages; they had long advocated partition of the Spanish possessions, which Austria as consistently resisted. St John hardly distinguished between the weapons of war and diplomacy, or between ally and enemy. Negotiations between France and the Allies in general session, meeting twice weekly at ten in the morning, lasted effectively only until mid-March. For the remaining nine months of 1712, negotiations ran through countless channels between the capitals of the great powers. But final agreement always depended on the concurrence of London and Versailles.

When the Congress opened, Britain's position was vulnerable in many respects. Her own commercial and territorial claims had been left in general terms; the exact disposition of the Spanish Crown and the geography of the Barrier had been left unsettled by the Mesnager Convention. Her plenipotentiaries, Strafford and Robinson, were instructed to work with the Dutch for a settlement. But the Congress suspended its sittings before serious negotiations could get under way. A demand by Buys, now a plenipotentiary from the province of Holland, for an elucidation of the Mesnager Convention, drew from Polignac and Huxelles an 'Explanation' which outraged the Dutch, and horrified St John, by its harshness. Admitting the extent of Britain's claims, the 'Explanation' cut back to a minimum the concessions France would make to all other powers. Thus the French appeared to be pushing hard to insert a wedge between Britain and her allies. The Allies replied with 'Specific Demands' to the Congress, individually, on 5 March. The English merely restated what France already admitted, claiming for their allies a 'just and reasonable satisfaction' in terms so general as to leave space for manoeuvre. The Dutch similarly concentrated on their own interests: a restoration of the favourable French tariff of 1664, a string of fortresses in the Netherlands and northern France in full sovereignty, with an additional demand for garrison rights in Huy, Liège and Bonn which could only be understood as a barrier against Austria and the Empire. The evasion in these demands of the central problem of Spain drew no concessions from Austria.

Sinzendorf had arrived as plenipotentiary, with orders to procure the whole Spanish inheritance and negotiate only from the basis of the Forty Articles of 1709. Since the announcement of the Congress, Austrian policy had been in a state of agitated paralysis. Gallas's indiscretions had led to his ejection from London, and Eugene's mission thither in January 1712 did nothing to improve Anglo-Austrian relations; his belated offer to send more troops to Spain only showed how wide was the gap between London and Vienna. Dynastic interests at Vienna were now fused in the single person of Charles III and VI; where Joseph I might ultimately have abandoned Spain in his scale of priorities, for the new emperor there could be no concessions. The Austrian 'Specific Demands' were entirely uncompromising. Both Sinzendorf and Eugene had advised Vienna strongly to approach either Britain or the Dutch for some alignment of views, but the Imperial Council objected to working with either. Even when both sides made private overtures to Austria, after the suspension of general sessions, Habsburg policy remained inflexible. Early in April, when Harley contemplated that Spain should pass to Savoy, Wratislaw saw the opportunity to work out some agreement from which Austria would gain Savoy and so consolidate her Italian holdings: he was angrily repudiated by the emperor because such a policy risked possible partition of the Spanish inheritance. The host of conflicting claims in the 'Specific Demands' of the German powers, led by Prussia's demand for the Orange inheritance, all served to lame the Congress. For Austria this raised the hope of a return to campaigning. But for Britain and France, equally happy to see the general conference in deadlock, it provided the chance to return to private diplomacy. When the French plenipotentiaries finally refused a written answer to the several 'Specific Demands', the general sessions were formally suspended on 9 April.

During the general sessions, the currents in the normal channels had hardly slackened in pace or complexity. In private negotiations with France during the first half of 1712, the English came near to achieving the great aim of 1709, the removal of the Bourbon from Spain. Once again this was to be cheated of success, this time by Philip V. Ten months after the death of the dauphin, his son the duke of Burgundy had died; and less than three weeks later, on 8 March 1712, Burgundy's son, the duke of Brittany, followed him to the grave. Brittany's younger brother, the duke of Anjou, now heir to the throne, was 'more sickly in appearance than he that died'. Had not 'God preserved this lamp which was almost exting-uished',[1] Philip V would have become heir to Louis XIV. Death might yet obtain for France what arms could not—the union of the two Crowns. But Louis was in no position to insist, against Allied fears, that Philip remain in that position: either he must leave Spain or renounce his French claims. The original English demand for a renunciation, made in March, was met by a rigid statement that the fundamental law by which 'the prince who is next to the throne is the necessary heir' would invali-date any such renunciation: Philip should make his choice of thrones if and when need arose. St John, seeing the futility of this and impatient of the doctrines of divinity, insisted that the renunciation be made now and the action coincide with it; if Philip chose France, he should leave Spain at once. To tempt him to leave Spain—which both powers assumed he would—St John took up the proposal consistently argued by the Dutch earlier: Naples, Sicily and the possessions of Savoy were to pass to him, thus opening the attractive prospect that if Philip ascended the French throne he would bring Savoy with him. This was sufficient to win Louis XIV, and Philip was enjoined to submit: 'Should gratitude and affection for your subjects be strong inducements with you to adhere to them, I can tell you that you owe the same sentiments to me, to your family and to your country, in preference to Spain.'[2] But Philip had not fought in Spain to live in France or Savoy as a prince of the blood. He hoped to inherit France by right, without renunciations, leaving Spain to his son. On 29 May after receiving the sacraments, he was fortified in his position:

By this step I give peace...to France, and I secure to her the alliance of a monarchy which otherwise might some time or other unite with her enemies to distress her:

[1] Torcy, *Memoirs*, vol. II, p. 282.
[2] Quoted A. Baudrillart, *Philippe V et la cour de France*, 2nd edn, 5 vols. (1890–1910), vol. I, p. 491.

and at the same time I embrace the resolution which appears most suitable to glory and to the welfare of my subjects whose zeal and attachment so greatly contributed to keep the crown on my head.[1]

In thus settling how the Spanish succession should finally be decided, Philip also ensured that there would now be little chance of Austria coming into a general agreement for peace. Louis perhaps, though disappointed, was not surprised. But St John possessed that same faith in the omnipotence of the French king which had deceived the Whigs in 1709–10; he had, while awaiting Philip's decision, called Maffei, the Savoyard envoy at Utrecht, to London, in readiness to hear that his master was to be made king of Spain. Nevertheless, St John had bound himself to accept Philip's choice and on 6/17 June the general peace terms were presented to parliament. After acceptance, parliament was prorogued until April 1713, when the treaties had been signed. The prerogative of peace-making thus removed government from the inquisition of the nation until the work was completed.

In these same six months, Anglo-Dutch relations deteriorated. Disputes about equal trading rights in the Indies and the Netherlands were brought to a head when, in February, ministers disclosed the terms of the 1709 Barrier Treaty. Parliament angrily repudiated it and voted Townshend an enemy of his country for signing its commercial concessions. The harvest of Dutch good faith, sown in trust of an ephemeral majority in parliament, was now reaped. An abortive Dutch attempt to draw closer to the Austrians had failed because Sinzendorf still had hopes from Eugene's mission in London. Now, with no supporters among the powers, the Dutch were at England's mercy and dropped their claim to an equivalent for the Asiento.[2] On 21 May, when the Restraining Orders to Ormonde effectively ended Anglo-French hostilities, St John wrote to Harley: 'Does it not make your blood curdle in your veins to hear it solemnly contested in Holland whether Britain shall enjoy the assiento, an advantage which the enemy have yielded to us?'[3] On 8 July, the Dutch were informed that the English had a two-months truce with France. This much reduced the Barrier and excluded the crucial commodities of woollens, whalebone and oil, fish, and refined sugar from the general return to the tariff of 1664 under which Dutch goods should be admitted into France. Finally concluded on 17 July, this armistice also provided for the occupation of Ghent and Bruges, as pledges of Dutch good behaviour, as well as

---

[1] Baudrillart, vol. I, p. 499.

[2] The Dutch agreed because it was understood the English were to receive nothing the French had not received—i.e. that the Spanish had made no trading concessions to the English. Geikie and Montgomery, p. 271, imply that the English deliberately deceived the Dutch on this point. In fact, the details of the Asiento, and the idea of including in it an annual 'permission ship', were not discussed until Lexington and Gilligan arrived in Madrid in October 1712 (G. Scelle, *La Traite négrière aux Indes de Castille*, vol. II, p. 541). See below, pp. 475–6.

[3] *Bolingbroke Corr.*, vol. II, p. 324. The letter is dated 10 May O.S.

Dunkirk. The Dutch decided to attempt yet another *rapprochement* with Austria, now once more isolated by Philip V's unexpected choice. Despite Sinzendorf's efforts, nothing came of this, largely because Villars's victory at Denain quenched Dutch willingness to fight on. Viscount Bolingbroke (as St John now was) feared that, in despair, the Dutch might turn to France before Britain had worked out the details of her North American settlement. Seeing the need for haste, he went in person to Fontainebleau in mid-August and remained there till September. The Anglo-French truce was extended for a further four months. As compensation for his disappointment over Spain, the duke of Savoy was to receive Sicily as a kingdom at the peace, with the reversion of Spain. Bolingbroke also agreed on Sardinia and a crown for Max Emmanuel. Yet he resisted a French attempt to persuade Britain to join in forcing her allies to peace, just as Louis XIV had resisted in 1709–10. In October, for fear the Dutch were themselves negotiating a return of the south Netherlands to Max Emmanuel, Britain suddenly stiffened her attitude to the Barrier, insisting now that it include Tournai. On 2 November Louis gave way, and three days later Philip V renounced his French rights before the Cortes in Madrid. Thus fortified, and with Tournai in reserve,[1] Bolingbroke faced the Dutch with these final terms on 8 December. After insisting on three weeks to consider them, all the Provinces except Groningen decided to accept.

Dutch preference for receiving unpalatable terms from the English, rather than from France later, signalled a general *sauve qui peut* among the smaller powers on both sides. Three of these could be secured for the peace because their affairs were separable from the impossible Austrian problem—Prussia, Portugal, Savoy. The smaller German powers, unrepresented at Utrecht except through the emperor or the French king, were to raise greater difficulties, especially Louis's Wittelsbach allies. But if peace was to be general, accommodation had to be found for various Allied claims, most awkwardly where these had been set aside in the earlier struggle to win over the Dutch.

Prussia's attitude was conditioned by her desires to gain French recognition of the royal title (which presented no difficulty) and Spanish Guelderland, which she had garrisoned in the name of the Allies since 1703 but which Britain had promised to the Dutch in the Barrier Treaty. Prussia also shared a claim to the Orange territories in France with the Dutch prince of Nassau-Friesland: lands in Burgundy, Franche-Comté and Provence had been offered to her by Britain in 1709 as compensation for Spanish Guelderland. Britain, now anxious to please the Dutch without alienating the French and no longer concerned to keep Prussia in the war, abandoned her support of Prussia's Orange claims. This revived Prussian agitation for Upper Guelderland. If France could not meet

---

[1] For the Barrier Treaty of January 1713, see below, pp. 476–8.

Prussian demands, the Republic must. In November 1712, when Leopold of Anhalt seized Moers, a fief of Cleves, Prussia followed by pushing the Guelderland claim with the French. The English accepted it; the Dutch could only protest; the Austrians concurred when they received Roermond (for joint garrison with the Dutch) to safeguard their communications with the Netherlands. By this same agreement, in March 1713, the Dutch obtained Stevensweert, Fort St Michael, Venlo, and free communications on the Meuse. In the final settlement Prussia also got the principality of Neuchâtel and its dependent county of Valengin.

The Portuguese were understandably ready to make peace. Every precaution had been taken to squeeze the maximum advantage from the Grand Alliance which King Peter had joined in May 1703. In the very treaty which first enunciated that all Spain should pass to Archduke Charles, this principle had been broken by the promise of a batch of Spanish frontier towns to Portugal. The Portuguese had no safeguards against their allies' defeat or desertion. Their highest prospects came when Louis XIV recognized their claims in the Forty Articles. With the break-up of the Grand Alliance after 1710, it only remained to salvage something from the wreck. Danger from Allied defeats in Spain was increased by the French capture of Rio de Janeiro on 23 September 1711. At Utrecht, the 'Specific Demands' of Portugal claimed fulfilment of the 1703 treaty and regulation of Brazil's disputed frontier with the French settlement of Cayenne. The bilateral Anglo-French discussions, ignoring the First Methuen Treaty, agreed on mutual territorial restitutions in the Peninsula, and concentrated on the American frontier. By 7 November, French concessions brought the Portuguese to a truce which was extended until the peace treaty of March 1713. France yielded in the New World to preserve the integrity of Spain in the Old. Philip V had thus secured by war what Charles III would have sacrificed by alliance.

The purchase of Savoy was more complicated. Victor Amadeus had joined the Allies on very favourable terms: he was recognized as heir to Spain if the Austrian line failed, and Montferrat was to be ceded to him, with part of the Milanese.[1] At Utrecht, Savoy was the only Italian State which counted and it suffered less than the other small powers. An attempt by France to limit herself to restitutions (Savoy and Nice)—hinting that Savoy should expand into the Milanese, with the title of king of Lombardy and a barrier against Austria—collapsed before the ability of the Savoyard diplomats, Bolingbroke's desire to erect an Italian barrier against France, and the tenderness of Queen Anne for a House which had been excluded from the English succession by the Act of Settlement. The possibility of the duke succeeding at once to Spain collapsed with Philip V's decision at the end of May 1712. Though the English would not support the Savoyard claim to the fort of Monaco, or to territory beyond Mont Genèvre, to the

[1] The Alessandrino as far as Valenza, with Lomellina and Valsesia.

466

Durance and to Fort Barraux on the Isère—'the very gates of France', as Torcy called them—Bolingbroke insisted that Sicily go to Savoy as compensation for Spain: this adjustment would also place a strategically important island in friendly hands. The French gave way when Bolingbroke agreed that Sardinia should go to Max Emmanuel. This support for Savoy's acquisition of Sicily, rather than an extended Alpine barrier, arose from Britain's decision to make peace with France, which virtually ruled out the pressing of claims against France, but not the granting away of territories belonging to allies. Sicily was claimed by Austria, which thus had notice that Britain was gradually isolating her by purchasing the small powers' adherence to a peace at the expense of a great power. The cession was accepted reluctantly by the emperor in January, and the elimination of Savoy from the war secured by the Italian truce of 14 March 1713. In the final settlement, the mountain tops between Savoy-Piedmont and Dauphiné were fixed as the frontier, the French surrendering (besides Exilles and Fenestrelle) the valleys of Oulx, Sezane, Bardonache and Château-Dauphin; Savoy ceded the valley of Barcelonnette, with its little fortress town, on the French side of the watershed. The reversion of Spain to Savoy, if the Bourbon line failed, was confirmed.

By the early spring of 1713 the United Provinces, Prussia, Portugal and Savoy had all been brought into a general settlement, but on terms which only hardened the difficulties of bringing the emperor to a conclusion. In the cases of the Dutch and Savoy the terms conflicted absolutely with Viennese claims. During the last six months of 1712, Austrian policy had offered practical concessions to hold the Alliance together, but without ever unequivocally abandoning the claim to at least part of Spain. The German members of the Secret Conference were indeed willing to abandon Spain; even before Denain reduced the hope of retaining Dutch support, Wratislaw and Seilern had converted the emperor to a partition or (as a last resort) to insistence on an independent Catalonia as reward for loyalty to the Habsburg cause. Renewed negotiations with Britain were not at once rebuffed. Bolingbroke hoped that sympathetic exchanges with Vienna could diminish the chances of Austria drawing off the United Provinces. At the same time, by his four-month truce with France, he neutralized British troops in Spain and cut the emperor's links with Barcelona, which depended on the British navy. In November, French agreement to the inclusion of Tournai in the Barrier proved the turning-point in the Dutch decision to accept terms. The Dutch ceased to support the Austrian demand for Strasbourg and to oppose the continued presence of Max Emmanuel in the Netherlands. This defection completed the emperor's isolation, and the French started to push up their price. The English, their own affairs all but settled, accepted French insistence that Max Emmanuel remain in Luxemburg and Namur until he should receive Sardinia with a kingly title. Adamant over Italy and Bavaria, Vienna now showed, too late, that elasticity over Spain which the Secret Conference had advised four months earlier. Hoffman, negotiating in London during November, indicated that the emperor would now be willing to abandon Spain and accept a republic for Catalonia, whose independence should be guaranteed by the powers. The English, knowing such an idea must delay peace, merely advised that the Catalans rely on Philip's mercy. More practically, they offered to negotiate a truce between Austria and her enemies in Italy and to arrange the evacuation of Austrian troops from Spain—a two-edged offer, because Charles VI, while worried about his wife's security in Barcelona, was unwilling to abandon his strong position in Italy. The emperor was also casting round for a private settlement with Max Emmanuel. But none of his moves could prevent the smaller powers from preferring the protection of English influence at Versailles. Having accepted the loss of Sicily in January 1713, Vienna worked out the evacuation of Spain and the truce in Italy through talks with the British envoys at The Hague in March. The effect of this blow to the Catalans was delayed because of English unwillingness to repatriate the Imperial troops for renewed action against France on the Rhine.

The nearest Austria came to inclusion in the general peace was with proposals for an overall settlement sent to London in February 1713. Only over Bavaria were the suggestions such that France refused them. The emperor was adamant that Max Emmanuel should be totally ex-cluded from his electorate, though his removal to Sardinia was now ad-mitted, and that the Upper Palatinate should not be returned to Bavaria. At this juncture, the French, knowing Bolingbroke eager to meet Parliament and consolidate his position as author of a general peace, and believing Britain would perforce support them, began to step up their claims against Austria once more, although Habsburg capacity for concession had already reached its limit. The French chose to champion the interests of 'that crowd of indolent droning Princes', as Bolingbroke called the smaller Italian powers,[1] with a view to separating Mantua, Mirandola and Commachio from Austria. The interests of the Italian princelings were not material to France and her military position could no longer sustain them. These moves and the new demand that Charles VI recognize Philip V, so extinguishing his own claim on Spain, can only be understood as attempts to humiliate the isolated Habsburg. The original instructions to the French plenipotentiaries at Utrecht had made clear that nothing would be attempted for the Italian princes, whose own timidity was blamed for their misfortunes. As late as 22 March, Sinzendorf agreed to join the peace if the latest demands were dropped, but now the French had left themselves no means of withdrawal: either the willingness of the English to support them—and Bolingbroke had given no support at

---

[1] To the British plenipotentiaries, 20 Feb./3 March 1713, quoted by O. Weber, *Der Friede von Utrecht* (Gotha, 1891), p. 376.

all—had been overestimated, or the pride of the Austrians underestimated. As the French plenipotentiaries openly admitted, 'If we had known how stubborn the emperor would be, we should not have drawn the bow so tight.'[1] Subsequent French rejection of the Austrian counter-proposals, which simply reiterated what had already been agreed, was the signal for resuming war.

In all these negotiations Bolingbroke played a major part. Much of his energies had been taken up with the settlement of disputes in which Britain had no direct interest. Only towards the end of the period in which the great patchwork quilt of tightly woven agreements took on its final shape did he return to complete that section which was, in the last resort, of most importance to him. His sense of timing was always superb, but he had left the detailed solution of Anglo-French problems until the latest possible moment. One of the original causes of the war, Louis's recognition of the Old Pretender, had been removed by the Mesnager Convention, but Louis had been less willing to expel the Pretender from French soil. The English politicians themselves were treading warily. There was no guarantee that the Pretender would not think the throne worth a Holy Communion; and the desertion of Austria would involve the desertion of Hanover, one of the emperor's staunchest allies, which did not augur well for Tory prospects after Anne's death. But although Harley, as late as the start of 1713, was hedging about whom he would support on Anne's death, the succession problem did not seriously obtrude into the peace negotiations. Louis XIV finally removed the Pretender to Lorraine in February 1713. Two outstanding issues remained: North America and a treaty of commerce. In America, the English could withhold concessions which France dearly wanted until they obtained terms for the revival of trade between the two countries. Bolingbroke was here looking to a future in which friendlier Anglo-French relations would be cemented by a commercial reciprocity reversing a generation of tariff war. The commercial treaty originated during Prior's first visit to France and took formal shape in March 1712, on English initiative. The assumption had been a most-favoured-nation treaty and a return to the tariff of 1664. Unfortunately, by the time Prior undertook detailed negotiations, the English had already agreed to exclude woollens and three other articles from the reductions that France was to offer the Dutch. Now Torcy insisted that the terms for Britain must be subject to the same limitations, to preserve most-favoured-nation treatment for the Dutch, with the consequence that the Treaty of Commerce as a whole was rejected by parliament in June 1713, after a fierce pamphlet war and the defection of the Tory sheep-raisers, led by Sir Thomas Hanmer. This treaty, from which Bolingbroke hoped so much, was perhaps his one real failure. However, the French

---

[1] Report of Heems, Austrian envoy in The Hague, 30 May 1713, quoted *ibid.* p. 390. For the Italian settlement at Rastatt, see below, p. 473.

and British economies were now more competitive than complementary: it is unlikely that closer political relations could have been promoted by commercial accord: the alliance of 1716 was largely the product of short-term dynastic weaknesses in both countries.[1] All that these negotiations achieved was to hold up agreement on differences in America.[2] There St John claimed the retention of Acadia, restoration of the Hudson's Bay forts, possession of Newfoundland and St Kitts in their entirety. Torcy's agreement depended on allowing French cod-fishermen the use of scheduled parts of the Newfoundland coasts for drying-stages. The failure of the Quebec expedition (known in England just as the Mesnager Convention was being concluded), with his desire for a general agreement before the two powers approached the Allies, led St John to ignore the Board of Trade, which feared French rivalry in the dry-fish trade and understood the truth of Torcy's remark to Prior that Newfoundland was as much the nursery for French as for English seamen. Even in December 1712, when final settlement of these issues was undertaken, it was as levers to procure a favourable commercial treaty that Prior and Shrewsbury in France dallied in reaching agreement about the fisheries, and continued to insist on Acadia and a partition of Cape Breton Isle. In the outcome, France was allowed the use of the Newfoundland coast from Bonavista north and west to Cape Rich, and retained full possession of the islands in the Gulf of St Lawrence. England recovered the Hudson's Bay forts and the whole of Newfoundland, while keeping Acadia (Nova Scotia) and all St Kitts.

Aware that the campaigning season was approaching with no preparations made, and uneasy at the continued prorogation of parliament, Bolingbroke stopped wranglings about the timing of tariff changes in the draft commercial treaty by an ultimatum of 28 February 1713. On 15 March he told Torcy he was ready to sign. On 11 April, at Utrecht, the plenipotentiaries of Britain, Savoy, Portugal, Prussia and (after midnight) the United Provinces signed the peace treaties with France. The Congress had completed the major part of its task. But the general pacification was still to seek. Austria and the German princes had not made peace with France. And no power had yet made peace with Spain, whose plenipotentiaries had only received passports in time to reach Utrecht as the French treaties were being signed.

The Anglo-French treaty secured Britain's major war aims: recognition of Queen Anne and the Protestant Succession, restoration of a balance of power by exclusion of Philip V from the French line. Bolingbroke has been rightly censured for his callous treatment of his allies. He should equally be praised for the clarity of his judgment and the effectiveness of his settlement. As the war had proceeded, Allied aims had diverged. As

[1] See vol. VII, pp. 194–5.
[2] For the Asiento see below, pp. 475–6.

he Dutch had been the first to recognize, the commitment to 'No peace
vithout Spain' took insufficient account of military practicability or
political implications. When Archduke Charles succeeded to the Habsburg
lominions in central Europe, only Austria had an interest in fighting to a
inish; nothing the British or Dutch could do would satisfy Austrian
imbition in Spain, even had it been their interest to attempt it. The conduct
of Anglo-Dutch relations was cordial while the friends of William III
emained in power in both countries, but the basic interests of the two
countries conflicted the moment common fear of France disintegrated.

With the war aims of the three main allies diverging, no common
agreement on when to make peace was possible. Of the two powers
eady to make peace, only Britain was in a position to take the initiative.
The Dutch could not abandon her because, should she continue the war,
hey would be at the mercy of France if their Barrier was not guaranteed
by their allies; but Britain's barrier needed no guarantor except the navy
which dominated it. In the last resort, the English could make peace without the Dutch; the Dutch could not safely make peace without the
English. Bolingbroke used this freedom of manoeuvre, not to make a
separate peace, but to secure a lasting settlement for Europe and a series
of exclusive advantages for Britain. As to these, all the Allies were concerned to get what they could. The emperor pitched his claims beyond
what he could make good. The Dutch paid the penalty of having relied on
extravagant promises from an English government concerned to hold
them to an impossible policy in 1709–10. Only that government's successors measured their aims to an attainable programme and, profiting from
Britain's indispensability, forced her allies to conform to it.

After the signature of the treaties of 11 April, Sinzendorf left Utrecht
within hours, his colleague Kirchner lingering another five weeks. The
emperor, now unhampered by the intelligent moderation of Wratislaw
(who died on 21 December 1712), but influenced by Spanish counsellors,
would neither recognize the Bourbon king of Spain nor agree to an
alternative endowment for the dispossessed elector of Bavaria. The
decision to continue the war, made easier by the empress's return from
Barcelona, was supported by the Diet at Ratisbon, which declared in
July that the French proposals would 'tarnish the glory of the German
nation'. It promised supplies for a new campaign, thus enabling the
emperor to borrow from Amsterdam. Yet these gestures could not conceal
a lack of common aim between emperor and Empire. All but Charles VI
wanted to restrict the campaign to the Rhine, where alone the emperor
had reached agreement with France. It was exactly this which the German
princes would most like to have upset. They were to succeed to their own
disadvantage. The emperor preferred territory in Italy and security for the
Catalans. Further misunderstanding lay in the ambitions of some States

to plunder the disintegrating Swedish empire in north Germany, which offered higher rewards than continued war against France: Hanover had already occupied Verden (August 1712) and the new king of Prussia, Frederick William I, had by June 1713 laid plans for acquiring Stettin.

The outcome of the new campaign was soon decided. After Villars's capture of Landau on 17 August, negotiations were resumed. Late in the month, Villars was given *pleins pouvoirs* and a series of alternatives to negotiate from, all including restitutions for the Italian princelings and the restoration to Max Emmanuel at least of his lands between the Inn and the Danube—in effect, Louis XIV's prized outpost in south Germany. In November, Freiburg-im-Breisgau fell. When the Circles meeting at Frankfurt announced that they could not continue the war, the emperor gave Eugene full powers. The two generals met in the palace of the margrave of Baden, at Rastatt, on 26 November.

The negotiations were not difficult. The plenipotentiaries were old friends; though Villars occupied the left and Eugene the right wing of the palace, they ate together and shared their reception rooms. Both wanted peace. But Villars, despite his army's commanding position, gave the advantage to Eugene, who played on Villars's nerves by threatening to sever the talks when they became difficult. Eager to appear the pacificator of Europe, Villars did not hesitate to blame Max Emmanuel, an old enemy, for delays. Argument centred on Italy and Catalonia, however. The French slowly retreated from demanding the eviction of the Habsburg from Italy, but maintained Philip V's right to do as he pleased with the Catalans. In January 1714 Villars and Eugene sent their own proposals to their respective governments. Here the claims of the Italian princes were met by a simple promise that justice be done 'but without holding up the peace'.[1] Villars also admitted Eugene's suggestion that the Austrians be allowed to continue military aid to the Catalans. Despite Torcy's bitter comments,[2] Villars thought he had won 'my final battle'. On the rejection of his proposals, he gladly accepted Eugene's idea that the Austrian send an ultimatum to Versailles. The campaigning season was in prospect and Villars exaggerated the possibility of renewed warfare. Eugene, while preparing for this, had little to hope from it. After the dispatch of the ultimatum, the plenipotentiaries parted on 6 February—Villars to Strasbourg, Eugene to Stuttgart, thus giving the appearance of rupture while allowing each to remain in touch with the other.

Villars had promised acceptance or rejection of the ultimatum. Perhaps fortunately, the negotiations were taken out of his hands. The delicate

[1] Marquis de Courcy, *La Coalition de 1701 contre la France* (2 vols. 1886), vol. II, p. 191.
[2] 'Our Commander, more in the habit of gathering laurels than olive-branches, thinks that a Soldier little knows how to disguise the truth, and places in Prince Eugene the same confidence as I have in Lord Bolingbroke': Torcy to Bolingbroke, 28 Jan. 1714, *Bolingbroke Corr.* vol. IV, p. 632.

mission of persuading Eugene to modify the ultimatum, without France's appearing to reject it, was entrusted to the marquis de Contades, a major-general and friend of Villars. In their talks at Stuttgart, by softening Louis XIV's objections to the ultimatum, Contades accepted that the emperor should use the title of King of Spain (with an explanatory article that this carried no recognition of rights), and that he should retain in Italy those places now or formerly possessed by Austria. Eugene agreed to simple silence on the Utrecht treaties, with their references to Philip V, instead of specifying formal repudiation. On 6 March, Louis XIV's acceptance of the final terms was known. The treaty was signed that day, at Rastatt, by Eugene and Villars.

The German settlement was based on the treaties of Westphalia, Nymegen and Ryswick. While Strasbourg and Alsace remained French, France yielded all her possessions on the right bank of the Rhine—Breisach, Kehl, Freiburg—and agreed to destroy fortifications on islands in the river. She retained Landau and its dependencies, ostensibly hers by the Peace of Ryswick but in fact her one real gain from the continuation of the war; Charles VI undertook to procure the Empire's agreement to its surrender. The simple and absolute restitution of the Wittelsbach electors of Bavaria and Cologne (reserving only the Imperial right to garrison Bonn in war-time) represented a retreat by both sides. The French demand for the kingly title of Sardinia for Max Emmanuel was dropped and the emperor himself took the Spanish Netherlands—the alternative proposed for Max Emmanuel and the one preferred by him. With the immediate danger of a Bavaro-Netherlands exchange removed, France agreed not to oppose such an arrangement in the future. The Dutch were accordingly to surrender the south Netherlands to Charles VI, less the territory ceded to Prussia and what should be agreed in a subsequent Austro-Dutch Barrier Treaty. The emperor kept Naples, Sardinia, and the Tuscan *presidii*. Contradictory conditions made nonsense of his obligation to 'render good and prompt justice' to the claims of Guastalla, Mirandola and the prince of Castiglione. Mantua, Mirandola and papal Comacchio were to remain Austrian. Vienna's claim to Parma and Piacenza as Imperial fiefs—a claim disputed by the papacy—was passed over in silence, to be the starting-point for later conflict with Spain, when Philip V married Elizabeth Farnese, niece of the childless duke of Parma, six months after the Treaty of Rastatt.

Fearing delays in the Diet, Eugene, without authority, had signed for the Empire and undertook to procure ratification at a subsequent congress. The emperor then invited the Diet either to nominate its own delegation to this new congress, as provided for in the Diet of 1709, or give him full powers. The Diet divided along religious lines. The Protestant States bitterly resisted taking the emperor's treaty with France at Ryswick as the basis of settlement. Article IV of that treaty had stipu-

lated that, in the lands of the *Réunions* outside Alsace which France wa
to surrender, 'the Roman Catholic religion is to remain...in the state i
which it is at present'. As a result whole areas, particularly in the Palati
nate, which had been forcibly converted to Catholicism, sometimes b
the mere passage of French troops, were retained for Catholicism—a clea
defiance of the Westphalian settlement. English and Prussian protests a
Utrecht had resulted only in an ambiguous promise, ignored at Rastatt, c
a return to Westphalia. Now only the Diet could save the Protestants. Bu
on 24 March, when the Catholic States, a majority, asked the emperor t
sign for the whole German body, the Protestant States could only reserv
their rights in a protesting postscript. The larger Protestant powers
willing to see peace delayed in order to divert attention from their activi
ties in the Northern crisis, in which Charles VI also was now eager t
intervene, vaguely offered to continue the war. The emperor, thoug
tempted, was not deceived. Indeed, French insistence on the retention o
Article IV had his full support.[1] He could anticipate only a further declin
in Habsburg power in Germany if he now relied on Protestant Hanoveria
or Prussian support.

The final Congress for the signing of peace between the Empire an
France opened at Baden in Aargau, Switzerland, on 18 June 1714. It ha
little to do beyond rendering into Latin what had been written in Frencl
at Rastatt. The host of disgruntled ministers from Italy, Lorraine, Bavari
and Cologne, even Spain, succeeded only in submitting *mémoires*. Villar
and Eugene, again their countries' representatives, made limp attempts t
produce a settlement between Vienna and Madrid; but the Austria
refusal to consider any territory for the princess des Ursins in the Nether
lands, until the Catalans were granted their liberties[2], prevented progress
Queen Anne's death on 12 August, the Northern crisis, and the Turkisl
situation[3] made both Louis XIV and Charles VI eager to conclude. Th
Treaty of Baden was signed on 7 September and ratified by the emperor
for the Imperial Diet, on 15 October.

The emperor's decision to fight on after Utrecht had brought valuabl
rewards. For the single loss of Landau, he had retained Sardinia—soon t
be the counter for gaining Sicily—secured the Netherlands, and won
free hand in Italy. If the restoration of the two Wittelsbach electors was
mortification to Habsburg pride, the alternatives would have been o
doubtful advantage. In Germany, however, the peace provided a les
stable settlement than elsewhere. The rivalry of Bourbon and Habsburg
separated by a frontier where political fragmentation was a constan
invitation to meddling, remained inevitable so long as French interest

---

[1] In a letter of 19 Oct. 1712 he had encouraged the pope to press Louis XIV to insist a
Utrecht on safeguards for the Catholic religion in Germany. Piety moved Louis agains
considerations of power, Catholics being a stronger support for the emperor in German
than the Protestants.

[2] Cf. above, pp. 376 ff.   [3] Below, pp. 637–8.

continued to be centred in Europe and until Austria, like France, needed protection in her rear to concentrate against a more dangerous rival, Prussia. At best, the German settlement did not worsen relations between Versailles and Vienna. The Austrian fear that a Bourbon on the Spanish throne would tip the balance of power in favour of France was only immediately true because of the marriage of Philip V to a wife who could, for her own interests, keep alive Spanish interest in Italy.

It had suited both Britain and France that Spain should be excluded from Utrecht, where they preferred to settle Spanish affairs between themselves. The French had bowed to commercial advantages for Britain in the Indies once these had been separated from demands for territory there. The South Sea Company, founded by Harley a month before the Mesnager Convention, was a Tory bid to win the commercial classes for peace. French resistance to Britain's demand for the Asiento was overcome by the threat to step up English bidding in North America. When the French agreed, the English yielded over the Newfoundland fisheries.

In October 1712 the English opened direct negotiations with Madrid. Philip V was not sorry to be offered an escape from tutelage to France. One of the inactive Spanish plenipotentiaries, Monteleon, was sent to London, while Lord Lexington and Manuel Manasses Gilligan, a commercial agent who had already been involved in the negotiation of an earlier Asiento, went to Madrid, to negotiate with Grimaldo and Bedmar. The main political problems were easily dealt with. Philip reaffirmed his renunciations and Savoy's rights to the reversion of his throne besides the grant of Sicily.[1] Spain recognized the Protestant Succession and Britain's retention of Gibraltar and Minorca. English attempts to save the Catalan liberties, however, were unavailing—Bolingbroke was unwilling to postpone peace for their sake. The political treaty was none the less delayed by the tortuous course of the commercial negotiations. The English claim to a 15 per cent reduction of duties on goods going through Cadiz for re-export to the Indies was abandoned when the Spanish insisted they would have to do the same for France and the United Provinces. As a brilliant equivalent, the English got the right to send an annual 'permission ship' of 500 tons for carrying on general trade—a breach in the colonial monopoly not admitted in the final treaty but held to be simply a favour conferred on Spain, so as to prevent other powers claiming what had been given to England alone. The Asiento Treaty, requiring a mini-

[1] Peace between Spain and Savoy came in July 1713, when the Spanish recognized that the duke should receive Sicily, with the reversion of the island to Spain. He was carried thither by the English admiral, Jennings, to be crowned as king in Palermo on 14 November, unrecognized by pope or emperor. The unnatural tenure of this strategic island by so weak a power—of interest only to England, who could control its affairs—was to last eight years only.

mum of 4,800 slaves a year (for 30 years) to be carried to the Indies and allowing a settlement of wooden buildings (open to Spanish inspection) on the Plate, was signed in Madrid on 26 March 1713, and peace preliminaries on the 27th, the final Anglo-Spanish peace treaty being sealed at Utrecht on 13 July. That same day a preliminary commercial treaty, in the form of an English memorial with Spanish answers, dealing with the reopening of trade with metropolitan Spain, was agreed. It promised much, but concluded little—a 'blind misshapen monster' Bolingbroke called it. It renewed the advantageous treaty of 1667, but through ignorance the new uniform tariff rates were fixed at the highest rate then prevailing in any port, while the important right of the English merchants to elect a special official, the *Juez Conservador*, to look after their interests was abandoned. The rectifying of the difficulties written into this agreement was to cause much bitterness later.

Dutch relations with Spain were bedevilled by reluctance to allow the English unilateral advantages in the Indies. About these Bolingbroke was adamant. Dutch unwillingness to risk the Barrier had finally, in May 1712, brought recognition of Britain's Asiento, at first on the understanding that it implied no general trading rights—which at that stage it did not. But further delays were caused by the Spanish demand that an appanage be found in the Netherlands for the princess des Ursins: Philip V only gave way when the French, alarmed by Queen Anne's illness and the possibility of renewed hostilities, withdrew their backing and withheld troops for the subjection of Catalonia until the peace. On 26 June 1713 Spain signed with the United Provinces. This treaty changed little in the relations between the two countries. Dutch trade was put on a most-favoured-nation basis, but the Provinces abandoned their claims to trade with the Spanish Indies and Spain agreed that no foreign nation should trade to her colonies—without prejudice to the Asiento.

The last of the Utrecht treaties, between Spain and Portugal (February 1715), had been delayed by Portuguese insistence on the Spanish towns promised in 1703 and by Spanish attempts to bring pressure on Portugal to use her good offices with the emperor. The treaty confirmed the mutual territorial restitutions in the Peninsula already settled between France and Portugal. In America, Spain ceded Sacramento, despite fears that a Portuguese colony across the Plate from Buenos Aires would become an English trading-post. This demarcated the southern extremity of Brazil as the French concessions between the Amazon and Oyapok had defined the northern. Britain mediated in these arrangements and now guaranteed them—a reminder of the value she placed on her Portuguese alliance.

The final problem was the Barrier. The 1709 treaty had been repudiated in February 1712; not until December did the English offer new terms, as a bait to bring the Dutch into a general peace. The Barrier Treaty of 1713 was signed on 30 January. The inner line of forts at Dendermonde, Lier and Hal—promised in 1709 and primarily of commercial significance— was excluded, and with it Lille, Condé, Valenciennes, Nieuwpoort and Maubeuge on the French frontier. To the east, Liège and Huy had gone. To offset these losses Mons was the only gain. This Barrier was less impressive than that of 1709, but a great improvement on Ryswick. The Dutch now had the promise of Furnes, Fort Knocke, Ypres, Menin, Tournai, Mons, Charleroi, Namur and Ghent, as well as the forts of Perle, Philippe and Damme, with the prospect of adequate revenues for proper maintenance of the Barrier, provided by the south Netherlands themselves. In their direct negotiations with France, beginning February 1713, the Dutch had to resign the territories surrounding Tournai and Ypres, while their claim to Upper Guelderland was upset by Prussian tenacity. British mediation brought instead a share in the garrisons of Roermond, Steven-sweert, Fort St Michael and Venlo, in return for the abandonment of Fort Damme. These adjustments apart, the Barrier incorporated in the Franco-Dutch peace treaty remained as the English had designed it. Nor did it ignore either British or Dutch interests in the exploitation of the south Netherlands. The Dutch were not to lay any new impositions which would have yielded unilateral advantage; Britain's troops were to stay until her 'trade and interests' were satisfied; and commercial regulations, yet to be worked out, should provide for equal treatment of both powers.

There remained the thorny problem of Austrian consent. As the Barrier clearly diminished the usefulness of the Netherlands to Vienna, negotiations were long and involved. They were also entangled by Anglo-Dutch jealousies. Britain, anxious to prevent the emperor from upsetting the Mediterranean settlement when he made peace with France, wanted Dutch support for Savoy's kingly title in Sicily, whereas the Dutch were unwilling to alienate Vienna before the Barrier was accepted there. The failure of the divided English government to exert any influence at Rastatt or Baden, where the Savoyard title was not recognized, together with the death of Queen Anne in August 1714, emphasized Britain's exposed position, now that the war was concluded. George I's administration decided to support Vienna rather than The Hague over the Barrier, partly because the new king had imperative need of Austrian support for Hanoverian ambitions to retain Bremen and Verden. This new friendliness blocked Eugene's pressures to abandon the Netherlands and forestalled the Spanish party at Vienna which, contrariwise, wished to occupy the Netherlands immediately. Either of these policies would have seriously damaged British and Dutch interests alike. The failure of Austro-Dutch talks at Antwerp in October allowed Britain to step in as mediator. In December, Stanhope visited Vienna to negotiate an alliance. There he supported Austrian resistance to Dutch proposals, which optimistically looked back to the Barrier of 1709, and in return got Habsburg agreement not to alienate the Netherlands. Final escape from deadlock, however, came only after a shrewd move by the Dutch. Article II of the 1713 Barrier Treaty pledged them to maintain the Hanoverian succession. In August 1715, the British government songht Dutch troops. The Dutch immediately agreed. As a result, the English lent a more sympathetic ear to Dutch arguments in the Barrier disputes. In effect, the Dutch now dropped their attempt once more to gain the 'commercial' barrier of Huy, Liège and Dendermonde, and on 15 November the Barrier Treaty between Austria and the United Provinces was signed. On the 16th, 6,000 Dutch troops sailed for England.

The Dutch now lost the right to garrison Mons, Ghent and Charleroi, but retained it in the other towns of the 1713 Barrier (as modified by the treaty with France) and were to share the garrison of Dendermonde. In the east, the emperor was to cede Venlo, Fort St Michael and Stevensweert. Of the 35,000 men who were to defend the Netherlands he was to provide three-fifths, with an annual subsidy of 500,000 crowns towards the cost of the Dutch forces. Commercially, the Dutch were entirely satisfied, not least because it suited the English to join with them in denying any advantage to Austria in her new provinces. Duties on goods of the Maritime Powers carried into the Austrian Netherlands were to be paid at the existing rates—fixed by the very favourable tariff of December 1680—pending a new commercial treaty, which the two powers perpetually obstructed. Quarrels about the Austrian subsidy and other details delayed final ratification of the treaty, with a British guarantee, until May 1719.

At the time, Britain once more appeared the main beneficiary. A balance of responsibility between Austrian and Dutch had been achieved that would apparently ensure security without letting either power predominate to her disadvantage. Time was to reveal that the treaty had, in fact, reduced the benefits of possession to the Austrians dangerously low. Dynastic interest, which accounted for the original Habsburg insistence on the Netherlands, gradually waned before Anglo-Dutch pressure for continued closure of the Scheldt and successful hostility to the Ostend Company, the one attempt made by the emperor (in 1722) to realize the economic potential of the Netherlands. The failure of the Barrier to hold up the French in 1745 was to frighten London into urging on Vienna a greater share of the burden of defence in the Netherlands; preoccupied with Prussia, Maria Theresa refused. After 1748, as it turned out, the area ceased to be a scene of international rivalry until the French Revolution.

When the series of treaties had been concluded at Utrecht a commemorative medal was struck carrying the motto *Spes Felicitatis Orbis, Pax Ultrajuctensis*.[1] The description was not unjustified. The war had challenged,

[1] 'The Peace of Utrecht, the hope of happiness for the world.'

and the peace had contained, the ambitions first of France, then of Austria. The Utrecht pacification was negative in its achievement, as the Grand Alliance had intended it should be. It had prevented a disruption of the balance of Europe and restored the principle of flexibility. The pacification ensured that as new problems and new powers emerged their demands would be met by new alliances and alignments freely arrived at, unimpeded by the overweening strength of any one power.

17-2

CHAPTER XV

FRANCE AND ENGLAND IN NORTH AMERICA, 1689–1713

BRITISH colonial policy in the months immediately following the landing of William of Orange was determined less by a change of objectives than by circumstances outside the control of London. The Lords of Trade, a Privy Council committee which had contributed since 1675 more constructive thought towards the political organization of the empire than either Charles II or James II, remained in being. But the loss of vigour occasioned by James's interference was never fully recovered. The king who had helped initially to create a favourable atmosphere for imperial centralization unwittingly did more than any other person to destroy it for ever. In addition, his flight thrust upon the Privy Council the grave task of ensuring that the accession of William and Mary did not precipitate a more radical revolution in the colonies. The speedy onset of war added to the distractions of government. Thus England was unfavourably placed to bargain with her colonies, let alone to impose her will. In particular, the imperial unity which war made imperative would be meaningless if Old and New England pursued sharply diverging paths.

For New England the Glorious Revolution provided the opportunity to overthrow a detested régime: with the imprisonment of General Governor Andros and Edward Randolph the short-lived Dominion of New England collapsed,[1] and men of perceptible imperial sentiment associated with it were discredited. There were revolutionary disturbances also in New York and in Maryland. Protestant hysteria was a feature common to them all, but is not a sufficient explanation of them in itself. Behind it festered the terror of Indian incursions—enlivened by recollections of King Philip's War and the massacres in Virginia during the mid-seventies.[2] Furthermore, each province had its own special background of distress, of factional jostling and individual contests for power; and all had witnessed or feared the end of provincial government which the vice-regal schemes of King James entailed. Since he had made no secret of his admiration for the French system of colonial government, the colonists not surprisingly associated schemes of centralization and consolidation with the external threat to their liberties posed by French Catholicism. Finally, the leading rôle of Boston as an instrument of political expression was a factor not to be ignored. The wave of colonial revolutions in 1689 revealed what for the next century was to be a fundamental reality, better

[1] See vol. v, pp. 351–3.   [2] See vol. v, p. 350.

understood than countered, namely, that England's Atlantic empire had two political capitals: Boston as well as London. Both were militantly anti-French and anti-Catholic. Though disparate in size, they contested, not unequally, to determine the political life of the eastern seaboard of North America. Boston was distinguished by the power of its Puritan tradition; official London was coming to be represented in America through the less effective force of Anglicanism. In 1689, London initiated and Boston merely exploited a revolution; but it was Boston, in part because of its own provincial function, which ensured that provincial autonomy would not disappear from the empire.

Massachusetts led the way in restoring provincial government north of the Delaware. The heavy-handed policies of Andros had brought a local shift in power. The moderate party, which in Wait Winthrop, Simon Bradstreet and others included influential colonists with interests ranging beyond the purity of the Puritan church, was confused and the 'faction' or theocrats, then skilfully represented in London by Increase Mather (1639–1723), one of the most articulate spokesmen of the Covenant tradition, had regained control of the province. The problems of the new government should not be underestimated. Few of its members possessed the confidence of an earlier generation that Massachusetts could act without heed of England's sanction. Because internal divisions might aid the French and Indians, the leaders of the revolution were compelled to compromise the colony's claim to independence. A counter-revolution seemed unlikely, but a major concern of the Council of Safety was to check the mobs which for months threatened its authority. Practically every responsible group now regarded legitimate government as something that required the concurrence of London. In recognizing this, republican notions were put aside; in their place, the common rights of all Englishmen were stressed. Further, it was tacitly conceded that constitutional monarchy deserved enthusiastic support: William and Mary were hailed as moral and divine instruments of delivery from popery. Thus the revolution in Boston could be skilfully defended as a selfless act of patriotic and Protestant devotion against the machinations of men branded as papists in the service of the French and Indians. This faced the newly installed administrators in London with a complex problem, for they could not easily reproach Boston without denying the major principles of their own Glorious Revolution. Nor was it a time to repudiate lightly a proffered acknowledgement of allegiance, following a half-century in which the will of Massachusetts had been bent only after protracted effort.

In New York the revolution was no less complex. The colony's disturbed state derived from many causes. Originally a Dutch trading post, it had moved rapidly to the status of a proprietary and then of a royal colony, confronted with the imposition of English administrative and legal codes, and with the effect of entry into the English colonial system. In addition it had suffered an economic depression which substantially lowered the value of property. These experiences, preceding the growth of popular belief in a Catholic plot involving French and Indians, had produced severe problems of adjustment. But the underlying malaise was probably the rigid barrier to preferment, resulting from the abolition of representative government and the colony's inclusion in the massive Dominion of New England. Among those shut out from activity in that government had been men of recognized ability, such as Abraham De Peyster and Jacob Leisler, and men socially only a little less influential than those who did participate.[1] Upon news of the invasion of England Francis Nicholson, the lieutenant-governor, invited the city council and military leaders to discuss avoidance of civil strife. He had a choice, denied to Andros, of putting himself at the head of the populace or of rallying the propertied elements in defence of law and order. But popular reaction, spurred on by events in Boston and London, rejected him as leader and opened the way for Leisler, a prosperous German-born merchant. Leisler was unable to maintain power for more than two years. His strenuous efforts to produce a war revenue undermined his position, and the failure of a projected land invasion of Canada induced New York to welcome in 1691 a royal governor selected in England. Colonel Henry Sloughter, sympathetic to the councillors ousted from power, was convinced that New York was in the hands of a rabble. His summary trial and execution of Leisler gave the latter's memory a more profound and consistent popularity with the underprivileged than Leisler had ever had alive.

In Maryland the revolutionary upheaval may be more simply represented. Again, fear of Roman Catholicism, real or affected, was rooted in fear of the French and Indians, but also in dissatisfaction with the proprietary government of the papist Lord Baltimore. As in New York, there was discontent among capable men unable to achieve the highest political offices. Yet beyond St Mary's and its neighbouring counties little support existed for rebellion, while initially a bipartisan group endeavoured to allay passions and counter the charge of conspiracy. John Coode, the revolutionary leader, dominated his government less openly than did Leisler and in August 1689 formally relinquished power to a representative assembly from which Roman Catholics had been specifically excluded. After a second convention had met, the Crown officially recognized the Protestant Association and in due course Lionel Copley arrived as royal governor. Although disturbances continued, the peaceful assumption of power by this post-revolutionary government enabled Maryland to avoid the bitterness from which New York politics long suffered by the martyrdom of Leisler.

The other colonies avoided revolution but did not entirely escape the political repercussion of events elsewhere. In Virginia Lord Howard of

[1] *The Glorious Revolution in America* (ed. M. Hall *et al.*, Chapel Hill, 1964), pp. 54–5.

Effingham, who had appointed certain Catholics to office, vacated his governorship. Surprisingly, East Jersey remained among the calmest provinces on news of James's abdication, despite its inclusion in the Dominion of New England, its significant proportion of New England settlers and long record of civil disturbance. Further north, the small colonies quietly exploited the confusion and resumed charter government, sheltering hopefully behind the vigorous diplomacy of Massachusetts.

In England the Massachusetts agents sought recognition of the fullest measure of provincial autonomy. Increase Mather had set his hopes on a restoration of the colonial charters vacated during the two previous reigns. The position of King William, who had formerly denounced the assault on the charters as arbitrary, was difficult. The character of the *de facto* governments and the behaviour of the New England colonists were subjected to continued criticism from Randolph on his return home, while it was clear that a reunification of the eastern seaboard, to which Massachusetts was opposed, would offer military advantages. But if the restoration of political fragmentation was accepted only with reluctance, the principle of representative government was unhesitatingly upheld. The outcome for Massachusetts was the charter of 1691. Mather, who at times had behaved as though he were a plenipotentiary from a State voluntarily joined in a confederal empire, was less than satisfied. Elisha Cooke, another of the agents in London and leader of the country party within the colony, believed that essential liberties were sacrificed. Yet concessions were by no means one-sided. England achieved the right to appoint the governor, but his discretionary power was limited and without consent of the General Court he could send no troops outside the province. The laws were subject to disallowance by the king, but the upper house, established as elective, escaped the interference to which an appointed royal council was exposed. Maine and New Plymouth remained under the control of Massachusetts, even if New Hampshire was given provincial status. Connecticut and Rhode Island continued as separate governments, although the former's military forces were commanded by the governor of New York and the latter's by Sir William Phips, the new royal governor of Massachusetts.

Outside New England similar compromises took place. The Maryland revolutionaries, initially approved by the Crown in 1690, were subsequently subjected, not to the proprietaryship of Lord Baltimore, but to a royal governor and a strengthened legislature. The first nominated council contained representatives of the Protestant Association and of the Puritans of Anne Arundel, besides two nominees of Lord Baltimore, who retained ownership of the soil. In New York, provision was made for a representative assembly and a nominated upper house under a royal governor. Because of the suspicion aroused by Penn's association with James II, Pennsylvania was placed under the executive control of the governor of New York. By 1692 the disturbances which had begun in the former reign were over, and a governmental system in being which was formally approved by England if only in part determined by her.

The small French communities of Quebec, Montreal and Trois Rivières, with their outlying farms along the St Lawrence and Richelieu rivers, were neither as politically articulate as the English settlements nor possessed of readily effective instruments for communicating their wishes to the home government. If France should be induced to make concessions it would be through the representations of leaders imposed by the monarchy, not through representatives of the people.[1] Apart from the onset of war itself, the significant event of 1689 was the return of Count Frontenac, at the age of 67, to take up his second governorship, in succession to Denonville. Next in importance to the governor, the bishop of Quebec, Saint-Vallier, had been selected by his strong-minded predecessor, Laval; wealthy and of high birth, he was at first held in great esteem by Louis XIV. Whereas Laval and Frontenac had clashed in personality and objectives, Denonville and Saint-Vallier had co-operated with relative ease. But after 1689 the relations of the Church with the political leaders of New France again deteriorated seriously. Despite Colbert's displeasure, Laval had firmly established the principle of an ultramontane Church determined to control the fur trade,[2] which challenged the missions as the first frontier of the empire. His views had triumphed in two royal edicts and in provincial ordinances, only to be defeated by forces within the colony contending for a free west. Saint-Vallier largely continued Laval's policies. At the council board in Quebec he joined with Champigny, intendant 1686–1702, to contest commercial expansion in favour of agricultural consolidation and Catholic virtue.[3] Although a match for Laval in vitality, Saint-Vallier's tactlessness rapidly disenchanted almost all with whom he came in contact and restricted his influence; throughout his prolonged absences from the colony it was Laval who, until his death in 1709, was consulted over the main problems. From the beginning of Frontenac's second administration theocratic power waned. Colbert in 1668 had predicted its decline when the population should increase, but the circumstances of prolonged warfare did much to bring it about. The Church, which had greatly aided the establishment of a civilized way of life in New France, was chronically hampered by inadequate revenues and a shortage of parish priests: even in 1700 there were less than seventy to serve a population of some 14,000, and few parishes had resident *curés*.

[1] For questioning of the feudal implications of the 'régime seigneurial', see M. F. Ouellet in *France et Canada Français du XVIe au XXe siècle* (ed. C. Galarneau and E. Lavoie, Quebec, 1966), pp. 159–60.   [2] See vol. v, p. 361.

[3] The development of an agricultural system as a basis for social order, rather than for imperial economic purposes, is discussed by J. Hamelin and F. Ouellet in *France et Canada Français*, pp. 84–5.

The strength of the Church, as of the political arm of the province, depended on royal support.

Under long-range control from Versailles government was cumbersome. Once a year all senior officials received from the king a statement of the general policies to be pursued, with minutely detailed information of decisions taken over the previous twelve months throughout the French colonial world. This *Mémoire du Roi* was the main instrument of administrative instruction. The official hierarchy through which it operated, however, was not perfectly symmetrical. In principle, the jurisdiction of the governor-general of New France extended over all the countries of 'la France Septentrionale', but in practice the governors of Acadia, Newfoundland and (after 1698) Louisiana had little direct contact with Quebec. The governor-general and intendant were assisted by a Sovereign Council which also included the bishop and seven others. Known from 1703 as the *Conseil Supérieur*, it was to become by 1713 essentially a court of appeal; within it the power of the bishop was limited to jurisdiction over the clergy and religious questions. At home the bureaucracy devoted to imperial administration was large and increasing. Before 1699 there was no single minister responsible for colonial commerce, internal administration and defence; but in September of that year, when the younger Pontchartrain succeeded as minister of marine, the navy's control over these matters was extended, although certain colonial questions remained under the Controller-General and the secretary for foreign affairs. Pontchartrain, a humane and hard-working organizer, retained control until 1715, while the king probably determined the main outlines of policy and the appointments of senior officials. For all Louis XIV's industry and eye for detail, the problem of communication, whether in peace or war, magnified the defects of personal judgment and helped to defeat the absolutist system which in theory appeared far more effective than the anarchic assemblage of English colonies. During the Spanish Succession War in particular, the Crown's authority was challenged by a growing lawlessness.[1]

The size of Canada's population was scarcely a match for New York alone, the marcher province of the English colonies, and it was scattered for 300 miles along the banks of the St Lawrence and Richelieu. It is difficult to assess the quality of the settlers and how far this offset the disparity of numbers. If the small seigneurial class has been castigated as lazy, improvident and poverty-stricken, the body of the *habitants* was described by Lahontan in his *Voyages* (1703) as enterprising and indefatigable; Denonville said they were tall and robust. However, they were also alleged to be extravagant, over-sensitive, dishonest, prone to

---

[1] J. C. Rule, 'The Old Regime in America: a review of recent interpretations of France in America', *William and Mary Qtly*, 3rd ser. XIX (1962), p. 580, indicates the sources of argument which support this view.

drunkenness and gambling, full of self-conceit. The young were regarded as especially idle, readily forsaking the settled areas for the unregulated attractions of the forest and Indian ways of life. The brandy trade was doubtless the source of many ills. Montreal, the centre of the trade, was known throughout America and even in western Europe for its debaucheries; at night bands of youths terrorized the citizens, and in 1694 a drunken orgy started a fire that destroyed the Sulpician Mission of the Mountain. Few were the communities not affected by the 'infinity of taverns'. At Trois Rivières there were 25 houses and in most of them drinks were sold; in Quebec and Villemarie the proportion was almost as high. Hard-drinking *coureurs de bois* were broken men before their fortieth year, and Denonville claimed that in twenty years alcohol had resulted in the death of 95 per cent of the christianized Iroquois living in the French settlements. Serious as was this problem, however, the population dispersal caused by the brandy and fur trade was graver still.[1]

In 1687 Denonville had sought to chastise the Senecas, one of the Five Nations whose ambition threatened this trade. His efforts were repaid in 1689 by the massacre of Lachine, 'the greatest single disaster in the history of the colony',[2] shattering French confidence and leading to a defection of Indian allies, most damaging in the case of the Ottawas, upon whose allegiance the fur trade north of the St Lawrence depended. Frontenac, bringing in September the news of Louis XIV's declaration of war, certainly inspired the colonists with a new spirit. Francis Parkman claimed that he also restored rapidly the system of Indian alliances, but a later historian has argued that his vain desire to appease the Iroquois prevented this and seriously jeopardized the French position in the west.[3] The resources at the governor's disposal were small: about 1,500 *troupes de la Marine* and somewhat more than 2,000 militia. The Iroquois alone could almost match these numbers. Champigny urged concentration against Albany, believing that its destruction would facilitate the crushing of the Five Nations and exploit the anarchy into which the Revolution had plunged New York, for Albany was held by anti-Leislerian forces. Frontenac preferred a combined naval and military attack on the port of New York. Lacking the necessary help from Europe, however, he substituted a series of stinging raids on the northern borders of the English settlements: against Schenectady in New York, Salmon Falls on the boundary between Maine and New Hampshire, Fort Loyal (Portland), and the settlements on Casco Bay. The French regained prestige in the eyes of their Indian associates; but it is doubtful if the unmolested Iroquois were much impressed.

[1] For the fur trade in these years, see below, pp. 850–1.
[2] D. G. Creighton, *Dominion of the North* (Boston, 1944), p. 97.
[3] W. J. Eccles, 'Frontenac's Military Policies, 1689–98: a reassessment', *Canadian Hist. Rev.* XXXVII (1956), pp. 201–24; cf. *idem*, *Canada under Louis XIV, 1663–1701* (1964), p. 170.

The English reacted by convening an inter-colonial conference at New York, in May 1690. Only delegates from Massachusetts, New Plymouth and Connecticut joined those of New York. Meanwhile Massachusetts, eager to protect her fisheries and to demonstrate her loyalty to the empire,[1] had already taken steps to secure herself from the French and Indian menace to the north-east: in Acadia an expedition of some 700 men under Sir William Phips captured Port Royal in May 1690 from a poorly prepared garrison. It was a success cheaply achieved in men and money, but the town was soon retaken. For the English, however, the capture of Port Royal was but a step towards the conquest of Canada. A plan was formulated by the inter-colonial conference which included the complete destruction of Quebec by a naval expedition of which Phips was again made leader. The project badly miscarried. New York and Connecticut forces, assembled for a diversionary overland attack on Montreal, proved unable to press beyond Lake George. News of their withdrawal permitted Frontenac to strengthen the feeble Quebec garrison, till now practically without ammunition. The delayed assault down the St Lawrence was then vigorously repulsed, the English being further demoralized by the onset of unusually severe autumn weather. A storm which scattered the fleet and sank three ships turned predictable success into shameful failure. The quality of Phips's leadership may well have deteriorated, although he has not reaped a major share of blame.[2] Cotton Mather (1663-1728), the scholarly eldest son of Increase who dedicated his life to interpreting God's plan for New England, regarded the fiasco as evidence of the hand of heaven. In *Pietas in Patriam*, a eulogistic biography of Phips, he indicated the dire consequences which followed from the exhaustion of New England's best spirits. If this were a true representation of the physical and moral state of Massachusetts, then she was fortunate to escape retaliatory action against her own capital. As it was, French privateers harassed her coasts and land-raids continued for the rest of the war: against York in 1692, Oyster River in 1694, Casco in 1696, Haverhill and Lancaster in 1697; even the newly-built, heavily-defended Fort William Henry at Pemaquid was overcome. Yet New England remained intact. Twice there had been a truce with the Abenaki Indians: in the winter of 1691, and again for a longer period in 1693, after the successful defence of the Maine frontier by Captain Converse and a force of 350 rangers.

On the Albany front New York alone was incapable of bearing the whole burden. In 1692 none but Virginia and Maryland sent financial help, and with such resources as he commanded the new governor, Benjamin Fletcher, felt unable to take the offensive. In February 1693,

---

[1] P. Miller, *The New England Mind: from Colony to Province* (Cambridge, Mass., 1953), p. 160.
[2] Cf. G. S. Graham, *Empire of the North Atlantic* (1958), p. 69.

however, Major Peter Schuyler, with a mixed European and Indian force of 550, inflicted heavy casualties on a slightly larger Canadian party that attacked the Mohawk towns, while Fletcher acted vigorously in bringing men from New York to Schenectady. Aid in both men and money had come from New Jersey, while by the end of the summer Virginia and Maryland between them had directly contributed £900 to the defence of the frontier province. There followed two years of relative quiet during which neither side had strength for spirited action. The difficulties of the French were no less severe than those of the English. If 1691 saw New England out of breath and downcast, New France was comparably depressed by the weakness of her resources. In the spring of that year, with a population swollen by refugees from the Newfoundland fisheries, food and ammunition were so scarce that troops and militia were unable to leave the forts to combat enemy raiders. Now, without hope of reinforcements from France, Frontenac felt obliged to turn the war of skirmishes into a system of assault. Borrowing the methods of the Iroquois, he developed a style of fighting costly in men and equipment, but suited to the Canadian genius and military predicament. On this foundation Pierre Le Moyne, Sieur d'Iberville, member of a gifted family and a brilliant tactician, added innovations of his own. But to Frontenac terroristic warfare remained a second-best. His original instructions had aimed at the ruin of New York by transporting its inhabitants to Pennsylvania or New England. Boston too, he believed, must be destroyed and the Hudson firmly secured for France. Ever since 1690 he had argued that the achievement of these objectives offered the best and perhaps the only way to finish the war and subdue the Iroquois. On no less than four occasions, he urged Louis to reconsider his earlier project as a means of bringing the fur trade and fisheries under undisputed control. New France alone lacked the strength for such ambitious schemes, which indeed required the use of sea power beyond French naval conceptions after Barfleur.[1] Neither parent power thought of weakening its position in Europe for the sake of a knock-out blow in North America.

The greatest of French successes by sea were achieved against the English fishing bases[2] and trading posts in Newfoundland and Hudson's Bay. The French population of Newfoundland, according to the census of 1687, was tiny: 687 colonists spread out between Placentia (Plaisance), Pointe-Verte, Fortune, Cap Nègre and L'Hermitage. The English possessed half as many more settlers, distributed in eleven communities. They won a temporary success in 1690 when Placentia was surprised by a raiding party from Ferryland; both town and port were taken with only trifling bloodshed, but not held. Two years later a second attack by three 60-gun ships and two smaller vessels under Commodore Williams failed, while a

[1] Cf. above, p. 244.
[2] On the French and English cod fisheries see below, pp. 848 ff.

yet more formidable assault commanded by Admiral Wheler was turned aside by bad weather and achieved no more than the pillage of the island of St Pierre. Neither side was strong enough locally to retain conquests for long. Frontenac's counter-measure was to send French privateers to harry the English settlements from Placentia. Ferryland was saved in 1694 thanks to the determined resistance of Captain William Holman; but in 1695 eight large privateers destroyed vessels and installations at many points, and in 1696 Ferryland fell to a privateering expedition from St Malo. Meanwhile Iberville, who commanded it, sent detachments to burn outposts along the eastern coast. In jealous emulation, the governor at Placentia, Brouillan, stormed several stations on the southern coast. In concert the two men had already seized the main English base, St John's, on 30 November 1696. The situation for England was serious. By 1697 she held only Trinity and Conception Bays, and every English settlement on the eastern coast save Bonavista and Carbonear had been annihilated. Alarm at this collapse produced a force of 1,500 soldiers and a large squadron under Commodore John Norris for the recovery of St John's. This devastated port the English expedition rebuilt and fortified, well enough to discourage a further attack by a more powerful squadron under the marquis de Nesmond, although they missed an opportunity to try conclusions with Baron de Pointis (laden with the booty of Cartagena)[1] after he had burnt Carbonear.

The contest for Hudson's Bay, and indirectly for the command of the beaver trade, centred about Fort York.[2] Although the English recaptured Fort Albany in 1693, the dispirited garrison of York capitulated next year to the ubiquitous Iberville. It was retained for three years and finally retaken by Iberville in 1697. The English thus paid the price for neglecting small local defences. This instance demonstrated how the intervention of brilliantly led metropolitan forces could radically affect the regional balance of power. By the Peace of Ryswick the boundaries and outposts of New France, New England and New York remained substantially unchanged; but in Newfoundland and Hudson's Bay, theatres in which decisive actions had been fought, French influence now predominated. William III, who had made the interests of the Bay Company a cause of war, was not prepared at the peace to hazard his European policy for the sake of their pursuit.

In Newfoundland France made the mistake of considering the destruction of the English settlements as final. Her success against the Iroquois Confederacy proved more enduring. The Indian chiefs had complained bitterly at English failure to send effective help to New York and by 1694, depressed by their losses and the apparent ability of New France to draw

---

[1] Above, pp. 355–6.
[2] See vol. v, p. 366. E. E. Rich, *The History of the Hudson's Bay Company, 1670–1870* (2 vols. 1958), vol. I, provides a detailed account of the fighting and diplomacy of this war and the next.

upon unseen resources in Europe, they sought a breathing space. But they approached the French only after Governor Fletcher had been fully apprised of their plight and military aid had not been sent. At this time loyalty to the English alliance was not in doubt. Frontenac's call for a general Indian peace to include the Ottowas, Miamis and other tribes received substantial support only among the Cayugas; the Onondagas, Oneidas and Mohawks rejected it. He then determined to crush the Confederacy, striking at the Onondagas and Oneidas in 1696 with a force of 2,000 Canadians, regulars, and Indians. The immediate consequence of this chastisement was limited. The French forced the Oneidas to make peace, but both tribes escaped the general destruction which had been hoped for. On the other hand, save for corn sent to prevent winter famine, English aid was negligible. The Peace of Ryswick brought no French acknowledgement of the English claim to sovereignty over the Confederacy. Frontenac rejected the overtures of the earl of Bellomont to include the Indians in the general European peace, although Bellomont commanded the resources of New England and New York, reunited under his governorship. Thus, with their strength now reduced to 1,300 warriors and apprehensive lest French and English combine against them, the Iroquois were obliged to open separate negotiations with Quebec. After Frontenac's death, on 28 November 1698, it was left to his experienced successor (1699–1703), the chevalier de Callières, governor of Montreal since 1684, to bring the protracted discussions to a successful conclusion. By the treaty of 1701 a general Indian peace was achieved. The Iroquois agreed to remain neutral in any future Anglo-French war. They accepted defeat of their endeavour to take control of the western fur trade from the French.

Before the Nine Years War ended the English undertook two important acts relating to the administration of their empire: the framing of the Navigation Law of 1696 and the establishment of a Board of Trade. English commerce had expanded in the years immediately after the Revolution, but within half a decade it was believed to be in decay and the future unassured.[1] As causes of this depression, two factors were considered uppermost: organized defiance of the Navigation Laws and the activities of Scottish interlopers. Already, before 1695, Bristol and Liverpool had petitioned parliament for the support of legitimate trade. In 1694 the Custom House declared that it was experiencing a revenue loss of £50,000 from trade illegalities. Randolph, who had hoped these difficulties would advance his own schemes for the political reorganization of the empire, contributed to but was not primarily responsible for the determination to make the old colonial system more effective. In January 1696 the Customs Commissioners, who blamed the proprietary and corporate colonies for many defects in the system, admitted to having

---

[1] Anglo-American trades are discussed below, ch. xxiii (1).

prepared a Bill to reinforce the Acts of 1660, 1663 and 1673. The matter was examined by a Privy Council committee which, like the Customs Commissioners, rejected as too radical Randolph's proposals for reorganizing the proprietary and corporate colonies. The main value of the Act of April 1696 was that it clarified the intention of earlier legislation, established administrative rules and new penalties for infringements, and further emphasized the governors' responsibility for enforcement. In addition, by extending the Statute of Frauds to America, it systematized the customs organization for the colonies. Of great importance, moreover, was the establishment of vice-admiralty courts with jurisdiction over the penal clauses in the Navigation Acts. To carry out the increased authority of the Crown and make good the decline in efficiency of the Lords of Trade, a new institution was created, the Board of Trade. Continuity was obtained through the personnel of the new body. The first president was the earl of Bridgewater and another member was William Blathwayt, former secretary to the Committee for Trade and Plantations; Randolph's influence also remained. The Board's function as a consultative body was widespread and valuable, but unlike its predecessor it lacked executive power, and save for its very early years it was dominated by the Treasury under Godolphin and by the secretaries of state.

The power of the colonial proprietors persisted, as is suggested by Randolph's failure to have attorneys-general appointed by the Crown in all the colonies. He also recommended that the government of the proprieties be invested in the king, but his dedicated efforts were not successful. In 1697 letters were sent to Rhode Island, Connecticut and Pennsylvania threatening forfeiture of charter and patent. It was recognized, however, that the government of the chartered colonies could not be arbitrarily assumed save by act of parliament or due process of law. Bills for the destruction of some or all the colonial charters, designed to set the plantations 'upon a more equal foot',[1] were subsequently introduced into the House of Commons on five occasions before the Peace of Utrecht. The earliest, in 1701, came nearest to success. This was backed in England by Anglicans, lay and clerical, and by leading figures in the colonies, including such influential administrators as Governor Nicholson and Robert Quary, surveyor-general of the customs. But the charter colonies were skilfully defended: the Carolinas by the earl of Bath; Connecticut, Rhode Island and Massachusetts by Sir Henry Ashurst, commercial magnate and leader of Dissent at Westminster; and Pennsylvania by the Penn family. The rôle of William Penn may well have been critical, despite Ashurst's claims to strong influence among the Lords. Yet the efforts of those who had striven to abolish the independent governments were not entirely void. Penn yielded all his political rights, as did the proprietors of the Jerseys, while Maryland remained in the hands of the Crown until

---

[1] *Calendar of State Papers Colonial, 1701*, no. 473.

after Anne's death. This was a poor substitute for the centralization envisaged by the Lords of Trade under the Restoration, but at least royal government had now become the rule and not the exception on the mainland.

New England's exposure to raids continued after the signing of the Peace and almost to the end of what had been one of the most testing decades in her history. The Indian terror communicated more than nervous expectations of direct attack and torture: it influenced the witchcraft accusations which engulfed the village of Salem in 1691–2. This notorious hysteria has been singled out as the darkest page in New England's history and has served to discredit the Puritan theocracy in the eyes of some recent historians.[1] It began when a number of young girls accused elderly members of the community of having bewitched them. Confessions of copulation with the devil and other enormities followed. A score of persons and two dogs were hanged. The leaders of the colony, instead of intervening, were afraid to deny charges levelled against the innocent lest they too be accused and their authority weakened. It was a failure of leadership, rather than the character of New England Puritanism in itself, that was responsible for these judicial murders. Nor should we forget that the province of Massachusetts was just emerging from a political struggle which had threatened its very existence and was currently engaged in a military struggle scarcely less tense. Moreover, the dread of witches, common to the western world, was intensified here by the proximity of heathen tribes universally supposed to be devil-worshippers. It was the combination of these circumstances which undermined the normally steady common sense of New Englanders.

The Quakers were loathed with near-equal intensity. Their incessant efforts to convert the frontier districts, where they met with some success, threatened to strip New England of its outer defence. Anger was further roused by 'a certain silly scribbler',[2] one Tom Maule, who sought to defend Indian savagery in war. But in the coastal areas, where Quaker ideas were resisted, molestation of Quaker by Puritan did not long outlive the Revolution. In 1691 the Friends were able to build their first brick meeting-house in Boston; fifteen years later their members had increased sufficiently to warrant a second. A further enemy within, the Church of England, feebly planted under Andros, had been viciously attacked with the overthrow of his régime. In 1690 only Boston possessed an Anglican congregation. Thereafter a more substantial period of growth affected the composition of many northern towns, measurably aided by the foundation in 1701 of the Society for the Propagation of the Gospel in Foreign

[1] Cf. S. E. Morison, *The Intellectual Life of Colonial New England* (New York, 1956), pp. 255–65, and Miller, ch. XIII.
[2] Cotton Mather, 'Decennium Luctuosum', *Narratives of the Indian Wars, 1675–99* (ed. C. H. Lincoln, New York, 1959), p. 278.

Parts, whose first object was to send clergymen into the plantations to instruct colonists in 'the principles of true Religion'. Although the S.P.G. was to prove the mainstay of Anglicanism in colonial America and has even been described as representing British imperialism in ecclesiastical guise,[1] its achievements were modest and diffuse. Even so, New England's orthodox ministers had good reason to regard their traditional values as in danger. The substitution by the charter of 1691 of a property franchise for one based on religion, together with acceptance of the principle of toleration, paved the way for the growth of dissenting sects and the end of the rule of the theocracy. The Puritan Church appeared to be further menaced by the growth of a progressive movement from within when, in 1699, a group of advanced thinkers founded the Brattle Street church in Boston. The counter-attack of the Mathers and other ministers led in 1705 to proposals for a reorganization on presbyterian lines. Under the influence of Solomon Stoddard and the synod of Saybrook, Connecticut adopted the 'consociation' principle in 1708; but in Massachusetts the model of centralization contained in *The Saybrook Platform* was thwarted by the democratic element, led by John Wise, and by the opposition of the British government, which feared a revival of theocratic power as detrimental to imperial interests.

Outside New England toleration had been upheld in the colonies since the Restoration. Its application was not always effective. For a while in New York the sects suffered more restriction than in the towns of New England, and their struggle in Charleston was a hard one. In all the mainland colonies from Maryland southwards the Church of England had become established by 1692. Yet it was not the church of the majority save in Virginia, and even there vestry control was already limiting the power of the clergy. In Maryland radical sects predominated; in North Carolina, as in East and West [New] Jersey, Quakerism was the dominant faith. Moreover, new types of immigrants added to the religious diversity that already marked colonial life before 1689. The most important were the Huguenots. Some settled in the interior of New York province, others along the Santee river in South Carolina, but mainly they went to the developing urban communities—Charleston, New York, New Rochelle, Salem, Boston and Oxford—where they readily associated with the Anglicans. The German sectaries began their historic entry in 1683 under Francis Daniel Pastorius. During the next two decades there followed many others from the Rhineland—Quakers, Mennonites, Baptist Brethren, River Brethren, Dunkers, New Mooners, and members of the Society of the Woman in the Wilderness. Emigrating mainly to Pennsylvania, they spread thence to Delaware and Maryland. Later came the Palatine Germans, mostly through Philadelphia, although some, after temporary refuge in England, were transported to New York to serve a dual imperial

---

[1] C. Bridenbaugh, *Mitre and Sceptre* (Oxford, 1962), p. 57.

purpose; the production of naval stores and the strengthening of the Albany frontier. A settlement of Swiss was formed under Baron de Graffenried at New Bern in North Carolina.

Religion, a vital if no longer a central factor in the life of most of the colonies, could hardly be expected to counter completely the disturbing influence on behaviour of a prolonged period of war. By 1690 crime was already a major problem and each colonial village made provision for nocturnal security. Inevitably the towns were worst affected. Danger came from many sources. In Newport, after 1707, privateersmen were the main cause of disturbance; the watch in Charleston was assaulted by sailors, sometimes of the navy; Philadelphia also suffered the crimes of seafaring men. In New York breaking into churches was a public scandal. Violence and rioting increased. By 1720 Boston, still regarded as the best-governed town in the English colonies, had a reputation for riots in which both sexes participated. Drunkenness, a universal vice despite numerous laws against it, contributed in particular to disorder in the seaboard areas, as did the readiness of citizens to trade with pirates and rescue them from gaol. The younger generation was probably more disturbed than any other segment of the population. In 1699 illicit relationships were common, and during the Spanish Succession War, when for the first time the colonists had widespread contact with European soldiers and sailors, a marked increase in adultery and illegitimacy took place. Not surprisingly, New England's sabbatarian code of 1692 was openly flouted; private organisations to combat the 'Leprosy of Sin' met with only limited success.[1]

The effect of the wars on education is more difficult to determine. The overturn of New England's educational system by Andros and the threat to transform Harvard into an Anglican seminary were for most New Englanders part of the alarming pattern of events preceding 1689. But there is evidence of a decline in the quality of undergraduate life at Harvard by 1680.[2] During the 1690s concern was often shown at a latitudinarianism which owed nothing to direct English interference, and at the influence on the university of 'morally degraded' Boston. Stoddard, the 'pope' of the Connecticut Valley and a critic of the Mathers but himself a Harvard graduate, preached in 1703 against centres of higher learning which had lost sight of their vocation to prepare men for public service. Perhaps the Puritan 'Jeremiad' purposefully exaggerated the decline. In any case Harvard could only gain in stimulation from the establishment of a second New England university. This was the constructive Puritan response to the soul-searching analysis of standards conducted by the leaders. The foundation of Yale was promoted by Harvard men, and Harvard uttered prayers for the success of the new

[1] C. Bridenbaugh, *Cities in the Wilderness* (New York, 1960), p. 228.
[2] *Journal of Jasper Danckaerts, 1679–80* (ed. B. B. James and J. F. Jameson, New York, 1959), pp. 266–8. Danckaerts was a Dutch Labadist agent in North America.

venture. Some erosion of New England's educational traditions may have taken place at a lower level. In the last twenty years of the seventeenth century almost the whole adult community was literate, but soon after Utrecht the General Court of Massachusetts could lament that some towns preferred to pay a fine rather than maintain a grammar school; in this respect frontier towns were particularly delinquent.

Virginia's traditions were less helpful in producing criticism of the quality of educational provisions. In 1671 Governor Berkeley, speaking against free schools and learning as parents of disobedience and heresy, expressed the views of many planters who regarded education as an individual responsibility. New England, by contrast, believed that its own exclusive qualities were best defended by facilitating the expression of thought at all levels. Virginia lacked this self-assurance and had yet to create its most effective traditions of aristocratic leadership. The College of William and Mary, it is true, was founded in 1693, with a gift of 20,000 acres from the provincial government and an annual income to be raised by an export tax on furs and skins. But the faculty, largely constituted of ministers of near-by parishes, lacked the brilliance which had distinguished Harvard. In South Carolina, understandably, organized education was even less developed, but legislation in 1710 proposed the creation of a free school in Charleston and the appointment of schoolmasters. In New York and Philadelphia, recognition that education was the joint concern of Church and State provided soil for more vigorous growth than the character of plantation economy could offer.

Resources for the dissemination of English culture, and for political instruction, were increasing steadily towards 1700, especially in the north. Boston, possessed of an active printing press continuously since 1639, was by 1690 the second largest printing and bookselling centre in the empire. After 1685 printing developed rapidly in Philadelphia. New England enterprise attempted in September 1690 a monthly newspaper 'designed to counter false reports'. Rigid censorship prevented a second issue and it was not until 1704 that a regular journal, the *Boston Newsletter*, was produced. Supervision, however, remained under the control of the governor's council. In the south there was no newspaper until the end of the colonial period, but enlightened planters were already collecting considerable libraries: William Byrd II possessed the equal of Cotton Mather's 4,000 volumes; Dr Thomas Bray, church commissary and founder of the S.P.G., established libraries in nearly all Maryland's thirty parishes. Here, more particularly in the Chesapeake Bay area, a planter aristocracy was rising which regarded the making of wealth and the fruitful employment of leisure in cultural pursuits as complementary objectives in the good life. Robert Carter of Corotoman, an astute Virginian businessman, avowed that his proudest office was the rectorship of William and Mary College.

Significant distinctions thus existed between the cultural equipment and even objectives of the English mainland colonies. Nevertheless, it is possible to exaggerate differences of social structure. Everywhere, even in New England, possession of land determined position in society. Beneath the landed aristocracy, which corresponded to the English gentry, were yeomen, tenants, artisans and servants. The commerce of New England had produced by the second generation a prosperous merchant class; in New York the opportunities of war aided the growth of fortunes, such as Robert Livingston's, in which agrarian and mercantile wealth were joined. War served also to accelerate the growth of urban consciousness. It is true that the population of Newport remained static, while that of Boston, despite an influx of refugees from the frontier, fell from 7,000 in 1690 to 6,700 in 1700, reaching only 9,000 by 1710; but Charleston and New York grew steadily. Few novel ideas not of English origin, indeed, emerged for dealing with social or administrative problems; and yet the communities improved their efficiency, became better paved and better policed. Above all, in the five main seaports a new civic pride and sense of identity was evident, marking them out as no longer colonial villages, but rather as towns closely related in character to those of Europe.[1]

New France witnessed no comparable urban development. The entire colony supported a white population less than double that of Boston alone; Quebec itself numbered little more than 1,800 persons even in 1713. Since 1678, moreover, there had been little to compare with the autonomy of the New England towns. The early *syndics*—representatives elected by the inhabitants of Quebec, Montreal and Trois Rivières—had not survived Frontenac's first governorship. Yet there was reason for pride in the social services, which were extended during this long period of war. Poor-relief offices had been established in the three main communities in 1688 to distribute alms and aid the unemployed to find work; each parish was empowered to erect similar offices. Four years later Jean François Charron founded a home for the aged and infirm in Montreal, and comparable facilities became available at Quebec's general hospital in 1693. In 1702 Trois Rivières was provided with a hospital by the Ursulines. Cultural life was conditioned by the climate, the demands of the soil, the constant fear of attack, the ribbon development of riparian parishes. The education of the colonists owed most to the devotion of the Jesuits, Sulpicians, Récollets and Ursulines, supported by the work of Laval and Saint-Vallier. In Quebec itself facilities for primary education were extended, while the needs of the surrounding countryside were served by the enlarged school at St Joachim; there were others at Pointe Levis, Sillery, Sainte-Foy, and Sainte-Famille (on the Ile d'Orléans). Montreal had two schools. There were establishments also at Fort Frontenac, La Prairie, Lachine, Pointe-aux-Trembles and Boucherville. The testimony of Crown representatives such as Raudot, Vaudreuil and Bégon suggests that rural

[1] See Bridenbaugh, *Cities*, pp. 138 ff.

education was handicapped by a shortage of schoolmasters, but evidence is conflicting on this point. Canadian women in this period were often better educated than the men, thanks to the work of the Ursuline communities at Quebec and Trois Rivières, and to the Sisters of the Congregation in Montreal and its district. In Acadia, where about 5,000 people were lightly ruled by governors whom Versailles ignored, schools for both sexes had long existed at La Hêve and Port Royal, although the latter's seminaries suffered fire and pillage in the Nine Years War. Throughout the educational system French practice was closely followed. The Jesuit college in Quebec, the only completely organized secondary school, is estimated to have held 130 to 140 scholars in 1699. There were also a number of Latin schools, Laval's 'junior seminary' at Quebec, and a few craft schools. St Joachim at one time offered hydrography, mathematics, wood-carving and probably painting. At Montreal navigation and fortification were also taught. War did not restrict the opportunities open to youth outside Acadia; they were expanded in spite of it.

In general, the cultural life of the French settlements was less rich than that of the English mainland settlements. There were no poets to compare with New England's Edward Taylor. After Saint-Vallier's quarrel with Frontenac over the production of *Tartuffe*, theatrical performances ceased. Personal libraries were no match for those of contemporary Virginia or Massachusetts: that of the royal hydrographer, Jean Deshayes, which in 1706 amounted to two score volumes, was exceptional. None but ecclesiastical bodies possessed libraries worthy of the name; the *habitants* rarely owned any books at all. French Canadian literature does not begin until after the conquest of 1759, although the appearance of major works describing the country and its expansion, such as Le Clercq's *Premier Establissement de la Foi dans la Nouvelle France* (1690) and Fr Louis Hennepin's *Nouvelle Découverte* (1697), stimulated interest. Yet this situation, partly reflecting the absence of a printing press, was not indicative of indifference to the printed word. Whether for pleasure or instruction, reading was an important feature of life and books circulated readily from hand to hand. As sculptors in wood and stone, Canadians already excelled. In this medium Noël and Pierre Levasseur were outstanding, while in Quebec Nicolas Bellin (or Blain) was distinguished for his graving of plaques of lead and copper.

The influence of the Church was not restricted to the St Lawrence and the maritime regions, but her strength in the furthest missions was partly wasted in fruitless quarrels. French penetration among the Indians was in any case more and more determined by political, military and commercial values. It is true that in 1696 Louis XIV ordered the abandonment of all military posts in the west, except Fort St Louis, and the practical termination of the western fur trade; but Frontenac and the traders he supported were able, as in Colbert's time, to win concessions from this policy, and under the persuasions of La Mothe-Cadillac, a skilful Gascon nobleman esteemed by Frontenac, it was decided to build a fort for the protection of the trade on the Detroit river. The discerning eye of Callières also recognized that French disengagement from the Illinois and Ohio country would soon place the western tribes within the English orbit, with the aid of Canadian malcontents. In outward appearance, however, the frontier remained a missionary one, stretching in a wide arc from northernmost Maine west to the Illinois country and southwards to the lower Mississippi basin, and radiating thence to the struggling new settlements of Biloxi and Mobile on the Gulf of Mexico.

In 1688 France retained only a foothold in Maine; the fortifications at Pentagoët (Castine) on the Penobscot had long been neglected. Denonville, who recognized the grave danger to Canada should the savage Abenaki fall under English influence, urged the establishment of missions from the Kennebec to the St John's river and placed his support solidly behind the Jesuits as the one body capable of controlling the minds of the Indians. In contrast to the Sulpicians, the Jesuits regarded the christianization of the Indians as a task best performed away from the white settlements, and they had gathered the Abenakis at Sillery. Subsequently they founded the mission of St Francis on the Chaudière and in 1688 revived their mission in Maine. Through Jesuit exertions the Kennebecs, Etchemins and Penobscots were gained as Catholic tribes. The parish at Pentagoët remained officially in the hands of the Seminary at Quebec, which also ministered to the Indians in Acadia; but it was relinquished to the Jesuits in 1699. Massachusetts, disturbed by Roman proselytizing within territory it claimed for its own, twice sent a commission in vain to induce the Indians to dismiss the missionaries. With the renewal of war an expedition ravaged the village, while another penetrated to Fr Sébastien Rasle's mission at Narantsouac and burned the church there. To the west, within the territory of New York, activity was declining: in 1689 the only Catholics among the Iroquois were the few converts made earlier and the sole priest Fr Pierre Milet, a prisoner of the Oneida but still very influential. In 1702, however, the cantons of their own volition requested the return of the missionaries; the veteran Fr Jacques de Lamberville was selected. His mission survived until Colonel Schuyler destroyed the church and Jesuit power there in 1709.

The greatest successes of the Roman Catholic religion were achieved in the upper Mississippi basin. By 1713 Vincennes had been founded on the Wabash, a mission-post established at St Joseph's for the Miamis and Pottawattomies, another at Peoria, a fourth among the Kaskaskias. Around these posts the French were slowly settling down, some taking wives from among the converted Indians. Their influence was perceptible, more especially on Illinois agriculture. Fr Jacques Gravier had succeeded the veteran Allouez in 1689 as supervisor of the missions and in 1690

Saint-Vallier appointed him vicar-general. Gravier planned missions to the Cahokia and Tamarois, both Illinois bands, and to the Osages and Missouris. After 1696 he devoted himself to more distant tribes. A complication was introduced when, with the bishop's support, the Seminary at Quebec—an offshoot of the *Missions Etrangères* at Paris and influential there—determined to participate in evangelizing the western tribes. Regarding the Tamarois as the necessary link with the more distant nations, it planted a mission among them first, despite the prior claims of the Jesuits. A residence among the Tonicas and another among the Taënsas extended the Seminary's influence to the Ounspik, the Yazoo and the Natchez on the lower Mississippi. But there Jesuit activity was also bearing fruit. From the fort at Biloxi, in 1700, Fr Paul Du Ru moved up the Mississippi, where his work was taken up by Fathers moving down from the north, Gravier and Joseph de Limoges, who built a chapel among the Oumas. The Jesuits now solicited Saint-Vallier and the king separately for exclusive direction of the Louisiana missions. But the French court and Saint-Vallier alike sided with the Seminary and conferred on it the powers of vicar-general over the entire Mississippi basin. While this decision formally preserved the authority of Quebec, it deprived the weak Louisiana settlements of the superior zeal and organizing resources of the Jesuits.[1] Despite continued support from France, on the other hand, the work of the Seminary failed to prosper. Its missionary Saint-Cosme was murdered in 1706; another, La Vente, unsuccessful in his relations with official Louisiana, returned to France in 1707 a dying man. Enemy action added to the difficulties. The Tonica mission was withdrawn to Mobile in 1708 because of the menace of war-parties of English and Indians; the church erected on Ile Dauphine by Lavigne Voisin in 1709 was destroyed next year. Alone of the Seminary missions, the station at Tamarois (Cahokia) showed promise of permanent results. By 1715 it had a French population of some 47 families.

More than any other possession in the New World, if exception be made of the definitive expulsion of the French from St Kitts in 1702, the fortunes of the nascent Louisiana were affected by war. After the murder of La Salle and the failure of his attempted settlement in 1684, French claims to the Mississippi were maintained by fur traders and by the assertion of the missionaries that there were Frenchmen like Michel Accault, companion of Hennepin, living and married among the Illinois. In 1689 Nicolas Perrot took possession in the king's name of the land between Lake Michigan and the Mississippi, on whose upper reaches, as on Lake Pepin, temporary forts were subsequently built. La Salle had warned Seignelay in 1684 that if foreigners got ahead of France in the Mississippi valley this would inevitably provoke the fall of New France. Within the French government Louis de Pontchartrain and his son showed a desire

[1] See M. Giraud, *Histoire de la Louisiane française*, vol. 1 (1953), pp. 217–23.

to substantiate French claims to the river's lower reaches. But it is doubtful if consideration of these claims, and of the need to ensure communication between New France and the Gulf of Mexico, much affected the negotiations at Ryswick. In 1696, on the contrary, French policy appeared to revert to Colbert's preference for no commitments beyond the St Lawrence. Nor was the king stirred to a radically new departure until after the publication at Utrecht of Hennepin's *Nouvelle Découverte*, which invited William III to take over this vast territory. Rémonville, an old friend of La Salle and a corsair with direct knowledge of the country, helped by influential associates like the parliamentary lawyer Argoud, then sought aid for a joint stock company charged with colonization. They drew attention to the menace of expanding British power and the imperative need to defend the highly vulnerable valley of the Ohio. Interest in France spread to members of the several Academies. Of particular value were the researches of the Abbé Dubos, one of the most widely travelled and geographically knowledgeable men in France. Two months after receiving proposals from Argoud, Pontchartrain took the first step towards preparing an expedition by selecting Le Moyne d'Iberville as its leader: information that Dr Daniel Coxe[1] in England was urging the settlement of French Protestants on the Gulf of Mexico spurred him on. The promoters escaped this danger, but the Spanish, fearing for the security of the Florida passage as well as the northern provinces of New Spain, in 1698 established a garrison in the Bay of Pensacola.

From the beginning, Louisiana's most serious problem was to obtain suitable colonists. Of the small initial force (120) which occupied several tentative sites east of the Mississippi outlets in 1699–1700, the Canadians formed the largest part. Many found the hot and humid climate difficult; for the *coureurs*, the discipline proved intolerable. The danger of population dispersal, which had so much threatened to enfeeble New France, Iberville hoped to prevent by grouping his settlements at selected points and forbidding a peltry trade with the Indians. To build up the population as speedily as possible he sought immigrants among the French poor and the families of garrison men. Plans for recruitment, inspired by Argoud and Vauban, were also drafted by Pontchartrain and the financier Antoine Crozat, whose interests extended to most French overseas trading companies. Not until the Regency, however, would the French government contemplate compulsory transportation. Iberville's aim was to stabilize the tiny colony's boundaries with outlying military posts as far as the Arkansas and Missouri. But in the shadow of renewed hostilities in Europe French merchants were unwilling to venture capital or ships. A plan for two large foundations near the Mobile river had to be shelved. By 1702, after the abandonment of the first settlement at Biloxi, the popula-

---

[1] For his vast colonizing projects see V. W. Crane, *The Southern Frontier, 1670–1732* (Ann Arbor reprint 1956), pp. 48 ff.

tion of Louisiana, thinly spread out between a fort on the Mobile and the Fort of the Mississippi, amounted to 140. Iberville complained bitterly of the poverty of French colonizing spirit, as had Vauban earlier. Yet this only partly explains why Louisiana was slow to develop. The natural attractions of the region were exaggerated, as in every colonial enterprise, and the underestimate of climatic difficulties proved a serious error. Food was the chief anxiety: livestock were insufficient, and some of the vegetable crops were destroyed by the heat, others by the very heavy rainfall. The inability of many immigrants to introduce techniques suited to these conditions led to despair and desertion. Lack of skilled labour thwarted plans for sugar and banana cultivation. Such modest success as was achieved owed most to Iberville's energetic leadership; but after 1702, distracted by the demands (and temptations) of war, he was unable to replenish the colony as he had intended. With his death in 1705 at Saint-Domingue, after a lucrative privateering expedition against the English Leeward Islands, the stripling Louisiana lost its source of inspiration.

For two years after the spring of 1706 Louisiana went altogether without aid from France. After February 1708, again, she depended on shipments from the Antilles or Pensacola for three more years. Even when ships did arrive, flour and other essential victuals were often not included, having been replaced by more profitable items or sold in the needy West Indies before Louisiana was reached. In 1707 the colony was denied competent leadership when Iberville's brother, Le Moyne de Bienville, was passed over in favour of the sieur de Muy, an officer from New France. But quality of leadership alone could not guarantee growth, as Iberville's experience had shown. Success depended above all upon the attitude of the king; and Louis, unable to provide the material support necessary to put the enterprise squarely on its feet, blamed the colonists for its shortcomings. A threat of abandonment indeed persisted throughout the war, although it was resisted by the younger Pontchartrain, who regarded the colony's strategic value as of more immediate concern than its questionable economic worth. Later, when Louis became reconciled to its continuance, Pontchartrain had no alternative but to fall back on private finance. By letters patent of 14 September 1712 a monopoly of the colony's trade, with property in any lands or mines that he could develop, was granted on easy terms to Crozat for 15 years, the Crown merely retaining the power to nominate the governor. This desperate remedy, which for Crozat was no more than another speculation, worked more oppressively than usefully. In 1717 Crozat sold out to the Crown, with recommendations that made Louisiana the nucleus of Law's Company of the West.[1]

Iroquois neutrality enabled New York to escape invasion during the Spanish Succession War, but in New England the pattern of the previous

[1] See Giraud, vol. II (1958), ch. VI.

conflict was repeated. The Maine communities were raided in August 1703, Winter Harbour in September 1707. On the Massachusetts border, Deerfield was brutally and dramatically destroyed in 1704. From their villages on the Saco, Kennebec, Penobscot and other northern rivers, the Abenakis were well placed to serve the objectives of French policy. France desired to counter dependence on English weapons and utensils by committing the Indians to ferocious raids that would incur retaliation where New France was least vulnerable. The Iroquois would thus be left undisturbed.

In 1703 the marquis de Vaudreuil became governor-general at Quebec. An accomplished soldier, with experience of the colony under three governors, he achieved a *rapport* with the Church and a unity of political leadership such as the St Lawrence settlements had not hitherto known. The cost of defending the English colonies against his form of attack was heavy. In the winter of 1703–4, 600 men patrolled the woods of northern New England without capturing a single Indian: by the following summer 2,000 men guarded 200 miles of frontier. Not only was this ineffective defence system highly unpopular with the more aggressive spirits, but the expense of killing had risen absurdly high. However, the native-born Governor Joseph Dudley of Massachusetts, who also commanded New Hampshire, was not wholly unsuccessful. In the winter of 1704 parties of rangers cleared the frontier of Indians, save for a raid on the Connecticut towns which was quickly beaten off. To ease his financial burden, Dudley was also ready to consider a treaty of neutrality. But Vaudreuil, although amenable for fear that the pacification of the Iroquois might break, set his terms too high: in seeking the exclusion of the English from fishing in the Gulf of St Lawrence and the Acadian seas, he proposed to New Englanders the unacceptable. Dudley's *démarche* was attacked in Boston itself. Men such as Samuel Sewall and the Mathers, staunchly loyal to their own corner of empire, preferred not to reassert New England independence at Vaudreuil's price. They accused Dudley, as formerly Andros, of harbouring pro-French designs. In any case, Vaudreuil's strategy had proved too successful, the wasp-like raids of his Indian allies having provoked vicious retaliation against the more exposed French settlements: hence the notion of compromise was unattractive.

Although intended also to undermine Abenaki striking power, such retaliation had little military value. Thus, in the summer of 1704, Major Benjamin Church with 550 Massachusetts men attacked Castine and burned Grand Pré in the Bay of Fundy. Port Royal, the main objective, had a garrison of only 185 under eight officers, but Church considered it too strong and the attack was postponed in hope of outside help. None was forthcoming as yet; but by 1707, with a force of over 1,000, including small contingents from New Hampshire and Rhode Island, Massachusetts was ready to try again. Its army, drawn from the rural militia and equal to two-thirds of the population of Acadia, failed badly before Port Royal, a fact which strengthened the influence of those who argued that competent military commanders were to be had only from the mother country.

In the Newfoundland theatre fortunes changed rapidly, but on the whole in French favour. In June 1702, Captain John Leake, governor at St John's, given a small force to secure the island, met immediate if short-lived success against French shipping and establishments at Trepassey and St Mary's. An opportunity to strike at Placentia itself was lost in 1703 by the refusal of Admiral Graydon to risk a force sent out primarily to protect the West Indies. This caution was to prove costly to the English. In 1706 a force of French Canadians, corsairs, and Abenaki, led by Governor Auger de Subercase of Acadia, left Placentia to attack St John's —a revival of Iberville's earlier proposal for the domination of Newfoundland. The town's impoverished inhabitants withstood a five-week siege, but the French went on to destroy Ferryland and ravage northwards to Bonavista. Further raids impressed on the British government the serious consequences of this French freedom of action, but not till the summer of 1708 were men directed to the capture of Placentia and the ultimate control of Newfoundland. Poor administration and inclement weather ruined that project. On the other hand, a privateering expedition mounted by Saint-Ovide, *lieutenant du roi* at Placentia, was able to destroy the fortifications of St John's and capture the governor in 1709, although the French withdrew next summer. An attack by land and sea on Carbonear in 1710, headed by Governor Pastour de Costebelle of Placentia, was less successful. Again and again, the French had kept the initiative, but without the local strength to consolidate their victories. To this kind of warfare privateering techniques were better adapted than naval power, which could not secure the English fishery so long as the French shared Newfoundland with it. The punishment here incurred by the British proved of value in publicizing the significance of the war in North America, and illuminates Bolingbroke's tough diplomatic insistence on sole possession of Newfoundland at the Peace.

Conflict for control of the Mississippi was first clearly joined on the southern frontier, where Iberville looked beyond Louisiana's immediate security to the Carolinian coast. Virginia, Maryland, and finally New York were also expected to fall as the outcome of a concerted drive from north and south. The first move in this continental plan was to be a joint Franco-Spanish land and sea expedition against Charleston, after which the Carolina English were to be repatriated and its Huguenots reconverted. But anticipating some convergence of French and Spanish objectives, Governor James Moore prepared an immediate offensive against the town and fort of St Augustine in Florida, whence forays on South Carolina were feared. In the autumn of 1702 a force of 500 Carolinians and 300 Indians swept away the northern Spanish missions and attempted to starve out St Augustine; after eight weeks, during which the morale of the besiegers deteriorated, Moore burned the town and retreated. He was now removed from the governorship. His aggression had contrasted with the defensive strategy initially adopted by New England, but the burden of its cost, falling on a less wealthy community, had been no less heavy. Even so, the Assembly at Charleston agreed to a military enterprise that was to bring more solid results than any other of the colonial war. At his own expense Moore raised an army of 1,000 Indians and 50 whites, and in 1704 laid waste the villages of the Spanish mission in western Florida, where the Apalache Indians could have been used against the Lower Creeks to destroy Carolina's defensive system of alliances. Many of the captured Apalache were moved to strengthen the struggling frontier town of Savannah, focus of Carolina's inland trade. Success followed success. The Timucua missions to the east, between Apalache and St Augustine, were next destroyed; by 1709 the Tocobaga Indians in southwest Florida had been broken.

The politically conscious Carolina traders had meanwhile taken precautions against attack from the direction of the Mississippi, where the Le Moyne brothers at Mobile succeeded only till 1706 in allaying the historic feud between the powerful Chickasaw, armed by the English, and the Choctaw, allies of France. The Alabama Indians had already deserted the French in 1703, while the Lower Creeks moved closer to the English after the conquest of Apalache. The foundations of Iberville's frontier policy were crumbling. With little or no help from France, the defence of Louisiana rested upon Bienville's masterly handling of the remaining alliances. The Franco-Spanish offensive was confined to an abortive attack on Charleston in 1706, which stimulated Carolina to improve its seaward security by a system of scout-boats, and to enlarge its military resources by sending officers to mobilize warriors among the Cherokee and Creeks. By 1707 English and Indians were burning and pillaging up to the walls of Pensacola—and action against Mobile itself, key to the lower Mississippi, was under consideration. Attempts to win over the Choctaw, Yazoo, Natchez and the other riverain allies of Mobile were made by Thomas Welch, trader and explorer, and by Thomas Nairne, Carolina's Indian agent, whose precocious strategic vision foresaw the need of concerted action by all the English colonies if they were not to be permanently restricted to the Atlantic seaboard. But for political vendettas in Charlestown and the dismissal of Nairne, the Carolinians might alone have completed the destruction of Louisiana at this time. As it was, their only major initiative for the rest of the war was to organize a huge expedition of Creeks and Chickasaw to accomplish the utter ruin of the Choctaw nation in 1712. In this crisis Bienville's forest diplomacy, which succeeded even in recovering the old Alabama allies, saved the French system from collapse.[1]

[1] For these events see Crane, ch. IV.

Governor Moore and Captain Nairne were not alone in their imperial vision. Among others, Governor Cornbury of New York, taking up the ideas of his predecessors, had urged at the outset that the French be driven from mainland America. By the end of 1708 the Board of Trade was convinced that this was necessary to safeguard the sources of West Indian food, thanks in particular to the lucid advocacy of Samuel Vetch, a survivor of the Darien disaster whose conception of conquest ran beyond the Spanish Caribbean to Canada, which he knew from his trading voyages. Colonial enthusiasm for the 'Glorious Enterprise' rose steadily. The northern governors pledged support and New Englanders sounded a note of urgency lest peace negotiations leave Canada, Nova Scotia, or even Newfoundland in French hands. According to Godolphin later, it was the progress of peace talks, as well as a diversion to Portugal of the naval squadron intended for Quebec, that led Britain to call off her aid in 1709; in 1710 Marlborough was opposed to it.[1] Instead, the aggrieved colonists had to be content with the acquisition of Port (Annapolis) Royal in October 1710. It was taken by a large expedition of New England militiamen and British marines commanded by Colonel Nicholson, Andros's former lieutenant, who left Vetch in charge of a small garrison to face the difficulties of winter in a hostile Acadia.

Despite the relief felt at the fall of 'the Dunkirk of North America', New Englanders saw it as a mere prelude to the conquest of Canada. In England, too, the new Tory ministers recognized the popularity of such a *coup*, especially as a bargaining counter for the conference table. St John in particular supported it and withdrew regiments from Marlborough's army for the purpose. It was he who supervised the somewhat hasty preparations, which left too much to the public spirit of Boston victuallers and others. Nor was the expedition fortunate in its leaders. The vigorous Colonel Vetch, in charge of the New England contingent, was subordinated to General Jack Hill, commander-in-chief of the land forces and brother of Abigail, with an undistinguished military record. The naval force—9 men-of-war, besides 60 transports and other vessels—was commanded by Sir Hovenden Walker, who had previously served in the Mediterranean. Hill and Walker had parity of command. Clashes between Englishman and New Englander occurred long before the expedition sighted the St Lawrence. Neither Walker nor Hill understood the complex political implications of managing an Anglo-American force. The quartermaster-general, equally ignorant, was even more outspoken in commenting on the 'ill-nature and sowerness' of the people and the 'indolence and indifference' of the Massachusetts government,[2] whose most grievous fault was its inability to provide competent pilots. In fact, besides contributing sub-

[1] G. M. Waller, *Samuel Vetch* (Chapel Hill, 1960), pp. 156 and 177 f. Cf. *ibid.* 114 ff. for the support of Sunderland and the Scottish peers.
[2] *The Walker Expedition to Quebec, 1711* (ed. G. S. Graham, Navy Rec. Soc. 1953), p. 25.

stantially to Nicholson's force of 2,300 at Albany for an overland strike at Montreal, the colony enlisted 10 per cent more men than it had promised for the naval prong of the great venture. At no other time, perhaps, was there closer identity of interests between Boston and London. In place of anticipated victory there occurred one of the most ignominious failures in British history. On the night of 20 August o.s., near Ile aux Oeufs in the St Lawrence estuary, a gross error of navigation caused the loss of 7 transports and 800 lives on the rocks of a lee shore.[1] Walker and Hill, supported by all the naval captains, chose to regard this disaster as decisive, though Vetch attempted to argue the harmful consequences of turning back. Blaming the pilots and the shortage of provisions, the expedition divided and returned home. In England, Massachusetts was made the scapegoat. The Board of Trade, which had earlier served as a balance wheel in colonial administration, publicizing the interests of the various parts of the empire and seeking reconciliation where they conflicted, avoided an enquiry. Nicholson, Vetch and Jeremiah Dummer, the agent for Massachusetts in London, were unable to convince the British public of the true causes of the débâcle. Equally futile were attempts by New York, Massachusetts and New Hampshire to renew the expedition. Pontchartrain correctly judged that the danger to New France had passed. The immediate consequence was a savage renewal of frontier attacks on New England.

The desire of English colonists for peace was tempered, especially in New England, by fear that their interests would be sacrificed to those of Britain in Europe, as their experience of the strategic emphasis of the Succession War, with its belated and half-hearted attention to the problem of Canada, rather strongly suggested. On the other hand, if war had brought no decisive example of the value of imperial co-operation, fewer colonists than in 1689 now questioned that it was better to be within than without the aggressive State which spanned the Atlantic. Superficially at least, there was one empire, unenthusiastically monarchical, emphatically Protestant, readily accepting the pursuit of wealth as a fundamental objective. Senior administrative servants alone noted with disquiet the absorption of colonists in parochial or at best provincial issues. While recognizing the seeds of imperial disintegration, however, they offered no real remedies to avert it, despite the opportunities which revolution and war provided. For them the collapse of the Dominion of New England had proved decisive. As the older administrators like Randolph, Blathwayt and the elder Povey passed away, their ideas of centralization, which had dominated the last quarter of the seventeenth century, withered. No future administrator was to match their influence, no statesman to emerge who would devote comparable thought to the underlying problem of an empire of the North Atlantic. Henceforth, in

[1] Graham, *Walker Expedition*, pp. 33 ff.

England, imperial thinking rarely moved far from bald economic objectives. It tended to regard political relationships in terms of fixed formulas, and political problems were confronted, if at all, on a provincial and not on an imperial level. It is suggestive that most of the men who had thought imperially in any constructive sense resided permanently or temporarily in North America itself: William Byrd II, Vetch and Nairne, and governors such as Joseph Dudley, Francis Nicholson and Robert Hunter. Their constant aim was to facilitate communication so that the English in Europe would better understand the problems and attitudes of their kinsmen overseas. In their hearts they also wanted the centre of imperial gravity to begin to move westwards from the eastern edge of the Atlantic. Growth of population and of urban centres nourished belief in the importance of North America; survival through a quarter-century of war gave assurance that the English settlements had a future.

The years since 1688 had brought one striking gain to the empire. New England no longer seemed seriously at odds with the mother country, even if Massachusetts retained exalted notions of the power of her General Court and a certain independence of outlook. Assembly powers which the circumstances of war had advanced elsewhere, particularly in New York, had been held in check by strong governors. Although Dummer kept himself closely informed of the peace negotiations, there was no claim to separate representation at Utrecht. Few New Englanders, indeed, were prepared to echo Dudley's claim that it was 'a happy peace'[1] until, like Sewall, they had studied its terms, but Sewall asked no more than just recognition of the contribution his province had made to victory. In part, this new if relative docility of official Massachusetts is explained by the serious domestic problems she now had on her hands. The frontier of New England had suffered severely. In Maine not a single town was founded between 1675 and 1713; over 100 miles of coast had become destitute of inhabitants. There had been practically no settlement in New Hampshire, and Connecticut had planted only a few towns. For this the loss of five or six thousand of their youth in a generation was partly responsible, although it is also significant that New Englanders on the move now preferred to settle elsewhere. In offering extravagant praise of the Peace, therefore, Cotton Mather was convinced that he had the support of all thinking men on both sides of the Atlantic. Yet he noted with unease that in this he divided from the multitude, who were convinced of betrayal, while Governor Nicholson of Newfoundland wrote of 'traitorous, factious and ill-natured pamphlets industriously spread abroad among the people' and called for loyal prints to counteract them.[2] In Maryland and Virginia economic distress overshadowed the joys of peace; William

---

[1] 'Sewall Diary', pt. I, *Mass. Hist. Soc. Coll.* 5th ser., vol. VI, p. 356. For the peace terms affecting North America, see above, p. 470.
[2] *Cal. S.P. Col., 1712–14*, nos. 523, 731.

Byrd II had noted indifferently the opening of negotiations. For the people of New York there remained apprehension at French plans for settlement along the Great Lakes and the Mississippi.

For the French communities the close of hostilities ended a fear of abandonment. Louisiana still struggled for survival, but the French were well placed to develop their hold on the interior lakes and rivers. Quebec, which had escaped conquest through good fortune, was further exposed by the cession of Acadia and Newfoundland at Utrecht. Yet the outworks of New France were not entirely destroyed. The boundaries of Acadia were left to be determined by a commission of the two powers which would not in fact meet for forty years, while the Ile Royale (Cape Breton) was retained and work on its fortification begun as soon as Placentia was surrendered. For her part, through the accession of Nova Scotia and the establishment of a British garrison at Annapolis Royal, New England had gained further protection on the Maine frontier, as did her fishermen on the Banks. In contrast to the neglect of Hudson's Bay at Ryswick, Bolingbroke had insisted on its total acquisition as a prerequisite of peace. On balance, however, French capacity to threaten the English had been shown to be more dangerous at the end of a quarter-century of war than before.

In the fighting on land English and French alike had suffered relatively light casualties, their Indian auxiliaries more severely. In the 1690s the tribes allied to the French lost perhaps only a hundred warriors, whereas over a thousand Iroquois perished by battle and disease; in the next war 800 Tuscaroras died in a single engagement. In the Nine Years War, 650 Anglo-Americans are estimated to have been killed or died in captivity.[1] Where a marked decrease in population took place—that of Albany county fell by a quarter—migration through fear of the enemy was the cause, not death by slaughter. For the Spanish Succession War the figures are even lower: New England suffered about 200 deaths, the Carolinians about 150; the French lost not more than 50 killed, compared with 300 in the previous war. These almost trifling losses were more than compensated for the French by a high birth-rate and for the English by immigration.[2] After prolonged conflict the population ratio of the two empires remained unchanged. Each had roughly doubled in size during the wars, New France to 19,000 and the English mainland colonies to 400,000. The most significant change was in the overwhelming absolute increase of English preponderance.

[1] H. H. Peckham, *The Colonial Wars, 1689–1762* (Chicago, 1964), p. 53.

[2] Immigration to New France practically ceased after 1680, but the annual rate of increase fell below 2 per cent only during the second half of the Spanish Succession War; in the 1690s it was for a time as high as 5 per cent. The census figures given by W. A. Riddell, *The Rise of Ecclesiastical Control in Quebec* (New York, 1916), p. 35, are as follows: *1681*: 9,677; *1688*: 10,303; *1692*: 11,075; *1695*: 12,786; *1698*: 13,815; *1706*: 16,417; *1712*: 18,440; *1716*: 20,531.

PORTUGAL AND HER EMPIRE, 1680–1720

I N the seventeenth century the Portuguese imperial economy revolved round sugar, tobacco and salt; in the eighteenth, without completely foresaking its old staples, it came to be based on gold, leather and wine. Its position, pivoted on the great entrepôt of Lisbon, lay somewhere between Anglo-Dutch capitalism, which dominated it in part, and the colonial economies which it was itself shaping and out of which a new national entity, Brazil, was slowly emerging. The dynamics of this profound structural transformation can most rapidly be grasped, and its phases demarcated, if we begin by looking at the course of prices.[1]

Until the peace of 1668 with Spain, some Portuguese prices had been rising gently while others remained stable. The very gradual increase in wheat prices levelled off at Evora from 1667, and in the Azores from 1670, until 1693; and this also happened at Viana do Castelo, though there the prices of rye and maize fell between 1680 and 1693. After 1693, prices in all three markets, as well as in Braganza—in the extreme north, beyond the mountains and isolated from imports—rose to a peak in 1710–11, home-grown cereals ahead of imported. There followed a cyclical decline which reached its lowest point in 1718—three years later in Braganza—and the long-term trend continued very slightly downwards or level until 1740. The price of rice—almost entirely imported, from Valencia, Genoa, Venice—fell in 1680–90, rose to a peak in 1709, then continued to fall until after 1728. What happened to the major export commodities[2] of metropolitan Portugal? The price of olive oil in Lisbon, after remaining constant until 1670, went down until about 1692 and then rose steadily to a peak in 1712 (apart from a cyclical depression about 1708, also affecting cereals, though more briefly); after 1712, a really marked downward trend set in until after 1728. Salt, the main export, was sold to the Dutch at a price which did not change between 1649 and 1690; 1,480 *reis* per *muid* f.o.b., duty (660–700 *reis*) paid.[3] Then suddenly the famine of 1693 doubled the price, which in 1709 reached the unprecedented figure of 6,000–7,000 *reis*. Thereafter the fever began to subside; in 1713 the *muid* sold for 2,650 *reis*, in 1714 for 3,650. In outline, therefore, the course of domestic prices may be schematized as depression, 1669–92; general recovery, 1693–1715; and a new fall, or no change, during the next two decades.

---

[1] See below, ch. XXIII (2) for the general movement of prices in Europe.

[2] Cf. vol. V, pp. 386–7.

[3] The *Misericórdia* (hospital) of Setúbal sold it at 978 *reis*, at least from 1660 to 1690. In Lisbon and Aveiro it was cheaper: 1,250 *reis* f.o.b. A *muid* (*moio*) of salt at Lisbon contained about 23 bushels; 400 *reis* = 1 *cruzado*, the silver crown worth roughly 2s. 6d. sterling.

Colonial re-exports fared differently: there was a spectacular collapse. Between 1668 and 1688, the price of cloves slumped by 72 per cent, tobacco by 65 per cent, and sugar—a much more important commodity, which began falling in 1660—by 41 per cent.[1] The arrival of large sugar convoys from Brazil in 1672 and 1675 caused immediate anxiety, in view of the large stocks already accumulated; in Brazil itself sugar-planting contracted, and in 1686 ships seeking freight in the Tagus turned back empty for lack of Brazilian sugars. All the Portuguese ports, indeed, slowly fell into a decline. Compared with the average for 1654–68, 20 per cent ships fewer entered Faro in 1669–83. Ships were not fully loaded and freight rates fell to unprofitable levels, according to the Tobacco Board (*Junta*) in 1682: before 1680, already, twists of tobacco had been rotting in the bonded warehouses of Oporto and Lisbon. By 1683 the French consul was painting a dramatic picture of the total ruin of the Lisbon exchange, 'there being no longer either the money or the merchants to buy the goods, with the result that one can sell them only to people who are likely to go bankrupt or to be caught by the Inquisition'.[2] As early as 1675, in fact, Lisbon had been shaken by a crop of bankruptcies. This long depression was not specifically Portuguese. The same phenomenon certainly existed in Venice[3] and there were symptoms of it in Spain. But what forces conditioned it in Portugal?

In 1666 a smallpox epidemic of unprecedented violence swept almost the whole of Brazil but especially the sugar-producing north-east, which suffered serious losses in manpower. This opened a prolonged production crisis. Moreover, Brazilian exports were now encountering a foreign competition[4] reinforced by systematic mercantilist policies and changes in the slave market. First England, then Colbert, erected barriers against foreign colonial produce; the French, English and Dutch still loaded sugar and tobacco in Lisbon and Oporto, but mainly for sale outside their national markets, which on the whole were lost to the Portuguese. The Dutch, in the Gulf of Guinea, aggravated the situation by hounding Portuguese slavers; in Angola, the littoral was drained of human life and the price of negroes rose as the manhunt extended into the interior. Taxes on the Brazilian plantations had been raised by the War of Independence and Catherine of Braganza's dowry. After 1660, in fact, lured by the higher profit rates of industry, the sugar planters increasingly went over to the production of spirits, investing more in crushing-mills and in the pastures required to feed the horses and oxen used in these *engenhos*. Hence the cane available for crushing diminished while sugar-mills multiplied and

---

[1] At Amsterdam, a major market, the price fluctuated around 0·69 guilders a pound during the 1650s, between 0·32 and 0·40 guilders 1660–70, and between 0·27 and 0·32 guilders 1671–82, finally reaching its lowest point of 0·23 in 1686–8.

[2] Des Granges, Lisbon, 7 June 1683 (Paris, Arch. Nat., Aff. Etr. B I, no. 646).

[3] Information from Prof. Cipolla; for Venice, cf. below, pp. 555–6.

[4] Cf. below, pp. 851 ff., for competition in sugar and tobacco.

ompetition between them intensified; and there were rises in the prices
of slaves—even more necessary in the mills than on the plantations—and
of timber and other supplies. In the case of tobacco, the soil was showing
clear signs of exhaustion about 1678. One difficulty and another drove the
owners of plantations and sugar-mills not only to borrow, but (as early as
1668) to sell their future produce to moneylenders at a discount of one-
third. In short, Brazilian profits were being curtailed by a pincer movement
constituted, on one hand, by the fall in market prices due to international
competition, especially from the West Indies, and on the other by inelastic
and even rising costs, due as much to international competition for slaves
as to the presence of too many producers in a limited market.

The trade between Cadiz and Spanish America was also passing through
a difficult stage. In 1675 no galleons returned from Cartagena; in 1676
they brought little 'because of the poor sale of merchandise' in the Indies.
More merchandise was steadily coming from China to Acapulco and the
prices of European goods collapsed. In 1682, 1684, 1686 and 1690, likewise, there was not enough trade to demand a Mexican *flota*; New Spain
was overflowing with too many unsold goods.[1] The arrivals of silver at
Cadiz continued to fall off. Together with the difficulties which Dutch
trade itself had been encountering since 1668, this impoverished the
circulation of money in Portugal, where the Mint registers record a fall
in arrivals from 1669–70, despite driblets derived from Spanish purchases
of sugar, tobacco, linens and negroes. For decades silver had been flowing
from Portuguese ports to northern Europe; but now, with smaller returns
in kind, foreigners were taking out still more in cash. In conditions of
restricted money supply, this 'bleeding' became serious after 1665; ten
years later, a third of the country's imports had to be paid for in specie.

The social and political environment intensified these conditions.[2] There
was a longstanding anti-capitalist reaction, widespread hostility towards
the merchant mentality itself, manifested in attacks on companies and
business circles suspect of Judaism by the Inquisition. This reaction had its
ups and downs, of course, and its influence on government was anything
but steady; but in the 1670s the Inquisition was again unleashed. The
French consul Des Granges, an impartial observer, in 1683 unhesitatingly
blamed it for completing the ruin of the Lisbon market. But perhaps his
explanation needs reversing in part. Was not the increasing pressure of
the Inquisition fed by an anti-mercantile feeling itself stimulated by the
commercial depression? From 1668 to about 1693, the imperial economy
had undergone a prolonged depression dominated by a crisis in the sugar,
tobacco, silver and slave trades.

What were the countervailing forces which eventually brought recovery?

[1] *Memorias de Raimundo de Lantery, mercader de India en Cadiz* (ed. A. Picardo y
Gómez, Cadiz, 1949), pp. 134, 162, 205, 267.
[2] On the reorganization of government after 1640, see vol. V, ch. XVI.

On 27 July 1671 the French ambassador in Lisbon, Saint-Romain, had written:

I learnt recently that the Portuguese, offended that we are imposing new taxes on sugar, were thinking more strongly than ever of ways and means of setting up factories to produce ribbons and most other goods in Portugal, and that Duarte Ribeiro had been ordered to find and send them again as many workers as he can for every kind of manufacture.[1]

It was no accident that one of the cardinal works of Portuguese economic thought in the seventeenth century, the *Discurso sobre a Introdução das Artes neste Reino* (1675), should have been written by an ambassador to France, Duarte Ribeiro de Macedo (1618–80), whose position had exposed him to the thinking of Colbert. The commercial crisis led to an elaboration of economic doctrine. Indeed, since exports to France, England and Holland consisted essentially of sugar, tobacco, Spanish wool, and brazil-wood, and since these nations were now refusing to continue to buy most of these commodities, the Portuguese—unable either to procure enough foreign exchange or to go on indefinitely paying silver for silks, woollens, baizes, ribbons, spirits, cod, and their other imports—could move only in one direction: they must undertake at home the production of goods hitherto imported.

From 1670–1, industrial investment projects spawned from the hands of merchants and manufacturers, Portuguese as well as foreign; and the State itself adopted a policy of industrial development under the influence of two ministers of finance—Count Torre (later marquis of Fronteira) and Count Ericeira, who was formally to receive the title of Super-intendent of the Workshops and Factories of the Realm. Master crafts-men and workers from France, England and Venice—with their looms, frames, tools and drawings—were attracted to Portugal to found the first factories there and train a skilled indigenous labour force. Ribeiro de Macedo, in Paris, himself took the leading part in this recruitment and in the ruses by which it was accomplished. In Turin, Bluteau, a French Theatine cleric who had turned Portuguese agent, pursued the same objects. At the end of 1670 two Portuguese entrepreneurs established in Lisbon a furnace to produce crystal and plate glass and glassware by Venetian methods. Venetian masters set it up and supervised production; the State provided a site, advanced money, exempted them from duties on the imported equipment and materials, and from other taxes, for ten years; the manufacturers, craftsmen and other staff received various personal privileges; and the undertaking enjoyed a monopoly throughout the kingdom and the Atlantic islands. In 1671 a master draper and eight female workers arrived from Rouen with looms for making serges, bolting-cloth and other light woollens at Estremoz, which had plentiful supplies of water and olive oil and easy access to supplies of Spanish wool:

[1] Paris, Arch. Nat., Aff. Etr. B I, no. 644.

founded by the State, this factory was handed over to private enterprise in 1672. In that year four master hatters came from Paris, but beaver had to be imported and the Portuguese dyes were of poor quality, with consequent delays in production, which came to an end when French emissaries contrived to send two of the masters home in 1672 and 1675. Better success attended silks and other fabrics. In 1676-8, a series of measures encouraged the raising of silkworms, for which Bluteau drew up instructions at Ericeira's instigation. Silk-manufacturing rights at Lisbon were farmed in 1677 to Roland Duclos, who soon had fifty English looms at work, with a large spinning-mill; most of the workers were foreigners, but over 300 Portuguese were spooling silk in Lisbon alone. In 1683-4 Benoît Duclos built a French-model calender for the finishing of raw silk and several machines based on French and Venetian models for the finishing of taffetas and linens, installed ten looms, and brought in foreign dyers. Woollen manufactures multiplied between 1671 and 1681 around Covilhã and Fundão. In 1680 the manufacturers in Covilhã, three Portuguese, established a factory at Manteigas for baizes and serges, with ten looms; in that year Ericeira listed five large establishments already producing baizes and a sixth which was being set up at Tomar. The production of Castilian-style bed coverlets (*cobertores de papa*) was stimulated in 1682 by a new management and protective measures. Cloth manufactures were also started in São Miguel (Azores), which by 1686 was selling regularly to Brazil. Finally, there was ironworking. Before 1654, owing to the War of Independence, which made it difficult to get iron from Biscay, the State had reopened the forges and foundries in Tomar and Figueró dos Vinhos, under the direction of a French official, Dufour, whose son obtained four masters from France. In 1687 and 1692 the State reorganized these two centres; a third, for casting ordnance, had already been set up at Arega, at the confluence of the Alge and Zêzere. Production of nails and wrought-iron articles in the *Ribeira* (port) of Lisbon began in 1680.

To protect this industrialization, itself partly designed to reduce imports, sumptuary laws were promulgated as a direct attack on imports, not on luxury clothing as such. Ministers had thought of raising tariffs, but that would have infringed international treaties. Instead, for example, the pragmatic of February 1677 prohibited the use and sale within the realm of French hats, ribbons and luxury lace, Italian brocades, and the more expensive English and Dutch cloths; the 'new draperies' (baizes and serges) and English stockings, which together made up the bulk of imports, were not affected. In August 1688 a similar ordinance was applied to all druggets, at first so severely that the dress of the Portuguese became monotonous and dull.

But industrial and commercial policies were bound up with monetary. While the unfavourable trade balance was 'bleeding' Portugal of specie, increasing difficulties were experienced in buying coin and bullion from Spain. It should be recalled that monetary chaos reigned in Castile from 1640 to 1686;[1] under the tidal wave of steadily depreciating copper coinage silver was always at a premium and there was a confused collapse of prices In October 1686, to stop the outflow of silver, Spain raised the face value of her currency by 25 per cent and correspondingly reduced the weight of newly minted coins, so that the gold-silver ratio was now 16·48:1 (compared with 15·39:1 in England). This devaluation made a similar change inevitable in Portugal. Ericeira aimed not only at keeping the national market supplied, but also at a stable currency. In October 1685 the government sought unsuccessfully to prohibit the circulation of old coin below legal weight, and in May and August 1686 to force them to bear a milled edge and stamp. In 1688 the problem was taken firmly in hand After a night of feverish discussion and military precautions, devaluation was decreed on 4 July. Pending collection and milling, the old coins were accepted on weight. Under popular pressure the Crown bore part of the loss, but it was estimated that private citizens incurred two-thirds of it This general recoinage more than halved the quantity of money in circulation. Merchants retorted by sending old coin to Holland for milling and stamping, and thereafter for return to Portugal below the new legal weight. To counter this fraud, and under pressure of the Spanish devaluation, a decree of 4 August raised the nominal value of all gold and silver specie. The main effect was to endow Portugal with a reliable currency that stood firm throughout the next decades. Ericeira explained that the revaluation would 'encourage the entry of *patacas* and doubloons from Castile, without which it seems impossible for the ordinary trade of this Kingdom to subsist'.[2] As early as 1690 an abundance of coin was already noticeable. In April 1691 a Portuguese vessel took in at Alicante and Cadiz 40,000 piastres for Lisbon merchants; in August, a Genoese vessel brought 80,000 more from Cadiz. In 1693, the same Genoese would have embarked 160,000 piastres there, for Lisbon, if the Customs had allowed more than 20,000; in August another Genoese brought 50,000–60,000 piastres, which would have been more but for fear of a French naval squadron. In January 1695, a Tuscan vessel came in with some 100,000 piastres from Cadiz. When, in August 1697, a Genoese arrived with only 12,000–15,000 and a month later two others brought nothing Lisbon complained that its trade would suffer 'if the galleons do not arrive soon' in Cadiz.[3]

The revival of the Portuguese slave trade also aided economic recovery

[1] See vol. v, pp. 371–2.
[2] 'Papel sobre se levantar a moeda': Lisbon National Library, Fundo Geral 748, fo. 266 The *pataca* was strictly the Portuguese silver dollar, but the term was freely used to denote the Spanish piastre or piece of eight. The gold doubloon was the two-escudo Spanish piece.
[3] Paris, Arch. Nat., Aff. Etr. B1, no. 650.

It had suffered badly from Dutch attacks in the Thirty Years War, and after 1640 the long War of Independence had cut off the Portuguese from the profitable supply of slaves to the Castilian Indies. As soon as peace made it possible, government and private business conducted a vigorous counter-offensive to recapture part of the Guinea trade and oust the Dutch from their now dominant place in supplying Spanish America. Freire de Andrade, governor of São Tomé island 1678–80, was ordered to build a fort on the Dahomey coast—São João Baptista de Ajudá (Whydah), a strong-point which made possible some years later a whole chain of trading factories eastward along the shores of the Gulf of Guinea. Meanwhile the 'Cacheo Company of the Guinea Rivers and Coast' was formed by the king (as to one-third), four Lisbon capitalists (one of them French) and an Azorean, with a capital of 150,000 *cruzados* and a royal guarantee to lend it up to 200,000 at 4 per cent at need. Turning on the island of Principe as chief entrepôt, the Company's activities duly spread to the whole of West Africa (including Angola, although it did not have a monopoly there), as was beginning to be apparent by 1690. In 1692 it contracted with the Crown to supply slaves for the Maranhão captaincy in north-western Brazil, and early in 1693 with the Spanish asientist, Marín de Guzmán to provide the Indies with 4,000 negroes per annum, at prices ranging from 55,000 to 70,000 *reis*,[1] the buying price in Africa (8,000 *reis*) being guaranteed by the king of Portugal, who authorized the Company to take annually up to 1,500 Angola slaves—a limitation intended to ensure that a reserve would remain for Brazil: an additional 1,500 were to be taken from Cape Verde and 1,000 from Cacheo[2] and the Gold Coast. The total turnover was estimated at 1·6 m. *patacas*. The Asiento itself was obtained in 1696 and the Company's capital increased to 468,000 *cruzados*. Its success is suggested by the fact that one of its ships from Cartagena and Havana reached Lisbon in 1698 with 400,000 *livres* in silver; in April–May 1699 two vessels entered the Tagus with 120,000 piastres (with cargoes of hides, cochineal and cacao for Cadiz), and in November a third unloaded in the Azores (for fear of Algerian corsairs) 20,000 piastres and 2,000 quintals of Campeache dyewood. Naturally the French and English went all out to share in these windfalls —by supplying the Company with regular stores, chartering ships to it, or even sharing in the capital. In 1697–8 the English ambassador in Lisbon made great efforts in this direction, in the name of London merchants, England being prepared to make even a disadvantageous agreement for the sake of access to the Indies.[3]

[1] The Spaniards were to pay 150 piastres (plus freight, food and 20 per cent insurance) for each *peça de Indias* (a negro of standard measurements and health, aged 15 to 25), half to be paid at Cumaná, half at Cadiz: G. Scelle, *La Traite négrière*, vol. ii, pp. 23–31.

[2] This settlement was the effective centre of Portuguese authority between the Gambia and Sierra Leone, the old 'Guinea of Cape Verde'.

[3] Arch. Nat., Aff. Etr. b i, no. 650: letters from Rouillé, Lisbon, 10 and 24 June 1698.

Some of the *patacas* earned by the Cacheo Company found their way to Goa,[1] and so helped to revive Portugal's trade by the Cape. During the great depression of their Atlantic economy the Portuguese had again begun to take an interest in this, not only to recapture their old share of Eastern trade, but also to divert the gold of the Monomotapa[2] to the Atlantic and to turn Mozambique into a source of slaves for Brazil, thereby making good the deficiencies of Guinea. Open trade between Brazil and the Indian Ocean had been advocated in 1671, but it was only in March 1680 that an *alvará* (decree) authorized it and then the expected flow of East African gold did not occur. Meanwhile, a new effort had been made to colonize South-East Africa. In October 1677 four ships left Lisbon for Mozambique with 600–700 men and 50 families; in April 1679 another two followed with 150 soldiers and 30 families; and in April 1680 a flyboat went out with men and women. The continuity of this effort is remarkable, considering the havoc wrought among the emigrants by disease. The government attached so much importance to it that the viceroy in Goa, Luís de Mendonça, was replaced so that he could supervise the establishment at Kilimane in person.

The trade between Lisbon, Goa and Macao had been languishing for decades. In 1672, it is true, three Indiamen had returned from China with pepper, calicoes, carpets, silk counterpanes and diamonds, worth more than 4 m. *cruzados*; but in 1673, when silver was short in Lisbon, the number of vessels outward had to be reduced; in 1675 it was intended to fit out five but only one sailed, although the three which returned from Goa were 'quite richly laden'. The two homeward Indiamen of 1680 brought little enough, however, and the two of 1689 so little that they had to seek a sugar freight at Bahia. The Indiaman of 1690 would have arrived empty had the English and Dutch not freighted it because of war risk to their own shipping—and even so it was necessary to load sugar and tobacco in Brazil, as was also done by the Indiaman of 1692. About 1675 two contrasted solutions had been under consideration in Portugal. Ribeiro de Macedo, supported by Fr António Vieira, proposed that cinnamon, cloves, pepper and other spices and drugs be introduced into Brazil from the East, as the best means of destroying Dutch trade there. Others thought more of imitating the Dutch by setting up an East India Company; on his return from Goa in 1689 the ex-viceroy, Count Alvor, returned to this idea with the backing of the secretary of state, Foios Pereira. But at that time the promise of Crown assistance did not suffice to overcome merchant apathy. Such a company was nevertheless established in 1693, with a capital of 500,000 *cruzados* wholly subscribed by private individuals,

---

[1] Arch. Nat., Aff. Etr. B I, no. 650, 8 April 1698. For the French Asiento, see above, p. 364.
[2] The dynastic name given to the paramount chiefs of the Bantu Makaranga confederacy and so to their 'empire', which (though already disintegrating) was believed to embrace the gold-bearing regions of what is now Rhodesia.

under eight Portuguese and four Genoese directors, the latter subscribing heavily. The king supplied the ships, charging only freight to the company, in which he had a share. Expectations centred on tobacco sales in the East. Economically the moment was propitious, for Dutch Eastern trade was stagnating[1] and in war-time Dutch and English alike were disposed to use Portuguese bottoms. The French East India Company went further, seeking participation in the Portuguese company in order to destroy the Dutch. Another company, with a capital of 600,000 *cruzados*, was founded at Goa in 1695 to trade within the East, at first without participation from metropolitan Portugal, although in 1698 it was compelled to admit this by the Crown, which in 1700 arranged for the merger of the two companies. Of their combined capital of 700,000 *cruzados* two-thirds belonged to Goanese; subscriptions also came from an influential Provençal, Pierre d'Oleolis, and two rich Italians.

It is noticeable that these companies were not launched till 1690 or later—when the recession had begun to give way to a recovery—and that the king took a personal interest in them. In 1698 the three ships for Goa took out more than 500,000 *patacas* in specie (60 per cent of the total value of the cargoes) and coral worth more than 200,000 *patacas* (25 per cent); the Indiaman of 1699 carried more than 300,000 *patacas* in specie and much merchandise. The Eastern trade was now regarded as flourishing. Net profits of 35 per cent were obtained by trade in goods, 30–40 per cent by trading in *patacas*. Outward cargoes were mainly specie and tobacco (on Company or Crown account), coral, Italian paper, Dutch woollens. Uncut diamonds constituted the most valuable imports, which also included cloth of gold and silver, damasks and other silks, brightly coloured piece goods for the Angola slave trade, quilted bed-covers, calicoes, porcelains, cabinets and chests, saltpetre, pepper, indigo, musk and ambergris.

This was a fragile prosperity nevertheless. On the Swahili coast of East Africa, thinly peopled by the Portuguese, Muslim resentments had long been accumulating. Convoys to India had been harassed in the 1660s by the maritime power of Pate (Patta), whose sultan had obtained Arab assistance for besieging Mozambique itself in 1670.[2] In 1698 the Omani Arabs, having taken possession of Pate and Zanzibar, captured Mombasa after three years' siege[3]—a severe blow to the ivory trade. Further south, Portuguese monopoly of the gold and slave trades of Zambesia still had substance, despite malaria, tribal war, and the occasional appearance of other European trading vessels, mainly English. The Zambesi delta yielded rice, wheat and sugar; to the south-west, producing cotton and timber,

---

[1] Cf. below, pp. 856 ff.

[2] E. Axelson, *Portuguese in South-East Africa, 1600–1700* (Johannesburg, 1960), pp. 141–3.

[3] See C. R. Boxer and C. de Azevedo, *Fort Jesus and the Portuguese in Mombasa* (1960), pp. 58–73.

Portuguese estates linked Sofala with Sena, the seat of government and home of the wealthiest slaving landholders. The Portuguese in these parts, while usually leasing Crown lands, were largely a law to themselves. 'Everybody in the Rivers wants to govern', wrote the viceroy at Goa in 1694,[1] at a time when Portuguese trading-posts in Karangaland were being overrun by the Rozvi chieftain Changamire, who had succeeded in detaching the Monomotapa himself from his normal allegiance; the trade and mission outpost of Tete was only spared by Changamire's death in 1695. At the end of the century the captaincy of Mozambique was a house divided against itself and against the Crown, whose captain-contractors, even when they had the qualities of a governor, stayed too briefly to reduce its half-caste feudatories and their private armies to obedience. Though new sources of gold were being reported, its once great prosperity, like the evangelical zeal of its missionaries, seemed a thing of the past. This stagnancy had implications for the towns of Portuguese India which traded with it, indeed for Portuguese power in the Indian Ocean as a whole.

Before 1700 the surviving Portuguese cities in India—in Gujarat and the Konkan—had fallen into decay. Diu and Chaul were already ruined by the rival European development of the ports of Surat and Bombay; Damão and Bassein suffered increasingly from Mahratta attacks upon the landed estates which now provided their only source of revenue; Goa itself, where the inhabitants could no longer afford to maintain their stately houses in repair, was 'largely abandoned' by 1687.[2] At that date the whole colonial population probably included less than 3,000 male whites and half-castes, consignments from the home country having dwindled in some years to as few as 150 men:[3] the bulk even of the urban upper classes consisted of 'Portuguesed' Indian Christians. Upon the loss or impoverishment of their own possessions large groups of Indo-Portuguese had migrated to, or remained from force of circumstances in, territories under foreign control. Many settled on the Coromandel coast—with the Danes at Tranquebar, the French at Pondicherry, and particularly the English at Madras, where their numbers increased from roughly 3,000 in the 1670s to 9,000 in the early 1700s. In Bengal, during the same period, the Portuguese-speaking element was assessed at between 20,000 and 34,000 persons, of whom about 8,000 were domiciled at Hugli, the precursor of modern Calcutta, and at least 2,000 at Chittagong. A total of several thousands continued to reside at Malacca, Colombo, Negapatam, and the Malabar ports, now occupied by the Dutch. The status of these expatriates varied widely. Some, in native principalities, held honourable posts as technicians, especially as artillerymen, in which capacity they

[1] Quoted by Axelson, p. 184.
[2] *O Chronista de Tissuary*, ed. J. H. Cunha Rivara (4 vols. 1865–6), vol. I, p. 229.
[3] India Office Library, Lisbon Transcripts, 'Noticias da India', MS. Engl. tr. vol. I, p. 389.

were supposed to excel: in the early eighteenth century Portuguese mercenaries in Mogul service at Chittagong are depicted as the 'domineering lords' of the place. Others figure as prominent merchants, as at Batavia and Madras, where the English Council reported in 1680 that 'our greatest income arises from the Customes upon their Commerce'.[1] At Hugli, by contrast, the majority were reduced to poverty, in such vocations as innkeeper, petty official and inferior artisan; the same was true in general of those in Malabar and Ceylon. Ethnically, these Indo-Portuguese minorities tended to be absorbed by intermarriage with natives or foreign Europeans, their complexion varying 'even from the Coal-black to a light Tawney'.[2] Culturally, however, they retained their corporate identity to a remarkable extent, even influencing those groups to which they were affiliated: among the Dutch this was so much the case that children reared in the colonies could scarcely use their own tongue, preferring a corrupt form of Portuguese. The Portuguese language was, in fact, the most lasting monument of Portuguese greatness, surviving throughout the eighteenth century as a medium of international trade, diplomacy and missionary activity on the Indian seaboards.[3]

The general economic recovery manifest after 1692 was more fundamentally connected with trades other than the East Indian. As soon as the Nine Years War broke out the Portuguese were sending their vessels to Dutch, English and French ports—with salt, sugar, tobacco, oranges, brazilwood and wool—to take advantage of the reluctance to ship under belligerent flags, the charterers being very often foreigners. In August 1689 not a single twist of tobacco remained in Lisbon and the price rose by more than 30 per cent: an association of New Christians[4] and rich merchants was soon formed which bought it up, good and bad, and controlled the entire market. At the end of 1689 the government considered it superfluous to lower the sugar duties to encourage sales: the arrival of the Brazilian convoy in 1690 caused no fall in prices, and when the French clapped a 15 per cent duty on Portuguese sugar unloaded in Marseilles and Brittany, the minister of finance, the marquis of Alegrete, explained that the French alone would suffer as the Italians would take it all. But all northern Europe was at this juncture seriously short of salt, oil, wine and wool. Portugal's remarkable recovery was not therefore based simply on the re-export of her colonial produce, but also on the export of metropolitan Portuguese and the re-export of Spanish (and Spanish American) commodities—Faro and Setúbal as well as Lisbon serving as entrepôts for this traffic. Whole convoys of France's enemies arrived in Portuguese

---

[1] *Notes and Extracts from the Government Records in Fort St George, Madras, 1670–81*, ed. W. Huddleston (4 vols. 1871–4), vol. IV, p. 14.

[2] Dampier, *Voyages and Discoveries*, ed. N. M. Penzer and C. Wilkinson (1931), p. 111.

[3] This paragraph has been contributed by Dr K. J. Crowther. Cf. vol. V, ch. XVII.

[4] Converted and/or crypto-Jewish: cf. Sp. *Marrano*.

ports and went away fully laden. The English in 1693 bought more Portuguese products than ever before, besides much silver. The Swedes and Danes also sent more merchantmen, though under armed escort. Portuguese shipping none the less continued to benefit. In 1694 the average price of food exports had quadrupled by comparison with pre-war, and French observers noted with envy that the English and Portuguese had grown very rich since then. This enormous boom so much stimulated production in Brazil that at the beginning of 1698 Portugal again experienced a glut of sugar, whose price collapsed, although both sugar and tobacco rose very high in 1699. Spain, Italy, Hamburg, Holland and England, in fact, continued to buy everything. Moreover, new outlets had opened up. Catalonia, for instance, was beginning to buy Portuguese salted fish, and Brazilian tobacco became one of the staple Catalan trades *ca.* 1700. Again, while in 1700 the Hamburg refineries were using raw sugar from many different sources, it was Brazil that provided the lion's share. With some interruptions this general prosperity lasted until 1714, when the French consul could still write that 'the volume of trade is increasing every day',[1] the average value of imports for the years 1708–13, from England, Holland and Hamburg alone, amounting to 16 m. *cruzados.*

Of the products of Portuguese soil, two were mainstays of this general recovery—olive oil and wine. The War of Independence had ravaged the olive groves of the Alentejo and slowed down planting in the Beira Baixa; but after 1668 replanting went on in the southern province and steadily spread north during the last third of the century, stimulated by demand from overseas and Baltic markets. In 1691 Lisbon alone sent to northern Europe (as far as Danzig) 10,000 pipes of olive oil, Oporto 5,000—a sixth and a seventh respectively of the total volumes of exports from each port. Oil-presses multiplied everywhere, particularly along the rivers, where advantage could be taken of water-power, and notably in Santarém (which had over 200 presses) and thence north and north-eastwards along the Tagus, the Zêzere and the Nabão up to Coimbra, while there were other concentrations around Vila Viçosa and Alcácer do Sal.

Still more important was the extension of vineyards, including vintage growths in several regions of mainland Portugal and in the islands. About 1715, 25,000 pipes of *vin ordinaire* and 5,000 of brandy were gathered every year on the islands of Pico and Fayal in the Azores, where wine production increased fivefold in some forty years; it was sold to Brazil, the Lesser Antilles, New England and even (at first in war-time but later regularly) to Northern Europe; with the growth of the Baltic market viticulture spread also to São Miguel, which produced *ca.* 4,000 pipes about 1725. But if in quantity the Azorean wines surpassed the Madeiran,

[1] Viganego, 30 Jan. 1714 (Paris, Arch. des Aff. Etr., Correspondance Politique, Portugal 46, fo. 18).

the value of the latter was greater. Towards 1718 Madeira produced *ca.* 20,000 pipes of Malmsey and 800 pipes of brandy a year—a tenfold increase compared with 1650—chiefly for New World markets. The English and Dutch were always the best customers for madeiras: in 1690 some fifty English merchantmen loaded them, for Barbados or England, and in 1693 more than sixty English and Dutch ships came to buy them; in the eighteenth century the West Indies and New England consumed on average *ca.* 9,000 pipes a year and the Dutch Antilles between 400 and 500, paid for with manufactures from England or food from Holland and North America. As Adam Smith later explained, 'Madeira wine, not being a European commodity, could be imported directly into America and the West Indies' without infringing the Navigation Acts.[1] A map of Portugal in 1700 shows almost no region without its vineyards. We find them even on high ground in the interior where they had later to be abandoned. During the previous quarter-century planting had continued to spread, as is strikingly illustrated by the erection of the famous *solares* —the country houses of the wealthier landowners—of the Basto country (near the river Tamega), which had been poor, underpopulated and lacking in any buildings worthy of mention before the Restoration; now the population increased, as the fame of their green wines, whose production became considerable, began to spread. Since the Middle Ages, of course, vines had been planted along the Douro and for many centuries they continued to conquer the slopes: yet it was only some time after 1600 that the luscious wine which would be called port was developed, and it was particularly after 1688 that so many vines were planted here, and that such serious efforts were made to improve the quality of the vintage. Colbert's 1667 tariff and the war of 1672 had led Dutch wine merchants to concentrate less on the Bordelais and to turn to Malaga, Alicante, Jerez, the Canaries, Setúbal and Lisbon. The English followed their example and the Nine Years War confirmed their preference for the Spanish and Portuguese markets.[2] In 1690, when at least 24 Portuguese vessels sailed from Oporto alone for England, they were buying *ca.* 14,000 pipes in all; in 1692 England imported 12,953 pipes of Portuguese wine, compared with 14,178 from Spain, whereas some years earlier imports of Portuguese had amounted to less than half of Spanish. From 1692 to 1712 imports of Portuguese were ten times those of French and three times those of Spanish wines. Holland, Hamburg and the Baltic seaboard remained more modest outlets. The production of the Upper Douro vineyards was to rise to 55,000–60,000 pipes, half exported and half consumed in metropolitan and overseas Portugal.

This far-reaching agricultural movement, which benefited from the

---

[1] *The Wealth of Nations* (ed. E. Cannan, 2 vols. 1904), vol. II, p. 4.
[2] Cf. below, pp. 845–6. By 6 Anne c. 27 the pipe was defined as 126 wine gallons—that is, exactly half a tun, although today it usually measures only 105 gallons.

trade recovery which it in turn encouraged, brought new social and political forces into play. The policy of industrialization suddenly collapsed. Ericeira, its moving spirit, committed suicide in 1692. It is true that the marquis of Fronteira, strictly the first promoter of a coherent policy of ship and factory construction, continued for some time yet to be one of the *Vèdores da Fazenda* (Lords of the Treasury); but his influence diminished, or rather, for he owned vineyards, his policy changed. The helm was taken over by other hands, which turned it to a different direction. As the manufacturing policy had been an answer to the trade depression, so it seemed to lose its *raison d'être* with the return of prosperity. The 'industrialists' yielded place to the great wine and olive growers. The marquis of Alegrete, a large landowner especially interested in vineyards, now became president of the Council of Finance, while the president of the Council of Justice was the duke of Cadaval, also a big wine grower. Although the duke was in high politics on and off from 1658 to his death in 1727, his influence suffered several eclipses and it is significant that one of these had corresponded precisely with the dominance of Ericeira.

In the seventeenth century and even at the beginning of the eighteenth, Portuguese wine producers and merchants found themselves in some ways at a competitive disadvantage. The quality of French and Spanish wines and brandies was more highly esteemed; they were bought indeed, notably from Bordeaux and Catalonia, for drinking even in Portugal and Brazil.[1] In 1685 the traditional freedom of entry was abandoned for the first time in favour of import restrictions, applied particularly to Spanish growths and fairly rigorously enforced for a few years, although forgotten during the 1690s and the early eighteenth century. During the Succession War, imports from France ceased and production in metropolitan Portugal and the Azores, under the tuition of French experts, increased considerably; but at the same time the high prices ruling for wines and brandies attracted increased quantities from Catalonia, Majorca and Castile. In face of this, the restrictions were again enforced in 1708, this time comprehensively, and solemnly renewed in August 1710. What is striking is the effectiveness of the Portuguese policy in this instance, in spite of strong foreign protests, by comparison with the short-lived enforcement of the earlier restrictions—proof that powerful interests were at work. In fact, customs policy was now shaped by Cadaval, Alegrete and Fronteira on behalf of the great landowners, enabling them to sell their wines at a much higher price, and on a much bigger scale, than before. After 1709 there were complaints that vineyards were displacing arable, and that cereal imports were increasing as a result. By then, however, the entire Portuguese nobility was interested in the enormous exports of wine, particularly to England.

[1] Beer also, recently introduced by foreigners and beginning to be brewed in the kingdom, was already alarming wine growers and merchants by the 1680s.

Thus, after 1692, the industrialization policy as a whole was abandoned; sumptuary laws fell into oblivion, and the import restrictions of 1687–8 on such industrial goods as pottery, tiles (*azulejos*) and glassware were lifted, as were the restrictions on beaver hats and black cloth. It is true that in November 1698 a new pragmatic went so far as to prescribe the form of male dress and prohibited for the first time the import of dyed cloth and woollen druggets, while allowing free entry to light silks and woollens, hats, silk ribbons and Breton linens, thus striking a blow at the English, whereas the earlier restrictions had been aimed at the French; but hardly had it been promulgated than it was generally assumed that it would be no more efficiently executed than the earlier ones. From 1692 onwards power was in the hands of the wine growers, the oil producers and the big merchants. The rise of manufacturing industry had proved only an interlude between two clearly defined periods in Portugal's economic and social history: the 'cycle' of sugar and tobacco from Brazil, of Setúbal salt and Cadiz silver, and the 'cycle' of port, madeira and Brazilian gold.

Following the increased duties on French wines in England in 1692–7,[1] the Portuguese paid less than half what their chief competitors paid on entry into that market—a preference that was to continue through the eighteenth century. In 1688 sales of port to England began to rise from an average of 572 pipes in the preceding decade to 6,668 in the next[2]—an increase over elevenfold. Not until 1718 was there such another jump. In total, Portuguese exports to England quadrupled between 1668–9 and 1699–1700, while imports from England doubled (and in the case of the new draperies trebled). The aggregate value of these imports rose to 250,000 *livres* in 1699, 277,190 in 1701, 460,465 in 1702, 714,241 in 1703. Thus, far from being checked by the pragmatic of 1698, imports from England almost trebled in 1699–1703: they reached a peak of 818,995 *livres* in 1705.

John Methuen, the brother of an English draper, as William III's envoy to Portugal till 1697, had witnessed the collapse of the policy of industrialization and seen the vineyard interest, with which he was on intimate terms, assume control. His son Paul succeeded him; but in 1702–3, when nothing less than Portugal's position in the Spanish Succession War was at stake, John Methuen himself returned to Lisbon, to seduce, if not to corrupt, her politicians. The economic treaty of 27 December 1703 stipulated two simple things. On her side, Portugal authorized the entry of

---

[1] As distinct from the prohibition on the import of French wines during the war.

[2] The annual averages are as follows: 6,668 pipes in 1688–97; 7,188 in 1698–1707; 9,644 in 1708–17; 17,692 in 1718–27. In 1704–12, port accounted for half of England's wine imports from Portugal. See A. Guerra Tenreiro, *O Douro. Esboços para sua história ecónomica: conclusões* (Oporto, 1944: separata dos *Anais do Instituto do Vinho do Porto*), pp. 105–8, which draws on C. Guerner, *Discurso analytico sobre o establecimento da Companhia Geral de Agricultura das Vinhas de Alto Douro* (Lisbon, 1920) [Ed.].

all English cloths, which had previously been imported more or less by stealth. In return, England granted preference to Portuguese over French wines, which were never to pay less than a third over and above the duties paid by the Portuguese—a concession, however, which lagged some way behind the actual proportion between the two sets of duties, for the Portuguese did not then pay (and were never to pay) more than half. The Commercial Treaty known after Methuen, therefore, did no more than set the seal of legality on two aspects of a *de facto* trading situation. Instead of itself revolutionizing anything, it was much rather the outcome of the Portuguese political somersault of 1692. On the other hand, while from one point of view the treaty was a by-product of the war, it must be said that the war itself delayed that development of the trade in wine and cloth to which the treaty gave its blessing.[1] Moreover, the Dutch also drew benefit from it, as in August 1705 the Council of Finance ordered the lifting of the duty on Dutch cloth notwithstanding the pragmatics, while a royal order of February 1706 formally removed other restrictions previously in force on the ground that the English already enjoyed such exemptions—a clever move to promote Anglo-Dutch competition.

During the seventeenth century Portugal always looked towards France, whose opposition to Spain had been one of the pillars of her independence. The threat which overhung Portugal remained a purely territorial one: hence it was on the support of a territorial power that she relied. The French, for their part, were only too happy to have a dagger permanently pointed at the Spanish flank, but other interests impelled them to support Portugal, especially from 1664. Thus, with the formation of the French East India Company Louis XIV's diplomacy aimed at the cession of a Portuguese factory in India and freedom of trade with Portugal's Eastern ports. This last objective was partly realized in 1669–70, except at Macao. When, however, the problem of the Spanish succession first became acute in 1670 and the French proposed a partition by which they should obtain Vigo or Mazagan (in Morocco), or a foothold in India, nobody in Portugal was tempted by the opportunity of a bargain except the queen (herself French) and two great nobles. Portugal preferred to adhere to a strictly defensive policy. She was satisfied to have avoided a war of succession of her own in 1668;[2] and in 1687 the future of her dynasty was secured by the second marriage of Peter II.

[1] In 1704 imports from England were 9 per cent higher than in 1703; in 1705, the peak year, they were less than 5 per cent higher than in 1704. Yet in 1703 there had been a 55 per cent rise above 1702; and in 1702 a rise of 65 per cent above 1701. From 1706 imports declined and did not pick up again until 1714. It was only in 1719 that they just managed to recover the 1705 level. Total wine shipments to England rose from an average of 16,252 pipes in 1700–3 to only 17,198 in 1704–7, while total exports to England in 1710 were lower than in 1700. Cf. A. D. Francis, *The Methuens and Portugal*, app. 3 (where the import figure for 1703 should read 19,906 pipes—Ed.).   [2] See vol. v, pp. 395–6.

Plans for the marriage of a Portuguese infanta with Carlos II, notably in 1689, were all smoke and no fire, like Peter II's candidature for the Spanish throne eleven years later. But two motives, at once politico-strategic and economic in character, led Portugal to interfere in Spanish affairs. First there was the definition of the southern frontier of Brazil, for which Portugal from 1679 claimed the River Plate, where her new colony of Sacramento ensured a plentiful supply of hides and served, thanks to its links with Buenos Aires and Tucumán, as a channel for procuring much-coveted silver. Second, the frontiers of Portugal herself could only be guaranteed by the transfer of such fortified places as Alcántara, Valencia de Alcántara, and Badajoz. These would also bring useful cornfields that already helped to feed Portugal. Obviously, too, she could not watch the Spanish throne go to a hostile dynasty without protest. Yet she took no part in the negotiations for either of the Partition Treaties, and only France sought even her *ex post facto* approval to them: this at least enabled the Portuguese to advance their claims, only to have them rejected out of hand by William III, whereas Louis XIV at least listened to them favourably, even though Lisbon had finally to consent without any formal compensation (15 October 1700). When the will of Carlos II reopened the entire question, France came into still closer contact with Portugal.

The traditional trend of her foreign policy, therefore, led Portugal to range herself on the side of France, the only power in any case interested in giving her the desired territorial guarantees, while Holland and England continued to make claims, which were considered excessive, for the liquidation of old debts. On the other hand, the English and Dutch navies were threatening to dominate the seas just as Brazilian gold was beginning to flow in. Caught between these conflicting forces, the government hesitated until William III recognized Philip V in April 1701. Then the ambassador to Versailles, Cunha Brochado, recommended it to follow suit and accept the French offers. The resulting treaties of 18 June 1701 with Spain and France were fairly favourable to Portugal. They gave definite recognition to her rights over Sacramento and support for her attitude to the debts claimed by Holland and England, as well as for her own claims to the restitution of the island of Mahim (which England had seized) and to the recovery of Cochin and Cananor from the Dutch in the event of war. In that event, however, Portugal undertook to close her ports to the English and Dutch.

In practice, this position, which seemed best to suit Portugal's interests, very soon proved untenable. This was because the whole of her economy and public finances depended on oceanic trade, while France was hardly capable of protecting the vital links of both Spanish and Portuguese empires as well as her own. In 1702 the returning treasure-fleet, convoyed by a French squadron, was surprised at Vigo. Though the Anglo-Dutch fleet, in spite of landing troops ashore, failed to lay hands on much of the precious metal, which had already been unloaded, it burnt or sank 20 French ships and 4 Spanish galleons and seized 9 other galleons and 8 ships. When it ran across the eight vessels of Villette's squadron after they had left the Tagus (where they had been since July 1701) to join the squadron in Galicia, this isolated force was easily destroyed. These victories and the frequent presence of powerful British forces off the coast of Portugal were irresistibly convincing arguments: Lisbon even feared a bombardment. Both John Methuen and a Dutch envoy had been in Lisbon since May, and the Englishman well knew how to play upon the interests of the wine growers. Public opinion accused the royal confessor, the secretary of state (Roque Monteiro), the minister of finance (Alegrete), and even Cadaval, of accepting substantial presents. Mendo de Foios Pereira, secretary of state since 1688, had been relieved of his post in 1702 and the ambassador to Versailles, Cunha Brochado, relegated to the background. If the balance of naval forces played the decisive part in the diplomatic volte-face which now took place, it should also be remembered that the Portuguese and French economies were more in rivalry, especially at a time when the vineyard interest was in power in Lisbon, than were the Portuguese and Anglo-Dutch economies. And yet it needed a full winter of negotiations to edge Portugal out of her neutrality to the Allied side. While the appearance of a squadron at the right moment was enough to destroy her pledges to King Philip, it was insufficient to drag a whole nation into war. Her strategic position indeed gave Portugal some trump cards. By the two treaties of 16 May 1703[1] she indeed committed herself to war and acknowledged her debt to the Dutch, who later agreed to reduce it only from 1 m. to 850,000 *cruzados*; but against this, besides receiving the supreme command in the Peninsula with auxiliaries, arms and subsidies for the war there (1·5 m. *cruzados* in the first and 1 m. every year thereafter), Portugal gained two essential points under secret clauses. First, Spain was to renounce her claim to the north shore of the Plate[2] and surrender not only the Estremaduran barrier-forts—Badajoz, Albuquerque and Valencia de Alcántara—but also the Galician towns of Tuy, La Guardia, Baiona and Vigo. Secondly and above all, King Peter refused point-blank to enter the war or to recognize 'Charles III' before the archduke arrived in Lisbon.

Another year passed before the opening of the new war-front in Spain. From 1704 to the summer of 1708 Portugal made great exertions. She had much to endure until the end of 1712. For the first five years she maintained a striking force of 20,000 infantry and 5,000 horse, in addition to defence troops in her most exposed provinces—the Alentejo, Beira and Minho. To assist her, there were on Portuguese soil about 10,000 English and Dutch infantry and 2,000 horse. What were her manpower resources?

---

[1] Above, p. 419 and note.
[2] The Brazilian frontier with Cayenne was also to be adjusted: cf. below, p. 531.

Her demographic position compared well with that of her much larger neighbour. From less than two millions in 1640 her population rose to 2,143,368 in 1732. It is safe to assume that in 1703 there were at least that many, and very probably rather more, since it is known that a number of towns and large villages contracted, sometimes considerably, as a result of the Spanish war and the Brazilian gold rush. Only Oporto expanded perceptibly after this date—rising from 14,909 (above age 11) to 20,737 in 1732.

Like the War of Independence, the Spanish Succession War ravaged large areas in the Alentejo and Beira. In May and June 1704 these provinces suffered an invasion by the duke of Berwick, followed by counter-offensives under the marquis das Minas in the north and under Count Galveias in the south, during which Salvaterra, Idanha, Penha Garcia, Monsanto, Castelo Branco, Portalegre and Castelo de Vide were captured and recaptured. This meant that areas rich in olives, vines and fruit, as well as very important textile centres, were affected. From spring 1707 to spring 1708 it was the turn of Serpa, Moura and Noudar to be invaded and recovered: cornfields, vineyards, orchards and olive-groves suffered, particularly the latter, which were systematically cut down by the Spaniards during their retreat. From 28 September to 29 October 1712 Campo Maior had to endure a bitter siege: indeed, this fertile frontier region, so rich in corn, was a theatre of operations throughout the war. Yet it was the Alentejo that harvested the fearful honour of being the main scene of the war on Portuguese soil after 1704, thanks to its crops, livestock, wine and oil, which facilitated the provisioning of armies.

The war had another very unfortunate economic consequence. As part of Portugal's regular grain supply normally came from Spanish Estremadura, the bakers' ovens had to slow down. During the great famine of 1694–5 the price of wheat in Lisbon had risen to 500–600 *reis* per *alqueire*,[1] instead of the normal 200–220; in December 1708 it stood at 700 *reis*, and a quarter of the horses in the Alentejo perished of starvation; in February 1709 it rose to 1,000 *reis*, at the beginning of April to 1,200. Most of this time the arrivals of enormous Allied convoys, bringing sacks of grain and barrels of dried cod, cheese and butter, were anxiously awaited: thanks to the arrival of an English convoy at the end of April 1709, the price of wheat fell to 960 *reis* and then to 720, at which level it could be pegged by the arrival of a still larger Dutch convoy: by November, however, these supplies were exhausted and famine began to spread, all the more as rain had destroyed the maize crop. It is therefore understandable that the Portuguese were anxious for a truce. In fact, a local armistice, arranged between the commanders-in-chief at the beginning of this year of misfortune,[2] did provide some relief by giving security to the farmers and their pastures in the Alentejo. Towards the end of 1709, when peace rumours

---

[1] Equivalent, at Lisbon, to 13·8 litres: 60 *alqueires* = 1 *moio*.
[2] Soares da Silva, *Gazeta em forma de carta, 1701–1716* (Lisbon, 1933), p. 186.

were current, quantities of Castilian corn came in through the Alentejo, and all the inland ports carried on their normal trade. In the autumn of 1712 this region experienced a renewal of hostilities; but by then, on the whole, stalemate had been reached.

The dependence of the Portuguese money market on American silver has already been stressed. During the last two decades of the seventeenth century the Cartagena *galeones* only made the return journey every five years and the Mexican *flotas* about every three years, bringing back on average 19–20 m. *patacas* in silver and 6–7 m. in merchandise.[1] This shrunken traffic was further impeded by the enemy's command of the Atlantic during the Succession War, when it became wholly dependent on French naval escorts. The *flota* of 1703, one of the richest ever known, arrived safely enough in Cadiz, but the English and the Dutch enjoyed the lion's share of it: significantly, as soon as it dropped anchor, the French pressed for effective action to prevent the silver leaking into Portugal. In spite of more or less clandestine trading with the Spaniards, the Portuguese market remained badly supplied with silver during these war years. Of more decisive importance, on the other hand, was the freedom of fleets or even single ships almost always to sail freely between Portuguese and Brazilian ports—the reward of the decision to side with the Maritime Powers. While the vital links of empire could thus be safeguarded, however, some overseas territories did not escape French attention. In 1709 the island of São Tomé was sacked, and in September 1711 Rio de Janeiro was held to ransom by the great privateering commander Duguay-Trouin.

In many respects the Succession War ended in paradox, and its results were also contradictory for Portugal. In recompense for the partial defeat of France and Spain, Portugal did obtain the renunciation of territory north of the Amazon as far as the Oyapok in French Guiana, while Spain abandoned her claims to the northern shore of the Plate. Yet, since Philip V retained the Spanish Crown, there could be no cession of the barrier-forts in Estremadura and Galicia which Portugal was to have received at the hands of Charles III. Moreover Portugal, like France, had to contribute to the costs of maritime victory by losing the profitable Asiento to the new ruler of the seas.

In the sixteenth century a trade route had been opened between the river Plate and Peru. Quick to participate, the Portuguese had shipped negroes for the Potosí mines to Buenos Aires, and so procured silver; in the next century, a third of the Buenos Aires population was Portuguese. This trade was halted by the War of Independence, but about 1670, when the mid-century crisis had produced a lasting depression, the Brazilians

---

[1] Paris, Arch. Nat., Marine B 7, no. 225 ('Moyens d'enrichir le royaume', 1701) and Aff. Etr. B 1, no. 649 (d'Estrées, Lisbon, 22 Dec. 1694). For the sailings of *galeones* and *flotas* from 1688, see above, p. 354, note 1.

renewed interest in it. Merchants from Rio de Janeiro and Bahia, and also the governor-general, sent cutters to the Plate, sure of finding even the highest authorities there complaisant, although specially licensed register ships from Seville tried to head off this competition. In 1671 the Portuguese Crown formally decreed an open trade between Brazil and Buenos Aires, thus cutting out the governor-general's attempt to corner it for himself. The stake was obvious: Sousa Freire wrote from Bahia that 'this country is being lost for lack of money, but the Castilians would fill our ships with it, if we found a way of entering their ports'.[1]

During the 1670s the Portuguese went one better by undertaking at last to realize Correia de Sá's old dream of a Brazil stretching to the Plate. In 1668 they established settlements near Lagoa dos Patos and Laguna, and in 1676 the king leased the territory north of the Plate to the sons and grandsons of Salvador de Sá. In that very year, when Rome created the bishopric of Rio with a jurisdiction extending down to the Plate, the town council (*Senado da Câmara*) of Rio asked the king to proclaim to all the world his right to these territories. In 1679 Dom Manoel Lobo, created governor of the south Brazilian captaincies,[2] was instructed to establish a frontier garrison of 200 soldiers opposite Buenos Aires. Thus, in January 1680, Colonia do Sacramento was founded. The first colony was destroyed by the governor of Buenos Aires, with the aid of the Paraguayan Jesuits, but by treaty of 7 May 1681 Spain agreed to provisional Portuguese occupation. Settlement and development, particularly of cattle-raising, went on with speed and determination until 1704. The possibilities of the new colony must be seen in relation to Buenos Aires, whence in May 1687 two ships reached Cadiz with 1·5 m. piastres and 60,000 hides worth 350,000 piastres—an event which defines the economic importance of the region clearly enough. But in April 1691 a ship arrived in Lisbon itself from Buenos Aires and Rio with 50,000 piastres and a cargo of hides (besides sugar); and on 7 September others came in with 5,500 hides and about 200,000 piastres—'a result of the slave trade which the Portuguese sometimes carry on in Buenos Aires via their fortress on the Island of St Gabriel'.[3] It was thought that this trade could be increased to a million piastres—say, £80,000—annually. Every year we find cargoes of hides and in 1699 we are told that the majority come from Buenos Aires. But the sheer number carried by the Rio convoys implies more than contraband with Spanish territory—namely, that the Portuguese were themselves rearing cattle and that their gauchos were hunting the wild herds fast multiplying in the interior. In 1704 the Spanish governor, Valdez, thanks to large contingents of Indians from the Jesuit

---

[1] Lisbon, Arquivo Histórico Ultramarino, Bahia, 11 June 1670.
[2] See D. Alden, *Royal Government in Colonial Brazil* (Berkeley–Los Angeles, 1968), pp. 36 ff. and 68.
[3] De Lescolle, 18 Sept. and 2 Oct. 1691 (Arch. Nat., Aff. Etr. B 1, no. 648).

missionary 'Reductions', again took Sacramento, which was recovered only at Utrecht; but after 1713 the Portuguese resumed their expansion in this area. The Buenos Aires trade itself was now much less restricted however, for in 1723 an English South Sea Company vessel shipped hides there for Lisbon. The Portuguese capital, indeed, now became a great leather market. Moreover, the silver trade between Peru and the Plate continued, because (as was noted in a memorandum of 1697)[1] it could be quicker to reach Buenos Aires from Lima by mule, down the Andean tracks and across the pampas, than to follow the official route by Callao and Panama to Portobello.

The Amazon, on the other hand, never became a link between the Atlantic and the high mining plateaus. In 1637–9 Pedro Teixeira had succeeded in getting from its mouth to Quito and back, and his journey was used by the Portuguese, despite earlier Spanish journeys, to claim sovereignty as far as the Upper Amazon. To explore and monopolize this immense space it was necessary to settle the region between the Amazon delta and Cape São Roque. About 1640 there were some 1,500 Portuguese and 40,000 loyal Indians in the captaincies of the Maranhão and Pará, exporting captured Indians to Pernambuco and cultivating tobacco and sugar, with hopes of cotton and spices also. The loss of Ceylon and Malabar to the Dutch forced Lisbon to look elsewhere for certain spices and drugs, and in 1669 cloves and cinnamon were actually discovered along the Tocantins, a tributary of the Amazon. The great depression provided a further stimulus. In 1671 the Crown made a concession to the governor of the Maranhão and Pará on conditions intended to promote indigo production; the municipal senate of Belém was to encourage vanilla and cacao. The idea of transplanting spices and drugs from Ceylon and India, and so ruining the trade of rivals via the Cape, was also taken up again. Trees, plants and seeds from the East were planted or sown, first in 1680 in Bahia, later in Pernambuco and the Maranhão; in 1683 Kannara[2] technicians were brought in. The experiment failed with pepper but succeeded with cinnamon. In 1690 the Maranhão and Grão Pará began to play a part in the Atlantic economy and so contribute to the general economic recovery. In that year they sent a vessel to Lisbon with 7,000 *arrobas*[3] of cloves, some cinnamon, cacao, sarsaparilla and tobacco, though the spices were still of very mediocre quality. Soon, instead of a single ship, there was a small fleet of three to five sailing every year for Portugal. The cloves were marketed chiefly in Italy, whence some reached Germany; the cacao remained inferior to Caracas cacao, but was already superior to that of the French Antilles; the vanilla was coarser than the Spanish American variety.

---

[1] Paris, Arch. Nat., Marine B7, no. 221.
[2] The west coast of India from Mangalore to Goa.
[3] An *arroba* = 32 lb. avd. or 14·688 kg.

All this presupposed population growth and the provision of labour. In 1675 sixty families from Madeira and the Azores settled in the Maranhão, while from 1682 the Cacheo Company had to supply 500 negroes a year for twenty years—a trade in which it was joined after 1685 by private merchants. Yet demand ran ahead of supply and the price of negroes was high. The Jesuits preferred that Africans should be imported, so as to minimize the enslavement of Indians, with whom they wanted to create a new Paraguay in the north. For this reason the Fathers were several times expelled by the settlers, as during local riots in 1661 and 1684–5. The Society's international position made it suspect. It was the Jesuits, after all, under the leadership of Fr Fritz,[1] who came down from the Andes in 1685 to push back the territory which the Portuguese were annexing in defiance of the Treaty of Tordesillas: the latter were already to be found on the rivers of Upper Amazonia, and in 1691 a military detachment established Portugal's sovereignty as far as the Rio Napo, without any reaction from the Spanish government before 1707. It is hardly surprising that the Portuguese government preferred to keep the Jesuit missions south of the Amazon, introducing in the north, along the Rio Negro, the Carmelites, whom it trusted. In 1709 Inácio Correia pushed back the Spanish Jesuits from the Upper Amazon and a Spanish military expedition from Quito was met by a victorious counter-offensive from the Maranhão.

Long since, in 1637, the Portuguese had asserted sovereignty over the 'Wild Coast' north of the Amazon as far as the Oyapok, later claimed by the French of Cayenne. In 1687, on the northern shore of the delta, the Portuguese built the fort of Macapá, which the French briefly occupied ten years later. By the treaty of 18 June 1701 Portugal ceded this territory to France, but the fortunes of the Succession War gave her a chance to recover it at Utrecht. Lisbon wanted to stop all trade between Guiana and the Maranhão, where the French bought horses for their sugar-mills.

While this far-reaching penetration of Amazonia was going on in the north and a powerful thrust towards the Plate proceeding in the south, the stockbreeders were slowly moving into the interior, behind the coastal strip filled with sugar and tobacco plantations, cassava and maize fields. Europe was using increasing quantities of hides, and along the Brazilian littoral itself livestock was an essential factor in industry and agriculture—in transport and above all in running the *engenhos*. But cattle could not well be reared in the heavily populated coastal strip, where life was too sedentary. Moreover, Indian labour was more easily employable in semi-nomadic pastoral activity than in the hard discipline of agriculture and industry; and as the small groups of cattlemen did not constitute a menace to the native villages they got on well together. From Bahia and Pernambuco the pastoralists and their beasts climbed the slopes and

[1] Above, p. 356.

531

followed the course of the São Francisco upstream, as far as Goyaz and the Mato Grosso plateau. Here they were joined by pastoralists and live-stock from São Vicente and São Paulo who occupied the Curitiba plateau in the south. In the extreme north, cattle were introduced at the outset of the eighteenth century on the island of Marajó, which became a consider-able breeding centre; earlier still, herds from the Maranhão had occupied the Parnahyba valley, linking up with those from the Rio São Francisco. Thus a whole society interested in leather stretched from the Amazon to the Plate, imparting value to the *sertão* (backwoods) and pioneering routes far into the interior. Farms as well as food and drink stores soon sprang up along these routes. The development of cattle-raising, more-over, set off a search for salt deposits: salt-mines were opened in the São Francisco valley and elsewhere which in turn made it possible to improve the preparation of hides.

A few great families acquired domains of unimaginable size in the interior and divided them up for cattle-raising, keeping a portion for themselves but leasing the larger part to dependants who each had between 200 and 1,000 animals: a great family itself would own up to 20,000. About 1710 there must have been more than 1·5 million head of cattle. In 1691 the three Brazilian convoys—from Rio, Bahia and Pernambuco—unloaded 100,000 hides in Portugal, though this was an exceptionally good year; in 1695 they brought only 5,000, 8,000–10,000, and 7,000–8,000 respectively, but this was an exceptionally poor year. In 1715 Lisbon alone received 60,000 hides. Henceforward Rio, Bahia and Pernambuco regularly sent each 20,000 per annum and often two or three times as many, while Buenos Aires was exporting up to 100,000.

Beyond the cattle country the frontiers of modern Brazil were gradually being drawn by the fantastic excursions of the Paulistas, from the Paraná and the Plate up to the Amazon and the foothills of the Andes. This movement, fanning outwards from the São Paulo plateau, is usually represented in summary fashion, as a series of expeditions in search of Indian slaves, led by uncouth Portuguese and half-castes of boundless greed who shrank from no cruelty. Such is the black legend created and fostered by the Jesuits, the adversaries of the *bandeirantes*. The archival evidence, notably as presented by the late Jaime Cortesão,[1] shows that the whole movement was far more complex, and that its objectives varied with time. The occupation of the São Paulo plateau, begun spontaneously by a few Portuguese who had forsaken civilization for the Indian way of life, became official policy, which aimed, like the first pioneers, at finding precious metal. Private and official efforts between them led to the forma-tion of *bandeiras*—para-military organizations, 700 to 2,000 strong, consisting of immigrant Portuguese, hardened settlers, half-castes (*mame-*

---

[1] *Manuscritos da colecção de Angelis: Jesuítas e Bandeirantes* (2 vols. Rio de Janeiro, 1951–2); cf. *idem, Introdução à História das Bandeiras* (Lisbon, 2 vols. 1964).

lucos) and Indian slaves, who followed navigable water and Indian paths in all directions. Soon the *bandeiras* took to rounding up Indians for labour on the plantations; but in the later sixteenth century, when the African slave trade was developing and Elmina gold beginning to fall off, the search for precious metal and stones was extended, although Indian slaves continued to be a main objective, especially when the Dutch occupied Angola and São Tomé (1641–8). Sometimes the *bandeiras* pursued political aims. They tried to destroy the independent theocratic State of the Jesuits in Paraguay, and to advance the frontiers of Brazil for the Crown by crossing the Tordesillas Line. This last had been the principal motive of Pedro Teixeira's journey, as it was of the extraordinary travels in 1648–51 of António Raposo Tavares across the Chaco to the foothills of the Andes, then down the river Mamoré to the Madeira, and so to the Amazon and finally Belém. In 1670 Lisbon made a pressing call to intensify the quest for gold, whose ratio to silver now fluctuated around 1:16, instead of 1:11 as before the Restoration: in other words, gold had become dear. This appeal came at an opportune moment, for the fall in sugar had reduced the demand for slaves and Indian-hunting was losing its *raison d'être*.[1]

The interior began to be systematically explored in 1674. On the governor's order, Brás Rodrigues Arazão explored the river Iguapé (south of Santos), with limited success. Pais Leme left São Paulo at the head of a *bandeira* which, after following the rivers Verde, Grande, Ibituruna and Paraopeba (a tributary of the São Francisco), established a first settlement at Santa Ana (near the future Ouro Preto) and a second, after following the Rio das Velhas, at São João (near the future Sabará). It was here that Leme's son-in-law, Borba Gato, in 1694 discovered some of the richest gold deposits, while Bueno de Sequeira and Miguel Garcia, also following in Leme's footsteps, struck gold at Santa Ana. In 1682 Bartolomeu Bueno, after pushing up the Parnahyba, crossed to the Araguayu river in the region of Goyaz and discovered gold on the plateau there, before going on to Amazonia and then retracing his steps. It was only some forty years later, however, that the Goyaz deposits began to be exploited. Until then attention was focused on the region called, because of this fact, Minas Gerais (General Mines). In 1693 António Arzão, setting out from Taubaté, found gold in the Casca, a tributary of the Rio Doce. And so, from 1674 to the end of the century, there was a great deal of feverish activity, most of it secret.

There remained, however, an obstacle. The gold-bearing region was several hundred miles from the coast, and the coastal mountains were backed by dense forests. The waterways were long, difficult to navigate, separated by substantial stretches of arid country. Only the most primitive forms of food were available—roots and wild fruit chiefly, a little game,

---

[1] A. Ellis Junior, *O Ouro e a Paulistânia* (São Paulo, 1948).

even reptiles. At the outset gold and food were carried on the heads of slaves—obviously a very limited means of transport. In 1697 the Paulistas cleared the first road through the forest, sowing maize and planting cacaa and fruit trees at regular intervals. Regular traffic started the following year. But the roads were very hard on horses during the dry season and impracticable during the wet, so that use of negro carriers long continued. It was only in 1701 that a direct road was opened between Rio de Janeiro and the mines. Soon, secretly but continuously, the towns of Bahia and Pernambuco were linked with them too, by the São Francisco.

Along the roads cultivated fields began to appear and, at regular halts, stores for the sale of food, drink and clothing. São Paulo and its plateau villages were almost emptied and thousands of immigrants poured in from metropolitan Portugal, while black Africa provided enormous contingents of slaves. By 1715, more than 80,000 negroes and about 20,000 whites were employed in mining and ancillary activities; between 1715 and 1718 alone, eight sites were promoted to the rank of *vilas* (something between a village and a town). The Rio Grande do Sul region was also beginning to be settled, for it reared the mules required for mining transport. During the first fifteen or twenty years of the new century, on the other hand, population moved from some of the coastal areas. The crisis in north-east and east began in 1697, when a very bad sugar and tobacco harvest came on top of a famine which had been felt since 1693: almost at once, many fields returned to fallow and quite a number of mills were abandoned. This crisis, moreover, coincided exactly with a renewal of the Inquisition's persecution of many of the sugar-masters. The economic centre of Brazil moved southwards, and Rio de Janeiro gained at the expense of Bahia.

When did Brazilian gold enter the international scene? It is difficult to be precise. Even before the great swarming of the *bandeirantes* some small bars had occasionally been unloaded at Lisbon: in 1691, besides a large quantity of silver from Buenos Aires, the Rio fleet brought 32 pounds of gold powder: but this must have been the result of gold-washings in the districts of Paranaguá, Curitiba and Iguapé, south of São Paulo. It was only in 1699 that Lisbon received the first noteworthy consignment of gold from the newly discovered mines: 514 kilograms were registered— something in excess of 734, if allowance is made for smuggling. This is surely connected with the fact that regular communications were established in 1698 between São Paulo and the mines. In 1701 the figure reached 1,909 kg., in 1703 considerably over 4,406. A first peak was reached with 14,500 kg. in 1712. There was a 50 per cent fall in the next year, followed by a rise to almost 9,000 in 1714 and to 12,400 in 1715; then a new fall in the next two years, to 3,000 and 1,000 respectively, and a further recovery in 1718–19 to 7,500–8,000—figures far surpassed in 1720 with a new peak of 25,000 kg. In 1721 and 1722 annual imports maintained the respectable level of 11,000 kg., but the next two years witnessed another fall. After 1731, however, imports only twice fell below 11,000 kg., and in 1740–55 only twice below 14,000. But in all this, of course, it would be foolish to forget contraband, variable and difficult to estimate as it is. In 1699, for example, 35 *arrobas* of gold were registered, but over 15 were smuggled in. British warships generally arrived in Lisbon at the same time as the Brazilian fleets, among which they often anchored; at night a good part of the undeclared gold was transferred to them. Many times other ships, English or French, on the Indies route, called at Brazilian ports and in spite of all controls found it easy to get a few kilos of gold. There was also some direct trade between foreign countries and Brazil, tolerated by governors who were soon dismissed. Later, all foreign commercial houses were to be expelled.

How important was this new source of gold? Quite early, certainly not later than 1703, it produced substantially more than all the gold Portugal and Spain had together received from Guinea and the Indies in any year of the sixteenth century; in ten to fifteen years, as much came from Brazil as Seville had received from America down to 1660. But Brazilian gold went from Lisbon by sea to London, Amsterdam and Genoa. The London mint alone struck gold coins to the value of £2,277,251 during the twelve years 1689–1700; £2,384,803 from 1701 to 1712;[1] and £8,884,477 from 1713 to 1724. These figures suggest that it took some thirteen years for Brazilian gold to find its way in quantity to the north; until the Succession War ended, a considerable fraction went to Genoa and on to Barcelona, to pay for the Portuguese intervention in Spain. But in the very first years of the new century substantial sums of minted Portuguese specie reached all three major markets mentioned above. Moreover, the rapid growth in Portuguese and Brazilian demand for manufactured goods between 1705 and 1714, swollen by the influx of gold and deprived of the Franco-Portuguese trade, stimulated the development of manufactures in England, Holland, Genoa, Turin, Florence, Lucca and Naples. Skilled French workers in England and Holland taught the processes of making the luxury materials which France had formerly exported to the Portuguese. Such large quantities of European goods were sent to Brazil that the market was already saturated by 1715 and prices tumbled below European levels.

The increase in the quantity of coin circulating in metropolitan Portugal seems at first sight to contradict the new fall in price levels which set in from 1712–14 till after 1730. But this reflected a trade depression, itself engendered partly by the end of the war, while in Brazil the decline of sugar and tobacco was hastened by the gold rush. To combat this depression, there were renewed attempts to develop industry. Although linen

---

[1] The figure of £1,249,520 for 1701 was quite exceptional; clearly the flood receded again in the following years.

manufacture had almost doubled during the war, when French linens were difficult to import, woollens had languished. The new industrial effort was chiefly the work of the marquis of Fronteira and the count of Ribeira. In 1716–17 the count established in the island of São Miguel a number of French families skilled in the making of silk and woollen stuffs of many kinds, and of fur hats. In 1716 he also tried to establish a glass manufactory at Lisbon with the aid of French artisans and capital, against the obstruction of the French authorities, who delayed its success until 1724. Yet Portugal had long to wait before acquiring an industrial sector of any significance.

During the first two decades of the new century, Brazilian gold not only reshaped the geography of Brazil and left its imprint on the economies of England, Holland and parts of Italy: it also provided the Portuguese State with a more powerful means of action. Since the fifteenth century that State had been cast in a commercial mould, depending essentially on its maritime trade. An analysis of public receipts in 1716[1] reveals its fiscal foundations:

	Contos (millions) of reis	Percentage
Customs on maritime trade (consular charges included)	1,260	31·9
Tobacco farm	760	19·2
Brazilian convoys and brazilwood monopoly	200	5
Quintos (one-fifth gold royalty)	345	8·7
Mint	200	5
Internal trade (duties and taxes)	667	16·9
Customs on overland trade	40	1
Taxes on production and other internal revenues	470	11·9
Total	3,942	99·6

The total annual revenue amounted to the equivalent of 8,789·85 kg. of gold in 1716, after which it remained between 4,410·59 and 6,065·56 kg. until 1760. In 1681 there had been no quintos and the maritime customs brought in only 683 contos[2] (84 per cent below 1716), the mint 4·76 contos (a difference of 4,077 per cent), the tobacco contracts 348 contos (121 per cent less), and customs on overland trade 28·84 contos (38 per cent less).

This was a mercantile monarchy, not only because the main State revenues were derived from trade, but also because the Crown itself took active part in it, even though some of its monopolies were farmed out. The king retained the monopoly of importing the red dyewood which gave its name to Brazil and of tobacco exports to India, and he had a one-third interest in the capital of the Cacheo Company. In 1663, moreover, the Trading Company of Brazil had been transformed into the *Junta do*

---

[1] Visconde de Santarém, *Quadro elementar das relações...de Portugal*, vol. v, pp. 248–9.
[2] In money of 1688, to make comparisons possible.

Comércio, a kind of royal trade tribunal which was also an organization of merchant fleets; we have seen how important to the State were the cargoes of the 'convoys', apart from the freights directly earned by royal ships. The king also, as we saw, took a considerable part in the formation of the East India Company, providing both capital and ships.

Landed wealth remained in the hands of Church and nobility. Out of Portugal's 2 m. people, over 25,000 were members of religious orders and over 30,000 were priests—that is, one in approximately every 36 inhabitants (as compared with 1 in 33 in Spain). The number of convents rose from 396 in 1600 to 450 between 1628 and 1652 and to 477 by 1739. It has been estimated that a third of the land in the kingdom belonged to the Church, which also enjoyed a tithe of all agricultural produce. Overseas its influence was relatively even greater. The Society of Jesus sought to erect not only a theocratic territorial empire there, but also a gigantic commercial association which should control the world's principal trades, from the silk of China to the maté tea of Paraguay. This is why it came into conflict with both State and society, bringing upon its head many riots in São Paulo, Santos, Rio, Maranhão and Pará—first signs of the movement which was to culminate in the expulsion by Pombal.[1] On the other hand, the king was Grand Master of the three military-religious orders, which provided him with a considerable income. But their social importance lay above all in the institution of the commanderies, which were entirely reserved for the nobles: 400 in the Order of Christ (which also had about 1,000 knights), 36 in the Order of Santiago (the richest) and 60 in the Order of Aviz. The commandery was granted by royal favour, usually for two generations, the income varying between 200 and 20,000 *cruzados*. The revenues of the orders came mainly from tithes, but they had other sources of income. Thus the Order of Christ owned the lands of Tomar and Soura, the Order of Santiago the ports of Setúbal and Alcácer, the Order of Aviz the lands of Benavente. We may take the priory of Crato as a good example of a lordship combining ecclesiastical and lay elements. Straddling the Tagus over a breadth of 9 leagues for a length of 18,[2] with 10 *vilas* and 29 *freguesias* (parishes), it had some 30,000 inhabitants above the age of 11. Its revenue consisted of tithes from all land, a quarter of the produce of all properties, perpetual quit-rents, the income of oil-presses and granaries, and the receipts of mills and ferries. The total income was 35,000 *cruzados*.

The wealth of the nobility was drawn from as great a variety of sources. In Peniche, for example, the count of Atouguia collected the tenths of the fish as well as of outward cargoes, bringing him *ca.* 5,000 *cruzados* a year,

---

[1] The Brazilian towns, whose senates (*câmaras*) retained more power than the town councils at home, were also more turbulent, although Lisbon, with over 165,000 inhabitants, could be riotous: see vol. v, ch. xvi. For Pombal and the Jesuits, see vol. vii, pp. 123–5.

[2] A Portuguese league = approximately 6 km. or 3¾ English miles.

besides an annual 'repast' offered by the Town Hall; at Redondo (in the Alentejo) he received 36 out of every 60 *alqueires* sown, the eighths of the wine, and 50,000 *reis* a year from tolls levied on entrance to the *vila*. The count of Castanheira received from his peasants the quarters of the wheat and the eighths of the wine, as did the duke of Cadaval. To the lord of Guardão were due the eighths of all the fruits; he also received *foros* (fixed rents) and gifts from 42 properties leased as emphyteuses. In this way the nobility were not only large producers of wine, oil and flour on their own demesnes, but also great warehousemen for the export of produce received in payment of seigneurial dues. In addition, they monopolized the highest posts in the public administration, at home and overseas, and so could enrich themselves further by direct participation in trade, or at least by dealing in licences and favours. In 1718 the Governor of the Mines of Brazil returned to Lisbon with 900,000 *cruzados* amassed from the trade he had carried on out there. From the East, too, many *fidalgos* (gentlemen) still drew considerable incomes year by year.

Economically, the nobility depended essentially on oceanic trade, but they could engage in it profitably because of their position as landowners. Utilization of the land was fashioned by three institutions: the commandery, the captaincy-donatary,[1] and primogeniture. This last, acquiring firm shape in the seventeenth century, had the effect of pushing younger sons into the religious orders. Moreover, a considerable number of landed estates and even chattels were burdened with chantries (*capelas*), so that the owner was in effect a trustee receiving from a fifth to a third of the income. At this point it is worth glancing at the different forms of property and rights over the land and its produce, bearing in mind that over three-quarters of the homeland was still waste. First came the *reguengos*, those royal estates whose tenants paid the king a quarter or fifth or some other fraction of the produce of the soil as well as the *laudémio* (fines on transfer). Then there were the Crown's much more important properties which took the form, in practice, of a variety of rights to levy dues, mostly ceded to donataries. The income of a commandery likewise consisted mainly of dues, including tithe, shared between the commander and his order. In the vast area of private property two basic categories are distinguishable: exempted properties, belonging to the Church (and subject to mortmain) or to the nobility, and taxed properties, belonging to commoners. Exempted and taxed properties alike could be directly exploited by the owner or leased—on tenancy, emphyteusis, or quit-rent (*censo*). The first and last paid no *laudémio* and carried no improvement obligations. The annuities payable as a rent-charge on emphyteutic leases were generally one-sixth below the rack-rent. Under

---

[1] Crown properties donated in usufruct to nobles, who thus became seigneurs, as had normally happened in the early stages of overseas colonization; but in Portugal itself the *donatario* seldom exercised jurisdiction over his captaincy.

such leases, juridically speaking, a 20-year annuity was supposed, in the aggregate, to equate with the capital value of the real estate, without the annual payment exceeding half the annual production (exclusive of what was needed for sowing); in practice, this consisted either of a portion of the produce (grains, wine, flax, etc.) varying from a fifth to a tenth (after deduction for tithe) and payable in kind or cash, or of fixed quantities of produce—in which case no commutation into money was permitted. While there were emphyteutic leases in perpetuity as well as leases for periods of ten years or more, contracts covering a period of three generations predominated. The *censo*, introduced into Portugal before the sixteenth century, usually represented the sale, perpetual or redeemable, of an annuity on the produce of a property itself retained by the owner (though sometimes leased or even alienated to a third party): the *censo* would be offered for sale at a certain price, normally by a proprietor in need of ready cash, and the buyer would have first claim on the produce of the land so secured for payment of his annuity, but with no right to possession of the land. The converse form of contract, under which the seller reserved for himself an annual rent on a property for sale, was almost invariably transformed into an emphyteutic lease.

The peasantry, while here and there enjoying the remnants of common rights, had to pay tithes to the Church, dues to the seigneurs, tolls and rent-charges, so that it retained only a minor fraction of the fruits of the soil, which went to fatten a swollen class of ecclesiastics and nobles. Yet it was not penetrated by the spirit of revolt. No doubt the possibility of emigrating overseas and the income which came back from there, as also the boom in agricultural exports, kept it quiet. Church and nobility were solidly based on the land and held the levers of State in their hands. And yet the State was an absolute monarchy.[1] After 1679–80 the Cortes met only in 1697–8, and then for the last time. Financially, the Crown depended hardly at all on the nobles or on the land, but on the nutritious sea and the merchant bourgeoisie, which it supported in times of depression by its policy of industrialization and the chartering of privileged companies. On the other hand, through its own commercial activities the State competed with private business, which the still powerful Inquisition attacked strongly whenever it could, under any pretext, thus preventing the flowering of a Portuguese capitalism. It is this opposition which partly explains the politico-social opportunities open to the landed nobility, face to face with a submerged and destitute peasantry. An analogous antithesis is to be noticed in the cultural sphere. There art and literature remained baroque, while a group of *estrangeirados*—people who had lived abroad and become aware of the birth of a modern culture and economy—made efforts to break through the scholastic shell of official teaching, and to open Portugal to the new currents stirring in Europe.

[1] Cf. vol. v, pp. 389–92.

CHAPTER XVII

THE MEDITERRANEAN

THE Mediterranean is unique among the seas of Europe. Its position as the meeting-place of three continents, which it at once joins and separates, has not only given it a commanding strategic and economic importance but made of it a world somewhat apart. Some of its distinctive features are of all time, others appear only at certain critical periods.[1] Both must be kept in mind if we are to understand how the region influenced and was in turn influenced by the Turkish and European wars between 1683 and 1718. Although its climate, roughly the same throughout, produces the harmony of sea and sky and landscape which delighted Homer, it also results in a certain leanness of agricultural resources which has forced people to look to the sea for a livelihood. But these physical similarities are contradicted by an exceptional diversity of culture and political style. In the course of its long history as a centre of civilization States of many kinds have grown up along its shores, with complex and often conflicting interests. Overshadowing all at this time was the great divide between the eastern Mediterranean, dominated politically by the Ottoman empire, and the western Mediterranean, a primary theatre of war in the struggle against Louis XIV, in which the leading rôle was played by the rising sea power of a non-Mediterranean nation.

By far the greater part of the sea was a watery desert, traversed only by an occasional long-distance convoy and by isolated vessels making all the running they could in fear of corsairs. Since astronomical navigation had not yet been generally adopted here and its seamen still liked to hug the coasts—relying on compass and plane chart, or simple cross-bearings on landmarks—there was a tremendous contrast between the empty expanses of open sea and the coastal lanes, which swarmed with traffic. There were the great arteries of trade, like the one running from Naples to Valencia, via Leghorn, Genoa and Marseilles; the less frequented routes along the North African coast; and the dense network of traffic-lanes in the Aegean, then known as the Archipelago—as if to suggest that the sea only mattered as a means of connecting one island with another. Shipping was particularly lively in the various straits and narrows which formed the crossroads of the sea-routes: the Straits of Gibraltar and Messina, the passage between Sicily and Malta, the Piombino channel between Tuscany and Elba, the entrance to the Adriatic commanded by Otranto, and the passage between Crete and the Morea controlled by the Venetian island of Cerigo, the ancient Kythera. These passages could be

---

[1] Readers may like to compare vol. x, ch. xvi.

really dangerous in war-time; even in time of peace sailors preferred to undertake them in summer, on account of the severe winter storms. Nor were vessels always safe in harbours and roadsteads, for these as a rule were poorly protected from the swell. Some shipwrecks were really catastrophic: in 1694 an Anglo-Dutch squadron lost eleven ships and a thousand men during a storm in the Straits of Gibraltar, where eight English ships were lost in the winter of 1703–4; and in the port of Barcelona itself 17 ships were destroyed by tempest in 1715.

The hazards of bad weather were increased by unfriendly coastal mountains, which often fall sheer to the water in great cliffs, as they do along the Ligurian riviera and the coasts of Dalmatia, the Morea, the Anatolian provinces of Pamphylia and Cilicia, and Kabylia (eastern Algeria). Coastal plains, where they exist, were often abandoned to livestock, malaria and visiting corsairs. The mountains and their forests offered refuge to man and shelter for his beasts. To the rocky spurs of their lower slopes and to hill-tops at their feet villages, with their watchtowers, had clung for centuries, in spite of a thin, friable and often excessively dry soil; not even the pressure of rising population could induce Mediterranean peoples to quit these historic homes for the unkempt plains. But the deeply fretted coasts sheltered innumerable ports, wherever the inhabitants could survive the incursions of enemies or the harshness of the land itself. Some of these ports were true capital cities, with an extensive trade and sometimes splendid buildings and wide cultural influence; nearly all the great centres of the Mediterranean world are ports. As it was costly and risky to transport goods by land, as much as possible went by water except when piracy or war made the sea even less secure. The major land-routes usually terminated at a port, though some towns, such as Aleppo, could best be described as caravan ports.[1] On the other hand, the great ports never completely turned their backs on their hinterlands, if only because the rural crafts and urban workshops of the interior provided most of the manufactured goods for exchange. That the economy of the great ports was nevertheless distinct from that of their hinterlands may be suggested by their differing experience of food supply. Because the countryside was preoccupied with its own production and the ports in general with far-flung commerce, there had existed ever since Roman times the organization known as the *Annona*, whose function was to ensure regular corn supplies to the towns. Its records provide evidence that these tended to claim larger populations than they really had, and that food was much scarcer in the country.

Some Mediterranean cities were certainly among the most crowded in Europe. Neither London nor Paris was more than half as populous as

---

[1] Aleppo was linked to the sea at Alexandretta (Iskanderun or Scanderoon) by a camel track notoriously exposed to robbers: see G. Ambrose, 'English Traders at Aleppo (1658–1756)', *Econ. Hist. Rev.* 1st ser. vol. III (1931), pp. 246–67.

Constantinople, which (with its suburbs) may have numbered as many as 800,000 inhabitants.[1] Cairo, the next largest Ottoman city, may have accommodated over 200,000, Smyrna and Aleppo (with Alexandretta) about 100,000 each, Damascus and Baghdad considerably less. The largest Christian town was undoubtedly Naples, with over 300,000 before the great plague of 1656, building up again to over 200,000 by 1700—a much higher total than Amsterdam or Vienna. Messina and Palermo had shrunk to no more than half this size, so that Venice with at least 150,000 came next, followed by Rome with about 135,000. Genoa, with nearly 80,000 inhabitants in 1688, had slowly recovered from the loss of half her population in 1656. Milan gradually recovered to 125,000 in 1688 but fell to 110,000 in 1710—little over half her population before the notorious plague of 1630. Bologna, the second city of the Papal States, was rising above 70,000—more than Florence or Turin, though the Piedmontese capital was growing apace. In the Iberian peninsula, the only towns to equal or surpass Milan were Seville and Lisbon, with about 165,000 each, and Madrid with nearly 140,000; the Iberian towns had in general been shrinking, especially (as was also true of Italy) the industrial towns; Segovia and Toledo had shrunk by half within a century. Finally, Marseilles was only a medium-sized town of 70,000–80,000—larger than Barcelona (40,000–50,000) and about the same size as Algiers.

These figures, however, afford no reliable guide to relative economic weight. Two of the busiest ports, Cadiz and Leghorn, had populations of little over 20,000. Yet Cadiz was in a position to influence not merely the Mediterranean but all European commerce. Apart from its capital rôle as a terminal of the Spanish-American traffic, it was an essential staging-point for the Anglo-Dutch convoys which every year or two plied between the North Sea and the Levant; the Genoese and Marseillais also went to Cadiz for silver. The most cosmopolitan market within the Straits was Leghorn. Unlike Marseilles and the Spanish ports, where the Inquisition was powerful, it admitted Jews and Levantines: the Jewish colony, in fact, was the most powerful in Leghorn, and its family correspondents in the Maghreb enabled it to handle most transactions with the North African coast. The grand dukes of Tuscany, who had created Leghorn late in the sixteenth century and found a fortune in it, were determined to maintain it as a free port, open to all in peace and war.

The trade of Genoa was in decline, notwithstanding that the wars favoured her as they favoured all neutral ports, and that her little tartans carried a good deal of corn and other commodities in the Gulf of Lyons. Her industry, not excepting luxury fabrics, was also decadent. On the other hand, her rôle as banker was still cosmopolitan; only the Venetian

---

[1] R. Mantran, *Istanbul dans la seconde moitié du XVIIe siècle* (1962), pp. 44–7. In what follows, the figures for European towns are largely based on R. Mols, *Introduction à la démographie historique des villes d'Europe* (Louvain, 3 vols. 1955–6), vol. II, pp. 47, 504–8.

Banco del Giro,[1] perhaps, could then be compared with the *Banco San Giorgio*; when Samuel Bernard wanted to remit piastres from Spain to the Flanders front, he sent them via Genoa and Geneva. Genoa's economic and strategic ties with Spain, in particular, were so intimate as to induce Louis XIV to order the terrible bombardment of 1684; some Genoese nobles owned large estates even in Naples. By contrast, Marseilles symbolized the supreme importance of the Levant trade to the French. Its activities also included the import of corn and such raw materials as leather and wool from Barbary, and of silver from Spain: the Marseillais always regarded Spain as their special preserve and by 1730 were including her among the *échelles*—a term used to describe those places, chiefly in the Levant, where they held trading supremacy. On the other hand, it had needed all Colbert's enthusiasm and patience to persuade them to enter the West India trade. In 1669, long after Leghorn, Marseilles had obtained the privileges of a free port, and it gradually pushed its way to the fore-front of the accepted Mediterranean trading centres.

Mediterranean trade was associated of old with two special features. First, the sea had come to be regarded as a more or less effective moat protecting Europe from the recurrent epidemics of the East. Since the sixteenth century a stern quarantine system had been evolved; any ship thought to be carrying disease was refused normal entry, if necessary by cannon shot, and at every port the authorities insisted on seeing a health certificate which covered the crew as did a bill of lading the cargo; ports like Marseilles and Malta which offered proper facilities for crews during quarantine attracted traffic. There were outbreaks of pest indeed, some of them calamitous—the plagues of 1630–1 in Spain and Italy, 1656 in Italy, 1691–2 along the Barbary coast, 1720 in Marseilles—but it is astonishing that they did not occur more often. Secondly, privateering was endemic, whereas in the Atlantic it now flourished only during a major war, except from the Moroccan base of Sallee (close to Rabat). To a greater extent than Morocco, the 'Regencies' of Algiers, Tunis and Tripoli along the Barbary coast lived by robbery; it was essential for the 'Algerines' at least always to be at war with at least one power whose ships they could seize. There were also centres of anti-Muslim privateering among the Christian ports, though none of them really specialized in it except Malta and (in a lesser degree) the Balearic islands of Majorca and Ibiza. Pirates proper— the outlawed and stateless *forbans*[2]—were also a common nuisance,

---

[1] The *Banco del Giro* of Venice (reorganized 1666) not only accepted deposits but provided credit, clearing and exchange facilities, and issued its own money, the *partita*, which was always covered up to 50 per cent at least by the Bank's reserves; it remained solvent until the reopening of the Turkish war in 1714. See G. Luzzatto, 'Les Banques publiques à Venise aux XVI-XVIII siècles', *Studi di storia veneziana* (Padua, 1954), pp. 225–58. On the decline of Venice cf. below, pp. 555–6.

[2] The distinction between Barbary corsairs and true pirates was no mere matter of form: between the black flag and that of a power to which consuls were properly

especially where the land could not support the population: thus the Dalmatian and Albanian coasts and islands were notorious for their pirates, as were Zante and Santa Maura (Leukas) until their reconquest by the Venetians in 1684, and sometimes the Archipelago itself. Piracy was widespread, as in the West Indies, for several years after a long war. War created a floating population of privateersmen who with luck might scoop big profits, quickly spent in good living: with the return of peace, their leaders, reluctant to become routine traders again, looked round for some belligerent State under whose flag they could continue their gambling career. Many a Christian corsair who preyed on the Muslims had learnt his trade in operations against the enemy of the moment—English, Dutch, French or Spanish—the most famous examples between 1680 and 1720 being Plannells from Majorca, the Englishman Plowman, and Manetta, a Genoese in Maltese service. There were also many instances of unemployed Christian privateersmen forswearing their religion and turning Barbary corsair, as an alternative to open piracy.

During the early seventeenth century, when their activity had received fresh impetus from the Morisco refugees, the Barbary corsairs had extended their range to preying on all Christian shipping. At that time Algiers maintained up to 100 warships, mostly very small; by 1700 it had only a quarter as many, but they were mainly powerful frigates. The naval forces of Algiers can be reckoned at about 25 vessels throughout the eighteenth century, when Tripoli and Tunis between them could not arm on average much more than half that number. About 1650, at the height of its prosperity, Algiers was at war with almost all the maritime powers. Their frigates were unmatched for speed and manoeuvrability; they were almost always able to avoid capture if chased, by taking advantage of their shallow draught to go so close inshore that no large ship could follow them. Algerine vessels and tactics, indeed, served as models for European privateers. It took a long time to develop methods of dealing with them, especially as their captains operated in waters they knew extremely well, having often sailed them as Christian seamen before turning corsair. At Algiers the Corporation of Corsair Captains (*Reis*) had acquired such wealth that it was reaching out for political power as well. Most of them being renegades, all forms of seafaring other than privateering were closed to them; to have traded in Christian waters would have been to give themselves up to the Inquisition. At the same time, Christian merchants did good business in prize goods with Algiers, through Jewish intermediaries. The grand dukes of Tuscany, traditionally astute men of business, not only allowed anti-Muslim corsairs to sail under their flag and to arm at Leghorn, but also provided a special enclosure there for the

accredited, there was also the real and practical difference that an ordinary pirate was hanged at the yardarm if captured, while corsair crews could at worst only be sent to the galleys.

Algerines themselves to unlade such prize goods as they could not dispose of at home. This was one channel by which the corsairs could turn their prizes into cash, although many sought to do without an intermediary at all: after raiding a coast they would fly a special flag, the 'banner of release', to indicate willingness to free freshly captured slaves for a prompt cash ransom; it was less usual to sell back a captured ship in this way, for that would have needed more time and might well have put the captor at the mercy of pursuers. At the same time the corsair ports, Algiers especially, were great entrepôts for slaves and all kinds of prize goods. The slaves were sold by auction to private individuals, not so much for immediate use as manual workers or galley slaves, or in harems, as in the hope of ransoms. Even if the captive could not himself raise the sum demanded by his owner, there was always the hope of obtaining release through one of the collective purchases made from time to time with alms gathered by the Christian clergy, notably by the Trinitarians, the Order of Mercy and the Lazarites. It is sometimes said that there were over 30,000 slaves simultaneously in Algiers;[1] the true figure, given the frequency of ransom, was probably nearer 10,000.

Treaties of peace with the Corsair States customarily provided for a mutual exchange of prisoners, except when they had been taken in the armed service of a permanent enemy: thus a seaman taken on board a Maltese corsair or a soldier from a Spanish *presidio* (fortified post) remained a slave in Barbary whatever his country of origin. However, since France and England were at peace with the Regencies at the end of the seventeenth century, there were now few slaves from these countries along the North African coast; by far the largest proportion were Italians and Spaniards. Besides wishing to protect their commerce from these half-legendary 'pirates', the great powers thought it worth while to solicit their assistance when at war against each other. When the Nine Years War broke out, the French nursed the hope of persuading Algiers to declare war on the English and Dutch and to wage it even in the English Channel, with access to French arsenals. These negotiations lasted until 1692. It is true that Ducasse and Pointis used freebooters in the West Indies during this war, but not as a result of negotiations between governments.

Although less is known about them, the Christian corsairs who operated against Muslim shipping were just as redoubtable as the Barbaresques and probably did more harm in the long run. About 1670 we find the Turks asking: 'Is France as powerful as Malta?' After 1704 the Knights of St John regularly armed three or four sailing-ships besides (as earlier) half a dozen galleys, working in two separate squadrons, against the sultan's

---

[1] An exaggeration apparently derived from a letter of Agi Chaban Dey to Louis XIV, 23 July 1691: E. Plantet (ed.), *Corresp. des Deys d'Alger avec la Cour de France, 1579–1833* (2 vols. 1889), vol. I, p. 310.

warships and merchantmen. Sometimes this was in collaboration with other Christian navies, notably the Venetian. Every year, in addition, a score of privateers were equipped with polyglot crews to hunt off the Barbary or Levantine coasts, under the flag of St John (sometimes illegitimately) or those of Tuscany, Poland, Monaco, Brandenburg, Spain and Portugal. In general, they were not out to destroy the Algerines so much as to prey upon the great merchantmen plying between Alexandria and Smyrna, which consequently dwindled in number towards the end of the seventeenth century. Chardin tells how the Archipelago was continually plundered about 1670 by forty Christian corsairs—'all very cruel'—and how Samos was virtually deserted by its terrified inhabitants.[1] Yet the collapse of the Ottoman merchant fleet, mainly due to these attacks, should not be exaggerated. In 1718, and again in 1750, the grand viziers made attempts to revive maritime trade by using large armed merchantmen ('caravellas'), although the strictly Turkish trade remained largely a coasting affair, carried on for the account of Ottoman merchants in Christian vessels. It is more significant that the Greek carriers, who were to flourish under Russian protection after 1770, benefited from the withdrawal of the Maltese *corso* from the eastern Mediterranean after 1720, partly because the Greeks were able to exploit differences between the Grand Master and the pope about the appeal of prize cases to Rome.[2] In 1700 they had been uncertain whether to rely on the patrols of the sultan's cruisers—a risky and merely provisional solution—or whether to put themselves under French protection, which could be dangerous when France was at war with enemies powerful at sea.

Christian or Barbaresque, the privateers relied on speed or gunpower or both. Immediately a war broke out, a swarm of small light raiders, in hopes of making a fortune by some sudden stroke, infested the more frequented coastal seaways—for example, in the neighbourhood of Ibiza, Oneglia, Elba and Porto Ercole. Any ship of light or medium tonnage would serve, for it could be rapidly armed and easily reconverted to ordinary trading as and when market conditions should invite; but most commonly they were galliots, whose proportionately enormous area of sail made them the fleetest of runners, while their flat keels and shallow draught enabled them to shave the shore in eluding pursuit. The larger and more highly gunned privateers did not appear till several months after the outbreak of war, but then sometimes in packs, when news of several lucrative hauls had got about. These too might be ordinary converted merchantmen, but also specially built light frigates such as those to which the Zeelanders (and the Algerines) owed their formidable

[1] *Voyages du Chevalier Chardin en Perse et autres lieux de l'Orient* (Amsterdam, 3 vols. 1711), vol. I, p. 2. The town of Sfax was exempted from taxes in these years on condition of maintaining six galliots, to be ready at all times to chase Christian privateers.
[2] R. Cavaliero, *The Last of the Crusaders* (1960), pp. 83–5.

efficiency, or even naval warships. In these cases a fairly heavy capital out-lay would be required, and so a handsome profit was expected.

The effect of privateering, on the outbreak of war, was to empty the seas of shipping—less because of the prizes taken as from fear of losses. Some merchant captains, like the Genoese, met the situation by fitting out substantial, heavily-armed vessels, with large crews to prevent boarding. Others relied on mobility, using lighter vessels with a larger sail area and with auxiliary oars, like the English 'galley'[1] of this time. Still others clamoured for naval protection, in the shape of counter-privateering squadrons, cruisers in certain shipping zones, or escorts: of these, the first method was the most effective, since reliance on cruisers limited the merchantman's range and time-table, while convoys, though safe enough as a rule, were slow and sometimes commercially disastrous. It was also the practice in war-time to split up the ownership of cargoes among a large number of consignors (or consignees) and insurers. In the last resort, if trade under a belligerent flag became too dangerous, one could always fall back on neutral bottoms or use flags of convenience. Thus neutral trade always expanded in time of war, which did not so much reduce the over-all volume of trade as change the flags under which it was carried; it was a general though by no means universal rule that an enemy cargo was protected by a neutral flag. Even this might not be respected, however: privateersmen were a rough set and out for hot money. Neutrality, in turn, implied the observance of certain recognized duties. Thus any belligerent merchantman leaving a neutral port was given 24 hours to get well away before the port authority allowed an enemy privateer to lift anchor in pursuit; in theory, no one was permitted to arm a privateer in a neutral port. Again, the custom of the sea required that a crew surrender-ing at first summons should not be ill treated, so most merchantmen gave in to avoid the fate of a garrison taken by storm.

The appearance of strong naval forces seems to have cleared all other shipping out of the way. Upon news of their approach, larger vessels ran for harbour while smaller ones hugged the coast as narrowly as they could. The squadrons were too large to pass unnoticed, and reports of their movements enabled shipping to dodge them fairly easily. But this situation held good only while the squadrons were operating, roughly from April to October, and then only the immediate area of operations was affected. It was much easier to keep out of their way than to avoid the ubiquitous and ever-dangerous privateers. When they were encountered, of course,

---

[1] Defined by their owners as follows: 'A galley is built to sail, and to row with oars, and measures twice her burthen or loading, and is broad and sharp, and carries twice the breadth in sail of common sailing ships that usually sail with convoy and is at double the charge in number of seamen...of force from 16 to 40 guns...': Hist. MSS. Comm., *House of Lords MSS.*, new ser. vol. VII, p. 182. Mediterranean seamen themselves still set a high value on the lateen sail, which enabled light vessels to sail closer to the wind, as corsairs needed to do.

everything turned on the respective speed, cunning, skill and courage of merchant captain and corsair, whose fortunes were so intimately interlocked.

By such improvisations trade contrived to flow even in war-time. The Mediterranean world was by no means an aggregate of small self-sufficient regions. From time immemorial its economy had been founded on wine, olives and corn, supplemented by migrant sheep-farming (transhumation) and by seafaring and the manufacturing industries indissolubly linked with it, such as pottery, weaving and leatherwork. The towns in particular had always relied on external trade to make good their food deficits. One great advantage of a generally dry climate was that corn could fairly easily be stored without going bad; yet the amount of cultivable land was limited and there were many mouths to feed, so that every year the surplus produce of the great 'granary regions' had to be brought to areas deficient in food crops. The hoarding of treasure, so often noticed in Muslim countries, sprang from a preoccupation with the need to guard against bad harvests. On the whole, the pattern remained the same year after year, Spain and Provence (for instance) almost always importing corn, while Languedoc, Barbary and the Levant were exporters. Wines and olive oil also bulked large in the internal commerce of the Mediterranean, while the ancient soap-making industry, which consumed large quantities of olive oil and potash, alone made relatively high demands on shipping. Long before the late sixteenth century, however, when Mediterranean lands began to enter the commercial orbits of the northern maritime powers, important links had developed with the rest of Europe: and since the 1590s, in times of shortage, even corn had been brought from the Baltic. Other major imports were timber, salted or smoked fish from the North Sea and Newfoundland, metals wrought and unwrought, arms and hardware. The commercial attraction of the Mediterranean, in turn, was that it offered exotic commodites sometimes difficult to obtain elsewhere: wines, fruit, dried currants, olive oil, leather, furs, drugs, spices, alum, sulphur, copper sulphate, and even salt. On the whole, the visible trade balance with the rest of Europe was favourable to the Mediterranean, which was a substantial importer of silver—a fact that may also have owed something to the superior skill of Mediterranean merchants, with their centuries of experience in handling money.

The Muslims were chiefly interested in overland trade, much of which they could enjoy without Christian competition. Besides regular use of the Nile and the Mesopotamian rivers, important caravan-routes linked Aleppo–Baghdad–Ispahan, Tripoli–Fezzan–Dar Fur, Morocco–Tripolitania–Egypt, Marrakesh–Sudan, to say nothing of the annual convergence of pilgrims by land and sea upon Mecca. On the other hand, owing to the Christian corsairs who lurked untiringly in the Archipelago and off the Barbary and Levant coasts,[1] the Ottoman merchant who risked his property on the Mediterranean resorted as a rule to European bottoms, especially those of Marseilles, the valuable business of whose numerous 'bazaar-ships' French statesmen sought anxiously to preserve throughout the *ancien régime*, while rival merchants did their best to engross it whenever war hampered French trade. It is impossible to calculate the loss to the Muslims resulting from foreign carriage of their own trade, but it must have been very considerable.

The Levant trade had been stimulated by the emergence of the Ottoman empire. It was characterised by developments less in maritime technique than of mercantile organization. Voyage-time—three or four months to Gibraltar and back—had changed little since the sixteenth century. The Ragusan argosies of that period still held the record for sheer size, smaller ships being more highly valued for their adaptability. It was the French who had first negotiated with the sultan for the necessary political framework; but between 1673 and 1681 the famous Capitulations, dating from 1579 though from time to time in abeyance, were renewed, clarified and extended in favour of the French, English and Dutch.[2] The Turks now discriminated against the Venetian trade, but this suffered most from the Cretan war and the equally prolonged hostilities of 1684–99. Only these four powers—effectively three when Venice was at war with Constantinople—could safely traffic in the Levant in the seventeenth and eighteenth centuries; merchants or merchantmen of other countries had to seek the protection of one of them, usually the French. The Capitulations promised freedom of trade (subject to the payment of fixed and limited dues) and the good behaviour of the local Turkish officials, and they authorized the maintenance of consuls in Levantine ports—the *échelles* of the French. Consuls enjoyed considerable authority and diplomatic immunities. The Muslims were often exasperated by the unscrupulousness of European agents and this was sometimes an occasion of victimization, although the victims were by no means always to blame. The consuls could provide information and protection on the spot more quickly and efficiently than could an ambassador resident at Constantinople. The brilliantly successful French system, recently improved by Seignelay, was the model for all subsequent consular organizations. However, in contrast to the *échelles*— where there were resident consuls and colonies of European merchants, organized by 'nations' when their number justified it—open roadsteads were also frequented by vessels from Europe, for there duties did not have to be paid and commodities could be shipped, such as corn and rice,

---

[1] Even the Red Sea, largely a Muslim preserve, was menaced by the Madagascar pirates, who hunted the Gulf of Aden for Indian shipping bound to or from Mocha and Jidda (the port of Mecca); only lack of water prevented Captain John Avery from establishing his base on the island of Perim itself in 1695.

[2] The Capitulations obtained by Genoa in 1666 and 1674 proved a false dawn: for the decline of her Levant trade and that of Ragusa see Mantran, *Istanbul*, pp. 519–22.

of which the export was forbidden. As this contraband was open to the risk of confiscation, most merchants tried to cover it by bribing Turkish officials.

While French trade was supreme at Sidon (in the Lebanon) and at Aleppo, the English and Dutch so far controlled the traffic of Smyrna as to dub their Levant trade 'the Smyrna convoy'. To Constantinople all Europeans regularly brought more than they took away, for it was above all a great centre of consumption, so that credits there partly set off debits at the other *échelles*. In 1701 the English obtained parity of treatment with the French for the first English consul at Cairo, which was then reviving economically, as were Alexandria and Damietta—exporters of corn (notably during the European scarcity of 1709) and cotton, but especially of Mocha coffee.[1] The Dutch, who had had their own consuls at Aleppo since 1613 and at Smyrna since 1628, traded under English or French protection in Egypt. Their Mediterranean trade, even at Leghorn, suffered badly from the wars, especially the Succession War, during which they never had a Straits convoy of their own.[2] From 1692 to 1702 they were also at war with Barbary, and with Algiers again in 1716–26; in 1716 most of the ships freighted from Amsterdam to the Straits were English and French. More ominously, Dutch woollens were being priced out of Levantine markets by English.[3] The successes of Zeeland privateers in the Mediterranean[4] can scarcely have compensated for this decline. The Marseillais, individualists to a man, conducted much of their Levant trade in single vessels even in war-time, whereas the English and Dutch traditionally sailed in convoy, in war and peace alike, and hence were better able to hold off enemy privateers. The cumbrous convoy system involved not only a risk of deterioration in the condition of cargoes but also lower selling prices in the *échelles*: large stocks were thrown on the market all at once, while prices of purchases for the return rose in response to an excess of demand. Yet the English and Dutch were able to reduce such handicaps by improving their commercial organization, buying in the Levant ahead of their outward cargoes and so making a profit each way on every voyage; their merchants had sufficient reserves of capital to spread sales and purchases over several months and so minimize the effects

---

[1] Below, pp. 858–9. Coffee-drinking became fashionable in Europe after an Ottoman embassy to Paris in 1669 and the capture of large stocks at the relief of Vienna in 1683. Cf. J. Leclant, 'Le Café et les cafés à Paris, 1644–93', *Annales (E.S.C.)*, 6ᵉ année (1951), pp. 1–14.

[2] According to the directors of the *Levantse Handel*, shipping insurances ran as high as 50 per cent of the value of the cargoes in 1711, when the French and English were paying only 14 per cent: K. Heeringa (ed.), *Bronnen tot de Geschiedenis van den Levantschen Handel*, vol. II (The Hague, 1917), pp. 6–7. Cf. *ibid.* p. 112 for the numbers of Dutch departures in 1697–1715. English shipping losses had been serious down to 1708, however.

[3] In 1702 the English calculated that Dutch cloth exports to the Levant had fallen by half in just over 20 years: A. C. Wood, *A History of the Levant Company* (Oxford, 1935), p. 100.

[4] See J. S. Bromley, 'Some Zeeland Privateering Instructions', in R. Hatton and J. S. Bromley (eds.), *William III and Louis XIV*, pp. 162–89.

of unfavourable price fluctuations. They had established their influence solidly between 1635 and 1654, and about 1680 held the upper hand in the Levant despite the much greater distances which their ships had to cover. Attributing their success to the existence of companies,[1] Colbert had tried to create a Levant Company in 1670, when the French trade was at its lowest ebb, and a Mediterranean Company in 1685. Better fortune attended the *Compagnie du Cap Nègre* and the older *Bastion de France* company, whose main function was now to arrange corn shipments from Barbary to Provence and Languedoc. These companies, which enjoyed a monopoly of the French trade with Barbary (including the coral fishery off Tunisia), were amalgamated in 1693, foundered in 1705, and were revived in 1706 as the *Compagnie d'Afrique*.

East-West traffic was undoubtedly less one-sided than used to be thought, as regards both aggregate values and the type of exchange. Not till the nineteenth century did it assume the classic 'colonial' pattern of an exchange of European manufactures for raw materials from the Middle East and North Africa. During the seventeenth and eighteenth centuries, in fact, many exchanges reversed this pattern: thus cochineal and fine wools from Segovia were essential raw materials for the Tunisian bonnets worn throughout the Levant. In the important Levantine towns, such as Damascus and Aleppo, there were many old-established industries, often exporting to Europe on a considerable scale: thus the traditional blue cotton fabrics made in Syria were commonly worn in Spain and elsewhere. The industrial decline of the Muslim countries would not be felt until the second half of the eighteenth century, nor completed until the age of steam-power. It is impossible, however, to assess the real balance of East-West trade owing to our very imperfect knowledge of the ultimate destinations of exports to the Levant. Some found their way to Persia and India, so that a proportion of the returns did not come through the Mediterranean at all but by the Cape route, which periodically competed with the Mediterranean. This was particularly true of expensive cargoes such as Caspian silk, which from time to time was diverted by the Indian Ocean.[2]

There was a long tradition of credit transactions in the Mediterranean, but the Italian towns which had developed instruments of credit were no longer flourishing by 1700, while Marseilles, the greatest Mediterranean

---

[1] The English Levant Company, reorganized in 1661, was much more rigid than its Dutch counterpart, which was merely a supervisory body, limited to the organization of convoys and controlling neither sales nor purchases. A convoy normally consisted of well up to 30 vessels.

[2] The question of the silk routes is a problem in itself. By *ca.* 1620 Leghorn had begun to supplant Venice and the land-routes. English imports of raw silk came mainly from Persia–Turkey (250,000 lb.) and Italy (110,000 lb.) in 1669; in 1700, out of a total of 440,000 lb., 280,000 came from Persia and Turkey, 110,000 from Italy, and 50,000 from Bengal. See R. Davis, 'Influences de l'Angleterre sur le déclin de Venise au 17ᵉ siècle', *Civiltà Veneziana Studi*, vol. IX (1961), pp. 207–8, and below, pp. 859–60.

mart in the eighteenth century, still nourished its Levant trade with 'barils de finance'. Colbert was always deeply troubled by this practice, which he put down to the bad disposition of the Marseillais: in fact, it was a natural result of the Ottoman customs regulations, which exempted importations in cash from the 5 per cent duty payable on all other merchandise. The coins in everyday use in Turkey were the Sevillian and Mexican piastres. Hence the Marseillais regarded the piastre as a commodity both easy to handle and certain to yield at least 5 per cent profit. It was possible to increase this profit considerably; the Dutch found they could make the specie trade yield 20 per cent by minting the *aboukel* piastres (*asselanis*), so called after the lion which they bore and which the Levantines took for a dog. Though made of a very inferior alloy, the 'dog' found a ready market in the Levant because of its handsome appearance and the high standard of craftsmanship which went into its production; the French at one time thought of imitating it.[1] Another widely employed means of payment, practicable only when there was cash to cover it, was the short-term 'mortgage' loan at high interest made by a captain to his freighter. One might have expected the comparative falling-off in arrivals of precious metal from the New World after 1630 to have had a singularly adverse effect on trade between the Christian West and the Muslim East: in reality, the reduced supply of silver had the happy effect of stimulating payment in manufactures. Here the English and the Dutch were the innovators. By the later seventeenth century, their cloth exports had reached a total which Colbert enviously reckoned at about 40,000 pieces a year for the English company alone—more than double the real figure.[2] The French government sought to emulate this success by encouraging the industries of Languedoc with loans, export subsidies and the aid of Dutch artisans. In this respect, indeed, a remarkable reversal of fortunes did take place. Whereas the French were exporting perhaps 5,000 pieces of cloth a year in 1680 (as against England's 20,000), this figure rose steadily after 1685 and spectacularly after 1708, exceeding 30,000 pieces in 1713–14. If these last years were exceptional, reflecting the return to peace, it remains true that by 1715–20 French trade in the Levant equalled, or

[1] Throughout the eighteenth century small clandestine mints thrived—e.g. in Monaco. Illegal practices played a big part in all Mediterranean trading, above all in the smuggling of piastres out of Spain, where the authorities usually turned a blind eye to fraud on a gigantic scale, in return for a surtax (indult) so widely accepted as to be a part of normal trading expenses. Spain had renounced the right to search French and English ships by the Treaty of the Pyrenees and the commercial treaty of 1667 respectively.

[2] The only convoy with such large cargoes was the convoy captured, in part, off Lagos in 1693; it was carrying 47,000 pieces of cloth, but this represented the total export for three years (R. Davis, *loc. cit.*). English woollen cloth was of two different sorts: a thick, warm cloth much in demand in the Levant, where the winters are severe in the interior; and a lighter cloth made in Devon and East Anglia for which there was not much of a market in the Ottoman empire (except at Alexandria, where cold is unknown), but which was bought in large quantities by Spain, Italy and Portugal.

even slightly surpassed, that of Great Britain;[1] and France was to hold first place among the trading powers of the Levant until the Revolution.

At the two ends of the Mediterranean, survivors of the ancient struggle between Cross and Crescent, lay the empires of Spain and Turkey. Although neither was exclusively a Mediterranean power, each had its nerve-centre within the Mediterranean world, in whose central area the Adriatic separated their possessions. Their methods of rule bear a striking resemblance. The Spanish viceroy was in many ways the counterpart of the Turkish bey, concerned to use the limited means at his disposal to the best advantage of his sovereign and himself; there were few attempts to change local customs, and both governments relied upon influential elements among the indigenous populations—the Orthodox priests in Greece, the baronage in Sicily. Alien merchants were allowed to profit from native commercial lethargy, although the Spanish empire was probably even more severely hit by alien penetration than Turkey. In each case the sluggishness of the economy was to some extent counteracted by large military expenditure; the building of watchtowers, castles, forts and military roads presented a brilliant but superficial air of activity which in the long run sterilized a large slice of capital resources. Both the Castilian mercenary soldier and the Anatolian janissary were of humble origin, their only loyalty a military one, their lives often spent wandering from one distant garrison to another. For both empires, again, maritime links were of such importance that large garrisons were maintained along the essential sea-routes, as in the little Turkish ports of the Archipelago or in the Tuscan *presidii* on the route from Naples to Genoa. In general, the ruling power was tolerable because fairly mild, although provincial particularism was as incompatible in principle with the centralizing drive of Ottoman 'Men of the Pen'[2] as with the more successful system of Castilian or Bourbon bureaucrats. The Catalans, who had sought foreign aid in 1640, did so again in 1705 in their desperate struggle to preserve their liberties; once defeated, a powerful fortress was built at Barcelona to dissuade them from ever rising again. By contrast, the Barbary Regencies perfected their growing autonomy by taking advantage of Ottoman weakness at the time of the Peace of Carlowitz.[3] The elected chief of the janissary *ojak* (Corps centre)—the dey at Algiers, the bey at Tunis and Tripoli—forbade the entry of any official sent by the Sublime Porte to exercise the functions of a pasha, and at Tunis a hereditary dynasty established itself in 1710. But every dey or bey, to heighten his own prestige, still requested the sultan to invest him with the caftan, the emblem of a pasha's office; the bey of Tunis received it regularly from

---

[1] Mantran, pp. 556–9; R. Romano, *Commerce et prix du blé à Marseille au XVIIIe siècle* (1956), p. 29 n.; cf. below, ch. XXIII (1).
[2] Below, p. 616.   [3] Below, pp. 626 ff.

1704, the dey of Algiers from 1711. This symbolized the real bond which, attenuated as it was, still subsisted between the sultan and the Regencies. In general, the subject peoples remained loyal to their overlord, even at a distance or of alien origin: the devotion of the Sicilians and Neapolitans to Carlos II and to Philip V was matched by that of the Orthodox Greeks to the sultan.[1] It was the Greeks, after all, who provided most of the crews for the Ottoman navy and they fought lustily against the Venetians, whom they detested as 'Latins'.

Morocco, the western portion of the Maghreb washed by the ocean swell, was hardly a Mediterranean power, but under the rule (1672–1727) of Sultan Muley Ismael she came to play an important part in Mediterranean affairs. The sultan's taste for ostentatious buildings, as at Meknes, and the length of his reign are alike reminiscent of Louis XIV, but his savage energy and sheer force of will remind one, rather, of Peter the Great. It was her ruler's personal qualities more than her corsairs that made Morocco a power to be respected. Moroccan corsairs were numerous enough at Sallee, but it is more significant that the sultan tried to bring them all under his control and take over their profits. A number of Christian outposts were rendered untenable and one by one evacuated: Tangier in 1684 by the English, La Mamora (1681), Larache (1689) and Arzila (1691) by the Spaniards. Others, such as Mazagan, Melilla, and the *peñones* (rock forts) of Alhucemas and Velez, were closely blockaded. Ceuta underwent a long though unsuccessful siege (1694–1720). Muley Ismael was also unable to carry through his designs on Tlemcen, for his black army was crushed on 28 April 1701 by the Algerian militia in the Chelif valley, which he had invaded. He was more fortunate in his search for better organization, especially of commerce, which was already more important to the country's economy than at Algiers or even Tunis. The sultan had a direct stake in it and Fez had become 'a kind of general warehouse for the whole of Barbary'.[2] Foreign trade was virtually monopolized by the Jews—perhaps 5,000 of them in Fez alone—and by the Christian merchants, mainly Frenchmen at first and often Huguenot refugees who tended to favour the English and the Dutch. Muley Ismael himself sought to maintain friendly relations with France; he concluded peace with her in 1682, and the arrival of a Moroccan embassy was the talk of Versailles in 1698. But Louis XIV was tactless and uncompromising in his attitude to Morocco. French trade and influence there lay in ruins by the end of his reign.[3] Only after Muley Ismael's death in 1727, however, did Morocco withdraw into herself again.

Fernand Braudel's distinction between 'narrow' and 'deep' countries—

---

[1] As a rule the sultans had non-Turkish, often Circassian, mothers; the mother of Mustafa II and Ahmed III was a Cretan.

[2] Pidou de Saint-Olon, *Estat présent de l'Empire du Maroc* (1694), p. 145.

[3] Cf. J. Caillé, 'Le Consul Jean-Baptiste Estelle et le commerce de la France au Maroc à la fin du XVIIᵉ siècle' in *Rev. française d'hist. d'outre-mer*, vol. XLVI (1959), pp. 7–48.

between mere coastal strips and territories with interior resources—is capital for Mediterranean history, especially perhaps because the deeper areas could recruit much larger armies than the bands of mercenaries upon which 'narrow' countries had to rely.[1] The developments of this period were working very much to the advantage of the former. The Mediterranean, like the rest of Europe, had been going through a period of deflation for nearly a century before 1720. Its countries, with the accumulated wealth and experience of centuries of profitable trading, should have been rich enough to survive bad times. Yet it was the countries of northern Europe, initially less well provided, which proved equal to the crisis, while old Mediterranean powers saw the culmination of a decline soon to appear incurable.

Why should it have been incurable? It is often said that the Atlantic had displaced the Mediterranean as the centre of world trade, although not before 1620;[2] that Venice was exhausted by the Cretan war (1645–69) and her subsequent wars with the Turks (1684–99, 1714–18); that in consequence the increasing competition of the northern powers short-circuited her in the Levant trade, in favour of Leghorn and Marseilles; and that she was troubled by the silting up of her lagoon, necessitating floating docks (*camelli*) to lighten incoming ships. All these are stock explanations, sound enough in their way. But surely remedies were to hand? Why was it that Venice failed to defend her position as the southern outlet for Germany and Central Europe? By 1700 Venetian trading influence was limited to Friuli, Cadore, Padua, Treviso, Rovigo and Bologna.[3] The half-deserted German factory, once so rich, was a standing reminder that most of their German trade, like that of Lombardy, had been lost by the Venetians—to the advantage of Ancona, Senigallia, Trieste, and even Genoa. The prosperity of Leghorn testified to the merits of a liberal customs policy in attracting trade and keeping it. But the haughty *Serenissima* regarded such a policy as the resort of weak new-comers, anxious to assure themselves a place in the sun. Even her very half-hearted attempt in 1661 to relax her customs regulations lasted only twenty years and was not resumed until the 1720s. This exaggerated traditionalism was all of a piece with the political orthodoxy of the governing oligarchy, so distrustful of foreign influences that from 1709 it needed a special permit from the Council of Ten for a patrician to travel abroad.

Equally harmful was the tradition which concentrated in Venice itself

---

[1] Cf. F. Braudel *et. al.* 'Aspetti e cause della decadenza economica veneziana nel secolo XVII', *Civiltà Veneziana Studi*, vol. IX (1961), pp. 81–3.

[2] G. Luzzatto, *Per una storia economica d'Italia* (1957), p. 68. From about 1620 Venice listed some Oriental commodities of which she had previously had the monopoly as 'products of the West'—a very convincing proof.

[3] G. Campos, 'Il Commercio estero veneziano', *Archivio Veneto*, vol. XIX (1936), pp. 145–83.

all the *arti* (craft gilds), tenacious of their privileges and hostile to every innovation. Nor on the whole did the mainland of Venezia, the *terraferma*, which had in any case the disadvantage of poor communications, provide a refuge for industries which found themselves embarrassed in the city. Colbert had created new industries to undercut Venetian products, in areas where there was cheap labour, local power and sometimes raw material resources. All these conditions were present in the *terraferma* but not fully exploited there, despite the protection extended to some local industries such as the woollens of Schio. In general, the Venetian textile industry was declining rapidly: whereas up to 30,000 pieces of cloth were exported at the beginning of the seventeenth century, by the end the number had dropped to 2,000; the export of silk fabrics fell from 10,000 to 6,000 in the same period, with a sharp dip to 2,300 about 1660. The export trade in hardware fared better, but even that suffered severely from the lively competition of similar articles made in Germany and the French Massif Central. Glassware remained an important prop of the Venetian economy. In another way, however, the *terraferma*, by contrast with the capital, was developing. It was expected to make good the decline in external trade and the loss of colonial possessions and later, when Ancona had the backing of the papacy and Trieste of the Habsburg, the loss of her predominance in the Adriatic itself, the 'Venetian Gulf'.[1] The capital accumulated by the Venetian aristocracy in sea-trade was increasingly invested in land, thus enabling Venice not only to meet her own very large food requirements but even to become an exporter of agricultural produce, notably rice and raw silk.

The sometime mistress of the Levant had become a regional port. After 1720 English and Dutch ships ceased to call at Venice, while few Venetian ships were to be found in Levantine ports. The substitution of the *terraferma* for the colonial empire, together with a condition of more or less permanent carnival which made Venice the gayest city in Europe, attracting an unending stream of spendthrift tourists and expatriates, only masked the decadence of the Most Serene Republic. And yet it is one of the stock ironies of cultural history that on the ruins of her imperial grandeur she was only at the threshold, with Sebastiano Ricci (1659–1734) and G. B. Piazzetta (1683–1734), of a second spring in painting.[2] The great Tiepolo was born in 1696, Canaletto in 1697, Guardi in 1712. They were the last of the great Italian masters.

Though by no means a unity, the Spanish dominions in Italy—the Two Sicilies, Sardinia and the Milanese—covered half the surface of the peninsula, more or less assuming the character of a 'deep' area, besides being able to rely on Genoa and Spain herself—still, after all, a great

[1] For Venetian jealousy of Ancona before it became a free port in 1732 (with Habsburg encouragement), see A. Caracciolo, *Le Port franc d'Ancône* (1965), pp. 33 ff.

[2] See M. Levey, *Painting in XVIII Century Venice* (1959) and F. Haskell, *Patrons and Painters* (1963), pt. III.

power. As a result of the Spanish Succession War, Austrian replaced Spanish rule in all these territories except Sicily, which at Utrecht went temporarily to the duke of Savoy, thus ending what had been in many ways a great record of imperial rule. Spain had protected Italy from the Ottoman expansion of the sixteenth century and largely maintained law and order there ever since. In so doing, she had shown considerable flexibility in her policies: thus in Sicily the baronage constituted her chief support and was allowed to control the island's affairs, whereas in the kingdom of Naples it had been stripped of all political power. The Neapolitan Estates had been practically suppressed in 1642, and the energies of the nobles deflected into petty quarrels over precedence—fostered by a proverbially ceremonious style of government—or into foreign war in Habsburg service or the patronage of artists. They were often the owners of vast *latifundia*, like the Spanish grandees, but the teeming cities of Naples, Palermo and Messina possessed a patrician class of their own, with a large and cultivated leaven of lawyers and office-holders. The Spaniards were tender towards the urban masses, whose temper was equally feared by the well-to-do, themselves generally loyal after the crushing of the Messinese revolt in 1678. It is true that the prince of Macchia's revolt (September 1701) was largely inspired by the demand for an independent monarch, but its failure is more significant; the general loyalty to Spain was personified in the prince of Montesarchio, who had been a leading rebel in 1647.[1] Philip V was welcomed by Naples in 1702, although his failure to live up to Neapolitan hopes was to facilitate the Austrian conquest in 1707. In the Milanese, the black legend of Spanish rule owes much to the ingratitude stimulated by the romanticism of Manzoni and others, who transposed the national sentiment of the nineteenth century two centuries back. The duchy furnished the Spanish army with a Lombard regiment as glorious as those of Naples and Sicily, and experienced nothing worse than fits of passive resistance which never amounted to rebellion. The peasants—perhaps more impoverished than elsewhere in north and central Italy—were apathetic, the town proletariat (as in Rome and Venice) appeased by charity. The nobility, despite continual intrigue, had begun to imitate Spanish ways. However reluctantly, the Spaniards themselves—merciless towards offenders, noble or plebeian, but otherwise content with remote control—allowed the local judicial and administrative organs to continue, each successive governor proclaiming on his arrival a *grida* which restated in effect the principles on which all Spanish administration had been based since the new constitution of Charles V in 1541. Any tendency towards more centralized government was compensated by a deliberate inflation of titles and of the

---

[1] Masaniello's revolt in 1647 had been directed against the bad municipal administration of Naples. Cf. the detailed article of P. Voltes Bou, 'Aportaciones a la historia de Cerdeña y Nápoles durante el dominio del Archiduque Don Carlos de Austria', *Estudios de Historia Moderna*, vol. I (1951), pp. 49–128.

formal dignity of declining institutions like the Senate, in such a way as to encourage harmless disputes among the aristocracy about lineage and so on.

On the other hand, while Spain succeeded in maintaining internal order, her policy of European greatness often meant that the Milanese was either a theatre of war or the object of its neighbours' covetousness. During the Nine Years War fighting in Italy was limited to Piedmont, but the eastern periphery of Lombard territory was the scene of Vendôme's campaigns against Eugene in 1701–5, while in 1707 the Montferrat, Alessandria, and Lomellina helped to pay for Savoy's vital intervention on the Allied side. What no one, even in Milan, seems to have thought of was independence for the Milanese. Vaudemont, the last Spanish governor, who evacuated the city after Eugene's victory in 1706, had a son who was already in the Imperial service. Economically, the duchy paid the price of its involvement in war, which set back such recovery as had been achieved since 1680, and which explains better than Spanish protectionism why it lost its historic importance as a transit zone for trade. In the countryside, however, where nobles and clergy retained two-thirds of the land, absenteeism led to more efficient management by middlemen, whose numbers had multiplied very fast since 1670. Again, the growth of industry in some of the smaller cities, such as Como, partially made good the tragic decline of industry in Milan itself—still, war and pestilence notwithstanding, one of the most striking of European cities. Fifty years later it could be said, half in jest, that not even two centuries of Austrian determination to ruin the region had succeeded, such was its natural wealth.

What is most to the credit of the later years of Spanish rule is that they did nothing to stifle Italy's creative genius. The last two viceroys in Naples even fostered it, and at no time did the Inquisition exert the same degree of censorship as it did over the intellectual life of Spain. Naples became the intellectual capital of Italy, as some of the greater names remind us: Pietro Giannone (1676–1748), the lawyer who was excommunicated for *The Civil History of the Kingdom of Naples* (1723),[1] a work much admired by Montesquieu; Domenico d'Aulesio (1639–1717), jurist, ancient historian, an authority on literature, philosophy, archaeology, medicine—one of the last of the great universal minds of the Renaissance; G. A. Borelli (1608–78), who ranks with Descartes and Harvey as a founder of modern physiology; Carlo Maiello (1665–1738), a canon of the cathedral and one of the foremost of the Cartesian philosophers in which Neapolitan society was so rich. The most illustrious name is that of Giambattista Vico (1668–1744), one of the most original thinkers of modern times, whose *Principles of a New Science of the Common Nature of Nations* (1725) founded the philosophy of history, although his thought did not begin to make its full impact until two generations later. Very different was the

---

[1] See vol. VII, pp. 120–2.

achievement of L. A. Muratori (1672–1750), the outstanding intellectual figure in northern Italy. A long and tranquil life passed almost entirely among the manuscripts and incunabula of the great ducal library in Modena, his birthplace, enabled him to produce a prodigious mass of writings of every kind, remarkable for their erudition and probably the largest output ever to flow from the pen of a single scholar: his irreplaceable *Rerum Italicarum Scriptores* (1723–51) or his *Antiquitates Italicae Medii Aevi*—a total of 34 folio volumes, printed at Milan 1738–42—would singly be monument enough to any man's labours.

It was also under the Spaniards that the great traditions of musical drama and the *commedia dell'arte* developed in Naples. In the eighteenth century the Neapolitan school of music was to influence the whole of Europe. In its four theatres and three concert halls—even Venice then boasted only five—flourished the genius of the Scarlattis, father and son, Giambattista Pergolesi (1710–36) and Domenico Cimarosa (1749–1801). Its painters, notably Luca Giordano (who died in Madrid in 1705) and Francesco Solimena (1657–1747), were the only Italian school to rival the Venetians in vitality and European influence after the glory of seventeenth-century Rome had departed. Solimena's Academy also trained some excellent architects, including Ferdinando Sanfelice (1675–1750), famous for his daring staircases. The most gifted architect of the period, Filippo Juvarra (1678–1736), came from Messina but found his opportunities in Turin.[1]

Of most pregnant consequence for the future of Italy was the remarkable change in the status of the duchy of Savoy-Piedmont.[2] Its transformation into the kingdom of Sardinia was the achievement of Victor Amadeus II (reigned 1675–1730). By 1713 this small State, regarded by a good judge in 1690[3] as a traditional French ally of less importance than the Swiss cantons, had won a European position. In contrast with the apathy of other Italian States, Victor Amadeus took advantage of the European balance of power to oust the French from Pinerolo and Casale in 1696, and later to gain certain Lombard provinces and the kingdom of Sicily. In the eighteenth century the strength of Savoy was to be reflected in the unique continuity of her dynasty. And yet her isolation in Italy and the presence of Austria in Lombardy formed effective checks to her longstanding hopes of expansion. The mistrust engendered by Victor Amadeus II's frequent changes of side exposed his fundamental weakness and forced him to accept Sardinia in exchange for Sicily as early as 1720.

[1] See R. Wittkower, *Art and Architecture in Italy, 1600–1750* (1958), pp. 258–82 and 305–8; cf. *ibid.* pp. 301–2 on the Neapolitan genius for Christmas cribs, one of the most brilliant folk arts of the eighteenth century, well displayed in the Bayerisches National-museum at Munich.

[2] The paragraphs on Savoy-Piedmont have been contributed by Dr Stuart J. Woolf.

[3] E. Spanheim, *Relation de la Cour de France en 1690* (ed. C. Schefer, 1872), pp. 373–7.

The two great wars clearly revealed the limitations of the duchy's resources in relation to her rulers' ambitions. Savoy itself and the county of Nice regularly fell into French hands; the principality of Piedmont, increasingly the nucleus of the duchy since the mid-sixteenth century, suffered heavily from ravagings. Financial disorder aggravated this geographical exposure: only one-ninth of the land paid taxes, according to a calculation of 1685. In 1702, when State revenues totalled 9·5 m. *lire*, the public debt already stood at 26 m. and required 1·5 m. in annual interest; in the Succession War, towards the 81 m. *lire* which military action cost in all, 43 m. came from Allied subsidies.[1] An agricultural economy remained predominant, developing slowly from about 1650, with a better average income than most of Italy and an increasing population: as elsewhere in Italy, however, conservative techniques, inadequate communications, government prohibitions, and above all disproportionately large noble and ecclesiastical possessions (increasingly tied down by *fedecommessi* and mortmain),[2] obstructed any major progress. Industry and commerce, though actively encouraged by the mercantilist policies of Duke Charles Emmanuel II (1637–75) and Victor Amadeus II, were hindered by lack of capital, restrictive craft-gilds, and confusion in government policies themselves; only the silk and (temporarily) the woollen manufacturers were comparable with Lombard industry. Despite sustained encouragement, the ports of Nice and Villafranca failed to rival Marseilles, Genoa or Leghorn. Piedmont, alone among the north Italian states, was not centred round an over-privileged capital. Turin, though unique among Italian cities in its steady demographic expansion in the seventeenth century, numbered only 56,000 inhabitants even in 1713.[3]

The urgent need to improve both the public finances and the army formed an impelling motive for Victor Amadeus's reforms. Equally important was his determination to establish the supremacy of royal authority, much weakened under the rule of two Regents (1637–61, 1675–84), and to enlarge the social basis upon which this authority rested. The rebellions of Mondovì against the salt *gabelle* (1680–6, 1699) were only the most manifest indications of underlying social tension. While still in his 'teens Victor Amadeus drew up a private memorandum outlining his

---

[1] L. Einaudi, *La Finanza sabauda all'aprirsi del secolo XVIII* (Turin, 1908), pp. 176–84, 277–319, 392–439. The acquisition of the Lombard provinces and Sardinia meant only a slight improvement for the public finances. The Montferrat, Alessandrino, Lomellina, Valenza and Valsesia yielded about 1·6 m. *lire* in total State revenues of about 12 m. in 1715; Sardinia (with an estimated capital value of 8 m. *lire*, as compared with 62·5 m. for Sicily) paid only 400,000 *lire* out of the total revenues of 15 m. *lire* in 1730.

[2] In Savoy-Piedmont the nobility and clergy (about 3·5 per cent of a total population of 1 m. in 1700) owned at least 25 per cent of all land in cultivation and received a third of all landed income. In Lombardy *ca.* 1700, these two classes owned 67 per cent of the land. *Fedecommessi* were very similar to entails, but generic rather than specific. Cf. S. J. Woolf, *Studi sulla nobilta piemontese nell' epoca dell' assolutismo* (Turin, 1963).

[3] G. Prato, 'Censimenti e popolazione in Piemonte nei secoli XVI, XVIII e XVIII', *Rivista italiana di sociologia*, vol. x (1906), pp. 349–55.

future reforms and a new land-survey was ordered as early as 1688, but reform was mostly delayed until after the wars; previous attempts had almost always failed because of the immense inherent difficulties and tenacious opposition. Beginning in 1717, the whole administration was reordered. Power was more logically distributed between the central councils, the numerous treasuries were unified and intendants established in all provinces. The wages of all offices were carefully regulated and venality suppressed. At the same time the old 'feudal' nobility, while retaining its virtual monopoly of diplomacy and the army, was almost wholly excluded from administrative posts: over 90 per cent were in non-noble hands between 1713 and 1740.[1] Taxation, based on the salt revenue and land tax (*tasso*), had long been vitiated by noble and ecclesiastical privilege and by continuous alienations of taxes: it was now simplified: when the great land-survey was completed in 1731, the tax-exempted lands of the two privileged classes were greatly reduced, while all feudal rights were attacked. The struggle against ecclesiastical jurisdiction, however, which accompanied the attack on Church patrimonies, was only partially won by the Concordat of 1727, although the Jesuit monopoly of education was limited by the reorganization of the university of Turin and the establishment of State schools. As elsewhere in Italy, the importance of political relations with Rome hindered ecclesiastical reforms. The anti-feudal policy knew no such restrictions. The determination of Victor Amadeus II was shown in the resumption of 172 illegally alienated fiefs in 1720; feudal jurisdictions were also carefully regulated, while an attempt was made to reorganize feudal finances and limit the local power of the feudatories. The donation or sale of titles on a large scale to non-noble bureaucrats, lawyers, financiers and industrialists assured greater obedience. Non-nobles were even to be found among the diplomats, while the development of the artillery under middle-class engineers encroached on the aristocratic monopoly of the army. The subjection of the magistracy and the publication of the Royal Constitutions (1723, 1729), partially annulling local liberties, further emphasized royal supremacy.

An ordered administration, balanced finances, an able diplomacy, and a large and efficient army, absorbing a third of State revenues in the 1730s, were the rewards of these changes. But the socio-economic structure of the country was only slightly modified. The middle class remained small and was easily attracted into the ranks of the nobility. Investments in land, the public debt, State and private taxes, even in industry, confirmed the disproportionate importance of some 3,000 families. In the countryside the nobility remained the most powerful element, particularly through its acquisition of communal and peasant debts. The very thorough-

[1] G. Quazza, *Le Riforme in Piemonte nella prima metà del Settecento* (Modena, 1957), pp. 91–5.

ness of Victor Amadeus II, indeed, which left his successors little more scope than to perfect his reforms, excluded any more radical solution. Moreover the bureaucratic, military and eminently practical nature of the reforms had the effect of suffocating intellectual activity, thus preventing Turin from coming to rival the brilliance of Milan, Naples, Modena or Florence. Count Radicati (1698–1737), the noted free-thinker, fled in the 1720s,[1] and was to be followed into exile by such distinguished figures as Lagrange, Denina, Baretti and Alfieri.

The Mediterranean has always presented acute problems for the supply of navies. Outside it, the maritime powers could get their ships built where timber was readily available or relatively cheap to import. Few Mediterranean states enjoyed this immense advantage. The Ottoman empire was the great exception, able to rely on materials within its own control, including timber of such quality as to arouse French envy. Timber for hulls and masts (as also for the building of Constantinople) was brought down to the Black Sea coast between the Danube mouths and Sinop;[2] hemp was grown from the Bosporus as far east as Trebizond, where the coast is too dangerous for loading timber; sailcloth was woven throughout the Aegean, so light in texture as to permit sails of enormous area, though too permeable to the wind for the highest efficiency; the best iron came from Salonica, some also (like tallow) from the Black Sea and the Crimea; Albania supplied the best pitch and tar; and there were ample supplies in Anatolia of saltpetre and copper for ordnance. Yet the Turks failed to make the best of these resources. From negligence and incompetence, or more likely because they were always in a hurry for new ships, they used unseasoned timber that deteriorated rapidly. Their ships were the laughing-stock of other nations, especially in Venice, whose resources (largely Dalmatian) were far inferior. Unlike the French, who in 1690 built 15 galleys at Rochefort for Mediterranean service, the Venetians had no access to Atlantic shipyards; nor could they build in American yards like the Spaniards, using strong and valuable hardwoods. Nevertheless, Venice made the best of what was available to her to keep on equal terms with the Ottoman. She had a smaller fleet, but it was better manned, commanded, constructed. Later, Venetian ships were often to remain 20 or even 50 years on the stocks; they were all the better for it, even if such delays point to a stagnation of building techniques and a crumbling of naval power.

Naval manpower was a still graver problem for Mediterranean ad-

---

[1] See F. Venturi, *Alberto Radicati di Passerano* (Turin, 1954).

[2] Dalmatian timber was not employed, doubtless because of the Venetian wars and the distance from Turkish naval shipyards. Egyptian shipbuilding depended entirely on imported timber, traditionally from the Lebanon but sometimes transhipped from the Antalya yards in Pamphylia; see the *mémoire* by the comte de Girardin, 14 Aug. 1686, Paris, Arch. Nat., Aff. Etr. B I, no. 379, fos. 433 ff.

miralties—a dual problem, in fact, since oarsmen had to be found for galleys as well as crews for sailing-ships. The recruitment of sailors was at least no more difficult than elsewhere, for in the more or less self-contained world of the Mediterranean seamen were a fairly close-knit as well as mobile community, so that every marine employed crews still more polyglot than in the Atlantic, especially during wars. The supply of galley-slaves was much more difficult. Naval galleys were fewer than in the sixteenth century, but the western Mediterranean powers still maintained nearly a hundred. The French galley corps had grown rapidly under Colbert and numbered nearly 50 vessels by 1690—larger than the Spanish or Venetian, let alone the half dozen operated respectively by Genoa, Tuscany, Malta and the Papal States. As late as 1716 the *Galères du Roi* required 6,000 oarsmen.[1] The sultan maintained about as many as all the Christian powers together. With each galley carrying from 250 to 300 oarsmen (besides soldiers and a few sailors), the demand for slaves, who constituted about a third of the rowing force, was insistent, all the more as wastage was high. Venetians and Turks went some way to meet it by enslaving their prisoners of war, some of whom were sold to other buyers. The French acquired large numbers of Balkan prisoners in 1690–2; during the Nine Years War, Louis XIV tried unsuccessfully to obtain the loan of twelve galleys, with their oarsmen, from Ahmed II, whose objections were partly religious. 'Turks' were more highly valued than other slaves and even in 1702 an average French galley carried fifty of them.[2] French consuls all had instructions 'to find slaves for His Majesty's galleys', contracting with specialized dealers like Franceschi of Leghorn, an *armateur* of anti-Muslim privateers, who delivered many hundreds of slaves to the king of France and was said to be worth 2 m. *écus*.[3] When their main supplies from Leghorn and Malta diminished in the 1680s, and when their peace with Algiers required the return of captives, the French experimented with Senegal negroes and even Iroquois. This was a dismal failure. It was the criminal courts which now provided the *Galères du Roi* with most of their manpower, often with salt-smugglers and military deserters but also a minority of Huguenots. When possible, paid voluntary oarsmen (*bonnevoglie*) were recruited from the dregs of the towns and of impoverished countries; but it was difficult to find them in time of prolonged war, when they preferred to sign on as sailors.

[1] Paris, Arch. Nat., Marine B5, no. 3. The duke of Tursi had seven galleys of his own which he leased for over thirty years, usually under his own command, first to Spain and then to France. He was Giovanni Andrea Doria del Canetto, a grandee of Spain who took his title from a duchy situated in the gulf of Taranto and belonged by family origin to the Genoese patriciate; he became lieutenant-general of the galleys of France in 1715.
[2] Paul W. Bamford, 'Slaves for the Galleys of France, 1665 to 1700', in J. Parker (ed.) *Merchants and Scholars* (Minneapolis, 1965), pp. 173–91; P. Masson, *Les Galères de France* (1938), pp. 275 ff.; J. Marteilhe, *Galley Slave* (ed. K. Fenwick, Folio Soc. 1957), p. 45.
[3] Arch. Nat., Aff. Etr. B1, no. 699, Livourne, 27 Aug. 1688.

This traffic in human beings, comparable only with the plantation slave trade and perhaps also the trade in mercenary soldiers, arose out of a special operational technique. Although the galley was still used occasionally as an auxiliary warship elsewhere, and was only at the beginning of its career in the Baltic,[1] it remained essentially an expression of Mediterranean circumstances, in which it had given distinguished service since ancient times. In the seventeenth century, however, not only was there no galley armada comparable with the fleets which had fought at Lepanto, but the naval value of the galley was more and more in question. It survived thanks to the aristocratic traditions, solidarity and prestige of its officers, who regarded the navy much as the cavalry did the rest of the army. Governments themselves were reluctant to acquiesce in the inevitable: thus the gigantic undertaking of the *Canal des deux mers* was seen by its creators, Colbert and Riquet, in part as a means of rectifying the regional balance of sea power by enabling galleys to be switched rapidly between Atlantic and Mediterranean. And yet, by the time this 'canal du Midi' was finished in 1681, the great battles won by Duquesne off Sicily had shown that the day of the fighting galley was over. Moreover, the galleys had very little freeboard and so were unsuitable for long cruises in the rough seas of winter, when they were generally laid up; their operational season extended only from May to early September at latest, except for the large and solidly constructed Maltese galleys. While galleys continued to figure in the navies, therefore, the tendency, at least in the western Mediterranean, was now to employ them only on such auxiliary duties as towing ships in and out of port (or out of the battle line), as coastguards and dispatch vessels, or for transporting precious cargoes.[2] Thus the Spanish *presidios* along the North African and Tuscan coasts were paid and victualled by galleys, which also carried the silks of Sicily to Genoa or Leghorn. Galleys retained some tactical value also for manoeuvre in flat calms or against the wind, and so for repressing privateers. That they were still of serious use in coastal waters, moreover, explains why they continued their career as warships in the Ottoman and Venetian fleets: they were notably of service in the Adriatic and Black Sea, and for river-work on the Danube and Dnieper. Even France did not abandon them completely for another generation. Spain revived them in 1749 and built her last in 1794.[3] Malta and the small Italian states remained faithful to them till the end of the eighteenth century. About 1730, they reappeared in a new form as the xebecs—small ships which could mount oars but were better armed and more robust than galleys. For long, indeed, the

---

[1] Tourville hoped to have 15 galleys with him before Beachy Head in 1690; Dunkirk had a small galley squadron throughout the Succession War. For the Baltic, cf. below, p. 806.

[2] Their service at Malaga in 1704 was to save the French men-of-war from being luffed by the English line of battle, which had the weather-gauge.

[3] G. Desdevises du Dézert, *L'Espagne de l'Ancien Régime*, vol. II (1899), p. 349.

Mediterranean peoples were to feel a nostalgia for these well-bred craft, so slender and elegant, and so much a part of their history.

During the thirty years which constitute the watershed between the seventeenth and eighteenth centuries, three developments modified the pattern of Mediterranean naval power: the collapse of Spanish sea power at one end, the revival of Ottoman at the other, and the irruption of the British.

Louis XIV had dealt Spanish sea power decisive blows from which it was to take half a century to recover. Duquesne's campaign against the Spanish and Dutch fleets off Sicily in 1676 resulted not only in the death of De Ruyter but in crippling losses for the Spaniards; after Palermo the Spanish navy was the ghost of its old self. Ironically, Louis was to gather the bitter fruit of this weakness when the whole weight of naval operations was thrown on the French during the Succession War. After 1714 Alberoni's first concern was to rebuild the navy as quickly as possible and resume Spain's previous imperial policy in the Mediterranean. His work was undone by English guns off Cape Passaro in 1718, followed by French attacks on the dockyards of Pasajes and Santona in 1719, when half a dozen ships were burnt on the stocks.

Louis XIV's wars, however, have tended to obscure the prolonged fighting in which the Ottoman navy was engaged over these years. The weight of the Christian offensive at sea was mainly borne by the Venetians, who were usually aided by the Knights of St John, less regularly by the naval forces of the pope and of Tuscany, and after 1715 by Spain and Portugal. In detail, the struggle was complicated and yet monotonous.[1] Both sides inflicted moderately heavy losses in men, little enough in ships or galleys. What is chiefly striking about their encounters is their indecisiveness, if not their infrequency. The truth is that the eastern half of the Mediterranean, like the western, offered only limited rewards for command of the sea in this period. Even when they held it, the Venetians lacked resources to exploit it systematically. They were able to cover the disembarkation of an army at limited range, as in the Morea in 1684–7 and 1714, and on Corfu in 1716; but their only long-range project, a landing on the island of Chios in 1694, was a disastrous failure. In spite of every setback, the Turks managed to get a fleet to sea each year and defend what was essential to them: the all-important Dardanelles, freedom of movement in the Archipelago, communications with Egypt. Even with the aid of a horde of Christian privateers, the Venetians could never disrupt Turkish lines of communication for long. Antonio Zeno, the Venetian commander defeated at Chios, was not comparable with his illustrious predecessor Morosini, whereas his adversary, the Kaptan Pasha Mezzomorto (1640?–1701), was a great seaman. In all his en-

[1] See R. C. Anderson, *Naval Wars in the Levant 1559–1853* (Liverpool, 1952), chs. VI and VIII. Cf. below, ch. XIX.

counters with the Lion of St Mark, from 1692, Mezzomorto was victorious; on two occasions, in 1695 and 1697, the Venetian squadrons narrowly escaped complete disaster. Mezzomorto, who virtually re-created the Ottoman navy, made a point of regularly reinforcing the number of his sailing-ships at the expense of the time-honoured galleys; he usually had at least 30 ships of the line under his command.[1] Having been born and bred on the Barbary coast, he had seen at first hand the greatly superior performance of sailing-ships. With the Venetians it was quite otherwise: they favoured the *armada sottile*, or galley fleet, rather than the *armada grossa* of sailing-ships, for a long while to come. The revival of Ottoman sea power seemed so secure by 1715, in fact, when the resumption of war with Venice led to the reconquest of the Morea, that an extension of the Turkish offensive was feared in southern Italy and Malta, for the defence of which France was begged urgently to lend auxiliary forces. The attack on Chios had been intended to strangle Constantinople: twenty years later the Turkish recovery was so spectacular that the Aegean became once more the *mare nostrum* of the Turks, until the advent of Russia (signalized by the battle of Tchesma in 1770) again changed the balance of power in the eastern Mediterranean.

Navally speaking, however, the Mediterranean was no longer simply the concern of the States that bordered it. The Nine Years War and still more its successor established England permanently as one of the great naval powers there. Without necessarily maintaining a standing squadron within the Straits, she was able to dispatch her ships thither at short notice from Cadiz or Lisbon, and to work them out there with a high degree of efficiency and safety; in 1704 and 1708 she acquired Gibraltar and Minorca, in excellent strategic positions. Although their naval penetration had begun half a century earlier, the English had been slow to realize that it was in their power to intervene aggressively in the Mediterranean for any length of time. The decision to abandon Tangier in 1683-4 had been favourably received in England,[2] and it needed all William III's forcefulness to persuade his admirals and ministers to base a winter fleet on Cadiz in 1694-5. Later, Gibraltar's strategic usefulness was less immediately appreciated than that of Port Mahon: the Straits were much too wide to be completely controlled from the Rock with the means available at that time, so that they did not provoke such persistent struggles as had been waged for the narrower Danish Sound. For many

[1] The first squadron of sailing-ships to work in the Mediterranean had been that of the duke of Osuna in 1617, but the Algerines had continued to make more consistent use of sail in the Mediterranean than the Spaniards. The Maltese decision to build four warships of 50 to 60 guns, two of them at Toulon, was taken in 1700: see Cavaliero, p. 106.

[2] Tangier had been a financial liability ever since its acquisition in 1662, and its naval value was slight. The regular squadrons maintained by Charles II in the Mediterranean for trade protection made use of Port Mahon in 1669-71: see the Introduction to John Baltharpe, *The Straights Voyage* (ed. J. S. Bromley, Luttrell Soc. Reprint, no. 20, Oxford, 1959).

years, Gibraltar was to remain an expensive symbol, and it would not have taken much to make George I and Stanhope restore it to the Spaniards in 1721; the invariable public outcry against such a step owed most to sentimental or commercial considerations.[1] After the Peace, France was the only great European power to station large naval forces in the Mediterranean, although for financial reasons her navy was slow to make good its losses. Nevertheless, in a war of any length, the English could soon make their presence felt. It is chiefly this contingency which must be taken into account when considering the new balance of power in the Mediterranean. The Mediterranean states themselves could aspire only to a secondary rôle.

In a sea so much more used for transport than the surrounding land, the destruction of enemy communications was the principal axiom of naval strategy. A second great principle was to emerge clearly when France found herself at war with both the English and Dutch. Since neither of the two principal French bases, Brest and Toulon, had facilities for sheltering the whole fleet for long, it had to be divided on the approach of winter and reassembled on the eve of the spring campaign, the divisions needing to arm as rapidly as possible in late March or early April to avoid being caught in their divided state by an enemy with all his forces concentrated at one point. During the Nine Years War at least, the almost invariable pattern preceding every campaign was the effort of the French divisions to effect their union, and that of the Allies to prevent it. In this way the Mediterranean influenced grand strategy even when the main theatre of operations lay outside it. In March 1689 Tourville managed to bring 20 ships of the Toulon division through to Brest. In 1690 Château-renault repeated this achievement with 17 ships—despite the squadrons under Papachino, Killigrew and Van Almonde which tried to blockade the Straits—and joined Tourville in time to take a distinguished part in the battle of Beachy Head. In 1691 the French fleet did not attempt concentration: one squadron assisted in the conquest of the Cerdaña (Cerdagne) and the county of Nice, while the core of the navy, too weak to try conclusions with the main Allied fleet, cruised evasively in the Channel Soundings under Tourville, inflicting such damage as it could. The attempt of 1692 to unite the fleets was a failure, despite the strenuous efforts of Estrées to get away from Toulon at the end of March and join Tourville at Brest as soon as possible: held back by persistent contrary winds in the Straits, the Toulon division was absent from the battle of La Hougue, with disastrous consequences for the French. During the first four years of the Nine Years War, therefore, the main fleets on either side operated in the Atlantic and the English Channel,

---

[1] D. Gómez Molleda, *Gibraltar: una contienda diplomática en el reinado de Felipe V* (Madrid, 1953), *passim*; W. F. Monk, *Britain in the Western Mediterranean* (1953), pp. 44, 70; B. Larsonneur, *Histoire de Gibraltar* (1955), pp. 44–61.

where Louis XIV hoped to strike the decisive blows. Not until June 1693 did one of them operate in strength in the Mediterranean. In the spring, with a squadron of 20 ships, Estrées had surprised the Spanish fleet while it was refitting in harbour at Baia,[1] but he let slip this chance of annihilating it. In June, after the débâcle of the Anglo-Dutch Smyrna fleet off Lagos, there was concentrated in the Mediterranean the largest French fleet ever seen, totalling 150 ships (including 90 of the line), 5,600 guns and 70,000 men. But this armada seemed bent more on harrying enemy commerce than seeking a strategic decision. It certainly succeeded in clearing Anglo-Dutch shipping from the Mediterranean for several months; but the vital Spanish communications between Spain and Italy, which would have been so vulnerable to its attack, were left unmolested.

In June 1694 the main Anglo-Dutch fleet appeared under Russell, the first admiral to command the English main fleet in the Mediterranean. His orders were simple: to support the Spaniards, then in imminent danger of collapse under the vigorous French offensive in Catalonia, and to prevent Savoy deserting the coalition. In August, Russell forced the French to raise the siege of Barcelona; Tourville, who had only 50 ships against Russell's 75, had to make for Toulon with all speed. King William then changed the entire pattern of English intervention by ordering Russell to winter at Cadiz with all his fleet. Hitherto it had been judged impracticable to take a fleet of any size through the Bay of Biscay between the autumn and spring equinoxes. Now, with the English main fleet at Cadiz for the winter, it became virtually impossible for Brest and Toulon to join forces, although William recognized that his initiative might draw the Brest squadron out of the Channel. Furthermore, Mediterranean operations might now last seven or eight months of the year instead of three or four. Thanks to William's momentous initiative, also, the envelopment of France herself became a possibility. In 1695 Russell played an active part in the siege of Palamos, but fell back precipitately on Cadiz after receiving false intelligence of the approach of a French squadron. It must be admitted that the campaigns of 1694–5 were a disappointment to the Allies. That of 1696 was even less rewarding. The concentration of French forces at Brest in the spring prevented the dispatch of an Allied fleet to Cadiz. Rooke, who had replaced Russell the previous October there, returned early in the year and took command at home against a threat of invasion, leaving only a small squadron at Cadiz under Mitchell and Evertsen.

Once more, therefore, the Mediterranean was left to the French navy, which could again support land operations without interference. Combined operations, military rather than naval in impact, led to notable results in Italy. In August 1696 the Treaty of Turin finally detached Savoy from the coalition, and by the convention at Vigevano in October

---

[1] 17 km. west of Naples, near Pozzuoli.

Austrian troops withdrew from Italy, which was thus completely neutralized. The exceptional honours bestowed by Louis XIV upon the envoy of Savoy showed what importance he attached to this success. The French were now free to concentrate on the Netherlands. The decisive breach in the Allied coalition had been made and it was possible to hasten the negotiations which led to the Peace of Ryswick. When Barcelona surrendered on 10 August 1697 to Vendôme and Estrées, after a two-month siege, Spain and the emperor gave way and the war was virtually at an end. Nevertheless, a striking warning of England's potential position as a Mediterranean power was given two years later when the Peace of Carlowitz was brought about by her mediation.

Throughout the crisis surrounding the death of Carlos II, the future of the Mediterranean was the major subject of anxiety with governments and peoples. 'In the eyes of contemporaries it was still the chief battlefield of commercial rivalry.'[1] Anything which threatened to upset the delicate balance established as the result of fifty years' competition between the Maritime Powers and the French provoked an immediate and violent reaction from the merchants concerned. Thus, in spring 1700, the suggestion that France might receive a share of the Spanish possessions in Italy seemed to constitute a threat to Leghorn, the 'miracle of the Medici' and hub of English Mediterranean trade. The project miscarried; but it was significant that it provoked uncompromising and immediate opposition in both English and Tuscan business circles.

The War of the Spanish Succession opened with Eugene's offensive in north Italy in the spring of 1701. A French squadron under Forbin tried to hold it up by attacking supplies from Trieste in the Gulf of Venice, while the sea connections between Spain, Italy and France remained secure. It was against these routes that William III wished to act in sending out the main Anglo-Dutch fleet in 1702, but this time Spain was no longer an ally and the problem of bases was immediate and acute: not till May 1703 did the First Methuen Treaty make it possible for Lisbon to provide a substitute for Cadiz. In March 1704 Châteaurenault was too weak to attempt interception of the Anglo-Dutch fleet which carried an expeditionary force to the Tagus to open the Peninsular struggle.

The Mediterranean war entered a more active phase in 1704 with the capture of Gibraltar and the indecisive battle of Malaga, when the contestants fired at each other for seven hours without attempt at manoeuvre: drawn up in parallel lines, each in turn let slip the opportunity to break the enemy's line and isolate his van. The French were left in control of the field of battle, but lack of ammunition prevented them pursuing the Allied forces. They never had such an opportunity again. This disappointment confirmed the hesitation of Louis XIV's government to use

[1] J. Meuvret, 'Les Intérêts économiques de la France dans la Succession d'Espagne', *Bull. de la Soc. d'hist. mod.*, 12e série, 56e année (numéro spécial Nov. 1957).

the fleet offensively as such. The Allies were free to sail the Mediterranean, in Tessé's famous phrase, 'like swans on the waters of Chantilly'. Marlborough, whose grand strategy followed the lines sketched out by William, made a great effort to achieve decisive victory in the Mediterranean between 1704 and 1708. Perhaps remembering De Ruyter's burning of the English fleet in the Medway in 1667, or the Spanish blockade of Toulon from the Iles de Lérins in 1635, he hoped to strike a final blow in 1707 at the very heart of French power in the Mediterranean, at Toulon itself—a daring scheme already meditated by William in 1695. The defence was very effectively organized, the ships of the line being protected from fires caused by the bombardment by half sinking them in the harbour itself, while the attack was badly co-ordinated. After this failure, which gave Philip V time to reorganize his forces in Spain, the Allied fleet abandoned all attempt to attack the periphery of the French position. The setback was bitterly resented by Marlborough, who in 1711 was to claim that an attempt on Toulon had been regarded 'from the beginning of this war...as one of the most effectual means to finish it'.[1] This was true enough, but served only to underline the indifferent outcome of an effort on sea and land which had been enormously costly in both money and men.

Although Spain lost her overseas possessions in the Mediterranean at the Peace, only the loss of Minorca and Sardinia—both occupied in 1708 by the English—could be ascribed to naval weakness. Her other losses, apart from Gibraltar itself, were due to military defeats by Imperialist forces: it was Eugene's victory at Turin in 1706 that drove the French out of Italy and opened the way to Naples in August 1707.[2] Even when Louis withdrew his own troops from Spain in the winter of 1709-10, leaving Philip V to rely on Spanish forces, the Allies were still unable to achieve decisive victory there. All Spain rallied to Philip except for Barcelona, which submitted only after a full-scale siege conducted by Berwick in person from July to September 1714.

Though their naval supremacy had been seldom disputed, the siege of Toulon had been the Allies' only serious attempt to take full advantage of the increased strategic flexibility that command of the Mediterranean should have given them. This, in turn, might have been established sooner than it was had Minorca been taken earlier: the Austrians advised this as early as 1704, and at least Minorca might have been taken at the same time as Majorca and Ibiza, instead of two years later, when it proved as easy to capture, under energetic leadership, as Gibraltar had been. More surprising still was the failure to heed the advice of Jean Cavalier, the

---

[1] Quoted Churchill, *Marlborough* (1947 edn.), vol. II, p. 789.

[2] Above, p. 429 and below, pp. 593–4. The Algerines took advantage of Spain's difficulties to seize Oran in 1707. Their previous attempt in 1694, when the siege of Palamos was at its height, had failed. The Spaniards recovered the place in 1732.

leader of the Camisard rebels, who from 1702 held down precious French regiments for years, at no great distance from the coast of Languedoc. The revolt was petering out when finally, in July 1710, a ludicrously small force of 700 was landed under a Huguenot, de Seissan, to attack Agde and Sète (Cette). Perhaps the Alliance, though prepared to use Huguenot services, drew the line at helping subjects in active revolt against their king? But if the answer is that the Allied fleets had no effective invasion force which they could have landed, then it is only another proof of the supremacy of military over naval power. Commercially, too, the results achieved by the Allies were scarcely impressive. So far from drying up, French exports to the Levant rose sharply; at the height of the war, the French were prospecting new markets—which did not, however, material- ize—in Persia and Ethiopia. Such 'blockade' of French coasts as the Allied squadrons were able to institute was quite easy to elude. And yet in the first half of the Succession War the Allies had concentrated the spearhead of their naval power in the Mediterranean, thereby possibly losing a chance of disrupting the Spanish empire in America.

The whole record of the fighting in these years seems to point to the same general conclusion. It was the war on land that saved Philip V's throne and made the Austrian Habsburgs Italian princes. It was the war on land that made Savoy a kingdom, the only Italian State to treat on almost equal terms with the great powers, and that strengthened her future ambitions as a sea power. It was the financially exhausting struggle on land that reduced the United Provinces to the status of a second-class power in the Mediterranean long before 1713. Finally, the maritime power of Venice faced the loss of much of her commercial hinterland in the Balkans to the Habsburgs, the land power which played the decisive rôle in forcing the first stages of the Ottoman retreat from Europe.

It was France, rather than convalescent Spain or far-away England, that emerged in 1715 as the leading power, even the leading commercial power, in the Mediterranean. This was not the least paradoxical result of two wars in which her record at sea had on the whole been undistinguished. It is true that Great Britain's political weight had vastly increased with her power to intervene in southern Europe by force, as the years of Stanhope's diplomacy were to show; but it would not for long remain dominant, as Stanhope himself understood, without French co-operation. The death of Louis XIV, however, marks the passing of the Mediterranean as a centre of world trade and power rivalries. As the seventeenth century gave way to the eighteenth, attention shifted further to the Atlantic and to the Cape route to the Indies. For a time at least, the great powers no longer saw the future primarily in terms of the Mediterranean.

CHAPTER XVIII

THE AUSTRIAN HABSBURGS

IN September 1683 the Turks fled from Vienna, in August 1684 the Emperor Leopold I returned there, and the elaborate mechanism of his court and government settled back into its traditional framework. In many ways this altered very little in the next 35 years. Several households, of the emperor, empress, the dowager empress or the emperor's sons, each with a corps of officials, had normally to coexist in the cramped accommodation of the Hofburg. In his private apartments, the *retirata*, the ruler discussed affairs in confidence: here was the ultimate source of authority. In a series of antechambers he dined publicly, held council, granted investitures and audiences: here that authority was formally displayed. Adjoining the Hofburg was an old irregular cluster of buildings and courtyards where most of the chanceries and councils had premises. Their archives were growing enormously as they recorded judgments or instructions which flowed out to the Empire and the hereditary Habsburg lands of Austria and Bohemia, to Hungary and (after 1700) to Italy, as well as to the ambassadors at foreign courts; but only gradually, from the early eighteenth century onwards, was a real distinction drawn between posts in the 'court' and in the 'government'. Then also, in 1723, Charles VI began his splendid and spacious reconstruction of the Imperial Chancery.

A little further from the Hofburg, the government of the Lower Austrian duchy had its administrative headquarters and the Estates their place of assembly. Elsewhere in the city, tightly surrounded by walls and bastions, the Vienna municipality was in control; but just as the common burghers had long lost their power to a small council of oligarchs, so this council elected its own members to office under the eye of the court. Vienna as a city had no political influence. An indication of this was the right of the Court-Marshal, one of the emperor's principal household dignitaries, to assign accommodation in the town to all persons connected with the court. The burghers complained bitterly and uselessly of the number of houses for which noblemen and others claimed exemption from this burden, which burghers had to shoulder. On the other hand the rents paid, and court expenditure generally, were an indispensable source of income to them. They rebuilt their houses on a larger scale, just as noblemen were doing. After 1683, beyond the glacis which the military authorities insisted on keeping clear, the suburbs also expanded. There, important families began to construct sumptuous country places. Two hundred of these were counted in 1720; and Prince Eugene's new Belvedere looked down towards his new town house a mile away. Without industrial activity or independent influence, the city grew as the appendage of court and government.

Civic history here appears to reflect the steady growth of an autocracy. In some respects this is confirmed by administrative developments. The central treasury, the *Hofkammer*, on Joseph I's accession in 1705, at length deprived the separate treasuries of Inner Austria at Graz and of Tyrol at Innsbruck of their old independence, against intense local opposition. Various attempts were made to improve the conduct of financial business at the court itself. Leopold's extravagant number of *Hofkammer* councillors was cut down after his death. The rule that important decisions must be taken at full meetings of the board was abandoned; smaller committees or commissions, of a few senior officials, were given greater responsibility; in 1717 one committee, the *Finanzkonferenz*, was appointed to supervise all the financial institutions of the empire. In the Austrian Court Chancery (*Hofkanzlei*), separate departments at Vienna already had considerable authority in Graz and Innsbruck; but they also tended to protect provincial interests too zealously, and another select committee now emerged to try and co-ordinate their work. In the longstanding struggle between this Court Chancery and the Imperial Chancery (*Reichskanzlei*)—which functioned in Vienna but was still perceptibly an organ of the Holy Roman Empire rather than of the emperor—the Habsburg institution gradually encroached on its rival's ground. The final battle took place in the decade after 1705, between Court Chancellor Philip Sinzendorf and Imperial Vice-Chancellor Friedrich Karl Schönborn, who was the nominee as well as the nephew of the elector-archbishop of Mainz, chancellor of the Empire. Sinzendorf won, because the balance of power at court favoured politicians for whom Habsburg interest predominated over those of the Empire. Schönborn found himself edged out of the inner councils of state. Another development was the appointment of a second court chancellor, again in 1705. This led in due course to the division of business into *juridica* and *politica*, the *politica* including above all the conduct of foreign affairs.[1] In fact, the *Hofkanzlei* was a formidable engine of government, with wider powers than before, even though it failed to penetrate the Habsburg Bohemian lands. The vital link between the emperors and their Bohemian kingdom remained the separate Bohemian Chancery at Vienna.

But the forces resisting centralization and administrative improvement of this kind were immensely strong. Control in the various principalities was divided at the local capitals between Habsburg office-holders and the

---

[1] Nevertheless, the Council of War (*Hofkriegsrat*) was responsible for diplomatic correspondence with Moscow until 1720, and with Constantinople until 1742. This body also, from 1705, attempted to secure greater control over the military authorities at Graz and Innsbruck. At the same time, the office of the war-commissariat (*Generalkriegskommissariat*) became gradually more important and 'depended' less and less on *Hofkammer* and *Hofkriegsrat*.

Estates of the privileged orders, even in Bohemia. Leopold's lieutenant (*Statthalter*) himself normally represented the local interest. The Estates had their periodic meetings, their permanent committees, their own office-holders. Political independence had been taken from them, but they preserved a stiff regional pride, based on historic rights and historic frontiers,[1] and their administrative importance remained paramount. Taxes voted by the Estates were collected by the Estates. Government military expenditure within an Austrian duchy, the cost of loans and advances raised there, or debts transferred to it, were often first deducted from such taxation. Inept accountancy, waste and delay then further reduced the amount reaching Habsburg treasuries. In any case, in their quality as landowners the Estates dominated the countryside. Their stewards, on whose goodwill and manipulation the collection of most local taxes depended, also helped to administer justice; and noblemen were often royal office-holders in Bohemian Circles and in Moravia where their lands lay. The unprivileged were subjects of theirs rather than of the Habsburg princes, whose edicts penetrated with difficulty to remote landscapes and illiterate peasantries. A bureaucracy of the type familiar in later Habsburg history—officials without local connections—did not exist.

Nor were the emperors personally able to weld together effectively the institutions of the central government. The autocrat, for whom in theory all those treasuries and chanceries and councils were advisory bodies only, rarely settled the endemic disputes which resulted from the traditional rivalry between them. Foreign ambassadors continually refer to the disorder of the Habsburg court. In this respect Leopold I (1658–1705), in his later years, was outstandingly weak. He loved taking advice, listened endlessly to contradictory recommendations, and was unable to come to a firm decision on any topic. By the 1690s, leaving aside the large number of merely titular councillors, he was surrounded by an incoherent collection of committees of active councillors. A small effective body of policy-makers was lacking. The experiment, begun in 1697, of a new 'Deputation' of office-holders from the chief departments to deal with the fundamental problems of war finance[2] and recruitment did little to improve matters. It is clear that the accession of Joseph I (1705–11) led to some useful reforms, but the system of counsel by collateral committees continued. At length, in 1709, these were subordinated to a small standing cabinet of greater authority, the *Konferenz*;[3] a supreme advisory body of this kind

---

[1] The magnificent study of local history and topography in *Die Ehre des Herzogtums Krain* (Nuremberg, 1689) by J. W. von Valvasor, a foreign member of the Royal Society of London, is the best memorial of this standpoint.

[2] Cf. above, pp. 305 ff.

[3] A small, responsible council of the most important ministers, the *Geheimkonferenz*, had functioned successfully for a few years from 1669 onwards; it still existed in 1700, but had little control over the network of committees.

was confirmed in its functions by an ordinance of 1721. The undeniable virtues of the government in the previous thirty years had depended rather on individual talents: on Ulrich Kinsky, the senior Bohemian chancellor between 1683 and 1699; on Gundaker Starhemberg and Prince Eugene, appointed to preside over the *Hofkammer* and *Hofkriegsrat* respectively in the great crisis of 1703; on Johann Seilern as one of the court chancellors from 1705 to 1715; and on Johann Wratislaw, the partner of Heinsius and Marlborough in the diplomacy of the Grand Alliance between 1701 and 1712. These men also owed much to a handful of hard-working higher officials. The fact remains that administrative disorder produced by overlapping and competitive bureaucratic institutions weakened the force of the government. It was a weakness clear to almost everyone under Leopold and, after an opening burst of reform, under Joseph. Charles VI (1711–40) showed greater energy; but his claims to the Spanish empire, which led to the appointment of Spanish advisory councils, and his clumsy if undeniable zeal in reorganizing the finances introduced yet further discords into the court at Vienna.

At heart these rulers did not believe that such a defect was a matter of fundamental importance. Their education moulded them to stress other values, among which constant religious exercise ranked first. Leopold and his younger son Charles were unwearied in attendance at the Court Chapel, and not only because they took an expert interest in its music. Both princes went enthusiastically on pilgrimage to shrines like Mariazell, considering it a solemn duty to publish in this way their profound sense of the union between the Habsburg family and the Catholic Church— a union which they had been taught from childhood to venerate as the great pillar of government. They sponsored directly two of the most powerful Catholic cults of their day, the Immaculate Conception and veneration for the Czech martyr John of Nepomuk. The elder son, Joseph, had been given tutors less clerical in bias and his temperament was worldly by comparison. As for recreation, all three princes would leave the Hofburg, or the Favorita on the edge of the city, for long stays at Laxenburg twenty miles away; here they hunted—Joseph with a peculiar frenzy—and more or less forgot the cares of administration. Wherever they were, they assumed that the government was immovably fixed in them by God through the virtues and status inherited from their ancestors. This confident assertion was a part of their theory of state and of politics.

The claim to authority was above all the claim of 'Our House', the 'illustrious House of Austria'. Its constitution and interests, its laws of succession, determined the fate of individual members of the family. Because Joseph had no direct heirs male, the claim by inheritance gave Leopold and his two sons in turn the lands of the Austrian duchies, with outposts in southern Germany and on the Adriatic. It gave them the lands of the Bohemian Crown, including Moravia and Silesia; a title to the

Crown of St Stephen of Hungary and all its historic dependencies, which in the Middle Ages had stretched across the Carpathians and into the Balkans; another title, when Carlos II died, to the dominions of the Spanish Crowns throughout the world; and a conviction, after the long sequence of Habsburgs who had won election as King of the Romans or Emperor, that the Imperial Crown was theirs by prescriptive right. On the one hand, historians and librarians employed by the bibliophile Leopold linked his genealogy with innumerable emperors, saint, and heroes, back to Noah; on the other, jurists in the Vienna chanceries manipulated legal instruments of every kind to defend the Habsburgs, or the Habsburgs as emperors, against rival dynasties. Not only the spiritual advisers, like the Capuchin Marco d'Aviano whose long series of letters consoled and exhorted Leopold throughout his Turkish wars, but a hard-headed politician like Wratislaw, who wrote often from Vienna to the young Charles at war in Spain (1704–11), accepted without question the extraordinary accumulation of inherited authority vested in their correspondent. These three Habsburg rulers in fact embodied a bid for power, in the flux of relations between States, which was one of the prime political factors of the period. It directly affected south-eastern Europe, Italy, Germany, Spain and the Netherlands.

At the same time, as they and their advisers were well aware, a bid for power of this kind, based on hereditary claims to widely scattered areas, involved profound difficulties. The most obvious, in 1688 and right down to 1718, was to decide the priority between east and west for the employment of limited military resources. Another was the conflict of interest between Spain—even Habsburg Spain—and the Austrian Habsburgs in Italy; or between the emperor, with a tradition of responsibility for the Empire behind him, and the emperor as Habsburg with increasing possessions elsewhere. There was also the problem of reconciling prescriptive claims with the demands of indispensable allies: the Austrian Netherlands of the eighteenth century were a memorial of Charles VI's determination to keep what the Habsburgs once had held, in spite of the limited sovereignty allowed him by the Barrier Treaty of 1715 and their remoteness from the main centres of Habsburg power. The dynastic character of Habsburg influence in Europe precluded empire-building on a compact geographical basis. Accumulation, rather than the increase of efficient authority, was the purpose in view.

In the 1680s the Ottoman power had once again taken the initiative south and west of the Carpathians. The Turks were defeated at Vienna, but at first they remained strong in Hungary. Both circumstances strengthened the case for attempting the reconquest of Hungary, and helped the politicians and churchmen who wanted to rescue the Christian populations of the Balkans from Turkish rule. This old idea had been pressed by

576

Innocent XI on Christian courts since 1676, but until 1683 Leopold's advisers were far more intent on resisting Louis XIV in the Empire than on checking the Turks. They now modified their views. By intense diplomatic activity, which sought to secure a truce with Louis over Germany and to consolidate an offensive alliance with Poland and Venice (and indirectly with Muscovy also), Vienna managed to concentrate on its military thrust eastwards. Between 1685 and 1688, one of the great landmarks of seventeenth-century Europe collapsed—the Turkish occupation of Hungary.[1] Imre Thököly, nominated 'king' of Hungary by Mehmed IV, was driven from his strongholds in Slovakia. Prince Michael Apafi and the Transylvanian Estates were forced by treaties of increasing severity in 1685-7 to admit Habsburg troops. Buda fell on 2 September 1686, and the victory at Nagyharsány on 12 August 1687 blocked the return of Turkish armies into the plain north of the Drava, the great right-bank tributary of the Danube. Other Habsburg troops pushed forward from Croatia into Bosnia. The Hungarian Estates, summoned to Pressburg, were unable to resist the first major political advance of the Habsburg government into the space thus cleared for it: the crowning of Leopold's son Joseph as king of Hungary, on 9 December 1687, formally closed negotiations which established the hereditary character of the title in the male line, revoked certain liberties previously enshrined in charters drafted when earlier kings were 'elected', and included in the coronation oath a formula hinting at reserve powers vested in the ruler which would permit him to disregard constitutional rights. This transaction rankled profoundly with the Magyars, all the more when they saw the reconquered territories provisionally administered by organs of the Vienna government —by military commanders on the spot and by the *Hofkriegsrat*, *Hofkammer*, and *Generalkriegskommissariat*. The *Hofkammer* soon had its regional officials at work, based on Buda, Košice[2] (Kassa) and Cakovec.

Such were the prospects for a revival of Habsburg power in Hungary when Belgrade fell on 4 September 1688. The Turks still held important points between Transylvania and the river Tisza, particularly Temesvár, but exciting news now came in from much further afield. There was chaos in the Ottoman camp after the deposition of Mehmed IV.[3] The Bulgarian Catholics had risen in rebellion and the bishop of Nicopolis arrived in Vienna to seek help. The Serbs were restive, encouraged by adventurers like George Brancovich[4] and his brother Sava, an Orthodox metropolitan

---

[1] Cf. vol. v, pp. 495-9, and below, pp. 619 ff.
[2] William Schröder (1640-88), in his 'Treasury of Princes' (*Fürstliche Schatz- und Rentkammer*, 1686) a champion of enlightened autocracy in finance and economics, received a *Hofkammer* appointment in northern Hungary in 1686; he was extremely unpopular with the Magyars.   [3] Below, p. 620.
[4] George Brancovich (1645-1711) was later arrested by the Austrians and exiled to Bohemia, where he died. His writings, particularly on Serbian history, considerably influenced his countrymen in the eighteenth century.

in Transylvania, who claimed descent from the medieval Serbian despots. Even more encouraging, General Veterani was able to put pressure on the prince of Wallachia, Serban Cantacuzene, by moving his troops in a wide arc through the Banat and Little Wallachia before returning to quarters in Transylvania; Cantacuzene sent a mission to Vienna to recognize Leopold's suzerainty. Meanwhile, in Moldavia the Polish campaign had been unsuccessful, so that the Habsburg could raise the convenient (but very ancient) claim of the kings of Hungary to this area. Far to the south, at the other end of the enormous battle-front, Habsburg forces were occupying points along the line of the river Sava, at Gradiska and Brod. In all these regions the Orthodox had their suspicions of a powerful Catholic ally and they negotiated tentatively in Moscow, but the Habsburg position had never been stronger. By the end of 1688 the outlines of a grandiose opportunity in war and politics had become clearly visible: an advance from Hungary and Transylvania into the predominantly Orthodox world beyond the Carpathians, beyond the Danube on its eastern course below Belgrade, and beyond the Sava and the Una. Ottoman envoys were already making their way slowly northwards to negotiate, with instructions as yet undisclosed.

At this point the complicated interests of the Austrian Habsburgs in western Europe began to assert themselves. Marco d'Aviano might talk of a move on Constantinople; but all the arguments which had brought into existence an alliance between emperor and Dutch in 1673 now pressed even more heavily. Louis XIV, aware that Habsburg military triumphs in the east affected the western theatre of politics and that the Turks proposed to negotiate, aimed at a speedy consolidation of French influence right up to the Rhine. Were he to succeed, it would settle a whole cluster of questions in which the Habsburgs—and the emperor—were deeply concerned. Among these was the fate of Lorraine—Charles V of Lorraine, Leopold's brother-in-law and general-lieutenant of the armies in Hungary, was determined not to accept the absorption of his duchy by France—and the complex matter of the duchess of Orléans's claim to a share in the Palatinate lands. No man could put greater personal pressure on Leopold than his father-in-law Philip William of Pfalz-Neuburg, the new elector palatine, who lobbied insistently through the empress, while a former minister of his, Stratmann, held the post of court chancellor in Vienna. There was also the crisis of the Cologne election.[1] If Louis XIV intruded his nominee Fürstenberg, it would be in the first instance at the expense of the Wittelsbachs, who had held the see—often with other sees, including the strategic point of Liège—for over a century; and Maximilian of Bavaria, victor at Belgrade and the emperor's son-in-law, an ally carefully decoyed away from the French connection of his father, was a Wittelsbach. Maximilian, moreover, had been promised through the good offices

[1] Above, pp. 224–5.

of Vienna the government of the Spanish Netherlands: increasing French pressure there would reduce the value of the offer. The Spaniards themselves clamoured for support, and the problem of the succession in Spain gave them a useful lever in Vienna. Finally, the States of the Empire were at last positively willing to collaborate in resisting French arms and diplomacy, so that it became inexpedient for the emperor to deny them support. He had to remember that his armament in Hungary depended to a considerable extent on their resources. In any case, at this date he himself could not accept the permanent alienation of Strasbourg from the Empire, or of the Breisgau from Habsburg rule. Nor could he afford to miss the chance, which his own offers of help made possible, of detaching Victor Amadeus II of Savoy from France.

In this way the western crisis and the eastern triumphs created an almost even balance, which determined the course of Austrian history down to the treaties of Ryswick and Carlowitz. Leopold, echoing the words of Kinsky, and of General Antonio Caraffa who directed the general War Commissariat in Hungary, at first agreed that to fight on both fronts would be, 'if not impossible, at least very difficult'. Yet, granted all that was at stake in the West, the Habsburgs could hardly surrender the fruits of victory along the Danube. The Habsburg ministers, in bargaining with the Turkish envoys now in Vienna,[1] gradually scaled down some of their original demands, but they still insisted on the complete surrender of Hungary and Transylvania and on the dismantling of Ottoman fortresses in Wallachia. The envoys were not empowered to accept such terms. In addition, Vienna's instructions to Lewis of Baden for the conduct of the next campaign in Hungary were too loosely drawn. They urged defensive tactics, but left the generals a sufficiently free hand; and in 1689 Lewis, with his subordinates Piccolomini and Veterani, went storming up the Morava valley deep into the Balkans. Their advance meant that Leopold lost all chance of contracting out of the Turkish war. A policy of moderation became more and more difficult to sustain. He had to accept conflict on both fronts, the ratification of a new alliance with the Maritime Powers and the final breakdown of discussions with the Turks. Young Eugene of Savoy and the Protestant politicians, who blamed the continuance of the Balkan war on clerical influence at court, were less than fair to Leopold himself.

At first the failure to make peace seemed providentially to open the chance of further gains far to the south. By moving from Nish to Üskub (Skopje) and thence to Prizren by November 1689, Piccolomini outbid the Venetians, who had been earlier in touch with the Serbs and Albanians of this region. He persuaded Arsenius III, the patriarch of Peć, who enjoyed great official authority under the Ottoman, to take an oath of loyalty to the emperor. Leopold's proclamation of 6 April 1690 appealed for the united support of all Balkan peoples against the tyrant and pro-

---

[1] Below, p. 621.

mised liberty under their lawful ruler, the new king of Hungary. During the same winter (1689–90) the other half of Lewis's army crossed over from the Morava to the Danube at a point below the Iron Gate and quartered in Little Wallachia, while troops also pushed down from Transylvania to Bucharest itself. General Heister concluded a pact with the dominant clique of boyars in Moldavia for tribute, provisions, and the maintenance of religious liberties.

These exploits marked the limit of the Habsburg advance. The Turkish power revived and 1690 was a year of retreat for the Imperialists—from the Principalities into Transylvania, from the Balkans back to Hungary. A new ruler in Wallachia, Constantine Brancovan, recovered his freedom of manoeuvre and negotiated impartially with both Constantinople and Vienna. Serbia became Turkish once more. The promised 'liberation of the Serbs' did not occur; instead, their patriarch had to lead an enforced migration of these people northward—by no means the first or the last of such migrations, but one of the most memorable. At Belgrade, the Ortho-dox clergy just had time to formulate demands to the emperor, on behalf of all members of their Church, before the city was recovered by the Turks. Arsenius set up his see at Carlowitz on the Drava, Leopold con-firming the rights of the Orthodox under his rule. A latter-day myth of some influence was to insist, mistakenly, that the Serbs were invited by the emperor to leave their homesteads and settle in Habsburg land on the promise of his favour. In fact, they came north as a consequence of his defeat.

Military deadlock followed. The Turks, after their resounding defeat at Zalánkemén in August 1691, could not advance beyond the Drava on the right bank of the Danube. They lost all points in Hungary north of the Maros, which flows into the Tisza (Theiss) from the east. For their part, the Habsburg commanders could neither take Temesvár, south of the Maros, nor recapture Belgrade. The fortifications of both Turkish Bel-grade and Habsburg Peterwardein (Pétervárad) were improved in 1692, and in the following years much ineffectual fighting took place in the area between them. The difficulty of communication across the rivers—and the enormous marshlands where the Drava, Tisza and Temes approach the Danube, and where in those days the Bega soaked its slow way past Temesvár into the Tisza—made contemporary problems of warfare in the Po valley or Flanders look insignificant by comparison. The campaigning here after 1692 was costly but indecisive. Vienna improved its galleys on the Danube, with the help of sea-captains and sailors recruited in Ham-burg or Holland, but to very little effect.

Imperial efforts in the Nine Years War, of course, contributed to this stalemate. The best commanders, as well as sufficient troops, were lacking along the Danube. In the end, it was the unfavourable course of war in the West, rather than a positive revision of policy, that persuaded Leopold to scale down his military commitments in Italy and the Empire. By accepting the ultimatum of Louis XIV and Victor Amadeus which ended the war in Italy in 1696,[1] he was able to transfer more regiments, and a first-class general in Eugene of Savoy, to the East. Eugene destroyed the Turkish army as it tried to cross the Tisza at Zenta on 11 September 1697. At last the Turks began seriously to treat for peace. William III's ambassadors smoothed the path for negotiations which led to the conference of powers at Carlowitz,[2] while Vienna compelled the Poles to join in. Muscovy apart, the belligerents finally agreed to keep what they held at the time, except that in order to make a defensible frontier between them the two major parties surrendered isolated points which they still occupied in territory dominated by the other. The Habsburgs, therefore, failed to gain Temesvár, Belgrade, or a footing in Wallachia. They kept Hungary, Transylvania, the area between them down to the Maros, and nearly the whole area down to the Sava. It was an immense new empire, even though western scholars or statesmen knew very little about great tracts of it. Significantly, it was one of the Habsburg commissioners in the difficult task of defining boundaries in this unmapped country, Count Luigi Marsigli, who was to publish in 1726 the first adequate account of the whole Danubian region in his *Danubius Panonico-mysicus...*[3]

Along the new frontier many rival institutions and populations were to jostle in the opening years of the eighteenth century. Expanding the system of defence which had protected Inner Austria and Croatia before 1683, the Habsburg government formed additional *Generalate*—military zones in which chains of small frontier posts and larger garrisons were set. Here a few regular soldiers reinforced colonists, themselves fighting men paid by land-holdings in return for military service, and often Serbs or members of one of the other migrant Slav peoples. Indeed, groups of families as well as individuals moved restlessly about, driven forward by poor harvests, epidemics, over-population or heavy taxation in their place of domicile, and attracted by news of better lands elsewhere. In 1715, for example, a particularly large number were to migrate towards the Danubian plain from western Croatia. Meanwhile, the *Hofkammer* constantly tried to whittle down the size of the areas administered by the *Hofkriegsrat*. The Magyar counties claimed to control the population along the Maros; but the military colonists protested, loath to be taxed like Hungarian peasants. The Croatian Estates at Zagreb, the *Ban* (Lieutenant) at their head, insisted on their rights over one part of the frontier, round Petrinje. The Catholic clergy sniped at the liberties recently granted to the Orthodox, liberties which Joseph wisely confirmed during the next Magyar rebellion. In short, there was little unity in the

---

[1] Above, p. 250. [2] Below, pp. 626–7.
[3] The Hague and Amsterdam, 6 volumes; the plan of this great work was complete by 1700.

southern region of the new Habsburg dominion. In 1718 the acquisition of Temesvár and the Banat, of Belgrade and strips of Serbia and Wallachia, gave it a greater apparent solidity. After the Peace of Passarowitz, colonization went forward faster than in the disturbed interim after Carlowitz.

Leopold had won a massive victory in the Danube valley, but he also kept his pretensions largely intact in western Europe. It was characteristic of his ambiguous but unyielding statesmanship that Vienna, although still at war with the Turks, was the last of the courts involved in the Nine Years War to accept the Peace of Ryswick.

Behind the moving frontier, military pressure had carried on the work of consolidation in Transylvania. The Estates there hoped for a settlement in which the principality would survive, with the prince (now Apafi's son, a minor) and the Estates merely recognizing the suzerain powers of the Habsburg in return for a generous guarantee of liberties. The Magyars meanwhile considered the country an indisputable part of the kingdom of Hungary. But Leopold, advised particularly by Caraffa, wanted a more absolute authority in Transylvania, available as a counterbalance to the Hungarian Estates. His policy was both purposeful and devious. The question of Michael Apafi's title was at first left open. The liberties of four religious denominations—Lutheran, Calvinist, Unitarian and Catholic—were safeguarded. Limits were set to annual taxation in peace and even in war. The respective powers of the civil government and of the Habsburg military commander were defined. Then, to the dismay of the Transylvanians, after long prevarication Leopold refused to recognize the younger Apafi's claim to succeed his father. The offices of a Transylvanian chancery and treasury began to function in Vienna, to the dismay and anger of the Magyars. In practice, the influence of the Habsburg military commanders remained paramount. When Apafi formally surrendered his claim, in April 1697, a distinct phase of Austrian expansion in this period was complete. Transylvania, as the great auxiliary of Ottoman domination in the plains, or of successful rebellion in Upper Hungary against the Habsburgs, had at length disappeared.

Hungary itself presented a different problem. A committee of advisers was set up under Cardinal Kollonich[1] to prepare detailed plans for a permanent settlement. On one hand they had to deal with current difficulties, such as the assorted evils of a military occupation, disputed or obscure claims to land long held by the Turks, the scarcity of labour. But they also debated fundamental questions of autocracy and constitutional

---

[1] Count Leopold, Cardinal Kollonich (1631–1707) joined the Order of St John at Malta in 1650, and after a period of military service in the Mediterranean held high office in the Habsburg lands for the rest of his life. In 1692–4 he was in charge of the *Hofkammer*, and from 1695 primate of Hungary. He must be reckoned one of the greatest representatives of militant Catholicism in the later seventeenth century.

right. Kollonich wanted to put in working order the basic administrative institution of the old Magyar polity, the *komitat* (county), with local interests entrenched there. He also wanted guarantees for the Habsburg government, its arms and revenues. Magyars like Paul Esterházy the Palatine (the highest office under the Crown recognized by the Hungarian constitution), who suffered in their pride and in their pockets under the existing military régime, pressed for the fullest possible restoration of ancient rights. Caraffa, who quarrelled bitterly with Kollonich, wished to repeat the authoritarian experiment unsuccessfully tried in the decade before 1681.[1] The cardinal attempted to hold a fair balance, except for his steady bias against the Protestant interest. The result of the discussions, the famous 'Memorandum for the Settlement of Hungary', was accordingly condemned by most Magyars as a blueprint for despotism, and by Habsburg officers and officials for its excessive tenderness towards archaic and anarchic Magyar concepts of liberty. Only fragments of the plan were adopted. The settlement of disputed titles went forward very slowly, and it seems that the sale of vacant lands did not begin before 1696. Immigration, an important point in the original drafts, first got under way long afterwards, and then on the initiative of individual landowners rather than of the government. The fierce arbitrary taxation of the War Commissariat, enforced by troops, continued. The Turkish war kept intact the military control which maintained the government. Peace with the Turks, followed by the Spanish Succession War (which drew off some of the regiments quartered in Hungary), set the stage for fresh uproars.

The one hint of real improvement made matters worse. In 1697 Leopold tried to settle the fundamental question of direct taxation. He wanted far more than the population could afford; but in order to lighten the overwhelming burden on the peasantry, long ago defined in Magyar law-books as the *misera plebs contribuens*, he decided to tax both magnates and gentry. He was unwilling to call a Diet but afterwards deferred to protests, drastically reducing the sums demanded from magnates and agreeing for the moment not to tax the lesser nobles. As a result, the squeezing of the peasants continued. Hosts of unattached soldiers were on the move. The Habsburg garrisons held the citadels but could only master the countryside by sporadic raiding. Markets, where poor men resisted the attempt to tax the necessities of life, were the scenes of rioting. Serious peasant unrest, inflamed by the combined demands of landlord and government, indeed a disorderly rejection of all authority, can be detected in most parts of Hungary by 1700. It proved the basis for a major political rebellion.

Agrarian unrest normally unites the landowner with the administration, but there were good reasons why this rule did not apply in Hungary. The

[1] See vol. v, pp. 492–6.

nobility cherished a political tradition which justified not only opposition to the king but appeals abroad for armed support—to Poland, France, and the sultan. They had quarrelled, in many areas, with Habsburg army officers. They feared the government's plan to tax them, especially if the Diet was never summoned. Leopold's refusal to call Hungarian representatives to the congress at Carlowitz was another affront to their ancient rights. The crisis broke when two notable figures intervened. One was Francis II Rákóczi (1675–1735).[1] His docile youth in court circles and a Jesuit academy could not obliterate, in the minds of the Magyars, the prestige bestowed upon him by the titles of his grandfather and great-grandfather, both princes of Transylvania, and of his stepfather Thököly; he was easily the most powerful magnate of north-east Hungary, a *grand seigneur* in possession of vast estates and hundreds of villages, with vineyards and salt-mines second to none. The other figure was Nicholas Berczényi, of lesser birth but a much stronger personality, who dominated Rákóczi; he was once described by an Austrian councillor as the 'new Hungarian Cromwell'.[2] These two corresponded with foreign powers and were detected. Berczényi fled to Poland. Rákóczi escaped from prison and joined him. They returned to Hungary in 1703 to head a rebellion. Hating the government, or preferring to lead mobs rather than to be threatened by them, men of importance soon joined in. Pre-eminent during the next few years was Alexander Károlyi, also a great landlord of the north-east and recently a senior officer in the Habsburg army. Protestants tended to follow these Catholic leaders, from whom the Catholic clergy tried to stand aloof. Leopold also had a party of Magyar supporters, especially magnates like Esterházy and the brothers John and Nicholas Pálffy, as well as the meagre military force which could be spared from western Europe.

It was no accident that Rákóczi prospered until 1704, prospered somewhat less for the next two years, and then began to lose ground: the victories of Blenheim and Turin had powerful repercussions in Hungary. Down to 1704 his opponents lost everything in the north. In Transylvania their authority shrivelled to a small area, so that an assembly of nobles declared Rákóczi prince of the country. His lieutenants occupied Hungary west of the Danube, raiding deep into Moravia, Lower Austria as far as the Wiener Wald, and Styria. Gradually, the leaders formulated the ideas to which they clung throughout repeated efforts at negotiation. They insisted on a guarantee by foreign States of any settlement in Hungary; Rákóczi himself became increasingly entangled in secret diplomacy with Louis XIV, Augustus of Poland and the tsar—all of whom duped him by empty promises of assistance. They insisted also that Vienna recognize Rákóczi's title to Transylvania. Above all, a solemn manifesto of February

---

[1] Spelt 'Ragotski' by·his English contemporaries.
[2] A. von Arneth, *Prinz Eugen von Savoyen*, vol. I (Vienna, 1858), p. 354.

1704 proclaimed that the settlement of 1687 was invalid, so that Joseph's claim as hereditary ruler of Hungary had no legal basis. With greater difficulty the rebels managed to agree with one another that Protestant grievances must be removed. Most of these views were still upheld at the meeting in Maros-Vasárkely (Târgul-Mures) in April 1707, when the Transylvanians swore homage to Rákóczi, and at the more important assembly near Onod in May and June 1707, when the Magyars dethroned Joseph by declaring an interregnum.

Unfortunately for them, it was already clear that Rákóczi could neither control his friends nor discipline his fighters. When the Protestants complained at Onod that earlier promises had been disregarded, two Protestant leaders were brutally killed. The privileged, as always, insisted on their right not to be taxed. Rákóczi, with the mining towns of northern Hungary in his hands, tried to fill the void by introducing a copper coinage, and then devalued it. Price inflation added to the miseries of the land. Meanwhile, his opponents grew slowly stronger. In the winter of 1703–4, on a lengthy visit to the eastern front, Eugene had almost despaired; he found the defences crippled by lack of men and, above all, of money. Then, after Blenheim, he was able to transfer cavalry regiments from Bavaria to Hungary. By a fine military feat in the autumn of 1705, an expeditionary force under Herbeville had marched right across the great plains from a camp below Pressburg to Transylvania. Rákóczi himself intercepted it but met with a crushing defeat at Zsibó on 11 November. Herbeville, joined by another Habsburg force under Rabutin which had long been isolated in this area, reconquered the country and gradually stripped the rebels of their influence in Transylvania. After the final occupation by the Habsburg of Milan and Naples by the end of 1707, still more regular troops were brought to Hungary. Under a relentless commander, old General Heister, they won an important victory at Trenčín (Trentschin) in August 1708, and made steady progress in the Carpathians. The right bank of the Danube was also cleared. John Pállfy, the Ban of Croatia, began to play an influential part, first as the Habsburg commander-in-chief from September 1710, then in unofficial negotiations. Károlyi and his friends considered seriously the case for a change of sides, just when Rákóczi was trapping himself deeper and deeper in a labyrinth of profitless diplomacy abroad. In a last bid for foreign aid, Rákóczi crossed into Poland in February 1711. When the Ottomans invited him to Constantinople in 1716, it was from Paris that he came.

The terms of peace were settled at Szatmár and (with few modifications) confirmed at the Diet of 1712–15. The Habsburgs secured two fundamental points. The hereditary character of their authority, so long as male heirs were forthcoming, was confirmed; and the Magyars accepted the automatic accession of Charles in Hungary on the death of Joseph in 1711.

Secondly, the old Hungarian claim that their constitution embraced borderlands like Transylvania, the Military Frontiers and Croatia was not confirmed by any positive enactment. The Croatian Estates, in particular, maintained their rights and looked to Vienna rather than Pressburg, as in the past. Direct supervision of the other areas from Vienna continued. For the Magyars, their great achievement was that an unsuccessful rebellion did not involve the usual whittling down of their liberties. Vienna finally gave up the autocratic programme once sponsored by men like Caraffa, and again recognized the rights of the Protestants, the privileges of the landowners, and the sacrosanctity of the Diet with the traditional offices of state. It was the reasonable price paid to many loyal Magyar noblemen who had followed the Crown against Rákóczi during the rebellion. Charles VI emphatically asserted the need for a policy of reconciliation when he came from Vienna to be crowned at Pressburg in the summer of 1712.

The Balkans had not been conquered, nor the Magyars reduced to complete subordination. But the future basis of a 'dual monarchy' was more firmly laid by the limits set to the great Habsburg expansion eastwards in this period.

In 1688 Louis XIV's aggression in the Rhineland had compelled Vienna to turn its attention westwards. The defence of the Empire, as in the past, seemed to it essential. But the politics of the next 25 years showed clearly that the limits of Habsburg power in Germany had already been reached and could not be extended. The more effective councillors preferred to concentrate on Hungary and the claim to the Spanish dominions. In retrospect, the general bias of 'Austrian' policy away from the Empire looks inevitable. Some contemporary statesmen regretted it, viewing the facts of the situation from a different standpoint; but they were defeated.

Between 1679 and 1688 France threatened the German princes directly, not only in the Rhineland but in Westphalia and Swabia. The majority turned for help to the Habsburg ruler who was also their emperor; they temporarily found it difficult to cavil at his authority, the limited authority sanctioned by the treaties of 1648 and later agreements. One sign of the times was the swift and easy election of Joseph as King of the Romans in 1690, in vivid contrast to the long struggle which preceded Leopold's election in 1658. Again, in 1711 when Joseph died, French manoeuvres to block the election of his brother Charles were quickly overcome. Vienna was stronger in Germany between 1688 and 1714 than in the decades immediately before or afterwards. Although the mass of small States in Swabia and Franconia displayed an impressive talent for raising, paying, and deploying a military force—through a confederation of the western Circles of the Empire[1]—to defend themselves during both the Nine Years

[1] For the Circles, see vol. v, pp. 447–9.

War and the Succession War, their combined resources were always inadequate. They were bound to look to Vienna for aid. Vienna certainly helped them in 1693 by transferring from Hungary Lewis of Baden, then at the height of his fame and powers, so that he could assume command in southern Germany. At the same time, Leopold's services to the anti-French coalition further north were immense. The bargain with Hanover in 1692, by which he gave Ernest Augustus the title of elector,[1] and the bargain with Brandenburg in 1700—the *Kron-Traktat* by which he acknowledged the Elector Frederick III's royal title[2]— helped to put more Hanoverian and Prussian troops into the field against Louis XIV, and to keep them there. These transactions revealed the peculiar character, the undeniable potency, of the emperor's influence in the Empire. Not surprisingly, a distinct party existed in Vienna which regarded it as both constitutional and realistic to emphasize the 'Imperial' aspects of Habsburg power. Its members were hostile to the court politicians of Bohemian, Italian, Spanish, and even Austrian extraction, who in their view were too ready to sacrifice the interests of the Empire, and of the emperor in Germany, in the broader context of Habsburg policy on other fronts. This party had always relied on the Imperial vice-chancellor, especially on Königsegg before his death in 1694 and on Schönborn after 1705. Its focus in these years was Joseph, first as king and later as emperor. His mentor and minister, Prince Salm, was its most influential spokesman. His fall in 1709 and the consequent ascendancy of Eugene of Savoy, the Bohemian Wratislaw, and the Austrian Starhemberg, together with the gradual elimination of Schönborn from the inner councils of state, was an epoch in the party-struggle at court. Less conspicuously, it involved the discredit of a policy. The constitutional relation of emperor and states, as fixed by treaties and charters of the Empire, had given Vienna influence in Germany, but inadequate direct powers.

That influence was due partly to Habsburg patronage. The court offered a career to men of talent from the Empire. Seilern and (later) Bartenstein were both Germans of comparatively humble origin. Conversely, other ministers belonged to families whose goodwill was worth having. Königsegg's father was a Swabian count. Schönborn and his relatives were influential in many ecclesiastical chapters of Franconia and the Rhineland. Families of the Imperial Knights, unrepresented in the Diet at Ratisbon, often concentrated on acquiring canonries and bishoprics, for which the emperor's support was valuable; they too were normally his allies and clients. Prince Salm was likewise connected closely with a number of important Rhineland and Westphalian families. In fact, the emperor patronized assiduously many interests in western and central Germany, and they relied on that patronage. Habsburg policy, on the other hand, took less account of them. The Hanover treaty of 1692 and

---

[1] Above, p. 166.   [2] See vol. v, pp. 556–7.

the acceptance of a truce in Italy in 1696 were both used, in the first instance, to secure more troops for the war in Hungary, not for operations in Germany. In the later stages of the Nine Years War, the directorate of the Franconian and Swabian Circles was less and less sympathetically treated by Vienna. Leopold's strongest minister at this period, Kinsky, was unfriendly both to the German States and to the Maritime Powers. The recovery of Freiburg, the Breisgau, and some Imperial territory on the left bank of the Rhine at Ryswick certainly owed very little to the meagre Habsburg war-effort in that area. The failure to recover Strasbourg was in part due to the Habsburg disinclination to regard this Imperial city as a priority of high importance.

The emperor, in the view of Kinsky and his associates, had to reckon with the unpalatable truth that his real authority in Germany never remotely corresponded with the prestige of his title. He could not legislate except with the consent of the Diet, and legislation could not be enforced on unwilling princely governments. In 1689 the Diet agreed to declare war against France: it voted war-taxes, along with measures which enhanced Leopold's ability to allocate the taxes collected in States which did not raise armies to those which did; and he was empowered to supervise the sharing out of winter-quarters between the princes. Yet in practice the 'armed' rulers of Germany kept control of their own bodies of troops. Their contribution, in troops or money, remained very small; they preferred to lend regiments in return for subsidies. Proposals of 1697–8 to maintain permanently in peace an Imperial army of 80,000, rising to 120,000 in war, were not finally accepted by the Diet. It is doubtful if there were ever more than 40,000 'Imperial' soldiers under arms during the Succession War, and they never acted as a unified force. Moreover, Leopold's decision to recognize the duke of Hanover as an elector had enraged some electors and almost all the princes. They disrupted the Diet, which did not function between 1693 and 1700. On that occasion, Catholic and Protestant rulers confederated together in protest. In 1697, Leopold's acceptance of Article IV[1] of the Franco-Imperial treaty of Ryswick led the Protestants to quarrel violently with the Catholics.

At the close of 1700 many Germans hoped to remain neutral in the struggle over Spain. Vienna countered by separate agreements with individual princes, who were persuaded by a variety of inducements to promise support. The new alliance with the Maritime Powers had a decisive effect on the waverers, although not on the electors of Bavaria and Cologne. The Diet, however, having declared war and voted measures similar to those of 1689, did not care to pursue it with any effectiveness; the deputies at Ratisbon were justifiably afraid of Max Emmanuel, who occupied the city from August 1703 to July 1704. Emperor and Empire,

---

[1] This safeguarded the rights and privileges of the Catholic Church in the territories restored by Louis XIV to the Empire. Cf. above, pp. 473–4.

their alliance paralysed by the constitutional relationship between them, were unable to resist the combined strategy of Bavaria and France. Then the victory of Blenheim, at a stroke, gave Vienna the hegemony in south Germany. For ten years, in spite of the desperate peasantries which rebelled in 1706 and were put down, the Bavarian countryside was squeezed for men, money and supplies. Joseph gave away some of its revenues to neighbouring Free Cities like Ulm and Augsburg, and he gave Bavarian lordships to his principal councillors—Sinzendorf, Lamberg, Seilern, Starhemberg, and others—in order to raise them to the dignity of princes of the Empire. Later, in 1713, there were negotiations with Max Emmanuel in which he was offered the southern Netherlands (or other territories) in exchange for the permanent surrender of Bavaria.[1] Individual Habsburg statesmen pressed the strategic and geographical arguments for taking over the lands so awkwardly wedged between Bohemia and Tyrol, but the Emperor Charles resisted them and preferred to respect the elector's hereditary right, preserving intact his own in the old Spanish dominions.

Viennese policy was also profoundly influenced by family ties with the Wittelsbach house of Pfalz-Neuburg. In 1685 Leopold championed Philip William's succession to the Palatinate, and was the faithful supporter of his son John William after 1690. But all electors palatine grudged the loss of territory and title which had been taken from them by Bavaria in the Thirty Years War; their goodwill was not easily to be reconciled with a Habsburg–Bavarian alliance. In 1688, it is true, Pfalz-Neuburg princes in the Cologne chapter took part in the struggle to defeat the French candidate in favour of Joseph Clement, Max Emmanuel's brother. Then the Austrian alliance with the Bavarian Wittelsbachs began to weaken. Maria Antonia[2] died in 1692. Leopold foolishly and unsuccessfully tried to frustrate Joseph Clement's desire for the bishopric of Liège: he backed a Pfalz-Neuburg candidate. The elector palatine's sister, Maria Anna, queen of Spain, opposed Max Emmanuel's interest at Madrid. As Max Emmanuel and Joseph Clement gravitated towards France, John William made himself indispensable to Leopold. He angled for the nomination as governor of the Netherlands, which were close neighbours of his own possessions, Jülich and Berg. He did much to stiffen the Habsburg party in the Empire after 1700; utterly opposed to the idea that Max Emmanuel should be won over by concessions, he must take some responsibility for Vienna's rigid policy during negotiations for a peaceful settlement with the Bavarian elector in 1702–3. Their failure led to the outbreak of war in south Germany. John William was one of the main beneficiaries of the victory at Blenheim. By 1708 he had acquired Max Emmanuel's title of elector—the first, in precedence, of the lay electors—

---

[1] Cf. above, pp. 465 and 473.
[2] Daughter of Leopold by his first wife and married to Max Emmanuel in 1685.

and he had been invested with the lands of the Upper Palatinate. The Imperial Ban proclaimed against Max Emmanuel and Joseph Clement made his favourable vote all the more decisive in the election of Charles as King of the Romans in 1711. However, Charles sacrificed him in 1714, when the two deposed rulers received back their titles and dominions at Rastatt. Another Pfalz-Neuburger became the archbishop-elector of Trier in 1716, but Charles and Max Emmanuel had come to terms. Bavarian troops played a useful part in the Turkish war of 1716–18.

The Habsburgs were unsympathetic to their greatest rival in north Germany, Brandenburg-Prussia.[1] The Imperial authority was consistently used to hamper the more ambitious designs of Frederick I. He was not permitted to monopolize the taxable resources of the 'unarmed' States for the benefit of his troops, nor to extend the areas on which he wished to quarter these regiments in Franconia and (after Blenheim) in the Upper Palatinate. Hohenzollern claims to a number of minor lordships in Germany were obstructed in the emperor's tribunals. Above all, the financial clauses of the *Kron-Traktat* and subsequent bargains were the source of perpetual friction. Exasperated, Frederick withdrew his troops from the upper Rhineland in 1705, and only the subsidies of the Maritime Powers retained them for service in Italy and the Netherlands. By contrast, Vienna favoured Hanover—a connection formally acknowledged by the marriages of Joseph in 1699 and of Charles in 1708 to princesses of the House of Brunswick. George of Hanover was given command of the Imperial army in 1706. As his English advisers discovered after 1714, he relied heavily on the emperor's support in Germany. Charles VI was able to use this reliance as a lever to influence British policy when the Barrier Treaty for the Netherlands and the future of Italy were discussed after the end of the great war.

All these transactions show Vienna manipulating, with fair success, the balance of power in north Germany. In the south, the permanent annexation of Bavaria was certainly possible after 1704, but the Habsburgs never took the project seriously. Nor were they concerned to hold out for the further recovery of territory in the Rhineland and Alsace, or for a 'Barrier' in that area, at the expense of France. They preferred to press dynastic claims elsewhere, and even to make greater use of the Imperial overlordship in Italy than in Germany: after all, the larger German states had long ago grown strong enough to shackle the emperor in the Empire with the law and practice of its constitution.

Accordingly, the forward policy adopted in Italy as the final crisis of the Spanish succession drew nearer in 1700 was of major importance. Leopold's councillors, however weak their diplomacy in Madrid or disordered their domestic administration, fully realized that his interest in Italy was far

---

[1] See vol. v, ch. xxiii.

greater than in Spain or the Netherlands. In Italy he enjoyed the real influence of a near neighbour. This remained true even though the Spaniards had turned down repeated proposals that the Archduke Charles be appointed viceroy in Milan during the life of Carlos II. The Nine Years War had shown that, with an army in Italy, the emperor's authority could be used to justify the collection of taxes from lands deemed 'Imperial' fiefs, and to take full advantage in diplomatic negotiations of his right to withhold the formal investiture of these fiefs, or of his power to confer royal status on such princes as the duke of Savoy and the grand duke of Tuscany. There were also small pro-Austrian factions in Milan and Naples.[1]

As early as July 1700, Leopold's ministers advised him to concentrate forces in Tyrol and Inner Austria. On 18 November, the day Leopold heard of Carlos II's death, he wrote: 'The troops destined for Italy... must march as soon as possible.'[2] The French reached Lombardy before them, but Eugene's descent into northern Italy was the first action of a new war in the west. This Habsburg initiative had a profound influence on the making of the Grand Alliance. By the treaty of 7 September 1701, only the Spanish dominions in Italy were to be ceded outright by the Bourbons. The stipulation satisfied most Austrian statesmen, because for them the crux of the Succession War was the Italian peninsula. They asserted this priority against English pressure for action in Spain. Vienna joined the Portuguese alliance in 1703 very reluctantly, with Wratislaw arguing for many months that the conquest of Italy must precede the conquest of Spain. The insistence of the Maritime Powers, at a time when the enemy began to mount their grand attack in central Europe, forced Leopold to give way; and there were no doubt secondary influences which pressed such a venture on him. The former Spanish ambassador at Vienna, Moles, was still an important politician there who wanted to take the initiative in Spain. Prince George of Hesse-Darmstadt, commander of the German troops in Catalonia during the Nine Years War and Carlos II's viceroy at Barcelona, had appeared in Vienna before going on to England in 1702. The courtiers around the young archduke did not wish to remain permanently overshadowed by those of his brother Joseph, and Charles himself soon showed that he had a will of his own. Yet, at bottom, the treaty finally ratified by Leopold in July 1703 was an unfortunate surrender to his allies. It could not help the Habsburg candidate for the Spanish throne that he had to agree, even though these articles remained secret, to the ultimate cession to Portugal of places in Estremadura, Galicia, and South America.[3]

[1] In 1700, through Leopold's representatives at the papal court, Neopolitan officers in the Habsburg army got into touch with the dissidents in Naples; the prince of Macchia's conspiracy next year, though quickly suppressed, was aided by the emperor's agents.
[2] *Feldzüge des Prinzen Eugens von Savoyen*, vol. III (1876), p. 406. Cf. above, p. 405.
[3] Cf. above, pp. 418–19 and 526 for the first Methuen treaties.

The immediate consequences were well appreciated at Vienna. The whole transaction implied that Leopold and Joseph (as the elder son) would transfer their claims to Charles, and recognize him as lawful heir in all the Spanish dominions; and also that Charles, heir presumptive in all the Austrian lands because Joseph had no sons, might soon become a hostage in the hands of uncertain allies and the champion of Spanish interests against Austria, or of his own family against Joseph's. It had become essential to settle the relationship of the two brothers in order to defend the future of the House of Austria as a whole. Hence the famous set of agreements sealed in September 1703. On 12 September Leopold and Joseph publicly renounced their rights to the Spanish inheritance, which therefore fell to Charles. They reserved the rights of the Empire over Imperial fiefs in the hands of the king of Spain, and the due order of succession in the Habsburg family. Charles accepted this; but seven days earlier he had already agreed secretly to the juridical argument that the original terms of enfiefment required the retrocession of Milan and Finale to the emperor upon Carlos's death. Leopold now chose to allot these to Joseph and his heirs. More frankly, the arguments of utility, proximity and expense were also put forward by the Austrian Habsburgs in taking from Spain what they wanted to keep for themselves. Finally, after the public act of 12 September, another secret instrument of the same date regulated the succession in both sets of dominions. Spanish law, as normally interpreted, declared that the ruler's eldest daughter should succeed him, if he had no sons; but the claim of a daughter to succeed Charles in Spain was now set aside in favour of Joseph and his heirs male—ultimately of any heir male from the Austrian side of the family. Equally, Charles and his sons were to precede Joseph's daughters in Austria and in Joseph's other dominions. In this way, by insisting on the precedence of all Habsburg princes over all Habsburg princesses, the Habsburg succession was 'restricted' and the unity of the whole House safeguarded. It was necessary to conceal from the Spaniards this characteristically Austrian version of a partition treaty, but the secret agreement must have been known to certain members of the Viennese court well before Charles VI disclosed it, in 1713, in order to settle the precedence of his sisters and nieces. His own first child, Leopold, was born and died in 1716. Maria Theresa was born in 1717.[1]

Charles's embarrassing promise to surrender Milan soon became entangled with a second promise. Like him, Leopold and Joseph had to make concessions. Negotiations had been going on with Victor Amadeus

---

[1] It is still a disputed question whether Charles VI's natural determination to give his daughter precedence over his nieces accorded with the original *Pactum Mutuae Successionis*. His Pragmatic Sanction, therefore, rested on an uncertain legal basis which was open to attack. Cf. the opposing arguments of G. Turba in *Archivalische Zeitung*, vol. XL (1931), pp. 65–119, and of W. Michael, *Zur Entstehung der Pragmatischen Sanktion Karls VI* (Basel, 1939). For the Pragmatic Sanction, see vol. VII, esp. pp. 393–4.

of Savoy since late in 1701, in order to win him over to the Allies. He came to terms in November 1703, and the price offered by the Habsburgs included certain areas in western Lombardy. In fact, Viennese policy now involved a double deception: the Spaniards were in due course to lose the whole duchy of Milan, and the citizens of Milan an important and fertile fraction of it.

Between 1704 and 1711 the history of Austrian expansion ran an intricate course of failure in Spain and success in Italy. Charles was enthusiastically welcomed in Barcelona, and firmly established there after October 1705, but his prospects slowly dwindled in spite of the increasing commitment of the Allies to this theatre. In any case, the military victories were theirs rather than his. He depended completely on the Maritime Powers for money and reinforcements, even for the transport of Habsburg troops (or his queen) from Italy, and for communication with his lieutenants in Majorca and Sardinia. He was also weakened by incessant difficulties with Joseph, and suspected that the emperor grudged him help while usurping his authority in Naples as well as in Milan. Civilian administrators took instructions from Barcelona, but the Austrian generals took theirs from Vienna. So, partially, did Guido Starhemberg in Catalonia—a good soldier but a poor substitute for Eugene, who refused to come to Spain in 1708. Yet the whole Spanish venture powerfully influenced its titular leader. After years of endeavour Charles believed with the utmost sincerity that he was the rightful king of Spain and all its dependencies. He grew less amenable to the advisers whom Leopold had chosen for him, and turned to a miscellaneous group of favourites: the Moravian nobleman Michael Althann, the Neapolitan soldier of fortune Count Rocco Stella, and a number of Spaniards and Catalans, of whom the ablest was the lawyer Ramón de Vilana Perlas, ennobled by Charles as the Marquis Rialp. The consequences were far-reaching. After the accident of Joseph's early death in 1711, Charles brought back to Vienna an obstinate devotion to his Spanish title and a circle of courtiers which together affected Habsburg policies deeply for several years. These men were reinforced by the inevitable tide of exiles, too closely committed to his cause to make their peace with Bourbon Spain.

The Austrian advance into Italy had been altogether more successful. At first, it is true, the government found it very difficult to support an aggressive policy with efficient military measures. In 1701 intervention south of the Alps was delayed for six months, to the chagrin of Eugene, who had been appointed to the Italian command in November 1700. Speedy mobilization was held up by disarray in the *Hofkriegsrat*. Its vice-president and the president (Rüdiger Starhemberg, the defender of Vienna in 1683) both died in the first half of 1701, and Leopold then appointed Prince Mansfeld as Starhemberg's unworthy successor. Leopold also blundered by putting Salaburg, another incompetent, in charge of the *Hofkammer*. The abrupt passage of Eugene's troops through the neutral territory of Venice in 1701, and the emperor's forthright decree deposing the enemy duke of Mantua, were followed by a number of inconclusive campaigns. The crisis of 1703, heightened by the temporary collapse of government credit,[1] compelled Vienna to deplete its armament in Italy, although not to withdraw it. These events drove Leopold to appoint Eugene president of the *Hofkriegsrat* and then Gundaker Starhemberg president of the *Hofkammer*, so that the direction of war and finance were at long last in capable hands.[2] After Blenheim, and a further stiffening of the government at Joseph I's accession, the statesmen turned their attention to Italy again: and after Eugene's triumph at Turin in September 1706, no amount of Allied argument shook for a moment the Austrians' determination to march down to Naples, which they occupied in July 1707. The fortress of Gaeta surrendered on 30 September. The most important of Habsburg ambitions, it may be asserted, was satisfied by this date, long before the Maritime Powers satisfied theirs. As a counterweight to any future surrenders of Milanese territory, Vienna also finally annexed the great strategic strongpoint of Mantua. The ruler of Castiglione, another ancient fief of the Empire, was deposed in 1708. Even while Daun's expeditionary force was moving towards Naples, military pressure and the whole armoury of legal argument applicable to ancient Imperial fiefs were combined in order to squeeze the Italian principalities. Tuscany, Genoa, Parma, Lucca, among others, paid in cash and kind about 2 m. florins in 1707 for the upkeep of Habsburg troops.[3] This contribution fluctuated in the later years of the war but always remained high.

The overwhelming strength of the Habsburgs in Italy after 1706 served to multiply the points already in dispute between Pope Clement XI and Vienna. Tension between Rome and Vienna was indeed a feature of the whole period, beginning during Alexander VIII's pontificate (1689–91) and increasing under that of Innocent XII, with whom Louis XIV's relations gradually improved. The most important ground of discord was Clement's refusal to recognize Charles's title to rule in the Spanish dominions; a vast amount of clerical taxation, normally at the king's disposal in Spain, Milan and Naples, was at stake. The Habsburgs countered with the publication of edicts in 1708, both at Milan and Naples, forbidding the transfer of ecclesiastical revenues to Rome. Another difficulty was the emperor's emphatic denial (supported by a number of the jurists in German uni-

---

[1] Above, p. 310.

[2] This crisis provides a clear example of the occasional influence of Leopold's confessors in politics: it was not until the Jesuit Engelbert Bischoff could be induced to speak up for Eugene and Starhemberg that they triumphed in the party-struggle at court. See M. Braubach, *Prinz Eugen von Savoyen*, vol. I (Munich, 1963), pp. 354–68.

[3] In 1707, for the purpose of calculating interest on Joseph I's English loan (above, p. 308) 8⅔ florins were taken as worth £1 sterling.

versities) of papal rights in the appointment to benefices, in the income from them, and in the government of fiefs which had at any time belonged to the Empire. Joseph, on his accession (1705), omitted to send the customary declaration of submission to the pope, and his advisers drew a very clear distinction between Rome as the supreme spiritual authority and as an Italian State. No one expressed himself more trenchantly on many of these topics, or caused greater fury in Rome, than George Adam Martinitz, Leopold's ambassador to the pope between 1696 and 1699; he had already raised the whole question of the fiefs in Italy. After 1706 this matter flared up again. No pope could agree that Parma was not a papal fief, for example: in a solemn public declaration of 26 June 1708 Joseph deemed it a fief of the Empire. Although war-taxation and winter quarters were the practical issues at stake, the struggle soon became entwined with the traditional enmity between papal and anti-clerical interests in Italy.

In any case, the Austrian military command was determined to enjoy the advantage, from which the French had profited before 1706, of quartering along the northern stretch of the Papal States; and it so happened that Duke Rinaldo of Modena, disappointed not to have secured the governorship of Milan which was given to Eugene, but with powerful connections in Vienna (and with the historian Muratori to write untiringly in his defence), had his eye on papal Ferrara and papal Comacchio—a small town commanding one of the mouths of the Po. Against the wishes of Eugene and Wratislaw, but with the blessing of Salm, Habsburg troops occupied Comacchio on 24 May 1708. The Emperor Joseph's ancient rights of possession were proclaimed there. This incident finally provoked Clement to begin a war which his meagre forces had no chance of winning without help from other Italian princes. The alliance proposed to them crumbled at once. He ended the hopeless struggle a year and a half later, when he recognized Charles as Catholic King. Joseph withdrew his declaration of 1708 and the other difficulties were left unresolved, but a pacification on these terms could not mask the Habsburg dominance of Italy.

It gradually became evident that the real threat to Habsburg pretensions south of the Alps would come from a different quarter. The relief of Turin and the conquest of Milan had been striking successes, but they posed difficult problems for Vienna. At once Victor Amadeus and the Maritime Powers demanded help for the invasion of France through the Alps. Joseph's advisers rather unwillingly tried to satisfy them by sending Eugene with 16,000 troops into Provence; but they kept 8,000 for the Naples expedition and they refused, in 1708, to commit Eugene to service in Spain, which also displeased Charles. Victor Amadeus had meanwhile claimed the immediate cession of the Lombard territories promised in 1703. Early in 1708 Joseph and Charles surrendered some, but not all, of the areas in dispute. The Habsburg statesmen were rightly convinced, none more emphatically than Eugene of Savoy, that Victor Amadeus had designs on the major part of Lombardy. He not only insisted that they must honour the treaty of 1703 in accordance with an interpretation which they did not accept: he also argued that they should compound for his financial aid to the Habsburg troops in Italy between 1704 and 1706 by ceding additional strips of the Milan duchy. During the next five years Eugene stressed the need to keep a large force in Lombardy, in spite of undoubted commitments elsewhere, in order to restrain his cousin. In fact, a determination to resist Piedmontese pressure in northern Italy now became a permanent feature of Austrian policy. But Victor Amadeus had other, less clearly defined ambitions. Already before 1700, his own claim on the Spanish succession led to the suggestion that Sicily (or Sicily and Naples) should fall to his share. In the successive peace conferences of 1709–10 and later at Utrecht, Victor Amadeus instructed his envoy to air this proposal again; and the treaties of 1713 gave him Sicily. Vienna, having failed to mount a successful attack on Sicily from Naples after 1707, protested sharply: yet it was confronted not merely by Victor Amadeus, but after 1710 by Great Britain, increasingly eager to find a counterweight to the Habsburgs in Italy, as well as an additional check on France. If the death of Joseph on 17 April 1711 appeared to promise (or to threaten) a revival of Charles V's empire, Charles VI had soon to learn that British sea power, on which Habsburg communications in the Mediterranean depended, made the prospect illusory.

When the news reached Spain that Joseph was dead, the court in Barcelona anxiously debated the problem caused by the failure of Charles and his wife, so far, to produce an heir or even a daughter. Six months later, it was agreed to leave Elizabeth Christina behind as a pledge to the Spaniards (on which the British also insisted), and her husband departed for Frankfurt and Vienna to secure the Empire and the old Austrian lands. He was at the same time absolutely determined to keep what he could of the whole Spanish inheritance. He believed that his lineage, his own career in the last eight years, and his allies all committed him to the defence of this claim. The politicians in Vienna, especially Wratislaw, were alarmed that he did not return home more speedily, and they were readier to contemplate the surrender of Spain. But the new emperor, not his advisers, determined the course and tempo of his diplomacy for the next few years. He clashed violently with the British when they no longer wanted him in Spain, and again when they wanted to use his Italian territories as counters in a general settlement of Europe. But he could not resist British naval pressure, which was used to detain his queen and isolate his troops in Catalonia, and then to compel their withdrawal. He still refused to recognize Philip and Victor Amadeus as the rightful rulers of Spain and Sicily respectively, or to surrender Mantua, Mirandola and

596

Comacchio. He dealt Victor Amadeus a shrewd blow in 1713 by selling the fief of Finale, a desirable port, to Genoa. Despite the total setback in Spain itself and the increased strength of Piedmont-Savoy, Charles VI and III had kept most of what he wanted in Italy. In 1720, he even secured Sicily in exchange for Sardinia.

Charles claimed to have inherited these lands, not to rule them by right of conquest. There could be no question of overturning the constitutional and social structure which earlier Spanish kings had accepted.[1] After 1714 they were still administered through the *Consejo d'Italia*, now settling into comfortable quarters in Vienna but with its customary Spanish and Italian councillors representing Milan, Naples and Sardinia. In Naples, the nobility continued to rely heavily on the government for the maintenance of their privileges. The new ruler rejected only the exaggerated demands of a small party headed by Tiberio Caraffa, who hoped that the expulsion of the Spanish viceroys would usher in a régime of untrammelled aristocracy; Caraffa was one in spirit with the Magyars of Hungary and Saint-Simon at Versailles. As before, lawyers (*togati*) ascended frequently to the ranks of the nobility, while the nobility dominated the provinces and the municipality of Naples itself. The finances remained in very poor shape, with the principal tax on property still based on the assessments of 1667–9; the relatively small extraordinary cost of reconquering Sicily from the Spaniards in 1720 was enough to cripple them. In Milan, signs of reform had been noted by disapproving citizens before 1706; the Bourbon viceroy, Vaudemont, tried to copy French administrative practice. After 1706, the Austrians also wanted an efficient government for war: there were plans for a new tax-census,[2] and in 1711 duties on imported raw materials were lowered to encourage Lombard industry. But this impulse soon flagged. Milan, both city and duchy, was left with its honeycomb of communes and councils and tribunals, each the vigilant watchdog of vested interests. These successfully counterbalanced the authority of the viceroys. Similar interests thwarted the very genuine desire of the Habsburg governor in Mantua to improve administration in that much-impoverished duchy.

The Austrian Habsburgs were settling down in Italy, therefore, without undue disturbance of the old Spanish framework of government. There was a shade more efficiency, and the viceroys did not enrich themselves in office, although members of the Spanish circle in Vienna drew generous incomes from both Lombardy and Naples. In turn, the new régime helped to preserve the old power of the Viennese court, and of individual

---

[1] See above, pp. 557–8.
[2] In 1718 a committee (*Giunta Censuaria*) was appointed to revise the whole system of direct taxation, and a serious effort was made to assess much landed property previously exempt from tax; but the practical enforcement of the scheme was delayed for thirty years. See S. Pugliese, *Condizioni economiche e finanziarie nella Lombardia nella prima metà del sec. XVIII* (Turin, 1924), pp. 310–13.

Habsburg noblemen, to draw men of talent from over the Alps. Charles VI welcomed Italian scholars to take charge of the Imperial Library, for instance, and the Italian musicians who became his *kapellmeister*. In many respects the Habsburg court remained Italianate for another generation.

In the Austrian Netherlands the general result of the change of sovereignty was no more sensational than in what had been Spanish Italy. Persisting grimly against his opponents, Charles wore down the Dutch after the signature of the 1715 Barrier Treaty until he recovered from them the northern part of Flanders, and he slightly eased the financial burden of Dutch garrisons on the country. There was no attempt to resume Bergeyck's programme of reform. De Prié,[1] plenipotentiary for the absentee governor-general Eugene of Savoy, disliked but confirmed the ancient liberties, except in places which had been annexed to France and administered on the French pattern, as at Ypres. In its new home at Vienna the Spanish *Consejo* for the Low Countries took on a fresh lease of life, although it depended on the *Hofkanzlei* a little more closely than did the *Consejo d'Italia*.

After all concessions, to enemies and allies alike, Charles VI was thus left with a fresh accumulation of interests in western Europe equal to his father's gains in Hungary. At first they absorbed most of the attention which he gave to foreign affairs. Then, in 1716, he was persuaded by Eugene, in one of the great moments of his career as a statesman, and by the clerical interest under Clement XI's enthusiastic guidance, to assist Venice against the Turk. He safeguarded his interests in the West by intense diplomatic activity, relying particularly on British support; but the change of policy was a disappointment to those councillors who still hoped to strengthen the Habsburg position in northern Italy at the expense of Victor Amadeus, and in the Netherlands at the expense of the Dutch. Meanwhile, Eugene's generalship led to further territorial acquisitions at Passarowitz in 1718.[2] Serbia, the Netherlands, and Sicily had all seemed very remote from the Hofburg when Mehmed IV's artillery began to bombard it in July 1683.

A leading Austrian historian has well summarized the whole process of expansion in the title of his work on the period: 'The Development of a Great Power.'[3] The process had its reverse aspect. Intent on war and diplomacy, Habsburg statesmen were far less inclined to examine the condition of the old possessions in Austria and Bohemia with a view to remedying signs of weakness. Partly because they took these for granted,

---

[1] Ercole di Turinetti, marquis de Prié (1658–1726), Victor Amadeus's envoy in Vienna until 1701, had been chiefly responsible for persuading Leopold to ratify, in 1704, the treaty of 1703 between the two courts. He then transferred into the emperor's service, helped to administer Milan, and negotiated the treaty with Clement XI in 1709. He was a distinguished example of the Italians who made a career for themselves under these emperors.

[2] Below, pp. 641–2.

[3] O. Redlich, *Das Werden einer Grossmacht: Österreich von 1700 bis 1740* (Vienna, 1938).

our knowledge of economic and social conditions in these countries is harder to obtain and is indeed still fragmentary.[1]

The main sources of wealth or subsistence—agriculture, pasture, forests, vineyards—supported a social structure which altered little in these forty years. In the whole Alpine region, including Tyrol and the Inner Austrian duchies and Upper Austria ('above the Enns'), and also in Silesia, the normal pattern of rural society included a powerful Estate of greater nobles, a Church which had recovered the losses of the previous century, a lesser nobility of knights always declining in numbers and importance, and a tenacious peasantry. Below these were many grades of smallholder and householder, itinerant cattle-drovers, horse-dealers and pedlars, and many destitute folk who also were often on the move. The income of nobility and Church derived from rents and dues of the most varied kinds. The peasantries were usually left in possession, after payment, of tenancies handed down from one generation to the next. In Bohemia and Moravia, increasingly in Lower Austria ('below the Enns'), and in old royal Hungary, the pattern was the same, except that here the lords relied more on direct exploitation. For this they needed the compulsory labour and plough-teams of their peasants, supervised by the very important class of stewards and bailiffs. But in both these great areas the lord, who was also a State tax-collector and exercised public as well as private jurisdiction, normally enjoyed a whole miscellany of supplementary rights—to buy at his own price from his subjects, to sell to them at his price, to profit from their use of his taverns, his mills and his market-places. The entire economy was tilted in his favour, so that the population's purchasing and taxpaying capacity always remained abysmally low. The tilt appears most evident in central Bohemia and Moravia. In the mountainous Austrian lands, although the soil was less fertile, prosperous peasant families could undoubtedly be found here and there. Sporadic disorders in Upper Austria were due more to irritation than despair, and a sturdy peasantry survived in Tyrol.

The Vienna government accepted the general position with few signs of disquiet. The régime of subjection and privilege was written into the law, as in the great revision of the Bohemian constitution of 1627 and the *Tractatus de Juribus Incorporalibus* of Lower Austria in 1679. A series of provincial ordinances tried to enforce the standing veto on the departure of peasants from their domicile: such Patents appeared for Bohemia in 1699, for Moravia in 1687, 1699 and 1712, and for Silesia in 1699, 1709, 1714 and 1720. It is noticeable that any promise of pacification in Hungary seems to have tempted men in the neighbouring provinces to leave home. There were also extradition treaties with Poland and Saxony. More important, legislation sanctioned a further decline in the condition of the Bohemian peasant. Serious agrarian trouble broke out in certain districts of Bohemia in 1679–80 and again in 1716. After each crisis Patents—two

---

[1] For conditions here after the Thirty Years War, see vol. v, pp. 478–85.

in 1680, one in 1717—attempted to define the obligations of lord and peasant. They forbade oppression, but provided quite ineffectively for appeals against it; after 1717 the first appeal had to be made to the lord himself. The result of the earlier Patents was to disallow rights claimed by peasants 'before the detestable rebellion', which could be interpreted to mean the rebellion of 1620 and so to abrogate rights of very long standing. These decrees also state that a maximum of three days' compulsory labour a week could be demanded by the lord, and this maximum tended more and more to become a standard, an inordinately high one compared with normal practice in the Austrian lands. It is true that the Patents of 1680 frowned on lords who bullied subjects into working excessively far from their own homes: in 1717, however, the idea was accepted that labour must be mobile at the lord's discretion, though not at the peasant's. The number of full peasant holdings had clearly declined in the previous forty years, but the 1717 Patent only reserved the government's right to tax those which the lord had annexed; it did not forbid the dispossession of the peasantry.

Great and continuous military expenditure made the position far worse in both Bohemia and Austria. It seems clear that high war taxes contributed as much to depress the peasants to the lowest levels of poverty—reached in the first half of the eighteenth century—as did the demands of the landlord for himself in rents and services, mainly because the structure of this society divided the double burden in so unequal a fashion. Excise and poll taxes all increased sharply. But the total 'ordinary', direct taxation of an estate would be calculated according to the number of its peasant holdings on the assessment rolls, the *Rustikal* lands: the remainder, including parts of the domain let out to peasants, was exempt. If the lord took over any of these *Rustikal* lands, the rest were often compelled to make good the difference, despite the 1717 Patent. In addition, 'extraordinary' demands, theoretically imposed on the domain or *Dominikal* lands of the lords, would also be assessed according to the number of scheduled peasant holdings and partly paid by them. Neither the unprivileged nor the government could get round the difficulty that the lord's officials collected the taxes as well as the rentals. Indeed, taxcollection could show a profit for the owner. In Upper Austria a surplus of this kind, the *Rustgeldüberschuss*, was a familiar item in estimating the value of estates for sale or purchase.

Excessive taxation also increased the chronic indebtedness of the agricultural classes. Unequal taxation left relatively untouched the assets of the propertied families. Impoverished populations and an improverished government were kept from contact with one another by an immensely wealthy aristocracy. The first starved; the second begged from the English or Dutch; the third lent at interest to the emperor instead of paying taxes in proportion to its wealth, and built magnificent new palaces, in war as in peace. The loans to the government of Hans Adam 'the Rich', head of the Liechtenstein family, totalled at least 905,000 florins between 1687 and 1710; but during the same period he spent more on buying property in Swabia, the Erzgebirge and Hungary. The great Fischer von Erlach (ennobled in 1696) was meanwhile 'engineer' and architect to the Habsburg court: but all his plans for building a more splendid version of Versailles at Schönbrunn, and for a grander Hofburg, had to be shelved during the wars. By contrast, what *Hofkanzler* Stratmann and the Liechtenstein or Dietrichstein families commissioned from him was put up without delay. Standards of noble expenditure, and of architectural magnificence, were no humbler in Graz and Prague. In Bohemian and Moravian country places the more modest work of the sixteenth century was often dramatically remodelled. Great double staircases now led up to triumphal halls and chapels. The servants' quarters and stables were much enlarged, or else the older building was allotted to the servants and to administrative offices, while overshadowing them rose the lord's new palace.

At the most, Habsburg rulers were able to regulate the system of nobility. Their capacity to ennoble by patent introduced new talents and fresh blood. The Chancellors Hocher, Stratmann and Seilern, from burgher families in the Empire, were conspicuous examples. The rulers' capacity to advance men from lower to higher degrees of nobility satisfied one of the strongest impulses of the age, and made their court the indispensable source of promotion. Earlier, they had compelled Estates to recognize and admit outsiders who had acquired titles within a duchy or kingdom, which now meant that the nobilities of all the Habsburg lands, with the ennobled office-holders and soldiers, were knitting together more closely: at this level, provincial barriers were breaking down. The rulers performed another useful service at the same time. For the greater families the distribution of widespread possessions among their individual members was a complex business, and the risk of alienation very real. The best safeguard against the splintering of an inheritance was the entail, or *Fideikommiss*, ratified by the ruler. What the Habsburg family secured by pacts of mutual succession they authorized their noble subjects to enjoy also.

The Church was as resolute in defence of a privileged position as the nobility. It appeared to be almost as strongly entrenched. By bequest and purchase, the accumulation of ecclesiastical property since the early seventeenth century had more than made good previous losses. Not only had the older Orders and the bishoprics rebuilt their prosperity, but an immense network of new foundations—Capuchin, Augustinian, Barnabite, Ursuline, Carmelite, Piarist, and above all Jesuit—came into existence. Occasional efforts to check the alienation of lay possessions to the Church were quite unsuccessful. Decrees against mortmain were enacted (1684, 1688, 1704, 1716 and 1720) and disregarded. The old and formidable arguments in favour of the secular ruler's lordship of churches had by no means been forgotten in Habsburg chanceries, but before 1720 they were largely ineffective. The piety of the court and countless members of great families, the interest which both enjoyed in nominations to episcopates and prebends, the authorized dominance of the Jesuits in universities and their powers of censorship—all this blocked the growth of anti-clericalism. What there was of it fastened on controversy with the pope, but the loud rattle of anti-papal argument during the Succession War did not diminish the influence of the Catholic Church in ordinary life; no more so did the surviving Protestantism of remote upland valleys in the Alps and northern Bohemia.[1] Even in Silesia, where there were Protestant churches tolerated by law and protected by international treaties,[2] the Catholic foundations remained powerful and very wealthy. Everywhere indeed in the Austrian dominions the higher clergy were one of the privileged Estates, so that the taxing of ecclesiastical assets by the ruler was always difficult, and somewhat unrewarding. The wealth of the Church, though not of the humbler clergy, continued to mount. Another great architect, Jakob Prandtauer, provided spectacular evidence of the fact by rebuilding on a grandiose scale, in the Danube valley, the church of the Benedictine monastery at Melk (1702–11), a good deal at St Florian from 1708 onwards, and at Göttweig after 1718.[3] The intellectual activity of these foundations, as of the universities, was less impressive. All the same, they were more vigorous after 1700 than before.

The dominance of the upper nobility and clergy in every quarter of the Habsburg lands must account in part for the static character of what was in any case a landlocked economy. Above all, this affected the towns adversely. The propertied classes bought their luxuries from western Europe. Raw materials like iron and flax were too often exported to the Empire, worked up there, and the manufactured goods imported again at heavy cost. But general purchasing power remained low and, in response, production in the towns was restricted by municipal oligarchies and rigid gild ordinances. These interests had been on the defensive for a hundred and fifty years against the landed interest, which encroached on the monopolies once stoutly defended by the medieval towns. The larger landowners dealt directly with foreign merchants from the Empire and favoured itinerant traders. They acquired more and more property inside the towns and this was gradually exempted from municipal taxes. As in Brandenburg-Prussia, they erected their own breweries—a bitter

---

[1] In 1717 Bernhard Raupach of Hamburg began to collect materials for his great history of Protestantism in Austria, *Evangelisches Oesterreich* (Hamburg, 1732). One dedication in the 1740 edition is to the Austrian Lutheran churches, 'wonderfully preserved to the present day—thanks to Almighty God—partly in public, partly in secret'.

[2] Cf. vol. v, p. 484 and above, p. 431.

[3] Conservative chapters nevertheless opposed the building projects of ambitious abbots because they involved heavy indebtedness.

grievance to townsmen. The larger estates produced not only food and timber: they organized domestic manufactures, completely overshadowing the burghers and their dependent artisans. The towns and the smaller nobility, whose interests were complementary, declined together.

The burghers, therefore, clung to a much restricted market, and also to a precarious monopoly within it, by tenaciously insisting on inherited rights within a tight gild-structure. Their attitude to technical innovations was profoundly hostile. Nor did government make any sustained effort to deal with this very difficult problem, although some statesmen realized that an unfavourable balance of trade between the Habsburg lands as a whole and their neighbours weakened State finances; more prosperous citizens would pay more taxes. In spite of their claim to scrutinize all gild ordinances, especially on the accession of a new ruler, the Habsburgs never ventured to amend them in essential particulars during this period. The expensive masterpiece, the *numerus clausus*, and other requirements continued to exclude from the ranks of the masters the journeymen who had served their time.[1] The first signs of serious government intervention in Austria—an attempt to improve the legal position of unauthorized craftsmen harried by the gilds—occur in the 1720s. Before that, the court contented itself with insisting merely on the freedom of its own purveyors from gild restrictions. There were about 500 of these *Hofbefreite* under Leopold I. Like the group of wholesale import merchants in Vienna (the staplers, or *Niederleger*), who benefited from longstanding privileges, they were often foreigners. The 'court Jews', who made themselves indispensable to many German rulers at this time,[2] were a special case of the same kind.

Leopold and his sons also issued, increasingly, *privilegia privativa* to projectors undertaking to introduce new techniques or trades into the country. Of this there were many examples, from the *Fabrik* for the manufacture of woollens at Linz (1672) to a cluster of workshops for various purposes set up in Wiener-Neustadt and Vienna in 1702–3. A characteristic episode was the arrival in 1717, from Meissen in Saxony, of a workman who brought with him the secrets of porcelain manufacture: next year, a group formerly connected with the War Commissariat secured a monopoly which initiated the splendid age of Viennese ceramics. In this way the Habsburg lands began to produce more of the luxuries they demanded. But the range of new business was small. It did not affect the smaller towns of the countryside, except where an enlightened landed proprietor took the initiative in promoting trades new to the neighbourhood.

Government, through the *Hofkammer*, had greater effective authority in controlling mineral resources. The results can be studied in the iron

---

[1] Hence the importance of the heiress in a narrow burgher society: she could transmit her father's privileged status to a husband who might otherwise fail to secure it.
[2] Cf. below, p. 788.

industry of Styria and Austria, one of the major assets of the Habsburg empire. The mines and the miners of Eisenerz, the smelters, forgers and dealers in the Enns valley, were nearly all associated in a single corporation, the *Innerberger Hauptgewerkschaft*, under the supervision of a government official. It used its wide powers to devise a complex set of agreements by which particular areas of forest were allocated to the various works, and particular agricultural areas obliged to sell their foodstuffs to the corporation, which resold them to its workmen at fixed prices. It controlled production generally, delivering iron to the towns privileged to market the metal, and handled foreign trade. These measures were directed to the defence of an industry which had collapsed in the early seventeenth century and came near to collapse some forty years later. The *Hauptgewerkschaft* still found the going hard at the end of the century, and depended excessively on advances of German capital. Far from helping it in this respect, the government even deprived it of resources, by anticipating revenue from the industry during the wars. Costs increased, partly because the company was compelled from 1693 to pay higher food prices which it could not recoup from the workmen. Technical skill, moreover, failed to keep pace with progress from abroad. The Estates at Linz agreed that English experts could be called in with advantage, but feared the repercussions this might have on the Protestant sympathies of their peasants. Although in 1690 less iron was mined than a century earlier, the figures crept up gradually during the next three decades; probably more of the increase was taken for manufacture at home than by higher exports.[1]

War with the Turks, followed by the prolonged disorders in Hungary, checked a promising revival of trade with south-east Europe. The Eastern Company of Vienna, founded in 1667, had collapsed in the 1680s. Despite the energy shown by one or two officials in 1698–9, and by individual foreign merchants, there was no real move forward until an agreement with the Turks had been negotiated in 1718 favouring Austrian commerce with the Balkans. Shortly afterwards, a new Vienna Eastern Company was founded. In 1719 Charles VI also succeeded (where his father had failed) in forcing Venice to surrender her historic claim to a monopoly of navigation in the Adriatic, and he declared Trieste and Fiume free ports. He improved road communications over the Semmering Pass from Vienna and Wiener-Neustadt to the sea: later, by building the 'Via Carolina' through Croatia, he gave Hungary access to the coast. In this southerly direction the treaties of Passarowitz ushered in a period of economic promise. Even so, progress remained very slow. The brilliant future of Trieste was barely visible. The further idea of a link between this trade and

---

[1] One of the best Austrian manufactures was the scythe, with a good market in many parts of eastern Europe; but for military reasons the *Hofkriegsrat* disapproved of its sale to the Turkish Balkans.

the overseas commerce of the Austrian Netherlands came to nothing, while the use of the Adriatic to by-pass Venetian tolls and stimulate exchange between Italy and the Austrian lands faced many difficulties. In all these matters Charles had a first-rate commercial adviser in Anselm Fleischmann, whose best work was done in Constantinople, at Passarowitz, and later in Italy.

Breslau in Silesia probably remained the most important business centre in the whole empire, although its trade with Hungary had languished. The obvious route for this led to Teschen (Creszyn) and over the Jablunka pass into Upper Hungary; but the tolls imposed at Teschen had been allowed to mount ever higher in the second half of the seventeenth century, while the staple rights of the towns of Prešov (Eperjes) and also Košice checked the movement of goods. Common robbers, too, were as troublesome to traders as those more imposing disturbers of the peace, Thököly and Rákóczi. Fortunately, the Polish commerce and the commerce westwards mattered much more to Silesia. All reports emphasize the scale of its dealings with the Dutch. The Great Elector's Elbe-Oder canal opened up a promising route to Hamburg, less choked by tolls than the lower Oder, and Silesian linens were sent to various parts of the world,[1] so that at least one Habsburg province gained something from the overseas expansion of Europe. Towards 1700, however, Leipzig was tending to capture more business from Breslau and the other Silesian towns.

Dutch and German dealers also bought direct from the peasants—and their lords—who grew and spun flax in a great arc stretching from Silesia across northern Bohemia. This had consequences for another corner of the Habsburg lands. There was an undoubted decline in the linen trades of Austria proper, an area which suffered more than most from an anarchic profusion of local tolls. Not only did these northern linens compete successfully with the Austrian product in German and Italian markets, but the course of trade now tended to avoid the middle Danube and to find an alternative route through Moravia and Bohemia into the Empire. It was also reported that merchandise in transit across the Alps paid lower toll and transport costs in the Swiss Grisons than in Habsburg Tyrol. The shifting of internal trade-routes in this way, of course, was not necessarily to the disadvantage of the Habsburg lands as a whole, provided that their commodities found a market somewhere, and the government did score one definite success in this respect. Salt from the Salzkammergut captured a larger share of the market in Bohemia and even made an entry into Silesia, partly because Leopold applied tariffs vigorously to discriminate against imports of Bavarian and Saxon salt. It proved more difficult to increase exports from the Salzkammergut into Germany, where Bavaria and Saxony barred the way. The stage was thus being set for the acute customs warfare of the eighteenth century, a

[1] See below, pp. 866–7.

warfare which forced Vienna to take the first steps towards freeing commerce between the Austrian duchies and Bohemia. Trade between Austria and Hungary was to remain much longer subordinate to, and a victim of, political considerations.

The government, it is true, considered many proposals for a reform of the economy, but it did so intermittently, and then usually laid them aside. This negative attitude is no doubt bound up with the character of contemporary statecraft. Politicians were preoccupied with war, and with ecclesiastical or juridical questions; politicians were courtiers, churchmen, jurists, or military commanders. But this dominant bias in turn helped to create a predicament in which reform really did appear impracticable. The greatest emergency was naturally the state of almost continuous war, fought on a grand scale. During the long series of campaigns in Hungary after 1683, the fiscal and commercial proposals made earlier by mercantilist thinkers and 'projectors' like Becher and Schröder were quietly shelved. Then, in 1698, when the pacification of east and west appeared nearly complete, Leopold called for a far-reaching survey of the whole economy, as the basis for a policy to stimulate it. In the short term, he wanted more money in circulation for the government to tap. The memoranda which he received from the authorities, in such territories as Bohemia, Upper Austria and Silesia, were the product of painstaking inquiry and covered a multiplicity of problems. Emphasis was laid on the disorder of weights, measures and currencies; the lamentable state of the roads, and the need for opening up the Elbe and Moldau (Vlatava) to shipping; the anarchy of official tariffs and private tolls both in the interior and on the frontiers of each principality, together with the archaic methods of valuing goods in transit. There was a call for permanent commissions to define and execute measures of economic reform. Yet the compilers largely repeat old facts and old arguments, expounded many years earlier by the first generation of 'Austrian' cameralists.[1] In any case, the Spanish Succession War broke out almost at once and the memoranda were set aside again. Except for the banking innovations of 1703 and 1706,[2] nothing was done, just as nothing was done before 1683. After 1714 and the treaties of peace, certain economic reforms were finally introduced. The mechanism for currency exchanges was improved from 1716 onwards, and a greater uniformity in weights and measures secured. Regional commissions were set up in Bohemia, Silesia and Inner Austria to encourage trade. Often against stiff local opposition and the protests of the *Hofkammer*, which feared to lose its sources of revenue, these committees began gradually to tackle the vested interests of toll-owners,

[1] These writers on political economy (cf. vol. v, pp. 45, 195, and vol. vii, p. 158), who all came to Leopold's court from the Empire, were dead by 1690. Significantly, they had no direct successors in the Austrian lands; nor was the subject introduced into Austrian universities until long after it was being regularly professed in Germany.
[2] Above, pp. 310 ff.

gilds and municipal oligarchies. No one, least of all the central government, dared to review the fundamental problems, taxation and the status
of the peasantry.

It is therefore only at the close of this period that the further development of the economy was somewhat falteringly encouraged. After 1720
it was a peculiar misfortune that Charles VI's personal enthusiasm for
the cause of internal reform declined, and that he failed to fulfil the
promise of his first ten years of rule. The House of Austria had made
many and far-flung conquests, in his and his father's time: effective
administration was as yet beyond its competence.

CHAPTER XIX

THE RETREAT OF THE TURKS, 1683–1730[1]

HE Ottoman empire attained its largest dimensions in Europe with
the conquest in 1672 of the fortress of Kamenets in Podolia
(Kamieniec Podolski), which extended the Domain of Islam as far
as the middle course of the Dniester. To the south-west, between this river
and the Danube, lay the two tributary principalities of Moldavia and
Wallachia, rich lowlands under palatine rulers chosen by the sultan.
Divided from these by the Carpathian mountains, the prince of Transylvania stood in a similar relation to the Porte. The greater part of Hungary, only about a fifth of which lay under Habsburg rule, was divided
into directly governed vilayets: Temesvár in the east; Nové Zamky
(Neuhäusel), Kaniza, and Varasdin in the far west; Eger (Erlau) and above
all Buda in the north. In the empire as a whole there were nearly forty
vilayets, subdivided into departments (*sanjaks*), more or less on a uniform
administrative plan but very variable in size, in which the sultan was
normally represented by a resident pasha, the *vali* and *sanjak-bey* respectively. South of the Danube and the Drava, the grand vilayet (*beyler-
beylik*) of Rumelia included all of what is now European Turkey, Bulgaria,
Thessaly, most of Yugoslavia, and Albania; but Bosnia and the Morea
had been formed into separate governments, while most of Croatia was
ruled by Vienna and portions of the Dalmatian coast by Venice; the
republic of Ragusa (Dubrovnik), like Salonica an important gateway to
Balkan trade, merely paid tribute to the sultan. The Greek Archipelago,
together with certain coastal districts of the Aegean (such as Gallipoli)
and the *sanjak* of the Morea and Lepanto, was directly administered by
the Kaptan Pasha of the imperial navy; Crete had been annexed to this
vilayet, from Venice, as recently as 1670. On the far side of the Mediterranean the 'regencies' of Barbary, where rule by Turkish garrisons did
not extend into the mountains or desert, acknowledged the sultan's
suzerainty;[2] they paid no tribute, but received presents of gunpowder and
took active part in his wars at sea.

In Asia the empire had contracted since 1612. The Peace of Zuhab
(1639) had consecrated the loss of six Persian provinces and of Georgia.
In Iraq the efficacy of Ottoman rule depended on the fluctuating success
of the pasha of Baghdad in repressing the desert Arabs, an increasingly

[1] Dr V. J. Parry, Mrs Nermin Streeter and the Rev. H. S. Deighton very kindly gave
advice on certain points in this chapter.
[2] Above, pp. 553–4. On Turkish methods of keeping the local population divided, cf.
M. Emerit, 'Les tribus privilégiées en Algérie dans la première moitié du XIXe siècle',
Annales (E.S.C.), 21e année (1966), pp. 44–58.

disturbing factor throughout the region of the Red Sea and even in Syria; in 1694, in alliance with the marsh Arabs, they captured Basra, which was only restored to the sultan after Persian intervention. Nomadic Arab or Turcoman pastoralists, as also the semi-nomadic Kurds, often threatened the caravan routes between Aleppo and Baghdad, so that trade was diverted northwards via Trebizond and Erzurum into Persia. Ottoman influence was stronger in Syria, but gravely compromised by annual changes in the person of the governor, who had to contend with strongly entrenched local factions without being able to rely on the garrison troops: only the emergence of dynastic pashaliks from these struggles was to offer some hope of stability in the eighteenth century. The turbulent region of Mount Lebanon was left largely to its own devices, though the governors of Sidon and Damascus were expected to ensure a flow of taxes and thus drawn into the quarrels of its complex tribal and religious divisions; from 1711 it was to be more or less dominated by the Shihab clan, which allowed Christian influences to increase.[1]

None of the Arab provinces was so thoroughly under control as were Anatolia and Rumelia, which bore a far larger share of the imperial burden. Despite reforms in 1695–6, Egypt remitted at most two-thirds of its estimated surplus, and often less, to the Ottoman treasury.[2] Since 1586 the viceroys in Cairo had had to handle many military revolts, but their situation was further complicated by the institutional survival of the Mamluk beylicate, a small order of grandees mainly Circassian in origin but now including emirs (beys) from Bosnia and elsewhere.[3] This aristocracy had been known to depose the sultan's representative and to intrigue at Constantinople against him, but it was deeply divided within itself. After the 'great insurrection' of 1711, when seventy days of bloodshed attended the attack on the janissaries by the six other military corps in Cairo, the struggle for power in Egypt was again, as in 1631–60, centred on the deadly rivalry between two great households, the Kasimiyye and the Fikariyye. Each created a following among artisans, peasants and even nomads, absorbing older lines of division as far as Upper Egypt, where the Fikariyye were often powerful. The viceroy could only govern by relying on one or other of these extensive clans—effectively the Kasimiyye from 1714 to 1730—in spite of their inherent tendency to split into sub-factions. Between 1692 and 1711, however, the frequent rioting in Cairo owed most to indiscipline among the janissaries and to the resentments they aroused: and to this restlessness, here as elsewhere, high food

[1] The ancient regional distribution of the Druze and Maronite communities also began to break up: see P. M. Holt, *Egypt and the Fertile Crescent, 1516–1922* (1966), p. 122.
[2] S. J. Shaw, *The Financial and Administrative Organization and Development of Ottoman Egypt, 1517–1798* (Princeton, 1962), pp. 6, 297, 304–5, 316, 400. Much of the Egyptian tribute took the form of gold from Abyssinia: R. Mantran, *Istanbul dans la seconde moitié du XVII siècle* (1962), pp. 234–5.
[3] Holt, pp. 73 ff.

prices (coupled with privileges and extortions) made a contribution which has yet to be investigated.

By 1700 the *sherif* of Mecca, ruler of the Hejaz, already defied the sultan, though the Red Sea ports, as far as Massawa and Kunfidha, still had Turkish governors and garrisons. Already, too, the arm of the central government had relaxed towards some of the hereditary Kurdish chieftains in the mountainous country between the Persian frontier and the Black Sea.[1] North of the Black Sea, however, the Porte exercised a strong suzerainty over the khanate of the Crimea, which in turn held sway over Circassia and Bessarabia. With that much justification was the Black Sea, even more than the Red, regarded as an Ottoman 'lake': yet the Turks had not forgotten how recently, while their navy was occupied in the Cretan war, the Cossack 'seagulls' had raided its coasts, nor how the Don Cossacks had captured Azak in 1637 and offered it to the tsar. The political instability of the southern steppes, like that of the Caucasus, was a prime factor in causing friction between the Ottomans and their neighbours—divided less by known frontiers than by the fluctuating homelands of the warlike and semi-nomadic tribes whom each in turn protected or sought to use. The Tatars were the chief suppliers of the Ottoman slave-markets.

The frontiers were defended, often in depth, by numerous fortresses and permanent garrisons of some size, especially in Hungary and along the Danube, whose lower course was commanded by Vidin, its upper by Buda and by Belgrade, the most remarkable specimen of Turkish mastery in the art of fortress-building, having a powerful citadel surrounded by three walls at the point where the Sava enters the Danube. This Holy House of War was linked with the capital by a military road running through Nish, Philippopolis and Adrianople, but the Danube itself was much used for the movement of supplies in the European campaigns, for which Bulgaria was the broad supply base, especially in horses. The heart of the empire was protected by the impregnable fortifications with which the first Köprülü had provided the Dardanelles, and by a system of fortresses north of the Black Sea: Kamenets and Chotin (Chocim) near and on the middle Dniester respectively, Bender (Tighina) on the lower Dniester, Ozü (Ochakov) near the mouth of the Bug, and Kilburun across the Dnieper estuary to the south. Further east, the keys of the Sea of Azov, whose integrity was considered vital to the empire, were held by Azak and Kerch.

Communication between the far from homogeneous regions of the empire depended principally on boats and baggage-animals. Where

---

[1] Sir W. Foster (ed.), *The Red Sea and Adjacent Countries at the Close of the Seventeenth Century*...(1949), p. xviii. On the confused situation in Ottoman Armenia, Kurdistan and Georgia, see H. A. R. Gibb and H. Bowen, *Islamic Society and the West*, vol. I (*Islamic Society in the Eighteenth Century*), pt. i (1950), pp. 162–5.

roads existed—chiefly in the Balkans—they were often, like the rivers and caravan-tracks, exposed to brigands or badly maintained by the villages or charities responsible for them. The movement of men—of couriers, soldiers, pilgrims, nomads and migrant peasants—was more in evidence than that of goods, and external commerce more than internal. Elaborate bureaucratic controls on the distributive trades (often geared to the supply of armies and the larger centres of population), with the piling up of in-direct taxes, fettered the enterprise of commercially-minded minorities like the Greeks and Jews, who owed most to the stimulus of external trade with the West. Within the empire the major routes converged by land and water on the capital, but such historic ports as Trebizond, Smyrna and Alexandria still sustained a considerable traffic between the Mediterranean, Persia, the Red Sea and Indian Ocean, while there was a vast amount of petty commerce along the many Muslim routes to Mecca. Much of the great variety of foreign coin[1] which flooded the Levant from the West found its way to Persia and India—not without adding to the monetary disequilibrium of the empire in its passage.

Since 1584 budgetary deficits, foreign speculation and American silver had contributed to successive devaluations of the Ottoman aspre[2] —a fate swiftly shared by the copper coinage and more slowly by the Turkish piastre, both introduced in 1687–8. Since most salaries were fixed, this huge inflation must be held to blame for much of the rapacity of officials and soldiers, some of whom expected a present with every message. Contrary to the experience of some other countries, the price revolution does not seem to have fostered the emergence of any significant new capitalist class in Turkey, where political and fiscal opportunities did more to found great fortunes than did the generally stagnant condition of trade.[3] In the eyes of an improving Westerner like Defoe, the Turks themselves were 'Enemies to Trade...distressedly poor!'[4] To the extent that it was not managed by Europeans—increasingly by French and English—external trade was largely in the hands of Jews, Armenians, Greeks and Lebanese. In the chief ports, Jewish intermediaries were indispensable to European merchants, but much of the overland trade from Persia and the East, in Turkey as in Russia, was Armenian; there were Armenian as well as Jewish colonies in Leghorn and Marseilles. Greek shipowners, with a brilliant career still to come, already dominated the Black Sea and grain trades; in the Mediterranean their freedom of movement received further impetus when the papal Curia espoused their

[1] Above, p. 552.
[2] This small silver piece (*akche*), weighing only a quarter of the finer coin of *ca.* 1570, survived only as a money of account; the silver Turkish piastre of 1687 was then worth 160 aspres. For the Ottoman currency see Mantran, pp. 233 ff.
[3] B. Lewis, 'Some Reflections on the Decline of the Ottoman Empire', *Studia Islamica*, vol. IX (1958), pp. 111–27.
[4] *A Plan of the English Commerce* (1728: repr. Oxford, 1928), pp. 10–11.

interests against the Maltese prize courts in 1702; and Greek business houses, often based on the rising Macedonian port of Salonica, were developing a commercial network in Italy as well as throughout the Ottoman empire by 1700.[1] Banking, such as it was, seems to have been very largely the preserve of the Jews but also, increasingly, of the ubiquitous Armenians: both, as short-term lenders, could strongly influence the local pashas. In the maze of Constantinople's alleys, the Jewish community was the largest in Europe. It included craftsmen, besides middlemen.

On the other hand, there was a most impressive range of traditional Turkish industrial crafts, subject to a high degree of marketing police and to a comprehensive gild system which maintained quality at the expense of competition. In the chief towns, large numbers of the Muslim gildsmen were also enrolled in the privileged military corps of the janissaries, who had thus a double organization for the expression of grievances: indeed, they had yet a third, for most of them belonged to the affiliated lodges of the Bektashi order of dervishes, the most influential of the many heterodox religious bodies which flourished among lower-class Muslims. This triple association served as a link between the great cities and provides a main clue to the domestic politics of the period, when the sultans had more to fear from a riot in the capital than from the rebellion of a whole province.

Town and country were even more sharply contrasted in the Ottoman empire than in Christendom. Besides containing in their numerous gilds and densely populated quarters (often characterized by common faith or racial origin)[2] ready-to-hand organizations for communal action, the towns were the active centres of religious teaching and of private and public spending. Only in their vicinity, where freeholds were commonest, does the cultivator seem to have produced a surplus not wholly absorbed by forced sales or payments in commutation thereof, taxes, dues and gratuities—the burden of these last deriving not only from the venality of officials but also from the frequency of administrative cross-postings. The surplus of the countryside at large was appropriated more and more by the extension of tax-farms in substitution for the old military service fiefs, *zimmet* and *timar*,[3] which tended increasingly to fall legally or illegally into the hands of courtiers and other speculators, who sometimes consolidated them into larger units. Some of these leaseholders, develop-

---

[1] R. E. Cavaliero, 'The Decline of the Maltese Corso in the XVIIIth Century', *Melita Historica*, vol. II (1959), pp. 224–38; Mantran, p. 56; N. G. Svoronos, *Le Commerce de Salonique au XVIII* siècle* (1956), pp. 193 ff.

[2] For the population of some Ottoman towns see above, p. 542; Mantran, pp. 37 ff. analyses that of Constantinople (with maps).

[3] The yearly income of a *zeamet* was 20,000–100,000 aspres, the more numerous *timar* anything below 20,000; a fief worth more than 100,000 was called a *hass*. Both *zeamet* and *timar* are enumerated for each *sanjak* as at *ca.* 1668 by Sir Paul Rycaut, *The History of the Present State of the Ottoman Empire* (5th edn, 1682), pp. 332 ff., with estimates of their military levies.

ing hereditary claims on their tax-farms, were beginning to form a new aristocracy of country notables, but there were many absentees; their bailiffs, as in other times and places, could be harsher and less far-sighted than the old resident sipahi class. The tax-farmers naturally strove to recoup their outlay—itself the result of competitive bidding, like the price of most public offices—without regard to the resilience of the cultivator. Although the introduction of life-contracts in 1692 supplied some corrective, there could be no more eloquent illustration of the weakness into which the central government had fallen, as well as of its growing cost.

The administrators and collectors of pious foundations (*evkaf*)—the economic basis of the Muslim religious institution and of many public services—notoriously exploited their peasants. The non-Muslims had also to pay a poll-tax and, if Orthodox Christians, to suffer the extortions of some of the Greek clergy. In any case, stagnancy, if not contraction, was the prevailing condition of an agriculture upon whose methods the weight of village custom and of the family pressed heavily, which aimed chiefly at local self-sufficiency, and in which animal-raising and barter exchange figured prominently. Few of the Balkan towns were anything more than centres for these purposes; those of the Hungarian Lowland had long since shrunk into small refuges for man and beast in a waste of forest, marsh and steppe country. More generally, Kochu Bey in 1630 had already noted the number of deserted villages, and an early eighteenth-century Turkish critic[1] was to emphasize the evil of peasant migration, which it was the sultan's traditional policy to prohibit.

These conditions told adversely on military manpower. In the first place, the burden of war-service and taxation fell mainly on Rumelia and Anatolia. The 'feudal' organization was principally characteristic of European Turkey and Asia Minor, and from this source came the largest single element in the army, including cavalry levies from the fiefs held by the provincial pasha himself and his subordinates—the nucleus of the private mercenary armies of the later eighteenth century. But the sipahi tenants-in-chief were both reduced in number and often unable to bear the strain of a long war, since ultimately their financial capacity came to reflect the fall in income from their peasants. Moreover, those who could best afford to honour their feudal obligation were precisely those who could bribe themselves out of it, while others feared that absence on campaign would allow rival claimants to their fiefs to collect the income

---

[1] Mehmed Pasha the *defterdar* (chief treasurer), whose work is translated by W. L. Wright in *Ottoman Statecraft: The Book of Counsel for Vezirs and Governors* (Princeton, 1935): see esp. p. 119. According to M. Pécsi and B. Sárfalvi, *The Geography of Hungary* (1964), p. 167, the number of Hungarian villages fell by over half during the Turkish occupation. Cf. H. Antoniadis-Bibicou, 'Villages désertés en Grèce', in R. Romano and P. Courbin (eds.), *Villages désertés et histoire économique, XI–XVIIIe siècle* (1965), pp. 379 ff.

from them.[1] Hence the pashas were increasingly driven to raising territorial troops out of the proceeds of tax-farms. On the other hand, a huge increase in the paid professional soldiery had long since reflected sixteenth-century changes in the art of war. Of this regular army, it is true, the standing sipahi cavalry, tainted by sedition, had been much thinned out[2] by the first Köprülü; and the efficiency of the janissary infantry, despite the hereditary character of its main cadres, had been diluted by the sale of exemptions from service and the admission of too many raw men. 'They never had so many Soldiers, nor such small Armies,' remarks Pitton de Tournefort, the sharp-eyed naturalist who travelled through Anatolia in 1701: 'the Officers...pass their own Domesticks for Soldiers, and put the Pay of those who ought to bear Arms...into their own Pockets. The Corruption which is introduc'd into this great Empire seems to threaten it with some strange Revolution.'[3] Many janissaries practised civilian trades, so that the Corps came to resemble a militia; and civilians might pay to be enrolled in it for the privilege of not being bullied by janissary neighbours in out-of-the-way places like Erzurum.[4] Rivalry between these locally enrolled auxiliaries and professional troops could be an important factor in the complex web of town-politics, as was jealousy between the leaders of the Corps and between its companies or 'hearths'. Although their religion and love of booty could make them brave in action—so that it needed a long period of peace to ruin their fighting efficiency altogether—the janissaries no longer compared favourably as soldiers with the garrison troops of European Turkey, which (despite absenteeism) were stiffened by some of the toughest elements in Ottoman service, Albanians and Bosniaks. It can almost be said that the janissaries were terrible only to their own sultan; even the grand vizier, who commanded the army in war, when his powers reached their fullest extent, had no power to punish offenders without their officers' concurrence. Some of the more subversive among them belonged strictly to the corps of armourers, transportmen and gunners. These last, provided with well-stocked arsenals, were still formidable in battering walls, but their field guns differed only in calibre from their huge siege guns.[5] Long before the reforms of Bonneval, however, Turkish military engineers had profited from other converts to

[1] Gibb and Bowen, vol. I, pt. i, p. 190. The terms 'feudal' and 'fief' are approximates only.
[2] *Ibid.* p. 185 n. for varying estimates, suggesting a figure between 15,000 and 26,000 in 1687–1703. Cf. A. N. Kurat (ed.), *The Despatches of Sir Robert Sutton, Ambassador in Constantinople (1710–1714)*, Camden Soc. 3rd ser., vol. LXXVIII (1953), p. 32. On the composition of the Ottoman forces generally, see below, p. 743.
[3] *A Voyage into the Levant* (tr. J. Ozell, London, 2 vols. 1718), vol. II, p. 35.
[4] *Ibid.* p. 195. For the large numbers of civilian artisans still levied by the gilds to accompany military expeditions, see O. L. Barkan, 'L'organisation du travail dans le chantier d'une grande mosquée à Istanbul au XVIe siècle', *Annales (E.S.C.)*, 17e année (1962), pp. 1097–8.
[5] See C. M. Cipolla, *Guns and Sails...1400–1700* (1965), p. 93 n. Turkish gunners and gun-founders were still valued in India (*ibid.* p. 128 n).

Islam; English and Dutch sappers had aided in the siege of Candia, and in 1705 the fortifications of Kerch and Bender were committed to a Modenese.[1]

The most striking application of imported skills was the adoption of sailing-ships by the navy, first during the Cretan war but above all under the impulse of a great Kapitan Pasha, Mezzomorto, in the 1690s, when European influences gained ground as fear of Europe took root. Mezzomorto's reforms were the most radical experienced by the Ottoman navy since the sixteenth century. Nevertheless, while enviably independent of foreign supplies and capable of impressing its enemies, the navy had serious weaknesses. Kara Mustafa had given it a reformed admiralty in 1681–2, and it had excellent arsenals at Antalya, Gallipoli, Sinop and Suez, above all at Constantinople; but the resources of the Kaptan Pasha's own vilayet, mainly the poll-tax on Christians there, no longer met the navy's needs in money or kind. One consequence was the sale of commissions, often to renegade Italian, English, French and Dutch captains, such as usually commanded the Barbary frigates—themselves often a powerful accession of strength to the sultan's fleet. Officers, from the Kaptan Pasha downwards, sought to recover their outlay by traffic in public stores and provisions. Like other Mediterranean powers, too, the Ottomans had difficulty in finding enough slaves for their galleys, which still had many uses. In the 1690s they could at times assemble a single force of a hundred galleys; but those of the Archipelago, theoretically in readiness all the year round, were seldom up to strength and their captains, less favourably placed financially than those of the summer squadron based on Constantinople, had a strong interest in avoiding loss by battle. The use of sailing-ships, including large armed merchantmen ('caravellas'), called for many more seamen and gunners. Of these there was no regular establishment, but only a summer strength largely recruited from the Greek coasts and islands, as refractory to discipline as the galley-soldiers known as 'levends'.[2] The Turks, though good oarsmen, were poor sailors and the Greeks anything but scientific pilots, while the only competent gunners seem to have been renegade Europeans.

The entire Ottoman State, as became its origins in a frontier organization, was primarily built for war against the infidel; even its domestic critics still urged preachers to proclaim 'the benefits of the Holy War'. The army was usually commanded by the grand vizier in person, with the provincial pashas at the head of the feudal levies. Occasionally the sultan still accompanied it, but the extreme seclusion in which heirs to the throne were now brought up engendered neither military nor political capacity in them. The main burdens of state were carried by the grand

[1] B. H. Sumner, *Peter the Great and the Ottoman Empire* (Oxford, 1949), p. 24.
[2] 'The Plague and the *Leventis*, next to Fire, are the two Scourges of Constantinople' (Tournefort, vol. I, p. 352). A western-style fire brigade was introduced in 1720.

vizier and the large personal secretariat of his chancery at the Porte. It was this able and loyal group of efendis or 'Men of the Pen', some of them trained in the palace-schools instead of in the college-mosques, that now held the empire together. The path of administrative promotion increasingly ran through this bureaucracy, rather than that of the treasury, and its chief writer (*Reis Efendi*) stood a good chance of appointment to a provincial government or even, as in the case of Mehmed Rami in 1703, to the grand vizierate itself.[1]

So long as he enjoyed the sultan's confidence, the powers of the grand vizier were limited only by the world of intrigue in which all business had to be conducted, by the necessity of humouring the janissaries, and by such interference as the Muslim Institution—the judicial as well as ecclesiastical organization—might bring to bear on all levels of civil and military administration. The higher ranks of the ulema, ultra-conservative custodians of law and education, still exercised a power of veto on all important policy decisions, and not simply because they were represented in the imperial Divan—a merely consultative body—and in the councils of the local pashas: the janissaries might overthrow a sultan now and then, but the ulema could bring daily pressure on him by dominance of Muslim opinion. Their chief spokesman, the Mufti of Istanbul, though formally subject to dismissal by the sultan, was either the grand vizier's necessary friend or his fatal enemy. Both, however, had most to fear from the chief of the black eunuchs. For the *Kizlar Agasi* not only disposed of an immense patronage as superintendent of the royal mosques:[2] from being master of the Harem he had become the tyrant of the whole Imperial Household (Seraglio), in which the sinister alliance of women and eunuchs formed the hub of all the wheels of court intrigue. These revolved without cease round every public position and source of profit, for which there was also a well-established tariff of presents. Fortunately, many efendis remained immune to victimization, if not to bribery. The higher officers, including the provincial pashas, were all vulnerable, and none more so than the grand vizier himself. Only a master of intrigue was likely to attain his position. Few held on to it for long. Between 1683 and 1702 there were no less than twelve grand viziers. All but the strongest had to manoeuvre between the largesse they must distribute and the extortions they could safely demand. Many of their adherents, knowing they might last no longer than their chief, naturally did their best to make hay while

---

[1] A. Hourani, 'The Changing Face of the Fertile Crescent in the XVIIIth Century', *Studia Islamica*, vol. VIII (1957), pp. 89–122; N. Itzkowitz, 'Eighteenth Century Ottoman Realities', *ibid.* vol. XVI (1962), pp. 73–94. Rycaut, who estimated the Grand Vizier's 'Court' at 'about 2,000 Officers and Servants', comments on the 'incredible' daily output of orders, etc. (*Present State*, 5th edn. pp. 81, 103).

[2] According to Tournefort (vol. I, pp. 363–4), these, with the educational and charitable organization dependent on them, consumed a third of the land tax; a surplus was available for the defence of religion, and hence for war.

the sun shone, not least if they had had to pay more for an office or a tax-farm than it or they were worth. It is arguable that the worst conse-quence of the abandonment of *devshirme*—the system of slave-enrolment from the sons of Christian subjects—was less the decadence of the free-born, married Muslim janissary than the opening of the civil offices of state to those who could intrigue most successfully for them, and very often to the highest bidder. In this special sense, however, the Ottoman polity did offer a *carrière ouverte aux talents*.

The Köprülü, father and son, had saved the empire from near-collapse in the third quarter of the seventeenth century, but they had not contem-plated any structural reform of its institutions. Critics of proved abuses— more numerous and penetrating than is generally realized—looked for remedy, unless they were Muslim converts with knowledge of the West, to a rejuvenation of morality and the drastic punishment of offenders, under the guidance of a Sacred Law which was supposed to have foreseen all requirements. Confident of the superiority of Islam and wilfully ignorant of the world outside its Domain, the Ottomans appreciated only the war techniques of the West; not until the French Revolution did western ideas make any deep impression on Islam.[1] What long remained lacking was the regenerative power of inductive reasoning. The ulema, with their virtual monopoly of higher education and learning, were profoundly hostile to what they understood of the infidel's 'rational' sciences and used their immense influence to forbid knowledge of Christian languages to the faithful. Even in the comparatively advanced study of medicine, though there were skilled Jewish and even Frankish physicians in Turkey, Muslim writers in the eighteenth century were only beginning to take account of European discoveries of the sixteenth.[2] Nepotism and venality also gave the religious hierarchy a large material stake in the established order, particularly as their property, unlike that of the sultan's secular servants (still technically 'slaves'), was both inheritable and safe from confiscation. This 'Learned Profession' was increasing in size.

Some of its failings, however, might also be imputed to many of the very numerous Greek Orthodox clergy. The Oecumenical Patriarchate, whose influence was recovering at Constantinople, was itself an incubus on fresh ideas, as well as on the purses of its following; bishops who failed to satisfy its fiscal demands might find their dioceses 'adjudg'd to the highest bidder'.[3] In general, its tributaries were on better terms with the contemptuously tolerant Muslims than with the Catholic minorities who lived uneasily beside them here and there, as in Turkish Croatia and some of the Greek islands, where the French Capuchins had established missions. Orthodox, not Muslim, persecution was to force the emigration of Abbot

---

[1] See B. Lewis, *The Emergence of Modern Turkey* (1961), pp. 53 ff.
[2] Something was known of western geographical science and the Turks were able to chart their own coasts (*ibid.* p. 44).
[3] Tournefort, vol. I, p. 79.

Mekhitar, whose foundation of a Catholic community in 1700 was the principal influence on the revival of Armenian culture.

It was at least as much the spirit of mountain tribesmen as of religious revolt, no doubt, that resisted the assimilation of some Slav, Georgian, and Armenian Christians to Ottoman rule. But this was a spirit working ultimately for anarchy, scarcely for improvements: the improvements conceivable to them were simple and not peculiarly the needs of Christians—less extortion and better justice. Such a ferment as Slav race-consciousness, too, in spite of the unsettling effect of alternating régimes in parts of the Balkans, was still far in the future. If the mass exodus of 'Rascian' Serbs to the southern marches of Hungary in 1690 was organized by Orthodox clergy, it also owed much to population pressure and the drive for larger pastures; it was a novel phenomenon only in its scale and speed. Muslim and Christian alike, the villages lived largely to themselves. Even the rebel Montenegrins, who did not lack leaders, never rose as one man at the call of Peter the Great.[1] Economic hardship had more to do in these years than ideological separatism with disturbances among the Christians, although the Turks were quick to suspect them of sympathy with hostile Christian States—an occasion of massacre in the long run, as in the 1730s. As for the Jews, it is enough to say that foreign ambassadors found their physicians an easier channel to the ears of the higher ranks of the ulema, and sometimes of the sultan himself, than were the Greek dragomans (interpreters) who were fast becoming normal intermediaries with the central bureaucracy at the Porte.

Only members of this last, the skilled 'Men of the Pen', could compete in education with the men of religion, Christian or Muslim. Their influence was growing, but the ulema in particular possessed an incomparable hold over the mentality of the mass of subjects. Hence, even if the limits of fatalism were sooner reached than is supposed, any constructive or even durable uprising from below was hardly to be expected. The repeated janissary risings, though they might champion the poor as well as express the grievances of one among many conservative gilds, were more properly mutinies, or strikes with violence, than real social revolutions. It remained to be seen whether the Ottoman polity would be changed by conquest from without.

Between 1683 and 1730 the Ottomans enjoyed less than twenty years of peace. The war which began with the siege of Vienna[2] was alone to last nearly as long—and severely to test that over-confidence which was responsible for the undertaking and for its failure alike. The rout of Kara Mustafa's vast army in September 1683 was followed by further serious losses during its crossing of the Danube at Párkány and by the abandonment of Gran (Esztergom) and other fortresses in Upper Hungary. On

---

[1] Below, p. 632.   [2] See vol. v, pp. 513–17.

25 December the grand vizier was strangled in Belgrade. The formation of the Holy League at Linz on 5 March 1684 meant that the Emperor Leopold, yielding to his generals and clergy, had turned aside from action against Louis XIV to rally German opinion behind Innocent XI's crusade. It is true that Leopold, suspecting John Sobieski of designs on Hungary, had cold-shouldered the saviour of Vienna and declined an all-out pursuit of the Turks in 1683. In succeeding years, moreover, his own domestic difficulties prevented the Polish king from mobilizing forces sufficient to recover Podolia or to realize his ambition of annexing the Rumanian principalities, although he attempted to do both.[1] On the other hand, the adherence to the Holy League of the sea power of Venice and Malta, together with the privateers of Greek islands under Venetian control, could seriously harass Ottoman commerce and divert forces from the Danube. The Venetians could stir up trouble among the Christians in Bosnia and Greece. In 1684, therefore, the Turks found themselves fighting on three fronts—in Hungary, the Polish Ukraine, and the Adriatic— besides having to defend vital routes across the Aegean. In October, the fierce Tatar horsemen of the Crimea broke a fresh Polish assault on Chotin, the scene of Sobieski's triumph in 1673; but the Venetians seized the Ionian island of Santa Maura (Leukas) and the Imperial commander, Duke Charles V of Lorraine, swept up more fortresses in northern Hungary.

It was in Hungary, which they had held sinçe 1526, that the Turks resisted most bitterly, in support of their vassal king Imre Thököly, leader of the Hungarian insurrection since 1678. In 1685 Charles of Lorraine mastered the great stronghold of Nové Zamky, only 200 surviving out of a garrison of 3,000. This blow was so sharply felt that the commander of the main Ottoman army, Ibrahim Pasha, opened parleys for a general peace. He was executed for acting without authority from the new grand vizier, himself dismissed soon afterwards. Such frequent changes of viziers and seraskers (commanders-in-chief) added to the confusion at the Porte and in the army. Strange indeed was the behaviour of the sultan himself, for Mehmed IV, in face of so many disasters, was obstinately absorbed in personal pleasures, notably hunting. Already murmurs could be heard about his blatant indifference to the developing crisis. This deepened in 1686 with the fall of Buda, the chief centre of Ottoman Hungary, 'the shield of Islam'. Abdi Pasha of Buda is still remembered in Turkey for his heroic 78-day defence against an army of 40,000; when the place was taken by storm on 2 September, nearly all the Turks perished, Abdi Pasha at their head. The whole Hungarian resistance broke down in consequence, and Thököly had to abandon his remaining towns to the judicial terror supervised by General Caraffa at Eperjes.[2]

---

[1] See below, pp. 683–4.
[2] Cf. vol. v, pp. 498–9 for the Habsburg advance down to 1691, and above, pp. 576 ff. Hungarian historians admit that the liberation of Hungarian soil by foreign forces aroused

While the main Turkish forces were thus engaged on the Danube, Francesco Morosini was able to use his command of the sea, not only to threaten important convoys from Egypt, upon which the Ottoman treasury greatly depended, but also to seize strongpoints on the coast of the Morea in 1685. Morosini's army of 11,000 was half composed of Hanoverian and Saxon troops, under Count Königsmark, which suffered badly from fever and complained of Morosini's firm discipline. His only significant success in 1686 was the capture of Nauplia (Napoli di Romania), which became his forward naval base. Next year, however, having lost control of the entrance to the Gulf of Corinth, the Turks were driven out of the Morea (though Malvasia held out till 1690), and then Athens itself[1] came under Venetian occupation; a Venetian bomb largely destroyed the Parthenon, then in use as a powder magazine.

These were not the only military misfortunes of 1687, a year also of drought and soaring food prices. Sobieski led his troops deep into Turkish territory as far as Jassy, capital of Moldavia, though once again his strength was unequal to the abstemious and mobile horsemen of the able Selim-Girei, four times khan of the Crimea.[2] The Turks themselves took the initiative on the Danube, where the grand vizier, Süleyman Pasha, hoped to recover Buda. Against all expectations he suffered a defeat costing some 20,000 men, while Imperial losses were trifling. This was on 12 August, at Nagyharsány (Berg Hasan), near Mohács. The news was carried to Vienna by a young and rather reserved cavalry officer, Eugene of Savoy, who received his military formation in these campaigns. On 9 December the Archduke Joseph received the Crown of St Stephen at Buda.

After these reverses the main Ottoman army revolted. It elected Siyavush Pasha general and asked the sultan to name him grand vizier; retiring from Belgrade to Adrianople, the troops called for the execution of Süleyman Pasha. Mehmed IV offered no resistance, but his acceptance of Siyavush as grand vizier was not enough to save him. His neglect of affairs had pushed resentment so far that on 8–9 November 1687 the ulema combined with the army to dethrone him.[3] So Mehmed 'the Hunter' was at last replaced by his half-brother Süleyman II, who was to show better qualities as a ruler (1687–91). He was at first hampered by the janissaries, now temporarily masters of the capital: in fact, their arbitrary government continued for four months, during which they appointed their

no enthusiasm in the local populations: cf. O. Jászi, *The Dissolution of the Habsburg Monarchy* (Chicago reprint, 1961), p. 41, and H. Marczali, *Hungary in the Eighteenth Century* (tr. H. Temperley, Cambridge, 1910), p. 2.

[1] Its population had shrunk since 1580, when it has been estimated at 17,000: O. L. Barkan, 'Essai sur les données statistiques des registres de recensement de l'empire ottoman aux XVe et XVIe siècles', *Journal of Econ. and Soc. Hist. of the Orient*, vol. I (1957), p. 27.

[2] 1671–8, 1684–91, 1692–9 and 1702–4.

[3] Cf vol. v, p. 518.

nominees to high posts, pillaged the Seraglio and behaved as in a conquered country. There were disturbances also in Anatolia, Crete and Belgrade. As was characteristic of the dramatic revolutions of Turkish politics, however, such excesses produced their own cure, at least for a time. With the help of an outraged civilian population, the new sultan's government contrived to put down the disorders, punish the janissaries, and execute some of their agas (officers).

During these troubles the main Habsburg army could advance without much opposition. Eger, to the north, was taken in December 1687. Southwards, under Elector Max Emmanuel of Bavaria, the Imperialists captured the key fortress of Peterwardein in the spring of 1688. The road to Belgrade thus lay open. It was expected that Belgrade itself would long hold out: it surrendered after only three weeks, on 6 September, probably after treason. As its fall threatened Serbia, Bulgaria and the Principalities —in all of which there were elements making contact with Vienna[1]—the Porte now attempted peace negotiations in earnest. Zulfikar, a senior official, and Alexander Mavrocordato, the highly influential First Dragoman of the Porte, were sent to Vienna, ostensibly to announce the accession of Süleyman II, in fact to probe the possibilities of agreement. The emperor's terms, which extended to the absorption of Transylvania as well as Hungary, were wholly unacceptable. To force the Habsburg to a more reasonable peace, therefore, the Turks mounted a new campaign in the late summer of 1689. It was hoped that the sultan's presence would fire the zeal of his troops to recover Belgrade. Instead, they lost the important city of Nish (150 miles further south) to Margrave Lewis of Baden on 24 September, and soon afterwards Vidin. This brought the enemy close to Adrianople, the summer residence of the sultans. Although the arrival of Selim-Girei Khan, with a great body of Tatars, saved Bulgaria and Thrace, some of Baden's troops penetrated Wallachia as far as Bucharest during the winter.[2]

With the whole military situation now so critical, public opinion in Constantinople, supported by the ulema, was calling for a strong personality (normally so unwelcome to court parasites) in the post of grand vizier—exactly as in 1656, when Köprülü Mehmed Pasha was given unlimited power. On 25 October 1689 the sultan nominated Fazil Mustafa Pasha, the youngest son of Köprülü Mehmed. Mustafa Pasha, entitled Fazil (the Virtuous) and one of the ablest grand viziers even known, was to be killed in battle less than two years later, but meanwhile he succeeded in putting some order into public business and the army's shaken discipline; offices were suppressed and salaries reduced, even in the Seraglio, and the aspre devalued by a third. There was also reason to expect that he might succeed in driving the enemy out of the Balkans. For the emperor's position was now complicated by the outbreak of the

---

[1] See above, pp. 577–8.   [2] Above, pp. 579–80.

Nine Years War. As Louis XIV intended, the French movement in 1688 to the Rhineland held down important Austrian forces which could otherwise have been employed in the east, where another ten years of Balkan fighting, in the event, were to bring them no further permanent gains. The Hungarians, moreover, were restless under Habsburg rule: the prince of Transylvania, Michael Apafi, formerly appointed by the Turks, had submitted to the emperor, but Thököly maintained the struggle for Hungary's independence. The fortunes of war in Greece had turned already, in 1688, when the Venetians evacuated Attica and failed against Negroponte; and control of northern Greece was more or less recovered in 1690 from the bandits who terrorized it—often Albanian and Dalmatian deserters from the Venetian army. In 1690, also, Fazil Mustafa scored notable successes in the Balkans, recapturing Nish on 9 September and Belgrade itself a month later. Serbia and part of Bosnia were again under Turkish rule. It was then that occurred one of the most celebrated episodes in Serbian history. Led by the patriarch of Peć, the holy place of Serb Orthodoxy, many thousands—some say as many as 200,000—moved into the depopulated lands of south Hungary, hoping to find better treatment from new overlords.[1] Nevertheless, Fazil Mustafa forbade punishment for their disloyalty, allowed the building of new Orthodox churches and the repair of old ones, stopped arbitrary oppression, and took what other steps he could to improve the lot of people who had inevitably suffered much by the passage of armies and the destruction of all normal life.

Süleyman II died in 1691 and was succeeded by his half-brother Ahmed II (1691–5). Of the five sultans who reigned between 1648 and 1730, these were the only two to escape deposition. Fazil Mustafa survived the change of sultan and personally led the army into Transylvania, but met a hero's death in the slaughter near Zalánkemén on 19 August 1691.[2] The Turks withdrew into the Banat, and there followed a standstill in operations of about a year, both sides weary of war. Before a new campaign opened, the British and Dutch representatives at Constantinople, Lord Paget and Jacobus Colijer,[3] offered their mediation. Britain and the United Provinces were naturally anxious to extricate their Imperial ally from what to William III was a diversion of sorely needed troops from the more important struggle against France. The Turkish demands were pitched too high, however, for mediation to succeed. The effort was repeated in 1693, but this time, as in 1688–9, it was again the Austrian demands which were

---

[1] V. L. Tapié, *Les Relations entre la France et l'Europe Centrale de 1661 à 1715* ('Cours de Sorbonne', 2 vols. 1958), vol. II, p. 187, calls attention also to the later migration from the Principalities into Transylvania; there had been a movement in the reverse direction after the Habsburg persecution of Hungarian Protestants in 1670. Cf. above, p. 580.

[2] See vol. V, p. 499 and above, p. 580 for the effects of this battle on Transylvania.

[3] Having gained experience under his father, Colijer had succeeded him as resident envoy in 1684 and remained at Constantinople till 1725. For much of this time he also acted as an unofficial Russian agent.

too stiff. So hostilities dragged on in face of the desire of both powers for peace. The Austrians made an unsuccessful attempt to retake Belgrade in September 1693; equally, the Turks failed against Peterwardein in 1694. The rivers and marshes between these places virtually imposed stalemate.

Presuming on the weakness of Ottoman sea power, however, in September 1694 the Venetian fleet crossed the Aegean to land some 8,000 troops in Chios (Scio), which was rapidly overcome. Such an occupation threatened a blockade of the Dardanelles (several times undertaken during the Cretan war), besides the loss of a rich island with a useful dockyard, regularly used as a way-station by the Alexandria-Constantinople convoys. For the sultan this might mean deposition or worse. As so often in the past, the Turks were able to concentrate a large fleet at the point and at the moment of extreme danger; in addition to their galleys, they now had a score of fast and powerful sailing-ships, supplemented by 16 Barbary privateers.[1] On the other hand, Antonio Zeno, who had succeeded to the Venetian command on Morosini's death in 1693, was short of men and money. Plunder embarrassed his relations with the Chiotes. His own commanders were not on good terms. His Maltese auxiliaries withdrew. There were rumours of a Turkish counter-attack on Argos, in the Morea. In fact, Zeno found himself in the predicament which the dying Morosini had advised his countryman at all costs to avoid: too far from his sources of supply, he had dispersed his limited manpower, thus endangering the Venetian hold on the Morea instead of seeking to protect it by clearing the Turks out of Negroponte. He had wasted the republic's carefully husbanded fighting resources on an easy conquest which could be retained only at Turkish discretion.[2] In February 1695 the Venetians evacuated Chios.

Under a new and energetic sultan, Mustafa II (1695–1703), the Turkish military offensive briefly flared up again. He insisted on taking personal part in it in June 1695; some small places were taken from the Austrians and Mustafa was hailed at home as 'Gazi', victor over unbelievers.

In view of their many crushing defeats and the loss of such extensive territories, it is remarkable indeed that the Turks still preserved so much of their old fighting spirit. After every forlorn battle the Porte succeeded each spring in furnishing a new army, guns, warships. But this was accomplished at the cost of much economic dislocation and the intensification of many social evils. Expenditure was met, or partly met, by higher taxes—notably on coffee, tobacco, official salaries—and by confiscating the fortunes of fallen officials. A courageous attempt was made in 1696–7

---

[1] The sailing-ships, unlike the galleys, remained in the Mediterranean when the Russians invaded the Sea of Azov. In each year after 1696 there were indecisive fleet-actions, in which the Venetians were slightly outnumbered. See R. C. Anderson, *Naval Wars in the Levant* (Liverpool, 1952), pp. 223 ff., and above, pp. 565–6.

[2] P. Argenti (ed.), *The Occupation of Chios by the Venetians, 1694* (1953), pp. xli ff.

to restore the currency by striking a new piastre and a new gold coin worth 300 aspres. In these years the treasury had more difficulty in making ends meet than at any time during the seventeenth or eighteenth centuries; in 1691, expenditure (about three-quarters military) had outstripped receipts by more than a quarter.[1] It is true that under Turkish practice the maintenance of many military services as well as virtually all public works was the responsibility of charitable trusts (*evkaf*): Ottoman piety endowed not only mosques, hospitals and almshouses, but roads, ships, and fortresses on 'the ever-victorious frontier'. But the administration of *evkaf* was an object of lively competition among the influential and much of the income was diverted, the property sometimes being converted into private ownership.[2] Similarly, a border garrison might find itself defrauded of its pay by the malversations of the agent who managed a government property alienated expressly to support it. Such properties often went out of cultivation, for lack of capital to maintain them or because the cultivators had fled, while unpaid garrison troops deserted.

As a chief treasurer (*defterdar*) later pointed out, the treasury was also the ultimate loser by maltreatment of the peasants, for 'the state exists through them and the treasure produced by them';[3] and since the treasury depended on 'abundance of subject people', it was not compassion alone that condemned the janissaries in these blistering lines:

Saying 'We are on campaign', they commit all sorts of shameful acts...Practising brigandage, they are not satisfied with free and gratuitous fodder for their horses and food for their own bellies from the villages they meet. They covet the horse-cloths and rags of the rayas, and if they can get their hands on the granaries they become joyful.[4]

Many normally quiet areas were now afflicted with bands of deserted soldiers, while in others (such as Thessaly) there was an increase of endemic brigandage. Many peasants found it best to join the brigands and even made their way into the *corps d'élite* itself, like those 'pretence janissaries' who drew their pay without going a day's journey from Constantinople.[5] The intrusion of these adventurers, sometimes as officers brought in over the heads of veterans, undoubtedly contributed to the decline of janissary discipline; and no item of expenditure strained the treasury so much as the quarterly sums—amounting to half the military budget—due to this swollen standing army, which could extort increases as well as arrears of pay under threat of mutiny. Since, also, the strength of the 'feudal' force

---

[1] Mantran, pp. 236, 240, 257–9.

[2] Many families converted their property (especially in and near a town) into *evkaf* to secure it from confiscation. It was a main aim of the great reforming sultan Mahmud II, after his destruction of the janissaries in 1826, to centralize administration of these pious foundations as well as to divert their revenues to himself (Lewis, *Modern Turkey*, pp. 91–4).

[3] Wright, p. 118.

[4] *Ibid.* p. 126.

[5] *Ibid.* p. 111.

could hardly fail to reflect the growing impoverishment, the empire had to fight for life with the aid of less disciplined volunteer levies.

At this difficult time a quite unexpected danger appeared from the north. The Turks habitually regarded Muscovite Russia with a certain disdain. In general, it was not the Porte but the khan of the Crimea who had direct dealings with the Muscovites; they indeed suffered mounting losses—in men, stock, and ransom-money—from the raids of Tatar horsemen, especially in the recently settled and ill-defended Slobodskaya Ukraine, centred on Kharkov. The insignificance of Russian military power appeared to be confirmed by the failure of V. V. Golitsyn's expeditions to the Isthmus of Perekop in 1687 and 1689. Although Sobieski had persuaded Muscovy to join the Holy League in 1686 (in return for the permanent cession of Kiev by Poland),[1] no serious danger arose from that quarter until 1695. Then the Russians, instead of another direct move on the Crimea, attacked Azak (Azov). The young tsar, Peter, opened a new era in Russo-Turkish relations as well as in Russian history. Besides Polish and Austrian appeals for aid, Peter had every reason to put a stop to Tatar raiding. He was also encouraged by spokesmen of the Balkan Orthodox, Serb and Rumanian as well as Greek, now thoroughly alarmed lest liberation from their Muslim masters should come from the Latin 'Swabians': as a Wallachian envoy in Moscow was to write in 1698, 'The secular war may finish some time, but the Jesuit war never.'[2] Beyond question, however, the tsar's leading motive was a thirst for 'warm seas'.

After the failure of his first attempt on Azak, which was reinforced by sea, Peter ordered warships to be built at Voronezh on the upper Don in the winter of 1695–6. The flotilla, which was commanded by the Swiss François Lefort, consisted of 17 galleys and 6 light sailing-ships in addition to fireships and some 40 Cossack small craft.[3] The Turks, taken by surprise, had neglected to repair the damage of the previous year. Azak fell in July. This was the first Russian victory over the Turks and it had far-reaching consequences. It was of immense importance as a demonstration of superiority over a power which the Muscovites had hitherto treated with all possible caution. At last they did reach the coasts of a sea, though not yet those of the Black Sea. At Taganrog, only 20 miles across the water to the north-west of Azov, Peter established a naval yard capable of building 14 ships-of-the-line by 1699. His troops were not very successful in other directions, however. In 1695 Boris Sheremeteyev had taken four small strongholds on the lower Dnieper and threatened Tatar communications with the west, but an advance on the Straits of Kerch, which give entry to the Black Sea itself, was frustrated. This is why Peter objected

---

[1] Cf. below, p. 683.   [2] Quoted Sumner, p. 34.
[3] For operations down the Dnieper and along the Black Sea Coast (as far as Akkerman), the Russians built a large number of small craft at Bryansk, on the river Desna, still further from the sea than Voronezh: Anderson, *Naval Wars*, pp. 239–40.

bitterly to the peace negotiations which Prince Eugene's first sensational victory against the Turk was to bring about, in unexpectedly decisive fashion, once Eugene had been released from the emperor's war in Italy by the Convention of Vigevano.[1]

Insisting that he again lead the army in person, Mustafa II took the military initiative for the recovery of Hungary in the summer of 1697. Yet the Turkish command acted without any definite plan and there were serious discords within it: while the grand vizier, now Elmas Mehmed Pasha, preferred to march north across the Banat, others wanted to go west in the direction of Peterwardein. The grand vizier prevailed and the army proceeded across the difficult swampy country of the lower Tisza, neglecting to watch the enemy's movements. Eugene, who had expected an attack on Peterwardein, made a remarkable forced march and caught the Turks just when most of their cavalry had crossed the Tisza eastwards and the infantry were still on the right bank. This was on 11 September, towards nightfall, near Zenta. Surprised by Eugene's appearance and immediate decision to attack, the Turks lost about 20,000 killed and perhaps 10,000 drowned, while the Imperialist losses were trifling. Mustafa II, who witnessed the slaughter across the river, fled. This 'frightful blood bath' (as Eugene himself called it) was accentuated by a mutiny of the janissaries, who in desperation killed the grand vizier and many high-ranking officers. By the end of October Eugene was deep in Bosnia, burning and plundering the important trading town of Sarajevo.

The sultan appointed Hüseyn Pasha, the fourth Köprülü, as grand vizier, hoping he would find means to halt the run of calamities. This was an appropriate juncture for the English and Dutch mediators to intervene again, especially as the imminent death of Carlos II threatened new complications for the Austrian Habsburg in the West. Both sides agreed to negotiate on the basis of *uti possidetis*, the territories actually occupied by each side to be left in its possession. This ruled out any Russian hope of winning the Straits of Kerch by diplomacy: the tsar's visit to Vienna in 1698 failed to renew the first Austro-Russian alliance against Turkey made only a year earlier. Eventually, at the small town of Carlowitz near Peterwardein, after 72 days' negotiation, with Mehmed Rami Efendi (afterwards grand vizier) and the experienced Alexander Mavrocordato as the Turkish plenipotentiaries, agreements were reached on 26 January 1699 with all but the Russians. With Russia an armistice of two years was concluded, to be followed by a peace for ten years in 1700, when the outbreak of the Great Northern War made it an urgent matter for Peter. But he never forgave the Habsburgs for their desertion at Carlowitz.

The Peace of Carlowitz is significant as the first agreement between the

---

[1] Above, p. 250. Nevertheless, money and supplies were too short for much to be hoped at Vienna from the 1697 campaign, which in fact began late and was regarded even by Eugene as defensive in purpose: M. Braubach, *Prinz Eugen von Savoyen*, vol. I (1963), pp. 248 ff.

Turks and a coalition of European powers, as the first occasion when the Turks accepted the mediation of neutrals, and as the first formal acknowledgement by the Ottoman empire of a defeat. It lost vast territories: Hungary and Transylvania (though not the heavily depopulated Banat of Temesvár) to the emperor;[1] Dalmatia and the magnificent Montenegrin harbour of Cattaro (Kotor), Santa Maura, the Morea and Aegina to Venice; Podolia, with Kamenets, to Poland. Further, by the Treaty of Constantinople in 1700, the Turks ceded the Azak area and accepted a regular Russian diplomatic mission for the first time—a right (lost in 1711 but regained in 1720) which gave Russia the same opportunity of studying and exploiting the inner convolutions of Turkish politics as was enjoyed by France, Britain, the Empire, the Netherlands and Venice. In addition, the Turks repudiated the Crimean khan's claim to an annual tribute, so much resented by the tsars: it had not been paid since 1683 and by 1700 the arrears amounted to perhaps a twelfth of Peter's revenue in that year.[2] Peter in turn agreed to destroy the four forts below the Dnieper cataracts which he had hitherto insisted on retaining, but the Turks did not recover them. The Russians also obtained recognition of an old demand for unhindered pilgrimage to the Holy Land. Together these treaties mark the beginning of Turkish retreat from European soil. Occasionally thereafter the Turks did recover some of their losses, as in the case of Azov (1711), the Morea and island of Aegina (1715). For a time, too, they were able to stabilize their Russian frontiers and even to extend their holdings in the Caucasus. It was only in 1774 that Russia obtained the freedom of the Black Sea for her navigation and recognition of a right to protect her Orthodox co-religionists in the Turkish Balkans, though Peter had staked out both claims at Carlowitz; and it was not until 1783 that Russia absorbed the Crimea. And yet, small as were the sacrifices of 1699–1700 by comparison with the vast area still under Ottoman rule, they were strategically and economically important. Above all, these losses gravely diminished Ottoman prestige as a great military power. It was evident that 'the Turkish menace' was a thing of the past.

In some ways the very survival of the empire was imperilled. The western approach to the Aegean was in Venetian hands and the Venetian fleet might again threaten the Dardanelles. In the north, the Sea of Azov had ceased to be a Turkish 'lake'; east of it the district of the lower Kuban river and parts of the northern Caucasus were coming under Russian influence, while the new fort of Kamenny Zaton on the left-bank Dnieper to the west was a reminder of the recent threat to the Tatar grazing and hunting grounds. The Crimea, the Dnieper mouth, the Black Sea itself were now shadowed by the tsar. Entry to the Black Sea, hitherto barred to the western nations that traded with Constantinople, might

---

[1] Cf. above, pp. 581 ff.
[2] Sumner, p. 77n. The Ottoman treasury also lost certain tributes.

soon be open to the Russians, who made no secret of their ambitions in this direction; it was seen as a portent when Ukraintsev, who came for the peace negotiations in 1700, arrived at the Bosporus in a 52-gun warship equipped at Taganrog. The Great Northern War by no means halted Peter's work of fortification and naval construction there and at Azov, for which a labour force of over 18,000[1] was demanded as late as 1709. The great uneasiness felt at Constantinople was occasioned, however, as much by the implications of the loss of a major frontier fortress as by any effective increase in the power of Muscovy. In the Russian south, this was slight enough when compared with Peter's acquisitions in the north; but what he accomplished in the south was of less significance than that he did it at all. The loss of Azak and the Dnieper forts had come as a violent shock to every good Osmanli. Henceforward the Turks were hypersensitive to every rumour of Russian moves.

In addition, the social and economic dislocation of war took years to put right. Many desperate peasants in Anatolia and other provinces had left their homes to become wanderers or brigands, or to pick up a living in the capital. In some areas corn reached famine prices, and in some the government was unequal to the maintenance of public order. The Grand Vizier Hüseyn Pasha worked hard from 1697 to redress both economy and administration. After the war he abolished many of the compulsory payments necessitated by it; in particular, by cancelling arrears of war contribution and otherwise, he sought to alleviate the deplorable condition of the Christian peasantry, who had suffered not only by the wide breakdown of local administration but above all by the campaigning in the Balkans.[2] Hüseyn even dared to attack the abuse of *timar*, for the long years of war had multiplied openings for the misuse of fiefs by persons who did not in practice perform military service; yet it was impossible in a short time to get rid of the thousands of illegal holders of these estates. He also tried to curb the janissaries by cutting down their numbers, with considerable savings to the treasury. Barracks were rebuilt, fortresses reconditioned. These were the years when naval efficiency made its greatest strides, notably by Mezzomorto's clarification of the chain of command and the increased building of square-rigged sailing-ships; Tournefort, who was favourably impressed by the organization of the dockyard at Constantinople, counted 28 fine ships there (from 100 to 60 guns) in 1701.[3] The combined strength of the standing army and navy was

---

[1] Already lower than this when the Cossack rebellion of 1706–8 (below, p. 732) had reduced it to a few hundreds. Construction continued in the yards up the Don and its tributaries.

[2] Ankara, Turkish National Archives, Mühimme Defteri, no. 145, p. 485. Gibb and Bowen vol. I, pt. ii (1957), p. 237 mention especially Bulgaria, which had always to endure the passage of armies leaving the capital for the Danube. Cf. Svoronos, p. 122, on the disruption of Salonica's Balkan trade.

[3] *A Voyage into the Levant*, vol. I, p. 374. A Venetian list of 1716 estimates Ottoman strength in sail at one ship of 112 guns, two of 88, one of 72, twenty-five of 64–50, and six of

estimated at 196,227 men, costing nearly 7 m. piastres a year. Writing in 1703–4, the *defterdar* Sari Mehmed Pasha placed the size of the standing army alone at 96,727, excluding another 70,000 in frontier garrisons or on pension and 23,500 'who have the duty of saying prayers'.[1]

More might have been achieved had not Hüseyn Pasha encountered a formidable obstacle in the wealthy and ambitious Mufti Feyzullah, a former tutor of Mustafa II who possessed great influence, placed his many sons in lucrative posts, and interfered constantly in public business. The position of the Mufti of Constantinople, the highest religious and therefore legal authority, whose rulings on points of sacred law included decisions of peace and war, commanded greater esteem than that of the grand vizier himself: disharmony between the two was fatal to the working of the higher administration. Feyzullah was a learned legist and did much to raise standards of religious discipline and teaching,[2] but he embodied the fierce opposition of the ulema to change. The grand vizier's health broke down and he resigned on 5 September 1702, shortly before his death. His successor, Daltaban Mustafa Pasha, a coarse and tyrannical creature of Feyzullah's, was neither able nor willing to continue his work, despite an improved administration of such *evkaf* as he controlled.[3]

Sultan Mustafa II, a man of culture and humanity but fond of his pleasures, now stayed permanently at Adrianople, so causing rumour to spread that he would make it his capital. Away from Constantinople, he could more easily escape the pressures of opinion in the college-mosques, coffee-houses and workshops, as well as in the palace itself. It was also a sinister fact that the chief janissary aga was mainly responsible for the police[4] of the capital. In 'the Adrianople affair' of August 1703, the armourers, angry about long arrears of pay, headed a military rising to compel the sultan's return. The army forced him to abdicate in favour of his brother, Ahmed III (1703–30), and it suborned the ulema into sanctioning this. As was doubtless foreseen, the confiscated estates of the fallen administration went far to provide the largest sum ever paid to the troops on such an occasion.[5] With less authority from precedent, the rapacious Feyzullah was abandoned to the fury of the mob, on the orders of his successor. Mavrocordato, who had been in his confidence, temporarily effaced himself.

48–28, exclusive of a Barbary squadron (Anderson, 248n.). The construction of three-decker galleons, first attempted in 1682, made rapid progress in these years.

[1] Wright, pp. 104–5.
[2] J. von Hammer, *Hist. de l'empire ottoman* (tr. J. J. Hellert, 18 vols. 1835–46), vol. XIII, p. 68.
[3] *Ibid.* vol. XIII, p. 83.
[4] Fully discussed by Mantran, pp. 148 ff.
[5] 3,688 purses or 1,537,666 piastres. The rest of the money was found by sales of offices and tax-farms. Another 1,000 purses went to the frontier garrisons in the shape of drafts on government properties. See Wright, p. 6.

The new sultan, then aged thirty, had spent his life in seclusion but with some freedom. Although fond of women and of verse, a distinguished calligrapher and flower-painter, he did not devote himself exclusively to the pleasures of the Seraglio. During the first part of his reign at least, from 1703 to 1714, Ahmed showed intelligent interest in public business, as was seen in a number of reforms in the judiciary and in the coinage. Unhappily, his morose, unsteady and ambitious character laid him open to the influence of favourites, although his early resolve was to trust no one too far and he concentrated on securing himself against conspirators. By causing or acquiescing in the deaths of thousands of suspected persons, he certainly filled the treasury but also deprived the empire of some of its ablest soldiers. While he shared the profound desire of many of his subjects to see the greatness of the empire restored, he understood well enough that its condition precluded any aggressive foreign policy. The first needs were to increase revenue and the efficiency of the armed forces. In pursuit of these objectives, Ahmed frequently changed his viziers until he found in Ali Pasha of Chorlu a man fitted for the task. Chorlulu Ali Pasha, grand vizier 1706–10, was a strong and intelligent statesman who had already done much to restore public order in Syria. His hand was soon felt by the provincial rulers. He removed restless elements from the Corps of Janissaries. He strengthened vital coast defences, notably on the Straits of Kerch, while the continued expansion of the fleet was such as to alarm other Mediterranean states. Desiring only peace, however, he made no attempt to exploit the Spanish Succession or Great Northern Wars, resisting persistent pressure from the French ambassador, Ferriol, to bring about a breach in Ottoman relations with the emperor and (from 1707) with the tsar. It is hardly too much to say that Chorlulu Ali's obstinate neutrality saved Russia from disaster in 1708–9.[1] When the turbulent Devlet-Girei II, thrice khan of the Crimea[2] and a fanatical Russophobe bitterly resentful of the drying-up of income from the tsar, wished to join the Swedes and Mazepa's Cossacks in July 1709, he received an order from the Sublime Porte to remain quiet—a good instance of the firm hand which the Turks still kept on their vassal. This restraint helped to make possible Peter's crushing victory at Poltava, whence Charles XII and Mazepa escaped to Ochakov, before being transferred soon afterwards to Bender, a Bessarabian fortress on the Dniester.

Poltava fundamentally altered the political balance of eastern Europe. Russia was now, incontestably, the strongest power there, as was quickly felt in Constantinople, where the new Russian legation under Tolstoy intrigued and bribed more extensively than ever, while preparations for

---

[1] For the Swedish invasion of Russia, see below, pp. 664 ff.

[2] In 1699–1702, 1707–13 and 1716. He was the most remarkable of the five sons of Selim-Girei between whom the khanate revolved from 1705 to 1736. In 1707 he replaced his brother Gazi-Girei, who had failed to repel an irruption by the Noghai Tatars from beyond the Kuban river. For a list of the Khans see Sumner, p. 13 n.

war were always to be feared at Azov and Taganrog. Alarming above all was the state of Poland, which swarmed with Russian troops. These had not hesitated to violate Turkish soil in pursuit of the fugitive Swedish king, whose presence now became a matter of critical importance in Russo-Turkish relations. The sultan accorded Charles an expensive hospitality and rejected the tsar's demand for his extradition. Turkish tradition demanded that asylum be granted to any who sought it, but here was an opportunity for bringing pressure on Peter to revise the treaty of 1700. This, since he was occupied with the Baltic war, Peter agreed to adjust in favour of the Turks by demolishing the small forts on the Lower Dnieper. In return the Porte undertook to send Charles XII away as soon as possible, through Poland or Russia, but with a Turkish escort of only 500 men so as not to alarm the powers. Here Chorlulu Ali was mistaken in his calculations. The 'Iron Head' refused to leave. Instead, he intrigued against the grand vizier, rightly seen as chief obstacle to his plan of using the Ottoman forces against Peter.

In this far-reaching plan the Swedish king came near to success. He was eagerly abetted by Devlet-Girei Khan, another redoubtable intriguer who attended sittings of the Divan, and by General Stanislas Poniatowski—an adherent of Stanislas Leszczyński, the exiled Polish king. Poniatowski had accompanied Charles to Bender and was able to influence the sultan through the latter's mother and doctor, Fonseca. This group of 'northerners' was ably supported by Mazepa's successor, Philip Orlik, whose objective was nothing less than the reconstitution of an independent Ukraine—a policy which his Polish collaborators, however, could like no better than his Russian enemies. These troublemakers contrived to harden anti-Russian feeling among the Turks. Their task was eased by the extreme nervousness aroused in governing circles by signs of war preparations at Azov and Taganrog and along the lower Dnieper, where the erection of new forts revived fears for the Crimea. It is true that Peter had no wish to try conclusions with the Ottomans at this juncture, when his troops were still engaged with the Swedes in Pomerania; but it was not difficult to represent his ultimate ambitions as immediately dangerous to Turkey, especially as the janissaries were not alone in Constantinople in thirsting to wipe out the dishonour of Azov. Though the mood of the capital generally did not favour another Russian campaign, the leaders of the ulema were sensitive to the propaganda of Devlet-Girei and it is symptomatic of their growing political influence that, against so much caution and faint-heartedness, they were to get their way. The position of the pacific grand vizier was rapidly undermined. His neutral foreign policy was now read as pro-Russian, and he was accused of showing a too independent attitude towards his sovereign: he had, notably, made a startling attempt to rid the harem of the negro eunuchs, whose chief was the channel of communication between grand vizier and sultan. In July

1710 Chorlulu Ali fell to a palace intrigue, his property being confiscated though his life was spared.

His successor was the cultivated Köprülü Numan Pasha, son of the hero of Zalánkemén. Like his predecessors of this family, he was a man of high principles and he tried to dispense impartial justice, especially in financial matters. But he lacked the ruthlessness of the first Köprülü and his honest methods incurred the sultan's disapproval. He held office for only 63 days. As his family still enjoyed considerable popularity, he was politely relegated to the governorship of Negroponte. By contrast, Baltaji Mehmed Pasha, 'the Woodcleaver', who attained the signet on 26 September 1710, had been brought up in the more athletic educational stream of the Seraglio known as the 'Foreign Boys'.[1] This is as much as to say that he understood obedience better than command, and yet he had recently been governor of Aleppo.

Although it had an unusually prolonged Egyptian rebellion on its hands,[2] the Porte finally made up its mind to declare war on 20 November and orders went out to the provincial pashas to join the main army in the spring of 1711. On receiving this news, Peter twice attempted to persuade the Porte to cancel its decision; as soon as it was clear that it was in earnest, he ordered an immediate march. Moreover, following the example of Leopold I,[3] he was willing to give this war a religious character. In imitation of Constantine the Great at the battle of Milvian Bridge in A.D. 311, he had the Cross inscribed on his Guards' standards with the words, 'Under this sign we conquer'. He proclaimed that his aim was to liberate the Balkan Christians from 'the yoke of the infidels'. For the first time Russia openly appealed to them to rise against their Muslim masters.

This historic pronouncement, an omen for the future, seems to have been composed by Sava Vladislavich *alias* Raguzinsky, a Serb from Ragusa who had been a Russian agent among the Serbs and Montenegrins. These tough peasants were virtually new material for tsarist policy. It is possible that Peter's chagrin over the Austrian desertion at Carlowitz was in part occasioned by the frustration of his ideas about the Balkans, and that his new-found distrust of the Habsburg made him listen more readily to Orthodox grievances against the Catholics. As early as 1687 the metropolitan of Skopje had visited Moscow to denounce the treatment of Orthodox bishops in Hungary; in 1698 the Serbian patriarch there made a similar appeal during Peter's stay at Vienna; and in 1702 Dositheus, patriarch of Jerusalem, wrote to him comparing Leopold I with Diocletian. Between 1704 and 1710 at least four Serb fighting leaders went to Moscow to offer their services 'on behalf of their Orthodox tsar', and to beg funds.[4] In the Black Mountain of Montenegro and in southern

---

[1] For the distinction between these and the 'Inside Boys', see Gibb and Bowen, vol. I, pt. i, pp. 56–7, and Tournefort, vol. II, pp. 8–14.   [2] Holt, pp. 88–90.
[3] Above, pp. 579–80.   [4] Sumner, p. 45 and Marczali, pp. 202–3.

Herzegovina, where banditry was always difficult to suppress, a sporadic guerrilla war had already begun with a massacre of Muslims at Christmas 1702. Its leader was the prince-bishop, Daniel Petrovich. In 1711 he was joined by a *haiduk* (bandit) chieftain from Herzegovina, Michael Milo-radovich. Poorly armed as they were, they were to inflict a defeat on the Turks as far to the east as Nish, but they were isolated from the Russian forces, with whose fate their own was bound up.

In many respects Peter himself was out of sympathy with the doctrines and practices of Orthodox religion, but Moscow had of course ancient and intimate ties with the Greek ecclesiastics. The seventeenth century had seen a thickening traffic in relics, pilgrims and erudition: the Greek patriarchs collaborated with Moscow in the revision of sacred rites and were to some extent dependent on Russian financial support.[1] If their strictly theological influence on Muscovy had declined in face of the 'Latin' culture transmitted by the Academy of Kiev, now the most vital centre of Russian Orthodoxy, the final condemnation in 1691 of the 'Calvinistic' doctrine of Cyril Lukaris once again brought the two hierar-chies together. Moreover, the Austrian and Venetian conquests had sharpened the antagonism between Orthodox and Catholic, as did the diplomacy of Louis XIV in protecting the stealthy formation of new Uniat communities by Jesuit and Franciscan missionaries in many parts of the Ottoman empire. A specially bitter blow fell in 1690, when French influence purchased the keys of the Holy Sepulchre for the Latins, thus compromising the normal preference of the Muslim authorities for the Orthodox. The return of the keys was placed formally on the Russian agenda in 1692, and the outraged feelings of the patriarch of Jerusalem were invaluable to Peter's information service. With good reason, however, the Russians were too wary to place much reliance on the Greek clergy. Rather different was the attitude of some of the great Rumanian land-owners, faction-ridden though they were. For half a century contacts between Muscovy and the Principalities had been developing. After Poltava the prince of Moldavia, Demetrius Cantemir (1673–1723), agreed in the event of a Russo-Turkish war to join the Russians, in return for acknowledgement as hereditary prince of Moldavia under Russian pro-tection; he promised to have food and forage ready for the invading troops. These undertakings were sanctioned by treaties in April 1711, which ensured Cantemir's safety in Russia in case of failure. Constantine Brancovan, prince of Wallachia and an enemy of the Cantemirs, had also been moving closer to Russia for some years but prudently decided to await the verdict of battle before deserting the sultan.[2]

The Russian army, a disciplined force of 40,000 infantry and 14,000 cavalry, set off through Polish territory towards Moldavia, with the

---

[1] Cf. vol. v, pp. 586–9.
[2] For earlier Wallachian intrigues with Vienna, see above, pp. 578 and 580.

confidence born of Poltava. It was accompanied by the tsar and his wife Catherine, by many of the generals' wives, and the busy Raguzinsky; the tsar's presence served only to impede the commander-in-chief, the aged Sheremeteyev. The cavalry was led by General Rönne, the infantry divisions by Ensberg, Janusch, Hallart, Bruce and Repnin—the only Russian among them. Before reaching the Dniester they began to suffer shortage of food and water as well as the surprise attacks of the Tatars, but they entered Moldavia—for the first time since the tenth century— without resistance and were in Jassy by June. Cantemir at once declared himself under Russian protection and called on his people to assist the tsar. Contrary to expectation, however, the Russians were not furnished with ample victuals and forage, for the crops had failed as a result of drought and locusts. This was the first serious setback. The second was the unexpected appearance of the whole Turkish army.

Peter had given orders to reach the Danube before the Turks crossed it. According to his intelligence, the Turks were afraid of him and reluctant to cross the river: their main force was thought to be some 60 miles away. Nobody in the Russian quarter was aware that Baltaji Mehmed Pasha was already close to the Russian army, which had had to be divided into three forces to ease provisioning. The Turks—reinforced by a large body of Tatars, with the Cossacks and Poles from Bender—advanced north along the right bank of the Pruth tributary, crossed it, and on 20 July moved against the Russians. The latter were already pulling back, but the Tatars blocked the road leading south from Jassy behind them. The Russians halted not far from Stanilesti, in a narrow plain with the river in their rear and an extensive marsh on one side. They were surrounded. Since the Turkish position was on hills that dominated theirs, so that the Turkish artillery could easily sweep them—and the river behind them—the tsar was completely at the mercy of his enemy. On 21 July 1711, Baltaji Mehmed was signing orders for a grand assault when the Russians hoisted white flags. Hungry, sick and tired, they could hardly resist an army at least twice as large; they must sue for peace or be annihilated. Peter, in his depression, scarcely knew what to do. At this critical moment Catherine was able to calm him and persuade him to ask for peace, which was supported by the Vice-chancellor Shafirov. It looked as if the calculations of Charles XII were to prove correct, for now the tsar expected to have to surrender most of his conquests from Sweden, though of course he offered much less. Lacking both confidence and foresight, however, Baltaji Mehmed was too easily content with the Russian proposals. He hurriedly granted terms: that Azov be retroceded, Taganrog, Kemenny Zaton and the new Dnieper fortresses entirely demolished; that the tsar no longer interfere in Polish affairs and no Russian reside in the quality of ambassador at the High Porte; that all Turkish prisoners be freed and the king of Sweden allowed safe passage. Baltaji Mehmed gave the Russians food and an unofficial promise to expel Charles XII. As hostages, the tsar sent Sheremeteyev's own grandson and Peter Shafirov, to whom he owed much.

The *dénouement* at the Pruth 'may deservedly be looked on as one of the most surprizing and extraordinary events that ever happened', wrote Sutton, British ambassador at the Porte (1701–16).[1] He regarded the victory as undeserved. Yet the fate of Peter and of his new Russia had depended within a hair's breadth upon the decision of the grand vizier, more ruthless action on whose part might have changed the course of East European history. Baltaji Mehmed seems to have been carried away by his own unexpected success, but it is only fair to add that the janissaries had little stomach for fighting in this country and that the impoverished sipahis were reluctant to face the cost of prolonged fighting at all. Moreover, the grand vizier's deep distrust of the whole Bender circle may have induced him to come to terms before Charles XII could appear on the scene.[2] The peace was certainly well received in Constantinople, except by the wavering sultan, who soon had Baltaji in prison. The victory was felt to have wiped out the disgraces of the previous war: in fact, the mercurial Turks were now able to convince themselves that the Russian menace could be held off quite easily. There was some justification for this illusion in the poor showing made by Peter's navy, said to have been carrying 35,000 soldiers and marines, when a powerful Turkish fleet appeared off Azov; a few months later, whatever remained of value in Peter's southern navy, including the stores at Taganrog, was sold to the Turks. Above all, it had been amply demonstrated that Russian and Balkan Christians were still incapable of effective combination. Though the Montenegrins held out till 1714, the tsar could do little for them, while the Principalities had done little enough to help the tsar.

From 1716 the government of the Principalities was regularly entrusted to the Mavrocordatos and a few other Greek families of the well-to-do Phanar quarter of Constantinople, where the Oecumenical Patriarch resided. Having paid highly for posts from which they always risked dismissal, the Phanariot governors and their numerous clients fleeced the Rumanians ruthlessly. Here indeed is a striking example of that working alliance between Greek and Ottoman which in some sense was to make European Turkey 'a Greco-Turkish régime'[3] and had already made the patriarchate itself a fiscal and police agent of the Porte. To the 'third Rome' of the tsars many educated Greeks preferred the hope of a new Byzantium, to be realized by improving their position in the Ottoman administration as a whole, where the posts of First Dragoman and Dragoman of the Fleet had become perquisites of the Phanariot commu-

---

[1] *Despatches*, p. 60: like Colijer, he was strongly pro-Russian.
[2] Thus Sumner, pp. 40–1, who doubts the charges of excessive bribery later levied against the grand vizier. Turkish opinion, not unnaturally, explained too much in such terms.
[3] D. Dakin, *British and American Philhellenes, 1821–1833* (Salonica, 1955), p. 10.

nity. The patronage thus acquired itself fertilized wealth and political influence. Moreover, the Porte, like the embassies accredited to it, had increasing technical need of the relatively westernized Greek aristocracy, now that it was coming to depend more on diplomacy to preserve its empire—against powers so often at odds with one another. Although nearly a century was to pass before regular Ottoman embassies were established in the West, it has been said that the plenipotentiaries at Carlowitz introduced something of the western diplomatic spirit into the Porte, largely animated in those years by the adroit Alexander Mavrocordato.[1]

By the Pruth treaty Russia had given up all that had been gained in 1700, but months of wrangling passed before practical effect was given to its rather general terms. Both sides desired to improve them, while doubting the other's sincerity. The tsar's initial dilatoriness, in fact, resulted in a new rupture on 2 October 1711 and the displacement of Baltaji Mehmed by the more bellicose Yüsuf Pasha. With the indispensable support of the Dutch and British representatives, Shafirov and Tolstoy worked hard for agreement against Swedish efforts, backed by the French and Venetians, to prevent it. Something was done to clarify the divided loyalties of the Cossacks and to establish responsibility for, if not to abolish, raiding and reprisals between Cossack and Tatar in the frontier zone of the Black Sea steppe and southern Ukraine. Here Peter formally withdrew to the line of the Dniester. But he was slower to recall his troops from Poland, where the continued presence of Russian garrisons caused the sultan, with French encouragement, to threaten further hostilities after a definitive agreement seemed to have been reached in April 1712. This question was linked with that of Charles XII's return across Polish or Russian territory, both sides fearing further complications were he given a Turkish escort strong enough to guarantee his safety. Reports from frontier commissions convinced the Ottomans of Peter's insincerity, and on 3 November the horse-tail was again hung in front of the Seraglio as a sign of war. Then, in March 1713, when the sultan had freed himself of any sense of obligation to his embarrassing guest, Charles was forcibly brought to Adrianople and Devlet-Girei was banished to Chios. Despite a further Turkish proclamation of war on 30 April (the fourth from 1710), encouraged by the Swedish success at Gadebusch in the previous December, these measures in fact removed the main obstacles to Russo-Turkish reconciliation. A 25-year peace was concluded with Peter at Adrianople on 5 June. Peter's southern frontier was now withdrawn—vaguely enough,

---

[1] See Von Hammer, vol. XIII, pp. 8–9. Son of a Chiote silk merchant, Mavrocordato (1636–1709) had been educated in medicine at Padua and professed it at the patriarchal college in Constantinople. His rise, which may have owed something to the protection of the Mufti Feyzullah, illustrates the special opportunities at court open to both physicians and those with a mastery of Christian languages. Wealthy Phanariots were frequently educated in Padua.

it is true—as far north as the river Orel, and he was to evacuate Poland within two months. Further, in April 1714 the sultan acknowledged Augustus II as ruler of the Polish Ukraine. In September Charles XII, Stanislas Poníatowski and Philip Orlik left Turkish soil to continue their struggles elsewhere.

A key to this decisive turn in Ottoman foreign relations is to be found in the preparations already going forward for a renewed trial of strength with Venice. With the Morea under the Venetians and a Venetian fleet in the Archipelago, no Turk could sleep quietly in Constantinople. The hardest sacrifice at Carlowitz had been the Morea; even during the vizierate of the peace-loving Chorlulu Ali there was talk of revenge. The Swedish king's refuge in Turkey, combined with Russian threats, had instead produced the war of 1711. The Morea appealed more than did war beyond the lower Danube to most Turkish politicians and to the janissaries, who disliked wintering in desolate country far from home but whose restlessness, according to some foreign observers,[1] was such as to tempt the authorities to find occupation for them. After the Russian danger had receded and the question of Poland been somewhat settled, the Porte decided on the recovery of the Morea. The war party was led by Silahdar Ali Pasha, the sultan's son-in-law and favourite, who had personal connections with the Morea and had been an active politician for some time already. It was he who had engineered the overthrow of Chorlulu Ali and Baltaji Mehmed, with the aid of two personages always dangerous to grand viziers, the Mufti and the *Kizlar Agasi*. In April 1713 he became grand vizier himself.

His policy accorded well with the interests of the Phanar, for the Venetian senate had deprived the patriarchate of its revenues from the Morea and switched to Venice what remained of Moreote export trade. The Venetian administration, despite good features,[2] had struck no deep root in the Morea itself, which it could only govern by creating a party on the brittle foundation of privileges and places. Injustices were done in its name by the native Greek primates, merchants and magistrates as well as by Venetian nobles—enough to curtail the benefits of the Venetian commune as the unit for a restored public order, of land resettlement, and of the conversion of State leases into freeholds. Nor did an improved educational provision compensate for an influx of Italian priests. The general-proveditor (governor) described the Moreotes in 1708 as unwearied in chicanery, inexorable in revenge.[3] When the Ottomans returned, there-

---

[1] *The Present State of Europe*, vol. xxv (1714), p. 483: advices from Turkey, 8 December.
[2] Notably in the restoration of agriculture, which seems to have been reflected in a three-fold population increase to 250,000 (H. Antoniadis-Bibicou, *loc. cit.* p. 391).
[3] G. Finlay, *A History of Greece* (1877 edn., 7 vols.), vol. v, p. 208. Cf. Tournefort's impression of the Greeks of the Archipelago (vol. i, p. 97): 'a Family-Quarrel cannot always be made up among them with Mony'.

fore, they were greeted as liberators, especially as they paid for food and forage. With a civilian population thus disaffected, a military establishment of some 8,000 was confronted by a Turkish army of over 70,000, supported by a much superior strength at sea. With reinforcements from Barbary and Egypt, the Kaptan Pasha, Jannum Hoja (Koggia), commanded 58 sail against 19 Venetian assisted by 4 Maltese.

A pretext for war, formally declared on 11 January 1715, was found in the assistance allegedly rendered by Venetian agents to the Montenegrin rebels, and in the refusal of the Bank of Venice to surrender the fortune deposited with it by Constantine Brancovan, the prince of Wallachia who had been executed in 1714. In June the Turkish fleet easily captured the islands of Aegina and Tine (Tinos, which the Venetians had held against attack for five centuries), while the grand vizier was still encamped on the plain of Thebes. Silahdar Ali's ability to enforce discipline on the march conciliated the Greek peasants, and his movements were not obstructed by shortage of provisions. Soon, on 7 July, he mastered the fortress of Corinth, after which the Ottomans proceeded to capture the other Moreote strongpoints—Argos, Nauplia, Koron, Navarino, and Methoni (Modon). This last might have been saved had the Venetian fleet given battle to the Kaptan Pasha, whose command of the coastal waters goes far to explain the weak resistance of the Venetian garrisons. There was no clash between armies. The campaign consisted entirely of sieges. It was completed in exactly a hundred days. In July 1716 the Turkish land and sea forces proceeded to attack Corfu itself, so often the rendezvous of Venetian fleets and now ably defended by Marshal Schulenberg, a Saxon who had fought with Eugene at Malplaquet. It looked as if Venice was facing collapse when Austria came to her rescue.

At the outset the emperor had tried mediation, although Louis XIV urged Vienna to war—an inversion of his earlier habit of encouraging the Porte against Vienna. Even in 1715 Charles VI was too much occupied with the legacies of the Spanish Succession War readily to resume Balkan campaigning, with Venice as his only ally; his Spanish entourage particularly favoured peace with the Ottoman, in opposition to Eugene, who threw his influence against any risk of some western enterprise diverting the concentration of Imperial strength against the Turk.[1] It was the threat to Dalmatia (and conceivably to Croatia and Styria) which led to the signature of a defensive alliance with Venice on 13 April 1716. The emperor demanded an indemnification for all the republic's losses. The interpretation of his ultimatum created difficulties at Constantinople: some of the Divan believed that it meant what it said, nothing less than restitution of the Morea, which had had nearly two and a half centuries of Turkish rule; others, that the emperor would be satisfied with the old Venetian possessions, Tine and Cerigo (Kythera). Contrary to reports

[1] Braubach, *Prinz Eugen*, vol. III (1964), pp. 309–10.

reaching Vienna,[1] it is certain that many of the viziers (ministers) were opposed to another war with the emperor. To avoid it had been a constant concern in their dealings with Charles XII; for this they had even refused asylum to Rákóczi's defeated followers; operations against Venice had been undertaken in reliance on Habsburg neutrality. Silahdar Ali, however, after his easy victory over the Venetians, flung caution to the winds. Regarding the Imperial intervention as a breach of the Peace of Carlowitz—though it was, rather, a reaction to the Ottoman disturbance of the balance of power erected by it—he persuaded the Divan to cut matters short by declaring war on Vienna. At the same time the Porte planned trouble by installing Francis II Rákóczi as king of Hungary: a messenger was sent to invite him from Paris to organize the struggle, and he came.

In the summer of 1716 a Turkish army of (at most) 120,000 began operations from Belgrade. Following Silahdar Ali's wishes, the council-of-war decided to attack the fortress of Peterwardein. Here, on 5 August, a major battle was fought. Eugene had 70,000 men, including 187 squadrons of cavalry. When Eugene ordered a cavalry charge, Silahdar Ali ignored advice to intervene at the point of danger; and when, finally, at the head of his officers he galloped into the thick of the battle, it was too late. He was struck by a bullet and died on the way to Belgrade. Others killed on this field included the governors of Anatolia and Adana, Türk Ahmed Pasha and Hüseyn Pasha. The loss of these leaders produced a rout. The whole Turkish camp, as at Vienna in 1683, fell into enemy hands—the grand vizier's magnificent ceremonial tent, 114 guns, 150 standards and 5 horsetails.[2] The Turkish casualties have been much exaggerated but were probably double those of the Imperialists, which are estimated at nearly 5,000 dead and wounded.[3] Impressed by the stout resistance of the janissaries, Eugene did not pursue the defeated army to Belgrade. Instead, he ordered a difficult march to Temesvár, the 'Gazi' (victorious) fortress which controlled the Banat and had resisted assault for 164 years. Its garrison of 10,000–15,000 held out fiercely, but troops sent to relieve it were beaten back and it capitulated on 12 October, with the honours of war. From fear of disturbances, its fall was not at once made public in Constantinople. Eugene placed the Banat under the command of his close friend Count Mercy, who sent a small force to raid Bucharest, capital of Wallachia since 1698. The siege of Corfu had already been called off after Peterwardein, when the Turkish forces were also withdrawn from Butrinto on the mainland and Santa Maura further south.

[1] The decisive impulse to the deliberations of the Wiener Hof was imparted by Fleischmann, the Austrian Resident at the Porte, who was convinced that the Turks intended a war of revenge against the emperor: *ibid.* p. 308.
[2] A badge of high rank suspended from a pole at the top of which was a golden ball; an ordinary bey had the right to one horse-tail, a *vali* or *beylerbey* to two, an ordinary vizier to three, the grand vizier to five.
[3] Braubach, vol. III, p. 320.

The death of Silahdar Ali had further consequences. For all his excessive self-confidence, he had been well fitted to restore the tarnished prestige of the empire and impose needful reforms. His successor, Halil Pasha, was ordered in July 1717 to the relief of Belgrade, to which key position Eugene and Mercy were already laying siege with a strength estimated at 80,000. The garrison of 30,000 under Mustafa Pasha prepared to resist while the Austrians dug trenches between the Danube and Sava, bridging both rivers. Halil Pasha, indecisive and incompetent, failed to use his initial advantage. Eugene was dangerously caught between a strong garrison in front and a field army twice the size of his own behind him. Instead of moving at once, Halil Pasha ordered his troops to entrench and open fire from high ground. Exploiting this indecision and a chance fog, Eugene surprised the Turkish lines in the early hours of 16 August. There ensued a good deal of confused fighting, during which a gap occurred in the Austrian centre; only when the fog cleared about 8 o'clock were the Austrians able to storm the Turkish artillery positions. At this point the grand vizier, who had had no clear idea of what was going on, ordered a retreat. The Turkish losses were more severe than at Peterwardein—perhaps 10,000 killed and as many wounded. The Imperialists suffered about 5,000 casualties. Besides 150 guns and 60 standards, a large supply of ammunition and food fell into their hands. On 18 August the battered citadel itself surrendered, and four days later the surviving two-thirds of the garrison marched out to freedom. After the fall of Belgrade the Turks evacuated their remaining outposts on the Sava river-line, but the garrisons of Zvornik (on the Drina) and of Bihach and Novi (on the Una) held out against strong attacks, with the result that Bosnia was not overrun as it had been in the aftermath of Zenta. And signs had already appeared of the malaria which was to cost the Imperialists thousands of their best troops in the next two years.

Meanwhile, the Venetians had reoccupied some of their lost Adriatic positions and resumed the offensive at sea, with the support of six well-armed Portuguese vessels in addition to Maltese and papal auxiliaries. An engagement off Cape Matapan in July 1717 was less disastrous to them than a three-day running battle near Cerigo a year later, when a superior Turkish fleet inflicted nearly 2,000 casualties on a Christian fighting-line of 26 sail, whose order was imperfectly preserved with the aid of galleys. Vienna was disappointed with the performance of its ally and no longer disposed to insist on the restitution of the Morea, which Venice lacked the strength to retain.[1]

As has been seen, many of the Divan had opposed the rupture with the emperor in the first place. At that time also British and Dutch diplomacy, at Vienna as well as Constantinople, had been strongly exerted to prevent it. Late in 1717 a new (and pro-Turkish) British ambassador to the Porte,

---

[1] Braubach, vol. III, pp. 335, 370, 372.

Edward Wortley Montagu, together with Colijer, again tried mediation. Vienna thought it could obtain better terms by direct negotiations. These were delayed because the Porte wanted first the restoration of Temesvár and then of Belgrade, the conquest of both of which was the essential Austrian war aim; also, a foreign statesman, this time Alberoni, intrigued to keep the Turks and the Hungarian malcontents engaged in what was for him a vital diversion.[1] Spain, which had landed troops in Sardinia, now seriously threatened the Habsburg position in Italy. For this very reason the emperor, while preparing another campaign in the Balkans, was anxious to settle his account with the Turks and willing to accept the mediation of the British, themselves also alarmed for the stability of the Utrecht settlement. Early in June, at Passarowitz, a small town near Semendria (Smederevo), the arduous task of mediation was again undertaken by Sutton, with Abraham Stanyan and Colijer in the offing.[2] Once more the principle of *uti possidetis* was adopted as the basis, though the Austrians repeatedly tried to go beyond it—successfully in the case of the Venetians, with whom the Turks were unwilling to treat at all. The treaty of 21 July provided for the cession of the districts of Temesvár, Semendria and Belgrade and for a new frontier along the Sava and Drina rivers, whence it ran eastwards just above Nish and then north to Orsova. To the loss in 1699 of Hungary, therefore, the Banat, Little Wallachia (as far as the Aluta), and the most fertile portion of Serbia were now added. Francis II Rákóczi and other Hungarians whom the Porte had supported were not to reside in the vicinity of the new frontier. The Austrian government more or less successfully handled the rehabilitation of the Banat, into which many German settlers, especially veteran soldiers, were introduced on Eugene's initiative; but it did little in Serbia beyond strengthening the fortress of Belgrade, which it was to lose in 1739. A commercial treaty was also signed with the emperor, who in 1719 chartered an Eastern Company at his new 'free port' of Trieste with an ambitious programme for developing his Balkan trade,[3] in some degree at the

---

[1] Cf. vol. VII, p. 197.

[2] D. B. Horn (ed.), *British Diplomatic Representatives, 1689-1789* (Camden Soc. 3rd ser. vol. XLVI, 1932), p. 152. Wortley's recall had been decided upon in London in September 1717, after Stanyan (then at Vienna) had informed Sunderland that the emperor, who in any case preferred to treat without mediators, would have nothing to do with him. Sutton, who had sailed from Constantinople in March, then hastened to Vienna. He told Addison that the Hanoverian minister, St Saphorin, had encouraged Stanyan to intrigue for the Turkish embassy. Stanyan was appointed to it in October without the usual prior consultation with the Levant Company, who still paid the ambassador's salary. See R. Halsband, *The Life of Lady Mary Wortley Montagu* (Oxford, 1956), pp. 77-9; W. Michael, *England under George I*, vol. I (1936), pp. 362-8; and Braubach, vol. III, p. 371.

[3] Some of Charles's advisers had argued for the acquisition of the Principalities and a Black Sea coast, in preference to Serbia: J. W. Stoye, 'Emperor Charles VI: the early years of the reign', *Trans. R. Hist. Soc.* 5th ser. vol. XII (1962), pp. 80-4; cf. above, p. 604. The commercial treaty gave the Austrians freedom of trade throughout the Ottoman empire, besides substantial tariff and consular concessions.

expense of Venice, another loser at Passarowitz. With her finances in ruin, Venice acquiesced in the surrender of the Morea (with Tine and Aegina), although she kept her conquests in Dalmatia, Santa Maura and the Gulf of Arta, and regained Cerigo. This island, with its redoubtable privateering record, remained her forward base, between the Ionian and Aegean seas; but Venice was never again at war with Turkey.

The Peace of Passarowitz proclaimed in effect that the Turks were no longer a military danger to their neighbours. The defeats at Peterwardein and Belgrade had shown how a much smaller but well-controlled army, at least under a commander of Eugene's cool presence of mind, could defeat Turkish forces far inferior in leadership and equipment. But there was more to it than this. The Turks had demonstrated, again and again, their powers of endurance and eagerness to give battle, and also what massive quantities of war material they could raise. They failed on the whole to make the best of these advantages because they were utterly outclassed in the efficient concentration of resources, in reconnaissance, in the adroit handling of cavalry and field-guns, and in the organization of a high command. Tactically, they relied too much on the terror of a mass assault and on hand-to-hand encounters, just as at sea they preferred ramming and boarding to an artillery engagement. Their high reputation as gunners was based on the big brass of sieges. They had not really caught up with the tactical revolution wrought by the mobile field-gun, let alone by the flintlock musket.[1] Their march as well as battle discipline was inferior to the German. No doubt the sheer size of their field armies added to the logistical problems of Balkan campaigning; although they had long experience of this and an elaborate supply organization, they moved with too many impedimenta and camp-followers. Of course there was a practical purpose for the treasure that was found after capture in the grand viziers' tents, but it required many hands to pitch and decorate these multi-chambered silken apartments, together with those of other pashas. Not the least striking fact about the débâcle at Zenta had been that the booty included 9,000 wagons and 60,000 camels.

The Turks now lost all hope of Hungary; they might be fortunate if they held on to their remaining possessions in Rumelia. No Turk, it is true, could reconcile himself to the loss of Belgrade, but the days of great expeditions seemed gone for ever. All classes longed for a durable peace. The newly-installed grand vizier, Ibrahim Pasha, from Nevshehir in Anatolia, to whose influence acceptance of the hard terms of the treaty was mainly due, was to respond fully to that longing and to the preference for rural retirement which the sultans had shown since the days of Hunter Mehmed. Brought up in the Seraglio, Ibrahim had been placed in Ahmed's service while the prince lived in seclusion—the Ottoman method of keep-

_____
[1] See below, pp. 746 ff.

ing heirs to the throne out of harm's way—and they were partners at chess. Upon his accession, Ahmed nominated Ibrahim Efendi as his secretary, and he was offered the post of grand vizier after Silahdar Ali's death; he refused it then, but was persuaded to become deputy (*Kahya*) when Halil Pasha proved unfit. An extremely supple courtier, he managed to keep himself afloat in the seas of palace intrigue and to preserve the sultan's confidence. His exceptionally long vizierate (1718–30) is remembered as *Lale Devri*, the 'Age of Tulips', for 'tulipomania' now became the characteristic passion of the court and of wealthy circles in Constantinople; no less than 1,200 varieties,[1] some very costly and objects of keen competition, imported as a rule from Holland or Persia, are said to have been cultivated; sale of a rare bulb outside the capital was even punishable with exile. Under the April moon, the sultan and all the higher dignitaries of the empire, attended by dancers and musicians, would abandon themselves to exquisite and extravagant festivals in the tulip-gardens, hung with lanterns and singing-birds, and with vases of Venetian glass for the finest tulips. In winter, there were helva parties, at which Chinese shadow-plays might be performed and philosophical discussion alternate with the distribution of sweets, jewels, and robes of honour. In summer, elaborate sea-fights and fireworks were staged. The most famous poet of the time, Nedim, glorified the beauties of the 'Palace of Felicity' (*Saadabad*)—the name given to Kagithane[2] on the northern side of the Golden Horn where pleasure-pavilions (kiosks) of the utmost luxury were built, often hinting at Chinese or French designs. For a brief spell faithful Osmanlis were shocked by the advent of the rococo, but it seemed as if their rulers were determined to forget their military humiliation in these fabulous gaieties and to demonstrate how profoundly they had now been converted into devotees of peace.

Besides these organized pleasures, Ibrahim Pasha promoted cultural activities of enduring value. Musicians, singers and poets found ample scope in the new atmosphere, as did the decorative arts. Although the celebrated Ahmed III fountain near Hagia Sophia is a monument to the foreign influence of the time, native Ottoman culture was still far from exhaustion. A vigorous historiographical tradition did not disappear with the death of its greatest representative, Naima, in 1716; not long afterwards, a learned commission was appointed to translate important works, above all of history, from Arabic and Persian. As had happened earlier in Spain, the decline of empire fostered self-criticism, in which contemporary Ottoman historians took the lead. The spread of knowledge

---

[1] B. Miller, *Beyond the SublimePorte: the Grand Seraglio of Stambul* (Yale, 1931), p. 124. On the powers of Ahmed III's new court officer, the Master of Flowers, see *ibid.* pp. 223–4.

[2] See the map of 'Istanbul and its environs' in A. D. Alderson, *The Structure of the Ottoman Dynasty* (Oxford, 1956), p. 78. It was on the meadows here that the ceremonial processions of the gilds and corporations of Constantinople traditionally took place; the great naval arsenal of Kasim Pasha lay immediately to the east (Mantran, pp. 68, 365).

was encouraged by the opening of five public libraries. In 1721 a Turkish envoy in Paris had instructions to 'make a thorough study of the means of civilization and education, and report on those capable of application' in Turkey; his son, Said Chelebi, returned with an enthusiasm for the art of printing.[1] The most striking innovation of this period, indeed, was the foundation in 1727 of the first Muslim printing press in Turkey by Ibrahim Muteferrika (1674–1745), a Hungarian by birth and a critic of Ottoman backwardness in many fields, who selected, edited and printed some thirty books—the incunabula of Turkish printed books—with the aid of presses and typographers imported from the West.[2] His achievement was only made possible by the support of the grand vizier, against strong opposition from the army of scribes who made their living as copyists, and from the ulema, who were able to prevent the printing of religious works and in 1742 to stop the enterprise altogether.

Ahmed III, whose love of pleasure and the arts fully matched that of his predecessor, was well content with his grand vizier, who became his son-in-law and so addressed as 'Damad'. But Damad Ibrahim had a free hand only at the cost of pandering to his master's avarice and concealing the true state of the empire. In these years the Venetian Residents reported a scarcity of hard money, much unemployment and severe annual epidemics. Pest-ridden Salonica, the largest town in the Balkans, was vacated by two-thirds of its population in 1719.[3] Food prices were exceptionally high; in 1719 the harvest failed in the Black Sea area and the provisioning of Constantinople, always a major concern of the authorities, caused pressure on alternative sources. There is reason to believe that the empire had already entered a new cycle of inflation.[4] At Cairo, which had rioted over the tombs of saints in 1711,[5] there were serious disturbances in 1721.

Even the sultan was slowly awakened to reality by the sensational revolution in Persia, where an Afghan invasion led rapidly to the downfall of the Safavi dynasty. Shah Husein asked for help at the end of 1720, but only his flight in 1722 stirred the Porte to action. It might not have reacted strongly even then had not the tsar moved his troops to Astrakhan in the summer. Peter had waited for no appeal before acting. He at once occupied Darband and proceeded to bar the Turks from approaching the Caspian. In 1723, Shah Tahmasp yielded to him all the provinces bordering that sea to the west and south. But Daghestan, Shirvan, and part of

---

[1] Lewis, *Modern Turkey*, pp. 45–6.

[2] Jewish, Greek and Armenian presses had long flourished in Salonica, Constantinople and other cities (*ibid*. pp. 47, 50–1).

[3] M. L. Shay, *The Ottoman Empire from 1720 to 1734 as revealed in the Dispatches of the Venetian Baili* (Urbana, Ill., 1944), pp. 20–4; cf. Svoronos, pp. 135–6.

[4] *Ibid*. pp. 86–7; Mantran, p. 279. On the elaborate organization for feeding the capital, see *ibid*. pp. 185 ff.

[5] All foreign visitors were impressed by the manifold cults and ceremonies of Egyptian piety: for a good later description see E. W. Lane, *An Account of the Manners and Customs of the Modern Egyptians* (3rd edn. 1842).

Azerbaijan had been under Ottoman rule before 1612: the Russian advance beyond the Caucasus therefore played into the hands of Turkish irredentists, still smarting from the humiliation of Passarowitz. So in 1723, when the Russians occupied Baku, the Turks seized Tiflis. From this year onwards, for a decade, Turkish policy abroad was dominated by the revolutions in Persia and the threat of a Russian Caspian.

The Porte had never ceased to be worried by the growth of Russian power. More than once it had had to call for the withdrawal of Russian troops from Poland, the maintenance of whose integrity was to remain an axiom of its policy down to the Russo-Turkish war of 1768, itself largely the result of Russian interference in Poland. It was also known that Peter was trying to cast the Georgian and Armenian Christians for the rôle formerly played in European Turkey by the Montenegrins. In 1721 there was news of Russian fort-construction in the Terek valley, of a Russian survey party on the Caspian coast.[1] Distrust of Peter was now, moreover, fostered by the British government, which had worked for a renewal of Russo-Turkish hostilities during the Passarowitz negotiations.[2] Stanyan, with Austrian support, had been authorized to spend 10,000 piastres to accomplish this. His efforts were cleverly countered by the Russian ambassador and his French colleague. These two finally succeeded in bringing the Porte to accept, in June 1724, Peter's novel proposal for a dismemberment of the Persian provinces. While the Porte acknowledged Russian occupation of the Caucasus and the south coast of the Caspian, the Russians recognized Turkish occupation of Georgia, Shirvan, Ardabil, Tabriz, Hamadan, and Kirmanshah. This was the first and last occasion on which the Russian and Ottoman empires agreed upon the partition of a neighbouring State—a Muslim State, though the only one which professed the Shi'a devotion. The partition proved of no lasting value to either beneficiary. With the appearance of Nadir Shah all their conquests were soon to be annihilated.[3] Quite early, in the summer of 1730, he forced the Turks out of Hamadan, Kirmanshah and Tabriz.

These reverses, crowned by rumours that peace talks were in progress after troops and taxes had been raised for war,[4] at a time when pro-

---

[1] L. Lockhart, *The Fall of the Safavi Dynasty and the Afghan Invasion of Persia* (Cambridge, 1958), p. 217. For the mapping activities of Soimonov and Van Verden, cf. *ibid.* pp. 239 ff.

[2] Michael, vol. I, p. 364. Britain was chiefly anxious to divert Peter from northern Europe, but she also feared Russian domination of the Persian trade: I. Jacob, *Beziehungen Englands zu Russland und zur Türkei in den Jahren 1718–1727* (Basel, 1945), esp. ch. VII.

[3] L. Lockhart, *Nadir Shah* (1938), pp. 24–106. From this time also dates the virtual independence of the great vilayet of Baghdad. Cf. below, p. 739.

[4] Shay, p. 27. In 1722 Stanyan had reported that the common people of Turkey hated the Persians for their persecution of Sunni Muslims (Lockhart, *Safavi Dynasty*, p. 215). A contemporary pamphlet, 'composed from Original Memorials drawn up in Constantinople' and first published in French at The Hague, states that the renewal of war with Persia, 'always disagreeable and often fatal to the Turks', was a cause of rebellion, not least

visions were dear, precipitated one of the bloodiest revolutions in Turkish history. It began on 28 September 1730 with a mutiny of a handful of janissaries in the capital, while the court was across the water at Scutari. Patrona Halil, by origin an Albanian seaman and later an attendant of the Common Bath near the Bayazid square, now a janissary and clothes-seller, gave a party for his friends and told how the overthrow of the tyranny of the sultan's ministers had been revealed to him. His movement was secretly sponsored by some of the ulema, but not joined by the chief janissary officers. In face of the inaction of the authorities,[1] and thanks to the obscure mechanics of a janissary rising, sedition soon spread through the soldiery. After two days the rebels were in control of the arsenal and able to cut off supplies of food and water to the Seraglio. The sultan tried appeasement by ordering the strangulation of his lifelong friend and son-in-law, whose body, with those of the deputy grand vizier and the Kaptan Pasha, was given to the crowd. Angry that these ministers had not been sent to them alive, the rebels called on the sultan to abdicate. On the night of 1 October, Ahmed III resigned the throne to his nephew Mahmud I, a prisoner of the Seraglio since his father's own abdication in 1703. The Chief Mufti went into exile; the *Reis Efendi* concealed himself.

Unassuaged by the new sultan's promised gratifications, the rioters put to the flames the summer-kiosks on the Golden Horn and pillaged the houses of proscripts in Constantinople itself. There are signs that the leaders tried to stop indiscriminate violence.[2] Some Jewish houses and Greek churches were plundered in Galata while it was without a district governor, but the rebels claimed also to be champions of the religious minorities against oppression. Nevertheless, the mutilated body of Damad Ibrahim Pasha, after a wholly exceptional vizierate of twelve years during which he had unlimited powers and immense fortunes in his hands,[3] was a terrible reminder of the licentiousness always present in the capital, for all its elaborate policing. Its narrow streets were full of unemployed immigrants. Yet Patrona's rebellion also sprang from deep forces in Turkish nature, hatred of the infidel and a habit of satirizing men in power. It was at once an outburst of xenophobia and a protest against the luxury and avarice of the higher Ottoman dignitaries. The insurgents

because the janissaries had shut up shop and incurred expenses for a march which was halted at Scutari, the rebel leader having himself laid out his savings in purchasing arms and clothes for resale during the campaign: *A Particular Account of the Two Rebellions, which happened at Constantinople in the Years MDCCXXX and MDCCXXI...* (London, 1737), pp. 2–5.

[1] Most of the responsible pashas were out of the city when the revolt broke out, or quickly fled from it, like the Aga of the Janissaries, whose own guard refused to act against the rebels. On the return of the court to the Seraglio there were divided counsels and bitter recriminations.

[2] *Ibid.* pp. 8, 15, 30, 38–41.

[3] The rebels are said to have found the hoards of the grand vizier and his deputy, amounting in cash alone to the equivalent of £1,350,000 and £1,875,000 respectively (*ibid.* pp. 26–7).

called not only for war on Russia but for domestic reforms, such as the abolition of leases for life. It seems prophetic that they adopted red turbans. They claimed to stand for the good and honour of the State, and it is unlikely that terrorism alone brought them their large if uncertain following.

For nearly two months Patrona Halil, still wearing his torn clothes, and his mate, an eloquent young fruit-vendor and fellow-janissary named Muslubeshe, held in their hands practically the supreme power in the State, living in the houses of deposed ministers and visiting the palace when they pleased. They vetoed high appointments and proscribed many judges. They tried to increase their janissary following from 40,000 to 70,000 men, and to get their own nominees elected as officers, with a lavish use of the money they had taken. As early as 13 October, however, when the new sultan ordered the reopening of the shops, some of the janissaries were becoming detached from the movement, partly under the influence of the ulema; and on 5 November Patrona admitted that he relied in the last resort on his 12,000 Albanians, some of whom had been put in charge of the prisons. Even his own companions complained of his greed. He demanded a palace for his concubine, the great office of Kaptan Pasha for himself, the rule of Moldavia for a Greek butcher who had supplied the rebels. Perhaps this swagger was not without a macabre sense of humour, for Patrona seems to have foreseen that his luck would not last.[1] The resistance of the court was stiffened by the return of Jannum Hoja as Kaptan Pasha, and by Kaplan-Girei, the new khan of the Crimea, who astutely advised concessions likely to provoke the janissaries. The end came when Patrona and his chief associates were summoned to the palace on pretext of a meeting with the Divan, ostensibly to debate their demand for war. There they were murdered in the sultan's presence on 25 November. It is reported that 7,000 of their accomplices were killed within three days, and that for weeks 'the Bosphorus was continually covered with Cadavars, agitated at the Pleasure of Winds and Waves'.[2]

For more than a year this counter-terror went on, costing many innocent lives and helping to precipitate in March 1731 a small janissary revolt, which the widow of Damad Ibrahim Pasha was suspected of having encouraged. Another plot was uncovered six months later. Cards were found in mosques denouncing the sultan's dependence on favourites. Repeatedly the public baths, taverns and coffee-shops were closed by the police.[3] Within a few years Constantinople is said to have been depleted, by death and banishment, of 50,000 people. The Bath near the Bayazid Square is still connected with the name of Patrona Halil and the restless days of his rule.

---

[1] *Ibid.* p. 53.
[2] *Ibid.* p. 79. The Venetian *bailo* stated that 10,000 janissaries lost their lives in 1730 (Shay, p. 32).   [3] Shay, pp. 36–7.

CHARLES XII AND THE GREAT NORTHERN WAR

IN the Great Northern War, Sweden and her young absolute king, Charles XII, had to meet a challenge which Swedish statesmen had long envisaged as a possibility but which hitherto, by good luck and good management, had been avoided: a simultaneous attack by a coalition of powers on the Swedish empire east and west. There had never been any false optimism in Stockholm as to the deep-rooted resentment aroused among her neighbours by Sweden's seemingly irresistible expansion since her secession from the Scandinavian Union of the later Middle Ages. The path of that expansion had been defined by strategic and economic necessities as well as by dynastic and religious considerations, but the whole dynamic process of empire-building had been conditioned nearly as much by the general Baltic and European situation, with its political tensions and local power-vacuums, as by Swedish initiatives. To throw off Denmark's stranglehold over Sweden's approaches to the west and to push Denmark out of the Scandinavian peninsula had been constant pre-occupations ever since the War of Liberation, in the same way as border unrest, engendering trouble with the Muscovites in the duchy of Finland, had led to the search for a defensible frontier in the north-east. Yet it had been an appeal for help from the dying Order of the Sword—whose territory was coveted by Denmark, Russia and Poland—that had first precipitated Sweden into ventures south of the Gulf of Finland, and the accident of a Polish marriage that had involved her both in Polish affairs and in the internal conflicts of the Holy Roman Empire.

Once involved in successful expansion on three fronts, a theory of empire evolved. Sweden's conquests along the eastern Baltic were, with good reason, regarded as the bastions of her great-power position, to be defended at all costs. Through the ports of Ingria, Estonia, and Swedish Livonia flowed much of the export trade of Russia and Poland, and it was hoped that ever more goods could be attracted or forced to come to Europe across these territories, so providing a money income in transit tolls and dues to swell the contribution to the Swedish budget of the eastern provinces themselves. Russia, in particular, was seen as a hinterland whose trade with Europe could be linked to Sweden's Baltic ports: that is why Swedish plans for the suppression of Archangel existed from an early date. Similarly, possession of Poland's West Prussian ports and the duchy of Courland were desirable because Polish trade was also inclined to by-pass the outlets under Swedish control at Narva, Reval and Riga. Beyond this ambition to filter Polish and Russian trade lay the dream of drawing traffic from Turkey and Persia, even the Far East, into a Baltic which would be a Swedish lake. In contrast to the mainly economic considerations thus dominating Swedish thought about the eastern Baltic—at a time when Denmark, having lost Gotland and Ösel, had ceased to count in the politics of that littoral, and when Russia and Poland seemed to have acquiesced in Swedish sovereignty there—Sweden's possessions in the Empire were regarded principally as safeguards of the religious (and therefore the dynastic) settlement of Westphalia, as were her seat in the Imperial Diet and her status as a guarantor of the peace of 1648. But they were also strongpoints of a European influence. Thanks to her garrisons in the Empire and her navy's ability to keep them supplied, Sweden could bring pressure on Brandenburg, manipulate the balance among the princes of the Lower Saxon Circle, and make her influence more widely felt among the great powers. In addition, her west German possessions of Bremen, Verden and Wismar provided an essential security check on Denmark, always vigilant to recover those Danish and Norwegian provinces on the Scandinavian peninsula that Sweden had taken. This Swedish containment of Denmark-Norway from the south was underwritten by a dynastic and political alliance with the duke of Holstein-Gottorp, aiming at a virtual protectorate over him: so long as that House could be prevented from coming to terms with Denmark, Sweden could enter the Jutland peninsula by a back door through the Holstein-Gottorp lands that lay scattered and intermingled with those of the king of Denmark in the duchies of Sleswig and Holstein. The standing threat of such an entry was regarded as the most valuable defence against direct Danish attacks on the Swedish peninsula; and it helped to neutralize the considerable Danish naval power in the Sound and western Baltic.

Swedish empire-building between 1560 and 1660 had been eased by the weakness of Russia and Poland at critical moments and by the co-operation, direct and indirect, of powers which shared Sweden's dislike of Danish control of both sides of the Sound or were partners in the anti-Habsburg struggle. With Sweden outdistancing Denmark as a Baltic power, however, this situation naturally changed. Towards the end of the wars of Charles X, which, if defensive in origin, developed into aggressive wars, the Dutch felt constrained to throw their weight against Sweden on behalf of Denmark in the interests of the northern balance. The French alliance lasted longer, an integral part of the French 'eastern barrier', but it could involve Sweden in French power-politics contrary to her own interests. Thus, when she was manoeuvred into hostilities with Brandenburg in 1675, Denmark seized the opportunity to attack her peninsular provinces. The experiences of 1675–9 led to a re-examination of the whole basis for

Sweden's great-power position, which had owed much to the nobility, Swedish and foreign-born, old and recently ennobled. They had been rewarded with Crown grants and with privileges, so generously that by 1680 the Crown found itself practically landless, while noble privileges caused increasing friction with the three non-noble Estates—clergy, burghers and peasants. During the long regencies after 1632 and 1660, moreover, the great nobles monopolized political power. The very policy of foreign subsidy treaties, regarded by them as necessary to defray part of the expenses of the armed forces and imperial administration, was now discredited as the occasion of involvement in a war generally regarded as contrary to Sweden's real interests. This disillusionment with foreign entanglements bred a determination to find means to make Sweden strong enough to safeguard her possessions alone. So it came about that Charles XI, who had shown unexpected qualities of leadership during the war, became the obvious focus for a movement of reform. Only his growing absolutism, condoned and even incited by the non-noble Estates and with powerful sympathizers even in the House of Nobility itself, enabled him to carry out the *reduktion* (resumption) that made possible a settled budget; the strengthening of the army, firmly rooted in traditional forms of service, but trained on European patterns and with such arrangements for exercise and mobilization as to merit the name of a standing army; the movement of the navy from Stockholm to the newly built Karlskrona, to facilitate defence of the empire in the south and west; and the modernization of the bureaucracy for its principal task as custodian of both branches of the armed forces.[1] Charles XII owed much to this reorganization in general, and also to the new military tactics developed during his father's reign by adaptation of European innovations to Swedish conditions, though naturally the experience of the Great Northern War itself was to bring some important modifications.

The positive legacy from the reign of the father was balanced by a negative factor, the consequences of which did not show themselves clearly till after 1697, when Charles XII succeeded to the throne. The desire for neutrality, not only to allow reorganization to proceed smoothly but, still more, to maintain the rôle of a 'balancing power', imprinted itself deeply on Swedish foreign policy in the 1680s and 1690s. Dislike of Louis XIV's preponderance, which momentarily brought Sweden into the anti-French camp, was qualified by fears aroused by the 'dynastic' union of the two Maritime Powers in 1688. The proper Swedish rôle now, in the opinion of the king and his advisers, was to remain outside the great-power struggle of the Nine Years War, thus reserving Swedish strength to make her acceptable to all belligerents as a mediator or else, if solid gains could be made, to enable her to enter the war at a decisive moment during its

---

[1] For a recent survey see M. Roberts, 'Charles XI', *History*, vol. L (1965), pp. 160–92. Cf. vol. v, pp. 531–8, and below, pp. 771–2 and 808.

final stages, meanwhile exploiting opportunities to increase the merchant marine and take over as much as possible of the trade usually carried by Dutch and English. Superficially Charles XI may be said to have succeeded in this policy. Trade and shipping showed spectacular growth: with 750 ships, the highest point of mercantile development in the 'great-power period' was reached. Moreover, Sweden was wooed by all the powers throughout the war and accepted as mediator for the Congress of Ryswick just before Charles XI's death in April 1697. Yet the seeds of distrust of Sweden had been sown. Her refusal to commit herself to either side was regarded as too self-centred a policy to deserve reward, and her mediation became a formal, empty honour far removed from the powerful balancing activity envisaged. Louis XIV, pessimistic about future positive support for France from Sweden, began to transfer his attentions to Denmark. The Maritime Powers, irritated both by Sweden's failure to merge herself in 'the common cause' and by her ambitions as a rival mercantile power, echoed the complaints of their diplomats about the 'treacherous' Swedes and prophesied ruin for a country that refused to co-operate with her real friends. What would become of a Sweden from which England and the Netherlands had withdrawn their support? The Dutch diplomat Van Heeckeren, at a moment of deep annoyance with the Swedes, answered his own rhetorical question with the picture of a Sweden ruined and confined once more to 'her rocks, woods and mountains'.[1] This distrust predisposed the powers to find alternatives for the alliance of an introverted Sweden.

On the other hand, the years of peace fostered confidence in Stockholm. Harvests were plentiful, a rise in population was noticeable, the rings on the Caroline pine had never been wider. Reforms went on apace in the economic, military and naval fields, the protective tariffs being backed by positive measures for mining and processing iron and steel, copper and tar. There was a momentary check during the winter of Charles XI's death. The harvest of 1696 had failed completely, and icebound waters prevented imports substantial or early enough to forestall misery and death for large numbers of the poor. Various portents in 1697—the burning of the Castle before Charles XI's body had been removed for burial, the crown slipping from Charles XII's head when he mounted his horse at the coronation procession—caused the superstitious to shudder. Above all, the accession of a 14-year-old king renewed the risk of a further noble challenge to the royal absolutism. Yet those who thought to profit by the situation were confounded by the boy-king's assertion in November of his majority.[2] The absolutists, headed by the king and the advisers he had

---

[1] To Heinsius, Stockholm, 22 Feb. 1696: H. J. van der Heim, *Het Archief van den Raadpensionaris Anthonie Heinsius*, vol. III (1880), pp. 182–3.

[2] For differing interpretations of the mixture of motives that led to the king being declared of age, see T. Höjer, *K[arolinska] F[örbundets] Å[rsbok]* (1942); G. Jonasson, *Karl XII och hans rådgivare* (Uppsala, 1960), pp. 48–74; and the exchanges between T. Höjer, G. Rystad and G. Jonasson in *H[istorisk] T[idskrift]* (1961–3).

inherited from his father, principally Wallerstedt and Piper, remained firm in the saddle, and hopes of a stop to the *reduktion* were disappointed.

Abroad, the affairs of Holstein-Gottorp pressed most urgently for attention. With the duke's marriage to Charles's elder sister Hedvig Sofia in the summer of 1698, the king prepared to defend the interests of his brother-in-law and of Sweden in the renewed controversy with Denmark over the duke's right to fortify places in his parts of Sleswig and Holstein.[1] The Danes understandably wanted to test how far they might proceed while the moment seemed opportune; they relied on exaggerated reports of an imminent revolt of the Swedish nobility. Stockholm feared that negotiations were afoot for Russian support of Danish pretensions in this dispute (though Russia was still at war with Turkey), but was completely misled as to the danger from another quarter. Unknown to Stockholm, negotiations between Denmark and Augustus of Saxony-Poland, Sobieski's successor, had reached an advanced stage. Sweden had adopted a neutral attitude to the Polish election of 1697[2] and knew of no cause for enmity between herself and the successful candidate, the elector of Saxony. Clever camouflage hid the full extent of the anti-Swedish coalition forged between Denmark, Saxony and Russia from 1698. Once Sweden had refused a speedy Danish marriage for Charles XII and thus made it obvious that she did not intend to sacrifice the Holstein-Gottorp alliance, Christian V entered into negotiations—continued with even greater urgency by his son Frederick IV (1699–1730)—with Augustus of Saxony-Poland and the tsar for a three-pronged attack on Sweden before her new ruler was secure. The Danes would enter the Holstein-Gottorp lands to force the duke out of Sleswig-Holstein, while Peter invaded Sweden's Baltic provinces and Augustus Swedish Livonia—a province which, once in his personal possession, might be used to convert the Poles to a hereditary Saxon kingship. In a Poland split between those who favoured Augustus as king and those who rejected his election as illegal, there were many of both parties who would be influenced by the prospect of Swedish Livonia becoming Polish. Discontented Livonian noblemen, hurt in their patriotic feelings and in their power by the imposition of Swedish absolutism, served as go-betweens in Denmark, Saxony-Poland and Russia alike, endeavouring to persuade any potential enemy of Sweden that an invasion of Livonia would be the signal for a rising of the nobility there in Augustus's favour, while yet hoping to use him to gain real independence.

The activities of one Livonian noble, Patkul, in Dresden and Warsaw, have drawn excessive attention to the initiative of Augustus in these negotiations. There is no doubt that the volatile Augustus was a less

[1] For an explanation of this dispute see P. Torntoft, 'William III and Denmark-Norway, 1697–1702', *Eng. Hist. Rev.* vol. LXXXI (1966), pp. 1–25.
[2] Below, pp. 686–7.

consistent enemy than Peter, who was determined to find outlets for Russian expansion. Fundamentally, however, the kings of Denmark, Christian V no less then Frederick IV, were the real driving force, urging the imperative need to seize the opportunity of Charles XI's death to realize an anti-Swedish coalition: for them the attack on Holstein-Gottorp was to serve only as a curtain-raiser to a descent on Scania, once Sweden became preoccupied with defending her east-Baltic provinces. Patkul's intrigues apart, the way in which so much of the Swedish war effort was in the event expended against Augustus also impressed him as the prime enemy on the minds of contemporaries; so shrewd an observer as Marshal Feuquières, as late as 1706, saw Augustus as the great adversary of Charles XII, mentioning the tsar only as his ally.[1] In one aspect only may Augustus be said to have represented a special danger to Sweden: it was his clever diplomacy that prevented her from understanding what was happening. Patkul's rôle as a messenger between the three anti-Swedish rulers was itself misunderstood; when he, a Swedish subject under sentence of death since 1694 for high treason, was discovered in Moscow by members of the Swedish embassy, Russian explanations of his presence were accepted at face value just because defective information as to the real state of affairs in Dresden and Warsaw blinded the Stockholm chancery. Yet it is difficult to see what ultimate difference a discovery of the coalition's plans could have made beyond saving Sweden the pain of having been Augustus's dupe. A split in the coalition could only have been bought with concessions to Denmark of a kind which no Swedish statesman, however pacific, could then have countenanced. The situation was further obscured for contemporaries, even Swedes, by the issue of the Holstein-Gottorp fortresses. Knowing nothing of the coalition negotiations, some critics argued that Charles XII's support for the duke, such as his loan of troops to rebuild razed fortresses in 1699, was dictated by dynastic considerations, or even mere whim, and hence that Denmark was provoked into an avoidable war. A further complication ensued from the circumstance that the Maritime Powers, bound by the Treaty of The Hague (23 January 1700) to render assistance in the specific Holstein-Gottorp issue, hoped by prompt action in this limited theatre to free Charles XII for entry on the anti-French side (under the same treaty) in the war now looming over the Spanish succession. Disappointment that such expectations were not fulfilled tended to make Allied statesmen forget that Sweden was fighting for her existence in the east, even when the threat from Denmark had momentarily been removed.

As soon as Augustus declared himself by attacking Livonia in February 1700, the magnitude of the defence problem was grasped by the Swedes

---

[1] Feuquières [sometimes spelt 'Feuquière'], *Memoirs Historical and Military*, vol. 1 (1736), p. 63. For Russian motives, cf. S. Svensson, 'Czar Peters motiv för kriget mot Sverige', *H.T.* (1931), and R. Wittram, *Peter I. Czar und Kaiser*, vol. 1 (Göttingen, 1964), pp. 191 ff.

who had served Charles XI. These men all had their share in the moulding of Charles XII as a military leader: Dahlberg, the old but still vigorous governor-general of Livonia, Rehnskiöld and Horn, the Guards officers who had been prominent in all the mock battles of the king's training period, and Stuart, who had taught him fortification. They had always reckoned with the possibility of a two-front war, with Denmark and Russia acting together, and they had also weighed the hypothesis that Poland might become hostile at the same time. The dilemma in the present situation arose from Augustus's claim to be acting as elector of Saxony: it was Saxon troops, not Polish, which attacked Livonia from Polish territory. The Polish-Lithuanian Commonwealth (*Rzeczpospolita*), indeed, while in reality split between supporters and opponents of their king's policy as elector, remained formally neutral. News of the attack reached Stockholm early in March; a few days later it became known that Denmark had sent troops into ducal Sleswig-Holstein. In spite of kind words from Moscow, Stockholm was now certain that Tsar Peter would sooner or later join forces with Frederick and Augustus. This appeal to the dice of war could not be refused by Sweden or by Charles XII. Though brought up to abhor aggression, he had been educated for the task of upholding the empire and was keen to measure himself in the Swedish tradition of personal royal leadership in war.

The Swedish defence plan against assault from east and west was an all-out attack on the nearer enemy, the more dangerous to the heart of Sweden. Mobilization went like clockwork, according to detailed regulations well rehearsed in peace. The navy of 38 of the line got ready to join the squadrons sent by the Maritime Powers in June for settling the Holstein-Gottorp dispute. With their help Charles counted on a naval superiority that would enable Sweden to annihilate the powerful Danish fleet of 40 ships and thus to acquire operational control of the Baltic. To achieve rapid junction with the English and Dutch squadrons he took risks, sending the Swedish fleet through the shallow Flintrännan—a course deplored by the architect of his navy, Admiral Wachtmeister, and in the event cheated of results by wind and weather and Danish disinclination to risk battle. The alternative of a descent upon Zealand, in the shelter of the combined fleets, for the purpose of capturing or destroying the Danish fleet in Copenhagen harbour, was successfully begun, but checked by Frederick IV's wise concessions to English, Dutch and Lüneburg diplomacy, anxious to pacify the North. The intervening powers saw their task principally as one of armed mediation, knowing little of the extent of Danish commitments to Augustus and Peter. It was even with some difficulty that Sweden persuaded the mediators of the need to include in the Peace of Travendal, which in August 1700 restored the duke to his 'former position', an article insisting that Denmark withdraw from hostilities against Sweden. This article was the real gain of the Zealand operation, brilliantly planned and executed by Stuart and Rehnskiöld. The guarantee of Travendal by the mediating powers would serve to protect Sweden's western and southern flanks while she turned against Augustus. It could therefore be regarded as a cheap alternative to the annihilation of the Danish armed forces which had been denied to the Swedes.

The best way to force the elector of Saxony to peace had been debated in Swedish circles in the summer of 1700. Some, including Charles himself, who had received his baptism of fire in the Zealand action and was already showing that predilection for radical solutions which was to be the despair of his more cautious advisers, favoured direct attack on the electorate. This plan was given up after urgent pleas by William III and Heinsius, who feared the repercussions of war in Germany on Louis XIV's adherence to the Second Partition Treaty, as well as on their own recruiting there in a possible war over the Spanish succession. Swedish gratitude for the Anglo-Dutch fleet was measured against disappointment at the ambiguous French attitude in the Holstein-Gottorp dispute: Louis had been sitting on the fence, unwilling to offend Frederick IV and quite content to see the North embroiled in war. Gratitude, besides fear of acting against the wishes of the powerful combination of the Maritime Powers, thus secured the reluctant but politic abandonment of a direct attack on Saxony. Instead, by mid-October, in great haste to avoid being foiled by the freezing of harbours, the Swedish army, fresh from its Zealand venture, was transported to Livonia to meet Augustus's 18,000 Saxons at their point of attack on the Swedish empire. On the news of its arrival, however, the Saxons, who had bargained on the main Swedish forces being occupied with the Danes for a considerable time, withdrew across the Dvina; and as the Russians had by now declared war and advanced into Ingria, besieging Narva, the most urgent task was to deal with Peter's challenge. The Swedes, as soon as the change of direction had been decided on, began forced marches towards Narva—cold and hungry at times, since there had been no time to perfect supplies, while Cossack troops had ravaged everything in their path of advance. Victory on 30 November over the huge Russian army—some 23,000 men, led by foreign officers who had little success in making their untrained levies resist—enormously enhanced the morale of those 8,000 Swedes who reached Narva in time to take part in the battle. The unexpectedness of the attack in foul weather, the parade-ground swiftness and precision of Swedish tactics, the brilliance of Rehnskiöld's battle-plan, all contributed to this success. The eye for terrain and the instinctive feeling for the decisive moment which Charles XII showed in this, his first big battle, in which he fought under Horn, augured well for a future when he might be expected to lead his army independently of his old teachers in the art of war: the talent for war had clearly been part of the birthright of this son and grandson of great generals. There was a note of relief in the victory celebrations in Stockholm, mirrored in the foreign diplomats' slightly patronizing references to 'our young hero'.

Narva rid the Baltic provinces of any immediate threat from the Russian side; but many arguments could be found for a rapid march on Moscow to knock Peter out of the war before dealing with Augustus, whose well-trained troops had a European reputation. Stuart drew up a plan for a winter campaign against Moscow; but difficulties of supply, equipment and recruits (who could not join the army till the spring), above all sickness among the soldiers after the brief but hard season of fighting, forced the Swedes into winter quarters. Ideally, an attack on two fronts against Russian and Saxon should have followed in the spring, when the army had been brought up to strength, but even then it would not have been large enough. Its peacetime strength had been some 30,000 as a mobile force, with about 15,000 allocated as garrison troops and frontier defence. This number was increased to a peak of 110,000, both by extra home levies and by the recruitment of paid foreign troops on a minor scale. Besides considerable subsidiary armies in Sweden-Finland, the Baltic provinces and Germany, these measures provided for an operational main army of 30,000 in 1702–6; of 40,000 in the 1707–9 campaign, excluding reserves left behind in Sweden-Finland, Swedish Pomerania and Poland; and of 65,000 in 1718. But any bisection of the main army, particularly in the early stages of the war, would have weakened the Swedish offensive and was considered too risky. Hence the Swedes, on breaking up in the spring of 1701, decided to go against Augustus first. It was not that they underestimated the Russian danger, for they knew that Peter was their more implacable enemy; but it was argued that the northern Baltic provinces could be defended by strong local garrisons while the main army dealt with the Saxons. A decisive battle was hoped for so that the king could then turn to the Russian front.

The crossing of the Dvina on 19 July, cleverly conceived by Dahlberg and Stuart but executed by Rehnskiöld and the king, with those feints and mock attacks which gained the inestimable advantage of surprise and shock for the main impact, was a great tactical victory. Yet the expected strategic gains were not achieved, since the Saxon army was able to reach sanctuary, first in Poland and then in the Empire, while the Swedes occupied Courland. In these circumstances, unable to march into Russia till Augustus had been defeated, and equally unable to attack Augustus so long as his army was hidden where Sweden could not reach him, Charles was unavoidably drawn into Polish and east European politics.

The alternative to violating the Empire, which would have risked alienating the Maritime Powers, lay so near after all: the dethronement of Augustus as king of Poland would rob him of any opportunity to send

Saxon troops into the Rzeczpospolita, with the connivance of his supporters there, and so solve the Swedish dilemma. This idea originated with those Polish groups who disapproved both of Augustus's plans for extending his powers at home and of his Russian alliance; it was urged by the powerful Sapieha family connection in Lithuania and others whom Augustus had neglected in the bestowal of offices and honours, because of their backing for the French candidate in the 1697 election. A demand for a Polish king —perhaps the eldest of the Sobieski brothers, James, who had received little support in 1697—was now raised as a means to achieve a national policy abroad and also a king at home who would prove less of a menace to the magnates. There seemed, therefore, a distinct possibility that the anti-Saxon Poles, given moral, monetary and military support, would themselves dethrone Augustus.[1] The Swedes entered into negotiations with James Sobieski in the winter of 1700–1. Wider schemes were discussed with Polish leaders: a Polish–Swedish alliance, containment of Russia by a joint offensive which might recover for Poland the lost provinces of Kiev and Smolensk, incitement of Turkey to declare war on Peter. Linked with the prospect of Polish gains in south-eastern Europe] lay the possibility of obtaining recompense for Sweden in the acquisition of Courland (over which Poland had an overlordship) or even of the West Prussian ports, as well as the hope of Polish support for rectifying the whole Swedish frontier with Russia, so as not only to improve its defensibility but to include Archangel on the Swedish side. The anti-Russian, anti-Saxon Sapieha family, who had kept up war against Augustus since 1697 with the ultimate aim of an independent Lithuania under a Sapieha dynasty, were the immediate military allies of Sweden inside Poland; but Charles XII made more significant political contacts with the commander of the Polish Crown army, Jabłonowski, and his son-in-law Rafael Leszczyński, experienced official and diplomat, influential especially at the Porte; and with Cardinal Radziejowski, whose vision for Poland also extended beyond the mere continuation of contested elections and offices. The unexpected deaths of Jabłonowski late in 1702 and of Leszczyński in January 1703 were serious blows to Swedish hopes. Leadership of the Polish patriots now tended to devolve upon the cardinal, a man less ambitious for reconquest of the provinces lost to Russia, and much more concerned with playing off all interested parties against each other till the issues should have been decided without active Polish participation. The cardinal's position was further strengthened by Augustus's clever if unscrupulous counter-move to the Sobieski candidature, the capture on Imperial soil in February 1704 of two of the three Sobieski brothers. The memory of Charles X's campaigns in Poland was still fresh, and the cry of foreign, heretic interference in the Commonwealth's domestic concerns could be used to effect. Augustus could hardly make capital out of

[1] Cf. below, pp. 693–4.

Charles's claim—made when he broke up from winter quarters in Courland in January 1702—to be permitted to pursue his Saxon enemies on Polish soil, although this demand was phrased in terms which showed that the Swedes supported the anti-Augustan parties in the Polish civil war. But Augustus could and did exploit Charles's demand, put forward in the late summer of 1701, that the Poles should dethrone him.

Most officials of the itinerant Swedish chancery-in-the-field deplored their king's political impetuosity in Poland. They would have preferred him to remain in the background and let the Poles settle their own differences, to encourage a better press in western Europe by showing a more pacific spirit, to match the innumerable appeals for mediation and protestations of willingness to make peace which Augustus spread far and wide. Some officials, particularly those left behind in Stockholm like old Bengt Oxenstierna, advocated peace with Augustus and Peter, however temporary, so that Sweden could make common cause with the Grand Alliance now taking shape against France, both with an eye to future gains in the Empire—Bremen, above all—and because the threat of French preponderance now seemed more real than during the Nine Years War. The Allies for their part, once war had broken out with Louis XIV, were anxious for the assistance of the victorious Swedish army and offered to mediate between Augustus and Charles. Sincere as were these offers, negotiations proved the hollowness of Augustus's will to peace. Swedes close to the royal headquarters came to accept, therefore, not only the primacy of the eastern theatre of war, where not even a truce could be got without sacrifice of Swedish territory, but also the need to go through with Charles's Polish policy of all-out support for a king other than Augustus.

After the capture of James and Constantine Sobieski, Charles failed to persuade their brother Alexander to submit himself for election as a caretaker king pending James's liberation. Yet agreement on a candidate outside the Sobieski family, acceptable both to the Polish anti-Saxon parties and to the Swedes, proved extremely difficult. Charles still insisted on a Polish (as opposed to a foreign) king to regenerate the Commonwealth, and on an active and pro-Swedish one at that, while in their turn the ambitions of the great Polish families and Cardinal Radziejowski's conscious temporizing—itself not untouched by personal and family ambition—had a paralysing effect on the negotiations. To end the deadlock Charles forced a Swedish choice on the anti-Saxon Poles. Hence the election in 1704 of Stanislas Leszczyński, without the cardinal's blessing.[1] Swedish arms then proceeded to get Stanislas accepted throughout Poland: wide military sweeps, aimed at the Saxon troops and the Russian

---

[1] Below, p. 697. Stanislas promised Alexander Sobieski that he would abdicate in favour of James Sobieski when Augustus should release him: V. D. Koroljuk, 'Der Eintritt der Rzeczpospolita in den Nordischen Krieg', in J. Kalisch and J. Gierowski (eds.), *Um die polnische Krone* (Berlin, 1962), p. 134.

auxiliaries brought in by Augustus, were also used to procure, by intimidation if necessary, Polish support in all districts and among all important family connections. By the end of 1705 this pressure had gone far enough for Stanislas to be crowned and for a treaty to be signed at Warsaw between Poland and Sweden, so ending that *de facto* war which had subsisted under the fiction that they were at peace. The treaty demonstrated the military, political and economic place of the Commonwealth in Charles's grand design for eastern Europe. It was reinforced by trade agreements in which the Poles undertook *inter alia* to recognize Riga's monopoly of Russian exports in transit to the West.[1]

The Polish campaigns of Charles XII have been variously judged. The need to defeat Augustus before turning against Peter has been generally admitted, even at the price of temporary Russian gains on the Baltic. Indeed it has been argued that there was a better road to Swedish security: if only Charles had come to terms with Prussia, Augustus could have been held by Frederick I; alternatively, Charles could have made a deal with Augustus and Frederick sufficiently satisfactory to both for him to invade Russia, without worry about attacks from the rear.[2] But each of these courses depended on a partition of Polish territory incompatible with Swedish plans for eastern Europe and also repugnant to Charles personally, as a betrayal of the Polish 'liberties' whose cause he had embraced on entering Poland. Moreover, even the most persistent negotiations showed how little Frederick would offer in return for Prussian expansion eastward: certainly not the clear-cut military alliance which, in Swedish eyes, would merit the sacrifice of any Polish territory (if compensated by Polish gains in other directions). Charles tested the alternatives, in fact, but found no way out of his Polish dilemma other than to adhere to his plan for a pro-Swedish Polish king, willing to co-operate in a venture against Russia and allow Poland to be the base from which that campaign was to be mounted—or at least a buffer-state strong enough to keep Augustus out.

Charles XII grew to maturity and self-reliance as military leader, politician and diplomat during these years in Poland. He showed himself more suspicious but also more realistic than his chancery advisers. He disliked virtuoso diplomacy and was not anxious to waste effort exploring opportunities that did not immediately concern him, but was never such a despiser of pen and conference-table as western accounts would make him. To them he seemed a hater of diplomacy because, in his efforts to keep freedom of action for Sweden in the east, and also to leave a loophole for Swedish initiative in the west if necessity and opportunity should coincide, he refused to let eastern and western theatres of war intersect more than he

[1] K. G. Hildebrand, 'Polen 1704–1709', *KFÅ* (1936), and 'Ekonomiska syften i svenska expansionsplaner, 1700–1709', *ibid.* (1949). Cf. below, p. 699.
[2] O. Haintz, *König Karl XII*, vol. I (rev. edn, Berlin, 1958), pp. 167–8.

could help. Inside his own sphere of interest he encouraged diplomatic feelers. Polish contacts with Ukraine, as with Tatars and Turks, had his blessing because they had a bearing on the fight with Russia: in fact, the kind of European-wide diplomacy which he embarked on later, in response to the growth of the anti-Swedish league, is foreshadowed by the way in which these Polish contacts from 1702 were made to serve Swedish purposes. Nor was he unaware of the value of propaganda; Hermelin, his 'Latin pen', was active in gaining Polish adherents by skilful manifestoes and pamphlets.[1] Of course, the propagandist picture presented to the capitals of Europe of a king who fought a just war, desiring only restitution of what had been taken from him, was not the whole truth. His grandiose though by no means unrealistic dreams of solving Sweden's eastern problem by absorption of Courland and Polish Livonia, and of creating a buffer-state between his empire and Russia in an enlarged Poland at Russia's expense, governed by a pro-Swedish king who should be tolerant in religious affairs and allow the trade of the East to be channelled through Swedish Baltic ports—these dreams, as typical of Charles XII as his sense of honour and justice, were purposely hidden from view.

As a warrior the king got plenty of opportunity to prove himself. The first major battle, at Kliszów in the summer of 1702, was his first victory as a commander sharing responsibility with Rehnskiöld. Charles's generalship was demonstrated when his quick responses to abrupt developments in the tactical situation materially helped 12,000 Swedes to defeat Augustus's 16,000 Saxons and 6,000 Poles. The siege of Toruń (Thorn) in 1703, though not technically directed by Charles—'I never did have much experience in siege-warfare', he once said,[2] implying also a slight distaste for it—illustrated his growing grasp of the operation from which most could be gained: defeat of a big Saxon garrison, influence on Prussian policy, speed and security of contact with Sweden to replace contacts imperilled by Russian activities in the Baltic provinces. The years 1704-6 further displayed his mature gifts for strategy and for economic deployment of his forces. He contained Augustus's Saxon troops in the Empire at the time when he needed a free hand in Poland to secure Stanislas's candidature. Later, simultaneous operations in east and west Poland were designed to relieve pressure on the Baltic provinces and prevent the ripening of Russo-Saxon plans for co-operation in the Polish theatre. Swedish moves were based on the hope of coming to grips either with the last and final army of Augustus, formed after Kliszów and Toruń, or else with Ogilvy's army sent by Peter to help his ally. Sound preparations and good reconnaissance, learnt in the hard school of experience, were finally crowned with success early in 1706. The Russians

[1] S. Olsson, *Olof Hermelin, en karolinsk kulturpersonlighet och statsman* (Lund, 1953), pp. 235 ff.
[2] 'Die Erinnerungen Axel von Löwens', ed. F. Adler and S. Bonnesen, *KFÅ* (1929), pp. 48-9.

escaped from the trap prepared for them at Grodno, but they were forced to retreat from Poland; and Rehnskiöld's great victory over the Saxons at Fraustadt (Wschowa) in Poznania, on 13 February, spelt the virtual end of Augustus's resistance to Swedish plans for the Rzeczpospolita.

The Polish years were not without setbacks; the very nature of the country, and Charles's precarious position in it, precluded that easy victory which Marshal de Saxe planned on paper for 'anyone engaged in a war in Poland'.[1] Setbacks, however, moulded the king's character no less than victories, which fed his natural optimism and deepened his religious convictions. A note of embittered hardness, at variance with his personal gentleness, sounds in his letters to Rehnskiöld and Magnus Stenbock at times when numbers of Swedish soldiers fell victims to guerrilla warfare.[2] Growing disillusion with the willingness of most Poles to change sides time and again—a 'treachery' whose motives he did not really understand—and the impossibility of achieving stable alliances with the Polish factions strengthened Charles's determination to act alone. The overriding need to surround all military plans with secrecy in a country of irregular warfare made him taciturn about the purpose of any given order, to the extent that his officers once or twice misunderstood his intentions. He would allow a good deal of frank criticism by the chancery-in-the-field, but the final decision was his. He was by nature obstinate once decisions had been made, but would at times change his mind if pressed strongly and for good reasons by Piper, Hermelin and Cederhielm, the three highest chancery officials at headquarters. He worked extremely hard, reconnaissance and inspection rides his only relaxation, with visits to old friends stationed at a distance. Social occasions—the wedding of a respected officer, the reception of an honoured guest—he attended only from politeness or a desire for news from home. He was affectionate by disposition; but the only private outlets for the emotional side of his personality came through correspondence with his sisters and concern for the well-being of some of the young volunteers who joined his army, notably Maximilian of Württemberg, entrusted to him at the age of 13. For the rest, 'I am married to the army' was his explanation of his continued bachelor status—'at least for the duration'. The attempt to follow the teaching of the Church and the need to set his men a good example help to explain the sexual abstinence which puzzled contemporaries and posterity. Those who knew him well declared that he was far from indifferent to women; but he seems on the one hand to have retained a youthful romantic conception of love which precluded promiscuity and, on the other, to have thought that his energies could best be concentrated

---

[1] *Reveries* (E. T. London, 1757), pp. 97 ff. Cf. below, pp. 700 ff.
[2] E. Carlson (ed.), *Konung Karl XII:s Egenhändiga Bref* (Stockholm, 1893; German transl. Berlin, 1894).

on his duties as a general if he remained celibate; the evidence we possess points rather to a control of natural appetites than to sexual abnormality. He taught himself to make do with little food and sleep, avoiding drink stronger than weak beer, and schooled himself to present a smooth, impassive countenance to the world, so that even officers who saw him daily could not judge his mood. He studied to instil into the army a self-control and courage, based on religious faith, that would steel it in battle and fire the offensive spirit. 'Married to the army', though said half in jest, held a deep truth. Charles's evident care for both the material and spiritual life of his soldiers, his obvious pride in his own professional reputation and theirs, the pithy sayings which became winged words or magic formulas to impress his will on them—these were outward manifestations of a mutual reliance and affection. It is hard to find a word of criticism of the king by anyone who ever served under him simply in the capacity of a soldier. By contrast, he was frequently criticized by those who served Sweden outside the army, a fact partly responsible for the superficial summary of him as a fine general but a poor statesman. Such criticisms occurred as a rule in private letters or official memoranda written at times when things were not going well, in fits of depression or with an eye to the writer's future career—for the king might well be killed and the writer would not like to be held responsible for his policies. These same people, when the king's policy succeeded, changed their tune. Discounting the ephemeral nature of some of this criticism and the natural resentment felt by pen-pushers for soldiers, a more constant element of friction remained. Charles was too apt to take extravagant risks, intent on radical solutions, unwilling to compromise and temporize, rigid in his preconceived ideas on the large scale for Sweden's future. Even in moments of triumph, the chancery officials, as patriotic as the king himself, feared that he 'tightened the bow too much'.[1]

A period of success, when all anxieties were stilled, followed the treaty with Poland and the victory at Fraustadt. Yet the treaty, so favourable to Swedish plans, would be valueless unless Augustus could be made to accept publicly his own dethronement. The only way of enforcing this was to invade his electorate. The Wars of the North and of the Spanish Succession had reached stages where a Swedish entry into the Empire might be, if not welcome to the Allies, at least not actively resented. Charles argued that he had refrained from disturbing the Empire as long as the war against France was going badly for the Allies, but that Blenheim and Ramillies now made such restraint unnecessary. In the early autumn of 1706, therefore, he marched into Saxony across Silesian territory, where he was implored by the Protestants to take up their grievances with the emperor, their churches having been closed contrary to the Peace of Westphalia. Such was the fear engendered by the Swedish

[1] N. Reuterholm to J. Cronstedt, 16 Feb. 1707 (*Personhist. Tidskr.* 1908, p. 137).

army that the Saxons hurried to make terms as soon as it reached the electoral frontier: the renunciation by Augustus of the Crown of Poland, the recognition of Stanislas, the handing over of Patkul, and permission for the Swedish army to stay in Saxony over the winter to rest, await recruits, and replace worn clothing and equipment. All this was embodied in the Treaty of Altranstädt on 24 September.[1]

The treaty was kept secret for a time and there was much uncertainty in Europe about Charles's intentions. Both sides in the western war sought his assistance. Marlborough's visit to Altranstädt in 1707 was in part to forestall any French recruitment of influential Swedes for a 'French party', in part to lessen friction between Charles XII and the emperor, and between Sweden and those countries that supplied the Grand Alliance with soldiers. There was also truth in the explanation openly given for the visit: Marlborough's desire to meet a royal master of his own craft. From Sweden's angle the Succession War could in 1706–7 look after itself; the two sides then seemed evenly matched, with no immediate prospect of peace.[2] This meant precious elbow-room for Swedish initiative in the East.

There never was much doubt in informed circles of Charles's next step. A campaign into Russia was to be prepared, militarily and diplomatically, during the stay in Saxony. Peter had asserted very forcefully that he would rather risk ten more years of war than give up Ingria with St Petersburg, whatever he might surrender from his conquests of 1704–5 in Estonia and Livonia. Although Augustus ratified his peace and even met Charles in a friendly enough way on several occasions, Charles was unwilling to leave Saxony before devising checks on Augustus's freedom during his absence in Russia. Having failed to get help from Prussia, in the form of auxiliaries stationed in Poland under Swedish command, Charles sought recognition of Stanislas by the Maritime Powers, preferably in the form of a guarantee for the peace with Saxony, as an obstacle to the return of Augustus. Marlborough promised to try to obtain this guarantee. The Dutch were unwilling to commit themselves before the Russian campaign; they had found Peter, in at least temporary control of Sweden's Baltic provinces, a generous host to Dutch shipping and felt that Russian competition with Sweden in the east Baltic would be preferable to Swedish monopoly. Such arguments had some effect also on English merchants, but in Whitehall a promise which Charles gave Marlborough, in return for an expected English guarantee, weighed more heavily. He confirmed his neutrality, but promised to assist the Allies as soon as practicable with Swedish troops. The sooner Charles could be encouraged to tackle Peter, the sooner he

---

[1] Cf. below, p. 701.

[2] Whenever one side had a setback, it is true, the long-term aims of mediation and balance tended to create a 'French' or an 'Allied' party at Swedish headquarters and then intervention was more seriously debated.

might be able to provide these. England at least recognized Stanislas in the spring of 1708.[1] The Dutch neither recognized Stanislas nor guaranteed the Saxon peace of 1706. There was thus a flaw, even before the Russian campaign started, in Swedish plans for safeguarding their rear. We know that it caused grave concern at Swedish headquarters.[2]

The offensive had been meticulously prepared. Recruits arrived from Sweden; German volunteers were formed into dragoon regiments of their own; and the army which began the march to Russia totalled some 40,000.[3] The direction of the thrust was a well-kept secret. Contacts were maintained through Polish intermediaries which would allow Charles to get into closer touch with Mazepa, hetman of the Cossacks of the Ukraine, or with the khan of the Crimea, Devlet-Girei, or his overlord the sultan, when the king deemed it advisable. This widespread net was as typical of the Swedish preparations as Charles XII's refusal to commit himself definitively 'until we get closer'. It is now realized that the rigidity of his eventual aims—to force Peter to give up the Swedish provinces and to rectify the Russian frontier in favour of both Sweden and Poland—was balanced by an extreme fluidity of means. Nevertheless, although discussion of Charles's methods in the Russian campaign now depends less than formerly on deductions from what actually happened, material for it remains scarce, most of the field-chancery papers having been destroyed on the king's orders on the night of 10–11 July 1709.[4]

The campaign began with impressive success. By keeping the Russians guessing as to his route and choosing the Masurian marshes and woods, never before traversed by a large army, Charles was able to avoid battle and yet force the Russians out of Poland. As soon as the Swedes had moved into Saxony in 1706 the Russians had streamed into Poland, hoping to make it the battlefield for Charles and Peter as it had been for Augustus and Charles, and endeavouring to get support for a candidate of Russian choosing—Rákóczi, the Hungarian prince.[5] 5,000 Swedish troops under Krassow were left in Poland to help Stanislas keep the country loyal and act as the nucleus for a reserve, Stanislas himself accompanying Charles's

---

[1] England, however, guaranteed neither of the Altranstädt treaties. The treaty with the emperor, confirming the rights of the Silesian Protestants, was signed on 1 Sept. 1707, nearly twelve months after the treaty with Augustus: K. G. Hildebrand, 'England och Sverige 1707', *KFÅ* (1937).

[2] R. M. Hatton (ed.), *Captain James Jefferyes's Letters from the Swedish Army, 1707–1709* (Stockholm, 1954), pp. 44–5.

[3] S. Waller, 'Den svenska huvudarméns styrka år 1707', *KFÅ* (1957), has shown that the army had 33,000 fighting men in the ranks; to these must be added officers and non-commissioned officers, civilians, wagoners and servants.

[4] E. Tarlé, *Severnaya voyna i shvedskoye nashestviye na Rossiyu* (Moscow, 1958), utilized all that fell into Russian hands, together with intercepts, etc.; but this material is clearly of secondary importance. Cf. K. G. Hildebrand, 'En relation om Mazepa våren 1707', *KFÅ* (1935).

[5] Cf. below, p. 701. Cf. G. Kiss, 'Frans Rákóczi, Peter der Grosse und der polnische Thron um 1717', *Jahrbücher für Geschichte Osteuropas* (1966), pp. 344–60.

army as far as Radoszkowice. Until the early summer of 1708 the Russians were left uncertain whether the Swedish blow would fall on the Baltic provinces or Muscovy itself. The provinces had been exhausted by the constant warfare of seven years and in part depopulated by Peter's transportation of civilians from their homes. A wish to spare them further suffering may have contributed to Charles XII's decision to march into Russia; but the main reason was that his whole plan for eastern Europe depended on such a decisive victory over the tsar as could only be achieved inside Russian territory. Moscow must be threatened in the way Copenhagen had been threatened by the Zealand descent of 1700 and Dresden by the invasion of Saxony in 1706.[1]

Four main routes to Moscow existed: one from the Baltic provinces by Narva and Novgorod; the second from Poland and Lithuania by Vilna (Wilno), Minsk and Smolensk; the third, further south, across Severia and the Ukraine by Kiev and Kaluga; and fourthly, the route from Tatary and Turkey, over the territory of the Zaporozhian Cossacks and their strongholds by Bjelgorod, Kursk and Tula. Muscovy proper lay protected by the big rivers which had to be crossed before one could get to Moscow, whichever route was chosen: the Beresina, Dnieper, Desna and their many tributaries. By keeping the defenders guessing, Charles forced Peter to be prepared to defend both northern routes; and there is evidence for supposing that the Swedish corps in Poland was intended not only as a reserve but also as an auxiliary army to break in along the southern (third) route—and so bring into action the Cossacks and the Tatars along the fourth route some time in 1708–9—or at least to feign such intervention in order to facilitate the main Swedish venture via Smolensk. Battles could be expected at the river-crossings, and it was Charles's design to manoeuvre the Russians into such a position that, while battle was avoided on the Vistula, Peter's troops should be tempted to stand as soon as the Swedes neared the Russian border.

The Swedish march was masterly and the early river crossings, effected with comparative ease after the Russians had been outflanked or drawn away by feints, have been judged models of generalship. But the Russian soldiers were no longer the untrained masses of the Narva period; they were well-organized veterans of the Baltic warfare, often with experience as auxiliaries in Poland. Above all, Peter and his generals had a well-conceived plan of defence. With so much at stake, with St Petersburg founded, heroic resistance was to be expected. A meeting at Zolkiev laid down a policy, as grimly determined as the Swedish, to conserve the army for a decisive battle: the Russians were to withdraw, risk battle only in the most favourable circumstances, and rob the Swedes of subsistence by destroying crops and farms—not only on Lithuanian and Polish soil but in

---

[1] It is certain that Charles also intended the capture of St Petersburg, from the side of Finland: H. Brulin, 'Domen över Georg Lybekers befälsföring', *KFÅ* (1934).

Muscovy itself.[1] At Hołowczyń (on the river Vabich, 14 July 1708) the Russians made their first serious, large-scale stand to stop Charles gaining command of the road to Smolensk. The Swedes gained a signal victory, but it cost them dear in men, particularly officers, and they could not properly exploit it when the Russians withdrew to new and strong positions. Charles had never underestimated the serious task ahead, but the Swedes learnt to their cost that the closer they got to the Russian border, the more did defence have the advantage over attack.

Charles was also handicapped in the late summer by having to await reinforcements from the Baltic provinces under Lewenhaupt, now freed by Peter's evacuation of the lands south of Ingria. These reinforcements were, besides 12,500 troops, a colossal moving supply-depôt to bring food, ammunition and equipment. The junction was to take effect in late July, but Lewenhaupt was delayed, principally by the difficult roads of an abnormally wet summer. After weeks of anxious waiting, occupied in marches and counter-marches to keep the Russians busy, and misled by false reports of his distance from Lewenhaupt, Charles decided to move south to Severia. Food was short for men and horses; reconnaissance showed that inside the Russian border 'the sun was hidden by smoke day after day';[2] there seemed no possibility of pushing ahead along the Smolensk road that autumn. In these circumstances, it made good sense to move south, to let Lewenhaupt join the main army in Severia, and to test the Russian defences for a quicker break-through: there also use could be made of Mazepa, who had been playing off Russians against Swedes and Poles to gain time, but who was known to want autonomy for the Ukraine. On 25 September, within a few miles of the Russian frontier, Charles turned south while Lewenhaupt was still on the wrong side of the Dnieper —a fact which the Russians with their more numerous reconnaissance parties soon realized. When Peter decided to draw his main army across Lewenhaupt's route before he could join Charles, the fate of the supply train was all but sealed; after the battle of Lesnája (9 October), though it could technically be reckoned a draw, all the Swedish wagons had to be left behind. Even this might not have presented more than a momentary check now that the southern route—with the fruitful Severia and Ukraine as bases—had been substituted for the northern attack on Russia, but for a further and graver setback that befell Charles even before he heard that Lewenhaupt was isolated by difficult wooded terrain which the king's army could not possibly recross in time to help him. Russian troops had seized the Severian passes and strongholds ahead of the Swedish advance-guard sent to do so. Thus the main Swedish army was compelled to take

---

[1] Along 1,500 kilometres of the border a zone 200 km. deep would be ruined and the population sent away, so that the Swedes should find 'neither forage nor food': V. E. Shutoy *Bor'ba narodnykh mass protiv nashestviya armii Karla XII, 1700–1709* (Moscow, 1958).

[2] Eyewitness cit. P. Engdahl, 'Karl XII', *KFÅ* (1930), p. 212.

the longer and more hazardous route of the Krissower woods into the Ukraine. As in a Greek tragedy, blow followed blow. Mazepa was not ready for the Swedes and wished Charles XII 'to the devil' for forcing his hand before the Swedish struggle with Peter had been decided. So the Russians were enabled to take Baturin, the Cossack capital, sack it of valuable supplies and make an example of all who favoured Mazepa's cause.

Charles prepared to renew the campaign, although he had only the most precarious contacts with Poland and Sweden now that the Russians were trying—with considerable temporary success—to cut his postal communications. Money was not a problem: the Swedes had brought money bills which found acceptance everywhere. Supplies could be got, contact with Tatars and Turks established, and the auxiliary corps of Stanislas and Krassow called on in the spring, with further reinforcements from Sweden if necessary. The winter of 1708–9, however, as destructive in the Ukraine as in western and northern Europe, was more costly than the fighting. On the night of 3–4 January[1] many Swedes, especially the wounded in the carriages held up in confusion at the gates of the town of Hadyach, froze to death or suffered injuries because they could not get a roof over their heads, though they had won the race for this town from the Russians. The first storming of the little fortress of Veprik on 17 January failed mainly because its walls had become solid ice; so many brilliant young officers lost their lives at Veprik that even its surrender (long after nightfall) scarcely relieved the sadness of the army. Once again, as in Poland, losses which seemed senseless brought forth a ruthless strain in Charles. Safe winter quarters were established under intense raiding, the Russian scorched-earth tactics being copied, though with more tenderness for civilian lives, to get a waste belt of territory round the camp.

Spring 1709 found the Swedish army, though smaller by 5/8,000 men, in better heart, besieging the fortified town of Poltava on the river Vorskla (a tributary of the lower Dnieper), negotiating with Tatars and Turks, and renewing contact with Sweden and Poland: Charles XII in virtual command of the land west of the Vorskla, Peter collecting his forces to the east. The momentum of Charles's campaign had undeniably slowed down. Lack of any startling success in 1708 revived the anti-Stanislas forces in Poland,[2] particularly as Russian troops had returned in the hope of reopening civil war and succeeded in tying down Stanislas and Krassow. Swedish negotiations with the Zaporozhian Cossacks brought them into co-operation by April; but in Constantinople the sultan was as reluctant to commit himself, before he could estimate Charles's prospects of success, as Mazepa had been the previous year. Piper and others in the chancery

---

[1] Christmas Eve by the Swedish calendar. E. Carlsson, 'Krasnokutsk-Gorodnoe-Kolomak', *KFÅ* (1947), refutes the view that this winter campaign was an attempt to break through to Moscow along the fourth route.

[2] See below, pp. 702–3.

advised temporary withdrawal to the Polish base as the safest course, peace-feelers showing Peter to be as adamant as in 1706–7 not to give up St Petersburg. On the other hand, Charles was seeking a prestige victory to win over Tatar and Turk: the timely fall of Poltava at the junction of the road-net, or a battle with the Russian army under conditions of his own choosing. Then would come the time for further advance. The Russians were also looking for a decisive victory; but cautiously, still in some awe of Charles, while attempting to deny him by diplomatic initiative the Turkish-Tatar help which Devlet-Girei agitated for at the Porte.

Accident helped to decide the issue. During skirmishes across the river made by both sides to test each other's positions, a stray shot wounded Charles XII in the foot. In these circumstances, when it was clear that the king could not in person lead his army, Peter decided to risk battle, not by attacking the Swedes, but by moving the whole Russian army across the Vorskla, digging in, and so inviting the Swedes to assault a defended camp. By 8 July these dispositions had succeeded so well that the Swedes were forced to take the initiative. Several misfortunes dislocated Charles's plan. The Russians had in the previous night built two new redoubts which Swedish reconnaissance did not discover till the last moment; a strong section of the infantry was delayed there, got separated from the main army, and was driven into retreat or cut down by Russian detachments. The main attack was held up in the vain hope of allowing the missing infantry to rejoin the battle-line; adjutants were killed before messages could be got through; and finally the Russians did what the Swedes had not expected—marched out of camp to attack of their own accord before the Swedish lines could be brought into proper order.[1] The Swedish generals blamed each other. The older officers were undoubtedly tired and did not relish the ultimate responsibility in battle which had for so long been the king's, but no single individual is to be blamed: it was rather the breaking of the bond between king and army by the shot of 8 July, still more perhaps the tremendous improvement in Russian tactics and morale. History usually speaks of the 'defeat' of Poltava, but the contemporary Swedish version of it, as an abortive attack on a fortified camp, contains a grain of truth,[2] although their losses in casualties and prisoners numbered over 10,000. What turned this unsuccessful attack into defeat was the surrender at Perevolochna on 11 July of another 15,000, the majority of the remaining army.

Charles, who took command of the retreat,[3] had first suggested offering battle at the spot where the Swedish baggage and artillery were collected, but agreed that a march south to get in touch with the Tatars and with

---

[1] G. Petri, 'Slaget vid Poltava', *KFÅ* (1958), summarizes Swedish research; for the Russian, cf. articles by W. Granberg, J. Hedberg and G. Medwedjev, *ibid.* (1961).

[2] C. Hallendorff (ed.), *Karl XII i Ukraina. En karolins berättelse* (Stockholm, 1915), p. 31; cf. E. Tengberg, 'Karl XII i Ukraine våren 1709', *KFÅ* (1948), pp. 135–6.

[3] E. Carlsson, 'Karl XII och kapitulationen vid Perevoltjna', *KFÅ* (1940).

Poland might be preferable. It was not easy to find transport across the Dnieper, since a Russian raid on the Zaporozhian strongholds in May had burnt nearly all the available boats. The king was urged to hasten ahead of the army to reach Ochakov, and from there to negotiate with the Tatar khan and the sultan for the army's return to Poland; he was to renew contact with Stanislas and Sweden as soon as possible—in short, to circumscribe the consequences of the Poltava fiasco by all available means, but also to remove himself from the danger of capture, since Peter was known to have sent out troops for that purpose. The army would have to take its chance of crossing the Vorskla at a wading-place known to some Tatars present with the Swedes, thence make its way to the Crimea and rejoin the king. This should have been possible, but irrational forces came into play. The senior officers, Lewenhaupt and Creutz—Rehnskiöld had been captured at Poltava, as had the chief chancery officials—were exhausted and nearly demoralized; they feared the Tatars and the unknown more than capture by the Russians, who were after all officered mainly by Germans. Many of the Swedes became listless or intent on saving their lives, especially after the king's departure with some 1,500 men—including Mazepa and the Cossacks, on whom Peter would be sure to wreak vengeance. Charles XII never forgave the surrender at Perevolochna. In his opinion, Lewenhaupt's duty was not to ask, still less to press, the colonels of the regiments to decide between capitulation or battle; he should either have ensured the army's escape or stood to fight the relatively small detachment of Russian cavalry that had caught up with the Swedes. Sincere as it doubtless was,[1] the argument shows a lack of insight into human motives which was perhaps the king's outstanding weakness as general and statesman. The link between Poltava and Perevolochna he could not or would not grasp.

From Turkish soil the Swedish king tried to repair the damage done by Poltava. With his help, many influential Turks and Tatars were for settling their accounts with the Russians at once; but Charles had at first no thought beyond establishing closer diplomatic contacts as a basis for future co-operation, while awaiting news of his armies in Russia and Poland and sending instructions to Sweden to make good his losses. His aim was to resume the struggle against Peter with the Krassow-Stanislas armies, reinforced by remnants of his own and by fresh forces from Sweden, based on Poland. He could not think of leaving Turkey till his foot was healed, but was sure that under the sultan's promised escort he could rejoin the Krassow corps in Poland before winter. Against all expectations, his stay in Turkey lasted over four years.[2] The opportunities energetically

---

[1] For conflicting views see L. Stavenow, *HT* (1910); E. Tarlé, *Karl XII och Poltava* (Swed. transl. 1951); and E. Carlsson, *loc. cit.*

[2] Cf. above, pp. 630–1 and 636–7.

grasped by his enemies tied him down. Russian troops at once flooded back into Poland as well as into the Baltic provinces; the capitulation of Perevolochna, which had promised the Swedish officers passage home on parole, was disregarded. Augustus returned to Poland and resumed the royal title, while Stanislas and Krassow had to retreat into Swedish Pomerania; and detachments of Polish troops hostile to Augustus took time to find their way through Hungary to Bender. The Swedes, Cossacks and Poles gathered there eventually numbered 4,000. The plague shut the frontier between Turkey and the Habsburg dominions from 1709 to 1714. Offers of transport to Sweden by sea, made by France and the Maritime Powers, were refused out of Charles's dislike of delivering his person so completely into the hands of any belligerent in the western war as to compromise his future freedom of action. He clung to the hope of a passage home through Poland, but this would now depend on landing a new Swedish army in the Empire. Meanwhile, he had to be content to work on the Turks to declare war on Peter for the reconquest of Azov.

In Stockholm the Council had its hands full with Denmark. Frederick IV had re-entered the war after Poltava. Before the close of 1709 Sweden was invaded from both Denmark and Norway. At the same time the lands of Holstein-Gottorp, administered by a paternal uncle on behalf of Duke Charles Frederick (born in Sweden in 1700 and brought up there),[1] were overrun. The guarantors of Travendal, exhausted by their own long war, felt themselves in no position to prevent this and argued that Charles should rather listen to peace than think of renewing his struggle with Peter. In the Hague Conventions of March and December 1710, the Maritime Powers guaranteed the neutrality of the Swedish possessions in the Empire, as the only way of keeping Germany at peace and so retaining Danish and Saxon troops against France. Though presented as a service to Sweden, the guarantee ruined Charles's scheme of using Swedish Pomerania as a base from which reinforcements from Sweden could reach Poland and himself. His disapproval opened a breach with the Maritime Powers that was never healed. A different attitude to them also fed misunderstandings between Charles and his Council, which regarded co-operation with them as essential.[2] King and Council were, of course, too distant to work well together. He expected the Council, reinforced before the Russian campaign with soldiers like Arvid Horn and Magnus Stenbock, to realize the primacy of supporting the larger war effort by sending him a new army; they, robbed of the king's drive, tended to see only immediate dangers and to take too pessimistic a view of Sweden's situation.

[1] His parents had taken refuge in Stockholm when the Danes began to destroy the fortifications on Duke Frederick IV's territory. The duke fell at Kliszów in 1702 and Hedvig Sofia died on 21 Dec. 1708. Her death was known in the Swedish camp before Poltava, but not to the king until he had reached Turkey.
[2] J. Rosén, *Det engelska anbudet om fredsmedling 1713* (Lund, 1946), pp. 7–95.

Badly shaken by the death of his favourite elder sister and only slowly recovering his mental balance through hobbies there was now time to resume—his correspondence with Tessin on architecture, his patronage of Swedish expeditions from Turkey to the Holy Land—Charles gradually lost patience with the majority of the Council and took up a new subject: economic and administrative reforms that would hasten mobilization of Sweden's undoubted resources for the war effort. Books were procured and discussions held with those best qualified in the entourage at Bender, principally Casten Feif, one of the chancery officials who was interested in the cameralist and mercantilist theories of the time; correspondence was also started with would-be reformers in Sweden, Feif acting as the king's secretary. Thus the foundations for Charles's reform activities after 1714 were laid in Turkey. At the same time experience of the Council and the Swedish administrative colleges while he was at Bender (e.g. over the issue of progressive taxation) made it unlikely that these institutions would be chosen to implement his will thereafter. Not till he had removed from the Council all responsibility for the army that was to support him on the Continent, and given full authority for it to an individual councillor, Magnus Stenbock, did his project of a landing in Germany acquire life.

Stenbock it was who saved Sweden in 1710 by driving the Danes from Scania. By the autumn of 1712 he had moved 16,000 men into the small strip of Swedish Pomerania which remained in Swedish control after the enemy offensive of 1711—an offensive condoned by the guarantors of the Hague neutrality conventions on the excuse that Charles XII had refused to accept them. But Stenbock's supply fleet was utterly destroyed by the Danish navy shortly after he landed. This has been judged the most fatal of all the reverses of the war. It forced Stenbock to keep near the coast in expectation of new supplies from home—a forlorn hope indeed without his own personal drive there to produce the money and the ships. Thus the victory he gained over combined Danish and Saxon troops at Gadebusch in December 1712 could not be properly exploited. Unable to break through into Poland as planned, Stenbock then attempted to force Denmark out of the war by an invasion of Jutland; but he was surrounded in the Holstein fortress of Tønning from January 1713 by a vastly superior army of Saxons, Danes and Russians. He had to surrender in May.

Before news of Gadebusch or its sad sequel could reach Turkey, Charles's position there had become precarious. He had watched three Ottoman declarations of war on Russia—to all of which Swedish diplomacy at the Porte had contributed—wasted from the point of view of Swedish interests, because of his own military weakness. Nor had he succeeded in getting an anti-Russian alliance with Augustus, now heartily tired of Peter's overlordship in Poland, or with Frederick I of Prussia, though he too was alarmed at Russian proximity. Charles was willing now to accept the sacrifice of Poland, if this would bring solid allies against Russia, but no agreement could be reached on specific terms. The obstacle was the old one of Charles insisting on 'guarantees' in the form of definite military commitments, while Augustus and Frederick—and from February 1713 his successor, Frederick William I—had in mind much less risky arrangements; they wanted Swedish concessions without pledging military co-operation in return. It was realized both at Bender and Stockholm that a disappointed Prussia might well join Sweden's enemies. There was uncertainty also—but less nervousness in view of traditional friendship—about Hanover's intentions: the elector, fearing a Danish conquest of Bremen and Verden, planned to occupy these Swedish possessions himself.

The most urgent problem in the winter of 1712–13, however, was the attitude of Charles's Turkish hosts. He had outstayed his welcome; his belligerent attitude to Turkey's neighbours accorded ill with military impotence; even his earlier supporters began to negotiate with emissaries of Augustus to have him removed. The Turkish escort at last materialized, but letters intercepted by the Swedes revealed a plot by Turkish and Tatar officials to leave Charles at the mercy of Augustus or the Russians, by the simple expedient of allowing the escort to melt away once the Polish border had been crossed. Hence Charles's last-ditch stand, the *Kalabalik* (tumult) of Bender, in February 1713: a deliberate opposition to the Turks and Tatars who had orders to make him begin his journey out of Turkey, 'if necessary by force'. Charles succeeded in exposing the intrigues between Augustus's diplomats and the sultan's officials.[1] For a moment, too, with news of Gadebusch and a consequent fourth Turkish declaration of war on Russia, his hopes of co-operation with the sultan on equal terms flickered into life again, only to be finally extinguished by the news of Stenbock's surrender at Tønning. The time had clearly come for Charles to go home of his own free will, to calm and sustain a Sweden made despondent by the long duration of the war and the scourge of plague, to counteract threats to her absolutist government, to mobilize her economic resources and find new ways of coming to grips with her enemies. After the initial difficulties of transition from peace to war in 1700–1, Charles had managed to 'let the war pay for the war' in 1701–9; but he and his advisers were now convinced that the king's immediate authority was essential to force sacrifices on the well-to-do, and to reform the country's economy in such manner that the Crown would get money and credit to continue the war—in face of the loss of the Baltic provinces and most of the German possessions, temporary as these losses were believed to be.

The Polish route home could no longer serve any useful purpose

---

[1] S. Bonnesen, 'Jan Sapieha. Ett bidrag till historien om kalabaliken i Bender', *KFÅ* (1954); I. Stafsing, *Kalabaliken vid Bender* (1960).

because the Porte, bent on war with Venice,[1] was making treaties with both Peter and Augustus. Discussions consequently began for Charles XII's return through Imperial territory; Charles VI agreed to let the king and his little army and court reach Germany. To make political propaganda for a Habsburg mediation in the Great Northern War, the emperor tried to arrange an official welcome for the Swedish king; for that very reason, Charles insisted on being allowed to travel incognito, ahead of the main body of Swedes, when he crossed the Turkish border. First by post-chaise, then on horseback, he sped the long miles to Stralsund in a fortnight, arriving at its gate late in the night of 10/21 November 1714. It was the only German port of any importance, along with Wismar, which remained in Swedish hands after the Hanoverians had sequestered Verden and the Prussians Stettin, between 1712 and 1714.

Charles's future policy had been outlined in letters from Turkey to his sister Ulrika Eleonora, whom he looked upon as co-regent during his absence. They were the frankest he ever penned on his intentions. A new army would have to be forged. Meanwhile the enemies must be divided by secret diplomacy, to gain time and probe how far a separate but also reasonable peace could be achieved with any one of them. He would not make peace with any mental reservation of breaking it: it must be durable. After his reverses, he was now willing to contemplate the surrender of Swedish territory in return for equivalents obtained with the help of the recipient; he would also consider temporary cessions of ports or lands, with their incomes, against military aid but not against mere money loans. The military situation, though grave, was not irreparable. Augustus need no longer be regarded as an important enemy; he was far too embroiled in Poland, where anti-Russian feeling ran strong after years of virtual occupation, and where also the pro-Swedes recovered on news of Charles's homecoming. Denmark was financially exhausted, no longer thought to be capable of mounting an independent invasion of Sweden. More dangerous was the semi-disguised enmity of Prussia and Hanover, each intent on keeping parts of the Swedish empire sequestered in the name of friendship, Hanover being potentially the more dangerous once its elector became George I of England. Russia remained the most formidable opponent, as tired of the war indeed as was Sweden but just as determined to pursue it to a successful conclusion. Finland had been conquered after prolonged campaigns and Sweden herself was threatened with raids from the Russian galley-fleet, which she could not match, though Charles had long since ordered the building of a squadron of galleys.[2]

With the king's return a period of intense activity began. A Hesse marriage for Ulrika Eleonora, long negotiated, now became a fact: in the ambitious Frederick of Hesse, son and heir of the landgrave, anxious to

---

[1] Above, p. 637.   [2] Cf. below, pp. 806–7.

emulate other German princes who had become kings outside the Empire, Charles got a confidant with more war experience than the brother-in-law he had lost at Kliszów in 1702. The improved prospect for Sweden also brought the administrator of Holstein-Gottorp back into the fold. One of his officials, the able Baron G. H. von Görtz, was lent to Charles as a man well versed in finance, willing to help raise money at home and abroad. Görtz's influence with Charles XII has been much exaggerated, partly because he was later made the scapegoat for all the king's measures that were resented in Sweden. In reality Charles was the originator of policy along broad lines, usually arrived at after consultation with all his trusted advisers, Swedish and foreign. Görtz was one instrument among many of that policy, though an exceptionally valuable one because of his devotion and capacity for work; he became also increasingly prominent in diplomacy thanks to his useful contacts inside the anti-Swedish coalition, gained in the involved and contradictory negotiations of 1709–14, when he had attempted to safeguard the interests of a Holstein-Gottorp bereft of Swedish support.

Charles was determined to defend Stralsund and Wismar as long as humanly possible, in order not only to keep the war away from the Swedish mainland and gain time for Frederick of Hesse to organize the defence of the Swedish east coast against Russia, but also to blot out the memory of Perevolochna and restore, if only by heroic defeat, the lustre of Swedish arms—a very real commodity in the battle of wits now beginning. Hanover and Prussia formally joined Sweden's enemies[1] in time to take part, respectively, in one or both of the sieges of her last two German possessions. It was during the year spent in the defence of Stralsund, on his return from Bender, that Charles first promulgated his decrees for more intensively mobilizing Swedish national resources. Having left the town at the last possible moment before its capitulation, the king set foot in southern Sweden on 13/24 December 1715. The fall of Stralsund was followed by that of Wismar in April 1716.

The reform of the central administration, which the king had planned in Turkey, was now put into effect: six 'expeditions', each with its departmental head, the *ombudsman*, to work in close contact with the king, were separated from the old unwieldy chancery, which now became a specialized office for the conduct of diplomacy. The administrative colleges were not suppressed, but they were rendered relatively powerless to resist reform by the creation of new bureaucratic units which controlled the economic life of the nation in unprecedented (and resented) ways. The most important of these new instruments of the royal will were the 'exchequer of contributions' (*kontributionsränteriet*), which implemented

---

[1] Prussia declared war in April, Hanover in October, 1715. But Frederick William I had made anti-Swedish treaties with Peter and George of Hanover, and the latter a similar treaty with Denmark, in the summer of 1714.

Charles's radical policy of progressive taxation, and the 'loan-deputation' (*upphandlingsdeputationen*),[1] a body charged with arranging and funding foreign and domestic loans. It was the second of these which decreed such unpopular measures as the compulsory sale of iron to the State (to permit highly profitable resale abroad) and which fixed maximum prices for commodities inside Sweden. By the summer of 1718 the reform of the local administration, designed to encourage initiative in the economies of the provincial districts, had also been completed. The monopoly position of Sweden's iron was used to drive its price on the European market sky-high, but such was the need of other countries for it that even Britain's prohibition of trade with Sweden in February 1717 failed in its purpose. Britain wished to retaliate against Charles's privateering war on ships trading with Russian-occupied Swedish ports and also against his intrigues with the Jacobites; but the English had to buy the iron through middlemen and pay even more for it,[2] while Charles persisted with his privateers and with the Jacobites. The Jacobite negotiations had been opened through French channels and continued partly because Görtz saw in them a means for obtaining money and ships for Sweden—though Charles himself returned money conditional upon any real commitment to Jacobite plans—and partly because of the king's desire to keep George I in suspense as to Swedish plans and unable to deploy Britain's navy fully against Sweden in the Baltic.

With a new Swedish army and navy still in the making, Charles's military initiative was necessarily circumscribed. In the winter and spring of 1715–16 a campaign was rapidly improvised against Norway, but abandoned in June. Norway offered several tempting possibilities: an equivalent for losses elsewhere, or at least the gain of a strategically favourable frontier—Charles had the river Glommen in mind—such as would prevent future Norwegian invasions, the mere prospect of which had helped to paralyse the Swedish Council in 1709–14: an admirable area also for feints to keep some enemies guessing, since Frederick of Denmark and George of Hanover-Britain could both be threatened in or from it— George as elector by invading Hanover from southern Norway and from Sweden through Jutland, George as king by invading Scotland from the Trondhjem area. On the European scale, negotiations were on foot to split the anti-Swedish coalition.[3] The two most formidable enemies, George and Peter, were the most courted, George through Hesse and

---

[1] See G. Lindeberg, *Krigsfinansiering och krigshushållning i Karl XII's Sverige* (Stockholm, 1946).
[2] G. Lindeberg, *Svensk ekonomisk politik under den Görtska perioden* (Lund, 1941), pp. 336 ff.; cf. R. Hatton, *Diplomatic Relations between Great Britain and the Dutch Republic, 1714–1721* (1950), pp. 147 ff.
[3] See S. Jägerskiöld, *Sverige och Europa, 1716–1718* (Ekenäs, 1937); S. Feygina, *Alandskiy Kongress* (Moscow, 1959); C. Nordmann, *La Crise du Nord au début du XVIIIe siècle* (1962).

Holstein channels, Peter through Görtz and Polish intermediaries. The overtures to Peter may have contributed to the abandonment of the invasion of Scania projected by the anti-Swedish league for the autumn of 1716. A large Russian army was already stationed in Denmark for this purpose, and ways had been found whereby the English navy could serve Hanoverian policy by co-operating in the descent, when Peter insisted on postponing it for a year: the usual explanation is that reconnaissance had convinced the tsar that Swedish defences were strong enough to make the invasion too hazardous, but there are indications that Swedish feelers for a separate peace also had some effect. Postponement meant virtual abandonment of the Scania project, since Frederick of Denmark professed himself unable to commandeer Danish merchantmen to serve as transports once more the following summer. In spite of George I's attempts to reconcile his allies, Peter's decision created lasting distrust between Danes and Russians. The league was further weakened by growing fear of the tsar's ambitions in Germany, where he insisted on quartering in the winter of 1716–17 the army which returned from Denmark, thus causing friction with George of Hanover. Swedish diplomacy took full advantage of these divisions and was not seriously hampered by the temporary arrest of Görtz by the States-General in 1717, at the request of George I, for his share in the 'Gyllenborg plot'. Soon two sets of negotiations were running in parallel: one between Charles XII and George I, conducted through confidential one-man missions sent to and from Hesse, Hanover, England and Sweden; the other set, more publicly displayed though its real discussions were concealed, at a congress on one of the Åland islands between Russian and Swedish official negotiators, of whom Görtz was the king's chief agent, communicating with him by letters opened only by Charles himself and burnt after perusal. Both sets of negotiations were meant to paralyse the military activities of Sweden's enemies at a time when her ruler was not yet ready to take the initiative in the field himself.

At the same time, in spite of the web of consciously exaggerated and purposely misleading 'official' letters that have rendered them so difficult to unravel, these were genuine peace negotiations, so far as honestly intended to discover conditions and 'equivalents' satisfactory to both sides. Neither set of negotiations was brought to conclusion in Charles's lifetime. The terms offered were not acceptable to a king who was perfecting the largest army he had ever commanded. Peter would not restore any Baltic port south of Viborg; George would not be satisfied with a temporary possession of parts of Bremen and Verden; no party was as yet exhausted enough to discontinue the appeal to arms. Succession problems, moreover, rendered the situation fluid; neither George nor Peter was very safe on his throne. Charles negotiated both with James Stuart and with the exiled Tsarevitch Alexis. When Alexis lost his life,[1] the prospect

---

[1] Below, p. 733.

remained that Peter would die and Russian terms become easier: already rumour ran that he was mortally sick.

In Sweden also there was a succession struggle. There, in the event of Charles dying childless, Görtz and the Holstein party favoured Charles Frederick of Holstein-Gottorp, son of the elder daughter of Charles XI, rather than Ulrika Eleonora, his younger daughter, who had married a Calvinist and was the candidate of the Hesse party. The king himself—fond equally of his young nephew, whom he was training much as he had once looked after Max of Württemberg, and of his sister, the beloved 'Ulla'—would not, indeed could not, admit the existence of this problem; he kept hinting at marriage and heirs of his own body once peace was achieved. Görtz was too sincere a king's man, and the young duke too inexperienced and devoted to his uncle, to allow a proper Holstein party to be formed in Charles's lifetime. But Frederick of Hesse began to collaborate with those whom the reforms of the post-1715 years had offended or incommoded. They were now forming a nucleus of opposition to absolutism, though Frederick himself hoped to retain as much as possible of this system.

By the autumn of 1718 all was ready for a fresh military offensive. Few forces were needed in the east, since the Åland negotiations were still kept spinning. The new army, reorganized into separate corps suitable for combined operations, moved west: one detachment of 7,500 towards Trondhjem, the main force of 36,000 into south-eastern Norway. Some 14,000 were kept in reserve in south Sweden. Magazines along the border were full. Siege-engineers and other experts, mainly French who had served in the Spanish Succession War, were with the army. The artillery had been rendered more mobile and its speed of fire accelerated since 1709 by the new principles of Cronstedt.[1] Horses and ships were ready for use, not in mountainous Norway, but for the second stage of the campaign. What that second stage was to have been can never be decided with certainty. Charles XII was killed by a stray bullet while taking part in the siege of Frederiksten fortress, on the night of 30 November o.s. 1718, at the very outset of the campaign.[2]

He had certainly visualized getting his army to the Continent, across Danish territory; it remained essential to find battlefields outside Sweden proper, and only in Germany and Poland could he have hoped to get to grips with his enemies. Denmark and Hanover could reasonably have been

[1] See T. Jacobsson, *Artilleriet under Karl XII:s tiden* (Stockholm, 1943).
[2] Swedish historians are still sharply divided on the issue whether Charles XII was murdered by someone on his own side, instigated by Frederick of Hesse, or killed by an enemy shot: see *Carl XII:s död*, ed. A. Sandklef (1940) and *Sanning och Sägen om Karl XII:s död*, ed. N. Ahnlund et al. (1941); also articles in *KFÅ* since that date. L. Thanner, *Revolutionen i Sverige efter Karl XII:s död* (Uppsala, 1953), pp. 73 ff., is firmly convinced of Frederick of Hesse's guilt; W. Holst, *Fredrik I* (1953) and *Ulrika Eleonora* (1956) considers the case not proved. The present writer holds the view that Charles XII was killed by what he himself might have called 'an honest enemy bullet': See *Charles XII of Sweden*, pp. 495 ff.

expected to make peace once Charles approached their territories. Peter, who could not be attacked frontally across the Baltic, where he was well prepared for defence on both land and sea, might be brought to battle once more in Poland or Lithuania, even in Russia. Yet it seems probable that Charles was thinking more of Germany. Many princes shared the emperor's alarm at the growth of Russian influence, and this would offer a rich field for diplomacy once Charles brought his army to Germany. There, as he reminded one of his generals—half grimly, half jokingly—a night or two before his death, 'we once fought a thirty years war, and we might yet fight a forty years one'.[1] Nothing, however, had been decided when the king was killed. Frederiksten would have fallen in a few more days: the offensive across the river Glommen had begun, and the king had indeed only postponed his departure for that sector of the front for a few days, to await Görtz with fresh reports from the Åland congress.

The difference in aim between Charles XII and his critics can easily be exaggerated. The Swedish diplomats and councillors who blamed his bellicosity were quite as strongly wedded to their country's great-power position. Frederick of Hesse, proclaimed king in 1720 after winning the succession struggle for his wife at the cost of the absolutist régime,[2] had called off the Norwegian campaign to concentrate on that struggle; nevertheless he continued Charles's policy of playing off the Hanoverians against the Russians. He had imbibed Charles's doctrine of sacrificing nothing before real guarantees were received. For several reasons, however, including his hope of founding a Hessian dynasty in Sweden (through Hanoverian support for his brother to succeed him should he die without issue), he let himself be outmanoeuvred by Anglo-Hanoverian diplomacy.[3] George I and his advisers genuinely wanted a reasonable peace for Sweden with Russia, leaving Sweden a foothold on the eastern Baltic, and were equally anxious to form a league that would scare Russia out of the Empire and Poland. But it was more urgent to get the *quid pro quo* in advance from Sweden: Bremen and Verden for Hanover, Stettin for Prussia, the duke of Holstein-Gottorp's lands in Sleswig for Denmark, as well as monetary compensation for giving up the Swedish territory held by Denmark round Wismar. These arrangements, which reflect the relative weight of members of the anti-Swedish league, were embodied in the Treaties of Stockholm and Frederiksborg, negotiated by George I with French diplomatic support in 1719–20. Augustus of Saxony was not included. Into the Treaty of Nystad, later, the tsar was to force a clause giving Russia the rôle of mediator with 'King Augustus and the Republic', but no peace was made between Sweden and Poland till 1731.[4]

---

[1] T. Westrin, 'Karl XII:s sista planer', *HT* (1895), pp. 341–2.
[2] See vol. VII, pp. 350–2.
[3] E. Carlsson, *Freden i Nystad* (1932), pp. 23–8, 297–330; O. Reinius, 'Sveriges utrikespolitiska läge, 1720–1721', *KFÅ* (1936).
[4] N. Ahnlund, 'Sveriges sista fred med Polen', *KFÅ* (1915).

The dilemma Charles XII had always seen so clearly—how to obtain real guarantees of military assistance from would-be allies—ensnared Frederick and the Swedes once they had signed away possessions against promises. They strove manfully to make George I implement his solemn assurances of naval support, but in a rapidly changing political and economic situation it was impossible to force him to go to war against Peter for Swedish objectives. The South Sea Bubble paralysed English initiative. The emperor became less anti-Russian as southern problems began to preoccupy him. The Swedes had been fighting the Russians at close quarters ever since Frederick had committed himself to George in the peace negotiations, the Russian fleet penetrating at times even into the Stockholm archipelago. By 1721, therefore, Sweden had to sue for peace. Under the treaty signed at Nystad during the night of 10–11 September, Finland was restored to Sweden, except for the important frontier district of Kexholm in the south-east and part of Karelia; but Ingria, Estonia and Swedish Livonia were lost in their entirety.

Sweden's great-power position was now at an end. Her remaining footholds in the Empire—Wismar, Stralsund and the Greifswald district of Pomerania, all of which were restored to her in 1719–20—were not enough to sustain it. There were Swedes who wished to reopen the struggle with Russia as soon as opportunity should offer, perhaps on Peter's death. There were others who hoped to regain the lost provinces in a more peaceful way through the offices of Charles Frederick, duke of Holstein-Gottorp, who, after Ulrika's victory over him in the succession struggle, had taken refuge in Russia and married a daughter of Peter: were he to become Sweden's king, might not the Baltic provinces come back as the dowry of a Russian-born Swedish queen? But most Swedes felt that the fight for the great-power position had been so long and so hard that it was a relief to be rid of it and of the 'Stora Ofreden [Great Unrest]' it had caused.

The reasons for the loss of Sweden's extraordinary empire have been debated ever since 1721. Was it the fault of Charles XII, who refused peace in the years when luck was with him? But it is questionable whether Augustus, Frederick of Denmark or Peter would have been satisfied with minor concessions from Sweden down to 1709; they too believed in a just cause and were as toughly determined to let the dice of war decide, under God, the issue. On the contrary, it can be argued that the only hope of keeping the great-power position died with Charles XII. With the disappearance of his personal drive and military genius, and with the reopening of all kinds of domestic issues, the war effort had to suffer, at least momentarily. The bold risks taken by the dead king could not be attempted by either of the contestants for his throne till some of these issues had been decided. Besides the disputed succession, there was controversy on absolutist versus constitutional government, socio-economic tension between noble and non-noble, a bitter struggle for office in general. Against such a background the momentum of the 1718 campaign was lost, the army called home, the war-chest divided to gain adherents. In the long run, however, the accident which removed Charles XII before the much more confidently expected death of Peter probably had less effect than the gigantic pressure of a new Russia. Unified at home, with revolts suppressed, a population of at least ten million and increasing technological knowledge, Russia was already a match for a Sweden of marvellous organization but with a population of not more than three million and a scattered empire, which, so experience proved, could not be defended against its natural enemies without the ties and sacrifices, as well as the advantages, of possessing an ally among the great powers.

THE ECLIPSE OF POLAND

'ECLIPSIS POLONIAE' was a phrase used by a leading statesman of the time, Stanislas Szczuka, vice-chancellor of Lithuania, to describe the condition of the Polish Commonwealth at the beginning of the eighteenth century. It would have been hard yet to talk of the 'collapse' of a State which still had a place in every European constellation, and whose favours were still courted by powers which themselves were facing great internal changes. This was not yet the period when Poland, narrowly controlled by powerful neighbours, would be the helpless butt of other people's politics. On the other hand, increasing anarchy was already preventing the Commonwealth (*Rzeczpospolita*) from exploiting such political opportunities as came its way. Contemporaries held that this was only the temporary eclipse of a State which until recently had been powerful. If by 1721 the long years of war were a thing of the past in this part of Europe, so too was the former balance of power between its various States. The Habsburgs were immensely strengthened by their control of Hungary and by their succession in Italy and the Low Countries. Russia, following the Petrine reforms and her conquests on the Baltic coast, had grown into the leading power in the North. In Prussia rigorous government was building the foundations of militarism. At the same time, Sweden had ceased to count and Turkey was capable of active policy only by fits and starts. Poland, restricted in scope for diplomatic manoeuvre and penalized by the interference of dominant neighbours, sank into the deepest gloom of the so-called Saxon era.

This was the result of a series of complicated processes reaching back to the beginning of the sixteenth century. It was compounded of the exceptionally privileged position of the gentry (*szlachta*), as against the underprivileged serfs and burghers, and of the virtual hegemony of the magnates, whose rivalries shattered the country's unity. The weakening of royal power, at a juncture when most European States were moving towards absolutism, was in itself significant, connected as it was with free elections and the accompanying covenants (*pacta conventa*) enforced on the king. The parliament (*Sejm*), which might have made good the defects of royal authority, was in turn beset by a serious disease, the *liberum veto*, which from 1652 had permitted individuals to protest against every bill presented, paralysed all efforts at reform, frustrated any systematic financial and military policy. The permanent taxes, raised mainly from Church and Crown possessions, barely supported the peacetime army, 12,000 men from 1678. Even the 'extraordinary' taxes of war-time, providing for the enlistment of necessary troops, were levied only with great difficulty: if a war dragged on, the Rzeczpospolita faced an unpaid and mutinous army. Furthermore, Poland's economic potential was decreasing. Based principally on agriculture, it was adversely affected by the decline in prices during the seventeenth century. Intensified exploitation of the peasantry, whereby the szlachta strove to compensate themselves for the decreasing profitability of their estates, served only to lower the efficiency and productivity of farming. Supposing that a mercantilist policy could have encouraged development, the paralysis of State decision-making ruled out its realization. The immense war damage already sustained in the middle of the century had in any case left deep scars on the whole economy.

In spite of all this, it is not sufficiently clear why a real breakdown occurred at the turn of the seventeenth century. Before that time the same basic malaise had not given rise to a serious crisis. So far, resources had been found to rectify reverses. Piławce was followed by Beresteczko, capitulation during the Swedish invasion of 1655 by a general mobilization of Polish society in the struggle for independence; Russian successes were answered by Cudnów and Połonka, the Treaty of Bučač (1672) by Chotin (Chocim) and Vienna; and Lubomirski's reactionary rebellion had been offset by the tentative reforms of 1673–8. But a new generation was growing up amidst the stream of violence. It possessed all the disruptive vices of its predecessors, without their determination or stamina. In its fierce defence of 'golden freedom' political prudence was lost. Private interests prevailed. Nor was there much belief in the possibility of a general improvement. The outlook of this generation was most exactly described in a tract, *De vanitate consiliorum* (1699), by Stanislas Heraclius Lubomirski, arguing that each and every State institution, however well organized, is soon corrupted into an instrument of evil: in consequence, no change can bring lasting benefit. Others, who did not look so deeply, placed their trust in Sarmatism—that boastful, conservative philosophy which exalted the Polish szlachta above all nations on earth. Sobieski's victory at Vienna, as recounted in the psalmody of Vespasian Kochowski, was to become for them a visible sign of their leading position in Christendom. They regarded the Polish constitution as unrivalled and thought of other peoples with condescension, as living in gross slavery.

In such circumstances the efforts of an individual, were he John III or Augustus II, did not count for much. Even Sobieski, a monarch in the classical Sarmatian mould, failed to inspire wide support for his political plans. His military talents, the appeal of a personality mingling the charms of French culture with flourishes of Turkish and Tatar style in his dress and in his new palace at Wilanów, which so well typifies the meeting of East and West—these advantages availed nothing in politics. All his initiatives were opposed by a majority of the magnates and by the szlachta who followed their lead. It was to be no different with Augustus Wettin, the first German to occupy the Polish throne. He had the benefit of wide political experience in his efforts to modernize both Saxony, which he had inherited, and Poland, to which he was elected; and it might have been hoped that the Poles would gain by closer contacts with the industrious and thrifty Saxons.[1] Yet here again the picture is presented, tragic at times, of an intelligent minority struggling against the noblemen and gentry who stubbornly defended the *status quo*.

To some extent this situation, like the state of Polish society in general, can be explained by the fact that the country was involved in two wars which made excessive demands on her strength, the War of the Holy League and the Great Northern War. In the wake of a quarter-century of military burdens, the recovery of stability depended largely on a long period of peace. The prolonged military and financial effort spent on fighting Cossacks, Russians, Swedes and Turks had weakened the framework of society; a renewal of the fighting could spell mortal danger. Yet only seven years passed after the Peace of Żórawno (1676) before Poland, by going to the relief of Vienna, entered on another protracted and costly war with the Ottoman.

The main object of the Holy League was to recover territories lost to the Turks. John III hoped to recover Podolia, gain Moldavia and Wallachia, and put an end once and for all to the Tatar raids which were mercilessly destroying the south-eastern region of the Rzeczpospolita. His expeditions brought no lasting results: Kamieniec Podolski was not recovered, Moldavia yielded only a couple of frontier fortresses. The Turks showed unexpected powers of resistance, while the szlachta, arguing that papal and imperial subsidies sufficed for their army's needs, refused to vote the requisite taxation. Poland was incapable of pursuing the war intensively. In this situation the court decided on an important withdrawal in the east. John III resigned himself to the conditions agreed in Moscow in 1686 for an alliance and perpetual peace between Russia and Poland, thus not only preventing Russia from taking sides against him but enlisting her aid in the Ottoman war. In return for the promise of further help against the Tatars, Poland finally renounced Smolensk, the Ukraine beyond the Dnieper, Kiev and Zaporoże. She also recognized the protectorate of the tsar over Orthodox Christians in the Rzeczpospolita. In this way the agreement of 1686 foreshadowed the political supremacy which Russia was to win during the years to follow in her relations with Poland. Ironically, it coincided with the peak of Polish cultural influence in Moscow. A wave of painters and sculptors, who had arrived there in the 1660s, left their mark on Russian art; Polish language and costume, radiating from the tsar's court, were also much in vogue.

[1] W. Konopczyński, 'The Early Saxon Period, 1697–1733', *Camb. Hist. of Poland*, vol. II (1941), p. 3.

At first, the military results of the alliance were meagre indeed. Golitsyn's expeditions into the Black Sea steppe all failed; not until 1696 was Peter able to occupy Azov. In 1686, with great effort, Sobieski put 40,000 men into the field. He reached the Danube delta, but could not hold his conquests. It was the Austrians who benefited, for at this juncture they conquered Buda. Succeeding Polish expeditions, including the largest one of all in 1691, were similarly fruitless, their only gains being Chotin and a few second-rate Moldavian forts. Worse, the Tatars raided Polish territory as far as Lwów, while the Turks maintained contact with their strong garrison in Kamieniec. Sobieski's failures were largely conditioned by lack of support from the szlachta. Of the seven Sejms summoned between 1685 and 1695, only two produced tangible results. The taxes voted were mean in proportion to the army's needs. In 1697 it claimed arrears of 26 m. Polish crowns—almost ten times the annual revenue. For years at a time the troops went unpaid. Paid badly, the soldiers fought badly and their numbers constantly fell off: in the 1690s scarcely 30,000 could be kept together. Only the king's personal authority restrained the army from forming a confederacy (*konfederacja*) to obtain its due.[1] This situation demanded a swift settlement with Turkey, which was not impossible. Through the mediation of the Tatars, the Turks announced their readiness to withdraw from Kamieniec and Podolia. French support too could be expected, since the outbreak of the Nine Years War increased Louis XIV's desire to detach Poland from the Austrian alliance. The main opposition would come from Poland's allies, who refused even to contemplate peace so long as Turkey did not acknowledge their conquests.

Like many an elected king before him, John III was intent on controlling the election of his successor, in the hope of permanently linking his dynasty to the throne. A useful move in this direction would have been to subject to Sobieski rule one of the principalities beyond the frontier—a principality to be connected to the Rzeczpospolita through the person of the ruler. In his first years John had thought of recovering the duchy of Prussia, and after 1683 of using Moldavia. These calculations no doubt prompted his repeated expeditions to the Balkans. The king specially favoured his eldest son James (Jakub). He took him to meetings of the Senate and gave him command over the army; they sat together under the royal canopy whenever ambassadors were received. Foreign support was

---

[1] The forming of confederacies in Poland was similar to the practice of 'covenanting' in seventeenth-century Scotland. The szlachta formed armed associations, bound under oath to fight together for the removal of any dangers to their liberties, or sometimes simply for the defence of the country. Often only small local groups were involved; but sometimes a 'General Confederacy', including all the szlachta of Poland, was declared. The confederates appointed a leader, governed themselves by majority voting—in contrast to the *liberum veto* of the Sejm—and were subjected to military discipline. The practice was in no sense illegal or rebellious. The right of confederacy was a well-established constitutional liberty which the king could not legally oppose.

sought for the dynastic plan in France and Austria. Louis XIV was readier to commit himself, but in the end hopes of the emperor's aid outweighed other considerations. It was decided to marry James to Elizabeth of Neuburg, Leopold's sister-in-law. James had competed for the hand of Ludwika Karolina Radziwiłł, heiress to a great fortune in Lithuania; but her guardian Frederick William, elector of Brandenburg, looked askance at the strengthening of the Sobieskis and gave her away first to his own son, then to Charles Philip, prince of Neuburg and brother to James Sobieski's future wife. Marriage to the Neuburg princess gave James possession of the rich Ohlau (Oława) lands in Silesia and the promise of Imperial support in the next Polish election. On the other hand, the marriage caused a rift within the Sobieski family itself. John III's French wife, Marie d'Arquien, whose influence grew with the king's illness, did not savour the prospect of losing control of policy when her husband should die. She began to work for the election either of one of her younger sons, still dependent on her, or else of some candidate who would dare to marry her. She outmanoeuvred James by knitting close ties with Versailles, signed a private agreement with Louis XIV in 1692, and supplied France with a large and vital consignment of corn. The rift in the royal family continued until John's death and effectively sealed the fate of his dynastic plan, all the more since there existed in Poland a strong opposition to the Sobieski family's continuance on the throne.

The centre of opposition lay in Lithuania, which in practice meant the Sapieha family. Early in his reign John had supported the Sapiehas, hoping thereby to curb the powerful Pac clan, and thanks to royal protection the Sapiehas had come to concentrate all available Lithuanian offices in their own hands. Casimir Sapieha became *Wielki Hetman*[1] and Benedict Sapieha treasurer of Lithuania. Controlling both army and treasury, they were able to conduct the business of the provincial *sejmiki* (dietines) as they wished and so to influence the choice of judges, elected annually in the *sejmiki*. The Sapiehas dreamed of the throne; if that were beyond their reach, then they would hold out for Lithuanian secession. Their sustained agitation against the king's dynasticism succeeded in winning most of the magnates of the Kingdom too. They even infiltrated the corridors of Berlin and Vienna, for Hohenzollern and Habsburg were

---

[1] In Poland, the title of Hetman referred to the highest army officers. There were four in all: a Grand Hetman and Field Hetman for the Kingdom of Poland (*Wielki Hetman Koronny* and *Hetman Polny Koronny*), also a Grand Hetman and Field Hetman for Lithuania (*Wielki Hetman Litewski* and *Hetman Polny Litewski*). They commanded the standing army, but not the general levy; the Field Hetmans were of lower rank. (In the Ukraine, among the Cossacks, 'Hetman' meant 'leader' or 'chieftain'.) 'Koronny' (translated 'Crown'), in such titles as Grand Hetman of the Crown, refers to offices of state of the Kingdom of Poland, as distinct from those of the Grand Duchy of Lithuania. The dual Polish-Lithuanian Commonwealth had two separate administrations, one for the Kingdom, the other for the Duchy. During the Saxon Union a third administration, with its own officers, was maintained in Saxony. For Polish institutions generally see vol. VII, ch. XVI.

alike uneasy about strengthening the Polish Crown. Already, in 1686, Brandenburg had signed treaties with Sweden and Austria guaranteeing the inviolability of the Polish constitution and the principle of free election. It was a simple matter in these conditions for the opposition to disturb the Sejm; they saw clearly enough how increasing anarchy would weaken the king's standing. Royal adherents among the magnates were few. The king could more hopefully have appealed to the middling szlachta; but when in the Sejm of 1689, owing to unprecedented attacks on him by the senators, the members demanded a 'Horseback-Sejm' (in which all the szlachta could have participated and confronted the magnates), John did not accede to their demands.[1] The king himself lacked determination, and perhaps could never bring himself to embark on a fratricidal struggle with the very circle of people from whom he originated. In any case the outcome of such a struggle, like the real wishes of the szlachta concerning royal power, was most uncertain. The opportunity passed, and the problem was never so sharply defined again in John's reign.

The lethargy of Sobieski's last years was followed by the longest interregnum in Polish history, 1696–7. It was caused by the violent quarrels between James Sobieski and his mother, which killed any chance of another Sobieski being elected. The queen did not hesitate even to break off the convocational Sejm (*konwokacja*)—the special Diet (in the form of a country-wide confederacy) summoned under the presidency of the Primate, as Interrex, to safeguard the State during a vacancy in the Crown and to prepare the time and place of the next election. Unpaid soldiery added to the chaos, helping themselves to arrears of pay by ravaging the countryside, especially the queen's estates; only with the greatest difficulty was some arrangement with them patched up before the election. These disturbances naturally laid Poland wide open to foreign interference in it. Her allies, particularly Russia, were opposed to any French-sponsored candidate who might sign a separate Polish peace with Turkey. To prevent this, Peter I began to concentrate a powerful force on the Lithuanian frontier. Meanwhile, however, some of the szlachta declared for the prince of Conti, the candidate of Versailles, while the French ambassador, the Abbé Melchior de Polignac, showered money and promises on all sides. On the electoral field itself, at Wola on 27 June, most of the szlachta chose Conti; the Sapiehas supported him; and the Cardinal Primate, Michael Radziejowski (1645–1705), declared him king. Nevertheless, after Conti's supporters had left the field, many members of the electoral assembly, won over by Russian threats or by papal and Imperial propaganda, called on Frederick Augustus Wettin, elector of Saxony, to assume the crown.

[1] K. Piwarski, 'Między Francją a Austrią, z dziejów polityki Jana III Sobieskiego w latach, 1687–90', in *Rozprawy Wydziału Historyczno—Filozoficznego*, 2nd ser., vol. XLIV, no. 1 (Cracow, 1933), pp. 96–100.

After this controversial double election, much depended on the speed with which the two competitors would act. Wettin displayed the greater energy. By 22 July 1697 he was on the Polish frontier, at Tarnowskie Góry, at the head of the Saxon army. There he was welcomed by a delegation led by the son of the Grand Hetman of the Crown, John Stanislas Jabłonowski, *wojewoda* (governor) of Ruthenia. Hastening from the banquet to Cracow, Augustus publicly heard Mass for the first time in the abbey of Piekary. There too he swore a covenant assimilating the constitutional rights of the Lithuanian szlachta to those of the Kingdom. In the first days of August he entered Cracow, where coronation preparations had already started. The opposition confederacy of Stephen Humiecki, which failed to gain control of the army, did not interrupt them. On 15 September 1697, in the cathedral on Wawel Hill in Cracow, Augustus was crowned king of Poland. Thus, in a manner foreseen by no one, a new era opened in Polish history—the era of the personal union with Saxony.

The Union offered large possibilities of economic and political development for both States. Economically, the junction of Saxon industry with Polish raw materials, timber and agricultural produce promised an important stimulus to output and trade. Saxon mercantilism, given access to the Baltic and to the trade-routes across Poland, might do much to restore the prosperity of the Polish towns. From the earliest months, Augustus II contemplated the creation of a Baltic trading company, the rebuilding of the port of Połąga (Polangen, north of Memel) and the consequential growth of Polish and Saxon sea power. This was the more significant because the treaty of 1686 gave Poland the right to conduct trade with Persia across Russian territory. It is only when one remembers these Baltic plans of Augustus II—further-reaching than his later attempt to recover all of Livonia—that it is possible to understand the stubborn determination of Charles XII to cut short the Polish-Saxon Union, which seriously threatened to alter the power structure of northern and central Europe. Obviously, the realization of these economic and political schemes would have been easier had Poland and Saxony possessed a common frontier; and it was not without relevance that the lands which divided them—Austrian Silesia and the Prussian Oder provinces—had once been Polish. Hopes were raised in Poland of recovering these lands, while in Saxony it was hoped to exploit the Union to play a larger part in German politics and check the growing power of Brandenburg. These hopes were crushed during the Great Northern War, which was fatally to weaken the Rzeczpospolita. Even before the war, in fact, elements of weakness in the Union became evident. Besides a mutual religious antagonism—Sàxony fearing the spread of Catholicism, Poland distrusting Protestantism—alarm was felt as to the implications of the new government. In his electorate Augustus had temporarily succeeded in weakening the Estates: the szlachta dreaded a similar policy in the Rzeczpospolita.[1]

The immediate problem was to defend the throne against Conti, who on 25 June 1697 approached Gdańsk (Danzig), a well-fortified city which supported Augustus and refused to admit the French squadron. Conti managed to get ashore at neighbouring Oliva, but was too weak to challenge the Saxon army, which attacked Oliva on 9 November. He then set sail for France. His supporters—Humiecki, Adam Nicholas Sieniawski, Radziejowski, the Sapiehas, the Lubomirskis—agreed to negotiate with Augustus and on 5 May 1698 terminated Humiecki's confederacy.

It was now possible to resume the Ottoman war, which, as conducted by Sobieski with large armies, had yielded neither Kamieniec nor significant gains in Moldavia or Wallachia, the object equally of Austrian and Russian ambitions. The stiffening of Polish cavalry with Saxon infantry and artillery augured better for a campaign here. As it happened, after being delayed by Humiecki's confederacy, it was held up by conflict between the Sapiehas and the szlachta in Lithuania. With the disappearance of Conti, however, the Sapiehas came over to the Saxon side with alacrity, and their return to royal favour disarmed the discontent of the Lithuanian szlachta: an agreement was patched up on 22 July 1698. This was already too late in the year for a distant campaign, so operations were confined to a further attempt on Kamieniec. More disappointing still, the Habsburgs now resolved to make peace with the Turks on the basis of *uti possidetis*[2]— a precept convenient for them but disastrous for Poland, since it would leave Kamieniec outside her frontiers. Hence it became urgent to achieve some positive military success before peace was concluded. Like Sobieski, Augustus wanted the Danubian principalities for dynastic reasons. Preparations for an expedition were under way shortly after his accession. His emissary at The Hague, Bose, collected arms and recruited miners and engineers qualified for siege-work; forage and food supplies were gathered in Poland; the experienced General Trautmansdorf was ordered to draw up a plan of campaign. In September 1698 the army concentrated round Lwów. Saxon regiments which had been engaged on the Austrian front also arrived. Yet the late season, which could turn roads into impassable mud, made success very doubtful. The army at last moved towards Kamieniec on 8 September and engaged in a victorious skirmish near Podhajce with Tatar cavalry; but on 17 September a meeting of the Senate decided to halt the expedition. The weather, new troubles in Lithuania, and the opening of peace talks explain this decision. A portion of the Polish army

---

[1] Contrary to the outlook of earlier German historians, attention has been given to the early awareness of the economic potential of the Union by R. Forberger, 'Zur wirtschaftlichen Neueinschätzung der säschsisch-polnischen Union', in J. Kalisch and J. Gierowski (eds.), *Um die polnische Krone* (Berlin, 1962), p. 209; cf. J. Kalisch, 'Sächsisch-polnische Pläne zur Gründung einer See- und Handelskompagnie am Ausgang des 17 Jh.', *ibid.* p. 45.

[2] For the peace at Carlowitz, cf. above, pp. 626–7.

THE ECLIPSE OF POLAND

was to be left to besiege Kamieniec, while some of the Saxon forces were detailed to stay in the Holy Trinity Trenches, to guard Poland against Tatar forays. The remaining Saxons were to be sent to Lithuania.

On 22 September a grand parade marked the end of the campaign. During this parade a quarrel broke out which all but caused an armed clash between Polish and Saxon soldiery. The incident began with an assault by Michael Potocki, *starosta* (bailiff) of Krasnostaw and son of the Crown Field Hetman, on the person of the king's trusted supporter Przebendowski, the *wojewoda* of Malbork (Marienburg). Struck down by several blows of a mace, Przebendowski none the less managed to escape, but Potocki then entreated the troops to join in expelling the Saxons. Any such thoughts were soon scotched by the prompt return of the two hetmans, who had been with the king in the Lithuanian encampment. The situation remained tense, however, with Augustus ordering an immediate court martial for the initiator of the outrage. A group of cavalry immediately broke loose, reproaching the Grand Hetman of the Crown for bringing the German king and his army into Poland. Augustus thereon resolved to suppress the rebels by force, bidding the hetmans at least remain neutral if they would give no practical assistance. The Grand Hetman Jabłonowski and other dignitaries undertook to punish Potocki, but declared that they would have to take up arms against the king if the Saxons attacked the Polish camp. Augustus had thus suffered a double setback. He had achieved nothing in the Turkish war, and he was made to feel most keenly the limitations of his powers as elected king of Poland.

In the course of the Balkan expedition news arrived of an attempt to seize Elbląg (Elbing) by the elector of Brandenburg. In October 1698 Prussian regiments had tried to surprise the old town on the Vistula delta; in November they threatened to bombard it. The Hohenzollern was forcibly bringing to notice a condition of the Treaty of Bydgoszcz (1657) by which Poland had promised either to cede the port, now much silted up, or to redeem it with 400,000 thalers. This condition had not been executed, but it was only in 1698 that Brandenburg chose to enforce it. In fact, the Elector Frederick III decided on the move only after secret conversations with Augustus at Jansborg in June. Among other matters, they discussed an exchange of the county of Mansfeld for the duchy of Krossen (Krosno), which stretched from Lausitz (Lużyce) to the Polish border and would have given Poland and Saxony a common frontier. In return for the promise of this exchange and of cash rewards totalling 250,000 thalers—100,000 on occupation, 150,000 when the next Sejm met —Augustus ceded Elbląg. Later, he undertook to reveal the most convenient date for the occupation. He settled for October 1698 as soon as he knew that the Moldavian expedition had been called off. It looks as if he wanted to have his hands free during the Prussian operation, although the documents of the Elbląg incident have yet to be thoroughly investigated:

we do not know whether Augustus's behaviour after the closing of the Turkish campaign was a deliberate attempt to exploit the Polish-Prussian dispute and so enforce the exchange of territory discussed at Jansborg. At all events he acted with great decision and proposed summoning the Estates of the duchy of Prussia to war with the elector.[1] He suggested that his own army take part and that the general levy be raised in Poland.[2] The Senate rejected these proposals: 'Cardinal Primate Radziejowski, the Hetman with his officers and the majority of the Senate...did not permit them, not wishing to involve the Rzeczpospolita in a war after fifty years of fighting.'[3] The senators had been influenced by Prussian thalers. At once public opinion reacted and broadsheets demanded Hohenzollern removal from ducal Prussia. The presence of the Polish army, slowly regrouping near Elbląg, encouraged the elector to negotiate, while Peter I brought pressure on him, not wishing to see the dispute spoil his projected anti-Swedish alliance, which was to include both Frederick and Augustus. Thus the elector consented to restore Elbląg in return for the 400,000 thalers. The Polish treasury did not possess such a sum, but Augustus wanted to offer it all the same, for it would have given him the right to occupy Elbląg with Saxon troops. The Senate saw this as a dangerous stiffening of the royal initiative, and dissented. Finally, after a year's negotiations, it was agreed to hand over the Crown jewels as a pledge of the debt, and in February 1700 Frederick surrendered Elbląg to the Polish commissioners, Stanislas Szczuka and Andrew Załuski.

During the months when the king's attention was concentrated on the Balkan expedition and the Elbląg affair, the contest with the Sapiehas in Lithuania once more came to a head. The agreement of July 1698 was superficial and civil war soon flared up. It was the Sapiehas who enjoyed the first blaze of success. Casimir Sapieha, son of the Grand Hetman and Lithuanian Steward of the Horse, shattered the szlachta assembled by Ogiński near Jorburg. The szlachta appealed in despair to the king. In August 1698 they formed a confederacy to resist the Sapiehas. Their aim was to disband the standing army, but they knew that the Sapiehas would never accept this without a fight, the general levy having been called to Grodno for 15 October. When the hetman and troops returned to Lithuania from the Turkish war, the conflict moved into a critical phase. The king could not ride to Lithuania in person owing to the Elbląg crisis, but he dispatched his army under General J. H. Flemming. The general levy of Lithuanian szlachta, assembled at Grodno, swore not to disperse until the Lithuanian army was disbanded. Augustus forestalled a clash by enjoining both sides to submit to his arbitration. At the same time he

---

[1] For opposition to Brandenburg sovereignty in this Polish fief, see vol. v, pp. 544–9.
[2] The szlachta were bound to present themselves in person when summoned by the king to defend the frontiers.
[3] Jan Stanisław Jabłonowski, *Pamiętnik* (Lwów, 1862), p. 17.

ordered Flemming to defend the szlachta in the event of a Sapieha attack. Unable to count on Flemming's neutrality, Casimir had to capitulate. A new agreement was signed on 20 December which disbanded 3,000 Lithuanian cavalry, leaving only 1,140 dragoons and 2,960 infantry. The influence of Augustus increased after this victory, but the szlachta remained wary of his intentions and soon requested that all foreign soldiers be withdrawn from the country. Thus deprived of their military forces, the Sapiehas nevertheless held on to their offices of state; nor was their economic power affected. The family continued to attract a powerful clientèle of people hostile to Augustus. Hence Augustus's position in the Grand Duchy, though much stronger than Sobieski's had been, did not justify the contemporary political squibs describing Lithuania as a country of 'absolutum dominium'.

In 1699 a Sejm was summoned with a view to calming the country and settling once and for all the consequences of Humiecki's confederacy. Besides business connected with the Peace of Carlowitz, which restored Kamieniec Podolski to Poland, the king invited discussion on the Elbląg affair, the Lithuanian situation, payment for the army, and the future of the Saxon forces in Poland. To the provincial *sejmiki*, reforms in the judiciary and in the monetary system were proposed. The szlachta rejected even minor changes in the existing law. They placed greatest emphasis on the problem of the Saxon forces. Most of their resolutions began by thanking the king for the favourable peace with Turkey but finished by demanding the unconditional withdrawal of Saxon troops from Poland. The szlachta from several provinces had instructed their representatives not even to debate the matter and to break up the Sejm if the king tried to retain the Saxons. This attitude was inspired by the conduct of the Saxon army, which subjected the population to many arbitrary acts and requisitioned supplies intended for the Polish army. The szlachta were outraged that this behaviour should go unpunished and feared the king might use his Saxons to destroy 'golden freedom'. This in turn alarmed the court, lest some confederacy inimical to the king be brewing, especially as Jabłonowski did contemplate moving the Crown army to Warsaw and only the king's urgent remonstrances prevented him from doing so. The opening of the Sejm on 16 June heightened tension, for at once the member for Chełm declared that he would not proceed with the election of the Speaker until the Saxon forces had withdrawn. Many others took the same stand and it looked as if the Sejm would have to be broken off. The situation was saved by Stanislas Szczuka, who argued that, there being no disagreement on the Saxon forces, it would be sensible to begin debate while still insisting on their withdrawal. This problem overshadowed the whole session, which lasted till 31 July. Eventually, the king signed a *pacta conventa* agreeing to withdraw the Saxons. By this concession Augustus strengthened his position in Poland and did something to heal the fracture caused by the double election. But it is also significant that the Saxon troops were removed to the vicinity of Połąga, in the direction of Livonia.

His plans for a victorious war with Turkey now wrecked, Augustus entered an anti-Swedish coalition for which the foundations had been laid in 1697–9. Denmark's had been the most active rôle. As early as 1697 Hainz, the Danish ambassador in Moscow, had been seeking to construct an alliance with Russia against Sweden. This mission had proved sterile owing to Peter's preoccupation with Turkey, but in 1698 the Carlowitz peace overtures changed the situation. Neither Peter nor Augustus felt able to prosecute the Turkish war without Habsburg help, but they saw a way of turning their attention to the North. Their plans were concerted at a meeting at Rawa Ruska on 8 August 1698. In that same month Augustus reached agreement with the Livonian nobles through their delegate Reinhold Patkul, who resolved to join Poland; a secret clause promised Livonia to the rule of Augustus in person, as distinct from that of the Rzeczpospolita. As elector of Saxony, Augustus had already become the ally of the Danes on 26 March. On 24 August Russo-Danish negotiations were concluded in Moscow, and in November an alliance between Russia and Saxony. Peter wished to draw in the elector of Brandenburg as well, but Frederick III, cautious as always, refused to commit himself formally. Nevertheless, it was widely believed that Brandenburg would enter the war, and Poland too. The date for the attack on Sweden waited on the ratification of the Peace of Carlowitz.

When war broke out in Livonia in February 1700, Augustus counted on his Saxon army mastering the province quickly, helped by the discontent of the population with Swedish rule.[1] As rulers of Livonia, the House of Wettin might be able not only to buttress its authority but even to reach for permanent possession of the Polish throne, while gaining an enormous revenue derived from Russian and Lithuanian trade through Riga. On the other hand, every extension of the war would complicate the king's position in the Rzeczpospolita, increasing the tension between court and dissident magnates. Augustus took a calculated risk, which in the light of the war of 1675–9 between Sweden and Brandenburg did not seem excessive; but his attempts to surprise and then to besiege Riga failed. On news that the Danes had sued for peace at Travendal, the Saxon forces, in spite of their numerical superiority, retreated beyond the Dvina and Augustus began to press France and Brandenburg to act as mediators with Sweden on his behalf. These negotiations were hastened by the Russian defeat at Narva. Augustus's policy had changed tack smartly. His ambassador in Paris, General Jordan, signed an alliance with Louis XIV providing that in the event of war over the Spanish succession Saxon regiments would help France in return for a fat subsidy. Augustus hoped that Louis would accordingly facilitate a peace with

---

[1] On the 'Swedification' of Livonia in the 1690s see vol. v, p. 537.

Sweden. His renewal of the Russian alliance at Birże in February 1701 was merely to insure himself against an expected Swedish attack: he refused to extend this agreement to include the Rzeczpospolita, a fact which further proves his desire to limit the conflict with Sweden.

Charles XII, however, was not inclined to compromise with Augustus. The Swedes recognized that the Union of Saxony and Poland could threaten their position both in Germany and on the Baltic. They were resolved to take the opportunity of breaking the Union. Prompted by the magnatial opposition in Poland, Charles planned to draw the Rzeczpospolita into the Swedish orbit by replacing Augustus by a weaker ruler there, on the pretext of protecting its freedom. It was even anticipated that Poland's eastern frontiers would be restored at Russian expense to make good the transference of Courland and Polish Livonia to Sweden. In practice, the scheme meant that Poland would become dependent on Sweden, politically and economically. The crucial factor here would be the resistance which the Poles might or might not show to Swedish pressure. The fundamental dilemma as to which was the more important, the liberty of the szlachta or the independence of the country, was not immediately evident. Many Polish minds were dominated, rather, by the notion that to defend their king would be to subject Polish interests to Saxon; there was no lack of magnates to exalt golden freedom in exaggerated terms and so dispel other people's doubts to the contrary. So it had been in the seventeenth century and so it was to remain to the end of the Rzeczpospolita. A pro-Swedish faction soon began to form, ready to co-operate in different ways with Charles XII.

Early in 1700, on the flank of the Livonian front, civil war in Lithuania flared up anew. The 'republican' szlachta wanted to abolish constitutional differences between Grand Duchy and Kingdom, and especially to limit the powers of the Lithuanian treasurer and grand hetman. In this struggle they enjoyed the sympathy of the Ogińskis and other great families whose position had been undermined by the Sapiehas. Under the magnate Michael Wiśniowiecki, the republicans defeated the Sapiehas at Olkienniki, near Vilna, and declared the Sapieha offices and possessions forfeit. They then sought the protection of Augustus, offering him their forces against the Swedes. But Augustus stood to gain little if he lost his rôle of arbiter in Lithuania. His relations with the Sapiehas had improved, after all, and they had furnished detachments for the Livonian campaign. By contrast, the republican forces—mainly a general levy equal only to an isolated engagement—were incapable of facing the well-drilled Swedish professionals. It soon became clear that Lithuania alone was in no position to contain the advance of Charles XII's army. The Grand Duchy was obliged to seek Russian help, later signing independent agreements with Peter, in 1702–3, by which the tsar promised reinforcements and subsidies in return for continued resistance to the Swede. These independent agreements shook the foundations of the Polish-Lithuanian Union and severely cramped the diplomacy of the Rzeczpospolita. A more immediate result of Olkienniki was that it prolonged the rift in Lithuania. It led to the murder of the captive Michael Sapieha and the utter devastation of the Sapieha estates. Attempts at reconciliation, by Augustus himself or by his senators, proved futile. The Sapiehas sought an external protector in Charles XII, binding their fortunes to his and setting up as managers of the pro-Swedish party. It was probably with them that the idea of deposing Augustus originated, for they regarded him as the hidden author of all their misfortunes.

There was no such open split as yet in the Kingdom itself. There the treasurer, Raphael Leszczyński, the greatest magnate of Wielkopolska (Greater Poland), leaned perhaps towards Charles XII, as did the primate, Radziejowski. But they were not men blindly to follow a Swedish lead. Radziejowski had far-reaching political ambitions, wanting to act as first minister, but he did not support the deposition of Augustus; he considered it necessary only to curtail what effective powers the king still held. He was ready to accept Sweden and Prussia as guarantors of such an arrangement, in which he as primate would control the king's initiative and any necessary consultations with the szlachta and the guarantors. This opposition group attached special weight to the backing of Prussia, where in that same year 1701 Frederick had been crowned king. The continued weakening of Polish influence in this region indeed opened fresh prospects for Prussia of winning Elbląg, of advancing into the 'royal way'—the belt of territory separating Brandenburg from East Prussia—and of securing Courland in succession to the Kettlers, with whom the Hohenzollerns had close family links. Nevertheless, Prussia could not be brought to intervene in the Northern War: the Spanish Succession War and Prussia's defensive agreement with Sweden of 1703 were limiting factors.

The most acute threat to Augustus came from James Sobieski, who was in close contact with Charles XII. The young Sobieski, now living in Silesia, saw that the moment had come for him to revive his pursuit of the throne. He was quite prepared to pay for his advancement by ceding territory to Sweden—Courland, for example. He began to muster his adherents and advised the Swedish king that 'il faut donner aux Polonais de bonnes paroles et se tenir à cet axiome, *fac et excusa*'.

The activities of the opposition took shape during the Sejm of 1701, summoned to take precautions against a Swedish invasion. The szlachta affirmed that Poland, dissociating herself from Augustus's policy, would remain neutral. The members again refused debate until the king had withdrawn his Saxon forces. They arranged to reassemble at the end of the year. Meanwhile Charles XII struck at the Saxon army, defeating them on the Dvina. Afterwards he broke into Courland and the Swedish cavalry raided deep into Lithuania. Charles rejected proposals of mediation put forward by the Polish senators. Instead, he advanced the deposition of Augustus as the only acceptable condition of a settlement. In spite of this menacing situation the Sejm, when it eventually reassembled, did not vote an increase in taxation or of the army. Its meetings were broken off through the action of the Sapieha party. Such was the state of unpreparedness in which Poland set about the task of repelling the Swedish invasion.

Augustus's efforts at making peace were still fruitless. Disillusioned with French mediation, he refused to ratify the alliance with Louis XIV and changed his attitude to the Spanish Succession War. His hope now was that an agreement with the emperor would open the way to an understanding with Charles XII, with the help of the Maritime Powers. The Swedish reaction was negative; the embassies of Countess Aurora Königsmark and of Friedrich von Eckstädt Vitzthum, whom Augustus sent to the Swedish camp, had no effect. The only result of the change of alliance was that French diplomacy now turned against Augustus. It encouraged Charles to attack Saxony and to depose Augustus from the Polish throne. Versailles no doubt hoped to gain an ally for the Spanish war. With that same object in view, however, Leopold I and the Maritime Powers obstructed a settlement in the Baltic.

In this plight, deprived of external aid and uncertain of his own subjects, Augustus in 1702 faced a campaign which would decide the future of the Swedish establishment in Poland. The Swedes occupied Vilna and Warsaw, defeated Augustus at Kliszów and took control of Cracow. In many parts of the country the population resisted the invader, especially in Lithuania, Podlesia and Mazovia; burghers and peasants fought alongside the szlachta in partisan bands. But a general mass resistance never occurred. The Crown army under Hieronymus Lubomirski, the new Grand Hetman appointed to soften his disgruntlement with the king, facilitated Swedish success by avoiding the battle of Kliszów. The general levy of Wielkopolska maintained strict neutrality. Augustus had insufficient forces for a counter-offensive. On the other hand, Charles XII lacked the military strength and civilian support needed for a decisive blow. Saxony was undefended, and the Swedes might well have turned in that direction but for the diplomatic warnings issued in their own interest by the anti-French allies. In Poland, the greater part of the szlachta were for Augustus. Immediately after the occupation of Cracow, the szlachta of Małopolska (Little Poland) met at Sandomierz and formed a confederacy in his defence. Later, elements of the szlachta of Wielkopolska and Lithuania did the same. Althcugh these confederacies did not much increase the armed strength of the Rzeczpospolita, they showed that the majority of the szlachta still recognized Augustus as lawful monarch and would not readily bow to foreign pressure.

Swedish successes nonetheless sufficed to quell any hopes Augustus still retained about strengthening his authority: a condition of szlachta support was that the king renounce all constitutional changes and solemnly guarantee the country's liberties. Yet Augustus did not flinch before the reproaches of the szlachta on account of the outbreak of a Cossack rising, the Palej rising in the Dnieper Ukraine in August 1702. During Sobieski's Turkish war, lands on the right-bank Dnieper had been appropriated for the Cossacks, because their military help was needed; but with the peace of 1699 the Sejm had ordered the disbandment of the Cossack militia. Magnates hoped to multiply the serfs available for estates lying near the Ottoman frontier and ravaged by the war. This prospect the Cossacks of course rejected, and an attempt to coerce them failed. The situation was the more tense since by 1700 the first steps for restraining Ukrainian separatism had already been taken. In 1696 Ruthenian was banned as an official language. Energetic measures were taken to eliminate the Orthodox Church and to receive her bishops into a new religious communion. So, when the Cossack commanders, Semen Palej and Ivan Samuś, turned against the supremacy of the szlachta, they had the general support of the Ukrainian townspeople and peasantry. The Cossacks captured the fortress of Biała Cerkiew and attempted to rouse their kinsfolk on the left-bank Dnieper. It looked as if the times of Chmel'nyćkyj[1] were returning, for the disturbances spread to the peasantry of White Russia, Podlesia and Podolia. At first the szlachta was unable to control the rising; the general levy scattered on news that the Cossacks were coming. Only when royal and private armies were concentrated under Joseph Potocki and Adam Sieniawski could the outbreak be contained to several smouldering localities. Fighting indeed continued in the Ukraine until 1704, when Russian intervention extinguished the remnants of the movement—an intervention, on behalf of the great Polish landowners, that was to encourage the formation of a tsarist party in Poland.

The Cossack operations had meanwhile detached important forces from the main theatre of war, thus reducing the Polish effort against the Swedes. Despite continual defeats, the Saxon army remained the heart of resistance. In spring 1703 the Swedes broke the Saxon cavalry at Pułtusk; in the autumn, after a difficult siege, they took Toruń, which was defended by sound Saxon infantry. Swedish and Saxon armies alike maintained themselves at the expense of the Rzeczpospolita by raising forced contributions, so that the burden of war fell on the Polish people. And yet the Poles entirely failed to sink their differences in order to repel the intruder. The Lublin Sejm of 1703 indeed manifested real support for Augustus: it voted a standing army of 48,000 and the requisite taxation. The realization of these dispositions was another matter, especially as the Swedes now occupied large areas of the country. Furthermore, the Lublin Sejm had excluded the opposition members from Wielkopolska and disregarded

[1] See vol. v, pp. 565–6, 572–4.

the recommendations of the Primate Radziejowski—two developments which crystallized a more determined pro-Swedish faction.

The szlachta of Wielkopolska, meeting at the *sejmiki* in Sroda, founded an anti-Saxon confederacy. It was patronized by Radziejowski and by Charles XII, who promised help in maintaining the ancient rights and privileges of the szlachta. On 14 January 1704 another assembly was convoked in Warsaw, under Radziejowski's own direction. It proclaimed a general confederacy, the deposition of Augustus II, and a new election. Its business was speeded by the increasing number of Polish territories daily falling into Swedish hands. It is true that members of the Warsaw Confederacy, notably Radziejowski, regarded it as a passing device for negotiating with Sweden and removing the Swedish troops. Charles XII, on the other hand, was working for a permanent arrangement. He wanted the guarantee of a submissive king on the Polish throne.

His original candidate, James Sobieski, had been captured near Breslau (Wrocław) on his way to Poland and was now in a Saxon prison. So Charles himself found a fresh candidate, the 27-year-old Stanislas Leszczyński, son of the recently deceased treasurer. In later years Stanislas was to be distinguished for breadth of vision, but for the time being family ambition dominated, pushing him towards the Crown at the cost of subservience to the Swede and great personal humiliation. Charles's choice was not approved by the other magnates. Radziejowski henceforth sought a new understanding with Augustus II. The Grand Hetman Lubomirski, originally a member of the Warsaw Confederacy, also detached himself from the Swedish cause. Indeed the whole confederate movement, which enjoyed little support outside Wielkopolska, was cracking. The election of Leszczyński, which took place in Warsaw on 12 July 1704, amid the Swedish soldiery, was a lamentable sight. The handful of szlachta assembled there were far from unanimous; the Podlesian members made lively protests. Nevertheless, for the first time in history, a Polish king had been deposed and a new one elected under the coercion of foreign troops. It is curious to note that the next time this occurred, in 1733, the same Leszczyński was involved as a national hero.

The election of Stanislas soon proved a political blunder. For the Swedes he was a liability. They met great trouble in their efforts to enforce recognition of the new king, completely dependent as he was on them and on their friends like the Sapiehas, without authority or armed force of his own. For Poland it was a fatal step. The country was split into two camps, the great majority of the szlachta denying the legality of the election, while Leszczyński was too weak to win control. The prospects for Augustus and stronger government were gravely compromised.

If most of the szlachta reacted against the Warsaw Confederacy, Augustus for his part shelved his absolutist aims. Even in Saxony, pressed by military and financial necessity, he rehabilitated the Estates. The turning-point there was the downfall, in 1703, of Beichling, the hitherto omnipotent minister who wanted to drive Saxony faster along the road to capitalist development and absolutism. Augustus was now better placed to exploit the loyalty of the szlachta. An incident in the army put this to the test. When Lubomirski went over to the Swedes, two-thirds of the Crown army turned against him, forming a confederacy at Opatów, at the head of which stood the officers sworn to Augustus. A new assembly, meeting on 20 May 1704 at Sandomierz, attracted senators and szlachta in great numbers. Under the direction of the Royal Swordbearer, Stanislas Denhoff, a general confederacy was proclaimed, committing the participants to fight the Swedes in defence of the legitimacy of Augustus II. The Warsaw Confederates were denounced as traitors, the Warsaw election as invalid; the pope was asked to excommunicate and deprive Radziejowski; the resolutions of the Lublin Sejm concerning finance and the army were renewed. Augustus once more pledged himself to uphold all rights and privileges, observe the *pacta conventa*, revive the Sejm, and when the war was over to withdraw all foreign troops from the Rzeczpospolita. He now had an opportunity of governing the country in co-operation with the General Confederacy of Sandomierz, which acted on the principle of majority voting and conferred wide powers on its leader, Denhoff. It was in this condition, threatened in her most fundamental right of free election, that the Rzeczpospolita herself at last declared war on Sweden.

When Poland took this step, she chose to ally with the tsar, who had been at grips with Sweden since 1700. Such an alliance had been proposed by the Russians in 1701, but then the Poles would only join the anti-Swedish camp if Kiev and Smolensk were returned to them. Peter had refused to bargain on those terms. In 1702–3 his diplomacy achieved agreements with the Lithuanian szlachta, whose hatred for the Swedish-backed Sapiehas had driven them into the war. On the Polish side, negotiations were only resumed after the election of Leszczyński. The Rzeczpospolita, now keenly interested in Russian help, was no longer able to set a high price on the conditions of co-operation and an alliance was signed on 30 August 1704, in Narva, after a month of negotiations.[1] The Poles were headed by Thomas Działyński, *wojewoda* of Chełmno, and Russia represented chiefly by F. A. Golovin; at Działyński's request there also participated Christopher Białłozor, canon of Vilna and Lithuanian resident at the tsar's court, but now attached to the Polish ambassador there. Działyński did not hesitate to reproach the Russians for the irregularity of parts of the Lithuanian agreements, and the Treaty of Narva was finally a work of compromise. The Russians declined to

---

[1] Moscow, Central State Archive of Ancient Documents [CSAAD], Polish documents, Collection 79, year 1704, no. 27, pp. 62–80: Działyński-Golovin negotiations. Golovin headed the Russian department (*prikaz*) of foreign affairs until his death in September 1706; he was succeeded by Count G. I. Golovkin, who in 1709 acquired the new title of Chancellor.

confirm the perpetual peace of 1686, but neither did they seduce the Poles to an open alliance, offensive and defensive, against all enemies: clearly they had the Turks and Tatars in mind. The Poles, for their part, failed to obtain the right to economic exploitation of those right-bank Dnieper lands which by the treaty of 1686 were to remain depopulated. What the Russians gained was an ally who would divert the bulk of the Swedish forces and leave Russia free to improve her position on the Baltic shore. The Poles, besides getting military and financial aid, succeeded in annulling the Russo-Lithuanian agreements and also in persuading the Russians to suppress the Cossack rising, which Działyński made a condition *sine qua non* of the alliance. Under this pressure the Russians ordered Ivan Mazepa, hetman of the left-bank Ukraine and an enemy of Palej, to capture the rebel Cossack. Palej was ambushed and sent to Siberia; later, after Mazepa's desertion, the tsar brought Palej back to the Ukraine, in time for him to take part in the battle of Poltava. The forts on the right-bank Dnieper, which Mazepa also captured, received Russian and Cossack garrisons, the Poles returning only in 1711, after Peter's surrender on the Pruth.

The Treaty of Narva boosted Augustus's fortunes at a time when fresh defeats were being heaped upon him. Charles XII overran Lwów, kept Augustus out of Warsaw and there, on 28 November 1705, imposed the signature of a treaty which subjected Poland to Sweden politically and economically. Sweden claimed to recruit on Polish soil and garrison Polish fortresses. The Rzeczpospolita must annul all treaties not approved by the Swedish king. Swedish merchants, exempted from most Polish customs and other duties, were authorized to settle and conduct their businesses throughout Poland. The port of Połąga was to be closed, its trade diverted through the Swedish ports of Livonia. This treaty, finally, was to be added to the list of *pacta conventa* solemnly accepted by all candidates for the Polish Crown. Even so, the Treaty of Warsaw did not include the Swedish claims in full, for these extended to Courland and Polish Livonia; in Stockholm the conquest of Gdańsk was recommended, and only the initiative of the Maritime Powers prevented the attack on that port contemplated by Stenbock in 1704. As it stood, however, the treaty demonstrated the utter dependence of the Leszczyński faction on Charles XII. It was to inhibit the later attempts at a *rapprochement* between Stanislas and the General Confederacy of Sandomierz.

It was now resolved in Moscow and Dresden to mount a combined Russo-Saxon-Polish assault on the forces of Charles XII. In February 1705 a Russian army 40,000 strong moved towards Vilna from Połock. Drawn into various engagements with Lewenhaupt's brigade, it was unable to prevent the coronation of Leszczyński in Warsaw on 4 October. General Pajkul also tried to obstruct the coronation, but his force of Saxon, Polish and Lithuanian cavalry was defeated on the outskirts of the capital on 31 July. So the plan for crushing Charles XII was postponed till next year. Yet Charles's situation at this time was not easy. To the east he faced a regular Russian army of 35,000, on the west 20,000 Saxons under Schulemburg. In Volhynia and the Lublin province lay detachments of over 20,000 Cossacks, ready to join the Saxons. The Polish Crown army had concentrated on the southern provinces, while Lithuanian banners waved over the line of the Bug. Over 100,000 soldiers were thus ranged against Charles, who controlled less than half that number—counting 12,000 raised by Leszczyński's adherents. Fearing above all the amalgamation of the allied forces, Charles as always sought salvation in attack. He detached Rehnskiöld's corps of 12,000 to the Silesian frontier and marched with the rest of his troops towards Grodno, where the Russians were dug in behind the town's fortifications. Rather than try to storm their positions, Charles decided to cut the line of communications linking Grodno to the Russian frontier, thereby making contact with the Swedish forces in Livonia and threatening Smolensk. Satisfied that Grodno was safe, Augustus left for Warsaw at the head of his cavalry. His aim was to organize, with Schulemburg, a grouping capable of destroying Rehnskiöld. But Schulemburg had taken the field alone at Wschowa (Fraustadt), where the Saxon army was shattered. The tsar therefore ordered his army to retire on Kiev. Interrupted by the stubborn defence of Nieświcz, Birże and Lachowice, the Swedish pursuit was unavailing and the Russians managed to join other forces assembled by Peter on the line of the Dnieper.

The Swedes, too few to control the whole countryside, occupied themselves in razing captured fortresses and burning the estates of Augustus's adherents. The ruin of their properties obliged several magnates to recognize Leszczyński—among them Charles Radziwiłł, chancellor of Lithuania, and John Stanislas Jabłonowski, uncle to Leszczyński and *wojewoda* of Ruthenia. But in general the Swedes gained little; they had to guard their recruits like prisoners to stop them deserting to Augustus. Eventually, the conquered lands were returned to their owners by the forces of Michael Wiśniowiecki and Gregory Ogiński, the Lithuanian hetman, loyal to Augustus. Seeing that the Russian frontier was well defended, Charles XII decided that the best way to destroy the Polish-Saxon Union, and to establish Leszczyński's rule on firmer foundations, was to overrun Saxony. From August 1706, therefore, the Swedish army began to move westwards from Volhynia, burning and destroying as it went; early in September, having combined with Rehnskiöld, it crossed Silesia into Saxony. Stripped of its forces, Saxony could offer no resistance: fortresses surrendered without a fight and towns opened their gates to the invader.

Meanwhile the Russians, together with a Polish army, crossed the Vistula and at Kalisz on 29 October defeated Mardefeld's Swedish division guarding Wielkopolska. Almost the whole of the Rzeczpospolita was thus restored to Augustus. Yet he could hardly forget his occupied electorate. In fact, Augustus had been in touch with Charles XII as soon as the Swedes entered Saxony; and before the turn of the tide at Kalisz, where only the Grand Hetman's insistence had forced a battle, his emissaries had accepted peace terms. On 24 September 1706 the Treaty of Altranstädt deprived Augustus of the Polish Crown, forced him to break with the tsar, and required the surrender not only of Russian units in the Saxon army but also of Peter's ambassador in Dresden, Patkul. Augustus was to recognize Leszczyński and pay a large cash indemnity. When his Russian ally proved disinclined to enter Saxony for a further confrontation with the Swedes, and when hopes of Habsburg intervention and an Austro-Swedish conflict had faded, Augustus left Poland altogether. Before departing, he assured the Polish senators and the Russian ambassador in Poland, Dolgoruki, that he would return when Saxony was evacuated.

The leaders of the General Confederacy of Sandomierz, having lost their king, did not for this reason consider abandoning the struggle. In place of Augustus they opted for James Sobieski. The son of the saviour of Vienna, freed now from the Saxon prison where he had been incarcerated, could attract wide support among the szlachta by the magic of his name; and if the election of Leszczyński were annulled, he might unite the two confederacies. This scheme appealed to the tsar, who promised support. Sobieski negotiated with the Confederates, but owing to the express hostility of [Charles XII did not dare claim the crown.[1] The Confederates then suggested other candidates to Peter: Eugene of Savoy or Francis Rákóczi II. The Savoyard candidature was calculated to cause an Austro-Swedish war; the alternative of Rákóczi was foreseen in the event of Louis XIV mediating in a Russo-Polish peace with Sweden. There would be one of two possible advantages: continued war in the company of a powerful new ally, or peace with Sweden and a tie with Hungary. The tsar, however, feared that the Confederates would turn to Leszczyński after all, once the expected Swedish offensive to the east materialized, and so Peter was anxious to see him replaced quickly; he therefore suggested Sieniawski, now Grand Hetman of the Crown and a leading magnate in his own right. Sieniawski discussed the offer with the tsar but did not accept it, having no wish to close the door on an understanding with Leszczyński or with Augustus, to whom the Confederates were again inclined after James Sobieski's withdrawal. Hence, so far as Peter was concerned, the Confederates failed to offer any serious alternative to Leszczyński, unless Augustus could be brought back. At the same time they sharply opposed tsarist annexations on the right-bank Dnieper and in Lithuania, where Russian troops had seized Bychów and Mohilev.

[1] Dolgoruki to Golovkin, 3 Feb. 1707, CSAAD, loc. cit. 1707, no. 25, p. 5; Potocka to Dolgoruki, 14 June 1707, ibid. no. 89, pp. 27-8.

Russo-Polish recriminations died down in 1707, when the Swedish army returned to Poland. The problem of a new election was deferred, the Russian alliance strengthened by a new military oath. Moreover, Charles XII's preparations for an eastward thrust obliged Peter to seek allies on the Swedish flank. The obvious choices were Denmark and Augustus of Saxony, still smarting from the humiliation of Altranstädt. Negotiations with Augustus were undertaken by two pro-Russian members of the Szembek family—Stanislas, the new primate, and John, the vice-chancellor—and by Constantine Szaniawski, bishop of Kujawy; on the Saxon side, by Flemming. Defying Peter's displeasure, the Szembeks travelled to Silesia at the end of 1707 to maintain better contact with Dresden. Yet Augustus, for all his repeated promises, could not bring himself to come back to Poland. Peter duly lost hope of his return: 'We have no news of Augustus's departure from Saxony, nor do we entertain any lively hopes concerning it.'[1] He would even have been prepared to allow the recognition of Leszczyński by the Sandomierz Confederates if thereby he could have ensured Leszczyński's neutrality in the Russian conflict with Sweden.

This conflict now developed swiftly. Early in 1708 Charles crossed the Vistula. After halts at Smorgony and Radoszkowice, he moved out on 17 June in the direction of Moscow, bursting through the Russian defences near Hołowczyń. Then dogged resistance along the Moscow road, with shortages of food and forage, pushed him south to the Ukraine, where Mazepa—in contact with Leszczyński since 1705—had decided to support the Swedes.

Leszczyński's forces took no part in this campaign, however, for on 16 June Stanislas retired from Radoszkowice into the heart of the Rzeczpospolita, intent on fortifying his own position—no easy undertaking now that the Confederates of Sandomierz were masters of much of Poland. The Grand Hetman Sieniawski made his headquarters at Lwów, whence the Crown army controlled the whole of Małopolska and parts of Wielkopolska and Mazovia. Bishop Szaniawski stayed in Cracow, acting as go-between for Moscow, Dresden and Lwów, and also between Sieniawski and the Szembeks. Denhoff was cultivating the szlachta of the Cracow and Sandomierz provinces, keeping them true to the Confederacy. In these circumstances, the Confederates had more reason than ever to lament Augustus's absence.[2] The arrival of Leszczyński and his army from Radoszkowice embarrassed them. Yet Augustus, whose appearance now at the head of his Saxon army could have changed matters decisively, constantly hesitated. The tsar, retreating before the Swedes, sent no help.

---

[1] Golovkin to Ukraincow, 27 July 1708, CSAAD, ibid. 1708, no. 16, p. 48.

[2] The basic sources for these developments are in the Czartoryski Library at Cracow (Sieniawski correspondence, nos. 5786, 5790, 5791, 5792, 5798, 5925, 5943, 5962; Szembek files 450, 451, 452) and in the Główne Archiwum Akt Dawnych, Warsaw (Radziwiłł archives, no. VI-II-79, files 4, 10, 95, 124, 142, 281, 288, 306).

Nevertheless, the Confederates were able to hold out against Leszczyński because they possessed a strong army and could exploit a rupture in Leszczyński's camp. Before his departure for Russia, Charles had forbidden his hireling to summon the Sejm or attempt a reconciliation with the opposition. Yet only a very small group of Leszczyński's collaborators approved his plans for war with Russia; most preferred neutrality and an understanding with the Sandomierz Confederates.[1] An armed showdown between the two sides was forced by Joseph Potocki, nominated Grand Hetman of the Crown by Leszczyński (in place of Sieniawski), *wojewoda* of Kiev and leader of the war party, who saw in Sieniawski a rival who deprived him of the full enjoyment of his authority. The battle occurred on 21 November 1708 at Koniecpol, where Sigismund Rybiński, chamberlain of Chełmno and Lewis Pociej, treasurer of Lithuania, defeated Potocki. At the same time Sieniawski approached Leszczyński with impossibly stiff conditions: the maintenance of the Russian alliance, declaration of a general peace, a free election. Leszczyński's entire dependence on the will of Charles XII, in turn, weakened his hand in discussions with Augustus's supporters. Sieniawski was playing for time, expecting that the tsar would either be victorious himself or assist the Confederates. In the New Year of 1709 a messenger reached Sieniawski with intelligence that Augustus was already in touch with Russian envoys in Leipzig: on conclusion of a treaty, he would return to Poland. This and the further news that three regiments of Russian regulars under General Inflant were drawing close to Poland markedly raised the spirits of the Confederates. Sieniawski marched to meet the Russians, while Denhoff rode to Silesia to assist the Szembeks hasten Augustus's return. Sieniawski's forces and Inflant's Russians, reinforced later by the corps of Field-Marshal Goltz near Czarny Ostróg, then wheeled to seek Leszczyński. Summoned by Charles XII to support the Swedes and unable to risk an engagement with Sieniawski and Goltz, Stanislas retired beyond the Vistula. In the end, already weakened by Lewenhaupt's defeat at Lesnaja, the Swedes received no assistance whatsoever from Poland in the crucial weeks preceding the climax of Poltava on 8 July 1709.

It was then, when news of Charles's flight reached Saxony, that Augustus at last made up his mind to return to Poland. The Russians advanced from the Ukraine; Sieniawski and Goltz expelled Leszczyński's forces; Leszczyński himself sought refuge in Swedish Pomerania; and in mid-August the Saxon army crossed the Polish frontier. Welcomed by the Sandomierz Confederates and Leszczyński's former adherents alike, Augustus hastened to reoccupy the throne which three years earlier he had abandoned. Poltava thus cancelled out Altranstädt. The Confederacy

---

[1] J. Gierowski, 'From Radoszkowice to Opatów: the History of the Decomposition of the Stanisław Leszczyński Camp', *Poland at the XIth International Congress of the Historical Sciences in Stockholm* (Warsaw, 1960), pp. 217–37.

24-2

of Sandomierz had played its part in the victory. It had prevented Leszczyński from uniting Poland in the Swedish cause and had contained his army when it tried to rescue the Swedes. Poland was now released from the fetters of the Treaty of Warsaw.[1]

In the backwash of the Swedish defeat, however, Russian power accumulated. Poltava transformed Russo-Polish relations. The phase of close collaboration, imposed by the common struggle against Sweden, came to an end. Instead, once re-established on the throne, Augustus II tried to win free control of his own policy. This became all the more difficult as pressures from Moscow mounted. Russia refused to withdraw her garrisons from the fortresses of the right-bank Ukraine, sent her troops deep into Polish territory, and began to interfere in Poland's internal affairs. The General Council of the Sandomierz Confederates, meeting at Warsaw in spring 1710 to annul the abdication of Augustus II and to vote necessary supply for the army, considered also measures for stemming Russian influence. Had Augustus's policy of independence indeed been consistently supported by the other authorities of the Rzeczpospolita, the tsar's interference might well have been curbed. A recurrence of the conflict between golden freedom and royal authority supervened to increase it.

Sweden's defeat and the restoration of Augustus opened a period of critical importance to Poland's destiny. In large measure it was to make her eventual collapse inevitable. During the wars of the 1650s a programme of reconstruction had been drawn up which should have enabled the country to hold its own against neighbouring military absolutisms. Fifty years later, its political independence had already been impaired. Hence aspirations for internal reform combined with efforts toward emancipation. The problem was posed in so many different shapes that no means was found of cutting the Gordian knot. And behind all the country's formidable political difficulties lay sheer exhaustion.

Poland certainly gathered the fruits of indecision. Long years of war, with the constant billetings and tramping of troops across the country, had brought widespread ruin. Saxony itself suffered seriously from Swedish occupation: in Poland, the Russian, Swedish and Saxon armies alike lived off the land over which they manoeuvred, falling mercilessly on village and town for contributions of money and supplies. It is estimated that 60 m. thalers were extorted in this way—more than triple the total revenue of the Rzeczpospolita throughout the Great Northern War. Gdańsk, the only city never to surrender to foreign arms, yet 'contributed' several hundred thousand thalers. The severest retribution was meted out to political opponents. For instance, in 1706 the Swedes gutted 140

---

[1] For a different evaluation of the rôle of the Sandomierz Confederates see J. Feldman, *Polska w dobie wojny północnej* (Cracow, 1924). Feldman discounted their rôle, but was not acquainted with the Russian material or with various Polish collections, such as the Sieniawski correspondence.

illages belonging to one of Augustus's supporters in Volhynia; next year he Russians behaved likewise in Wielkopolska; and in 1716 the Saxon rmy burned the estates of the king's opponents. In the wake of this lestruction, whose proportions have never been explored, came pestilence nd famine. A vast epidemic of the bubonic plague, spreading through he whole country between 1706 and 1713, thinned out the population; everal towns—Wschowa, Sieradz, Łęczyca—were virtually depopulated. High mortality also occurred in years of poor harvest, especially 1709–10 n Lithuania and 1714–15 in Małopolska. The population of the Rzecz-ospolita, which had reached about 10 million ca. 1650, fell to scarcely million. It is not surprising that whole villages and even towns lay mpty. The survey of Crown properties undertaken in 1710–15 constantly eported heavy losses of population, buildings destroyed, untilled fields, bsence of estate inventories and lack of corn for sowing. In some areas— he Grodno lands in Lithuania and the Libus lands near Cracow—up to o per cent of the farms were desolate.

These reverses did not alter the relation of szlachta and serfs. The ormer high level of the *corvée* was maintained; personal restrictions on he peasant were not relaxed. It was hard to reconstruct an estate in hese circumstances, or even to re-create conditions of minimum prosperity. Only in the next generation did the countryside rise above the catastrophe. The towns presented an even sorrier picture. They had suffered in the tream of wars for over half a century. Previously, in the unfavourable nvironment of a manorial economy based on serf labour, the towns had t least managed to keep going; the new misfortunes brought ruin. Nowhere, perhaps, in the Europe of the time was the plight of the towns o pitiable. Burned, sacked, depopulated, overburdened by debts to lergy and magnates, subject to anarchistic exploitation by the court bailiffs (*starostas*) of royal towns or by the owners of private towns four-fifths of the total), they had no resources for reconstruction, let lone development. Urban craftsmanship, competing with rural crafts upported by the szlachta, was reduced to minimal production. Commerce tagnated; except at Gdańsk, the more important purchases were made beyond the frontiers—at Breslau, Leipzig, Frankfurt-am-Oder, Riga. Many towns were ruralized, most of their citizens occupied not in urban rades but in agriculture, and depressed like serfs to the *corvée*. The urban niddle class, already weak, became quite incapable of any significant rôle n Poland's political or economic life; and the task of modernizing the State was rendered that much more difficult.

The misfortunes of war hit the nobility too, both the middling sort and he magnates. The armies had no respect for aristocratic immunity: and noblemen's estates, once devastated, never produced the same revenue as before. The magnates, often with many estates scattered through different provinces, escaped more lightly, but the middling szlachta was exposed to full catastrophe. They sought asylum with more powerful neighbours, crowding the magnatial retinues. Rivalry between magnates and gentry thus ceased to be a major factor in the politics of the Rzeczpospolita It was replaced by the more frequent contests of competing magnates and their clientèles, who habitually obstructed the formation of the royal party desired by patriots—for, after so much grim experience, some of the szlachta were indeed interested in reform, if only partial reform.

The first decade of the eighteenth century witnessed a creeping disintegration of the State. The Sejm met only in 1701 and 1703; from 1704 only the councils of confederacies ever met. Royal authority was doubly compromised by the foreign imposition of a dethronement, then of a new election. Administration was disorganized by Stanislas's appointments to offices already held by Augustus's nominees. By contrast, the hetmans powers attained unprecedented proportions; besides command of the army, they took control of finance and conducted foreign policies of their own. Shrunken revenue hindered the enlistment of sufficient troops; it did not allow even for the repair of equipment. The powers of the *sejmik* were distended, moreover, in the vacuum left by central authority. They took independent decisions on matters affecting taxation, recruitment, the principles of internal and external policy. Thanks to self-instituted prorogations, they would meet without the accustomed royal writs. Many of their resolutions were influenced by whatever faction was dominant at the moment and by the pressures of foreign and Polish military. The only workable substitute for the royal power lay in the authority of the general confederacies: but the split between the Warsaw Confederacy and the Sandomierz Confederacy, added to the interference of alien protectors, effectively curtailed their capacity for directing the country's affairs.

From the disintegration of government followed the demoralization and political bewilderment of the szlachta. Corruption was practised by even the highest dignitaries. The politicians switched from one faction to another and back again, sometimes for casual profit, sometimes to safeguard their properties. It was an exceptional man indeed who achieved political consistency. And yet, paradoxically, it was among elements of the szlachta who preserved their public spirit that there appeared a movement to obstruct military and financial reforms. For these depended on a strengthening of the royal power, whereas that of the Sejm was preferred.

Republican tendencies in reform were represented by Stanislas Szczuka, vice-chancellor of Lithuania, who was connected with the gentry of Mazovia, and by Stanislas Dunin Karwicki, steward of Sandomierz, a Calvinist and an experienced parliamentarian. Szczuka's ideas were published under the pseudonym 'Candidus Veronensis' in *Eclipsis Poloniae, orbi publico demonstrata* (1709). Karwicki's work 'De ordinanda Republica' was not printed, but numerous hand-written copies testify to its wide popularity. Both writers proposed to finance the army by permanent property taxes and to appropriate Crown revenue exclusively to that purpose; Szczuka also suggested tapping ecclesiastical wealth, though hypothetically and without real conviction. These writers also wanted to curtail the hetmans' powers, making those offices elective; they agreed, too, on the need to reorganize the armed forces, Szczuka thinking of an army of 36,000, Karwicki of a somewhat smaller force. Szczuka laid great stress on keeping the szlachta politically informed, envisaging for instance a postal information service. Karwicki proposed an annual Sejm in permanent session, able to prorogue itself and renew its debates without change of membership—something new to Polish practice. He also conceived a drastic limitation of the opportunities for dissolving the Sejm, but did not attack the principle of the *liberum veto*. The reformed Sejm was to assume the royal patronage. Finally, Karwicki suggested a change in the procedure of royal elections whereby voting would be by provinces. Many of these ideas were later discussed by such eminent political writers as Leszczyński himself and Stanislas Konarski.

The restoration of Augustus II improved the prospect for fundamental constitutional changes, which lay in fact within the court's own interest, although the king's personal plans went further. The debates of the General Council of Warsaw of 1710 tended in the same direction: it voted a standing army of 36,000 and appropriated to it important revenues, including the customs and excise, whose disbursement was confided to the Treasurer. These resolutions 'marked the highest flight of reform in the period of the two Saxon kings'.[1] In the Rzeczpospolita, however, a resolution voted was far from being a resolution carried out. The szlachta, incited by the propaganda of Leszczyński's adherents, refused to act on the resolutions of the General Council; the clergy referred their attitude to Rome; and the *sejmiki* manipulated the legislation according to their own sweet will.

Meanwhile the Russo-Turkish war, on which Leszczyński's following had pinned great hopes,[2] had ended; although Peter came out of it badly, it had no repercussions on the Polish Crown. Diversionary operations were wound up in Swedish Pomerania, whither the Saxon army had gone to win Stettin and Stralsund for Augustus. The Sejm summoned in 1712 was not especially productive of reform. It rejected royal proposals to support the army out of permanent taxes. But it saved itself from dissolution by declaring a prorogation, a device whereby all resolutions previously voted were upheld: a premature dissolution, on the other hand, would have nullified them. This procedural novelty aroused fears lest 'an English type of parliament was being introduced'—that is, one more

---

[1] M. Nycz, *Geneza reform skarbowych sejmu niemego* (Poznańskie Towarzystwo Przyjaciół Nauk: Prace Komisji Historycznej, vol. XIII, no. 1, Poznań, 1938), p. 180.

[2] Above, pp. 631 ff.

easily controlled by the king.[1] Ultimately, this Sejm was dissolved on the great question of limiting the hetmans' powers. The members greeted the dissolution by recording that 'Your Royal Majesty has returned to us the right of veto in these parliaments'. In this way the first wave of reforming energy was wasted. Argument itself never escaped the orbit of financial and military reform; but basically the rupture was due to the opposition of the Leszczyński faction, and to anxiety about the growth of Saxon influence and continuing Russian intervention.

After Poltava, Russian troops had filled the Rzeczpospolita and Tsar Peter dominated its politics. The tsar tried to impose on his ally a significant portion of his military expenses so as to spare his own exhausted country. With contributions falling on towns and villages, together with the proscription of Leszczyński's adherents, the ascendancy of the pro-Russian party was well assured. In the Kingdom, Hetman Sieniawski retained his strong position with the tsar's assistance, as did Hetman Pociej in Lithuania, Augustus acceding on this point to Peter's wishes. Each hetman consolidated a conservative party firmly wedded to szlachta liberties. Augustus, after all, owed his restoration to a Russian victory, and also to the tsar's decision to abandon an agreement, reached in Dresden before Poltava, whereby Augustus's son was to have been elected to the throne during his father's life, following a precedent of Sigismund I's reign. Threatened by a movement in favour of Constantine Sobieski, Augustus had later signed another agreement with Peter, at Toruń on 20 October 1709, undertaking to continue the Swedish war at Russia's side until final victory and accepting limitations on his diplomatic freedom. All the main power-centres in Poland thus depended on Peter. Furthermore, uninhibited by his obligations to the Rzeczpospolita and to Augustus, Peter proceeded to conquer Livonia, forbidding the Poles to approach Riga. On the other hand, he strongly rejected Prussian suggestions for partitioning Poland. A weak Poland was both a comfortable neighbour and a convenient bridge for Russian activities in Germany. By exploiting the antagonism between king and hetman, Peter could count on perpetuating his ascendancy.

Tsarist policy, nevertheless, did not run smoothly in Poland. The szlachta, who had welcomed the removal of the Swedes and been prepared to see the tsar as the defender of their rights, now turned against the presence of his auxiliary regiments and gradually against Augustus himself, whom they came to regard as a tsarist instrument. This was the background to the revival of the Leszczyński party. Many of its prominent members had emigrated, some settling with Stanislas himself in Stettin, others joining Charles XII at Bender. Inside Poland, however, a conspiracy was organized by Stanislas Jabłonowski, *wojewoda* of Ruthenia

[1] J. Gierowski, *Między saskim absolutyzmem a złotą wolnością, z dziejów wewnętrznych Rzeczpospolitej w latach 1712–15* (Wrocław, 1959), p. 159.

and Leszczyński's former chancellor. When war broke out between Russia and Turkey in 1711, the Polish court was in no hurry to take the Russian side; at Jaroslav, on 9 June, Augustus agreed only to mount a diversion in Pomerania. The Treaty of the Pruth changed Peter's relations with Poland once again. He now promised to pull out of the Rzeczpospolita, whose integrity was of first importance to the Turks.[1] It was two years before these promises were honoured. Then Ottoman statecraft ensured that the benefit should accrue not to Leszczyński or the Swedes but to Augustus, thus giving his policy of emancipation another lease of life.

Augustus's emancipation policy was entwined with his intention of strengthening royal power and, in particular, of ensuring the Polish succession to his son. This being so, the plans of Karwicki and others for republican reform played into the hands of the court's absolutist schemes, whose chief authors were the Saxon ministers, especially Flemming. Support for a strong monarchy was weaker among leading Polish figures, although at moments some of them—for instance, the Crown Treasurer Przebendowski, Bishop Szaniawski of Kujawy, and Sigismund Rybiński, *wojewoda* of Chełmno—seemed favourably inclined to it. There was in any case no question of introducing a thorough-paced absolutism in Poland. Augustus himself made it clear that the most he could expect was to curtail the powers of the Sejm and of the *sejmiki*. No more than in Saxony did he expect to overthrow the established order. In this sense the so-called Flemming plan, said to have envisaged a *coup d'état* to revolutionize the entire system of government, was certainly apocryphal. Setting aside a Prussian scheme combining the destruction of szlachta powers with a limited partition—a scheme discussed with Flemming in June 1715 but rejected by him because of its territorial clauses—the court's projects can be reduced to four points: an enlargement of the royal authority to ensure the Wettin succession; the abolition of the *liberum veto* and the creation of Sejm committees acting in conjunction with the Crown; the institution of secret councils for determining the distribution of offices and for encouraging the formation of a court party; and finally, a closer union between Poland and Saxony—by reducing the Polish army and transferring part of the more reliable Saxon army to the purse of the Rzeczpospolita, by opening a common frontier through the conquest of Silesian territory, and by permitting the Saxon nobility to acquire lands and offices in Poland.[2]

None of these plans enjoyed wide support in Poland, while in Saxony Augustus's promotion of Catholicism lengthened the odds against their

---

[1] Above, p. 645.

[2] The vast majority of these propositions are included in a memorandum of 14 Oct. 1715, certainly by Flemming and prepared after news of the outbreak of fighting between the Polish Crown Army and the Saxons: Dresden, Landeshauptarchiv, loc. 3492, v, pp. 51–4.

acceptance.[1] In Poland, they were regarded as a means whereby courtiers would ingratiate themselves with Germans, 'who always wanted to hold our Republic in tribute and never to see her in a prosperous condition'.[2] What was more, Augustus meant to achieve his objectives by using the Saxon army or by soliciting foreign help, if necessary at the cost of territorial concessions to his neighbours.

In 1713, the re-entry of Saxon troops into the Rzeczpospolita was made possible by a Turkish threat to restore Leszczyński. The king therefore had fresh excuse to proscribe the Leszczyński faction; Jabłonowski was imprisoned in the Saxon fortress of Königstein. On pretext of continuing danger from the Ottomans Augustus retained the Saxons. But they exacted large contributions of food and supplies and thus provoked a ferment of protest throughout Poland. This the king chose to ignore. At the same time he set about seeking foreign support. Among Poland's neighbours, Austria and Russia alike rejected the idea of strengthening the Polish Crown, even in return for territorial gains. On the contrary, Russia held on to Livonia in the knowledge that its restitution would be used to ensure the Wettin succession. Only Prussia might have encouraged the plans of the Polish court, though at the price of acquiring Eastern Pomerania and Courland—a sacrifice which would have cut Poland from the sea. The court was obliged, therefore, to seek more distant allies, for whom a stronger Crown in Poland was of no immediate concern. The worsening of relations with Britain, where Queen Anne's circle had tried to prevent the conversion of Augustus's son to Roman Catholicism, indicated that France was the likeliest choice. The Warsaw court calculated that Versailles could act as mediator in arranging a northern settlement, whilst Versailles no doubt thought of using Augustus as a means of hastening peace in the West. Following the eclipse of Swedish power, France had either to find a new strong ally in the North or to recon-stitute a pro-French block of minor States—Sweden, Poland, Saxony and perhaps Prussia. Such was the background to the signing at Rydzyna on 20 August 1714 of a treaty of friendship, intended to precede agreement on a French marriage for Augustus's son and the assurance of French support at the next royal election.

Augustus's plans came to grief on the inflexibility of Charles XII, who had rejected an understanding reached between Augustus and Stanislas at Mecklenburg in 1712. After his return from Bender Charles prepared in Stralsund to carry on the war. Fearing another Swedish invasion, Augustus resumed military operations against him, along with Denmark and Prussia. French mediation was not forthcoming; indeed, Louis XIV sided with Charles XII. In effect, Charles's unyielding stand rang the death

---

[1] For the relations of Frederick Augustus I with the Estates of Saxony, see F. L. Carsten, *Princes and Parliaments in Germany* (Oxford, 1959), pp. 242 ff. Cf. vol. v, pp. 453–4.

[2] *Przestroga generalna stanów Rzplitej z doczieczonej na zgubę wolności u dworu rady*, ed. J. Gierowski in *Rzeczpospolita w dobie upadku* (Wrocław, 1955), p. 202.

knell of Augustus's plans, for Augustus now found himself isolated in the centre of a dangerous storm which broke around him in the Rzeczpospolita. The extremist policy of Charles XII was to thrust Poland, as well as Sweden, into the abyss.

Augustus's attempt at a *rapprochement* with France aroused suspicion both in Poland and among his allies. It alarmed the Russians, lest he quit the Northern League and even, in deference to Swedish wishes, take up arms against Peter himself. This fear was misplaced, but Peter resolved to paralyse Augustus's initiative by exploiting Polish discontent with him. Originating with the Saxon contributions, which coincided with a run of bad harvests, Polish distrust of the king was accentuated by his drift towards Versailles, which was identified with an absolutist plot. The hetmans, in particular, scented danger when they discovered the royal project to clip their authority and even to remove their influence from the army. In the autumn of 1714 Sieniawski and Pociej urged the szlachta to move against the Saxons, promising military aid. The court managed to crush this resistance for the time being, but without resolving the basic problem. For behind the principle of szlachta liberties stood Peter I, calling for the departure of the Saxons from Poland. The tsarist resident in Warsaw, Dashkov, promised Russian support against Augustus not only to the hetmans but also to the chief of the Leszczyński party, Janusz Wiśniowiecki, *wojewoda* of Cracow. The Rzeczpospolita thus stood once again on the brink of civil war.

The first move came from Lithuania. Hetman Pociej, fearing dismissal, summoned the szlachta to assemble at Vilna in the summer of 1715. Here it was agreed to refuse payment of the Saxon contribution and drive the Saxon army out of the country. When the Russians appeared in Lithuania, heading towards Stralsund to succour the Danes and Prussians, the situation must have looked grave indeed to the Polish court; but it was soon apparent that the Russians did not intend to give Pociej military help, with the result that the hetman reached a compromise with General Weisenfels on 22 September, allowing the Saxons to keep their winter billets in Lithuania. Elsewhere, however, fresh Saxon contributions set off disturbances in September. In the southern districts of Cracow province skirmishes occurred between the szlachta and Saxon detachments sent to gather contributions. Agitation in other provinces and in the army led on 1 October to the formation by a section of the Crown army of a new confederacy at Gorzyce. Shortly afterwards, a Saxon regiment in the province of Sandomierz was defeated at Radogoszcz; thus emboldened, the szlachta there too proceeded to organize a confederacy, before Flemming could counter-attack. Throughout Małopolska the struggle flared up: burghers and peasants, driven to desperation by Saxon vandalism, fought alongside the szlachta. On 26 November 1715 a General Confederacy was formed in the little town of Tarnogród. The szlachta, from whom it had been impossible to extract money for the Crown army, now spontaneously raised its own taxes and unfurled its banners. Even those who had stood aloof from the Swedish war now joined the common cause.

Saxon military superiority was nevertheless so marked that Flemming was able to repel the Tarnogród Confederates south-eastwards into Volhynia; treachery yielded the important castle of Zamość. The mediation of Sieniawski and the senators close to him patched up a treaty at Rawa Ruska, granting the Saxons a single contribution and fixing their departure at an unspecified date; but this arrangement was rejected by the Confederate leadership, which was expecting Lithuanian reinforcements and Russian diplomatic intervention. At first the Russians remained neutral; indeed, by holding their forces from moving to Pomerania, they positively facilitated concentration of the Saxon army. They sought in reality to arbitrate in the dispute between 'Majesty and Liberty', Peter reckoning to insure against any strengthening of Polish majesty by posing as champion of golden freedom. Maintenance of the existing constitution guaranteed Russia against Polish action aimed at recovering the lands lost in the seventeenth century. It also gave time for Russia to absorb her newly conquered Baltic lands and eliminate Polish claims to Livonia. Understanding perfectly well that the tsar's mediation would embarrass his constitutional plans, Augustus essayed direct negotiations with the Confederates. They, on the other hand, were deluded into believing that Peter would advance no claims on the Rzeczpospolita and called for a mediator; a section indeed hoped that he would enable them to depose Augustus, marry Constantine Sobieski to Peter's niece and raise him to the throne. In these circumstances, Augustus bowed to the idea of mediation and arranged to meet Peter at Gdańsk. Meanwhile civil war continued. The Confederates forced their way into Wielkopolska, where another confederacy was declared, and they overcame Poznań. Lithuania now supported them. Nevertheless, the decision was eventually made to negotiate with Augustus. Peace talks dragged on from June to November, first at Lublin, then at Kazimierz Dolny and Warsaw. There, on 4 November 1716, almost a year since the formation of the Confederacy of Tarnogród, a treaty was signed.

It was signed in the shadow cast by Russian troops. Relations between Peter and the Confederates, originally so friendly, had deteriorated when he realized that their leader, Stanislas Leduchowski, chamberlain of Krzemieniec, was bent on an independent policy. Leduchowski had suggested seeking aid from Vienna, even from Turk or Tatar. The Austro-Turkish war of 1716 blighted these hopes. Instead, Russian forces crossed into the Kingdom of Poland at the request of Augustus. The treaty of 4 November, along with later agreements made at Warsaw without the good offices of Gregory Dolgoruki, the Russian ambassador, was confirmed by the so-called Silent Sejm, which met on 1 February 1717 and dispersed without discussion. But contrary to the repeated opinions of historians, neither the Treaty of Warsaw nor the resolutions of the Silent Sejm were dictated by Dolgoruki, who confined himself in general to the rôle of chairman. Despite Peter's explicit wishes, he did not succeed in inserting a Russian guarantee, to which both Augustus and the Confederates were hostile.[1] Hence Russian diplomacy missed the very object for which it had consented to mediate in the first place.

The treaty certainly excluded any possibility of Augustus moving towards absolutism with the support of the Saxon army. It ordered the Saxons to leave the Rzeczpospolita, leaving Augustus with only his personal Saxon guard of 1,200 men. The Saxon officials were also expelled, except for six members of the Saxon chancery who were expressly forbidden to interfere in Polish business: Polish diplomacy was thus to be detached to a large extent from Saxon. Other clauses, however, clearly enhanced the king's position in the State—so much so that the Prussian ambassador, Lölhöffel, anxiously informed Frederick William I that 'a beautiful foundation has been laid for an absolutum dominium'. It is true that a section of the Confederates under Leduchowski worked with Augustus to use the negotiations as a lever for introducing certain reforms. The competence of the *sejmiki* was reduced, the formation of confederacies banned. Most important, the standing army was fixed at 24,000, supported for the first time by permanent taxes, including those raised from the properties of the szlachta. State revenue was to reach the annual figure of 10 m. *zlotys*, a sum too small for military needs but limited by the economic ruin of the country. To ensure that this money went to the army, it was to be paid direct to the various regiments, by-passing the treasury—a ruling which had a fatal effect on this particular reform. The power of the hetmans was curbed, the duties of other high officials precisely defined. Special courts were instituted for persons prosecuted for contact with the enemies of king or Rzeczpospolita. Finally, the king persuaded the hetmans to place the finest elements of the army, including infantry and dragoons, in the hands of Flemming.

The court's following was convinced that the first step towards fundamental reform had been taken. Bishop Szaniawski, one of the authors of the treaty and of the resolutions of the Silent Sejm, confided to Lölhöffel that it would be better for Poland if she returned to hereditary succession, and that the *liberum veto* was absurd: 'England manages much better with majority voting.'[2] At the next Sejm, in 1718, the court suggested an extension of military reform which would have financed the artillery and upkeep of fortresses; an increase in the size of the army was also considered. At the same time the State launched a mercantilist programme,

---

[1] Dolgoruki to Golovkin, 20 Nov. 1716.: CSAAD, loc. cit. 1716, no. 11, pp. 470–1.
[2] Memorandum of Lölhöffel, 23 Feb. 1717: Mersburg, Deutsches Zentralarchiv, Rep. 9, no. 27, p. 1, k.2.

envisaging the encouragement of urban growth, abrogation of private customs duties, protection of mining, prohibition of the export of wool, regularization of the Vistula navigation, monetary reform and other innovations. Adjustments in Church–State relations were also proposed: an increase of tax liability on ecclesiastical property, limitation of bequests to the Church, confiscation of Church estates occupied in defiance of the 1635 constitution, a reduction in ecclesiastical fees and in the competence of ecclesiastical courts. Yet Augustus, notwithstanding the recent improvement in his authority, failed to get these further reforms through. Once again, only a timely prorogation saved the Sejm from breaking up altogether.

At the root of the king's troubles lay renewed collaboration between the hetmans and Peter the Great. Russian forces were kept in Poland after the Silent Sejm of 1717 and helped to organize a faction opposed to the court. Dolgoruki even played with the idea of a confederacy of magnates aimed at removing Augustus.[1] Protests by the szlachta sufficed, it is true, to effect a Russian withdrawal in 1719; but old suspicions of the king revived as the immediate Russian threat relaxed. The proclamation of the conversion of Augustus's son to Rome and his marriage to a Habsburg princess had given the impression that the king was still planning an attack on free election. In consequence, the Sejm of 1720 was dissolved, as were three more Sejms after it. The opposition of the hetmans crushed all further reformist initiatives. In 1720, moreover, Peter reached agreement in Potsdam with Frederick William of Prussia to confirm the immutability of the Polish constitution and the principle of free election. Given the existing balance of power, this meant that no reform could be effected without foreign permission. And so Poland sank into a legislative lethargy which was to last until 1764. The resolutions of the Silent Sejm remained half-completed—a monument to the wiser aspirations of these tormented years, to be evoked from time to time as the military weakness of the Rzeczpospolita became ever more ominous.

In this way Poland became, after Sweden, the second major victim of the Great Northern War. Military failures, a ravaged countryside and political disintegration worsened the anarchy already announced in John Sobieski's last years. The opportunity offered to the Polish–Lithuanian State by the personal union with Saxony was squandered. In part, one must blame the szlachta and the magnates, who refused to abandon their privileges and who feared a Saxon supremacy. In part it was the fault of Augustus himself and of his advisers, who were sometimes guilty of exaggerated ambitions and who failed to stem mounting difficulties, often of their own making. The visionary idealism of Charles XII, too, must answer for much of the catastrophe. His far-fetched, unrealistic plans hoisted his puppet Leszczyński on to the throne, fostered Polish

[1] Dolgoruki to Golovkin, 30 Nov. 1718: CSAAD, loc. cit. 1718, no. 8, pp. 244–5.

divisions and at no time invited a *rapprochement* with Augustus II. The Swedish attitude in turn opened the way to Russian domination. These circumstances cut short the promise of reforms widely acknowledged as vital to the safety of the Rzeczpospolita, and so prevented a solution to the conflict of 'Majesty and Liberty' which was beginning to be well understood. Hence, in the course of two wars which fettered her autonomy, the degradation of Poland became a European byword. Twice in succession Poland emerged from war nominally among the victors, in reality a ruined and a second-rate power.

CHAPTER XXI

RUSSIA UNDER PETER THE GREAT AND THE CHANGED RELATIONS OF EAST AND WEST

THE Russia into which the Tsarevich Peter was born in 1672, and of which he became joint ruler ten years later, was a poor, thinly populated and backward country. She had few towns of any size, no large-scale industry; her economic life was based on the production of timber, furs and salt, and on an inefficient agriculture. Vast areas were still undeveloped and virtually uninhabited. The only direct geographical outlet to the West was the port of Archangel, frozen for half the year; from the Baltic Russia was severed by Sweden's possession of Finland, Ingria, Estonia and Livonia; her frontiers were as yet several hundred miles from the Black Sea, the Crimea being a tributary state of the Ottoman empire and the raids of its Tatar inhabitants still a serious menace to the security of south Russia and the Ukraine. From the second half of the fifteenth century, however, soldiers, doctors and skilled workers of many kinds from western Europe had been active in Russia, and western ideas and techniques slowly taking root there. In the seventeenth century this process was accelerating,[1] but even in its last decades Russia was far from being a part of Europe in any true sense. She was isolated not merely by geography but also by her distinctive and in many respects unfortunate history, by a national pride so intense and arrogant as to attract the comment of almost all foreign visitors, and above all by deep-rooted religious differences. The Orthodox Church, her wealthiest and most powerful institution, had inherited from Byzantium a profound feeling of superiority to western Christendom and was in general a most formidable opponent of foreign influence. To observers in the West the Russians seemed an Asiatic people, the autocracy of the tsars comparable to the despotism of sultan or shah rather than to the absolutism of any European monarch. To the economic life of Europe the country contributed little save a few raw materials; to its political life she was hardly more important.

The formal education arranged for Peter by his mother—his father, the Tsar Alexis, died in 1676—differed little from that marked out by precedent as suitable for members of the ruling family; it consisted largely of reading, elementary arithmetic, a knowledge of the liturgy and service-books of Orthodoxy, but no formal instruction in foreign languages. Peter was never a lover of books, which he valued only as sources of

[1] Cf. vol. v, ch. xxv.

716

useful information; indeed, he always tended to despise literature—
'useless tales which merely waste time'. To the end of his life his spelling
remained wild and irregular. On the other hand, he showed from boyhood
keen interest in tools and machines, in skilled manual work of all kinds.
Education of this sort he received, not from the teachers chosen by his
mother, but from working craftsmen, above all foreigners in the 'German
suburb' of Moscow. The neglect from which he and his mother suffered
after the *strel'tsy* revolt of 1682,[1] his exclusion from all real power during
the regency of the Tsarevna Sophia (1682–9), helped him to acquire an
education of this unprecedentedly wide and practical kind by freeing him
from the trammels of convention that would otherwise have enclosed him
in the Kremlin. The physical energy, the materialistic approach to problems of all kinds, the indifference if not outright hostility to abstractions,
of which he gave evidence in these early years, were to remain characteristic
all his life. He had always a surer touch with things than with people, as his
relations with his wife and son were to show. By the later 1680s he was
displaying an interest that was to dominate his life: still in his 'teens, he
had begun to create from the numerous servants and subordinates at his
disposal considerable bodies of organized troops, the 'toy regiments',
supplied with arms and even cannon from the arsenal in Moscow, and to
employ them in manoeuvres, mock battles and sieges. Perhaps without
any conscious purpose, he was forming the nucleus of a modernized
army. The idea of constructing a navy was also taking shape in his mind,
though as yet he had never seen the sea and had little idea of where or for
what a Russian fleet could or should be used. By comparison, the marriage
his mother arranged for him in 1689 to the dull and worthy Evdokia
Lopukhina meant little to him. Nine years later he forced her to withdraw
into a nunnery, and though she lived till 1731 she had never any political
significance. In 1707, with typical disregard for tradition, he was to take
as his second wife a former servant-girl and a foreigner, the future
Catherine I, whom in 1724 he crowned as empress.

As he approached manhood it became clear that Peter I, resolute and
energetic, was an increasing threat to the power of Sophia, who had
dominated the government since the revolution of 1682. His half-brother
Ivan, who had been proclaimed joint tsar with him in 1682 and who died in
1696, was so deficient in body and mind that he was never a serious factor
in the situation. In the developing struggle for power Sophia was supported
by her lover and chief minister, Prince V. V. Golitsyn, and by the *strel'tsy*,
Peter by the adherents of his mother's family, the Naryshkins. It came to a
head in 1689. At the end of August, terrified by a false report that the
strel'tsy were on their way to seize him, Peter took refuge in the great

---

[1] The *strel'tsy* (archers or shooters) were a part of the army, stationed mainly in Moscow,
which acted as a palace guard and had great political influence. In 1682 they rebelled,
murdered a number of leading nobles, and established Peter's half-sister Sophia as regent.

Troitskaya monastery near Moscow. The news was false, but his action made open conflict unavoidable. It was decided by the willingness of a number of foreign officers, notably the Scotsman Patrick Gordon, to come out in favour of Peter. Within a few days Golitsyn was exiled to the wastes of northern Russia and Sophia immured in a convent, where she died fifteen years later. But the success of Peter and his supporters was by no means a victory for the forces of progress. Golitsyn was at this time far more conscious of the necessity for radical change in almost every department of Russian life: for a standing army, permanent diplomatic relations with foreign States, some freedom of religious belief, education of children abroad. That his fall debarred him from contributing to the reforms of the following generation makes him one of the most tragic figures in Russian history. By contrast, the men who governed Russia for the next six years in Peter's name—Prince Boris Golitsyn (a cousin and opponent of the exile), together with the boyars L. K. Naryshkin and T. N. Streshnev—were little more than typical representatives of the upper bureaucracy of the day; and his mother, who retained considerable influence over him until her death in 1694, was in many ways deeply conservative. Moreover, the young tsar continued for several years to be interested more in drilling his 'toy regiments', acquiring knowledge of shipbuilding, and drinking with his boon companions of the German Suburb, than in the problems of day-to-day administration. It was then that he cemented those friendships, with the much older Patrick Gordon and notably with the Genevan adventurer François Lefort, that so considerably influenced the development of his ideas. Although both these men died in 1699 and their places were taken by new advisers and favourites —especially by the able if corrupt A. D. Menshikov, who received the title of prince in 1705—Peter never forgot his debt to them.

When in 1695, at the age of 24, he began to take the reins of government into his own hands, his first enterprise was an attack on the Turkish fortress of Azak (Azov), which controlled the mouth of the river Don. Its capture would show Russia capable of playing an important part in the war which Austria, Poland and Venice had long been waging with the Ottoman, wipe out the disgrace of two futile attacks made by Golitsyn on the Crimea in 1687 and 1689, and above all go far towards giving Peter an outlet to the Black Sea and the possibility of a navy. The first Russian attack on Azak failed. Peter had still no fleet capable of preventing the Turks from throwing reinforcements into the town by sea, no engineers fit to conduct such a siege, no real unity of command in his forces. In 1696, equipped with a large flotilla of shallow-draught vessels and a squadron of warships built around Voronezh on the Don, and helped by engineers sent by the Emperor Leopold, he renewed the attack and on 18 July the town was captured, its fall being celebrated by a triumphal procession in Moscow in which the tsar himself took part. If Russia could seize the Straits of Kerch, which control the entry from the Sea of Azov to the Black Sea proper, the way would be open for the creation of a permanent Black Sea squadron and perhaps to further gains at Ottoman expense. In these ambitions, however, the tsar was thwarted. The Austrians, Poles and Venetians were all, for various reasons, anxious for a quick peace with Turkey; and when that peace was made at Carlowitz in 1699 Peter found himself isolated and Russian interests, as he bitterly complained, completely ignored. In 1700 events in the Baltic forced him also to make peace with the Porte. A striking exhibition of Russian power had been given, but as yet Russia had no secure access to the Black Sea.

A few months later came the most striking of Peter's breaches with the past, his 'great embassy' to western Europe. Ostensibly led by Lefort, F. A. Golovin and P. B. Voznitsyn, a large cavalcade of Russians—with servants, guards and translators—left the country in March 1697, the tsar accompanying them under an easily penetrated incognito as 'Peter Mikhailov'. Travelling through Swedish Livonia and the duchy of Courland, East Prussia and Brandenburg, Peter reached the Netherlands in August. After working as a shipwright at Zaandam (Saardam) and Amsterdam, he crossed over to England in January 1698 and remained there four months. He then travelled by way of the Netherlands, Halle, Leipzig, Dresden and Prague to Vienna, which he reached in June and where he stayed five weeks. This remarkable journey, quite unprecedented in the history of the Russian monarchy, was inspired by two motives. The first and probably the more important was to acquire knowledge of a variety of technical skills, above all of shipbuilding and navigation. In this aspiration Peter was remarkably successful. In Prussia he was able to study gunnery, in the Netherlands and England shipbuilding and other trades; and he constantly displayed a devouring curiosity about the technical establishments of the countries he visited. As an immediate result of the tsar's travels, moreover, Russia acquired the services of nearly a thousand foreign experts—seamen, gunners, shipwrights, mathematicians, surgeons, engineers and skilled workers of many kinds, with their books and instruments. Peter also began to realize that the wealth and efficiency which he so much admired in the West could not be transplanted to Russia without the adoption of new and westernized institutions. The second objective of his journey, however, the idea of constructing a great new coalition against the Turks, proved impracticable. The policies of William III, the States-General and the emperor were all dominated by the question, now obviously approaching a crisis, of the Spanish succession.

From Vienna Peter was hastily recalled to Moscow by news of a serious new outbreak of the *strel'tsy*. Alarmed by his partiality for foreigners and foreign ideas, irritated by the distrust he had shown in sending the *strel'tsy* away from Moscow to Azov and the Polish frontier, a number of these regiments revolted in June 1698 and attempted to march on the capital. The revolt lacked any real leader and had been effectively crushed, largely by the quick action of Gordon, before the tsar's return; but Peter was determined to free himself once and for all from this turbulent, undisciplined, would-be praetorian guard. By torture and executions—some of which he was alleged, probably wrongly, to have carried out with his own hand—and by banishment to Siberia, he destroyed the *strel'tsy* for ever as a political force, disregarding the efforts of the Patriarch Adrian to secure more merciful treatment for them.

By the end of 1698, therefore, Peter was in a position to inaugurate a series of great innovations which for Russia had almost the effect of a revolution. They were often introduced without plan or system and achieved stable form only in the last years of his reign. In particular, they were distorted by the great struggle with Sweden which opened in 1700. Nevertheless, they mark a watershed in Russian and indeed in European history. The most urgent, spectacular and in some ways most significant were the reorganization of the army and the creation of a navy. Both involved far-reaching administrative, psychological, and to a lesser extent social changes; both made a deep impression on foreign observers; both were essential if Russia was to become a real factor in European politics.

Improvement in the quality and organization of the Russian army had begun long before Peter's accession. Since the 1630s it had become steadily less feudal in composition and larger, with foreign influences and models counting for more and more. Yet it remained inefficient and antiquated: otherwise, it is doubtful whether the Swedes could have overcome numerically superior Russian forces with ease in the early years of the Great Northern War. Neither the *strel'tsy* nor the surviving feudal levies were a reliable fighting force; the artillery was out-of-date; above all, there was a great lack of well-trained officers.[1] Peter's youthful interest in military affairs, sharpened if anything by foreign travel, bore fruit in a drastic reorganization of the entire structure. At the end of 1699, 29 new regiments of infantry and two of dragoons, composed partly of volunteers and partly of conscripts, were created; in little more than three months a new and relatively efficient force of 32,000 was thus formed. At the same time, a start was made on the improvement of the central organization of the army by the establishment of a series of new posts: those of the *General-Kommissar*, who supervised much of its administration; the *General-Proviant*, who controlled supplies; and the *General-Feldtseikhmeister*, who commanded the artillery. Nine more dragoon regiments came into existence in 1700–1, largely as a reaction to the catastrophic failure of the 1700 campaign, and the first Russian artillery regiment was set up. The casting of guns, helped by the growth of iron production in the Urals, was

---

[1] Cf. vol. v, pp. 577–8 and below, p. 777.

developed on such a scale that Vockerodt, the well-informed secretary to the Prussian minister in St Petersburg, estimated that by 1713 the country possessed 13,000 brass and iron cannon. In 1705 the system of recruiting was extended and intensified: a levy of recruits was ordered at the rate of one man from each twenty peasant households. In 1705–9, the most critical years of the Northern War, up to 168,000 men were raised in this way. From 1705, also, the infantry and dragoon regiments which made up the bulk of the army began to be grouped in brigades and divisions, though these were not permanent units. Simultaneously, strenuous efforts were made to reduce Russia's dependence on foreign countries, notably on the Netherlands, for supplies of small arms, with the result that after 1712 such imports ceased.

The problem of obtaining an adequate supply of trained officers proved much harder to solve. At first Peter depended heavily for his officers, especially in the higher ranks, on foreigners and above all Germans; the organization of the new regiments of 1699 was largely the work of a German, General Weide, and not even one of their colonels was a Russian. But the tsar never intended this dependence to last: almost from the start, he was doing what he could to procure enough properly trained Russian officers. The first military school in Russia, that of the famous Pre-obrazhensky regiment, had come into existence before the end of the seventeenth century, and from this humble beginning grew a structure of training establishments imposing in theory if not always very efficient in practice. Artillery schools were founded in 1701, 1712, 1721; engineering schools in 1709 and 1719; a school for army surgeons in 1707. More important in many ways were the Guards regiments, for it was by service in these, as common soldiers, that the bulk of Russian infantry officers received their training. Peter made strenuous efforts to ensure that no young member of the landowning class should obtain a commission without having served in them or undergone some other appropriate form of training. He was thus able by degrees to replace unsatisfactory or unnecessary foreign officers by trained Russians—a process accelerated after 1709, when the crisis of the war had clearly passed.

More than any other activity, however, it was the construction of a fleet which, throughout his reign, engaged the tsar's close personal interest. Himself a shipwright of ability, he considered himself competent to interfere even in quite technical matters of naval organization and administration. For example, as early as 1694 he had worked out a system of signals for the use of the few small craft which as yet constituted his whole fleet; later, he frequently examined in person, on their return, the many young Russians whom he sent to western and southern Europe to study seamanship. Information about foreign navies was always welcome and under his instructions a large collection of foreign naval regulations was compiled in Russia. After his journey in the West

Peter's desire for a powerful fleet was directed, in default of any other outlet, to the development of a squadron for use in the Black Sea. In November 1696 it had been decided to force the landowning class to contribute to the building of new ships; in 1697 his wealthier subjects were ordered to group themselves in companies for this purpose, each to contribute one or more vessels. By the spring of 1698 over 50 ships were ready. Many of them, badly designed and hastily built, proved unserviceable. Yet their construction was a major innovation, for it was intended to provide Russia with a permanent fleet of relatively large men-of-war—a far more substantial force than that improvised in 1695-6. The acquisition of a foothold on the Baltic opened a new and more rewarding area of naval expansion. As early as 1702 Peter ordered frigates to be built on the river Syas, which flows into the southern end of Lake Ladoga; the first ship of the Baltic fleet was launched in August 1703; a year later there was a squadron of six frigates and a considerable number of galleys. The growth of a Baltic fleet was rapid, even spectacular: 10 ships of the line by 1710; 17 by 1714 and 32 by 1724. This called for new organs of administration, supply and training. In 1700 a special admiralty department was set up, an admiralty chancery in 1712, and finally a college of admiralty in 1718. A navigation school had been established at Moscow in 1701: in 1715 a much more important and lasting institution, the Naval Academy, began to train officers in St Petersburg. It was in 1705, for the first time, that recruits were conscripted specially for the navy: hitherto the ships had been manned largely by soldiers transferred to them. A set of regulations for the fleet was drawn up in 1710, a more elaborate one in 1720-2. The new navy nevertheless proved a much more fragile creation than the modernized army and was much slower to take permanent root. It was weakened by the surrender of Azov and the dismantling of the Black Sea fleet as a result of the disastrous Pruth campaign in 1711.[1] Moreover, it remained always the tsar's personal creation, almost his private toy, deeply unpopular with the country as a whole, so that foreign officers and experts continued to dominate it long after they had been relegated to a more or less secondary position in the army.[2] The unpopularity of the fleet also meant that, as an effective instrument of war, it scarcely survived its creator. After his death it fell at once into a neglect from which it did not emerge till the reign of Catherine II. The most cherished of Peter's creations, it was also one of the least enduring.

The growth of these powerful fighting forces was made possible by a corresponding development of the economic life of Russia. It is an exaggeration to think that this was the product merely of the war with

[1] Above, pp. 634-6.
[2] Cf. M. S. Anderson, 'Great Britain and the Growth of the Russian Navy in the Eighteenth Century', *The Mariner's Mirror*, vol. XLII (1956), pp. 132-46.

Sweden, or that Peter was completely indifferent to economic problems before that struggle began. Nevertheless, the demands of the armed services for weapons, gunpowder, uniforms, ship-timbers and other supplies strongly influenced much of the industrial development of the reign, acting as a powerful stimulus to increased production. Public finance and taxation were almost completely dominated by the burden of war, which in 1702–3 accounted for 76–77 per cent of all government expenditure and in 1705—the most critical year for the Russians—almost 96 per cent. In these very difficult years the cost of war could be met only by debasing the coinage, which yielded considerable profits in 1700–3, and by imposing a very wide range of burdensome indirect taxes. These, however, when supplemented by the seizure of monastic estates, the proceeds of customs duties, of State monopolies, above all of the poll-tax introduced in 1718, meant that by the end of the reign the government's financial position was stronger than ever before.[1] If allowance is made for changes in the purchasing power of the rouble, government income in 1724 was perhaps three times what it had been in 1680 and over twice that of 1701.

Was Peter a 'mercantilist' in the usual sense of that vague term? Undoubtedly he had some knowledge of the economic ideas and prejudices characteristic of most western countries, and it is not difficult to find aspects of his policies that have a mercantilist air. The best-known work on economic affairs produced during his reign, the *Kniga o skudosti i bogatstve*[2] of I. T. Pososhkov, shows many similarities to contemporary western writings, not least in the barely concealed xenophobia underlying many of its arguments. On the other hand, large-scale government interference with the national economic life, of the type of which Peter made use, had been well established in Russia long before his time and even before the ideas of mercantilism had been fully elaborated in western Europe. Moreover, in a number of important respects—in the relatively slight emphasis on increasing exports, in the appreciable attention given to agriculture—the tsar's record does not easily fit the conventional mould of western mercantilism. In the value which he attached to industry and trade, however, as in the means by which he attempted to develop them, he appears at many points as an East European equivalent of Colbert.

Industry was stimulated in the first place by setting up State factories for a wide variety of products: iron and copper hardware, small arms and cannon, woollen textiles and sailcloth, sulphur, gunpowder and paper. 86 such factories are known to have been set up during Peter's reign—not far short of half the total of new industrial enterprises then created in Russia. Many, it is true, especially in his last years, were eventually leased

[1] Cf. vol. VII, p. 320.
[2] 'Book about poverty and wealth' (1724). The author came of a family of Crown peasants in the Moscow area and was by trade originally a silversmith working for the arsenal there. He was then concerned with the minting of coins, finally becoming a manufacturer in his own right and the owner of houses and even villages.

or sold to individuals or companies. Nevertheless, government influence played throughout a greater part in Russian industrial life than in that of any West European country. Even factories set up by individual entrepreneurs normally relied heavily on tax exemptions or monopolies granted by government, cheap forced labour provided by it, and government demand for the goods they produced.[1] Labour for the new industries came from many different sources. Some was provided by free men working for hire; some by criminals, runaway peasants, and even army recruits, who were put to work in factories very much as was done in most other European states; some, particularly in government-owned factories, by 'ascribing' for work in or for these factories considerable numbers of State peasants. According to one calculation, there were in 1719 over 31,000 men who had been ascribed in this way, and by 1725 over 54,000. Finally, an *ukaz* of 1721 allowed industrialists, irrespective of class origin, to buy villages and use in their establishments the labour of the peasants over whom they thus acquired control. Such coercive or semi-coercive measures ensured an adequate flow of unskilled workers, but skilled labour of many kinds remained very scarce. Although strenuous efforts were made to train craftsmen in Russia as well as to recruit more from abroad —German miners and Italian silk-workers, for example—a shortage of skills was to be a fundamental weakness of all Russian economic life long after Peter's death. Many of his industrial schemes themselves proved to be premature, shallow-rooted, and consequently short-lived. In spite of a protective tariff introduced in 1724, the factories producing textiles, paper, chemicals, leather, and consumer goods generally, were doomed to speedy decay by incompetent management, lack of skilled workers, and the decline of the artificial demand created by war. One major sector, however, the smelting and working of iron, developed rapidly in this period, mainly because of the exploitation for the first time of the great deposits of high-quality ore in the southern Ural area. By 1725 Russia had become a major exporter of iron to western Europe, notably to Great Britain.[2]

Peter's efforts to develop a merchant marine, and to fit Russians to trade actively with the outside world, were almost completely unsuccessful. Ambitions of this kind were already in his mind during his 'great embassy'; but it was not until after the crisis of the struggle with Sweden that he could do much to translate them into practice, and then the ineffectiveness of his measures soon became apparent. Commercial treaties with foreign States, the creation of trading companies, grants of privileges to individuals for the construction of a merchant marine—none of these could

---

[1] For a discussion of Russian views on this subject, many aspects of which are still obscure, see R. Portal, 'Manufactures et classes sociales en Russie au XVIIIᵉ siècle', *Rev. Hist.* vol. CCI (1949), pp. 160–85, and vol. CCII (1949), pp. 1–23.

[2] Cf. vol. VII, pp. 318–19, and R. Portal, *L'Oural au XVIIIᵉ siècle* (1951), chs. i–iii.

make much impression on the problem. Peter's inability to think in truly economic terms, his reliance (not always misplaced) on purely administrative and even coercive measures to produce permanent economic results, is well illustrated by his handling of commercial questions, and particularly by his efforts to divert the foreign trade of Archangel[1] to his new capital of St Petersburg by discriminatory customs duties and other means.

On agriculture also the tsar's impact was very limited. Attempts were made to improve stockbreeding, to encourage the growing of silk, flax and hemp, and to spread the use of the scythe instead of the less efficient sickle. There was certainly a considerable extension of the area under cultivation, a filling up of unoccupied lands in border areas and in south-central Russia. To the end, however, Russian agriculture remained highly resistant to change, adhering to various traditional systems of cultivation (mainly a three-field rotation), and relatively inefficient.

Peter's economic policies were thus in many ways unsuccessful. They present a picture of incessant government activity, but one which, at least until late in his reign, was chaotic and disorganized—a series of unplanned responses to immediate necessities, of *ad hoc* improvisations.

Side by side with these military, naval and economic initiatives went a series of complicated administrative changes. The structure of government inherited by Peter was the product of generations of haphazard growth.[2] At the centre were the *Boyarskaya Duma*, an advisory council of representatives of the upper nobility, and over forty departments (*prikazy*), whose functions varied very widely in importance and geographical scope, and whose jurisdictions often intersected each other in a highly irrational way. Local administration was dominated by the provincial governors, the military voivodes. Peter's reign saw a continual struggle to overhaul this system and transform it into an efficient machine for placing Russia's resources at his disposal.

At an early stage the *Boyarskaya Duma* was replaced by much smaller and less formal bodies, the Privy Chancery and the Council of Ministers, able to act as more effective and flexible organs of central control. At the same time a series of changes was made in the organization of the *prikazy*, especially in 1699–1701. Some were suppressed or allowed to fall into disuse, others established expressly to supervise the execution of the tsar's new policies, like the admiralty *prikaz*, set up to control building for the new fleet: the most important was the *Preobrazhenskii prikaz*, created to detect and repress opposition of any kind to government. A more radical departure was the establishment in 1699 of a new administrative organ, the *Ratusha*, to develop trade and industry, to control the towns—

---

[1] Below, pp. 842–4.　　　　　　　　　　[2] Cf. vol. v, pp. 581–6.

which would thus be withdrawn from the jurisdiction of provincial governors—and to collect indirect taxation and act as a central government treasury. It did not justify all the hopes placed in it, but for the next decade it was one of the most important institutions in Russia and did a good deal to centralize administration, above all in financial matters. Nevertheless, until well into the second half of Peter's reign the machinery of government remained essentially a collection of expedients designed to raise men and money for the war, of executive extensions of the tsar's will. Only after victory over Sweden had freed his hands for more leisurely and systematic reforms did he introduce permanent changes on a large scale. The first was the creation of a new central controlling body, the Senate, in 1711. Its nine members included none of Peter's most important subordinates, and one of them was illiterate, but it was not thereby prevented from becoming in many ways the most important organ of central government. Later, from 1718, the outdated *prikaz* system was replaced by nine administrative colleges. Three of these dealt with various aspects of finance, the others with commerce, mines and manufactures, foreign affairs, the army, navy, and justice. Like the other reforms of Peter's later years, these colleges—composed of a president, a vice-president, and a number of assessors, chiefly after the Swedish model—were the fruit of prolonged forethought and discussion. They differed from the *prikazy* in both their limited number and the relatively logical way in which the functions of government were divided between them, and also in the fact that each, unlike many of the *prikazy*, had a jurisdiction covering the whole of Russia.

The tendency of the reforms introduced into the provincial administration[1] during Peter's reign, especially towards the end, was to strengthen central control by subjecting local officials to the Senate and later to the colleges. The result, however, was not only a clearer definition than hitherto of the duties of these officials, but also the creation of large numbers of new government agents with specialized functions, such as supervisors of Crown lands and *waldmeistery* for the protection of woodlands. In other words, there was a great bureaucratization of the provinces. On paper at least, in little over two decades, Russia had thus been endowed with an administrative system more highly centralized than before.

Accompanying these far-reaching material and institutional changes went an effort to widen the scope and raise the level of Russian intellectual life. His travels had brought home very forcibly to Peter his country's limitations in this respect, and his reforms created an unprecedented and increasing demand for educated men in many fields. As early as October 1699, in a conversation with the Patriarch Adrian, the tsar had expressed very freely his dissatisfaction with the inadequacies of Russian education

[1] See vol. VII, p. 324.

and outlined a number of ways in which it might be improved; but the Swedish war meant that for many years his energies and resources had to be concentrated on projects likely to have some immediate usefulness, such as the military and naval schools, the School of Languages (1701) designed to supply translators for the conduct of foreign affairs, and the School of Mines (1716). Not until 1714 was some effort made to lay an adequate foundation for such institutions by developing primary education. In that year Peter ordered the establishment in each province of a 'ciphering school', intended mainly to teach arithmetic and a little geometry to the sons of local landowners and officials. Over forty such schools were set up during the reign. Their effect was nevertheless very limited: education was not desired by the majority of the class which they were meant to serve; few of the students completed their courses, and within little more than a year of Peter's death the schools still in existence could muster between them scarcely 500 pupils. Other methods were tried, but they too were limited in scope and success. In 1721 orders were given to open a school in each diocese for the sons of clergy; neither these nor the garrison schools, which gave elementary instruction to the sons of soldiers, went very far towards equipping Russia with an educational system.

The country's intellectual life received a much greater stimulus from the increasing production and importation of books. The translation of suitable foreign works, above all in technology and the physical sciences, was encouraged by the government, though as yet the Russian market for such literature, except at a fairly elementary level, was very small. Grammars, dictionaries, almanacs, and text-books of all kinds began to be available in hitherto unprecedented numbers, equipping students more adequately than ever before with the basic tools of learning. In 1703 appeared the first issue of what is usually considered the earliest Russian newspaper, the *Vedomosti*. It was purely a government gazette, used by Peter to defend reforms and publicize successes; it appeared irregularly and its circulation was small; yet it was another indication of the growing modernization of Russian life. The theatre also obtained a foothold in Russia, though a very precarious one, owing most to the support of members of the royal family. Perhaps the most promising institutional result of foreign intellectual influences was the Academy of Sciences, planned by Peter but not established until some months after his death. A more indirect but often powerful stimulus, at least to the upper ranks of the Russian people, was furnished by a whole series of minor revolutions: the adoption in 1700 of the Julian calendar; the systematic use of Arabic numerals; the legislation of 1699-1700 ordering all Russians save peasants and clergy to shave their beards and wear European dress; and the institution at St Petersburg in Peter's later years of 'assemblies', where men and woman could engage in civilized conversation on the French model, perhaps interspersed with Polish or German dances. It was certainly not the least far-reaching of Peter's innovations that he waged war on the historic seclusion of women in Russia.

Indeed, his personal attitude to western culture changed somewhat in his last decade. Conscious after years of strain of greater strength and security, he became less materialistic in outlook, more willing to borrow from the West not merely its military, naval and industrial techniques but also its art, architecture and literature. Thus in 1716 he was buying pictures on a large scale in Amsterdam and sending young Russians to study at the *Accademia di Disegno* in Florence; in 1718 he was acquiring statues and paintings in Rome, and trying to engage Italian artists and sculptors for work in Russia. Architects from western Europe had begun to enter his service in the early 1700s—the Peter and Paul fortress in the new capital was built to plans drawn up by a pupil of Vauban—and their numbers and importance increased considerably towards the end of the reign. The building of St Petersburg, largely in the German-Dutch style of Baltic baroque, was directed successively by Domenico Trezzini (Tresini) of Lugano, Andreas Schlüter of Berlin, G. J. Mattarnovy (another German), and N. F. Härbel of Basel.[1]

By far the greatest obstacle to an intellectual revolution was the Orthodox Church. That Peter himself was a devout man is clear from the interest he took in religious matters on his travels abroad, the numerous biblical allusions and quotations scattered through his letters and speeches, the crusading element prominent in his attitude to the Ottoman, and his encouragement of missionary work among the non-Christian peoples of his empire. Yet, from the outset of his reforming activities, he was compelled to regard the Church in Russia as an enemy. This was essentially because it and its leaders, as the expression of the xenophobic conservatism still so strong in the country, appeared as the only force powerful enough to frustrate his plans, despite the breaking (in 1666) of Patriarch Nikon's bid for ecclesiastical supremacy.[2] Peter's own failure in 1690 to secure the elevation of his candidate for the patriarchate of Moscow certainly annoyed and perhaps alarmed him; it may have contributed to the foundation, probably in 1692, of the 'Most Drunken Synod', a body of the tsar's boon companions whose purpose is still debated, but whose blasphemous parodies of religious rites continued to the end of his reign. Peter also disliked the Church for the wealth which it diverted from more useful purposes, as well as for the laziness and ignorance of its monks and clergy. The result was a renewed and sustained effort to reduce clerical power and independence.

[1] See C. Marsden, *Palmyra of the North: the First Days of St Petersburg* (1942), ch. II, and R. Wittram, *Peter I. Czar und Kaiser* (2 vols. Göttingen, 1964), vol. II, pp. 57–79.

[2] For the conflicts engendered by the claims and reforms of Nikon, see vol. V, pp. 586–91. Western influences, mainly through the school of Kiev, are reconsidered by Simone Blanc, 'L'Eglise russe à l'aube du "Siècle des Lumières"', *Annales* (*E.S.C.*), 20e année (1965), pp. 442–64.

The essential step in this process, which began at least as early as 1696, was taken in 1700: on the death of Patriarch Adrian no successor was appointed. This deprived the Church of a formal head and opened the way to more direct State influence in its affairs. In 1701 the Monastery *prikaz* was founded to supervise Church property; a large proportion of the Church's revenues was soon being diverted towards the growing cost of the war with Sweden. There was a simultaneous drive to reduce the number of monks, force them to work and practise asceticism, and prevent the building of new monasteries. Finally, in 1721, the patriarchate itself was formally abolished. In its place, with the advice from 1716 of the erastian Feofan Prokopovich, later archbishop of Novgorod, a boldly 'philosophic' theologian who had lived in Switzerland and introduced science into his courses at Kiev, Peter set up the Most Holy Directing Synod, a body of ten churchmen intended to be superior in standing to any of the colleges—in fact, though itself collegiate in form, the equivalent in spiritual affairs of the Senate in secular.[1] In theory it wielded all the powers of the patriarch, but only as the subordinate agent of the tsar. The autonomy so long enjoyed by the Church was thus destroyed and its political power decisively broken: an innovation pregnant with consequences for the whole future of Russia.

Underlying all these developments, and in part resulting from them, changes were taking place in the structure of Russian society which Peter had not planned and whose full implications he could not foresee, but which were none the less one of his most historic legacies.[2] They affected above all the peasantry and landowners, neither of whom had been a homogeneous or legally unified social class but embraced, rather, a variety of fairly well-marked groups, each with its distinct legal rights and obligations, so that Russian society presented a picture of remarkable complexity and diversity. The peasantry ranged, at one extreme, from the *kholopy*, who were in effect slaves (though a relatively minor element in Muscovite society), through various groups of serfs and small freeholders to the *odnodvortsy*, a class of semi-military colonists in central and south Russia, sometimes esteemed as the lowest stratum of the nobility and not peasants at all. The landowners and serf-owners included a group of great boyar houses, some of which could claim to be more ancient than the Romanovs themselves, and beneath them a complex hierarchy of ranks and families—a hierarchy maintained until 1682 by *mestnichestvo*, the officially recognized custom governing the precedence of different noble families. The landowners had also been divided, at least formally, by the existence of two different forms of estate in Russia; but the distinction

---

[1] Cf. vol. VII, p. 325.
[2] The best account in English of these social changes, which have been much discussed by Russian historians, is to be found in V. Klyuchevsky, *Peter the Great* (1959)—a translation of part of his *Kurs Russkoi Istorii* (Moscow, 5 vols. 1904–21). Cf. vol. VII, pp. 320–2.

between *votchiny* and *pomest'ya* was now virtually meaningless, since in practice all estates had become hereditary.[1]

The effect of Peter's innovations was to create out of this subtly graded social system two large and, in law, relatively homogeneous classes: the tax-paying peasants—both serfs on private estates and State peasants—and the privileged landowners. The peasant class, as it existed by 1724, had been created largely by the systematic recruiting of large numbers for the army, and by the imposition after 1718 of the poll-tax. Under the continual pressure to raise as many recruits and as much money as possible, both liabilities tended to fall on an increasing proportion of the population, so that the old legal and economic distinctions within the peasant mass—nine-tenths of the population—lost much of their relevance. This levelling and consolidating process is clearly seen in the decline of the *odnodvortsy* to the status of a mere group of State peasants and, in a different direction, in the disappearance in 1723 of slavery (*kholopstvo*) as a legal status. In the same way, at the other end of the social scale, a more homogeneous and self-conscious landowning class (*dvoryanstvo*) was emerging, largely as a result of the increasingly effective imposition on all landlord groups of the burden of State service. Throughout, Peter made strenuous efforts to compel all landowners to serve the State in army, navy or administration—and to prevent and punish all attempts to evade such service. Thus the important and highly unpopular decree of 1714, ordering that estates henceforth be inherited by only one of the owner's children and not divided as had hitherto been normal, was designed to drive young members of the landowning class into State service. The considerable success achieved in this purpose meant that official rank, rather than descent or even wealth, more and more became the criterion by which the importance of a Russian landowner or nobleman was judged. As a result, the outlook of the upper class tended increasingly to become dominated by the idea of society as a bureaucratic hierarchy—an attitude strengthened by the issue in 1722 of the 'Table of Ranks', which divided army and navy officers into 14 distinct grades and assigned to each an equivalent in the civil service. Any of these grades conferred hereditary nobility, as did the eight highest equivalents in the bureaucracy. By 1724, therefore, the 'nobility' was rapidly becoming a relatively numerous class with very strong official connections, akin in some ways to that which Frederick William I was now creating in Prussia.

How far were all these schemes stimulated by the impact of Western ideas? Some historians have seen Peter's rule as the Russian equivalent of the increasingly centralized and efficient absolute monarchies now evolving in most of western and northern Europe. Certainly, foreign ideas on forms of government and methods of administration circulated freely in his entourage during most of the reign, and he was influenced by the

[1] See vol. v, pp. 578–9.

advice of foreigners, notably the Holsteiner Fick and the Saxon Luberas. Undoubtedly, also, several innovations—above all, the creation of the administrative colleges and of the navy, the reorganization of the army—were inspired by foreign practice. Equally clearly, such foreign influences were confined to questions of means and methods. The ends which Peter's policies were designed to serve—increased military strength, a more developed economic life, the acquisition of outlets to the sea—were inherent in the previous history and geographical position of Russia: they were not suggested to him by foreign advisers or the experience of foreign travel.[1] Indeed, for all the changes he introduced, except the outright abolition of the patriarchate, some precedent can be found during the reigns of his immediate predecessors. Even a Russian navy, in some ways the most striking and most unpopular of his innovations, had been faintly foreshadowed in the 1660s. Peter's reign saw Russia, under an autocratic and even brutal master, evolving with unheard-of speed at the cost of almost unbearable social and psychological tensions. She was undergoing, however, a process of forced evolution rather than of true revolution.

Peter's reforms gained him the enthusiastic support of a small number of westernized young Russians, but were carried out in face of the uncomprehending hostility of the vast majority of his subjects. Some of this was merely the instinctive repulsion which an uneducated people, dominated by religious conservatism, felt for the external signs of growing foreign influence—shaving, the wearing of western clothes, smoking, the new calendar. Yet behind these feelings lay more substantial and enduring grievances. The greatest and most widely felt was the sometimes unbearable physical and financial burden that the reign placed on the peasant: most obviously the heavy taxation and levying of great numbers of recruits, but harder still perhaps the constant conscription of peasant labour and resources for public works such as the building of ships, harbours, fortifications, canals—further levies often on a very large scale. The construction of St Petersburg notoriously consumed enormous drafts of peasant labour. From its foundation in 1703 until 1718, conscripted workers, some from as far as Siberia, struggled, suffered and died in the marshes at the mouth of the Neva, while with infinite labour and great losses from hunger and disease the city slowly rose. Even after 1718 the peasants of the St Petersburg province continued to provide labour for

---

[1] The part played by foreign influences in Peter's reforms is still debated. Among many discussions of it may be mentioned W. Leontiev, 'Peter der Grosse: seine Wirtschaftspolitik und sein angeblicher Merkantilismus', *Jahrbücher für Geschichte Osteuropas*, vol. II (1937), pp. 234–71; P. Milyukov, *Gosudarstvennoe khozyaistvo Rossii v pervoi chetverti XVIII stoletiya i reforma Pyotra Velikogo* (St Petersburg, 1905); W. Hinz, 'Peters des Grossen Antheil an der wissenschaftlichen und künstlerischen Kultur seiner Zeit', *Jahrbücher für Kultur und Geschichte der Slaven*, neue Folge, vol. VIII (1932), pp. 349–447; and B. I. Syromyatnikov, '*Regulyarnoe*' *gosudarstvo Pyotra pervogo i ego ideologiya*, vol. I (Moscow–Leningrad, 1943).

this purpose; elsewhere the compulsion was not abolished but merely commuted for a cash payment. The sufferings of the men who built the new capital are recorded in more than one folksong. When to burdens of this kind are added the obligations to provide workers for the new factories, food and forage for the army, and a wide variety of carrying services, the widespread and bitter unpopularity of Peter's régime is easily comprehensible. It has been estimated that the average peasant household during most of his reign was forced at different times to contribute to the State—in cash, services and kind—the equivalent of between 125 and 187 days' labour a year. Even the tsar's sister Maria was driven to complain of the endless war and the consequent ruin of the people. Against these burdens, intolerable in years of bad harvest and food shortage like 1704–6 and 1722–3, the peasant's only effective protest was flight—to thinly populated frontier areas, to the Cossacks, or to non-Russian peoples like the Bashkirs. Peter complained as early as 1707 of the numbers taking refuge with the Don Cossacks. The phenomenon increased in scope as his reign drew to a close, and in 1719–27 nearly 200,000 cases of flight of this kind were officially registered. The tsar's last years saw intensified efforts to stamp out so dangerous a tendency.

The Cossacks, besides serving as a refuge for discontented or despairing peasants, also provided on occasion more active opposition.[1] In 1706–8 those of the Don area rebelled on a considerable scale, under Kondrat Bulavin, against the foreign influences the tsar was believed to represent, and especially against the forced labour in the shipyards of Azov, Taganrog and Voronezh which he was now increasingly demanding. Coming just when Swedish pressure on Russia's western frontiers was at a climax, the revolt marked one of the most dangerous moments of the reign. Nor did its savage suppression in the summer of 1708 end Peter's difficulties with discontented elements on his southern frontier. The Zaporozhian Cossacks —a group of unruly freebooters settled on the river Dnieper—joined Charles XII and Mazepa, the rebellious hetman of the Ukraine, in 1709. Their military value was slight and they were immediately punished by the destruction of the *sech'*—the fortified settlement on the middle Dnieper which had for almost a century been their headquarters. Yet for many years after Poltava Cossack refugees, led by Philip Orlik, Mazepa's successor, continued to harass the tsar. Though too few and weak to be in themselves a serious threat, the influence they could sometimes exert at Constantinople long made them a factor of importance in the usually strained relations between Russia and the Porte.

Above all, Peter had to face within Russia a powerful religious opposition

---

[1] See vol. v, pp. 566–8, 572–6, and 584–5 for their importance in the relations of Muscovy with its neighbours. Cf. D. Eeckaute, 'Les Brigands en Russie du XVIIe au XIXe siècle: mythe et réalité', *Rev. d'hist. mod. et contemp.* vol. XII (1965), pp. 161–202, on the background of endemic crime in the frontier zones and along trade routes which Peter's many measures failed to stamp out.

that could take actively dangerous forms. The feeling that the tsar and his ambitions were a danger to the traditions of Holy Russia, even to the Orthodox faith itself, had considerably influenced the *strel'tsy* revolt of 1698. Its suppression, the abolition of the patriarchate, Peter's open adherence to foreign methods and ideas, all stimulated these fears, which often assumed the form of grotesque beliefs about him—that he was really the son of Lefort, a foreigner substituted for the true tsar who had been murdered on his travels abroad, or even Antichrist himself, whose rule foretold the end of the world. Such notions were common, notably among the *raskol'niki*, members of the very widespread dissenting movement which had reacted against Nikon's Graecophil reforms of Russian rites in the 1660s[1] and which, despite Peter's relative toleration of it, remained intensely distrustful of him. Religious emotions were important in stimulating a considerable revolt in Astrakhan, in 1705–6, and influenced that of Bulavin a year later. Opposition of this type was most strikingly seen in the tragic career of Peter's son Alexis, the product of his short-lived marriage to Evdokia Lopukhina. Devout, studious, pious and weak, Alexis had nothing in common with the terrible father whom he feared and hated, and with whom he had never any real personal contact. As time passed and the hopeless antagonism between the two became clearer, Peter's anger and disappointment, like Alexis's fear and hatred, were intensified. The tsarevich had a natural interest in theology and ritual, and under the influence of conservative advisers came to the conclusion that his father's policies were ruinous to Russia. He meant when he came to the throne—as he afterwards admitted—to abandon the fleet, restore the capital at Moscow, and fight no aggressive wars. The father-son antagonism came to a head in the autumn of 1716 when Alexis fled abroad, first to the Habsburg lands, then to Naples. His return in February 1718 under a promise of personal safety, the arrest and condemnation of many of his alleged supporters, his interrogation and torture, his death in July—this is one of the most famous tragedies of the century. The exact causes of his death are still unknown, but that Peter bears the responsibility for it is beyond doubt. That he was willing to proceed to such extremes, in defence of what he considered essential reforms, is striking proof both of his sense of duty to the State and of the streak of ferocity in his character. Four years later, in 1722, he assumed the right to nominate his own successor; but it was never used. On his death-bed, in January 1725, weakness frustrated his last effort to make known his will on this matter, and the succession was left to be determined by the Guards regiments and a handful of great officials.

Poltava is an unmistakable turning-point in Russia's relations with the rest of Europe. Until the catastrophic defeat of Charles XII in the Ukraine,

---

[1] See vol. v, pp. 589–90.

Peter and his country had occupied a relatively minor place in the calculations of Western statesmen.

It is true that Russia's entry into the Great Northern War had brought her into closer political contact than ever before with other States. The Maritime Powers, anxious to end the war and so use Swedish troops in their imminent struggle with France, offered mediation in 1700 to both Peter and Charles. Such offers, repeated more than once in after years, were consistently accepted by the tsar and as consistently refused by the king of Sweden, flushed with success and inspired by the idea of a righteous vengeance to be exacted from the States which had attacked him. Charles's stubbornness, however, served to increase the interest which the anti-French powers were now compelled to take in events in the North. In 1702, for example, Keyserlingk, the Prussian representative at Moscow, proposed that Peter should ally with the emperor and the Maritime Powers, while in May and June 1707 A. A. Matveev, the very able Russian minister at The Hague, was in London negotiating for a possible Russian adhesion to the Grand Alliance—negotiations not finally abandoned until autumn 1708. Meanwhile, France had also hoped to obtain Swedish troops for the Spanish Succession War. When Peter and Augustus II met at Birże early in 1701, the French ambassador to Poland, du Héron, proposed a peace with Charles XII: then Russia, Poland, Sweden and Turkey should all join France in a great coalition against the emperor and the Maritime Powers. A year later, Patkul, the Livonian nobleman who had done so much to create the anti-Swedish coalition of 1699–1700,[1] suggested an alliance of France with Russia, Denmark and 'other northern states'. In the spring of 1707, hard pressed by the Swedish victories in Poland and mounting discontent at home, Peter offered to supply Louis XIV with a considerable body of troops in return for his mediation to end the Northern War. Louis accepted this proposal. But Charles XII's demand for the restitution of all former Swedish territory, together with Peter's equally adamant refusal to give up his newly created St Petersburg, meant that there was as yet no real possibility of peace. These negotiations, however, never seemed of really fundamental importance to the English or French statesmen concerned, none of whom attached any great significance to Russian support. In February 1706, Torcy refused to make a bid for the tsar's goodwill even at the comparatively trivial cost of returning two Russian ships seized by Dunkirk privateers; at the end of August, he rejected a proposal for a commercial treaty with Russia on the grounds that the war precluded any development of trade between the two countries. Similarly, in England, Godolphin argued in 1707 that the Northern War 'may be without much affecting our war, unless the Turk takes the advantage, when Muscovy and Poland can give him no diversion, to fall upon the Emperor and the Venetians'.[2]

[1] Cf. above, pp. 652–3. [2] Hist. MSS. Comm. Bath MSS. vol. I, p. 184.

Poltava, which transformed Charles XII from a conqueror into a fugitive, revolutionized the whole position. It made possible a resurrection of the anti-Swedish coalition of 1699–1700, thus threatening Britain and the Netherlands with the recall of the auxiliary troops they had hired from Denmark and Saxony. It destroyed the position of Stanislas Leszczyński and made Russian influence dominant in Poland. It opened the prospect of Russian occupation of much of the Baltic coastline and even of northern Germany. In these ways it enormously increased Peter's influence in western Europe, besides endowing him with the prestige which military success alone could give. 'Now', wrote Urbich (the Russian minister in Vienna) to Leibniz in August 1709, 'people begin to fear the Tsar as formerly they feared Sweden.' The philosopher agreed that 'it is commonly said that the Tsar will be formidable to all Europe, and that he will be a kind of northern Turk', and a few weeks later advised his employer, the elector of Hanover, to take pains to keep on good terms with Peter.[1] In 1710, during the negotiations with Britain and France at Geertruidenburg, Torcy suggested that the Spanish Succession War should be ended by Russian mediation: he hoped, as he admitted, to use Peter for French purposes as Richelieu had used Gustavus Adolphus. Poltava had thus produced an immediate recognition of Russia's new standing in European affairs. It also made clear that the other States of northern Europe had now far more to fear from her than from the decaying empire of Sweden. In 1711 a Prussian diplomat proposed that Denmark, Prussia and Augustus II of Saxony-Poland should form an alliance, which might later be joined by Charles XII, to restrain the now menacing expansion of Russian power. This was only one of a number of similar suggestions put forward in the years following the Russian victory.

Active intervention in the North by the major western powers was nevertheless impossible until 1713 or later. The British government indeed regarded with uneasiness the conquest of Livonia, the irruption of Russian troops into Germany, the growth of Russian naval power in the Baltic, and the possibility that Peter might soon come to monopolize the supply of some types of naval stores; but until peace had been made with France its hands were tied. 'We have our eyes intently fixed on the Northern Affairs,' wrote Bolingbroke in February 1713, 'but like People who gaze on a storm at Sea, we are rather filled with horror at the sight, and compassion for those that suffer, than with hopes of being able, at least immediately, to contribute to save them.'[2] In 1714, with the accession of a king who was already, as elector of Hanover, a member of the anti-Swedish alliance, the prospect of British action to restrain Russian expansion became still more remote.[3] The United Provinces also, linked

---

[1] V. I. Guer'e, *Sbornik pisem i memoryalov Leibnitsa otnosyashchikhsya k Rossii i Petru Velikomu* (St Petersburg, 1873), pp. 115, 120, 139.
[2] To Scott, minister to Saxony-Poland, 3 Feb. 1713 (London, P.R.O., S.P. 104/123).
[3] Cf. above, pp. 673, 675–6.

to Russia by the desire of many Amsterdam merchants to preserve and extend their profitable trading connections there, were unlikely to offer her any effective opposition. Louis XIV and his ministers, though strongly influenced by the pro-Swedish tradition still powerful in France, had hoped to use Russia against the victorious coalition, believing in particular that Peter might be persuaded to support the Hungarian nationalists under Rákóczi against the emperor. After Poltava, therefore, Peter was able to complete the conquest of Livonia without interference, while Denmark, Hanover and Prussia expelled the Swedes from all their German possessions.

It was also during this period that Peter undertook the most spectacular and dangerous adventure of his reign, the Turkish campaign of 1711. The war declared by the Porte in November 1710 had not been sought by the tsar, whose hands were still tied by the need to consolidate his conquests on the Baltic and make peace with Sweden. The Russo-Turkish war of 1711 was the work of Charles XII, of Poniatowski and his other agents at Constantinople, and above all of the khan of the Crimea.[1] Peter would have been willing to accept mediation by one of the great powers in order to avoid the dispersal of his energies by a conflict on his southern borders: not until March 1711 was a formal and public declaration of war issued in Moscow. Once declared, however, war was pressed forward with energy. The tsar now dreamed of a victorious advance to the Danube, supported by a general revolt of the Balkan Christians against Muslim rule. The offensive was nevertheless a catastrophic failure. The loss of Russia's new and hard-won foothold on the Black Sea was a bitter blow, but the outcome of the campaign was less disastrous than at one time seemed likely. It did not result in the destruction of Peter's army or the loss of his personal liberty, and it left him free to complete the overthrow of Swedish power in the Baltic. Not even the belated return of Charles XII in 1714 from exile in Turkey could prevent this taking place. With the fall of Wismar in 1716, the last of Sweden's continental possessions had been lost: by the summer it seemed that a Russo-Danish army, supported by British and Dutch squadrons, was about to land in southern Sweden.

The crisis which followed—the sudden decision of the tsar to abandon the invasion, the quartering in Mecklenburg during the winter of 1716–17 of much of the Russian force which had been collected for it, the alarm of Peter's allies and the consequent dissolution of the anti-Swedish coalition —this was the most serious diplomatic complication in which Russia had yet been involved.[2] The events of 1716, by the very intensity of the anti-Russian feeling they stimulated in Britain, Denmark and Hanover, made

[1] Above, pp. 631 ff.
[2] See above, pp. 675–7. Cf. J. J. Murray, 'Scania and the end of the Northern Alliance', *Journal of Mod. Hist.* vol. XVI (1944), pp. 81–92, and W. Mediger, *Russlands Weg nach Europa* (Brunswick, 1952), pp. 32–5.

it clear—more, perhaps, even than Poltava—that Russia was now politically a part of Europe. The fears of complete Russian domination of the Baltic and of north Germany then aroused were slow to die down. Peter appears to have thought of seeking compensation in Livonia, or at the expense of Hanover, for the tyrannical duke of Mecklenburg, who had been expelled by his Estates with the support of a Hanoverian force; and in 1722 there were fears that the tsar might seize Mecklenburg and Danzig for himself. In the last years of his reign the possibility that his son-in-law, Duke Charles Frederick of Holstein-Gottorp, might be established as king of Sweden, with Russian backing, fed distrust in the chancelleries of western Europe. Disliked, feared, in some respects still despised, Russia could no longer be ignored. The strangeness and barbarity of many aspects of her national life, the incomprehensibility of her language, the superstitions of her Church, could not disguise the fact that she now played a growing part in moulding the policies of the European states.

Peter was soon to emphasize this in unmistakable manner. In 1717 he undertook his second journey to the West, a journey which included visits to Hamburg and Amsterdam and culminated in Paris where, not surprisingly, the Gobelins factory and the *Jardin du Roi* held a peculiar fascination for him. He now appeared, however, no longer as a pupil travelling incognito in search of new ideas and techniques, but as a political innovator and military conqueror, to many eyes the greatest ruler of the age. At the same time, the results of this journey were negligible in terms of immediate political advantage. Peter hoped for a French alliance, an idea that was to influence much of his foreign policy until his death: 'I come', he told Marshal Tessé, who had been appointed to negotiate with him, 'to offer myself to France, to take for her the place of Sweden.'[1] This offer, made with typical frankness and wholeheartedness, was sterile. The French government, now bound to Britain by the Triple Alliance of 1717, was to some extent caught up in its hostility to Russia and remained obstinately loyal to Sweden, France's traditional ally. The Regent Orléans was unable to offer Peter either the subsidy or the guarantee of his conquests for which he asked. The tsar had to be content merely with the signature in August, at Amsterdam, of a treaty with France and Prussia by which the former agreed to mediate in the Baltic and make no new agreement contrary to Russian interests. Ineffective as it was, the treaty nevertheless constituted a still further recognition of Russia's new European status.

This was recognized in other ways. Diplomatic relations with the European states were now far more continuous and systematic than ever before. By the end of Peter's reign representatives of the major powers

---

[1] *Sbornik Imperatorskogo Russkogo Istoricheskogo Obshchestva*, vol. XXXIV (1881), p. 198.

were established in Russia on a permanent basis, and a value unknown in the seventeenth century was attached to their negotiations and reports. On his side, Peter did much to accelerate this growth of contact. In 1699, with the dispatch of A. A. Matveev to The Hague, he inaugurated a Russian diplomatic service of a modern kind. Russian embassies to the West ceased to be the short-lived, *ad hoc* episodes of the two preceding centuries. Furthermore, from 1707, Russia began to acquire for the first time a system of consular representation in western Europe. By 1725 she was equipped with a diplomatic service comparable with that of any other European state. The enhancement of her international standing can also be seen in the hitherto unheard-of willingness of many ruling families to contemplate marriage alliances with the Romanovs. As early as 1701 the Emperor Leopold hinted at a possible marriage of his son to Peter's sister Nataliya, or to one of his nieces, though it is unlikely that this project was ever taken very seriously in Vienna. Of more practical importance was the marriage in 1710 of the tsar's niece Anna to the duke of Courland; she was the first Russian princess for two centuries to marry a foreigner, and six years later another niece, Catherine, became duchess of Mecklenburg. The Tsarevich Alexis married in 1711 Charlotte of Brunswick-Wolfenbüttel. Philip V appears to have considered marrying his son to a Russian princess in Peter's last years, when the tsar was able on more than one occasion seriously to suggest that one of his daughters marry into the French royal family—a striking demonstration indeed of how highly the standing of the Romanovs had improved. When, on the conclusion of a victorious peace with Sweden in 1721, he assumed the title of *Imperator*, the gesture struck Western statesmen as an appropriate assertion of Russia's new place in the world.

His position on the Baltic finally secured at Nystad, Peter's last years were spent largely in pursuit of expansion in Asia. With Peking a regular caravan trade from Moscow had been organized since 1698, but no attempt was made to reoccupy the Amur valley—despite its proven value as a granary for the Russian colonies on the Siberian rivers—after the assertion of Manchu influence over it by the Treaty of Nerchinsk in 1689. Russian resources were not likely to be diverted to this region while they were strained in Europe, although Peter gave considerable support to missionary activity in Siberia and was much concerned to halt the abuses of the local Siberian administrators, not least in the interest of his treasury, which still drew a useful revenue from the profits of the State-controlled fur trade.[1] From 1714 a series of somewhat unsuccessful missions—part military, part scientific—were sent to the khanates of central Asia, and in

---

[1] Wittram, vol. II, pp. 480–3; G. V. Lantzeff, *Siberia in the Seventeenth Century: a Study of the Colonial Administration* (Univ. of California Publications in History, vol. 30, 1943), pp. 151–4. Cf. R. Portal, 'Les Russes en Sibérie au XVIIᵉ siècle', *Rev. d'Hist. Mod. et Contemp.* vol. V (1958), pp. 5–38, for a general assessment of Siberia and its problems.

1717 a commercial treaty was signed with Persia. In 1721, tempted after Nystad by the approaching collapse of the Safavi dynasty, Peter began a systematic campaign to seize Persia's Caspian provinces, rich in silk and apparently easy to conquer. Disease, difficulties of communication, lack of help from the Christians of Georgia, the threat of Turkish intervention, all made the war unexpectedly difficult and expensive. Nevertheless Darband and Resht were occupied in 1722, Baku in 1723; and in 1724, after much complicated diplomacy, Russia found herself possessed of a long strip of territory on the west and south coasts of the Caspian.[1] This, Peter's last conquest, proved neither valuable nor permanent. Russian troops stationed in the conquered area, much of which was never effectively occupied, continued to lose many men by disease; and in 1732, under the rule of the Empress Anna, the territories acquired less than a decade earlier were abandoned.

Russia's new power naturally had intellectual and psychological repercussions abroad, requiring a drastic revision of the contemptuous indifference long current in the West. Even before Poltava there were signs that Peter's activities were beginning to win the respect, if not the admiration, of western observers; the great Leibniz, deeply interested in Russia as a field for scientific and linguistic study and as an intermediary between the civilizations of Europe and China, had already been impressed by the opportunities which a largely undeveloped country appeared to present to such a ruler. It was, however, her military successes against Sweden which above all won for Russia the attention of western Europe. Mainly for this reason, the second half of Peter's reign saw a steady increase in the output of books on Russia, and in the notice allotted to Russian affairs by western newspapers and periodicals. Peter himself understood the importance of a good press abroad. As early as 1703 he maintained at Paris an agent whose duty was to spread news of his victories and reforms, while the major German political journal of the time, the *Europäische Fama*, was strongly influenced by him and gave favourable publicity to what he did. It is true that knowledge of Russia and her tsar remained, even after Poltava, remarkably limited in some respects. As late as 1717, on his visit to Paris, a good many of the citizens who flocked to see Peter were uncertain even of his exact name or title. To the end of his reign, and indeed for long after, many of the most significant aspects of Russian life—the problems created by the consolidation and extension of serfdom, by bureaucratic inefficiency and corruption, by religious dissent—were almost a closed book to western Europe. As yet no writer had succeeded in presenting to the West a truly balanced and realistic picture of Russian society. Nevertheless, it was widely felt that what had been the obscurantist and semi-barbaric Muscovy was now beginning to belong to Europe in more than a merely political sense. This awareness is symbolized by

[1] Above, pp. 644–5.

the appearance of Russia in 1716, for the first time, in the list of European powers printed in the French *Almanach Royal*.

The growing respect thus felt for Russia reflected in large degree, of course, the admiration, sometimes amounting to adulation, lavished on her ruler personally. Even before Louis XIV died, Peter had become for many observers by far the greatest of living monarchs. His energy, his open-mindedness, his regard for knowledge (at least for certain types of knowledge), his self-sacrifice in the cause of national greatness—these qualities seemed irrefutable proofs of the benefits to be obtained from the rule of an intelligent and public-spirited autocrat. Peter appealed almost irresistibly to the growing taste of the Enlightenment for constructive rulers willing to follow the dictates of reason and nature. 'His Piety is visible', wrote the chaplain of the British factory at St Petersburg, 'in his noble Attempt to reform the Manners of his People, his Resolution great in thwarting their Inclinations, and obliging them to relinquish their long-espoused Errors and superstitious Practices which they were born and bred in.'[1] His death produced a flood of laudatory comments and epitaphs, at least one of which, the *Eloge* delivered to the French Academy by Fontenelle, was profoundly to influence future Western views of his reign: this somewhat uncritical admiration was to be given even more influential form a generation later by Voltaire, notably in his *Histoire de l'Empire de Russie sous Pierre le Grand* (1759–63). Whatever reservations Peter's contemporaries may have felt about welcoming Russia as a European State, they had none in his later years about accepting him as a great man. In spite of his brutalities, his over-confidence, his miscalculations and occasional catastrophic defeats, Peter's place in the Pantheon of those who have 'made history' was even then secure.

[1] T. Consett, *The Present State and Regulations of the Church of Russia* (1729), p. xiv.

CHAPTER XXII

ARMIES AND NAVIES

I. THE ART OF WAR ON LAND

BY the last decade of the seventeenth century the attitude of influential European opinion towards warfare was undergoing radical change. The intolerance that embittered the wars of religion had largely ebbed away, except in regions exposed to the Ottoman; and although the increasing scope of hostilities led to the ever deeper commitment of available national resources, only the desperate French war effort after 1708, and the Homeric sacrifices borne by the Swedes in their protracted struggle with Russia, looked forward in any way to that patriotic inspiration destined, from 1793, to produce the *levée en masse* and 'total' warfare. Between the eras of religious and national wars the conduct of military operations tended to become 'limited',[1] less perhaps in the sense that objectives were restricted to dynastic or commercial ambitions as that the fighting itself was increasingly regarded as a relatively gentlemanly affair governed by firm conventions. In any case, the impact of war on the civilian populations of Europe was still restrained by poor communications, which tended to channel campaigns to certain well-fought-over areas. Although the economic consequences were widely felt, wars varied considerably in the amount of direct misery they inflicted. The Great Northern War earned a reputation for ferocity, whilst in the South-East Turkish atrocities were occasionally avenged by Austrian reprisals. In the West, the two sackings of the Palatinate by the French forces, in 1674 and 1688, and the Allies' ravaging of Bavaria in 1704 are often cited as examples of the horrors of war; but the widespread contemporary outcry about these excesses suggests that they shocked the conscience of the age.

Nevertheless, the most striking feature of war during this period was the gradual growth in the size of certain armies, even though most armed forces remained small. At Rocroi, widely regarded in 1643 as a large battle, 23,000 French troops defeated approximately 27,000 Spaniards; sixty-six years later 80,000 Frenchmen fought 110,000 Allied troops on the gory field of Malplaquet. This reflected a general growth of military manpower as governments improved their financial and administrative systems. Between 1691 and 1693 it is estimated that France controlled some 440,000 soldiers; in war-time, however, the total fluctuated considerably according to national fortunes and in 1705 this number had shrunk to 250,000, although it subsequently recovered. Even in peace-time the French establishment rarely fell below 150,000 effectives. The Swedish

---

[1] Cf. above, pp. 229–31 and below, pp. 784 ff.

empire, with a population of two and a half million, supported an army of 110,000 at its peak. Peter the Great built up a regular army (excluding Cossacks) of twice this size. The Austrian and Imperial forces varied between 100,000 and 140,000. These figures were matched, if not exceeded, by the Ottomans. England continued to pursue her incalculable way and her army differed in size at different periods: the lowest ebb was reached in 1698, when parliament restricted the strength to 7,000 on English soil and 17,000 in Ireland and overseas, but at the height of the Succession War a total of 75,000 native-born troops was attained. The forces of the United Provinces were of that order.[1]

These larger armies must not be regarded necessarily as 'national' forces of home extraction. Large elements were made up of hired mercenaries. Thus the French employed Swiss, Scots, Irish and other foreign regiments to form no less than an eighth of their army in 1677; the Dutch used Danes and Brandenburgers, the English Hanoverians and Hessians; and the Austrians relied on large numbers of troops provided on contract by the States of the Empire, besides contingents of irregular infantry and cavalry supplied by the Croats and other inhabitants of the military frontiers (*Militärgrenze*). This 'international' appearance of many armies was made possible in part by the professional attitude of the adventurer element in all of them. The Irishman Peter Drake served in both Allied and French armies during the same war without embarrassment; the Flemish cavalry general, the count of Mérode-Westerloo, switched from the Franco-Spanish to the Habsburg army and rose to high rank in both. Scorned by the rest of society as a wastrel, the professional soldier felt little compunction about changing sides if it suited his advantage. Yet this did not prevent individual units from acquiring a very high *esprit de corps*—the *Maison du Roi*, the English Guards, the Swedish Drabants being outstanding examples—and the great commanders often inspired a high degree of personal loyalty in their men. Deeds of great gallantry were never lacking on the field of battle.

Transfers of service by soldiers of fortune were facilitated by the large similarity existing between armies. This was often more than superficial, for a series of strong influences, long-term and immediate, ensured that they developed along the same broad lines as regards tactics, equipment and theories of warfare. Throughout the second half of the seventeenth century, the influence of France predominated. Her forces were the largest, the best organized and (until Blenheim) patently the most successful in Europe. French military terms (or their derivatives), such as battalion and platoon, were incorporated in many languages. Charles II sent young officers to study their profession under Turenne: one was John Churchill, destined as the first duke of Marlborough to become the scourge of his old French colleagues. Goaded by William of Orange, the United Pro-

---

[1] See below, ch. xxii (2), for the recruitment and social composition of armies.

vinces slowly reformed their forces on the French model. Peter always relied heavily on German officers, especially in the higher ranks.[1] The Austrians and Swedes developed their military systems more independently under Montecuccoli and Charles XI, but in most ways they reproduced the standard French pattern. Gallic influence was more marked in Germany, although Sweden was copied in Brandenburg-Prussia.[2]

One major protagonist in the wars of this period continued to employ the organization and methods of a much earlier age. While the Ottoman navy was already adopting certain western techniques, modernization of the army was not seriously undertaken before the time of Bombardier Ahmed Pasha, *alias* Claude Alexandre de Bonneval (1675–1747), who entered the sultan's service in 1729.[3] The Turks still relied on weight of numbers, their field-armies being the largest in Europe. The well-informed Count Marsigli, who was in Turkey in 1678–9 and 1690–1, placed the number of second-line infantry, sappers and pioneers (*müsellems*), raised by the provincial pashas and known generically as 'Seratculi' (*serhadd kullari*, slaves of the frontier), at 100,000, in addition to a maximum of about 54,000 janissaries, organized in three corps. With the other regular arms—janissary novices, cannoneers, armourers, water-carriers— the janissaries were described as 'Capiculi' (*kapi kullari*, slaves of the Porte). The standing ('Capiculi') cavalry of over 15,000 sipahis, senior and junior, was supplemented by something like 50,000 horsemen from the provinces, raised as tribute or under various forms of service related to the holding of public offices, tax-farms and land. Tributary contingents were provided by Transylvania (until its conquest), the Rumanian principalities, and the Crimea, whose Tatar horsemen played a notable part in Ottoman campaigning. The old 'feudal' host, based on *zeamet* and *timar* tenures, was yielding in importance to the several types of 'Seratculi' cavalry—*gönülüs* (heavy), *beshlis* (light) and *delis* (scouts)—originally concerned with frontier defence but now recruited increasingly by all provincial governors out of the proceeds of tax-farms and by forced levies.[4]

Many features of the new-style French military machine were not of native origin, but it was the development of borrowed ideas by a series of great French generals and administrators that ensured their eventual incorporation into practically every European army. Most notable, after the tactical innovations of Maurice of Nassau (d. 1625) was the influence of Gustavus Adolphus, whose reforms amounted to a new type of warfare

---

[1] See above, pp. 720–1, and below, p. 777, for Peter's army reforms.
[2] See vol. v, p. 552.
[3] Exception might be made of the sappers, who gained from English and Dutch instruction during the Cretan war of 1664–9 (Gibb and Bowen, *Islamic Society and the West*, vol. I, pt. i, p. 187). Like Bonneval's new-style bombardiers, many were of Greek or Bosnian extraction.
[4] L. F. Marsigli, *L'Etat militaire de l'empire ottoman: son progrès et sa décadence*, pt. I (Amsterdam, 1732), pp. 61–143; Gibb and Bowen, vol. I, pt. i, pp. 192–3, 314–28. Cf. above, pp. 613–15.

based on exploiting the higher fire-power achieved by an improved 'wheel-lock' musket, by increasing the ratio of musketeers to pikemen, and by careful standardization of artillery calibres into the three main groups—siege, field and regimental. Gustavus was the first to realize the full implications of the improved artillery arm and he evolved his battle tactics round a complex fire-plan. Further, his new and compact tactical units, 400–500 men strong, increased mobility. Many countries imitated his innovations. Thus Cromwell and Rupert adopted the 'cold-steel' cavalry charge; Montecuccoli replaced the unwieldy Habsburg *tercio* by the six-rank battalion. Most significantly, Richelieu absorbed the entire army of Bernard of Saxe-Weimar into the French forces and sent promising officers to serve under others among Gustavus's old comrades. As applied by Turenne, Condé and Luxembourg, the Swedish system provided one basis for French martial predominance. Unfortunately for France, her generals later misapplied Swedish principles, and it was left to Marlborough, Eugene of Savoy and Charles XII to redevelop Gustavus's doctrines. Hence Sweden had introduced a 'military revolution' that left a lasting imprint on the armies of the century after Gustavus.[1]

It was in the reshaping of military administration that France made her greatest original contribution. Richelieu, again, began the process, by creating a war secretariat to co-ordinate supply and organization. His work was continued by Michel Le Tellier (1603–85) and his son Louvois (1641–91), who between them transformed an ill-trained rabble into the finest standing army in Europe, and whose reforms were imitated far and wide. They imposed close government supervision at all levels, although there was often a world of difference between practice and precept. A revised court-martial system dealt ruthlessly with cases of indiscipline and overt corruption. Irregular formations were suppressed and attempts made to end financial speculation in recruitment. Many abuses were eliminated by the careful allocation and supervision of funds, although the troops were still paid months in arrears.[2] Colonels of regiments received regular visitations by inspectors-general; drill, training and equipment were standardized as far as possible; distinctive uniforms were gradually introduced between 1672 and 1700. Precise regulations settled the numbers of battalions in the various regiments, the strength of cavalry squadrons, and many other points. The reorganization of the supply services particularly engaged the attention of Louvois. A body of war commissaries was set up to supervise the different branches of the Quartermaster's department, which included the artillery, munitions,

[1] M. Roberts, *The Military Revolution, 1560–1660* (Belfast, 1956). For the innovations of Charles XII, see R. M. Hatton, *Charles XII of Sweden,* pp. 465 ff. and 525–6.

[2] The French private soldier received 5 *sous* a day, a dragoon 11, a cavalryman 15. The English infantryman was paid 6*d.* a day subsistence and 2*d.* off-reckonings (less several deductions), the cavalry trooper 2*s.* 6*d.* in all (including forage allowance). In the Dutch service, the foot-soldier received 12½ guilders a month, the mounted soldier 28.

commissariat, remount, transport and ambulance services. The civilian intendants were to relieve the field commanders of as many supply problems as possible and report independently to Versailles on the conduct of operations. A comprehensive series of depôts (*étapes*) was established behind the frontiers to replenish supply-trains. All this greatly lessened the need to live off the countryside—a practice condemned by contemporary opinion and in any case inefficient, owing to the high desertion rates encouraged by sending men out to forage. Similar reforms improved the logistics of other European forces. The Austrian *Generalkriegskommissariat*[1] existed as early as 1650, but the General Supply Department (*Generalproviantamt*) became responsible for details of supply in the field. In England, the ancient Board of Ordnance provided many war materials besides artillery, but was supplemented in 1703 by the office of Comptroller of Army and Accounts to ensure that soldiers were issued with good equipment and regular subsistence money; the historic Royal Warrant of 1707 prescribed a scale of the correct clothing and equipment to be issued to each soldier. Such improvements were near to Marlborough's heart and it was his influence that procured them.

The French command-structure was thoroughly revised. The celebrated *Ordre du Tableau*, first issued in 1675, minutely regulated the military hierarchy, clearly defining the privileges of each grade and the requirements for promotion. The ancient custom whereby generals of equal rank commanded in the field on alternate days was finally replaced by the principles that seniority was firmly based on date of commission to the rank, and that the highest commands were solely in the royal gift and subject to continuous review.[2] Thenceforward the social status of the

[1] Cf. above, p. 573 n.
[2] Three representative chains of command showing approximately equivalent ranks are as follows:

FRANCE	ENGLAND	AUSTRIA
Maréchal de France	Captain-General	Feldmarschall
Maréchal-général des logis	Quartermaster-General	Feldzeugmeister
Lieutenant-général	Lieutenant-General	Feldmarschall-Lieutenant
Maréchal de camp	Major-General	General-Feldwachtmeister
Brigadier	Brigadier-General	(no equivalent)
Colonel	Colonel	Obrist
Lieutenant-colonel	Lieutenant-Colonel	Obristlieutenant
Major	Major	Obristwachtmeister
Lieutenant	Lieutenant	Lieutenant
Enseigne (infantry); Cornette (cavalry)	Ensign; Cornet	Fähndrich; Cornet
Sergent	Sergeant; Corporal of Horse	Feldwebel
Caporal	Corporal	Kaporal
Anspessade	Senior Soldier	Gefreite

These lists are not exhaustive: thus there were additional grades of general officer. The Quartermaster-General frequently carried out the functions of an unofficial Chief of Staff—a post not yet created—but he might be an officer of relatively junior rank.

French officer became theoretically less important than the rank he held. Old posts of dubious value, including that of *colonel-général*, were discontinued and new ones substituted, the most important being that of brigadier-general. Similar rank structures appeared throughout Europe, mostly owing something to the French, despite local variations and the strength of Austrian influence in Germany and Russia. Commissions in the intermediate and lower ranks were still bought and sold. In France they remained largely a noble perquisite, especially after 1715, although Louvois had attempted to make qualifying tests compulsory and set up training cadres for aspiring noblemen. Several European countries followed his lead.[1]

By these means the Le Tellier and their imitators founded efficient standing armies. At the same time, a tendency towards over-regulation encouraged a deadening stress on correct procedures that afflicted the French and other armies at the turn of the century. Many field-forces, moreover, continued to suffer great hardships from corrupt contractors and war profiteers.

Certain developments in types of infantry weapons also transformed the art of war. The flintlock musket and socket-bayonet were fast replacing the old combination of matchlock and pike. The new musket incorporated many improvements. It was still a heavy weapon[2] but considerably lighter than the matchlock, so that the musketeer no longer required a rest to support the barrel. A second improvement was a reduction in the calibre, increasing the number of musket balls from 12 to 16 to the pound, and in the case of one French model to 24; as a general rule, each soldier carried 25 rounds. The firing mechanism was easier to operate, the powder being ignited by a spark produced through the action of flint on steel. Although misfires were still experienced, this mechanism was more convenient than the use of the burning slow-match, which had to be manually applied to the touch-hole and was frequently put out of action by dampness. The effective range of the flintlock did not noticeably increase beyond 75 to 100 yards, but the rate of fire, assisted by the growing use of paper cartridges, was almost doubled; a good marksman could loose off several rounds a minute. One weakness persisted: the ramrod continued to be made of wood and tended to snap in the excitement of battle. Yet the flintlock represented a considerable advance in weapon technology: 'Firearms and not cold steel', Puységur (1655–1743) was to write, 'now decide battles.'[3] The flintlock was soon adopted as the

---

[1] Cf. below, pp. 780–2.

[2] The standard English version weighed a little under 10 lb. without the bayonet fixed, the Swedish version about 5 kg.; the matchlock weighed 15 lb. and more.

[3] *L'Art de la guerre par principes et par règles* (1748), quoted in G. B. Turner, *A History of Military Affairs in Western Society* (1953), p. 23. J. F. Puységur was a *maréchal général des logis* in 1690, a Marshal of France in 1734.

standard infantry weapon. Part of Feversham's army had it at Sedgemoor in 1685; by 1700 the English, Dutch and French forces were almost completely rearmed with it, although matchlocks were still issued to French second-line troops as late as 1703. The Swedish government approved the pattern for a flintlock musket in 1692 and began distribution in 1696, but many Swedish units long retained the peculiar 'combination-lock' musket of older design, embodying features of both match- and flintlock. This weapon was also widely used by the Austrians, but they gradually replaced it by the *flinte* during the early years of the new century. Only in the Russian and Ottoman forces did the matchlock remain for a further period the standard firearm for most musketeers. Ottoman troops were very unevenly armed; the janissaries carried good muskets, but many of the territorial formations still fought with javelins, bows and arrows, and *coupies* (lances).

The transition from pike to bayonet, as the weapon of personal protection, came more slowly, for the 'queen of weapons' had many champions: for instance, d'Artagnan strongly resisted Vauban's attempt to arm the French infantry exclusively with the musket. The proportion of one pikeman to five or six musketeers was retained by all armies to the end of the seventeenth century. Gradually, however, the disadvantages of the pike came to be widely recognized. Its great weight and unwieldy length (14 to 18 feet) severely restricted the mobility of the battalions, whilst the musketry experts coveted the unit manpower the pike employed. Even before an effective alternative had been discovered, the emperor in 1689 ordered the substitution of the *Schweinsfeder* (boar spear)[1] against the Turk. The pike's value as a defensive weapon was also in doubt after the battle of Fleurus (1690), where it was widely remarked that certain German battalions armed only with the musket had repulsed French cavalry attacks more effectively than other units conventionally armed with a proportion of pikes; in 1690 also, Catinat abandoned his pikes before undertaking his Alpine campaign against Savoy. Yet the development of a satisfactory replacement was very gradual. The *Schweinsfeder* was still an awkward weapon to convey, needing special carts. Attempts to fix a knife-blade or bayonet to the musket itself were not at first very successful. The 'plug' bayonet was in service in England as early as 1663 and on issue to certain French and Imperial units within the next twenty years, but this weapon's drawback, when fitted into the muzzle of the musket, was that it obstructed firing. As General Hugh Mackay, defeated at Killiecrankie (1689), pointed out: 'The Highlanders are of such quick motion that if a Battalion keep up his fire until they be near to make sure of [hitting] them, they are upon it before our men can come to the second

---

[1] This too was a Swedish invention; shorter than the pike, it was customarily planted in the ground in front of the soldier or incorporated in *chevaux de frise* (barricades of steel points set in wood)—a device widely employed by Continental armies.

defence, which is the bayonet in the musle of the musket.'[1] The difficulty was eventually overcome by the ring and socket bayonets, fitted round the muzzle. Different authorities credit both Mackay and Vauban with this invention, the effect of which was to ban the pike from the field of battle. The Swedish Guards received the bayonet in 1700, and the changeover was completed in most armies three years later, although the French regulations of 1703 still refer to 'le combat à la pique et au mousquet'. Different armies produced their own versions—thus the Austrian model was shorter and squatter than the French bayonet which it originally copied—but the tactical implications were the same. The ancient and puissant pike disappeared from European armies, although its small brothers, the half-pike, the *spontone* and halberd, were retained for more than another century as the personal weapons of sergeants and junior officers, proving invaluable for correcting the alignment of the rank and file.

The effects of the improved weapons were far-reaching. The importance of the infantry soldier on the battlefield was greatly enhanced, the rôle of the cavalry became correspondingly less vital. New formations were gradually created to make the most of the increased fire-power; infantry lines were extended to provide a wider unit frontage, but battalions were reduced in size. At the battle of the Dunes (1658), the French battalions consisted of 1,200 men apiece drawn up eight ranks deep: forty years later it was 700, in four or five ranks. The English battalion averaged approximately 500 men in 1702, drawn up in three ranks only, to achieve the maximum fire frontage. The Swedish units commonly contained 600 men in four ranks, covering an area in open order 185 metres long and 6 metres deep. In the Austrian army the regiment remained the basic major unit, but was grouped into battalions for tactical convenience; its size varied at different periods, consisting in 1695 of 2,300 men grouped in four battalions, but reduced by Eugene's reforms in 1711 to three battalions of five companies, each with a nominal strength of 140 men.

These changes encouraged a more aggressive employment of the infantry arm by commanders able to understand the true implications. At the same time tactics remained rigid. To secure maximum efficiency in firing and reloading, elaborate drill-movements were evolved. This inevitably meant the retention of strict linear formations and shoulder-to-shoulder drill. Both William III and Marlborough insisted on frequent exercises to develop disciplined fire-power. Many of the English were trained to fire by platoons in three firings, instead of by line, company, or even battalion volleys—the continued practice of the French and their allies. The English innovation had grown almost unnoticed over the years, but Marlborough recognized its tactical importance. Platoon fire conferred several marked advantages: greater continuity and accuracy

---

[1] *Memoirs, Letters, and Short Relations* (Edinburgh, Bannatyne Club, 1833), p. 52.

was achieved by entrusting fire control to the subordinate officers; the opposing line received no respite from the rippling fire of the English platoons, for one third of the battalion was always in the act of firing; and equally important from a defensive standpoint, a further third of a battalion's strength was always loaded and available to repulse an unexpected attack. To beat off enemy cavalry, a battalion formed a hollow square, each division or quarter-battalion wheeling into position to form one face. The English infantry were trained to move as well as to stand and fight, and gradually the modern principle of fire and movement was evolved. After wearing down the enemy with platoon fire at 70 yards' range, the English battalions poured in a single, delayed volley, followed by a bayonet charge into the reeling enemy line. The French were less imaginative in their employment of infantry fire-power. Their battalions were expected to provide chiefly a static base behind which the cavalry could re-form after the charge. The retention of four- and five-men-deep formations from the days of the pike wasted fire-potential and hindered fast redeployment; but Louvois had unimaginatively encouraged these concepts and it was not until Villars took command that the superior Allied techniques were partially adopted. The Swedes employed their infantry more effectively than the Russians. Charles XI introduced many improvements of drill in 1680; his son made few original contributions in this respect, but produced revised manuals in 1701 and 1708. The importance of the attack was constantly stressed. The Swedish infantry were ordered to counter-attack as soon as the enemy were reported advancing: at forty paces the two rear ranks fired a volley; advancing through the protective smoke, the two front ranks reserved their fire 'until one could reach the enemy with the bayonet'.[1] The Russian levies could rarely withstand such pressure.

One consequence of the association of linear formations and higher fire-power was a general increase in casualty rates. Steenkerk (1692), an action in which both armies were still largely armed with pike and match-lock, was widely regarded at the time as the severest infantry battle ever fought, each side losing some 4,000 killed and as many wounded out of 150,000 present; the brunt of the Allied casualties was borne by the advance guard of infantry. At Blenheim, after the change of weapons, there were over 30,000 casualties (besides prisoners) out of a joint total of 108,000 men; at Malplaquet the Allies lost one man in four; and at Poltava the Swedes suffered almost 4,000 casualties out of some 13,000 sent into battle. Exceptional losses on this scale evoked widespread outcry, and it is small wonder that many commanders preferred wars of manoeuvre. At the same time, sieges could be extremely costly: the capture of Lille, for example, cost the Allies at least 12,000 casualties.

[1] General Magnus Stenbock's 'Instructions' (Waxjö, 24 Jan. 1710), quoted in *General-stabens Krigshistoriska*, vol. III (Stockholm, 1919), p. 521.

By the last quarter of the seventeenth century, the science of defensive engineering had far outstripped the power of the cumbrous and short-ranged artillery. Rather ironically, Vauban never intended his fortifications to become the central focus of military operations: they were to conserve troops for offensives on other fronts. Nevertheless, an obsession for fortification and its associated operations gripped both France and the United Provinces, inevitably inducing defensive thinking and a preference for limited wars. Vauban's 'regulation of the frontier towns' (1678–98) resulted in the building of 33 new fortresses and the renovation of several hundred more near the French frontiers. His Dutch counterpart, Coehoorn, also developed a formidable fortress barrier. The emperor somewhat ineffectively attempted to renovate the defences of the upper Danube (Villingen, Ulm) and north Italy (Milan, Mantua) against French incursions, besides setting in order the fortresses of the Iron Gate (Old and New Orsova, Mehadia) against the Turk. After the French, the Turks were originally the most renowned for siege warfare; but their failure before Vienna in 1683 reduced their prestige as besiegers,[1] whilst Eugene's capture of Belgrade in 1717 irreparably damaged their reputation for invincibility in defence. Vauban's influence really dominated both aspects of such operations.

The measure of impregnability that his 'three orders' of defence-works conferred on fortresses compelled generals to concentrate on sieges and on operations in support or relief of them. His system, in the simplest terms, was to make the widest possible use of enfilading fire, defence in depth, and sally-ports for sudden sorties by the defenders. Vauban perfected the system of Pagan (1604–65), which hinged on the bastion; he reinforced vulnerable salients with outworks and ravelins, and based all his fortifications on the natural configuration of the ground. Thus, employing night-raids and mining to delay the progress of a siege, the defence often possessed the upper hand until supplies and morale ran low. But Vauban also perfected the techniques of siegecraft, regularizing the sciences of 'contravallation' and 'circumvallation'.[2] As a contemporary saying ran, 'a town defended by Vauban is a town held; a town invested by Vauban is a town taken'. He regarded each of the 53 sieges he personally conducted as an entirely separate problem, but his general principles were copied throughout Europe. After carefully siting their camp and making a full reconnaissance of a town's defences to determine the weakest sector, the attackers sapped forward by digging three 'parallels'—elaborate earthworks linked by indirect approach trenches and

---

[1] Technically their siege-work was excellent on this occasion but too time-consuming, while Kara Mustafa failed to safeguard the besieging army from outside relief: J. W. Stoye, *The Siege of Vienna* (1964), esp. pp. 150–73 and 235–64.

[2] Lines of 'contravallation' were trench-systems directed against the besieged town, those of 'circumvallation' designed to protect the besiegers against possible attack by relieving armies.

designed to hold troops for local defence and ultimately for the assault—until the edge of the enemy's glacis was reached. These pioneers were supported by small batteries employing direct or ricochet fire to make a breach through the selected sector of the parapet, whilst mortars swept the hostile defences. Once undertaken, the progress of sieges of this type could be almost mathematically calculated; one stage followed another until the defending commander, caught in the toils of Euclid, faced the alternatives of honourable surrender or a direct assault through the breach—with the potential consequences of fire and sword for both garrison and townsfolk. Such stormings were indeed rare, for they could entail enormous loss of life, while convention permitted defenders to capitulate on terms after a 48-day period or in face of an imminent assault; but all sieges involved much preparation of material, consumed a great deal of manpower and time, and so constituted a drag on active warfare.

Regular fortresses were sometimes supplemented by permanent lines where conditions of terrain made these advisable. The Lines of Stollhofen, constructed in 1703 to command the ten-mile interval between the Rhine and the Black Forest, exemplified the more elaborate variety. Simpler specimens consisted of inundations, natural obstacles and fortified posts, designed to delay rather than forbid the advance of hostile forces. The difficulty of manoeuvring eighteenth-century armies made it hard to turn such positions, whilst a frontal attack was at a decided disadvantage owing to the inadequacy of the preliminary bombardment by the artillery of the day. Although, by consummate artistry, Marlborough forced the 70-mile-long Lines of Brabant in 1705 and the Lines of 'Ne Plus Ultra' six years later, and Villars surprised Stollhofen in 1707, the use of fortified lines encouraged defensive warfare and justified Defoe's complaint that 'now it is frequent to have armies of 50,000 men of a side standing at bay within view of one another, and spend a whole campaign in dodging, or, as it is genteelly called, observing one another, and then march off into winter quarters'.[1]

Under these general conditions, victory or defeat or stalemate rested on the quality of individual generalship and on the size of the armies—otherwise so similar as a rule in equipment, weapons and tactical ideas. A few leaders were bold, but most were cautious, allowing the developments that favoured defensive war to dictate their style. Often, however, it was their governments who imposed this on them. From 1676 defensive warfare had appealed strongly to Louis XIV, influenced after the death of Turenne by Louvois and his assistant Chamlay, who waged war as administrators and moved armies like pawns on a chessboard. 'Journals' of detailed instructions were issued for every campaign; frequent reminders to avoid risks were sent to the front. 'Conduct yourself in such a way

---

[1] Quoted H. Morley, *The Earlier Life and Works of Daniel Defoe* (1889), p. 135.

as not to compromise the reputation of my army', wrote the king. 'I know there is no need to tell you what pain an unfortunate defeat would cause His Majesty', reiterated the minister,[1] whose successors Barbezieux and Chamillart, constantly sounded similar notes of caution. Even the great Luxembourg fought brilliant campaigns of evasion during the Nine Years War, continually thwarting the efforts of the ailing William III to force a decisive action. Small wonder that lesser generals of the next generation such as Tallard and Vendôme hesitated to fight battles. Even when action was authorized by Versailles, royal directives restricted the initiative of the commander; in 1706, Louis ordered Villeroi 'to pay special attention to that part of the line which will endure the first shock of the English troops'[2]—advice which substantially contributed to the defeat of Ramillies. Cautious Allied governments might hamper their generals with similar trammels. Through their field-deputies, the States-General frequently obstructed Marlborough's designs for battle: so did the Tory outcry at the 'butcher's bill' of Malplaquet.[3] The Habsburg Council of War (*Hofkriegsrat*),[4] to its credit, never attempted to dictate courses of action to commanders in the field, but some Imperial generals—Styrum and later Bayreuth—tended to favour siege operations. The Swedish army, of course, led in person by its soldier-monarch, enjoyed a comparatively free hand for the war of movement in which Charles XII delighted.

The preference for limited war was not shared by the truly great generals. Like Charles XII, probably the most daring soldier of his times, Marlborough, Eugene and Villars were often able to escape the deadening military customs of the day and to revive the spirit of movement and decision known to Gustavus Adolphus and Turenne before them. 'Make few sieges and fight plenty of battles', Turenne had advised Condé; 'when you are master of the countryside the villages will give us the towns.'[5] As a general rule, the Turks shared this eagerness to give battle. Marlborough's four great victories proclaim his belief in the importance of the major action, even when undertaken at considerable risk. After Oudenarde, where the Allied army ran the peril of being divided and annihilated in detail as it crossed the Scheldt in close proximity to the French, Marlborough wrote: 'I was positively resolved to endeavour by all means a battle, thinking nothing else would make the Queen's business

[1] Quoted H. Weygand, *Histoire de l'armée française* (1938), p. 155.
[2] Quoted F. E. de Vault and J. G. Pelet, *Mémoires militaires relatifs à la Succession d'Espagne* (11 vols. and atlas, 1835–64), vol. VI, p. 19.
[3] See the comments of G. M. Trevelyan, *England under Queen Anne*, vol. III (1934), pp. 19–20.
[4] The Instructions of 1675 declared it the principal medium of orders between the emperor and his generals. An independent branch of the Council at Graz dealt with the Turkish fronts until its dissolution by Eugene in 1705; thereafter a single *Hofkriegsrat* conducted all military activities.
[5] Quoted Weygand, p. 155.

go on well. This reason only made me venture the battle yesterday, otherwise I did give them too much advantage.'[1] Eugene was similarly dedicated to action. In spite of his failure before Toulon (1707) and his inability to master Villars in the years following Marlborough's dismissal, he merits fame for his many victories against the Turk, the defeat of Marsin at Turin (1706), and his masterly co-operation with his English colleague. On the French side, Villars had the unique distinction of confining Marlborough and Eugene to a technical victory at Malplaquet: rallying the demoralized French forces, Villars enabled France to continue the struggle and win a not unfavourable peace after his culminating triumph at Denain.

As in every age, conditions of terrain and climate had much to do with determining the type of operations conducted in the various theatres of war. Shortage of green fodder and the bad state of the winter roads normally confined the campaigning season to the summer months, and even then the generally low agricultural yield of Europe tied the larger armies to the distances they could carry their bread. Hot weather brought dysentery to ravage the ranks; winter's cold produced frostbite, starvation or sickness in billets.

In western Europe wars were fought over four main theatres. First in importance was the 'cockpit of Europe', contained within the quadrilateral formed by Antwerp, Dunkirk, Namur and Maastricht, and largely dominated by the river basins of the Meuse and Scheldt. The comparatively high fertility, the facilities for attack and defence offered by the numerous intersecting waterways, and the wealth of its many towns made the southern Netherlands a good area for soldiering, besides its strategic situation for protecting the respective approaches to Paris and the Rhine. The many fortresses there made it a general's first preoccupation to protect his lines of communication. Beyond Luxemburg and the Moselle forts was a second front, the upper Rhine, which saw much fighting in the Spanish Succession War as it had done in the days of Gustavus and Turenne. The rich agricultural lands of Alsace and Lorraine were now protected by the fortresses of Strasbourg and Landau on the left bank, while the Stollhofen Lines shielded the approaches to the upper Danube and lower Rhine; the Black Forest area was mountainous and barren, armies having to convoy supplies through narrow passes before emerging into the plains of Franconia. North Italy, thirdly, figured prominently in both of Louis XIV's later wars. Here the Po valley, with its fertile acres, many cities and tributary watercourses, bore certain resemblances to the Netherlands. Operations frequently turned on control of the four fortresses of 'the Quadrilateral' north of the valley: Mantua, Verona, Peschiera, Legnano. From the north and west, enclosed by the

[1] To Godolphin, 12 July 1708, W. Coxe, *Memoirs of the Duke of Marlborough* (3rd edn. 1847), vol. II, p. 265.

Alps, the only means of easy access from France lay along the narrow Ligurian coast, which was exposed to seaborne operations; also vital to the French were certain passes: the Bochette, running north from Genoa, the valleys of the rivers Bormida and Stura, and the Colle di Tenda. The Brenner and Semmering passes similarly linked Italy and south Austria. Except in the mountains, summers were hot and winters mild. Very different was the Spanish theatre. The arid mountains dividing Portugal from Spain severely limited operations in the west of the Peninsula after 1704; most of the fighting took place in the east, in Catalonia (as in the Nine Years War) and Valencia, but even there the inhospitality of much of the countryside and the great heat of the summer months rendered effective operations difficult.

The Great Northern War ranged from the Baltic lands through Poland to the Ukrainian steppe beyond the Dnieper. In 1701–7 the focal area was Poland, where the Swedes fought hard campaigns along the Niemen and Vistula against the elector of Saxony. The swampy nature of much of this region (particularly the Pripet marshes), which presented a major obstacle in spring and summer, induced Charles XII to undertake several unconventional winter campaigns. His invasion of Russia meant traversing vast distances of forest and rolling plains besides a series of great river obstacles, and then the Russian 'scorched earth' plan forced him to strike south to the friendlier areas of the Ukraine, there to meet disaster after surviving the bitter frosts of early 1709. The tides of the Turkish wars flowed over half a dozen different regions of the Balkans. Three zones along the Danube are worth distinguishing in particular. The area of the middle Danube and the Hungarian plain saw Vienna besieged by the Turks in 1683 and the Magyar revolt two decades later; here the north bank of the river opened on to fertile regions, but to the south lay more barren areas. Further down, the confluence of the Danube and Sava formed a second theatre, the scene of the battle of Zalánkemén (1691) and successive contests for the key citadel of Belgrade, below which the dry hills of Serbia and Wallachia closed to the fortresses of the Iron Gate; away to the south-east, through the open country round Nish, stretched the high road to Adrianople. A great deal of fighting, including the battle of Zenta (1697), took place north of Belgrade, in the Banat of Temesvár,[1] which linked the Danube with Transylvania and with the key Wallachian passes, the Vulcan and Red Tower.

It remains to describe the general features of field operations, including those tactical and administrative adaptations which distinguished different forces and which, though often small in themselves, frequently swung the fortunes of war between armies in other respects basically similar.

---

[1] On the difficult terrain of the Tisza tributary and its marshes, see above, p. 580. For the Turkish defence system on the Danube, cf. above, p. 610.

Details of drill and minor tactics varied considerably from army to army, and even from regiment to regiment.

The troops normally assembled for a campaign in the vicinity of a fortress, carefully stocked with munitions and supplies during the previous winter. Such preparations were difficult to conceal from the enemy's spies; an army's broad intentions could often be deduced from the areas reconnoitred and the fortresses supplied. To achieve surprise, therefore, generals had to resort to deception. In the winter of 1703–4 the Allies made elaborate preparations at Coblentz and Philippsburg in order to deceive Versailles into believing that their main attack would be launched up the Moselle or against Alsace, not towards the Danube; in 1707, Villars lulled the margrave of Bayreuth into a false sense of security by attending a ball in Strasbourg at the very time the French forces were secretly converging on Stollhofen. The area chosen for the assembly-camp was surveyed by a senior officer accompanied by representatives of all arms; outposts were established and the site carefully subdivided. The camp plan invariably reproduced the order of battle. The flanks were normally allocated to the cavalry, each squadron receiving a frontage of fifty paces with a similar distance dividing it from the next lines. The infantry were placed in a double line of cantonments, each battalion usually receiving a sector 100 yards broad with similar intervals. The artillery was generally parked in front or at the rear of the main position under the protection of a special guard; and the commissariat wagons were drawn up in an easily accessible area ready to issue supplies every four days. Junior officers laid out the lines of the regimental camps within the allotted areas before the main body of the army arrived. On reaching the appointed bivouac, the colours or standards were planted in the front centre of the unit area to provide a rallying-point and the men dismissed to prepare their meal. For protection from the weather, the rank and file often had to build rude shelters from whatever materials they could procure, but after 1700 tents were increasingly provided. Main guards and picquets were mounted, grand guards of infantry and cavalry were sent to the outposts a mile or more from the camp. These were under the command of the *maréchal de camp* or *General-Feldwachtmeister*, appointed each day from a roster and responsible to the commander-in-chief for security and discipline. If the camp was to be permanent, palisades and earthworks were constructed around the perimeter. Fortified camps could play decisive rôles: in July 1704 Marlborough and Baden were not strong enough to attack the elector of Bavaria's entrenchments outside Ulm; in 1709 Peter fought the Swedes at Poltava close to a large encampment supported by a line of fortified outposts.[1]

[1] Compared with the European, Ottoman camps were notorious for their disorder, partly because they accommodated so many camp-followers, who occasionally outnumbered the combatants by as many as 4 to 1; it is said that there was an executioner present for every 300 men.

This elaborate procedure was followed every time an army halted on the completion of the day's march. The camp survey party rode at least half-a-day ahead of the army, searching for a site with fresh water and protected flanks, and it was not unknown for it to run unexpectedly into the enemy; in 1706, Cadogan discovered Villeroi's army already camped on the very site round Ramillies that the Allies had intended to select. The plan for the following day's march was prepared jointly by the lieutenant-general of the day and the camp-commandant, for the commander's approval. Within range of the enemy, armies always marched in battle-order. The formation adopted would depend on the direction of the foe: if he was reported ahead, the army marched by 'wings'; if on the flank, by 'lines'.[1] The reserve, artillery and supply-trains were commonly placed in the centre along the best available road, under the orders of the wagon-master and his detachments of provosts or *archers*. The other columns used parallel tracks or struck off across country, headed by detachments of dragoons carrying fascines or straw-trusses for bridging streams or marshy ground, whilst groups of engineers laboured to improve the way. The battalions normally marched by column of platoons, temporarily narrowing the front by dropping files to the rear when necessary, but resuming formation as soon as possible so that the battle-line could be formed by a simple wheel of platoons.

An army rarely progressed more than ten miles in one day. On the march to the Danube, Marlborough's forces took more than five weeks to cover the 250 miles to the rendezvous with Baden at Launsheim. The main limitation was the weight of the cumbersome field-guns; the current practice of harnessing the horses in tandem, and of hiring civilian con-tractors to supply transport and drivers, did little to improve their general performance over the mud roads of Europe. The successful performance of long marches depended on the quality of the field administration. In many cases this left much to be desired, and nothing is more revealing than the contrast between the French and British forces in this respect during the campaign of 1704. On his first march to reinforce Bavaria, Tallard lost a third of his effective strength through desertion and straggling in the Black Forest; before the second operation in July, half his cavalry horses contracted a murrain and had to be kept in quarantine. By comparison, the Allied army's longer march from the Netherlands to the Danube was conducted far more efficiently; advance preparations ranged from the provision of a new pair of shoes for the infantry at Heidelberg to an alternative set of communications. Measures of this type enabled Marlborough to execute a daring march down the flank of superior enemy forces, and to bring his men to the Danube fit enough to win the

---

[1] Marching by 'wings', the horse of the right flank formed one column, those of the left a second, the foot and guns a third column between them; advancing by 'lines', each column formed a complete battle-line, cavalry at each extremity and foot in the centre.

bitter struggle for the Schellenberg Heights; the English cavalry, in particularly fine fettle after the long march, earned Eugene's unstinted admiration. Painstaking administration and care for the men and horses were indeed two secrets of the high morale prevalent in the British forces, who dubbed Marlborough 'Corporal John', a reputation that enabled him to make calls on his men's endurance that few other generals would contemplate. Although Charles XII was equally popular with his men, his administrative talent was not so high; the loss of Lewenhaupt's single convoy at Lesnaja in October 1708 compromised the entire invasion of Russia. But it would be erroneous to believe that the British forces were invariably well equipped. The army that served in Spain under Peterborough, and later Galway, suffered terrible privations through mismanagement, seriously affecting its battle-power and contributing to the defeat at Almanza.

Most generals marched at sunrise and camped at dusk, but another secret of Marlborough's success was his use of night-marches to conceal his movements and save his army from the heat of the day. Captain Parker wrote of the Danube march: 'We generally began our march about three in the morning, proceeded four leagues or four and a half by day, and reached our ground about nine.'[1] This stratagem of advancing under cover of darkness was also used in tactical operations. Baden marched by night to attack the rear of the Turkish position at Nish, and Marlborough forced action upon unwilling adversaries at both Blenheim and Oudenarde by adopting similar measures. 'If they are there, the devil must have carried them. Such marching is impossible!': such was Vendôme's reaction to reports of the Allied army deploying over the Scheldt on the latter occasion.[2] An advance into battle was made in several columns to facilitate tactical deployment. Five was the number most frequently used; but Marlborough marched on Blenheim in nine columns, and at Poltava Charles XII let Rehnskiöld and Lewenhaupt advance with six of cavalry and four of infantry respectively. By deploying his men on as broad a front as possible, a general attempted to envelop his adversary's flanks; but over-extension had to be avoided to prevent units being cut off and crushed in detail. At Ramillies, Marlborough made the fullest use of interior lines against Villeroi's over-extended position, and employed the cover of a reverse slope to conceal the transfer of the British troops from the right flank to the centre at the crisis of the battle. An eye for country was, of course, an essential attribute in a commander; the key to many actions lay in the proper exploitation of the natural advantages a position offered, or of the weather. At Narva (1700) the Swedes attacked the more numerous Russians under cover of a snow blizzard.

The development of formalized tactics materially restricted the possi-

[1] Robert Parker, *Memoirs...1683–1718, in Ireland and Flanders* (Dublin, 1746), p. 80.
[2] Quoted by Churchill, *Marlborough* (1947 edn.), vol. II, p. 360.

bilities of the battlefield. The elaborate battle-arrays needed much time to prepare: unless taken by surprise, either side had time to refuse action by withdrawing to some inaccessible position. Once battle was joined, a general's first preoccupation was to preserve his battle-order intact, for an unbroken line of battle was considered as important on land as at sea. This was no easy matter when the slightest irregularity of terrain could throw the carefully aligned battalions and even whole armies into confusion. The largest formation then in existence was the brigade, and this factor further complicated the deployment and handling of armies in action. Charles XII formed part of his army into self-contained corps in 1718, but this was a unique experiment. No army possessed even a divisional organization at the end of this period.

Before battle, each army formed up in two or more parallel lines, 300 to 600 yards apart, thus permitting mutual support without unduly exposing the rear to the enemy's fire. General officers took post in a predetermined order according to rank, the station of greatest honour being the front line's right flank; the junior general present commanded the left of the second line. Brigadiers served with their own groups of battalions or squadrons, but all higher command posts were decided by seniority. In other respects, the principles governing battle-formations varied between nations. The standard seventeenth-century practice of drawing up infantry and cavalry units in alternate succession was continued by the Imperial armies, whose rectangular battle-formations, drawn up behind barricades of *chevaux de frise*, proved effective in checking the loosely controlled attacks of the Turkish masses. The French, on the other hand, stationed their cavalry on the flanks, employing them throughout the battle. By contrast, Marlborough and Charles XII placed much of their cavalry in reserve for use at the moment of crisis or decision, and left the preliminary fighting to the lines of infantry battalions supported by smaller detachments of horsemen. Similarly, the Turk kept his regular sipahis in reserve for the *coup de grâce*. Eighteenth-century authorities were to consider a well-planned battle-formation a major secret of victory. Turpin de Crissé, for example, wrote that 'Battles are won not by numbers but by the manner of forming your troops together and their order and discipline.'[1]

Once formed, the battle-line advanced directly to the front, halting frequently to rectify the alignments. Over-haste was considered fatal, 'slow but sure' was the rule. The theory was commonly held that the side that fired first was often defeated before it had time to reload; consequently the infantry was trained to hold its fire until the last practicable moment. At Blenheim, Rowe reserved his brigade's first fire until he was within sword's reach of the enemy palisades. Restraint of this order required a highly developed discipline. The tactical deployment of the

---

[1] *Essai sur l'art de la guerre* (1754), quoted in Turner, p. 24.

British, French and Swedish infantry in battle has already been considered in connection with the changes in weapons. The other European armies conformed to the general pattern with a few individual idiosyncrasies. The Imperial regiments were notorious for their lack of uniform training, but most of their tactics were conventional and the 'firings' generally performed on a battalion basis. In one unique respect, however, the Habsburg infantry were ahead of the times—in using the Croats as a light infantry screen ahead of the main battle-formation. Turenne had experimented with the use of individual skirmishers, but the practice had been temporarily abandoned on the grounds that it obstructed the battalion fields of fire. The stolid discipline of the Imperial infantry indeed contrasted strikingly with the fighting methods of their Turkish opponents. Ottoman commanders relied on massed rushes to win infantry battles. The large numbers of irregular troops they commonly employed made more sophisticated tactics impossible. At this period the Turk rarely triumphed in open battle, provided the Imperialists preserved their battle-order and were not lured into premature pursuits in their eagerness to loot the viziers' rich encampments.

Despite the increased importance of European infantry as a battle-winning arm, the cavalry retained much of its ancient prestige and size, normally a fifth to a third of an army's strength. A total of 60,000 horse were in action at Malplaquet—by far the largest cavalry engagement of the age. The regiment remained the standard administrative unit, but for action the cavalry served in two or more squadrons of three troops apiece, fifty soldiers forming a troop. There were two main types of cavalry. The heavy cuirassier was armed with sword and pistols; wore breast- and back-plates, sometimes a steel cap—the last vestiges of functional armour. The dragoon was expected to fight on foot or on horseback as occasion demanded, and was additionally armed with a carbine. The Austrian army contained a third type in the hussar. Light cavalry of Magyar origin had been employed for centuries, but the first regular regiments were raised in 1688. These hussars had no place in the line of battle, but were used for raids, foraging and reconnaissance, in much the same way as the Turks employed the *beshlis* of the territorial cavalry.[1] The hussars were not universally admired: Colonel de la Colonie described them as 'properly speaking, nothing but bandits on horseback who carry on an irregular warfare'.[2] Similarly, the Swedish forces adopted a type of light cavalry from the Poles, and the Russians made great use of the mounted Cossack bands.

The tactical employment of the *arme blanche* (sword or sabre) varied considerably from army to army. The French tended to exaggerate the

[1] Marsigli, pt. I, p. 99.
[2] De la Colonie, *The Chronicles of an Old Campaigner, 1692–1717* (tr. W. C. Horsley, 1904), p. 159.

use of cavalry as an instrument of sophisticated fire-power, although both Turenne and Condé had believed in 'la charge sauvage'. The parade-ground manoeuvres of the French cavalry, firing their pistols or carbines at the halt, troop after troop, made them extremely vulnerable to the 'knee by knee' twin-squadron charges of the English horse. Marlborough was insistent on the use of cavalry as a shock force: cold steel was the specified weapon and on campaign the English were issued with only three rounds of pistol ammunition—for personal protection while foraging. Similarly, Charles XII permitted attack only with the sword. A Swedish tactical innovation was the use of a wedge or arrow-shaped formation, three ranks deep, the troopers riding 'knee behind knee'. The Turk often employed his territorial horse in loosely co-ordinated attacks ahead of his foot soldiers, the Crimean Tatar being renowned for his superb individual horsemanship and ability to fire accurately from the saddle at full gallop, although he more than met his match in the well-handled Austrian cavalry, which under Baden and Eugene formed the finest arm of the Imperial forces.

The artillery included a variety of calibres, but there was little to choose between the different armies so far as the types and ranges of guns were concerned. The field and regimental artillery which regularly accom-panied an army included small three-pounders, 'sakers' (six-pounders), 'demi-culverins' (eight-pounders), and larger pieces firing 16-pound and 24-pound cannon-balls. Effective ranges varied between 450 and 600 yards according to type, and armies were provided with guns on a scale of one or two for each thousand men. Heavier metal was required for siege work: these pieces ranged from 36- to 60-pounders, supported by an array of mortars and brass petards; the Ottomans boasted a cannon that fired stone balls of 120 pounds, but it was unique. The 'train' was a vast, complex organization embracing engineers, pioneers and supply services as well as gunners, though it varied in size from one campaign to another. The heavy guns were organized into separate 'siege trains': these did not accompany the armies but moved independently from fort to fort as the campaign progressed, the protection of the guns being entrusted to companies of infantry specially detached from the line battalions. Guns most influenced the conduct of wars, indeed, by their bulk and weight. The slow rate of march which they imposed was fatal to schemes of rapid or daring movement, although the increasing use of two-wheeled trails slightly improved their speed.

All things considered, the artillery arm made little progress. Certain armies ignored the professional gunner as belonging to an inferior social class, but the most important reason for this eclipse of the artillery was that the organizations responsible for providing and serving the guns were not usually integral parts of the regular army authorities. The English Board of Ordnance was a completely autonomous body; the

Austrian *Büchsenmeister* (trained artillerists) regarded themselves as gildsmen rather than soldiers. Louvois slightly improved the organization of the French artillery, reducing the number of calibres to six in 1679, but no real corps existed, despite the exertions of Claude du Metz. Once again, it was differences, not in the kind or quality of equipment, but of its correct employment, that distinguished the hostile batteries. During the Succession War the English guns were the best served in Europe, partly because Marlborough combined the post of Captain-General with that of Master-General of the Ordnance and paid the closest attention to the component parts of the artillery. In action he frequently sited the guns in person, as at Blenheim and Malplaquet; he insisted on the use of prepared powder-charges; he introduced a well-sprung cart for easier and faster movement of supplies and munitions. Above all, he nursed the professional interests of his gunners and engineers, assuring them their fair share of promotions and honours. Of much tactical significance was the English practice, originally Swedish, of attaching two light guns to each infantry battalion to provide close fire support. The Dutch and Austrians soon followed suit, and Eugene issued 'galloper guns' to the Imperial cavalry. The Turks experimented with firing small cannons from the backs of camels, but the results were not very satisfactory to man or beast. The French made rather less effective use of their guns on the battlefield, brigading them into rough groups of four, eight or ten pieces; but the terrible carnage inflicted on the Dutch Guards at Malplaquet was caused by a cunningly concealed French battery. On the whole, however, the artillery created more limitations than advantages. By reducing mobility to a minimum, it generally reinforced the unimaginative handling of armies.

Effective control of the various arms during operations was made more difficult by the virtual absence of any staff organization. Louvois attempted to form the first rudiments of a staff system after Nymegen, but it failed to develop. Most commanders packed their staffs with relatives or sycophants. Marlborough planned and executed his great designs with the assistance of a mere handful of confidants—his secretary Cardonnel, Quartermaster-General Cadogan, and Henry Davenant, the financial agent. These men gave the duke skilled assistance based on experience. Marlborough was also exceptional in his careful training of the aides-de-camp, who were expected to assess and report on local military situations as well as carry messages through the smoke of battle. Charles XII relied on advisers of the calibre of Stuart, Rehnskiöld and the wily Gyllenkrook, who was responsible for all aspects of supply and the production of maps and routes. With no intermediary divisional or corps headquarters, and only a few subordinate generals in charge of the various sectors of the battlefield, the commander-in-chief bore a very personal responsibility for every decision. Orders were often issued to colonels by word of mouth, but it was exceptionally difficult for a commander to keep a balanced view of the over-all progress of a battle, owing to the clouds of coarse-powder smoke that soon obliterated the scene. Success, then, was won by a general's ability to overcome the many limitations of the time, especially in co-ordinating the efforts of his men to make the fullest use of the advantages of improved fire-power.

The endeavours of the great captains attracted considerable attention from contemporary essayists and diarists. A few, like Defoe or Goslinga, the Dutch colonel, were openly critical, but most of the chroniclers—themselves serving soldiers—appreciated the problems their leaders faced. The Count of Mérode-Westerloo has left an interesting description of service in the French armies, complementing Captain Parker's reminiscences of campaigning under William III and Marlborough.[1] Colonel Blackader of the Cameronians betrays in his journal the conflict between his Presbyterian conscience, which condemned the loose talk and behaviour of many of his fellows, and pride in their martial achievements;[2] Captain Drake, Private Deane, Corporal Bishop and Sergeant Millner speak for Marlborough's rank and file.[3] Count Marsigli made a comprehensive survey of the Ottoman army. The 'Old Campaigner', De la Colonie, painted a graphic picture of life in the Bavarian and Imperial forces. At a critical stage, Captain James Jeffereyes reported at length Charles XII's operations.[4] Richard Kane was to lay the foundations for deeper studies of the military art in *The Campaigns of King William and Queen Anne* (1745). Vauban's works on military engineering and Puységur's *L'Art de la Guerre* remain classics of military writing. These sources reveal that the last decades of the seventeenth century and the early years of the eighteenth were a period of military transition and general mediocrity, enlivened by only a few men of genius. Yet the period clearly foreshadowed major developments in equipment and tactics, and it proved that the profession of arms could be relatively humane as well as honourable.

2. SOLDIERS AND CIVILIANS

THE seasonal rhythm of warfare and politics in Europe at this period was rarely broken. Year after year armies had to wait for the thaw to dry out, and the earth to grow fresh forage, before they could move. The great majority of battles and sieges took place in summer and autumn. If in Spain fighting paused in the July heat, if in Poland Swedish

[1] A selection from the *Memoirs* of both Mérode-Westerloo (first published, Brussels, 1840) and Parker (Dublin, 1746) was published in 1968 (ed. D. G. Chandler); the introduction examines the authenticity of the latter's work.

[2] *Life and Diary of Lt.-Colonel J. Blackader* (ed. A. Crichton, 1824).

[3] *Amiable Renegade: the Memoirs of Capt. Peter Drake* (ed. S. Burrell, 1960); J. M. Deane, *Journal of a Campaign in Flanders* (privately printed, 1846); C. T. Atkinson, 'One of Marlborough's men: Matthew Bishop', *J. Army Hist. Research*, vol. XXIII (1945), p. 157; J. Millner, *A Compendious Journal of all the marches, famous battles, sieges, etc.* (1733).

[4] *Letters from the Swedish Army, 1707–1709* (ed. R. Hatton, Stockholm, 1954).

commanders manoeuvred with remarkable speed across snow-covered plains in winter, the normal timetable nevertheless repeated itself in most areas with monotonous punctuality. By late November armies were going into winter quarters. The political season now began, of diplomatic and financial preparation for the next campaign. In the English House of Commons detailed estimates of the cost of land and sea forces for the following year—a new device in 1690—were introduced in November or December. In a dozen assemblies of Estates in the Habsburg lands, the ritual bargaining over war-taxation took place between December and March. At the same time, the size of the forces to be hired from smaller States by the principal belligerents was with more or less difficulty settled. Many French officers returned to Paris where Louis XIV's quartermaster-general, the marquis de Chamlay, set about his annual task of drafting Bourbon plans for the next year's campaign.

Equally, winter was the main recruiting season. From the widely scattered quarters of many armies, often from each troop or company in a regiment, an officer or two came home to find recruits; they were due back punctually in the spring with contingents of fresh manpower. By then, in the Spanish Succession War, Scotsmen had joined the Scots brigade in Dutch employ, Brandenburgers had reached Frederick I's troops in Flanders or Italy, and more Englishmen were expected in Spain. From northern Sweden, along the well-organized routes to Stockholm and Karlskrona and then over the sea, as well as from Finland, conscripts were brought to the forces stationed in the Baltic dependencies and Poland. Less methodically, in some winters between 1683 and 1699, the main Otto-man army would be stiffened by fresh troops from Asia Minor and Egypt. Such annual transfers of manpower to distant theatres of war, after 1700, were made easier in western and northern Europe by intensive 'drafting' from regiments or battalions at home to regiments or battalions on service abroad; but most of the gaps so caused were filled during the winter.

No doubt military conditions dictated the timing of this seasonal drive for recruits: when armies cannot move to fight, the opportunity must be taken to replace men, horses and equipment. Yet the season was also determined by the whole structure and economy of civilian society. The hardships of life for the poorer classes, always severe, were aggravated in winter by a shrinkage of employment on the land and in many trades. Intense activity during the harvests was succeeded by widespread idleness and indigence in the worst time of the year, so that captains in southern Europe reckoned it wise to collect their recruits before the vineyards took on extra hands in spring; and Marlborough, in January 1709, could say of officers anxious to go back to England: '. . . in this hard winter in all probability they may get more men in a day than in a week hereafter'.[1] Civilian hardship explains why most armies continued to depend on

[1] *Letters and Despatches of. . .Marlborough* (ed. Sir G. Murray, 5 vols. 1845), vol. IV, p. 397.

enlistment by volunteers. The heavy taxes enabled recruiting officers to proffer money and clothing to secure the men they needed. If more were needed, a government usually raised the value of the bounty offered to potential recruits. It also regarded leniently those company-captains and sergeants who increasingly relied on unlawful methods of coercion to fill the ranks. If numbers still lagged, compulsory enlistment authorized by law became necessary, but even conscription was often made more tolerable by the general poverty. Men in distress were bound to consider the traditional alternative of service in the wars. Apart from the promises of cash, drink, food and clothing, there was the direct appeal of adventure and possible booty. There was also the fact that enlistment on a momentary impulse settled the matter: according to the law of most countries, it made a soldier for life or until his company was disbanded by the sovereign. Although conditions of service were known to be hard, the common remedy of desertion was available.

Such pressures and allurements meant little enough to youths from the families of French *laboureurs* or the *Grossbauern* in some German lands or the successful stratum of English yeomanry, all with sound tenures and sufficient reserves of stock; or to the sons of master craftsmen inheriting a place in tight municipal gild structures. But there were large numbers of peasants and artisans low down on the economic ladder, casually employed, incessantly moving through the countryside to the bigger towns and out again, especially when wages were low, with prices and rents and taxation high in proportion. This situation occurred frequently and over wide areas in the later seventeenth century. Many parts of France were affected by an over-all decline in the local economy, and the population fell. Across the Rhine, it is true, population began to recover the losses of the Thirty Years War, but it did so without the general economic upswing needed to support an increase in numbers. Moreover, within this long span of depression, the 1690s suffered unusually long and cold winters. In societies overwhelmingly agricultural, but with unimproved methods of tillage, two poor harvests in sequence spelt catastrophe; the progressive husbandry of an area like the Pays de Waes, south of the Scheldt, was quite exceptional. In France the harvest failed in 1692 and 1693 successively. Scotland endured seven 'hungry years' between 1695 and 1701. The Swedish government, alarmed by similar conditions—Finland lost a third of its population in the famine of 1696–7—cut to a minimum the export of grain to western Europe from its eastern Baltic ports in 1695–9. In England, where Gregory King's estimates point to a very large number of families below the level of a decent subsistence, there was a sharp rise in the Poor Rates. In fact, words published by William Penn in 1693—'the poor turn soldiers, or thieve, or starve'[1]—reflect fairly enough the prevailing background of civilian hardship everywhere. So do contemporary

[1] *Essay towards the Present and Future Peace of Europe*, ch. I.

engravings of Watteau's drawing, 'The Recruit', showing a handful of tattered men tramping through a desolate landscape as if from a hopeless past to an uncertain future.

Such conditions, clearly, did not end at the frontiers of belligerent States. Great wars drew impartially on the population everywhere. In neutral regions poor folk were equally needy and, where there was a long tradition of foreign service, equally aware that the profession of arms offered an escape. The army of the States-General included German regiments hired to the Dutch; but there were also many north Germans in Dutch regiments. The French had both Swiss regiments raised under the aegis of the cantonal governments and Swiss contingents recruited without their authorization.

The Swiss cantons, indeed, provide a case-study of how mountain economies influenced the composition of the greater European armies; similar conditions reappear in Savoy-Piedmont, the Pyrenees and Scotland. Switzerland had more people than could be sustained by a mountainous region with few minerals and with archaic methods of cattle-raising, forest economy and tillage. In some of the valleys ruled by the Berne government, for instance, although a substantial peasantry continued to prosper, the numbers with only a minute holding of ground and cattle or none at all had increased since the mid-century agrarian risings. They tried to encroach on the forests and communal meadows, but were resisted; they drifted away from their homesteads, only to be harried by poor-law legislation of growing severity (1676, 1678, 1690), which made the villages more reluctant to admit strangers. Countrymen found it equally difficult to settle in Swiss towns, where demand for labour remained small and vested interests correspondingly exclusive. As a result, roving bands of beggars were common enough, very like the contemporary 'sorners' of Scotland. There were three ways out of the Swiss predicament. Emigration was one: after 1650 a number of families had moved into south Germany and Alsace, a few from the Grisons to Venice; the beginnings of Swiss settlement in North America occurred during the Succession War. A second remedy was increased industrial activity at home. Slowly the textile manufactures of northern Switzerland expanded at the very end of the seventeenth century, and the argument could already be heard that the Zürich government was reluctant to allow recruitment for service abroad because artisans were needed. Yet industrial Zürich suffered acutely from crises of dearth and unemployment. A Dutch envoy there vividly described the high cost of goods during the winter of 1692, the beggars and workers dying of hunger in the streets, the disappointment caused by the failure of an English negotiation to recruit men, and the consequent success with which he himself raised a battalion immediately afterwards.[1] War service was the third and most obvious possibility open

---

[1] C. Hoiningen-Huene, *Beiträge zur Geschichte der Beziehungen zwischen der Schweiz und Holland* (Berlin, 1899), pp. 71–82.

to the Swiss. To the long-standing connection of many cantons with France and Spain was added service for the Dutch in the wars of 1689–1714, which salved the conscience of the Protestant cantons. The needs of belligerents ensured attractive terms. Foreign money, filtering through the hands of the oligarchs in control of the various administrations, reached colonels and captains eager for employment and profit—and they raised the men. Evidence that the yearly replacements were hard to find is rare.[1] The main contingents in French and Dutch service, together with the smaller numbers employed by Spain, Venice and Piedmont, certainly exceeded 30,000 in several of the war years. In 1698, when the Dutch and French had begun reducing the size and pay of their armies to a peace footing, irritation in the cantons was profound.

Poverty and unemployment, and deeply rooted military traditions, did not provide a stimulus to recruitment potent enough to maintain the increasingly large forces now required. From the great crisis of 1688–9 until the pacification of 1713–14, conscription by governments played an important part in the warfare of western Europe. It rested in theory on two distinct ideas, often merged in practice. One was a claim to recruit by compulsion dissolute or idle persons. English legislation from 1704, for instance, authorized the pressing of 'able bodied men without lawful calling or visible means of support'. The other claim was to conscript for home or local defence. Although now overshadowed by professional armies, territorial and municipal militias survived in one form or another in many parts of Europe. Their periodic musters and exercises might be neglected, but militia service was still in theory a duty laid upon certain classes of subject or citizen, in contrast with the freely chosen profession of arms. In some areas the militias safeguarded law and property against local disorder, but a threat of invasion was enough for governments to reckon on them as auxiliary to the standing regiments. The relationship between the two became one of the great administrative problems of these years.

A good example is the experience of Piedmont, so often a theatre of war in this period. Here the ruler enforced the subject population's obligation to defend the country. The 'peasant militias' were merged with the duke's own regiments, raised originally by voluntary recruitment at home or in Switzerland. With the enemy at the door, from 1690, outright conscription became the rule. Orders went out to every township to provide its quota and were repeated at steady intervals. The syndic and other notables in the Piedmontese communes tried every device, from the drawing of lots to arbitrary arrest, to find recruits without prejudicing their private interests. Their victims often disappeared, before enlistment or immediately after-

---

[1] This applies even to Venetian recruitment in Switzerland in 1692 for service in the Morea—least inviting of all the possible theatres of war.

wards; the population of one district would be abruptly depleted by flight or abruptly swollen by the arrival of fugitives from another.[1] Yet Victor Amadeus II's administration was effective, and its measures gradually gained in precision and equity during the next twenty-five years.[2]

They were dwarfed in significance, however, by those of France, where the great change distinguishing Louis XIV's land forces after 1688 was the introduction of conscription.[3] Government left intact and unused the old militias but conscripted new militia regiments, and from 1693 some of these were employed as such in Catalonia, Piedmont and Flanders. The further step of fusion with regular troops had already been advised in 1688 by Chamlay, who favoured conscription with that very object in mind, but this was not followed up till 1701, when the disaster to Villeroi's army in northern Italy gave point to his argument; some of the conscripted militiamen were immediately ordered across the Alps and absorbed into the ordinary field-regiments. The resulting increase in numbers helped to meet the need for a more continuous flow of men from France to a distant theatre of war than could be supplied by the traditional system of recruitment. Thereafter, every year until 1712, the king issued an *ordonnance de levée*. The numbers called for varied from 33,000 in 1701 to 9,800 in 1708, with an average of 20,000, very unequally distributed between the *généralités*. The original ordinance of 1688 had required each parish to find an unmarried *milicien* by majority vote; in December 1691 it was ordered that lots be drawn. After 1703 married men were also taken.

Meanwhile the old system of recruitment continued, but army officers and their agents bullied the civilian population more openly, with disquieting results. As early as 1690, the Controller-General stated that their violence frightened the peasants from fairs and markets, which diminished the revenue from consumption taxes. Resistance to both forms of recruitment increased illicit trading; the bands of salt-smugglers were swollen by deserters of all kinds. Vauban, who believed that the profession of arms should be made attractive by good pay and short terms of service, was appalled by such disorders and he detested conscription. So did other regular soldiers, but their particular grievance was the common practice of paying a voluntary substitute to replace the conscript, because such volunteers were the very persons who normally offered themselves to the recruiting officer. First individuals in the larger cities, then whole parishes, took to paying the unlucky conscript's expenses, and this led gradually but inevitably to the payment of substitutes. Such friction between two overlapping methods of recruiting suggests that conscription, though it

[1] E. Mosca, 'La provincia di Alba...durante la guerra di successione spagnola, 1703, 1706', *Bolletino storico bibliografico subalpino*, vol. LV (1957), pp. 67–101.
[2] Cf. above, pp. 560–1.
[3] For the naval conscription introduced by Colbert, see below, pp. 821 ff.

helped to enlarge the French armed forces, did not alter their social basis. The long list of persons legally exempted from the *milice* points to the same conclusion. Exemption, which could be procured by purchasing one of a wide variety of offices, was a privilege almost as attractive as freedom from the burden of billeting or of *taille*, but as the petty office-holders multiplied the pressure on poorer unprivileged householders grew worse. More vulnerable still were the miscellaneous beggars and loiterers who were delivered up for war-service by the intendants, occasionally with men convicted of minor criminal offences.

The position in some States of the Empire was very similar. Ernest Augustus of Hanover conscripted for the first time in January 1689: suitable peasant lads and vagrants were both taken. In the same winter Frederick of Brandenburg-Prussia approved a scheme that was to be amplified by the important *Reglement* of 24 November 1693. His government, informed of the regiments' needs, fixed the number to be raised in each province; the province conscripted and turned over the men to neighbouring garrisons, from which they were ultimately transferred to regiments in the field. Later it became customary to impose a quota on each village, and on groups of trades or gilds in towns. If a village defaulted, a heavy fine was added to the ordinary taxes; but artisans in Berlin and elsewhere preferred to tax themselves in order to hire recruits, and so to be quit of the obligation to serve. This use of compulsory powers by provincial commissaries to find a specific number of recruits was novel, and variations in procedure abound during the next twenty years. In the Hohenzollern lands as in France, conscription overlapped and interfered with the traditional method of recruitment. Government tried one method or the other, or both simultaneously.

Evidence from this part of Europe discloses another reason why military men disliked conscription. They felt themselves fobbed off with unsuitable recruits—because civilians wanted to keep their farms and trades going with competent workmen and to get rid of criminals, vagabonds and other unemployables. Conscription could be regarded, paradoxically, as a defence against military pressure, for those in charge of it were more likely than recruiting officers to recognize the claims of 'domiciled' burghers and peasants not to be disturbed, and to appease landowners anxious to keep subjects or tenants. But resistance by civilian interests could take other forms. The elector of Saxony's many conscription ordinances, between 1702 and 1711, were increasingly clogged by a detailed schedule of exempt professions; his mining population, in particular, belonged to the list of reserved occupations. In ecclesiastical principalities, the bishop was often compelled to admit the claim of the chapter not to contribute recruits from its property. In Brandenburg an ordinance of 1703 summoned all unmarried men of 18–40 years to join local militia units: the policy was to enlarge the forces available for service abroad by entrusting home defence to the resident population,[1] but once enrolled in the militia a man was judged exempt from any other kind of military service. Frederick I also wanted retired officers to command the militia troops, but civil commissaries and burgomasters soon took their place. Crown Prince Frederick William, his enthusiasm for military matters stimulated for the rest of his life by the Spanish Succession War, disliked every one of these limitations on an efficient army's need for the best and tallest men to be found, and he swept the limitations away after 1713. The return of his troops from abroad ushered in a short period of quasi-military rule in certain areas, where recruiting officers terrorized the population by the violence of their competition for men.[2]

Elsewhere in Germany, in spite of the honeycomb structure of privilege existing in even the smallest principality, the lesser rulers raised regiments which were leased to greater powers like Saxony, Hanover, Denmark and the emperor himself; or they allowed these powers to recruit directly in their territories. In the Free Cities, burgher oligarchies bargained away to military states the right to recruit within their walls from the many casual immigrants. Documents in Cologne reveal a bewildering series of agreements by which recruiting officers from Denmark to Venice were authorized to pick up men willing to go.[3]

Resistance to military pressure in England was more effective. The crisis of 1688–9 did not destroy the standing army built up by James II. William III was able to add to it the English and Scottish regiments formerly in Dutch service, the forces raised by the gentry in England at the Revolution, the regiments raised at Enniskillen and Londonderry against Tyrconnel, and others in Scotland. He also maintained in English pay some of the Dutch troops that accompanied him in 1688, and German and Danish forces were to be employed by the English government in Flanders. Additional regiments were recruited in England in 1689. The numbers raised at home were large but not excessive. While the unsettled economic conditions of William's reign persisted, the traditional method of finding volunteers 'by beat of drum or otherwise' worked sufficiently well. In fact, the important innovations in personnel during the Nine Years War were the definite exclusion of Papists, the inclusion of a few extreme Protestant elements like the Cameronians (though from the more moderate of them) and some of the northern Irish, and the addition of Huguenot officers. Only during the Succession War, in that prosperous period between 1700 and 1708 when Defoe discerned a 'want of People,

[1] By 1709 there were 23,000 Prussian troops in Flanders and 8,000 in Italy, out of a complement of 43,756 in the army: C. Jany, *Geschichte der Königlich Preussischen Armee* (4 vols. Berlin, 1928–33), vol. I, p. 503.
[2] For the reforms which mitigated these conditions after 1720, see vol. VII, pp. 295–6.
[3] Cf. T. Heuel, *Werbungen in der Reichsstadt Köln von 1700–1750* (Bonn, 1911).

not of Employment',[1] did parliament begin to sanction the annual conscription by mayors, justices and constables of vagrants and their like. These, with imprisoned debtors and some convicted felons released for the purpose, helped to fill a few gaps; but while corn prices fell and farmers complained, the poor were better off and not easily tempted 'to be knocked o' th' head for 3s. 6d. per week',[2] which compared unfavourably with normal wages when steady ordinary work was available. Defoe, no doubt, underestimated the chronic problem of 'the poor' about which there was so much contemporary discussion, and the ordinary flow of recruits into the army continued. A real shortage of manpower later compelled Marlborough and his government to consider more positive action. During his captain-generalship, normal wastage and an increased number of regiments required the annual recruitment of some 12,000 infantrymen in Great Britain.[3] The enormous effort in the Spanish Peninsula, and the losses there, aggravated the whole problem by comparison with William III's campaigning. Even so, no mention appears of the French device of fusing new bodies of militia with standing regiments. The English militia belonged to the privileged interest, and conscription for service abroad could not possibly be applied to it. The alternative, a quota of conscripts from each county or parish, was dropped early in 1708: it might have involved tenants and employees whom the parliamentary interests would never willingly release, and it was mooted at a time when the war was less popular. Instead, a royal proclamation doubled the bounty of £2 payable to volunteers who came forward immediately. This procedure was incorporated into the Conscription Act of 1709, but with the important innovation of an allowance payable to the parish for each conscript, to help it maintain his family. The Land Tax Commissioners, who administered the new Act, were fairly successful in finding men. It was to their advantage that food prices shot up in 1709, remained high in 1710, and in 1711 were still well above the level of 1704–7.

In England, as everywhere else in western Europe, the recruitment of cavalry and dragoons caused far less difficulty. Their pay was higher; conscription ordinances did not apply to them; volunteers came forward in sufficient numbers. They or their families commanded some cash or credit, like the farmers' sons from parts of Hanover and Oldenburg, riding the horses reared there. It may also be that the influence of substantial landed families, from which members of the younger generation would step out into the great world ambitious to cut a figure in the wars, was exerted most easily on their humbler relatives and more prosperous

[1] 'Giving Arms no Charity', in *A Second Volume of the Writings of the Author of the True-Born Englishman* (1705), p. 426.

[2] *Ibid.* p. 445; cf. Defoe's *Review*, 31 March 1705 and 31 Jan. 1706, and *A Plan of the English Commerce* (1728), pp. 69–74. On the English poor, cf. above, pp. 259–60.

[3] I. F. Burton, 'The Supply of Infantry for the War in the Peninsula, 1703–1707', *Bull. Inst. Hist. Research*, vol. XXVIII (1955), pp. 35–62.

tenants, as happened in England when gentlemen raised troops in 1688: the circumstances were exceptional, but many who then volunteered remained under arms for service in Ireland and Flanders. Later, after 1701, it was noticed that the recruitment of dragoons was a simple matter in Midland areas where such troops had been quartered during the years of peace after 1697. The worst misfortune of an English recruiting officer was to arrive in a good neighbourhood after other officers had taken the best cavalrymen.

By contrast, the raising of foot-soldiers in sufficient numbers presented all the western States with one of their fundamental administrative problems. Their task was eased by the difficulties of ordinary people in finding a bare livelihood, but much intensified for a few years after 1688, and again after 1701, by the need to find even more men; possibly, in the concluding stages of both wars, it was eased again by the added impoverishment which the strain of war itself ultimately produced—with the result that the supply of manpower tended to outlast the supply of taxable resources. A more active economy, in the generation after 1714, would pose a new problem for statesmen who wished to recruit large armies.

In northern Europe conscription had long since been imposed, doubtless owing in part to an endemic scarcity of manpower and currency. By 1700, the native forces of Sweden (including Finland) and Denmark (including Norway) were based on the allocation of specified lands and their revenues for the upkeep of regiments, and on the liability of groups of peasant-holdings to produce a foot-soldier and his equipment. The strain of war and military setbacks had contributed to the constitutional changes of 1660 in Copenhagen and of 1680 in Stockholm. In each case the monarchy emerged with more autocratic powers, and it was able to strengthen the military system.[1]

In Sweden, during the war of 1675–9, conscription for the infantry was peculiarly obnoxious to most peasants because servants and tenants of the nobility were often exempted. After 1680 Charles XI disallowed these exemptions. He approved the practice, adopted earlier in parts of Sweden, by which the inhabitants of a district themselves undertook to maintain a regiment; this accorded with his need for a standing force in time of peace and the other provinces of 'old' Sweden[2] were induced to follow suit. In a series of detailed agreements between Stockholm and local authorities, the general claim to conscript was substantially modified by an undertaking to the Crown that each district should keep its own regiment at full strength—usually 1,200 men. The older schedules of peasantry responsible for finding a soldier were revised, and the lands assigned for

[1] See vol. v, ch. xxii.
[2] The provinces in the south, taken from Denmark by the Treaty of Roskilde in 1658, were excluded from the reform, so far as infantry regiments were concerned. The war of 1675–9 had shown that the loyalty of the population there was very uncertain.

the support of officers and men meticulously listed. There was no violent breach with the past, the government by no means surrendered its powers to conscript on a grander scale in an emergency; but ordinary peasants felt that their obligations were fixed, and hoped that they were limited, by the terms of their contract. For the cavalry a similar system was worked out. Troopers had never been difficult to find, but the cost of equipping and maintaining a permanent force of cavalry severely strained a poor countryside; in any case, some of the lands set aside for the upkeep of cavalry were no longer so employed. Together with the alienation of much royal property and the taxes due from it, this meant that the government's military resources were correspondingly diminished. Charles XI reversed these trends. Step by step with the *Reduktion*, he assigned lands and revenues (the *indelningsverk*) to his cavalry regiments, as well as to the infantry. The allocations to officers were scaled according to rank, the holdings grouped to maintain the troopers, and the peasants working them no longer required to serve in the provincial infantry regiments. It followed that resources and manpower formerly feeding the revenues of privileged families were, by the close of Charles XI's reign in 1697, supplying the Swedish army; but members of the lesser nobility, particularly the third 'order' of noblemen who had supported the king in 1680, along with those members of the senior orders who were impoverished by the *Reduktion*, could expect from army service itself the livelihood afforded by an improved system of endowment. The obligation of noblemen to serve the Crown in any case remained intact, although some preferred to follow the profession of arms abroad, like the officers of the *Royal-Suédois* regiment in France or of the Swedish regiments in the Dutch army.

In Denmark, conscription of the unprivileged for military service had long been familiar. In the war of 1676–9 provincial regiments of conscripted infantry were raised, but they included men recruited in the normal way, by the proffer of bounty-money, and many foreigners. During the next twenty years these regiments became barely distinguishable, except in name, from Christian V's other standing regiments. On Christian's death, in August 1699, the eleven regiments (including Guards and Marines) and three miscellaneous units of the 'Danish' infantry were manned predominantly by volunteers, though local authorities had been encouraged to take up beggars and unsatisfactory workmen. At least a third of the nominal complement of 16,000 were Germans and Holsteiners. The government also relied on a fluctuating number of troops raised in the Empire, but often hired them out again to other rulers. In raising and in maintaining infantry, it followed French and German practice more closely than did the Swedes. On the other hand, the Danes developed their own system of 'cavalry lands', where the peasants' taxes and services were replaced by the burden of supporting the soldiers quartered on them. As

772

in Sweden, though less decisively, the earlier alienation of royal domain was checked between 1680 and 1720, because the government wanted to enlarge the area assigned to the cavalry. This reached its maximum extent in 1717, afterwards gradually diminishing again: the contributions in kind, and other services to the troops, were then commuted for cash. The Danish kings never relied as heavily as Charles XI and Charles XII on the direct transfer of goods and services from civilians to soldiers.

The Northern Crowns controlled many other troops. Norwegian peasants—normally freeholders, unlike the Danish—were still chosen by lot at regular intervals to form six provincial regiments of foot; the cavalry were assigned to various properties. Sweden also kept forces in Finland, where the *Reduktion* helped to provide the territorial basis for a new personnel of military and civil officers—the 'service' nobility whose families dominated Finland for two centuries. Other forces, on the eve of the Great Northern War, were stationed across the Baltic.[1] In Livonia and Estonia the military system involved the rigorous assessment of estates: severe taxes in money and corn, partly required for the troops, were collected by local landowners acting as the reluctant agents of government. Moreover, Baltic noble families had long figured conspicuously in the Swedish army—just as Mecklenburgers and other north Germans flocked into Danish service. The *Reduktion*, first carried out in Livonia and Estonia at the expense of absentee Swedish magnates, began by firing the hopes of native landlords. When they too were forced to make substantial surrenders of property, Charles XI stirred up great bitterness. It was an open question, by the time Patkul became their spokesman in Riga, whether he would undermine their loyalty to the Swedish Crown. In fact, the great majority stood firmly by Charles XII and a quarter of his Baltic officers died in the campaigning after 1700. When Riga and then Reval fell, in 1710, a new phase began. Peter recognized the privileges of the Estates in that region and shrewdly mitigated the *Reduktion*: the Baltic Germans, their old sphere of honourable employment denied them but their need for it as pressing as ever after the devastations of a long war, turned to the Russian service. It was a momentous transfer, even though the extension of the tsar's sovereignty westward made it inevitable. Just beyond his new frontier the gentry of Courland, in the following decades, tended to enter the Prussian, not the Russian army.

---

[1] The total ordinary complement of the Swedish army in 1700 was the following: in Sweden and Finland, 178 companies of infantry (25,217 men) and 95 troops of cavalry (11,459 men) were raised by the system of 'contracts' and allocations of land to the forces. Those recruited by individual enlistment at home and abroad, mostly stationed in southern Sweden and overseas, reached a nominal total of 8,444 cavalry and 21,992 infantry; but the real figures must have been very considerably lower. See C. O. Nordensvan, 'Svenska armén åren 1700–1709', *Karolinska Förbundets Årsbok* (1916), pp. 171 ff.

An estimate of 25 August 1699 gives a complement of some 23,000 troops available in Denmark, 10,500 in Norway: *Bidrag til den store nordiske Krigs Historie* (Danish General Staff, 10 vols. 1899–1934), vol. I, pp. 88 ff.

However, discontent in the Baltic States had been a minor flaw in the Swedish defences. After 1700 the whole structure of military organization in Sweden was adapted, though not destroyed, during the long emergency. Already in the first year of tension Charles XII needed a reserve force at home while he prepared for action overseas. The 'contracts' were duly overstepped: every three of the groups that had previously supplied a man for the regiments had to find one more. In Finland the liability was doubled. Once Charles became involved in Poland these new troops were moved also, so that in 1702 he called for a 'fourth' and yet a 'fifth' man— one from every four or five of the groups—in order to raise more regiments. Meanwhile the losses of every company in the older regiments had to be made good under the old agreements. Officers crossed the Baltic to supervise the contingents due, thus keeping a regiment in touch with its real base and paymaster at home, the province. The strain on the Swedish countryside was serious, but mitigated until 1708 by decent harvests and gently rising prices. After Poltava the position grew much worse. Charles XI's system was now supplemented by outright conscription; and the economy suffered because its manpower was withdrawn, at a time when a recurrence of the plague was in any case causing frightful mortality in the whole Baltic region (1709–12). During the earlier period, moreover, heavy requisitioning in foreign territory had lessened the expenses of the Swedish government. The contribution squeezed from Saxony in 1706–7, and the conscription there, were comparable with Habsburg pressure in Bavaria or in some of the Italian principalities at the same date. On the other hand, no subsidies could be expected from the western States, whom Charles XII refused to assist, and foreign loans were kept to a minimum. He spent less on recruiting foreign volunteers than Gustavus Adolphus had done. The impressive resilience of Sweden's military power owed much to the efficient linking of regiments and provinces, and to the modest cost to Sweden of warfare waged at the expense of a wide tract between Elbe and Dvina.

In a less spectacular way the Danish Crown kept abreast of Charles XII. After the humiliating episode of 1699–1700 in Holstein, Frederick IV behaved with the utmost caution in Baltic affairs, preferring to buy a promise of naval support in any emergency by hiring 12,000 men to the Dutch and English governments. Ironically, although not a belligerent, he was then faced by the same difficulty which worried States like Sweden, France and Brandenburg: his troops had gone, he needed a territorial defence. His order of 24 February 1701 for the resurrection of the *Vaern* appeared for the same reason as the organization of a militia in Brandenburg. The Danish measure obliged all property, 'cavalry lands' excepted, to find its quota of peasants. A few other exemptions were allowed, on home farms or the like, and landlords were permitted to find substitutes for conscripted tenants. This was a true militia, trained periodically, ready to defend the country. Its members were therefore forbidden to leave their home district during the compulsory six years of service—a prohibition that was to have profound repercussions for Danish society, since the government's reasons for disallowing freedom of movement accorded with the landlords' interest in tying labourers to their estates. Certainly, the lord suffered in moments of crisis. After the Danish attempt to recover Scania in 1710 had broken down, the standing regiments were filled up without ceremony from the militias. But in peace-time the legal restriction of the militiaman's right to move mainly served a different purpose, culminating in the *Stavnsbaand* ordinance of 1733 which confined any peasant of military age (14 to 36) to his district.[1]

Such a coincidence of public and private interests was not a characteristic of Peter I's Muscovy, although something like it existed after his death, when Russian landowners partially recovered control of the countryside from the military institutions which he had created. Instead, his mobilization of manpower after 1700 dislocated the traditional order of society at its lower levels.[2] Apart from the peasantries which the tsars directly controlled, Peter laid violent hands on the serfs of propertied men, on the personnel normally engaged in working or administering Church lands, and above all on the very large numbers unattached to a lord, the latter greatly diminished in number. The subjects of nobles or Church all now became the tsar's subjects as well, permanently liable for service in his army.[3] Finally, in connection with the registration of souls for a universal poll-tax (1718–24), intended to pay for a massive standing army, the country was divided into 'regimental districts'. In these the different regiments were quartered and the officers, normally strangers to the district, dominated its administration. They took what they judged necessary in manpower, labour-service, billets, taxes. For many Russians the end of the Great Northern War meant, above all, occupation of their country by the new Russian army.

Conditions were somewhat different over a wide band of frontier lands. In the old Muslim khanate of Kazan, already in Russian possession for a century and a half, Peter abruptly reduced the subject population from tribute-payers to conscripts who also paid the poll-tax; and Tatar families of quality were made liable to labour service. From Astrakhan northwards, and then west across the Don, garrisons and border militias continued to subsist on lands allotted to them. In the Ukraine, however, the old organization of the Cossack 'regiments' was already breaking down under internal pressure. Their colonels had appropriated more and

[1] See vol. vii, pp. 342–3. In effect, the ordinance reversed that of 1702 giving the peasant freedom of movement except during his six years of service.
[2] See above, pp. 729 ff.
[3] Equally, the great expansion of mining and metallurgy in the Urals after 1697, for the supply of sufficient armaments, depended on the industrial conscription of both the tsar's peasants and the subject population of lords and convents.

more land within the territory occupied by each regiment; the lesser families grew poorer. Peter, who did not rate Cossack troops highly in the struggle against western armies and mistrusted most of the Cossack leaders after Mazepa's desertion, hastened the decadence of this ancient military society after 1709 by intensive conscription in the Ukraine for labour-service in other parts of Russia. The new hetman, Skoropadsky, judged it prudent to give away large tracts of land to Muscovite generals and politicians. Peter also destroyed the *sech'*, stronghold of the independent Cossacks of the Dnieper. The military colonies of eastern Europe, based on a division of the land between the fighting men, nevertheless remained important. They helped to hold the frontier of Christendom against the Muslim world across southern Russia and in the Balkans.[1] Here, between the Adriatic coast and the middle Danube, they formed the basis of that 'Military Frontier' which Marshal Marmont, a century later, was to describe as a masterpiece of modern government.

On the great arc drawn through Scandinavia, Russia and southern Hungary the State tended to act with crushing authority upon the local populations. Yet within the arc, despite all the raw material available for an imposing armed force, the elective monarchy of Poland was fading away. After the fiasco of Sobieski's expedition of 1686 into Moldavia, weakened in any case by the independent commands of the Hetman (general-in-chief) of the Crown and the Hetman of Lithuania, the Polish army faithfully reflected the paralysis of the Polish constitution. In the individual palatinates respectable numbers of heavy cavalry, hussars and light cavalry, dragoons and infantry—the infantry more numerous in western Poland and Mazovia, the heavy cavalry in the central area around Sandomierz and in the south—could be raised by magnates who fused territorial influence with official titles of authority. But they feared royal authority and each other more than Russia, Sweden or the Tatars. In consequence, the war-taxes were inadequate or not collected; and the army's arrears of pay in both Lithuania and Poland help to explain the corruptibility of military leaders and politicians when electing a new king in 1696–7. Afterwards, Poland simply became a battleground on which Polish forces played an auxiliary part. If the settlement in 1717 created on paper a standing army (with a disproportionate number of officers) and a tax to pay these officers and their men,[2] it was an inferior replica of the peace-time army constituted by the Sejm and Sobieski in 1677. The social structure of Poland appears to have altered little between these dates; but

[1] After 1711, also, Peter invited a number of Serb 'officers' from the Ottoman empire to form a military colony on the right bank of the Dnieper; in 1726 they were followed by Serbs from Habsburg territory: B. Nolde, *La Formation de l'empire russe* (2 vols. 1952–3), vol. II, pp. 32–3.
[2] See above, pp. 713–14. Significantly, Münnich, a very able soldier of fortune from Oldenburg, found his post in the Polish army intolerable and transferred to the service of Peter the Great in 1721.

the State itself, although still maintained by the balance and counter-balance of foreign powers, had approached the point of collapse.

The pressure on propertied men to serve in the armies of this period took various forms: compulsion by the State, economic motives, a military ethic and tradition. The autocrats pulled hardest in Russia, before 1725, and in Brandenburg-Prussia, after 1713.

Peter above all required rapid military expansion. To raise enough experienced officers from abroad quickly proved impossible; efforts were made by strenuous advertising in Germany and a promise of religious tolerance, but it was very difficult to pay those who came. So he proceeded on the assumption that his landowners were all permanently and personally liable for service; the size of a property did not affect the personal obligation. The result was that men of this type, even if many tried to conceal themselves in the depths of the Russian landscape, were forced into military service more generally than under his predecessors or successors. The bond between the Russian army and landowning families of all sorts remained direct and tight until after 1720. It was perhaps the most spectacular change of the reign, and exerted a profound influence on the later history of eastern Europe. But Peter had to subordinate the old social order to a somewhat different hierarchy in the armed forces. Because systematic training was needed to produce disciplined officers, it followed that even the sons of princely families had to rise from an apprenticeship in junior ranks, and it seemed equally to follow that good men of low birth should be promoted. The bias of the tsar's autocracy against vested interests in court or country was evident. Nevertheless, the upshot was to compel the landowning classes to serve in his army (or elsewhere) without necessarily degrading them. Although he prised open the barriers of an intensely hieratic society, the barriers were later moved back into position to ring round a new privileged order. This reaction proved irresistible after Peter's death, but already before 1725 there were signs that the then existing nobility would remain dominant in the army. Youths of suitable family, scheduled in elaborate registers which were scrutinized each winter, had to serve as ordinary soldiers in the Pre-obrazhensky or Semonovsky Guards before receiving commissions in other regiments. What had once been the 'toy regiments' of Peter's boyhood became increasingly exclusive; when a third Guards' regiment emerged in 1719, it was authorized to accept recruits of good family only.

In Brandenburg-Prussia, a vigorous autocracy began forcing the native landed class into the army with the accession of Frederick William I. He too had his lists of suitable recruits from each province, and kept them up to date. He too developed an institution, the Cadet Corps in Berlin, through which he could effectively train and supervise the Junkers. The cadet companies, earlier attached to some of the regiments which took part in the Nine Years War, were first converted into training establishments at home and finally amalgamated in one body by 1720.[1] In 1688 a majority of officers in the Hohenzollern army already came from Hohenzollern nobilities; but in Brandenburg, and even more in East Prussia, strong conservative tendencies at first held back many potential officers. Not all gentry circles accepted the elector's increased authority. Some clung to old-fashioned habits of mind in other respects; they remained in the countryside, often poor, not very different in outlook from groups of the *szlachta* in parts of Poland who spent their lives splitting and resplitting small family heritages, or from the debt-ridden section of the *Ritterschaft* (the privileged Estate) in Sleswig. A few families were proud and substantial enough to feel genuinely independent. Their members, if they chose a military career, in many cases preferred to serve foreign princes. Yet the desire for employment was a powerful impulse in Brandenburg, as everywhere else, and the elector's was a large army. It could hardly escape attention that his most successful commanders were generously rewarded with territorial grants, or that any rank from the captain's upwards promised a livelihood; for the captain, besides pay and allowances, had the profits of his company—the difference between the costs of recruiting, equipping and paying his men, and the sums paid him by the State; a colonel equally drew pay and allowances and enjoyed the sundry profits of managing a regiment, but in addition kept his company in the regiment; generals and general officers often kept the profits of both their regiments and their companies. This inducement gained in substance between 1688 and 1713. The military activity of the north German states was then paid for by Dutch and English subsidies, and by contributions from occupied areas, as well as by heavy taxation at home. In spite of arrears, the war pay of officers compared well with the scanty income of many German gentry.

Moreover, a strong military tradition stretched back in certain families to the Thirty Years War. Many young gentlemen from northern Germany hurried south to fight in the Turkish wars after 1683, and astonishing numbers, principally from Mecklenburg and Holstein, joined the Danish army.[2] Brandenburgers were bound to enter their elector's own force from the same motives. The Great Elector, for his part, employed them without any intention either of insisting on their service or of allowing them a monopoly. He welcomed foreign soldiers and promoted his commoners. Above all, he recruited Huguenots: in 1688, out of 1,030 commissioned officers in his total force, at least 300 were Huguenot. But after 1700 King Frederick I's army was largely though not exclusively officered by his

---

[1] As early as March 1704 a proposal was made in the War Council, probably by the Crown Prince, that arrangements should be made for 'all youths of the nobility in the country' to enlist in cadet companies: C. Hinrichs, *Friedrich Wilhelm I. Jugend und Aufstieg* (Hamburg, 1941), p. 98.

[2] In 1699, 410 Germans as against 136 Danes are believed to have officered 22 out of the 27 Danish regiments: *Bidrag til den store nordiske Krigs Historie*, vol. I, pp. 108–9.

own nobles, and the same was true of the forces raised by princes of the House of Brunswick, including Hanover. It must be remembered that in the Protestant States of the Empire (and in Scandinavia) the alternative of a career in the Church, common enough in Catholic Europe, hardly existed for men of quality. Further south, however, the proportion of noblemen serving Max Emmanuel of Bavaria who did not come from Wittelsbach lands,[1] or of those in the emperor's army who were not Habsburg subjects, was substantially higher.

On the other hand, the strain of war helped to keep entry into the officers' ranks, in Brandenburg and elsewhere, fairly open. Every army increased in size. Exercising the troops grew more meticulous in the better units.[2] Military organization became more complex: regiments were split into battalions in garrison and abroad, and they were joined together in brigades while on campaign. For these reasons more officers were needed. Colonel-lieutenants, majors, staff captains and second lieutenants became common appointments. All this compelled German governments to encourage able commoners. In 1704 Frederick I promised formally that in his Guards they should stand an equal chance of promotion with their colleagues of privileged origin; he also ennobled freely, unlike his successor. Hence German armies still provided a career reasonably open to talent. After 1713, however, the proportion of non-noble officers gradually ebbed away, though very gradually indeed in the more technical services. In another respect the situation changed even during the war years. Very quickly the Huguenot officers of the Brandenburg, Hanoverian, Dutch and British armies merged into German, Dutch, English and Anglo-Irish society; rigidly Lutheran Saxony never admitted them. Before the Spanish war ended Frederick William expressed a wish to replace Huguenot by German officers, and in 1714 he dismissed far more commoners than noble officers; but the general movement of the nobility into war-service had already anticipated his policy. The conscription of young noblemen into the Cadet Corps was to stiffen the traditional structure of society, and their sense of exclusiveness increased as the king excluded all but native noblemen. A cadet sent from Berlin to his next phase of training as a *Gefreite-korporal* in the army itself could no longer be confused with his social inferiors, who had less and less chance of promotion into the ranks of the *Oberoffiziere*. In 1700 some gentlemen still served for long periods as private soldiers or sergeants, unable to rise, while com-

---

[1] Of the 430 officers in his army on 10 Nov. 1705, 131 were Bavarian, 61 German, 23 Austrian, 3 Swiss, 34 French, 16 Lorrainers, 42 Walloon or Flemish, 31 Italian, and 35 Irish: K. Staudinger, *Geschichte des kurbayerischen Heeres unter Kurfürst Max II Emmanuel, 1680–1726* (Munich, 2 vols. 1904–5), vol. II, app. 6. The list is incomplete.

[2] The rigour and uniformity of Prussian infantry drill can be traced to Philip William (1669–1711), the Great Elector's eldest son by his second marriage. He inspired his brother-in-law Leopold of Anhalt-Dessau and his nephew Frederick William I. The *Exercise* used in his regiment was, by order of the War Council in 1702, printed for adoption by all the Prussian foot-regiments.

moners did rise. Twenty or thirty years later social relations in the army had been tidied up. They mirrored more faithfully civil society itself.

Westwards, the same interlocking of royal pressure with the search for employment, and many of the same institutions, reappear. As an Englishman wrote in 1695, pondering his son's prospects: '...he is qualified for any civil employ but the only way of attaining to them in due time for a young man under such a prince is by arms in his youth...';[1] and William III did indeed promise the future Earl Stanhope a commission in his Guards for valour shown at Namur that very year. William shared a deep conviction that war was the profession of a ruler—and therefore of his trusted servants—with Peter the Great, Charles XII, Victor Amadeus II, George of Hanover and even Augustus of Saxony. These princes surrounded themselves with their 'Household' and 'Guards', who enjoyed special privileges. From 1691 Guards officers in England, even the lieutenants, ranked with officers a step or sometimes two steps higher in all other regiments; later in their careers they tended to monopolize the best posts in the British army. But William's Guards could never be used by the ruler as the instrument of radical social change, as in Russia, nor was there any development in England comparable with the rise of the Prussian Cadet Corps.

The magnificent military section of Louis XIV's *Maison du Roi*, 8,500 strong in 1690, was relatively more important. The favoured section of the French nobility, normally combining the advantages of lineage and fortune, streamed out from it to dominate the army under the king's approving gaze; and to a certain extent Louis used it to supervise and restrict the aristocratic monopoly. Saint-Simon, for example, resented the compulsory period of service in the *Mousquetaires* at court imposed on men of his stamp: he assumed that a nobleman had a right to follow the wars, to volunteer and to secure a commission through relatives or friends without government's active interference. He also complained that the rule of promotion by seniority, based on the *Ordre du Tableau*, was used to impede the advancement of able men of good family. This had certainly been intended to fortify royal control over the army; but the king made exceptions to the rule, and in fact followed it less closely in the Succession War than earlier. He had also abolished venality in the four companies of his bodyguard below the captain's rank; to these, non-noble troopers were admitted.[2] Between 1701 and 1714 the number of commissions issued to 'bons bourgeois vivant noblement', in the French army as a whole, undoubtedly increased. This was due to the shortage of suitable men in an emergency. After the war, bourgeois officers were dismissed in

---

[1] Quoted in B. Williams, *Stanhope* (Oxford, 1932), p. 7.
[2] Cf. above, p. 340. Recruiting for the cadet companies founded by Louvois (above, pp. 223–4) was not continued after 1691: service with the *Mousquetaires* or with the *Régiment du Roi* helped to replace them.

larger numbers than their noble colleagues. On the other hand, the older nobility of the sword was being joined by the offspring of more recently ennobled families, some of which had prospered in administration or the law; and this in turn gradually affected the personnel who held senior military posts.[1] Marshal d'Huxelles sprang on his mother's side from the *noblesse de robe* and Catinat belonged to a *parlementaire* family of not more than moderate eminence. Vauban's radical suggestion[2]—that soldiers themselves should qualify for noble status of ascending degrees by promotion and long service in the king's army—never stood a chance of acceptance; even the military Order of St Louis, created in 1693, with its various classes of award, did not confer noble status. The social order, changing though it might be, was not to be remodelled in accordance with the hierarchy of military ranks; nor was military rank, unlike war finance and prosperity in the law, to prove an instrument of social change.

Moreover, the conviction was still strong everywhere in the West that the bearing of arms meant two things, the armorial and the sword, one involving the other. It had been one of Louis XIV's great triumphs, in his years of success before 1688, to entwine with these a sense of military obligations to the State. By 1700 a set pattern was decisively worked into the fabric of countless French family histories: of a gentleman's sons, one or more served in Louis's army, one or more entered the Church. By then it was hardly possible to distinguish royal pressure from that of a potent convention. The underlying circumstances are clear enough. An income which depended more on rents than on demesne farming, combined with exclusion from local administration by royal officialdom, implied leisure and freedom of movement. So did the *droit d'aînesse* in many areas and the desire to preserve patrimonies intact, which tended to delay the marriages of younger sons. The very idea of a *noblesse d'épée* debarred it from other activities, and the sanctions against *dérogeance* should have helped to confine noblemen to the profession of arms. The temptation (or the necessity) to 'derogate' did become stronger, indeed, if a family's economic resources declined sharply, and a decline at this level of society has certainly been traced in regions like Anjou, Briançon and Dauphiné between 1670 and the early eighteenth century;[3] impoverished men drew up wills empowering their children to learn trades and to forfeit their status. But commercial or professional openings were often hard to find, and sheer force of custom kept most of the nobility true to their military tradition.

---

[1] Of the 276 lieutenant-generals appointed by Louis XIV, the social origins of 164 have been traced. Of these, 43 came from families ennobled in the sixteenth and seventeenth centuries, 114 from a more ancient nobility; only 7 can be described as of non-noble origin. See A. Corvisier, 'Les Généraux de Louis XIV et leur origine sociale', *XVIIᵉ Siècle*, nos. 42–3 (1959), p. 41.

[2] 'Des moyens à tenir pour faire une excellente noblesse par les services', *Vauban, sa famille et ses écrits*...(ed. Rochas d'Aiglun, 2 vols. 1910), vol. i, pp. 642–6.

[3] 'Famille et population au XVIIᵉ siècle', *XVIIᵉ Siècle*, no. 15 (1952), p. 454.

If they could, they bought commissions. The more modest rural gentry applied to relatives, or to local patrons already possessed of an interest in the king's regiments. The administration helped them by maintaining a distinction between commissions which had to be purchased (with royal approval) from the previous holder and those which did not: the second lieutenant, lieutenant, *aide-major*, major and lieutenant-colonel all belonged to the second category. Louis's grants and pensions, occasionally, also assisted good soldiers at the bottom of the hierarchy to climb it. On the other hand, in many cases the claim of merit or seniority was overbid by that of property or patronage, and the running expenses of the non-venal ranks below lieutenant-colonel could with difficulty be met out of pay alone. The intendants' reports in the Succession War show that surplus revenue belonging to landed families commonly flowed out of the countryside to support relatives away on military service. Without these extra funds, or extraordinary luck, their lives were barely endurable. The economic basis of an officer's career under Louis XIV was therefore provided by adding official pay to family resources. The greater a man's private means, the better his prospect of rising in the army; but if he rose high enough, then his rank became profitable.

Many of these characteristics were repeated outside France, others not. The refusal to countenance derogation was considered partly responsible for the nobility's impoverishment in Savoy by 1700;[1] yet in neighbouring Piedmont, where there were no legal sanctions against other careers, Piedmontese noblemen normally chose one of the classic alternatives, Church or army. Elsewhere in Italy, and in Spain, it was the element of autocratic pressure that was missing. Italian noblemen sometimes joined the Habsburg and Bourbon armies, and the great Montecuccoli had successors who likewise became distinguished Imperial commanders; but Italian society no longer contained a definite military class.[2] There were noblemen who raised followers for conspiracy, but few signs of military organization. Venice owed the recovery of the Morea largely to German mercenaries. The militias of the north Italian cities were mere spectators of the fighting in Lombardy between 1701 and 1706. In Spain, the privileged—the humble *hidalgos*, most numerous in the northern kingdoms from Guipúzcoa to León, or the more select classes of grandees and other titled noblemen, found mainly south of the Ebro and Douro—did not spurn arms, but they spurned armies. They preferred civil and court offices, attaching little prestige to the military service of the Crown. This attitude of mind, certainly associated with the decay of Spanish power

[1] M. Bruchet, 'Les Instructions de Victor-Amédée II sur le gouvernement de son Duché de Savoie en 1721', *Bull. hist. et philol. du Comité des travaux historiques et scientifiques*, anneé *1900* (1901), p. 286.
[2] R. Filamondo, *Il Genio bellicoso di Napoli* (1694), containing some fifty biographies of Neapolitan officers, was one of the last literary echoes of an old military tradition.

after 1660, altered during the long crisis of the civil war after 1704. Many of the highest nobility of Castile and Aragon, alarmed by what they considered the autocratic administration of Philip V, fought for the Archduke Charles. Philip's edict of 8 November 1704, in turn, was an important attempt to revive the military force of Castile and other areas under his control. It expressed the king's wish that his regiments serve as a 'school for the nobility of my kingdoms', by training cadets; it also opened the junior commissioned ranks to those who 'lived nobly' and to the sons of merchants; and it decreed the liability of nearly all classes to conscription.[1]

In England a new legal device, the 'strict settlement', made it possible to bestow on younger sons fixed monetary revenues from family estates otherwise kept intact for the principal heir. These men could move freely; they had some income but not enough. The steadily growing military force of the later Stuarts consequently attracted its fair share of the large numbers seeking preferment. The county militias were officered by resident gentry, the standing army—at the level of lieutenant and captain—by non-resident gentry, apparently with a smaller but still definite stake in the country: in this respect the distinction between army and militia was by no means as clear-cut as politicians declared. One view put forward in 1692 was that 'Our officers are men of Estates, to subdue the Enemy and not make a Trade of the War'.[2] Meanwhile the historic influx of Scottish gentry into the British army had begun. No more than the English were they debarred from trade and other occupations, but their country as a whole was far too poor to keep them. Now, instead of serving under a foreign flag, the same sort of young adventurer turned naturally to the British forces serving abroad. Outside the Scots regiments proper, often raised by great men and lesser lairds from their tenantry, the number of Scots officers in English regiments grew astonishingly. A quarter of all the regimental officers in the British army between 1714 and 1763 were to be Scotsmen.[3]

In England, also, there are clear signs of a development that was important everywhere else: the commissioned ranks of the army were coming to regard themselves as a great permanent 'interest', defending a mass of smaller private interests and so involving the livelihood of thousands. The proprietary element in commissions was one aspect of this, half-pay another. Military service looked its most attractive in wartime, thanks to the ease of entry into new regiments; but after a commission had been granted for the first time, the post acquired a cash value, so that promotion became bound up with purchase. This was especially true of

[1] A. Domínguez Ortiz, *La Sociedad española en el siglo XVIII* (Madrid, 1955), p. 372. Cf. above, pp. 347–8 and 366–7.
[2] *Debates of the House of Commons 1667–94* (ed. Anchitell Grey, 1769), vol. x, p. 263.
[3] J. Hayes, 'Scottish officers in the British Army, 1714–63', *Scottish Hist. Rev.* vol. xxxvii (1958), pp. 25–7.

the older regiments, which stood a better chance of survival when hostilities ended; the seniority of regiments, more strictly determined by William in 1693, was important partly for this reason. The difference between the amount payable when someone became an ensign or lieutenant or captain, and so on upward, and the amount he received for his previous post, was therefore a factor affecting countless military careers by this period. The purchase of a commission might represent the savings of a lifetime, its sale an income for the widow. The system had obvious drawbacks, but Marlborough for one sharply defended it in 1711 against an attempt at reform; until the closing years of the war, in fact, there were many opportunities for promotion without purchase. George I, with a stiffer autocratic tradition behind him, felt strongly that the practice limited the monarch's right to decide promotion and kept good men down; but the regulations of 1720 show that he was powerless to do more than fix an official tariff of maximum prices for each commissioned rank, although he was able to insist on a respectable period of service before junior officers could qualify for a captaincy.

'Half-pay', a retaining fee for supernumerary officers on disbanding, was granted by various governments at the close of the Nine Years War. Occasionally, it took the form of a pension for the old and disabled. Irregularity and arrears in payment, rather than its modest scale, caused grave hardship to many officers during the interval of peace. Even this much was never projected for the rank and file. When regiments were disbanded or reduced, privates were dismissed with a few weeks' subsistence money. Except in the general sense that unemployed or casually employed old soldiers were also willing recruits when the next round of warfare began, they did not form part of the military 'interest' which had grown up with the standing armies. Revenues set aside by certain States to care for those invalided in war assisted only a small minority of private soldiers.[1]

Just as the military business of a government went far beyond the raising of large numbers of men and officers, so the contribution of a civilian population was not confined to producing them. The course of great wars depended ultimately on civilian capacity to stand the over-all strain of hostilities, and to support large permanent forces stationed at home in time of peace. During this period there are signs of improved adminis-

[1] The Commissioners for Sick and Wounded figure largely in the military correspondence of Anne's reign, but part of their outlay, as for Chelsea Hospital, was borne by stoppages from pay; gratuities and pensions to wounded private soldiers were rare. In Prussia, a separate fund for the disabled (*Invalidenkasse*) was set up in 1705, assisting about 2,000 men by 1709; and in 1722 Frederick William I began to build the great Potsdam military orphanage. In Paris the *Hôtel Royal des Invalides* was said to accommodate up to 7,000 officers and men, but Louis XIV's later wars showed its inadequacy. Many governments also organized companies of disabled men fit enough for garrison duty.

trative skills, and of a calculated readiness to limit the destructiveness of war in order to diminish that strain. There are signs, too, that certain social groups not only adapted themselves easily but prospered.

The importance of first-class administration was shown by the intendants of the French frontier provinces. It is hardly exaggerating to say that the intendant at Lille was King William's and Marlborough's most formidable opponent. With his subordinate *commissaires de guerre* (and the more senior *commissaires ordonnateurs* after 1700), he provided French armies in the north-east with essential supplies. He negotiated with all local authorities over the quartering of officers and men, except in the field, and decided what expenditure under this head they could set off against taxes. He assessed compensation when land was expropriated for military works and fortifications. He could forbid private building, to make carpenters and masons available. He dealt with the various types of contractors—builders, hospital administrators, suppliers of bread and forage. He controlled the prices charged by *cantiniers* (sutlers) to the troops. He would fix responsibility on the ordinary magistrates of town and country: ways and means, contracts fulfilled by additional local taxes or by direct requisitioning, were their affair, but he had the last word. The provincial intendant was also an *intendant de guerre*, an important official in the army itself. He had some responsibility for the arrangements to pay it. Sometimes he sent in confidential reports on the generals. By contrast, the navy had its own *intendants de marine*.

As in Flanders and Artois, so in Alsace the administration contrived to exploit the resources of a fertile frontier zone without bleeding it intolerably. Here the intendants were above all occupied in working out the detailed terms on which the inhabitants and great military installations could exist together. The load was enormous. Besides garrisons for the extensive new fortifications erected on the Rhine since 1681, a field-army had to be maintained to oppose Imperial forces in south-western Germany. The effects upon the province were intricate and contradictory. Peremptory conscription of manpower, and not least of carts and draught animals, strained the economy of peasant families to the limit, notwithstanding the decision to take no militiamen from the frontier provinces after 1702. Troops quartered for the winter, in addition to the permanent garrisons, sent up prices, which hurt many but of course suited others. Some Strasbourg burghers and some landowners did very well out of contracts, the burghers buying up property near the city; rentals in kind provided more foodstuffs for disposal to the magazines.[1] The administration tried to temper the effects of excessive demand by regulating prices, requisitioning, storing and releasing its reserves at the

---

[1] Closely comparable were those families of Chambéry (afterwards rising to territorial dignity) who supplied French forces on the route to Italy: see F. Vermale, *Les Classes rurales en Savoie au XVIIIe siècle* (1911), p. 64.

right moment. The inhabitants recouped part of their taxes, too, in payment for wages and supplies. To build the fortresses or do the spadework in siege warfare men had to be raised and paid by village communities, but this gave a livelihood to many casual labourers; for some a golden period of full employment ended with the completion of the works at Neuf-Breisach in 1701. On the whole, pressure of this controlled type avoided the depression of fertile lands adjoining major war-zones to the level of misery experienced in some regions of the interior.[1]

In the southern Netherlands the situation was still more complex. Here, and to a lesser extent also in western Germany, an extraordinary network of fortified points or lines tended to pin down the field-armies. Troops could not range freely, as in eastern Europe, to live off the country. On the other hand, the fortifications were by no means continuous enough to stop strong bands of partisans or dragoons from slipping past enemy forces to raid the countryside far behind them and then returning. Equally, the supply of armies from behind their own fronts was a matter of great difficulty. A well-developed system of water transport could not wholly compensate for bad roads. During the war of 1672–8, a number of 'contribution treaties' had been negotiated locally by the intendants most nearly concerned: they agreed to recognize each belligerent's claim to levy contributions from areas which it had not fully conquered but which the other could not effectively defend. Such levies, in cash or goods, were collected by the local administration of the area defined in the treaty, to avoid requisitioning by force of arms. In the Nine Years War no such treaty was made until 1694. The desultory course of battles and sieges was overshadowed by the brutal raids carried out by the combatants in two main areas: between the Scheldt estuary and Artois, and between the Meuse and Rhine. This particularly ruinous warfare had been anticipated by French efforts in the winter of 1688–9 to ravage Württemberg, the Palatinate, and parts of the lower Rhineland. The intentions were strategic, the consequences for civilians appalling. The Succession War in this part of Europe caused less hardship to non-combatants. In the Netherlands contribution-treaties were arranged as if it were now understood that no better method existed for tapping extra resources from enemy country, and indeed of avoiding the waste through devastation which would halve the benefit of a conquest later on. These notions harmonized with the natural desire of a countryside to compromise with the enemy rather than expose property to military 'execution'. As a result, in the great triangle bounded by the Pays de Waes and the bishopric of Liège and French Artois, a cluster of local governments (*châtellenies*), municipalities and Estates maintained themselves intact throughout the wars. A small world of magistrates and contractors—the taxes imposed by the magistrates paying the contractors—ministered alike to the needs of

---

[1] For the effects of war on food and money supplies there, see above, pp. 320–1.

opposing armies and their own pockets. Opposing sovereigns, for their part, rarely failed to recognize the historic privileges of cities, nobilities and clergy when they conquered fresh territory; nor did cities, nobilities and clergy delay in recognizing a transfer of sovereignty. Cities, too, often asked a besieging commander not to associate them with the garrison defending the citadel in their midst. It was in this respect, among others, that wars were dynastic. At least in the Netherlands, Germany and north Italy, the intention was always to defeat the enemy sovereign, not to disrupt the social order on which his sovereignty rested. The fighting in Ireland between 1689 and 1691, and in Catalonia two decades later, were important exceptions to the more or less general rule.

In this way the burdens of war in the West were mitigated. Hardly less important, when the wars were over, improved administration made a standing army less irksome to the population at home. Taxation and contracting were gradually substituted for direct military rule and requisitioning. The *ustensile* or *Serviz*—the old claim of officers and men, to various amenities in kind from their civilian hosts—was increasingly redeemed by cash payments under official tariffs, which were in turn replaced by a tax spreading the liability fairly over larger numbers of households in wider areas. Cities financed the building of barracks to avoid the evils of billeting in private houses and stables, although the quartering of cavalrymen on the countryside continued in most States. Sometimes the lack of any accommodation at all, as in Ireland before 1700 and Scotland after 1715, would force government itself to construct barracks.

Besides the small groups already identified who contrived to prosper in the very shadow of military activity, there were others who thrived remote from the theatres of war. The most fortunate were the creditors of the Dutch and English governments. In France the sale of offices increased the number of families who were more or less sheltered from the worst impositions of a powerful government at bay, although they had often to repurchase their privileges. Many such office-holders were connected with the organization of military supplies; a wide gulf separated soldier and *milicien* from the municipal oligarchs who commanded their own burgher militias, guarded conscripts passing through their towns, and had interests in common with contractors supplying the local magazines. Yet another gulf divided these minor privileged interests from the greater tax-farmers, financiers and administrators. Of the last, perhaps the most spectacular example in all Europe was Queen Anne's Paymaster of the Forces Abroad, James Brydges, son of an impoverished nobleman and a Turkey merchant's daughter. A judicious use of his office in 1705-13 enabled him to put the balances of public money passing through his hands to profitable use, so that his income increased enormously. He enlarged it still further by currency manipulation and speculating in stock.

War paid for the buildings and artistic collections of this civilian, as it paid for Eugene's Belvedere in Vienna and Lewis of Baden's palace at Rastatt.

Business men turned easily to war contracts and financing, even to military administration. Johann Andreas Kraut of Berlin dealt in luxury textiles until 1686, entered the Great Elector's *Kommissariat* and became for 25 years a principal administrator of the Hohenzollern War Treasury, officially authorized to use his firm's resources in combination with official ones; through his hands went both taxes and Allied subsidies; and later he organized the *Lagerhaus* which manufactured the army's clothing. A number of Huguenot emigrants followed a similar course. The Huguetan brothers, refugees from Lyons to Amsterdam, were still selling books in the 1690s, but from 1701 they appear as agents for remittances to both the British and French forces; after 1703 Jean Henri Huguetan at Geneva diverted on loan to the French government money which had normally flowed into business.[1] To the embitterment of the poorer classes there, a number of his rivals in Geneva also switched from silk, salt and corn merchandising to banking; they organized the movement of French funds to Italy or Allied funds to Piedmont. From 1704, after various efforts to employ their large bullion reserve to encourage industry at home, the Bernese government found it more profitable to advance loans to the Dutch; the private Malacrida bank in Berne followed suit. Swiss investment in both Holland and England began its long history. Meanwhile the 'Court Jews' of the German princes, often beginning as purveyors of luxuries, became financiers and contractors to their armed forces. Leffmann Behrens of Hanover handled Louis XIV's great subsidy to Ernest Augustus in 1690, and later the flow of Allied subsidies to the bishop of Münster. Behrend Lehmann of Halberstadt, who had played a key rôle in the election of Augustus the Strong, kept the Saxon army in Poland in boots and clothing after 1701. Still more important was Samuel Oppenheimer, in the 1670s an army contractor to the Habsburg, by 1700 its indispensable banker. His great contemporary in Paris, Samuel Bernard, similarly found his business expanding prodigiously with the increased scale of French expenditure in distant theatres of war. All these men depended on their ability to tap a wide circle of partners or investors in order to make available the advances required promptly, and in the right places, by governments. They struggled, sometimes against unfavourable odds, to maintain those resources of cash and credit which enabled them to wait for the tardy though profitable repayments ultimately due from taxes or subsidies.

The fundamental soundness of this type of business was often suspect. In France the investigations of the *Chambre de Justice* during the Regency led to the confiscation of some wartime fortunes. Many other speculators

[1] Cf. above, pp. 303-4.

had already burnt their fingers badly, when too many borrowed too much in order to invest in reckless schemes. In 1703, on Oppenheimer's death, the Habsburg government was rocked by the temporary failure of his heirs and by its own dangerous attempt to repudiate them. In 1705 Huguetan left his creditors in the lurch, and in 1709 Bernard temporarily failed to settle outstanding obligations in the Lyons money market. But the fortunes of the Oppenheimer family, and of their relatives the Wertheimers, were nevertheless placed on foundations sound enough to allow them an immense prosperity in the eighteenth century. Bernard lived to enjoy his wealth into a green old age. Nor was business of their kind extinguished by the peace, for armies were now permanent institutions. A classic example is the firm of Splitgerber, Daum and Company of Berlin (1713), which built the works at Potsdam and Spandau and supplied munitions to the Prussian army for generations.

In broadest outline, the armed forces mirrored the general structure of society. They were directed and sometimes commanded by sovereign princes, normally officered by representatives of the very various degrees of gentry and nobility. The numbers of noblemen following a military career without a commission, and of non-nobles promoted to senior commissioned posts, if exception be made of the artillery and other technical services, alike diminished fast after 1714. The ranks were overwhelmingly filled by the unprivileged, who could rise to become corporals and sergeants—but no higher. This common basis of armies and civil society cannot be taken for granted in all periods. The decayed relics of a very different system were still just visible in eastern Europe, for neither the janissaries nor the *strel'tsy* had at any time been representative of the rural classes. Conversely, as was still true of the Ottoman sipahis, armies and civil society could sometimes be fused together on the basis of military tenures. But Louis XIV summoned his nobles to arms in virtue of their fiefs for the last time in 1693, and the king of Prussia finally commuted the same obsolete liability into a tax in 1717. Even so, one important legacy did survive from the feudal past of the West: the idea that a nobility of the sword owed their status to a duty to bear arms. It carried them to a favoured position in the new standing armies.

All the same, men became increasingly conscious of a distinction between military organization and civil society. The greater rigour of military law, discipline and training, together with the larger scale of this military organization, helped to divide the two. It was now an accepted function of governments to settle the relations between soldiers and civilians so that neither suffered unduly to the detriment of the State. For this purpose administrative techniques were worked out and applied with varying effectiveness. In some respects soldiers and civilians both gained, for their interdependence was understood; but the civilian interest was easier to appreciate in western Europe, where the economy was more vigorous and sensitive than further east. There, at any rate in Russia, and to a lesser degree in Brandenburg-Prussia after 1713, it is possible to speak of society's new military foundations in the early eighteenth century, laid by the State's autocratic power. Elsewhere, governments were unable to transform the social foundations of armed forces. More modestly, they sought to adjust the stresses caused by their own desire for sufficient armament in a world of eager rivals.

3. NAVIES

IN 1688 the most powerful European navies were the French, English and Dutch. Spanish and Portuguese sea power had suffered a serious decline in the seventeenth century. The Ottoman, Algerine, Venetian and Maltese fleets, though no longer limited to galleys, did not count outside the Mediterranean (ch. xvii) and none of them dominated it. Denmark-Norway and Sweden maintained larger and more efficient fleets than did any of the Mediterranean states except France, but neither was able to win hegemony in the Baltic or forbid the intervention of outside navies there. By 1721 decisive changes had taken place. The Danish and Swedish navies were weaker, and Russian warships were cruising in the Baltic for the first time (ch. xxi). The Ottoman fleet had undergone the reforms of Mezzomorto (ch. xix). The great tradition of Spanish naval shipbuilding had been revived by Admiral Antonio de Gastañeta and Josef Patiño. As was shown in 1718 by the battle of Cape Passaro, however, Britain had the will and the means to delay the recovery of Sicily and Naples, which had made Spanish warships and galleys an undeniable nuisance to the French in the 1690s. Her new control of Gibraltar and Minorca signified Britain's status as the predominant European naval power. The Dutch, who in 1689 had contested English command of the combined sea forces, were hard pressed to get eight ships together in 1714 as an escort for King George I: their contribution to the confederate line of battle had fallen from a third to a fifth between 1702 and 1710, from which year they could no longer afford a North Sea squadron at all.[1] By contrast, the newer and more resilient naval might of France, with a matchless bureaucracy behind it, was beginning in 1721 to make good two decades of gathering decay. A survey of her fleet in 1716 (or a little later) reveals a total strength of 69 rated vessels, nine of them prizes and three-fifths of the remainder built before 1702, when 84 *vaisseaux* had been commissioned out of 135 described as *effectifs*.[2] Unlike these navies,

[1] J. H. Owen, *War at Sea under Queen Anne*, app. c, p. 277.
[2] Paris, A[rchives] N[ationales], Marine B5, no. 3, and G13, fos. 11, 24–31. In 1689 the French had only 113 *vaisseaux effectifs*, including 35 third and 28 fourth rates (ibid. G9, fo. 23), as compared with 54 of the third (60–46 guns) and only 17 of the fourth (44–36) in 1702. These figures exclude galleys, of which there were 25 in 1716: cf. above, p. 563.

as late as 1709, when the naval hostilities of the Spanish Succession War had begun to wane, the English line of battle was as strong as it had been in 1689 or 1702.[1] With a hundred sail of the line, it was stronger than all the Baltic fleets together.

The term 'ship of the line' belongs to the 1690s, when considerations of cost, timber supply and winter sea-keeping told against the building of the three-decker leviathans developed since the 1630s. The line-ahead formation itself, deriving from the seventeenth-century preference for artillery duels to the old line-abreast mêlée of hand-to-hand fighting, had acquired a degree of sophistication during the Anglo-Dutch wars which achieved classic form in the English Fighting Instructions of 1691, probably drafted by Torrington, and in the mathematician Paul Hoste's *L'Art des armées navales* (1697), based indirectly on English practice.[2] The line put a premium on short-range gunnery and stout ship construction. The English so far excelled in both these respects as habitually to sacrifice sailing qualities to them; the dimensions of a French or Spanish man-of-war were larger in relation to the same fire-power.[3] But the line also imposed equal standards of performance on belligerents, with important consequences for the standardization and distribution of guns, the classification of warships by gun-power, and the demarcation of 'capital ships' from others. The capital ships were those judged sufficiently powerful to lie in the line, as distinct from the multifarious routine services, notably commerce protection and naval reconnaissance, for which numerous frigates, sloops, yachts and other vessels were required by every maritime country. An English or Dutch capital ship would carry at least 50 guns, the French (mounting heavier pieces) a minimum of about 40. Before the mid-seventeenth century, on the other hand, armed merchantmen could serve in battle and governments were free to maintain relatively small forces of regular warships. The inadequacy of hired or impressed merchantmen—except as fireships to consummate an action—had been finally demonstrated during the Anglo-Dutch wars, after which they were

Their firsts and seconds corresponded broadly with the first three English rates, whereas an English fourth rate was roughly equivalent to a French third. All powers modified such ratings from time to time, but the definitive French classification dates from the *Ordonnance* of 15 April 1689.

[1] Owen, pp. 273–7; J. Ehrman, *The Navy in the War of William III*, p. 4.

[2] J. S. Corbett (ed.), *Fighting Instructions, 1530–1816* (N[avy] R[ec.] S[oc.], 1905), pp. 175–94. On the interdependent evolution of ships, guns and the line of battle in this century, see Ehrman, ch. I, and F. L. Robertson, *The Evolution of Naval Armament* (1921), pp. 15 ff. The line (as even its opponents admitted) suited the rough ballistics of the day, but required discipline in manoeuvre, tactical control and a comprehensive code of signals—a matter in which the French are said to have profited by the exile of James II (L. E. Holland in *The Mariner's Mirror*, vol. XXXIX, 1953, pp. 5 ff.). The formalism of line tactics, which echoes contemporary trends in land warfare (above, ch. XXII (1)), is discussed by M. Lewis in *The Navy of Britain* (1948), pp. 455 ff.

[3] Robertson, p. 41, refers to the case of the English-built *Pembroke*, which on recapture from the French was found to bear only 50 guns instead of the original 64.

relegated to auxiliary duties such as the transport of troops and stores, if not commissioned as privateers, sometimes to combine trade with privateering. It is noticeable that hired ships disappeared from the Swedish fleet after 1679.

By 1688, professional standing navies were not only more carefully articulated but also larger and stronger than ever before. More English naval tonnage was built in 1670–5 than in any previous quinquennium, and in 1677, when the English fleet was first comprehensively classified, a new land tax was created 'for the speedy building of thirty men-of-war'— a programme without comparable sequel, however, till an Act of 1691, which reflected the astonishment aroused by Tourville's appearance at Beachy Head with 70 great ships.[1] It is a rough measure of the achievement of Colbert and Seignelay that forty years earlier the entire naval resources of France barely added up to a score of battleships, all but three mounting less than 50 pieces; of the relatively formidable fleet bequeathed by Richelieu, the strongest survivor in 1648 bore only 52.[2] The United Provinces, influenced by their stadholder, resolved in 1684 to build up to a total of 96 sail of the line, comparable with the French and English; they were some thirty units short of this at the end of 1688, even counting those of 40–50 guns, but of the 27 battleships turned out by their yards in 1682–8 no less than seven were in the 90-gun class, well above the armament hitherto dictated by the shallow home waters of the Netherlands. This output may be contrasted with the sixty-odd warships built by the Dutch in 1665–7. They proved capable of a comparable volume of construction through the Nine Years War, as did the English and French. The following table shows the new construction of capital ships by these powers from 1689 to 1698 inclusive:[3]

	Dutch	English	French
(1) Over 76 guns	8	4	25
(2) 76–60 guns	31	23	14
(3) 60–36 guns	39	42	35
	78	69	74

Contemporary respect for Louis XIV's war marine, so easily overlooked in the light of his subsequent failure to use it effectively, can be inferred from these simple statistics; but they conceal a rapid falling-off in French

[1] Ehrman, pp. 372, 430–2; J. C. M. Warnsinck, *De Vloot van den Koning-Stadhouder, 1689–1690* (Amsterdam, 1934), chs. 13–14. Tourville commanded 7 ships of 80 guns or more, including the *Dauphin Royal* (110) and *Soleil Royal* (98).

[2] R. Mémain, *Le Matériel de la Marine de Guerre sous Louis XIV* (1936), pp. 3–4n. Cf. Soc[iety for] Naut[ical] Res[earch], Occas[ional] Pub[licatio]ns, no. 5, pt. II: *French Ships, 1648–1700* (compiled P. Le Conte, Cambridge, 1935).

[3] Based on *ibid.* pt. IV: *Ships of the United Netherlands, 1648–1702* (comp. A. Vreugdenhil, 1938); Ehrman, app. II; and P. Le Conte, *loc. cit.* The tables in J. C. de Jonge, *Het Nederlandsche Zeewezen* (3rd edn. Zwolle, 5 vols. 1858–69), vol. III, app. VII, yield a Dutch total of 55 ships built for 52 to 92 pieces in the same years.

naval building after 1693. In 1695–8, when the English launched 44 of their total and the Dutch 24, France produced only 19—i.e., 2 first rates, 9 thirds and 8 fourths. It is clear, however, that the lower rates were now universally favoured and that French construction never came to a dead halt in the Nine Years War, as it did after 1707.

By 1650 the build of warships had come to vary only in detail from one country to another, although the differences were important enough to excite contemporary study, especially in France. The English developed a shorter stem and a deeper draught than the Dutch, whose heaviest ships of the line sometimes had difficulty in working out to sea on ordinary tides; with their flatter bottoms and fuller bellies, they were the slowest of all navies. By the end of the century French ships in general, with their sharp lines and more spacious distribution of guns, had the reputation of being the finest sailers. This was not Colbert's opinion in 1671, when he set up a *conseil de construction* at each of the three great arsenals of Brest, Toulon and Rochefort.[1] Since then, however, Dutch shipbuilding had become highly conservative, whereas Colbert had persisted in the search for a theory of construction, not so much by the application of the new science to practice as by an effort to derive agreed theoretical principles from the performances of ships. Master carpenters could be secretive about their art and reluctant to change their methods. It needed the advent to Rochefort of the clever Neapolitan, Biaggo Pangalo, known as Blaise, backed by Tourville and the minister, to shake the dominance of Etienne Hubac of Brest, with his preference for beam over length. Colbert forced them to debate with each other and to listen to the observations of sea-going officers, who in turn were required to attend lectures and demonstrations given by the more articulate shipwrights. Out of this restless discussion came the new ship proportions laid down in the *Ordonnance* of 1689 which were to hold good for a century, although dynasties of carpenters preserved a wide latitude of 'secrets'. By contrast, the resistance of Dutch masters to any kind of theoretical explanation led the Tsar Peter, a pupil who wanted value for his time, to compare Zaandam unfavourably with Deptford.[2] In his *Théorie de la Construction des Vaisseaux* of 1697—the most celebrated contribution to a large French output in this genre—Fr Hoste nevertheless conceded that the best ships were often the work of illiterates, no doubt because ship science was still obsessed with problems of proportion to the neglect of other dynamic factors, like the profile of a vessel's sides, which might with luck be well judged by an experienced eye. In all countries, moreover, designers worked under similar limitations of materials and tools. Community of practice was also furthered by the imitation of foreign models; thus the Dutch once tried to

[1] Mémain, pp. 664–6.
[2] S. C. van Kampen, *De Rotterdamse particuliere scheepsbouw in de tijd van de Republiek* (Assen, 1953), p. 65.

copy the new fast frigates, complete with oars, which Dunkirk was turning out from 1695.[1] Before 1670 the French had borrowed from the Dutch and the Danes. As the example of Blaise reminds us, shipwrights could often sell their skill abroad. Both Dutch and English found employment in Scandinavia, although it was not until 1727 that the Dutch admiralties could bring themselves to follow a suggestion made by Rotterdam in 1695 of placing their yards under an English director.[2] The most notable borrower, of course, was Peter the Great.

Another levelling influence was provided by contemporary naval tactics. In the hands of a competent commander the fleet in line, given no serious numerical inferiority, could thwart the efforts of an offensively minded opponent to bring on a decisive engagement. On many occasions in the eighteenth century the French made skilful use of the line for this very purpose, but there was nothing essentially defensive about it. Most tacticians indeed emphasized strict preservation of the line and discouraged displays of initiative by individual captains: yet the value of independent action by squadrons in isolating and containing portions of the enemy fleet was stressed, so long as it did not compromise control by the commander-in-chief. A superior force might double the enemy's line, but an equal force was advised not to try to break it—a lesson of the Anglo-Dutch wars. If the Spanish Succession War introduced an era of indecisive engagements, the reasons must not be sought exclusively in the use of the line. The ships were cumbersome and leewardly, gunnery inaccurate, signalling systems inadequate. Hence the annihilation of an enemy fleet was virtually beyond reach of the navies. The levelling influences could be outweighed only by numerical superiority. 'Experience has taught me', wrote Shovell, 'that, where men are equally inured and disciplined in war, 'tis, without a miracle, number that gains the victory.'[3] There were three occasions between 1689 and 1721 when a battle in the open sea resulted in the disorderly retreat of the defeated fleet: Beachy Head, La Hougue, and off Kolberg in 1715, when the Swedish fleet was decisively defeated by the Danish. In each case the victor possessed a marked numerical superiority. The greater the massed fighting strength, the greater the chance of victory. But no power could concentrate on the construction of great numbers of the largest and most heavily gunned ships of the line, to the exclusion of all considerations except size and quantity.

The size and structure of a naval establishment were determined by a government's own assessment of the value of naval power to State interests, by the strength of possible rivals and not least by the resources available

[1] J. J. Backer Dirks, *De Nederlandse Zeemacht in hare verschillende tijdperken geschetst* (The Hague, 2 vols. 1890), vol. I, p. 810. For English indebtedness to France and Tuscany in the 1670s see J. R. Tanner (ed.), *A Descriptive Catalogue of the Naval Manuscripts in the Pepysian Library*, vol. I (N.R.S. 1903), pp. 225 ff.
[2] Van Kampen, pp. 65–6.   [3] Quoted Owen, p. 74.

to it, both in skilled manpower and in a wide range of materials. The Ottoman, Russian and Baltic states were the only powers able to provide their own timber and naval stores. Under the pressure of war, moreover, initial estimations of requirements would inevitably be modified by the course of events, not only by the war at sea itself or by the opening of fresh strategic theatres, but by developing shortages of men or supplies and above all by the handling of public credit, on which the frequent refitting of ships and the feeding of thousands of men placed a burden heavier than did any other branch of administration. Navies therefore fluctuated in strength, whether or not they declined over the years. In any case, it was easier to bow to the necessity of a strong navy than to know what to do with it when the test came. Every winter, statesmen and sea-men—the latter understandably more cautious than the former—must decide the scale and direction of operations amid the conflicting claims of soldiers and shipowners, foreign courts and colonial authorities. There were always land operations to support, convoys to be arranged, allies or neutrals or even rebels to be humoured or seduced. How were the available ships to be distributed among different stations? Should a main fleet be prepared, with all that this implied for co-ordination between allies or, in the French case, between the divisions of the Levant and of the Ponant (ch. VII)? Beyond safeguarding the movements of armies, the only obvious tasks were simply an intensification of peacetime work, to prevent invasion and to protect commerce, and neither dictated a line of battle unless a rival had one. In this respect the naval race of the late seventeenth century added a new dimension to warfare, an artificial game of hide-and-seek which devoured money and energy with few dramatic results for years on end. For example, it is hard to exaggerate the dead weight on English initiative of the presence of even a squadron in Brest harbour; significantly, the principle of blockading it by means of a cruising watch in the Channel Soundings was sketched by Godolphin, at the very time when William III wished to increase the Anglo-Dutch commitment to the Mediterranean.[1] A French 'fleet in being' was a major factor in the warfare of the period long after Versailles had ceased to believe in its aggressive potential. Nor was this loss of interest itself a ready inference from the losses of La Hougue, for these could be attributed to the accidents of weather and geography, the unlucky culmination of an engagement whose first stage (Barfleur) can be claimed as a tactical victory for Tourville. More instruc-tive in some French eyes was the futility of a major success. When Tour-ville commanded the Channel in 1690 he had wanted to concentrate on the Mediterranean, while Jean Bart (who had been with De Ruyter in 1667) recommended a blockade of the Thames: after Beachy Head, with many

[1] Although not immediately effective, this doctrine long anticipated Edward Vernon, to whom it is usually accredited: A. N. Ryan, 'William III and the Brest Fleet', in R. Hatton and J. S. Bromley (eds.), *William III and Louis XIV*, pp. 49–67.

sick on board, Tourville could find nothing better to do than fire Teign-mouth.[1] Priorities were easier to settle when the enemy held the initiative. However it might decide to apply its naval resources, not even an absolute government could ignore the pressures of mercantile opinion. In the event, by switching his naval effort to commerce destruction, Louis XIV harnessed the interests of his subjects to his own. In England and the Netherlands, more reliant on oceanic trade, the value of a fleet was never questioned. Quite small Dutch towns felt it their business to examine the causes of a naval defeat, while promotions to flag rank could tax the ingenuity of the Amsterdam town council. Even when the Provinces were not at war naval matters were constantly on their agenda, if only because of Baltic politics and Mediterranean corsairs (ch. XVII). Armed convoys to 'the bottom of the Straits' were also the price of England's Levant trade, in which so many squires and villagers as well as merchants and manu-facturers had a relatively big stake in late Stuart times. Lord Halifax spoke for his countrymen when he declared, 'The first Article of an Englishman's political creed must be that he believeth in the sea'.[2] Besides offering the only effective shield against invasion, the wooden walls were vital to the interests of a politically influential section of society. How sensitive and influential it could be was demonstrated by the outcry which followed the mauling of the 'Smyrna convoy' in 1693. Admirals were called to explain their conduct to the House of Commons and in 1694 legislation already anti-cipated the Cruisers and Convoys Act of 1708, also a response to 'mis-carriages at sea', which required 'that over and above ships of war for the line of battle and for convoys to remote parts, at least forty-three ships of war be employed as cruisers in proper stations...for securing of the merchants' ships in their going out and returning home'. In effect, this was an angry criticism of the deployment of naval force in the Mediter-ranean at the expense of the security of the Sea of England, sovereignty over which had been proclaimed since the thirteenth century and had deeply penetrated the English psyche during the seventeenth. Englishmen were agreed that a powerful navy was indispensable, but they differed violently about its positive uses.

The classical eighteenth-century arguments for an American as opposed to a European strategy were first formulated in the 1690s. It was argued that England should devote her war effort to the sea, with the object of eliminating French trade and overseas empire; this of itself would maim Louis XIV's ability to sustain full-scale war in Europe. After Louis's acceptance of the will of Carlos II, the dispatch of Benbow to search for the treasure fleet in the Caribbean, where a sizeable English squadron was to be retained for several years, showed how quick to

[1] Warnsinck, p. 85. For a French view of Barfleur, as distinct from La Hougue, cf. J. de la Vaernde, *Le Maréchal de Tourville* (1943), p. 220.

[2] H. C. Foxcroft, *A Character of the Trimmer* (Cambridge, 1946), p. 26.

revive was the deeply-rooted popular myth of easy pickings at Spanish expense. These notions appealed to an expanding commercial society, anxious to increase its supply of silver and to open new markets for home industries, and to vocal elements in the colonies, from Jamaica to New England (ch. xv). The political and personal opponents of William III and Marlborough were also ardent supporters of a 'blue-water' policy, which came to be identified with Tories. They greeted Rooke's lucky capture of a treasure-fleet in Vigo Bay with extravagant praises, and regarded an invasion of Canada as more of a national interest than a campaign in Flanders. In fact, as previous chapters in this volume have shown, the grand strategy of the age aimed almost entirely at predominance in Europe and on land. How maritime power could influence that might be clear enough in the comparatively localized context of the Baltic or eastern Mediterranean. For the Western belligerents it posed entirely fresh problems. William III's ultimate decision to encircle France by water was the most interesting answer. Whatever his early hesitation, much of which was due to the battle of Ireland and to administrative difficulties, the king-stadholder, as early as 1692, was well on the way to resolving the conflict between England's defensive needs and his personal conviction that the war must be decided ultimately on the Continent. His solution resulted from a growing insight into the importance of secure maritime communications between the different theatres of war. This was obvious enough in the case of England's links with Ireland and the Low Countries. William, and after him Marlborough, also saw that a fleet in the Mediterranean could directly influence the European war by controlling the sea-routes from France to Spain and Italy, by threatening southern France in conjunction with the armies, and by stiffening Allied diplomacy among the vacillating Italian states. If the net results fell short of expectation, it can still be claimed that Anglo-Dutch control of the western Mediterranean, besides securing a vital trading artery and (for better or worse) facilitating Allied intervention in the Iberian Peninsula, limited the offensive potential of the French in a region even more crucial to them. Indeed, the repercussions extended to the whole maritime war. The only large-scale movement by the French navy after 1694, apart from the bid to relieve Gibraltar in 1704, was the attempt to cover a Jacobite invasion of Scotland in 1708—interesting in naval annals as a prime example of the ability of French ships to outsail their pursuers. All in all, therefore, it must be confessed that the European navies were distinctly subordinate to the armies in the strategy of this period. William III and Marlborough were right when they calculated that France must be defeated on land. Between 1689 and 1713 England had to learn the best methods of fighting an enemy who could not be made to yield by naval strength unsupported by military action. Criticism of the continental strategy, superficial though much of it was, reflected the dilemma of a maritime power faced with the hostility of a great land power, able to continue the struggle despite eclipse at sea.

England was an exception, like Venice and the Knights of Malta, to the rule that the naval powers of the time relied primarily on their soldiers for defence. This rule applied now to England's naval ally. It is true that the Dutch depended even more upon their far-flung commerce and fisheries, which the enemy often ravaged. They had to import large quantities of food and the raw materials needed by their industries, including the many finishing industries which fed their exports. Reasonably safe sea-routes were necessary for their survival, and their national heroes were mostly seamen. Yet the admirers of Piet Hein, 'Dad' Tromp and De Ruyter had since 1672 become almost pathologically sensitive about their vulnerable land frontier, at the same time as they had reluctantly come to accept a leading rôle in European politics.[1] The search for a 'barrier' and a European 'balance' entailed full participation in the war on land against Louis XIV, which in the event proved incompatible with the maintenance even of the subordinate naval presence assigned to the Dutch in the two-power negotiations of 1689 (ch. VII): the ratio of Dutch to English capital ships, fixed at 3:4 in the defensive treaty of 1678, was then lowered to 3:5. In absolute numbers the quotas were reviewed each autumn, when the Maritime Powers started their sometimes prolonged discussion of the next year's strategy, and there was room for misunderstanding about the inclusion of convoy detachments in the States' contribution. At a favourable estimate, it fell short of quota by an average of some twenty ships a year (or more than half) during the Spanish Succession War;[2] and those fitted out were often late. This dilatoriness wrecked English hopes of a grand strike at the Spanish Indies in 1702, while in June 1703 the Dutch Mediterranean fleet set out too late for the planned capture of Naples. No more than William III did Heinsius display an eye for conquests in America; on the contrary, Amsterdamers had had a stake in the silver-fleet destroyed at Vigo. In the Mediterranean, however, Dutch trading interests coincided well with William's strategy—so much so that the decision to winter the fleet there in 1694–5 owes more than is recognized to the advice of the Amsterdam admiralty and its experienced secretary, Job de Wildt (1637–1704).[3] Even in 1710–11, when they could no longer afford a home fleet and had long given up their Levant convoys, the States-General retained a dozen battleships in the Mediterranean.

In 1712 a Tory House of Commons summed up the accumulated resentment of the English at recent Dutch naval shortcomings:

---

[1] For a fresh examination of their hesitations, see the contribution by J. W. Smit to *Britain and the Netherlands in Europe and Asia* (ed. J. S. Bromley and E. H. Kossman, 1968), pp. 13–36.

[2] De Jonge, vol. IV, pp. 87–8; F. Snapper, *Oorlogsinvloeden op de overzee handel van Holland, 1551–1719* (Amsterdam, 1959), pp. 268–70.

[3] *Ibid.* pp. 194 ff.

Hence your Majesty hath been obliged to supply these deficiences with additional reinforcements of your own ships, and your Majesty's ships have been forced in greater numbers to continue in remote seas, and at unseasonable times of the year, to the great damage of the navy. This also hath straitened the convoys for trade; the coasts have been exposed for want of cruisers; and you have been disabled from annoying the enemy in their most beneficial commerce with the West Indies, whence they received those vast supplies of treasure, without which they could not have supported the expenses of the war.[1]

Such criticism undoubtedly helped to clear the path for Bolingbroke's diplomatic betrayal of an ally, as indeed it conditioned Stanhope's one-sided commercial treaty with the Archduke Charles in 1708.[2] And yet Bolingbroke, who seems genuinely to have felt that the Dutch neglected the sea, 'which is our frontier, whilst we are exhausting ourselves...to secure their Barrier', well knew the reason for it: 'the government there grown poor, whatever private men may be'.[3] By the end of 1707 Heinsius was already writing miserably to Marlborough of the 'horrible expenses' of the war.[4] In 1710 Dutch maritime trade was to feel the full impact of the Great Northern War, having resisted the stresses of the Spanish Succession less successfully than it did those of the Nine Years War (at least down to 1695). There is reason to think that the convoy system functioned less effectively. Escort ships saw harder fighting than the cruising squadrons, and losses were no longer replaced by new building.[5]

Another difference between the war of 1689–97 and that of 1702–13, for the Dutch, was that the second was fought without such unifying direction as the stadholderate could provide. William had been captain-general on sea as well as land; the House of Orange also commanded the loyalties of recalcitrant provinces, especially Zeeland, as no Grand Pensionary of Holland ever could, even if Heinsius had been free to take the same professional interest in naval matters as the seagoing John de Witt. The Stadholder Frederick Henry had wanted to get rid of the fragmented and cumbersome constitution of 1597 which committed not only regional safety but federal sea power to five independent *admiraliteits-collegiën* (admiralty boards), each jealous of its status and of the interests of the provincial States and towns which elected its members. Neither De Witt, 'the perfect Hollander', nor William III, so often at loggerheads with Amsterdam, had been willing or able to do more than work this loose machinery by personal leadership, negotiation and patronage.[6] Some degree of concentration was afforded by the facts that three of the

---

[1] Quoted A. T. Mahan, *The Influence of Sea Power upon History, 1660–1783* (5th edn. 1890), p. 218.
[2] Above, p. 430; cf. Snapper, p. 231.
[3] Letters to Townshend and Drummond, 6 Feb. and 30 March O.S. 1711, quoted *ibid.* pp. 338, 264.
[4] B. van't Hoff (ed.), *The Correspondence of Marlborough and Heinsius*, p. 354.
[5] Snapper, pp. 203, 231, 242–4.
[6] J. K. Oudendijk, *Johan de Witt en de Zeemacht* (Amsterdam, 1944), esp. p. 7.

admiralties—the Maze (Maas), Amsterdam, and the Northern Quarter with West Friesland—depended on the States of Holland and were responsible for two-thirds of naval expenditure, as compared with one-sixth each for Zeeland and Friesland (with Groningen): to these quotas the landward ('non-equiperende') provinces were expected to contribute about a fifth of the total—i.e. more than double Zeeland's obligation—but they were always behindhand. When a fleet was to be set out, all the colleges sent deputies to discuss their respective quotas with representatives of the States-General at The Hague—the so-called *Secreet Besogne*, an advisory body which could act only through the good pleasure of the colleges and such influence as the States-General might bring to bear on them, financially or politically. It was the States-General who nominated and instructed a naval commander-in-chief. They had a useful instrument also in their right to select all naval captains. But the lieutenant-admiral, vice-admiral and rear-admiral (*schout-bij-nacht*) 'under' each college were appointed by it, with or without external advice, the senior board at Rotterdam having a prescriptive claim to possess the commander-in-chief and the States of Holland the right to propose a candidate when the general command fell vacant—in the past, usually as a result of death in action. Failing a stadholder, the Grand Pensionary's more limited authority was exerted primarily through his membership of the States of Holland and their naval committee, the *Commissie tot de Zeezaken*. Standing between three admiralties and the States-General, these bodies were the best substitute the Dutch had for the focal power of the English Lord High Admiral (or more often after 1690 the Lords Commissioners of the Admiralty) and that of the French Secretary of State 'ayant le département de la marine'. Not surprisingly, however, the British ambassador spent much time discussing details of command and recruitment with the provinces themselves.

The intercollegiate system of the Netherlands had always been uneconomic of time and money. As soon as the country's finances came under strain it broke down. Zeeland, in particular, a fierce nurse of seamen but monotonously prone to plead abject poverty and state rights, was inclined to go her own way once the stadholder-king had died. The admiralty at Middelburg had a duty to protect its coasts and inland waters against the prying of corsairs from neighbouring Dunkirk, Ostend and Nieuwpoort. It was also concerned to maintain the prosperity of its own 'commissievaarders', as terrible to the French as were the Dunkirkers to the Maritime Powers—but in more than one sea, for from 1695 the Zeelanders ranged the Mediterranean. Between 1688 and 1715 prize sales in Middelburg and Flushing realized nearly 20 m. guilders[1]—enough to

---

[1] The gross proceeds of prize sales for the Nine Years War are given in G. N. Clark, *The Dutch Alliance and the War against French Trade*, p. 148: those for the later years are based on the same source and were kindly communicated by Mr M. P. de Bruin, of the Provinciale

cover the entire cost of the navy for three years. To this must be added large sums for prizes sold abroad and for the premiums paid by the States-General on the capture or destruction of enemy warships. These *premie* help to explain why 'les Flessinguois', unlike most other corsairs, enjoyed a fighting reputation, although it is true that the courage of Dutch seamen generally was admired by ally and enemy alike. It was by a doubling of the *premie* in July 1705 that the Zeeland States were persuaded to endorse stricter rules of prize procedure. Hitherto they had upheld the readiness of their admiralty to condemn neutral and friendly vessels trading with the enemy—an old Holland practice virtuously resented in Zeeland—and so to embroil the States-General in diplomatic disputes with the Scandinavian and Allied governments.[1] To make for further friction with The Hague, the privateers encroached on naval manpower. It was a good year when Zeeland contributed 3,000 men to the fleet, as in 1702. When it was capable of arming over forty vessels with a thousand guns between them, as at the end of 1703, the privateering interest needed more than 5,000 men, for a crew of 180 was not uncommon for a 32-gun frigate. Privateering was always a lottery, and manpower everywhere set limits to investment in it; but the *Commissievaart* of Middelburg and Flushing, dominated by some thirty families, did well enough in these wars to remain the true expression of Zeeland patriotism. Only in narrow provincial terms, however, was it still the right way to make war pay for itself.

All the maritime countries—even Savoy, when Oneglia was its only port—commissioned privateers, if only for tip-and-run raids on enemy coasters which could ease local impoverishment. During the Nine Years War, Zeeland's Captain Credo and England's Captain Plowman created a stir in the Mediterranean, but the Majorcans did most to send up insurance rates at Marseilles. The British government was protesting at Swedish seizures months before Charles XII's Privateering Ordinance of 19 Feb-

Bibliotheek van Zeeland. Excluding the minor ports of Veere and Zierikzee and disregarding minor complications, they may be tabulated as follows:

Years	Flushing	Middelburg	Total	Annual Average
	(Flemish pounds: £1 vl. = 6 guilders)			(war years)
1689–98	840,897	665,719	1,506,616	167,402
1698/9–1702	78,076	35,094	113,170	—
1703–7	510,148	645,657	1,155,805	231,161
1708–12	261,337	259,259	520,596	104,019
1713–15/17	1,895	21,108	23,003	—
	1,692,353	1,626,837	3,319,190	

It will be seen that, although the annual average for 1703–12 is minimally higher than for 1689–98, receipts during the second half of the Spanish Succession War amounted to less than half those of the first. In 1702–13 over 300 commissions were issued: J. S. Bromley, 'Some Zeeland Privateering Instructions: Jacob Sautijn to Salomon Reynders, 1707', in *William III and Louis XIV*, p. 165 n.

[1] *Ibid.* pp. 169–74, and idem, 'Les Corsaires zélandais et la navigation scandinave', in M. Mollat (ed.), *Le Navire et l'économie maritime du Nord de l'Europe* (1960), pp. 93–109.

ruary 1715, which unleashed thirty 'capers' from Stockholm, twenty from Gothenburg, others from Wismar and Stralsund.[1] In 1689–97, 420 letters-of-marque were declared in the admiralty court at London, which accepted bonds for as many as 1,540 in 1702–12.[2] The *Conseil des Prises* at Versailles condemned more than 4,000 prizes taken into European ports alone between June 1702 and December 1713, besides ratifying half as many ransoms: when sinkings, illicit disposals and captures in colonial waters are added, the English merchants' estimated loss of 3,600 ships during the first half of the Spanish Succession War acquires credibility, especially as the French *course* was past its peak by 1708 and the energies of St Malo, in particular, had turned to the more remunerative South Sea trade. The best years of the Malouin corsairs, who cruised mainly in the English Channel, were 1694–7—a total of 246 armaments in spite of peace negotiations, which tended to discourage them. Dunkirk armed as many *capres* within 28 months in 1693–5, principally for the North Sea, in addition to the royal squadrons commanded by Jean Bart (1650–1702), the most brilliant of the Flemish seamen who used against the Dutch the tactics they had learnt from De Ruyter. Although Allied squadrons were often tied down in attempts to blockade its many sinuous approaches, Dunkirk increased its takings by 25 per cent in the following war and earned a place to itself in the peace treaties.[3] It was superbly well placed to interfere with that major portion of English trade which converged on the Thames, and with Dutch convoys returning between Scotland and Norway or through the Danish Sound, not to mention the long-suffering northern fisheries. An even wider radius of action lay open from Brest, the base used from 1702 by René Trouin, sieur du Guay (1673–1736), who nevertheless continued to rely on his native St Malo for funds and crews. But he and Jean Bart, with Jacques Cassard of Nantes (1672–1740) and the proud chevalier Claude de Forbin (1656–1733), are only the best remembered of the many captains of this age who made French privateering into something of a legend, a national institution with a strategic doctrine of its own.

Like other fresh impulses in the France of Louis XIV's later years, the

[1] J. F. Chance, *George I and the Northern War* (1909), pp. 46–8, 65–8.

[2] Clark, *Dutch Alliance*, pp. 150–1; London, Public Record Office, H.C.A. 26/13–21. A preponderance of these commissions was for armed traders. The increase is none the less striking. It is partly accounted for by the repeal in 1696 of the Act of 1689 which prohibited the import of all French goods, prize included. The Channel Islands took out only 55 commissions in 1689–97 but no less than 759 in 1702–11: J. S. Bromley, 'The Channel Island Privateers in the War of the Spanish Succession', *Trans Soc. Guernesiaise*, vol. XIV, pt. 4 (1950), pp. 447 f., 450–1.

[3] Idem, 'The Trade and Privateering of Saint-Malo during the War of the Spanish Succession', *ibid.* vol. XVII, pt. 5 (1964), pp. 631–47, and 'The French Privateering War, 1702–13', in H. E. Bell and R. L. Ollard (eds.), *Historical Essays 1600–1750 presented to David Ogg* (1963), pp. 213–16, 229; A. Morel, *La Guerre de course à Saint-Malo, 1681–1715* (Acad. de Marine, n.d.), pp. 132–73; H. Malo, *Les Corsaires dunkerquois et Jean Bart* (2 vols. 1913–14), vol. II, p. 418, and *Dunkerque, ville héroïque* (1918), pp. 75–6.

classical case for a privateering war (*la course*) was made by Marshal Vauban, who knew Dunkirk well and personally inspired some of its armaments. His celebrated 'Mémoire concernant la caprerie', dated 30 November 1695,[1] made two capital assumptions: Anglo-Dutch war-making was founded on a vast but vulnerable commerce, while a large navy served no good purpose unless it was master of the seas. In the circumstances, salvation lay in a ruthless and intelligent maximization of 'a subtle and stealthy maritime war', which would force the enemy to break under the financial strain of protecting the merchantmen vital to his survival. Private capital would carry the main burden of attacking them, provided that the king's lower rates and frigates—again with the participation of private investors—were used in squadron strength against major targets, and provided also that more were done to accelerate prize litigation, reduce discouragements to prize sales from the General Farmers, and improve the morale of privateering crews, who were notoriously prone to desert and to shirk combat, largely because they received (and often spent) most of their wages or prize shares before sailing. Royal legislation failed to stop the abuse of these *avances*, which were inflated by competition between employers, and others of Vauban's desiderata were never fulfilled. Sixteen years later the well-informed Trousset de Valincour, secretary to the Admiral of France and of his prize jurisdiction, castigated the dishonesty of the treasurers of privateering armaments as well as the chicanery of the lawyers and the pillage of vessels by their captors—all factors in the decline of the *course*.[2] Meanwhile, nevertheless, Vauban's programme was realized in part, notably through the lease of the king's ships to private syndicates, themselves often promoted by unemployed naval officers; alternatively, the king sought backing for his own expeditions, as he had done for getting his ambassadors through to Denmark and Sweden early in 1693. Such arrangements were bargains scrutinized by his naval intendants and the minister's sanction was never a foregone conclusion, but the result was an intimate union of public and private resources which had no counterpart in Europe. It goes far to explain why the French *course* as a whole enjoyed a higher domestic standing than privateering elsewhere, especially as ministers and courtiers sometimes invested in it; early in 1689 Seignelay was already arming four frigates, one of them in partnership with Louvois. The king himself encouraged this, and made a virtue of necessity when he decided to reduce the naval budget in 1695. In a sense he had only modified the Colbertist purpose for which Seignelay and the navalists had argued the case for a fleet against Louvois, Chamillart and eventually Madame de Maintenon:

[1] Printed by Rochas d'Aiglun, *Vauban, sa famille et ses écrits; "ses Oisivetés" et sa Correspondance*, vol. I, pp. 454–61. Vauban had matured his ideas in earlier years: cf. Malo, *Jean Bart*, vol. II, pp. 327–38.

[2] Mémoire sur la course par M. de Valincourt (1711), AN, Marine G 144.

the wresting of world trade from the Maritime Powers.[1] But Richelieu and Colbert had both believed in strong striking forces as a condition of commercial and colonial growth. Commerce and colonies continued to be directed by the naval minister. Active, off and on, moreover, as were the small privateers of Saint-Domingue and Martinique, the governors and intendants of the islands would all have preferred half a dozen of the king's cruisers. The neglect of French overseas commerce was honestly accepted 'for a time' in Vauban's memoir itself. What he miscalculated was at once the ability of the *course* to compensate for this (although it responded more deeply than the navy to French motivation) and the resilience of the enemy in face of heavy losses, which at times amounted to a political war of nerves. Having committed themselves to the commercial war, the French were confronted with the fact that naval supremacy was in the last resort essential to it.

The idea of economic warfare was prevalent in England even before that supremacy was attained. It is seen in repeated English attempts to stop the important Dutch trade with France, as in 1703–4, and above all in William III's efforts to stop the Northern neutrals from so trading in 1689–90. In 1693, when corn was short in France, William unilaterally added it to the list of contraband of war—a subject of many treaties in the late seventeenth century (ch. v). He had to withdraw, but in 1703–5 further arrests renewed the bitter complaints of Stockholm and Copenhagen. On this occasion much trouble was allegedly due to defects in the papers carried by neutral vessels, some of which were undoubtedly forged to conceal the property of Allied subjects forbidden to trade with the enemy. Such 'colouring' of cargoes was widely practised by all belligerents, so that the movements of neutral shipping were restricted by many rules. Like the exact form of a passport, they provided many pretexts for arrest and legal pedantry. Disputes arose over visitation and search at sea, the definition of contraband, and the very competency of belligerent prize courts to adjudicate in cases involving neutrals. All this contributed to international hatred and was to bring privateering into disrepute with eighteenth-century humanitarians, who would like to have spared all non-combatants, even the subjects of belligerent States. The powers did invoke certain principles in support of their claims; but agreement, such as it was, rested upon a corpus of bilateral and somewhat contradictory treaties. The attitude of a power was affected by its status as neutral or belligerent, and if a belligerent by its ability to impose its wishes or, alternatively, by its dependence on the services of neutral carriers.[2] Hostile to each other

[1] L. Rothkrug, *Opposition to Louis XIV* (Princeton, 1905), pp. 377–85.
[2] See Clark, *Dutch Alliance*, ch. v and idem, 'Neutral Commerce in the War of the Spanish Succession', *The British Year Book of International Law* (1928), pp. 69–83; C. J. Kulsrud, *Maritime Neutrality to 1780* (Boston, Mass., 1936), pp. 123 ff.; P. C. Jessup and F. Deák, *Neutrality*, vol. I, *passim*. English and French documents may be studied in

as they were, Denmark and Sweden formed 'armed neutralities' in 1691–3; they succeeded in obtaining some financial compensation for losses incurred. Yet the question of neutral rights also flared up in the Great Northern War, when there was in effect an Anglo-Dutch armed neutrality. The Danish and Swedish prize regulations of 1710 and 1715 were at variance with the policy of these Crowns in the Nine Years War, while Anglo-Dutch disapproval of Swedish attempts to prevent all trade with Russian-occupied ports was inconsistent with belligerent rights as defined in the Anglo-Dutch Convention of London of 1689.

Neutrality clearly had its hazards as well as rights, but to defend them the Northern Crowns disposed of relatively small navies, mainly intended for use against each other and within the Baltic. Both had the solid advantages of a proud seafaring tradition and laborious seafaring populations, especially Denmark, which drew her best seamen from Norway. They were also rich in shipbuilding materials, among which Norwegian masts, Finnish tar and Swedish iron were exported to the West. But neither power rested as yet on a very broad foundation of merchant shipping. At least two-thirds of Sweden's foreign trade was conducted from Stockholm; Gothenburg (Göteborg) was still a small place, though its share of iron exports was fast increasing. It is true that both Crowns had long since encouraged the private building of defence ships by substantial customs exemptions; but these had been overtaken by the new scale of naval armaments and Charles XII in fact abolished the system (helfrihet). On the other hand, the English Navigation Acts had stimulated the growth of Scandinavian tonnage at the cost of the Dutch. In the 1690s it was booming. Although allowance must be made for foreign ownership, seeking the protection of neutral flags, Sweden's mercantile fleet (750 vessels) was then larger than it was to be throughout the eighteenth century. The Danish mercantile fleet was smaller, but Danish naval construction was noticeably more active in the 1690s. In 1692 Christian V already had nine ships of 76 guns or more, with another twenty mounting 70–34; another eight were added to the line of battle in 1692–9, including the Fredericus Quartus (110). Even so, it was then unequal in strength or quality to the Swedish line of nearly forty sail. Lists of the two fleets in 1703 amount to about fifty sail each, but the Swedes had 2,872 guns as compared with 2,414 Danish.[1]

Within the Baltic, as within the Mediterranean, secure communications

R. G. Marsden, Law and Custom of the Sea, vol. II (N.R.S. 1916); R. J. Valin, Nouveau Commentaire sur l'Ordonnance de la Marine de 1681 (La Rochelle, 2 vols. 1776), vol. II, pp. 213 ff.; Lebeau, Nouveau Code des Prises, vol. I (An VII [1799]).

[1] E. F. Heckscher, An Economic History of Sweden (Cambridge, Mass., 1954), pp. 97, 111–14; [R. Molesworth,] An Account of Denmark: as it was in the Year 1692 (4th edn. 1738), pp. 88–9; Soc. Naut. Res., Occas. Pubns. no. 5, pt. III (comp. H. Börjeson and P. Holck, 1936); G. de Lamberty, Mémoires pour servir à l'histoire du XVIIIᵉ siècle, vol. XII (The Hague, 1734), pp. 134–7. Cf. J. H. P. Barfod, Danmark-Norges Handelsflåde, 1650–1700 (Kronborg, 1967).

by water were politically important. The Swedish empire was in a real sense a maritime empire, its integrity resting largely upon freedom to move troops and supplies between Sweden, Finland, Estonia, Livonia and northern Germany. Denmark's communications with Norway were vulnerable also. In 1700 Denmark was temporarily eliminated from the Northern War by her failure to keep command of the Sound itself, against a Swedish descent supported by an Anglo-Dutch fleet under Rooke, although this action illustrates the difficulties of manoeuvring large ships among the shallows ('Flats') north and south of Copenhagen, especially when all marks of navigation had been removed.[1] Between 1700 and 1709 the Swedes could move freely across the Baltic in support of their king's campaigns. After 1709 the situation changed. Emboldened by the Swedish defeat at Poltava, Denmark re-entered the war and Russia began to emerge as a new naval factor in the Baltic. By 1710 Karelia, Ingria, Estonia and Livonia had all fallen to Peter. Swedish difficulties were the greater because combat with his forces required a different type of vessel and fighting technique from those traditionally employed against the Danes in the open Baltic. In the waters around the islands which fringe the Finnish coast and extend westwards towards Sweden, the Russians used the oar-driven, shallow-draught galleys first launched in 1704. At a time when the fighting galley was losing its historic importance in the Mediterranean, a century of fresh influence was opened to it in the Baltic, owing to the strategic position of Finland in the Russo-Swedish wars and the possibility of moving galley flotillas along her coasts even without command of the Baltic. Sweden had 37 capital ships and 21 frigates, but only five galleys, in 1709. Into his first galley action, at Hangö Udd (Gangut) in 1714, Peter was able to bring a hundred galleys.[2] In 1719–21 he used them to harry Sweden's own coasts, from Piteå in the far north to Norrköping well south of Stockholm. Nevertheless, Sweden's loss of her trans-Baltic provinces was in some respects cause rather than consequence of her failure to retain control of the Baltic. Possession of the Gulf of Finland had been intended by Eric XIV and his successors to cut off the Russians from the Baltic. Peter's conquest of the southern shore of the Gulf, essentially a military achievement, necessarily accompanied the foundation of Russian sea power in the Baltic. In contrast, the campaigns in Germany which culminated in the fall of Swedish Pomerania were influenced decisively by the maritime campaigns. Because the Swedish navy was unequal to a war on two fronts, the Russians and Danes obtained the initiative. The inability of the Swedish navy to maintain even a local superiority over the Danish between 1712 and 1716 isolated the Swedish garrisons in Germany and led to their capitulation. Later, when

---

[1] O. Browning (ed.), The *Journal of Sir George Rooke* (N.R.S. 1907), pp. xi ff.
[2] R. C. Anderson, 'Mediterranean Galley-Fleets in 1725', *The Mariner's Mirror*, vol. XLII (1958), p. 179. Cf. idem, *Naval Wars in the Baltic* (1910), ch. VIII.

Sweden's own coasts were raided, the Russians penetrated almost to Stockholm. That invasion did not occur may be attributed to lack of Russo-Danish co-operation and to British determination to preserve some balance of power in the North, if necessary by force. On the other hand, Charles XII's attempts to redress his losses by the conquest of Norway had been checked by Danish control of the sea communications between Sweden and Norway.

The land campaigns of the Great Northern War dominate its history (ch. xx), but it was also a war, particularly in its second half, of short, sharp naval campaigns in Finnish, Swedish, German and Norwegian coastal waters in support of the armies. The main fleets were generally held in reserve, employed only for some specific object judged worth the risk and expense. The growing weakness of the Scandinavian navies coincided with the astonishingly rapid rise of Russian sea power. Although Russian pine-built ships had short lives and Russians themselves disliked naval service, so that it depended on the tsar's will, this novel development certainly contributed to Sweden's fall from great-power status.

Apart from damage incurred in action the endurance of warships was limited, of course, by the strain upon them and their crews of the elements. Foul or leaking hulls, sprung masts, tattered rigging and parted cables were commonplaces of navigation. Although wonders of first-aid (and mutual aid) were accomplished at sea, ships were too heavily encumbered to stow spare topmasts, yards, canvas, cordage and other tackle in quantity. Sides and bottoms must occasionally be retimbered and, above all, regularly careened for cleaning and recaulking. Water-casks needed constant replenishment, as did stores of victuals, ammunition and fuel. Hence a direct connection between operational efficiency and facilities for refit and refreshment near to the theatres of war. Inevitably, suitable harbours were not always to be found where they were strategically wanted. A fleet required space and depth of water, secure from enemy attack and from the worst the weather could do to it.

Of the two Scandinavian states, Denmark had certain natural advantages over Sweden in the matter of bases. Besides the well-fortified harbour of Copenhagen, whence a fleet could normally dominate the Sound and southern Baltic, and where much work was done after 1680 to accommodate the bigger warships, the Danes had dockyards at Glückstadt and Christiansand—the latter to service the small squadron employed in the Kattegat to protect commerce and the Norwegian coast. The Danes were anxious to establish a base within the Baltic also, on the island of Bornholm. It had no suitable harbour, but it was possible to develop one between the two rocky islets known as the Ertholmene, north-east of Bornholm. Warships cruising up the Baltic could take refuge there in bad weather; and lying near a focus of Baltic trade-routes they made an obvious privateering stronghold. A Swedish base on the Sound was impracticable so long as the Danes occupied the southern provinces of Skåne (Scania) and Blekinge. After 1658, however, a base was founded on the Blekinge coast and given the name of Karlskrona. The decision to replace Stockholm by Karlskrona was prudent, for Karlskrona was better placed to curb the Danes and to protect communications between Sweden and her German provinces. During the Great Northern War, however, it proved a disappointment. It was far from the Gulf of Finland and the coast of Livonia, and with the foundation of the Russian arsenal at Kronstadt it was found to point in the wrong direction. After 1710 Stockholm regained some of its earlier importance, although its neglect since 1682 limited its usefulness now. Swedish warships operating in the Kattegat and Skagerrak were based on Gothenburg.

Although English and Dutch squadrons regularly visited the Baltic, usually but not always on convoy duties, neither power had a base there. The Baltic was near home, however, and its campaigning season relatively short, so that the ships could return at the end of autumn without serious detriment to the economic and political interests which they were sent to safeguard. Very different was their situation in the Mediterranean, where the confederate fleet was hampered for want of an adequate base until the capture of Minorca in 1708. The ports of Naples and Sicily offered certain facilities in the Nine Years War and again after 1707, while English ships had long been accustomed to using the Mediterranean harbours of Spain herself to obtain wood and water, fresh food and wine. Yet, so far as bases went, the French possessed an unrivalled asset in Toulon. Until the winter of 1694–5, and sometimes afterwards, Toulon was left in almost undisputed command of the Mediterranean naval scene for half the year. When William III ordered Russell to winter in the Mediterranean, the best he could do was to borrow the facilities of Cadiz, the regular terminus of Straits convoys under Charles II, which also made use of the Balearics. When Spain was no longer an ally, the superb anchorage of the Tagus promised the best substitute: it was secured by the diplomacy of the Methuens, profiting from the impression made on Lisbon by the victory at Vigo, but not before the Allied forces had failed to seize Cadiz (ch. xiii). At Lisbon as at Cadiz, the English appointed their own agents for the procurement of supplies and attendance of the seamen, prisoners, sick and wounded. At Cadiz especially, this was done on such a scale and required so much technical gear and supervision, together with special arrangements for credit and remittances, as to constitute one of the most remarkable administrative feats of the day: 'the nucleus of an English dockyard had in fact to be set up, at short notice, 1100 miles from England and in a foreign state'.[1] There was need of private firms as agents for buying what was locally available—although Dutch captains at any rate

[1] Ehrman, p. 526.

had often to pledge their personal credit—and of the ambassadors to appease local susceptibilities. Yet the value of Cadiz and Lisbon, subject in any case to the vicissitudes of Peninsular politics, was reduced by their distance from Toulon and the war theatre of Catalonia. The weather in the Straits caused delays and sometimes shipwrecks. The roadstead of Gibraltar, when captured in 1704, offered little protection or accommodation. Only when they were free to develop Port Mahon did the Allies possess a base free from these disadvantages, and one very well situated for the policing of the western Mediterranean.

Minorca was not England's first naval base overseas. In modern times that priority belongs to Tangier and Bombay, if not to Madras. Tangier, however, a place of refuge unsuited for heavy ships and constantly besieged by hordes of Moroccan horsemen, was abandoned in 1684 for financial and political reasons,[1] while East Indiamen were expected to dispense with naval protection beyond St Helena or the Cape of Good Hope, the 'tavern of two seas' where foreign vessels were more welcome than at Batavia or other nerve-centres of the Dutch East. On the other hand, England's American convoys were escorted the whole way and guardships were appointed to some of the colonies—at times as many as half a dozen for the summer fishery at Newfoundland, a favourite target of the French corsairs (ch. xv). More ambitious and frustrating was the stationing of a comparable force all the year round at Kingston, Jamaica. The chief virtue of this base, as the buccaneers well knew, was its commodious harbour and natural defences, only excelled in the Caribbean of this time by Cartagena and Havana—the key-points, with Vera Cruz, of the Spanish fleet system. Another merit of Kingston—or rather of Port Royal at its entrance, where the batteries were sited—was its forward position in relation to Spanish trade-routes. As such, its naval importance dates from the Spanish Succession War, when several expeditions were made to intercept the galleons from Cartagena, though none so strong as Benbow's squadron of 22 warships in 1701. Similarly, the only large naval force to reach the Caribbean from France in this period was the expedition of Baron de Pointis which captured Cartagena in 1697 (ch. xi).

The main preoccupation of all governments in this area was nevertheless with the defence of their shipping (which for the French after 1700 included escort of the Spanish convoys) and above all of the islands themselves, whose inhabitants dwelt in chronic terror of raids on their plantations and their slaves, themselves a source of insecurity. The ubiquitous small corsairs of Jamaica, Saint-Domingue and Martinique did not confine their attentions to captures at sea, and from time to time major raids added to the distress caused by hurricane, earthquake, hunger and fever. The French captured the English portions of St Kitts (St-Christophe) in 1689, and the English turned the table there in 1690 and 1702. It

---

[1] E. Chappell (ed.), *The Tangier Papers of Samuel Pepys* (N.R.S. 1935), pp. xx–xxix.

is true that the English were no more successful at Guadeloupe in 1691 or 1703 than they were at Fort-Royal (the administrative centre) of Martinique in 1693; in fact, West Indians were reluctant to absorb competitive sugar-islands into their own national systems and lukewarm about attacking them. Plunder, however, was another matter. Ducasse did great damage during a six-week stay in Jamaica in 1694; Le Moyne d'Iberville, the hero of Hudson's Bay and Louisiana, had Nevis and St Kitts at his mercy in 1706; and in 1712 Cassard ruined the other Leeward Islands, Montserrat and Antigua, before going on to ransom the Dutch in Surinam, St Eustatius and Curaçao. These were lucrative successes for Ducasse's *flibustiers*, and later for privateering squadrons from La Rochelle and Marseilles-Toulon, but any part played by French naval units was merely incidental.[1] Unless the loading of the *galeones* or *flota* demanded it, the French cruisers did not linger in the Caribbean to await the autumn hurricanes or increase the ravages of shipworm. Small English squadrons began wintering there in 1690, but there was no regular squadron based on Jamaica while Spain was an ally. Nor could Queen Anne's governments spare more than a frigate or two for what later became the Leeward Islands station, despite pressure since the 1660s from governors and assemblies, who could hardly feel secure when it took many weeks to beat up to Antigua from Jamaica, in the teeth of the trade wind.[2] As a naval base, moreover, Port Royal was still rudimentary even in 1739, when it boasted a heaving-down wharf and storehouses. In the days of Brigadier Thomas Handasyd, effectively governor of Jamaica 1702–11 and an able one, cleaning facilities were limited to a hulk and stores always short.[3] These handicaps were aggravated by sailing conditions in the Caribbean, high rates of sickness and desertion, the tendency of colonists to put up their prices to the navy and the fecklessness of civilian agents.[4]

[1] Fr Labat, *Nouveau Voyage aux Isles d'Amérique* (The Hague, 2 vols. 1724), vol. II, p. 213, says that Ducasse in 1694 made use of four royal ships on visit to the Coast (St-Domingue) and of 1,500 or 1,600 *flibustiers*. Impressed on first arrival in Martinique by their readiness to attend Mass and share their good fortunes with the Church, Labat praises the piety as well as the bravery of the *flibustiers* (vol. I, pp. 72–6). This is consistent with the fraternal spirit which governed the distribution of 'pillage' ('à compagnon bon lot') and compensation for wounded men in their 'charterparties', but colonial officials were more inclined to dilate on their incorrigible 'libertinage'. Even Ducasse, who sometimes took their part and in 1689 regretted that his government had been suppressing them, found them recalcitrant, largely because they controlled their elected captains by majority voting and disobeyed orders to return from sea when urgently needed for home defence. They also lured *engagés* (indentured servants), artisans and merchant seamen to join them. AN, Colonies C9A/2, fos. 52, 465–6, and C8A/16 (Mémoire sur l'estat présent des Isles remis par M. Mithon, 10 May 1706).
[2] A. P. Thornton, *West-India Policy under the Restoration* (Oxford, 1956), pp. 239–44.
[3] D. A. Baugh, *British Naval Administration in the Age of Walpole* (Princeton, 1965), p. 353; R. Bourne, *Queen Anne's Navy in the West Indies* (New Haven, 1939), pp. 72–4.
[4] *Ibid.* p. 83. Much friction was caused by disagreements over the rate of discount on navy bills. For similar disputes about the value of 'country money' at Boston, see G. S. Graham (ed.), *The Walker Expedition to Quebec, 1711*, pp. 319 f., 336.

After a spell of fifteen months on the Jamaica station, warships were much decayed. Some were unfit when they set out. For defective overhaul captains and dockyard officials blamed each other. There was doubtless negligence on both sides, but the many calls on cruisers did not always allow time for a proper refit, while the dockyards at home were overstrained. It was on their efficiency that that of the navies, even in overseas theatres, most of all depended. In 1689 it was evident that English capacity had not kept pace with the growth of the fleet, and that Portsmouth alone was well situated for a war with France. A dry dock and two basins were added to it by 1698, although Chatham retained its pre-eminence and Sheerness was re-commissioned; Deptford and Woolwich declined. The major innovation was the decision in 1690 to create a dockyard at Plymouth, homogeneously planned and sufficiently advanced by 1693 to clinch the arguments against a similar development of Falmouth.[1] The need of westerly bases was also reflected in the appointment in 1694 of a naval commissioner to Kinsale, already a victualling port like Cork but better defended and equipped for refits, at least of the rates which could clear its shoal at half tide. Portsmouth and Plymouth are to leeward of Brest in the prevailing Channel westerlies, but this strategic disadvantage was offset by the fact that the same wind made it difficult for ships to work out of Brest; or they might have to stand off Ushant for a wind that would carry them up the Channel. Given an easterly, however, English forces could not reach the Atlantic—or Ireland—so quickly. Trade defence in the Soundings was handicapped by this circumstance, especially as the hazardous and wearing technique of blockading Brest was not perfected for another century. With the shift of the focal area of maritime war from the North Sea, moreover, the position of the Dutch bases, generally to leeward of the enemy during the wars with England, became still less favourable, except for meeting convoys from the north and blockading Dunkirk. Flushing, near the mouth of the Scheldt, acquired a new dock at this time.

The absence of a deep-water port on the English Channel had worried Cardinal Richelieu, who wanted to develop Le Havre. Had it possessed an adequate roadstead, a major base on the Seine estuary would have offered many advantages and perhaps have made French governments as sea-conscious as were ministers on the Thames. Like other secondary French ports, Le Havre served the navy chiefly for the building and refitting of the lower rates. Vauban, who inspected the coasts systematically as military *Commissaire Général des Fortifications* from 1678, advocated the substitution of Cherbourg, 'l'auberge de la Manche', as a frigate base; designs were drafted accordingly, but little was spent on it or on neighbouring La Hougue, the alternative favoured by the Chevalier de Clerville, the chief engineer responsible for the reconstruction of Brest. The system

---

[1] Ehrman, pp. 416 ff.

of defence and harbour works at Dunkirk, including a dike admired by the Dutch, was among Vauban's masterpieces, although the basin (and the Bergues canal by which it was reached) needed constant dredging. It could accept 60-gun ships, but was overcrowded by the corsairs and their prizes. Dunkirk in 1706 had a smaller resident population than that which managed to survive on the malarial marshes of the lower Charente where the wholly new dockyard of Rochefort had been constructed, under great difficulties and at huge cost, since 1666.[1] Brest and Toulon were virtually re-created as arsenals by Colbert, but Rochefort was intended to be the grand model, with a storehouse for each ship attached to it, a gun foundry of its own, the first dry dock in France, an immense ropewalk designed by Blondel. Duquesne distrusted its dangerous approaches and it earned the reputation of being late in delivery, partly because it was long before solid quays were erected on ground where every stone building rested on piles, partly because its ships had to complete their outfit in the roadstead twenty miles down river.[2] Nevertheless, in the eyes of its chief creator, Colbert de Terron (1618–84), who also did much as general intendant of the *Marine du Ponant* for the rehabilitation of Brest, Rochefort offered the great advantages of being inaccessible without a local pilot and of lying near good provision country—two supreme merits in the France of that time, so recently subject to civil troubles that compromised the security of her coasts, so frequently racked by harvest shortages (ch. x). Rochefort also had river access to building timber and the iron of Périgord and Angoumois. Situated near La Rochelle, between Loire and Gironde, Rochefort became the usual provider of escorts to the Antilles (the East India Company having its own base at Lorient); and lying between Bayonne and Brest it acted as a collecting-point for the tar of the Landes and masts from the Pyrenees, while procuring good Breton sailcloth and hemp from Nantes.

Brest, with its poor hinterland, drew most of its supplies by sea; and since enemy corsairs habitually frequented Breton coasts, the arsenal depended on convoy movements, themselves exposed to weather variations and the delays incident to all convoys. Its strength consisted in the numbers and quality of the seamen available to it, the best of which came from the 'department' of St Malo, whereas Toulon in 1689 could not arm a score of capital ships without borrowing manpower from the Ponant.[3] Yet Toulon, the base of the Levant division, could obtain many

---

[1] P. Faulconnier, *Description historique de Dunkerque*, vol. ii (Bruges, 1730), p. 130, cites a *dénombrement* of April 1706, which excluded the mass of sea-folk in lodgings or on shipboard, as follows: 2,682 heads of family, 3,098 married women and widows, 937 girls over 12, 5,847 children, 742 servants and 277 clergy—a total of 14,274 in 1,639 houses. The population of Rochefort in 1690 did not exceed 30,000 and made shift in wooden 'cayennes' until an ordered town was taken in hand by Bégon: Mémain, pp. 33, 164 ff. Cf. Y. Bézard, *Fonctionnaires maritimes et coloniaux sous Louis XIV: les Bégon* (1932), pp. 107 ff.

[2] Mémain, pp. 65 ff., 967 ff.   [3] AN, Marine B3/59, fo. 25.

requirements with relative ease. It had only to guarantee transport from the Rhône at Arles to receive coal, iron, small arms and much of its timber from the forests and forges of Burgundy, Franche-Comté, Nivernais, Forez and Dauphiné, although the collection of hemp from Burgundy and Dauphiné could be disrupted by winter roads and, as elsewhere, by mercantile competition. Wines, beans, salted pork and beef were available from Languedoc, oxen and sheep from Dauphiné and Languedoc, cheeses from Burgundy or Switzerland, rice and wines in Provence itself. Like the rest of southern France, however, Toulon relied on corn from the Levant, Tunisia or southern Italy; one of its functions was indeed with the safeguard of these imports. Here, as in the business of privateering and counter-privateering, it worked closely with Marseilles. The proximity of Marseilles, a highly sophisticated shipping and capital market, was an advantage; Brest, by contrast, was poorly served by the Malouin capitalists and Nantes was not yet wealthy. Nor were building and refits as often interrupted by heavy rains at Toulon as in the western shipyards. On the other hand, its supply of home-grown timber was already an anxiety. In 1702 it was having to look to Piedmont-Savoy and Catalonia for masts, to the Romagna and Tuscany for oak.[1] Stocks of northern masts accumulated before 1689 lasted at Toulon till 1696, but they could not so easily be replenished as Baltic tar, and perhaps other stores, at neutral Genoa and Leghorn. To obtain mast or other timber from the Spanish Pyrenees implied control of the Ebro and its mouth, denied to the French from 1705.[2] The Spaniards themselves appreciated varieties of Italian oak tougher and more crooked than the northern, but maladministration and faulty selection made it suspect in France as yet.

The increased scale of naval war inspired energetic measures after 1660 to preserve and extend timber resources in France and England. Colbert's forest code (1669) was supplemented by much piecemeal legislation, itself consolidated by decree in 1700, which gave the navy powers of census and pre-emption in private forests near coasts and rivers. English statutes, in 1668 and 1698, were confined to the enclosure and replanting of royal forests, in any case less extensive than those of the French Crown; more valuable, as a long-term corrective of a century's spoliation, was the private planting advocated in John Evelyn's classical *Sylva* (1664). English landowners were thus in a stronger position to call their own prices or refuse to sell, especially as navies competed with many other purchasers. Yet the French system of reserving *arbres d'espérance* in private woodlands, in addition to compulsory felling of *arbres de service*

---

[1] P. W. Bamford, *Forests and French Sea Power, 1660–1789* (Toronto, 1956), pp. 95 ff.
[2] AN, Marine B3/95, fo. 145 and B3/118, fo. 333. Northern masts might serve thirty years, compared with only six for one of Dauphiné. On the Ebro delta, where tar and hemp were also plentiful, Geronymo de Uztari(t)z argued in 1724 for a new dockyard. His work was translated into English as *The Theory and Practice of Commerce and Maritime Affairs* (2 vols. 1751): see esp. ch. LXXII.

at bitterly disputed prices, disheartened proprietors, at the same time as a venal forestry service (the *Eaux et Fôrets*) failed to replenish Crown woods after overcutting. Its elaborate bureaucracy, dominated by lawyers, came into conflict with naval intendants, as both did with the encroachments and evasiveness of lord and peasant. The very fluctuations of naval demand also diminished observance of Colbertian forest discipline, and not until the Napoleonic empire was French forest practice to learn the superior technique of the Rhenish states.[1] Nevertheless, by 1700 the Dutch, who got most of their oak and some pine from Germany, were reaching into the Vosges. From 1686 the English admitted East Country oak for planking the hulls of warships, as well as deck deals, but they could still rely on home-grown oak (or elm) for both curved pieces (compass timber) and straight, used in constructing the frame. Since 1652, moreover, they had increasingly obtained mainmasts, bowsprits and the heavier yards from their colonies, though their main sources were still the Baltic and Norway.[2] The Massachusetts charter of 1691 reserved to the Crown trees of 24 inches diameter, but so devouring were the sawmills of New England that in 1722 all white pines from New Jersey to Nova Scotia were placed under the 'broad arrow'. This attempt to stop 'the waste of the woods' went further than Colbert's selective *martelage* of privately owned trees and would not have been tolerated by English landowners.

With no reserves at home outside the royal forests, the navy of William III and Anne must have fared worse had English mercantile tonnage continued to expand after 1689 or been unable to recoup its losses with vessels built in New England and with prizes. In fact, the naval programme of the 1690s was partly met by recourse to private builders, especially on Southampton Water, where prices were lower than on the Thames. Later, much as the navy preferred its own facilities, private shipyards had capacity to spare for laying down small warships on speculation.[3] Dutch shipyards, on the contrary, were still working at full stretch in 1707, when the Zaan district (*Zaanstreek*), with 307 vessels simultaneously on the stocks,

---

[1] R. G. Albion, *Forests and Sea Power* (Cambridge, Mass., 1926), ch. III; Bamford, pp. 23 ff., 82 ff.; A. Peyriat, 'Problèmes forestiers en Provence', *Provence Historique*, vol. XV (1965), pp. 229–44, and vol. XVI (1966), pp. 42–71. Cf. M. Devèze *et al.*, *Actes du Colloque sur la Forêt* (1967), esp. pp. 141 ff. and 219 ff.

[2] Norwegian oak was reserved by the Danes, but the English took increasing quantities of red deals and other sawn produce which, unlike spars, did not interest the Dutch: H. S. K. Kent, 'The Anglo-Norwegian Timber Trade in the Eighteenth Century', *Econ. Hist. Rev.* 2nd ser. vol. VIII (1955–6), pp. 65–7. The correct diameter of an English mainmast was an inch to a yard and the tallest were 38 yards long, weighing about 18 tons and costing several times one of 28 yards; elasticity and durability, as well as fine proportions, were qualities sought for. Cf. J. J. Malone, *Pine Trees and Politics: The Naval Stores and Forest Policy in Colonial New England, 1691–1775* (1964), chs. IV–V, and below, pp. 839 ff.

[3] R. Davis, *The Rise of the English Shipping Industry* (1962), pp. 25 ff., 61 ff.; B. Pool, *Navy Board Contracts, 1660–1832* (1966), pp. 49–61; Ehrman, pp. 433–9. Cf. A. J. Holland in *The Mariner's Mirror*, vol. XLIX (1953), pp. 21–7, 275–87.

achieved its all-time record: such overcrowding was to encourage a revival among the higher-cost yards on the Maas. The Dutch admiralties habitually made more use of contract work for building and refits than the English Navy Board was willing to risk, but only because the colleges could exercise supervision on the spot, while the *scheepsbouwmeesters* commanded more capital and manpower than most English builders.[1] In England such contracts were centralized in London, like the annual contracts for major stores, so that the resident dockyard commissioners (though formally members of the Navy Board) enjoyed much less freedom of action than an *intendant de marine* or *admiraliteitscollegie*. There were also 'standing' contracts for the provision of miscellaneous services like plumbing and cooperage, or of manufactured items such as blocks, ironwork and compasses. Much of this work was performed within the dockyard, but the Board itself made the arrangements, as in the general contracts for anchors with Isaac Loader from 1686: his ground tackle failed sadly under the test of the 'great storm' of December 1703, but more (it seems) because of contemporary welding methods than 'from Mr Loader's having undertaken so great a work as the making of anchors for the whole Navy'.[2] Sailcloth, though not always the sails themselves, was also subject to central contracting in England until 1716—and another subject of angry complaint from captains, who had more sailing to do (and more fore-and-aft sails) than in the Dutch wars, without the trusted canvas of Brittany. Even Brest set up its own workship in 1687, but the nascent British industry was only beginning by 1713, with a statutory bonus, to hold its own with Hamburg sailcloth and 'Hollands duck'.

Not least in France, where most was done to equip the main dockyards with forges and ovens and workshops of their own, was naval administration dependent on the skill, credit and patience of many contractors. There the State might assist with capital and privileges—as Colbert encouraged the production of arms and ironware by the companies formed in Nivernais and Dauphiné by the Dalliez brothers—or establish a monopoly, like the gunpowder farm negotiated with the financier François Berthelot from 1664. The State might also support contractors (*fournisseurs*) against third parties, such as mineowners or the numerous interests involved in the cutting and carriage of timber, and protect them from creditors. On the other hand, industries were subject to inspection and the navy attached its own agents (*commissaires* or *écrivains*) to private gun-foundries and powder-mills, while the *intendants de province* could be invoked in aid of the *intendants de marine*, whose arms were long: Michel Bégon even combined the intendancy of Rochefort (1688–1710) with that

---

[1] For all but Amsterdam and the Northern Quarter, the advantages of proximity, including technical and quality control, outweighed the lower costs of Zaandam: Van Kampen, pp. 91 ff., 113 ff. The Navy Board, consisting of four Principal Commissioners responsible to the Admiralty for supply, preferred Thames builders for the same reason.
[2] R. D. Merriman (ed.), *Queen Anne's Navy* (N.R.S. 1961), pp. 141, 155 ff.

of the new *généralité* of La Rochelle from 1694. Requisitioning was uncommon, but Berthelot's private powder-magazines were occupied on Seignelay's orders during the armaments rush of 1689.[1] Contract procedure was rigidly laid down in the great naval *Ordonnance* of that year, following a *règlement* of 1674, the work of Colbert de Terron. It provided, as in England, for open tender at frequent intervals and for a thorough inspection of quantities and qualities delivered to the dockyard, where the *capitaine de port*, the *contrôleur*, the storekeeper, and the commissary in charge of general stores had a duty to assist the intendant on these occasions, together with the master carpenter or others directly concerned. Intendants reported all the 'detail of the port' to the naval minister and sought his approval before using exceptional measures. Although they placed all contracts except for victuals—handled by agents (*commis*) of the victualling farmers (*munitionnaires*) in Paris—naval bargaining was as tough as that of the Navy Board, which enjoyed the advantage of being situated at the hub of the English business world and could more easily look into market trends before inviting bids.

If only because they had to work with chronically insufficient financial means, and within strict accounting procedures, neither type of purchasing authority could afford soft favours. A contractor was expected to buy more cheaply than could a public authority direct. Yet everything depended on his ability to deliver goods of the right quality on time. In practice, this meant that rigorously open tender was impracticable for many supplies, although monopolies as a rule were avoided. Capital, connections and experience were obviously requisite for the negotiation of large amounts of timber, hemp and tar in the East Country: whereas 34 merchants contracted with the Navy Board for domestic timber in 1689–97, only 15 were concerned in Baltic wood and masts, and three of them also supplied hemp and tar.[2] French arsenals undertook comparatively little foreign buying on a large scale, but they too tended to rely year after year on the *fournisseurs* they could best trust. As in England, these were merchants who could wait for payment, who preferably commanded hard cash and knew how to turn navy bills into cash, or whose credit was good enough to persuade others to do the same. When the financial market was difficult, however, as in England under William III and in France through most of the Spanish Succession War, willing contractors were harder to find. In the early 1690s, when ready money was scarce and relations with the Scandinavians strained, the Navy Board had difficulty in persuading East Country merchants to tender and contracts were drawn several months late, February being preferred.[3] By the spring of 1707, the delicate economy of Brest had so far broken down that it was

---

[1] Mémain, pp. 881 f., 898.
[2] Ehrman, pp. 59 ff. The principal mast contractor, John Taylor, also imported from New England.   [3] Pool, pp. 66–8.

asking the minister to find a contractor for all supplies. Local merchants would no longer contract for bills on Paris payable months in arrear (and sometimes protested), even for longer contract periods at higher prices, while the humble sailcloth *fournisseurs* of Locronan and Ploudaniel, holding paper 8 months old and persecuted by creditors, could no longer buy thread or pay their workers. It was feared that this industry would be permanently damaged, and that the peasants of the Lannion and Tréguier areas would stop growing hemp. The experience of Brest, whose many small suppliers could not always perform their undertakings, was an extreme case; but as early as 1702 the intendant at Toulon was telling his minister that hemp could not be bought with paper, and that the service suffered when contractors made a loss.[1]

Such stresses told even more on the intricate network of producers, contractors and correspondents who provided the enormous quantities of food and drink consumed by the navies at home, at sea and abroad—at a time when preservation techniques were limited to salting and pickling, when summer-brewed beer tended to 'fox', when farms and herds were small, harvests particularly unreliable and ready money scarce. Stores might have to be imported and reserves run low sometimes, as of tar and hemp in France and England; but with proper care they did not perish nor have to be stocked at many ports, nor compete in hard times with civilian subsistence. Ships could be victualled at home for up to five months at best, assuming the reduced diet scale of two-thirds—what the English termed 'short allowance', for which money in lieu was payable to the crew—and the probability of scurvy, for lack of vitamin C. In practice, the virtue of fresh meat, though not of lime juice, was beginning to be stressed; there was no stowing all the strong beer an English crew, with unlimited access to the casks, could put down in three months; and even official estimates of spoilt provisions went as high as one-fifth. Hence replenishment on foreign stations was a necessity, besides the desirability of adapting drink and diet to changes of climate—a transition to rice, raisins, olive oil, beef-suet and wine in the Mediterranean, for instance. Yet the problems of large-scale replenishment could not be mastered all at once at a new victualling base, as Admirals Norris and Byng discovered at Copenhagen in 1715–21: Danish officialdom and production costs were only partly overcome by an experienced agent from Gibraltar, by then a major victualling centre.[2]

An English victualling agent was normally present only at a naval base, but the two functions did not necessarily overlap: ships anchoring in

[1] Brest, Archives du Port, 1E458, fos. 412–13, 750–1, and 1E460, fos. 541, 879–81; AN, Marine B3/118, fos. 495, 502.

[2] Danish beer proved surprisingly small and was supplemented in 1720–1 with French brandy; hitherto the only spirit allowed was rum—for tropical voyages: D. D. Aldridge, 'The Victualling of the British Naval Expeditions to the Baltic Sea between 1715 and 1729', *Scand. Econ. Hist. Rev.* vol. XII (1964), pp. 1–25.

the Downs—as common a rendezvous as Spithead—were victualled by Dover. At other 'by-ports', provisions might be got from the stock of a standing contractor or negotiated in the local market by an authorized dealer. The French navy did not need so many delivery-points away from home, but an established consular organization served it well in the Mediterranean. The Dutch also relied heavily on their consuls at Lisbon, Leghorn and elsewhere, although their admiralties incurred debts to their captains which often went unpaid for years.[1] The multiplication of victualling depôts created problems of accountancy that were never satisfactorily overcome in this period, although the English parliament and admiralty were sensitive to them and there was some improvement in 1702–13. Yet the worst difficulties of England's victualling commissioners were inherent in the size and timing of the calls made on them, in purchases and processing as well as distribution. Although narrow in range compared with stores, the victualling requirements of a naval year had to be prepared during the preceding winter—the right season for salting provisions but not for buying dairy produce—with every precaution against spoilage, over-ordering and the disturbance of market prices. For this purpose the Victualling Board enjoyed the great advantage over the *munitionnaires* in Paris that London already dominated the national market and was much nearer the dockyards; Plymouth was the exception and resembled a French arsenal in relying mainly on regional resources.

The bulk of English provisions could not only be bought but also processed centrally, even if the hiring of numerous coasting hoys and their safe-conduct to the dockyards were not accomplished without delays and losses. Before 1684 the navy had contracted with a merchant syndicate for the supply of all victuals, as the French government still did. Colbert, who created the naval *munitionnaire* in 1670, did so in order to stop the easy profits earned by captains who did their own purchasing, as all captains would when they could. It is not clear how this contract system functioned in 1689–1713, except that by 1708, like the administration itself, it was utterly discredited by the dearth of hard cash.[2] Long before this, however, it is noticeable that when the king leased ships to privateering armaments he provided the guns but not the victuals, and that often prize victuals were bought by the navy. In principle, the English system of direct government management made for closer control over suppliers and relatively efficient deliveries, while retaining a degree of protection for the State against abrupt price movements. The Victuallers did their buying at home contractually, through a very small number of commodity specialists and usually for given quantities, supplemented by limited local dockyard

---

[1] On 2 June 1710 Zeeland owed Captain Nosse £vl.5,086 for bills outstanding since 1705 and £vl.37,490 to twelve other captains: The Hague, Algemeen Rijksarchief, Adm. 2536.

[2] In April 1704, already, the intendant at Brest was having to pledge his own credit to keep the local butchers in funds, at the same time as the small masters of wine-barques from Bordeaux were begging for their freights: Arch. du port de Brest, 1 E452, fos. 383, 419.

arrangements in which graft, as the Board feared, was likelier to occur.[1] That the Victualling Debt proved so intractable—and that its more insistent calls on cash helped to pinch other services—was not the result of this method in itself, but of rises in food costs, civilian competition, and emergency demands from the ships for supplementary provisions, sometimes in unforeseen places. Poor accountancy and the dishonesty of ships' pursers did the rest, admittedly with the connivance of captains and of dealers ashore.

All these supplies and services implied a sophisticated division of labour, as well as a substantial capital investment, in the dockyards, half factory and half warehouse, with diverse skills and inventories controlled by a mass of warrants, imprest bills, paysheets and vouchers. A nucleus of administrative and technical officers stayed on through war and peace, and the need was recognized for reserves of labour and material to meet any emergency: for Colbert, an arsenal should stock enough to fit twice over the ships attached to it. In practice, when war brought work to fever-pitch, improvisation and shoddy workmanship had to be tolerated. This was the price of Tourville's grand fleet in 1689–90, for instance, the arsenals having been depleted since 1683 so that a third of the navy was unfit for sea by 1688—an anticipation of the run-down after 1694. To expand its labour to a war-footing was easier for a dockyard near comparatively dense population centres, as was the case of Chatham but not of Portsmouth in 1689. It is remarkable that Portsmouth, with a labour force of 400 in 1688, surpassed the employment figures at Chatham by 1696, when both exceeded 1,200; by 1711, when Chatham was falling below this level and Plymouth had grown to 700, Portsmouth reached 2,000. In 1689 England's total dockyard labour did not much exceed this figure: by 1697 it was almost double, and by 1711 H.M. Dockyards had 6,369 'tradesmen' on their books, half being shipwrights, carpenters and sawyers.[2]

An increase of this magnitude was not achieved without friction, extending to the use of press warrants for some categories of labour, especially riggers, recruited from the seamen of ships laid up. French crews were consistently used for refitting and disarming, whereas the English ones were reluctant even to shift their stores from ship to shore unless bribed with double pay—a device resisted by the Navy Board. In

[1] Thomas Ridge, M.P., a big Portsmouth brewer, was expelled from the House in February 1710 for selling short to pursers, who gave receipts for undelivered sea-beer and shared the difference. Brewers at Harwich, Chatham, Rochester and Deal were also found guilty of fraud by the House of Commons Committee, while the Agent-Victuallers of Dover and Portsmouth were shown to have been lax in certifying deliveries. Cf. P. Mathias, *The Brewing Industry in England, 1700–1830*, pp. 197 ff.

[2] Ehrman, pp. 636–7; Merriman, p. 373. Employment was highest in winter, but seasonal fluctuations were not so sharp in 1702–13 as earlier, probably because more ships came home in the summer from overseas and more were engaged in commerce protection (*ibid.* p. 104).

1708 the experiment was tried of selecting senior captains as dockyard 'superintendents' with powers of discipline over crews in harbour, such as resident commissioners did not enjoy till 1712, unlike the *intendants de marine*, who could also threaten at need a *lettre de cachet*. At Copenhagen the work of the dockyard was carried out in peace-time by a reserve of 3,000 seamen (supplemented by convicts), who were fed and housed at the king's expense; but the hiring of labour, like the purchase of materials, became progressively more difficult there as finance dried up after 1709. Similar problems in Sweden were aggravated by outbreaks of plague at Karlskrona. Dockyard authorities everywhere had to deal with restlessness among their working forces, none the less tenacious of old working practices when their pay was a year or more in arrears, which in itself meant undernourishment and a fall in output. Such arrears caused the Copenhagen seamen to mutiny in spite of their weekly allowance of provisions. Even when pays were regular, an English commissioner was confronted with endemic malingering, embezzlement and wrangling about overtime. The tragedy of dockyard towns in general was their complete dependence on a public employer as uncertain as the navy. At Brest, five months' arrears were enough to force working families into selling or pawning their possessions in 1704, and a delay of only two months in 1706 precipitated a strike. Even when the men were docile, their wives were not. Their distresses were compounded by compulsory billeting and by the inability of lodgers to pay cash. Well before the great famine of 1709, bakers refused to supply the families of arsenal employees cast off by cuts in naval spending. Latent sedition turned into arson at Rochefort in 1706. By 1710 it was feared that the naval police, the last guarantee of public order in the arsenals, were about to mutiny.[1]

Irregular pay, often a mere IOU cashed at a high discount by professional ticket-buyers or assigned to innkeepers and slopsellers, was the burning grievance of seamen in all navies, together with the unwholesome diet and harsh discipline of shipboard. It cancelled such incentives as the chance of a minute share of prize money, ephemeral security from the debtors' prison, modest welfare schemes for the invalided and widowed. This was the more true since wages in most merchant ships doubled or trebled in the intense competition of war-time for experienced ('able' or 'prime') seamen, and even for landsmen willing to go to sea. Privateering was a stronger counter-attraction still in some places, so much so that in 1697 the English admiralty wished to suspend it. The French tried to limit corsair campaigns in the same way as long trading voyages, by stipulating a date for the return home. Occasionally they clapped an embargo on all sailings from certain ports, as the English more frequently

---

[1] Arch. du port de Brest, I E453, fos. 253, 721, 821; I E457, fos. 154–6, 220, 536; I E458, fos. 3 f., 173, 859. Cf. M. Giraud, 'Marins et ouvriers des ports', *Éventail de l'histoire vivante: hommage à Lucien Febvre*, vol. II (1953), pp. 343–52.

did, for a fortnight or so, in all ports. In Dutch ports this device apparently succeeded in enabling naval ships to complete their complements by taking, in principle, one man in five out of merchant and fishing vessels, notably at the expense of the Arctic fisheries, which employed 14,000 men at the end of the century.[1] In England, where the spring port-closures reinforced the indiscriminate manhunt known as a 'hot press' and in 1702 robbed the merchantmen of two-thirds of their crews while the rest went into hiding, it was an admitted failure. For the French it was simply a 'sovereign remedy' for local defects in the *Inscription Maritime*, the most remarkable administrative innovation of the age.

Introduced in 1668–73 and consolidated in 1689, this 'system of the classes' was intended to man the navy quickly, spread the obligation of service equitably, and avoid the violence which accompanied 'pressing'. It was based on the compulsory registration of all seamen and fishermen and on their division into classes, each liable for call-up every fourth— for Rochefort and Toulon every third—year, masters and pilots being exempted because they were expected to breed new seamen. As conceived by Colbert, it was also a welfare system, providing above all for payment of a portion of naval wages to a seaman's dependants in his absence—a point not effectively conceded in Britain before 1792, until when wives and children were all too often on the poor rate, if not reduced to vagrant alms-gathering. The intendants' dispatches show that care was taken to observe this rule so long as money lasted.[2] Unfortunately, half-pay (*demi-solde*) for the reserve ceased in 1683, so that a man might be hard hit during his year of service if not called up. Another setback, especially for Rochefort, was the emigration of Protestants. Total registrations, which rose from 29,000 in 1677 to 59,494 in 1686, fell to 55,790 by 1690.[3] Allowing for *exempts* and those at sea or abroad, this did not prove enough to meet a line-of-battle requirement for 23,175 in 1690—a number already lower by 10,000 than the entire English requirement that summer, but about the same as the maximum Dutch requirement during the Nine Years War, which oscillated between 16,000 and 24,000. French needs in 1690 would have been somewhat larger when account is taken of con-

---

[1] C. R. Boxer, 'Sedentary Workers and Seafaring Folk in the Dutch Republic', *Britain and the Netherlands*, vol. II (ed. J. S. Bromley and E. H. Kossmann, Groningen, 1964), p. 149. Sailings to Greenland, averaging 198 per annum in 1680–9, fell to an average of 94 in 1690–9: G. van Sante (ed.), *Alphab. Naam-Lyst van alle de Groenlandsche en Straat-Davissche Commandeurs...*(Haarlem, 1770), pp. xxvi–xxvii. Cf. below, p. 848.

[2] See (e.g.) AN, Marine B3/131, fo. 317 (Toulon, 30 Aug. 1705).

[3] The 1687 reviews show the following distribution (AN, Marine G9, fos. 81–2):

Dunkirk to Dieppe	3,818	Basque ports	1,831
Le Havre to Granville	5,501	Languedoc	2,092
Brittany	14,991	Arles to Antibes	12,068
Poitou to Guyenne	10,178		

Total (excl. 7,388 *exempts*) 50,479

Cf. R. Mémain, *Matelots et soldats des Vaisseaux du Roi...1661–1690* (1937), p. 209.

voys, coastguards and the galley corps, though the latter was served principally by slaves and convicts (ch. XVII). On the other hand, 1690 was a peak year for the French naval effort, whereas the English navy bore some 48,000 men in 1694–6 and sometimes rather more after 1702— certainly more than half the country's native seamen.[1]

One answer to the deficit of the *Inscription Maritime* in 1690 was the organization of eighty 'compagnies franches de la Marine', each of a hundred men. William III revived James II's 'maritime regiment' in the same year and De Witt's Marines nine years later, but the confederate navies made less use of sea-soldiers than did the French, a third of whose naval force was to consist of them. Recruited and clothed by their own majors, they were distinct from the naval police (*archers de la Marine*) and coastguard *milices*. They were expected to perform certain shipboard and dockyard tasks and so constitute a 'nursery of seamen', although their specific virtue was as trained marksmen, particularly useful to the corsairs. The English regiments were primarily intended to produce fore-mast hands. Quartered near the dockyards, they were spent in small change to complete the complements of ships and even to replace men pressed out of homeward-bound merchantmen.[2]

Too little is known of the functioning of the *Inscription Maritime*. Pierre Arnoul, who toured the ports as *intendant des classes* (1692–1710), claimed that the system was producing more men than were needed in 1693, after some tightening of the rules; but he wanted more co-operation between the *commissaires* in charge of the many *départements*—some situated inland so as to gather novices from the numerous river boatmen— and between their agents in the *quartiers*, groups of country parishes or segments of a large town.[3] At that level much depended on how intimately a *commis* knew his men, their homes and hiding-places, and on his ability to stand up to local notables, gentry and shipowners, inclined like most English merchants and magistrates to prefer their own interests. Some *commis* won confidence because they understood 'the manner of governing' mariners. Some let their registers fall into disorder as war laid its toll

[1] E. L. Asher, *The Resistance to the Maritime Classes* (Univ. of California Publications in History, vol. 66, 1960), p. 91; C. R. Boxer, *loc. cit.* p. 153; Ehrman, p. 110.

[2] Disbanded in 1699, the English marines were re-established in 1702, in six regiments totalling not more than 8,000 men (Merriman, pp. 41, 177–9, 207 ff.). The regiment created by the States of Holland in 1665 (see Oudendijk, pp. 142–4) was disbanded after 1679; but when parliament dismissed his Dutch Guards William III was able to organize three regiments against the penny-wise opposition of the admiralty colleges, which had proved pound-foolish in the Nine Years War, for enemy musketeers often drove their seamen below deck and so got a chance to board: J. R. J. P. Cambier, *De Nederlandsche Mariniers van 1665 tot 1900* (Helder, 1899), pp. 78–9. Cf. H. W. Richmond, *The Navy in the War of 1739–48* (3 vols. Cambridge, 1920), vol. I, pp. 267–75.

[3] Thus the department of Marseilles was divided into four *quartiers* (with a fifth in the adjacent countryside); Duclos, for many years the commissary in charge there, denied that he ever resorted to force, thanks to an intimate knowledge of the streets and *cabarets:* AN, Marine B3/71, fos. 706–9. For Arnoul's reports in 1693 cf. ibid. B3/78.

of casualties and dispersals. Such *commis* had to be kept up to the mark by their fellow *écrivains* in the arsenals, where the *Bureaux des Armements* checked the ships' muster-books (*rôles d'équipage*) as was done by the Clerk of the Cheque in English dockyards, but with a general register to collate in addition. Whether or not the *commis* took bribes, he was often overworked and in some roadsteads hard put to carry out his duty of inspecting every little barque as it came in or before it went out. There were notorious centres of resistance, such as Martigues and St Tropez, as well as places like Cherbourg (and all of Languedoc) said to produce mediocre sailors. Many escaped for the duration to foreign parts, such as Italy or the Aegean, one estimate of these 'fuyards' for 1706–8 being as high as 30,000.[1] Conversely, foreign seamen were welcomed in France but were nothing like so numerous as in the Netherlands. Desertions, commonest in foreign ports of call, might also occur from squads in overland transit to the arsenals. Yet it is remarkable that Toulon and Brest could exchange large detachments overland without serious loss. On the whole, whatever pressures were exercised, the arsenals got their levies on time and distributed them between the ships with an eye to origin and therefore quality, apparently with fewer unfit men than were swept up by the English press gangs in this period, despite cases of self-induced injury.

Recruitment was less often accompanied by riots than in England, where pressmasters ashore had to proceed warily to avoid charges of trespass. 'Jean le matelot', above all, was allowed more leave. He was less often switched from ship to ship before pay-off than was the English sailor, and he normally received two months' advance pay (*avances*) before leaving home—an obligation given the highest priority so long as there was any money about, since more than anything else it affected willingness to serve. As everywhere, even in Holland, recruits were harder to find as arrears of pay lengthened, all the more when manifest injustices occurred in the methods of payment—unhappily most common in England, where in 1699 the seamen had even to petition parliament against the practice of treating sick men as deserters unless they were lucky enough to rejoin their former ship after convalescence. The relative efficiency of the *Inscription*, however, suffered from the conversion of its salaried commissariat into office-holders, in 1704, and from the later demoralization. Under the stress of a major war it was never expected that the classes would serve in rotation, although efforts were made to reward the deserving, refresh tired crews and spread the burden between departments, backed by marginal port closures and other compulsions. Abuses were denounced and sometimes punished. Yet wherever musters and registers fell into confusion the system was deprived of its essential virtue as one of controlled conscription.

Whatever the shortcomings of French impressment, contemporary

---

[1] AN, G7/1830 (Creslé to Controller-General, 10 Dec. 1708).

critics of England's more haphazard and openly provocative methods saw it as a model of smooth and punctual manning. Even had service pay and conditions been more attractive, a peace establishment of 10,000 could not have been quadrupled by volunteers alone, even with a 'bounty' larger than the wages advanced to all French recruits. Press gangs, afloat and ashore, employing two or three hundred lieutenants, worked now on an unprecedented scale, none the less because conservative seamen resented the novel practice of keeping the great ships in pay throughout the winter from 1692. Originally intended to reduce the cost of spring pressing and synchronized with 'staggered' leave, this innovation hardened into a series of precautions against the desertions which it stimulated. The necessities of the winter cruisers, in turn, increased the numbers who were 'turned over' from ship to ship, thus confusing pay-books and postponing pay-off. With the conjoint evils of payment by 'recalls' and the ticket trade, these 'big-bellied miseries...that beget more miseries'[1] excited more humane anger than pressing itself, which was criticized by Defoe and others chiefly on economic grounds—such as the indirect costs to trade of frightening mariners from the ports and of undermanned merchantmen, besides inflated wages. Naval authorities were neither blind nor indifferent: advocates of a register included St Lo, a dockyard commissioner, and the admiralty secretary Burchett. In 1696, indeed, parliament set up a voluntary register. It was abolished in 1710, an acknowledged failure. Instead of a reserve of 30,000 names by 1698, there were only 17,000 by the end of 1702, many of uncertain domicile. The scheme was discredited when a certificate of registry, which protected the holder from pressing, was seen to be vendible. Only a compulsory registration, with penalties, could have stemmed this traffic; but England's naval bureaucracy was too small for that, even with the help of the Customs in checking crew lists. As became their very different institutions, the English relied far more than the French on the willing co-operation of civilian magistrates, which usually left much to be desired.

If the English and Dutch could ultimately call on relatively vast pools of seafaring manpower, by fair means or foul, Denmark and Sweden had to husband their resources with foresight. Like the French, the Danes tried to ensure the readiness of men for immediate service by the compilation of a register, though they differed in making registration voluntary. Registration was open to Danish, Norwegian and foreign mariners. They were freed from all compulsory service and shipowners were instructed to give priority in employment to those whose names were on the muster-rolls. Originally introduced in 1679 and revised after 1700, this *Indrullering*,

---

[1] [William Hodges,] *Great Britain's Groans: or, an Account of the Oppression, Ruin and Destruction of the Loyal Seamen of England*...(1695), p. 2. On re-calls—deferred payments due to men not present at a 'general pay' on discharge—and payment problems generally, see Merriman, pp. 173–5. Once he had 'RUN' against his name, a man forfeited all arrears of wages.

though insufficient for the total demands of the fleet, did provide a hard core of men and justified itself in practice. The Swedes were less successful. The nucleus of their crews was provided by the *båtsmanshåll* and the *båtsmansindelning*. The *båtsmanshåll* dated from the time of Gustavus Adolphus: specified coastal districts were exempted from conscription and certain taxes on condition of providing for the upkeep of a fixed number of men who would join the fleet when needed. The *båtsmansindelning*, first established by Charles XI in the country round Karlskrona, meant that men were appointed to small farms which, with some Crown aid, sufficed to maintain them. They were required to train periodically, and when war began could be transported quickly and cheaply to their ships at Karlskrona. The weakness of the Swedish system was that it was based on the land. It made some use of volunteers, including foreigners, but Swedish warships were inadequately manned because too many of the servicemen had insufficient maritime experience.

Rooted in the universal horror of naval service—likened by contemporaries to the old terror of Barbary—the manning problem particularly reflected losses by sickness, which far exceeded casualties in action and sometimes affected the outcome of an action. In 1701 Benbow lost a quarter of his men by death and desertion in the West Indies. Desertions there were notoriously high, but it was the 'distemper' which cost the English a thousand men at Martinique in 1693, as it did the Spanish plate fleet in one month of 1706. Scurvy in temperate waters was only less deadly than the fevers and fluxes of the tropics. Venereal and pulmonary diseases, sunstroke and rheumatism, also contributed heavily to 'this kind of stewing to death in Ships',[1] crowded and poorly ventilated between decks. Typhus was introduced by soldiers and pressed men—'*Shacome-filthies, Ragga-muffings* and *Scrovies*'[2]—and liquor caused many accidents. To meet these daily enemies most ships carried a surgeon, often inadequately assisted, and in 1691 the English followed Dutch example by adding a physician. Dutch practice in this and cognate matters had been much improved by John de Witt, the only leading statesman (apart from James II) to sail with a fighting fleet. But the best standards were set much earlier by the Spaniards, the first to employ hospital ships. Tourville had several of these at Beachy Head and they were sorely needed; by 1703, when certain rules of sick-care were better understood, the English had five in commission. Spain and France were furthest ahead in the provision of naval hospitals ashore. The Dutch relied on excellent civilian hospitals, while the English admiralty used its powers to requisition beds in the reluctant London hospitals. Plymouth was the only English dockyard with its own hospital, the sick otherwise being at the mercy of lodging-

[1] *Great Britain's Groans*, p. 11.
[2] George St Lo, *England's Interest* (1694), p. 43. Cf. J. J. Keevil, *Medicine and the Navy, 1200–1900*, vol. II (1958), pp. 245, 264, and C. Lloyd (ed.), *The Health of Seamen* (N.R.S. 1965), pp. 28 ff.

houses overseen by the Commissioners of Sick and Wounded, who had agencies in most ports. The Royal Hospital at Greenwich, founded in memory of William's queen, became serviceable in the Spanish Succession War, as an infirmary for disabled pensioners; and 'smart money' was available from the much older Chatham Chest, fed by prize money, officers' contributions and wage-deductions. Colbert's *Caisse des Invalides*, financed by a tax on imports and prizes to provide half-pay for cripples and pensions for widows, made a more generous provision, especially as it was open to all registered men. On the other hand, the Seamens' Hospital at Copenhagen, which depended on church collections and other donations, was reserved from 1682 for naval casualties only. English philanthropy, so prolific in founding almshouses and friendly societies, was directed less towards the condition of seamen than to educating boys for sea-service. The Keelmen's Hospital at Newcastle, erected in 1701, was a rare case of mutual aid. But in England there was more care for prisoners-of-war in 1702–13 than formerly, besides evidence that the needs of sick and wounded were better understood by the officials directly concerned than could be met by limited funds, incompetent practitioners or the harassed Commissioners of the Navy[1]

It was already true, as Dr Thomas Trotter observed in 1804, that 'a well-regulated ship soon reconciles all disaffection'.[2] If the average seaman was profane, feckless, and quick to resentment, equally he responded to leadership. Much depended on the characters of the masters, pilots, boatswains and other warrant officers who managed the routine work of a ship and had complete charge of its navigation. At his best, however, the captain understood the duties of every man under his command, besides the special responsibilities that fell to him in combat and foreign ports. He received the essence of his formation at an early age, either in merchantmen or as the *protégé* of a naval commander, with fair expectations of being commissioned lieutenant by the age of twenty. In De Ruyter's time there were captains in the Dutch fleet not many years older, one of them being his own son, but this was commoner among corsair and merchant captains. After 1660 governments became less willing to rely wholly on traditional forms of apprenticeship, which lent themselves to nepotism without guaranteeing competence. As early as 1663 Denmark established a training corps whose members were sent into foreign navies or made ocean voyages on merchantmen. Swedish officer cadets underwent similar training. A more methodical education was introduced in Denmark in 1701 with the formation of the Sea Cadet Company: besides maritime experience, the cadets were given regular instruction in nautical

---

[1] Keevil, pp. 235 ff. Cf. O. Anderson, 'The Impact on the Fleet of the Disposal of Prisoners of War in Distant Waters, 1689–1783', *The Mariner's Mirror*, vol. XLV (1959), pp. 243–9.

[2] *Medicina Nautica*, reprinted in Lloyd, *The Health of Seamen*, p. 267.

and military subjects at a school on the Bremerholm at Copenhagen. Did it owe anything to d'Usson de Bonrepaus, Seignelay's right hand, who was sent ambassador to Denmark in 1692? At all events, the most systematic naval training was that required of the training corps formed by Colbert in 1669, for which a number of special colleges were created in subsequent years to teach navigation and the accomplishments of the *honnête homme*. These *gardes de la marine*, of whom there were 634 in 1696,[1] benefited from the State's interest in the practical applications of science, especially to the making of up-to-date charts. England and the Netherlands, for all their leadership in marine surveying,[2] as yet offered no formal training to intending officers; the essential foundation was service 'midships'. In 1677, however, in his long war against dilettantism, Pepys introduced an examination in practical seamanship as a condition of appointment as lieutenant. Conversely, when a naval school was created at Cadiz in 1717, aristocratic prejudice saw to it that there was no entrance examination.

Arrangements of this kind, however one-sided, proclaim the emergence of the regular naval officer, product of the permanent fleets. Not only did they provide more continuous employment: the need to multiply ships in commission on the outbreak of war, and so for a reserve of officers, led to the improvisation of half-pay schemes for a number who were unemployed. In 1694 England extended this principle, introduced for senior officers in 1668–75, by an order-in-council which also cut the number of 'servants' allowed to admirals and captains at public expense. When in 1700 half-pay was limited to 50 captains, 100 lieutenants and 30 masters, it became necessary to evolve a seniority list. In this way the modern conception of whole-time rank began, though slowly, to supersede part-time post-holding. It did not follow that each command held was senior to the previous one. An English flag officer might find himself rear-admiral after he had worn a vice-admiral's flag, although he would not be demoted captain. These nuances were complicated by the traditional hierarchy of the Red, White and Blue squadrons, as was flag rank in the Netherlands by the seniority of the Rotterdam admiralty—a delicate matter when the lieutenant-admiral-general wished to live in Amsterdam, as De Ruyter did.[3] In 1689 the Dutch agreed that the confederate fleets or squadrons should be commanded by the senior English officer present. It was a large concession, the effect of which on Dutch morale is hard to measure; that it was made to work, despite occasional tensions, is a tribute to the tact of Dutch commanders, especially Van Almonde, of

---

[1] A total of 706 if their officers are included, divided into three companies—at Rochefort, Brest, Toulon. By 1712 this figure had dropped to 467, including 413 *gardes* (AN, Marine G11 and 19).

[2] See A. H. W. Robinson, *Marine Cartography in Britain* (Leicester, 1962), ch. 3.

[3] G. Brandt, *La Vie de Michel de Ruiter* (Fr. tr. Amsterdam, 1698), pp. 336–7. In 1665 the younger Tromp's objection to serving under De Ruyter was only overcome by attaching three civilian deputies to the fleet, one of whom was De Witt (*ibid.* pp. 290 ff.).

whom William III had the highest opinion.[1] By 1702 England had more flag officers than the nine active appointments available: hence 'dormant commisions' to enable unemployed admirals to draw half-pay. In 1689 France had eleven *officiers généraux*, including a vice-admiral for the Ponant and another for the Levant but excluding the Admiral of France, whose office had been shorn by Richelieu of its naval significance, although in 1704 the life-holder did take nominal command of the fleet which fought at Malaga. By 1712 the three lieutenants-general had increased to five and there were twelve *chefs d'escadre*. The highest rank open to them was a military one, that of Marshal of France; army service was more highly rated socially and in fact produced a number of naval officers. Some of the most illustrious names in the French navy, moreover, especially of its élite galley corps, were those of Knights Hospitallers. Tourville began as a *chevalier de Malte* and ended as a *maréchal de France*.

With the development of a professional *esprit de corps*, a naval career attracted more sons of 'good family', especially as the wars of 1689–1713 produced some fortunes in prize money. The recruitment of 'gentlemen', indeed, was one object of Charles II's innovation compelling captains to accept admiralty nominees—'volunteers per order'. Colbert displayed a similar preference, on the assumption that seamanship could be acquired by the traditional military class more easily than their qualities could be transmitted to seamen. A French officer could not even marry without the king's approval. This also implied a regard for dowries, since an officer without private means was considered more open to the temptations offered by the service to private trading, the pillage or improper disposal of prizes, manipulation of muster-rolls and other illicit practices. Such offences continued to be common. French naval ethics understandably declined under the financial pressures of Louis XIV's later years, when officers were sternly reprimanded for brutality as well as dishonesty by the younger Pontchartrain.[2] English court-martial records suggest that brutality was condoned whilst cowardice was severely punished. There was plenty of both in the West Indies, where commanders were constantly at loggerheads with civilians, 'huffing and hectoring the governor and the whole island as if each of those little commanders were a petty king...'[3] In reply to frequent complaints from the Board of Trade, the Admiralty merely drew attention to the instructions enjoining officers to co-operate with the governors, although it must have known the trouble caused to dockyard commissioners at home by the individualism of

---

[1] His English colleagues recognized that 'one line from Almonde to the King' was more efficacious than prolonged entreaties on their part: A. L. van Schelven, *Philips van Almonde, Admiraal in de gecombineerde vloot, 1644–1711* (Amsterdam, 1947), p. 135.

[2] M. Giraud, 'Crise de conscience et d'autorité à la fin du règne de Louis XIV', *Annales* (*E.S.C.*), 7ᵉ année (1952), pp. 172–90, and 'Tendances humanitaires à la fin du règne de Louis XIV', *Rev. Hist.* vol. CCIX (1953), pp. 217–37.

[3] Jamaica merchants' petition, 1696, quoted Bourne, p. 214; cf. *ibid.* p. 287.

captains. More humility on their part could have assisted the yards in detecting the defects of their ships. At the disarmament of 1697, the Chatham commissioner sarcastically suggested finding jobs for them by laying aside 'all such old-fashioned fellows as I am, that way may be found for these modish sparks to New Model the Navy, and erect a Babel of their own'.[1]

Here is a resonance of old jealousies between 'gentleman' and 'tarpaulin'. They were still strong enough in 1702 to produce a mutiny against Benbow, although it is significant that social connections did not save the ringleaders from execution. As late as 1703–12, the Navy Board certified 303 former members of the merchant service as competent for a lieutenant's post—only thirty less than the number of volunteers per order. The percentage of these was rising, however, and they stood a much better chance of becoming captains.[2] 'Tarpaulins' were likelier to achieve rank in the lower rates or as commanders of fireships, transports and the like. French 'officiers bleus', like Bart, more rarely broke the monopoly of the noble 'officiers rouges', largely Provençal and Breton, especially as naval commissions were never open to purchase like military ones. Openings to commissioned rank, clearly, were most numerous at the start of hostilities. Thus the *Abrégés de la Marine du Roy* list only 589 officers in 1689 but 1,138 in 1696, a drop to 952 in 1702 but a rise to 1,068 in 1712—including 153 captains of *vaisseaux*, 54 of frigates and 6 of bomb vessels, 41 of fireships and 18 of storeships (*flûtes*).[3] But it would be mistaken to draw too firm a line between commissioned and warrant officers at this date. Even had the quarterdeck always been beyond the ambition of a master, his wages on an English first rate were those of the captain of a sixth, while those of a lieutenant did not much exceed the boatswain's on any ship. Masters, pilots and boatswains were more important to its working than all lieutenants and many captains. If a captain had the power of life and death, a purser (*écrivain, schrijver*) possessed an independent authority of his own. At different times all these sea officers conspired together or opposed each other. But their complementary functions drew them together more than differential pay or social standing divided them. The real dividing line lay between them and their miscellaneous crews—the *matelots* as distinct from the *mariniers*.

Another line ran between sea officers and the civilians now determined to control them. Naval officers were certainly not excluded from administrative posts. They provided many of England's dockyard commissioners, while the French chose active officers for their ten port-captains, described by the younger Pontchartrain as 'the soul' of a port. During the Nine Years War Russell was simultaneously commander-in-chief, a member of

---

[1] R. D. Merriman (ed.), *The Sergison Papers* (N.R.S. 1950), p. 272: cf. *ibid*. pp. 131–6.
[2] Baugh, p. 98.
[3] AN, Marine G9 to G19. At any one time, about fifty officers would be serving in the colonies, including a couple at Pondicherry.

the Board of Admiralty and Treasurer of the Navy. Hans Wachtmeister, the able admiral-general of the Swedish navy, exercised immense authority between 1689 and 1713 as president of the admiralty college and as head of the *amiralitets stats- och kammarkontoret*, which was responsible for naval finance. Even his energy, however, did not prevent him becoming progressively dependent on professional bureaucrats, who managed the navy themselves after his retirement. By 1721, the age was long past when naval business was the affair of a few clerks and a dominant personality deriving his prestige from successes at sea. The civilian administrators had acquired an authority of their own, even if the social standing of some of them had not kept pace with their developing responsibilities, as was true of the dockyard commissioners in England though not by any means of the *intendants de marine*.

Specialized knowledge was already so much at a premium as to limit the capacity of politicians to hold their own with the experts. This may explain why the weekly meetings of Admiralty and Navy Board became a formality in Anne's reign, and why Louis XIV never obtained a grasp of naval business. Technocracy was also furthered by length of service. Bégon's two decades at Rochefort were more than matched by Girardin de Vauvré, who ruled Toulon from 1680 to 1715. Pepys served the best part of thirty years, as Clerk of the Acts 1660–73, then Admiralty Secretary 1673–9 and 1684–90; Charles Sergison, who joined the Navy Board from a dockyard clerkship in 1675, was Clerk of the Acts from 1690 to 1719; and Josiah Burchett, a nominee of Russell in 1694, remained Admiralty Secretary, alone or in partnership, till 1742. Colbert de Seignelay had been apprenticed to 'le détail de la Marine' for many years before inheriting his father's secretaryship in 1683, while Jérôme Phélypeaux de Pontchartrain worked beside his father before taking over the secretaryship in 1699. It is true that the elder Pontchartrain entered office in 1690 with no such background: the logical successor to Seignelay was thought to be d'Usson de Bonrepaus, part author of the 1689 *Ordonnance*, the French navy's fundamental statute, but he could not afford the purchase money. The result, significantly, was to elevate the influence of the *commis* attached to Pontchartrain—to the indignation of sea-officers and of French naval historians, who mostly adopt their standpoint. Given aristocratic prejudice towards Louis XIV's ministerial despotism, their contempt of men like La Touche and Salaberry, heads of the Ponant and Levant *bureaux* 1688–1709, calls for reserve. In no country had more been done to define the respective spheres of pen and sword. The Pontchartrain family certainly upheld the civilian predominance laid down by Colbert, and lectured their subordinates quite as much. But their influence was modified by the coming of age in 1695 of Toulouse, the king's natural son, who had been made Admiral of France at the age of two with the object of weakening the chief representative of the sword. He also headed the port *Amirautés*, with their prize jurisdiction and control of merchant shipping; between these office-holders and the naval bureaucracy no love was lost. A further blow was the advent to the *Contrôle-Général* in 1699 of Chamillart, protégé of Madame de Maintenon, who had instructed him to draft a reduced naval budget five years earlier. Under pressure from the Controller-General, two hundred naval commissaries had either to purchase their posts in 1702–4 or go. Experienced men were thus lost to the service, if only a minority.

Whereas political influences tended to starve naval finance in France and the Netherlands—where the admiralties resented bitterly the unfulfilled 'consents' of the landward provinces to subsidize them in the Succession War—English naval credit benefited in the long run from the upheaval of 1688–9, even though party politics created friction among officers and increased the weight of patronage in their careers. The superiority of the English fleet, which absorbed roughly a quarter of the State's wartime expenditure,[1] was above all that of Godolphin's finance. As explained elsewhere (ch. IX), the Nine Years War was in this respect more difficult than its successor, which began with an unfunded naval debt large enough to have paid for the navy in 1702. This was paid off by 1704, but by 1711 the accumulated debt stood at nearly £4 m. and the Victuallers' bills at one-third discount—as high as long-dated obligations in 1697. In nine years the Victualling had exceeded its parliamentary vote by £2·6 m., thus forcing other departments to go short. Such a vote, in any case, did not mean ready money, for supply was tied to the proceeds of taxes yet to come in and habitually overestimated. French naval revenues, 'assigned' to the product of the general farm, poll-taxes, mint-profits and so on, invariably came to considerably less than the totals annually authorized for the navy.[2] Delayed receipts were made good by private borrowing on the part of the *Trésoriers de la Marine*, of whom three took a year's 'exercise' in turn—unlike the army's 'Extraordinaire des Guerres', handled by a company and said to be less exposed to the fragile credit of single financiers.[3] 'Here we are in March 1705 and I've still to pay about 12 millions for 1704', wrote one of them, Louis de Lubert: 'People are persuaded that it is I who hold back the salaries [*appointments*] of the principal officers and the wages of the seamen.'[4] Not the least anguished

---

[1] For rough estimates year by year, ranging from 34 per cent in 1696–7 to 15 per cent in 1710–11, see D. C. Coleman, 'Naval Dockyards under the Later Stuarts', *Econ. Hist. Rev.* 2nd ser. vol. VI (1953–4), p. 136.

[2] AN, G7/1830. From 1708 to 1713 the *ordonnances expédiées* oscillated between 14 m. and 16 m. *livres*, but *ordonnances assignées* between 4 m. and 12 m. There was less of a discrepancy in these figures in the case of the galleys, costing nearly 3 m. per annum.

[3] *Trés-gén. de Marine* to Controller-Gen. 8 Jan. 1704: ibid. 1828.

[4] Ibid. 1829. By 11 November Lubert was dead, owing nearly 7 m. on which no *fonds* had yet been obtained, and in 1711 his heirs still held over 1 m. in unpaid assignations (ibid. 1838). Not only had 1704 been an unusually expensive *exercice*: it had opened with a deduction of 5 m. (from a total authorization of 18 m.) to meet debts incurred by the

hours of these treasury scapegoats were spent in arranging cash remittances from one part of France to another—a function requiring much virtuosity in itself at a time of extreme monetary confusion. England's more unified money market was as great an advantage as her State loans. It was necessary on one occasion for the intendant Vauvré to visit Lyons himself and make a sleepless return to Toulon with bags of money; fortunately perhaps, he and Bégon both had family links with the banking world.

The fiscal ordeal of the Dutch admiralties may be illustrated from the case of the Maas, a less obstructive college than that of Middelburg. The cost of the Rotterdam armaments in 1701–12 totalled 13,035,763 florins, of which by 1713 only half had been raised—6,317,975 fl. by Holland, a mere 245,274 fl. by the 'non-equipping' provinces. They still owed 1·4 m. and Holland 5·1 m., which shows that the failure of Utrecht and the landward provinces, although demoralizing to the others, was not the preponderant deficit.[1] Duties available locally, chiefly 'convoys and licences', sufficed only for routine defence costs. Rotterdam had therefore to borrow the price of half its war effort—the 'Extraordinary'—and that was not the effort the English expected. In January 1709 Dutch loans were running as high as 9 per cent, while deposits in the Bank of Amsterdam fell lower than they had ever been during these wars.[2] Even with Amsterdam's lending facilities and higher taxes, the Netherlands could not sustain two long wars in rapid succession simultaneously on land and sea (ch. IX, XIII). Still less were Sweden and Denmark able to maintain even their relatively modest fleets for long. Swedish Crown revenues were largely in kind from the royal estates. They had been restored by Charles XI (ch. XX (I)), but foreign loans were harder to get and foreign exchange reserves shrank with a fall in copper output. Nor could a navy subsist on occupied countries, unlike the Swedish army before 1709. Denmark's weaker economic base and revenues forced her desperately to seek loans abroad. There were long but fruitless negotiations with the financier Isaac Liebmann, who was offered a contract for all war-materials purchased inside Denmark against a loan of 800,000 *rixdalers*. No reliance could be placed on irregularly paid Russian subsidies.

Merely to sketch the financial limitations within which the naval administrators worked, with their improved but still rudimentary accountancy and record-keeping, is enough to suggest why 'abuses' were central to their thinking. Innovations, as often as not, were attempts to prevent abuses. The naval correspondence of the time abounds in reprimands, even if the hands of those who wrote them may not always have been clean by later standards. French naval ministers were particularly prone to cast

previous treasurer, who himself had taken over 2·5 m. owing for 1702. Half the wage arrears in the Brest arsenal for 1704 were assigned to the sale of coastguard captaincies in Brittany, when Chamillart told Pontchartrain that the deduction of 5 m. must be covered by office-sales (ibid. 1829, Lubert to Chamillart, 6 Sept. 1706).

[1] Algemeen Rijksarchief, Adm. XXXVII/37, fo. 145.   [2] Below, p. 896.

reproaches, as if to expect the impossible from their men-of-all-work. It is clear, finally, that the central authorities insisted on knowing everything. The English Admiralty and Navy Board could correspond about the sailing qualities of a yacht or the illness of a master caulker. The *intendants de marine*, who wrote several times a week to their minister, overlooked neither the cargo of a prize nor the eccentricities of an officer's wife. The Zeeland admiralty was much occupied at times with rebutting the complaints of ambassadors, while the omission of a privateer to salute a naval captain was reported to the States-General by the Maas. Even in the decentralized Netherlands, the navy depended ultimately on the will and ingenuity of statesmen.

It was the statesmen, however slender their acquaintance with naval technicalities, who had to determine ultimate priorities. They had to decide, in particular, whether they could afford to spend on so costly an arm resources needed for other military commitments. In doing so, they could not ignore the complaints and aspirations of influential groups. A navy was therefore likely to flourish best in a society whose economy was dominated by maritime trade and whose security utterly depended on maritime power. Both these conditions were satisfied most incontrovertibly by the nature of English society after 1650 and by its political structure after 1688. England's navy was universally accepted as a primary need, while a standing army was felt to threaten liberty. The naval policies of the continental States, even of the Netherlands, were more vulnerable to rival interests and multiple necessities.

CHAPTER XXIII

ECONOMIC ACTIVITY

I. THE MAP OF COMMERCE, 1683–1721

A NY synthesis of the economic history of a continent over a short
period is bound to be a somewhat arbitrary artifact, moulded by
the historian's necessarily personal assessment of the relative claims
to importance of the local *vis-à-vis* the general, of the shorter and the
longer term, of spectacular versus less visible changes. This essay cannot do
justice to all aspects of making and getting and consuming, even in Europe,
between the death of Colbert and the end of the Great Northern War. It
is focused on international aspects of European production and exchange,
to the relative neglect of those that were merely local,[1] not because the
former were absolutely more important but because the latter, as our
knowledge stands, are difficult to interpret on a continental scale. On the
other hand, since it is important to suggest, above all, the distinctive
character of a relatively short period of economic time, attention must be
given to more immediate and conspicuous phenomena, notably to the
effects of wars and to the business cycle, at the expense of the more slowly
changing though in a sense more fundamental factors in economic life,
such as population, patterns of consumption, technology, and economic
institutions generally.[2]

During the great wars men had as at other times to live. Far and sometimes not so far from the scenes of glory there were crops to be harvested,
furnaces to be charged, bills to be collected, and that vast loom of
transportation and communication kept working that wove into one
fabric the economic life of Europe. Few were unaffected by the wars, if
only in the price of their daily bread. While statesmen turned trade into
war, entrepreneurs found business in war: great government loans to
float, munitions and naval stores to be contracted for, armies to be clothed
and fed and paid, opportunities to be taken in that continuing battle of
privateers and merchantmen which year after year involved more ships,
men and guns than all the naval battles put together. But for most
businessmen war was still an extraordinary situation in which one divided
one's risks, insured where one could, made every allowance for abnormal
price and demand levels and, above all, hedged against the return of peace.

In such times, economic policy could hardly have been one of the more
static elements of institutional life. Yet, amidst all its vagaries, there was

---

[1] Some of the national and local factors are treated above, chs. VIII–XI, XVI–XIX, and XXI.
[2] Cf. vol. V, ch. II, and below, ch. XXIII (2).

little to distinguish it in this age. Mercantilism, in the sense of government regulation of the economy in the interests of State power, had reached its apogee in western Europe in the half-century preceding 1683; though it was still a new force in the less advanced areas of Europe like the Russia of Peter, and was to retain great vitality in Germany and Scandinavia for another century, it was in obvious decay in the West. The Dutch were turning away from the monopolistic chartered company and experimenting with new forms of organization for regulating foreign trade, such as the compulsory, State-supervised but open societies of merchants trading to Russia or the Baltic; old regulations, like those for the herring fishery, were slow to go after they had outlived their usefulness, but few new ones were added. In France, it is true, routine and vested interest triumphed after Colbert, piling regulation upon regulation, without critical self-evaluation or innovation, till war shook the whole edifice. Though Colbert's domestic legacy on the whole withstood the strains of war and famine, his foreign trading companies collapsed, their revival by John Law belonging to the history more of public finance than of international trade. The universally critical memorials submitted to the revived *Conseil de Commerce* in 1701 reveal most starkly the extent to which forty years of Colbertism had turned the French upper bourgeoisie against State controls. In England, the hostility to monopoly endemic throughout the seventeenth century was able to end within a generation the effective privileges of the Africa, Russia, and Merchant Adventurers Companies; and the 'old' East India Company was for a time challenged by interlopers, although economic and political self-interest induced old and new Companies to merge their trade in 1702 and their identities in 1709. It was geographical and military factors, combined with a much more limited trade, that preserved the privilege of the Hudson's Bay Company. At home, in destroying the last legal props of conciliar government, the Revolution completed the destruction of the only controls that could make the internal regulation of industry effective and uniform in England. Henceforth, where continuing or new legislation was needed, it was in parliament and not in council chambers that the battles between rival interests were to be fought.

The history of public finance in some of the belligerent countries has been discussed above (ch. IX). The basic structure of private credit did not change significantly, except perhaps in Britain, where the foundation of the Bank of England was ultimately to give the London money market considerable advantages over Amsterdam. Whereas the Bank of Amsterdam was primarily a bank of deposit and exchange, whose most valuable function was probably that of facilitating monetary transfers between merchants all over Europe, the Bank of England's discount and loan services marked a tentative advance towards the functions of both the modern commercial and modern central bank. The generation that saw the flotation of the Bank, the New East India and South Sea Companies in

England, and of Law's companies in France, was clearly much given to experiment, though more original in financial than in commercial technique. In England particularly, the years after 1688 saw the floating of hundreds of companies for foreign trade, mining, manufacturing and finance, until finally joint-stock organization was curtailed by the 'Bubble' Act of 1720: thereafter, only the three great moneyed companies holding public debt, some new joint-stock companies for fire and life insurance, and a few others remained as memorials of the speculative creativeness of the years before 1720. During the flood of experiment, however, stock exchange and speculative techniques first developed in Holland were speedily acclimatized in England. Indeed, financial operations in general were becoming more and more international, with Swiss money active in France and Holland and Dutch money in France, England, eastern and northern Europe.

Behind the international movement of money and credit flowed the goods and commodities, by land but above all by sea, whose exchange was of all economic phenomena the one most present to the minds of contemporary policy-makers and business leaders alike. Under the impact of war, profound if not always permanent transformations were wrought in the volume and direction of virtually every important inter-regional exchange in Europe, and very often also of such exchanges as Europe then practised with other continents. Most governments now felt the need to watch fluctuations in their import-export trade as they occurred and, so far as their means permitted, to measure them. Their statistics certainly leave much to be desired, but if cautiously used they afford us the readiest clue, not only to the condition of individual branches of the economy in different countries, but to those dynamic elements in the economy of Europe and Europe overseas which best define the period. Its economic character will be most clearly related to its history in general, therefore, if we proceed to map the main inter-regional exchanges, with special attention to what was new in them and to what was dying or temporarily in eclipse. In this way, it should also be possible to suggest how far the wars of the time were responsible for changes in the patterns of consumption and production as well as of distribution.

One of the most striking features of the early modern as compared to the high medieval economy was the relatively large place of bulky grain-stuffs in inter-regional trade. The leading producer-exporter was the Polish-Lithuanian commonwealth, whose greater and lesser landowners sent their grain (usually as private ventures) down the Vistula and Niemen to Danzig (Gdańsk) and Königsberg—Danzig being twice as active as Königsberg and accounting for roughly half the grain shipped through the Sound. Little as yet reached the Baltic from Russia proper, while the quantities moving from the German Baltic ports were small compared with the Polish shipments. At Riga, a poor third in the grain trade, cereals were relatively unimportant—14·2 per cent of its exports in 1685–99, 4·2 per cent in 1700–18—and came almost exclusively from southern Livonia, Courland and inner Lithuania.[1] Rye had always predominated in the Baltic generally, although wheat had been growing in importance as cultivation for export increased in Volhynia and the newly developing provinces of south-east Poland towards the Ukraine. Thanks to geography, Danzig shipped 70 per cent of the wheat exported from the Baltic from 1670 to 1730, but even there wheat was only half as important as rye in the last quarter of the seventeenth century—and even less so in the next quarter-century. By contrast, Riga, Reval and the other Livonian-Estonian ports were far too northerly to tap any but negligible quantities of wheat; barley, oats and peas followed rye in the 1680s, but were declining by the 1690s. The great days of the Baltic grain trade had lain in the first half of the seventeenth century, when at Danzig alone cereal exports averaged 100,000 lasts[2] per annum. The wars of the mid-century almost ruined it; even with peace, Danzig exports had recovered to an average of barely 36,000 lasts by the last quarter of the century. During the Great Northern War shipments there fell again, averaging only 20,000 lasts a year in 1700–19 (and recovering to an average of only 31,000 for 1720–62); at Riga and Reval, which suffered much more from this war, grain exports became quite negligible in 1700–20. Königsberg was relatively less affected, in some years even surpassing Danzig in rye shipments through the Sound. With the return of peace, however, the relative lead of Danzig over Königsberg and the other ports was actually greater than before the war.

Except for small shipments from the Swedish Baltic provinces to the mother country, virtually all the grain loaded at the Baltic ports was shipped to the United Provinces, about four-fifths in Dutch vessels. Of the grain moving to the great Amsterdam market in the seventeenth century, an average of 43·5 per cent was re-exported. Although the grain trade was almost universally regulated by European States to prevent local dearths, only in the famine year 1698 did the States-General ever prohibit even briefly the export of cereals. In time of local scarcity, grain from Amsterdam might be sent to any corner of western Europe—in great quantities to France on occasion, more regularly to Iberia and Italy; the only constant markets, however, were in the United Provinces and up the Rhine. Not only were the two Netherlands the most densely populated section of Europe, but relatively little of their surfaces was available for cereal cultivation. Much of their land could only be used for pasture and hay, while the great Dutch cattle-raising and fattening in-

---

[1] E. Dunsdorfs, 'The Riga Grain Trade in the Seventeenth Century', *Baltic and Scandinavian Countries*, vol. III (1937), pp. 27–8, 32, 35.
[2] A last of grain was two tons or ten quarters.

dustry itself increased the demand for imported feeds as for imported cattle. At the same time, much other land suitable for breadstuffs had long been attracted to the more profitable crops required by Dutch industry—barley, hops, tobacco, hemp, flax, madder, weld and woad—or to market gardening for an increasingly urbanized population. Thus, in gin and beer, bread and meat, the Dutch consumed the surplus product of the great Polish plain.

The other significant corn-exporting areas were of lesser importance. They included North Africa and Syria, Tunisian corn sometimes appearing even in northern Europe; but the Mediterranean as a whole was a corn-importer. England, on the other hand, was rapidly changing her status in the international corn market. Before 1674, her exports were insignificant and her internal market poorly organized, London down to about 1688 frequently having to import corn, though the country as a whole was more than self-sufficient. By 1700 the metropolis was consuming in bread, drink, fodder and ships' stores almost $1\frac{1}{2}$ m. quarters a year—more than the entire Baltic export. Yet even London's imports ceased after 1688 as England, from being an occasional importer, turned into a considerable exporter. Temporary export bounties in 1674 and 1689 led to brief export flings, but a much more solid and extensive export trade had developed by 1700. From 1697 to 1731, England exported an average of 353,353 quarters of corn a year (slightly more than Danzig after 1720), primarily to Iberia and the Mediterranean but also to Ireland, Norway and America, as local conditions demanded. English cereal exports, however, were not of the same composition as Baltic. Rye and even wheat tended to be less important than barley and malt; from 1710 malt usually equalled all other grains combined; together, malt and barley formed about two-thirds of total exports. In Scotland, whose cereal exports were only about one-fifth the English, malt and barley also predominated.[1]

The greatest corn-producer in Europe, and the greatest market, was France. Like Germany, Spain, and even England, France was not so much a grain market as a congeries of overlapping marketing areas: some quite large, like the Paris market, which drew widely from the basins of the upper Seine and the Oise;[2] others quite small—a market town and its *pays* or immediate area of influence, cut off by poor roads from the ordinary effects of external supply and demand fluctuations. Only in years of exceptionally high prices, when transportation costs declined in relative importance, did these remote inland markets lose with a jolt their isolation from ordinary world price-fluctuations. Coastal areas, by contrast, never enjoyed any such isolation (unless artificially imposed), and

[1] [London,] P[ublic] R[ecord] O[ffice], T. 64/274/66, 68.
[2] J. Meuvret, 'Le Commerce des grains et des farines à Paris et les marchands parisiens à l'époque de Louis XIV', *Rev. d'hist. mod. et contemp.* vol. III (1956), pp. 169–203.

grain prices tended to fluctuate consistently throughout the whole Mediterranean and Atlantic littorals. Market conditions in France during the very difficult war and famine years between 1688 and 1713 are summarized below (ch. xxiii(2)), but it should be noticed here that the agricultural developments of these years were not all of one piece. Thus Provençal agriculture was in decline all through the seventeenth century and an area that had once exported was now forced to import regularly from Languedoc, whereas in the south-west grain (particularly wheat) cultivation was expanding. In the first half of the century, on balance, the Bordelais had imported grain from as far as Danzig; but considerable investment in draining the swamps round Bordeaux and the floodable low-lying lands along the middle Garonne later made this area more than self-sufficient, although further expansion in the interior was inhibited by the greater profitability of stock-raising. Very good prices were obtainable in Spain for French cattle, sheep, horses and mules; but this livestock trade, which supplied silver ultimately for all France, was disturbed by bad harvests on both sides of the Pyrenees and came to a halt when French merchants were expelled from Spain in 1694. Thereafter, there was an extensive spread of cereal cultivation throughout the south-west. Thanks in part to army victualling, wheat here became as sure a cash crop as livestock had been; the peasantry were prepared to eat maize and millet and save their wheat for cash. After 1713, areas like Lower Quercy continued to specialize in wheat production, based now upon the demand at Bordeaux for first-quality flour for the West Indies.[1]

Much more important than cereals as a bulk commodity in inter-regional trade, and much more troublesome in war-time, was the almost exclusively water-borne commerce in forest products and naval stores. Europe as a whole was far more thickly forested in 1700 than at any subsequent date. Since wood, however cut, was relatively expensive to move, transport being usually several times prime cost in final sales, most Europeans supplied themselves with timber for building and wood for burning (domestically or industrially) from sources close at hand. Ship-building, however, created highly specialized demands for particular types, shapes and qualities. In time of war, indeed, when regular supplies might be interrupted and both mercantile and naval demands on reserves were at a peak, timber became a major problem.[2]

In 1692 the six English royal dockyards used 19 loads of ash, 48 of beech, 705 of fir, 1,129 of elm and 6,780 of oak. The oak came almost exclusively from English forests, particularly in Hampshire, Kent and Sussex. New England oak, though tried, was considered too tender, too liable to decay, for naval use. German and south Baltic oak was better: if the rather

---

[1] In these same years, the trade with Ireland also provided western France with increasingly important supplies of salt beef, butter, etc. for re-export to the Antilles.

[2] Cf. above, pp. 813–14.

cautious English navy accepted it only for planking and deals, never for frames, English mercantile shipbuilders used it extensively. The larger Dutch merchant marine got its oak (and much pine) from Germany and to a lesser extent the south Baltic ports as far as Königsberg: Dutch merchants not only bought at the key river-marts (Emden, Bremen, Hamburg) but penetrated the interior, buying whole standing forests and having them cut to order. Yet the Dutch, unlike the English, did not insist that the hulls of their merchantmen be exclusively of oak: the famous flyboat, the workhorse of the northern seas, hundreds of which were put down every year, was generally built entirely of softwoods, making up in economy of construction and efficiency of handling what it lacked in sturdiness. For softwood of all varieties, the Dutch depended in part on the Baltic but especially on Norway, whose trade they in great part dominated. The English, five-sixths of whose ship-timber needs in 1686 were met by importation, also depended on Norway for up to 80 per cent of their imported timber.[1] There was less scope for an entrepôt in timber than in cereals, largely because of the expense of loading, unloading and storage. Although very great stores of timber were constantly on hand at the great shipbuilding centre of Zaandam, that area was not properly a timber market. Though timber remained a significant Dutch re-export, particularly to France and Spain, it seems that Dutch predominance was slipping at the Baltic, if not at the Norwegian and German ends of the trade: by 1721, barely 40 per cent of the timber going out of the Baltic (chiefly from Narva and Finland) went in Dutch bottoms or to a Dutch destination. Increasingly common were direct shipments to England and France, occasionally to Spain and Portugal, though timber for the last three destinations was almost never carried in ships of the importing countries.

The bulk of timber products in inter-regional commerce were ordinary ship-timbers, including deals and planking, and barrel-staves of every description. A problem was set by the great straight conifers suitable for masts—fir preferably, spruce for smaller types. Masts of varying qualities and quantities were available throughout the North. The best came from Riga, but they were limited in size and quantity and this source almost dried up during the Northern War, when Riga was cut off from the inland forests. Norwegian masts of ordinary size were much more plentiful, if not quite as good. For the largest masts it was becoming necessary to go to North America, though the French were not happy with the quality of those they received from Canada. Since mast timber was so rare and so necessary, its conservation and control were matters of state. The export of the largest sizes was controlled in Norway and at Riga, while Tsar Peter's grants of mast (and tar) monopolies to Dutch syndicates, shipping only to Holland, led to regular English protests. Whitworth, the first

[1] P.R.O., C.O. 390/8/G, H, I.

resident English envoy to Russia (1705–12), also strove with only partial success to get Peter to permit masts for England to be sent down the Dvina, through the Russian lines, to Riga. In New England, from 1685, the government worked somewhat ineffectively to pre-empt accessible mast timber for naval use. The French government was no more successful in making the mountaineers of the Pyrenees conservation-minded. The English tried a bounty for colonial masts and naval stores after 1705, but not until 1718–23 did they get as much as 40 per cent of their great masts from their own plantations, compared with only 12 per cent in 1708–13. They continued to depend heavily on Norway for small and medium masts, but in the Spanish Succession War had been able to supplement supplies of great masts from Norway and New England with irregular supplies from Archangel and Riga and (1707–14) more important supplies from Sweden.[1]

No navy could operate without flax for sailcloth, hemp for cables and cordage, as well as pitch, tar, rosin and turpentine: over the life of the average vessel, expenditures on such stores would exceed the costs of the original hull and of replacements for masts, spars, etc.[2] Pitch and tar had been virtually a Swedish monopoly. Taking advantage of the dependence of maritime Europe upon these products of the Bothnian and Finnish forests, the Swedish government sought economic, fiscal, and occasionally political advantages. Starting in 1648, a series of chartered companies monopolized the tar trade in Sweden despite objections from the Maritime Powers; although the third in this series was killed (1682) by a combination of English and Dutch diplomatic pressure and of resentment expressed in the Diet, a new company regained the monopoly in 1689. The government obliged it not to raise prices so high as to stimulate competition. Nevertheless, by monopolizing the export trade to Holland and selling there only through their own factors, the company did force Dutch prices high enough to produce some counter-activity. Holland was the principal mart and consumption centre for pitch and tar: an estimate of 1703 attributed two-thirds of European consumption to the Dutch market and its re-exports to Spain, Portugal and the Mediterranean—the English taking a sixth, the French and German ports a twelfth respectively.[3] In the 1690s the Dutch tapped new sources in Norway, Courland and particularly Russia. The Swedish monopolists soon lowered their prices defensively, but these new channels were not stopped. Russian tar, the product of the 'governments' of Vologda and Vyatka, floated hundreds of

---

[1] Ibid.; C.O. 388/6/A.7 and 390/6, pp. 225–42. Cf. P. W. Bamford, *Forests and French Sea Power, 1660–1789* (Toronto, 1956) and J. J. Malone, *Pine Trees and Politics: The Naval Stores and Forest Policy in Colonial New England, 1691–1775* (1964).

[2] In 1702–6 (inclusive) the English navy spent more on hemp and canvas alone than on timber and masts: P.R.O., Adm. 20/77, 80, 83, 86, 89.

[3] P.R.O., S.P. 9/206/10, fos. 324ᵛ–5 estimates European consumption of pitch and tar in 1674 at 8,100 lasts per annum of which Dutch domestic use accounted for 3,000, Britain for 1,800.

miles down the Dvina to Archangel, was both good and cheap. Imports of Archangel tar at Amsterdam alone reached 18,000 tons in 1698 and 60,000 in 1713, compared with a mere 6,100 tons passing through the Sound in 1714.[1] Over 80 per cent of the tar coming out of the Baltic still came from Sweden or Finland, but Archangel had smashed the Swedish tar monopoly for ever.

English merchants were by the Navigation Acts normally obliged to import tar directly from the producing lands instead of Holland. Anglo-Swedish relations often turned on such humble articles of commerce. With England in 1700 still basically dependent on Sweden, the coincidence of the Northern and Spanish Succession Wars brought on a crisis. As English needs soared, Russian incursions into Finland disrupted supplies at the source. The Swedish monopolists reacted by raising prices and refusing thenceforth to sell tar in Sweden, marketing all of it instead through their own factors abroad. When English naval needs were most acute in 1702-3, the Swedish company, even while shipping to France, cut off England with virtually no tar at all. This was corrected at the time, but from 1705 Swedish tar shipments to England declined steadily as Anglo-Swedish relations deteriorated. Slightly increased shipments from Norway could not make up the deficiency; little could be got from the eastern Baltic; the vast supplies of Archangel were monopolized by syndicates who shipped only to Holland, diplomatic pressure obtaining mere erratic driblets for England. The Bounty Act of 1705, however, so stimulated supplies from New England and the Carolinas that by 1718-25 England was receiving over four-fifths of her pitch and tar from them. Although Sweden abandoned the monopoly after the death of Charles XII, her tar trade had to wait till the American Revolution for another bout of real prosperity.

The French, like their neighbours, were obliged to the Dutch for most of their pitch and tar; but in the pine forests of the Landes, south of Bordeaux, they had the principal European source of turpentine and rosin, on which even the English and Dutch depended. The English were developing an alternative source of turpentine in New England adequate for war-time, but rosin was more difficult, especially when Spanish supplies also were cut off. The Dutch had developed new sources in Russia in the 1690s; the English got by with odd lots from New England, Russia, prizes, smuggling (via the Channel Islands), and later from parts of Spain subject to the Archduke, but primarily with speculative imports in 1701-2.[2] Ultimately, the French were to lose their command over these articles as the Swedes lost theirs, partly because the winter of 1709 killed most of the trees in the Petites Landes.

[1] Cf. P.R.O., C.O. 388/6/A.7; A. J. Alanen, *Der Außenhandel und die Schiffahrt Finnlands im 18. Jahrhundert* (*Annales Academiae Scientiarum Fennicae*, ser. B, tom 103, Helsinki, 1957), pp. 97-8, 105-6.   [2] P.R.O., C.O. 390/6, pp. 223-42.

The most valuable naval supplies from northern Europe were flax, hemp and their products. Before 1689 the sailcloth most esteemed was that of Brittany. It was only with difficulty that the Maritime Powers developed wartime substitutes from the newer manufactures of England, Holland and northern Germany.[1] Hemp, more exclusively a naval store than flax, was grown everywhere from south-west France to northern Russia, but especially in the east Baltic river basins, where Riga hemp was esteemed the best and sold for a premium over that of Narva and Königsberg. At least two-thirds of the hemp passing out of the Baltic before 1700 came from Riga, where hemp and flax accounted for 61 per cent of exports in 1655–99 and 69 per cent in 1700–18; in addition, hemp seed and linseed came to 14·7 per cent and 17·7 per cent in these periods. The Riga trade was at peak volume during the 1690s but declined with the Great Northern War, particularly after 1704. In 1699, fully 75 per cent of Riga hemp came from the White Russian or easternmost sections of the Polish-Lithuanian Commonwealth[2]—precisely the areas most subject to foreign incursions, lying in effect behind the Russian lines before the fall of Riga itself in 1710.

Hemp as the constituent of rope was vital to all maritime powers. The Dutch had a minor supply in their own 'inland' hemp, but their rope-works consumed vast quantities from the Baltic. The English never were able to produce much at home or in America, despite bounties. Thus hemp was rivalled only by iron as the most valuable commodity imported into England from the North. Sheer need perhaps made the English compete against the Dutch more successfully in this than in any other branch of Baltic trade. They also developed a major alternative source at Archangel. As late as 1698, the half-dozen annual ships of the moribund Muscovy Company at Archangel were overshadowed by some 30 Dutch arrivals. The opening of the Muscovy Company in 1699, followed by the Northern War, sharply stimulated the Archangel trade: total ship arrivals there rose from 54 in 1698 to 149 in 1702, and in 1703 the English alone sent some 70 ships. Hemp was the basis of this trade, not only in bulk but in value, soon constituting half England's imports from Russia. From 1704 Russia supplied from two-thirds to nine-tenths of English hemp imports. After 1721, however, with Peter discriminating against Archangel, the trade shifted back to Riga, while St Petersburg emerged as the second Baltic hemp port and centre of the English trade.

Though pearl ash commonly came from Germany, only the unlimited forests of northern Europe could supply the enormous quantities of the commoner ash and potash needed by western soapmakers.[3] The Dutch almost monopolized the Baltic export trade in ash (centred at Danzig and Königsberg), but from about 1699 the English took out most of the potash.

[1] See below, pp. 866–7, for the linen trade.
[2] E. Dunsdorfs, 'Der Außenhandel Rigas im 17. Jahrhundert', *Conventus primus historicorum Balticorum Rigae, 16–20. viii. 1937. Acta et relata* (Riga, 1938), pp. 461–80.
[3] Cf. P.R.O., C.O. 390/5, fo. 53.

Both were big buyers of these commodities at Archangel. The Dutch, in particular, also brought from the Baltic for their soapmakers considerable quantities of tallow—inferior in quality, however, to their own or the German—and for their candlemakers and the export trade to Catholic Europe lesser quantities of wax, 'chiefly the produce of *Poland* and *Muscovy*, Countries where the Bees seem to have chosen principally to reside'.[1]

Except for metals[2] and such luxuries as caviare, rhubarb and amber, these were the principal products of northern Europe in inter-regional trade—in general, much more necessary than valuable. In return, the North customarily received equally bulky commodities: salt, wines and fish.

The principal sources of salt for the Baltic lands were the west coast of France, Setúbal and the bay of Cadiz (notably at San Lucar). Spanish salt came also from the coast of Valencia and the mines of Catalonia. The salt of Sardinia and Sicily, too, began to enter Atlantic commerce in the early eighteenth century. The evaporation works in Languedoc supplied the south of France, Savoy-Piedmont and parts of Switzerland; the mines at Wieliczka and Bochnia (near Cracow) met much of the internal demand in Poland; and there were also important mines in Hungary and Austria. The older works at Lüneburg were in decay, but new works opened at Halle in 1699 reduced the dependence of eastern Germany on overseas supplies. The evaporation works in the west of Scotland supplied a small export surplus, while the opening of the Cheshire mines in 1670 was to free the English market from dependence on foreign supplies besides providing outward ballast for the nascent port of Liverpool. Some Cheshire salt went to the North American colonies, but the fishing industry there preferred Caribbean or Portuguese salt of higher salinity.

Dutch dominance of the north European salt trade rested on the huge quantities consumed in their fisheries, on their important refineries, and on the share of Baltic imports carried by their vessels: 74 per cent in 1681–90, dropping to 42 per cent in 1691–1700, recovering to 58 per cent in 1701–20 but slipping to 45 per cent in 1721–40.[3] Their Baltic salt trade was not based upon a home entrepôt or manufacture; they carried the salt direct from France and Portugal. It is sometimes asserted that the wars destroyed the French 'salt monopoly' by driving the Dutch and English to Portugal. In fact, although Portuguese salt pulled ahead of

---

[1] [Pierre Daniel Huet], *Memoirs of the Dutch trade...translated from the French* (2nd edn. London, 1719), p. 56.

[2] Below, pp. 869–70.

[3] The low Dutch share (42 per cent) of the 1690s was not very significant: many, perhaps most, of the Danish, Swedish, Lübeck and other north German vessels which then moved into the 'Bay Trade' (Biscay) were owned by invisible Dutchmen. Scandinavian vessels, in part similarly disguised, were also very important in English trade in this decade.

French in the wildly fluctuating war years, in 1720 as in 1683 French salt exceeded Portuguese at the Sound by better than two to one. Only after 1720 did the French lose ground.

The ancient wine trade is a much better example of a trade permanently disrupted by war. In this period viticulture extended over a fairly broad area from Portugal to Hungary. The most northerly of the important vineyards were those by the Rhine and Moselle, on which large quantities of wine were floated to Holland for common consumption and export. With these wines declining in international importance, however, and with the Portuguese still awaiting a wider market, the European trade in the 1670s was dominated by Spanish and still more by French growths.

Although burgundies were well known in the Paris of Louis XIV, their penetration even that far was restricted until new canals were opened after 1720 and they played no significant part in the world market, where French wines were still Bordeaux wines.[1] The wines of the Rhône and Midi were shipped out of the Mediterranean after 1700, but at first only in modest quantities. At Bordeaux, the *grands crus* of today had yet to be developed in the mid-seventeenth century. Exports then consisted almost exclusively of the un-aged *vin ordinaire* grown in the immediate vicinity of the town. Since the Dutch, however, had less use than the English for this 'claret', their agents moved out from Bordeaux north along the coast and into the *haut pays* of the interior, looking for hitherto unexported local wines attractive to Dutch taste: white wines, sweet wines, more heavily bodied wines, sugared wines, muscatels, the *vins forts* of Gaillac and Cahors, the white wines of Saintonge, Aunis and Périgord, and the new white Sauternes developed for Dutch palates. For the first time there was a considerable commercial production of spirits, which the Dutch wanted for fortifying their wines. Thus, with Dutch orders and advances, the viticulture of the south-west had been transformed into the export-oriented, rather prosperous trade that existed in 1672. Its only serious rivals in the world market were the wines of the Canaries and of Jerez, preferred by the English, and of Alicante and Malaga, generally preferred by the Dutch. But the Spanish vineyards did not significantly expand after the 1680s. By contrast, the international rôle of the Portuguese, including the vineyards of Madeira and the Azores, was dynamic. Portuguese wines hitherto, like some Spanish, had been considered local wines. The Dutch imported their first fortified wine from Oporto in 1675, the English in 1678. Thereafter the growth in the Alto Douro was to be extraordinary, encouraged alike by a highly artificial foreign demand and by a government dominated by vineyard landlords.

[1] H. Enjalbert, 'Comment naissent les grands crus: Bordeaux, Porto, Cognac', *Annales* (*E.S.C.*), 8ᵉ année (1953), pp. 315–28, 457–74; idem, 'Le Commerce de Bordeaux et la vie économique dans le bassin aquitain au XVIIᵉ siècle', *Ann. du Midi*, t. 62 (1950), pp. 21–35. Cf. R. Dion, *Histoire de la vigne et du vin en France* (1959), pp. 576–90, and Paris, Arch. Nat. F 12: 1834A.

Nevertheless, it did not prove easy to challenge the French hold on the north European market. In England, during the 'normal' years 1675–8, imports of French wines at London (almost four-fifths of the English market) averaged 8,535 tuns a year, compared with 5,008 Spanish, less than 1,000 Rhenish, and under 100 each of Portuguese and Florentine. When, however, all imports from France were prohibited from 1679 till 1685, the opportunity was exploited primarily by Portugal, whence imports rose from almost nothing to 16,772 tuns in the peak year, 1683. As soon as 'normal' market conditions were restored, however, the French ascendancy was even more pronounced than before. In 1685–9, London imports of French wines averaged 13,402 tuns compared with only 434 from Portugal, while imports of Spanish wines declined below their level of the 1670s to 3,915. The wars of 1689–1713 were much more damaging to Bordeaux's English market than the boycott of 1679–85. During the Nine Years War the importation of French wines at London ceased altogether, their place being again taken by Spanish (about 70 per cent from the Canaries) and Portuguese.[1] These changes were to be more permanent than those of the earlier boycott years. Thanks to an improving quality at Oporto, shifts in English taste, and above all the high duties still imposed on French wines, Bordeaux did not recover its market at the peace; in the official statistics French wines even figured behind Italian. The final victory of Oporto was the work of the war of 1702–13.[2] Since all Spain was under Philip V's authority until 1704, Spanish wines were as effectively excluded as French; although both the situation in Spain and the English attitude towards trading with the enemy changed soon afterwards, the dominant position consolidated by Portugal in the English market in 1702–4 was retained. With a duty on Portuguese (and Spanish) wines after 1697 less than half that on French, this primacy was well defended. From 1711 to 1750, English imports of Portuguese wines were to run at about double the rate of Spanish,[3] and at about ten times the rate of French.

Besides England, however, there was the much greater Dutch market. If pre-1672 Amsterdam took less Spanish wine than London, it took several times as much French. By 1721, though total wine exports from Bordeaux were only half what they had been in the 1660s, 34,138 tuns were shipped to Dutch destinations—almost six times the quantity shipped for England, Scotland and (especially) Ireland—mostly for drinking in the Netherlands and places adjacent, although a substantial fraction was re-exported, particularly to the North. There the market for southern wines had been relatively small before 1688 and was diminished by the wars, but by 1714 it reached a level double that of the 1680s and it was to double again

---

[1] P.R.O., C.O. 388/6/B.49; T. 64/274/111, 115.
[2] Cf. above, pp. 523–4.
[3] Spanish wines seem in general to have been losing their hold on northern Europe, though Scotland was supplied almost entirely from Spain in the post-Utrecht years: P.R.O., T. 64/274/113; T. 36/13.

between 1714 and 1725. This was particularly fortunate for Bordeaux, for the North was taking more than the great London market of the golden years before 1678; at least three-quarters of the wines passing through the Sound now came directly from France, apart from what may have come indirectly. After 1721, too, Danish and Swedish vessels became very active in this trade: in 1725, only about 18 per cent of southern wines going through the Sound went in Dutch bottoms, as against 40 per cent in 1714.

The war years, so critical for the wine trade generally, were particularly difficult for the vineyards of south-west France. There was a temporary reversion to subsistence economy in many areas. To preserve vast quantities of unsaleable wine, a great stimulus was given to the distilling of brandy; army victualling offered a temporary market, but later the south-west had to embark on a more arduous course of salvation. The era of the undifferentiated and un-aged product was past; the time for the *grands crus* had come. The ordinary *Graves rouges* could not pay a duty in England thirteen times their prime cost in France; hence, while the Dutch took cheap wines worth 100 *livres* per tun at Bordeaux, the wines shipped thence to England, averaging 180 *livres* in 1717, increased in average value to 600 *livres* in 1724. The founding of the house of Martell in 1713 can be taken as a symbol of the same process of quality specialization in the brandy distillation of the south-west. As far as Riga, with its almost exclusive preference for French wines, we find regular imports of French brandy growing steadily from the 1680s. Its biggest markets before 1689 had been Holland and England; but in England its place was now usurped by the native distilling industry itself. English spirits production, steady at something over half a million gallons a year in the 1680s, started upon a rapid growth in 1691, exceeding 1 m. gallons in 1700, 2 m. in 1710, and 3 m. in 1722. With the 4 m. gallons of 1727, the 'Gin Craze' proper had well begun.[1]

The Dutch herring fleet with its thousand and more busses and tens of thousands of sailors, snatching the stuff of empire from off the British coasts, was thought to furnish directly and indirectly the means of subsistence to some 450,000 souls in Holland alone. The Dutch were thought in the 1690s to take yearly some 300,000 tons of fish worth some £20 per ton. At £6 m. a year, this would easily have been the greatest branch of European commerce. Much of this herring was consumed at home and in the countries reached by the Maas (Meuse) and Rhine. Other great vents existed in France and the Catholic countries of the Mediterranean, especially Spain, with important secondary markets at Hamburg, Bremen

---

[1] Much more important than wine as an industrial product and item of consumption in northern Europe was beer; consumption in England, for example, generally exceeded a barrel a head per annum (P.R.O., C.O. 390/3, fo. 16). But it was an item of small, even diminishing, importance in inter-regional trade, as it was easier to ship barley than beer.

and in the Baltic, where the Dutch accounted for three-quarters of the herring imported in the 1680s and almost as much during the peace of 1697–1702. During the wars, however, their fishing fleets and carriers were ravaged by the Dunkirk privateers—to the partial advantage of the Scots, whose shipments into the Baltic exceeded those of the Dutch both then and in the immediate post-war years. Though the Dutch resumed the lead in a reduced Baltic market after 1722, British political pressure after 1713 opened to Scots herring the hitherto reserved Dutch markets at Hamburg and Bremen. Together, foreign competition, the movement of the fish, the ravages of two wars, and the inflexibility of Dutch entrepôt regulations were by 1750 to reduce the historic Dutch herring fishery to little less than a fifth of what it had been in its prime.

Despite constant efforts by government, the English herring trade was more decayed at the end of the seventeenth century than at the beginning. Similar disappointments befell the various efforts—the last being a special monopoly company chartered in 1692—to break the Dutch grip on the Greenland whale fishery, for which, in the peak years of the early 1680s, up to 240 or more Dutch vessels sailed annually, killing over 1,400 whales and returning with up to 60,000 tons of blubber. During the Nine Years War, because of higher insurance and labour costs and a temporary prohibition of the trade by the States-General, sailings dropped to less than half the pre-war average and the price of whale products fluctuated wildly at Amsterdam. Though again restricted by the State, sailings were more regular in the following war, but catches were sometimes bad and returns fluctuated as wildly. After each war, however, the Dutch were able to reassert their absolute position at roughly the level of the 1680s, though catches were growing smaller in proportion to the number of ships sent out. By the 1720s, a substantial proportion of the Dutch effort was turning to the newly developed Davis Strait fisheries. In 1721, of the 355 vessels employed in the whale fishery to Greenland and the Davis Strait, 251 were Dutch—the rest being from Hamburg (55), Bremen (24), Biscayan ports (20), and Bergen (5). The whale oil was used primarily for inexpensive lamp oil and soap.

In the North Atlantic, the Dutch had also a very successful cod fishery, employing 350 busses in the 1690s, between Scotland and Iceland. The Danes and Norwegians, however, were active here and by the 1720s the Norwegians had supplanted the Dutch as suppliers of cod to the Baltic; in fact, the Dutch shipped only herring through the Sound after the wars, and by 1750 their cod fishery was to shrink to a fifth its size of the 1690s. While the Dutch fisheries still flourished, the English and French had concentrated on the more distant North American cod grounds. From a very promising start, however, the English West Country fishery had declined to less than 100 vessels in 1680, owing partly to French competition but also to the growth of a residential fishery—first in New

848

England, then in Newfoundland. The dynamic New England fishery was expanding not only in the Gulf of Maine but over the banks off Nova Scotia and Newfoundland as well: by 1700, it was already considerably larger than the fleet from the West Country. Most of the large winter-cured New England fish were shipped to Bilbao, the smaller varieties to Lisbon and Oporto, the slightly inferior to the Canaries, Madeira, Azores and Jamaica, and 'refuse fish' to Barbados and the Leeward Islands as food for slaves. Much of the proceeds so earned in Europe went as coin or bills of exchange to England, to buy the growing New England imports of European manufactured goods; part was used to pay for the fishery's Iberian salt and for brandy, wine and fruit imported directly into New England. Fish shipped to the West Indies (along with New England timber, provisions, etc.) bought sugar, molasses and salt, but again some of the proceeds ultimately went to England in goods or bills to buy more manufactures. With ample supplies of the salt, rum, provisions, tackle and other goods in demand on the fishing banks, the New Englanders were also able to expand their purely commercial operations in Newfoundland. The West Country vessels carried most of their Newfoundland fish to Spain and Portugal, returning with salt, wine, fruit, olive oil or wool to their bases in England.

The once great French herring fishery had languished under Dutch competition. As late as 1700 the French imported from Holland almost 50 per cent more salted herring than their own fishery produced. This situation their government had tried to discourage, especially as the readiest means of bringing pressure on the Dutch was to raise the tariff on their herring, but the very establishment of customs duties gave the Farmers-General a counter-interest in importation; there was also an opposition of interest here between the trading towns like Rouen and the fishing ports, especially Dieppe. The French fishery was not to be saved by State action, however, for the Franco-Dutch treaty at Utrecht forbade prohibitions and reduced import duties to the level of 1664. With the herring trade in decline, the ports west of Dieppe concentrated more on the cod fishery. At a peak between 1678 and 1688, the French Newfoundland fishery employed 300 vessels and 20,000 men in a typical year—considerably more than the English. Its very scale, however, made it highly vulnerable to war, if only because the navy competed for the fishermen. In 1702 sailings from St Malo and Granville numbered five score, but from 1703 to 1712 seldom approached as many as 30 per annum; during the Nine Years War, after 113 sailings in 1688, the average was only 18.[1] The French fishery was more simply organized than the English: it was

[1] Rennes, Arch. Dép. d'Ille-et-Vilaine, Amirauté 9B, 402–7; J. Delumeau, *Le Mouvement du port de Saint-Malo à la fin du XVIIᵉ siècle* (Rennes, 1966), pp. 272–3. The movements of these vessels on return to Europe, which were complex and prolonged, are analysed in idem, 'Les terreneuviers malouins à la fin du XVIIᵉ Siècle', *Annales* (*E.S.C.*), 16ᵉ année (1961), pp. 665–85.

largely a 'wet' fishery in war-time and to that extent less in need of local drying-stages and settlements ashore. Moreover, attempts to develop multilateral trade between Placentia, Canada, the West Indies and France met with little success. Thus the French cod fishery, even in prosperity, was not the empire-building force that was the English; it was more important as the basis of a carrying trade in the Mediterranean, where Marseilles in particular had close links with St Malo. At Utrecht the French lost Placentia and all claims to territorial sovereignty in Newfoundland: they might land on designated sections of the coast to dry their catch, but could not build permanent structures or stay the winter there; Louisbourg, on Cape Breton Island, displaced Placentia in the defensive system, but was little used by fishing vessels. Yet the French cod fishery recovered quickly after the war. In 1719 it employed 500 vessels, and it grew continuously until in 1740 its gross annual earnings attained the startling equivalent of £1 m.

So far we have been dealing with commodities rooted in the old north European economy and important as much for bulk as value. When we look beyond the seas, we come to classes of commodities much more valuable in proportion to their bulk and of much newer importance in the European economy. Though cod had been the first commodity to draw the French and English regularly to North America, it now represented only a small part of North America's economic relations with Europe, while other important branches of North American trade concerned Europe only indirectly, if at all: thus the rapidly developing economies of New England, New York and Pennsylvania depended largely on exporting provisions and timber to the West Indies. North America and the West Indies taken as a whole, however, were able to buy what they needed in Europe thanks to furs, tobacco, and above all sugar.

Furs may be divided into the luxury furs used on the pelt for garments and the staple furs used by hatters or felt-makers (beaver, musk-rat, coney, hare). The principal source of luxury furs was now Siberia, and eastern (with central) Europe was the chief centre of consumption. In western Europe staple furs were of much greater importance: virtually everyone wore a hat, whereas luxury furs were going out of fashion. Cheap felts could be made from local or imported coney and hare, but the best required beaver; in the early eighteenth century, 65 per cent of English fur imports were staple furs and over 50 per cent beaver alone. By this time, of the English colonies, only New York, with its superior water communications into the interior, still had an important fur trade. From Canada, where the river systems of the St Lawrence and Hudson's Bay tapped seemingly inexhaustible sources of beaver, fur remained the only significant export. Since North America produced much more beaver and coney than England or France could use, considerable quantities—

70 per cent in the case of England—were re-exported to the great fur marts of Amsterdam and Hamburg. During these years, moreover, warfare in Hudson's Bay threw on to the market great stores of pelts taken as spoils. Much of this *castor sec* or 'parchment' beaver—unsoftened, that is, by the sweat of Indians—ultimately found its way to Russia, where artisans used a secret process to comb out the underfur (*duvet*), leaving only the long guard hairs on the skin. These combed pelts usually came back to Hamburg for use in garments, the beaver wool as frequently returning to Holland and France for use by feltmakers. In the short run, however, shipments to Russia tended to stabilize western fur markets.[1] Military successes and the St Lawrence route to the interior gave the French a permanent edge over the English in the importation of beaver pelts. Yet the English had certain advantages. The Indians in general preferred English manufactures. The Hudson's Bay Company did not have to support a colonial government; and when Britain recovered the Bay at Utrecht, the Company had passed its time of greatest trial and emerged with a sure supply of superior pelts. Improvements in western combing techniques by 1713 made it no longer necessary to send the difficult *castor sec* to Russia. The immigration of Huguenot felt-makers was giving the London hat industry a technological pre-eminence which enabled it to treble its exports in 1700–25—about 70 per cent to Europe (largely Spain and Portugal), the rest to North America and the West Indies. This was a classic entrepôt industry: by 1725, hat exports were worth almost six times as much as fur imports.

Several times more important than fur was tobacco. By the 1680s, large-scale commercial cultivation for the European market had contracted primarily to Brazil, Virginia and Maryland. In the West Indies tobacco was yielding to more profitable crops, while the production of 'Varinas'—grown in small patches by the Indians along the Venezuelan coast and worth several times as much per pound as the commoner Brazilian or Chesapeake leaf—seems to have been relatively static; much of it was acquired surreptitiously by the Dutch. The later seventeenth century saw a most dynamic growth of the more progressive sections of the European tobacco trade. If the Spanish stagnated at high prices and the Brazilian was seriously hurt by declining prices, the Chesapeake trade continued to thrive, for all that it suffered from the slump in prices. London imports rose from 7·37 m. lb. in 1662–3 to 25 m. in the glut years 1696–7 and 1700–1; total English imports more than doubled between 1672 and 1700 (37·8 m. lb.). Tobacco, like fur, was an almost ideal colonial commodity in that as imports grew a rising surplus became available for re-export, buttressing the nation's 'balance of trade'. As a

---

[1] E. E. Rich, 'Russia and the Colonial Fur Trade', *Econ. Hist. Rev.* 2nd ser. vol. VII (1954–5), pp. 307–28; M. G. Lawson, *Fur: a Study in British Mercantilism, 1700–1775* (1943). Cf. R. H. Fisher, *The Russian Fur Trade, 1550–1700* (Univ. of Calif. Publications in History, vol. 31, 1943).

whole, English re-exports tended to grow much more rapidly than imports: in 1668–9 re-exports stood at over half the level of imports, but *ca.* 1700 at almost two-thirds. Nearly as high a proportion of Portuguese imports was probably re-exported.

The great re-export mart for English, Portuguese and Spanish tobacco alike was Holland; even in 1697–1701, after a decline, the percentage of English tobacco going to Holland was nearly 40 per cent. Amsterdam was the tobacco-manufacturing as well as the tobacco-trading centre of Europe. Dutch manufacturers mixed expensive leaf from all the colonies with inexpensive leaf grown in the Low Countries and Germany, to produce moderately priced blends of cut and roll tobacco that could not be matched elsewhere. They supplied much of Germany and all northern Europe, much to the embarrassment of the English manufacturers, who, confined to Virginia and Maryland leaf, found themselves underpriced all through the North. Dutch tobacco cultivation was centred about Amersfoort, spreading east into Gelderland, Overijssel and the Hohenzollern duchy of Cleves. There was also an extensive cultivation of an inferior leaf in Brandenburg and Pomerania, and some at scattered inland places between Alsace and Hungary. By far the most important was the Dutch growth. Its greatest stimulus came from the wars of 1689–1713, when colonial deliveries were irregular and the price of Virginia rose at least 50 per cent at Amsterdam: the price advantage of 'Amersfoort' or 'Inland', previously rather tenuous, now became decisive and production soared. Hence, by the middle of the Succession War, English re-exports of 15–20 m. pounds a year had to compete on the Continent with a production in the United Provinces and Cleves of at least 15 m. lb., with Brandenburg-Pomerania adding perhaps 13 m., France 6–8 m., to say nothing of an 'Interior' production (Alsace to Hungary) of up to 20 m. lb. and about 6–7 m. from Brazil. Not until the 1720s did England regain (and in fact exceed) the export levels of 1697–1701.

Tobacco consumption had gradually been spreading for a century from small urban and courtly coteries to the populations at large. The last area to be conquered was Russia, where the Church forbade tobacco to all but foreigners. In 1697, for reasons fiscal and ideological, Peter authorized it and made its importation a State monopoly. As a consequence of the tsar's visit to London, this was farmed to a syndicate of English merchants who hoped to supply all Russia from Virginia. They had to give up their contract after two years, when the Russian government proved unwilling or unable to stop the smuggling into Russia proper of duty-free tobacco from the Cossack territories.[1] An even greater market for foreign tobacco was to develop in France. Despite Colbert's vision of self-sufficiency and of an export trade to the North, the greater ease of collecting duty on

[1] J. M. Price, *The Tobacco Adventure to Russia* (Trans. Amer. Phil. Soc. new ser. vol. 51, pt. 1, Philadelphia, 1961.)

imported leaf induced him to confine the cultivation within France to a few small areas, mostly along the middle Garonne. John Law, with more rigorous Scots logic, suppressed these plantations in 1719–20. In the French Antilles production had almost ceased by 1700, partly because the succeeding monopolists in France would not pay a sufficiently high price, and France increasingly depended on Amsterdam supplies of foreign tobacco, even in war. In 1697–1702, however, the French mono-polists began to make major purchases directly in England. After 1713 France became the second most important market for British tobacco; and after 1730, the first.

If tobacco was esteemed as an entrepôt commodity, sugar was still more highly valued as an empire-builder, for it employed more hundreds of ships and more capital. Further, whereas tobacco consumption in western Europe had reached something of a plateau by 1700, sugar con-sumption was still increasing rapidly. It was by then a significant index of colonial success that the British sugar colonies led in production, followed by those of Portugal, France and Holland. The older Brazilian production declined from 27,200 tons in 1670 to 21,800 in 1710.[1] This was higher than the output of the French West Indies, estimated to have risen from 18 m. lb. in 1682 to 30 m. in 1701. The Dutch were vigorously developing their much smaller cultivation, particularly in Surinam, but the marketing of British and French sugar passed out of their immediate control.

By 1701 the British West Indies were sending home 52 m. lb. and exporting to North America besides. English sugar imports were worth more than double the tobacco. In the last third of the seventeenth century production more than doubled. It grew henceforward at a more modest pace—less fast, indeed, than home consumption, so that what might have been an ideal trade pattern was distorted. While British sugar before 1688 had frequently gone to Curaçao or St Eustatius for direct shipment to Holland, after 1713 French and Dutch was slipped into the British islands for shipment as British, to an increasingly desirable English market. More important, re-exports—as late as 1698–1700 still 37·5 per cent of imports—were by 1733–7 to drop to a mere 4·2 per cent. It is said that British sugars could not compete in price with French and Dutch in foreign markets (principally the Netherlands and Germany): it is truer to say that British consumption tended to outstrip production, thus leaving the protected home market with less of an exportable surplus and hence less dependent on sales to the Continent, with the result that English prices rose significantly above continental levels. Manufacturing costs in England were irrelevant, for virtually all re-exports (except to Ireland) were unmanufactured.[2]

Sugar had developed rapidly in Martinique, Guadeloupe and St Chris-

[1] Cf. above, pp. 510 and 534.
[2] P.R.O., C.O. 390/5/47, fos. 83ᵛ–87; T. 64/276B/361, 364, 368, 371.

topher, though not at first in Saint-Domingue, where tobacco and indigo persisted longer. An increased supply of slaves from the 1690s gave further impetus to sugar, especially at Saint-Domingue, which after 1713 became the major French producer. The future was with the French: at Nantes alone, despite the ups and downs of war,[1] sugar imports in 1714 were about 150 per cent above the level of 1698, by 1733 four times better. French production, therefore, was accelerating after 1697, just when the British rate of growth was beginning to slacken and the Portuguese was in full decline. This increase eventually created a huge surplus for re-export. In the late 1690s France had only some 5 m. lb. available for re-export, while England was re-exporting almost 20 m. As late as 1714, indeed, re-exports at Nantes were only 14 per cent of imports; but by 1730 after a sevenfold increase in quantity, they formed over 70 per cent. These cargoes went mainly to Holland: it was the failure of the French to develop surer direct markets in Germany and the North for their colonial produce that explains why, as late as 1721–6, fully 63 per cent of the colonial produce passing the Sound came from Holland. The greatest of French entrepôt trades, moreover, owed much to the self-denial of the French consumer himself. In the late 1690s England and Ireland, with perhaps a third the population of France, consumed at least a third more sugar; and while their consumption was to increase at least 166 per cent in the next 30 years, French consumption, heavily taxed, seems to have been relatively static.

The remaining American produce may be quickly surveyed. In the 1690s rice culture became firmly established in South Carolina (with seed from Madagascar) and soon provided a useful re-export—about three-quarters of the rice imported by England from 1709—primarily to Holland and Germany,[2] although most of the crop was consumed locally or shipped to the West Indies. Far more important were the dyestuffs indispensable to the European textile trades. The insect cochineal was almost exclusively the product of the Spanish Indies. The Spaniards also had a natural monopoly of the much prized logwood which grew wild in the Yucatan peninsula and adjacent coasts to the south, although English loggers had penetrated the cutting trade in Campeche, Honduras and Nicaragua, satisfying English wants and bringing down prices from the heights earlier reached by Spanish monopoly: a more effective enforcement of Spanish restrictiveness drove the cutters from Campeche, only to increase their activities round Belize in the Gulf of Honduras and on the Moskito Shore of Nicaragua. The northern colonial powers had been much more successful in developing their own autarkic supplies of indigo: the Dutch in Java and Surinam, the French in Saint-Domingue,

---

[1] Shipping departures for the French islands from Nantes, Bordeaux and La Rochelle, 1702–12, are tabled in *Ann. du Midi*, t. 65 (1953), p. 66, where the La Rochelle figures for 1705 and 1711 should be corrected respectively to 38 and 34 [Ed.].

[2] P.R.O., T. 64/276B/320.

the English in Jamaica. After 1713, however, English industry became increasingly dependent on French supplies.

The rapid growth of nearly every branch of the American trade in this period was largely based upon the expanding African slave trade. The heavy labour of planting, harvesting and grinding sugar, above all, was best done by gangs of Africans, who gradually took over from white immigrants most of the skilled tasks as well. The Spanish colonists continued to depend on illegal importations from English and Dutch colonies (especially Curaçao) as well as on licensed foreign asientists—Genoese, Portuguese, French and English.[1] The considerable Portuguese and still greater Dutch slave trades continued on an important scale throughout this period, each carrying more Africans than the colonies of either nation required, thus providing surpluses for sale to the Spaniards and (in the case of the Dutch) to the French. Companies chartered in Denmark and Brandenburg were also taking a modest part in the slave trade; both made use of the Danish island of St Thomas, perhaps the most active centre of clandestine traffic in the Antilles during the wars, not least for trading between belligerents. The English slave trade, more recent in origin, was now the most dynamic. The Royal African Company of 1672 enjoyed a fairly effective monopoly until 1689, but in depriving the Company of its right to seize interlopers the Revolution left it impotent before the influx of 'free traders'. Parliament recognized the need to keep up the forts on the West African coast and by an Act of 1698 obliged the free traders to pay the Company a 10 per cent toll on goods exported thither. After 1712, when this ran out, the Company was commercially moribund except for a brief revival in the 1720s. Its defeat can be ascribed to the political weight of the interlopers and of the outports excluded by the London monopoly; the hostility of hardware and other manufacturers against a privileged buyer; and the irritation of colonists in the smaller islands and North America at the alleged neglect of their interests. It was also due to financial mismanagement at home, heavy and uncontrolled expenses in Africa, and the difficulty of collecting debts quickly from the planters who bought the slaves. In the nine years 1680–8, the Company delivered an annual average of 5,155 slaves to the West Indies; in 1690–8, only about 1,400 yearly; in the ten years after 1698, about 1,800 a year, as compared with about 7,500 for the so-called Separate Traders. The English thus came to outdistance all competitors. While London alone sent an average of over 50 ships a year to Africa (37 free, 13 Company) *ca.* 1698–1707,[2] the Dutch now sent only 12 or 14. Compared with English deliveries in this war decade of over 9,000 slaves a year, annual French deliveries even in 1716–18 are estimated at only

[1] Cf. above, pp. 364, 475–6 and 514–15.

[2] P.R.O., C.O. 388/10/H.108 and 388/11/I.8; T.70/1205/A.43. Cf. K. G. Davies, *The Royal African Company* (1957), pp. 310–12, 361–3.

1,800–2,000—insufficient for the French Antilles alone, which complained constantly of labour shortage. Thus French planters had also to depend on surreptitious trade with the Dutch and English: by 1716, when the Dutch had dropped out, the English were supplying the French with about 1,500 slaves a year. Yet the French slave trade was on the eve of a great expansion. In 1713, after the loss of the Asiento, it was effectively thrown open; by 1723–30 deliveries were to average over 7,200 yearly.[1]

Certain trades were valued in the seventeenth century for the shipping employed; others for the strategic commodities supplied; others for the many hands kept employed at home; still others for the favourable balances of trade produced on paper. The great East India trade fulfilled none of these desiderata. Since its cargoes were not bulky, shipping needs were small. Except saltpetre, it brought no strategic commodity to Europe. Although it brought raw silk to be worked up in Europe, it also brought silk and cotton fabrics that competed painfully with Western industry. Finally, its unfavourable commodity balance of trade produced the greatest and most continuous drain of specie and bullion out of Europe. For all that, it was heavily capitalized, politically powerful, highly if spasmodically profitable, and a major empire-building factor.

The Dutch had dominated all branches of the trade.[2] Though precise data are lacking, the evidence for 1683–1721 suggests that, while yielding primacy to the English in India proper, they retained a lead, if only a slight one, in the East India trade as a whole. In 1720–3 they sent an average of 39 ships a year compared with 20 English.[3] Moreover, the annual sale proceeds of the Dutch Company in the ten years 1709–19 averaged £1,326,000 compared with £979,000 for the English in 1708–17. But afterwards the Dutch lead narrowed, with average sales of £1,571,000 (1719–29) compared with £1,470,000 for the English (1718–27). Before the 1720s French trade was on a small scale. Colbert's State enterprise, never very successful, suffered seriously during the Nine Years War from the loss of Pondicherry and of many vessels. Even during the prosperous interlude of 1698–1702, the *Compagnie* sent out an average of less than 5 vessels a year (compared with 21 for the two English companies), and the average number of East Indiamen returning to France was then less than 4—compared with 19 Dutch. Early losses in the succeeding war were too much for the *Compagnie*, which dispatched no vessels after 1703 but entrusted the trade to licensed private merchants—from 1709 the Malouins.

---

[1] Paris, Bibl. de l'Institut, MS. 2387, fo. 243. Cf. Gaston Martin, *Nantes au XVIIIᵉ siècle: l'ère des négriers, 1714–1774* (1931).

[2] Much in this and the following paragraphs is based on K. Glamann, *Dutch-Asiatic Trade, 1620–1740* (Copenhagen, 1958). For the Portuguese, see above, pp. 516 ff. Cf. vol. v, ch. XVII (ii) and L. Dermigny, *La Chine et l'Occident: le commerce à Canton au XVIIIᵉ siècle* (4 vols. 1965), vol. I, pt. I.

[3] Cf. P.R.O., C.O. 390/6, pp. 183–95.

In the last years of its privilege (1715–19), scarcely one or two French vessels sailed yearly for the East:[1] exports were then estimated at under £200,000 per annum (compared with over £500,000 for the English), imports at £400,000 (compared with *ca.* £1,200,000 for the Dutch). As with so many other branches of French commerce, however, this trade was transformed during the Regency period. The new *Compagnie des Indes* of 1719, once it had the chaos of Law's conversion schemes behind it, was to push ahead with vigour.

Commodities from the East were many and varied, but generally more valuable than bulky. Only a few of the primary commodities competed with production nearer home. Both English and Dutch had substantially reduced shipments of indigo from India, depending respectively on the rising West Indian cultivation and on a new source in Java. Sugar was widely cultivated from Bengal to Taiwan; in Java commercially important plantations had been developed by Chinese planters and refiners. Before 1688 the Amsterdam price was usually too low to make it worth while to ship much of this production home; instead, the Dutch sold it in Japan in competition with Chinese sugar, and in north-west India and Persia in competition with Bengali. During the wars and after, however, higher European prices and mounting supplies encouraged them to send home more Javan sugar, first as ballast, then after 1715 as a commercial cargo, though trifling compared with the quantities from America.

Of enormously greater importance were commodities peculiar to Asia. The most famous was Malabar pepper, now overshadowed by the vaster supplies of Sumatra and Java (particularly of Bantam) developed by the Dutch. The Dutch monopoly was not complete. Rather than follow a restrictive buy-cheap and sell-dear policy, they preferred to buy more than they needed and to sell liberally in Europe and the East to discourage foreign competition. The English, after losing Bantam, developed alternative supplies at Benkulen in southern Sumatra and clung to the Malabar footholds from which they now obtained two-thirds of their pepper. Yet, in what was altogether a contracting trade, the Dutch improved their lead to better than two to one in 1715–20. No other nation supplied Europe with much pepper till the French and Ostend companies became active in the 1720s. The Dutch enjoyed a more valuable advantage in their monopolization of the clove, nutmegs, mace and cinnamon of the 'Spice Islands' of eastern Indonesia. Though sometimes exaggerated in the popular image of Dutch eastern trade, this monopoly was important for their Company's profits: in 1698–1700, although spices formed only 11·7 per cent of the invoice value of goods sent back from the East, they formed almost 25 per cent of Amsterdam sales receipts—a proportion

---

[1] P. Kaeppelin, *La Compagnie des Indes Orientales et François Martin*...(1908), appendix, pp. 657–61; B. Krishna, *Commercial Relations between India and England, 1601–1757* (1924), pp. 289–90, 323–4.

which remained strikingly constant, unlike the shrinking share of pepper. Between 1683 and 1721 the Company was usually able to maintain a fixed price for spices at home based on large reserve stocks, letting European demand adjust itself to this price. In Asia it generally sold at prices slightly below European to encourage consumption, but not so far below as to make it worth while for anyone to buy up spices in the open market there for Europe. This policy was not maintained without difficulty. The Company was constantly threatened by over-production in the East and frequently resorted to destruction of trees and crops; in Europe, too, its reserves sometimes proved excessive and after the peace of 1713 much over-age stock was burned. In general, European consumption declined perceptibly as Dutch price-fixing became established in the second half of the seventeenth century. Though the directors were aware of this elasticity of demand, they did not experiment with lower prices to see whether it could be exploited for larger gross profits at a higher level of consumption.

Far newer in Euro-Asian trade at this period were tea and coffee. Their real importance dates only from the 1690s. By 1698–1700, they accounted for 4·1 per cent of Amsterdam sales; by 1738–40, for almost 25 per cent. Unlike spices, they were commodities which the Dutch, at least before 1720, had to purchase and sell competitively on the open market.

Coffee was grown primarily in the hills of the Yemen and (an inferior variety) across the Red Sea in Ethiopia. The great mart was the Yemeni port of Mocha, whence coffee was distributed by ship and caravan throughout the coffee-drinking world, stretching from north-west India and Persia to the West. The major movement was up the Red Sea and overland to Egypt's Mediterranean ports, then by sea throughout the Mediterranean: when the coffee-drinking rage hit Europe in the 1690s, the French in particular were able to supply western Europe with great quantities through their Levant trade, and as late as the early 1700s the Dutch were still buying much of their coffee at Leghorn and Genoa. After 1700, however, this route was increasingly obstructed by privateers, Arab disturbances, and the exactions of the Egyptian and Red Sea pashas. Coinciding with increased demand in Europe, this forced the development of more direct European connections with Arabia. Already, the English and Dutch were sending from India coffee purchased at factories specially established at Mocha; in the new century English, Dutch and French purchasers penetrated inland from Mocha to the Yemeni hill country to buy nearer the source. By about 1710, all three nations were sending special ships to Mocha to bring coffee to Europe without transhipping in India or Ceylon. During the next ten years the Mocha coffee trade was at its height. In general, the English took the lead, imports rising from 213,444 lb. per annum in 1685–8 to 552,235 lb. in 1699–1701 (about half of this direct from the East) and to 1,350,689 lb. by 1713–15 (about three-quarters direct).[1] The Dutch, however, followed quickly: by the peak years 1717–21 they were sending from Mocha more than twice the English quantities, which had fallen off slightly. At that point the trade was revolutionized. The new demand for coffee had led to the introduction (or revitalization) of its cultivation not only in the Ile Bourbon (Réunion) and Java, but in Brazil, Surinam and the Antilles. None of the plantations there was at first very important. As late as 1721, 90 per cent of the coffee imported by the Dutch East India Company came from Mocha, only 10 per cent from Java. Within five years the proportions were reversed. This extraordinary new production enabled the Company to force down the price of coffee, and to leave the difficult Mocha trade to the English, French and Arab caravaneers. The 1730s saw the large-scale introduction of French West Indian coffee to complicate further the European market. By that time, however, popular preference had switched to tea.

In the 1680s, China tea was still an exotic and excessively expensive commodity in Europe—a medicine to many, a fashionable drink in court circles. The modest quantities so consumed could be picked up here and there in Asia without direct trade to China. In the 1680s the English gained access to Amoy; by 1700 both English and French were admitted to Canton. In the new century, with a direct supply assured, the trade blossomed, though not as rapidly as coffee. Average English imports of 16,000 lb. (1685–1700) increased to 197,000 lb. by 1711–17, then trebled in the next decade—to increase fivefold more by mid-century. The Dutch did not trade directly to Canton before 1728, but depended on supplies brought to Batavia by Chinese junks. This had the great advantage of avoiding a further silver drain to China, but meant that the Dutch purchased only limited quantities of tea and at relatively high prices.

The commodity which first drew the English to Canton and Amoy, however, was not tea but silk. Chinese raw silk had long been known in Europe, where it competed with the Italian product and the great output of Persia, carried overland from Ispahan to Aleppo or Smyrna. The silk trade was a royal monopoly in Persia, and whenever political conditions were right—generally when Persia was hostile to Turkey—schemes were set afoot by the European companies to redirect it to the Persian Gulf for shipment—with only short-lived success. In the later seventeenth century, a new and increasingly important source for both western and eastern trade developed in Bengal. When the parliamentary ban of 1678–85 on all imports from France stimulated English silk-weaving, the English East India supplanted the Levant Company as the principal importer by ordering immense quantities of raw silk from Bengal; after 1685 the Levant Company resumed its dominance. Meanwhile the Dutch had built up a much more solid trade in Bengal silk, based on good markets in Japan and Holland. In 1698–1700 they imported about two and a half

---

[1] P.R.O., C.O. 390/5, fo. 59 and Finch MSS., vol. xvi (F.T.3).

times as much Bengali silk as the English: while the English were still getting the bulk of their silk via Turkey and twice as much from Italy as from Bengal,[1] Dutch imports were 75 per cent Bengali, 16 per cent Persian, 9 per cent Chinese. The Persia–Turkey trade remained the predominant supplier of English raw silk—as Italy did of thrown silk—in the generation after 1713, though raw silk shipments from Bengal were gradually to increase with the extension of British trading strength there.

Though the textile group (raw materials and finished goods) declined from 43 per cent of Amsterdam sales *ca.* 1700 to 28 per cent in 1738–40, it remained the most important Dutch return from the East, thanks not so much to raw silk as to silk and cotton piece-goods. The Dutch had always prized their trade on the Coromandel Coast for its textiles, particularly cottons, which they could exchange for pepper and spices in Indonesia (so saving currency) and which they also sent home with Chinese and other Indian silks. Here the inter-Asian country trade was the more important until a great revolution occurred in European taste in the 1680s. Bizarrely printed and painted cotton and silk fabrics suddenly became the fashionable rage for both men and women. Sales of cottons at Amsterdam almost trebled. The English, having greater difficulty in obtaining returns from the East, had already been pushing textile purchases at Surat—the great international coastal vent for the manufacturing area about Ahmedabad, where local cotton and Persian raw silk were worked up. Even when political disturbances at the end of the century forced the English to transfer their main base to Madras, a major portion of their piece-goods continued to come from Surat. Indeed, English imports were still rather evenly divided between Surat, Coromandel and Bengal, whereas Dutch piece-goods imports had shifted more radically: 55 per cent from Bengal, 26 per cent from the Coromandel Coast, little from Surat. Nevertheless, the English trade was to grow much more rapidly in the new century.

Wrought silks and cottons, alone of East India goods, competed with native European industries. The competition was very sharp, for the English and Dutch Companies sent out both artisans and patterns for the direction of Indian workmen and eliminated middlemen, to ensure a production suitable for the European market. Indian competition, and the resulting social pressures, reached crisis level in the generation immediately following the 'Indian' craze of the 1680s—first in France, where all the difficulties of the textile manufactures (arising out of the international crisis of 1686 and the Huguenot emigration) were conveniently blamed on the importation of oriental silks and painted calicoes. A series of decrees in 1686 (not fully effective till 1689) prohibited the importation of eastern silks, cloth of silver and gold, and painted cottons. In 1700 a comprehensive code finally prohibited the importation of even white

[1] Cf. above, p. 551, n. 3.

calicoes, except by the *Compagnie* and the merchants of Marseilles, and then only for re-export. This calico ban lasted till 1759, but it was very difficult to enforce in a country where fashion still demanded *toiles peintes* and where fashion was king. Similar bans were adopted in Spain and Brandenburg. In Holland and Switzerland, however, the printing of white calicoes—much of it by French Huguenot émigrés—flourished, largely to meet an export smuggling demand. In England, the battle was rather prolonged; but in 1700 parliament finally forbade the use of wrought silks manufactured in India, Persia or China, and of calicoes 'painted, dyed, printed or stained there'. The English companies could, like the French, still store vast quantities of these fabrics in sealed warehouses for re-export, to the embarrassment of the Dutch. This warehouse trade was most considerable: even before the Act, half the calicoes imported into England had been re-exported. Unlike the French legislation of 1700, moreover, the Act allowed importation of white calicoes, so giving tremendous impetus to the English textile-printing industry until an Act of 1721 prohibited their use also. The English ban like the French was hard to enforce. It is doubtful whether the woollen industry in either country gained much by these prohibitions; the silk industries probably benefited more, but the principal beneficiaries were the smugglers.

An even greater problem posed by the East India trade to conventional commercial policy was that of shipments outward. Nowhere in the East was the demand for European produce sufficient to pay for all that Europeans wanted to buy. Despite an almost universal prejudice against it, there was no real alternative to the exportation of coin and bullion. Specie, in fact, formed over 80 per cent of English exports to the East (1708–30),[1] more like 90 per cent of Dutch (1714–28), and 76 per cent even of the much smaller French outward cargoes of 1716. In general, each Company could only expand its trade by further shipments of specie. Every device was tried to circumvent this drain. To avoid spending cash, Indonesian pepper and spices could be sold to the Chinese, Indian piece-goods to the Indonesians, and so on. The most hopeful trade was to Japan, for there cash could be obtained. The exclusive Dutch entry to Japan was one of the hinges of their dominant trade position: in some years they had got more specie from Japan than was sent from Holland. When the Japanese banned the export of silver in 1668, gold took its place in Dutch shipments thence. Successive Japanese depreciations of the gold content of their coins, however, made this trade less and less attractive. After the debasement of 1696, it was no longer profitable to export the gold *coubang* from Japan, though the Dutch kept on nevertheless, prepared to take a loss on the exchange to get the coins needed in India for buying the textiles which bought the spices of Indonesia. Fortunately for them,

---

[1] P.R.O., C.O. 390/6, pp. 183–95 Seventy per cent of English exports of precious metal, 1698–1719, went to the East Indies.

Japanese copper was available in large quantities after silver was cut off and gold depreciated. This crucial trade was at its height in 1681–2, when over 3 m. lb. of copper was exported in each year by the Dutch. Thereafter the trade declined slowly, owing in part to Japanese restrictions, in part to the increasing difficulty of selling silk in Japan after 1690 as the Japanese developed their own manufactures. Most of the copper, like the gold and silver, eventually went to India, but a surplus was sent home as ballast in spice ships, helping to free the Dutch in Europe from an exclusive dependence on Swedish copper and serving to moderate European copper prices.

The Levant trade[1]—here considered as an alternative routing for the Eastern trade—was also a considerable specie drain for the European nations engaged in it, particularly the French. Much, however, of the gold and silver expended by the Europeans in the Levant, for such commodities as Mocha coffee and Persian silk, was carried by the caravaneers eastward and southward to the homelands of those commodities. Hence the Dutch and others, trading to ports along the Arabian Sea and Persian Gulf, were able to tap large sources of this 'Moorish' gold and silver and bring it back into the course of European trade. There were thus counter-eddies in the great drain of specie from west to east.

As silver was worth more in the East than in Europe (in relation to gold), the English sent only silver; the Dutch sent chiefly silver, with only modest shipments of gold. The English and Dutch got their silver primarily by trade in and about Cadiz, where the Dutch had traditionally a great edge; the French got a good deal too by trade across the Pyrenees. Much Spanish silver also reached central Europe through Genoa. After 1660, however, though all the old silver distribution mechanisms continued to function, the supply of Spanish silver reaching Europe was only a fraction of what it had been. Credit stringency and sagging prices were generally characteristic of the peace years in the next two generations. On the other hand, the extraordinarily rapid development of the Brazilian gold mines altered the monetary situation in Europe after 1700.[2] England, the northern country with the major commercial connection with Portugal, was able to attract the greatest part of this gold; some of it went on to Holland or France,[3] but enough stayed in England to make possible the widespread substitution of gold for silver (undervalued and in short supply) in commercial transactions.

No European State liked the drain of specie to the East. The English were rather better situated in this respect than the French. Woollens rose from 58 per cent of English *merchandise* exports to the East in 1698–1710 to 70 per cent in 1710–30—iron and lead being the only other important cargoes besides silver—but for climatic reasons woollens could make

[1] Cf. above, ch. XVII and pp. 551–2.
[2] Above, pp. 534–5.
[3] P.R.O., T. 64/276B/391.

only a very limited contribution to eastward remittances. In the Levant, however, the market for English woollens and other goods made it unnecessary to send specie. The Marseilles merchants, by contrast, supported their much greater Levant trade by heavy shipments of specie. Only in the money-starved years after 1708 did cloth shipments from Marseilles become really substantial: after the war they actually exceeded those of the English.[1]

The slowness with which the French expanded cloth exports to the Levant was partly due to the generally depressed condition of their woollen industry in the generation after Colbert. Since the wools of Champagne, Berry, Languedoc and Provence did not suffice for French manufactures, the industry depended on imported material, especially when military demands rose. The best wools were Castilian, imported over the Pyrenees and forwarded by sea from Bayonne for the manufactures of Elbeuf, Abbeville and Sedan. Adding the less fine wools of Aragon and the coarse wools of Navarre, French imports of Spanish wools *ca.* 1700 were worth 9 m. or 10 m. *livres* annually. French industry was therefore peculiarly susceptible to wartime interruptions of Spanish supplies; the coarse wools of the Levant and Africa were used only in the cruder peasant handicrafts and not permitted in military uniforms, while Baltic supplies or those smuggled out of England and Ireland by the 'owlers' were only a drop in the bucket of French needs.

Although small independent handicraft manufactures survived in the Cévennes and Pyrenees, most of the French industry, as in other advanced countries, was organized on the putting-out system, particularly in Normandy (dependent on the merchant-manufacturers of Rouen), Picardy and French Flanders. Around Lille a single clothier kept over 3,000 outworkers busy in 1700: this quality industry was only temporarily hurt by the siege of 1708 and enemy occupation. The manufacture of Picardy, centred on Amiens, used a greater variety of wools to make a wider variety of cloths and in general suffered less from the war. More important was the great Norman manufacture. It is true that the manufacture around Elbeuf, employing over 8,000 persons working up Segovia wool into *draperies fines* to resemble English and Dutch products, had passed its peak by the 1690s and was on the decline; but the lesser centres in Normandy, either imitating Elbeuf styles more cheaply or making serges and *draps communs*, held their own better. Not so the recently important Champagne manufacture, now far behind that of Normandy: Sedan in particular was hurt by the emigration of Huguenot masters,

[1] Cf. above, p. 552. French *returns* from the Levant were dominated by textile raw materials: 24·3 per cent silk and 15·3 per cent cotton *ca.* 1700–2. In the ensuing decades, silk shipments stagnated. By the 1720s they were surpassed by those of cotton, which had steadily and rapidly increased. See R. Paris, *De 1660 à 1789: Le Levant* (G. Rambert, ed. *Histoire du commerce de Marseille* vol. v, 1957), pp. 505–11.

which left 2,000 artisans unemployed in the town; at Rheims and Rethel, the number of workshops was halved between 1686 and 1699 by the wool shortage and emigration. Other centres suffered even more, although at Châlons and Langres the development of new qualities of cloth mitigated the effects of the adverse commercial climate and the decay of older lines. Elsewhere, all over France, there were scattered manufactures mostly working for the local market but sometimes quite important. Romorantin in the Orléanais specialized in cloth for army uniforms and Châteauroux in Berry employed over 10,000 persons. There were also important manufactures in Provence, Dauphiné and especially Languedoc, producing cheap cloths for the Levant, North Africa and the Antilles. A more concentrated type of production was encouraged by the State for special purposes. In Languedoc the privileged *manufactures royales* at Carcassonne, Conques, Saptes and elsewhere employed several hundred workers under one roof. Much more famous was the Van Robais undertaking at Abbeville, employing 1,500 workers by 1700. At that time only scouring, shearing and fulling took place in company-owned buildings, but between 1708 and 1714 the firm consolidated all operations from spinning onwards in its own extended buildings. The resistance of the workers to this new discipline forced government strike-breaking intervention in 1716. So vast an undertaking, employing 3,000 to 5,000 workers by the 1720s, was nevertheless a freak in the textile world of that time. The putting-out system still had great vitality. It was indeed growing throughout Europe.

In general, the French woollen industry had by 1708–10 reached the end of the long slump following the revocation of the Edict of Nantes: despite signs of over-production *ca.* 1715, the industry as a whole continued to grow. The Dutch, by contrast, remained depressed. The great Leiden industry, which in 1661–71 had produced 129,000 cloths a year, turned out only 83,000 on average in 1699–1701; after very difficult times during the ensuing war, it recovered to only 72,500 per annum in 1717–26. Leiden's wartime difficulties owed much to the shortage of Spanish and other imported wools. Of more permanent injury was the growth of highly protected manufactures in former markets like France and Prussia and the loss to the French after 1713 of the open market in the Ottoman empire. In southern Germany and the Habsburg lands, Dutch and English cloth sales were both impeded by high transport costs, river tolls and protective duties.[1] Moreover, the growth of indigenous manufactures in Silesia and Lusatia, utilizing the good raw wool of Silesia, satisfied much of the demand locally and in southern Germany, besides sending several thousand pieces yearly to Poland and Russia *ca.* 1715. Though some houses reputedly vended cloth as good as the English, Silesian woollens,

---

[1] On Habsburg commercial policy and the economy of the Habsburg lands, see above, pp. 602 ff.

worsteds, fustians, etc. were usually of the commonest grade. A better sort was available in Germany from the manufacture around Aachen (Aix-la-Chapelle).

Much greater than the German, indeed ten times greater than even Leiden in value of output, was the extensive English cloth industry—probably the greatest industry of any description in Europe. Though constantly lamenting one affliction or another, its production was moderately increasing in this period. Wool consumed in manufacturing in England and Wales increased from about 40 m. lb. *ca.* 1695 to about 57 m. *ca.* 1741. The native wool itself was a tremendous national asset: of the approximately £2 m. worth of raw wool used by the English and Welsh industry in the 1690s, roughly nine-tenths came from England and Wales, the remainder primarily from Ireland, secondarily from Spain.[1] The West Country—classic home of the putting-out system, from stagnating Wiltshire and Gloucester to rising Devon—manufactured the finest cloth, was more likely to use Spanish wool, and was in general more export-oriented than the other cloth-making areas. War protected it from changes in foreign fashion, and not until the 1720s did its serges feel the full force of competition from Norfolk stuffs,[2] said to have employed 120,000 persons (at lower wages) near Norwich alone. Potentially the most dynamic area, however, was the West Riding of Yorkshire, home *par excellence* of the smaller independent master employing only a few apprentices and journeymen, although the putting-out system existed there too on a limited scale. The north traditionally produced coarser cloths, notably kerseys, essentially for the domestic market: the new element *ca.* 1700 was the revivification of the worsted industry round Bradford—ultimately the most serious challenge to Norfolk. In the newer worsted trade, the entrepreneurs were more substantial and the putting-out system more widely used.

About 1700, two-fifths or more of all English woollens and worsteds were exported, providing indeed about five-sixths of English exports of native manufactures and three-fifths of aggregate English exports, though this last proportion would diminish to only a third by 1750. Woollen exports had increased only about a third in value between the 1660s and 1700 (then valued at about £3 m.) and took till 1750 to increase by another third. The trade had experienced great difficulties in Charles II's reign from new foreign rivals and hostile foreign duties, but recovered by 1688. The wars created military and speculative demands abroad but also disrupted foreign markets, bringing both very bad periods (e.g. 1696–7) and very good (e.g. 1708–10). The post-Utrecht years were erratic and marked no real advance till the middle twenties. Holland and Germany—though their share dropped from 44 per cent of the English foreign market in

[1] T. 64/275/147.
[2] W. G. Hoskins, *Industry, Trade and People in Exeter, 1688–1800* (Manchester, 1935), pp. 74–7.

1699–1701 to 36 per cent in 1716—remained the major single market area, especially for the outports, which had no Levant or Eastern trade. Then came southern Europe, particularly gold-rich Portugal (17 per cent in 1716) and Spain (11 per cent), the Ottoman empire, the Northern countries and the American plantations (both below 5 per cent), and Flanders; for all the trouble they gave, the East Indies were a relatively small market, while France bought only smuggled wool.[1] Woollen exports had been encumbered by the monopolies of the Hamburg Company (the old Merchant Adventurers) and other chartered companies, but an Act of 1689 removed all restrictions saving only the privileges of the Levant, Africa, Russia and Eastland Companies; by 1699 the last three trades were in effect open to all. Thereafter, instead of the Merchant Adventurers exporting cloth to a staple abroad, Dutch and German merchants increasingly bought direct through agents in London and the cloth ports;[2] these factors, at first English, were gradually supplanted by foreign buyers sent over expressly, like the Barings of Bremen at Exeter. Thus the staple at which English sellers met foreign buyers was in part shifting to England, though great London merchants continued to export on their own account, especially to southern Europe.

The linen trade was more evenly spread over northern Europe than the woollen. Flax was grown everywhere and the necessary technical skills were not difficult to come by. In general, both quality and price declined from west to east, the finest and dearest linens coming from France, the coarsest and cheapest from Russia. Since, however, there was a great and growing demand for inexpensive linens, especially in the West Indies and North America, the underlying dynamic of the industry in this period was the eastward shift towards cheaper raw materials and labour.

The substantial French industry had markets in Britain, Italy, Spain and Spanish America for a wide range of its products, ranging from the canvas, lockrams and dowlas of Brittany and Normandy to the cambrics and lawns of Picardy, Artois and French Flanders. In 1686–8 the English perhaps imported £700,000 worth of French linens each year, while Cadiz alone took more than £450,000 per annum for the Indies. Yet the French position in both these markets, even in the eighties, was challenged by the newer imitative manufactures of Holland and Brabant, and by even newer ones in Saxony and elsewhere in Germany. During the wars German linens acquired a large and permanent share of the Spanish and American markets, while German imitation lockrams, dowlas and 'French' canvas did well in England. With the aid of Britain's temporary prohibitions and permanent discriminatory duties against the French, Saxon and Dutch linens were permanently to replace French there: in the decade after 1713, besides the cheaper linens from Germany, England

---

[1] P.R.O., C.O. 388/15/20; 390/5, fo. 37ᵛ; 390/7/36; 390/12, pp. 2 ff.; cf. T. 64/275/146.
[2] P.R.O., C.O. 388/11/76.

got its lawns almost entirely from Holland, its cambrics mainly from Holland and Flanders. Outside France the trade was centred in Holland. There a complex pattern had evolved in which the brown (unfinished) linens of the southern Netherlands, Westphalia and the modern Lower Saxony were brought to the bleaching-grounds at Haarlem—in great measure for re-export by Amsterdam to England, Spain and Portugal. By 1700, this complex included the linen-producing areas of Upper Saxony, Bohemia and Silesia; but the greatest days of Haarlem were already in the past, for bleacheries were being erected in Westphalia and deeper in Germany. Even in the 1680s, the English Merchant Adventurers imported considerable quantities of Westphalian linens direct from Hamburg; with the end of that Company's privileges, Bremen became the outlet for the direct shipment of Westphalian linens and yarn to England, though Hamburg remained the chief supplier to Spain.[1]

Further east, linen manufacture for export was spreading in Polish and Russian villages. Modest Russian exports from Archangel in the 1670s grew substantially in Peter's reign as Dutch agents diffused an improved technology among the peasantry. The amount of linen cloth exported from the Baltic quadrupled between 1680 and 1700. The new industry suffered seriously during the Great Northern War but surpassed its 1700 level in the 1720s. While Danzig had almost monopolized this trade before 1700, followed far behind by Königsberg, the spread of the craft from Poland into Russia revolutionized its trade pattern: by 1721–5, 71 per cent of the linen leaving the Baltic came from St Petersburg and only 29 per cent from Danzig. In the 1720s as in the 1680s a good three-quarters went to England. Hence this new branch of the industry grew up independent of the Dutch entrepôt.

Another new branch was to develop in the British Isles. Attempts to establish a linen industry in England had on the whole failed, in part owing to labour costs, though there was greater success with sailcloth; but Ireland was an underdeveloped country with a cheap labour force also experienced in textiles. Since official policy restricted Irish woollen exports after 1699, linen manufacture provided a convenient alternative employment. Further, the best French linen technology had been introduced by Huguenot refugees from St Quentin after 1685. From 1696, Irish linen and yarn were imported into England duty-free. To encourage the manufacture the Irish government set up a Linen Board in 1711. Under its aegis, exports almost doubled between 1711 and 1721 and were to double again by 1734. The linen industry in Scotland also developed rapidly, particularly after the Union.

A somewhat less important manufacture in Europe was silk, long established in northern Italy, Switzerland, the papal territories of Avignon and the Comtat Venaissin, besides Paris, Tours and the Rhône valley. The

---

[1] P.R.O., C.O. 388/7, fo. 14 and 388/11/76; cf. T. 64/275/164.

French industry depended for its raw material primarily upon Italy, but Persian silk from Smyrna made an increasing contribution. Italian silk for the Lyons manufactures was already 'thrown' (i.e. in the form of thread); for weaving elsewhere, the centre for working the raw Levantine silk was Avignon. By a decree of 1687, however, foreign silk entering France, whether raw silk through Marseilles or silk thread from Avignon, had to pass through the staple at Lyons and pay toll there. The obligatory transportation up the Rhône and down again was felt as a special burden by the Languedoc silk industry around Nîmes. Yet Avignon remained a major silk-throwing centre until the plague of 1721–2 scattered the workmen to Lyons and Nîmes, giving a great stimulus to silk-throwing in France proper. In the last years of Louis XIV renewed efforts were made to establish mulberry groves in the south, particularly in Dauphiné and round Nîmes; with the success of this new raw silk production by the 1720s, silk-throwing and weaving tended to become more widely diffused throughout the countryside. The French silk-weaving industry had been considerably advanced by Colbert, particularly at Nîmes, whither a ban on foreign fabric had encouraged the immigration of weavers from nearby Avignon. But while the Lyons trade was tightly organized in gilds open only to Catholics, Nîmes was relatively unregulated and many of its masters were Protestants, so that the anti-Huguenot measures proved particularly unsettling there. The emigration of the masters led to considerable unemployment: some workers followed them, others returned to Avignon. The silk industry at Lausanne was formed entirely of artisans from Nîmes, as were to a lesser extent those at Amsterdam and London.

England had provided almost as good a market for French silks as linens. Despite the boycott of 1679–85, the English weaving industry made only limited headway until reinvigorated by skilled immigrants and the wartime interruptions of French trade. Between 1689 and 1713 a well-protected, well-entrenched industry came into existence, strong enough to join effectively in the fight against Bolingbroke's Anglo-French commercial treaty of 1713. It depended for thrown silk on Italy, for raw silk on the Persia–Turkey trade (later on Bengal). The English had considerable difficulty in converting raw silk into thread strong enough for warp until the Lombe brothers, in 1716, mastered the technique of the Piedmontese throwing machine—jealously guarded in their factory at Derby.

Textiles were the great industries of this time in capital, labour force and output alike. The 'heavy industry' we know was much less important, vital as were its products in war. England exported considerable quantities of tin and lead—to France above all in peace, to Holland in war—but coal was her chief mineral and she was Europe's chief coal producer: it has been doubted[1] 'whether the entire annual production of the Continent [ca. 1700] amounted to more than a sixth of the annual

---

[1] J. U. Nef, *The Rise of the British Coal Industry* (2 vols. 1932), vol. I, p. 129.

production of Great Britain'. Output in the 1680s, estimated at about 3 m. tons per annum was increasing steadily, especially with the advent of Newcomen's pumping engine. About 16 per cent was raised in Scotland, 41 per cent in Northumberland and Durham, 29 per cent in the Midlands. Coal raised close to navigable waters, as in Northumberland and Durham, could be carried long distances; the rest had to be consumed within fifteen miles of the pithead—the economic limit of hauling by cart. London was the chief consumer of waterborne coal, though the price there was never less than four or five times the pithead price. The Thames valley consumed about 460,000 tons annually, as compared with 160,000 exported—three-fifths to Holland, about a tenth each to France and Germany. Despite Colbert, total French production in 1715 was less than that of a single Tyneside manor. The principal mining areas were Forez (round St Etienne), whence coal could be shipped down the Loire, and the nearby Rive-de-Gier in the Lyonnais from which it went by water to Lyons and down the Rhône. The larger German production was centred in 1700 round Aachen and in Saxony, but above all in the Ruhr. Only in the zone from Liège to Mons did exploitation remotely resemble the English; yet it is doubtful whether Belgian production in all was more than a third that of Durham-Northumberland, although it did support a thriving metallurgical industry and provide an important export to France and Holland by water.

Iron ore and charcoal were sufficiently available to maintain in most countries an iron industry just adequate for domestic needs, as (notably) in France; only a few areas, such as the bishopric of Liège, had resources of their own to support an ironware manufacture for export. Chief exceptions were England and Sweden—England as the only significant iron-importer, Sweden as a large exporter. The commonplace that the English iron industry stagnated from 1660 to 1760, because of forest 'exhaustion', is inaccurate: the industry grew steadily if modestly, particularly in the war years. Forests were far too valuable in England for timber to be chopped down for firewood: charcoal came, rather, from coppices of not more than twenty years' growth or the thinnings of timber plantations, and these were well enough planned to keep the industry going, without allowing for rapid expansion.[1] More decisive perhaps was the high cost of English labour—reflected in both the price of charcoal and the processing costs in iron-making. Therefore, with her iron-using trades expanding much faster than her iron-making, England increasingly depended on imported iron. In 1699–1701, about four-fifths was Swedish; indeed, about two-thirds of all the iron shipped out of the Baltic in 1720 was for England. Within the Baltic, Sweden's pre-eminence seemed unassailable. Not only was her industry technologically the most advanced

---

[1] Abraham Darby started smelting iron ore with coke at Coalbrookdale in 1709, but his process long remained secret.

in Europe; it used an exceptionally pure ore, abundant forests close to the forges, and remarkably cheap (because often seasonal) labour. The government's attempts, however, to conserve the forests for primary production, by moving the bar-iron forges to regions remote from the pig-iron furnaces, was a portent that the second of these advantages would not endure.[1] In the eighteenth century the industry grew much more slowly than in the seventeenth, production increasing only 27 per cent between 1697 and 1747. Exports, which absorbed at least three-quarters of production, ceased to grow after 1740. By then Russian exports, only 2 per cent of shipments out of the Baltic in 1721–5, were beginning to count.

These separate trades would be much more readily comprehensible in their entirety if we could add them all up and allot to each trade, country and year its share in the total activity of the European economy. Only for English and French foreign trade can we make even the most tentative over-all calculations and comparisons. Of the two, England's was the more active, particularly in re-exports—£2 m. in 1699–1701, compared with only £1·2 m. for the French in 1716.[2] Both countries exported far more manufactures than they imported, and both imported more industrial raw materials than they exported—the normal condition for 'industrialized' States and the desideratum of mercantilist planners. In both countries, too, manufactures were dominated by textiles. These constituted 87 per cent of English imports and exports, 69 per cent of French exports.

French foreign trade was directed principally towards Spain, Italy, Switzerland and the two Netherlands. Italy and Spain between them took three-quarters of French manufactures exported within Europe, mainly in return for silk and silver respectively; by contrast, the United Provinces —the greatest mart for French produce—took almost no manufactures. The next important French trades were with Germany, French America and Great Britain, in that order. British trade was heavily orientated (46 per cent in 1699–1701) towards Germany, the two Netherlands and France, exports here exceeding imports in the ratio of 15:7. Over half the imports were linens; the exports were dominated by woollens (45 per cent), followed by the re-export of calicoes, sugar and tobacco. Within this area the Dutch trade was the most important, though relatively static between 1700 and 1725; the German trade was much more dynamic, particularly after 1720, when direct English exports to Germany became relatively commoner. Next was England's trade with southern Europe (23 per cent in 1699–1701), the principal import being Italian and Turkish silk, the principal export woollens: it was silk that enabled Italy to replace Spain

---

[1] E. F. Heckscher, *An Economic History of Sweden* (Harvard edn. 1954), pp. 97–8.

[2] One reason for the increase in French exports after 1710 may be the substantial devaluations of the *livre* between 1709 and 1726, when it was stabilized at one-third below its value in 1693–1700. Cf. [Alfred de Foville], 'Le Commerce extérieur de la France depuis 1716', *Bulletin de statistique et de législation comparée*, vol. XIII (1893), pp. 48–51.

by 1715 as the principal source of English imports from the south; Portugal had replaced Spain by 1705 as the principal destination of English exports thither. In third place came the English colonies (16 per cent in 1699–1701), imports being dominated by sugar and tobacco, exports mostly by manufactures, both English (notably woollens) and foreign (notably linens). The East Indies accounted for only 7 per cent of English trade: for the Dutch it was closer to 10 per cent.

Viewing all the European exchanges together, we are struck by the persistence of that late medieval 'map of commerce', whose principal artery ran from the Baltic, by way of the Low Countries, to the Bay of Biscay and the Iberian coasts. Important links connected it with Norway, the British Isles and the Mediterranean. The sixteenth century had added remoter connections to northern Russia, the Americas and the Far East, but the Baltic–Cadiz route remained the greatest employer of shipping. Upon it was based the continued maritime pre-eminence of the United Provinces. The following table[1] shows the annual average number of ships passing the Sound in the decades before and after the wars:

Nationality	1681–1690	1721–1730
United Provinces	1,902 (47 %)	1,612 (42 %)
England and Scotland	592 (15 %)	791 (20 %)
Danish-Norwegian	538 (13 %)	489 (13 %)
Swedish	470 (12 %)	390 (10 %)
Total	4,011	3,796

In reality, the Dutch lead over the British in the Baltic was much more pronounced, yet diminishing much more rapidly, than these figures suggest. The average Dutch vessel here was still bigger, but Dutch vessels were getting smaller and the English larger: at Danzig, in 1688, the average Dutch ship was almost four times larger than the average English-Scots ship; by 1729, it was only twice as large.[2] That the lead of the Dutch here was narrowing was one of their lesser worries. Far more serious was the dubious health of their general trade complex, many branches of which were now contracting: Cadiz silver, Bordeaux wine, Danzig grain, and with them the Dutch manufactures they supported and the Dutch entrepôt generally.

That the Dutch were nevertheless to remain strong in their accustomed trades is shown by a calculation of their shipping in 1740 (excluding coastal and fishing craft and the East Indies fleets):[3]

---

[1] These and all other Sound traffic data from N. E. Bang and K. Korst, *Tabeller over Skibsfart og Varetransport gennem Øresund, 1661–1783* (2 vols. in 4, Copenhagen-Leipzig, 1930–53). Cf. below, p. 893.

[2] W. Vogel, 'Beiträge zur Statistik der deutschen Seeschiffart im 17. und 18. Jahrhundert, II', *Hansische Geschichtsblätter*, Jg. 57 (1932–3), pp. 78–151.

[3] Amsterdam, Gemeente Archief: Archief Burgemeester, no. 137, cited in M. Gideonse, 'Dutch Baltic Trade in the Eighteenth Century' (MS. thesis, Harvard, 1932), p. 45.

Trade	Ships	Lasts
Baltic and Norwegian	870	130,500
Archangel	33	7,590
Greenland fisheries	146	—
English and Channel	81	2,196
French and Biscayan	248	17,360
Spanish, Portuguese and Mediterranean	216	24,840
Guinea and West Indies	80	8,000

This calculation might have been made a century earlier, so familiar are all its proportions. A similar calculation made in 1670 (excluding the Greenland fishery) shows the European and Mediterranean trades combined as scarcely smaller: 1,160 ships totalling 164,000 lasts, against 1,448 and 182,486.[1] More startling conclusions emerge for the Guinea and West Indies trade, estimated to employ 100 vessels totalling 20,000 lasts in 1670, compared with 80 of only 8,000 lasts in 1740: even though this estimated halving of average tonnage capacity may be exaggerated, we are faced here with an ominous decline in what was a rising section of the shipping economy at large.

This fixity of interest becomes more striking when we compare Dutch with English data.[2] The entire European and Mediterranean trades employed only 56 per cent of English merchant tonnage in 1686, compared with about 77 per cent for the Dutch in 1670 and rather more in 1740. On the other hand, in contrast with the decline of Dutch shipping in the African and American trades (10 per cent in 1670, *ca.* 4 per cent in 1740), as much as 38 per cent of English tonnage was already employed here in 1686—and that percentage was rising. Such a marked difference of focus would not in itself matter much were it not for the fact that the Dutch focus was on the declining, the English on the rising section of the international shipping economy.

The direction of effort being different, it is not surprising that the overall development of English, Dutch and French gross tonnage varied. The total shipping (including fishing fleets) of the principal powers in 1670 has been estimated[3] as follows:

United Provinces	284,000 lasts (568,000 tons)
England 47,000 } Scotland 5,000 }	52,000 lasts (104,000 tons)
France	40,000 lasts (80,000 tons)

With a lead of this magnitude, it is not difficult to understand that the Dutch were still leading in 1720, even perhaps as late as 1750. Their growth pattern, however, differed from that of their competitors. Despite

[1] W. Vogel, in *Forschungen und Versuche zur Geschichte des Mittelalters und der Neuzeit: Festschrift Dietrich Schäfer* (Jena, 1915), p. 319.

[2] R. Davis, 'Merchant Shipping in the Economy of the Late Seventeenth Century', *Econ. Hist. Rev.* 2nd ser. vol. IX (1956–7), p. 70.

[3] W. Vogel, *loc. cit.* p. 331.

the Nine Years War, Dutch shipping continued to expand in the last decade of the century, reaching a peak about 1700: Amsterdam tonnage alone was 50 per cent higher in 1694–1702 than in 1667–71. However, with the coincidence of the Northern and Spanish wars, to which the Dutch trading pattern was peculiarly sensitive, a significant contraction, at least in Amsterdam shipping, took place.[1] The 1720s did not see a recovery to the levels of 1700. On the other hand, English shipping activity, after increasing very rapidly in the generation before 1688, stagnated during the wars and resumed growth after 1713 at a much slower, though still impressive, rate. Similarly, the French merchant marine barely held its own during the wars, but resumed its growth afterwards: in 1730 it was to consist of 1,657 high-seas vessels and 3,707 *barques* (used in the coastal and fishing fleets), compared with 757 and 3,226 in 1686.[2] Even in 1730, however, it was still only two-fifths the size of the English merchant fleet, which by then, indeed, had a greater lead over it than in 1670. Yet in the growing world trades it was, like the English, better represented than the Dutch.

In every branch of trade in these decades, war was the most obvious but by no means the exclusive controlling factor. The international business cycle reflected most clearly the alternations of war and peace. In general, the volume of international trade had been very high after the Franco-Dutch peace in 1678, but that post-war boom had faded by 1682 as competition increased: the difficulties of individual trades were generalized in the international crisis of 1686, and the later eighties saw only a partial recovery, aided by such circumstances as the restoration of Anglo-French trading after 1685. In the uncertain early years of the Nine Years War, the volume of international trade was generally down, although the Dutch recovered by 1693 and continued prosperous till 1700. English trade remained much more sluggish and started upwards again only with the peace—owing in part, perhaps, to the greater exposure of English shipping to French privateers. The fairly widespread financial difficulties of 1696–7 seem to have had relatively little effect on a generally reviving trade (except on English woollens). Volume stayed high in the inter-war years, but the outbreak of the Great Northern War meant a temporary setback for the Dutch.

Unlike its predecessor, the Spanish Succession War at first saw a fairly high volume of international trade, at least for England and Holland.

---

[1] The advantages scored by the Scandinavians from neutrality in the 1690s, when the Swedes alone counted 750 vessels, were more than cancelled by the Northern War. The Dutch northern trade was almost entirely in Amsterdam hands. Rotterdam, though relatively unimportant in the seventeenth century, was much more dynamic than Amsterdam in the eighteenth: it was important in the Bay and Iberian trades, and from the 1720s in the English tobacco trade. Generalizations based on Amsterdam data thus need some qualification.

[2] P. J. Charliat, *Trois siècles d'économie maritime française* (1931), pp. 32, 35–6, 42–4, 52–3.

After 1704, trade became more sluggish till the Peace Preliminaries of 1711. The worst years were 1705–7, relieved only by the resumption of trade between Holland and France, England and Spain. Modest recovery in 1708 led to a boom in individual lines like English woollens, and to a heightened speculative activity which culminated in an international crisis in 1710–11. This was primarily a financial crisis, aggravated by loss of confidence in the war-ruined finances of the Western belligerents—the first of a series of similar crises that hit different sections of Europe in the difficult years of 1711–15. From 1711, however, the physical volume of trade increased quite rapidly in both France and England, to be checked only slightly and temporarily by the financial difficulties of 1720–1. Holland and the North, on the other hand, failed to share in this advance because the second decade of the Northern War involved more intensive hostilities in the Baltic itself than had the first and dislocated many ports.

In sum, then, the wars had stimulated some sectors of the European international economy, temporarily annihilated others, and distorted or re-directed still others. Nevertheless, in the 1720s the general map of commerce was substantially what it had been in the 1680s. In the North, the most striking changes were the increasing importance of Russia compared with the relatively stagnant rôle of Sweden as an exporter; hemp and particularly linen bulked larger as export staples, while cereals declined. In the West, Dutch shipping was still first in tonnage, though not growing significantly, while the Dutch fisheries were in full and ominous decline. English commerce had grown more rapidly in the war decades than it was to grow in the first generation of full peace. The most striking new element on the map, however, was the speed with which the remoter branches of French enterprise were now growing after the atrophy of the wars.

2. PRICES, POPULATION AND ECONOMIC ACTIVITIES IN EUROPE, 1688–1715: A NOTE

A direct attack on the history of economic activity postulates indices of production, distribution and consumption. Unfortunately, only a very few indices of this kind exist for the remote past, even for the late seventeenth century, so that we are forced to recur to a method of indirect approach, such as the analysis of price series. These, however incomplete they may be, are relatively numerous, continuous and precise.

The short phase here surveyed must first of all be situated in a wider chronological framework. For this purpose use may be made of the table of weighted indices of various prices worked out by the late N. W. Posthumus, on the basis of dealings quoted on the Amsterdam commodity exchange.[1] In the following table a new base (= 100) has been

[1] *Nederlandsche Prijsgeschiedenis* (Leiden, 1943), p. CIV. These figures may be collated with the English cost of living index established by E. H. Phelps Brown and Sheila V.

substituted for his, in accordance with the data available simply for the years 1680–9:

Years	Harvest produce	Other products
1680–4	99	100
1685–9	101	100
1690–4	152	119
1695–9	[*lacuna*]	[*lacuna*]
1700–4	133	118
1705–9	131	100
1710–14	167	104
1715–19	114	119
1720–4	100	108

These indices assemble the prices of a fairly large and varied range of items, each specified in monetary units of a constant weight in silver. Admittedly, they are the resultant of both highly fluctuating and remarkably rigid prices, so that there is some danger of diluting and even of forgetting the definite impressions which the principal series can leave on one's mind as soon as one looks at each series in turn, one by one. Another disadvantage is that the breakdown into fixed five-year periods forbids the exact dating of changes in the direction of movement, to say nothing of the regrettable break in continuity for the quinquennium 1695–9. With these qualifications, certain broad facts, comprehending a fairly large international zone, stand out clearly. The first is that the whole phase 1690–1714, which corresponds nearly enough with the period of this survey, is marked by a prevailing level of relatively high prices in comparison with both the preceding and the following years. For 'harvest' produce, the mean price established during the years 1690–1714 reaches 146, against an average of 100 for the decade 1680–9: this same index falls to 107 for the decade 1715–24. The mean price of other products for 1690–1714 as a whole, however, rising to no more than 110, remains after 1714 at almost the same level (113·5). As perceived thus from the unique observation post of the Amsterdam Bourse, the collective appearance of the years 1690–1714 contrasts with the generally downward trend of prices and the stagnation of economic activity which, for a long while, had characterized the seventeenth century. Should this be interpreted as a return to normal and a revival of business? Only a detailed stocktaking could sustain so positive a conclusion, for which other proofs are needed, and it is only by examining individual price series that we can hope to come nearer to the truth.

The place of cereals in the diet of the time, and especially the place of rye, constitutes a first claim on our attention. From the fairly numerous series available to us under this head let us select the markets of Amster-

Hopkins, 'Seven Centuries of the Prices of Consumables, compared with Builders' Wage-rates', *Economica*, 2nd ser. vol. XXIII (1956), pp. 296–314. Taking the years 1681–9 as the base (= 100), this index gives 112 for 1690–9, 101 for 1700–9 and 121 for 1710–15. For a survey of certain price movements in Portugal, see above, pp. 509–10.

dam, Lyons and Carpentras. Rye prices at these three centres lend themselves to calculations comparable with those of Posthumus once they are grouped by harvest years, translated into weight of silver and expressed as indices,[1] using the decade 1680–9 again as base = 100: see below, Table A. Thus, at Amsterdam, the mean index figure for rye over the whole period 1690–1714 works out at 154, thereby confirming the rise already noticed in food prices generally. This occurs again, though far more emphatically, when we move to Lyons, where the corresponding index is 176. Inversely, the figure for Carpentras is only 122. These results are worth underlining in themselves. They point, in effect, to the existence of a differential geography of prices which is most distinctly reflected in cereals.[2]

Furthermore, not only geographical differences but also fluctuations within the same series are much more strongly accentuated when viewed across a brief period of years, in the short or medium term. For example, if we take the mean of the ten highest annual prices in a single series between 1690 and 1714 and then the mean of the ten lowest, using the latter as a new base (= 100) and expressing the former as an index in relation to it, we can measure after a fashion the mean amplitude of the fluctuations involved. On this scale, the average of the ten highest prices for rye at Amsterdam becomes 173, at Lyons 259 and at Carpentras 157. More striking still is a direct confrontation between maximum and minimum annual prices. From this angle, returning to the indices based on 1680–9 (= 100), contrast a maximum of 316 for the harvest-year 1698–9 at Amsterdam with a minimum of 105 for 1691–2 (or 95 if we go back to 1688–9); in 1709–10 this index touched 263 even though only three years earlier, in 1706–7, it had fallen again to 95. But what is to be said of the fluctuations in rye at Lyons? In 1693–4 this index climbs as high as 400, although it had stood at only 83 in 1688–9 and was to climb down to 103 from 1695–6; the year 1708–9, however, brought the record figure of 457 after the same commodity, in the same market, had stood at only 87 two years earlier—a mere fifth of the price ruling in 1708–9. By comparison, the widest fluctuations to be noticed at Carpentras appear modest: 151 in 1691–2 and again in 1692–3, against 58 in 1689–90 and 91 in 1690–1; even the harvest year 1709–10, the year of the hard winter ('le grand hiver'), brought the index at Carpentras only up to 214, as opposed to 81 in 1701–2 and 93 in 1711–12. These typical examples, of course, are confirmed in their dissimilarities as well as in their resemblances by the data gathered from neighbouring regions.

[1] Posthumus, p. 574; Lyons, Archives Communales, séries BB and HH; Carpentras, Arch. Comm. These and other indices are printed below, pp. 898–902.

[2] The geographical diversity of grain prices renders any composite index in this field unreliable for interpretation, at least over the short and medium term. Beveridge's index in 'Wheat and Harvest cycles', Econ. Journal, vol. XXXI (1921), was useful in its own day; that of Usher, for French wheat, in Rev. of Econ. Statistics, vol. XII (1930), is altogether debatable.

Such contrasts in amplitude of fluctuation, however, like the time-lags evident in the short-term movements of the series just mentioned, need not conceal a degree of synchronization, approximately at least, in their general shape. And this synchronism, in greater or less degree, holds good as far as central Europe, in Saxony and in Austria.[1] At first sight, an objection to the universal character of the price-rise which our indices so far seem to bear out might appear to arise from the experience of Barcelona,[2] where the calm tenor of the corn market—a phenomenon characteristic of the Mediterranean—is accompanied by a low mobility of prices over the long term. But this difficulty falls to the ground when, instead of considering corn prices in isolation, we reckon with other agricultural commodities like olive oil and wine.

Nevertheless, tempting as it is to draw conclusions from the wealth of data available for cereals, this is a temptation to resist if it means reconstructing long-term price movements from these series alone, which would in any case call for a good deal of learned manipulation. It is doubtless wiser to extend the investigation to other agricultural produce whenever we can. In certain cases, as we have just seen, oil and wine enable us to correct the general picture of agricultural prices to be derived from cereals alone, or they may confirm it. In a country like France wines had a place of honour. Obviously, like cereals and at times even more than cereals, wines were vulnerable to vicissitudes of weather which caused strong oscillations in their prices. Those of burgundies, ex-vineyard, underwent extreme swings from year to year.[3] This makes it still more remarkable that they so clearly record from 1686 onwards, after thirty years of progressive decline, a movement lifting them all to a high level which, despite momentary reverses, was maintained until 1715 and beyond. The quotations for Bordeaux wines sold at Amsterdam,[4] though more tranquil, confirm this general movement.

Spices, the classical merchandise of international trade if ever there was one, can be convincingly represented by the course of pepper. In fact, once converted into their equivalent weight in silver, these prices also, in widely scattered places, present the same common features. In Bavaria as in New Castile, we again find about 1689 and 1690, after the low levels of 1680 and the next years, an almost identical and simultaneous upswing which is then prolonged.[5] Measuring this rise in accordance with the procedure used above for the years 1690–1714, an index of 133 is obtained for

[1] O. Dittmann, *Die Getreidepreise in der Stadt Leipzig* (Leipzig, 1889) and M. J. Elsas, *Umriss einer Geschichte der Preise und Löhne in Deutschland*, vol. IIA (Leiden, 1940), p. 517; A. F. Pribram, *Materialen zur Geschichte der Preise und Löhne in Österreich*, vol. I (Vienna, 1938), p. 529.
[2] P. Vilar, *La Catalogne dans l'Espagne moderne* (3 vols. 1962), vol. I, p. 642.
[3] Arch. Comm. of Beaune and Nuits; similarly at Arbois, in the Jura.
[4] Posthumus, p. 226.
[5] Elsas, vol. I (1936), p. 659; E. J. Hamilton, *War and Prices in Spain, 1651–1800* (1947), pp. 241 and 246.

New Castile and 137 at Würzburg. At Amsterdam, the gaps in the series of published data[1] make it preferable to compare median rather than mean figures: if this is done for black pepper, we get a median level of 131—very close, therefore, to the mean levels of Spain and Bavaria. In another direction, the purchases of white pepper made in England by the Lord Steward[2] furnish an index consistent with the above but rising higher, to a figure of 166. This concordance between different markets, however, is far from reappearing if sought among the detailed prices quoted during each year, or even among the mean prices for short runs of years. For instance, the unusually high levels at which the English government bought pepper in 1695-7 were matched neither at Madrid nor at Würzburg; the much lower prices paid by the same administration from 1702 to 1708 can be interpreted as corresponding with those obtaining during these years in south Germany, but not with the Spanish quotations nor even (so far as gaps in the evidence allow of comparison) with those of Amsterdam.

The prices of the commodities so far mentioned—cereals, wines, peppers—exhibit strong or very strong annual variations, with well-marked curves, long or short. But the prices of non-foodstuffs and of labour present as a rule quite another aspect. Raw material prices and above all the prices of every kind of manufactured product vary little if at all. A limiting case is the rigidity characteristic of wages: what is to be said of all those columns in which the same figure repeats itself for several years on end, sometimes for whole decades? Examples of price rigidity are not far to seek even in the relatively elastic world of textiles. Alongside fine-quality (*alto*) cloth, typical of products highly sensitive to the economic weather, the accounts of the *Misericordia* of Milan supply a table for coarse (*basso*) cloth which is absolutely without price variation from 1688 to 1707.[3] The prices of towelling cloth which figure in the classical study of Thorold Rogers are identical from 1691 to 1701.[4] In the collection of studies directed by Charles Verlinden, the price of linen at Zottegem (Flanders) shows no change from the beginning of the series in 1692 down to 1788![5] This example is particularly significant as it comes from an unimpeachable source, which is often not the case when one is dealing with the accounts of public establishments, owing to cut prices and auctions. The unchanging price at Zottegem summarizes observations made on a local market. While linen there remained stable, the same source in fact reveals fairly sensitive variations in the prices of wheat,

---

[1] Posthumus, p. 175.

[2] W. H. Beveridge *et al.*, *Prices and Wages in England* (1st edn. 1939; repr. 1965), p. 430.

[3] A. de Maddalena, *Prezzi e aspetti di mercato in Milano durante il secolo XVII* (Milan, 1950), p. 175.

[4] *A History of Agriculture and Prices in England* (7 vols. Oxford, 1866–1902), vol. VI, p. 547.

[5] *Dokumenten voor de Geschiedenis van Prijzen en Lonen in Vlaanderen en Brabant*, vol. II (Brugge, 1965), pp. 495–7.

maslin (a mixture of wheat and rye), barley, oats, straw, capons, goslings, oil and butter.

A like inelasticity applies to a sector whose importance needs no underlining, the building industry, the data for which are so frequently used in studies of price history. We possess indeed many accounts of institutions responsible for building or for the repair of buildings, featuring both materials and wages of skilled and unskilled labour, often in abundance. But there is always the same phenomenon: the same monotony characterizes the mason's remuneration and the price of bricks.[1] In many other cases, price oscillations, which can sometimes be quite lively in the course of a year, have very likely no economic implication, corresponding in all probability with differences in quality impossible to detect in the documents.

Over and above all this, however, there is one major obstacle to the utilization of price series for the study of economic climate in our period. The end of the seventeenth century and the first years of the eighteenth, in most European countries, saw changes in the nominal value of the metal coinage in circulation. Questions are always being raised about the procedure adopted for getting round this difficulty—that is to say, by converting values expressed in a money of account, such as the *livre tournois*, into weight of precious metal. Such conversion is none the less acceptable so long as one is dealing with the price of merchandise whose specific value varies more than the course of the money market. But when it is a matter of products whose intrinsic variations are narrow, the arbitrariness of such a monetary adjustment becomes obvious: if mutations in money values, which one is obliged to reckon with, overwhelm the importance of 'natural' price movements, there is the danger that our calculations will culminate crudely in the shift of a purely monetary mutation to the price figures. Conversely, nominal prices can react so promptly to changes in money values that these last are at once translated in the price series into a money of account: in this event, as soon as the reconversion is made, we rediscover a price inertia which the monetary phenomena have masked. A good example is the case of sailcloth bought by the naval administration at Toulon.[2] Fixed by contracts of supply for several years at a time, these prices, expressed in *sous tournois*, move abruptly like the steps of a staircase when projected on a graph. They were subject to a first upturn between 1689 and 1694, then to a new one in 1701 and another, more violent, in 1708 and 1709. But these rises explain themselves in the light of modifica-

---

[1] Numerous examples of this rigidity, amounting to identity, in Elsas, *Umriss einer Geschichte der Preise und Löhne*. Thus English scarlet cloth in the Munich accounts stood at the same price from 1671 to 1710 (*ibid.* vol. I, pp. 552–3); similarly, bricks showed no change in price from 1665 to 1713. At Augsburg, the wages of masons' assistants remained steady from 1693 to 1712 and those of journeymen masons from 1672 to 1712 (*ibid.* vol. I, pp. 728, 731), as also those of other building labour from 1695 to 1712.

[2] Toulon, Archives du Port, I L, pp. 253–306.

tions in the value of the *livre tournois*, which fell by the same magnitudes. It scarcely seems too audacious to infer that the contractors, but for these same modifications, would have agreed to deal virtually at the same prices throughout.

There remain the countries whose money can be regarded as a stable, or almost stable, standard of measurement between 1688 and 1715. There are not many of them. Here, since Posthumus's work contains some very large gaps, we shall content ourselves with a single table of textile prices (Table B below), using two English series and one Milanese, although Houghton's contemporary investigation of wool prices in different English districts[1] extends only from 1691 to 1702, while the Milanese series for *alto* cloth stops in 1706;[2] only the prices of hemp purchased by the English Navy Board cover the whole phase under review.[3] Houghton's wool prices, when expressed in indices of annual averages, show a clear rise from 1691 to 1695 and then a level which stays high down to 1702, the end of his series. These indices are necessarily calculated in relation to a base furnished by the prices of the years 1691–1702 themselves; but with this reservation they are in over-all agreement with the other indices already examined, if not really so in detail. The other two series permit of direct comparison on the same base (1680–9) with the general indices established by Posthumus. Since they remain constantly above 100, it is clear that they confirm the evidence of a general rise. As regards the indices for English hemp purchases, moreover, the interdecennial rise which they display is much more pronounced than that of our general indices. The difficulties of extending this part of the enquiry to other series have been indicated. Too much should not be expected from the apparent wealth of publications on price history.

When all is said, the most instructive facts remain those which result from confronting cereal prices with the prices of non-foodstuffs in the same places, at the same dates, and consequently within the same monetary system. In a general way, the relative rigidity of the non-foodstuffs, by contrast with contemporaneous and sometimes violent oscillations in cereals, points to a reciprocal failure of integration between the different sectors of economic life. Inelastic wages, like the cost rigidity of many manufactured products, certainly embarrassed the situation of the principal agricultural producers in such years as 1688–9 or 1706–7, when corn was selling at a loss.[4] Yet soaring rises in the prices of foodstuffs were a far more serious matter. If only because of the rigidity of other prices, dear food in itself meant hardship to artisans and wage-earners; and when such

---

[1] Assembled by Thorold Rogers, vol. v, p. 416; for John Houghton, F.R.S. (d. 1705), see *Dictionary of National Biography*, vol. XXVII, p. 422.

[2] Maddalena, pp. 173–4.   [3] Beveridge, p. 676.

[4] For minimum wheat prices at Winchester after the 1688 harvest and the low level of prices ruling there during the harvest-years 1705 and 1706, see Beveridge, 81–2; there are numerous examples of these depressions in the French price-currents.

rises exceeded a certain level, it could even happen that a downturn of prices would reveal itself in those sectors where consumption, and consequently activity, was contracting most. The study of these acute crises, indeed, presupposes a clear understanding of what may truly be called a retrospective economic geography. Many historians, having too narrow a field of observation, tend to underrate the real harshness of these events.

The 1692–4 crisis, a tragedy for France as a whole (ch. x), was felt elsewhere to a lesser extent. Even within the French kingdom it was greatly attenuated in the west and on the Mediterranean coast. Far more European in scope, the 1709–10 crisis was nevertheless not of the same intensity everywhere. Another crisis, undoubtedly as serious, afflicted Scandinavia and other Baltic countries from 1696 to 1698 (and Scotland in 1698–9).[1] It had its repercussion on Amsterdam and was felt even in French markets, but its effects were much less severe in western Europe than in the North.

As an illustration of what has been said above, two test cases will suffice. The first is taken from the course of prices for raw wool quoted at Castelnaudary, in the south of France but well away from the Mediterranean.[2] At Castelnaudary corn went up in 1693–4 to index 214 and in 1709–10 to 302—extraordinarily high for that area, though well below the maxima recorded at Lyons and elsewhere, as we have seen. Untreated wool (*laine surge*), besides being a rural product *par excellence*, found its way to an industry which was also in part rural and which, as we know from other sources, suffered from the low agricultural prices that ensued upon the big cereal rises. Here, therefore, we are able to confront corn prices with those of a raw material recorded in the same documentation. The comparison is conclusive. It can surely be no accident that the corn *maxima* should have coincided (but for a lag not exceeding a few months) in 1694 with a *minimum* touched by raw wool (index 76) and in 1709–10, more revealing still, with a wool index of only 61 (Table C). Such diverse indices for wool and corn suggest not only that the manufacturers were failing to replenish their stocks of wool for lack of demand, but also that the peasants were under pressure to sell it.

Our second test case is provided by the pewter objects which feature in the estate inventories of deceased persons. They were valued in these inventories by weight, the quality being habitually distinguished simply as 'common' or 'fine', thus facilitating classification. In normal times these prices varied hardly at all, but in time of severe crisis they fell perceptibly. This is because pewter services played the same rôle among the less well-

[1] E. Jutikkala, 'The Great Finnish Famine, 1695–1697', *Scandinavian Econ. Hist. Rev.* vol. III (1955), pp. 48–63. In Estonia the rise in rye attained its maximum in autumn 1698: O. Liiv, *Die Wirtschaftliche Lage des estnischen Gebieten am Ausgang des XVII Jahrhunderts*, vol. I (Tartu, 1935), pp. 281–94. For oatmeal prices in several Scottish counties cf. R. Mitchison, 'The Movements of Scottish Corn Prices in the Seventeenth and Eighteenth Centuries', *Econ. Hist. Rev.* 2nd ser. vol. XVIII (1965), pp. 278 ff.
[2] Castelnaudary (Aude), Arch. Comm., HH2 and 3.

off as did silverwork for the better-to-do classes. In times when good metallic money was scarce enough and often hoarded, pewter constituted a savings reserve that could be sold, or preferably pledged, if one needed ready cash or credit. Yet this could not be done without loss during a severe general crisis, so that a conclusive symptom of what was happening in 1693–4 appears in the collapse of pewter valuations in the Paris region: the index fell to 83 in 1693 and to 80 in 1694—just when the Paris *mercuriale* (price current) takes the wheat index up to 306 (Table D).[1] The subsequent rise in the pewter indices is easily explained by the increasingly lively demand which arose precisely out of its monetary function. Accordingly in 1709, when wheat goes up to index 509, pewter turns downwards to 99, from the figure of 123 at which it stood in the years immediately before and afterwards.

Attention has already been drawn to the 'rigidity' of wages. Emphasis should once again be laid upon it. The multisecular index of building wages in southern England established by Phelps Brown and Hopkins[2] rests essentially on the data collected by Thorold Rogers. A glance at their graphs suffices to show how wages rose in successive vertical steps, each of them lasting unchanged for years on end. The curve of real wages—the result of dividing money wages by an artificially constructed cost-of-living index—reproduces (inversely for distant epochs) the short- and long-term vicissitudes of the cost of living. As regards the period which concerns us here, Thorold Rogers gives a maximum daily wage rate of 2s. 6d. for carpenters and masons in 1689–90 and the same for 1697–9, 1701–2 and 1702–3.[3] For certain years a mass of unpublished information about wages is available in the archives of the *Hôpital des Incurables* in Paris.[4] Allowing for seasonal deviations and others due to various professional qualifications, one can at most discern a rise in the dominant entries from 15–17 *sous* at the start of our period to 17–18 *sous* towards the end, around 1715. This is less than the contemporaneous devaluation of the money of account.

Documents survive from the end of the seventeenth century which serve, up to a point, to make good the lack of comprehensive and periodical population censuses. There are limited enumerations and evaluations to be extracted from administrative sources. Most of them were compiled for fiscal reasons and so allow us to know the number of taxpayers rather than

[1] Pewter prices in notarial minutes: Paris, Archives Nationales, série zz, and Versailles, Arch. Départementales of Seine-et-Oise. For wheat prices down to 1698, see M. Baulant and J. Meuvret, *Prix des céréales extraits de la mercuriale de Paris*, vol. II (1952), p. 135; for the years 1699–1715, see H. Hauser, *Recherches et documents sur l'histoire des prix en France* (1936).

[2] Brown and Hopkins, 'Seven Centuries of Building Wages', *Economica*, 2nd ser. vol. XXII (1955), pp. 195–206.   [3] *A History of Agriculture and Prices*, vol. V, p. 671.

[4] Paris, Archives de l'Assistance Publique, Fonds des Incurables, pièces comptables.

that of inhabitants. Ecclesiastical archives, thanks to certain diocesan visitations, yield the number of communicants, which in France is almost equivalent to that of the adult population. But all this material calls for classification and criticism—in short, for an amount of research which has so far been very inadequate. Of contemporary estimates, the well-known statistical effort of Gregory King, remarkable for its time, allows us to estimate the total population of England and Wales about 1695 at 5½ millions.[1] The inquiry launched with the French provincial *intendants* in 1697, and carried out over the next three years, is far from yielding reliable results; at best these are a pretty crude approximation. Vauban, who studied them, attributes to the kingdom as a whole a population of 19 millions.[2] But indications of this nature remain static. One wants to know about the movement of a population and its age-structure, its composition in terms of social categories and by localities. In principle, these questions should be capable of answers, in a fairly large number of places, from the registers kept by the parish clergy recording baptisms, marriages and burials.[3] In fact, the very end of the seventeenth century did see a considerable growth in the number, and an improvement in the quality, of the registers which have come down to us. But systematic investigation of them is still in its infancy. The majority of historians, in any case, have concentrated on seeking to determine the evolution of population in broad outlines and over long periods. Even when their findings are sound, they hardly allow the characteristics of a relatively short phase to be discerned in any exact sense. Those monographs are still few and far between which enable us to consider the problem within a comparatively precise chronological framework.

Demographic facts clarify history under different heads, some being the result of short and violent crises, other of a slow and progressive evolution. So far, it has been this second group which has attracted most attention. Now, there is a certain lag between the time during which durable transformations are produced in the coefficients of birth, death and marriage rates and the influence which these transformations exert on the total size of a population—or rather, what is undoubtedly still more important, on the size of the active population. On the other hand, no more than in the matter of prices have different countries and different social groups lived simultaneously at the same rhythm. For these reasons, any attempt to draw general inferences from a few specific series of vital statistics is bound to be especially hazardous.

If one is to take the plunge, however, it seems reasonable to describe the years 1688–1715, comparatively and negatively, in terms of relatively low rates of growth and decline; in other words, there was no demo-

[1] D. V. Glass and D. E. C. Eversley (eds.), *Population in History* (1965), pp. 159–220.
[2] Vauban, *Projet d'une Dixme Royale* (ed. E. Coornaert, 1933), p. 159.
[3] Numerous indications in the articles collected in Glass and Eversley.

graphic revolution. Although estimates of the English population in the eighteenth century are still controversial, experts are agreed on the broad outline of its development. So far as we are concerned, it is accepted that the first years of the century saw a certain growth, but a rather small one. Three different estimates acknowledge an increase between 1700 and 1720: one of 136,000, another of 175,000, a third of 212,000. For a total population of $5\frac{1}{2}$ to 6 millions, a rise of this order over twenty years—i.e. about 1·75 per cent a year—is nothing spectacular. These same estimates agree on figures for 1740 which are very close to those of 1700, after a regression between 1720 and 1740, while allowing a growth from 1740 to 1760 variously placed at 567,000, 622,000 and 657,000 inhabitants. Even the lowest of these three figures, however, is more than two and a half times the highest estimate of increase in 1700–20—567,000 against 212,000—and yet the growth in 1740–60 is modest by comparison with the calculations made for 1750–1801, when the so-called industrial revolution was beginning.[1]

Venice underwent a sensational population decline in the course of the seventeenth century, and was to experience a further marked fall in the eighteenth. Between these two catastrophic phases, however, the years which concern us here may be called a plateau. Daniele Beltrami's study in depth of births and deaths within the city, over the decades 1690–9 and 1700–9, reveal a negative balance (-372) for the first decade, but this is in part compensated by an excess of births over deaths ($+257$) in the second.[2] The Venetian mainland (*terraferma*) was in effect demographically stable from 1680 to 1719. The earlier researches of K. J. Beloch, which applied to the whole of Italy, leave the same impression. His hypothetical estimates for Sicily show a slight fall (from 1,171,000 to 1,143,000) between 1681 and 1713, but this is partly attributable to a very special occurrence, the earthquake of 1693.[3]

This relatively stationary situation seems to characterize the demography of the age in general, disregarding short-run oscillations. Thus the population of Munich has been put at 23,000 in 1680, at 25,000 in 1690 and 24,000 in 1700; that of Augsburg at 26,000 in 1681–90, at 27,000 in 1691–1700, at 26,000 in 1701–10 and 27,000 in 1711–20.[4] In the same years the population of Zürich settled at *ca.* 11,000—almost exactly the figure which reappears in 1762.[5] Catalonia, where births declined considerably between 1630 and 1670, had recovered the lost ground by 1686–90; the

[1] J. D. Chambers, *The Vale of Trent, 1670–1800* (Econ. Hist. Rev. Supplement, no. 3, 1957), p. 23.

[2] *Storia della popolazione di Venezia dalla fine del secolo XVI alla caduta della Repubblica* (Padua, 1954), p. 140.

[3] *Bevölkerungsgeschichte Italiens*, vol. I (Berlin, 1937), pp. 152–3.

[4] Elsas, vol. I, p. 79.

[5] W. Bickel, *Bevölkerungsgeschichte und Bevölkerungspolitik der Schweiz* (Zürich, 1947), p. 42.

quinquennial figures for 1691–5 and 1696–1700 denote no great change.[1] In central Sweden, the birth rate of the province of Närke fluctuated quinquennially between 28·5 per cent and 35·4 per cent from 1691 to 1715: the balance of births over deaths is alternately positive and negative.[2]

The general impression of a relatively stable demographic situation is not contradicted by specialist studies, based on the parish registers, in England and France. The investigations conducted for Nottinghamshire between 1670 and 1800 indeed show an upsurge of baptisms and burials during the second half of the eighteenth century, the first predominating by an ever wider margin; but only a slight predominance of baptisms and an insignificant slope in the population curve are observable during the reigns of William and Anne. A slight fall in burials, while baptisms remain 'stagnant', is to be noticed in the 'agricultural' villages: in the 'industrial' villages, burials also diminish slightly but baptisms have a slight tendency to rise.[3] When one turns to France, if episodic but particularly violent swings may be discounted for the moment, the over-all results obtained by Pierre Goubert for northern France lead to a similar conclusion.[4] At Crulai, in Normandy, the mean number of baptisms was 36·7 a year from 1681 to 1690 and 37 during the next twenty-five years.[5] It is true that in the countryside of Languedoc the depopulation trend beginning in 1680 continued on its inexorable way, but in this same province the towns were expanding.[6]

Nevertheless, it is important not to claim too much for this impression of the general situation. It leaves scope, indeed, for some very different hypotheses concerning the mechanism of the phenomena that have been summarized. Quite possibly, there may have been no real dynamic force in them; and it is also possible that strong movements, working in opposite directions, may have cancelled each other out in time and space. At all events, it is right to examine briefly the factors which could have determined the population movements of the age. A distinction may first be made between the causes which could develop or restrict fertility and those which promoted mortality. One notion which is still widespread must be rejected out of hand. This amounts to the assumption that before the late eighteenth century the birth rate was subject to no control, whether arising out of social conditions or from the preferences of individuals. The age at which the majority of marriages were performed is a factor whose importance has been underlined with good reason: it

---

[1] J. Nadal, *La población española* (Barcelona, 1966), p. 60; for Spain generally, cf. above, p. 345.

[2] G. Utterström, 'An outline of some population change in Sweden *ca*. 1660–1750', *Population in History*, pp. 538–48. On the drastic decline in Poland see above, p. 705.

[3] Chambers, pp. 34–5.

[4] *Beauvais et le Beauvaisis*, vol. II: *Cartes et graphiques* (1960), pp. 50–1.

[5] E. Gautier and L. Henry, *La Population de Crulai, paroisse normande* (1958), p. 243.

[6] E. Le Roy Ladurie, *Les Paysans de Languedoc* (2 vols. 1966), vol. I, pp. 541–7.

certainly varies with the period and type of society under consideration. On the other hand, it would be naïve to imagine that the men even of a distant past did not know how to restrain their progenitiveness when they so wished.[1] The hypothesis which looks most convincing postulates a variety of reactions, collective or individual, aimed at maintaining a certain equilibrium in face of the causes of death.

Losses due to war, without being altogether negligible, had only a moderately damaging effect on the demography of the age. While armies had become larger since the mid-seventeenth century, they did not compare in size with those of the late eighteenth century and after. Recruitment affected no more than a small slice of the population; in spite of the new militias in France and elsewhere, systematic conscription was still in the future. Battles could be murderous, but they were not fought every day. There were times when the troops had more to endure from disease.

Diseases of various kinds, even in countries with the best provision for health, were the standing cause of a huge wastage, especially among infants. The distinction between 'endemic' and 'epidemic' diseases is an elusive one, although the doctors of the day discussed it a good deal.[2] But the great epidemics were distinguishable by their extensive spread and by their gravity. In this connection, at least in western Europe, one terrible scourge had largely disappeared in the course of the seventeenth century: bubonic plague (the *peste*). Its last notorious appearance there was in England in 1665–6, and this outbreak had hovered over France in the following years; but it was the last, apart from the Spanish visitations of 1676–85 and those in Marseilles and Provence of 1720–2.[3] Outside western Europe, however, from Scandinavia as also from eastern Europe, the plague had not withdrawn.[4] Nor did these areas command as efficient an administration for defeating it as was now available in France, which owed her preservation in 1668 to the energetic measures displayed by the public authorities: in the ports, too, the quarantine regulations were increasingly respected and efficient. Far more difficult was it to bar the road to other diseases, less imposing in their onset but insidiously propagated, besides being poorly understood.[5] The medicine of the age

[1] E. A. Wrigley, 'Family Limitation in Pre-Industrial England', *Econ. Hist. Rev.* 2nd ser. vol. XIX (1966), pp. 82–109.

[2] See C. Creighton, *A History of Epidemics* (2 vols. Cambridge, 1891–4), vol. I.

[3] C. F. Mullet, *The Bubonic Plague and England* (Lexington, 1956), p. 266; C. Carrière M. Courdurié and F. Rebuffat, *Marseille Ville Morte; la peste de 1720* (n.d. [1968]).

[4] Mullet, pp. 262–4, notes the presence of plague at Warsaw in 1707, Danzig 1709, and Copenhagen 1711, in which year it ravaged Brandenburg (215,000 dead) and Austria (300,000). Between 1709 and 1712 a whole series of measures were taken in England to quarantine shipping from the Baltic. In the Habsburg lands, the monumental columns erected to the Holy Trinity in recognition of deliverance from the plague record six epidemic years, 1691–2 and 1711–14 inclusive: A. Grünberg, *Pestäulen in Österreich* (Vienna, 1960).

[5] Among the many contemporary writings which display the bewilderment of the keenest minds concerning the origins of disease, the reader may be referred to Robert Boyle's essay,

employed a vocabulary which leaves the historian guessing. Even when it becomes more precise and corresponds with recognizable clinical observations, it remains to be seen whether it is the same as the language used by the majority of inexpert witnesses. For instance, was the 'purple' fever (the *pourpre*, mentioned in many a letter of the time) really what the doctors themselves would allow us to identify as the typhus known to us?[1] As then currently used, the term more often gives the impression that it is being applied to eruptive distempers like smallpox or scarlet fever. The word 'dysentery', in turn, could designate every kind of intestinal complaint. This uncertainty is all the more vexatious to the historian because a by no means negligible aspect of collective psychology would be illuminated by knowledge of the manner in which disease was propagated. The towns went on living under the nightmare of 'contagion', and this was the principal reason for their harshness towards poor refugees from the countryside suspected of carrying disease.

Morbidity in England and its consequences were long ago the subject of a precocious study. In the eighteenth century a doctor named Thomas Short had the idea of studying the question in the parish registers of a number of districts, notably in the counties of York, Nottingham, Derby and Kent.[2] Basing himself on 150–60 rural parishes (in addition to a few towns), Short counted year by year the number which he considered 'sickly', on the ground that burials there had exceeded baptisms. In the sickly parishes he added up the total figures of burials and of baptisms.[3] Some of his findings, translated into percentages, are reproduced below (Table E). The first comment suggested by this table is that the years 1688–1715 were years of relatively good health. In none of these years does the percentage of sick parishes reach the figure of 20 per cent, which is the mean for 1680–9, still less the figure of 25 per cent attained in 1680. The second remark to be made is that the highest figures of 18 or 19 per cent at no point coincide with the years of cereal price-rises in England. Disease, as it is here recorded, does not coincide with dear food.[4]

This is a statement of capital importance but it cannot be extended to other countries, least of all to France, where the late seventeenth and early eighteenth centuries were still periods of disastrous food shortages. Let us be quite clear what is at issue here. We are not now considering the influence of food scarcity, prolonged through many years, on the misery of a section of the lower classes, nor the corrosion of the life of these classes

'Causes of the Wholesomeness and Unwholesomeness of the Air', in *Philosophical Works*, ed. Peter Shaw (3 vols. 1725), vol. III, pp. 521–44. Cf. J. P. Peter, 'Malades et maladies à la fin du XVIIIe siècle', *Annales* (*E.S.C.*), 22e année (1967), pp. 711–51.

[1] P. Harsin and E. Hélin (eds.), *Problèmes de mortalité: méthodes, sources et bibliographie...Actes du Colloque international de démographie historique* (Liège, 1965), pp. 26–7.

[2] *New Observations...on City, Town and Country Bills of Mortality* (London, 1750).

[3] *Ibid.* p. 85, table 4.

[4] Cf. wheat prices at Winchester in Beveridge, pp. 81–2.

in the long run. That is another problem. In the present state of our knowledge, no decisive judgment on this subject, except in the case of Languedoc,[1] is warranted by what has been said above about the general price-rise—itself moderate enough when viewed over a period of 25 or 30 years—and on the other hand about the stationary character of the demographic situation during the same period. And yet we cannot escape the conclusion—so often apparent from the behaviour of the quinquennial and *a fortiori* of the decennial averages—that there were veritable demographic dramas, short but violent, which corresponded with equally violent upswings in food prices.[2] To detect them, certainly, requires data both numerous and continuous enough to enable us to follow, in close chronological detail, the course of cereals simultaneously with the variations in births and deaths. The context of the calendar year is the major obstruction to this analysis: in many cases, the year from 1 January to 31 December reduces from the outset the scope of phenomena whose dimensions would be better grasped if grouped between one harvest and the next.[3] Moreover, the abnormal mortality that we are forced to recognize in the years of exceptionally dear food presents some complex features. It is possible that the impact of scarcity was superimposed on that of diseases independent of it. Hard winters, for instance, could in themselves have been responsible for an increase in deaths at the same time as they froze the seed in the ground. In fact, if an autonomous malady precedes a dearth it may well obscure it: raging in advance of the food crisis, it will have taken its pick of the population and left the most resistant element in its wake. Perhaps this is what happened in England in 1708–9. Most often, however, hunger and disease are associated. There is a mortality set in train by hunger, whatever the causal link between the two. In addition, we must take account of the displacement of beggars towards the towns where they hoped to find succour. The urban mortality of these tragic years, indeed, is partly composed of these same refugees who came to town to die, and partly of deaths among the townspeople themselves by disease brought in from outside.

Violent crises in the death rate, but also in the birth rate: that births declined is as plain a fact as that deaths rose in time of dearth. It is the combination of these two phenomena that produces the percentages of disaster to be seen in Table F below, drawn up to indicate the demographic effects of the 1693–4 dearth in a number of places scattered through different regions of France.[4] Closer observation of the movement of

[1] Cf. Le Roy Ladurie, *passim.*
[2] For an analysis of this type of crisis see Goubert, vol. I, p. 45.
[3] On all these questions of method cf. J. Meuvret, 'Les Crises de subsistance et la démographie de la France d'ancien régime', *Population* (1946), p. 643.
[4] Based on parish registers for Rouen (parishes of St Godard, St Maclou, and St Patrice) and all other places listed except Crulai (cf. Gautier and Henry, *La Population de Crulai*) and Saint-Mézard, for which see C. Bourgeat, *Famine et Peste dans un coin du Lecturois*

births than is practicable here shows that it dips several months after a rise in the death rate. This lag has been attributed to the impact of disease or death on pregnant women. The proportions and suddenness of the drop in *conceptions*, however, fit in better with a different hypothesis—family limitation. For the rest, the rapid recovery of conceptions immediately after catastrophe, along with a fall in deaths, completes the contours characteristic of these dramatic but ephemeral episodes. Their place in history is none the less significant for their brevity.

Nevertheless, without going beyond the frontiers of France, some very obvious geographical differences in the incidence of scarcity strike the eye in reading Table F. First of all, the immunity of the places chosen in Mediterranean Provence: conceptions predominate at Tarascon and Cassis. The position in neighbouring Languedoc is more finely graded: at Lodève the balance is nearly equal; at La Tour sur Orbe, not very far from Lodève, deaths were more than double conceptions (223 per cent) whereas at Frontignan, more surprisingly, they amounted to nearly three times as many. The fact is that in the last two cases account has to be taken of poor refugees from the mountains. The most striking contrast to be drawn is perhaps between Valence, in the Rhône valley, and the figures for Tarascon in Provence. In a general way, the severity of the crisis is mitigated as one approaches the lands of the Midi from the central areas of France, where the death rate was at a peak. It is mitigated too as one moves westwards from the Paris region or from Normandy. All these facts of demographic geography are clarified by the geography of prices.

The demographic geography of other countries, where nothing like this is noticeable, nothing at least of the same order of magnitude, may nevertheless have been affected by scarcity to some lesser extent. Naturally it is harder to notice phenomena which are much less visible. The Turin price-current records a maximum, though a fairly moderate one, in 1695.[1] If the subsistence crisis made itself felt there at all, one would expect it to have been felt later and more mildly: and yet soundings undertaken on the frontier of Dauphiné and Piedmont reveal a slight excess of deaths in 1693 which disappears in 1694 and 1695.[2] Even in London, it is to be noted that the mortality peak, in relation to the whole phase 1687–1700, occurs in 1694: not that it was much of a peak—24,109 against a trough of 18,638 in 1696.[3] Was it a mere accident? A more serious comparison could be made between the crises in France and in the Baltic: in one area of

(Auch, 1929). The registers were all consulted in the respective Archives Communales (Viglain being supplemented by Villemurlin), except for Tarascon and Cassis (at Marseilles, Arch. Dép. Bouches-du-Rhône), Auvers-sur-Oise (with two neighbour parishes) and Rambouillet (with six neighbour parishes), for all of which counterparts of the registers are deposited at Versailles, Arch. Dép. Seine-et-Oise.

[1] Turin, Archivio Comunale.
[2] Parish registers of Cesare and Bousson (Suse valley): information kindly communicated by Mademoiselle Davico.
[3] Creighton, vol. II, p. 43.

Finland, between 1695 and 1697, the population contracted by as much as 39 per cent.[1]

The contrast between the demographical rhythms of England and France is, in reality, the contrast between two Europes, situated in differing natural conditions and evolving at different stages of commercial development.

To ascertain the annual returns of the different branches of agricultural production in different countries at this time is certainly out of the question. Recently, however, the methodical study of tithes has been taken in hand in France;[2] and tithes being levied as a fixed proportion of the harvests, we may be able to estimate harvests from this angle. Similarly, we can try to take advantage of the figures furnished for estates leased under *métayage*, which divided the harvests between owner and share-cropper (*métayer*). Here, unhappily, the surviving fragments of accounts come from the biggest tithe-owners and landowners and almost always passed through the hands of middlemen-lessors, who undertook the collection of what was due from the tenants in return for a rent fixed in advance and so based on rough forecasts. Decisive evidence could only be provided by continuous and detailed accounts kept by those who directly exploited the soil. There were landowners who lived on their estates and saw to their own cultivation: from their domestic day-books valuable information can be derived, but the entries are sporadic and seldom amount to a statistical series. Very few peasant cultivators, naturally, were capable of keeping such records or indeed had any use for them.

Nevertheless, here is an example, rare in its precision though unfortunately it concerns an altogether abnormal case—that of a very large farm situated in the great plain extending from the *banlieue*[3] north of Paris, beyond Saint-Denis. The soil is rich and the proximity of the Paris market made for a flourishing grain trade. The farmer paid the proprietor a substantial rent in money, while himself owning his working equipment and the livestock: in other words, he was an entrepreneur in the modern sense of that term. Now it happens that we have his accounts of corn sent to market, giving figures for quantities and prices at each sale from the autumn of 1690 to the summer of 1695—including therefore the crisis of 1693–4 (Table G below).[4] The first comment to be raised is that the biggest receipts occur exactly in the year of scarcity 1693–4. They exceed 22,000 *livres tournois*. At the opposite end of the scale, the minimum return throughout the four harvest-years in question was only 8,883 *livres*, in 1691–2. And yet the quantities sold in this year aggregate 745 *setiers*, as

---

[1] Jutikkala, p. 51.   [2] Le Roy Ladurie, vol. I, pp. 227–35.
[3] The administrative circle extending round Paris to a distance of 25 or 30 miles.
[4] Arch. Dép. Seine-et-Oise, J 67: *registre de comptes* kept by Chartier, farmer of Choisy aux Bœufs. The *setier* was a measure of account equivalent to 12 bushels of corn at Paris.

compared with 585 *setiers* in 1693–4. This difference of 160 *setiers* is relatively mild—21·5 per cent: when account is taken of deductions made for the sowing, for tithe and the farmer's own consumption, the diminution of sales in 1693–4 by comparison with 1691–2 implies a reduction in the harvest yield of at most 10 to 15 per cent. During the interval, however, prices have almost quadrupled. It can be said that this rise favoured the very big grower; but it goes without saying, too, that these data could be very misleading as a guide to the situation of cultivators in general. Even those who were regularly sellers, if only of modest surpluses (not always as much as the 10–15 per cent differential noticed here), had nothing at all to sell when the harvest was really poor. From another angle, the enormous difference financially between the maximum and minimum results obtained by our corn-grower can be interpreted in a contrary sense. If the year of scarcity shows up as relatively favourable to this exceptional type of producer, the years of low prices were years of poor sales (*mévente*) and the present case shows what implications these could have. A rent paid to the proprietor of 6,000 *livres* per annum and a direct tax (the *taille*) of 1,600 *livres*—these two liabilities alone were almost equivalent to the total receipts noted for 1691. It is true that our farmer had certain other sources of income, but he had also to meet other expenses in cash. Moreover, the fact that his accounts begin in 1690 is due, significantly, to the surrender of their lease at this moment by predecessors who had done very poorly in 1688 and 1689, when corn was selling at 8 *livres* per *setier* and at times for less.[1]

But low prices, if they hit the biggest producers hard, left only very mediocre margins to the small and medium growers. In the region of Paris prices could hold up, more or less, thanks to the enormous consumption at close hand. In the distant provinces, a superabundance of produce fell to very low prices and was even difficult to dispose of.[2] The Tables to which reference has been made need interpreting from this point of view. The base chosen, that of the years 1680–9, is a low-price phase, so that consecutive indices around 100 (and *a fortiori* indices below 100) correspond in fact with years of poor sales. In this connection special notice may be taken of the years 1702–7, when the French authorities were flooded from all sides with complaints of the harm done by an accumulation of excessively good harvests.[3] In a country like England the range of price variation was most certainly narrower than in France, but still very much wider than it was to become later. Thus it was not by chance, though

---

[1] Baulant and Meuvret, vol. II, p. 40.

[2] A curious document on this subject comes from Anjou in 1688. The peasants would not give a day's work for a bushel of corn, saying that 'bread and wine counted for nothing and they would rather have 8 or 10 sous in money than a bushel of corn': René Lehoreau, *Cérémonial de l'Eglise d'Angers*, ed. F. Lebrun (1967), p. 186.

[3] See (e.g.) the correspondence of the *intendants de province* with the Controller-General in Arch. Nat., série G7.

it happens to have been in this period, when changes in the volume of production were measured on a simple arithmetical scale, that Gregory King should have formulated his famous law on the geometrical progression or diminution of prices.[1]

Industrial production in those days was very closely bound up with the rural world. Raw materials were not merely gathered in or extracted: they were the object of trimming and dressing procedures up to the stage of the semi-finished product, which furnished the countryside with important sources of income. These, as we have seen, contracted when dear bread reduced industrial demand. But even finished goods were worked up in a rustic setting. Thus the village of Wigston, in the English Midlands, had an artisan component the like of which could be found, at the same time, in numerous parts of the Continent. Apart from the 16 per cent of its inhabitants described as 'poor', W. G. Hoskins has discovered '30 per cent in various crafts and trades, who also depended on agriculture to a varying degree; 17 per cent dependent on framework-knitting. . .'.[2] In many other industrial sectors besides knitting, and without even the appearance of new tools, villagers worked in their homes at the most diverse manufactures, complementing but also competing with the old urban crafts.

In order to gauge the activity of these last, a few direct indications can occasionally be obtained. For instance, we are not entirely without information of the numbers of apprentices, which may be estimated by a patient search of notarial records, or about the number of tools in active use. But information of this kind is usually incomplete and valid for one type of industry or for one locality alone; it is very hard to distinguish from it any tendency common to several industries or several countries, especially since we may find ourselves in the presence of a veritable kaleidoscope of trading and manufacturing patterns.[3] Well before our period, the seventeenth century had witnessed the advent of technical innovations whose general purport at least is discernible. No doubt one may be tempted to take note of facts like the precocious appearance during these years of coke-smelting in the blast furnaces of the first Abraham Darby, although it is as well to understand that we are not yet dealing with mass production; the problem was merely to find a cheap substitute for charcoal now that wood was becoming scarce. A parallel tendency is particularly obvious in the case of textiles, but again this is a qualitative transformation which implies no jump in output. The new tissue takes the place of the old and thereby ruins manufactures no longer adapted to meet changes—changes, however, which it is perhaps an over-simplifica-

---

[1] King did not publish his work on this question: we know of it through Charles Davenant, *An essay upon the...making a people gainers in the balance of trade* (1699), p. 83.

[2] *The Midland Peasant* (1957, reprint 1965), p. 212.

[3] Charles Wilson, 'Cloth Production and International Competition in the Seventeenth Century', *Econ. Hist. Rev.* 2nd ser. vol. XIII (1960–1), p. 221.

tion to attribute to fashion alone, without taking account of the incomes of users. The old textile industry of Leiden was notably prosperous in 1664, when 144,000 pieces of cloth, of every sort, were sold: in 1700, no more than 85,000 were sold.[1] Decadence here was probably the penalty for a traditionally high quality of manufacture. At Beauvais, the making of serges offers a striking contrast with that of broadcloth. After a long decline in both, followed by an interruption in the records, they reappear after 1695 in totally different situations: in the case of serges, the numbers of looms and of masters alike are perceptibly reviving, whilst broadcloth finally collapses.[2] This contrast points to the 'lowering in the purchase power of a clientèle...which has fallen back on cheaper clothstuffs'.[3]

The Sound tolls established by Denmark at the mouth of the Baltic serve to clarify the course taken by an important section of international trade (ch. XXIII (1)), although the published tables of these precious quantitative series have given rise to fairly strong criticism,[4] while the exemptions enjoyed by Sweden until 1710 limit the value of the statistics for our purpose. Nevertheless, the round totals of shipping in these returns retain a certain significance. Whereas the gross number of ships had fallen very low from 1661 to 1679, with an annual average of about 2,500, and then recovered from 1680 to 1689 with over 4,000, the mean figure for 1690–9 works out at 3,700—still a fairly high level. From 1700 to 1710 the drop is much more noticeable: from a maximum of 3,193 vessels, in 1701, we reach a minimum of only 1,413 in 1710.[5]

The considerable share taken by the Dutch in this trade makes it useful to compare the Sound statistics with those furnished by the duties levied on entering and leaving the port of Amsterdam.[6] Here the annual average revenue from 1661 to 1679 amounts to 966 m. florins, as compared with 1,095 m. for 1680–9 and nearly 1,200 m. for 1690–9: finally, from 1700 to 1710, when this revenue fluctuated a good deal, the annual average remains around 1,000 m. Dutch trade, of course, enjoyed many zones of activity. The East India Company's sales in the Netherlands did not decline in these years. Kristof Glamann's examination of its accounts shows sales aggregating approximately 102 m. florins from 1679 to 1688; 124 m. in 1689–98; and 137 m. from 1699 to 1708.[7]

[1] N. W. Posthumus (ed.), *Bronnen tot de geschiedenis van de Leidsche textielnijverheid*, vol. V (The Hague, 1918), p. viii.
[2] Goubert, *Cartes et graphiques*, p. 117.   [3] *Ibid.* p. 588.
[4] N. E. Bang and K. Korst, *Tabeller over Skibsfart og Varetransport gennem Øresund*. Cf. Pierre Jeannin, 'Les Comptes du Sund comme source pour la construction d'indices généraux de l'activité économique en Europe (XVIe–XVIIIe siècle)', *Rev. Hist.* vol. CCXXXI (April–June, 1964), pp. 55–102, 307–40.
[5] Bang and Korst, vol. II, p. 1. Cf. above, p. 871.
[6] J. C. Westermann, 'Statistische gegevens over den handel van Amsterdam in de zeventiende eeuw', *Tijdschrift voor Geschiedenis*, 61e jg. (1948).
[7] *Dutch Asiatic Trade, 1620–1740* (Copenhagen, 1958), p. 16, table 3.

English foreign trade underwent a profound transformation during the second half of the seventeenth century. Tropical goods and re-exports came to occupy an even larger place in it.[1] Taking the whole of Britain's maritime traffic together, including Scotland and Ireland, over the years 1699–1701, north-western Europe (from Hamburg to the south of France), accounted for 46 per cent by value, southern Europe and the Mediterranean for 23 per cent. But relations with North America and the West Indies were of growing importance, sugar constituting 23 per cent and tobacco 15 per cent of the value of total English imports, although wines (chiefly Spanish and Portuguese) still kept ahead with 24 per cent.[2] Similarly, the Portuguese economy, whose development has been outlined above (ch. XVI), was intimately linked with the Anglo-Atlantic trade. In the Mediterranean the English continued to share with the Dutch the advantages of the free port of Leghorn and the profits of the Levant trade: the idea of associating the economy of the Maritime Powers with their own was a steady attraction to the court of Turin.[3] The economic growth of England was already connected with her overseas commerce. From 1697 onwards we possess official evaluations of her aggregate exports. In 1697 they add up to a total of £2,257,000. In 1708 they reached £5,069,000.[4]

Before the wars, French external trade had shown a buoyancy in exactly the same direction, as may be illustrated by the striking progress registered in shipping departures from Nantes to the Antilles: 35 ships in 1674, aggregating less than 3,000 tons, but 73 in 1687—or 7,675 tons. The impact of the Nine Years War is reflected in a fall to 1,485 tons in 1696 and a recovery to 5,365 tons in 1697.[5] Nevertheless, even in a France whose maritime trade was handicapped, it was towards the sea that her boldest and on the whole most effective initiatives were directed. As soon as peace returns, shipping movements become vigorous. Even in war-time there was more than one innovation: notably the South Sea trade, but also the rise of the China trade. By 1701 already, the cheaper China silks were stimulating the manufacture of new textiles at Rouen, not without protest from Lyons.[6] A good example of how imports might continue to

[1] Ralph Davis, 'English Foreign Trade, 1660–1700', *Econ. Hist. Rev.* 2nd ser. vol. VII (1954–5), pp. 150–66.
[2] Idem, 'Merchant Shipping in the Economy of the Late Seventeenth Century', *Econ. Hist. Rev.* 2nd ser. vol. IX (1956–7), pp. 59–73.
[3] F. Venturi, 'Il Piemonte dei primi decenni del settecento nelle relazioni dei diplomatici inglese', *Bollettino storico-bibliografico Subalpino*, vol. LIV (1956), fasc. 2.
[4] P. Deane and W. A. Cole, *British Economic Growth, 1688–1959* (Cambridge, 1962), p. 319; cf. G. N. Clark, *Guide to English Commercial Statistics, 1696–1782* (1938).
[5] J. Delumeau, 'Le Commerce extérieur français au XVIIᵉ siècle', *XVIIᵉ Siècle*, nos. 70–71 (1966), p. 81; cf. idem, *Le Mouvement du port de Saint-Malo, 1681–1720*, and J. S. Bromley, 'The Trade and Privateering of Saint-Malo during the War of the Spanish Succession', *Trans. Société Guernesiaise*, vol. XVII (1964), pp. 631–47.
[6] Arch. Nat. G7, Matières de commerce—Indes Orientales (1701).

grow in spite of war is the case of Roman alum: average annual exports from Civita Vecchia to Marseilles, which stood at 2,856 cantars in 1683-9, rose to 7,357 in 1689-95 and to 8,039 in 1695-1707.[1]

On the other hand, it looks as though continental centres remote from the sea suffered more, not only from the violent crises discussed earlier, but from the latent crisis which embraces the entire age. Geneva can supply a test case. From about 1680 Genevan trade experienced a real boom. Difficulties were apparent in the spring of 1689. In the following years crises appeared—subsistence crises to start with, but finally a general crisis of long duration from which Genevan trade did not recover. Surrounded on all sides by States which curtailed or prohibited exchange, the small republic was one of the spots most sensitive to all European recessions.[2]

Tight money, of which we hear so much in this period and in so many different contexts, is it a commonplace of all times and places? Between 1689 and 1715 this kind of 'penury' seems to be contradicted by the progressive rise in the prices of a large number of goods, as we see it occurring in the great international markets such as Amsterdam. Such a rise, modest as it was in contradistinction to the extreme upward thrusts in cereals, how could it have taken place at all if the means of payment had been defective? Various forms of inflation might be the answer, for there is no ground to suppose that the Brazilian gold discoveries added significantly to European stocks of precious metals before 1715.[3] But could a more active circulation have satisfied the growing calls on money? At this point, unquestionably, something must be allowed for the abnormal expenditure of many States during wars which, in the West alone, lasted nine and twelve years.

Here again we return to the contrast, more than once noticed already, between the Maritime and Continental powers. On what credit could the State or individuals rely in France? It assumed many forms, all still short of perfection. People who possessed solid property, which could serve as security, continued to make wide use of the private contract of loan (*constitution de rente*), thus obtaining the sums they needed at relatively moderate interest. The mass of such contracts, arranged before a notary, has so far been very insufficiently examined by historians, and the limited sample presented below (Table H) cannot be taken as more than a rough foretaste of the results to be obtained from more systematic research. It comes from Rouen in Normandy,[4] a province where the legal rate of interest was over 5½ per cent (*au denier* 18) and so higher than in the rest

[1] J. Delumeau, *L'Alun de Rome* (1962), p. 274, table XXVIII. The cantar at Rome = 50 kg. approx.
[2] A. M. Piuz, *Recherches sur le commerce de Genève au XVII* siècle* (1964), esp. p. 382 (graph of the *ferme des halles*). [3] Cf. above, pp. 534-5.
[4] Rouen, Arch. Dép. Seine-Marit., Minutes des notaires, Pochon and Grebeuval.

of the kingdom (*au denier* 20 = 5 per cent). A low rate on safe investments is no symptom of economic expansion. When business does not offer substantial gains, or when the prospects of gain are too risky, prudent men prefer to use their savings in the safest manner open to them and are glad enough to accept a lower income. Thus it is not uncommon to come across contracts of loan at rates below the legal rate—except, of course, in times of severe crisis, when it was difficult to borrow by this regular and well-supervised medium. At such times short-dated cash alone was in fashion, and it rose to usurious levels of interest. Economic crisis was reflected less in the straining of the interest rate towards the legal maximum, in nearly all contracts, than in the shrinking of the number of such contracts.

Business men were already thoroughly familiar with the use of bills of exchange, but this method of settlement had then an unchallenged international centre in the *Wisselbank* of Amsterdam. With the practice of endorsement, a vast network had developed in which a large portion of the most important international bills were finally drawn on this Exchange Bank, particularly well organized as it was for underwriting this kind of claim and for offering maximum guarantees of the safeguard of balances. So it seems useful to reproduce below (Table I) some of the data drawn from the archives of this famous bank.[1] It will be seen that from 1688 to 1697 the number of account-holders shows an increase on the pre-war years. The total of balances at the bank has also grown and during the three years of peace, 1698–1700, continues to multiply. After that it descends gently till 1708 and 1709, when the drop becomes more marked. Nevertheless, the institution holds up well down to the end of the long phase of the Spanish Succession War. Metal deposits should theoretically have constituted a 100 per cent cover for the balances held by the bank, and in fact the reserves were very strong. In 1712 they fell to a minimum cover of 66 per cent (6,801,000 against balances totalling 10,284,000 florins); but from 1713 the cover returns to 84 per cent and in 1715 to over 93 per cent. Such solidity as this was no merely private accomplishment. It presupposes a real spirit of confidence spread throughout the State.

The English coinage had been consolidated in 1696, after some hesitation, at its traditional parity. Thus the government could not have met its growing expenses had it not succeeded in obtaining a large amount of credit from the public. In this instance, the development of the National Debt (Table J) heralds the modern style of public finance.[2] France and the majority of other Continental States, placed in the same circumstances, could do no better than fall back on expedients. Easiest of all was the

---

[1] Based on J. G. van Dillen, *Bronnen tot de Geschiedenis der Wisselbanken*, vol. II (The Hague, 1925), p. 985.

[2] A. Browning (ed.), *English Historical Documents, 1660–1714* (1953), pp. 355–6, citing *Accounts of the net Public Income and Expenditure of Great Britain*, vol. II (1869), p. 298. Cf. above, ch. IX and P. G. M. Dickson, *The Financial Revolution in England, 1688–1756* (1967), esp. pp. 39 ff. and 341 ff.

monetary expedient. An augmentation of the nominal value of the metal currencies enabled people to put up better with an ascending scale of prices measured in money of account.

All in all, over the short term, the economic climate of this age in many countries was inescapably stamped by brutal up-and-down movements. Over a longer term and on the international plane, the moderate and comparatively regular rise in prices, as it is to be observed in a market like Amsterdam, is only a contradiction in appearance of the over-all downward trend to be noticed at least from the middle of the seventeenth century and to be prolonged far into the eighteenth. Our interdecennial phase of relatively high prices marks only a temporary breach in the continuity of a secular movement. It is, above all, the effect of a tension which arose primarily out of the wars and which is perhaps wholly to be identified with them.[1]

[1] For Tables A–J see below, pp. 898–902.

TABLE A. *Indices of Rye Prices* (1680–9 = 100)

Years	Amsterdam	Lyons	Carpentras	Years	Amsterdam	Lyons	Carpentras
1688–9	95	83	76	1702–3	100	93	93
1689–90	115	108	58	1703–4	118	103	102
1690–1	115	178	91	1704–5	103	100	98
1691–2	105	132	151	1705–6	103	91	118
1692–3	170	230	151	1706–7	95	87	112
1693–4	186	400	135	1707–8	97	105	102
1694–5	155	151	135	1708–9	200	457	214
1695–6	141	103	145	1709–10	263	288	174
1696–7	159	115	112	1710–11	178	120	93
1697–8	200	159	148	1711–12	129	123	93
1698–9	316	316	141	1712–13	129	209	129
1699–1700	214	224	112	1713–14	159	237	112
1700–1	145	123	102	1714–15	151	126	112
1701–2	118	135	81	1715–16	138	89	68

TABLE B. *Indices of Textile Prices*

	Hemp (English Navy Board)	English wools (Houghton)	Fine (*alto*) cloth (Milan)		Hemp (English Navy Board)	English wools (Houghton)	Fine (*alto*) cloth (Milan)
1680–9	100	—	100				
1691–1702	—	100	—				
1688–9	127	—	102	1702–3	159	101	115
1689–90	132	—	104	1703–4	159	—	115
1690–1	130	—	131	1704–5	133	—	110
1691–2	123	75	131	1705–6	108	—	111
1692–3	127	80	103	1706–7	141	—	107
1693–4	128	79	135	1707–8	141	—	—
1694–5	132	89	111	1708–9	153	—	—
1695–6	153	119	113	1709–10	168	—	—
1696–7	169	112	116	1710–11	188	—	—
1697–8	147	112	114	1711–12	176	—	—
1698–9	128	106	121	1712–13	147	—	—
1699–1700	141	106	122	1713–14	136	—	—
1700–1	159	101	127	1714–15	126	—	—
1701–2	158	102	124	1715–16	131	—	—

TABLE C. *Indices of Corn and Raw Wool Prices at Castelnaudary*
(*in* livres tournois)

	Corn	Raw wool		Corn	Raw wool
1682–8	100	100			
1688–9	66	101	1702–3	124	94
1689–90	62	—	1703–4	115	108
1690–1	113	96	1704–5	135	93
1691–2	142	112	1705–6	108	108
1692–3	135	129	1706–7	110	108
1693–4	214	139	1707–8	113	89
1694–5	118	76	1708–9	209	109
1695–6	113	106	1709–10	302	61
1696–7	132	121	1710–11	121	61
1697–8	152	135	1711–12	148	85
1698–99	139	153	1712–13	270	84
1699–1700	155	129	1713–14	148	81
1700–1	163	171	1714–15	115	118
1701–2	121	118	1715–16	115	103

TABLE D. *Indices of Wheat Prices at Paris and of Pewter in
the Paris Region* (*in* livres tournois)

	Wheat	Pewter		Wheat	Pewter
1680–8	100	100			
1688–9	66	111	1700–1	137	123
1689–90	87	111	1701–2	115	143
1690–1	78	111	1702–3	94	136
1691–2	104	99	1703–4	94	136
1692–3	156	86	1704–5	86	111
1693–4	306	83	1705–6	74	143
1694–5	134	80	1706–7	65	123
1695–6	121	86	1707–8	70	123
1696–7	129	80	1708–9	141	123
1697–8	154	80	1709–10	509	99
1698–9	206	111	1710–11	155	123
1699–1700	113	123	1711–12	164	123

TABLE E. *Demographic Incidence of Disease in England*
(*from T. Short*, New Observations...)

	Percentages of parishes where burials preponderated	Percentages of burials in relation to baptisms in the same parishes		Percentages of parishes where burials preponderated	Percentages of burials in relation to baptisms in the same parishes
1680–9	20	144			
1688	8	122	1702	8	110
1689	19	120	1703	9	123
1690	12	164	1704	4	128
1691	11	187	1705	8	115
1692	7	147	1706	16	135
1693	18	153	1707	10	135
1694	12	134	1708	10	136
1695	15	132	1709	6	125
1696	13	145	1710	10	117
1697	14	137	1711	10	169
1698	8	137	1712	13	149
1699	13	136	1713	10	120
1700	18	122	1714	15	118
1701	18	133	1715	9	133

TABLE F. *Dearth of 1693–4 in France:*
Percentages of deaths in relation to conceptions

Locality	Region	Percentage
Rouen	Normandy	407
Crulai	Normandy	431
Digny	Perche	357
Dinan	Brittany	110
Auvers-sur-Oise	North of Paris	518
Rambouillet	South-West of Paris	478
Gien	Orléanais	457
Viglain	Sologne	421
Issoudun	Berry	736
Belabre	Poitou	491
Saint-Mézard	Armagnac	251
La Tour sur Orbe	Languedoc	223
Frontignan	Languedoc	282
Lodève	Languedoc	93
Romans	Dauphiné	161
Valence	Rhône valley	307
Tarascon	Mediterranean Provence	46
Cassis	Mediterranean Provence	50

TABLE G. *Corn sold by a large farm north of Paris, 1691–5*

	Quantities (*setiers de Paris*)	Mean price (*livres tournois*)	Receipts (*livres tournois*)
Half-years			
February–July 1691	451	9·47	4,271
August 1691–January 1692	227	10·37	2,346
February–July 1692	518	12·56	6,507
August 1692–January 1693	314	18·56	5,821
February–July 1693	583	22·06	12,859
August 1693–January 1694	339	37·13	12,587
February–July 1694	246	40·05	9,851
August 1694–January 1695	232	18·83	4,369
February–July 1695	930	12·98	12,069
Harvest years			
1691–2	745	11·88	8,853
1692–3	897	20·82	18,680
1693–4	585	38·36	22,448
1694–5	1,162	14·66	16,438

TABLE H. *Interest rates on* rentes (*Rouen notaries*)

Three-year moving averages	Percentages of rates below 5 per cent	Indices of number of contracts		Percentages of rates below 5 per cent	Indices of number of contracts
1687–9	64	100	1701–3	63	98
1688–90	64	150	1702–4	75	91
1689–91	56	164	1703–5	76	77
1690–2	68	160	1704–6	74	59
1691–3	79	110	1705–7	76	43
1692–4	84	78	1706–8	80	34
1693–5	86	62	1707–9	100	28
1694–6	72	48	1708–10	100	36
1695–7	78	55	1709–11	84	48
1696–8	82	66	1710–12	60	43
1697–9	81	74	1711–13	55	57
1698–1700	63	90	1712–14	48	47
1699–1701	47	91	1713–15	63	47
1700–2	71	102	1714–16	50	38

TABLE I. *Activity of the Bank of Amsterdam*

No. of account-holders per annum (averages)	Years	Total balances (1,000 florins)		Metal reserve (1,000 florins)
2,034	1681–90	9,360	(average per annum)	8,309
	1688	10,752		9,947
	1689	12,715		11,831
	1690	12,604		11,742
	1691	13,557		12,708
	1692	13,181		12,322
2,510	1693	13,525		12,602
	1694	11,479		10,377
	1695	12,013		10,405
	1696	10,207		8,649
	1697	10,263		9,110
2,640	1698	15,234		12,384
	1699	16,751		13,716
	1700	16,285		13,365
	1701	14,830		12,038
	1702	14,783		11,542
2,698	1703	12,578		10,006
	1704	10,964		9,477
	1705	11,524		9,054
	1706	11,299		10,106
	1707	10,089		8,733
2,755	1708	9,319		8,177
	1709	8,182		7,058
	1710	11,386		9,385
	1711	10,206		7,857
	1712	10,284		6,801
2,475	1713	11,772		10,090
	1714	10,666		8,544
	1715	12,991		12,113
2,656	1716–20			

TABLE. J. *English National Debt (funded and unfunded), 1691–1714*

Years	Totals (£ m.)	Years	Totals (£ m.)
1691	3·1	1703	12·3
1692	3·3	1704	12·4
1693	5·9	1705	12·1
1694	6·7	1706	12·4
1695	8·4	1707	15·2
1696	11·6	1708	15·5
1697	14·5	1709	18·9
1698	15·4	1710	21·3
1699	13·8	1711	22·4
1700	12·6	1712	34·9
1701	12·6	1713	34·7
1702	12·8	1714	36·2

INDEX

(The reader should refer to the analytical list of contents for the treatment of major themes)

Aachen, woollens, 865
coal, 869
Aargau, 474
Abbadie, Jacques, Huguenot theologian, 145
Abbeville, woollens, 863-4
Abdi Pasha, Turkish commander, 619
Aberdeen, golf, 151-2
Académie Française, 76
de Musique, 106
des Sciences, 38, 40=1, 43, 65, 76
Acadia, 12, 13, 251, 442, 470, 485, 487, 497-8, 502, 508; *see also* Nova Scotia
Acapulco, China trade, 511
Accault, Michel, of Illinois, 499
Adanson, Michel, French botanist, 59
Addison, Joseph, writer, 32-3, 146, 282, 315
Cato, 83
Spectator, 94, 282
Adige, the, 405, 429
Adler, Guido, musicologist, 103
Adrian, patriarch of Russia, 720, 726, 729
Adrianople, 610, 621, 754
'the affair', 629
Peace of (1713), 636-7
Adriatic, 564, 619, 776
and Venice, 604
Aegean (the Archipelago), 2, 540, 544, 546, 548, 608, 615, 627, 823
sailcloth, 562
Affirmation Act (1696), 264
Afghanistan, and Persia, 644-5
Africa
East, 516-18
North, 277, 385, 551, 564, 838, 864
West, 12, 261, 515, 855
see also Barbary Coast, slavery
African Company, Royal, 261, 855
Afrique, Compagnie d', 551
Agde, 571
Aguirre, Cardinal José Sáenz de, Spanish historian, 134, 343
Ahmed II, sultan, 563, 622
Ahmed III, sultan, 629, 642-4
abdicated, 646
Ahmedabad, 860
Aire, fortress taken by English (1710), 437, 440
Åland Islands, congress (1717-19), 676-8
Alassio, 403

Albania, 544, 562, 608, 622, 646-7
Albany (New York), 486-7, 489, 494
Albarazin, bishop of, 379
Alberoni, Cardinal Giulio, of Parma, Spanish statesman, 164, 380, 565, 641
Albuquerque, fortress, 526
Alcácer do Sal, 520, 537
Alcántara, fortress, 525
Alegrete, Manuel Teles da Silva, 1st marquis of, Portuguese finance minister, 519, 522, 526
Alembert, Jean le Rond d', French mathematician, 43, 52
Alentejo, province, 520, 526-8, 538
Aleppo, caravan route, 541, 548, 550-1, 859
population, 542
Alessandria, 418, 466 n., 558, 560 n.
Alexander VIII (Pietro Ottoboni), pope, 131, 161, 594
Alexandre de Rhodes, S.J., missionary in Far East, 129
Alexandre, Noël, Dominican historian, 132
Alexandretta, 542
Alexandria, 546, 550, 611, 623
Alexis, tsar, 716
Alexis, tsarevich, son of Peter the Great, 676, 733, 738
Alfieri, Count Vittorio, Italian poet, 562
Algiers
population, 542
corsairs, 227, 391, 515, 543-6
wars with Dutch, 550
power of dey, 553-4
captives, 563
see also Barbary Coast
Alhucemas, fortress, 554
Alicante, 370, 438, 514
wine, 521, 845
Allin, Sir Thomas, British admiral, 391
Allouez (Alloues), Claude Jean, S.J., missionary, 498
Almanza, battle of (1707), 373, 433, 438, 447, 757
Almenara, battle of (1710), 440
Alost, fortress, 252
Alsace, 8, 223, 765, 852
religion, 120
war, 304, 421, 753, 755, 785
and Utrecht, 454, 473, 590

Althann, Count Michael Johann, adviser to Charles VI, 593
Altona, Treaty of (1689), 3, 154
Altranstädt, 4, 432, 633
  Treaty (1706), 431, 701
Alvor, Francisco de Tavora, 1st count of, viceroy of Goa, 516
Amazonia
  missions, 129, 356, 531
Ambros, August Wilhelm, German musicologist, 101
Ameller, Francesc, Catalonian fiscal, 379
Amelot, Michel Jean, French diplomat, 183, 186–7, 370–1, 373–4, 376–9
America, North
  and Europe, 11–13, 56, 95, 128, 195–6, 506–8
  Philosophic Society, 42
  Nine Years War, 251–2, 486–90
  Succession War, 441, 501–6
  Utrecht, 13–14, 469–70, 507
  trade, 256, 490–1, 840, 842, 850–3, 855, 866, 871, 894
  immigrants, 493–4, 765
  see also New France and separate colonies
American Indians, 13, 96, 99–100, 128–9, 486, 492
  Abenaki (Canada), 487, 498, 502–3
  Alabamas (Louisiana), 504
  Apalache (Florida), 504
  Araucanians (Chile), 356
  Cahokia (Illinois), 499
  Cayugas (Iroquois), 490
  Chickasaws (Louisiana), 504
  Choctaws (Louisiana), 504
  Creeks (Florida), 504
  Etchemins (Canada), 498
  Jurimaguas (Amazon), 356
  Kaskaskias (Illinois), 498
  Kennebecs (Acadia), 498
  Lake Peten (Mexico), 356
  Miamis (Illinois), 490, 498
  Mohawks (Iroquois), 490
  Natchez (Louisiana), 499, 501, 504
  Omaguas (Amazon), 356
  Oneidas (Iroquois), 490, 498
  Onondagas (Iroquois), 490
  Osages (Illinois), 499
  Ottawas (Canada), 486, 490
  Ounspik (Louisiana), 499
  Penobscots (Acadia), 498, 502
  Pottawattomies (Illinois), 498
  Pueblos (New Mexico), 356
  Senecas (Iroquois), 486
  Taensas (Louisiana), 499
  Tamarois (Illinois), 499
  Timucuas (Florida), 504
  Tocobagas (Florida), 504
  Tonicas (Louisiana), 499
  Tuscaroras (Iroquois), 508
  Yazoos (Louisiana), 499, 504
Amersfoort, tobacco, 852
Amiens, woollens, 863
Amsterdam, 15, 51, 75, 105, 176–7, 187, 195, 200, 262, 727, 737, 796
  finance and war, 23, 297–8, 303–4, 307, 314, 420, 471; see Banks
  admiralty, 21, 295, 800
  population, 542
  trade, 295, 535, 550, 736, 846, 851–2, 857, 860, 873, 875, 877, 893
  corn market, 322, 837, 876–8, 898
Anatolia, 541, 553, 567, 609, 621, 628, 639, 642; see also Turkey
Ancona, trade, 555–6
Andalusia, 349, 353, 366–7, 369, 375
Andes, 531–2
Andrade, Freire de, governor of São Tomé, 515
Andros, Sir Edmund, governor of Dominion of New England, 480, 492, 494, 505
Angola, slaves, 515, 533
Angoumois, iron, 812
Anna, duchess of Courland, 738–9
Anne, queen of Great Britain, 17, 29, 102, 108, 121, 169–70, 190, 255, 268–9, 381
  as princess, 201, 204–5, 207–9
  and Tories, 270
  accession, 414
  and Savoy, 466
  and Augustus II, 710
  death, 474, 477
Ansbach, troops, 404
Antalya, Turkish naval arsenal, 615
Antigua, 810
Antilles, see West Indies, flibustiers, and separate islands
Anton Ulrich, duke of Brunswick-Wolfenbüttel, 74, 166, 202, 246, 402, 407
Antonio, Nicolás, Spanish bibliographer, 343
Antwerp, 87, 390, 398–9, 416, 426–7, 435, 445, 477, 753
  Bank of England office, 293
  defence, 404, 413
Apafi, Michael, prince of Transylvania, 577, 582, 608, 622
Aragon, 9, 347, 348, 353, 363, 368, 373–4, 375
  civil war, 370, 373, 425, 433, 783
  wool, 863
Arbuthnot, Dr John, Scottish wit, 48, 107
  John Bull, 443
Archangel, 657, 716
  trade, 648, 725, 841–4, 867
Ardabil, occupied by Turks, 645
Arega, 513

Argos, retaken by Turks, 638
Argoud, sieur, Louisiana promoter, 500
Argyle, Archibald Campbell, 9th earl, 196
Argyle, John Campbell, 2nd duke, 271
Arias, Manuel de, Spanish minister, 352, 361
Arizona, 356
Arles, 813
Armenians, 186, 618, 642, 645, 811
Arminianism, 122, 142
Arnauld, Antoine, Jansenist, 132, 135, 139
Arnoul, Pierre, intendant des classes, 822
Arras, fortress, 440
Arsenius III, patriarch of Peć, 579–80
Artagnan, Pierre de Montesquiou d', marshal of France, 747
Artois, linens, 866
Arundel, Anne, of Maryland, 483
Arzão, António, Brazilian explorer, 533
Arzila, fortress, 554
Asam, Cosmos Damian and Egid Quirin, Bavarian architect–decorators, 144
Asfeld, Jacques Vincent, baron d', French diplomat, 160
Ashurst, Sir Henry, colonial agent, 491
Asiento, the, 349–50, 367, 376
  and France, 10, 15, 364, 367, 376, 415, 856
  and England, 434, 439, 442, 448, 460, 464, 475–6, 528
  and Portugal, 364, 515
  see also slaves
Asselijn, Thomas, Dutch dramatist, 75
Assendelft, Jean Deutz van, Dutch banker, 307
Astrakhan, 644, 733, 775
Astruc, Jean, French scholar, 67, 141
Asunción, 357
Ath, fortress, 252, 381
Athens, bombarded by Venetians (1687), 620
Atouguia, Jeronimo Casimiro de Atáide, 9th count of, 537
Atterbury, Francis, bishop of Rochester, 127
Aubusson, 325
Auersperg, Count Leopold von, imperial ambassador to Britain, 383
Aughrim, battle of (1691), 242
Augsburg, 238, 421, 589
  League of, 120, 223
  population, 884
Augustus II, king of Poland and elector of Saxony, 2–3, 116, 184, 402, 406, 584
  conversion to Rome, 121, 188, 687, 709–10
  elected king (1697), 652, 686–7
  surrenders crown (1706), 663, 701
  abdication annulled (1710), 704
  absolutist aims, 2, 697–8, 707, 709, 713
  Polish reforms, 687, 691, 707–8, 713–14

opposition in Poland, 654, 657–9, 686–9, 697, 711–12, 714
support from Poles, 654, 695–6, 698, 700, 702–3
and Turkey, 637, 672–3, 688–9, 692
and Lithuania, 690–1, 693–4, 711
and Courland, 694
and Livonia, 2, 652–3, 655, 687, 692, 712
and Charles XII, 652 ff., 662–3, 671–3, 678, 692 ff.
and Russia, 184, 636, 654–6, 660–1, 678, 692, 693, 698–9, 701–2, 704, 708–15, 734–5
and Brandenburg-Prussia, 2, 689–90, 694, 708, 709, 710, 735
and France, 406–7, 692, 695, 710–11
and Maritime Powers, 655, 670, 695, 699
and Habsburg, 695, 710
army, 237, 241, 768
Aulisio, Domenico d', Neapolitan jurist, 558
Aunis, wines, 845
Aurangzeb, Mughal emperor of India, 35
Austria, duchies of, 572–3, 591, 599 ff.
Austria, house of
  conflicting interests, 4–6, 157, 162, 228, 238, 412, 576, 578–9, 586, 621–2
  and papacy, 131, 434, 448, 594–5
  and Turkey, 162, 195, 225–7, 232–4, 238–42, 253, 383, 402, 572, 576 ff., 618 ff., 625 ff., 638 ff.
  and Spanish succession, 8, 157, 351–2, 357–9, 384 ff., 393 ff., 448, 449–50, 454–5, 462–3, 468, 471 ff., 590 ff.
  family law, 575–6, 592, 597
  see also Habsburg monarchy, Vienna
Avaux, Jean Antoine de Mesmes, comte d', 172, 178, 186, 200, 203, 246, 400–1
  in Ireland, 213
Aviano, Marco d', Austrian Capuchin, 576, 578
Avignon, silk manufacture, 867–8
Ayloffe, Captain William, 145
Azerbaijan, 645
Azores, the, 509, 513, 520, 531, 849
Azov (Azak), fortress, 6, 610, 625–8, 631, 634–5, 684, 718–22, 732

Bach, Carl Philipp Emanuel, musician, 118
Bach, Johann Sebastian, musician, 105, 115–18, 144
Bacon, Francis, philosopher, 37–8, 43, 71, 84
Badajoz, fortress, 525–6
Baden, 5, 167, 402, 477
  Grand Alliance, 411
  Treaty of (1714), 446, 474
  see also Lewis, margrave of Baden
Baden-Durlach, margrave of, 166

Baghdad, 548, 608–9
  population, 542
Bahamas, 372
Bahia, 128, 516, 529, 531–2, 534
Baia, naval engagement (1693), 568
Baiona (Galicia), 526
Baku, occupied by Russians (1723), 645, 739
Balance of power, concept of, 155–7, 395
Balkans, the, 1, 7, 29, 563, 571
  wars in, 5, 30, 579–80, 628, 684, 689, 754
  Christians, 167, 576, 625, 632, 754, 776
  see also Turkey and separate territories
Baltaji Mehmed Pasha, grand vizier, 632, 634–7
Baltimore, Charles Calvert, 3rd baron, 482–3
Bamberg, bishop of, 407
Bangor (Ireland), 237
Banister, John, English musician, 104
Banks
  Amsterdam, Wisselbank, 832, 835, 896, 902
  of England, 23, 249, 288–93, 314, 457, 835
  Genoa, Banco San Giorgio, 543
  Paris, Caisse des Emprunts (1674, 1702), 302
  Rouen, Caisse Legendre, 302, 305
  Venice, Banco del Giro, 543
  Vienna, Giro Bank (1703), 311–12, 606;
    City Bank (1706), 311–12, 314, 606
  see also Berne, Geneva, Lyons
Bantam, pepper, 857
Bantry Bay, naval battle (1689), 236
Baptist Brethren, 493
Barbados, 251, 521, 849
Barbary Coast, 178, 543–6, 548, 550, 553–4, 566, 608, 615, 638
  corsairs, 6, 224, 357, 543 ff., 615, 623
  see also Algiers, Morocco, Tripoli, Tunis
Barbezieux, Louis François Marie le Tellier, marquis de, French war minister, 752
Barcelona, 16, 252, 362, 368, 441, 444, 541, 553, 591
  French navy at, 243, 248
  population, 357, 542
  sieges (1697), 358, 423, 568–9; (1705), 419, 455, 429; (1714), 377–8, 444–5, 467, 570
  corn market, 877
Barcelonette valley, 159, 245, 467
Barclay, Robert, Quaker apologist, 150
Barcos, Abbé Martin de, Jansenist, 133
Baretti, Giuseppe, Italian critic, 562
Barfleur, naval battle, see La Hougue
Baring, John, clothier, 866
Baron, Michel, French dramatist, 90
Barrier, Dutch, 16, 384, 391, 395, 400, 406, 427, 431

Anglo-Dutch Treaty (1709), 438–9, 441–2, 447–52, 455, 460, 462–7, 471, 750; (1713), 444, 476–7
Austro-Dutch (1715), 445, 473, 478, 576, 598
Bart, Jean, Dunkirk corsair, 19, 244, 248, 795, 802, 829
Bartenstein, Johann Christoph von, baron, 587
Bashkirs, 732
Basle, 223
Basnage, Jacques, Huguenot writer, 123, 337
Basra, 609
Bassein (Baçaim), Mahratta attacks, 518
Basto, 521
Basville, Nicolas de Lamoignon, marquis de, intendant of Languedoc, 335
Batavia, 519, 809, 859
Bath, John Grenville, earl of, 491
Baturin, cossack headquarters, 667
Bavaria
  and Austria, 237, 241, 243, 450, 468, 589–90
  and France, 167, 203, 215, 402, 404, 407, 411, 588, 756
  after Blenheim, 30, 422–3, 589, 741
  Utrecht, 473–4
  price levels, 877
  see also Maximilian Emmanuel
Baxter, Richard, presbyterian divine, 142, 146, 153
Bay, Alexandre Maître, marquis de, French officer, 438
Bayle, Pierre, philosopher, 24–5, 36, 77–8, 91, 123–4, 139, 142–3, 218
  République des Lettres, 33, 46, 76
  Dictionnaire, 47, 88, 136–7, 341
Bayonne, 175, 812, 863
Bayreuth, 402
  margrave of, 432, 752, 755
Beachy Head, battle of (1690), 215, 239, 567, 792, 794–5, 825
Beauchesne, Gouin de, French captain, 359
Beauvais, textiles, 893
Beauval, Basnage de, Huguenot pastor, 329
Beauvillier, Paul de Saint-Aignan, duc de, minister of state, 189, 326–8, 365
Becher, Johann Joachim, Austrian economist, 54, 310, 313, 606
Beckford, William, English writer, 97
Bedmar, I. J. J. Domingo de la Cueva de Benavides, marquis of, governor of the Spanish Netherlands, 365, 398, 475
Beeston, Sir William, governor of Jamaica, 355
Beethoven, Ludwig van, 105, 116
Bégon, Michel, intendant of Rochefort, 21, 815–16, 830, 832

Bégon, Michel, son of preceding, intendant of Canada, 496
Behrens, Leffmann, Hanoverian banker, 788
Beichling, Wolf Dietrich von, Saxon minister, 698
Beira Baixa, province, 520, 527
Bekker, Balthasar, Dutch scholar, 123, 142
Belém, see Pará
Belgrade, 6, 7, 610, 754
  taken by Austrians (1688), 225, 577–8, 621; (1717), 582, 640–2, 750
  taken by Turks (1690), 241, 580–1, 619–20, 622–3; (1739), 627
Belhaven, John Hamilton, 2nd baron, Scottish independent, 276
Belize, 354
Bellin (Blain), Nicolas, French-Canadian engraver, 497
Bellomont, Richard Coote, 2nd earl of, governor of New York, 490
Benbow, John, British vice-admiral, 372, 796, 825, 829
Bender, fortress, 610, 615
  Charles XII at, 630, 634–5, 669–70, 673–4, 708
Benevente, 537
Bengal, 518, 857, 859–60
Benkulen, 857
Benoist, Elie, Huguenot divine, 123
Benserade, Isaac de, French musician, 106
Bentley, Richard, English scholar, 82
Berczényi, Count Nicholas, Hungarian rebel leader, 584
Beresteczko, battle of (1651), 682
Berg, duchy of, 589
Bergen, whale-fishermen, 848
Bergeyck, Count Jan van Brouchoven, reformer of the Spanish Netherlands, 374, 390, 395, 398, 413, 426, 428, 435, 446, 598
Bergen-op-Zoom, 399
Bergh, Johan van den, Dutch minister in Brussels (1706–16), 428, 445
Bergues canal (Dunkirk), 812
Berka, Franciscus Antonius, count of Havora, imperial envoy at The Hague, 171
Berkeley, George, bishop of Cloyne, philosopher, 50, 55, 126
Berkeley, Sir William, governor of Virginia, 495
Berlin, 31, 768
  Academy of Sciences, 42, 45, 76
Bernard, Samuel, French banker, 23, 303–5, 314, 336–7, 339, 543, 788–9
Berne, 31, 288
  Malacrida bank, 788
Bernier, François, French traveller, 95, 99

Bernini, Giovanni Lorenzo, Italian sculptor and architect, 144
Bernoulli, Daniel, Swiss scientist, 42, 66
Berry, wool, 863
Berthelot, François, French financier and war contractor, 815–16
Berwick, James Fitz-James, 1st duke of, marshal of France
  Ireland (1689), 237
  Nice (1704), 426
  Portugal invaded (1704), 527
  Madrid (1706), 372, 429–30
  the Moselle (1708), 434
  Barcelona (1714), 378–9, 570
  see also Almanza
Bessarabia, 630
Béthune, fortress taken by English (1710), 440
Biała Cerkiew, fortress, 696
Białozor, Christopher, canon of Vilna, 698
Bielke, Count Nils, Swedish senator, 184
Bienville, Jean-Baptiste le Moyne, sieur de, 501, 504
Bignon, Abbé Jérôme, 40–1, 45
Bihach, Turkish garrison, 640
Bilbao, 849
Biloxi, 360, 365, 498–500
Birże (Birzha), 693, 700, 734
Bishop, Corporal Matthew, English soldier, 762
Blackadder, Colonel John, 762
Black Forest, 237, 417, 753, 756
Black Sea, 1, 3, 31, 562–4, 611, 627, 644, 716, 736
Blaise (Biaggio Pangalo), French shipbuilder, 21, 793
Blasphemy Act (1698), 265
Blathwayt, William, secretary at war and to Board of Trade, 176, 491, 506
Blécourt, Jean Denis, marquis de, French diplomat, 361
Blekinge, 808
Blenheim, battle of (1704), 269, 277, 421–2, 449, 756–7, 758
  results, 167, 169, 302, 304, 449, 584, 589–90, 594, 662
  casualties, 749
Blondel, Nicolas François, French architect and engineer, 40, 812
Bluteau, Fr, Portuguese agent, 512–13
Bochette, the, Alpine pass, 754
Bochnia, salt mines, 844
Boerhaave, Herman, Dutch physiologist, 34, 44, 65–6
Bohemia
  religion, 120, 602
  constitution, 573–5, 599
  lord and peasant, 599–600
  economic, 605–6

Boileau-Despréaux, Nicolas, French critic and poet, 24, 73, 81, 83
Boisguilbert, Pierre le Pesant de, French economist, 329–30
Bolingbroke, Henry St John, 1st viscount, 221, 430, 735, 799
  colonial policy, 13–14, 16, 503, 505, 508
  commercial treaty with France, 17, 261, 469–70, 868
  in power, 254, 270, 281, 441
  Schism Act, 273–4
  Utrecht negotiations, 442–3, 457–71
Bolivia, 357
Bologna, 10, 555
  population, 542
Bombay, 518, 809
Bonn, fortress, 225, 237, 413, 451, 462, 473
  taken by Allies (1703), 416
Bonnet, Charles, Swiss naturalist, 64 n.
Bonneval, Claude Alexandre (Ahmed Pasha, 'the Bombardier'), 614, 743
Bonrepaus, François d'Usson de, French naval intendant and diplomat, 186, 830
Bordeaux, 42, 335, 341, 522, 839, 842
  wines, 845, 871, 877
Boreel, Jacob, burgomaster of Amsterdam, 170, 249, 388
Borelli, Gian Alfonso, Neapolitan scientist, 558
Bornholm, island, 807
Bose, Christoph Dietrich, Saxon envoy at The Hague, 688
Bosnia, 1, 577, 608–9, 619, 626
Bosporus, the, 562
Bossuet, Jacques Bénigne, bishop of Meaux, 25, 72, 87, 94, 124–5, 136, 216 n., 218, 343
  Gallicanism, 132, 334
  and Richard Simon, 140–1
  and Mme Guyon, 147–8
  death, 334
Boston (Mass.), 12, 14, 480–1, 488, 492–6
  Succession War, 502, 505–6, 810 n.
Bouchain, fortress, 440, 444
Boucherville (New France), 496
Boufflers, Louis François, duc de, marshal of France, 324, 398
  Ryswick, 170, 252, 388
  Nine Years War, 232, 239, 242, 247, 249
  Succession War, 404, 409, 436
Bouhier, Jean, magistrate of Dijon, 340
Bouhours, Dominique, S.J. critic, 78
Boulainvilliers, Henri, comte de, French historian, 329
Bounty Act (1705), 842
Boyle, Robert, English scientist, 34, 47, 51, 53
Boyne, battle of the (1690), 214, 240

Brabant, 415; States of, 426, 428
  Lines of, 413, 417, 424, 751
Bradford, worsteds, 865
Bradley, James, astronomer royal, 40, 43, 52
Bradstreet, Simon, of Massachusetts, 481
Braganza, corn prices, 509
Brancovan, Constantine, prince of Wallachia, 580, 633, 638
Brancovich, George, Serbian historian, 577
Brancovich, Sava, Orthodox metropolitan in Transylvania, brother of preceding, 577–8
Brandenburg-Culmbach, margrave of, 166
Brandenburg-Prussia, 2, 154, 241, 719
  Huguenots welcomed, 121, 779
  army, 20–1, 202–3, 228, 232, 239, 244, 404, 742–3, 768, 777, 779
  Nine Years War, 195, 215, 225, 232, 239
  Grand Alliance, 404, 406, 410, 425, 432
  Utrecht, 465–6, 477
  and Habsburgs, 587, 590
  and Augustus II, 689–90, 694, 708–10
  plague, 886 n.
  see also Frederick III, Frederick William, Great Northern War
Bray, Thomas, founder of S.P.G., 152
Brazil
  missions in, 128–9, 356, 531, 537
  gold discoveries, 163, 533–5, 862, 895
  Buenos Aires trade, 350, 528–30
  production crises, 510–11, 534
  sugar, 510–11, 516, 519, 520, 530, 531, 534, 853
  tobacco, 510–11, 516, 520, 530, 534, 851–2
  cattle, 531–2
  Paulistas, 532–3
  Trading Company, 536–7
  see also Cayenne, Maranhão, Pará, Sacramento, slavery
Breda, Treaty of (1667), 387
Breisach, 252, 473
Breisgau, the, 579, 588
Breitkopf, J. G. I., Leipzig music-printer, 105
Bremen, 477, 649, 658, 672, 678, 840
  trade, 847–8, 866–7
Brenner Pass, 417, 754
Breslau (Wrocław), 605, 697, 705
Brest, arsenal, 20, 256, 793, 811, 812–13, 820, 823
  squadron, 18, 22, 203–4, 236, 250, 408, 423, 567–8, 795
  Allied attack (1694), 215, 248
Bridgewater, John Egerton, 3rd earl of, president of Board of Trade, 491
Brihuega, battle of (1710), 375, 440, 458
Briord, Gabriel, comte de, French diplomat, 181

Bristol, 70, 490
Brittany, Louis of France, duke of, 463
Brittany, 335, 519, 523, 829
  sailcloth, 812, 815, 843, 866
Britton, Thomas, concert promoter, 104
Brochado, Cunha, Portuguese minister to
  France, 525–6
Brouillan, Jacques François de, governor at
  Placentia, 489
Bruce, James Daniel, Russian general, 634
Bruges, 436, 443, 464
Brunswick-Lüneburg, 61, 404; see Ernest
  Augustus
Brunswick-Wolfenbüttel, see Anton Ulrich
  of and Charlotte of
Brussels, 242, 247, 249, 388, 397, 424, 426,
  428, 436
Brydges, James, 1st duke of Chandos, Pay-
  master of the Forces Abroad, 107, 787–8
Bubble Act (1719), 836
Bučač, Treaty of (1672), 682
Buccaneers, see flibustiers
Buchanan, George, Scottish scholar, 217
Bucharest, 580, 639
Buckingham, John Sheffield, 1st duke of,
  79, 254
Buda, 6, 7, 608, 610
  taken by Austrians (1686), 577, 618–20, 684
Bücken, Ernst, German musicologist, 102
Buenos Aires, 372, 476
  trade, 350, 364, 376, 525, 528–9, 534
Buffon, Georges Louis Leclerc, comte de,
  French naturalist, 35, 62–4
Bug, the, 610, 700
Bukofzer, Manfred, musicologist, 103
Bulavin, Kondrat, leader of the Don
  Cossacks (1706–8), 732
Bulgaria, 608, 610, 621
Bunyan, John, 79, 146
Buonanni, Filippo, S.J., Italian botanist, 64
Buononcini, Giovanni Battista, Italian
  musician, 110
Burchett, Josiah, British admiralty secre-
  tary, 824, 830
Burckhardt, Jakob, Swiss historian, 103
Burgundy, Louis of France, duke of, grand-
  son of Louis XIV, 148, 189, 327–8, 435
  death, 463
Burnet, Gilbert, bishop of Salisbury, 119,
  125, 138, 140, 201 n., 217–18
Burnet, Thomas, divine, 86, 141
Burney, Dr Charles, musicologist, 101, 107
Butler, Samuel, English satirist, 79
Butrinto, 639
Buys, Willem, pensionary of Amsterdam,
  425–6, 438–9
  peace negotiations (1709–11), 450–1,
  459–62

Bychów, occupied by Russians, 701
Bydgoszcz, Treaty of (1657), 689
Byng, George, later Viscount Torrington,
  British admiral, 817
Bynkershoek, Cornelius van, Dutch jurist,
  173
Byrd II, William, Virginian planter, 495, 507

Cacheo Company (Guinea), 364, 515–16,
  531, 536
Cadaval, Nuno Alvares Pereira de Melo,
  1st duke of, Portuguese minister, 522,
  526, 528
Cadillac, Antoine de La Mothe de, French
  naval captain in Canada, 498
Cadiz, 345, 408
  naval base, 11, 22, 238, 249, 566–9, 808–9
  Allied attack (1702), 369, 418, 423
  trade, 371–2, 385, 475, 511, 514, 528–9,
  844, 866, 871
  population, 542
  naval school, 827
Cadogan, William, 1st Earl Cadogan,
  quartermaster-general, 428, 756, 761
Cadore, Venetian trade, 555
Cahors, wines, 845
Cairo, 11, 609, 632, 644
  population, 542
  English consul, 550
Cakovec, 577
Calais, bombarded (1695), 249
Calandrini family, Genevan bankers, 303
Calcinato, battle of (1706), 429
Caldara, Antonio, Venetian musician, 111
Calderón de la Barca, Pedro, Spanish
  dramatist, 72, 343
California, missions, 35, 129, 354, 356, 373
Calixtus, Georg, Lutheran theologian, 122
Callao, 530
Callenburgh, Gerald, Dutch vice-admiral,
  423
Callières, François de, French diplomat,
  170, 172–3, 179–80, 249, 388
Callières, Louis Hector, chevalier de,
  governor of Montreal, 490, 498
Calvinism, 24, 119–23, 149, 150, 218, 582
Camaret Bay (Brest), 248
Cambodia, Dominican mission, 357
Cambridge, university, 43
  Platonists, 92, 138, 142
  Dissenters, 274
Camden, William, English antiquary, 87
Camerarius, R. J., German botanist, 64
Cameronians, 278
Camisards, 169, 325, 414, 571
Campeche, 350, 354–6, 372, 515, 854
Campo Maior, siege of (1712), 527
Camprodon, surrender of (1689), 235

Canada, *see* New France
Canaletto (Antonio Canale), Venetian painter, 556
Cananor, 525
Canary Islands, 349, 353, 372–3, 387, 521
  trade, 845, 849
Candamo, Francisco Bances, Spanish dramatist, 343
Candia, 615
Canitz, F. R. von, Prussian poet, 73
Cantacuzene, Serban, prince of Wallachia, 578
Cantemir, Demetrius, prince of Moldavia, 633–4
Canton, 11, 15, 35, 96
Cap Français (St-Domingue), 355
Cap Nègre (Newfoundland), 488
Cape Breton Isle, 470, 508, 850
Cape of Good Hope, 809
Cape Matapan, 640
Cape Passaro, naval battle (1718), 565, 790
Cape São Roque, 530
Cape Verde, slavery, 515
Capitulations, the Ottoman, 549
Caprara, Aeneas, Austrian general, 245
Capuchins, 129, 146, 576, 617
Caracas, cacao, 530
Caraffa, Antonio, imperial general, 243
  in Hungary, 579, 582–3, 586, 597, 619
Carbonear (Newfoundland), 503
Carcassonne, woollens, 864
Cardonnel, Adam, secretary to Marlborough, 761
Careri, Gemelli, traveller to China, 96
Caribbean, *see* Cartagena, Vera Cruz, West Indies and separate islands
Carignano, 247
Carinthia, 386
Carlos II, king of Spain, 8, 9, 162, 168, 296, 344, 352–3, 358, 391, 591, 626
  will, 10, 163, 360–1, 394, 400, 796
  character, 348–9
  marriages, 348, 351, 525
  succession, 385–8, 410
  death, 4, 181, 361–2, 569, 576
  see also Partition Treaties, Spain
Carlowitz, Peace of (1699), 1, 2, 6, 158, 162, 394, 553, 581, 632, 637, 639, 719
  British mediation, 569, 580
  the terms, 518–2, 626–7, 691–2
  Hungarians and, 584
Carmelites, 531
Carnero, Alonso, Spanish minister, 352
Carniola, 386
Carolinas, 491, 493
  South 12, 350, 372, 495
  rice, 854
Carpentras, rye prices, 876

Carpi, battle of (1700), 405
Carrickfergus, captured (1689), 237
Cartagena (Indies), 12, 251, 349, 354, 372, 511, 515, 528, 809
  taken by French (1696), 355, 489
Cartagena (Spain), 370
Carter, Robert, Virginian planter, 495
Cartesianism, 43, 46, 49–51, 73, 84–6, 122, 136
Casale, 27, 160, 223, 238, 240, 248, 250, 559
Casca river, gold, 533
Casco Bay, 486–7
Caspian Sea, 1, 2, 551, 644–5, 739
Cassano, battle of (1705), 425
Cassard, Jacques, French corsair, 20, 810
Cassini, Giovanni Domenico, astronomer, 41, 73, 77
Castanheira, counts of, 538
Castel Branco, 527
Castel dos Rios (Castelldosrius), Manuel de Oms y de Santa Pau, 1st marquis of, viceroy of Peru, 372
Castelnaudary, corn and wool prices, 881, 899
Castiglione, prince of, 473, 594
Castile, 343–4, 783
  government, 9, 348, 353, 371, 374, 377–8, 425, 553
  finances, 346, 366, 514
  loyal to Philip V, 369, 371, 430
  trade, 522, 528, 877–8
Castine (Acadia), 502; *see* Pentagoët
Catalonia, 7, 11, 30, 343, 396, 430, 553, 787
  and Archduke Charles, 8, 370–1, 425, 430, 437, 593, 596
  French in, 235, 242–3, 247–50, 351, 357, 374, 389–90, 444, 767
  government, 347–8, 357, 362, 368, 378–80, 382, 390, 425, 445
  guerrillas (Miqueletes), 371, 429
  Utrecht, 444, 467–8, 472
  Rastatt, 472, 474
  trade, 370, 379 n., 520, 522, 813, 844
  population, 884–5
Catherine I, empress of Russia, 617, 634
Catherine II, empress of Russia, 722
Catherine, duchess of Mecklenburg, 738
Catholics, 8, 10, 25, 149, 474
  Congregation of Propaganda, 128–30
  in Asia, 129–30
  in United Provinces, 135
  in Germany, 120–1, 188, 252, 473–4, 588
  in Britain, 135, 194 ff., 201, 264; *see* James II
  and British colonies, 480 ff., 492
  in Transylvania, 582
  see also Jansenism, missions, papacy, Quietist controversy

Catinat, Nicolas de, marshal of France, 19, 747, 781
  in Italy, 233, 241, 243, 245, 404–5, 414
Cattaro (Kotor), 627
Caucasus, 610, 627, 645
Cavalier, Jean, Camisard leader, 570–1
Cavalli, Pietro Francesco, Italian musician, 104
Cayenne, 41, 466, 531
Cederhielm, Josias, Swedish chancery official, 184, 661
Celle, duchy of, 188, 226, 407
Cerdaña (Cerdagne), 567
Cerigo, Venetian base, 540, 638, 640, 642
Cervera, university, 379
Cesti, Marc'Antonio, Tuscan musician, 110
Ceuta, Moorish attacks, 359, 390, 554
Cévennes, 325, 338, 863
Ceylon, 519, 530, 858
Châlons, woollens, 864
Chambers, Ephraim, encyclopaedist, 47
Chamillart, Michel, controller-general and secretary for war, 284, 298, 331, 363, 752, 803, 831
Chamlay, Jules Louis Bolé, marquis de, quartermaster-general, 751, 763, 767
Chamoy, Rousseau de, French diplomat, 173
Champagne, woollen manufacture, 863–4
Champigny, Bochart de, intendant of New France, 484, 486
Changamire, Rozvi chieftain, 518
Channel Islands, 20, 842
Chantilly, 40, 570
Chardin, Sir John, traveller, 95, 98, 546
Charente, the, 812
Charlemont, fortress, captured by Schomberg (1690), 238
Charleroi, fortress, 248, 252, 381, 477–8
Charles, archduke of Austria; successively Charles III of Spain and Charles VI, emperor; proposed for Milan (1697), 161, 393, 426, 591
  Spanish succession, 164–5, 358, 388, 418–19, 433, 437, 446 ff., 592, 596–7
  Succession War, 296, 370–1, 422–3, 425, 429–30, 440, 444, 575, 593
  Stanhope treaty (1708), 434, 439, 464, 799
  and Clement XI, 164, 376, 434
  emperor, 164, 441–2, 459, 462, 593
  king of Hungary (1711), 585
  and Turks, 638–42
  Habsburg administration, 597–607
Charles II, king of Great Britain, 102, 106, 183, 193, 221, 254, 269, 480, 742, 808
  and House of Commons, 193–4
  character, 193–4, 209
  foreign policy, 193, 225

finance, 285, 291
  army, 197; navy, 792 ff., 828
Charles V, duke of Lorraine, 225, 234, 237, 396, 578
  in Hungary, 619
  death, 241
Charles VI, duke of Lorraine, 5, 252, 397, 424
Charles V, emperor, 5, 308, 368, 387, 557
Charles VI, emperor, see Charles, archduke of Austria
Charles X, king of Sweden, 649
Charles XI, king of Sweden, 172, 183–4, 650, 650, 743, 749, 771, 773, 825, 832
  death, 651
Charles XII, king of Sweden, 2–4, 154, 167, 169, 182, 184, 188, 402–3
  accession, 650–1
  military qualities, 655–6, 660, 744, 749, 752, 757–8, 760, 761
  character, 659–60, 661–2, 714
  Polish policy, 631, 656–9, 693 ff., 714–15
  invades Russia, 663–8, 702
  exile in Turkey, 630–1, 635–6, 669–72
  return to Baltic (1714), 673, 710
  later policies, 673–7
  death, 677
  see also Augustus II, Russia, Sweden
Charles Emmanuel II, duke of Savoy, 243, 560
Charles Frederick, duke of Holstein-Gottorp, 670, 677, 679, 737
Charles Philip, prince of Pfalz-Neuberg, 685
Charleston, 12, 493–6, 503–4
Charlotte of Brunswick-Wolfenbüttel, 738
Charron, Jean François, philanthropist of Montreal, 496
Châteaurenault, François Louis Rousselet de, vice-admiral and marshal of France, 418, 567, 569
Châteauroux, woollens, 864
Chatham dockyard, 229, 811, 819
  Chest, 826
Chaucer, Geoffrey, poet, 79
Chaudière, the, mission, 498
Chaul, decay of, 518
Chaussée, Nivelle de la, dramatist, 95
Chełm, 691
Chełmno (Culm), 698, 703
Cherbourg, 811, 823
Chesapeake Bay, 495, 851
Cheshire, salt mines, 844
Chevreuse, Charles Honoré d'Albert, duc de, French minister of state, 326–9
Chiari, battle of (1700), 405
Child, Sir Josiah, merchant, 15, 260
Chile, 15, 350, 359, 376
Chimay, fortress, 252

China, 36
    trade, 24, 139, 511, 516, 537, 856–60, 894
    missions, 96, 130
Chios, 565–6, 623
Chiquitos missions, 356–7
Chittagong, Indo-Portuguese, 519
Chmel'nyćkyj, Bogdan, cossack hetman, 696
Chorlulu Ali Pasha, grand vizier, 630–2, 637
Chotin (Chocim), 610, 619, 682, 684
Christian V, king of Denmark, 166, 652–3, 772, 805
Christiansand, dockyard, 807
Christina, queen of Sweden, 73
Church, Major Benjamin, of Massachusetts, 502
Churchill, John, see Marlborough
Cibber, Colley, playwright, 94
Cilicia, 541
Cimarosa, Domenico, Neapolitan musician, 559
Circassia, 609–10
Civita Vecchia, alum, 895
Clairaut, Alexis Claude, French mathematician, 41, 52
Clarendon, Edward Hyde, 1st earl of, 87, 91
Clarendon, Henry Hyde, 2nd earl, 198, 209
Clarke, Samuel, metaphysician, 51, 138
Claverhouse, James Graham of, 1st Viscount Dundee, 212
Clement IX (Giulio Rospigliosi), pope, 132
Clement XI (Giovanni Francesco Albani), pope, 9, 131, 140, 163, 598
    Jansenism, 131–2, 162
    Archduke Charles recognized, 164, 376, 434, 448
    Philip V recognized, 414
    dispute with Vienna, 594–5
Clerville, Louis Nicolas, chevalier de, French military engineer, 811
Cleves, 225, 242, 466, 852
Clyde, the, 256
Coalbrookdale, iron, 70, 869 n.
Coblentz, 223, 225, 232, 755
Codde, Peter, archbishop of Utrecht, 135
Codrington, Christopher, governor of the Leeward Islands, 251
Coehoorn, Menno van, baron, Dutch military engineer, 236, 250, 416, 750
Coello, Claudio, Spanish painter, 343
Coëtlogon, Alain Emmanuel, marquis de, lieut.-general in French navy, 363–4
Coimbra, 520
Colasse, Pascal, secretary to Lully, 108
Colbert, Jean-Baptiste ('le grand'), marquis de Seignelay, 40, 96–7, 103, 826
    naval, 13, 22, 563–4, 792–3, 803–4, 812, 818–21, 827–8

economic, 28, 510, 521, 543, 551, 835, 852, 856
financial, 298–9, 302, 317–20
colonial, 484, 497, 500
industrial, 556, 723, 813–15, 863, 868–9
death, 15, 316
Colbert de Terron, intendant of marine, 812, 816
Colijer, Jacobus, Dutch resident in Constantinople, 185, 622, 641
Collegiants, 123
Colle di Tenda, Alpine pass, 754
Collier, Jeremy, nonjuror, 94, 140
Cologne, 161, 171, 237, 399
    disputed election, 5, 202–3, 224–5, 393, 398, 578, 588
    Succession War, 407, 411–14, 473–4
Colombo, Indo-Portuguese, 518
Colonia do Sacramento, see Sacramento
Colonie, Colonel Jean Martin de la, officer, 759, 762
Comacchio, 468, 473; war of, 595–7
Comenius, Jan Amos, Bohemian educationalist, 121
Compton, Henry, bishop of London, 125, 197–8
Condé, fortress, 438, 451, 477
Condé, Louis II de Bourbon, prince of, 744, 752, 760
Condominium, see Spanish Netherlands
Condorcet, marquis de, philosopher, 71
Confederacies, in Poland-Lithuania
    defined, 684 n.; praised by Rousseau, 2 n.
    Sapiehas, 685–6, 690–1
    Lithuanian anti-Sapieha, 657, 690–1, 693, 695
    convocational Sejm (1696–7), 686
    Łowicz (pro-French 1697–8), see Humiecki
    Sandomierz (1702), 695, 697; (1704–10), 698, 701–4; see also Augustus II
    Warsaw (1704), 697–8, 701
    Gorzyce (anti-Saxon, 1715), 711
    Tarnogród (anti-Saxon, 1715), 711–12
Confucius, 96, 130
Congreve, William, dramatist, 89
Connecticut, 483, 487, 507
Conques, woollens, 864
Conscription Act (1709), 770
Constantine the Great, 632
Constantinople, 2, 130, 178, 181, 185, 549, 566, 578, 602, 623, 628–9, 732
    population, 542
    trades, 550, 611–12, 623, 644
    Mufti, 616, 629, 646
    Treaty of (1700), 627
    riots (1730–1), 645–7
Contades, Georges Gaspard, marquis de, French major-general, 473

Conti, François Louis de Bourbon, prince of, and Poland, 686, 688
Converse, Captain James, of Maine, 487
Coode, John, Maryland leader, 482
Cooke, Elisha, agent of Massachusetts, 483
Copenhagen, 3, 42, 654, 804–7, 817
  dockyard, 820
  Seamen's Hospital, 826
  Sea Cadets, 826–7
  plague, 886 n.
Copernicus, Nicolaus, astronomer, 84–5
Copley, Lionel, governor of Maryland, 482
Corelli, Archangelo, musician, 102, 105, 116
Corfu, siege (1716), 565, 638–9
Cork, 240
Cornbury, Henry Hyde, 1st viscount, governor of New York, 505
Corneille, Pierre, dramatist, 110, 329
Coromandel coast, 518, 860
Corresponding Princes, 246, 399, 402, 406–7
Corsairs, see privateering
Cosimo III, grand duke of Tuscany, 131, 151
Cossacks, 31, 610, 630, 634, 636, 665–70, 683, 732, 759, 775–6
  and the Poles, 696, 699, 759
  and Peter the Great, 732, 775–6
  see also Bulavin, Don, Mazepa, Orlik, Palej, Samuś, Ukraine
Coste, Pierre, translator of Newton, 78
Costebelle, Pastour de, governor at Placentia, 503
Côte d'Or (Burgundy), 31, 335
Cotentin, the, 243
Cotes, Roger, English mathematician, 43, 47
Couperin, François, musician, 103
Courland, 656–7, 660, 693–4, 699, 710, 719, 773
  and Augustus II, 694
  trade, 648–9, 837
Courtilz de Sandras, Gatien de, French writer, 91
Courtrai, fortress, 252, 381
Covilhã, woollen manufacture, 513
Coxe, Dr Daniel, colonial propagandist, 500
Coymans, Balthasar, Dutch asientist, 350
Crab Island (Caribbean), 354
Cracow, 695, 702, 705
Crato, priory of, 537
Crébillon, Prosper Jolyot, sieur de, French dramatist, 95
Credo, Willem, Zeeland corsair, 801
Cremona, fortress, 409
Creutz, Karl Gustaf, Swedish general, 669
Crimea, 562, 610, 619–20, 625, 647, 664, 669, 716, 718, 736
Crisp, Tobias, antinomian, 142
Crissé, Turpin de, French military writer, 758

Croatia, 7, 242, 577, 581, 586, 604, 608, 617, 638
Cromwell, Oliver, 197, 744
Cronstedt, Karl, Swedish artillerist, 677, 808
Crozat, Antoine, French financier, 13, 500–1
Cruizers and Convoys Act (1708), 796
Crulai, population, 885, 900
Cruz, Sor Juana Inés de la, nun-poetess, 343
Cuba, 355, 372
Cudnów, battle of (1660), 682
Cudworth, Ralph, Platonist, 93, 139, 142–3
Curaçao, 12, 350
Curitiba, gold-washings, 534
Cussy, Pierre Paul Tarin, sieur de, governor of St-Domingue, 633
Czarny Ostróg, 703

Daghestan, 644–5
Dahlberg, Count Erik, governor of Livonia, 654, 656
Dahomey, 515
Dalliez, the brothers (de la Tour and de Réalville), French ironmasters, 815
Dalmatia, 541, 544, 608, 627, 638, 642
Daltaban Mustafa Pasha, grand vizier, 629
Damão, Mahratta attacks, 518
Damascus, 551, 609
  population, 542
Damietta, 550
Dampier, William, explorer and corsair, 15, 35, 56, 96, 372
Danby, Thomas Osborne, 1st earl of, 204–5, 207, 209, 215, 264
Dancourt, Florent Carton (sieur d'Ancourt), French dramatist, 32, 90, 340
Danube, the, 4, 5, 7, 223, 241–2, 422, 562, 564, 577, 605, 610, 640, 753–5, 776
Danycan, Noël, merchant of St Malo and company promoter, 15, 359, 364
Danzig (Gdańsk), 10, 186, 520, 688, 699, 704–5, 712, 737
  trade, 836–7, 843, 867, 871
Darband, occupied by Russians (1722), 644, 739
Darby, Abraham, ironmaster, 70, 869 n., 892
Dardanelles, the, 565, 610, 623
Dar Fur, 548
Darien, Isthmus of, 35, 350
  Company, 15, 212, 275, 277, 360, 392, 505
Dartmouth, William Legge, 1st earl of, 460
Darwin, Charles, 64
Dashkov, Aleksei Ivanovich, Russian resident ambassador in Warsaw, 711
Das Minas, see Minas
Daubenton, Louis Jean Marie, scientist, 41
Daun, Count Lorenz Wierich von, Austrian general, 433, 594

Dauphiné, 231, 240, 245, 336, 390, 433, 467, 781, 813, 815, 864, 889
silk, 868
Davenant, Charles, economist, 157, 260, 284
Davenant, Henry, financial agent to Marlborough, 761
Davis Strait, whale-fishery, 848
Deane, Private J. M., British soldier, 762
Declaration of Rights (1689), 208, 220, 382
Deerfield (Mass.), 502
Defoe, Daniel, 15, 24, 32, 36, 153, 157, 281–2, 315, 611, 751, 762, 769–70, 824
  Robinson Crusoe, 91, 97
  Shortest-way, 281
  True-born Englishman, 281–2
Deists, 86, 99, 136–9
Delaware, 493
Denain, battle of (1712), 19, 444, 467, 753
Dendermonde, 426, 431, 447, 455, 477–8
Denhoff, Stanislas, leader of Sandomierz Confederacy, 698, 702–3
Denmark
  and Sleswig-Holstein, 3–4, 402, 652–5, 678, 774
  army, 3–4, 227, 237, 410, 426, 742, 772–3, 774–5
  and Russia, 1, 158, 652–4, 676, 692, 736, 806, 832
  and France, 3–4, 183, 187, 651, 827
  and William III, 3–4, 227, 246 n.; see also Corresponding Princes, Neutral rights
  trade, 174, 234–5, 420, 520, 804; slave-trade, 855
  West Indies (St Thomas), 350
  India (Tranquebar), 128, 518
  Norway, 648, 649, 670, 675–7, 773, 806, 824
  in eastern Baltic, 649
  navy, 184, 654, 671, 805–8, 820, 824–5, 826–7, 831
  see also Christian V, Frederick IV, Great Northern War, Sweden, Travendal
Denonville, Jacques René de Brisay, marquis de, governor of New France, 484, 486, 498
Denys, Pierre, canon, Jansenist, 135
Deptford, dockyard, 21, 229, 793, 811
Derbyshire, population, 887
Derham, William, English divine, 85
De Ruyter, Michiel Adrianszoon, admiral, 236, 565, 570, 795, 798, 802, 826–7
Desaguliers, John Theophilus, Huguenot scientist, 47
Descartes, René, 24, 32, 34, 37, 55, 61, 65, 67, 70–1, 79, 92, 126, 139, 558
Des Granges, Louis, French consul in Portugal, 511
Deshayes, Jean, French hydrographer, 497
Desideri, Hippolyte, S.J., missionary, 130

Desmarets (Desmaretz), Nicolas, controller-general, 298, 302, 305, 331, 336, 365
Devlet-Girei II, khan of the Crimea, 630–1, 636, 664, 668, 736
De Witt, Johan, Dutch statesman, 48, 799, 822, 825
Diderot, Denis, 43, 71, 93, 97, 100
  Encyclopédie, 34–5
Dieppe, bombarded (1695), 249
Dijkvelt, Everard van Weede, baron, Dutch envoy to England, 170, 172, 198, 200, 249, 388
Dijon, 335, 340
Dinant, fortress, 223, 252
Dissenters (Nonconformists), English, 123, 198 ff., 259, 264, 270, 273–4, 281, 288
  Occasional Conformity Act (1711), 273, 274 n., 461; Schism Act (1714), 273–4
Diu, decay of, 518
Dixmude, surrender to French (1693), 247
Dnieper, the 3, 564, 627–8, 631, 665–6, 699, 732, 754, 776
Dniester, the, 610
Dolgoruki, Count Gregory Feodorovich, Russian ambassador in Poland, 701, 712–13
Don Steppe, 7
  river, 625, 718
  Cossacks, 610, 636, 732
Donauwörth, 421
Dort (Dordrecht), Synod of, 121–2
Dositheus, patriarch of Jerusalem, 632
Douai, fortress, taken by English (1710), 437, 440, 444
Douro, the, 521, 782
  wines, 845
Drake, Captain Peter, soldier-of-fortune, 742, 762
Drava, the, 577, 580, 608
Dresden, 31, 652–3, 701–2, 719
Drina, the, 641
Dryden, John, 33, 70, 79, 81, 83, 106, 113–14, 282–3
Dublin, 240
Dubos, Abbé Jean-Baptiste, traveller, 500
Ducasse, Jean-Baptiste, governor of St-Domingue, 355–6, 372, 545, 810
Duclos, Benoît and Roland, Portuguese silk manufacture, 513
Dudley, Joseph, governor of Massachusetts, 502, 507
Düsseldorf (Lower Palatinate), 31
Dufay, Charles, French electrician, 53
Dufour, French ironmaster in Portugal, 513
Dufresny, Charles Rivière, dramatist, 340
Dugdale, Sir William, antiquary, 87
Duguay-Trouin, René, corsair of St Malo, later naval captain, 19, 244, 528, 802

Du Hamel, Jean-Baptiste, Cartesian, 84
Dumas, Alexandre, novelist, 91
Dummer, Jeremiah, agent for Massachusetts, 506–7
Dundalk, 237
Dunes, battle of the (1658), 343
Dunin-Karwicki, see Karwicki
Dunkers, 493
Dunkirk, 19, 244, 248–9, 257, 435, 442–3, 451, 452, 460, 753, 794, 803, 811–12
privateers, 734, 800, 802, 812, 848
Duquesne, Abraham, marquis and admiral, 564–5, 812
Durham, coal, 869
Du Ru, Paul, S.J., French missionary, 499
Dussen, Bruno van der, pensionary of Gouda, 439, 446–7, 450–1
Dutch, see United Provinces
Duverney, Joseph, French anatomist, 41, 47, 56
Dvina, the, 655–6, 692, 694, 842
Dzialyński, Thomas, Polish diplomat, 698–9

East India Companies
English, 40, 262, 288, 360, 392, 457, 517, 835, 856 ff.
Dutch, 298, 516, 856–62, 893
Portuguese, 516–17
French, 517, 524, 812, 856–7, 861
Danish, 518
Ostend, 352, 390, 478, 857
Eberenburg, 245
Eberhard Ludwig, duke of Württemberg, 121
Ebro, the, naval stores, 813
Ecuador, 356
Edinburgh, 42, 67
Edwards, John, Calvinist divine, 141
Eger (Erlau), fortress, 608, 621
Egypt, 548, 565, 609–10, 620, 632, 638
Eisenerz, iron mines, 604
Ekeren, battle of (1703), 416
Elba, 540, 546
Elbe, the, 605–6
Elbeuf, woollens, 863
Elbląg (Elbing), 689–90, 694
Element, Moitrel d', French scientist, 46
Elizabeth Christina, wife of Charles VI, 596
Elizabeth Farnese, queen of Spain, 9, 377–8, 380, 473
Elizabeth of Pfalz-Neuberg, 685
Elmas Mehmed Pasha, grand vizier, 626
Embrun, fortress, 245
Emden, timber market, 840
Empire, the Holy Roman
military organization, 5, 20, 411, 588, 742, 764, 768–9, 777–8
and emperor, 8, 166–7, 225, 402, 450, 471–2, 578–9, 586 ff.

religion, 120–1, 189, 252, 383, 473–4, 588
mercenaries, 165–6, 404–5, 411, 742, 769, 772, 778
and foreign diplomacy, 165–7, 203, 227, 399, 401–7, 414–15, 586
Nine Years War, 225, 228, 232 ff., 586–7
Ryswick, 252, 381, 383, 473–4, 588
Grand Alliance of 1701, 407, 410–11, 588
Succession War, 416 ff.
Treaty of Baden (1714), 444, 474–5
and Sweden, 154, 184–5, 431–2, 649, 656, 658, 660, 662–3, 670, 673 ff.
Corresponding Princes, 246, 399, 402, 406, 407
Magdeburg Concert, 232
Circles, 165–6, 250, 402, 405, 407, 409, 586, 588
imperial fiefs, see Italy
see also Leopold I, Joseph I, Charles VI
England
seapower, 4, 11–13, 18–19, 21–2, 155, 204, 215, 229, 234 ff., 292, 355, 370, 382, 387, 391–2, 404, 407, 411 ff., 488–9, 503, 505–6, 525–6, 566 ff., 654, 790 ff.
trade, 10, 14–17, 19, 185–8, 238, 244, 246, 252–3, 257, 261–2, 282, 382, 387, 391–2, 395, 412, 414, 418–20, 428, 431, 434, 438–9, 441–2, 459, 460, 469–70, 475–6, 490–1, 510, 513, 519 ff., 535, 549–53, 611, 675, 796–7, 802, 805, 809, 816–19, 833, 835 ff., 870–4, 894
and Americas, 12 ff., 35, 56, 95 ff., 128, 195–6, 251–2, 255, 261, 349, 354, 372–3, 385, 391–2, 410, 434, 441, 459 ff., 480 ff., 535–6, 796–7, 809–11, 814, 848 ff., 849; see also Asiento, West Indies
foreign policy, 15 ff., 26–7, 155 ff., 193, 266–7, 432, 622, 641, 645, 654, 658, 663–4, 670, 675–6, 735; see Barrier, Bolingbroke, Grand Alliance, Portugal, William III
army, 18–21, 196–7, 198, 201, 204–5, 208, 228 ff., 293, 382–3, 411 ff., 505, 742 ff., 763–4, 766, 769–71, 783–4
finance, 22–3, 26, 208, 209, 251, 255, 260, 274, 277, 285–94, 299, 313–15, 382, 401, 440, 535, 787, 816–19, 831–2, 836, 896, 902
religion, 25–6, 85–7, 92–3, 99, 123 ff., 136–9, 140, 149 ff., 197 ff., 209–10, 212, 215, 264, 270, 285; see also Dissenters, James II
constitution, 25–6, 193 ff., 206–11, 216 ff., 253, 255, 264–75; see also Scotland
society, 29, 31–3, 89, 93–4, 151–3, 219–21, 258–60, 262–3, 279–82, 769–71, 783–4, 823 ff.
music, 32, 104, 107–8, 110, 113–15

England (*cont.*)
  literature, 32–3, 72, 78 ff., 263, 280–2
  science, 33–5, 37 ff., 84–5; technology,
    68–70, 259, 719, 747–9, 815, 867, 868,
    892
  industries, 69–70, 259, 814, 819, 865 ff.
  population, 883 f., 885–7, 889, 900
  agriculture, 68–9, 257–8, 763, 813, 818–19,
    865
Enlightenment, the, 70, 72, 96, 150, 740
Enniskillen, 213, 769
Eperjes (Prešov), 605, 619
Epicurus, 24, 146
Eric IV, king of Sweden, 806
Ericeira, Luís de Meneses, 3rd count of,
  Portuguese minister of finance, 514,
  522
Erlach, Johann Reinhold Fischer von,
  Austrian architect, 144, 601
Ernest Augustus, duke of Brunswick-
  Lüneberg, 166, 183–4, 202, 241, 232,
  246, 735
  elector of Hanover, 587–8, 768
Ertholomene, Baltic islets, 807
Erzurum, 609, 614
Esterházy, Count Paul, palatine of Hungary,
  583–4
Estonia, 648, 663, 679, 773, 806
  trade, 648, 837 ff.
Estrées, César d', cardinal, 369
Estrées, Jean d', abbé, nephew of preceding,
  369
Estrées, Victor Marie, comte d', vice-
  admiral, marshal of France, 390, 567–9
Estremadura, 163, 366, 438, 526–8, 591
Estremoz, 512
Ethiopia, 571, 858
Eugene, prince of Savoy-Carignan
  Rastatt, negotiations at, 5, 171, 444, 472–3
  as soldier, 18, 744, 752–3, 760–1
  Blenheim, 19, 421–2
  Turks, 21, 164, 251, 383, 581, 598, 626,
    638–42
  war profits, 23, 572–3, 788
  Italy, 243, 247, 250, 405–6, 409, 412, 417,
    425, 428–9, 558, 570, 593–6
  Toulon, 5, 433
  Oudenarde, 434–6
  Malplaquet, 438
  London mission, 443, 462, 464
  Utrecht negotiations, 450
  Hungary, 579, 585, 620
Euler, Leonhard, Swiss scientist, 42, 52
Evdokia Lopukhina, tsaritsa, 717, 733
Evelyn, John, *Sylva*, 813
Evertsen, Cornelis, lieut.-admiral of Zee-
  land, 568
Evora, wheat prices, 509

Exeter, cloth sales, 866
Exquemelin, Alexandre Olivier (*alias* John
  Esquemeling), buccaneer, 96

Fagel, Gaspar, grand pensionary, 176
Fahrenheit, Gabriel Daniel, Prussian phy-
  sicist, 54
Falmouth, 811
Faro, 510, 519
Farquhar, George, British dramatist, 89
Fatio family, Genevan bankers, 303
Fayal (Azores), wine and brandy, 520
Feif, Casten, secretary to Charles XII, 671
Feijóo y Montenegro, Benito Jerónimo,
  Spanish Benedictine critic, 72
Feitama, Sybrand, Dutch dramatist, 75
Fénelon, François Salignac de la Mothe de,
  archbishop of Cambrai, 27, 72, 126,
  135, 142, 146, 153, 156, 339
  Télémaque, 32, 93, 327–9
  and Mme Guyon, 147–9
  Letter to Louis XIV and *Les Maximes*, 327
Fenestrelle, Alpine fortress, 467
Ferrara, 595
Ferriol, Charles de, baron d'Argental,
  French ambassador to Turkey, 630
Ferryland (Newfoundland), 488–9, 503
Fétis, François Joseph, musicologist, 101
Feuquière(s), Issac du Pas, marquis de,
  French diplomat, 160, 180
Feuquière(s), Antoine du Pas, marquis de,
  marshal of France, 653
Feversham, Louis Duras, 2nd earl of, 747
Feyzullah, mufti of Constantinople, 629
Fez, entrepôt of Barbary, 548
Fezzan, 548
Fick, Heinrich, of Holstein, 731
Fikaiyye, Egyptian political clan, 609
Filmer, Sir Robert, political writer, 25, 216,
  219–20
Finale, marquisate of, imperial fief, 386–7,
  395, 401, 403, 592, 597
Finland, 4, 656, 673, 716, 773–4, 806, 808
  famine, 764
  population, 889–90
Fiume, free port, 604
Flamsteed, John, first astronomer royal, 52
Flanders, Spanish, *see* Spanish Netherlands
  French, 543, 785, 866
  States of, 426, 428
Fleetwood, William, bishop and numis-
  matist, 48
Fleischmann, Anselm, Austrian economist,
  605
Flemming, Count Jakob Heinrich von, Saxon
  field-marshal, 690–1, 702, 709, 711–13
Fletcher of Saltoun, Andrew, Scottish
  independent, 276

Fletcher, Benjamin, governor of New York, 487
Fletcher, John, English dramatist, 79
Fleurus, battle of (1690), 239, 241, 747
Fleury, Cardinal André Hercule de, 27
Flibustiers, 12, 15, 349, 350, 354, 356, 809–10
Florence, 106, 109, 535, 562
  population, 542
Florida, 129, 350, 500
  Succession War, 503–4
Flushing, 20, 800–1, 811
Foigny, Gabriel, Franciscan novelist, 98
Fontana, Carlo, Italian architect, 144
Fontenelle, Bernard le Bovier, sieur de, philosopher, 32, 41, 61–2, 70, 88, 104, 137, 740
Forbin, Claude, chevalier de, squadron commander, 19, 244, 257, 435, 569, 802
Forez, production of, 813, 869
Forkel, J. N., musicologist, 117
Fort Frontenac, 496
Fort Knocke, 477
Fort Louis (Rhine), 252
Fort Loyal (Portland), 486
Fort Royal (Martinique), 810
Fort St Louis (New France), 497
Fort St Michael, 477–8
Fort William Henry, 487
Forth, Firth of, 256
Fortune (Newfoundland), 488
Fox, George, Quaker, 150
France: general survey, 316–42
  religion, 10, 85, 93, 98–9, 119–20, 131 ff., 147–9, 189, 333–4; see also Huguenots
  trade, 10, 14–15, 185–7, 320–1, 329–30, 359, 385, 549–53, 571, 839 ff., 894; fisheries, 13–14, 470, 488–9, 503, 849–50; vineyards, 335, 521, 845–7, 877; industries, 69, 323, 329, 512–13, 536, 552, 737, 793–4, 812, 815, 843, 850, 860–1, 863 ff., 879, 881, 893, 894
  navy, 19, 21–2, 224, 234 ff., 283–4, 412, 550–1, 568–71, 790 ff.
  army, 20, 223–4, 232 ff., 319, 325–6, 340, 373–5, 412 ff., 741 ff., 763–7, 780–2, 785–9
  foreign policy, see Louis XIV; preponderance, 26–7, 74–5, 154 ff., 230, 254–5
  food crises, 29–30, 320 ff., 764, 838–9, 875 ff., 898–9
  culture, 32–3, 72 ff., 220–1, 340–2
  science, 33–5, 38 ff., 84–5, 88–9
  society, 28–32, 89–91, 94–5, 332 ff., 338–42, 780–1, 785–6, 829
  finance, 298–305, 317–18, 321, 323–4, 325–6, 330–3, 335–8, 788, 831–2
  population, 883 ff., 900
  see also Colbert, Louis XIV, Paris

Franceschi, slave trader of Leghorn, 563
Franche-Comté, 223, 387, 438, 452, 454, 465, 813
Francke, August Hermann, German theologian, 150–1
François de Sales, Saint, 146, 149
Franconia, 237, 245, 250, 402, 405, 432, 586–8, 590, 752
Frankenthal, fortress, 225
Frankfurt-am-Main, 225, 232, 237, 421, 596
Frankfurt-am-Oder, 705
Franklin, Benjamin, 42
Frauds, Statute of (1677), 491
Fraustadt, battle of (1706), 661–2, 700, 705
Frederick Augustus I, elector of Saxony, see Augustus II
Frederick II, the Great, of Prussia, 42
Frederick III, elector of Brandenburg-Prussia, and from 1701 Frederick I, king in Prussia, 28, 44, 130, 168, 225, 232, 237, 249, 402
  Grand Alliance, 406, 411, 439, 583, 659, 671, 689–90, 692, 694, 763, 768–9
Frederick IV, king of Denmark, 652–3, 655, 670, 676, 679, 774
Frederick of Hesse, 673, 677
  king of Sweden, 677
Frederick Henry, prince of Orange, 799
Frederick William of Brandenburg-Prussia, the Great Elector, 158, 198, 232, 685, 778–9
Frederick William I, king in Prussia, 151, 471, 672, 713–14, 730, 769
Frederiksborg, Treaty of (1720), 678
Frederikssten, fortress, 677–8
Freiburg-im-Breisgau, 252, 472–3, 588
Freire, Sousa, governor-general of Brazil, 529
Frescobaldi, Girolamo, Italian musician, 115
Friesland, 800
Fritz, Samuel, S.J., missionary in Amazonia, 356, 531
Friuli, Venetian trade, 555
Fronteira, Fernando Mascarenhas, 2nd marquis of, 438, 512, 522, 536
Frontenac, Louis de Buade, comte de, governor of New France, 12, 13, 484, 486, 488, 490, 497
Fuensalida, Antonio de Velasco, count of, governor of Milan, 241
Fürstenberg, Cardinal Wilhelm Egon von, bishop of Strasbourg, 202, 224, 578
Fuggers, imperial bankers, 308
Fundão, woollens, 513
Fundy, Bay of, 502
Furnes, fortress, 247, 451, 477
Furnese, Sir Henry, banker, 293, 314

Gadesbusch, battle of (1712), 636, 671–2
Gaeta, 433, 594
Gaillac, wines, 845
Galicia, 163, 366, 526, 528, 591
Galileo, astronomer, 24, 37, 57, 68, 73
Gallas, Count Johann Wenzel Avon, imperial ambassador to Britain, 458, 460, 462
Gallicanism, 131–4, 334, 376
Gallois, Abbé Jean, French geometer, 41
Galveias, Dinis de Melo e Castro, 1st count of, Portuguese general, 527
Galway, 242
Galway, Henri de Massue de Ruvigny, 1st earl of
  in Spain, 371, 425, 429–30
  Almanza, 373, 433, 438, 447, 757
Game Act (1670), 258
Gap, 245
Garcia, Miguel, Brazilian explorer, 533
Garonne, the, tobacco-growing, 853
Gassendi, Pierre, philosopher, 95
Gastañaga, Francisco Antonio Agurto, marquis of, governor of Spanish Netherlands, 242
Gato, Borbo, Brazilian explorer, 533
Gaulli, Giovan Battista, painter, 145
Gaultier, Abbé François de, chaplain at the French embassy in London, 175, 458–9
Gdańsk, see Danzig
Gedoyn, Abbé Nicolas, French writer, 342
Geertruidenberg, negotiations (1710), 375, 439–40, 454–8, 596, 735
Gelderland, Dutch province, 439, 852
Geneva, 120, 221
  religion, 121–2, 151
  bankers, 23, 303–4, 314, 543, 788
Gennes, J.-B. de, French naval captain, 15
Genoa, republic of, 9, 28, 168, 224, 379, 509, 556, 594, 597, 754
  bankers, 23, 345, 543
  population, 542
  galleys, 563
  trade, 509, 535, 540, 547, 555, 564, 813, 858, 862
Geoffroy, Etienne, French chemist, 41
George I, king of Great Britain, 155, 272, 434, 676, 784
  his relatives, 168
  accession, 477, 790
  and Sweden, 673–6
George, prince of Denmark, 204
George, prince of Hesse-Darmstadt, 5, 249, 370, 390, 423
  viceroy of Catalonia, 357–8, 362, 382, 390, 591
Georgia, Christians in, 645, 739
  Turkish occupation, 645

Germany
  science, 42–5, 53–4, 61, 65–7
  culture, 31–2, 73–4, 87, 172, 728
  music, 101–3, 105, 110–11, 114–18
  see also Empire and separate states
Gerona, 248
Ghent, 404, 408
  and French, 431, 435–6
  and British, 443, 464
  and Dutch, 477–8
Giannone, Pietro, Neapolitan lawyer, 558
Gibraltar, 162, 371, 397, 442, 540, 549, 817
  taken by British, 11, 248, 419, 444, 448, 460, 475, 566–70, 809
  French and Spanish attempt to recover, 19, 366, 423, 797
Gibson, Edmund, bishop of London, 127
Gilligan, Manuel Manasses, Spanish commercial agent, 475
Ginkel, Godert de, 1st earl of Athlone, 242
Giordano, Luca, Neapolitan painter, 343, 559
Giovan Gastone, grand duke of Tuscany, 73
Gironde, the, 812
Giudice, Cardinal Francisco del, Spanish inquisitor-general, 378
Givet, fortress, 247, 250
Glasgow, 256
Glencoe, massacre of (1689), 212
Glommen, river in Norway, 675, 678
Gloucester, woollens, 865
Gluck, Christoph Willibald, musician, 103, 111, 116
Glückstadt, dockyard, 807
Goa, 516–17
Godolphin, Sidney, 1st earl of, lord treasurer, 17, 23, 256, 267, 269, 284–5, 291–4, 414, 430, 437, 795
  and William of Orange, 205
  dismissed, 270, 294, 441
  and Scotland, 275–7
  and peace, 280
  and Northern War, 734
Görtz, Georg Heinrich, baron von, Swedish envoy at The Hague, 180, 674, 676–7
Goes, Count Johann Peter, imperial ambassador at The Hague, 409
Goethe, Johann Wolfgang von, 118
Göttingen, university, 42, 44–5, 65, 71
Göttweig, monastery, 602
Gold Coast, 515
Golden Horn, 643
Goldoni, Carlo, Italian dramatist, 73
Golitsyn, Prince Boris, Russian statesman, 718
Golitsyn, Prince Vasily Vasilyevich, Russian statesman, 625, 684, 717–18

Golovin, Feodor Alexeyvich, Russian minister, 698, 719
Golovkin, G. I., Russian chancellor, 698 n.
Goltz, Heinrich von der, Russian marshal, 703
González, Tirso, Jesuit general, 147
Gordon, Patrick, friend of Tsar Peter, 718, 720
Gorzyce, confederacy (1715), 711
Gothenburg, 802, 808
  trade, 805
Gotland, 649
Gott, Pierre, Dutch financier, 303
Gottsched, Johann Christoph, German critic, 74
Gouda, 446
Goyaz, 532-3
Graaf, Regnier de, Dutch biologist, 64
Grabu, Louis, French musician, 106-7
Gradiska, 578
Gran (Esztergom), fortress, 618
Grand Alliance, 157, 162, 165, 188, 388-9, 419, 446, 449 ff., 591, 658
  Treaty (1701), 406, 410, 427, 431, 591
  Utrecht, 442 ff., 461 ff.
Grand Pré (Bay of Fundy), 502
Granville, bombarded (1695), 249
  codfishermen, 849
Graunt, John, statistician, 48
Gravesande, Willem Jakob van 's, Dutch scientist, 46
Gravier, Jacques, S.J., missionary among Illinois, 498-9
Gray, Stephen, English scientist, 53
Graydon, John, British vice-admiral, 503
Graz, 573, 601
Great Britain, see England, Ireland, Scotland
Great Northern War
  character, 2-3, 19, 21, 154, 157-8, 648, 714-15, 742-3, 754, 807
  causation, 649-54, 687, 692-3
  and Denmark, 652-5, 670-1, 673, 676, 677-8, 679, 692, 735, 736, 774-5
  and Saxony-Poland, see Augustus II
  and Russia, 652 ff., 663 ff., 673 ff., 692 ff., 698 ff., 708 ff., 722-3, 733-5
  and Brandenburg-Prussia, 671-4, 678, 710
  and Hanover, 673, 674, 675-6, 677-8
  and Turkey, 630-2, 635-7, 645, 669-73, 710
  and the West, 154, 402-3, 410, 431-2, 654-5, 656, 662, 670
  in Baltic provinces, 653-6, 673, 674, 676, 692, 708-9, 736, 773, 806
  in Poland, 656-63, 669-70, 670-1, 673, 695 ff., 704 ff.
  in Saxony, 662-3, 701, 704
  in Ukraine, 666-9, 702-3

  in Sweden, 670-1, 774, 806-7
  in Denmark, 654-5, 671
  in Norway, 675, 677-8
  naval aspects, 654, 671, 673, 679, 721-2, 806-7
  economic effects, 672, 673-5, 704-6, 714, 722 ff., 772 ff., 832, 837 ff., 873
  peace efforts, 154, 158, 676, 678-9, 692-3, 694, 710-11, 735-7
  see also Charles XII, Holstein-Gottorp, Peter I, Polish-Lithuania, Poltava
Greeks
  as traders, 186, 546, 611-12
  as sailors, 544, 554, 615, 619
  Orthodox Church, see Turkey
  see also Aegean, Corfu, Morea
Greenland, whale-fishery, 848, 872
Greenock, 256
Greenwich, Banqueting Hall, 32
  Observatory, 68
  Hospital, 826
Greg, William, Harley's clerk, 269
Grenoble, 336
Gresham College, 39
Grew, Nehemiah, English naturalist, 56, 64
Grimaldo, José de, secretary of Spanish Despacho Universal, 370, 475
Grimmelshausen, Johann Jakob Christoffel von, German novelist, 73
Grodno, 661, 690, 700, 705
Groningen, 465, 800
Gropello, Giambattista, count of Borgone, Savoyard finance minister, 171
Grotius, Hugo, Dutch jurist, 173
Grüber, Johann, S.J., missionary, 130
Guadalajara, 430
Guadeloupe, 251, 810, 853
Guardão, lord of, revenues, 538
Guardi, Francesco, Venetian painter, 556
Guastalla, duchy of, 473
Guatemala, 356
Guayaquil, 356, 373
Guelderland, Upper (Spanish)
  Utrecht, 439, 444, 451, 465-6, 477
Guelders, fortress, 399, 404, 416
Guiana, 350, 528, 531; see Cayenne, Surinam
Guiger family, Genevan bankers, 303
Guillestre, fortress, 245
Guinea, Gulf of, and Portuguese, 510, 515
  French Company of, 364
  Dutch trade, 510, 872
Guipúzcoa, 175, 363, 393
Guiscard, Antoine, comte de, 457
Gustavus Adolphus, king of Sweden, 735, 743-4, 752-3
Guyon, Jeanne Marie Bouvier, dame de la Motte, French mystic, 147-9
Guzmán, Marín de, Spanish asientist, 515

Gyllenborg, Count Karl, Swedish diplomat and writer, 180, 676
Gyllenkrook, Axel, Swedish general, 761

Haarlem, linen-bleaching, 867
Haas, Robert, musicologist, 102–3
Habeas Corpus Amendment Act (1679), 265
Habsburg monarchy
  organization of government, 7–8, 155, 177, 228, 449–50, 572–6, 598 ff., 752
  finance, 22, 305–14, 383
  armies, 228, 642, 742, 745, 747–8, 752, 759, 761, 782
  and Italy, 5, 9, 163–4, 368, 386–7, 405–6, 409, 412, 428, 432–3, 557–8, 569–71, 576, 581, 590 ff.
  and southern Netherlands, 444–5, 472–3, 477–8, 576, 579, 598
  and Venice, 577, 638 ff.
  and Poland, 581, 683–5, 695, 701, 710
  and Bavaria, 588–90
  and Savoy, 159, 241, 250–1, 417–18, 462, 466–7, 559, 595–6
  economy of Habsburg lands, 599 ff.
  social structure, 599 ff.
  buildings, 601–2
  church, 601–2
  towns, 602–3, 605
  plague, 670, 886 n.
  see also Austria, Bohemia, Bosnia, Croatia, Empire, Hungary, Silesia, Transylvania, Turkey
Hadow, Sir Henry, musician, 101
Härbel, Nikolaus Friedrich, Swiss architect, 728
Hague, The, 420, 734, 738, 800
  Congress, 171–2, 237
  Treaty (1700), 653
  Conventions of (1710), 439, 670–1
  peace negotiations (1709), 450
Hainault, province, 426, 446
Haines, Richard, inventor, 152
Hainz (Heins), Paul, Danish ambassador to Russia, 692
Hales, Stephen, physiologist, 40, 54, 65–6
Halifax, Charles Montagu, 1st earl of, 216, 266, 270
  Chancellor of the Exchequer, 286
Halifax, Sir George Saville, marquis of, 195, 199, 205, 214–17, 263
  Trimmer, 208
  Dissenter, 211
Halil Pasha, grand vizier, 640, 643
Hall, Chester Moor, inventor, 54
Hallart, Ludwig Nikolaus von, Russian general, 634
Halle, 719
  university, 44, 65, 150

saltworks, 844
Pietists, 128
Haller, Albrecht von, physiologist, 45, 65–7
Halley, Edmund, astronomer royal, 39, 40, 52, 68
Hamadan, occupied by Turks, 645
Hamburg, 168, 186, 605, 737
  trade, 520–1, 847–8, 894
  seamen, 580
  sailcloth, 815
  fur market, 851
  Company, 866
Hamilton, James Douglas, 4th duke of, 276
Handasyd, Thomas, lieut.-governor of Jamaica, 810
Handel, George Frederick, musician, 32, 101–7, 114–15
Hangö Udd (Gangut), battle of (1714), 806
Hanmer, Sir Thomas, Speaker of the House of Commons, 469
Hanover, 44, 61, 87, 154–5, 469, 737
  Catholics, 188
  mercenaries, 237, 742, 769–70
  electorate (1692), 246, 383, 587–8
  Succession War, 402, 407, 410, 472
  Utrecht, 477
  Great Northern War, 672–4
  French subsidy, 788
Harcourt, Henri, duc d', marshal of France, diplomat, 357, 361, 363, 365, 368, 389
Harlay de Champvallon, François de, archbishop of Paris, 133
Harley, Robert, 1st earl of Oxford, 18, 430
  South Sea Company, 15–16, 288, 475
  lord treasurer, 269–70, 281, 441, 443, 460
  attempted assassination, 457
  and the succession, 469
Harrach, Count Ferdinand Bonaventura von, imperial ambassador to Spain, 359
Harrington, James, political theorist, 289
Harris, John, scientific writer, 47
Harrison, John, clockmaker, 68
Hartsoeker, Nicolas, microscopist, 64
Harvard, college, 494
Harvey, William, physician, 44, 65, 558
Hasse, Johann, German musician, 111
Havana, 186, 361, 392, 515, 809
Haverhill (Mass.), 487
Hawkins, Sir John, musicologist, 101
Hawksbee, Francis, English scientist, 53
Haydn, Franz Joseph, 102, 105, 117
Hayes, William, professor of music, 104
Hearne, Thomas, antiquary, 33
Hedges, Sir Charles, secretary of state, 430
Hedvig Sofia, duchess of Holstein-Gottorp and elder sister of Charles XII, 652, 670 n.

Heeckeren, Walraven van, Dutch diplomat, 651

Heidelberg, fortress, 225, 756
sacks of, 233, 247

Hein, Piet, Dutch seaman, 252, 798

Heinsius, Anthonie, grand pensionary, 17, 171, 172, 183, 283, 425, 443
and Marlborough, 17, 162, 176–7, 409, 415, 421, 446, 575
and William III, 156, 162, 165, 170, 178, 183, 228, 266, 392, 400–1, 655, 798
and neutral commerce, 174
Barrier, 439, 449
Preliminary Articles (1709), 437, 448, 451 ff.
Utrecht, 459

Heister, Count Sigbert von, Austrian field-marshal, 580, 585

Hejaz, 610

Héliodore, Fr, French Capuchin, 146

Hennepin, Fr Louis, Récollet historian, 497, 500

Herbeville, Count Ludwig von, Austrian general, 585

Hermelin, Olof, Swedish chancery official, 184, 660–1

Herne, Sir Joseph, financier, 314

Héron, Charles de Caradas, marquis du, French ambassador in Poland, 634

Hesse-Cassel, 202, 232, 237, 244, 250, 402, 404, 406, 410, 675–6, 742
see also Frederick of Hesse

Hesse-Darmstadt, see George, prince of troops, 402, 405, 742

Hickes, George, nonjuror scholar, 127, 140

Hill, Abigail, Lady Masham, 254, 269, 505

Hill, Colonel John, general, 505–6

Hill, Richard, British envoy at Turin, 284

Hirschl, Lazarus, Viennese financier, 309

Hispaniola, 350, 364–5; see also Santo-Domingo and Saint-Domingue

Hobbes, Thomas, 92, 135–6, 139, 219

Hocher, Johann Paul von, Austrian chancellor, 601

Höchstädt, see Blenheim

Hoffman, Friedrich, physiologist, 65

Hoffman, Johann Philipp von, Austrian envoy in London, 468

Hofmannswaldau, C. Hofmann von, Silesian poet, 73

Hogguer family, French war contractors, 304

Holbach, baron d', encyclopaedist, 137

Holland, see United Provinces

Holman, Captain William, of Ferryland, 489

Hołowczyń, battle of (1708), 666, 702

Holstein, duchy of, 166, 702, 772

Holstein-Gottorp, duchy of, 3, 158, 182, 407, 447, 737, 774
and Sweden, 649, 653–4, 670, 674, 677

Holt, Sir John, chief justice, 265

Holy League (1684), 2, 158, 203, 577, 619, 625, 683

Honduras, logwood, 854

Hooke, Robert, scientist, 39, 51, 57, 62

Hooker, Richard, theologian, 138, 217

Hop, Jacob, Dutch diplomat, 396

Horn, Count Arvid, Swedish general, 654–5, 670

Hoste, Fr Paul, French mathematician and naval theorist, 791, 793

Howard of Effingham, Francis, baron, governor of Virginia, 482–3

Hubac, Etienne, French shipbuilder, 793

Hudson, the, 251, 488

Hudson's Bay, 12–14, 26, 252, 460, 470, 488–9, 508, 810, 850
Company, 261–2, 489, 835, 851
trade, 850

Hüningen, fortress, 223, 241

Huet, Pierre Daniel, bishop of Avranches, 140

Hugli, Indo-Portuguese, 519

Huguenots, 124–5, 186, 188, 195, 198, 218, 274, 288, 337–8, 821
bankers, 23, 293, 303–5, 336–7
emigration, 33, 220–1, 860
spread of French culture, 76–7, 137
emigration of skills, 121–2, 259, 293, 788, 851, 861, 863–4, 867
in Allied armies, 238, 243, 769, 778–9; see also Galway, Schomberg
in N. America, 493, 503
in Morocco, 554
see also Camisards, Nantes

Huguetan, Jean Henri, financier, 23, 293, 303, 788
flight to England, 304, 789

Humfrey, Pelham, musician, 106

Humiecki, Stephen, Polish patriot, 687–8, 691

Humières, Louis de Crevant, duc d', marshal of France, 235

Hungary, crown of St Stephen, 7, 576, 585
rebellion, 5, 7, 154, 412, 434, 583–5, 754
religion, 120, 582–3, 586
taxation, 306, 583
and Turks, 576–81, 608, 610, 618–23, 642
Habsburg reorganization, 581–6, 599
Carlowitz, 584, 626–7

Hunter, Robert, governor of New York, 507

Husein, shah of Persia, 644

Hüseyn Pasha, grand vizier, see Köprülü

Huxelles, Nicolas de Laye du Blé, marquis d', marshal of France, 237, 439, 462, 781

Huy, fortress, 248, 413, 451, 478
taken by Allies (1703), 416
Huygens, Christiaan, Dutch physicist, 49–50, 53, 69, 77
Hyde, see Clarendon and Rochester

Iberville, Pierre le Moyne, sieur d', 12, 20, 360, 500–1, 503–4, 810
Ibiza, 370, 387, 543, 546, 570
Ibrahim Pasha, grand vizier, 619, 642–3
murdered, 656–7
Idanha, 527
Idria, mercury mines, 228 n., 307
Iguapé, gold-washings, 533–4
Ile Dauphine (Louisiana), 499
Iles de Lérins, 570
India, 95, 524, 551, 611
Indo-Portuguese, 518–19
see also East India Companies
Indulgence, Declarations of (1687), 198–9, 201, 204
Inflant, Nikolaus, Russian general, 703
Ingolstadt, fortress, 421
Ingria, 648, 655, 663, 679, 716, 806
Innocent XI (Benedetto Odescalchi), pope, 130–1
and James II, 194–5, 199
and Louis XIV, 161, 203, 225
and the Turks, 130, 576–7, 619
Innocent XII (Antonio Pignatelli), pope, 131, 161–2, 396, 594
Innsbruck, 417, 573
Inquisition, the, 346, 353–4, 363, 376, 378, 511, 534, 544
Insurance companies, in England, 289, 836
Iraq, 608
Ireland
Jacobites, 30, 255, 257
religion, 126, 213–14, 256
James II and, 197, 201, 206
James II in, 213–14, 235–6, 238, 240–2
Treaty of Limerick (1691), 214, 242
mercenaries, 742
economy, 256, 846, 867, 894
Iroquois confederacy, see American Indians
Isabella, infanta of Portugal, 183
Ispahan, 548, 859
Istanbul, mufti of, 616, 629, 646
Italy
Habsburg interest, see Habsburg monarchy
French interest, see Casale, Louis XIV, Pinerolo
Italian states, 9–10, see also separate states
Spanish interest, see Spain
culture, 10, 32, 46, 72–3, 144, 556, 558–9
music, 108, 109–13, 114

Stato dei Presidii, 387 n., 393, 395, 473
imperial fiefs, 163, 386, 473, 594–5
trade, 520, 530, 597; see also Leghorn and separate states
Papal States, see Innocent XI, Alexander VIII, Innocent XII, Clement XI
Nine Years War, 240–1, 243, 245, 247, 250–1, 558
Succession War, 405–6, 409, 417–18, 422, 425, 428–9, 432–3, 558, 569, 570, 594
War of Comacchio, 595
the Quadrilateral, 753; see also Mantua, Po
Ivan V, co-tsar with Peter the Great, 717

Jabłonowski, John Stanislas, Leszczyński's chancellor, 687, 700, 708, 710
Jabłonowski, Stanislas, Polish crown hetman, father of preceding, 657, 689, 691
Jablonski, Daniel Ernst, religious leader, 121–2
Jacobites, 209, 210, 215, 255, 257, 261, 264, 273, 275–6, 278, 289, 408, 675, 797
rising (1715), 257, 272, 279
Jamaica, 12, 20, 22, 349–50, 355, 392, 797, 809–11
trade, 849, 855
James I, king of Great Britain, 266
James II, king of Great Britain, 17, 27, 168, 183, 480
religion, 25, 123, 125, 194–201, 225, 265
character, 194–5
and Louis XIV, 195, 200, 203, 205, 213, 243, 250
death, 408
see also Ireland
James Stuart, the Old Pretender, 162, 271
birth, 201–2
recognized by Louis XIV, 169, 281, 408, 414
abortive expedition (1707), 435
leaves France, 452, 460
Charles XII and, 675–6
Janissaries
discipline, 6–7, 614, 624, 630, 637, 639, 642
organization, 553, 612, 628, 743, 789
revolts, 31, 618; (1687), 620–1; (1703), 629; (1730–1), 646–7; (Cairo, 1711), 609, 632
Jannum Hoja, Turkish kaptan pasha, 647
Jansborg, 689–90
Jansenism, 10, 24, 128, 132–6, 146, 149, 161–2
Unigenitus, 132–4, 135, 334
in Spanish Netherlands, 413
Janson, Toussaint de Forbin, Cardinal, 131
Janssen, Sir Theodore, financier, 243
Janusch von Eberstedt, Lebrecht Gottfried, Russian general, 634

Japan, Dutch trade with, 859, 861–2
Jassy (Moldavia), 620, 634
Jativa, destroyed, 373
Java, trade, 854, 857, 859
Jean-Baptiste de la Salle, Saint, 151
Jeffereyes, Captain James, 762
Jeffreys, George, 1st baron, lord chancellor, 195, 197, 265
Jennings, Sir John, vice-admiral, 372
Jerez, 521, 845
Jersey, Edward Villiers, 1st earl of, 459
Jersey, East and West, 14, 483, 488, 491, 493, 814
Jerusalem, 632
Jesuits, 25, 35, 128, 133, 134, 139, 145, 147, 153, 625
  Bollandists, 87, 140
  in China, 96, 98
  in America, 128–9, 496, 498, 529–33
  and world commerce, 346, 537
  in Habsburg lands, 601
  and Uniat churches, 633
Jews
  in Turkey, 186, 611–12, 617–18
  financiers, 309–12, 602, 788
  in Spain, 345, 511
  in Morocco, 554
John of Nepomuk, Saint, Czech martyr, 576
John III, king of Poland, see Sobieski
John George III, elector of Saxony, 232, 246, 756
John William, of Pfalz-Neuburg, elector palatine, 189, 402, 589
Jommelli, Niccolò, Neapolitan musician, 111
Jordan(s), General, Polish ambassador to France, 692
Joseph I, emperor, 5, 167, 412, 587, 589–90
  as archduke, 388, 575
  King of Hungary (1687), 577, 585
  King of the Romans (1690), 162, 238, 586–7
  marriage (1699), 590
  elected emperor (1705) 423, 573
  and Italy, 163, 440, 447, 449, 592–5
  and Netherlands, 440
  and Spain, 419, 440
  reforms, 311, 574–5
  death, 7, 441, 585–6, 593, 596
Joseph Clement of Wittelsbach, bishop of Liège and archbishop-elector of Cologne, 135, 167, 169, 203, 224, 393, 408, 413, 416
  ban of empire, 423, 589–90
Joseph Ferdinand, electoral prince of Bavaria, 353, 358, 390, 393
  death, 394
Jourdan, Jean, French financier, 15, 359
Jülich, duchy of, 409, 589

Junto, the whig, 267–9
Jurieu, Pierre, Huguenot polemicist, 123–5, 218–19, 341
Jussieu, Antoine Laurent de, botanist, 59
Jussieu, Bernard de, biologist, 41
Jutland, peninsula, 649, 675
Juvarra, Filippo, architect at Turin, 559

Kabylia, 541
Kaiserslautern, taken by French (1688), 232
Kaiserswerth, fortress, 224–5, 237, 399, 409, 413
  taken by Allies (1702), 416
Kalisz, battle of (1706), 700–1
Kamenny Zaton, fortress, 627, 634
Kamieniec Podolski (Kamenets), 608, 610, 627, 684, 688–9, 691
Kane, Richard, military writer, 762
K'ang-hsi, Manchu emperor, 130
Kaniza, Turkish vilayet, 608
Kannara, spice-growers, 530
Kaplan-Girei, khan of the Crimea, 647
Kara Mustafa, grand vizier, 615
  siege of Vienna, 618–19
Karangaland, 518
Karlskrona, dockyard, 650, 763, 808, 825
  plague at, 820
Károlyi, Count Alexander, 584–5
Karwicki, Stanislas Dunin, Polish patriot, 706–7, 709
Kasimierz Dolny, 712
Kasimiyye, Egyptian political clan, 609
Kassa, see Košice, 577, 605
Kazan, khanate, 775
Kehl, fortress, 223, 252, 417, 473
Keill, John, Oxford scientist, 47
Kennebec, the, 498, 502
Kent, population, 887
Kerch, Straits of, 610, 615, 625–6, 630, 719
Kettler family, of Courland, 694
Kexholm, 679
Keyserlingk, Johann Georg von, Prussian envoy at Moscow, 734
Kharkov, 625
Kidd, Captain William, 12
Kiev, 625, 633, 657, 683, 698, 700, 729
Kilburun, fortress, 610
Killiecrankie, battle of (1698), 212, 747
Killigrew, Henry, British admiral, 238, 567
King, Gregory, statistician, 47, 260, 764, 883
King, William, bishop of Derry, 143
Kino, Eusebio Francisco, S.J., missionary, 356
Kinsale, 235, 240, 811
Kinsky, Count Franz Ulrich von, Bohemian chancellor, 177, 575, 579, 588
Kirchner, Michael Achaz von, baron, Austrian diplomat, 471

Kirke, Percy, British colonel, 237
Kirmanshah, occupied by Turks, 645
Kliszów, battle of (1702), 660, 674, 695
Kneller, Sir Godfrey, English painter, 32
Kochowski, Vespasian, Polish psalmodist, 682
Kochu Bey, Turkish writer, 613
König, J. U. von, Saxon poet, 73
Königsberg, 402
trade, 836–7, 840, 843, 867
Königsegg, Count Leopold Wilhelm von, imperial vice-chancellor, 587
Königsmark, Countess Aurora von, 695
Königsmark, Count Otto Wilhelm von, Swedish soldier-of-fortune, 620
Köprülü, family of Turkey, 610, 617
Köprülü, Fazil Mustafa Pasha, grand vizier, 621–2
Köprülü, Hüseyn Pasha, grand vizier, 626, 628, 629
Köprülü, Mehmed Pasha, grand vizier, 621
Köprülü, Numan Pasha, grand vizier, 632
Kolberg, naval battle (1715), 794
Kollonich, Count Leopold, Cardinal primate of Hungary, 582–3
Konarski, Stanislas, Polish political writer, 707
Koniecpol, battle of (1708), 703
Koron, retaken by Turks, 638
Košice (Kassa), 577, 605
Krassow, Ernst Detlow von, Swedish general, 667, 669–70
Kraut, Johann Andreas, contractor and Hohenzollern war treasury official, 788
Kronstadt, Russian arsenal, 808
Krossen (Krosno), duchy of, 689
Kuban, the, 627
Kunfidha, 610
Kusser, Johann, German musician, 106

Labadie, Jean de, religious leader, 150
La Bassée, Lines of, 437–8, 440
Labat, Fr Jean-Baptiste, missionary, 355
La Bruyère, Jean de, 90, 109, 147, 322, 341
La Calprenède, Gauthier de Costes de, playwright and novelist, 91
Lachine (New France), 486, 496
Lachowice, 700
La Fayette, Marie Madeleine, comtesse de, novelist, 72
La Feuillade, Louis d'Aubusson, comte de, marshal of France, 429
La Fontaine, Jean de, poet and fabulist, 72
Lagoa dos Patos, 529
Lagos (Portugal), 246, 568
Lagrange, Joseph Louis, comte de, mathematician, 52, 562
La Guardia (Galicia), 526

Laguna, 529
La Hêve (Acadia), 497
La Hire, Philippe de, astronomer, 40–1
Lahontan, Louis Armand, baron de, Canadian traveller, 100, 485
La Hougue, naval battle (1692), 18, 19, 215, 231, 243–4, 567, 794–5, 811
Lake George, 487
Lake Ladoga, 722
La Laguna, mission, 356
Lallemant, Jacques Philippe, S.J., 334
La Mamora, fortress, 554
Lamarck, Jean-Baptiste de Monet, French scientist, 64
Lamberg, Count Johann Philipp von, bishop of Passau and Austrian councillor, 589
Lambert, Anne Thérèse, marquise de, French society hostess, 342
Lamberville, Fr Jacques de, French missionary, 498
La Monnoye, Bernard de, of Dijon, 340
La Mothe-Cadillac, see Cadillac
La Motte-Houdar(d), Antoine, dramatist, 95
Lancaster (New England), 487
Landau, fortress, 422, 472–3, 473–4, 753
Landen, battle of (1693), 231, 247
Landrecies, siege of (1712), 443
Lange, Lorenz, Swiss engineer, 96
Langendijk, Pieter, Dutch dramatist, 75
Langres, woollens, 864
Languedoc, 119, 325, 328, 335, 375, 552, 570, 813, 823
corn, 548, 839; see also Castelnaudary
salt, 844
woollens, 552, 863–4; see Castelnaudary
silk, 868
population, 885, 889, 900
Languet de Gergy, Jean Joseph, bishop of Soissons, 134
Lannion, hemp, 817
La Pile, Rhine fortress, 252
Laplace, Pierre Simon, marquis de, mathematician, 52
Lapland, 41
La Prairie (New France), 496
Larache, fortress, 554
Largillière, Nicolas de, French painter, 32
La Rochefoucauld, François, duc de, moralist, 72, 84, 91, 149
La Rochelle, 354, 810
La Salle, Robert Cavelier, sieur de, French explorer, 13, 356, 499
La Touche, French naval administrator, 830
La Tour sur Orbe, population, 889, 900
Lausanne, silk industry, 868
Laval, François Xavier, de Montmorency, bishop of Quebec, 484, 496–7
La Vente, Fr Henry Roulleaux de, 499

Lavoisier, Antoine Laurent, chemist, 54
Law, John, financier and statesman, 305, 337, 352, 501, 835–6, 853, 857
Laxenburg, 575
Lazarites, 545
Leake, Sir John, British admiral, 429
  takes Sardinia, 434
  governor at St John's, 503
Lebanon, 609, 611
Lebret, Pierre Cardin, father and son, intendants of Provence, 335
Le Clerc, Daniel, French historian, 71
Le Clerc, Jean, Huguenot scholar and publicist, 76 n., 123, 137, 140–1, 143
Le Clerq, Fr Chrétien, historian of Canada, 497
Le Comte, Louis, S.J., in China, 96, 139
Łęczya, 705
Leduchowski, Stanislas, Polish statesman, 712
Lee, Nathaniel, British dramatist, 79
Leeuwenhoek, Anthonie van, microscopist, 57, 64
Leeward Islands, 251, 501, 810, 849
Lefort, François, friend of Tsar Peter, 625, 718–19
Legendre, Thomas, French financier, 23, 329, 336–7, 339
Leghorn, 10, 174, 540, 542–4, 550, 555, 563–4, 569, 611, 813, 818, 858, 894
  population, 542
Legnano, fortress, 753
Le Havre, 248, 811
Lehmann, Behrend, financier of Halberstadt, 788
Leibniz, Gottfried Wilhelm, 24, 34, 37, 42, 45, 50, 60–2, 74, 77, 86, 96, 128, 143, 173, 735, 739
  calculus, 55
  history of Hanover, 87
Leiden, 44, 122
  cloth, 864, 893
Leipzig, 45, 74, 76, 105, 605, 703, 719
Leisler, Jacob, of New York, 482, 486
Leme, Pais, Brazilian explorer, 533
Lémery, Nicolas, French chemist, 41
León, 782
Leopold I, emperor, 5, 119–20, 162, 166–7, 203
  methods of government, 8–9, 177, 572 ff.
  relatives, 168–9, 224, 388, 578, 685
  character, 177, 574–5
  death, 309, 423
  Spanish succession, 159, 386–8, 393–6, 399, 401 ff., 410, 417, 419, 420, 591–3
  see also Austria, Empire, Habsburg monarchy, Nine Years War, Turkey
Leopold of Anhalt, 466

Lepanto, 608
  naval battle (1571), 564
Le Pelletier, Claude, controller-general, 298
Le Quesnoy, fortress, 443–4
Lérida, surrender of (1707), 373
Lesage, Alain René, French writer, 32, 90, 92, 97, 340
Lesnaja, battle of (1708), 666, 703, 757
Leszczyński, Philotheus, metropolitan of Tobolsk, 128
Leszczyński, Raphael, Polish treasurer, 657, 694, 697
Leszczyński, Stanislas, son of Raphael, puppet-king of Poland (1704), 658, 663–4, 667, 697–9
  after Poltava, 669–70, 700
  withdraws, 703, 707–10, 714, 735
Le Tellier, Michel, French statesman, 744, 746
Levant, the, 215, 246
  trade, 236, 249, 262, 385, 549–53, 611, 862–3, 866
  French in, 549–53, 858, 864
  see also Marseilles, Smyrna, Turkey
Levasseur, Noël and Pierre, wood-carvers of New France, 497
Lewenhaupt, Count Adam Ludwig, Swedish commander, 666, 669, 699, 757
Lewis, margrave of Baden, 243, 250
  in Balkans, 5, 579, 621
  imperial commander against France, 403, 409, 417, 421, 755, 757
  death, 432
  Rastatt palace, 788
Lexington, Robert Sutton, 2nd baron, British envoy to Spain, 475
Lhasa, mission to, 130
L'Hermitage (Newfoundland), 488
Lhuyd, Edward, English geologist, 61
Licensing Act (1685), not renewed (1695), 211
Liebmann, Isaac, financier, 832
Liechtenstein, Hans Adam, prince of, 310–11, 601
Liège, bishopric of, 223–4, 242, 252, 393, 408, 413, 414, 451, 462, 477–8, 578, 786
  armaments production, 224, 869
  fortress taken by Allies (1702), 416
Lierre, fortress, 398
Liguria, 541, 754
Lille, 426, 438, 451, 477
  taken by Allies (1708), 436
  intendant of, 785
  industry, 863
Lillieroot, Count Nils, Swedish envoy at The Hague, 172
Lillingston, Colonel Luke, 355
Lima, 376, 530

Limburg, fortress, 416
Limerick, 240, 242
    Treaty of (1691), 214, 256
Limoges, Joseph de, S.J., missionary, 499
Linnaeus, Carl, Swedish botanist, 35, 57–60,
    62–3
Linz, 603–4, 619
Lions, Gulf of, 248, 542
Lisbon, 16–19, 30, 261, 418
    Allied base, 418–19, 526, 566, 569, 808–9,
    818
    population, 542
    trade, 509–10, 513 ff., 527, 529, 535–6, 849
Lister, Martin, English zoologist, 56
Lithuania, grand duchy of, 2, 3, 665, 678,
    695, 700, 703, 705, 776, 837
    opposition to Sobieskis, 685–6
    civil war, 657, 690–1, 693–4
    Russians and, 693–4, 698–9, 708, 711
    see also Polish-Lithuanian Common-
    wealth, Radziwiłł, Sapieha
Littlecote, 205
Littleton, James, naval commodore, 372
Liverpool, 490
Livingston, Robert, of New York, 496
Livonia, Polish, 660, 699
Livonia, Swedish, 2, 687, 716, 806, 808
    invaded by Augustus, 652–5, 692
    and Russia, 403, 663, 708, 710, 712, 735–7
    Treaty of Nystad, 679
    trade, 648, 699, 837 ff.
Lloyd, William, bishop of St Asaph, 125
Loader, Issac, British anchorsmith, 815
Lobkowitz, Wenzel Eusebius, prince of, im-
    perial ambassador to Spain, 353
Lobo, Dom Manuel, governor of S.Brazil
    529
Locke, John, philosopher, 24–5, 36, 47, 88,
    121, 126, 136–8, 260
    Human Understanding, 78, 96
    Toleration, 124
    Government, 219–22
Locronan, sailcloth, 817
Lodève, population, 889, 900
Lölhöffel, Georg Friedrich von, Prussian
    ambassador at Warsaw, 713
Loire, the, 812, 869
Lombardy, 7, 410, 557, 593, 597, 782
    French in, 591
    Victor Amadeus claims, 595–6
Lombe brothers, John and Thomas, silks,
    868
Lomellina, 466 n., 558, 560 n.
Lomonosov, Mikhail, Russian chemist, 42
London
    Bank of England, 23, 249, 288–93, 314, 835
    concerts, 32, 104–7, 114–15
    theatre, 89, 94

St Paul's cathedral, 108, 125, 262
religion, 128, 144, 270
newspapers, 26, 211, 280
Revolution of 1688–9, 205–6
City institutions, 262, 289, 835–6
Mint, 290, 535, 896
Navy Board, 22, 292, 815, 816, 826, 830,
    833, 880, 898
Victualling Board, 292, 818–19
population, 262, 541, 889
imports of coal, 31, 869; of wines, 846
corn trade and ships' stores, 838
compared with Boston, 481
Londonderry, siege of (1689), 213–14, 235–7
troops, 769
Loreto, Californian mission, 356
Lorge, Guy de Durfort, duc de, marshal of
    France, 245
Lorient, 812
Lorraine, 9, 161, 252, 474, 578, 753; see also
    Charles V and VI, dukes of Lorraine
Louis, dauphin of France, 385
Louis XIII, king of France, 41, 84
Louis XIV, king of France
    outlook, 17, 147, 156, 169–70, 189–90
    authority, 26–8, 216–18, 221, 316–18,
    333–8
    criticisms of absolutism, 32–3, 156, 218,
    326 ff.
    patronage of letters, 77
    ballet and music, 104, 106, 108, 110, 114
    religious policies, 10, 119–20, 130–4, 161–
    2, 333–4, 337–8
    military affairs, 316, 340, 751–2, 780–2, 789
    conduct of foreign policy, 169–71, 175 ff.,
    316
    dynastic ties, 168, 385, 388
    and English Revolution, 18, 26; see also
    James II
    and Italy, 9, 159–61, 164–5, 223, 468, 569;
    see also separate states
    and Rákóczi, 154, 169, 701
    and Habsburg monarchy, 8, 157–8, 160,
    165–7, 387; see also Partition Treaties
    and Spain, 10, 15, 159–61, 163–4, 215,
    235, 350–1, 357–9, 381–2, 384, 397 ff.,
    408, 451–6, 570; see also Orry, Philip V
    and Portugal, 159–60, 163–4, 407, 524–5
    and Barbary states, 224, 545, 554
    and North America, 13, 485, 500–1
    and Poland, 4, 686, 692–3, 695, 710–11
    and Russia, 158, 734–5
    Nine Years War, 154, 160 ff., 202–3, 215,
    223 ff.
    War of Spanish Succession, 26, 360 ff.,
    397 ff., 412 ff., 446 ff.
    death, 27
    see also France, Paris, William III

Louis XV, king of France, 27, 168, 463
Louisbourg, fortress, 850
Louisiana, 12, 485, 499–501
Louvain, 247, 424, 426
Louville, Charles Auguste d'Allonville, marquis de, adviser to Philip V, 365, 368
Louvois, François Michel le Tellier, Marquis de, French war minister, 40, 230, 803
　death, 243, 316
　army, 223–4, 319, 744–51, 761
Luberas, Ludwig, Saxon adviser to Peter the Great, 731
Lubert, Louis de, French naval treasurer, 831
Lubomirski, Hieronymus, Polish crown hetman, 688, 695, 697–8
Lubomirski, Stanislas Heraclius, Polish writer, 682, 844
Lucca, republic of, 535, 594
Lukaris, Cyril, patriarch of Constantinople, 128, 633
Lully, Jean-Baptiste, musician, 79, 106–10, 113–15, 118, 131–3
Lusatia, woollens, 864
Lutheranism, 119–20, 150, 188, 582; see also Silesia
Luxembourg, François Henri de Montmorency-Bouteville, duc de, marshal of France, 19, 232, 239, 242, 244, 247–8, 744, 752
　death, 249
Luxemburg, duchy and fortress, 161, 223, 232, 252, 381, 400, 426, 438, 467, 753
Luzzara, battle of (1702), 417
Lwów, 684, 688, 699, 702
Lyonet, Pierre, French zoologist, 57
Lyonnais, coal, 869
Lyons, financiers, 23, 303, 789
　Payments of Lyons, 304–5
　silk, 868, 894
　corn prices, 876, 898
Lys, the, 381

Maas, the, admiralty of, 800, 815, 832–3, 847
Maastricht, fortress, 249, 400, 404, 753
Mabillon, Dom Jean, historian, 33, 87, 140
Macanaz, Rafael Melchor de, Spanish lawyer, 9, 373–4
Macao, 130, 516, 524
Macapá, Guyanese fort, 531
Macaulay, Thomas Babington, 26
Macchia, Gaetano Gambacorta, prince of, 368 n., 557
Mackay, Hugh, British general, 747
Maclaurin, Colin, British mathematician, 39
Madagascar, 11, 12, 854
Madeira, 520–1, 531, 849; river, 533
Madras, 518–19, 809, 860

Madrid, 343, 348, 352, 359, 361, 365, 367, 369, 373, 377, 389, 408, 423, 475–6
　Real Academia, 76, 343
　population, 357, 542
　Philip V in, 361, 369, 372, 425, 430
　Galway in (1706), 371, 429
　Charles III in (1710), 375, 440
Maffei, Count Annibale di, Savoyard envoy at Utrecht, 464
Maffei, Scipione, Italian dramatist, 73, 140
Magdeburg Concert (1688), 232
Magliabecchi, Antonio, Florentine scholar, 77
Magnol, Pierre, Montpellier botanist, 58
Mahim, island, 525
Mahmud I, sultan, 646
Mahrattas, 518
Maiello, Carlo, Neapolitan philosopher, 558
Maine, 483, 486–7, 498
　Succession War, 502, 507–8
Maintenon, Françoise d'Aubigné, marquise de, 2nd wife of Louis XIV, 326–7, 363, 369, 803, 831
Mainz, 225, 237
　archbishop-elector, Lothar Franz von Schönborn, 407, 573
Majorca, 370, 379, 387, 391, 522, 543–4, 570, 593, 801
Malabar ports, 518–19, 857
Malacca, Indo-Portuguese, 518
Malaga
　naval battle (1704), 423, 569
　trade, 521, 845
Malebranche, Nicolas, Oratorian philosopher, 25, 73, 136–7, 143, 145–6
Małopolska, 695, 702, 711–12
Malpighi, Marcello, biologist, 56, 64, 73
Malplaquet, battle of (1709), 20, 280, 438, 741, 753, 759, 761
　casualties, 749, 752
Malta, 11, 540, 566, 838
　quarantine, 543
　corso, 545–6, 563–4, 619
　and Greeks, 546, 611–12
　and Venice, 640
Malvasia, taken by Venetians (1690), 620
Mamluks, 609
Mandeville, Bernard de, moralist, 152
Manetta, Genoese corsair, 544
Manila, galleon, 373; see Acapulco
Mannheim (Upper Palatinate), 225, 421
Mansfeld, Count Heinrich von, Austrian statesman, 593
Manteigas, woollens, 513
Mantua, duchy and fortress, 160, 240, 468, 473, 594, 596–7, 750, 753
Mantua, Charles IV Gonzaga, duke of, 164, 169, 223, 403, 414, 594

Manzoni, Alessandro, novelist, 557
Mar, John Erskine, earl of, Jacobite leader, 272
Marais, Marin, French musician, 108
Maranhão, Brazilian captaincy, 530–1, 537
Marchand, Jean Louis, French musician, 116
Mardefeld, Arvid Axel, Swedish general, 700
Mardyck, peace negotiations (1719), 456
Margaret Theresa, 1st wife of Leopold I, 386
Maria, sister of Peter the Great, 732
Maria Anna of Pfalz-Neuberg, 2nd wife of Carlos II, 351, 358, 361, 371, 390
Maria Antonia, Austrian archduchess and electress of Bavaria, 353, 388
  death, 589
Maria Luisa of Savoy, 1st wife of Philip V, 367–70, 377
Maria Theresa, queen of France, 385
Maria Theresa, empress queen, 312–13, 478, 592
Mariana of Austria, mother of Carlos II, 348
Marianas (Ladrone Is.), mission to, 349
Mariazell, shrine, 575
Marie d'Arquien, wife of John III, 685
Marie Louise d'Orléans, 1st wife of Carlos II, 160, 348, 350
Marine regiments, 822
Marino, Giambattista, Italian poet, 73
Mariotte, Edmé, French scientist, 40
Marivaux, Pierre de, French writer, 92, 95
Marlborough, John Churchill, 1st duke of
  and Swedes, 4, 184, 432, 633
  and Eugene, 5, 19, 421–2, 435, 438, 443
  and Heinsius, 17, 176–7, 415
  as commander, 18, 19, 21, 169, 742, 748, 751–3, 756–8, 760–1, 763, 770, 784
  war profits, 23, 186, 280, 427
  deserts James II, 204, 209
  in Ireland, 240
  commander-in-chief, 406, 415
  dismissed (1711), 270, 443, 461
  reinstated (1714), 272
  Swift's attack on, 280–1
  and peace terms, 439, 449, 451, 455, 456
  campaigns, 416 ff., see separate battles
Marlborough, Sarah, duchess of, 204, 269, 441
Maronites, 128
Maros, the, 580–1
Maros-Vasárkely, 585
Marrakesh, 548
Marsaglia, battle of (1693), 247
Marseilles, Levant trade, 249, 385, 540, 543, 549–52, 560, 611, 801, 862–3, 868
  Galley Corps, 390, 563, 790 n.
  and Toulon, 20, 813

population, 542
quarantine, 543
plague, 543, 886
sugar imports, 519; cod, 850; alum, 895
Marsigli, Count Luigi, geographer of the Balkans, 581, 743, 762
Marsin (Marcin), Ferdinand, comte de, marshal of France, 408, 421–2, 429
Martell brandy, 847
Martí, Manuel, Spanish scholar, 343
Martigues, seamen, 823
Martinitz, Count Georg Adam von, Austrian statesman, 311
Martinique, 12, 251, 804, 809–10, 825
  trade, 853–4
Mary II, queen of Great Britain, 198
  the throne, 207–9
  during William's absence, 215
  as princess, 217
Mary Beatrice of Modena, 2nd wife of James II, 194, 255 n.
Maryland, 480, 482–3, 487–8, 493, 507–8
  Succession War, 503
  trade, 851–2
Maskelyne, Neville, astronomer royal, 68
Massachusetts, 12, 487, 502, 506, 814
  and the Glorious Revolution, 481, 814
  charter of 1691, 483, 491, 493
  religion and culture, 492–6, 498
Massawa, 610
Mather, Cotton, New England divine, 487, 493–5, 502, 507
Mather, Increase, father of preceding, 481, 483, 493–4, 502
Mato Grosso plateau, 532
Mattarnovy, Georg Johann, German architect, 728
Matveev, Andrey Artamonovich, Russian minister at The Hague, 734, 738
Maubeuge, fortress, 438, 451, 477
Maule, Tom, American writer, 492
Maupertuis, Pierre Louis Moreau de, mathematician, 35, 41–2, 47, 52, 62, 64
Maurice of Nassau, prince, 743
Mavrocordato, Alexander, first dragoman at the Porte, 621, 626, 629, 635–6
Maximilian Emmanuel, elector of Bavaria
  ally of France, 167, 407, 413, 417
  relatives, 168, 386, 390–1
  governor of the Spanish Netherlands, 242, 352–3, 395, 397, 398, 400, 412–13, 422, 436, 578–9
  Spanish succession, 352, 381, 386–8, 390–1, 393, 394, 397, 402
  Blenheim, 422, 588–9
  ban of empire, 423, 590
  Ramillies, 426
  Malplaquet, 438

Maximilian Emmanuel (*cont.*)
and Marlborough, 446
Utrecht, 472–3
in Hungary, 621
Maximilian Henry, of Wittelsbach, arch-bishop-elector of Cologne, 224
Mazagan, fortress, 524–54
Mazarin, Cardinal, 103, 108, 165, 225, 243
Mazepa, Ivan Stepanovich, hetman of the Ukraine cossacks, 630, 664, 666–9, 699, 702, 732, 776
Mazovia, 695, 702, 706, 776
Mecca, 548, 610–11
Mechlin (Malines), 247
Mecklenburg, duchy of, 404, 710, 736–7, 773, 778
Medici, Cosimo III de, grand duke of Tus-cany, 131, 151
Medici, Francesco Maria de, cardinal, 131
Medici, Giovan Gastone, grand duke of Tuscany, 73
Medina de Rioseco, Juan Enríquez de Cabrera, duke of, admiral of Castile, 351, 353, 370
Medinaceli, Luis Francesco de la Cerda, duke of, 374–5
Mehadia, fortress, 750
Mehmed IV, sultan, 577, 598, 619, 620
Mehmed Rami Efendi, grand vizier, 616, 626
Meichl, Simon, Viennese financier, 309–10
Meissen, porcelain, 603
Mekhitar of Sebaste, abbot, 617–18
Meknes, 554
Melilla, fortress, 554
Melk, Benedictine monastery, 602
Melkites, 128
Mendonça, Luís de, viceroy of Goa, 516
Mendoza, Balthazar, bishop of Segovia, 361, 376
Menin, fortress, 451, 477
Mennonites, 493
Menshikov, Prince Alexander Danilovich, adviser to Peter the Great, 718
Merchant Adventurers, 262, 866–7
Mercy, Claude Florimond, comte de, im-perial general, 639
Merian, Maria Sibylla, entomologist, 46
Merlat, Elie, Huguenot writer, 218
Mérode-Westerloo, Eugène Jean Philippe, comte de, soldier-of-fortune, 742, 762
Méry, Jean, French anatomist, 41
Mesnager, Nicolas le Baillif, 186, 337, 447, 462, 469–70, 475
Messina, 540, 557, 559
population, 542
Metastasio, Pietro, librettist, 73, 111
Methoni (Modon), 638

Methuen, John
treaties with Portugal (1703), 16, 163–4, 418–19, 466, 523–6, 569, 591, 808
Methuen, Paul, son of preceding, 523, 808
Metz, Claude du, French artillery expert, 761
Meuse, the, 224, 248, 400, 404, 413, 753; *see also* Maas
Mexico, 13, 129, 350, 355–61, 511
Gulf of, 498, 500
flotas, 349, 354 n., 511, 528
Mezzomorto Pasha, Turkish admiral, 565–6, 615, 628, 790
Middelburg, privateers, 20, 800–1
Milan, duchy and city of, 9, 31, 223, 240, 562, 594, 595
under Austria, 5, 9, 447, 585, 595, 597, 750
rival claims, 164, 250, 389, 401, 426, 446–7, 466, 591–3, 594, 596
Partitions, 386, 393, 396
Succession War, 369, 404, 414, 417, 429
Treaty (1707), 432
population of city, 542
under Spain, 557–8
Milet, Pierre, S.J., missionary, 498
Millner, Sergeant J., English soldier, 762
Miloradovich, Michael, Herzegovinian chieftain, 633
Milton, John, 79, 138, 142
Minas, António Luís de Sousa, 2nd mar-quis das, Portuguese general, 429, 433, 527
Minho, province, 526
Minorca, 11, 22, 162, 387, 391, 419, 439, 442
taken by English, 370, 434, 444, 448, 566, 570, 808–9
Utrecht, 448, 460, 475
Mirandola, duchy of, 403, 468, 473, 596
Missions
Protestant, 128, 152, 492–3, 495; *see also* Pietism
Orthodox, 128, 738
Congregation of Propaganda, 128–30
New France, 128–9, 497–9
South America, 129, 356, 503–4, 531, 533, 537
Far East, 96, 129–30, 139, 537
Philippines, 129, 357
Marianas, 349
Barbary coast, 545
Mississippi, the, 13, 498–9, 500–1, 503–4
Mitchell, Sir David, vice-admiral, 568
Mobile (Louisiana), 360, 365, 498–501, 504
Mocha, coffee, 11, 35, 550, 858–9, 862
Modena, 160, 559, 562
Modena, Rinaldo d'Este, duke of, 595
Mohilev, occupied by Russians, 701

Moivre, Abraham de, Huguenot mathematician, 39
Moldavia, 2, 578, 608, 619, 620, 633–6, 647, 683–4, 689, 776
Molière, 72, 75, 79, 81, 84, 89, 90, 106–8
Molina, Luis de, Spanish Jesuit, 135 n.
Molinos, Miguel de, Spanish mystic, 146
Mombasa, taken by Omani, 11, 517
Monaco, 403, 466
    privateers, 546
Monclova, Melchor Portocarrero Lasso de la Vega, count of, viceroy of Peru, 356
Mondovì, rebellions, 560
Monmouth, James Scott, duke of, 196–8, 202
Monomotapa, the, 516
Mons, fortress, 242, 252, 381, 400, 426, 438, 477–8
    coal, 869
Monsanto, 527
Montagu, Edward Wortley, British diplomat, 641
Montagu, Lady Mary, wife of preceding, 40
Montaigne, Michel, 70
Montalto, Ferdinand de Moncada d'Aragon, duke of, 351, 353
Montecuccoli, Raimondo, Austrian general, 743, 744, 782
Monteiro, Roque, Portuguese statesman, 526
Monteleon, Isidoro Cassado de Azevedo, marquis of, 475
Montenegro, 618, 632, 635
Montesarchio, prince of, 557
Montesquieu, Charles Louis de Secondat, baron de, 33, 100–1, 221–2, 294, 341, 558
Monteverdi, Claudio, musician, 103, 108
Montfaucon, Dom Bernard de, scholar, 87
Montferrat, the, 159, 164, 418, 466, 558, 560 n.
    duke of, 447
Montmélian, 243
Montpellier, 58, 67
Montreal, 251, 484, 486–7, 496–7
Mont-Royal, see Trarbach
Montserrat, 810
Montucla, J. E., historian of mathematics, 71
Moore, James, governor of Carolina, 503–5
Morava, the, 579–80
Moravia, 7, 575, 584, 599, 605
Morea, the, 164, 540
    under Venice, 2, 158, 565, 620, 623, 627, 782
    under the Turks, 566, 608, 637–8
    ceded by Venice, 640, 642
Moreri, Louis, lexicographer, 88
Morin, Jean, Oratorian, 140

Morocco, 359, 548, 554
Morosini, Francesco, Venetian commander, 560, 620
    death, 623
Moscow, 576, 632–3, 654, 665, 702, 718, 738
Moselle, the, 223, 225, 404, 755
    wines, 845
Moura, 527
Mozambique, 516
Mozart, W. A., 105, 111, 113, 116
Müteferrika, Ibrahim, Turkish printer, 644
Münster, bishop of, 166, 182, 250, 410
    Peace of (1648), 439
Muffat, Georg, German musician, 106, 116
Mughals, 11
Muley Ismael, sultan of Morocco, 11, 554
Munich, population, 884
Muralt, Beat Ludwig von, Swiss writer, 221
Muratori, Ludovico Antonio, historian, 33, 87, 559, 595
Muscovy Company, 262, 843
Muslebeshe, Turkish rebel, 647
Muslims, 6, 20, 517, 614, 633, 775–6
    overland trade, 548–9
    Bektashi sect, 612
    Shi'a devotion, 645
    Koran, 6, 97, 617
Musschenbroek, Pieter van, physicist, 46–7
Mustafa II, sultan, 623, 626, 629
Mustafa Pasha, grand vizier, 640
Mutiny Act (1689), 208
Muy, sieur de, Canadian officer, 501

Nadir Shah, conqueror of Persia, 645
Nagyharsány, battle of (1687), 577, 620
Naima, Turkish historian, 643
Nairne, Captain Thomas, Indian agent, 504–5, 507
Namur, fortress and province, 223, 400, 404, 426, 753
    sieges of (1691, 1695), 244, 249
    Barrier, 381, 399, 413, 477
    Maximilian of Bavaria, 438, 467
Nanking, Portuguese diocese, 130
Nantes
    Revocation of the Edict of (1685), 77, 105, 119, 196, 220, 337; see also Huguenots
    trade, 812–13, 894
Naples, kingdom and city
    Austria and, 5, 9, 433, 570, 585, 591–7, 808
    culture, 32–3, 558–9, 562
    Spain and, 164, 368, 370, 557
    Philip V in, 368, 557
    France and, 387, 393, 395–6, 426
    Utrecht, 447, 451–3, 463, 473
    trade, 535, 540
Narantsouac, mission, 498

Närke, population, 885

Narva, battle of (1700), 403, 649, 655–6, 692, 698

Naryshkin, Leo Kirilovich, Russian boyar, 717–18

Nassau, Johan Willem Friso, prince of, stadholder of Friesland, 415, 465

Nataliya, sister of Peter the Great, 738

Nauplia (Napoli di Romania), 620, 638

Navarino, 638

Navarre, 9, 353, 363, 375, 387, 389, 440, 862

Navarrete, Pedro Fernández de, Spanish naval commander, 364

Navigation Acts, 805, 842; (1696), 261, 490–1

Nedim, Turkish poet, 643

Neerwinden, *see* Landen

Negapatam, Indo-Portuguese, 518

Negroponte, 622–3, 632

Ne Plus Ultra Lines, 440, 460, 751

Nerchinsk, Treaty of (1689), 738

Nesmond, André, marquis de, French squadron commander, 489

Nestorians, 128

Netherlands, *see* Spanish Netherlands, United Provinces

Neuhäusel, *see* Nové Zamky

Neutral Rights, 4, 174–5, 187, 234–5, 804–5

Neville, John, British vice-admiral, 251

Nevis, 810

Newcastle, Keelmen's Hospital, 826

Newcomen, Thomas, engineer, 69, 869

New Edinburgh, 360; *see also* Darien

New England, 13, 483, 492–6, 506–8
    Dominion of, 14, 480
    Nine Years War, 12–13, 30, 486–8, 492
    Succession War, 12–13, 30, 501–3, 505–7
    trade, 814, 842, 849
    see also Connecticut, Massachusetts, New Hampshire, Maine, Rhode Island

Newfoundland
    codfishery, 14, 261, 548, 809, 849–50
    Nine Years War, 251, 488–9
    Succession War, 503
    Utrecht, 442, 460, 470, 505, 508

New France, 12–13 ff., 251, 484 ff., 496 ff.
    trade, 488, 840, 850–1
    population, 485, 496, 508
    see also America, Missions, Quebec

New Hampshire, 483, 488, 491, 493, 814

New Jersey, 14, 483, 488, 491, 493, 814

New Mooners, 493

New Plymouth, 483, 487

Newport (Rhode Island), 495–6

New Rochelle (New York province), 493

Newry, 233

New Spain, 500, 511; *see also* Mexico

Newton, Sir Isaac, 24, 37–40, 49 ff., 86, 88, 156, 260, 343
    Principia, 34, 37, 50–3, 70, 137
    Opticks, 39, 52–3, 70, 78
    calculus, 55
    Chronology, 99

New York, 12, 14, 480–90, 493–5, 498, 501

Nicaise, Abbé Claude, French scholar, 77

Nicaragua, logwood, 350, 854

Nice, county of, 243, 425, 426, 560, 567

Nicholson, Sir Francis, of New England, 491, 505–7

Nicolas, Jean, French banker, 304

Nicole, Pierre, Jansenist, 132

Nieswicz, 700

Nieuwpoort, 381, 400, 436, 447, 477, 800

Nikon, patriarch of Moscow, 728, 733

Nîmes, silk manufacture, 868

Nine Years War, 5, 182, 586–7; causes, 202–6, 224–6
    characteristics, 11–13, 18, 154, 160, 174–5, 184, 227–32, 741 ff., 766 ff., 790 ff.
    campaigns, 19, 213–16, 232 ff., 354–7, 486–9, 558, 566–9, 795–8
    economic effects, 174, 244, 314–15, 320, 327, 354 n., 814, 839 ff., 849, 856, 873, 875, 894, 897

Nish (Niš), 579, 610, 621–2, 633, 641, 754, 757

Nithard, Eberhard, Spanish Jesuit, 351

Nivernais, 813, 815

Noailles, Anne-Jules, duc de, marshal of France, 235, 248–9

Noailles, Adrien Maurice, duc de, son of preceding, 375

Noailles, Louis Antoine, cardinal archbishop of Paris, 133, 147

Nollet, Abbé Jean Antoine, scientist, 46–7

Nonjurors, English, 123, 127, 209, 212, 215

Norbis, Abbé, of Vienna, 311

Norfolk, serges, 865

Normandy, 325, 329, 863, 866, 900

Norris, Sir John, vice-admiral, 489, 817

Norrköping, 806

Northumberland, coal, 869

Norway, *see* Denmark

Nottingham, Daniel Finch, 2nd earl of, 169, 205, 216, 392

Nottinghamshire, population 885, 887

Noudar, 527

Nourse, Timothy, English moralist, 145

Nova Scotia, 505, 814; *see* Acadia

Nové Zamky, vilayet and fortress, 608, 619

Novi, Turkish garrison, 640

Nuremberg, 45, 421

Nymegen, Treaties of (1678–9), 171, 223, 383, 411, 473, 761

Nystad, Peace of (1721), 1, 3, 171, 678–9, 738–9

Oates, Titus, English conspirator, 270
Occasional Conformity Act (1711), 273, 461
Ochakov, fortress, 610, 630
Oder, the, 2, 605
Ösel, island, 649
Ogilvy, George, Russian general, 660
Ogiński family, of Lithuania, 690, 693
Ogiński, Gregory, hetman, 700
Ohio, protection of valley, 500
Old Pretender, see James Stuart
Oldenburg, Henry, science publicist, 40
Oleolis, Pierre d', French merchant, 517
Oliva, battle of (1697), 688
Olivares, Gaspar de Guzmán, count-duke of, Spanish statesman, 366
Olkienniki, battle of (1700), 693-4
Omani Arabs, 11, 517
Omerique, Antonio Hugo de, Spanish geometer, 343
Oneglia, privateers, 546, 801
Onod, rebel Magyar assembly (1707), 585
Opatów, military confederacy, 698
Oporto, 510, 520-1, 849
  port-wine, 521, 523, 845-6
Oppenheimer, Samuel, Viennese banker, 309, 311-12, 788-9
Oran, Moorish attacks, 390
Order of Aviz, 537
Order of Christ, 537
Order of Mercy, 545
Order of Santiago, 537
Orel, the, as Russian frontier, 637
Orinoco, the, 356
Orléans, see Philip, duke of, and Marie Louise
Orlik, Philip, cossack leader, 633, 637, 732
Ormonde, James Butler, 2nd duke of, 418
  Restraining Orders of 1712, 443, 464
Oropesa, Manuel Joaquín, count of, Spanish statesman, 351, 358-9, 361
Orry, Jean, French financial adviser to Spain, 365-6, 369-72, 376, 377, 378
  recalled to Versailles (1704), 369; (1706), 371
  returns to Spain (1713), 377
  dismissed (1714), 380
Orsova, 641
Orthodox Church, 128, 188
  in Greece, 553, 554, 633, 637
  in Serbia, 580, 632
  in Ruthenia, 696
  at Constantinople, 617, 635
  see also Russia, Turkey
Osnabrück, bishop of, 405
Ossian (James Macpherson), pseudo-Gaelic bard, 93
Ostend, 248, 390, 400, 436, 439, 447
  taken by Allies (1706), 426-7

Company, 390, 478, 857
corsairs, 800
Osuna, F. M. de P. Acuña Pacheco y Tellez-Giron, duke of, 352
Otranto, strategic position of, 540
Ottoman empire, see Turkey
Oudenarde, fortress, 381
  battle of (1707), 435, 752, 757
Oulx valley, 467
Ouro Preto, 533
Ouwerkerk, Hendrik, count of Nassau, Dutch field-marshal, 415, 422
Overijssel, tobacco cultivation, 852
Oxenstierna, Bengt, Swedish, 172, 184, 658
Oxford, university, 43, 78, 125, 152, 216, 262
  Bodleian collection of manuscripts, 87
  Magdalen College, 125, 199
  Dissenters, 274
Oxford, earl of, see Harley
Oyapok, the, 528, 531
Oyster River (New England), 487
Ozü, see Ochakov

Pac, Lithuanian clan, 685
Padua, 555, 636 n.
Pagan, Blaise François de, comte de Merveilles, French military engineer, 750
Paget, William, 6th baron, British envoy at Constantinople, 622
Pajkul, Otto Arnold von, Livonian officer, 699
Palamos, sieges of (1694-5), 248, 568
Palatinate, the, 5, 30, 120, 166-7, 189, 578, 589-90
  devastation of (1688), 233, 741, 786
  refugees (Palatines), 274, 493-4
  troops, 404
  Succession War, 408, 410
  Utrecht, 468
  see also John William and Philip William of Pfalz-Neuberg
Palej, Semen, cossack leader, 696, 699
Palermo, 557
  population, 542
  naval battle (1676), 565
Palestrina, G. P. da, musician, 102
Paley, William, English theologian, 85
Pálffy, Counts John and Nicholas, Hungarian magnates, 584-5
Palma, Luis António Tomas, count of, viceroy of Catalonia, 362
Pamphylia, 541
Panama, 376, 530
Papachino, Victorio, Spanish corsair, 567
Papacy, see Innocent XI, Alexander VIII, Innocent XII, Clement XI
Papenbroeck, Daniel van, Bollandist, 140
Pará (Belém), 530, 537

Paracelsus (T. B. von Hohenheim), sixteenth-century scientist, 54
Paraguay, Jesuit missions, 129, 357, 529, 533, 537
Paranaguá, gold-washings, 534
Paris
Louvre, 40–1
Observatory, 41
Jardin du Roi, 41–2, 56
science, 47, 84; *see also* Académie des Sciences
Académie Française, 76
publishing, 78, 105
court and town, 81, 341
Hôtel de Nevers, 342
theatre, 32, 89–90, 106, 109
music, 32, 104–7, 108–9, 324
Port-Royal, 132, 334
Parlement, 132, 335
university, 43, 47, 132
St-Germains-des-Prés, 87
archbishop, 133, 147
Issy, theologians' conference, 147–8
Charenton, Protestant church, 336
population, 541
food supply, 31, 323, 882, 890–1, 899, 901
General Farmers, 300
Hôtel de Ville, 301
building employment, 323, 882
police, 324
army recruitment, 326
taxation, 332
Missions Etrangères, 499
Peter the Great at, 737
Gobelins, 737
silk manufacture, 867
trade, 867, 890
pewter valuations, 882, 899
Paris la Masse, Dauphiné contractor, 336
Paris la Montagne, son of preceding, 336
Párkány, 618
Parker, Captain Robert, British soldier, 757, 762
Parker, Samuel, bishop of Oxford, 199
Parma, duchy of, 160, 164, 473, 594–5
Parry, Sir Hubert, British musician, 102
Partition Treaties, 154, 156–7, 161–3, 186–7, 191, 266, 268, 447, 525
first (1698), 176, 358, 393–4
second (1700), 154, 360, 395–6, 400, 402, 655
secret (1668), 387
Pasajes, Spanish dockyard, 565
Pascal, Blaise, 144, 147, 341
Passarowitz, Peace of (1718), 1, 2, 158, 581, 604, 641–2, 645
Passau, taken by Bavarians (1703), 417

Pastorius, Francis Daniel, German emigrant leader, 493
Pate (Patta), taken by Omani, 517
Paterson, William, Scots financier, 15, 360
Patiño, José, Spanish statesman, 379
Patkul, Johann Reinhold von, Livonian nobleman, 652–3, 663, 701, 734, 773, 775
Patrona Halil, janissary leader, 646–7
Paxton, Peter, physician and historian, 33
Pecquet, Antoine, political theorist, 173
Peking, 1, 35, 96, 130, 738
Pelew Islands (Palaos), 357
Pellegrin, Abbé Simon Joseph, librettist, 107
Pels, Andreas, Dutch merchant, 303
Peniche, 537
Penn, William, Quaker, 123–4, 483, 491, 764
Pennsylvania, 483–4, 488, 491, 493
Pensacola, bay of, 356, 360, 364–5, 500–4
Pentagoët, fort and mission, 498; *see* Castine
Pepusch, John Christopher, professor of music, 104, 107
Pepys, Samuel, admiralty secretary, 827, 830
Pereira, Mendo de Foios, Portuguese secretary of state, 516, 526
Perekop, isthmus of, 625
Perevolochna, battle of (1709), 1, 668–70, 674
Pergolesi, Giovanni Battista, Neapolitan musician, 113, 559
Peri, Jacopo, Florentine musician, 109
Périgord, iron, 812
wines, 845
Perle, fortress, 477
Pernambuco, 530–2, 534
Perrault, Charles, poet and critic, 342
Perrault, Claude, architect and physician, 40, 51, 56
Perrin, Pierre, French librettist, 106
Perrot, Nicolas, Canadian explorer, 499
Persia, 95, 551, 571, 608–9, 611, 649, 687
Afghan invasion, 644
Russo-Turkish partition, 645, 739
trade, 551 n., 857, 859–62, 868
Peru, 13, 15, 41, 350, 354, 359, 376, 528, 530
Peschiera, fortress, 753
Peter I, the Great, tsar of Russia
character and upbringing, 188, 633, 716–18
armed forces, 718–19, 720–3, 775–7
travels, 21, 75, 172, 719, 737
state service, 29, 730, 775, 777
economic policy, 723–5
administrative reforms, 725–6
education and culture, 726–7
ecclesiastical changes, 728–9
opposition to, 719–20, 731–3

Peter I, the Great (*cont.*)
death, 733
see also Great Northern War, Poltava, Pruth, Russia, St Petersburg
Peter II, king of Portugal, 168, 395
Grand Alliance, 163–4, 418, 466, 525
Peterborough, Charles Mordaunt, 3rd earl of, in Spain, 425, 430, 757
Peterwardein, fortress, 580, 621, 623, 626
battle of (1716), 639–40, 642
Petkum, Hermann, Holstein-Gottorp resident at The Hague, 182–3, 447, 456
Petre, Edward, Jesuit confessor to James II, 195, 197, 200, 204
Petrinje, 581
Petrovich, Daniel, Serbian bishop, 633
Petty, Sir William, economist, 48
Peyssonel, J. A., French naturalist, 57
Peyster, Abraham de, of New York, 482
Pforzheim, taken by French (1692), 245
Philadelphia, 42, 493–4
Philip William, of Pfalz-Neuburg, elector palatine, 168, 578, 589
Philip III, king of Spain, 386
Philip IV, king of Spain, 384, 388
Philip V, king of Spain, duke of Anjou, 8, 9, 19, 369, 372, 425, 430, 440
relatives, 168, 388
heir to Carlos II, 360–1, 396–7
arrival in Spain, 361–2
character, 362–3
and Louis XIV, 16, 161, 164, 361–4, 373–7, 446, 451–6
in Naples, 368, 557
marriages, 367, 380, 404
recognition of, 397, 400, 414, 441, 448, 451–2, 459, 463–4, 470, 475–6
see also Orry, Partition Treaties, Spain
Philip, duke of Orléans, 429, 737
Philippines, the, 129, 346, 349, 357, 387
Philippopolis, 610
Philippsburg, fortress, 203, 215, 225, 755
occupied by French (1688–97), 232, 237, 252
Phip(p)s, Sir William, governor of Massachusetts, 251, 483, 487
Piacenza, imperial fief, 473, 595
Piazzetta, Giovanni Battista, Venetian painter, 556
Picard, Jean, French astronomer, 40
Picardy, 438, 863, 866
Piccolomini, Count Aeneas Silvius, imperial general, 579
Pico (Azores), wine and brandy, 520
Piedmont, *see* Savoy-Piedmont
Piekary, abbey, 687
Pietism, 24, 120, 125, 128, 146, 149–51
Piławce, battle of (1648), 682

Pinerolo, fortress, 160, 238–41, 245–52, 559
Piombino, channel of, 540
Piper, Count Carl, Swedish chancery official, 184, 652, 661, 667
Piracy, 11, 12, 31, 349, 541, 544
Piteå, 806
Placentia (Plaisance), 488–9, 503, 850
Plague, visitations of,
Italy (1630–1), 542, 543; (1656), 542, 543
Spain (1630–1), 543; (1676–85), 345, 886
London (1665–6), 283, 886
France (1666), 886
Barbary Coast (1691–2), 543
Habsburg lands (1691–2, 1709–14), 670, 886 n.
Poland (1706–13), 705, 886 n.
Baltic region (1709–12), 774
Brandenburg (1711), 886 n.
Copenhagen (1711), 886 n.
Sweden (1710–12), 672; Karlskrona, 820
Salonica (1719), 644
Marseilles, Provence (1720–3), 868, 886
Plate, the (Rio Plata), 350, 365, 476, 525–32
Ploudaniel, sailcloth, 817
Plowman, William, corsair, 544, 801
Pluche, Abbé Noël Antoine, popularizer of scientific knowledge, 85
Plymouth, dockyard, 22, 229, 811, 818
naval hospital, 825
Po, the, 223, 595, 753
Pociej, Lewis, treasurer and later hetman of Lithuania, 703, 708, 711
Podhajce, skirmish (1698), 688
Podlesia, 695–6
Podolia, 2, 608, 619, 627, 683–4, 696
Pointe-aux-Trembles (New France), 496
Pointe Levis (New France), 496
Pointe-Verte (Newfoundland), 488
Pointis, Bernard Louis Desjean, baron de, French squadron commander, 251, 355, 489, 545, 809
Połąga (Polangen), 687, 692, 699
Polignac, Abbé Melchior de, French ambassador to Poland, 439, 462, 686
Polish-Lithuanian Commonwealth (Rzeczpospolita)
population, 705
religion, 119, 128, 188, 714
disintegration, 2, 681–3, 704–6, 714–15
Union with Saxony, 2, 683, 687–8, 689, 693, 700, 709–10, 713–14
Saxon troops in, 689, 691, 694, 696, 704–5, 710–13
Crown army, 21, 696, 707, 709–10, 713, 776
disposal of crown, 656–9, 663, 684–7, 688, 697, 699, 701–2, 703–4, 707, 709
Charles XII and, 2, 631, 656 ff., 661, 693 ff., 698–700, 704–5, 714

Polish-Lithuanian Commonwealth (*cont.*)
and Habsburgs, 581, 683–5, 695, 701, 710
and Turkey, 619, 620, 627, 631, 634, 636–7, 645, 672, 683–4, 688–9, 692, 709, 710
and Cossacks, 696, 699, 759
economy, 682, 704–5, 714, 836 ff.
finance, 184, 690, 704, 706, 713–14
royal power, 177, 681, 691–2, 698, 709
hetmans' powers, 685 n., 706, 708, 711, 713–14
liberum veto, 681, 707, 709
plague, 705, 886 n.
Sejm, 177, 681, 686, 691–2, 694–5, 698, 703, 707–8, 709, 712–14
sejmiki, 685, 691, 709, 713
'golden freedom', 682–3, 691, 693, 706, 711–12
see also Augustus II, Confederacies, Leszczyński, Lithuania, Sobieski
Połonka, battle of (1660), 682
Poltava, battle of (1709), 1–5, 185, 439, 630, 667–9, 699, 703, 708, 732, 755
a turning-point, 733–9, 755, 757, 744, 806
casualties, 749
Pomerania, Eastern (Polish), 710
Pomerania, Swedish, 631, 656, 670–1, 679, 703, 707, 712, 806, 852
Pomponne, Simon Arnaud, marquis de, French foreign minister, 161, 389, 397
Ponant, the (French oceanic ports), 234, 812
Pondicherry, 252, 518, 856
Poniatowski, Count Stanislas, Polish officer, adherent of Charles XII, 631, 637, 736
Pontchartrain, Jérôme Phélypeaux de, French minister of marine and colonies, 13, 499–501, 506, 828, 829, 830
Pontchartrain, Louis Phélypeaux de, father of preceding, controller general and minister of marine and colonies, 40, 242–3, 298, 331, 485, 499, 830
Pope, Alexander, poet, 80–2, 86, 107
Popish Plot (1678), 196, 211, 273, 279
Porcio, Nicolás, Spanish asientist, 350
Porpora, Nicola Antonio, Neopolitan musician, 111
Portalegre, 527
Portland, Hans Willem Bentinck, 1st earl of, 156, 161, 170, 202, 226, 266, 388–9, 395
Ryswick, 252, 388
Port Mahon, *see* Minorca
Portobello, 350, 376, 530
Portocarrero, Luis Emmanuel Fernández Boccanegra, Cardinal archbishop of Toledo, 9, 358, 361, 365, 367, 371, 396
Porto Ercole, 387 n., 546
Port-Paix, 355
Port-Royal, convent, 132, 334

Port Royal (Annapolis), 12, 487, 497, 502, 505, 508
Port Royal (Jamaica), 810
Port St Mary, 418
Portsmouth, dockyard, 229, 811, 819
Portugal
and England, 16–17, 163–4, 261, 418–20, 466, 512 ff., 521 ff., 535, 569, 808
and Spain, 365, 466, 476, 511, 514, 519, 524 ff.
and France, 163–4, 183, 364, 365, 407, 466, 512–13, 519–20, 522 ff., 528, 531, 535
finance, 347, 511, 514, 517, 526, 536
wine exports, 261, 419, 520 ff., 538, 845–6
Succession War, 418–19, 422, 465, 429–30, 433, 438, 808
course of prices, 509 ff., 519–20, 527, 535
agriculture, 509, 520 ff., 527–8, 537–9
salt, 509, 519, 532, 844–5
religion, 511, 531, 532–3, 537–9
industry, 512–13, 523, 524, 535–6
silver, 511, 514, 517, 520, 528, 529, 533
gold, 261, 533–5
sugar, 510, 517, 519–20, 531, 534
hides, 529–30, 532
East Africa, 516–18
social structure, 522–3, 537–9
see also Angola, Azores, Brazil, India, Macao, Madeira, Peter II, slavery
Pososhkov, I. T., Russian economist, 723
Potocki, Joseph, grand hetman of King Stanislas, 696, 703
Potocki, Michael, son of preceding, 689
Potosí, silver mines, 528
Povey, Thomas, London merchant and colonial adviser, 506
Poznań (Posen), 712
Pozzo, Andrea, Italian painter, 145
Pragmatic Sanction (1713), 7, 156, 592
Prague, 601, 719
Prandtauer, Jakob, German architect, 602
Preobrazhensky Guards, Russia, 721, 777
Presidii, Stato dei, *see* Tuscany
Prešov, *see* Eperjes
Pressburg, 306, 577, 585–6
Prévost, Abbé Antoine François, French novelist, 32, 92, 95
Prié, Ercole di Turinetti, marquis of, envoy of Savoy in Vienna, 598
Principe island, slave entrepôt, 515
Prior, Matthew, English poet and diplomat, 186, 459–61, 469–70
Privateering, 6, 12, 19–20, 174, 187, 349, 354, 792, 801–4, 809, 820, 834
Zeelander, 20, 174, 187, 420, 427, 546–7, 550, 800–1
French, 487, 489, 503, 528, 802–4

Privateering (*cont.*)
  Mediterranean, 357, 390, 515, 543, 544–8, 558, 619; *see also* Barbary Coast
  Dunkirk, 734, 800, 802, 812, 848
  Caribbean, *see* flibustiers
  Baltic, 4, 675, 802, 808
Probabilism, 147, 153
Prokopovich, Feofan, Russian bishop, 729
Protestantism, 7, 14, 25, 76–7, 119 ff., 138, 141 ff., 188–9, 193 ff., 259, 273, 506, 604
  Poland, 119, 687
  Savoy, 238
  Ryswick, 189, 252, 383, 473–4, 588
  Bohemia, 602; Hungary, 583, 586
  see also Calvinism, Dissenters, Huguenots, Lutheranism, Pietism
Provence, 240, 465, 829, 889
  agriculture, 548, 839; corn supply, 548, 813
  industry, 863–4
  population, 889, 900
Prussia, *see* Brandenburg-Prussia
Pruth, the, Russian surrender at (1711), 1, 185, 634–5, 736
  Treaty (1711), 636, 709
Przebendowski, Jan Jerzy, Polish treasurer, 689, 709
Pufendorf, Samuel von, German jurist, 74, 173
Pułtusk, battle of (1703), 696
Purcell, Henry, 102–4, 107–8, 113–14, 144
Puységur, Jacques François de Chastenet, marquis de, marshal of France, 746, 762
Pyrenees, Treaty of the (1659), 234, 246

Quadruple Alliance (1718), 27
Quakers, 25, 140, 146, 149–51, 210, 259, 264
  in North America, 492–3
Quary, Robert, surveyor-general of the customs in N. America. 491
Quebec
  expeditions against, 13; (1690), 251, 487; (1711), 441, 457, 470, 505–6, 508
  bishopric, 128, 484–5, 497, 499
  council, 484–5
  population, 496
  schools, 496–7
  Seminary of Foreign Missions, 499
Queensberry, James Douglas, 2nd duke of, 276
Quercy, Lower, wheat, 839
Quesnel, Pasquier, Jansenist, 132–3, 334
Quietist controversy, 24, 128, 137, 147–50, 327
Quinault, Philippe, French librettist, 110, 112
Quito, 356, 530–1

Rabutin [-Bussy], Count Ludwig von, imperial general, 585
Racine, Jean, 33, 72, 82–3, 106–8, 110–12
Radicati, Count Alberto, free-thinker, 562
Radogoszcz, battle of (1715), 711
Radosczkowice, 665, 702
Radziejowski, Michael, cardinal primate of Poland, 657–8, 686, 688, 690, 694–8
Radziwiłł, Charles, chancellor of Lithuania, 700
Radziwiłł, Ludwika Karolina, Lithuanian heiress, 685
Ragusa (Dubrovnik), 549, 608, 632
Raguzinsky, *see* Vladislavich
Rákóczi, Count Francis Leopold, Hungarian rebel, 5, 7, 154, 169, 412, 584–6, 605, 639
  and Poland, 585, 664, 701
Rameau, Jean Philippe, musician, 107–8
Ramillies, battle of (1706), 164, 176, 370, 426–9, 446, 752, 756–7
  repercussions, 662
Randolph, Edward, surveyor-general in North America, 480, 483, 490, 506
Rapin, René, S.J., French critic, 78
Rasle, Sébastien, S.J., missionary, 498
Rastatt, Peace of (1714), 5, 167, 171
  negotiations, 444, 446, 472–4
Ratisbon (Regensburg), Truce of (1684), 17, 182, 202–3, 343, 588
  Diet (1713), 182, 471, 473–4, 587–8
Raudot, Jacques, intendant of New France, 496
Ravensberg, county of, 225
Rawa Ruska, treaties of (1698, 1716), 692, 712
Ray, John, English naturalist, 35, 40, 56, 58–60, 85, 142–3
Réaumur, René Antoine Ferchault de, French scientist, 41, 47, 54, 57, 61, 65–7
Rébenac, François de Pas, comte de, French diplomat, 160
Red Sea, 11, 610–11
Redi, Francesco, Italian physician, 64
Redondo, 538
Regensburg, bishop of, 399; *see* Ratisbon
Régis, Pierre Sylvain, Cartesian, 84
Regnard, Jean François, dramatist, 90
Rehnskiöld, Count Karl Gustaf, Swedish marshal, 654–6, 660–1, 700, 757, 761
  captured at Poltava, 669
Rémonville, sieur de, of Louisiana, 500
Rennes, parlement, 335
Repnin, Prince Nikita Ivanovich, Russian marshal, 634
Resht, occupied by Russians (1722), 739
Rethel, woollens, 864

Retz, Jean François Paul de Gondi, cardinal de, memoirs, 91
Reval, trade, 649, 773, 837
Reventlau, Count Christian Ditlev von, Austrian general, 429
Rheims, woollens, 864
Rheinberg, fortress, 224, 237, 413, 416
Rhine, the, 4, 6, 9, 17, 223–4, 245, 405, 417, 753, 845–7
Rhode Island, 483, 491, 502
Rhône, the, 813, 889
  trade, 845, 867–8
Rialp, Ramón de Vilana Perlas, marquis of, Spanish lawyer, 593
Ribeira, Luis Manoel da Camara, 3rd count of, Azorean industrialist, 536
Ribeiro de Macedo, Duarte, Portuguese ambassador to France, 512, 516
Ricci, Sebastiano, Venetian painter, 556
Richelieu, Cardinal, 165, 735, 744
  and the navy, 792, 804, 822
Richerism, 134
Ricous, Louis Gaspard de, diplomat, 182
Riga, 2, 10, 30, 649, 659, 692, 708, 773
  naval supplies, 840–3
  other trade, 837, 847
Rights, Bill of (1689), 265
Rio Grande do Sul, 534
Rio de Janeiro, 466, 528–9, 532, 534, 537
Rio Napo, Jesuit mission, 356, 531
Rio Negro, Carmelite mission, 531
Riquet, Pierre Paul, canal-builder, 564
River Brethren, 493
Roberti, G. Frigimelica, librettist, 112
Robinson, Dr John, dean of Windsor (1707) and bishop of Bristol (1710), diplomat, 186, 462
Robinson, Sir Tancred, naturalist, 96
Roche, Michel de la, Huguenot publicist, 78
Rochefort, arsenal, 22, 390, 562, 793, 812, 815, 820–1
Rochester, Laurence Hyde, 1st earl of, 195, 198, 209, 215, 267–8
Rocroi, battle of (1643), 239, 343, 744
Roemer, Olaus, Danish astronomer, 40
Roermond, fortress, 416, 477
Roger, Estienne, Dutch printer, 105, 116
Rogers, Captain Woodes, corsair and circumnavigator, 96–7, 373
Rohault, Jacques, Cartesian, 51, 84
Romagna, oak, 813
Romorantin, army uniforms, 864
Ronquillo, Francisco, Spanish statesman, 359, 373, 377
Rooke, Sir George, British admiral, 418, 423, 569, 797, 806
Rosas, taken by French (1693), 247
Rossi, Luigi, Italian musician, 109

Rotgans, Lucas, Dutch dramatist, 75
Rotterdam, 218, 329, 794, 800, 832
Rouen, 23, 336–7, 512, 895, 900–1
  textiles, 863, 894
Rouillé, Pierre, French diplomat, 446
  negotiations of 1709, 450–1, 453–6
Rousseau, Jean-Jacques, 2 n., 95, 100, 221
Rousseau de Chamoy, 173
Roussillon, 375, 390
Rovigo, Venetian trade, 555
Rowe, Charles, British general, 758
Royal Society, the, 37–40, 43, 45, 51, 76–7, 84, 96
Ruhr, the, coal, 869
Rumania, see Moldavia, Wallachia
Rumelia, 608–9, 642; see also Turkey
Russell, Edward, earl of Orford, admiral, 200, 216, 244, 248, 391, 568, 808, 829
Russia
  and the West, 3, 154, 157–8, 676, 678, 716 ff., 727–8, 733–40
  and Turks, 1, 6, 31, 158, 185, 227, 394, 566, 625–8, 630–7, 644–5, 669–70, 671–2, 718–19, 722, 736
  and Cossacks, 31, 610, 630–1, 634, 636, 665–8, 669–70, 685 n., 696, 699, 732, 759, 775–6
  and Tatars, 31, 610, 625, 627, 634, 636, 667–8, 672, 683–4, 688, 760, 775
  and Poland, see Augustus II
  and Sweden, 1–3, 158, 402–3, 630–1, 634–5, 636, 648–9, 652 ff., 663 ff., 679–80, 692 ff., 716, 720–2, 733 ff.
  and Denmark, see Denmark
  and Persia, 644–5, 739
  religion, 3, 128, 716, 728–9, 732–3, 738
  culture, 42, 726–9, 739
  government, 718–19, 725–6, 730–1
  economy, 716, 723–5, 836–44; see also Archangel, Riga
  finance, 723, 726, 730–2
  social changes, 729–32, 775, 777
  see also Peter I, St Petersburg, Siberia
Ruthenia, 687, 696, 708
Ruvigny, Huguenot general, see Galway
Rybiński, Sigismund James, Polish governor, 703, 709
Rycaut, Sir Paul, historian of Turkey, 97
Rydzyna, Treaty of (1714), 710
Rymer, Thomas, historian, 33, 79, 82, 87
Ryswick, Peace of (1697), 26, 161, 167, 169–70, 252, 262–3, 291, 332, 337, 381–5, 388, 392, 411, 477, 569, 579, 582
  North America, 13–14, 489–90, 500, 508
  Sweden, 172, 246, 651
  religious clause IV, 189, 252, 383, 473–4, 588
  Dutch trade, 185–6, 187, 252

Rzeczpospolita Polska, *see* Polish-Lithuanian Commonwealth

Sabará, gold, 533
Sacheverell, Dr Henry, English divine, 125, 152, 220, 270, 441, 457
Sacramento, 350, 372, 476, 525, 529–30
Safavi dynasty of Persia, 644
Said Chelebi, and Turkish printing, 644
St Augustine (Florida), 372, 503
Saint-Cosme, Fr Jean François Buisson de, French missionary, 499
Saint-Cyran, Jean du Vergier de Hauranne, abbé de, Jansenist, 133
Santo-Domingo, 354–5, 390
Saint-Domingue, 350, 501
  privateers 12, 251, 349, 356, 804, 810
  attacks on (1691, 1695), 251, 355
  sugar, 854
St Eustatius, 810, 853
St Florian, Austrian monastery, 602
St Germains, 255, 275
St Helena, 809
Saint-Hilaire, Geoffroy, French biologist, 64
St Joachim (New France), 496–7
St John, knights of, 545–6, 828; *see* Malta
St John, Henry, *see* Bolingbroke
St John's (Newfoundland), 489, 498, 503
St Kitt's (St Christophe)
  French in, 251, 499, 809–10
  English in, 13, 470, 809
St Lawrence, the, 13, 470, 500, 502, 506
  fur trade, 850–1
St Lo, Captain George, British dockyard commissioner and pamphleteer, 824
St Malo, 246, 249, 812
  privateers, 19, 489, 802
  trade, 15, 364, 375–6, 849–50, 856–7
St Mary's, codfishery base, 503
Saint-Ovide, sieur de, French officer, 503
St Petersburg, 3, 42, 663, 665, 668, 734
  building of, 31, 725, 728, 731
  trade, 867
Saint-Prest, Jean Yves de, archivist, 178, 182
St Quentin, Huguenot refugees, 867
Saint-Romain, Melchior de Harod de Senevas, marquis de, French envoy in Lisbon, 512
St Ruth (Ruhe, Rhue), Charles Chalmot de, French general, 242
Saint-Simon, Louis de Rouvroy, duc de, 28, 327, 329, 339, 597, 780
St Stephen, crown of, *see* Hungary
St Tropez, seamen, 823
Saint-Vallier, Jean Baptiste de, bishop of Quebec, 484, 496–7, 499
St Venant, fortress taken by English (1710), 440

Sainte-Famille (New France), 496
Sainte-Foy (New France), 496
Saintonge, wines, 845
Salaberry, French naval administrator, 830
Salaburg, Count Gotthard Heinrich von, Austrian minister, 309
Saladin family, Genevan bankers, 303
Salem (Mass.), witchcraft trials, 492
Sallee, corsairs, 390, 554
Salm, Karl Theodor Otto, prince of, Austrian minister, 450 n., 487
Salmon Falls, 486
Salonica, 562, 608, 612, 644
Saluzzo, 241, 245
Salvaterra, 527
Salvatierra, Juan María de, S.J., 353
Salzkammergut, salt exports, 605
Samuś, Ivan, cossack leader, 696
Sancroft, William, archbishop of Canterbury, 197, 201, 209
Sandomierz Confederates, *see* Confederacies
Sanfelice, Ferdinando, Neapolitan architect, 559
Santa Ana (Brazil), 553
Santa Maura, 544, 619, 627, 639, 642
Santarém, oil presses, 520
Santiago de los Caballeros, 355
Santona, Spanish dockyard, 565
Santos, 537
São Francisco valley (Brazil), cattle, 532–4
São Miguel (Azores), wines, 520
São Paulo, 532–4, 537
São Tomé, island, 515, 528, 533
São Vicente, 532
Sapieha family, of Lithuania, 657, 685, 688, 690, 693–5, 697–8
Sapieha, Benedict, Lithuanian treasurer, 685, 688
Sapieha, John Casimir, grand hetman of Lithuania, 685, 688, 690–1
Sapieha, Michael, son of preceding, 694
Saptes, woollens, 864
Saragossa, 368, 370, 440
Sarajevo, 626
Sardinia, 159, 161, 164, 375, 387, 439, 556, 570, 593, 597, 641
  taken by Allies (1708), 370, 433–4
  Utrecht, 467, 473
  Victor Amadeus and, 559
  salt, 844
Sari Mehmed Pasha, Turkish treasurer, 629
Sarsfield, Patrick, Irish soldier, 242
Sas van Ghent, 408
Sauveur, Joseph, French scientist, 40
Sava, the, 578, 581, 610, 640–1
Savannah, the, 504
Savery, Thomas, English engineer, 69

Savoy-Piedmont, duchy of, 6, 9 11, 18, 29, 159, 161, 163–4, 591, 596, 747, 788
  religion, 119–20, 188, 560–2
  Nine Years War, 231–3, 240–1, 243, 245–7, 250–1, 558
  Succession War, 417–18, 422, 425, 428–9
  Utrecht, 159, 164, 444, 447, 463–7, 571
  army, 238, 560–1, 766–7
  finance, 560–1
  economy, 560, 844
  population, 889
  see also Turin, Victor Amadeus II
Saxe, Maurice, comte de, marshal of France, 661
Saxe-Gotha, duke of, 246 n., 402, 407
Saxony, 2, 232, 246
  Nine Years War, 237, 241
  Northern War, 411, 431, 652 ff., 754
  Charles XII in, 431, 654, 662–3, 700–1, 704, 774
  economy, 605, 867, 869
  Estates, 687–8, 697–8
  Union with Poland, 2, 683, 687–9, 691–3, 697, 700, 709–10, 713–14
  see also Altranstädt, Augustus II, Empire
Saybrook (Conn.), 493
Scania, 3, 653, 671, 775, 808
Scarlatti, Alessandro, Neapolitan musician, 101–2, 104, 109–13, 115–16, 559
Scarlatti, Domenico, son of preceding, 109, 559
Scarron, Paul, French writer, 75
Scheldt, the, 249, 381, 395, 413, 436, 447, 478, 752–3, 757, 764, 786, 811
Schellenberg, the, fortress of Donauwörth, 421, 757
Schenectady, 251, 486
Scheuchzer, J. J., Swiss geologist, 61–2
Schio, woollens, 556
Schism Act (1714), 273–4
Schlüter, Andreas, German architect, 728
Schönborn, Count Friedrich Karl von, imperial vice-chancellor, 573, 587
Schomberg, Frederick Herman, 1st duke of, marshal, 236–9
Schröder, Wilhelm von, Austrian economist, 310, 313, 606
Schulenberg, Johann Matthias von der, Saxon marshal, 638, 700
Schuyler, Colonel Peter, of New York, 488, 498
Scotland
  Union (1706–7), 26, 220, 275–9, 431
  universities, 43, 279
  religion, 123, 149, 198, 211–12, 276–8
  population, 211, 254
  William III, 211–13, 275–6, 769

economy, 211–12, 255–6, 392, 420, 765, 844, 846, 869, 881, 894
  and Charles XII, 675
  mercenaries, 742; regiments, 769, 783
  Jacobites, 255, 257, 272, 275–6, 279, 797
Scudéry, Madeleine de, French novelist, 91
Seafield, James Ogilvy, 1st earl of, chancellor of Scotland, 276–8
Seckendorff, Veit von, historian of Lutheranism, 121
Security, Scotttish Act of (1704), 276–7
Sedan, woollens, 863
Sedgemoor, battle of (1685), 747
Segovia, 542, 551, 863
Seignelay, Jean-Baptiste Colbert, marquis de, French naval minister, 239, 499, 549, 792, 803, 830
Seilern, Johann Friedrich Edler von, Austrian chancellor, 467, 575, 587, 689, 601
Selim-Girei, khan of the Crimea, 620–1
Selkirk, Alexander, castaway, 97
Semendria (Smederevo), 641
Semmering Pass, 604, 754
Semonovsky Guards, Russia, 777
Sena, 518
Senegal, 563
Senesino [Francesco Bernardi], male mezzo-soprano, 107
Senigallia, 555
Septennial Act (1716), 220, 275
Sequeira, Bueno de, Brazilian explorer, 533
Serbia, 1, 7, 577, 621, 625, 754
  Turks, 580, 598, 618
  Austria, 30, 582
  Orthodoxy, 580, 632–3
Sergison, Charles, of the Navy Board, 830
Serpa, 527
Sète (Cette), 571
Settlement, Act of (Irish, 1662), 214
  (1701), 220, 254 n., 266, 466
Setúbal, 519, 521, 537, 844
Severia, 666
Seville, 11, 42, 343, 368
  population, 542
Sewall, Samuel, Massachusetts judge, 502, 507
Sezane valley, 467
Shadwell, Thomas, English dramatist, 113
Shafirov, Peter Pavlovich, baron, Russian statesman, 185, 634–6
Shaftesbury, Anthony Ashley Cooper, 3rd earl of, 29, 93, 127–8, 142, 219
Shakespeare, William, 79, 111, 114
Sharp, James, archbishop of St Andrews, 152
Sharp, James, archbishop of St Andrews, 152
Sheerness, dockyard, 811
Sheffield, John, 3rd earl of Mulgrave, 79
Sheremeteyev, Count Boris Petrovitch, Russian marshal, 634–5, 655

Sherlock, William, dean of St Paul's, 125
Shirvan, occupied by Turks, 644–5
Short, Dr Thomas, statistician, 887, 900
Shovell, Sir Cloudesley, British admiral, 19, 425, 433, 794
Shrewsbury, Charles Talbot, duke of, 216, 271–2, 457–60
Siam, 95, 130
Siberia, 128, 731, 738
Sicily
  and Austria, 9, 406, 426–7, 596–7
  and Savoy, 159, 465, 467, 477, 559
  and France, 385, 387, 395
  and Spain, 164, 370, 556–7
  and Philip V, 161, 375, 439, 447, 451–2, 463
  baronage, 553, 557
  salt, 844
  earthquakes and population, 884
Sidon (Saida), 550, 609
Sieniawski, Adam Nicholas, crown hetman of Poland, 688, 696, 701–3, 708, 711–12
Sieradz, 705
Silahdar Ali Pasha, grand vizier, 637–40, 643
Silent Sejm (1717), the, 712–13
Silesia, 8, 432, 575, 599, 605–6, 662, 685, 687, 703
  Lutherans, 188, 432, 602
  trade, 605–6, 864, 867
Sillery (New France), mission, 496, 498
Simon, Richard, Oratorian scholar, 24, 36, 88, 140–1, 341
Sinop(e), 562, 615
Sinzendorf, Count Philip Ludwig von, imperial chancellor, 450, 452, 454–5, 464–5, 468, 471, 573, 589
Sisters of the Congregation, 497
Siyavush Pasha, grand vizier, 620
Skopje (Üskub), 632
Skoropadsky, Ivan, hetman of the Ukraine, 776
Slangenburg, Frederik Johan van Baer, baron, Dutch general, 416, 424
Slavery and slave-trade, 12, 24, 533–4
  Portuguese, 349–50, 514–16, 517, 529, 531, 533, 855
  Brazil, 510, 515, 531–4
  Zambesi, 518
  Algiers, 545
  Mediterranean galleys, 563–4, 615, 822
  Danish and Prussian, 855
  French, 855–6
  English, 260–1, 855–6
  Dutch, 855–6, 872
  see also Asiento
Sleswig-Holstein, 2, 3, 652, 654, 678
  Danish invasion (1700), 654

Sloane, Sir Hans, English naturalist, 38–40
Sloughter, Colonel Henry, governor of New York, 482
Slovakia, 7, 577
Smolensk, 657, 665–6, 683, 698, 700
Smorgony, 702
Smyrna,
  population, 542
  the convoy (1693), 215, 246, 550, 568, 796
  trade, 10, 546, 611, 859, 868
Soames, Sir William, translator, 78
Sobieski, Alexander, 658
Sobieski, Constantine, 657–8, 708, 712
Sobieski, James, 667, 684–6, 694, 701
  captured by Augustus II, 657–8, 697
Sobieski, John III, king of Poland, father of three preceding, 168, 183, 619, 620, 625, 682–6, 696, 714, 776
  relief of Vienna, 619–20, 696
Society for Promoting Christian Knowledge, 128, 152
Society for Propagation of the Gospel, 128, 152, 492–3, 495
Socinianism, 136–7; see also Unitarians
Sofala, 518
Solimena, Francesco, Neapolitan painter, 559
Solms [-Braunfels], Count Hendrik Trajectinus van, Dutch general, 245
Somers, John, baron, lord chancellor, 216, 266–7, 270, 277
Somerset, Charles Seymour, 6th duke of, 271
Sophia, electress of Hanover, 266
Sophia, tsarevna, 717–18
Soura, 537
Southampton Water, 814
South Sea, Company, 15, 288–9, 291, 475, 530, 679, 835
  French in, 15, 359, 364, 385
Southwell, Sir Robert, 38
Spain
  government, 8–9, 348–9, 351–2, 353, 357–9, 361 ff.; see also Castile, Orry
  nobility, 8–9, 347–8, 352, 361–2, 365, 370, 371, 375
  religion, 9, 131, 346–7, 363, 376; see also Inquisition
  in Italy, 9, 159 ff., 368, 370, 385 ff., 397, 409, 419, 425, 428–9, 432–3, 439, 447, 451 ff., 556–9, 590–4
  overseas, 12, 13, 128–9, 349–50, 354–7, 359–60, 364–5, 372–3, 375–6, 385 ff., 395, 406, 410, 511, 528 ff., 798, 809
  culture, 72, 343
  army, 20, 231, 353, 363, 366–7, 374, 782–3
  navy, 21, 565, 567–8, 790, 813

Spain (*cont.*)
  succession problem, 159, 161–3, 168, 172, 178, 270, 348, 350–1, 357–9, 360–1, 370 ff., 384–98, 418–19, 437–9, 447 ff., 590 ff.
  problem of decadence, 343–5
  finance, 345, 346, 351, 353, 366, 370, 376
  economy, 251, 345 ff., 352, 511, 514, 520, 548, 863
  Nine Years War, 235, 247–9, 251–2, 354–7
  Succession War, 369–75, 418–19, 422–3, 425, 429–30, 432–4, 438, 440–1, 444–5
  population, 345, 542
  Utrecht, 376–7, 453–4, 461–3, 467–8, 476
  see also Asiento, Carlos II, Catalonia, Louis XIV, Philip V, Portugal
Spanish (southern) Netherlands, 398–400, 408, 445, 473
  strategic factors, 18–19, 231, 750–1, 753, 786–7
  and France, 161, 385, 397–9, 400, 404–5, 412–13
  and Dutch, *see* Barrier
  and Spain, 352–3, 366, 398; *see also* Bergeyck, Maximilian Emmanuel
  Nine Years War, 232–3, 239, 241, 242, 244 ff.
  Ryswick, 252, 381–2
  Partitions, 384, 387, 391, 393–5, 398, 400, 406, 427
  Succession War, 411, 416–17, 422, 424, 426–7, 432, 435–6, 438, 440, 752
  and Marlborough, 427, 435
  Condominium, 428, 445
  Austrian, 427, 441, 445, 598
  Utrecht, *see* Barrier
  economy, 293–4, 352, 390, 413
Spanish Succession War, 5, 19, 154, 169, 172, 287 ff., 369 ff., 591 ff., 663, 763, 769, 842, 852, 873–4, 896
  campaigns, 370 ff., 405, 409, 416 ff., 501 ff., 527, 569–71, 593–4, 741 ff., 770, 782–3, 794 ff.
  peace efforts, (1705) 425–6, 446 n.; (1706) 374, 430, 446–7; (1708) 431, 447–8; (1709) 374–5, 436–7, 450 ff.; (1710) 161, 439–40, 458; (1711–14) 270, 376–7, 441 ff., 459 ff., 528
Spee, Friedrich von, S.J., poet, 150
Speirbach, battle of (1692), 231
Spener, Philipp Jakob, German pietist, 25, 150
Spenser, Edmund, English poet, 79
Speyer, archbishopric, 203, 225, 233
Spice Islands, 857
Spinoza, Benedictus de, 36, 88, 136, 139–40
Spitzbergen, whale-fishery, 19

Splitgerber, Daum and Company, Berlin war contractors, 789
Staffarda, battle of (1690), 231, 241
Stahl, Georg Ernst, German chemist and physician, 54, 65–6
Stanhope, Hon. Alexander, diplomat, 352
Stanhope, James, 1st earl, son of preceding, 434, 440, 477, 567, 571
  commercial treaty (1708), 434, 439, 799
Stanislas I, king of Poland, *see* Leszczyński
Stanyan, Abraham, British diplomat, 645
Starhemberg, Count Guido von, Austrian general, 310, 434, 438, 440, 593
Starhemberg, Count Gundaker von, vice-president of Austrian cabinet, 309, 312–13, 575, 587, 589, 594
Starhemberg, Count Ernst Rüdiger von, defender of Vienna, 593
Stavnsband ordinance (Denmark), 775
Steele, Richard, nonconformist divine, 153
Steele, Sir Richard, politician and essayist, 32, 94, 145
Steenkerk, battle of (1692), 20, 245, 247
Stella, Count Rocco, of Naples, 593
Stenbock, Count Magnus, Swedish general, 661, 670–1, 699
Steno (Stensen), Niels, Danish naturalist, 61, 64
Stettin, 673, 678, 707
Stevensweert, fortress, 416, 477–8
Stiernhök, Olaf, Swedish envoy in Vienna, 183
Stillingfleet, Edward, English divine, 125, 140
Stockholm, 4, 42, 186, 650, 651, 652, 653, 658, 670, 672, 679, 763, 802, 806, 808
  Treaty of (1719), 678
  trade, 804–5
Stoddard, Solomon, of Connecticut, 493–4
Stöcken, Johann Heinrich von, Danish envoy, 182–3
Stollhofen, Lines of, 237, 417, 421, 432, 751, 753, 755
Strafford, Thomas Wentworth, 3rd earl of, 460, 462
Stralsund, 673–4, 679, 707, 710–11, 802
Strasbourg, 237, 467, 579, 753, 755, 785
  held by French, 26, 161, 223–4, 252, 421, 473, 588
Stratmann, Count Theodor Heinrich von, Austrian chancellor, 383, 578, 601
Streshnev, Tihone Nikitich, Russian boyar, 718
Stuart, Karl Magnus, Swedish general, 654–6, 761
Styria, 584, 604, 638
Styrum, Frederick Willem, count of Limburg-Styrum, imperial general, 752

Subercase, Auger de, governor of Acadia, 503
Sudan, 548
Suez, 615
Süleyman II, sultan, 620-1
  death, 622
Süleyman Pasha, grand vizier, 620
Sulpicians, 496, 498
Sumatra, pepper, 857
Sunderland, Charles Spencer, 3rd earl of, 268-9, 430, 547
Sunderland, Robert Spencer, 2nd earl of, 195, 199, 204, 216, 266-7, 271, 382
Surat, 518, 860
Surinam, 810, 854, 859
Susa, 241, 245
Sutton, Sir Robert, British ambassador to the Porte, 185, 635
Swabia, 237, 245, 402, 405, 432, 587-8, 601
  French threat to, 586
Sweden
  empire, 1-2, 648-9, 679-80
  and Denmark, 1-4, 402, 648-9, 652-5, 670, 673, 676-9, 692, 774-5
  army, 20, 228, 650, 655 ff., 661-9, 677, 743, 744, 747-8, 757-8, 760-1, 771-4, 780
  nobility, 28-9; *Reduktion*, 650, 772-3
  religion, 126
  and Louis XIV, 154, 158, 182-5, 227, 246, 402-3, 734
  and William III, 154, 172, 174, 184, 227
  government, 650-1, 661-2, 674-5, 677
  trade, 174, 234-5, 251, 420, 520, 648-9, 651, 659, 675, 699, 840-2
  navy, 654, 671, 805-8, 824-5, 830, 831
  plague, 672, 774
  see also Augustus II, Charles XII, Empire, Great Northern War, Holstein-Gottorp, Russia
Swift, Jonathan, 36, 81, 98, 126, 139, 153, 286, 315
  Conduct of the Allies, 274, 281, 442-3, 460
Switzerland
  mercenaries, 20, 243, 742, 765-6
  religion, 120-2, 189
  Villmergen war (1712), 120
  neutrality, 174-5
  economy, 605, 765, 813, 844, 895
  see also Berne, Geneva, Zürich
Sydenham, Thomas, English physician, 47
Syria, 128, 609, 630
  trade, 551, 838
Szaniawski, Constantine Felix, bishop of Kujawy, 702, 709, 713
Szatmár, peace of (1711), 585
Szczuka, Stanislas, vice-chancellor of Lithuania, 681, 690-1, 706-7

Szembek, John, vice-chancellor of Poland, 702-3
Szembek, Stanislas, primate of Poland, 702, 703

Tabriz, occupied by Turks, 645
Taganrog, dockyard, 625, 628-9, 634-5, 732
Tahmasp II, shah of Persia, 644
Taiwan (Formosa), sugar, 857
Tallard, Camille d'Hostun, comte de, marshal of France, 165, 175, 178, 186, 389, 395, 752, 400-1
  Succession War, 404, 421-2, 458
  Blenheim, 756
Tamarois, mission to, 499
Tangier, 391, 554, 566, 809
Tarascon, population, 889, 900
Tarnogród confederacy (1715), 711-12
Tasso, Torquato, Italian poet, 75
Tatars, *see* Crimea, Kazan, Russia
Tate, Nahum, Irish poet, 113
Tavares, António Raposo, Brazilian explorer, 533
Tavernier, Jean-Baptiste, French traveller, 95, 98
Taylor, Edward, New England poet, 497
Taylor, Jeremy, English divine, 146
Tchesma, battle of (1770), 566
Teignmouth, 239, 796
Teixeira, Pedro, Amazon explorer, 530, 533
Temesvár, Banat of, 6, 7, 581-2, 608, 622, 626-7, 639, 641, 754
  fortress, 577, 580, 639
Ter, the, battle of (1694), 248
Terek valley, 645
Terranova, Juana d'Aragon Cortés, duchess of, camarera mayor, 348
Teschen (Creszyn), 605
Tessé, René de Froullay, comte de, diplomat and marshal of France, 171, 247, 369, 372, 403
  Savoy, 418, 433
  Gibraltar, 423, 570
  and Peter the Great, 737
Tessin, Count Nicodemus, Swedish architect, 671
Test Acts, (1673, 1678), 196-200, 210
Tete, 518
Texas, 129, 356
Thessaly, 608, 624
Thévenot, Melchisedec, French scientist, 40
Thököly, Count Imre, Hungarian rebel, 577, 584, 605, 619, 622
Thomasius, Christian, Leipzig professor, 74
Thornhill, Sir James, English painter, 32
Tibet, Jesuit mission, 130
Tiepolo, Giambattista, Venetian painter, 556

Tiflis, seized by Turks, 645
Tilbury, fort, 205
Tillemont, Le Nain de, Jansenist, 132
Tillotson, John, archbishop of Canterbury, 138, 142, 152
Tilly, Claude Tserclaes, count of, general in Dutch service, 416
Tine (Tinos), Venetian base, 638, 642
Tisza, the, 577, 580–1, 626
Tlemcen, battle for (1701), 554
Tønning, fortress, 671–2
Toland, John, deist, 136, 140
Toledo, 371, 542
Toleration Act (1689), 210, 256, 259, 264
Tolstoy, Count Peter Andreyevich, Russian minister in Constantinople, 185, 636
Tomar, 513, 537
Tonking, 130
Torbay, 204
Torcy, Jean-Baptiste Colbert, marquis de, French foreign secretary, 165, 182, 365, 389, 397, 408
    peace negotiations (1709–12), 436–7, 441–2, 450–4, 459–61, 469, 470, 472
    and Russia, 734–5
Tordesillas, Treaty of (1494), 531, 533
Torelli, Giacomo, stage designer, 109, 116
Tories, 201, 208, 261, 267–8, 273–5
    Jacobitism, 273
    Church of England, 215, 270, 273–4, 280
    October Club, 275
    in opposition, 216, 275, 281, 437, 439
    in office, 16–17, 215, 270 ff., 441, 457 ff.
    see also Bolingbroke, Harley, Nottingham
Torre, Count da, see Fronteira
Torrington, Arthur Herbert, earl of, British admiral, 201, 226, 236–9, 791
Toruń (Thorn), 660
Toulon
    Allied attack (1707), 5, 19, 432–3, 570
    French naval base, 20–2, 236, 240, 403, 419, 567–8, 793, 808–13, 817, 832, 879
    squadron, 234, 246, 248, 250, 423
    seamen, 821, 823
Toulouse, Louis Alexandre de Bourbon, comte de, admiral of France, 423, 830–1
Tournai, fortress, 249, 436–8, 451, 465–7, 477
Tournefort, Joseph Pitton de, botanist and traveller, 41, 56, 58, 614, 628
Tournon, Charles Thomas Maillard de, papal legate in the East Indies, 130
Tours, silk, 323, 867
Tourton family, Genevan bankers, 303
Tourville, Anne Hilarion de Costentin, comte de, French admiral, 21, 568, 793, 819
    Beachy Head, 239, 795–6
    La Hougue, 215, 243–4, 567, 792, 795, 828

Townshend, Charles, 2nd viscount
    Barrier Treaty (1709), 439–42, 464
Traetta, Tommaso, Italian musician, 111
Tranquebar, Danish factory, 128, 518
Transylvania, 1, 7, 242, 424, 577–82, 584–6, 608, 621–2, 627, 754
Transylvania, prince of, see Apafi, Michael
Trapani, Michelangelo Fardella da, Paduan philosopher, 73
Trarbach, fortress, 27, 223, 252, 422
Trautmansdorf, Johann Sigismund, Saxon general, 688
Travendal, Treaty of (1700), 402, 654–5, 670, 692
Treason, English statutes, 265
Trebizond, 562, 609, 611
Tréguier, hemp, 817
Trembley, Abraham, microscopist, 64 n.
Trenchard, John, religious polemicist, 137
Trenčin, battle of (1708), 434, 585
Trent (Tyrol), 417
Trepassey, codfishing base, 503
Treviso, Venetian trade, 555
Trezzini, Domenico, Italian architect, 728
Triennial Act (1694), 220
Trier, city of, 223, 225, 233, 422, 424
    archbishop-elector, 225, 407, 590
Trieste, 7, 164, 404, 417, 555–6, 569
    free port, 604
    Eastern Company, 641
Trinidad (Cuba), 372
Triple Alliance (1717), 737
Tripoli (Barbary), 224, 227, 543–4, 548, 553
Trois Rivières, 484, 486, 496–7
Troitskaya, monastery, 718
Tromp, Maarten Harpetszoon, admiral, 798
Trondhjem, 675, 677
Trotter, Thomas, naval physician, 826
Trouin, René, sieur du Guay, see Duguay-Trouin
Tschernin (Czernin), Count Jacob von, 309
Tucumán, 525
Türk Ahmed Pasha, governor of Anatolia, 639
Tull, Jethro, English agriculturist, 68–9
Tunis, 227, 543–4, 551, 553, 813, 838
    see also Barbary Coast
Turenne, Henri de la Tour d'Auvergne, vicomte de, marshal of France, 233, 243
    military ideas, 742, 744, 751–3, 760
Turin, 31, 284, 418, 422, 425, 512, 535, 559, 560–2, 568, 584, 894
    Treaty of (1696), 160, 171–2, 175, 179, 250–1, 447
    taken by Eugene (1706), 5, 429, 570, 594, 753
    population, 542, 560
    university, 561
    corn prices, 889

Turkey
extent of Ottoman empire, 1–2, 6, 608–10;
see also Carlowitz, Passarowitz
ulema, 616–17, 620, 629, 631, 644, 646
Orthodox church, 3, 128, 554, 578–9, 613,
617–18, 625, 627, 632–3, 635–6, 637, 736
and Russia, see Russia
and West, 6, 614–15, 617–18, 635–7, 644
foreign views, 7, 95, 97, 611, 614
grand vizierate, 6, 614 ff., 629
army, 21, 553, 612–15, 642, 741, 743, 752,
759, 761, 789; see also Janissaries
navy, 21, 554, 562–6, 615, 623, 628, 630,
790; see also Barbary Coast
and Innocent XI, see Holy League
and Venice, 2, 6, 154, 227, 555, 562, 565,
619–23, 627, 637–42
Habsburg wars, 195, 223–4, 225–7, 232,
238, 241, 242–3, 251, 253, 383, 402, 572,
576 ff., 618 ff., 638–42
and Hungary, 576–81, 618–23, 626–7; see
also Transylvania
and Charles XII, 2, 630–1, 635–6, 669–70,
673, 703
and Arab provinces, 608 ff.; see Egypt
and Tatars, see Crimea, Russia
and Persia, 609, 643–5
and Cossacks, 31, 610, 625, 630–1, 634,
636
economy, 546, 549–52, 611–12, 623–5,
628, 644
finance, 552, 611–12, 613, 623–4, 628–9
government, 553–4, 608 ff., 615–18, 628,
630, 635–6, 643 ff.
Age of Tulips, 643–6
Turrettini, J. A., Genevan theologian, 122
Tuscany, 9, 151, 160, 174, 404, 473, 540–4,
591, 813
rupture with Venice, 171
presidii, 387, 393, 395, 473
privateers, 546; galleys, 563
Tuy (Galicia), 526
Tyrconnel, Richard Talbot, earl of, 198,
206, 213, 769
Tyrol, 167, 386, 417, 591, 599, 605
Tyson, Edward, English anatomist, 56, 60, 62

Ukraine
war in, 30, 619, 666–9, 754
Turks, 619, 631, 636
separatism, 631, 664, 696, 732
Charles XII, 631, 660, 666–9
Poland, 683, 696, 699
Russia, 683, 696, 699, 732, 775–6
see also Mazepa, Orlik, Palej, Samuś,
Zaporozhian Cossacks
Ukraintsev, Emel'an Ignat'evich, Russian
envoy to Constantinople, 628

Ulm, 422, 589, 750, 755
Ulrika Eleonora, duchess of Hesse and
queen of Sweden (1718), 673, 677, 679
Ulster, 213, 235–7, 256
Uniat Church, 128, 633
Uniformity, Act of (1662), 264
Unigenitus, papal bull, see Jansenism
Unitarians, 582; see also Socinianism
United Provinces
navy, 3, 4, 16, 21, 234, 295, 382, 790, 798–
800, 808–9, 811, 814–15, 821, 822, 825,
826, 827–8, 832
army, 20, 202, 228, 382, 404, 411, 415 ff.,
742, 747, 750
stadholderate, 176, 195, 415, 799
economy, 29, 69, 385, 390–1, 415, 510,
520–1, 523, 535, 549–50, 799, 835 ff., 893
culture, 32, 34–5; religion, 122–3, 135
and America, 235, 350, 359, 406, 410,
434, 464, 515
war finance, 294–8, 314, 411, 799–801,
831–2, 896
and Marlborough, 406, 416–17, 420–1,
424, 427, 435–6; see Heinsius
Utrecht, 442–4, 448–51, 460 ff.
see also Amsterdam, Barrier, East
India, Heinsius, privateering, slavery,
William III
Uppsala, academy, 42
Urals, industries, 724
Urbich, Johann Christoph von, baron,
Russian minister in Vienna, 735
Urgal, taken by French (1691), 243
Ursins, Anne Marie de la Trémoïlle-
Noirmoutier, princesse des, camarera
mayor, 367, 371–3, 377–9, 380, 474, 476
Ursulines, in Canada, 496–7
Ushant, 811
Utrecht, Peace of (1713), 6, 14, 16, 17, 26,
108, 131, 155, 164–5, 170, 186, 337, 376–
7, 443–4, 461–7, 491, 507, 528, 557,
641, 832, 849–50
Congress, 186, 337, 443, 446, 461 ff., 507,
596
see also Spanish Succession War (peace
efforts)

Vairasse (Veiras), Denis, novelist, 98
Valence, population, 889, 900
Valencia, 9, 347, 754
civil war, 370–1, 373, 425, 429–30
government, 9, 348, 353, 363, 373–4
trade, 509, 540, 844
Valencia de Alcántara, fortress, 525–6
Valenciennes, fortress, 438, 477
Valenza, 418, 466 n., 560 n.
Valenzuela, Fernando de, Spanish minister,
351

Valincour, J.-B. Henri du Trousset de, secretary to Admiral of France, 803
Valladolid, 346, 375, 440
Vallisneri, Antonio, Italian scientist, 61, 64
Valsesia, 418, 466 n., 560 n.
Vanbrugh, Sir John, English dramatist and architect, 26, 89, 281 n.
Van Robais, family of Abbeville, 864
Varasdin, Turkish vilayet, 608
Vargas, governor of New Mexico, 356
Varignon, Pierre, French geometer, 41
Vattel, Emmerich de, jurist, 173
Vauban, Sébastien le Prestre, marshal of France, military engineer and statistician, 29, 728, 762
    fortresses, 18, 223, 230-1, 248, 750, 812
    population studies, 47, 330, 883
    on taxes, 329-31, 332
    siegecraft, 416, 750-1
    on colonization, 500-1
    on army, 747-8, 767, 781
    on privateering, 803-4
    harbour works, 811-12
Vaudemont, Charles Henri de Lorraine, prince of, governor of Milan, 250, 397, 403, 558, 597
Vaudois, 119-20, 188
Vaudreuil, Philippe Rigaud, chevalier de, governor-general at Quebec, 496, 502
Vauvré, Louis Girardin de, intendant of Toulon, 830, 832
Velez, fortress, 554
Vendôme, Louis Joseph, duc de, marshal of France
    in Spain, 249, 357, 375, 440, 569
    in north Italy, 417, 425, 429, 558
    in Tyrol, 417, 422
    in Netherlands, 432, 435, 757
    Oudenarde, 435-6
    cautiousness, 752
Venezuela, 129, 350, 851; see also Caracas
Venice, republic of, 131, 155, 168, 173, 180, 186, 386, 394, 594, 604, 608
    Turkish wars, see Turkey
    culture, 10, 32, 76, 109, 556
    and the Morea, 2, 158, 164, 184, 565-6, 620, 623, 627, 637-8, 640, 642, 782
    rupture with Tuscany, 171
    economy, 509, 510, 543, 549, 555-6, 571, 604-5
    population, 542, 884
    navy, 546, 562, 565, 620, 623, 638
    Cretan war, 549, 555
    Negroponte, 622-3
    see also Carlowitz, Passarowitz
Venlo, fortress, 399, 466, 478
    taken by Allies (1702), 416

Veprik, fortress taken by Swedes (1709), 667
Vera Cruz, 349, 354, 361, 372; see also Mexico (flotas)
Verbiest, Ferdinand, S.J., in China, 130
Verden, 472, 477, 649, 673, 678
Verger, Dame du, French agent in Portugal, 183
Verona, fortress, 753
Verrio, Antonio, painter, 32
Vetch, Samuel, New England colonel, 505-7
Veterani, Count Friedrich von, imperial general, 578-9
Via Carolina, 604
Viana do Castelo, corn prices, 509
Viborg, 676
Vico, Giambattista, philosopher, 33, 73, 558
Victor Amadeus II of Savoy, 9, 169, 188, 238, 432, 598
    and France, 160-3, 215, 238, 243, 247, 250, 403-4, 414, 579, 581
    Grand Alliance, 163, 240-1, 245, 248-9, 417-18, 422, 425, 429, 433, 592-3
    Sardinia for Sicily (1720), 159, 559, 597
    his reforms, 560-2, 766-7
    claims to Lombardy, 418, 466 n., 560 n., 595-7
    see also Savoy-Piedmont, Sicily, Turin
Vidin, Turkish fortress, 610, 621
Vieira, António, S.J., Brazilian missionary, 129, 516
Vienna
    siege of (1683), 5, 572, 618, 683
    threat to (1704), 19, 417, 420; see also Blenheim
    building growth, 31, 572-3, 601
    Allied conference, 172
    municipality, 311-12, 572
    City bank, 311-13, 314, 606
    population, 542
    Hofburg, 572, 573-5, 601
    chancery of Transylvania, 582
    Consejo d'Italia, 597
    industries, 603
    Niederleger, 603
    Peter the Great at, 626, 719
Vigarani, Carlo and Gaspare, Italian stage designers, 109
Vigevano, 418, 466 n., 560 n.
    Convention of (1696), 175, 250, 568, 626
Vigo, 372, 418, 525-6, 797-8, 808
Vila Viçosa, 520
Villafranca, 243, 560
Villa Viciosa, battle of (1710), 375, 440
Villars, Claude Louis Hector, duc de, marshal of France, 177-8, 314, 428, 456
    at Rastatt, 5, 171, 444, 472-3
    Camisards, 325

Villars (*cont.*)
  Succession War, 19, 417, 421, 424, 428, 432, 437–8, 440–1, 443–4, 472
  as soldier, 432, 437, 749, 751–3, 755
Villemarie, 486
Villeroi, François de Neufville, duc de, marshal of France
  Netherlands, 249, 421
  Italy, 405, 409, 767
  Ramillies, 426, 432, 532, 752, 756
Villette, Philippe de Valois, marquis de, French squadron commander, 526
Villmergen, war of (1712), 120
Vilna, 693, 695, 699
Vincennes (Wabash), 498
Vinhos, Figueró dos, iron-making, 513
Virginia, 480, 487–8
  College of William and Mary, 495
  Succession War, 503, 507–8
  tobacco, 851–2
Visé, Donneau de, French journalist, 76
Vistula, the, 2, 665, 700–3, 754
Vitringa, Campegius, Dutch Calvinist, 141
Vitzthum, Friedrich von Eckstädt, Saxon diplomat, 695
Vivaldi, Antonio, musician, 105, 115–16
Vladislavich, Sava (*alias* Raguzinsky), 632, 634
Voetians, 122
Voisin, Lavigne, French missionary, 499
Volhynia, 700, 705, 712, 837
Vologda, tar, 841
Voltaire, 32–3, 40, 46, 62, 83, 97, 108, 111, 137
  Lettres Philosophiques, 52, 221
  Louis XIV, 70–1; *L'Empire de Russie*, 740
Vondel, Joost van den, Dutch poet, 74, 142
Voronezh, dockyard, 625, 718
Vorskla, the, 667; *see also* Poltava
Vosges, timber, 814
Voznitsyn, Prokofy, companion of Peter the Great, 719
Vuillart, Germain, Jansenist, 132
Vyatka, tar, 841

Wachtmeister, Count Hans, Swedish admiral, 654, 830
Wager, Sir Charles, naval commodore, 372
Wake, William, archbishop of Canterbury, 127
Walcourt, cavalry engagement (1689), 235
Waldeck, Georg Friedrich, prince of, diplomat and general, 156, 207 n., 235
  Fleurus, 239; Steenkerk, 245
Walker, Sir Hovenden, rear-admiral, 505–6
Wallachia, 1, 2, 578–82, 608, 619, 621, 625, 633, 635, 639, 641, 683, 688, 754
Wallachia, Little, 1, 578, 580, 641

Wallerstedt, Count Lars, Swedish statesman, 652
Wallis, John, mathematiciain, 37, 42, 179
Walther, J. G., German musicologist, 117
Wanley, Humfrey, English antiquary, 87
Wars, *see* Algiers, Comacchio, Cossacks, Great Northern War, Holy League, Hungary, Malta, Morea, Morocco, Nine Years War, Omani, Persia, Pruth, Sacramento, Spanish Succession War, Villmergen; and for Habsburg–Ottoman wars, *see under* Turkey
Warsaw, 2, 652–3, 691, 695–7
  Confederacy of (1704), 697–8, 701
  Polish–Swedish treaty (1705), 659, 699
  Russo-Polish treaty (1716), 712–13
Waterford, 240
Watteau, Antoine, French painter, 32, 765
Webb, John Richmond, British general, 436
Weide, Adam Adamovich, German general in Russia, 721
Welch, Thomas, American explorer, 504
Wellekens, J. B., Dutch translator, 75
Wertheimer, Samson, war financier, 309, 739
Wesley, John, religious leader, 151–2
West Indies, 11, 20, 231, 392, 501, 812
  buccaneers, *see* flibustiers
  Nine Years War, 251, 355, 809–10, 825
  Succession War, 372, 503, 505, 809–10, 825
  trade, 839, 849–51, 853–7, 859, 864, 866, 872, 894
Westphalia, 586, 587
  Peace of (1648), 162, 234, 246, 473, 649, 662
  linens, 867
Wharton, Henry, divine and scholar, 87, 140
Wharton, Thomas, 1st marquis of, 268
Wheler, Sir Francis, British admiral, 251, 489
Whigs, 201, 208, 273–5
  in office, 216, 267–9, 437, 439, 448–9
  out of office, 215, 270, 440–1
Whiston, William, Cambridge divine and scientist, 47, 51
White, Thomas, English philosopher, 135
Whitworth, Charles, baron, English envoy to Russia, 840–1
Whydah (S. João Baptista de Ajudá), slaving entrepôt, 515
Whytt, Robert, Scottish physiologist, 67
Wicquefort, Abraham de, historian, 173, 179
Wieliczka, salt mines, 844
Wielkopolska, 695–7, 700–2, 705, 712
Wigston, occupations at, 892
Wijnendaal, battle of (1708), 436
Wilanów, palace near Warsaw, 682

Wildt, Job de, secretary of Amsterdam admiralty, 798

William III, of Orange, king of Great Britain
character, 17, 190–2, 208, 232
and European common weal, 17, 156–7, 192
religion, 122, 169, 188, 190–1, 210, 395
confidants, 156, 170, 176, 192, 388
dynastic ties, 168
and Louis XIV, 18, 156, 189–90, 195, 392, 400
and James II, 198–9, 211 ff., 250
invasion of England, 200–6, 226–7
attitude to crown, 169–70, 206–8, 249
prerogative, 208, 215, 265–8
and Scotland, 212–13, 275–6, 392, 769, 783
and Ireland, 213–14, 235 ff., 240, 242
war aims, 162, 246, 249, 253
Nine Years War, 223, 242 ff., 247, 249
Hague Congress, 171–2, 237–8, 239
Ryswick, 26, 169–70, 187, 252, 381
Spanish succession, 191, 388 ff., 400–1, 406; see Partition Treaties
and Max Emmanuel, 353, 390, 393–4, 395
and German states, 165–6, 226, 237, 404, 408–9
and Baltic powers, 154, 165, 172, 174, 184
neutral trade, 174, 187, 235
and Savoy, 238, 250–1
and Turks, 233
on trade and colonies, 13, 15, 186, 187
conduct of foreign policy, 176, 187, 191, 266–7, 415
as strategist, 11, 17, 18
on sea power, 11, 18, 19, 162, 236, 239, 248–9, 391–2, 568, 569, 797
and army, 748, 769–70, 784
death, 409, 414

Willughby, Francis, English naturalist, 59

Wilmot, Robert, British naval captain, 251, 355

Wiltshire, woollens, 865

Winter Harbour (Maine), 502

Winthrop, Wait Still, chief justice, Massachusetts, 481

Wismar, 649, 673–4, 678–9, 736

Wiśniowiecki, Janusz, governor of Cracow, 711

Wiśniowiecki, Michael, Lithuanian magnate, 693, 700

Wittelsbach, house of, 167, 169, 224, 578, 589
see also Joseph Clement, Maximilian Emmanuel

Wolff, Christian, German philosopher, 74

Woodward, John, English geologist, 40, 61

Woolwich, dockyard, 229, 811

Worms, French in (1688–9), 225, 233

Wotton, William, English scholar, 70

Woudenberg, Cornelis, count of Nassau, Dutch general, 436

Wratislaw, Count Johann Wenzel von, imperial ambassador to Britain, 575, 587, 591
and Marlborough, 420
Utrecht, 450, 455, 462, 467
and Archduke Charles, 576, 591, 596
and Eugene, 587, 595
death, 471

Wren, Sir Christopher, architect, 106, 262

Wrenn, Ralph, British naval captain, 251

Wschowa, see Fraustadt

Württemburg, duke of, 121, 245, 402
ravaged (1688–9), 786

Würzburg, bishop of, 405
prices, 878

Wycherley, William, English dramatist, 89

Yale, foundation of college (1701), 494–5

Yavorsky, Stefan, Russian churchman, 127

Yemen, coffee, 858

Yorkshire, population, 887

Ypres, fortress, 249, 451, 477

Yucatan, 356

Yugoslavia, 608

Yüsüf Pasha, grand vizier, 636

Zaandam (Saardam), 21, 719, 793, 814, 840

Zagreb, 581

Zalánkemén, battle of (1691), 580, 622, 631, 754

Załuski, Andrew Chrysostom, bishop of Ermland, chancellor of Poland, 690

Zambesi, the, 517

Zamość, fortress, 712

Zante, pirates, 544

Zanzibar, taken by Omani, 517

Zaporozhian Cossacks, 665–9, 683, 696, 699, 732, 775–6

Zeeland, 174, 187, 546, 655, 833
privateers, 20, 174, 187, 420, 550, 799–801

Zeno, Antonio, Venetian admiral, 565, 623

Zeno, Apostolo, Venetian librettist, 110–11

Zenta, battle of (1697), 5, 383, 581, 626, 754

Ziegler, H. A. von, German novelist, 74

Zinzendorf, see Sinzendorf

Zolkiev, 665

Żórawno, Peace of (1676), 683

Zottegem, prices, 878

Zoutleeuw, 424

Zsibó, battle of (1705), 424, 585

Zürich, population, 765, 884

Zuhab, Peace of (1639), 608

Zulfikar, Turkish official, 621

Zvornik, Turkish garrison, 640